Lecture Notes in Computer Science 13941

Founding Editors

Gerhard Goos
Juris Hartmanis

Editorial Board Members

The series Lecture Notes in Computer Science (LNCS), including its subseries Lecture Notes in Artificial Intelligence (LNAI) and Lecture Notes in Bioinformatics (LNBI), has established itself as a medium for the publication of new developments in computer science and information technology research, teaching, and education.

LNCS enjoys close cooperation with the computer science R & D community, the series counts many renowned academics among its volume editors and paper authors, and collaborates with prestigious societies. Its mission is to serve this international community by providing an invaluable service, mainly focused on the publication of conference and workshop proceedings and postproceedings. LNCS commenced publication in 1973.

Alexandra Boldyreva · Vladimir Kolesnikov
Editors

Public-Key Cryptography – PKC 2023

26th IACR International Conference
on Practice and Theory of Public-Key Cryptography
Atlanta, GA, USA, May 7–10, 2023
Proceedings, Part II

 Springer

Editors
Alexandra Boldyreva
Georgia Institute of Technology
Atlanta, GA, USA

Vladimir Kolesnikov 🆔
Georgia Institute of Technology
Atlanta, GA, USA

ISSN 0302-9743   ISSN 1611-3349 (electronic)
Lecture Notes in Computer Science
ISBN 978-3-031-31370-7   ISBN 978-3-031-31371-4 (eBook)
https://doi.org/10.1007/978-3-031-31371-4

This Springer imprint is published by the registered company Springer Nature Switzerland AG
The registered company address is: Gewerbestrasse 11, 6330 Cham, Switzerland

Preface

The 26th International Conference on Practice and Theory of Public-Key Cryptography (PKC 2023) was held in Atlanta, Georgia, USA on May 7–10, 2023. It was sponsored by the International Association for Cryptologic Research (IACR).

The conference received 183 submissions, reviewed by the Program Committee of 49 cryptography experts working with 142 external reviewers. The reviewing process took 2.5 months and resulted in selecting 50 papers to appear in PKC 2023.

Papers were reviewed in the usual double-blind fashion. Program committee members were limited to two submissions, and their submissions were scrutinized more closely. The two program chairs were not allowed to submit papers.

The Program Committee recognized two papers and their authors. "The Hidden Number Problem with Small Unknown Multipliers: Cryptanalyzing MEGA in Six Queries and Other Applications," by Nadia Heninger and Keegan Ryan, and "Post-Quantum Anonymity of Kyber", by Varun Maram and Keita Xagawa, were selected Best Papers of the conference.

PKC 2023 welcomed Chris Peikert (University of Michigan) as the invited speaker.

The PKC Test-of-Time Award (ToT) recognizes outstanding and influential papers published in PKC about 15 years prior. The inaugural PKC Test of Time Award was given in PKC 2019 for papers published in the conference's initial years of the early 2000s and late 1990s. In 2023, the ToT committee, consisting of Alexandra Boldyreva, Goichiro Hanaoka, Vlad Kolesnikov, Moti Yung, and Yuliang Zheng, considered papers published in PKC 2006–2008 for the award. The committee selected the PKC 2008 paper "Unidirectional Chosen-Ciphertext Secure Proxy Re-encryption" by Benoît Libert and Damien Vergnaud for the Test-of-Time award.

PKC is the main IACR-sponsored conference with an explicit focus on public-key cryptography. It is a remarkable undertaking, only possible due to the hard work and significant contributions of many people. We would like to express our sincere gratitude to the authors of all submitted works, as well as to the PC and external reviewers, session chairs and presenters. Additionally, we would like to thank the following people and organizations for helping make PKC 2023 a success:

- Joseph Jaeger and Daniel Genkin – PKC 2023 General Chairs,
- Chris Peikert – invited speaker,
- Kay McKelly and Kevin McCurley – all things technical behind the scenes,
- Ellen Kolesnikova – design of the PKC 2023 logo,
- the team at Springer,
- Georgia Tech Hotel and Conference Center,
- Georgia Aquarium,
- School of Cybersecurity and Privacy at Georgia Tech - the academic home of the PKC 2023 Program and General Chairs.

We would also like to thank our sponsors: Google (platinum), Starkware (silver), Amazon AWS (silver), and Algorand (bronze). 2022 and 2023 were difficult years in the tech industry, making sponsors' contributions ever more valued. Their generous support covered several student travel stipends and helped minimize registration fees, including half-priced registration for all students.

Lastly, a big thanks to everyone who attended PKC 2023 in Atlanta. We hope you enjoyed the conference and the warm welcome of our city and university.

May 2023   Alexandra Boldyreva
                                                               Vlad Kolesnikov

Organization

General Chairs

Daniel Genkin   Georgia Tech, USA
Joseph Jaeger   Georgia Tech, USA

Program Committee Chairs

Alexandra Boldyreva   Georgia Tech, USA
Vladimir Kolesnikov   Georgia Tech, USA

Steering Committee

Masayuki Abe   NTT, Japan
Jung Hee Cheon   Seoul National University, Korea
Yvo Desmedt   University of Texas at Dallas, USA
Goichiro Hanaoka   AIST, Japan
Aggelos Kiayias   University of Edinburgh, UK
Tanja Lange   Eindhoven University of Technology, Netherlands
David Pointcheval   École Normale Supérieure, France
Moti Yung (Secretary)   Google Inc. & Columbia University, USA
Yuliang Zheng (Chair)   University of Alabama at Birmingham, USA

Program Committee

Ghada Almashaqbeh   University of Connecticut, USA
Nuttapong Attrapadung   AIST, Japan
Carlo Blundo   Università degli Studi di Salerno, Italy
Katharina Boudgoust   Aarhus University, Denmark
Dario Catalano   Università di Catania, Italy
Suvradip Chakraborty   ETH Zurich, Switzerland
Shan Chen   Southern University of Science & Technology, China
Jean Paul Degabriele   Technology Innovation Institute, UAE
Chaya Ganesh   Indian Institute of Science, India

Additional Reviewers

Behzad Abdolmaleki
Calvin Abou Haidar
Ojaswi Acharya
Gorjan Alagic
Gennaro Avitabile
Arnab Bag
Shi Bai
Magali Bardet
Hugo Beguinet
Fabrice Benhamouda
Loris Bergerat
Ward Beullens
Olivier Blazy
Maxime Bombar
Cecilia Boschini
Vincenzo Botta
Samuel Bouaziz-Ermann
Charles Bouillaguet
Nicholas Brandt
Lennart Braun
Matteo Campanelli
André Chailloux
Rohit Chatterjee
Jesus-Javier Chi-Dominguez
Hien Chu
Heewon Chung
Michele Ciampi
Jean-Sébastien Coron
Anamaria Costache
Baptiste Cottier
Jan-Pieter D'Anvers
Pratish Datta
Gareth T. Davies
Paola De Perthuis
Jean-Christophe Deneuville
Julien Devevey
Mario Di Raimondo
Javad Doliskani
Keita Emura
Andreas Erwig
Daniel Escudero
Andre Esser
Pouria Fallahpour

Antonio Faonio
Joël Felderhoff
Weiqi Feng
Rune Fiedler
Georgios Fotiadis
Tako Boris Fouotsa
Georg Fuchsbauer
Clemente Galdi
Romain Gay
Robin Geelen
Paul Gerhart
Lenaïck Gouriou
Mohammad Hajiabadi
Erin Hales
Mickaël Hamdad
Patrick Harasser
Keitaro Hashimoto
Sorina Ionica
Vincenzo Iovino
Aayush Jain
Christian Janson
Corentin Jeudy
Saqib Kakvi
Daniel Kales
Harish Karthikeyan
Julia Kastner
Mojtaba Khalili
Hamidreza Khoshakhlagh
Ryo Kikuchi
Dongwoo Kim
Elena Kirshanova
Fuyuki Kitagawa
David Kohel
Sebastian Kolby
Walter Krawec
Mikhail Kudinov
Péter Kutas
Roman Langrehr
Mario Larangeira
Changmin Lee
Antonin Leroux
Andrea Lesavourey
Varun Madathil

Lorenzo Magliocco
Jules Maire
Monosij Maitra
Takahiro Matsuda
Liam Medley
Kelsey Melissaris
Hart Montgomery
Ngoc Khanh Nguyen
Ky Nguyen
Thi Thu Quyen Nguyen
Phong Nguyen
Ruben Niederhagen
Koji Nuida
Tapas Pal
Kunjal Panchal
Mahak Pancholi
Lorenz Panny
Robi Pedersen
Lucas Prabel
Thomas Prest
Sihang Pu
Krijn Reijnders
Mahshid Riahinia
Doreen Riepel
Felix Rohrbach
Mélissa Rossi
Olga Sanina
Paolo Santini

André Schrottenloher
Robert Schädlich
Yixin Shen
Mark Simkin
Animesh Singh
Sayani Sinha
Luisa Siniscalchi
Christoph Striecks
Atsushi Takayasu
Debadrita Talapatra
Aravind Thyagarajan
Junichi Tomida
Toi Tomita
Monika Trimoska
Damien Vidal
Chenkai Wang
Yohei Watanabe
Christian Weinert
Weiqiang Wen
Keita Xagawa
Shota Yamada
Takashi Yamakawa
Yibin Yang
Kazuki Yoneyama
Yusuke Yoshida
Bor de Kock
Rafael del Pino
Wessel van Woerden

Contents – Part II

Encryption

ZK I

IO and ZK II

Contents – Part I

Isogenies

Crypto for Crypto

Homomorphic Cryptography and Other Topics

On Homomorphic Secret Sharing
from Polynomial-Modulus LWE

Thomas Attema[1,2,3], Pedro Capitão[1,2(✉)], and Lisa Kohl[1]

[1] Cryptology Group, CWI, Amsterdam, The Netherlands
{pedro,lisa.kohl}@cwi.nl
[2] Mathematical Institute, Leiden University, Leiden, The Netherlands
[3] Cyber Security and Robustness, TNO, The Hague, The Netherlands
thomas.attema@tno.nl

Abstract. Homomorphic secret sharing (HSS) is a form of secret sharing that supports the local evaluation of functions on the shares, with applications to multi-server private information retrieval, secure computation, and more.

Insisting on additive reconstruction, all known instantiations of HSS from "Learning with Error (LWE)"-type assumptions either have to rely on LWE with superpolynomial modulus, come with non-negligible error probability, and/or have to perform expensive ciphertext multiplications, resulting in bad concrete efficiency.

In this work, we present a new 2-party local share conversion procedure, which allows to *locally* convert noise encoded shares to non-noise plaintext shares such that the parties can detect whenever a (potential) error occurs and in that case resort to an alternative conversion procedure.

Building on this technique, we present the first HSS for branching programs from (Ring-)LWE with polynomial input share size which can make use of the efficient multiplication procedure of Boyle et al. (Eurocrypt 2019) and has no correctness error. Our construction comes at the cost of a – on expectation – slightly increased output share size (which is insignificant compared to the input share size) and a more involved reconstruction procedure.

More concretely, we show that in the setting of 2-server private information retrieval we can choose ciphertext sizes of only a quarter of the size of the scheme of Boyle et al. at essentially no extra cost.

1 Introduction

In 1979, Shamir introduced the concept of secret sharing information in his seminal paper *How to Share a Secret* [31]. In the two-party setting, secret sharing allows to split up a secret value into two secret shares, such that each share individually hides the secret, whereas the shares together allow to recover it. The simplest secret-sharing scheme is *additive secret sharing*, where a value x in an additive group $\mathbb{G}$ is split into x_0, x_1, such that x_0, x_1 are distributed uniformly at random conditioned on $x_0 + x_1 = x$. Despite its simplicity, additive secret

© International Association for Cryptologic Research 2023
A. Boldyreva and V. Kolesnikov (Eds.): PKC 2023, LNCS 13941, pp. 3–32, 2023.
https://doi.org/10.1007/978-3-031-31371-4_1

sharing comes with a number of nice properties. For example, it allows the *local* evaluation of linear functions on the shares.

In 2019, Boyle, Gilboa and Ishai [10] extended this notion to *homomorphic secret sharing (HSS)*, which allows the *local* evaluation of larger classes of function on the shares, while keeping the nice properties of additive secret sharing (so far possible). More precisely, a homomorphic secret-sharing scheme for a function class $\mathcal{F}$ (over some input space $\mathbb{G}$) has the following properties:

- The secret shares individually hide the message (*computationally*).
- The secret shares are succinct, i.e., they are *polynomial* in the size of the secret to be shared (in particular, they are independent of the complexity of the function class $\mathcal{F}$).
- The secret shares allow local evaluation of all functions $f \in \mathcal{F}$. More precisely, there exists an evaluation procedure Eval, such that given secret shares x_0, x_1 of $x \in \mathbb{G}$, it holds $\mathsf{Eval}(f, x_0) + \mathsf{Eval}(f, x_1) = f(x)$.

Note that the last condition explicitly requires *additive reconstruction*, i.e., evaluation results in an additive secret sharing of the output. While this requirement can be relaxed to more general reconstruction functions (as we will do in this work), it has a number of useful features, such as allowing the local postprocessing with linear functions.

Since their introduction, homomorphic secret sharing has found numerous applications, including 2-server private-information retrieval [9,11,19,24,32], low-communication secure computation [8,10,12,20], and succinct generation of correlated (pseudo-)randomness [6,7].

In [10], Boyle et al. presented a homomorphic secret-sharing scheme from the decisional Diffie-Hellman assumption for the class of *restricted multiplication straight-line (RMS) programs*. These programs are restricted in that they only allow multiplication between an input value and a memory value (where a memory value is an intermediate value in the computation), but not a multiplication between two memory values. It can be shown that this captures the class of polynomial-size branching programs, and circuits of constant fan-out and logarithmic depth (i.e., circuits in the complexity class NC^1).

Since then, further HSS constructions for RMS programs have been proposed based on the decisional Diffie-Hellman assumption [8], the Paillier assumption [23,28,30], and based on the learning with errors (LWE) assumption [14,16,22]. All schemes, however, come with some efficiency bottleneck: either the evaluation is computationally expensive [8,10,16,22,23,28,30] and/or the input shares have high concrete overhead resulting in bad communication complexity [14,16,22].

In particular, while the scheme of Boyle et al. BKS [14] comes with desirable properties such as (plausible) post-quantum security and (comparatively) efficient multiplication on ciphertexts, it inherently has to rely on LWE with (double-)superpolynomial modulus (and thus large ciphertexts) in order to keep the error probability negligible. The reason for their (double-)superpolynomial modulus is a share conversion procedure to locally convert noise encoded shares modulo q to non-noisy shares modulo q. In order to achieve negligible error probability, they need to choose moduli p, q with $1 \ll p \ll q$, where each $\ll$ denotes a superpolynomial gap. The starting point for our work can thus be phrased as follows.

Is it possible to design a share-conversion procedure for polynomial-sized p, q without introducing a non-negligible error?

1.1   Our Contribution

In this paper, we answer this question (somewhat) affirmatively and present an HSS scheme from LWE for RMS programs with polynomial modulus, which otherwise inherits the nice properties from BKS. Our core technique is a share conversion which allows to locally detect and tentatively correct potential errors. On the downside, we have to relax additive reconstruction to a more involved reconstruction procedure, where the parties choose the output from an expected constant-size list of potential output values. In the following we give a high-level overview of our main results, which we discuss in more detail in the technical overview.

Our Core Lemmas. Our core technique can be captured in the following two lemmas for *share conversion*, a crucial step in the homomorphic evaluation of multiplications. Informally, the lemma states that (for rounding) there exist *local* conversion procedures that return shares flag_0, z_0 and $\mathsf{flag}_1, z_1, z'_1$, respectively, such that either $z_0 = z_1 \mod p$ or $z_0 = z'_1 \mod p$, where the latter holds if and only if $\mathsf{flag}_0 = \mathsf{flag}_1 = 1$. This extends the technique of BKS, who only consider the case $\mathsf{flag}_0 = \mathsf{flag}_1 = 0$ and choose parameters to ensure that this holds except with negligible probability.

Lemma 1 (Rounding with correction [Lemmas 5, 6]). *Let $p, q \in \mathbb{N}$ with $p|q$. Then, there exist efficient procedures $\mathsf{Round}_0 \colon \mathbb{Z}_q \to \{0,1\} \times \mathbb{Z}_p$ and $\mathsf{Round}_1 \colon \mathbb{Z}_q \to \{0,1\} \times \mathbb{Z}_p^2$ such that the following holds:*
For any $x \in \mathbb{Z}_p$, any $e \in \mathbb{Z}$ with $|e| < q/(4p)$, and any t_0, t_1 with

$$t_0 + t_1 = \frac{q}{p} \cdot x + e \mod q,$$

it holds

$$x = \begin{cases} z_0 + z_1 \mod p & \text{if } \mathsf{flag}_0 = 0 \lor \mathsf{flag}_1 = 0, \\ z_0 + z'_1 \mod p & \text{if } \mathsf{flag}_0 = \mathsf{flag}_1 = 1, \end{cases}$$

where $(\mathsf{flag}_0, z_0) \leftarrow \mathsf{Round}_0(t_0)$ and $(\mathsf{flag}_1, z_1, z'_1) \leftarrow \mathsf{Round}_1(t_1)$.
Further, for t_0, t_1 chosen at random, it holds $\mathsf{flag}_0 = \mathsf{flag}_1 = 0$ with probability at least $1 - (4 \cdot |e| \cdot p)/q$.

Similarly, we extend their lemma for lifting.

Lemma 2 (Lifting with correction [Lemmas 8, 9]). *Let $p, q \in \mathbb{N}$ with $p|q$. Then, there exist efficient procedures $\mathsf{Lift}_0 \colon \mathbb{Z}_p \to \{0,1\} \times \mathbb{Z}_q$ and $\mathsf{Lift}_1 \colon \mathbb{Z}_p \to \{0,1\} \times \mathbb{Z}_q^2$ such that the following holds:*

For any $x \in \mathbb{Z}_p$, with $|x| < p/6$, and any z_0, z_1 with

$$z_0 + z_1 = x \mod p,$$

it holds

$$x = \begin{cases} v_0 + v_1 \mod q & \text{if } \mathsf{flag}_0 = 0 \vee \mathsf{flag}_1 = 0, \\ v_0 + v_1' \mod q & \text{if } \mathsf{flag}_0 = \mathsf{flag}_1 = 1, \end{cases}$$

where $(\mathsf{flag}_0, v_0) \leftarrow \mathsf{Lift}_0(z_0)$ *and* $(\mathsf{flag}_1, v_1, v_1') \leftarrow \mathsf{Lift}_1(z_1)$.

Further, for z_0, z_1 chosen at random it holds $\mathsf{flag}_0 = \mathsf{flag}_1 = 0$ with probability at least $1 - (4 \cdot |x|)/p$.

Our HSS. We show that building on the core lemma, we obtain an HSS with one-sided error correction. More precisely, $\mathcal{P}_0$ will follow a fixed computation path (remembering the wires where $\mathsf{flag}_0 = 1$). Party $\mathcal{P}_1$ on the other hand, continues the computation for z_1 and z_1' whenever $\mathsf{flag}_1 = 1$ for some wire. In the end, the parties can reconstruct the value by choosing the computation path that resorts to the alternative computation for $\mathcal{P}_1$ whenever $\mathsf{flag}_0 = 1$ and $\mathsf{flag}_1 = 1$ for some wire. Note that this potentially results in *exponential* computation time for $\mathcal{P}_1$. We resolve this by choosing the parameters depending on the number of multiplications to be performed, such that the *overall* number of expected errors is 1 (or less). This means that on expectation $\mathcal{P}_1$ has to perform the computation twice (from some point in the program on) and finally obtains two output shares. We want to stress that the output shares (corresponding to plaintext values) are typically several orders of magnitude smaller than the input shares (corresponding to ciphertext values). The increase in output values is therefore insignificant compared to the savings in input shares.

For instantiating our HSS, we present a trade-off between ciphertext size (equaling the input share size) and expected number of output shares. More precisely, instantiating the underlying public-key encryption scheme PKE with the Ring-LWE based encryption scheme of Lyubashevsky, Peikert and Regev [27] over the ring $\mathcal{R} = \mathbb{Z}[X]/(X^N + 1)$, we obtain the following.

Lemma 3 (Corollary of Lemma 11). *Let $\gamma > 1$. Let P be a branching program with multiplicative size $|P|$ (i.e., number of load and multiplication operations) and magnitude bound B_{max} (i.e., upper bound on all intermediary computation values). Then, setting $p \geq 8 \cdot B_{\mathsf{max}} \cdot N \cdot |P| / \ln \gamma$ and $q \geq 8 \cdot p \cdot N \cdot |P| / \ln \gamma$ in our HSS construction party $\mathcal{P}_1$ obtains at most γ output shares on expectation.*

Setting $\gamma = 1 + \lambda^{-\omega(\log \lambda)}$ (and thus obtaining $1/\ln \gamma \approx \lambda^{\omega(\log \lambda)}$) we can recover the negligible error probability at the cost of superpolynomial ciphertext sizes of BKS.

HSS with Perfect Correctness. As a corollary of our techniques, we can obtain an HSS for RMS programs that satisfies *perfect* correctness, since the parties can *always* detect and correct the errors.

Table 1. Our HSS parameters for program size $|P| = 2^{20}$, $\gamma = 2$.

B_{max}	N	$\log q$
2	2048	71
2^{16}	2048	86
2^{32}	4096	104
2^{64}	4096	136
2^{128}	8192	202
2^{256}	8192	330

Table 2. BKS HSS parameters with *per gate* error probability 2^{-40}.

B_{max}	N	$\log q$
2	4096	137
2^{16}	4096	167
2^{32}	8192	203
2^{64}	8192	267
2^{128}	16384	399
2^{256}	16384	655

Concrete Efficiency. In Tables 1 and 2, we give concrete parameter sizes in comparison with the scheme of BKS, depending on the program size $|P|$. Note that the parameters of the BKS HSS scheme also have to grow with the program size of the underlying program $|P|$ to ensure a fixed error probability, similarly to our scheme. Even without taking this into account (i.e., considering an error probability of 2^{-40} after one operation rather than $|P|$), it can be seen that our scheme can achieve a factor 4 shorter ciphertexts.

HSS with Expected Constant-Time Evaluation. The focus of our paper are applications where there is no privacy requirement for reconstruction, and thus *expected* constant-time evaluation can be dealt with by cutting off the computation after a fixed certain number of operations. We note though that the expected running time of the evaluation algorithms imposes challenges in applications such as secure two-party computation, where party $\mathcal{P}_0$ can potentially derive information about the input from the response time of $\mathcal{P}_1$. We leave dealing with this issue as an interesting open question.

Share Reconstruction with Privacy. We note that (apart from the above described problem concerning run-time leakage) the problem of share reconstruction with privacy can be viewed as (one-server) private information retrieval by keywords [17] satisfying a strong notion of database privacy, where the client (here party $\mathcal{P}_0$) is not allowed to learn anything about the number and content of the database held by the server (here party $\mathcal{P}_1$), except for the queried entry. This can be viewed as a special case of labelled private-set intersection [15,18] and can be instantiated by relying on somewhat homomorphic encryption. (Note here that the database for share reconstruction is very small on expectation, and thus even using expensive ciphertext multiplication for the final reconstruction would in typical applications not have a significant impact on the overall run time.)

Impossibility of Fully Local Share Conversion. To complement our result, we show that *no* direct local share conversion (i.e., not resorting to an alternative conversion procedure) can achieve negligible error, showing that the BKS HSS scheme inherently requires either superpolynomial ciphertext or some postprocessing on the outputs.

Limitation to 2-Party HSS. As for BKS, our techniques are inherently limited to the two-party case, since we use some "symmetry" properties between the two shares. More precisely, we rely on the fact that if $t_0 + t_1 = \frac{q}{p} \cdot x + e$, then the distance of t_0 and t_1 to the next (potentially different) multiple of $\frac{q}{p}$ differs only by $|e|$. This is no longer true for three or more parties, where local rounding results in a constant error probability (independent of p and q). Going beyond the two-party case therefore inherently requires new techniques.

Beyond HSS. A corollary of our core lemma is that the secure reconstruction of $x \mod p$ given $t_0 + t_1 = \frac{q}{p} \cdot x + e$ can be performed using a single string-OT, where party $\mathcal{P}_0$ acts as the sender with input-bit flag_0 and $\mathcal{P}_1$ acts as the receiver inputting (z_1, z_1) if $\mathsf{flag}_1 = 0$ and (z_1, z_1') else. This might have applications to encryption with 2-party distributed decryption, as used, e.g., in lattice-based electronic voting schemes.

HSS Rounding vs. Learning with Rounding (LWR). The rounding function which underlies [14] and this paper is essentially the same as the rounding function used for LWR [4]. While [4] uses non-distributed rounding to reduce the hardness of LWR to LWE (essentially building on the fact that the LWE error is "rounded away" with high probability), the line of work on constructing HSS via rounding needs a stronger property on distributed rounding towards achieving correctness. In particular, the techniques to reduce the modulus in the reduction from LWR to LWE from super-polynomial to polynomial [2,5] do not appear to help in reducing the modulus for LWE-based HSS constructions.

1.2   Technical Overview

In the following, we give an overview of the idea behind our core lemma and our HSS construction. For the purpose of the technical overview, we assume $\mathcal{R} = \mathbb{Z}$, $n \in \mathbb{N}$, and $p = p(\lambda), q = q(\lambda) \in \mathbb{N}$ such that $p|q$. By writing $p \ll q$, we denote that $q/p \in \lambda^{\omega(1)}$.

Restricted Multiplication Straight-Line Programs (RMS). Recall that for RMS programs there is a distinction between *input values* (inputs to the program) and *memory values* (intermediary computation values) and the following operations are supported:

- Loading an input value into memory;
- Adding two memory values;
- Multiplying an input value with a memory value;
- Outputting a memory value.

The HSS Scheme of [14]. Our starting point is the HSS scheme of [14]. The basis of their construction is an encryption scheme with nearly linear encryption. More precisely, let $\mathsf{PKE} = (\mathsf{Gen}, \mathsf{Enc}, \mathsf{Dec})$ be a public-key encryption scheme over message space $\mathbb{Z}_p$, such that the secret key and ciphertext space is $\mathbb{Z}_q^d$. Recall that PKE satisfies *nearly linear decryption*, if for all secret keys $\mathbf{s}$, all messages $m \in \mathbb{Z}_p$, and all encryptions $\mathbf{c}$ of m, it holds

$$\langle \mathbf{s}, \mathbf{c} \rangle \approx \frac{q}{p} \cdot m \quad \mathrm{mod}\ q.$$

Further, BKS requires that $\mathbf{s}$ has only entries in $\{-1, 0, 1\}$ (or otherwise small bounded values). As observed in [14], these requirements are indeed satisfied by (variants of) many lattice-based encryption schemes [3,4,25,26,29].

Now, if $B_{\max} \in \mathbb{N}$ with $B_{\max} \ll p \ll q/B_{\max}$, then an HSS for RMS programs with magnitude bound $B_{\max}$ can be obtained as follows.

Key generation. The HSS key generation generates a key pair according to the key generation algorithm $\mathsf{PKE.Enc}$ and outputs secret key shares $\mathsf{ek}_0 := \mathbf{s}_0$ to $\mathcal{P}_0$ and $\mathsf{ek}_1 := \mathbf{s}_1$ to $\mathcal{P}_1$, s.t., $\mathbf{s}_0 + \mathbf{s}_1 = \mathbf{s}$ for the secret key $\mathbf{s} \in \{0,1\}^d$.

Input and memory values. Values are stored as follows.

– **Input values:** Input values $|x| \leq B$ are encrypted as $\{\mathsf{Enc}(x \cdot s_i)\}_{i \in [d]}$, where s_i is the i-th component of $\mathbf{s}$. (Note that by the techniques of BKS this is possible given knowledge only of the public key of the underlying encryption scheme. We will give more details on this in the main body of the paper.)

– **Memory values:** Memory values $|y| \leq B$ are secret shared as $\mathbf{t}_0, \mathbf{t}_1$, such that $\mathbf{t}_0 + \mathbf{t}_1 = y \cdot \mathbf{s} \quad \mathrm{mod}\ q$.

Note that adding two memory values is straightforward by the linearity of additive secret sharing. Further, assuming that the first component of the secret key $\mathbf{s}$ is always one (which is straightforward to achieve), outputting a memory value mod q can be done by simply outputting the first entry of the corresponding share. Finally, loading an input value is equivalent to multiplying an input value by 1. We therefore restrict to describing the restricted multiplication in the following.

To perform a multiplication of an input value x encrypted as $\{\mathbf{c}_i\}_{i \in [d]}$ with a memory value y shared as $(\mathbf{t}_0, \mathbf{t}_1)$, the idea is for the parties to locally compute t_b^{pre} as $t_{b,i}^{\mathsf{pre}} := \langle \mathbf{c}_i, \mathbf{t}_b \rangle$. By the property of nearly linear decryption, this yields:

$$t_{0,i}^{\mathsf{pre}} + t_{1,i}^{\mathsf{pre}} = \langle \mathbf{c}_i, y \cdot \mathbf{s} \rangle = y \cdot \langle \mathbf{c}_i, \mathbf{s} \rangle \approx \frac{q}{p} \cdot x \cdot y \cdot s_i \quad \mathrm{mod}\ q,$$

and thus

$$t_0^{\mathsf{pre}} + t_1^{\mathsf{pre}} \approx \frac{q}{p} \cdot x \cdot y \cdot \mathbf{s} \quad \mathrm{mod}\ q.$$

The challenging part is to *locally* convert the shares t_b^{pre} into memory values, i.e., $\mathbf{t}_0^{\mathsf{out}} + \mathbf{t}_1^{\mathsf{out}} = x \cdot y \cdot \mathbf{s} \mod q$. To that end, BKS [14] introduce the *rounding* and *lifting* technique, which allow local share conversion. In the following, we will focus on the *rounding* technique, since the *lifting* technique (to lift shares modulo p to shares modulo q) can be adapted similarly.

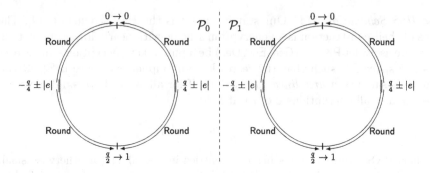

Fig. 1. Depiction of the local rounding procedure. If both shares are *outside* the area highlighted in red, then no rounding error occurs. (Color figure online)

Lemma 4 (Rounding [BKS [14]]). *Let $p, q \in \mathbb{N}$ such that $p|q$. Let $x \in \mathbb{Z}_p$ and let $e \in \mathbb{Z}$ with $|e| \ll q/p$. Let $t_0, t_1 \in \mathbb{Z}_q$ be sampled uniformly at random subject to*

$$t_0 + t_1 = \frac{q}{p} \cdot x + e \mod q.$$

Then there exists an efficient deterministic procedure Round *such that*

$$\mathsf{Round}(t_0) + \mathsf{Round}(t_1) = x \mod p$$

except with negligible probability.

Towards HSS from Polynomial-Modulus LWE. A straightforward approach towards HSS with polynomial modulus is to choose p, q of polynomial-size and handle the resulting non-negligible error with the generic error correction techniques of [10] introduced towards HSS from decisional Diffie-Hellman (where a non-negligible error is inherent [21]). These generic error correcting techniques come with a high concrete overhead though: If the error probability is a constant, then $\omega(\log \lambda)$-repetitions are necessary to achieve negligible error-probability via a majority vote. Thus, both the evaluation time and the size of the output shares are increased by a factor of $\omega(\log \lambda)$.

This work: HSS from polynomial-modulus LWE with fine-grained error correction. In this work, we show that in the case of LWE – and unlike decisional Diffie-Hellman – it is actually possible to detect (potential) errors, and therefore only correct if an error really occurs (or is very likely to occur). In order to outline our techniques, in the following we take a closer look at the rounding procedure from above.

To simplify presentation, for the rounding technique we assume $p = 2$ and $4|q$ (to ensure $\frac{q}{2}$ and $\frac{q}{4}$ are integers). We give a depiction of the rounding procedure in Fig. 1, where $\mathsf{Round}: \mathbb{Z}_q \to \mathbb{Z}_2$ is defined as

$$\mathsf{Round}(y) := \left\lfloor \frac{2}{q} \cdot y \right\rceil \mod 2.$$

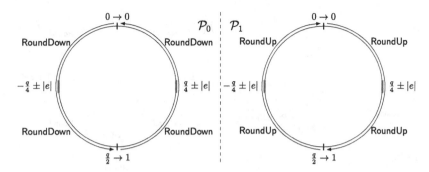

Fig. 2. Depiction of the alternative local rounding procedure. If at least one of the shares is *inside* the area highlighted in red, then no rounding error occurs. (Color figure online)

Now, assume to be given shares t_0, t_1 chosen at random conditioned on

$$t_0 + t_1 = \frac{q}{2} \cdot x + e,$$

where $x \in \{0, 1\}$ and e is some error. Then, as observed in BKS [14], if at least one of the shares t_0, t_1 is *outside* the *red area* $\left[-\frac{q}{4} \pm |e|\right] \cup \left[\frac{q}{4} \pm |e|\right]$,[1] then no rounding error occurs, i.e.,

$$\left\lfloor \frac{2}{q} \cdot t_0 \right\rceil + \left\lfloor \frac{2}{q} \cdot t_1 \right\rceil = x \mod 2.$$

This crucially relies on the fact that for the shares it holds that $t_0 + t_1 = e$ mod q or $t_0 + t_1 = \frac{q}{2} + e$ mod q. Now, assume t_0 is outside the red area and $\mathsf{Round}(t_0) = 0$ (the other cases are similar). Then, it must hold that t_0 has distance $< \frac{q}{4} - |e|$ from 0. Thus, if $t_0 + t_1 = e$, it must hold that t_1 has distance $< \frac{q}{4}$ from 0, and thus $\mathsf{Round}(t_1) = 0$ as required. On the other hand, if $t_0 + t_1 = \frac{q}{2} + e$ mod q, then t_1 must have distance $< \frac{q}{4}$ from $\frac{q}{2}$, and thus $\mathsf{Round}(t_1) = 1$ as required.

If $|e| \ll \frac{q}{2}$, then the probability of a random element $y \xleftarrow{\$} \mathbb{Z}_q$ lying in the red area is negligible, and thus by the above considerations no rounding error occurs except with negligible probability.

Towards correcting the error, we observe that – on the other hand – if at least one of the shares t_0, t_1 is *inside* one of the bad areas, then following an alternative procedure (depicted in Fig. 2) no rounding error occurs. The alternative rounding procedures $\mathsf{RoundDown}, \mathsf{RoundUp}$ are defined as

$$\mathsf{RoundDown}(x) := \left\lfloor \frac{2}{q} \cdot x \right\rfloor \mod 2, \quad \mathsf{RoundUp}(x) := \left\lceil \frac{2}{q} \cdot x \right\rceil \mod 2.$$

---

[1] Here, we consider $\mathbb{Z}_q$ to be represented as integers in the interval $\left(-\frac{q}{2}, \frac{q}{2}\right]$. For $y \in \left\{-\frac{q}{4}, \frac{q}{4}\right\}$, by $[y \pm |e|]$ we denote the interval containing all $z \in \mathbb{Z}_q$ having at most distance $|e|$ from y (considered as integer).

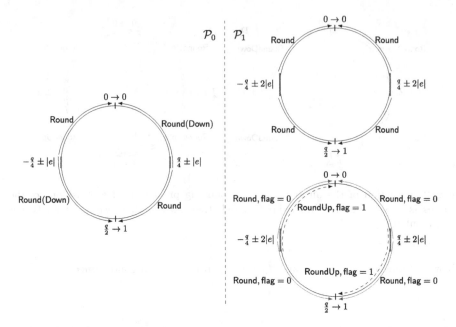

Fig. 3. Depiction of the asymmetric local rounding procedure, where party $\mathcal{P}_1$ is fully in charge of the error correction. (Color figure online)

In other words, party $\mathcal{P}_0$ rounds all negative numbers $\left(-\frac{q}{2}, -1\right]$ to $-1 = 1$ mod 2, and all positive number $\left[1, \frac{q}{2}\right]$ to 0, and $\mathcal{P}_1$ rounds all negative numbers $\left(-\frac{q}{2}, -1\right]$ to 0, and all positive numbers $\left[1, \frac{q}{2}\right]$ to 1 (and 0 is always rounded to 0).

The idea here is that if at least one of the shares t_0, t_1 is *inside* the red area, then the other share is also $|e|$-close to the red area, and therefore one party rounding up and the other party rounding down always yields the correct result (as long as $|e| < \frac{q}{4}$). More precisely, assume that t_0 is in the red area and Round$'(0, t_0) = 0$, i.e., $t_0 \in \left[\frac{q}{4} \pm |e|\right]$ (the other cases are similar). Now, if $t_0 + t_1 = e$ mod q, then $t_1 \in \left[-\frac{q}{4} \pm 2 \cdot |e|\right]$, and thus Round$'(1, t_1) = 0$. If $t_0 + t_1 = \frac{q}{2} + e$ mod q, on the other hand, it holds $t_1 \in \left[\frac{q}{4} \pm |e|\right]$ and thus Round$'(1, t_1) = 1$ as required.

Given these two observations, we obtain our first core lemma (Lemma 1). We present the corresponding rounding procedures in Fig. 3. Here, $\mathcal{P}_0$ always follows a fixed rounding procedure, where $\mathcal{P}_0$ uses the normal rounding procedure *outside* the red area, and the rounding procedure RoundDown *inside* the red area. If its share is within the red area, it sets flag $= 1$ for the corresponding wire, and flag $= 0$ otherwise. If the share of $\mathcal{P}_1$ is *outside* the (now larger) red area, it follows the standard rounding procedure, and sets flag $= 0$. If the share of $\mathcal{P}_1$ is *inside* the larger red area, it follows both the standard rounding procedure (depicted by the blue arrows) and the RoundUp rounding procedure (depicted by the dashed arrows) and sets the flags to 0 and 1, respectively. For reconstruction, the parties resort to the alternative ("dashed") computation path whenever both parties set flag $= 1$ on the corresponding wire.

Together with our new lifting lemma, this yields our HSS scheme. A crucial part of our construction is carefully taking account of the gates with flag $= 1$, which we explain in the main body.

2 Preliminaries

In this section we define the HSS primitive as well as the computational model for programs supported by our construction. We begin by introducing some notation. For $n \in \mathbb{N}$, $[n]$ denotes the set $\{1, \ldots, n\}$. We denote by λ the security parameter.

We will work with the ring $\mathcal{R} = \mathbb{Z}[X]/(X^N + 1)$, where $N \leq \text{poly}(\lambda)$ is a power of 2. The infinity norm on $\mathcal{R}$ is defined as $\|x\|_\infty = \max_{i \in [n]} |x_i|$ for $x \in \mathcal{R}$ with coefficients $x_1, \ldots, x_n$. For $q \in \mathbb{N}$, let $\mathcal{R}_q = \mathcal{R}/q\mathcal{R}$, where we consider elements of $\mathcal{R}_q$ to have all their coefficients in the interval $(-q/2, \ldots, q/2]$.

2.1 Homomorphic Secret Sharing

We consider homomorphic secret sharing with a general decoding algorithm for the reconstruction of shares, as defined by Boyle et al. [13], in the public-key setting. We note that HSS is commonly defined with the stronger requirement of additive reconstruction, which enjoys several useful properties. By considering the more general definition, our scheme is able to forego some of those properties for efficiency. Moreover, we show that the decoding functionality can be easily and securely realized, depending on the application setting.

Definition 1 (Homomorphic Secret Sharing). *A 2-party public-key homomorphic secret sharing (HSS) scheme for a class of programs $\mathcal{P}$ consists of algorithms* (Gen, Enc, Eval, Dec) *with the following syntax:*

- Gen(1^λ) : *On input a security parameter 1^λ, the key generation algorithm outputs a public key* pk *and a pair of evaluation keys* (ek_0, ek_1).
- Enc(pk, x) : *On input the public key* pk *and an input value x, the encryption algorithm outputs a ciphertext* **c**.
- Eval(σ, ek_σ, ($\mathbf{c}_1, \ldots, \mathbf{c}_n$), P, β) : *On input a party index $\sigma \in \{0, 1\}$, evaluation key ek_σ, a vector of n ciphertexts, a program $P \in \mathcal{P}$ with n input values, and an output modulus β, the homomorphic evaluation algorithm outputs a share y_σ.*
- Dec(y_0, y_1, β) : *On input shares y_0, y_1 and an output modulus β, the decoding algorithm outputs a value y.*

The algorithms (Gen, Enc, Eval, Dec) *should satisfy the following correctness and security requirements:*

Perfect Correctness. *For all $\lambda \in \mathbb{N}$, inputs $x_1, \ldots, x_n$, program $P \in \mathcal{P}$, and integer $\beta \geq 2$, we have*

$$\text{Dec}(y_0, y_1, \beta) = P(x_1, \ldots, x_n),$$

where $(\mathsf{pk}, \mathsf{ek}_0, \mathsf{ek}_1) \leftarrow \mathsf{Gen}(1^\lambda)$, $\mathbf{c}_i \leftarrow \mathsf{Enc}(\mathsf{pk}, x_i)$ *for* $i \in [n]$ *and* $y_\sigma \leftarrow \mathsf{Eval}(\sigma, \mathsf{ek}_\sigma, (\mathbf{c}_1, \ldots, \mathbf{c}_n), P, \beta)$ *for* $\sigma \in \{0, 1\}$.

Security. *For all* $\lambda \in \mathbb{N}$ *and for all PPT adversaries* $\mathcal{A}$,

$$\Pr\left[\mathcal{A}(\mathsf{state}, \mathsf{pk}, \mathsf{ek}_\sigma, \mathbf{c}) = b \left| \begin{array}{l} (\sigma, x_0, x_1, \mathsf{state}) \leftarrow \mathcal{A}(1^\lambda) \\ b \leftarrow \{0, 1\} \\ (\mathsf{pk}, \mathsf{ek}_0, \mathsf{ek}_1) \leftarrow \mathsf{Gen}(1^\lambda) \\ \mathbf{c} \leftarrow \mathsf{Enc}(\mathsf{pk}, x_b) \end{array} \right. \right] - \frac{1}{2} \leq \mathsf{negl}(\lambda).$$

Remark 1. We relax the definition of HSS by not requiring the Eval algorithm to run in polynomial time, but only *expected* polynomial time, which will be the case in our construction. This can be converted into polynomial time by halting the computation after some fixed number of steps.

2.2 Restricted Multiplication Straight-Line Programs

Our HSS scheme supports homomorphic evaluation of the class of Restricted Multiplication Straight-line (RMS) programs. These are a restricted form of arithmetic circuits in which multiplication of intermediate values is not possible; only multiplication of an input value by an intermediate value (or *memory value*) is allowed.

Definition 2 (RMS programs). *An RMS program over the ring* $\mathcal{R}$ *consists of a magnitude bound* B_{max} *and a sequence of instructions of the four types below, each indicating its ingoing and outgoing wires and ordered by a unique identifier* $\mathsf{id} \in \mathbb{N}$.

- *Load input into memory: instruction* $(\mathsf{load}, \mathsf{id}, x, w)$ *sets input* x *as a memory value in wire* w *($\hat{y}_w \leftarrow \hat{x}$).*
- *Add values in memory: instruction* $(\mathsf{add}, \mathsf{id}, u, v, w)$ *adds the values in wires* u *and* v *($\hat{y}_w \leftarrow \hat{y}_u + \hat{y}_v$).*[2]
- *Multiply input by memory value: instruction* $(\mathsf{mult}, \mathsf{id}, x, v, w)$ *multiplies the input* x *and the memory value in wire* v *($\hat{y}_w \leftarrow \hat{x} \cdot \hat{y}_v$).*
- *Output from memory: instruction* $(\mathsf{out}, \mathsf{id}, w)$ *outputs the value in wire* w *as an element of* $\mathcal{R}_\beta$.

If at any step of execution the magnitude of a memory value exceeds the bound B_{max} *(i.e.* $\|\hat{y}_w\|_\infty > B_{\mathsf{max}}$*), the output of the program on the corresponding input is defined to be* $\bot$. *Otherwise the output is the sequence of values given by the* out *instruction.*

We define the multiplicative size *of an RMS program* P *as its number of* load *and* mult *instructions, and we denote it by* $|P|$.

---

[2] We assume that for every instruction $(\mathsf{add}, \mathsf{id}, u, v, w)$ such that u (resp. v) is the output wire of a previous instruction with id id_u (resp. id_v) we have $\mathsf{id}_u < \mathsf{id}_v$. This ensures that shares corresponding to u are computed before shares corresponding to v in our evaluation algorithm.

Note the distinction between the magnitude bound $B_{\max}$ and the output modulus β. For example, in an RMS program computing a Boolean function $f : \{0,1\}^k \to \{0,1\}$, the input values 0 and 1 would be interpreted as integers, $B_{\max}$ would be a bound on the greatest integer appearing as the result of an operation, and the output modulus would be $\beta = 2$. Our HSS scheme will require $\beta \leq B_{\max} < p < q$, where p and q are, respectively, the plaintext modulus and ciphertext modulus of the underlying encryption scheme.

Remark 2 The definition of RMS program in [14] includes an additional operation type which allows input values to be added. The class of functions computable with this additional operation is the same, but it allows some functions to be computed using fewer multiplications, which may result in a more efficient homomorphic evaluation. We omit this operation from our definition, but we note that our HSS also supports it, in identical fashion to the BKS scheme. In both constructions this feature requires adjusting the bound on the ciphertext noise according to the maximum number of input additions, which influences the parameters of the scheme.

3   The Homomorphic Secret Sharing Scheme

In this section, we describe our homomorphic secret sharing scheme. Our HSS is an adaptation of the BKS scheme [14]. It supports homomorphic evaluations of the same class of functions: *Restricted Multiplication Straight-Line* (RMS) programs. Informally, we adapt the original BKS scheme by incorporating a new error reconciliation procedure. The protocol parameters of the BKS scheme are chosen such that correctness errors only occur with negligible probability. By contrast, our reconciliation procedure allows for smaller protocol parameters, since potential errors occurring during the homomorphic evaluations are corrected by the error reconciliation procedure. As a result the internal protocol parameters can to chosen to be polynomial in the security parameter, whereas BKS scheme requires superpolynomial protocol parameters, thereby reducing the communication complexity.

3.1   The Protocol

Both the BKS scheme and our adaptation crucially rely on a public-key encryption scheme $\mathsf{PKE} = (\mathsf{PKE.Gen}, \mathsf{PKE.Enc}, \mathsf{PKE.Dec})$ with *nearly linear decryption*, i.e., for all key-pairs $(\mathsf{pk}, \mathbf{s}) \leftarrow \mathsf{PKE.Gen}(1^\lambda)$, messages $m \in \mathbb{Z}_p$ and ciphertexts $\mathbf{c} \leftarrow \mathsf{PKE.Enc}_{\mathsf{pk}}(m)$, it holds that

$$\langle \mathbf{c}, \mathbf{s} \rangle = \frac{q}{p} \cdot m + e \mod q\,,$$

for some "small" noise term $|e| \leq B_{\mathsf{err}}$.

HSS.Gen(1^λ):   Generate $(\mathsf{pk}, \mathbf{s}) \leftarrow \mathsf{PKE.Gen}(1^\lambda)$ and sample a PRF key $K \leftarrow \{0,1\}^\lambda$ uniformly at random. Sample $\mathbf{s}_0 \leftarrow \mathbb{Z}_q^d$ and define

$$\mathbf{s}_1 := \mathbf{s} - \mathbf{s}_0 \mod q.$$

Output $(\mathsf{pk}, \mathsf{ek}_0, \mathsf{ek}_1)$, where $\mathsf{ek}_0 := (K, \mathbf{s}_0), \mathsf{ek}_1 := (K, \mathbf{s}_1) \in \{0,1\}^\lambda \times \mathbb{Z}_q^d$.

Fig. 4. Homomorphic Secret Sharing - Key Generation.

Since the PKE has nearly linear decryption, the decryption procedure simply rounds the inner-product $\langle \mathbf{c}, \mathbf{s} \rangle$ of the ciphertext and the secret key, multiplied by $0 < p/q < 1$, to the nearest integer, i.e.,

$$\mathsf{PKE.Dec}(\mathbf{c}, \mathbf{s}) = \left\lceil \frac{p}{q} \cdot \langle \mathbf{c}, \mathbf{s} \rangle \right\rfloor \mod p.$$

We assume that the first coefficient of the secret key $\mathbf{s} \in \mathbb{Z}^d$ equals 1. This property is crucially required by the HSS construction, and it is satisfied by most PKE schemes with nearly linear decryption.

Further, for simplicity, we assume PKE to be defined over $\mathbb{Z}$. For this reason, our homomorphic secret sharing scheme will also be defined over $\mathbb{Z}$. However, all techniques and results have a straightforward generalization to rings of the form $\mathcal{R} = \mathbb{Z}[X]/(X^N + 1)$ for N a power of 2, namely, the rounding and lifting procedures are applied to each of the N coordinates of elements of $\mathcal{R}$.

As shown in [14], if PKE has nearly linear decryption and pseudorandom ciphertexts, there exists a *Key Dependent Message* (KDM) oracle PKE.OKDM that, without knowledge of the secret key, outputs encryptions of scalar multiples of the secret key ([14], Lemma 3). More precisely, for all $j \in \{1, \ldots, d\}$ and $x \in \mathbb{Z}$,

$$\mathbf{c}_j \leftarrow \mathsf{PKE.OKDM}(\mathsf{pk}, x, j) \quad \text{s.t.} \quad \langle \mathbf{c}_j, \mathbf{s} \rangle = x \cdot s_j + e \mod q,$$

where $\mathbf{s} = (s_1, \ldots, s_d)$ and $|e| \leq B_{\mathsf{err}}$. By linearity, the KDM oracle allows encryptions of arbitrary linear combinations of the secret key to be generated.

Let us now continue to describe our 2-party homomorphic secret sharing scheme HSS. Besides a PKE scheme with the above properties, the HSS construction also requires a keyed pseudorandom function PRF. The key-generation of our HSS scheme, described in Fig. 4, is identical to that of the BKS scheme. The HSS public key is simply a public key for the PKE scheme and each evaluation key contains an additive secret share $\mathbf{s}_\sigma$ of the secret key together with a PRF key K.

The second functionality of the HSS is encryption. It allows parties to encrypt the inputs to the RMS program that is to be evaluated. However, an HSS encryption of an input value $x \in \mathbb{Z}$ is different from a standard PKE encryption of x. Instead, it is an encryption of the key-dependent vector $x \cdot \mathbf{s} \in \mathbb{Z}_q^d$, where $\mathbf{s} \in \mathbb{Z}_q^d$ is the secret key corresponding to the public key pk generated in the key generation. Hence, the HSS encryption of x is a vector of d PKE encryptions, each

---

HSS.Enc(pk, x):   Compute $c_j \leftarrow$ PKE.OKDM(pk, x, j) for $j = 1, \ldots, d$.
Output the ciphertext $\mathbf{C} := (c_1, \ldots, c_d)$.

Fig. 5. Homomorphic Secret Sharing - Encryption.

to a different key-dependent message $x \cdot s_i$ for $i \in \{1, \ldots, d\}$. Note that, since $\mathbf{s} = (1, s_2, \ldots, s_d) \in \mathbb{Z}_q^d$, the first component of an HSS encryption is a standard PKE encryption of $x \cdot 1 = x$. The HSS encryption functionality, again identical to the one used by the BKS scheme, is described in Fig. 5. Intuitively, security of our HSS scheme follows from the security of OKDM and from each share $\mathbf{s}_\sigma$ individually hiding $\mathbf{s}$.

The reason for using this "key-dependent" encryption is that, by deploying a distributed decryption, the two parties can take encrypted input values and obtain additive secret shares of the vector $x \cdot \mathbf{s}$. The BKS scheme shows how to perform certain operations on secret shares of key-dependent messages of this form. More precisely, it shows that the following operations can be performed *locally* (i.e., without requiring interaction between the two parties):

- **Addition**: given a secret share of $x \cdot \mathbf{s}$ and a secret share $y \cdot \mathbf{s}$, obtain a secret share of $(x + y) \cdot \mathbf{s}$.
- **Multiplication by Input Value**: given an HSS encryption of x and a secret share of $y \cdot \mathbf{s}$, obtain a secret share of $xy \cdot \mathbf{s}$.

The HSS scheme thus distinguishes between (encrypted) input values and intermediate computation values, also referred to as *memory* values. The above functionalities immediately imply an HSS for RMS programs.

Our scheme deviates from BKS in how it performs the above HSS operations. In the BKS scheme these operations involve a distributed decryption, which in turn involves the rounding of a noisy value followed by a "lifting" of shares mod p to shares mod q. Both of these steps may fail, causing a correctness error, and the BKS scheme chooses its parameters such that such errors only occur with negligible probability. In our approach, we employ procedures Round and Lift (defined in Sect. 3.2) which indicate whether an error may have occurred and correct it if necessary.

In more detail, for party $\mathcal{P}_0$, the output of Round is of the form $(\mathsf{flag}_0, z_0) \in \{0, 1\} \times \mathbb{Z}_p$. If $\mathsf{flag}_0 = 0$ (no error can occur), then z_0 is obtained by rounding as usual, while if $\mathsf{flag}_0 = 1$ (an error may occur), then z_0 is the result of an alternative "error-correcting" rounding.

Before describing the procedure for party $\mathcal{P}_1$, note that, since the parties cannot communicate, there is no guarantee that their flags will coincide. Moreover, the error-correcting requires the two parties to be in sync, i.e. correctness is not guaranteed if one party follows the usual rounding and the other the alternative rounding. Therefore, it may seem necessary that each party computes both the usual and alternative values when their flag is positive, in order to use one of them depending on the flag of the other party. However, we are able to define

---

HSS.Eval$(0, \mathsf{ek}_0, (\mathbf{C}^1, \ldots, \mathbf{C}^n), P, \beta)$:   Parse $\mathsf{ek}_0 = (K, \mathsf{s}_0)$ and P as a sequence of RMS instructions. Initialize pos_0 as the empty binary string. Proceed as follows for each instruction in P.

- *Load input into memory:* On instruction $(\mathsf{load}, \mathsf{id}, \mathbf{C}, w)$, compute

$$(\mathbf{t}_0^w, \mathsf{pos}_0) \leftarrow \mathsf{Mult}_0(K, \mathsf{id}, \mathbf{C}, \mathsf{s}_0, \mathsf{pos}_0),$$

  where Mult_0 is the algorithm described in Figure 8.
- *Add values in memory:* On instruction $(\mathsf{add}, \mathsf{id}, u, v, w)$, set

$$\mathbf{t}_0^w := \mathbf{t}_0^u + \mathbf{t}_0^v \mod q.$$

- *Multiply input by memory value:* On instruction $(\mathsf{mult}, \mathsf{id}, \mathbf{C}, v, w)$, compute

$$(\mathbf{t}_0^w, \mathsf{pos}_0) \leftarrow \mathsf{Mult}_0(K, \mathsf{id}, \mathbf{C}, \mathbf{t}_0^v, \mathsf{pos}_0),$$

  where Mult_0 is the algorithm described in Figure 8.
- *Output from memory:* On instruction $(\mathsf{out}, \mathsf{id}, w)$, parse $\mathbf{t}_0^w$ as $\mathbf{t}_0^w = (x_0, \hat{\mathbf{t}}_0)$ for some $x_0 \in \mathbb{Z}_q, \hat{\mathbf{t}}_0 \in \mathbb{Z}_q^{d-1}$ and output

$$y_0 := (H(\mathsf{pos}_0), x_0 \mod \beta),$$

  where $H(a_1, \ldots, a_k) = \{i \in [k] \mid a_i = 1\}$.

Fig. 6. Homomorphic Secret Sharing - Evaluation for party $\mathcal{P}_0$.

Round in a way such that whenever $\mathsf{flag}_0 = 1$ we have $\mathsf{flag}_1 = 1$ as well. This allows us to define Round for $\mathcal{P}_0$ as described above, always computing a single value z_0, and have only $\mathcal{P}_1$ compute two different values when $\mathsf{flag}_1 = 1$.

For $\mathcal{P}_1$, Round either outputs $\mathsf{flag}_1 = 0$ and z_1, or $\mathsf{flag}_1 = 1$ and (z_1, z_1'), where z_1 and z_1' denote the outputs of the usual and alternative rounding, respectively. The following table displays the 3 different scenarios that may occur, and whether the parties should use corrected values or not.

		Flag of $\mathcal{P}_0$	
		0	1
Flag of $\mathcal{P}_1$	0	No Correction	——
	1	No Correction	Error Correction

Similarly, errors can occur and be mitigated in the so-called lifting step, which always follows rounding.

The homomorphic evaluation procedure for party $\mathcal{P}_0$ is presented in Fig. 6. For every wire w in the RMS program P we compute a vector $\mathbf{t}_0^w \in \mathbb{Z}_q^d$ which is $\mathcal{P}_0$'s additive share of x^ws, where x^w is the value of P at w. Throughout this algorithm we keep track of the variable $\mathsf{pos}_0 \in \{0,1\}^*$ which denotes the sequence of flags of $\mathcal{P}_0$. After each "multiplicative" operation (i.e. load or mult

---

HSS.Eval$(1, \mathsf{ek}_1, (\mathbf{C}^1, \ldots, \mathbf{C}^n), P, \beta)$:   Parse $\mathsf{ek}_1 = (K, \mathbf{s}_1)$ and P as a sequence of RMS instructions. Initialize L_1 as an empty list. Proceed as follows for each instruction in P.

- *Load input into memory:* On instruction $(\mathsf{load}, \mathsf{id}, \mathbf{C}, w)$, compute

$$(T_1^w, L_1) \leftarrow \mathsf{Mult}_1(K, \mathsf{id}, \mathbf{C}, \{(\epsilon, \mathbf{s}_1)\}, L_1),$$

  where Mult_1 is the algorithm described in Figure 9 and ϵ denotes the empty binary string.
- *Add values in memory:* On instruction $(\mathsf{add}, \mathsf{id}, u, v, w)$, set

$$T_1^w := \big\{ (\mathsf{pos}_1, \mathbf{t}_1^u + \mathbf{t}_1^v \bmod q) \,\big|\, \mathsf{pos}_1 \in L_1, (\mathsf{pos}_1^u, \mathbf{t}_1^u) \in T_1^u,$$
$$(\mathsf{pos}_1^v, \mathbf{t}_1^v) \in T_1^v, \mathsf{pos}_1^u \subseteq \mathsf{pos}_1^v \subseteq \mathsf{pos}_1 \big\}.$$

- *Multiply input by memory value:* On instruction $(\mathsf{mult}, \mathsf{id}, \mathbf{C}, v, w)$, compute

$$(T_1^w, L_1) \leftarrow \mathsf{Mult}_1(K, \mathsf{id}, \mathbf{C}, T_1^v, L_1),$$

  where Mult_1 is the algorithm described in Figure 9.
- *Output from memory:* On instruction $(\mathsf{out}, \mathsf{id}, w)$, output the list

$$y_1 := \big\{ (H(\mathsf{pos}), x_1 \bmod \beta) \,\big|\, (\mathsf{pos}, \mathbf{t}_1) \in T_1^w,$$
$$\mathbf{t}_1 = (x_1, \hat{\mathbf{t}}_1), x_1 \in \mathbb{Z}_q, \hat{\mathbf{t}}_1 \in \mathbb{Z}_q^{d-1} \big\},$$

  where $H(a_1, \ldots, a_k) = \{i \in [k] \,|\, a_i = 1\}$.

Fig. 7. Homomorphic Secret Sharing - Evaluation for party $\mathcal{P}_1$.

instruction), the flags generated during that operation are appended to the string $\mathsf{pos}_0 \in \{0,1\}^*$. Adding a pseudorandom value $\mathsf{PRF}(K, \mathsf{id})$ before each rounding step guarantees that the shares are always close to uniform, and therefore the occurrences of positive flags are independent from one instruction to another. Finally, the output of Eval consists of a compression $H(\mathsf{pos}_0)$ of the flag sequence of $\mathcal{P}_0$ and the first component of $\mathbf{t}_0^w$, which is an additive share of $P(x_1, \ldots, x_n)$. The compression function H simply outputs the list of indices with a flag set to 1 (which will be constant in number). The use of H is crucial in obtaining succinct output shares, as the size of pos_0 is proportional to the size $|P|$ of the program.

In Fig. 7 we present the homomorphic evaluation procedure for party $\mathcal{P}_1$, which is similar to that of $\mathcal{P}_0$ but has an added degree of complexity, since $\mathcal{P}_1$ generates two different possible values for its additive share whenever it gets a positive flag, and must keep track of all possible combinations. The global variable L_1 in this algorithm is the list of binary strings which includes all possible sequences of flags of $\mathcal{P}_0$ – recall that whenever $\mathcal{P}_1$ has $\mathsf{flag}_1 = 0$ it knows that $\mathsf{flag}_0 = 0$, but if $\mathsf{flag}_1 = 1$ then flag_0 can be either 0 or 1. To each wire

---

Input $(K, \mathrm{id}, \mathbf{C}, \mathbf{t}, \mathrm{pos})$

Parse $\mathbf{C} = (\mathbf{c}_1, \ldots, \mathbf{c}_d)$
For each $i \in [d]$:
    $(\mathrm{flag}_i, z_i) \leftarrow \mathsf{Round}(0, \langle \mathbf{t}, \mathbf{c}_i \rangle + \mathsf{PRF}(K, (\mathrm{id}, i)) \mod q)$
    $(\mathrm{flag}'_i, v_i) \leftarrow \mathsf{Lift}(0, z_i)$
$\mathbf{t}' \leftarrow (v_1, \ldots, v_d)$
$\mathrm{pos}' \leftarrow \mathrm{pos}\|\mathrm{flag}_1\|\mathrm{flag}'_1\| \ldots \|\mathrm{flag}_d\|\mathrm{flag}'_d$

Output $(\mathbf{t}', \mathrm{pos}')$

Fig. 8. Algorithm Mult_0, employed by party $\mathcal{P}_0$ on loading and multiplication instructions.

Input $(K, \mathrm{id}, \mathbf{C}, T, L)$

Parse $\mathbf{C} = (\mathbf{c}_1, \ldots, \mathbf{c}_d)$, $T = ((\mathrm{pos}_1, \mathbf{t}_1), \ldots, (\mathrm{pos}_\ell, \mathbf{t}_\ell))$
For each $(i, j) \in [d] \times [\ell]$:
    $V_{ij} \leftarrow \emptyset$
    $(\mathrm{flag}_{ij}, z_{ij}^0, z_{ij}^1) \leftarrow \mathsf{Round}(1, \langle \mathbf{t}_j, \mathbf{c}_i \rangle - \mathsf{PRF}(K, (\mathrm{id}, i)) \mod q)$
    $(\mathrm{flag}_{ij}^0, v_{ij}^{00}, v_{ij}^{01}) \leftarrow \mathsf{Lift}(1, z_{ij}^0)$
    $V_{ij} \leftarrow V_{ij} \cup \{(00, v_{ij}^{00})\}$
    If $\mathrm{flag}_{ij}^0 = 1$:
        $V_{ij} \leftarrow V_{ij} \cup \{(01, v_{ij}^{01})\}$
    If $\mathrm{flag}_{ij} = 1$:
        $(\mathrm{flag}_{ij}^1, v_{ij}^{10}, v_{ij}^{11}) \leftarrow \mathsf{Lift}(1, z_{ij}^1)$
        $V_{ij} \leftarrow V_{ij} \cup \{(10, v_{ij}^{10})\}$
        If $\mathrm{flag}_{ij}^1 = 1$:
            $V_{ij} \leftarrow V_{ij} \cup \{(11, v_{ij}^{11})\}$
$T' \leftarrow \big\{ \big(\mathrm{pos}\|a_1\| \ldots \|a_d, (v_1, \ldots, v_d)\big) \,\big|\, j \in [\ell], \mathrm{pos} \in L,$
$\hspace{6cm} \mathrm{pos}_j \subseteq \mathrm{pos}, (a_i, v_i) \in V_{ij} \big\}$

$L' \leftarrow \big\{ \mathrm{pos} \,\big|\, (\mathrm{pos}, \mathbf{t}) \in T' \big\}$

Output (T', L')

Fig. 9. Algorithm Mult_1, employed by party $\mathcal{P}_1$ on loading and multiplication instructions.

$\mathsf{HSS.Dec}(y_0, y_1, \beta)$:   Parse the shares as $y_0 = (u_0, x_0)$ and $y_1 = \{(u_1^{(1)}, x_1^{(1)}), \ldots, (u_1^{(k)}, x_1^{(k)})\}$. Output $x_0 + x_1^{(i)} \mod \beta$, where i is the unique index such that $u_0 = u_1^{(i)}$.

Fig. 10. Homomorphic Secret Sharing - Decoding.

w in P we associate a list T_1^w of pairs of the form $(\mathsf{pos}_1, \mathbf{t}_1^w)$, where $\mathbf{t}_1^w$ is the additive share corresponding to the value of P at w and pos_1 is the corresponding sequence of flags. The output of the evaluation algorithm for $\mathcal{P}_1$ is a list of pairs of the same form as the output for $\mathcal{P}_0$, one for each possible flag sequence.

Finally, in the decoding algorithm, depicted in Fig. 10, we identify the additive shares x_0, x_1 which correspond to the same sequence of flags and add them to obtain $P(x_1, \ldots, x_n)$.

Remark 3. We omit an optimization step consisting of checking if the two values associated with a positive flag for $\mathcal{P}_1$ are the same, which provides a reduction of the flag probability by a factor of 2 in both rounding and lifting.

Remark 4. Like the BKS scheme, our protocol can also be converted into a secret-key HSS version, which is more efficient for those applications which do not require the public-key capabilities.

3.2   Rounding and Lifting

Below we present our rounding procedure and analyse its properties. The corresponding step in the BKS protocol consists of multiplying the share $v \in \mathbb{Z}_q$ by p/q and rounding it to the nearest integer to obtain a share in $\mathbb{Z}_p$. This introduces a correctness error with probability proportional to p/q (see Lemma 7). Our approach solves this issue by flagging instances in which an error could occur if both parties were to round their shares to the nearest integer and correcting it by having one party round up and the other round down in those instances.

Recall that we consider the representation $\mathbb{Z}_n = \{-\lceil (n-1)/2 \rceil, \ldots, \lfloor (n-1)/2 \rfloor\}$ for any $n \in \mathbb{N}$. We first define the operations RoundDown, RoundUp and RoundNear, which map a value v from $\mathbb{Z}_q$ to $\mathbb{Z}_p$ by scaling and then rounding it down, up, or to the nearest integer, respectively:

$$\mathsf{RoundDown}(v) = \lfloor (p/q) \cdot v \rfloor \quad \bmod p,$$
$$\mathsf{RoundUp}(v) = \lceil (p/q) \cdot v \rceil \quad \bmod p,$$
$$\mathsf{RoundNear}(v) = \lceil (p/q) \cdot v \rfloor \quad \bmod p.$$

The deterministic procedure Round, which takes as input a party identifier $\sigma \in \{0, 1\}$ and a value $v \in \mathbb{Z}_q$, is defined as follows:

$$\mathsf{Round}(0, v) = \begin{cases} (1, \mathsf{RoundDown}(v)), & \text{if } v \in \mathsf{bad}_{B_{\text{err}}}, \\ (0, \mathsf{RoundNear}(v)), & \text{otherwise,} \end{cases}$$

$$\mathsf{Round}(1, v) = \begin{cases} (1, \mathsf{RoundNear}(v), \mathsf{RoundUp}(v)), & \text{if } v \in \mathsf{bad}_{2B_{\text{err}}}, \\ (0, \mathsf{RoundNear}(v), \bot), & \text{otherwise,} \end{cases}$$

where $\mathsf{bad}_{B_{\text{err}}} = \{v \in \mathbb{Z}_q \mid |v \bmod (q/p)| \geq q/(2p) - B_{\text{err}}\}$ and $\mathsf{bad}_{2B_{\text{err}}}$ is analogously defined.

Lemma 5 (Rounding correctness). *Let $p, q, B_{err} \in \mathbb{N}$ be such that q is a multiple of p and $B_{err} < q/(4p)$. Then, for any $v_0, v_1 \in \mathbb{Z}_q$, $m \in \mathbb{Z}_p$ and $e \in \mathbb{Z}$ such that $|e| \leq B_{err}$ and*

$$v_0 + v_1 = (q/p) \cdot m + e \mod q,$$

the outputs $(\mathsf{flag}_0, z_0) \leftarrow \mathsf{Round}(0, v_0)$, $(\mathsf{flag}_1, z_1, z_1') \leftarrow \mathsf{Round}(1, v_1)$ satisfy the following:

(i) If $\mathsf{flag}_0 = 0$, then $z_0 + z_1 = m \mod p$.
(ii) If $\mathsf{flag}_0 = 1$, then $\mathsf{flag}_1 = 1$ and $z_0 + z_1' = m \mod p$.

Proof. Let v_0, v_1, m, e be such that $v_0 + v_1 = (q/p) \cdot m + e \mod q$ and $|e| \leq B_{err}$, and let $(\mathsf{flag}_0, z_0) \leftarrow \mathsf{Round}(0, v_0)$, $(\mathsf{flag}_1, z_1, z_1') \leftarrow \mathsf{Round}(1, v_1)$. To prove the first claim, assume that $\mathsf{flag}_0 = 0$. Then there exist $k, r \in \mathbb{Z}$ such that $v_0 = (q/p) \cdot k + r$ and $|r| < q/(2p) - B_{err}$. Therefore

$$v_1 = (q/p) \cdot (m - k) + e - r \mod q$$

and $|e - r| \leq |e| + |r| < q/(2p)$. It follows that

$$z_0 = \lceil (p/q) \cdot v_0 \rfloor = \lceil k + \underbrace{(p/q) \cdot r}_{\in (-1/2, 1/2)} \rfloor = k \mod p,$$

$$z_1 = \lceil (p/q) \cdot v_1 \rfloor = \lceil m - k + \underbrace{(p/q) \cdot (e - r)}_{\in (-1/2, 1/2)} \rfloor = m - k \mod p,$$

which shows that $z_0 + z_1 = m \mod p$.

We now prove the second claim. If $\mathsf{flag}_0 = 1$, there exist $k, r \in \mathbb{Z}$ such that $v_0 = (q/p) \cdot k + r$ and $q/(2p) - B_{err} \leq r \leq q/(2p) + B_{err}$. The other share is then $v_1 = (q/p) \cdot (m - k) + e - r \mod q$, where $q/(2p) - 2B_{err} \leq e - r \leq q/(2p) + 2B_{err}$, since $|e| \leq B_{err}$. Therefore $|v_1 \mod (q/p)| \geq q/(2p) - 2B_{err}$ and $\mathsf{flag}_1 = 1$. Moreover, observe that $e < r$ and $(p/q) \cdot (r - e) < 1$, since

$$r \leq q/(2p) + B_{err} < q/p - B_{err} \leq q/p + e.$$

It follows that

$$z_0 = \lfloor (p/q) \cdot v_0 \rfloor = \lfloor k + \underbrace{(p/q) \cdot r}_{\in [0, 1)} \rfloor = k \mod p,$$

$$z_1' = \lceil (p/q) \cdot v_1 \rceil = \lceil m - k + \underbrace{(p/q) \cdot (e - r)}_{\in (-1, 0]} \rceil = m - k \mod p,$$

and therefore $z_0 + z_1' = m \mod p$. $\qquad\square$

Lemma 6 (Rounding flag probability). *Let $p, q, B_{err} \in \mathbb{N}$ be such that q is a multiple of p and $B_{err} < q/(4p)$. Let $v_0, v_1 \in \mathbb{Z}_q$ be uniformly random subject to*

$$v_0 + v_1 = (q/p) \cdot m + e \mod q,$$

where $m \in \mathbb{Z}_p$ *and* $|e| \leq B_{\text{err}}$ *are fixed. Let also* $(\text{flag}_1, z_1, z_1') \leftarrow \text{Round}(1, v_1)$. *Then*

$$\Pr[\text{flag}_1 = 1 \text{ and } z_1 \neq z_1'] = 2B_{\text{err}} \cdot (p/q).$$

Proof. Let $u_1 = v_1 \mod (q/p)$ and note that u_1 is uniformly distributed in $\mathbb{Z}_{q/p}$. Recall that $\text{flag}_1 = 1$ if and only if $|u_1| \geq q/(2p) - 2B_{\text{err}}$. Moreover, $\text{RoundNear}(v_1) \neq \text{RoundUp}(v_1)$ if and only if the fractional part of $(p/q) \cdot v_1$ is in the interval $(0, 1/2)$, which holds if and only if $0 < u_1 < q/(2p)$. Define the set

$$S = \left\{ u \in \mathbb{Z}_{q/p} \,\middle|\, q/(2p) - 2B_{\text{err}} \leq u < q/(2p) \right\}.$$

If $q/p = 2k + 1$ for some $k \in \mathbb{N}$, then $S = \{k - 2B_{\text{err}} + 1, \ldots, k\}$, while if $q/p = 2k$ then $S = \{k - 2B_{\text{err}}, \ldots, k - 1\}$. In both cases $|S| = 2B_{\text{err}}$. Therefore $\Pr[\text{flag}_1 = 1 \text{ and } z_1 \neq z_1'] = \Pr[u_1 \in S] = |S| \cdot (p/q) = 2B_{\text{err}} \cdot (p/q)$.   □

Lemma 7 (Rounding error probability). *Let* $p, q, B_{\text{err}} \in \mathbb{N}$ *be such that* q *is a multiple of* p *and* $B_{\text{err}} < q/(4p)$. *Let* $v_0, v_1 \in \mathbb{Z}_q$ *be random subject to*

$$v_0 + v_1 = (q/p) \cdot m + e \mod q,$$

where $m \in \mathbb{Z}_p$ *and* $|e| \leq B_{\text{err}}$ *are fixed. Then*

$$\Pr[\text{RoundNear}(v_0) + \text{RoundNear}(v_1) \neq m \mod p] \geq (|e| - 1) \cdot (p/q).$$

Proof. Define $u_\sigma = v_\sigma \mod (q/p)$, for $\sigma = 0, 1$, and assume first that $e < 0$. Observe that, if $u_0, u_1 \in (0, q/(2p))$, then a rounding error occurs: since $e = u_0 + u_1 \mod (q/p)$ and $-(q/p) < e < 0$, it must be the case that $e = u_0 + u_1 - (q/p)$, and therefore $\text{RoundNear}(v_0) + \text{RoundNear}(v_1) = m - 1$. If $q/p = 2k + 1$ for some $k \in \mathbb{N}$, then

$$\Pr[u_0, u_1 \in (0, q/(2p))] = \Pr[u_0 \in \{k + e + 1, \ldots, k\}] = |e| \cdot (p/q).$$

Alternatively, if $q/p = 2k$, then

$$\Pr[u_0, u_1 \in (0, q/(2p))] = \Pr[u_0 \in \{k + e + 1, \ldots, k - 1\}] = (|e| - 1) \cdot (p/q).$$

By a similar reasoning it can be seen that in the case $e \geq 0$ a rounding error occurs with probability at least $|e| \cdot (p/q)$, if q/p is odd, or $(|e| + 1) \cdot (p/q)$, if q/p is even.   □

Now we present the lifting procedure, which always follows rounding. In the BKS protocol this step is simply an inclusion: a share $z \in \mathbb{Z}_q$ becomes $z \in \mathbb{Z}_p$. However, as shown in Lemma 10, a correctness error occurs with probability proportional to $1/p$. Again, our new procedure overcomes this issue by predicting and correcting possible errors to guarantee that additive shares modulo p are always converted into shares modulo q of the same secret value.

The deterministic procedure Lift, which takes as input a party identifier $\sigma \in \{0,1\}$ and a value $z \in \mathbb{Z}_p$, is defined as follows:

$$\mathsf{Lift}(0,z) = \begin{cases} (1,z), & \text{if } z \in \mathsf{bad}^+_{B_{\max}}, \\ (1,z+p), & \text{if } z \in \mathsf{bad}^-_{B_{\max}}, \\ (0,z), & \text{otherwise,} \end{cases}$$

$$\mathsf{Lift}(1,z) = \begin{cases} (1,z,z-p), & \text{if } z \in \mathsf{bad}^+_{2B_{\max}}, \\ (1,z,z), & \text{if } z \in \mathsf{bad}^-_{2B_{\max}}, \\ (0,z,\bot), & \text{otherwise,} \end{cases}$$

where $\mathsf{bad}^+_{B_{\max}} = [p/2 - B, p/2)$, $\mathsf{bad}^-_{B_{\max}} = [-p/2, -p/2 + B]$, and $\mathsf{bad}^+_{2B_{\max}}$, $\mathsf{bad}^-_{2B_{\max}}$ are analogously defined. The proofs of the following three lemmas can be found in the full version of this paper.

Lemma 8 (Lifting correctness). *Let* $p, B_{\max} \in \mathbb{N}$ *be such that* $B_{\max} < p/6$. *Then, for any* $z_0, z_1 \in \mathbb{Z}_p$, $m \in \mathbb{Z}$ *such that* $|m| \leq B_{\max}$ *and*

$$z_0 + z_1 = m \mod p,$$

the outputs $(\mathsf{flag}_0, v_0) \leftarrow \mathsf{Lift}(0, z_0)$, $(\mathsf{flag}_1, v_1, v_1') \leftarrow \mathsf{Lift}(1, z_1)$ *satisfy the following:*

(i) If $\mathsf{flag}_0 = 0$, *then* $v_0 + v_1 = m$ *over* $\mathbb{Z}$.
(ii) If $\mathsf{flag}_0 = 1$, *then* $\mathsf{flag}_1 = 1$ *and* $v_0 + v_1' = m$ *over* $\mathbb{Z}$.

Lemma 9 (Lifting flag probability). *Let* $p, B_{\max} \in \mathbb{N}$ *be such that* $B_{\max} < p/6$. *Let* $z_0, z_1 \in \mathbb{Z}_p$ *be random subject to*

$$z_0 + z_1 = m \mod p,$$

where $m \in \mathbb{Z}_p$. *Let also* $(\mathsf{flag}_1, v_1, v_1') \leftarrow \mathsf{Lift}(1, z_1)$. *Then*

$$\Pr[\mathsf{flag}_1 = 1 \text{ and } v_1 \neq v_1'] = 2B_{\max}/p.$$

Lemma 10 (Lifting error probability). *Let* $p, B_{\max} \in \mathbb{N}$ *be such that* $B_{\max} < p/6$. *Let* $z_0, z_1 \in \mathbb{Z}_p$ *be random subject to*

$$z_0 + z_1 = m \mod p,$$

where $m \in \mathbb{Z}_p$. *Then*

$$\Pr[z_0 + z_1 \neq m] \geq (|m| - 1)/p.$$

We can now prove our main result.

Theorem 1. (HSS correctness and security). *Let* PKE *be a public-key encryption scheme with plaintext space* $\mathcal{R}_p$ *and ciphertext space* $\mathcal{R}_q^d$, *satisfying the properties of nearly linear decryption (with error bound* B_{err}*) and pseudorandom ciphertexts, such that* $B_{\mathsf{err}} < q/(4p)$. *Let also* PRF *be a pseudorandom function taking values in* $\mathcal{R}_q$. *Then the 2-party homomorphic secret sharing* *scheme described in Figs. 4, 5, 6, 7, 8, 9 and 10 is perfectly correct and secure, as per Definition 1, and supports homomorphic evaluation of polynomial-sized RMS programs with magnitude bound B_{max} and output modulus β such that $\beta \leq B_{\mathsf{max}} < p/6$.*

Proof. Security follows immediately from the security of the BKS HSS [14], as the algorithms Gen and Enc are identical in the two schemes and the security definition is independent of the Eval algorithm. Note that this is a consequence of KDM security and of the fact that the evaluation keys individually hide the secret encryption key.

We will now show that our scheme satisfies perfect correctness. Let $y_0 = (H(\mathsf{pos}_0), z_0)$ and $y_1 = \{(H(\mathsf{pos}_1^{(1)}), z_1^{(1)}), \ldots, (H(\mathsf{pos}_1^{(k)}), z_1^{(k)})\}$ be the evaluated shares corresponding to an RMS program P on input $x_1, \ldots, x_n$.

Observe that, according to the definition of the algorithms Mult_0 and Mult_1, there always exists $i^* \in [k]$ such that $\mathsf{pos}_1^{(i^*)} = \mathsf{pos}_0$. This follows from the fact that, at any rounding or lifting step with position tag pos, party $\mathcal{P}_1$ always computes a value associated to $\mathsf{pos}\|0$ and, by part (ii) of Lemmas 5 and 8, if $\mathcal{P}_0$ has a value associated to $\mathsf{pos}\|1$ then so does $\mathcal{P}_1$. Furthermore, the index i^* is unique, since the binary strings $\mathsf{pos}_1^{(j)}$ are all distinct. Since the compression function H is injective, the only index i such that $H(\mathsf{pos}_1^{(i)}) = H(\mathsf{pos}_0)$ is i^*.

We will show below that, during homomorphic evaluation of P, for all wires w we have

$$\mathbf{t}_0^w + \mathbf{t}_1^w = x^w \mathbf{s} \quad \bmod q \tag{1}$$

whenever $(\mathsf{pos}_1, \mathbf{t}_1^w) \in T_1^w$ and $\mathsf{pos}_1^w = \mathsf{pos}_0^w$, where pos_0^w is the flag sequence pos_0 of $\mathcal{P}_0$ at the time wire w is evaluated, $x^w \in \mathcal{R}$ denotes the value of P at w and $\mathbf{s} = (1, \hat{\mathbf{s}}) \in \mathcal{R} \times \mathcal{R}^{d-1}$ is the PKE secret key.

The final output will be $\mathsf{Dec}(y_0, y_1, \beta) = z_0 + z_1^{(i^*)} \bmod \beta$, where $(z_0, \hat{\mathbf{t}}_0) = \mathbf{t}_0^w$, $(z_1^{(i^*)}, \hat{\mathbf{t}}_1) = \mathbf{t}_1^w$, $(\mathsf{pos}_1^{(i^*)}, \mathbf{t}_1^w) \in T_1^w$ for an output wire w and $\mathsf{pos}_1^{(i^*)} = \mathsf{pos}_0$. If Eq. (1) holds, then by looking only at the first component of each vector in the equation we see

$$z_0 + z_1^{(i^*)} = x^w \cdot 1 = P(x_1, \ldots, x_n) \quad \bmod q,$$

hence $\mathsf{Dec}(y_0, y_1, \beta) = P(x_1, \ldots, x_n)$ with probability 1.[3]

It remains only to check that Eq. (1) holds for every instruction in P of type load, add or mult.

- For instruction $(\mathsf{load}, \mathsf{id}, (\mathbf{c}_1, \ldots, \mathbf{c}_d), w)$, where $\mathbf{c}_i \leftarrow \mathsf{PKE.OKDM}(\mathsf{pk}, y, i)$, by the nearly linear decryption property we have

$$(\mathbf{t}_0^w)_i + (\mathbf{t}_1^w)_i = \langle \mathbf{s}_0, \mathbf{c}_i \rangle + \mathsf{PRF}(K, (\mathsf{id}, i)) + \langle \mathbf{s}_1, \mathbf{c}_j \rangle - \mathsf{PRF}(K, (\mathsf{id}, i))$$
$$= \langle \mathbf{s}, \mathbf{c}_i \rangle = (q/p) \cdot y \cdot s_i + e_i \quad \bmod q$$

---

[3] We assume here that β divides q, so that shares mod q are also shares mod β. If we wish to avoid this assumption, we can simply perform a lifting step to obtain shares over $\mathbb{Z}$ before reducing them mod β.

for some $|e_i| \leq B_{\mathsf{err}}.$[4] We can thus apply Lemma 5 followed by Lemma 8 to conclude that, for the matching flags (i.e. $\mathsf{pos}_1^w = \mathsf{pos}_0^w$), the corresponding shares $\mathbf{t}_0^w, \mathbf{t}_1^w$ satisfy $\mathbf{t}_0^w + \mathbf{t}_1^w = y\mathbf{s} \mod q$.

- For instruction $(\mathsf{add}, \mathsf{id}, u, v, w)$, assume Eq. (1) holds for $(\mathbf{t}_0^u, \mathbf{t}_1^u)$ and $(\mathbf{t}_0^v, \mathbf{t}_1^v)$, where $\mathsf{pos}_1^u \subseteq \mathsf{pos}_1^v \subseteq \mathsf{pos}_1^w$ and $\mathsf{pos}_0^\tau = \mathsf{pos}_1^\tau$ for $\tau \in \{u, v, w\}$. Then

$$\mathbf{t}_0^w + \mathbf{t}_1^w = \mathbf{t}_0^u + \mathbf{t}_0^v + \mathbf{t}_1^u + \mathbf{t}_1^v = x^u\mathbf{s} + x^v\mathbf{s} = x^w\mathbf{s} \mod q.$$

- For instruction $(\mathsf{mult}, \mathsf{id}, (\mathbf{c}_1, \ldots, \mathbf{c}_d), v, w)$, assuming Eq. (1) holds for $(\mathbf{t}_0^v, \mathbf{t}_1^v)$ we have

$$(\mathbf{t}_0^w)_i + (\mathbf{t}_1^w)_i = \langle \mathbf{t}_0^v, \mathbf{c}_i \rangle + \mathsf{PRF}(K, (\mathsf{id}, i)) + \langle \mathbf{t}_1^v, \mathbf{c}_j \rangle - \mathsf{PRF}(K, (\mathsf{id}, i))$$
$$= x^v \langle \mathbf{s}, \mathbf{c}_i \rangle = (q/p)x^v \cdot y \cdot s_i + e_i \mod q$$

and as in the load instruction we conclude that $\mathbf{t}_0^w + \mathbf{t}_1^w = x^v\, y\, \mathbf{s} \mod q$.

$\square$

3.3   Impossibility of Local Share Conversion

The next theorem shows that the local share conversion procedure that lies at the heart of lattice-based HSS cannot achieve perfect correctness with additive reconstruction. Therefore one must either allow correctness error (which can only be made negligible with a superpolynomial modulus) or relax the requirement for reconstruction.

Theorem 2 (Correctness error of share conversion). *Let* $m \in \mathbb{Z}_p$ *and* $e \in D$, *where* $\{0, 1, -1\} \subseteq D \subseteq (-q/(2p), q/(2p))$. *Let also* $v_0, v_1 \in \mathbb{Z}_q$ *be sampled uniformly subject to*

$$v_0 + v_1 = (q/p) \cdot m + e \mod q.$$

Then, for any local share conversion functions $g_0, g_1 : \mathbb{Z}_q \to \mathbb{Z}_q$, *there exist* $m \in \mathbb{Z}_p$ *and* $e \in D$ *such that*

$$\Pr[g_0(v_0) + g_1(v_1) \neq m \mod q] \geq p/(3q).$$

Proof. We show that in each interval $I_k \subseteq \mathbb{Z}_q$ of the form $I_k := [k \cdot q/p, (k+1) \cdot q/p)$ there exists $v_0 \in I_k$ such that an error $g_0(v_0) + g_1(v_1) \neq m$ occurs for at least one of the pairs $(m, e) := (0, 0)$, $(m, e) := (1, -1)$ or $(m, e) := (0, 1)$. Since there are p disjoint intervals I_k, one of these three choices of (m, e) must have at least $p/3$ values v_0 in the above conditions and the result follows from the fact that v_0 is uniform.

To prove the above claim, consider $v_0 := k \cdot q/p$ and $v_1 := -v_0$. If $g_0(v_0) + g_1(v_1) \neq 0$ we have found an error for $(m, e) := (0, 0)$, as $v_0 + v_1 = 0$ and $v_0 \in I_k$. Meanwhile, $v_0' := (k+1) \cdot q/p - 1$ satisfies $v_0' + v_1 = q/p \cdot 1 - 1$, hence

---

[4] Here we again consider the case $\mathcal{R} = \mathbb{Z}$ for simplicity. For $\mathcal{R}$ of dimension N, the equation applies to each coordinate of y.

if $g_0(v_0') + g_1(v_1) \neq 1$ we have found an error for $(m, e) := (1, -1)$. Suppose now that $g_0(v_0) + g_1(v_1) = 0$ and $g_0(v_0') + g_1(v_1) = 1$. Then $g_0(v_0) \neq g_0(v_0')$ and there must exist $\tilde{v}_0 \in [v_0, v_0')$ such that $g_0(\tilde{v}_0) \neq g_0(\tilde{v}_0 + 1)$. Note that $\tilde{v}_0, \tilde{v}_0 + 1 \in I_k$. Then, unless an error occurs with $\tilde{v}_0$ and $(m, e) := (0, 0)$ or $\tilde{v}_0 + 1$ and $(m, e) := (0, 1)$, by taking $\tilde{v}_1 := -\tilde{v}_0$ we obtain

$$g_0(\tilde{v}_0) + g_1(\tilde{v}_1) = g_0(\tilde{v}_0 + 1) + g_1(\tilde{v}_1) = 0,$$

since $\tilde{v}_0 + \tilde{v}_1 = 0$ and $(\tilde{v}_0 + 1) + \tilde{v}_1 = 1$. This contradicts the assumption $g_0(\tilde{v}_0) \neq g_0(\tilde{v}_0 + 1)$. □

4   Efficiency and Parameters

In this section we compute concrete parameters for our HSS scheme and compare them with the BKS scheme [14]. The next lemma gives us an expression for the average number of elements of the list that constitutes the share y_1 of party $\mathcal{P}_1$ after evaluating a program P. We are then able to choose parameters such that this number is bounded by a constant. Since the running time of the evaluation algorithm of $\mathcal{P}_1$ is proportional to this quantity, the lemma also implies that it runs in expected polynomial time.

Lemma 11 (Expected share size). *Consider the HSS scheme described above, with ciphertext space $\mathcal{R}_q^d$, where $\mathcal{R} = \mathbb{Z}[X]/(X^N + 1)$. Let P be an RMS program of multiplicative size $|P|$. Denote by p_{round}, p_{lift} the probabilities of party $\mathcal{P}_1$ having a positive flag in a single rounding or lifting step, respectively. Then the expected total number E of terminal values in the homomorphic evaluation of P by $\mathcal{P}_1$ is*

$$E = \left((1 + p_{\mathsf{round}})(1 + p_{\mathsf{lift}})\right)^{dN|P|}.$$

We defer the proof of Lemma 11 to the full version. As a consequence of Lemmas 6, 9 and 11, we obtain the following bound, which we can use to choose parameters for the HSS scheme:

$$E \leq \left((1 + 2B_{\mathsf{err}}p/q)(1 + 2B_{\mathsf{max}}/p)\right)^{dN|P|}.$$

We instantiate PKE with the Ring-LWE based encryption scheme of Lyubashevsky, Peikert and Regev [27] over the ring $\mathcal{R} = \mathbb{Z}[X]/(X^N + 1)$, giving us $B_{\mathsf{err}} = 1$, $d = 2$. Then, if we wish to bound the expected number of terminal values E by some value $\gamma > 1$, setting $p \geq 8B_{\mathsf{max}}N|P|/\ln\gamma$ and $q \geq 8pN|P|/\ln\gamma$ gives

$$E \leq (1 + \ln\gamma/(4N|P|))^{4N|P|} \leq \gamma,$$

which justifies that γ is indeed an upper bound. For instance, if we choose $\gamma = 2$, party $\mathcal{P}_1$ will have, on average, a single positive flag throughout the homomorphic evaluation and two terminal values on which to perform reconstruction.

Table 3. HSS parameters for $|P| = 2^{10}$, $\gamma = 2$.

$B_{\max}$	N	$\log q$	Security
2	2048	51	147.3
2^{16}	2048	66	109.4
2^{32}	2048	82	86.0
2^{64}	4096	116	122.9
2^{128}	8192	182	159.5
2^{256}	8192	310	89.1

Table 4. HSS parameters for $|P| = 2^{20}$, $\gamma = 2$.

$B_{\max}$	N	$\log q$	Security
2	2048	71	100.9
2^{16}	2048	86	81.6
2^{32}	4096	104	139.0
2^{64}	4096	136	103.0
2^{128}	8192	202	141.7
2^{256}	8192	330	83.6

Table 5. BKS HSS parameters, with error probability 2^{-40}.

$B_{\max}$	N	$\log q$	Security
2	4096	137	103.3
2^{16}	4096	167	83.7
2^{32}	8192	203	142.0
2^{64}	8192	267	104.9
2^{128}	16384	399	143.9
2^{256}	16384	655	84.6

In Tables 3 and 4 we present parameters of our scheme in this RLWE instantiation, namely the ring dimension N and the ciphertext modulus q, when we choose the bound $\gamma = 2$ for the expected number of terminal values and maximum program sizes 2^{10} and 2^{20}, respectively. These are given in function of the magnitude bound $B_{\max}$ of plaintexts during the computation. For comparison, Table 5 shows the parameters for the corresponding instantiation of the BKS HSS scheme. We observe that our scheme reduces the size of the modulus q by nearly a factor of 2 for programs with up to 2^{20} operations (or by a greater factor, if we further restrict the program size) while also reducing N by a factor of 2 and attaining similarly high estimated computational security.

The security estimates on Tables 3, 4 and 5 were obtained by computing, for magnitude bound $B_{\max}$, the smallest pair (N, q) with at least 80 bits of computational security, as predicted by the lattice estimator tool of Albrecht et al. [1]. Note that the parameters of the BKS HSS scheme are also dependent on the size of the program P. The parameters on Table 5 correspond to a correctness error probability of 2^{-40} for *each* (multiplicative) operation in P.

The parameter γ can be adjusted to reduce the frequency of raised flags for a relatively small cost in the size of lattice parameters. For instance, setting $\gamma = 1.01$ boosts the probability that there are no raised flags in the entire computation to at least $1 - (\gamma - 1) = 0.99$, at the price of increasing the modulus q by a factor of $(\ln 2/\ln 1.01)^2 \approx 2^{12}$, compared to the choice $\gamma = 2$.

On the other hand, since the size of the input shares is much larger than the size of the output shares, it can make sense to choose larger parameter γ for certain applications. One should note though, that if the parties wish to execute linear postprocessing on the output shares (e.g., a counting query over a large database), then the total expected number of shares scales with 2^{γ}.

5   Applications

Our scheme retains most of the standard applications of HSS, even without having the usual property of additive reconstruction. It is particularly suited for scenarios where there is asymmetry between the parties performing the computation (e.g. two servers of different sizes).

Private Database Queries. We explore in detail one of the applications of the BKS HSS scheme and show that our construction provides an overall improvement in efficiency. A 2-server private database query protocol involves two non-colluding servers, each holding a copy of a public database DB, and a client, who can issue queries on the database. The protocol should allow the client to obtain the answer of its query while hiding both the query and the answer from the servers. HSS gives a simple solution to this problem with only one round of communication: in this protocol the client sends an encryption of its query to both servers, who then homomorphically compute shares of the answer and return them to the client. HSS for branching programs supports many expressive queries, such as conjunctive keyword search and pattern matching.

Remark 5. Unlike with secure 2-party computation, in this setting there are no concerns with the security of the reconstruction procedure. We can simply have both servers send their shares to the client, who evaluates the decoding algorithm directly with minimal computational cost.

Linear Post-processing of Shares. There are scenarios in which the additive reconstruction property of other HSS schemes is quite useful, such as when computing a counting query. This type of query returns the number of elements of the database satisfying some predicate Q, which can be written as $\sum_{x \in \text{DB}} Q(x)$, where $Q(x) = 1$ if x satisfies Q and $Q(x) = 0$ otherwise. Because of this additive representation, instead of homomorphically evaluating the query on the database at once, the servers can evaluate the predicate individually on each database element. The shares q_σ^x corresponding to each element x can then be locally summed to obtain $q_\sigma = \sum_{x \in \text{DB}} q_\sigma^x$ and this value sent to the client, who recovers the result of the query as $q_0 + q_1 \mod \beta$. In the BKS HSS scheme, this approach allows using the optimal case of $B_{\text{max}} = 2$ on the individual HSS evaluations, even though the query output is not bounded by 2.

Although our construction does not benefit from the additive reconstruction property, we can employ a similar technique and show that even in this setting we obtain a performance improvement. Recall that, in our scheme, a share evaluated by party $\mathcal{P}_0$ is of the form (u, q) where u is the compression of the flag sequence of $\mathcal{P}_0$ and q is the additive share of the result, while a share evaluated by $\mathcal{P}_1$ is a list of pairs of the same form. $\mathcal{P}_0$ can homomorphically evaluate Q on each $x \in \text{DB}$ to obtain (u_0^x, q_0^x) and then send $y_0 = (u_0^{x_1}, \ldots, u_0^{x_M}, q_0 := \sum_{x \in \text{DB}} q_0^x)$ as its final share to the client, where $M = |\text{DB}|$ is the database size. Similarly, $\mathcal{P}_1$ obtains M lists from evaluating Q on every database element and its output to the client is a list of shares of the same form as y_0, one for each possible choice of a single element from each of the M lists. The client can then reconstruct by summing q_0 and the corresponding value from $\mathcal{P}_1$'s share. This solution may look terribly inefficient for the fact that the size of $\mathcal{P}_1$'s output is proportional to the product of the number of elements of all M lists, but we can set the probability of any list having more than one element to be very low.

A Concrete Example. Consider a database DB with entries of the form (x, W_x) where x is a document and W_x is a list of keywords. Given a target list of keywords W, we wish to count the number of documents containing all the keywords in W. That is, we consider a counting query for the predicate $Q_W(x, W_x) = 1$ if $W \subseteq W_x$. Suppose the database size is $M = 1024$, the client's query consists of 4 keywords, and each document has 10 keywords with 128 bits of length. This can be achieved by an RMS program P with around $|P| = 5120$ multiplications. For this application the BKS scheme requires as parameters $N = 4096$ and $\log q = 137$, which gives a share size of $3N \log q \approx 210 \, \text{kB}$ for each input bit, for a total of $107 \, \text{MB}$ of communication to each server. In our scheme, choosing $\gamma = 1.0001$ allows us to use $N = 2048$, $\log q = 81$. This results in an input share size of $60.7 \, \text{kB}$ and a total of $31 \, \text{MB}$ sent from client to server. Since the (expected) size of the compressed flag sequence is $|H(\mathsf{pos})| = \gamma \log |\mathsf{pos}|$ and the output modulus of the query should be $\beta = M$, the size of the first output share is $|y_0| = M\gamma \log(4N|P|) + \log \beta \approx 3.2 \, \text{kB}$ and the size of the second output share is $|y_1| = \gamma^M |y_0| \approx 3.5 \, \text{kB}$. Meanwhile, the output share size in BKS is only $\log \beta \approx 1.2B$ for both servers. Note that only a single output share is sent from each server to the client, so the bulk of communication lies in the input sharing step for both approaches.

A drawback of our solution is that the size of the output shares grows with the size of the database (linearly for $\mathcal{P}_0$, and exponentially with base γ for $\mathcal{P}_1$). However, the communication bottleneck is still the size of the input shares and not of the output, as illustrated in the example above. For more general queries, for which this technique relying on additive reconstruction is not applicable, our scheme again provides an improvement over BKS HSS in both computation and communication costs.

Acknowledgments. Thomas Attema was supported by the Vraaggestuurd Programma Cyber Security & Resilience, part of the Dutch Top Sector High Tech Systems and Materials program. Pedro Capitão and Lisa Kohl have been supported by the NWO Gravitation project QSC.

References

1. Albrecht, M.R., Player, R., Scott, S.: On the concrete hardness of learning with errors. Cryptology ePrint Archive, Report 2015/046 (2015). https://eprint.iacr.org/2015/046
2. Alwen, J., Krenn, S., Pietrzak, K., Wichs, D.: Learning with rounding, revisited. In: Canetti, R., Garay, J.A. (eds.) CRYPTO 2013, Part I. LNCS, vol. 8042, pp. 57–74. Springer, Heidelberg (2013). https://doi.org/10.1007/978-3-642-40041-4_4
3. Applebaum, B., Cash, D., Peikert, C., Sahai, A.: Fast cryptographic primitives and circular-secure encryption based on hard learning problems. In: Halevi, S. (ed.) CRYPTO 2009. LNCS, vol. 5677, pp. 595–618. Springer, Heidelberg (2009). https://doi.org/10.1007/978-3-642-03356-8_35
4. Banerjee, A., Peikert, C., Rosen, A.: Pseudorandom functions and lattices. In: Pointcheval, D., Johansson, T. (eds.) EUROCRYPT 2012. LNCS, vol. 7237, pp. 719–737. Springer, Heidelberg (2012). https://doi.org/10.1007/978-3-642-29011-4_42

5. Bogdanov, A., Guo, S., Masny, D., Richelson, S., Rosen, A.: On the hardness of learning with rounding over small modulus. In: Kushilevitz, E., Malkin, T. (eds.) TCC 2016-A, Part I. LNCS, vol. 9562, pp. 209–224. Springer, Heidelberg (2016). https://doi.org/10.1007/978-3-662-49096-9_9
6. Boyle, E., Couteau, G., Gilboa, N., Ishai, Y.: Compressing vector OLE. In: Lie, D., Mannan, M., Backes, M., Wang, X. (eds.) ACM CCS 2018, pp. 896–912. ACM Press, October 2018
7. Boyle, E., Couteau, G., Gilboa, N., Ishai, Y., Kohl, L., Scholl, P.: Efficient pseudorandom correlation generators: silent OT extension and more. In: Boldyreva, A., Micciancio, D. (eds.) CRYPTO 2019, Part III. LNCS, vol. 11694, pp. 489–518. Springer, Heidelberg (2019). https://doi.org/10.1007/978-3-030-26954-8_16
8. Boyle, E., Couteau, G., Gilboa, N., Ishai, Y., Orrù, M.: Homomorphic secret sharing: optimizations and applications. In: Thuraisingham, B.M., Evans, D., Malkin, T., Xu, D. (eds.) ACM CCS 2017, pp. 2105–2122. ACM Press, October/November 2017
9. Boyle, E., Gilboa, N., Ishai, Y.: Function secret sharing. In: Oswald, E., Fischlin, M. (eds.) EUROCRYPT 2015, Part II. LNCS, vol. 9057, pp. 337–367. Springer, Heidelberg (2015). https://doi.org/10.1007/978-3-662-46803-6_12
10. Boyle, E., Gilboa, N., Ishai, Y.: Breaking the circuit size barrier for secure computation under DDH. In: Robshaw, M., Katz, J. (eds.) CRYPTO 2016, Part I. LNCS, vol. 9814, pp. 509–539. Springer, Heidelberg (2016). https://doi.org/10.1007/978-3-662-53018-4_19
11. Boyle, E., Gilboa, N., Ishai, Y.: Function secret sharing: improvements and extensions. In: Weippl, E.R., Katzenbeisser, S., Kruegel, C., Myers, A.C., Halevi, S. (eds.) ACM CCS 2016, pp. 1292–1303. ACM Press, October 2016
12. Boyle, E., Gilboa, N., Ishai, Y.: Group-Based Secure Computation: Optimizing Rounds, Communication, and Computation. In: Coron, J.-S., Nielsen, J.B. (eds.) EUROCRYPT 2017, Part II. LNCS, vol. 10211, pp. 163–193. Springer, Cham (2017). https://doi.org/10.1007/978-3-319-56614-6_6
13. Boyle, E., Gilboa, N., Ishai, Y., Lin, H., Tessaro, S.: Foundations of homomorphic secret sharing. In: Karlin, A.R. (ed.) ITCS 2018, vol. 94, pp. 21:1–21:21. LIPIcs, January 2018
14. Boyle, E., Kohl, L., Scholl, P.: Homomorphic secret sharing from lattices without FHE. In: Ishai, Y., Rijmen, V. (eds.) EUROCRYPT 2019, Part II. LNCS, vol. 11477, pp. 3–33. Springer, Cham (2019). https://doi.org/10.1007/978-3-030-17656-3_1
15. Chen, H., Huang, Z., Laine, K., Rindal, P.: Labeled PSI from fully homomorphic encryption with malicious security. In: Lie, D., Mannan, M., Backes, M., Wang, X. (eds.) ACM CCS 2018, pp. 1223–1237. ACM Press, October 2018
16. Chillotti, I., Orsini, E., Scholl, P., Smart, N.P., Van Leeuwen, B.: Scooby: improved multi-party homomorphic secret sharing based on FHE. In: Galdi, C., Jarecki, S. (eds.) International Conference on Security and Cryptography for Networks, pp. 540–563. Springer, Cham (2022). https://doi.org/10.1007/978-3-031-14791-3_24
17. Chor, B., Gilboa, N., Naor, M.: Private information retrieval by keywords. Citeseer (1997)
18. Cong, K., et al.: Labeled PSI from homomorphic encryption with reduced computation and communication, pp. 1135–1150. ACM Press (2021)
19. Corrigan-Gibbs, H., Boneh, D., Mazières, D.: Riposte: an anonymous messaging system handling millions of users. In: 2015 IEEE Symposium on Security and Privacy, pp. 321–338. IEEE Computer Society Press, May 2015

20. Couteau, G., Meyer, P.: Breaking the circuit size barrier for secure computation under Quasi-Polynomial LPN. In: Canteaut, A., Standaert, F.X. (eds.) EURO-CRYPT 2021, Part II. LNCS, vol. 12697, pp. 842–870. Springer, Heidelberg (2021). https://doi.org/10.1007/978-3-030-77886-6_29

21. Dinur, I., Keller, N., Klein, O.: An optimal distributed discrete log protocol with applications to homomorphic secret sharing. In: Shacham, H., Boldyreva, A. (eds.) CRYPTO 2018, Part III. LNCS, vol. 10993, pp. 213–242. Springer, Heidelberg (2018). https://doi.org/10.1007/978-3-319-96878-0_8

22. Dodis, Y., Halevi, S., Rothblum, R.D., Wichs, D.: Spooky encryption and its applications. In: Robshaw, M., Katz, J. (eds.) CRYPTO 2016, Part III. LNCS, vol. 9816, pp. 93–122. Springer, Heidelberg (2016). https://doi.org/10.1007/978-3-662-53015-3_4

23. Fazio, N., Gennaro, R., Jafarikhah, T., Skeith III, W.E.: Homomorphic secret sharing from Paillier encryption. In: Okamoto, T., Yu, Y., Au, M.H., Li, Y. (eds.) ProvSec 2017. LNCS, vol. 10592, pp. 381–399. Springer, Heidelberg (2017). https://doi.org/10.1007/978-3-319-68637-0_23

24. Gilboa, N., Ishai, Y.: Distributed point functions and their applications. In: Nguyen, P.Q., Oswald, E. (eds.) EUROCRYPT 2014. LNCS, vol. 8441, pp. 640–658. Springer, Heidelberg (2014). https://doi.org/10.1007/978-3-642-55220-5_35

25. Langlois, A., Stehlé, D.: Worst-case to average-case reductions for module lattices. Des. Codes Crypt. **75**(3), 565–599 (2015)

26. Lyubashevsky, V., Peikert, C., Regev, O.: On ideal lattices and learning with errors over rings. In: Gilbert, H. (ed.) EUROCRYPT 2010. LNCS, vol. 6110, pp. 1–23. Springer, Heidelberg (2010). https://doi.org/10.1007/978-3-642-13190-5_1

27. Lyubashevsky, V., Peikert, C., Regev, O.: A toolkit for ring-LWE cryptography. In: Johansson, T., Nguyen, P.Q. (eds.) EUROCRYPT 2013. LNCS, vol. 7881, pp. 35–54. Springer, Heidelberg (2013). https://doi.org/10.1007/978-3-642-38348-9_3

28. Orlandi, C., Scholl, P., Yakoubov, S.: The rise of Paillier: homomorphic secret sharing and public-key silent OT. In: Canteaut, A., Standaert, F.X. (eds.) EURO-CRYPT 2021, Part I. LNCS, vol. 12696, pp. 678–708. Springer, Heidelberg (2021). https://doi.org/10.1007/978-3-030-77870-5_24

29. Regev, O.: On lattices, learning with errors, random linear codes, and cryptography. In: Gabow, H.N., Fagin, R. (eds.) 37th ACM STOC, pp. 84–93. ACM Press, May 2005

30. Roy, L., Singh, J.: Large message homomorphic secret sharing from DCR and applications. In: Malkin, T., Peikert, C. (eds.) CRYPTO 2021, Virtual Event, Part III. LNCS, vol. 12827, pp. 687–717. Springer, Heidelberg (2021). https://doi.org/10.1007/978-3-030-84252-9_23

31. Shamir, A.: How to share a secret. Commun. Assoc. Comput. Mach. **22**(11), 612–613 (1979)

32. Wang, F., Yun, C., Goldwasser, S., Vaikuntanathan, V., Zaharia, M.: Splinter: practical private queries on public data. In: 14th USENIX Symposium on Networked Systems Design and Implementation (NSDI 2017), pp. 299–313 (2017)

Discretization Error Reduction for High Precision Torus Fully Homomorphic Encryption

Kang Hoon Lee and Ji Won Yoon[✉]

School of CyberSecurity, Korea University, Seoul, South Korea
{hoot55,jiwon_yoon}@korea.ac.kr

Abstract. In recent history of fully homomorphic encryption, bootstrapping has been actively studied throughout many HE schemes. As bootstrapping is an essential process to transform somewhat homomorphic encryption schemes into fully homomorphic, enhancing its performance is one of the key factors of improving the utility of homomorphic encryption.

In this paper, we propose an extended bootstrapping for TFHE, which we name it by EBS. One of the main drawback of TFHE bootstrapping was that the precision of bootstrapping is mainly decided by the polynomial dimension N. Thus if one wants to bootstrap with high precision, one must enlarge N, or take alternative method. Our EBS enables to use small N for parameter selection, but to bootstrap in higher dimension to keep high precision. Moreover, it can be easily parallelized for faster computation. Also, the EBS can be easily adapted to other known variants of TFHE bootstrappings based on the original bootstrapping algorithm.

We implement our EBS along with the full domain bootstrapping methods known (FDFB, TOTA, Comp), and show how much our EBS can improve the precision for those bootstrapping methods. We provide experimental results and thorough analysis with our EBS, and show that EBS is capable of bootstrapping with high precision even with small N, thus small key size, and small complexity than selecting large N by birth.

Keywords: Homomorphic encryption · TFHE · Precision

1 Introduction

Fully homomorphic encryption (FHE) is a powerful cryptographic scheme that allows to compute on encrypted data with unlimited depth, without leaking any information about it. Nonetheless, performing homomorphic operations on ciphertext accumulates noise or consumes certain amount of levels, and can only evaluate circuits with bounded depth. Thus to support unlimited level of computation,

© IACR 2023. This article is the final version submitted by the authors to the IACR and to Springer-Verlag on 17th February 2023. The version published by Springer-Verlag is available at https://doi.org/00.00000/0000000000.

© International Association for Cryptologic Research 2023
A. Boldyreva and V. Kolesnikov (Eds.): PKC 2023, LNCS 13941, pp. 33–62, 2023.
https://doi.org/10.1007/978-3-031-31371-4_2

these schemes come with an operation called *bootstrapping*, which follows from the blueprint of Gentry [18]. Bootstrapping refreshes a possibly noisy, or level-consumed ciphertext into a fresh ciphertext, and allows further computation.

The FHEW/TFHE [11,16] style bootstrapping methods are still known to be one of the most efficient bootstrapping methods. These algorithms refers to the *blind rotation* algorithm, which refreshes the noisy ciphertext, and evaluates pre-computed lookup table at the same time. From its name, the blind rotate algorithm rotates a polynomial of degree N, power-of-2, by certain amount blind-folded, over $2N$-th cyclotomic ring. The LUT of a function is encoded as the coefficients of the polynomial, and the blind rotation homomorphically selects the value from the encoded LUT by rotating the polynomial. The amount of rotation is decided by the message encrypted inside the ciphertext, with rounding error added due to the scaling-and-rounding of $(n+1)$ coefficients in $\mathbb{T}$ into $\mathbb{Z}_{2N}$. Due to this rounding, bootstrapping in FHEW/TFHE style can only preserve at most $(\log_2 N + 1)$-bits of precision of the input ciphertext, and the precision is actually much smaller in practice due to the summation of those rounding errors, restricting the high precision usage of these schemes. Thus, it is believed that one should select huge N to bootstrap with high precision.

To manage real world applications with low precision ciphertexts, the most familiar, but powerful solution is to decompose the message by some base, and encrypt each of the decomposed message in a single ciphertext. The original binary logic of TFHE is a special case of this decomposition, where the base is 2. Clearly, the smaller the base is, the number of bootstrapping increases for performing arithmetic operations on decomposed ciphertexts. If larger base is used to decrease the number of bootstrapping, the bootstrapping precision works as an upper-bound of the size of the base, as the bootstrapping must preserve precision at least $\log_2(\text{base})$. This forces to use larger N, where one can gain 1 bit of precision by doubling N. Nonetheless, quasi-linear growth in bootstrapping time is accompanied, and the public key size also doubles. Thus, the most efficient usage of TFHE for large precision and corresponding parameter selection is still an open problem.

1.1   Our Contributions and Technical Overview

In this paper, we propose a large precision bootstrapping algorithm for TFHE, which we name it by EBS. Compared to the previous literature of TFHE bootstrapping with large precision, our EBS can bootstrap TFHE ciphertext without enlarging the ring dimension N. Rather, we can keep N as small as possible as long as the (bootstrapping) error doesn't damage the message in the MSB part. Working with small N has lots of advantage in TFHE literature since the time complexity of bootstrapping grows quasi-linearly by N, and the public key size grows linearly. Thus, it is recommended to use small N for efficiency, and our EBS can solve that problem, while still preserving the precision.

Our EBS inherits the idea to use larger N to hold larger information of the ciphertext. Nonetheless, rather than increasing N itself, we use the fact that N is selected as a power of 2 in TFHE and its variants. We induce a homomorphism to a larger ring from dimension N to $2^\nu N$, where we call $\nu \in \mathbb{N}$ the extension factor. The homomorphism is actually a zero padding, and does not affect the security, nor the information of the ciphertext. With the homomorphism, the bits extracted from the ciphertext increases by $(\log_2 N + 1)$ bits to $(\log_2 N + \nu + 1)$ bits, and thus we can bootstrap with additional ν bits of precision.

For efficiency reasons, we also use the fact that our induced homomorphism is actually a zero padding. Thanks to the zeros, the bootstrapping in dimension $2^\nu N$ can be converted to 2^ν times of parallel bootstrappings in dimension N. The advantage in this is that we can perform the bootstrappings simultaneously, where we can save much time with proper parallelization. Also, the asymptotic complexity decreases compared to when performing the bootstrapping in dimension $2^\nu N$.

Also, we provide a proof-of-concept implementation over the TFHE library [12] along with the three variants of the state-of-the-art full-domain functional bootstrapping algorithms. With our implementation, we provide detailed noise analysis, benchmarks with eight sets of parameters with $N = 1024, 2048$ and 4096 that achieves $\lambda = 80$ or 128 bits of security. We also evaluate functions over the torus and provide detailed precision improvements with four sets of parameters. With our EBS, we show that even with $N = 1024$ and 2048, it is possible to achieve *over* 8 bits of precision, which is known to be possible with at least $N = 2^{14} = 16386$. Thus, with our EBS, we can enhance not only the exact computation of TFHE, but also the approximate computation combined with other homomorphic encryption schemes like in [30].

1.2   Related Works

High precision bootstrapping is a common problem throughout homomorphic encryption literature. For approximate homomorphic encryption schemes, the high precision bootstrapping is required to evaluate huge depth circuits such as deep neural network training and inference [25,26], or retrieve statistical information from a dataset. Starting from the dawn of CKKS bootstrapping of 10 to 15 bit of precision [9], many optimizations and better approximations have been studied, and reached 90 to 110 bit of precision [27], or even higher precision of 420 bits which takes 903 seconds [2]. The bootstrapping in CKKS takes much longer than FHEW/TFHE style bootstrappings, but their SIMD (Single Instruction, Multiple Data) structure enables them to bootstrap multiple messages, and usually presented in terms of amortized latency.

Nonetheless, the FHEW/TFHE style bootstrapping still has its own advantages, its significantly low latency, and its capability to evaluate even nonlinear functions with lookup table evaluation. These versatility even brought bridges to approximate homomorphic encryption schemes, to evaluate polynomial functions by approximate schemes, and bring them to TFHE to evaluate nonlinear functions [5,30]. The enhancements in the usage of FHEW/TFHE itself has also been studied throughout many works, including the extension of binary keys to general keys (ternary, Gaussian, etc.) [20,32], or improved FHEW bootstrapping with ring automorphisms [28]. When it come to high precision TFHE, most of the works select decomposition of plaintext message [15,19,22,29,34], with low precision TFHE bootstrapping, and no algorithm was known to bootstrap a single ciphertext with large precision except using large N. Recently, Bergerat et al. [3] proposed an algorithm called WoP-PBS (WithOut Padding - Programmable BootStrapping), to extract each bit of the message as a RGSW ciphertext with circuit bootstrapping [10] and evaluate function with vertically packed lookup table. They did not provide any implementations or noise variance in their work, but it is estimated that their WoP-PBS has noise variance bound larger than our EBS by factor of at least $O(\kappa N)$ when they bootstrap with κ-bits of precision. Nonetheless, their time complexity is linear to κ while our EBS is exponential. This makes their bootstrapping more efficient when κ is sufficiently large. But until certain level, our EBS is more efficient as the circuit bootstrapping is itself quite costly.

2 Preliminaries

2.1 Notations

We introduce the notations used throughout this paper. The real torus $\mathbb{T}$ denotes the real set $\mathbb{R}/\mathbb{Z}$, which is also interpreted as a half open interval $\left[-\frac{1}{2}, \frac{1}{2}\right)$. Each set $\mathbb{R}_N[X]$, $\mathbb{Z}_N[X]$, and $\mathbb{T}_N[X]$ denote the set $\mathbb{R}[X]/\langle X^N + 1\rangle$, $\mathbb{Z}[X]/\langle X^N + 1\rangle$, and $\mathbb{T}[X]/\langle X^N + 1\rangle$.

For a set $\mathcal{S}$, $x \xleftarrow{\$} \mathcal{S}$ implies that x is sampled from $\mathcal{S}$ from uniform distribution. Also, for a distribution $\mathcal{D}$, $x \leftarrow \mathcal{D}$ implies that x is sampled from a distribution $\mathcal{D}$. Next, $\mathsf{Err}\,(c)$ represents the error in the ciphertext c, and $\mathsf{Var}\,(\mathsf{Err}\,(c))$ denotes the variance of error of the ciphertext c. The parentheses $[\![a, b]\!]$ for $a, b \in \mathbb{Z}$ denotes the set $\{x \in \mathbb{Z} \mid a \leq x \leq b\}$. All indices starts with 0 unless mentioned otherwise.

2.2 TFHE Ciphertext

The security of TFHE is based on the hardness of the Learning with Errors (LWE) problem [35] and its ring variant, Ring-Learning with Errors (RLWE) [31,36]. More precisely, the generalization of those problems over the real torus $\mathbb{T}$.

TLWE. Let $n \in \mathbb{N}$ be the TLWE dimension, and σ_{TLWE} be the standard deviation. Then for a discrete message space $\mathcal{M} \subset \mathbb{T}$, the TLWE encryption of a message $m \in \mathcal{M}$ under the key $\mathbf{s} \in \mathbb{B}^n$ is

$$\mathsf{TLWE}_{\mathbf{s}}(m) = (\mathbf{a}, b) \in \mathbb{T}^{n+1},$$

with $\mathbf{a} \xleftarrow{\$} \mathbb{T}^n$, and $b = \langle \mathbf{a}, \mathbf{s} \rangle + m + e$ where $e \leftarrow \mathcal{N}(0, \sigma_{\mathsf{TLWE}})$. Given arbitrarily many TLWE samples with the key $\mathbf{s}$, the (torus) LWE problem [11] assures that if it is λ-secure, it requires at least 2^λ operations to distinguish TLWE samples from uniform distribution over $\mathbb{T}^{n+1}$, or to find $\mathbf{s}$. We now denote that the parameter achieves λ-bit of security if it is λ-secure.

The decryption of a TLWE ciphertext first begins with calculating its phase

$$\varphi_{\mathbf{s}}((\mathbf{a}, b)) = b - \langle \mathbf{a}, \mathbf{s} \rangle,$$

and round it to its closest element in $\mathcal{M}$.

TRLWE. For $N = 2^\beta, k \in \mathbb{N}$, and the standard deviation σ_{TRLWE}, the TRLWE encryption of a message $m(X)$ in a discrete message space $\mathcal{M} \subset \mathbb{T}_N[X]$ under the key $\mathcal{K} \in \mathbb{B}_N[X]^k$ is

$$\mathsf{TRLWE}_{\mathcal{K}}(m(X)) = (A_0(X), \cdots, A_{k-1}(X), B(X)) \in \mathbb{T}_N[X]^k \times \mathbb{T}_N[X],$$

where $A_i(X) \stackrel{\$}{\leftarrow} \mathbb{T}_N[X]$, $B(X) = \langle (A_0(X), \cdots, A_{k-1}(X)), \mathcal{K} \rangle + m(X) + e(X)$, with each coefficients of $e(X)$, $e_i \leftarrow \mathcal{N}(0, \sigma_{\mathsf{TRLWE}})$. The decryption of a TRLWE ciphertext rounds its phase $\varphi_{\mathcal{K}}((A_0(X), \cdots, A_{k-1}(X), B(X)))$ to the closest element in $\mathcal{M}$.

TRGSW. Given an integer base $B_{\mathsf{G}} = 2^\gamma \in \mathbb{N}$ and decomposition length $\ell_{\mathsf{G}} \in \mathbb{N}$, first define the gadget matrix $\mathbf{H}$.

Definition 1 (Gadget Matrix). *For an integer base $B_{\mathsf{G}} = 2^\gamma \in \mathbb{N}$ and decomposition length $\ell_{\mathsf{G}} \in \mathbb{N}$, we call $\mathbf{H}$ the gadget matrix given as*

$$\mathbf{H} = \begin{pmatrix} 1/B_{\mathsf{G}} & \cdots & 0 \\ \vdots & \ddots & \vdots \\ 1/B_{\mathsf{G}}^{\ell_{\mathsf{G}}} & \cdots & 0 \\ \hline \vdots & \ddots & \vdots \\ 0 & \cdots & 1/B_{\mathsf{G}} \\ \vdots & \ddots & \vdots \\ 0 & \cdots & 1/B_{\mathsf{G}}^{\ell_{\mathsf{G}}} \end{pmatrix} \in \mathbb{T}_N[X]^{(k+1)\ell_{\mathsf{G}} \times (k+1)}$$

The TRGSW ciphertext encrypts a integer polynomial $q(X) \in \mathbb{Z}_N[X]$. The TRGSW encryption of $q(X)$ under the key $\mathcal{K} \in \mathbb{B}_N[X]^k$ is

$$\mathsf{TRGSW}_{\mathcal{K}}(p(X)) = \mathbf{Z} + \mathbf{H} \cdot q(X) \in \mathbb{T}_N[X]^{(k+1)\ell_{\mathsf{G}} \times (k+1)},$$

where $\mathbf{Z}$ is a vector of $(k + 1)\ell_{\mathsf{G}}$-$\mathsf{TRLWE}_{\mathcal{K}}(0)$'s. Chillotti et al. [11] defined an external product $\boxdot$ between $\mathsf{TRGSW}_{\mathcal{K}}(m_a)$ and $\mathsf{TRLWE}_{\mathcal{K}}(m_b)$ ciphertext, which gives

$$\mathsf{TRGSW}_{\mathcal{K}}(m_a) \boxdot \mathsf{TRLWE}_{\mathcal{K}}(m_b) = \mathsf{TRLWE}_{\mathcal{K}}(m_a \cdot m_b),$$

for $m_a \in \mathbb{Z}_N[X]$, and $m_b \in \mathbb{T}_N[X]$.

2.3 Bootstrapping in TFHE

The *bootstrapping* in TFHE is a homomorphic calculation of (discretized) phase of the TLWE ciphertext, and aims to reduce internal noise of the ciphertext. Moreover, it simultaneously evaluates a look-up table (LUT) of a function over the torus, and is also known as the *functional bootstrapping* [4], or *programmable bootstrapping* [13].

To bootstrap a ciphertext, one needs two kinds of public key, namely the bootstrapping key, and the keyswitch key. We will denote each of them as BSK, and KSK. For two secret keys $\mathbf{s} \in \mathbb{B}^n$ (TLWE key), $\mathcal{K} \in \mathbb{B}_N^k[X]$ (TRLWE, TRGSW key), the two public keys are defined as follows:

$$\mathsf{BSK} = \{\mathsf{TRGSW}_{\mathcal{K}}(\mathbf{s}_i)\}_{i \in [\![0, n-1]\!]},$$

$$\mathsf{KSK} = \left\{ \mathsf{TLWE}_{\mathbf{s}} \left(\frac{\mathcal{K}_i}{B_{\mathsf{KS}}^j} \cdot k \right) \right\}_{i \in [\![0, N-1]\!], j \in [\![1, \ell_{\mathsf{KS}}]\!], k \in [\![0, B_{\mathsf{KS}}-1]\!]},$$

where $B_{\mathsf{KS}}, \ell_{\mathsf{KS}}$ is the decomposition base, and the length of the keyswitch key. Starting from $\mathsf{TLWE}_{\mathbf{s}}$ ciphertext $c = (\mathbf{a}, b)$, bootstrapping consists of four consecutive procedures.

- ModSwitch: transforms $c = (\mathbf{a}, b) \in \mathbb{T}^{n+1}$ into $\bar{c} = (\bar{\mathbf{a}}, \bar{b}) \in \mathbb{Z}_{2N}^{n+1}$ by computing $\bar{\mathbf{a}}_i = \lfloor 2N\mathbf{a}_i \rceil$ for $i \in [\![0, n-1]\!]$, and $\bar{b} = \lfloor 2Nb \rceil$. From [11,22], the variance after ModSwitch comes with

$$\mathsf{Var}\left(\mathsf{Err}\left(\frac{\bar{\mathbf{a}}}{2N}, \frac{\bar{b}}{2N} \right) \right) \leq \mathsf{Var}\left(\mathsf{Err}\left(\mathbf{a}, b \right) \right) + \frac{n+1}{48N^2},$$

and we denote

$$V_{\mathsf{MS}} = \frac{n+1}{48N^2}.$$

- BlindRotate: homomorphically rotates the (possibly noiseless) TRLWE encryption of the test polynomial $tv \in \mathbb{T}_N[X]$ by $-\tilde{m} = \langle \bar{\mathbf{a}}, \mathbf{s} \rangle - \bar{b} \pmod{2N}$. This process be viewed as a function evaluator for a function $f : \mathbb{Z}_{2N} \to \mathbb{T}$ by setting $tv_i = f(i)$ for $i \in [\![0, N-1]\!]$. The rotation is done by computing the controlled MUX (CMux) n times:

$$\mathsf{ACC} \leftarrow \mathsf{TRGSW}_{\mathcal{K}}(\mathbf{s}_i) \boxdot (X^{\bar{\mathbf{a}}_i} - 1) \cdot \mathsf{ACC} + \mathsf{ACC}.$$

Each execution of the CMux multiplies $X^{\bar{\mathbf{a}}_i \mathbf{s}_i}$ to the accumulator with a certain level of noise growth. Thus, after the BlindRotate, the accumulator is multiplied by $X^{\langle \bar{\mathbf{a}}, \mathbf{s} \rangle \pmod{2N}}$ blindfolded, and outputs the rotated TRLWE ciphertext $\mathsf{TRLWE}(X^{-\tilde{m}} \cdot tv)$. After BlindRotate, the variance of ACC is bounded by

$$\mathsf{Var}\left(\mathsf{Err}\left(\mathsf{ACC} \right) \right) \leq \mathsf{Var}\left(\mathsf{Err}\left(\mathsf{ACC}_{init} \right) \right)$$
$$+ n \left((k+1)N\ell_{\mathsf{BS}} \left(\frac{B_{\mathsf{BS}}}{2} \right)^2 \mathsf{Var}(\mathsf{Err}(\mathsf{BSK})) + \frac{1+kN}{4 \cdot B_{\mathsf{BS}}^{2\ell_{\mathsf{BS}}}} \right),$$

where the result comes from [11]. Note that $B_{\mathsf{BS}}, \ell_{\mathsf{BS}}$ is the decomposition base, and the length of the bootstrapping key. Usually, we start off with a noiseless accumulator with $\mathsf{Var}\left(\mathsf{Err}\left(\mathsf{ACC}_{init}\right)\right) = 0$. We now denote

$$V_{\mathsf{BR}} = n\left((k+1)N\ell_{\mathsf{BS}}\left(\frac{B_{\mathsf{BS}}}{2}\right)^2 \mathsf{Var}(\mathsf{Err}(\mathsf{BSK})) + \frac{1+kN}{4 \cdot B_{\mathsf{BS}}^{2\ell_{\mathsf{BS}}}}\right).$$

- SampleExtract: extracts TLWE ciphertext from the rotated TRLWE accumulator ACC. Considering tv_i as the i-th coefficient of tv, it gives $\mathsf{TLWE}_{\mathcal{K}'}(tv_{\bar{m}}) = \mathsf{TLWE}_{\mathcal{K}'}(f(\bar{m}))$ (resp. $\mathsf{TLWE}_{\mathcal{K}'}(-tv_{\bar{m}-N}) = \mathsf{TLWE}_{\mathcal{K}'}(f(m - N)))$ if $\bar{m} \in [\![0, N-1]\!]$ (resp. $\bar{m} \in [\![N, 2N-1]\!]$) under the key $\mathcal{K}' \in \mathbb{B}^{kN}$. The SampleExtract does not accumulate any noise to the ciphertext, so the variance maintains the same.
- KeySwitch: converts the key $\mathcal{K}'$ of extracted $c' = \mathsf{TLWE}_{\mathcal{K}'}(m)$ into $\mathbf{s}$, and gives $c = \mathsf{TLWE}_{\mathbf{s}}(m)$ that encrypts the same message. Since the KeySwitch adds noise to the ciphertext, there have been attempts to remove the KeySwitch error by eliminating the need for KeySwitch by using $\mathbf{s} = \mathcal{K}'$ [22], or by moving around the KeySwitch before BlindRotate [3,6]. Here, we refer to the TLWE-to-TLWE KeySwitch, and the error accumulation is given as

$$\mathsf{Var}\left(\mathsf{Err}\left(c\right)\right) \le R^2\mathsf{Var}\left(\mathsf{Err}\left(c'\right)\right) + kN\ell_{\mathsf{KS}}\mathsf{Var}(\mathsf{Err}(\mathsf{KSK})) + \frac{1}{12}kNB_{\mathsf{KS}}^{-2\ell_{\mathsf{KS}}},$$

where R is the Lipschitz constant for functional public keyswitching (in our work, $R = 1$). We now denote

$$V_{\mathsf{KS}} = kN\ell_{\mathsf{KS}}\mathsf{Var}(\mathsf{Err}(\mathsf{KSK})) + \frac{1}{12}kNB_{\mathsf{KS}}^{-2\ell_{\mathsf{KS}}}.$$

Algorithm 1 sums up the gate bootstrapping procedure from [11], mainly used to refresh the ciphertext after homomorphic operations (e.g. Homomorphic NAND). From Algorithm 1, the variance of the error of the output ciphertext c is given by

$$\mathsf{Var}\left(\mathsf{Err}\left(c\right)\right) \le V_{\mathsf{BR}} + V_{\mathsf{KS}},$$

and we denote $V_{\mathsf{BS}} = V_{\mathsf{BR}} + V_{\mathsf{KS}}$.

3   Modified TFHE Bootstrapping

3.1   Functional Bootstrapping

Functional bootstrapping, which is the generalization of the gate bootstrapping in Algorithm 1, evaluates the LUT of the target function $f : \mathbb{T} \to \mathbb{T}$, and gives the $\mathsf{TLWE}_{\mathbf{s}}$ encryption of $f(\frac{\bar{m}}{2N})$ for $\bar{m} \in [0, N-1]$. The procedure is depicted in Algorithm 2. Here, we name it by the *half-domain* functional bootstrapping since it only uses the half of the torus $[0, \frac{1}{2})$ due to the negacyclic BlindRotate (i.e., it gives the encryption of $-f\left(\frac{\bar{m}-N}{2N}\right)$ if $\bar{m} \in [N, 2N-1]$). Thus, the domain

---

Algorithm 1: Gate Bootstrapping Algorithm (from [11])

Input: TLWE ciphertext $(a, b) \in \mathsf{TLWE_s}\left(m \cdot \frac{1}{2}\right)$ with $m \in \mathbb{B}$
Input: Bootstrapping key BSK
Input: Keyswitch key KSK
Output: Refreshed TLWE ciphertext $\mathsf{TLWE_s}\left((-1)^m \cdot \mu\right)$

1 $\bar{\mathbf{a}}_i = \lfloor 2N\mathbf{a}_i \rceil$ for $i \in [\![0, n-1]\!]$, and $\bar{b} = \lfloor 2Nb \rceil$ ▷ ModSwitch $((a,b), 2N)$
2 Let $tv = X^{\frac{N}{2}} \cdot (1 + X + \cdots + X^{N-1}) \cdot \mu$ for $\mu \in \mathbb{T}$
3 Let $\mathsf{ACC}_{init} = (\mathbf{0}, tv) \in \mathsf{TRLWE}_\mathcal{K}(tv)$
4 $\mathsf{ACC_{BR}} \leftarrow \mathsf{BlindRotate}((\bar{\mathbf{a}}, \bar{b}), \mathsf{BSK}, \mathsf{ACC}_{init})$
5 $c' \leftarrow \mathsf{SampleExtract}(\mathsf{ACC_{BR}})$ ▷ Extract $\mathsf{TLWE}_\mathcal{K}((-1)^m \cdot \mu)$
6 **return** $c = \mathsf{KeySwitch}(c', \mathsf{KSK})$ ▷ $\mathsf{TLWE_s}((-1)^m \cdot \mu)$

Algorithm 2: Half-Domain Functional Bootstrapping (from [4,19])

Input: TLWE ciphertext $(a, b) \in \mathsf{TLWE_s}(m)$ with $m \in \left[0, \frac{1}{2}\right)$
Input: A $\mathcal{L}$-Lipschitz morphism $f : \mathbb{T} \to \mathbb{T}$
Input: Bootstrapping key BSK
Input: Keyswitch key KSK
Output: Refreshed TLWE ciphertext $\mathsf{TLWE_s}\left(f\left(\frac{\bar{m}}{2N}\right)\right)$

1 $(\bar{\mathbf{a}}, \bar{b}) = \mathsf{ModSwitch}\left((a, b), 2N\right)$ ▷ $\bar{m} = \bar{b} - \langle \bar{\mathbf{a}}, \mathbf{s} \rangle \bmod 2N$
2 Let $tv = \Sigma_{i=0}^{N-1} f\left(\frac{i}{2N}\right) X^i$
3 Let $\mathsf{ACC}_{init} = (\mathbf{0}, tv) \in \mathsf{TRLWE}_\mathcal{K}(tv)$
4 $\mathsf{ACC_{BR}} \leftarrow \mathsf{BlindRotate}((\bar{\mathbf{a}}, \bar{b}), \mathsf{BSK}, \mathsf{ACC}_{init})$ ▷ $\mathsf{ACC_{BR}} = \mathsf{TRLWE}(X^{-\bar{m}} \cdot tv)$
5 $c' \leftarrow \mathsf{SampleExtract}(\mathsf{ACC_{BR}})$ ▷ Extract $\mathsf{TLWE}_\mathcal{K}\left(f\left(\frac{\bar{m}}{2N}\right)\right)$
6 **return** $c = \mathsf{KeySwitch}(c', \mathsf{KSK})$ ▷ $\mathsf{TLWE_s}\left(f\left(\frac{\bar{m}}{2N}\right)\right)$

---

can be naturally extended to the full torus for any negacyclic function $h(x) = -h\left(x + \frac{1}{2}\right)$.

In Proposition 1, we analyze the error of the functionally bootstrapped ciphertext with $\mathcal{L}$-Lipschitz function f evaluated on an arbitrary message $m \in [0, \frac{1}{2})$. From the result, we observe that the rounding error from the ModSwitch affects the value of the function itself by directly changing the message of the original ciphertext. The rounding error is thus highly related to the maximal precision a ciphertext can have, and has been pointed out to be the major reason for the severe precision loss in TFHE based applications [13, 22].

Nonetheless, this rounding error was not a serious problem for the *gate* bootstrapping since it only needed 1-bit of precision after the ModSwitch to assure its correctness. However, functional bootstrapping works on larger plaintext space

$\mathcal{M}$, which usually has the size of power of 2 (i.e., $|\mathcal{M}| = 2^{\pi}$). Thus, to correctly bootstrap a ciphertext $\mathsf{TLWE_s}(m)$ with full precision π (with high probability), the errors should satisfy

$$\epsilon_{pre}, \epsilon_{\mathsf{BS}} \leq \frac{1}{2|\mathcal{M}|},$$

with high probability for pre-BootStrap and BootStrap errors $\epsilon_{pre}, \epsilon_{\mathsf{BS}}$.

Proposition 1 (Functional Bootstrapping Error). *Let c be the output of functional bootstrapping with a $\mathcal{L}$-Lipschitz morphism $f : \mathbb{T} \to \mathbb{T}$. Then the variance of the error between $\varphi_{\mathbf{s}}(c) = f(m + \epsilon_r) + \epsilon_{\mathsf{BS}}$ and $f(m)$ is bounded by*

$$\mathsf{Var}\left(\varphi_{\mathbf{s}}(c) - f(m)\right) \leq \mathcal{L}^2 V_{\mathsf{MS}} + V_{\mathsf{BS}}.$$

Proof. During the ModSwitch, the message m is rounded into $\frac{\tilde{m}}{2N} = m + \epsilon_{\mathsf{MS}}$, where ϵ_{MS} is the rounding error. Then during the BlindRotate, the function f is evaluated on $\frac{\tilde{m}}{2N}$, with the BlindRotate error ϵ_{BR}. Thus, after the KeySwitch, the phase of the output ciphertext c from line 6 of Algorithm 2 will be

$$\varphi_{\mathbf{s}}(c) = f(m + \epsilon_{\mathsf{MS}}) + \epsilon_{\mathsf{BR}} + \epsilon_{\mathsf{KS}},$$

where ϵ_{KS} is the error from the KeySwitch. Then by the $\mathcal{L}$-Lipschitz condition, we have

$$\begin{aligned}
\mathsf{Var}\left(\varphi_{\mathbf{s}}(c) - f(m)\right) &\leq \mathsf{Var}\left(f(m + \epsilon_{\mathsf{MS}}) - f(m)\right) + \mathsf{Var}\left(\epsilon_{\mathsf{BR}}\right) + \mathsf{Var}\left(\epsilon_{\mathsf{KS}}\right) \\
&\leq \mathsf{Var}\left(\mathcal{L}\epsilon_{\mathsf{MS}}\right) + V_{\mathsf{BR}} + V_{\mathsf{KS}} \\
&\leq \mathcal{L}^2 \mathsf{Var}\left(\epsilon_{\mathsf{MS}}\right) + V_{\mathsf{BS}} \\
&\leq \mathcal{L}^2 V_{\mathsf{MS}} + V_{\mathsf{BS}}.
\end{aligned}$$

3.2   Large Precision TFHE with Functional Bootstrapping

We revise the major branches of TFHE based applications which attempts to operate with large precision. The functional bootstrapping plays an essential role in all of these works, and sometimes appropriately modified to fulfill their required functionality.

Radix-Based Decomposition with Multiple Ciphertexts. In this branch, the plaintext m is decomposed into several digits $(m_0, m_1, \cdots, m_d)$ of certain base(s) B, and each m_i's are encrypted as a single TLWE ciphertext. Usually, small power-of-2 integers ($2^{\pi} = 2^1, 2^2$) are used as a base [3,7,11,15,19,37], or decomposed by co-prime integer bases for the CRT representation [3,24].

To collaborate with the vector of ciphertexts (i.e., addition, multiplication, function evaluation), *tree-based* [19] and *chaining* [7] method are known as two major solutions. Both methods lookup to huge LUT (encoded in multiple TRLWE ciphertexts) by applying the functional bootstrapping consecutively. The *chaining* method is known to have lower complexity and output noise compared to the *tree-based* method, but can only evaluate restricted types of function. Recently, Clet et al. [15] generalized the *chaining* method and enabled to evaluate any function by the cost of larger plaintext modulus (i.e., $3 \cdot \lceil \log_2 B \rceil + 1$ bits, or $2 \cdot \lceil \log_2 B \rceil + 1$ bits with additional bootstrapping) to work with base B.

Using Larger N. As the variance of the rounding error was bounded by $\mathsf{Var}(\epsilon_{\mathsf{MS}}) \leq \frac{n+1}{48N^2}$, if we double N, the bound halves [7,22,24,30]. However, using large N brings superlinear growth in BlindRotate due to the expensive polynomial multiplication with complexity $O(N \log N)$. Moreover by doubling N, the size of the public key (e.g., BSK, KSK, etc.) exactly doubles which can be a burden for both the client and the server using TFHE based applications.

Small Hamming Weight $\mathsf{Ham}(\mathbf{s})$. Similar to the case of using large N, by restricting the hamming weight of $h = \mathsf{Ham}(\mathbf{s})$, the rounding error gets bounded by $\epsilon_r \leq \frac{h+1}{4N}$ [8,24]. Nonetheless, large TLWE dimension n is required to achieve the same security level with small hamming weight compared to when using uniform binary key, worsening the performance of bootstrapping as well as its output noise.

VP-LUT Evaluation and Circuit Bootstrapping. Recent approach of Bergerat et al. [3] employed the TLWE-to-TRGSW *circuit bootstrapping* from Chillotti et al. [10]. For ciphertext(s) with total κ bit of precision, their method extracts a single bit TLWE encryption with κ functional bootstrappings (i.e., $m = \sum_{i=0}^{\kappa-1} m_i \cdot 2^i$ extracted into $\mathsf{TLWE_s}\left(\frac{m_i}{2^{\kappa-i}}\right)$'s). Then the circuit bootstrapping transforms each ciphertexts into $\mathsf{TRGSW}_{\mathcal{K}}(m_i)$'s. These TRGSW ciphertexts are used to evaluate the VP-LUT (Vertical Packing LUT), which costs $\frac{2^\kappa}{N} + \log_2 N - 1$ CMux evaluations. Note that the circuit bootstrapping before the VP-LUT is a costly operation that contains multiple functional bootstrappings, and the output error of the VP-LUT evaluation can be larger than works featured above.

Aforementioned approaches can be combined together for further improvements if needed (e.g., selecting larger N to attain larger plaintext modulus for the *chaining* method). However, this can reduce the overall usability of TFHE, and should be selected with care.

3.3 Extended BlindRotate for Larger Precision

In this section, we introduce a strategy that can be adapted during the BlindRotate that allows to attain full precision a single ciphertext can have, even when using small N. In other words, our method can make the error from the ModSwitch quite negligible without using larger N, and enlarge the precision as long as it is affected the after-bootstrap error, ϵ_{BS}.

The main idea of our algorithm is to *crank up* the BlindRotate into a larger auxiliary ring dimension of $2^\nu N$ using a homomorphism, which is actually sent back to 2^ν-rings of dimension N for efficient calculation. We first investigate on how to *crank up* the BlindRotate into a larger space. Note that here, we use an uppercase to clarify the polynomial dimension of TRLWE ciphertext. To be specific, $\mathsf{TRLWE}_\mathcal{K}^N$ implies that each of the polynomial elements in this TRLWE ciphertext is an element of $\mathbb{T}_N[X]$, while $\mathsf{TRLWE}_\mathcal{K}^{2^\nu N}$ comes from $\mathbb{T}_{2^\nu N}[X]$.

BlindRotate in Larger Dimension. Recall that the main precision drop comes from the ModSwitch, where the elements of $\mathsf{TLWE}_\mathbf{s}(m) = (\mathbf{a}, b)$ are rounded into $\mathbb{Z}_{2N}$. A simple intuition is to *pretend* we are using $2^\nu N$ instead of N for $\nu \in \mathbb{N} \cup \{0\}$, and round the coefficients into $\mathbb{Z}_{2^{\nu+1}N}$. The variance of error from the ModSwitch can now be written as

$$\mathsf{Var}\left(\mathsf{Err}\left(\frac{\bar{\mathbf{a}}}{2^{\nu+1}N}, \frac{\bar{b}}{2^{\nu+1}N}\right)\right) \leq \mathsf{Var}\left(\mathsf{Err}\left(\mathbf{a}, b\right)\right) + \frac{n+1}{48 \cdot 2^{2\nu}N^2},$$

where the variance decreased by $V_{\mathsf{MS}}/2^{2\nu}$. What is left is on how to evaluate the BlindRotate on dimension $2^\nu N$. Thus, we induce a module homomorphism $\iota : \mathbb{T}_N[X] \to \mathbb{T}_{2^\nu N}[X]$ by

$$\iota : \mathbb{T}_N[X] \longrightarrow \mathbb{T}_{2^\nu N}[X],$$

$$p(x) = \sum_{i=0}^{N-1} p_i X^i \longmapsto p_{\mathsf{ext}}(X) = \sum_{i=0}^{N-1} p_i X^{2^\nu i},$$

which is actually a zero padding. We now write the undercase ext to denote the polynomials zero-padded in a similar way. By applying ι on each torus polynomials of ciphertext, which we denote by $\iota\left(\mathsf{TRLWE}_\mathcal{K}(p(X))\right)$ and $\iota\left(\mathsf{TRGSW}_\mathcal{K}(q(X))\right)$, are also extended to

$$\iota\left(\mathsf{TRLWE}_\mathcal{K}^N(p(X))\right) = \mathsf{TRLWE}_{\mathcal{K}_{\mathsf{ext}}}^{2^\nu N}(p_{\mathsf{ext}}(X)) \text{ for } p(X) \in \mathbb{T}_N[X],$$

$$\iota\left(\mathsf{TRGSW}_\mathcal{K}^N(q(X))\right) = \mathsf{TRGSW}_{\mathcal{K}_{\mathsf{ext}}}^{2^\nu N}(q_{\mathsf{ext}}(X)) \text{ for } q(X) \in \mathbb{Z}_N[X],$$

for extended key $\mathcal{K}_{\mathsf{ext}} \in \mathbb{B}_{2^\nu N}[X]$. Also, since ι does not add any noise, the noise variance of the ciphertext stays the same. The external product $\boxdot$ follows naturally

$$\mathsf{TRGSW}_{\mathcal{K}_{\mathsf{ext}}}^{2^\nu N}(q_{\mathsf{ext}}(X)) \boxdot \mathsf{TRLWE}_{\mathcal{K}_{\mathsf{ext}}}^{2^\nu N}(p(X))$$
$$= \mathsf{TRLWE}_{\mathcal{K}_{\mathsf{ext}}}^{2^\nu N}(p(X) \cdot q_{\mathsf{ext}}(X)).$$

Thanks to the zero padding in TRGSW ciphertext, the error propagation of the external product is exactly the same with computing the external product in dimension N whether the TRLWE message $p(X)$ is an extended polynomial or not. Thus, by extending the bootstrapping key BSK with ι, we can evaluate the BlindRotate with reduced ModSwitch error with exactly same error propagation, i.e., V_{BR}. Note that the test vector of the accumulator should be generated in $\mathbb{T}_{2^\nu N}[X]$, so the accumulator is a TRLWE encryption under the key $\mathcal{K}_{\mathsf{ext}}$, but the message is not an extended torus polynomial.

After the extended BlindRotate, the SampleExtract follows. However, due to the extension, the SampleExtract now gives $\mathsf{TLWE}_{\mathcal{K}'_{\mathsf{ext}}} = (\mathbf{a}, b) \in \mathbb{T}^{2^{\nu}kN} \times \mathbb{T}$. Notice that the key $\mathcal{K}'_{\mathsf{ext}} \in \mathbb{B}^{2^{\nu}kN}$ is just a TLWE representation of the extended key $\mathcal{K}_{\mathsf{ext}}$, and are all 0 except for the indices multiple of 2^{ν}. Thus we extract only the $2^{\nu}i$-th coefficients from $\mathbf{a}$ for $i \in [\![0, kN-1]\!]$ and attain $\mathsf{TLWE}_{\mathcal{K}'}$, which can now be keyswitched. The full Algorithm is depicted in Algorithm 3.

Algorithm 3: Large Precision Bootstrapping (without parallelization)

Input: TLWE ciphertext $(\mathbf{a}, b) \in \mathsf{TLWE}_{\mathbf{s}}(m)$ with $m \in [0, \frac{1}{2})$

Input: extension factor $\nu \in \mathbb{N} \cup \{0\}$

Input: A $\mathcal{L}$-Lipschitz morphism $f : \mathbb{T} \to \mathbb{T}$

Input: *Extended* Bootstrapping key $\mathsf{BSK}_{\mathsf{ext}} = \left\{ \mathsf{TRGSW}^{2^{\nu}N}_{\mathcal{K}_{\mathsf{ext}}}(\mathbf{s}_i) \right\}_{i \in [\![0, n-1]\!]}$

Input: Keyswitch key KSK

Output: Refreshed TLWE ciphertext $\mathsf{TLWE}_{\mathbf{s}} \left(f \left(\frac{\bar{m}}{2^{\nu+1}N} \right) \right)$

1 $(\bar{\mathbf{a}}, \bar{b}) = \mathsf{ModSwitch}((\mathbf{a}, b), 2^{\nu+1}N)$ ▷ $\bar{m} = \bar{b} - \langle \bar{\mathbf{a}}, \mathbf{s} \rangle \bmod 2^{\nu+1}N$

2 Let $tv = \Sigma^{2^{\nu}N-1}_{i=0} f \left(\frac{i}{2^{\nu+1}N} \right) X^i$

3 Let $\mathsf{ACC} = (0, tv) \in \mathsf{TRLWE}^{2^{\nu}N}_{\mathcal{K}_{\mathsf{ext}}}(tv)$

4 $\mathsf{ACC}_{\mathsf{BR}} \leftarrow \mathsf{BlindRotate}((\bar{\mathbf{a}}, \bar{b}), \mathsf{BSK}_{\mathsf{ext}}, \mathsf{ACC})$ ▷ $\mathsf{ACC}_{\mathsf{BR}} = \mathsf{TRLWE}^{2^{\nu}N}_{\mathcal{K}_{\mathsf{ext}}}(X^{-\bar{m}} \cdot tv)$

5 $c' \leftarrow \mathsf{SampleExtract}(\mathsf{ACC}_{\mathsf{BR}})$

6 **return** $c = \mathsf{KeySwitch}(c', \mathsf{KSK})$ ▷ $\mathsf{TLWE}_{\mathbf{s}} \left(f \left(\frac{\bar{m}}{2^{\nu+1}N} \right) \right)$

Parallelization of Extended BlindRotate. Still, the extended BlindRotate contains lots of polynomial multiplications in dimension $2^{\nu}N$, which is quite costly. Therefore, we bring back the calculation of BlindRotate multiple polynomial multiplications in dimension N, which can be easily parallelized. First, we introduce a module isomorphism $\tau : \mathbb{T}_{2^{\nu}N}[X] \to \mathbb{T}^{2^{\nu}}_N[X]$ defined by

$$\tau : \mathbb{T}_{2^{\nu}N}[X] \to \mathbb{T}^{2^{\nu}}_N[X]$$

$$p(x) = \sum_{i=0}^{2^{\nu}N-1} p_i X^i \longmapsto \left(p^{(0)}(X), \cdots, p^{(2^{\nu}-1)}(X) \right)$$

$$= \left(\sum_{i=0}^{N-1} p_{2^{\nu}i} X^i, \cdots, \sum_{i=0}^{N-1} p_{2^{\nu}i+2^{\nu}-1} X^i \right).$$

Then for $\mathsf{TRLWE}^{2^{\nu}N}_{\mathcal{K}_{\mathsf{ext}}}$ ciphertext encrypted under extended key $\mathcal{K}_{\mathsf{ext}}$, we apply τ on each torus polynomial elements in $\mathbb{T}_{2^{\nu}N}[X]$, creating $(k+1)$ vectors of torus polynomials in $\mathbb{T}^{2^{\nu}}_N[X]$. Due to the zero padding in $\mathcal{K}_{\mathsf{ext}}$, collecting i-th entries from the $(k+1)$ vectors naturally induces a $\mathsf{TRLWE}^N_{\mathcal{K}}$ ciphertext for $i \in [\![0, 2^{\nu} - 1]\!]$. We denote the whole process by $\tau \left(\mathsf{TRLWE}^{2^{\nu}N}_{\mathcal{K}_{\mathsf{ext}}}(m) \right)$:

$$\tau \left(\mathsf{TRLWE}^{2^{\nu}N}_{\mathcal{K}_{\mathsf{ext}}}(m) \right) = \left(\mathsf{TRLWE}^N_{\mathcal{K}}(m_0), \cdots, \mathsf{TRLWE}^N_{\mathcal{K}}(m_{2^{\nu}-1}) \right).$$

for $m \in \mathbb{T}_{2^\nu N}[X]$ and $\tau(m) = (m_0, \cdots, m_{2^\nu - 1})$. Since τ is rearrangement of coefficients, the noise variance of TRLWE ciphertexts generated by τ is at most the noise variance of original ciphertext $\mathsf{TRLWE}_{\mathcal{K}_{\mathrm{ext}}}^{2^\nu N}(m)$.

Then with two constraints that the $\mathsf{TRGSW}_{\mathcal{K}}^{N}(z)$ encrypts an integer $z \in \mathbb{Z}$ (which is quite common in TFHE literature) and that the $\mathsf{TRGSW}_{\mathcal{K}_{\mathrm{ext}}}^{2^\nu N}(z)$ is extended from $\mathsf{TRGSW}_{\mathcal{K}}^{N}(z)$, we can perform the parallel external product on the decomposed TRLWE ciphertext by

$$\mathsf{TRGSW}_{\mathcal{K}_{\mathrm{ext}}}^{2^\nu N}(z) \boxdot \mathsf{TRLWE}_{\mathcal{K}_{\mathrm{ext}}}^{2^\nu N}(m)$$

$$\cong \left(\mathsf{TRGSW}_{\mathcal{K}}^{N}(z) \boxdot \mathsf{TRLWE}_{\mathcal{K}}^{N}(m_0), \cdots, \right.$$

$$\left. \mathsf{TRGSW}_{\mathcal{K}}^{N}(z) \boxdot \mathsf{TRLWE}_{\mathcal{K}}^{N}(m_{2^\nu - 1})\right)$$

$$\cong \left(\mathsf{TRLWE}_{\mathcal{K}}^{N}(z \cdot m_0), \cdots, \mathsf{TRLWE}_{\mathcal{K}}^{N}(z \cdot m_{2^\nu - 1})\right),$$

where each external product in dimension N can be all performed in parallel. Moreover, with the inverse mapping τ^{-1}, the output exactly maps to

$$\tau^{-1}\left(\mathsf{TRLWE}_{\mathcal{K}}^{N}(z \cdot m_0), \cdots, \mathsf{TRLWE}_{\mathcal{K}}^{N}(z \cdot m_{2^\nu - 1})\right) = \mathsf{TRLWE}_{\mathcal{K}_{\mathrm{ext}}}^{2^\nu N}(z \cdot m),$$

for $z \in \mathbb{Z}$ and $m \in \mathbb{T}_{2^\nu N}[X]$. Keeping this in mind, we now suggest a parallelized extended BlindRotate, which we now denote as ExtBlindRotate in Algorithm 4. From our construction, the 2^k external products in line 6 used to compute the CMux gate can be computed in parallel.

Remark 1. In Algorithm 4, the rotation of the accumulator was represented by rotating in large dimension, and sending back to its vector of dimension N with the isomorphism τ. We used this representation for simplification, which in practice can actually be *rotated* by changing the order of polynomial vector, and rotating the polynomials.

With the parallel ExtBlindRotate, we now present our final extended bootstrapping algorithm EBS in Algorithm 5.

Proposition 2 (EBS). *The EBS in Algorithm 5 with the extension factor $\nu \in \mathbb{N} \cup \{0\}$ allows to bootstrap a ciphertext with reduced ModSwitch error with variance $\frac{1}{2^{2\nu}}V_{\mathsf{MS}}$. The variance of error of the bootstrapped ciphertext is exactly same as V_{BS}.*

Proof. From line 1 and 2 of Algorithm 5, the reduced ModSwitch error variance naturally follows

$$\mathsf{Var}\left(\mathsf{Err}\left(\frac{\bar{\mathbf{a}}}{2^{\nu+1}N}, \frac{\bar{b}}{2^{\nu+1}N}\right)\right) \leq \mathsf{Var}\left(\mathsf{Err}\left(\mathbf{a}, b\right)\right) + \frac{n+1}{48 \cdot 2^{2\nu} N^2}$$

$$\leq \mathsf{Var}\left(\mathsf{Err}\left(\mathbf{a}, b\right)\right) + \frac{V_{\mathsf{MS}}}{2^{2\nu}}.$$

Algorithm 4: Parallel ExtBlindRotate

Input: $(\bar{\mathbf{a}}, \bar{b}) \in \mathbb{Z}_{2^{\nu+1}N}^n \times \mathbb{Z}_{2^{\nu+1}N}$

Input: extension factor $\nu \in \mathbb{N} \cup \{0\}$

Input: A $\mathcal{L}$-Lipschitz morphism $f : \mathbb{T} \to \mathbb{T}$

Input: Bootstrapping key BSK

Output: $\overrightarrow{\mathsf{ACC}}$ with $\tau^{-1}\left(\overrightarrow{\mathsf{ACC}}\right) = \mathsf{TRLWE}_{\mathcal{K}_{\text{ext}}}^{2^\nu N}(X^{-\bar{b}+\langle \bar{\mathbf{a}}, \mathbf{s}\rangle \bmod 2^{\nu+1}N} \cdot tv)$

1 Let $tv = \Sigma_{i=0}^{2^\nu N - 1} f\left(\frac{i}{2^{\nu+1}N}\right) X^i$

2 $\overrightarrow{\mathsf{ACC}} \leftarrow \tau\left(\mathsf{TRLWE}_{\mathcal{K}_{\text{ext}}}^{2^k N}(X^{-\bar{b}} \cdot tv)\right)$

3 **for** $i \in [\![0, n-1]\!]$ **do**

4      $\overrightarrow{\mathsf{RotACC}} \leftarrow \tau\left(X^{\bar{a}_i} \cdot \tau^{-1}\left(\overrightarrow{\mathsf{ACC}}\right)\right)$

5   **for** $j \in [\![0, 2^\nu - 1]\!]$ **do**

6          $\overrightarrow{\mathsf{ACC}}_j \leftarrow \mathsf{BSK}_i \boxdot \left(\overrightarrow{\mathsf{RotACC}}_j - \overrightarrow{\mathsf{ACC}}_j\right) + \overrightarrow{\mathsf{ACC}}_j$ ▷ Parallel comp.

7   **end**

8 **end**

9 **return** $\overrightarrow{\mathsf{ACC}}$

Now we show the correctness of ExtBlindRotate in Algorithm 4 and analyze its error propagation. Starting from line 4 of Algorithm 4, we see that it is a rotation of $\overrightarrow{\mathsf{ACC}}$ by $\bar{a}_i$ in $\mathbb{T}_{2^\nu N}[X]$ and does not add any noise since it only rearranges the coefficients.

In line 6 of Algorithm 4, the CMux gate is evaluated on each row of the accumulator using the external product. Thus if BSK_i encrypts 1, the $\bar{a}_i$-rotated accumulator $\overrightarrow{\mathsf{RotACC}}$ is selected for the next accumulator. If not (i.e., if BSK_i encrypts 0), $\overrightarrow{\mathsf{ACC}}$ is selected. Thus after each i-th loop, the merged accumulator $\tau^{-1}\left(\overrightarrow{\mathsf{ACC}}\right)$ is rotated by $X^{\bar{a}_i \cdot \mathbf{s}_i}$, and hence encrypts $X^{-\bar{b}+\sum_{p=0}^{i} \bar{a}_i \cdot \mathbf{s}_i} \cdot tv$ for $i \in [\![0, n-1]\!]$.

For the error propagation of ExtBlindRotate, the errors only comes from the CMux evaluation. More specifically, from the decomposition of the TRLWE ciphertext for the external product, and the external product itself. Thus the error propagation for a single CMux evaluation is exactly the same as the BlindRotate error V_{BR}. After the ExtBlindRotate, the error is once more accumulated from the KeySwitch in line 5 of Algorithm 5, whose variance is same as V_{KS}. Thus the variance of error after bootstrapping is exactly bounded by V_{BS}.

Remark 2. The homomorphism ι and isomorphism τ was defined on module since $\mathbb{T}_N[X]$, $\mathbb{T}_{2^\nu N}[X]$ are not rings. Nonetheless, this can be easily associated to rings, using the isomorphism between $\mathbb{Z}_q$ and $\frac{1}{q}\mathbb{Z}_q \subset \mathbb{T}$. Thus, our method can naturally be used in ring-based TFHE bootstrapping implementations like in [24, 30, 37].

Algorithm 5: EBS

Input: TLWE ciphertext $(a, b) \in \text{TLWE}_s(m)$ with $m \in [0, \frac{1}{2})$

Input: extension factor $\nu \in \mathbb{N} \cup \{0\}$

Input: A $\mathcal{L}$-Lipschitz morphism $f : \mathbb{T} \to \mathbb{T}$

Input: Bootstrapping key BSK

Input: Keyswitch key KSK

Output: Refreshed TLWE ciphertext $\text{TLWE}_s\left(f\left(\frac{\bar{m}}{2^{\nu+1}N}\right)\right)$

1 $(\bar{a}, \bar{b}) = \text{ModSwitch}\left((a, b), 2^{\nu+1}N\right)$ $\triangleright \bar{m} = \bar{b} - \langle \bar{a}, s \rangle \bmod 2^{\nu+1}N$

2 $\overrightarrow{\text{ACC}} \leftarrow \text{ExtBlindRotate}((\bar{a}, \bar{b}), \nu, f, \text{BSK})$

3 $c' \leftarrow \text{SampleExtract}(\overrightarrow{\text{ACC}}_0)$ $\triangleright$ Extract $\text{TLWE}_{\mathcal{K}'}\left(f\left(\frac{\bar{m}}{2^{\nu+1}N}\right)\right)$

4 **return** $c = \text{KeySwitch}(c', \text{KSK})$ $\triangleright$ $\text{TLWE}_s\left(f\left(\frac{\bar{m}}{2^{\nu+1}N}\right)\right)$

3.4 Large Precision in Full Domain TFHE Bootstrapping

Recall that the aforementioned functional bootstrapping algorithms (including our EBS) only works with half domain of the torus $[0, \frac{1}{2})$ to evaluate arbitrary function $f : \mathbb{T} \to \mathbb{T}$. These algorithms consumes 1 additional bit in front of the MSB of the message, and bootstrapping requires $p + 1$ bits of precision to successfully bootstrap messages of p bit precision.

Luckily, it is always possible to evaluate arbitrary function $f : \mathbb{T} \to \mathbb{T}$ in the *full* domain of the torus with extra operations. From the state-of-the-art full domain functional bootstrapping algorithms, we observed that our EBS can cooperate with most of these algorithms [14,15,24,37], as they all contain the ModSwitch to $2N$ or N. The WoP-PBS from [3] uses the functional bootstrapping for extracting bits from the ciphertext and during the circuit bootstrapping. Nonetheless, neither the bit extraction nor the the circuit bootstrapping require high precision. As a result, even if our EBS is adaptable, there would be no need to adapt it to their method. Thus, we first briefly explain and compare three full domain bootstrapping algorithms from [15,24,37].

FDFB. The idea of full domain bootstrapping of FDFB [24] is to select between two test vectors $p_+, p_- \in \mathbb{T}_N[X]$ based on the sign of message ct encrypts. The selection is done by public Mux evaluation, PubMux, with the external product. First, the sign of ct is first encrypted in a TRGSW-like ciphertext with the circuit bootstrapping [11] (like) procedure. We refer to it as a (T)RLev ciphertext [14], which equals to the last ℓ_{PM} rows of the TRGSW ciphertext. Note that the multiplication between a torus polynomial $p(X)$ and a TRLev encryption of $q(X) \in \mathbb{Z}_N[X]$ outputs a TRLWE encryption of $q(X) \cdot p(X)$.

The transformation to TRLev starts with ℓ_{PM}-functional bootstrappings to extract the sign from ct. Then each ciphertexts are TLWE-to-TRLWE keyswitched, which we denote it as RS. For specific information about the algorithm, refer to Algorithm 2 of [11]. This ends the conversion to TRLev, and the error in TRLev is bounded by

$$\mathsf{Var}\left(\mathsf{Err}\left(\mathsf{TRLev}(\mathsf{sign}(\mathsf{ct}))\right)\right) \leq V_{\mathsf{BS}} + V_{\mathsf{RS}},$$

and where V_{RS} denotes

$$V_{\mathsf{RS}} = n\ell_{\mathsf{RS}}\mathsf{Var}(\mathsf{Err}(\mathsf{RSK})) + \frac{1}{12}nB_{\mathsf{RS}}^{-2\ell_{\mathsf{RS}}}.$$

The TRGSW' encrypts 1 (resp. 0) if the sign of ct is positive (resp. negative). Then the evaluation of the PubMux follows by

$$\mathsf{ACC} = (\mathbf{0}, p_+ - p_-) \boxdot' \mathsf{TRLev}(\mathsf{sign}(\mathsf{ct})) + (\mathbf{0}, p_-).$$

Then ACC is initialized as a $\mathsf{TRLWE}_{\mathcal{K}}$ encryption of p_+ or p_- according to the sign of the input ciphertext ct. The error of ACC is given as

$$\mathsf{Var}\left(\mathsf{Err}\left(\mathsf{ACC}\right)\right) \leq N\ell_{\mathsf{PM}}\left(\frac{B_{\mathsf{PM}}}{2}\right)^2 (V_{\mathsf{BS}} + V_{\mathsf{RS}}) + \frac{1 + kN}{4 \cdot B_{\mathsf{PM}}^{2\ell_{\mathsf{PM}}}},$$

which we will now denote it as $V_{\mathsf{FDFB-ACC}}$. What is left is to bootstrap ct with the accumulator, and the final error after bootstrap is bounded by

$$V_{\mathsf{FDFB-ACC}} + V_{\mathsf{BS}}.$$

The full algorithm of FDFB(-EBS) is shown in Algorithm 6.

TOTA. The main intuition for TOTA [37] bootstrapping is the ModSwitch to $\mathbb{Z}_N$, since N is the maximal number of coefficients a test vector $tv \in \mathbb{T}_N[X]$ can hold. This makes the quadruple growth to the variance of ModSwitch (i.e., $4V_{\mathsf{MS}}$). Also, the decryption in $\mathbb{Z}_{2N}$ during BlindRotate with elements that lied in $\mathbb{Z}_N$ adds unwanted term pN to the message, for $p \in \{0, 1\}$. Thus TOTA computes the pN with the sign bootstrapping. The term pN is removed by subtracting the ModSwitch-ed sign bootstrapped ciphertext, which adds additional ModSwitch error V_{MS} and the bootstrapping error V_{BS} before the final bootstrapping. After removing the pN, the ciphertext is then finally bootstrapped with the test vector encoding the function f.

To sum up, TOTA involves two bootstrappings. First bootstrapping to calculate pN with pre-bootstrapping error variance

$$\leq V_{\mathsf{ct}} + 4V_{\mathsf{MS}},$$

followed by the second bootstrapping to evaluate the function f, with pre-bootstrapping error variance

$$\leq V_{\mathsf{BS}} + V_{\mathsf{ct}} + 5V_{\mathsf{MS}}.$$

The variance of error of the output ciphertext is bounded by V_{BS}. The full algorithm of TOTA-EBS is shown in Algorithm 7. For the EBS in line 3 of Algorithm 7, the ciphertext $(\bar{\mathbf{a}}, \bar{b})$ is already in $\mathbb{Z}_{2^{\nu+1}N}$, and we assume that ModSwitch is skipped during the EBS in Algorithm 5.

Algorithm 6: FDFB-EBS

Input: TLWE ciphertext $(\mathbf{a}, b) \in \mathsf{TLWE_s}\,(m)$
Input: extension factor $\nu \in \mathbb{N} \cup \{0\}$
Input: A $\mathcal{L}$-Lipschitz morphism $f : \mathbb{T} \to \mathbb{T}$
Input: Bootstrapping key BSK
Input: Keyswitch key KSK
Input: TLWE-to-TRLWE Keyswitch key RSK
Input: PubMux parameter $\ell_{\mathsf{PM}}, B_{\mathsf{PM}}$
Output: Refreshed TLWE ciphertext $\mathsf{TLWE_s}\left(f\left(\frac{\widehat{m}}{2^{\nu+1}N}\right)\right)$

1 **for** $i \in [\![1, \ell_{\mathsf{PM}}]\!]$ **do**

2 $\quad (\mathbf{a}^i, b^i) \leftarrow \mathsf{EBS}\left((\mathbf{a}, b), \nu, \frac{1}{2B_{\mathsf{PM}}^i} f_{\mathsf{sign}}, \mathsf{BSK}, \mathsf{KSK}\right) + \left(\mathbf{0}, \frac{1}{2B_{\mathsf{PM}}^i}\right)$

$\qquad\qquad\qquad\qquad\qquad\qquad \triangleright\ (\mathbf{a}^i, b^i) = \mathsf{TLWE_s}\left(\frac{\mathsf{sign}(ct)}{B_{\mathsf{PM}}^i}\right)$

3 $\quad \mathsf{PubACC}_i \leftarrow \mathsf{RS}_{\mathbf{s} \to \mathcal{K}}\left((\mathbf{a}^i, b^i), \mathsf{RSK}\right) \quad \triangleright\ \mathsf{PubACC} = \mathsf{TRLev}_{\mathcal{K}}\left(\mathsf{sign}(ct)\right)$

4 **end**

5 $\overrightarrow{\mathsf{ACC}} \leftarrow \mathsf{PubMux}\left(\mathsf{PubACC}, f(x), -f\left(x - \frac{1}{2}\right)\right)$

$\qquad\qquad\qquad\qquad \triangleright\ \tau^{-1}\left(\overrightarrow{\mathsf{ACC}}\right) = \mathsf{TRLWE}_{\mathcal{K}_{\mathrm{ext}}}^{2^\nu N}\left(tv_{\mathsf{sign}(ct)}\right)$

6 **for** $i \in [\![0, n-1]\!]$ **do**

7 $\quad \overrightarrow{\mathsf{RotACC}} \leftarrow \tau\left(X^{\bar{a}_i} \cdot \tau^{-1}\left(\overrightarrow{\mathsf{ACC}}\right)\right)$

8 $\quad$ **for** $j \in [\![0, 2^\nu - 1]\!]$ **do**

9 $\qquad \overrightarrow{\mathsf{ACC}}_j \leftarrow \mathsf{BSK}_i \boxdot \left(\overrightarrow{\mathsf{RotACC}}_j - \overrightarrow{\mathsf{ACC}}_j\right) + \overrightarrow{\mathsf{ACC}}_j$

10 $\quad$ **end**

11 **end**

12 $c' \leftarrow \mathsf{SampleExtract}(\overrightarrow{\mathsf{ACC}}_0)$

13 **return** $c = \mathsf{KeySwitch}(c', \mathsf{KSK})$

Comp. Using the fact that every function f can be written as the sum of (pseudo) odd and even functions, the Comp method [15] decomposes a function f as the sum of odd and even functions f_g, and f_h. They aim to compute odd/even functions within 2 bootstrappings each, which can be performed in parallel, and combine them together with simple addition. In total, they can compute any function with 4 functional bootstrappings. The first bootstrapping contains pre-bootstrapping error bounded by

$$\leq V_{\mathsf{ct}} + V_{\mathsf{MS}},$$

and the second bootstrapping bounded by

$$\leq V_{\mathsf{BS}} + V_{\mathsf{MS}}.$$

Due to the addition of two ciphertexts encrypting the value of the odd/even function, the final error of the Comp method is bounded by $2V_{\mathsf{BS}}$. The full algorithm of Comp(-EBS) is shown in Algorithm 8.

Algorithm 7: TOTA-EBS

Input: TLWE ciphertext $(\mathbf{a}, b) \in \mathsf{TLWE}_\mathbf{s}(m)$
Input: extension factor $\nu \in \mathbb{N} \cup \{0\}$
Input: A $\mathcal{L}$-Lipschitz morphism $f : \mathbb{T} \to \mathbb{T}$
Input: Bootstrapping key BSK
Input: Keyswitch key KSK
Output: Refreshed TLWE ciphertext $\mathsf{TLWE}_\mathbf{s}\left(f\left(\frac{\widehat{m}}{2^\nu N}\right)\right)$

1 $(\bar{\mathbf{a}}', \bar{b}') = \mathsf{ModSwitch}\left((\mathbf{a}, b), 2^\nu N\right)$ $\triangleright\ \widehat{m} = \bar{b}' - \langle \bar{\mathbf{a}}', \mathbf{s} \rangle \bmod 2^\nu N$

2 $(\bar{\mathbf{a}}, \bar{b}) = \mathsf{ModRaise}_{2^\nu N \to 2^{\nu+1} N}\left((\bar{\mathbf{a}}', \bar{b}')\right)$ $\triangleright\ \bar{m} = \widehat{m} + p 2^\nu N\ (\text{in } \mathbb{Z}_{2^{\nu+1}N})$

3 $\mathsf{ct}_{\mathsf{sgn}} \leftarrow \mathsf{EBS}\left((\bar{\mathbf{a}}, \bar{b}), \nu, \frac{1}{4} f_{\mathsf{sign}}, \mathsf{BSK}, \mathsf{KSK}\right) + \left(\mathbf{0}, \frac{1}{4}\right)$ $\triangleright\ \mathsf{ct}_{\mathsf{sgn}} = \mathsf{TLWE}_\mathbf{s}\left(\frac{p}{2}\right)$

4 $(\mathbf{a}', b') \leftarrow \mathsf{ModSwitch}\left(\mathsf{ct}_{\mathsf{sgn}}, 2^{\nu+1} N\right)$ $\triangleright\ b' - \langle \mathbf{a}', \mathbf{s} \rangle \bmod 2^{\nu+1} N = p 2^\nu N$

5 $(\mathfrak{a}, b) = (\mathbf{a}', b') + (\bar{\mathbf{a}}, \bar{b})$ $\triangleright\ b - \langle \mathfrak{a}, \mathbf{s} \rangle \bmod 2^{\nu+1} N = \bar{m}$

6 **return** $c = \mathsf{EBS}\left((\mathfrak{a}, b), \nu, f, \mathsf{BSK}, \mathsf{KSK}\right)$

The whole comparison of three full domain bootstrapping algorithms is shown in Table 1, and the functional bootstrapping is denoted as BS, and the keyswitch as KS. Among the three full domain bootstrapping algorithms, TOTA [37] outperforms other two works in terms of number of operations needed, and also the error after the bootstrapping. However, the variance of error from the ModSwitch nearly quadraples, and quintuples compared to other two. This can be effectively mitigated by our EBS, without changing any of the structure of TOTA. Still, our EBS can also be adapted to other two methods as they all inevitably bootstrap with ModSwitch error added.

3.5 Probability of Correct Bootstrapping with EBS

As formerly mentioned, TFHE based applications usually works on plaintext space of $\mathbb{Z}_p$, with p an integer [15,23,33]. Using the isomorphism between $\mathbb{Z}_p$ and $\frac{1}{p}\mathbb{Z}_p$, the elements $m \in \mathbb{Z}_p$ is encoded as $\frac{m}{p} \in \mathbb{T}$ ($\frac{m}{2p}$ for half domain). Then, to correctly bootstrap a ciphertext, both pre-bootstrap error and the error after bootstrapping must be smaller than $\frac{1}{2p}$. For a ciphertext whose error variance is V and plaintext space $\mathbb{Z}_p$, the probability of correct decryption is estimated by

$$p\left(|\mathsf{Err}\,(\mathsf{ct})| \leq \frac{1}{2p}\right) = \mathsf{erf}\left(\frac{1}{2p\sqrt{2V}}\right),$$

where erf is the error function. Thus, starting from the half-domain EBS with extension factor ν, the probability of correct bootstrapping is given as

$$p(\mathsf{HDEBS}) \geq \mathsf{erf}\left(\frac{1}{4p\sqrt{2V_{\mathsf{ct}} + \frac{1}{2^{2\nu-1}} V_{\mathsf{MS}}}}\right) \cdot \mathsf{erf}\left(\frac{1}{4p\sqrt{2V_{\mathsf{BS}}}}\right),$$

Table 1. Comparison of 3 full-domain functional bootstrapping algorithms. Here, $V_{\mathsf{MS}} = \frac{n+1}{48N^2}$, V_{ct} is the variance of error of input ciphertext ct. The BS denotes bootstrapping, RS denotes the TLWE-to-TRLWE KeySwitch.

	FDFB [24]	TOTA [37]	Comp [15]
Pre-bootstrap error	$V_{\mathsf{ct}} + V_{\mathsf{MS}}$	$V_{\mathsf{ct}} + 4V_{\mathsf{MS}}$ $V_{\mathsf{ct}} + V_{\mathsf{BS}} + 5V_{\mathsf{MS}}$	$V_{\mathsf{ct}} + V_{\mathsf{MS}}$ $V_{\mathsf{BS}} + V_{\mathsf{MS}}$
# of operations	$(\ell_{\mathsf{PM}} + 1)$-BS $+ \ell_{\mathsf{PM}}$-RS $+ 1$-PubMux	2-BS	4-BS
Error after Bootstrap	$V_{\mathsf{FDFB-ACC}} + V_{\mathsf{BS}}$	V_{BS}	$2V_{\mathsf{BS}}$
Parallel Computing	Partial	✗	✓
Compatible with EBS	✓	✓	✓

as for successful bootstrapping, both the pre-bootstrap error, and the after-bootstrap error must both be smaller than $\frac{1}{2p}$. Thus, for other three bootstrappings, FDFB-EBS, TOTA-EBS, Comp-EBS, we have

$$p(\mathsf{FDFB\text{-}EBS}) \geq \mathtt{erf}\left(\frac{1}{2p\sqrt{2V_{\mathsf{ct}} + \frac{1}{2^{2\nu-1}}V_{\mathsf{MS}}}}\right) \cdot \mathtt{erf}\left(\frac{1}{2p\sqrt{2V_{\mathsf{FDFB-ACC}} + 2V_{\mathsf{BS}}}}\right),$$

$$p(\mathsf{TOTA\text{-}EBS}) \geq \mathtt{erf}\left(\frac{1}{2p\sqrt{2V_{\mathsf{ct}} + \frac{1}{2^{2\nu-3}}V_{\mathsf{MS}}}}\right) \cdot \mathtt{erf}\left(\frac{1}{2p\sqrt{2V_{\mathsf{ct}} + 2V_{\mathsf{BS}} + \frac{5}{2^{2\nu-1}}V_{\mathsf{MS}}}}\right) \cdot \mathtt{erf}\left(\frac{1}{2p\sqrt{2V_{\mathsf{BS}}}}\right),$$

$$p(\mathsf{Comp\text{-}EBS}) \geq \mathtt{erf}\left(\frac{1}{2p\sqrt{2V_{\mathsf{ct}} + \frac{1}{2^{2\nu-1}}V_{\mathsf{MS}}}}\right) \cdot \mathtt{erf}\left(\frac{1}{2p\sqrt{2V_{\mathsf{BS}} + \frac{1}{2^{2\nu-1}}V_{\mathsf{MS}}}}\right)^2 \cdot \mathtt{erf}\left(\frac{1}{2p\sqrt{4V_{\mathsf{BS}}}}\right).$$

Then, the probability of failure is calculated by subtracting the success rate from 1, e.g., $p_{err}(\mathsf{HDEBS}) \leq 1 - p(\mathsf{HDEBS})$.

Remark 3. The above estimation is for when fixed-point arithmetic is used (in which is IND-CPA^{D} secure), using $\mathbb{Z}_p$ as a plaintext space. Thus, the functions are encoded in a staircase-like manner, i.e., $\sum_i f\left(\lfloor \frac{p}{2^\nu N} \cdot i \rfloor\right)$ for $f : \mathbb{Z}_p \to \mathbb{Z}_p$, that works like a breakwater to prevent pre-bootstrap noise flooding out.

4   Experimental Results

We implemented our (HD)EBS along with the adaptation of EBS to three full-domain bootstrappings, FDFB-EBS, TOTA-EBS, Comp-EBS. Our implementations were built upon TFHE library [12], where the torus elements $\mathbb{T}$ are represented as 32-bit integer, $\mathbb{Z}_{2^{32}}$. Our experiments were executed with Intel i9-13900K running at 5.80 GHz with 24 cores (8 performance cores, 16 efficient

---

Algorithm 8: Comp-EBS (Modular)

Input: TLWE ciphertext $(\mathbf{a}, b) \in \mathsf{TLWE_s}(m)$

Input: extension factor $\nu \in \mathbb{N} \cup \{0\}$

Input: A $\mathcal{L}$-Lipschitz morphism $f : \mathbb{T} \to \mathbb{T}$

Input: Bootstrapping key BSK

Input: Keyswitch key KSK

Input: Plaintext modulus $\mathcal{P}$

Output: Refreshed TLWE ciphertext $\mathsf{TLWE_s}\left(f\left(\frac{\widehat{m}}{2^\nu N}\right)\right)$

1 $c_1 = \mathsf{EBS}\left((\mathbf{a}, b), \nu, \frac{1}{2\mathcal{P}} + \frac{1}{\mathcal{P}}\lfloor 2^\nu N\mathcal{P}x\rfloor, \mathsf{BSK}, \mathsf{KSK}\right) - \left(\mathbf{0}, \frac{1}{2\mathcal{P}}\right)$

2 $c_2 = \mathsf{EBS}\left((\mathbf{a}, b), \nu, \frac{1}{2\mathcal{P}} + \frac{1}{4} + \frac{1}{\mathcal{P}}\lfloor 2^\nu N\mathcal{P}x\rfloor, \mathsf{BSK}, \mathsf{KSK}\right) - \left(\mathbf{0}, \frac{1}{2\mathcal{P}} + \frac{1}{4}\right)$

3 $c_3 = \mathsf{EBS}\left(c_1, \nu, \frac{f(x)-f(-x-\frac{1}{\mathcal{P}})}{2}, \mathsf{BSK}, \mathsf{KSK}\right)$

4 $c_4 = \mathsf{EBS}\left(c_2, \nu, \frac{f(x)+f(-x-\frac{1}{\mathcal{P}})}{2}, \mathsf{BSK}, \mathsf{KSK}\right)$

5 **return** $c_3 + c_4$

---

cores) and 32 threads, 128 GB RAM, and with 64-bit Ubuntu 22.04 environment. We compiled our experiment with g++ 11.3.0 with flags `-ltfhe-spqlios-fma -fopenmp -lquadmath`, using `spqlios` FFT in TFHE for fast polynomial multiplication, and multi-threading for our parallel EBS. The code we used for experiment is publicly available at https://github.com/Stirling75/Extended-BootStrapping.

4.1   TFHE Parameters

As the security of TFHE scheme has its roots in the hardness of (R)LWE problem, its security level is decided by the dimension of ciphertext (i.e., n, kN), and its corresponding standard deviation of errors added during encryption (i.e., $\sigma_{\mathsf{TLWE}}, \sigma_{\mathsf{TRLWE}}$). The security of TRGSW is guaranteed by the security of TRLWE, as it is a vector of TRLWE ciphertexts. We estimated the cost of attack models for various instances $(n, \sigma_{\mathsf{TLWE}})$, and $(N, \sigma_{\mathsf{TRLWE}})$ with the lattice estimator [1]. For most of our instances, the cost of the dual-hybrid attack [17] were estimated to be the cheapest.

In Table 2, we present eight TFHE parameter sets satisfying $\lambda = 80, 128$ bits of security, which implies it requires at least 2^λ operations for the attack models to succeed their attacks. As can been seen from parameter set I_1 and III_1, T(R)LWE ciphertexts with same dimension, decreasing the security parameter λ enables to use small standard deviation for the error which decreases the error after bootstrapping. Notice that for parameter sets (I_1, I_2, I_3) and (III_1, III_2, III_3), we used exactly the same parameters except for the ring dimension N, to observe the effect of using larger N. Nonetheless, the native TFHE library only supports FFT of dimension 1024, and we made slight changes in their library to enable FFT on dimension 2048 and 4096 to support fast polynomial multiplication.

Table 2. TFHE parameter sets. λ indicates the security level of given parameter set.

Param Set	λ	TLWE		TRLWE			KSK		BSK	
		n	σ_{TLWE} $(\log_2)$	N	k	σ_{TRLWE} $(\log_2)$	ℓ_{KS}	B_{KS}	ℓ_{BS}	B_{BS}
I_1	80	750	-21.2	1024	1	-29.3	3	2^8	7	2^4
I_2	80	750	-21.2	2048	1	-32	3	2^8	7	2^4
I_3	80	750	-21.2	4096	1	-32	3	2^8	7	2^4
II	80	900	-25.7	2048	1	-32	5	2^6	7	2^4
III_1	128	670	-12.4	1024	1	-20.1	3	2^5	8	2^3
III_2	128	670	-12.4	2048	1	-32	3	2^5	8	2^3
III_3	128	670	-12.4	4096	1	-32	3	2^5	8	2^3
IV	128	1300	-26.1	2048	1	-32	5	2^6	7	2^4

However, this modified FFT still uses 64-bit `double` with 53 bits of precision, accumulating non-negligible noise during polynomial multiplication when $N \geq 2048$. We found this inhibits exact noise analysis for cases where polynomial multiplication over dimension $N \geq 2048$ is used. Further details on noise accumulation during FFT and polynomial multiplication can be found in Proposition 1 of [21].

We also describe FDFB parameters in Table 3. These parameters are only used for FDFB and has no effect on other bootstrapping methods. Using these parameters, FDFB runs with $\ell_{\mathsf{PM}} + 1 = 6$ (functional) bootstrappings, $\ell_{\mathsf{PM}} = 5$ RS and 1 PubMux operations.

Table 3. Parameters for RSK and PubMux for FDFB.

Parameter Set	RSK		PubMux	
	ℓ_{RS}	B_{RS}	ℓ_{PM}	B_{PM}
I_1, I_2, I_3	6	2^5	5	2^5
II	4	2^6		
III_1, III_2, III_3	4	2^6		
IV	6	2^5		

4.2 Performance Results

With the parameters we suggested in Sect. 4.1, we make a thorough analysis in terms of public key size, latency, and noise.

Public Key Size. Following the footsteps of [11], we measure the size of the public keys (BSK, KSK, RSK) published for homomorphic operations. First we measure the size of TLWE, TRLWE, TRGSW ciphertexts and then calculate the size of each public keys. For example, the size of TLWE ciphertext of parameter set I_1 is $(n + 1) \times 32 = 24\,032$ bits ≈ 3.004 KB. Also, since KSK is composed of $N \times \ell_{KS} \times B_{KS}$ TLWE ciphertexts, the size of the KSK is 2.36 GB.

Likewise, we evaluate the key size for every parameter set and present the result in Fig. 1. As we can observe from the result of parameter sets (I_1, I_2, I_3) and (III_1, III_2, III_3), the key size doubles as N doubles. Still, with proper adjustment of parameters, we can make the public key size '*sufficiently small*' (see BSK and KSK of parameter I_1 and II) even with large N.

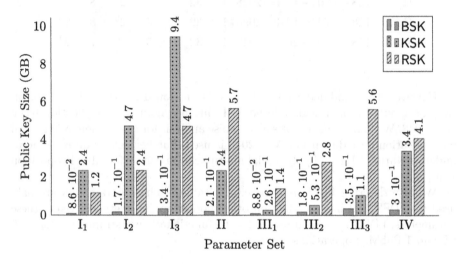

Fig. 1. Public key (BSK, KSK, RSK) sizes for our parameters.

Noise Analysis. Next, we examine the variance of noise for our parameters. As our work heavily relies on the noise estimates of variety of algorithms, we found it necessary to show experimental validation of our estimations proposed in previous sections. We present our results in Table 4. We calculated (with label $^{(c)}$) the standard deviations with our variance estimations, and experimentally validated it (with label $^{(E)}$) by observing 2^{15} samples for each case. For bootstrappings, we set the test vector as identity function and calculated the standard deviations.

For ModSwitch, we calculated two standard deviations with the conventional V_{MS} formula $\frac{n+1}{48N^2}$, and with the hamming weight of the TLWE key s, $\frac{\mathsf{Ham}(s)+1}{48N^2}$. Our result shows that the experimental error nearly corresponds to the standard deviation calculated with the hamming weight for all cases. For bootstrapping (including TOTA and Comp), we observe that for parameter sets I_2, I_3, II and IV, their experimental bootstrapping error are larger than expected due to the non-negligible FFT error accumulated during polynomial multiplication. Nonetheless, for parameter set III_2 and III_3, their main error standard deviations are dominated by the keyswitching error and seems to follow the estimation well. We provide detailed error analysis of BlindRotate and KeySwitch in Appendix A.1, Table 5.

To only observe the output noise of each bootstrapping method, we first pre-computed the rotated amount (during BlindRotate) for given ciphertext. Then we bootstrapped the ciphertext with each bootstrapping methods, and then subtracted the rotated test vector from the accumulator, thereby eliminating the effect of the ModSwitch. From the result, FDFB shows larger noise standard deviation compared to other bootstrapping methods due to the PubMux operation. Moreover, from the result of Proposition 1, we claim that until $\mathcal{L}\sigma_{\mathsf{MS}}$, where $\mathcal{L}$ is the Lipschitz constant of the function f, is larger than the output bootstrapping noise standard deviation, there will be room for improvement with our EBS (Fig. 2).

Table 4. Estimated noise standard deviation (with label $^{(c)}$) and experimental noise standard deviation (with label $^{(E)}$) of ModSwitch and four bootstrapping methods. The standard deviations are presented in the form of $\log_2$.

		I_1	I_2	I_3	II	III_1	III_2	III_3	IV
ModSwitch	$\sigma_{\mathsf{MS}}^{(c)}$	-8.016	-9.016	-10.016	-8.885	-8.097	-9.097	-10.097	-8.620
	$\mathsf{Ham}(s)$	379	379	379	448	330	330	330	645
	$\sigma_{\mathsf{MS}}^{(c,\mathsf{Ham})}$	-8.508	-9.508	-10.508	-9.387	-8.607	-9.607	-10.607	-9.125
	$\sigma_{\mathsf{MS}}^{(E)}$	-8.509	-9.506	-10.507	-9.385	-8.601	-9.591	-10.544	-9.116
Bootstrap	$\sigma_{\mathsf{BS}}^{(c)}$	-14.411	-14.855	-14.355	-16.614	-6.000	-6.107	-5.607	-16.364
	$\sigma_{\mathsf{BS}}^{(E,\mathsf{id})}$	-14.882	-14.663	-14.033	-15.293	-6.369	-6.157	-5.654	-15.128
FDFB	$\sigma_{\mathsf{FDFB}}^{(c)}$	-4.250	-4.194	-3.193	-5.951	4.161	4.554	5.554	-5.703
	$\sigma_{\mathsf{FDFB}}^{(E,\mathsf{id})}$	-10.196	-10.010	-8.524	-9.882	-2.152	-1.830	-1.750	-9.753
TOTA	$\sigma_{\mathsf{TOTA}}^{(c)}$	-14.411	-14.855	-14.355	-16.614	-6.000	-6.107	-5.607	-16.364
	$\sigma_{\mathsf{TOTA}}^{(E,\mathsf{id})}$	-14.879	-14.639	-14.063	-15.628	-6.371	-6.160	-5.649	-14.992
Comp	$\sigma_{\mathsf{Comp}}^{(c)}$	-13.911	-14.355	-13.855	-16.114	-5.500	-5.607	-5.107	-15.864
	$\sigma_{\mathsf{Comp}}^{(E,\mathsf{id})}$	-14.581	-14.460	-13.611	-14.796	-6.163	-6.149	-5.645	-14.533

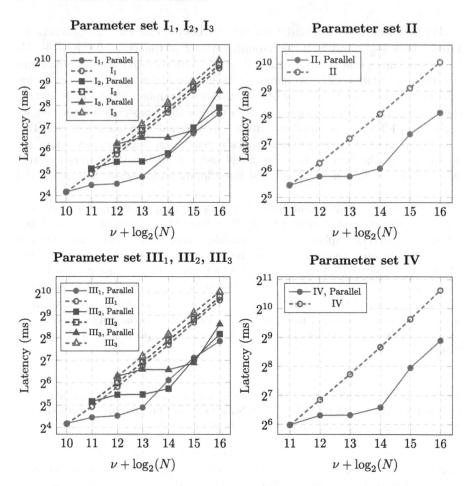

Fig. 2. Latency for EBS with eight sets of parameters given in Table 2. The x-axis represents $\nu + \log_2(N)$ for each parameter set, and the y-axis represents the latency in milliseconds in logarithmic scale of base 2.

Benchmarks. We now present benchmarks for EBS, and precision growth when adapted to full-domain bootstrapping methods. We first measure the latency for computing a single conventional TFHE bootstrapping with EBS. Note that when the extension factor $\nu = 0$, the EBS becomes exactly same as original bootstrapping. From the results, we can see that for non-parallelized settings (depicted in dashed line), using $N' = 2^\nu N$ with $\nu > 0$ is slower than using EBS with dimension N and extension factor ν. Also, since the EBS increases the number of external products by the factor of 2^ν, it is easy to see the exponential increase in latency with respect to the extension factor ν. For parallelized version of EBS (depicted in solid line), we found that we lose full parallelization from $\nu = 3$ due to computational limitations. Thus, our results show exponential growth after $\nu = 3$.

Precision. We finally turn to our major contribution of EBS, the precision enhancement. For three full-domain bootstrapping methods we introduced, we measured the output noise standard deviations for two functions, the identity function (with Lipschitz constant $\mathcal{L}_1 = 1$) and $f(x) = 43\sin(x/32)$ (with Lipschitz constant $\mathcal{L}_2 \approx 33.772$) by matching the torus $\left[-\frac{1}{2}, \frac{1}{2}\right)$ to $[-64, 64]$. With the three sigma rule, we measured the bit precision of the results and presented them in Fig. 3 for four parameter sets I_1, II, III_1, IV. With the experimental results from Table 4 and some additional experiments, we also calculated the (ideal)

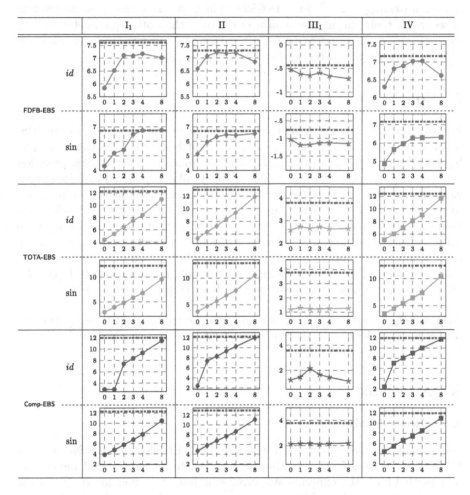

Fig. 3. Experimental output precision of three full-domain bootstrapping methods (FDFB, TOTA, Comp) with EBS evaluated with the four parameter sets I_1, II, III_1, and IV. The *id* and sin stands for the identity function and the function $f(x) = 43\sin(x/32)$, by mapping the torus to $[-64, 64]$. The x-axis represents the extension factor ν, and the y-axis represents the output bit precision. The red dash-dot line represents the maximum precision for each parameter and bootstrapping method.

maximum precision of each parameter set and depicted it as a dash-dot line in all of the figures. We noticed that the change of function (which changes the test vector) introduces noticeable changes to the maximum precision to FDFB due to their PubMux, but is quite negligible to other two full-domain bootstrapping methods.

From our results, we can see for both parameter sets I_1, II and IV, the precision improvement is significantly clear for TOTA and Comp. Nonetheless, due to the PubMux in FDFB, the maximum precision for their method is lower than other two methods. For parameter set III_1, due to its large noise standard deviation ($\sigma_{TRLWE} = 2^{-20.1}$) for TRGSW ciphertext (since they achieve 128 bits of security), their output precision is quite lower than other parameter sets. In this case, it is suggested to increase the size of N and use smaller standard deviation, like in parameter set IV ($N = 2048, \sigma_{TRLWE} = 2^{-32}$).

5   Conclusion

In this paper, we suggested a high precision TFHE bootstrapping algorithm EBS, which can almost remove the affect of ModSwitch during bootstrapping. The biggest advantage in our scheme is that it allows to bootstrap with large precision with small public key size compared to when enlarging N. Also, EBS can be naturally parallelized for fast computation, where no known algorithm is known to parallelize TFHE bootstrapping. Thus, we can even bootstrap much faster than previous literature of using large N. We show that our EBS is compatible with both modular, and approximate arithmetic, as well as previously known full domain bootstrapping algorithms. We also believe EBS can be one of the solution for bridging other homomorphic encryption schemes with TFHE, by allowing high precision, nonlinear function bootstrapping with small cost.

Acknowledgements. This work was supported by the National Research Foundation of Korea (NRF) grant funded by the Korea government (MSIT) (No.2022R1 F1A1074291).

A   Appendix

A.1   Noise Analysis

We present detailed analysis of noise for the BlindRotate, KeySwitch, and FDFB-ACC in Table 5. Due to the error added during polynomial multiplication (with FFT), the experimental error standard deviation for $N \geq 2048$ is larger than estimated results.

Table 5. Estimated noise standard deviation (with label $^{(c)}$) and experimental noise standard deviation (with label $^{(E)}$). The standard deviations are presented in the form of $\log_2$.

		I_1	I_2	I_3	II	III_1	III_2	III_3	IV
Bootstrap	$\sigma_{BR}^{(c)}$	−14.620	−16.771	−16.271	−16.640	−6.406	−14.794	−14.295	−16.374
	$\sigma_{BR}^{(E,\mathrm{id})}$	**−15.355**	**−15.539**	**−14.675**	**−15.297**	**−7.181**	**−11.539**	**−10.682**	**−15.129**
	$\sigma_{KS}^{(c)}$	−15.407	−14.907	−14.407	−19.039	−6.607	−6.107	−5.607	−19.439
	$\sigma_{KS}^{(E)}$	**−15.413**	**−14.910**	**−14.419**	**−19.068**	**−6.657**	**−6.157**	**−5.655**	**−19.472**
	$\sigma_{BS}^{(c)}$	−14.411	−14.855	−14.355	−16.614	−6.000	−6.107	−5.607	−16.364
	$\sigma_{BS}^{(E,\mathrm{id})}$	**−14.882**	**−14.663**	**−14.033**	**−15.293**	**−6.369**	**−6.157**	**−5.654**	**−15.128**
FDFB	$\sigma_{ACC}^{(c)}$	−4.250	−4.194	−3.194	−5.951	4.161	4.554	5.554	−5.703
	$\sigma_{ACC}^{(E,\mathrm{id})}$	**−10.207**	**−10.004**	**−8.546**	**−9.892**	**−2.155**	**−1.838**	**−1.751**	**−9.764**
	$\sigma_{FDFB}^{(c)}$	−4.250	−4.194	−3.193	−5.951	4.161	4.554	5.554	−5.703
	$\sigma_{FDFB}^{(E,\mathrm{id})}$	**−10.196**	**−10.010**	**−8.524**	**−9.882**	**−2.152**	**−1.830**	**−1.750**	**−9.753**

A.2   Benchmarks

In this section, we present the benchmark results for our parallelized and non-parallelized EBS along with the benchmarks for three full-domain bootstrapping methods. Note that none of the operations except the EBS were parallelized for fair comparison (Table 6).

Table 6. Benchmark results for EBS and three full-domain bootstrapping methods. The **NP** is for non-parallelized, and **P** denotes parallelized results. All results are presented in milliseconds (ms).

		ν	I_1	I_2	I_3	II	III_1	III_2	III_3	IV
HDEBS	NP	0	17.88	36.44	79.28	43.98	18.08	35.84	77.88	62.72
		1	31.38	64.4	146.24	77.88	30.58	63.7	145.5	114.74
		2	57.04	120.02	284	148.42	56.32	119.88	286.42	211.9
		3	107	233.82	537.98	280.32	107.52	236.54	556.74	405.54
		4	207.98	458.46	1050.92	550.52	207.48	457.56	1061.12	792.28
		5	412.86	910.26	–	1088.24	414.1	904.76	–	1580.92
		6	825.16	–	–	–	819.8	–	–	–
	P	0	17.895	36.67	78.4	43.94	18.205	35.85	78.1	63.21
		1	22.12	45.205	96.28	55.16	21.98	44.15	96.12	79.015
		2	23.015	45.6	96.62	55.2	23.15	44.55	95.53	79.64
		3	28.465	59.235	120.6	67.8	29.79	53.42	118.055	95.545
		4	55.305	131.64	406.12	166.36	69.47	132.765	392.385	246.675
		5	110.225	243.07	–	290.92	138.865	288.21	–	475.665
		6	201.275	–	–	–	232.34	–	–	–

(continued)

Table 6. (*continued*)

		ν	I_1	I_2	I_3	II	III_1	III_2	III_3	IV
FDFB-EBS	P	0	130.22	253.78	543.57	303.67	123.02	243.8	529.18	457.89
		1	154.42	298.65	605.84	355.07	146.28	295.92	600.24	520.72
		2	157.94	307.18	639.79	365.77	150.76	294.27	626.65	532.28
		3	239.23	432.24	1016.78	478.13	193.35	443.41	957.79	821.15
		4	410.85	854.58	2561.31	1012.06	438.65	833.93	2522.98	1484.04
TOTA-EBS	P	0	37.98	75.1	162.64	92.84	37.15	74.9	166.33	134.13
		1	44.06	88.56	191.68	113.51	45.33	91.87	193.88	157.56
		2	46.77	91.86	196.31	113.15	46.52	91.47	196.84	159.61
		3	83.1	134.62	275.54	155.91	59.89	131.12	307.76	258.35
		4	153.99	273.6	827	330.39	139.47	268.45	822.79	474.7
Comp-EBS	P	0	74.67	150.25	325.02	184.9	74.12	149.96	332.31	267.24
		1	89.31	181.11	384.38	226.16	89.9	181.79	394.74	317.37
		2	93.24	184.26	391.46	225.2	93.5	182.38	392.45	318.85
		3	171.22	308.43	561.69	321.24	152.34	271.53	595.7	460.4
		4	303.01	544.15	1650.39	657.29	281.76	541.95	1669.71	964.52

References

1. Albrecht, M.R., Player, R., Scott, S.: On the concrete hardness of learning with errors. Cryptology ePrint Archive, Paper 2015/046 (2015). https://eprint.iacr.org/2015/046, https://eprint.iacr.org/2015/046
2. Bae, Y., Cheon, J.H., Cho, W., Kim, J., Kim, T.: Meta-BTS: bootstrapping precision beyond the limit. Cryptology ePrint Archive (2022)
3. Bergerat, L., et al.: Parameter optimization & larger precision for (T) FHE. Cryptology ePrint Archive (2022)
4. Boura, C., Gama, N., Georgieva, M., Jetchev, D.: Simulating homomorphic evaluation of deep learning predictions. In: Dolev, S., Hendler, D., Lodha, S., Yung, M. (eds.) CSCML 2019. LNCS, vol. 11527, pp. 212–230. Springer, Cham (2019). https://doi.org/10.1007/978-3-030-20951-3_20
5. Boura, C., Gama, N., Georgieva, M., Jetchev, D.: CHIMERA: combining ring-LWE-based fully homomorphic encryption schemes. J. Math. Cryptol. **14**(1), 316–338 (2020)
6. Bourse, F., Minelli, M., Minihold, M., Paillier, P.: Fast homomorphic evaluation of deep discretized neural networks. In: Shacham, H., Boldyreva, A. (eds.) CRYPTO 2018. LNCS, vol. 10993, pp. 483–512. Springer, Cham (2018). https://doi.org/10.1007/978-3-319-96878-0_17
7. Bourse, F., Sanders, O., Traoré, J.: Improved secure integer comparison via homomorphic encryption. In: Jarecki, S. (ed.) CT-RSA 2020. LNCS, vol. 12006, pp. 391–416. Springer, Cham (2020). https://doi.org/10.1007/978-3-030-40186-3_17
8. Carpov, S., Izabachène, M., Mollimard, V.: New techniques for multi-value input homomorphic evaluation and applications. In: Matsui, M. (ed.) CT-RSA 2019. LNCS, vol. 11405, pp. 106–126. Springer, Cham (2019). https://doi.org/10.1007/978-3-030-12612-4_6

9. Cheon, J.H., Han, K., Kim, A., Kim, M., Song, Y.: Bootstrapping for approximate homomorphic encryption. In: Nielsen, J.B., Rijmen, V. (eds.) EUROCRYPT 2018. LNCS, vol. 10820, pp. 360–384. Springer, Cham (2018). https://doi.org/10.1007/978-3-319-78381-9_14

10. Chillotti, I., Gama, N., Georgieva, M., Izabachène, M.: Faster packed homomorphic operations and efficient circuit bootstrapping for TFHE. In: Takagi, T., Peyrin, T. (eds.) ASIACRYPT 2017. LNCS, vol. 10624, pp. 377–408. Springer, Cham (2017). https://doi.org/10.1007/978-3-319-70694-8_14

11. Chillotti, I., Gama, N., Georgieva, M., Izabachène, M.: TFHE: fast fully homomorphic encryption over the torus. J. Cryptol. 33(1), 34–91 (2020)

12. Chillotti, I., Gama, N., Georgieva, M., Izabachène, M.: TFHE: fast fully homomorphic encryption library (2016). https://tfhe.github.io/tfhe/

13. Chillotti, I., Joye, M., Paillier, P.: Programmable bootstrapping enables efficient homomorphic inference of deep neural networks. In: Dolev, S., Margalit, O., Pinkas, B., Schwarzmann, A. (eds.) CSCML 2021. LNCS, vol. 12716, pp. 1–19. Springer, Cham (2021). https://doi.org/10.1007/978-3-030-78086-9_1

14. Chillotti, I., Ligier, D., Orfila, J.B., Tap, S.: Improved programmable bootstrapping with larger precision and efficient arithmetic circuits for TFHE. In: Tibouchi, M., Wang, H. (eds.) ASIACRYPT 2021. LNCS, vol. 13092, pp. 670–699. Springer, Cham (2021). https://doi.org/10.1007/978-3-030-92078-4_23

15. Clet, P.E., Zuber, M., Boudguiga, A., Sirdey, R., Gouy-Pailler, C.: Putting up the swiss army knife of homomorphic calculations by means of TFHE functional bootstrapping (2022). https://eprint.iacr.org/2022/149

16. Ducas, L., Micciancio, D.: FHEW: bootstrapping homomorphic encryption in less than a second. In: Oswald, E., Fischlin, M. (eds.) EUROCRYPT 2015. LNCS, vol. 9056, pp. 617–640. Springer, Heidelberg (2015). https://doi.org/10.1007/978-3-662-46800-5_24

17. Espitau, T., Joux, A., Kharchenko, N.: On a dual/hybrid approach to small secret LWE. In: Bhargavan, K., Oswald, E., Prabhakaran, M. (eds.) INDOCRYPT 2020. LNCS, vol. 12578, pp. 440–462. Springer, Cham (2020). https://doi.org/10.1007/978-3-030-65277-7_20

18. Gentry, C.: A fully homomorphic encryption scheme. Stanford university (2009)

19. Guimaraes, A., Borin, E., Aranha, D.F.: Revisiting the functional bootstrap in TFHE. IACR Trans. Cryptogr. Hardw. Embed. Syst. 2021(2), 229–253 (2021)

20. Joye, M., Paillier, P.: Blind rotation in fully homomorphic encryption with extended keys. In: Dolev, S., Katz, J., Meisels, A. (eds.) CSCML 2022. LNCS, vol. 13301, pp. 1–18. Springer, Cham (2022). https://doi.org/10.1007/978-3-031-07689-3_1

21. Klemsa, J.: Fast and error-free negacyclic integer convolution using extended Fourier transform. In: Dolev, S., Margalit, O., Pinkas, B., Schwarzmann, A. (eds.) CSCML 2021. LNCS, vol. 12716, pp. 282–300. Springer, Cham (2021). https://doi.org/10.1007/978-3-030-78086-9_22

22. Klemsa, J.: Setting up efficient TFHE parameters for multivalue plaintexts and multiple additions. Cryptology ePrint Archive (2021)

23. Klemsa, J., Önen, M.: Parallel operations over TFHE-encrypted multi-digit integers. In: Proceedings of the Twelveth ACM Conference on Data and Application Security and Privacy, pp. 288–299 (2022)

24. Kluczniak, K., Schild, L.: FDFB: full domain functional bootstrapping towards practical fully homomorphic encryption. arXiv preprint arXiv:2109.02731 (2021)

25. Lee, E., et al.: Low-complexity deep convolutional neural networks on fully homomorphic encryption using multiplexed parallel convolutions. In: International Conference on Machine Learning, pp. 12403–12422. PMLR (2022)
26. Lee, J.W., et al.: Privacy-preserving machine learning with fully homomorphic encryption for deep neural network. IEEE Access **10**, 30039–30054 (2022)
27. Lee, Y., Lee, J.W., Kim, Y.S., Kim, Y., No, J.S., Kang, H.: High-precision bootstrapping for approximate homomorphic encryption by error variance minimization. In: Dunkelman, O., Dziembowski, S. (eds.) EUROCRYPT 2022. LNCS, vol. 13275, pp. 551–580. Springer, Cham (2022). https://doi.org/10.1007/978-3-031-06944-4_19
28. Lee, Y., et al.: Efficient FHEW bootstrapping with small evaluation keys, and applications to threshold homomorphic encryption. Cryptology ePrint Archive (2022)
29. Liu, Z., Micciancio, D., Polyakov, Y.: Large-precision homomorphic sign evaluation using FHEW/TFHE bootstrapping. Cryptology ePrint Archive (2021)
30. Lu, W.J., Huang, Z., Hong, C., Ma, Y., Qu, H.: PEGASUS: bridging polynomial and non-polynomial evaluations in homomorphic encryption. In: 2021 IEEE Symposium on Security and Privacy (SP), pp. 1057–1073. IEEE (2021)
31. Lyubashevsky, V., Peikert, C., Regev, O.: On ideal lattices and learning with errors over rings. J. ACM (JACM) **60**(6), 1–35 (2013)
32. Micciancio, D., Polyakov, Y.: Bootstrapping in FHEW-like cryptosystems. In: Proceedings of the 9th on Workshop on Encrypted Computing & Applied Homomorphic Cryptography, pp. 17–28 (2021)
33. Okada, H., Kiyomoto, S., Cid, C.: Integer-wise functional bootstrapping on TFHE: applications in secure integer arithmetics. Information **12**(8), 297 (2021)
34. Paul, J., Tan, B.H.M., Veeravalli, B., Aung, K.M.M.: Non-interactive decision trees and applications with multi-bit TFHE. Algorithms **15**(9), 333 (2022)
35. Regev, O.: On lattices, learning with errors, random linear codes, and cryptography. J. ACM (JACM) **56**(6), 1–40 (2009)
36. Stehlé, D., Steinfeld, R., Tanaka, K., Xagawa, K.: Efficient public key encryption based on ideal lattices. In: Matsui, M. (ed.) ASIACRYPT 2009. LNCS, vol. 5912, pp. 617–635. Springer, Heidelberg (2009). https://doi.org/10.1007/978-3-642-10366-7_36
37. Yang, Z., Xie, X., Shen, H., Chen, S., Zhou, J.: TOTA: fully homomorphic encryption with smaller parameters and stronger security. Cryptology ePrint Archive (2021)

Verifiable Capacity-Bound Functions: A New Primitive from Kolmogorov Complexity

(Revisiting Space-Based Security in the Adaptive Setting)

Giuseppe Ateniese[1], Long Chen[2], Danilo Francati[3(✉)],
Dimitrios Papadopoulos[4], and Qiang Tang[5]

[1] George Mason University, Virginia, USA
ateniese@gmu.edu
[2] Institute of Software, Chinese Academy of Sciences, Beijing, China
chenlong@iscas.ac.cn
[3] Aarhus University, Aarhus, Denmark
dfrancati@cs.au.dk
[4] Hong Kong University of Science and Technology, Kowloon, Hong Kong
dipapado@cse.ust.hk
[5] The University of Sydney, Sydney, Australia
qiang.tang@sydney.edu.au

Abstract. We initiate the study of *verifiable capacity-bound function* (VCBF). The main VCBF property imposes a strict lower bound on the number of bits read from memory during evaluation (referred to as minimum capacity). No adversary, even with unbounded computational resources, should produce an output without spending this minimum memory capacity. Moreover, a VCBF allows for an efficient public verification process: Given a proof of correctness, checking the validity of the output takes significantly fewer memory resources, sublinear in the target minimum capacity. Finally, it achieves soundness, i.e., no computationally bounded adversary can produce a proof that passes verification for a false output. With these properties, we believe a VCBF can be viewed as a "space" analog of a verifiable delay function. We then propose the first VCBF construction relying on evaluating a degree-d polynomial f from $\mathbb{F}_p[x]$ at a random point. We leverage ideas from *Kolmogorov complexity* to prove that sampling f from a large set (i.e., for high-enough d) ensures that evaluation must entail reading a number of bits proportional to the size of its coefficients. Moreover, our construction benefits from existing verifiable polynomial evaluation schemes to realize our efficient verification requirements. In practice, for a field of order $O(2^\lambda)$ our VCBF achieves $O((d+1)\lambda)$ minimum capacity, whereas verification requires just $O(\lambda)$. The minimum capacity of our VCBF construction holds against adversaries that perform a constant number of random memory accesses during evaluation. This poses the natural question of whether a VCBF with high minimum capacity guarantees exists when dealing with adversaries that perform non-constant (e.g., polynomial) number of random accesses.

The authors are listed alphabetically.

© International Association for Cryptologic Research 2023
A. Boldyreva and V. Kolesnikov (Eds.): PKC 2023, LNCS 13941, pp. 63–93, 2023.
https://doi.org/10.1007/978-3-031-31371-4_3

Keywords: Kolmogorov complexity · Adaptive security · Polynomial evaluation · Verifiable computation · Verifiable delay function

1 Introduction

Time and space complexity are functions that measure the efficiency of algorithms. These two functions are related (sometimes appear in the same setting) but distinct. For instance, "time" may refer to the number of memory accesses performed by an algorithm, while "space" refers to the amount of memory needed. In general, we try to minimize these functions, i.e., an ideal algorithm is one that is fast and tight. However, in cryptography, we are also interested in algorithms that are deliberately slow or capacious with the idea that, if the adversary must run them, the attack will be slow and costly. This has found numerous applications, e.g., in the context of proof-of-work for distributed consensus [46], and anti-spam mechanisms [9,27]; and password hashing or key derivations to be used against offline brute-force [38,52].

The most prominent definitions for "space-demanding" functions proposed in the literature are memory-hardness [2–6,19,21,49], and bandwidth-hardness [15,54]. While they share the same initial motivation, these notions vary in their formalization and achieved security guarantees. Memory-hardness, as originally defined [49], guarantees a lower bound in the memory/time product required to compute the function. Informally, a function is memory-hard if the product of the evaluation memory cost m and time t for any adversary cannot be less than $mt \in \Omega(n^2)$, where $O(n)$ is the time for an honest party. This has been widely proposed as a countermeasure against attackers that aim to gain an unfair advantage by using customized hardware, such as an ASIC, as it forces one to dedicate a significant area of memory to avoid being too slow. Thus, the cost of ASIC manufacturing would grow proportionally. Bandwidth-hardness guarantees that the *energy cost* for evaluating the function does not differ much across different platforms with variable computing energy costs (e.g., CPU vs. ASIC). In practice, this is based on the observation that although ASICs may have superior energy consumption for specific tasks, off-chip memory accesses incur comparable energy costs on ASICs and CPUs. Thus, energy consumption is enforced by ensuring a substantial amount of off-chip memory accesses.

None of these provides a strict bound on the amount of distinct bits read: The former allows for a trade-off between memory block accesses and computing, whereas the latter bounds the ratio of energy consumption benefits for ASIC adversaries. A different notion, predating memory and bandwidth-hardness, is that of memory-bound functions [1,26,28] that do impose an expected lower bound on the number of memory accesses, expressed as cache misses.

All these notions have "symmetric" hardness in the following sense. Given a candidate input-output pair (x, y) for function f, verifying whether $f(x) = y$ is, at best, achieved by evaluating f. In that sense, evaluation and checking require the same amount of resources. In many applications, it would be desirable to have an *efficient public verification* algorithm that can check the correctness of an evaluation using significantly fewer resources, after the party that evaluates f provides a proof of correctness π for y. In practice, considering a cryptographic puzzle application [27,36,43], a challenger receiving multiple candidate puzzle solutions from different parties should be able to verify their correctness with much less effort than it took to compute them. Even considering egalitarian proofs of work [12], checking the validity of a proposed evaluation with considerably smaller memory requirements allows for easy validation by numerous lightweight clients.

In the context of time-demanding functions, verifiable delay functions (VDFs) introduced by Boneh et al. [18] achieve such a property: any observer can verify that the computation of the function was performed correctly and can do so efficiently. The scope of this paper is to introduce an analogous function but for capacious/space-hungry algorithms. However, "space" or memory functions appear to be more intricate. Indeed, space-hardness does cover the memory needed by an algorithm for instructions, data, and inputs. Still, as discussed above, hardness often involves a trade-off between space and time, i.e., an algorithm is allowed to use more time to make up for a smaller memory footprint.

This Work: Verifiable Capacity-Bound Functions. In this work, we initiate the study of *verifiable capacity-bound functions (VCBF)*. At a high level, a VCBF guarantees: (a) a strict lower bound m in the necessary number of *distinct bits read* from memory in order to evaluate the function each time (referred to as *minimum capacity* complexity), (b) a public verification process that given a proof π can check the correctness of an evaluation by reading only $o(m)$ bits, and (c) soundness, i.e., no computationally-bounded adversary should be able to produce a convincing proof for an incorrect evaluation. The space notion of VCBF differs significantly from other space-related functions: It provides a strict lower bound on the number of distinct bits read at each evaluation of the function (minimum capacity) even if an adversary adaptively chooses its strategy after the function is instatiated. In addition, it does not present any time/space trade-off on evaluation, i.e., the only way to compute the VCBF's output is to satisfy its minimum capacity complexity unless the VCBF is heavily precomputed. Note that every function inevitably presents a time/space trade-off under heavy precomputation, e.g., evaluate the function on all inputs and store the outputs into an ordered dictionary. This differs from other space functions [1,4,6,28,54] in which an evaluator can tune the memory usage at the price of computing the function in more time, even if the function has not been preprocessed.

Also, unlike the notion of asymmetric hardness [13] which allows parties with access to a secret trapdoor to evaluate f quickly, we aim for public verifiability. Hence, a VCBF is a publicly verifiable function that does not present a time/space trade-off on evaluation. In that sense, it can be viewed as a space-analog of a VDF.

Comparison Between VCBF and Other "Space-Demanding" Functions. We provide a more detailed discussion of the relation between VCBFs and other primitives that attempt to bound the resources used when evaluating a function.

Table 1. Comparison summary between VCBF and existing space-demanding functions. We exclude from the comparison any primitive that deviates from our objectives: (*i*) primitives based on heuristics or enforce memory/space usage on expectation, i.e., no strict lower bound on the memory/space usage (e.g., [1] and puzzle-based constructions [26,28]) or, (*ii*) primitives that require interaction (e.g., [7,29,53]). Publicly verifiable means that the correctness of the function's output can be publicly verified with significantly fewer space-units than evaluating the function. We use the term "memory" to denote the total space required to evaluate the function (this does not guarantee a lower bound on the number of bits read).

	Space-unit per execution	Security analysis	Publicly verifiable
Code-hard functions [13]	Memory	Ideal cipher	✗
Memory-hard functions [4,6,49]	Time/Memory trade-off	ROM & Pebbling	✗
Bandwidth-hard functions [54]	Time/Cache-miss trade-off	ROM & Pebbling	✗
VCBF (this work)	Bits read	Standard	✓

See Table 1 for a comparison summary between VCBF and the most prominent functions and the corresponding space flavors.

Minimum Number of Computation Steps. Such primitives provide a lower bound on the minimum number of *sequential steps* necessary. Notable examples include classic time-locked puzzles [55], key-derivation function PBKDF2 [38], and the recently proposed verifiable delay functions mentioned above [18,50,59]. Another related notion is proof-of-sequential-work (PoSW) [23,25,42], which is similar to VDF except PoSW is not a function. Typically, these enforce a repeated operation (hashing or squaring in the group with an unknown order). As discussed, our VCBF shares the same spirit as VDF but for space/energy consumption.

Minimum Number of Memory Access. As explained above, memory-bound functions provide an expectation of the lower bound on the number of cache misses for any polynomial-time bounded adversary. In [1,26] a subset of a large random table (thus incompressible) is accessed during evaluation. However, they do not meet our requirement of the strict capacity lower bound on the number of bits read for each evaluation (like VDF for the time setting) since their lower bound is only a statistical expectation.

Follow-up work [28] suggests a construction with a time/space trade-off for the process of constructing the table from a representation, but this permits us to easily trade memory accesses for computation workload. We stress that [26,28] leverage a puzzle-based approach: They reach the desired number of cache misses by evaluating the function multiple times. Hence, they cannot be considered functions due to their puzzle-based nature (similarly to the analogy between VDF and PoW in the time setting). Lastly, [1] leverages an inner function f whose inverse f^{-1} cannot be evaluated in less time than accessing the memory. Hence, their construction presents a time/space trade-off: A malicious adversary may choose to involve more time to reduce the number of memory accesses.

Code-Hard Functions. Code-hard algorithms [13] require that a minimum amount of memory is used in order to store the code (generated using block ciphers). This has found different applications, e.g., white box encryption [11,16,17,34] or big-key encryption [10]. The key difference between a code-hard function and VCBF is that while a large amount of memory space must be dedicated for storing the code-hard function, it is possible that only a small fraction of those stored bits must be retrieved during evaluation (i.e., using memory does not imply reading bits). A VCBF imposes a non-trivial strict lower bound on bits read from memory during each evaluation.

Memory and Bandwidth-Hard Functions. These functions adaptively read/write from/in the memory to achieve two different objectives: Memory-hard functions require evaluators to use a large amount of memory while bandwidth-hard functions produce a high number of cache misses.[1] These functions [4,6,49,54] allow adversaries to dynamically trade additional computation for reduced memory usage on evaluation (even without precomputation); thus, they do not meet our strict lower bound guarantee.[2] Moreover, the existing formalizations are highly reliant on the random oracle model, e.g., [54] for bandwidth hardness and [4,6,49] for memory hardness (in the parallel random oracle model). This comes naturally, as many of these works use variations of a graph-pebbling game to model their computation, heuristically estimating the energy cost for each unit computation and memory access operations. On the other hand, our VCBF definition does not rely on the random oracle model (this does not preclude the possibility of specific VCBFs operating in this model). Another impact of relying on the random oracle model is that it makes it harder to design an efficient verification algorithm as it "destroys" any algebraic structures between inputs and outputs.

We stress that a VCBF's lower bound in memory bits accessed can be used to infer a lower bound in energy consumption, analogous to the motivation behind bandwidth-hard functions. E.g., considering an ASIC-based adversary with on-chip memory of size s bits (such as a hardware cache) a VCBF that guarantees to access m bits from main memory imposes a $u(m - s)$ lower energy consumption, where u is the atomic cost for reading one bit from memory.

In a recent work [31], the first memory-hard VDF construction was proposed by combining a SNARK with a parallelizable prover with a memory-hard "sequential" function. Although this result is close in spirit with what a VCBF tries to achieve, we do not aim for an explicit time lower bound, whereas

---

[1] We stress that, in the setting of memory-hard functions, the term "memory" is used to denote the number of memory blocks required to correctly evaluate (in a given time) the function. This differs from the VCBF objective of forcing the evaluator to read a fixed number of distinct bits (requiring n memory blocks of size w on evaluation does not imply reading nw distinct bits since multiple memory blocks may present a redundant pattern that may be compressed).

[2] We stress that memory-hard functions present a time/space trade-off on evaluation that varies according to the notion of memory hardness considered (e.g., time-space complexity [49], cumulative space complexity [6], sustained space complexity [4]).

the memory-bound we achieve is strict without leaving room for time/space trade-offs, as explained above.

Proof of Space (PoSpace). PoSpace [7,29,53] extends memory-hard functions with efficient verification and adopts the graph pebbling framework and the random oracle model. The prover convinces a verifier that it consumed its space capacity to store data while allowing for efficient verification in both space and time. Like memory-hard functions, the PoSpace constructions can only guarantee a time/space trade-off, thus cannot enforce a space lower bound. Also, the security analysis is based on the heuristic (parallel) random oracle model.

Overview of Techniques. The main challenge in building a VCBF is finding a function that has a natural strict lower bound on the space necessary for evaluation while still allowing for efficient verification. Past works [2,3,5,6,15, 19,21,54] achieve the first property only on expectation (i.e., expected lower bound) by relying on assumptions such as the random oracle or ideal cipher. Hence, this approach fails to achieve a strict lower bound and makes it harder to achieve the second property as it dismantles structured relations between the function's inputs and outputs that could be used for efficient verification.

In this work, we deviate from previous techniques significantly. To model the inability of an adaptive space-based adversary to compute an output without reading enough data from memory, we turn our attention to *Kolmogorov complexity* [40], which measures the complexity (in an absolute sense) of an object in terms of the minimum number of bits necessary to represent it. Kolmogorov complexity is viewed as a fundamental theory of computer science and has been shown connected with multiple areas in cryptography [41,45,56]. (The most recent work of Liu and Pass [41] proves the equivalence of a computational bounded version of the Kolmogorov complexity and the existence of one-way functions.) Somewhat more formally, the Kolmogorov complexity of object x is the minimum number of bits needed to represent *any description* (T, α) where T is a Turing machine and α is a string such that $\mathsf{T}(\alpha)$ outputs x. One can view T as an adaptive decompressing algorithm and α as a "compression" computed adaptively from x. Based on this, our first observation is that if an algorithm *depends* on an object x (e.g., x could be the description of the algorithm itself or the algorithm's input), then its execution *cannot require reading fewer bits than the Kolmogorov complexity of x*. In that sense, Kolmogorov complexity is the right tool for us; choosing a function with high Kolmogorov complexity readily provides an arguably loose bound for the minimum capacity of a VCBF even in the presence of an adaptive adversary that chooses its strategy (that determines how memory is read and organized) after the function is instatiated (see Sect. 1.1 for a discussion about adaptive security in the space setting).

On the other hand, when building our VCBF we need to identify a function that is amenable to verification; ideally, it should preserve an efficiently checkable (algebraic) relation between inputs and outputs. One candidate function is *polynomial evaluation* for single-variable polynomial $f(X) \in \mathbb{F}_p[x]$ of degree d of the form $f(X) = \sum_{i=0}^{d} a_i \cdot x^i$. The good news is that there exist numerous works in the literature for verifiable polynomial evaluation (e.g., [30,32,48,61]). In order to use such a scheme for a VCBF we need to ensure it is *publicly verifiable* (anyone can verify it using public parameters) and *publicly delegatable* (anyone can query it on an evaluation point). In our construction, we use the lightweight scheme of Elkhiyaoui et al. [30]. Its verification process requires a constant number of operations among a constant number of elliptic curve elements. This is important for us since we want VCBF to have verification capacity complexity *sublinear* in its evaluation's minimum capacity. Using [30], the latter is $O((d+1)\lambda)$ whereas the former is $O(\lambda)$ (where λ is the security parameter), i.e., the gap is linear in the degree of the polynomial.

The "honest" way of evaluating polynomial $f(X)$ is by reading its coefficients a_i, so by fixing $|(a_0, \ldots, a_d)| \geq m$ (where $|x|$ denotes the bit length of x) one would hope to get a VCBF with minimum capacity m. However, this is not the case as every polynomial has multiple alternative representations that an adversary may try to exploit in order to bypass the memory capacity bound. For example, all lists of the form $(x_0, \ldots, x_d)$, $(f(x_0), \ldots, f(x_d))$, for any choice of $d+1$ distinct x_i, completely determine the coefficients $(a_0, \ldots, a_d)$ of $f(X)$ (by interpolating the points). Here is where Kolmogorov complexity comes in handy: The above evaluations and points together with a Turing machine that performs polynomial interpolation are a valid description, in terms of Kolmogorov complexity, of the coefficients $(a_0, \ldots, a_d)$. As a consequence, it *cannot be significantly shorter* than the Kolmogorov complexity $C(a_0, \ldots, a_d)$ of the coefficients of the polynomial $f(X)$ (Theorem 5).

What remains is to find a way to sample a polynomial $f(X)$ with high Kolmogorov complexity. For any large-enough set, most of its elements have sufficiently high Kolmogorov complexity. Since this holds for arbitrary sets, sampling at random from a large-enough set of polynomials guarantees that the chosen polynomial is of high Kolmogorov complexity with high-enough probability.

As discussed above, many previous works inherently adopt non-standard models in their definitions to capture the fact that a function is memory-heavy (e.g., random-oracle, ideal cipher, or heuristic assumptions about graph pebbling). Instead, we want to base our security definition in the standard setting, and we regard our paper on VCBF as a foundational one. Our approach is to model adversaries as Turing machines that read (at most) a fixed number of distinct bits m (whose value is estimated using the Kolmogorov complexity) from a precomputed memory τ of size $n \geq m$ (Sect. 4). We stress that it is crucial to consider the memory of size n larger than m since an adversary can leverage a large memory to increase its advantage ϵ while, at the same time, minimizing the number m of distinct bits it must read to answer a particular challenge (for example, it can store a large dictionary containing several evaluations of the polynomial $f(X)$). However, this introduces the new challenge of estimating the adversary's advantage ϵ with respect to the memory size n: A particularly challenging task when working in the standard model with black-box access to the adversary. In more detail, it is hard to provide a strict bound on the number of (partial) information that can be stored in a memory of size n since their space requirement highly depends on the precomputation strategy (e.g., the entropy of the precomputed values) and the encoding (e.g., memory organization, memory access patterns) that can be adaptively chosen by an adversary after some parameters are revealed (e.g., the object to compress). Still, we show that it is possible to give a positive, meaningful estimation of ϵ and n when considering adversaries that perform a constant number $v \in O(1)$ of random accesses (e.g., conditional jumps) in order to read discontinuous bits from memory. We discuss the formulation of our definition and our results in Sect. 4 and Sect. 5.1, respectively.

Summary of our Contributions. Our contributions in this work can be summarized as follows:

1. We build a cryptographic framework that combines the notion of Kolmogorov complexity and randomized Turing machines and use it to bound the minimum amount of bits required in order to evaluate a polynomial (Sect. 3).
2. We propose a formal definition of verifiable capacity-bound functions VCBFs that captures (a) a lower bound m on the number of bits read from memory (of bounded size) for evaluation (minimum capacity), (b) efficient verification of outputs with minimum capacity that is sublinear in m with respect to any malicious evaluator, and (c) soundness, i.e., no computationally bounded adversary can produce an incorrect output that passes verification (Sect. 4). We stress that the minimum capacity definition of VCBF (Sect. 4) significantly changes the perspective about how adversaries are usually modeled in cryptography. In our setting, the power of an adversary is solely dependent on the space it uses, i.e., the adversary has unbounded computational power, but it has limitations in the space it uses.[3] In a nutshell, an adversary is only limited to the size of available (precomputed) memory and the number of bits it reads from it. Considering space-only adversaries requires rethinking the meaning of adaptive security. As we will discuss next, adaptiveness refers to the ability of choosing the precomputation strategy (that sets the memory of the adversary) and the evaluation strategy (that sets the reading strategy during evaluation) after the VCBF's public parameters (i.e., the coefficients of the polynomial) are revealed. To work with such a space adaptive setting, Kolmogorov Complexity is essential and succeeds where any other standard entropy measure fails (see Sect. 1.1 for a detailed discussion).
3. We propose the first VCBF construction that satisfies our definition, based on single-variable polynomial evaluation for polynomial $f(X) \in \mathbb{F}_p[x]$ of degree d. To achieve efficient verification, we employ the publicly verifiable and publicly delegatable verifiable computation scheme of [30]. For a target minimum capacity $m \in O((d+1)\lambda)$, it suffices to set the size of the polynomial to

---

[3] Considering unbounded adversaries is fundamental in order to capture the (concrete) strict lower bound on the number of distinct bits read that a VCBF must guarantee (i.e., a VCBF does not present any time/bits read trade-off). We provide a more detailed discussion in Sect. 4 and Remark 2.

$(d + 1)\lambda$, where λ is the security parameter. Hence, to achieve large capacity bounds, we need to set $d \gg \lambda$, e.g., $d \in \Omega(\lambda^c)$ for $c > 1$ constant. On the other hand the capacity complexity of the verification is $O(\lambda)$, i.e., independent of d hence verification remains efficient (Sect. 5).

4. In the full version of this work, we provide an estimation of the concrete parameters for our construction. For an elliptic curve group of order p of size 1024 bits, a polynomial of size $1\,\mathrm{GB}$ ($d = 78.20 \cdot 10^5 \approx \lambda^{2.29}$) guarantees a minimum capacity m of $0.82\,\mathrm{GB}$, even with respect to an unbounded adversary that can spend an exponential amount of computational resources.

We stress that a target minimum capacity m of a VCBF is guaranteed only in the presence of adversaries with a limited memory size n. As explained, the estimation of n is a major challenge when working in the standard setting (this work). Along this line, we initiate a fine-grained study on the memory size n estimation according to the number v of adaptive random accesses performed by the adversary (denoted by the set $\mathcal{A}^{v\text{-access}}$). In particular, we prove (in the concrete setting) that the evaluation of a polynomial $f(X) \in \mathbb{F}_p[x]$ guarantees a target capacity $m \in O((d+1)\lambda)$ even if an adversary $\mathsf{A} \in \mathcal{A}^{1\text{-access}}$ has access to a memory whose size n is proportional to the cardinality of the input space of the polynomial $f(X)$, i.e., super-polynomial. Our results can be extended to the asymptotic setting for the class $\mathcal{A}^{O(1)\text{-access}}$ (Corollary 1). This result implies the security of our construction against adversarial strategies primarily used in practice (e.g., pre-computed dictionaries) or strategies executed on limited devices that have a bound on the number of random accesses (e.g., for energy efficiency) that they can perform. In Sect. 4 and Sect. 5.1, we discuss our results in more detail.

Regarding the larger class of adversaries $\mathcal{A}^{\omega(1)\text{-access}}$, the minimum capacity of our polynomial-based VCBF construction deteriorates when n gets closer to $d^{1+\delta}\lambda^{1+o(1)}$ for a constant $\delta > 0$. This is due to the work of Kedlaya and Umans [39]: They shows how to build a data structure D of size at most $d^{1+\delta}\lambda^{1+o(1)}$ (only from the coefficients of $f(X) \in \mathbb{F}_p[x]$) that allows them to evaluate $f(X)$ over any of the points. This evaluation requires reading a non-constant number of elements from D (using $\omega(1)$ random accesses) whose total size is at most $O(\log(d)^{s_1}\lambda^{s_2})$ for some positive $s_1, s_2 \in O(1)$. Hence, the plain evaluation of a polynomial of degree d can not guarantee a minimum capacity of $m \in \omega(\log(d)^{s_1}\lambda^{s_2})$ when an adversary $\mathsf{A} \in \mathcal{A}^{\omega(1)\text{-access}}$ has access to a memory of size n, close to or greater than $d^{1+\delta}\lambda^{1+o(1)}$ (see Sect. 5.1 for more details).

1.1 Adaptive Security and Kolmogorov Complexity (vs. Selective Security and Other Entropy Measures)

Here, we provide an answer to two natural questions about the meaning of adaptive security (in the space setting) and Kolmogorov complexity. These points significantly differentiate the techniques used in this work from previous ones.

Adaptive Security in the Space Setting. In the standard computational time cryptographic setting, adaptive security refers to the ability of an adversary of changing its behavior according to the scheme's parameters with the objective of increasing its advantage in breaking the scheme's security. An example is the adaptive CCA security of public encryption in which an adversary wants to increase its advantage in distinguishing between two encryptions by adaptively choosing both the two challenge messages and the next query for the decryption oracle after seeing the public key and the answers received from previous decryption queries. The natural question we pose is "What does adaptive security mean for the minimum capacity definition of VCBF?". To give a concrete answer to this question, it is necessary to rethink the meaning of adaptive security against adversaries whose power is measured by solely considering the memory used/read (as done in this work). Jumping ahead, the minimum capacity of VCBF (Sect. 4) guarantees that an adversary needs to read at least m bits from its memory τ (of size n) when asked to correctly evaluate the function on a random point. This must hold even if the adversary is computationally unbounded, and it is allowed to generate/organize its memory τ by precomputing the VCBF according to its parameters (i.e., polynomial). In such a setting, the objective of an adversary is to break the security of VCBF by minimizing the number of distinct bits m read from the precomputed memory. To achieve this, an adversary may think of changing its compression/precomputation strategy after the VCBF's parameters (i.e., the polynomial coefficients) are revealed.[4] This is analogous to the CCA public key encryption example in which an adversary changes its two challenge messages after seeing the public key and the answers of the decryption oracle. To formally define the intuitive security of VCBF (i.e., a strict lower bound on the number m of distinct bits read), it is fundamental to cover adaptive space-based adversaries (as described above). Indeed, if an adversary can change its precomputation/compression strategy after seeing the VCBF's parameters and reduce, for example, m by $\log(\lambda)$ bits then the strict lower bound is not strict anymore. For this reason, the natural definition of minimum capacity (Definition 4) requires that the function remains secure for any possible space-based adversary sampled after the instantiation of VCBF, i.e., the precomputation and evaluation strategy (i.e., the memory and the bits read) of the adversary can depend on the VCBF itself. Such a model of adaptive security requires the usage of Kolmogorov complexity (see next).

Why Kolmogorov complexity? Conventional entropy measures (including Yao entropy that leverages the notion of compression and Shannon) consider the incompressibility of objects only on expectation. It implicitly means that the compression strategy does not depend on the object (i.e., our polynomial of our VCBF construction) sampled from a distribution. The typical example is on [35, Page 10] (quoting): "Consider the ensemble consisting of all binary strings of

---

[4] For example, a particular (hard to guess) compressible pattern may be revealed after the polynomial coefficients are chosen. Note that this may happen (with a certain probability) even if the polynomial is sampled at random.

length 9999999999999999. By Shannon's measure, we require 9999999999999999 bits on the average to encode a string in such an ensemble. However, the string consisting of 9999999999999999 1's can be encoded in about 55 bits by expressing 9999999999999999 in binary and adding the repeated pattern 1". Note that the above argument applies also to the Rényi family of entropies (e.g., min-entropy).[5] The Kolmogorov complexity overcomes these limitations by considering the worst-case scenario: It measures incompressibility in an absolute sense, i.e., the compression strategy can depend on the object. Hence, lower-bounds derived through Kolmogorov complexity are universal, and they do not hold only on expectation. Also, quoting [58]: "The Kolmogorov complexity of an object is a form of absolute information of the individual object. This is not possible to do by C.E. Shannon's information theory. Unlike Kolmogorov complexity, information theory is only concerned with the average information of a random source".

In the VCBF setting, these concepts translate into adaptive vs. selective security. Kolmogorov complexity allows us to bound the minimum capacity of VCBF in the adaptive setting in which the adversarial compression/precomputation strategy can depend on the VCBF's parameters (this mimic the adversarial behavior of changing strategy after the parameters are revealed). As already discussed, this is fundamental in order to have strict (universal) lower bound on the number of bits m that an adversary needs to read to evaluate a VCBF. Adaptive security remains unachievable if we consider standard entropy measures: This is because Information Theory studies the average information in objects, i.e., compression/precomputation strategies are fixed before the object (i.e., polynomial) is revealed/sampled. Hence, Kolmogorov complexity remains a fundamental tool in order to deal with space-based adaptive security and, in turn, to prove the security of our polynomial-based VCBF.

1.2   Applications of VCBF

Since VCBF can be seen as a space-analog of VDF, replacing minimum sequential steps with a minimum number of bits retrieved from memory, we believe they can find applications in various settings where memory usage needs to be enforced. In this direction, we describe how VCBF can be used as an *energy-consumption function* to achieve fairness among ASIC and CPU participants. We then briefly discuss other promising VCBF applications. We emphasize that the objective of this work is to lay the foundation for VCBFs, providing an initial study about publicly verifiable asymmetric memory/space hardness in the standard model. Naturally, depending on the application, ad-hoc properties and/or slightly different flavors of VCBF may be required, opening interesting directions for subsequent works.

---

[5] This can also be seen by observing that the Rényi family of entropies is equivalent to Shannon entropy when considering uniform distributions (as considered in this work, e.g., polynomial's coefficients are sampled at random).

Energy-Consumption Function. Juels and Brainard [37] proposed client-puzzles as a solution to mitigate denial of service attacks (the concept of cryptographic puzzles can be traced back to Merkle's key exchange [43] and Dwork and Naor's pricing function [27]). The general idea of such puzzles is to associate a cost to each resource allocation request by requiring the client to complete a task before the server performs any expensive operation, thus making large-scale attacks infeasible. Classic client-puzzles [8,20,22,37,57] will force adversaries to consume certain CPU cycles as the cost for attacks. However, state-of-the-art hash engines [14,54] could be $200,000\times$ faster and $40,000\times$ more energy-efficient than a state-of-art multi-core CPU. Hence, denial-of-service attacks may still be feasible for ASIC-equipped adversaries, even when such client puzzles are deployed as counter-mechanisms.

Motivated by this, we propose to replace CPU cycles with alternative resources, i.e., energy consumption using a VCBF. Classic ASIC-resistant methods follow the memory-hard function approach, i.e., ensuring that solving the puzzle "costs" much memory. In this manner, the cost of manufacturing an ASIC for puzzle solving would increase proportionally to the chip area devoted to memory. However, as argued in [54], memory hardness only partially solves the problem since it does not address the energy aspect of ASIC advantage. Indeed, energy consumption can be more important than the one-shot ASIC manufacturing cost since the corresponding cost (due to electricity consumption) keeps accumulating with time. Hence, a function with a strict lower bound on energy consumption, due to off-chip memory accesses enforced via VCBF, could fill in a critical but often overlooked gap in ASIC resistance.

Our VCBF can be used as an energy-consumption function in the following protocol between a server S and a client C:

- C contacts server S, requesting permission to use some service such as establishing TLS connection [24] or accepting an email [27].
- S returns a fresh challenge x to the client C.
- C evaluates VCBF f on x, and returns the output and proof π to S.
- The server S verifies the correctness of $f(x)$. If the verification succeeds, it allows C to use the service.

Jumping ahead, from Theorem 7, we can easily find a set of parameters so that an adversary needs to invest a sufficiently large amount of energy in computing the function. Observe that the client is required to compute the VCBF f on a (honest) challenge x chosen by the server. Another option is to allow the client to choose multiple challenges on its own as is usually done in client-puzzles. In this case, it is fundamental that f can not be amortized, i.e., the puzzle's total energy-cost increases proportionally to the number of parallel evaluations (on different challenges) of f. We stress that this work does not study amortization but this is not an inherent limitation of VCBF as a primitive. Non-amortizable VCBFs can be studied in future works.

The above protocol can be extended to blockchain systems that support smart contracts. For example, a client C may be required to evaluate the VCBF f on input $x = \mathsf{H}(s,t)$ in order to trigger the execution of a smart contract S.

Here, inside the hash function H, we place s which is the current state of the smart contract and t a counter used to randomize the challenge $x = H(s, t)$ (e.g., t is incremented after each invocation of the contract or after a block is mined).[6] In this way, an adversary is desisted from monopolizing the service offered by the smart contract S for specific malicious purposes. For instance, if the smart contract runs a decentralized auction system, the adversary will not be able to produce spamming bids to delay the acceptance of valid bids from competitors. We stress that efficient public verification is essential in blockchain systems since verifiers, that check the correctness of executions, have limited resources.

Real-Time Services (and VCBF vs. VDF). Although VCBF and VDF are both efficiently verifiable, there are applications in which VDFs can not be used, whereas VCBFs can. Consider a server S that offers a real-time service in which it is a requirement to receive requests within a precise time frame (e.g., within 1 minute). Clearly, using a VDF to block denial of service attacks is not an option since the time required to evaluate the VDF will delay all users' requests and affect the quality of the real-time service. A concrete example is an auction service: Bids must be received before the end of the auction or within a given time frame. Hence, VCBFs offer a unique solution in scenarios in which creating a delay is not acceptable.

The Filecoin Network. Protocol Labs is working on Filecoin [51], a blockchain-based decentralized storage system that has gathered much visibility in the last few years (it raised over \$250 million through an ICO in 2017). In Filecoin, miners earn coins by offering their storage to clients interested in storing and replicating files. The mining power in Filecoin is proportional to the active storage offered by a miner. Thanks to its public and capacity efficient verification, a VCBF can play an important role in improving *proof of useful space* (a fundamental primitive in the Filecoin protocol), i.e., a primitive that allows miners to prove that they are using a significant amount of space to store (multiple) files. In particular, Filecoin is interested in designing a proof of useful space in the cost model [44]. However, a common problem of proof of useful space constructions (e.g., [33]) is the possibility of trading space for computation: An evaluator may erase some data and reconstruct it on the fly when needed. A VCBF can tremendously improve proof of useful space by enforcing rationality during the computation when working in the cost model (e.g., by replacing the RO with a VCBF in graph-labeling based constructions). For example, the minimum capacity of VCBFs may increase the costs (e.g., energy consumption) of regeneration of the erased data. This encourages evaluators to store the data in its entirety. Also, the VCBF public verification does not introduce any additional cost to verifiers with minimal resources in terms of space and energy.

---

[6] The challenge $x = H(s, t)$ has this format since smart contracts cannot generate secret randomness to sample a random challenge.

2 Preliminaries

Notation. We assume the reader to be familiar with standard cryptographic notation.

2.1 Publicly Verifiable Computation for Polynomial Evaluation

A publicly verifiable computation scheme (VC) for polynomial evaluation allows a client to outsource the computation of a polynomial f to an untrusted server. We are interested in VC schemes that are both *publicly delegatable* and *publicly verifiable*. The former allows any querier to submit input to the server, while the latter allows any verifier to check the computation's correctness. Formally, a VC scheme for a family of polynomials $\mathcal{F}$ with input space $\mathcal{X}$ is composed of the following algorithms:

Setup($1^\lambda, f$): Upon input the security parameter 1^λ and a polynomial $f \in \mathcal{F}$, the randomized setup algorithm returns the evaluation key ek_f and the verification key vk_f for the polynomial f.

ProbGen(vk_f, x): Upon input the verification key vk_f for a polynomial $f \in \mathcal{F}$ and an input $x \in \mathcal{X}$, the deterministic problem generation algorithm outputs an encoding σ_x and the verification key vk_x for the input x.

Compute(ek_f, σ_x): Upon input the evaluation key ek_f for a polynomial $f \in \mathcal{F}$ and an encoding σ_x for input $x \in \mathcal{X}$, the deterministic computation algorithm returns a value y and a proof π_y.[7]

Verify(vk_x, y, π_y): Upon input the verification key vk_x for an input $x \in \mathcal{X}$, a value $y \in \mathcal{Y}$, and a proof π_y, the deterministic verification algorithm returns a decisional bit b.

Correctness of a publicly VC scheme captures the fact that an honest execution of the computation to evaluate a polynomial $f \in \mathcal{F}$ on input $x \in \mathcal{X}$ produces the correct output $y = f(x)$ along with a proof π_y that correctly verifies. As for security, a malicious evaluator cannot convince an honest verifier that $y^* \neq f(x^*)$ is the correct evaluation of $f(x^*)$ on an arbitrary input $x^* \in \mathcal{X}$ (*soundness*). For the formal definitions, we refer the reader to [30].

In this work, we are interested in single-variable polynomials $f(X) \in \mathbb{F}_p[x]$ of degree d of the form $f(X) = \sum_{i=0}^{d} a_i \cdot x^i$. An example of such a VC scheme has been proposed by Elkhiyaoui et al. [30]. It uses an asymmetric bilinear pairing $e : \mathbb{G}_1 \times \mathbb{G}_2 \to \mathbb{G}_T$ where $\mathbb{G}_1, \mathbb{G}_2$, and $\mathbb{G}_T$ are groups of prime order p, and its security follows from the $(d/2)$-Strong Diffie-Hellman assumption $((d/2)$-SDH).

VC schemes allow verifiers to check the computation's correctness more efficiently than the work required to evaluate the polynomial honestly. By leveraging the $(d/2)$-SDH assumption, the publicly VC scheme proposed in [30] yields a constant time $O(1)$ verification. This gives to our VCBF an efficient capacity verification when using the VC scheme of Elkhiyaoui et al. [30] (see Sect. 5.1).

---

[7] We explicitly detached y from its proof π_y. Several works define the output of the computation algorithm Compute as a singleton σ_y (the encoding of the output y) defined as $\sigma_y = (y, \pi_y)$.

2.2 Kolmogorov Complexity

The Kolmogorov complexity [40] aims to measure the complexity of objects in terms of the minimum amount of bits required to represent them. We say that (T, α) is a (possibly inefficient) description of a string $x \in \{0,1\}^*$ (in terms of algorithmic complexity) if $\mathsf{T}(\alpha) = x$. We can look at T as a decoding algorithm and $\alpha \in \{0,1\}^*$ as an encoding of x. The minimum amount of bits needed to represent a fixed bit string x is measured by the Kolmogorov complexity $C_\mathsf{T}(x)$. In more detail, the Kolmogorov complexity $C_\mathsf{T}(x)$ of a bit string $x \in \{0,1\}^*$ with respect to a deterministic Turing machine T (called reference Turing machine) is defined as $C_\mathsf{T}(x) = \min_{\alpha \in \{0,1\}^*} \{|\alpha| : \mathsf{T}(\alpha) = x\}$. Similarly, the conditional Kolmogorov complexity measures the complexity of x given some auxiliary information $y \in \{0,1\}^*$, i.e., $C_\mathsf{T}(x|y) = \min_{\alpha \in \{0,1\}^*} \{|\alpha| : \mathsf{T}(\langle \alpha, y \rangle) = x\}$ where $\langle a, b \rangle$ denotes the self-delimiting coding of strings a and b.[8] The above definitions of Kolmogorov complexity are known as *plain* Kolmogorov complexity. The name comes from the fact that no constraints are put on the input α of the Turing machine T. Another type of complexity, called *prefix-free* Kolmogorov complexity [40, Sect. 3], focuses only on prefix-free programs, i.e., Turing machines that only take in input strings encoded in a prefix-free fashion. In this work, we focus on the plain version, and we refer the reader to [40, Sect. 3] for a more detailed discussion about the prefix-free version.

The definition of plain Kolmogorov complexity can be made independent from the reference Turing machine. Indeed, Turing machines are enumerable. The code of any Turing machine T can be interpreted as a binary string i.[9] Therefore, we can define a *universal* Turing machine U as $\mathsf{U}(i, \alpha) = \mathsf{T}_i(\alpha)$. In other words, U simulates all possible computations that Turing machines perform by taking in input $\alpha \in \{0,1\}^*$ and the code i of the i-th Turing machine T_i and executes the computation $\mathsf{T}_i(\alpha)$. Based on this observation, it has been proved that the Kolmogorov complexity with respect to different Turing machines is invariant only up to a constant that depends on the reference Turing machine.

Theorem 1 (Invariance Theorem [40, Theorem 2.1.1]). *There is a universal deterministic Turing machine* U *such that for any deterministic Turing machine* T, *there is a constant* c_T *that only depends on* T, *such that for any string* $x, y \in \{0,1\}^*$ *we have* $C_\mathsf{U}(x) \leq C_\mathsf{T}(x) + c_\mathsf{T}$.[10]

Since the choice of the reference Turing machine does not significantly change the Kolmogorov complexity of any string, we express the Kolmogorov complexity using the universal Turing machine U as a reference machine.

Definition 1. The Kolmogorov complexity of a string x is defined as $C(x) \overset{\text{def}}{=} C_\mathsf{U}(x)$ and $C(x|y) \overset{\text{def}}{=} C_\mathsf{U}(x|y)$ for the universal Turing machine U.

---

[8] As we will discuss later, Kolmogorov Complexity considers constant-size Turing machines. This requires the use of a self-delimiting code to encode multiple inputs.

[9] Note that not all binary strings are valid Turing machines.

[10] The constant c_T corresponds to the self-delimiting description of the Turing machine T.

It is fundamental to restrict the definition of Kolmogorov complexity to constant-size Turing machines in order to rule out any ambiguity. Indeed, as mentioned in [40, Sect. 2.1.4], by removing the size constraint of T, it is possible to assign low complexity to any string by simply selecting a reference Turing machine with large complexity (i.e., hardcode the string into the code of the Turing machine). Still, the size constraint does not reduce the number of languages recognizable by a Turing machine. For example, it was shown the existence of a universal Turing machine with 15 states, 2 symbols, and 30 state-symbol product (transition function) [47,60], with a polynomial slowdown of $O(t^6)$.

String Incompressibility. A crucial notion derived from the Kolmogorov complexity is the incompressibility of a string [40, Definition 2.2.1] with respect to unbounded deterministic Turing machines.

Definition 2 (Deterministic c-incompressibility [40, Definition 2.2.1]). A string $x \in \{0,1\}^*$ is c-DET-incompressible if $C(x) \geq |x| - c$.

We will refer to the above definition as *deterministic c-incompressibility* (c-DET-incompressibility in short) since it covers deterministic Turing machines, i.e., the reference Turing machine of the Kolmogorov complexity is deterministic.

The following theorem provides a lower-bound on the number of c-DET-incompressible elements in a given set $\mathcal{X}$.

Theorem 2 ([40, Theorem 2.2.1]). *Let $c \geq 0$ be a positive constant. For each $y \in \{0,1\}^*$, every finite set $\mathcal{X}$ of cardinality m has at least $m(1 - 2^{-c}) + 1$ elements $x \in \mathcal{X}$ such that $C(x|y) \geq \log(m) - c$.*

By leveraging Theorem 2, we can easily calculate the probability of sampling a c-DET-incompressible string from $\mathcal{X}$. The proof is deferred to full version.

Theorem 3. *Let $\mathcal{X}$ be a finite set of cardinality m, then the following probability holds: $\Pr[x$ is c-DET-incompressible $\mid x \leftarrow_\$ \mathcal{X}] \geq 1 - 2^{-c} + 1/m$.*

String Incompressibility in the Randomized Setting. In cryptography, we deal with randomized adversaries represented by randomized Turing machines. However, the c-DET-incompressibility only covers deterministic Turing machines since the reference Turing machine (used to measure the Kolmogorov complexity) is deterministic. Accordingly, we extend the notion of incompressibility to randomized Turing machines.

Definition 3 (Randomized (c, ℓ_{rnd})-incompressibility). A string $x \in \{0,1\}^*$ is (c, ℓ_{rnd})-RND-incompressible if for all constant-size unbounded randomized Turing machine T with randomness space $\{0,1\}^{\ell_{rnd}}$, for all $r \in \{0,1\}^{\ell_{rnd}}$, and for all $\alpha \in \{0,1\}^{|x|-c-1}$, we have $\Pr[\mathsf{T}(\alpha; r) = x] = 0$.

Naturally, there is an obvious connection between the two definitions of incompressibility. Indeed, the randomness of a randomized Turing machine can be seen as part of the input of a deterministic one. The following Theorem 4 reports the formal result, whose proof is deferred to full version.

Theorem 4. *Let $x \in \{0,1\}^*$ be a string. If x is c-DET-incompressible (Definition 2) then x is (c', ℓ_{rnd})-RND-incompressibile (Definition 3) where $c' = c + \ell_{rnd} + 2\log(\ell_{rnd}) + 1 + O(1)$.*

The factor $\ell_{rnd} + 2\log(\ell_{rnd}) + 1$ is due to the need of using a self-delimiting δ-encoding (Elias delta coding) to encode the randomness $r \in \{0,1\}^{\ell_{rnd}}$. Also, the relation between the two incompressibility definitions is up to a constant $O(1)$ because of the invariance theorem (Theorem 1), i.e., any equality holds up to a constant factor.

3   Kolmogorov-Bound for Polynomial Evaluation

At each evaluation, a VCBF scheme forces the evaluator to read at least m distinct bits from its main memory. To achieve this functionality, our construction leverages a single variable polynomial $f(X) = \sum_{i=0}^{d} a_i \cdot x^i \in \mathbb{F}_p[x]$ of degree d. Intuitively, on receiving a challenge $x \in \{0,1\}^{\ell_{in}}$, an honest evaluator needs to read the coefficients $(a_0, \ldots, a_d) \in \mathbb{F}_p^{d+1}$ that determine the polynomial $f(X)$ in order to compute $y = f(x)$. In this case, we obtain the desired functionality by setting $|(a_0, \ldots, a_d)| \geq m$. However, a malicious evaluator may find an alternative strategy to compute $y = f(x)$ and read fewer than m bits. In this section, we prove the lower bound on the number of bits read during the polynomial evaluation by leveraging the Kolmogorov complexity. Next, we provide some examples of strategies a malicious evaluator could adopt:

1. Compress the coefficients $(a_0, \ldots, a_d)$ into a smaller string α. In this way, the evaluator just needs to read α, decompress it into $(a_0, \ldots, a_d)$, and evaluate $f(X)$ on the desired point x.
2. Precompute a dictionary $T \stackrel{\text{def}}{=} (f(x_0), \ldots, f(x_n))$ composed of the evaluation of $f(X)$ on points $(x_0, \ldots, x_n)$. By accessing T, the malicious evaluator can simply read and return $y_i = f(x_i)$ if the challenge x_i is one of the precomputed points. In this case, the malicious evaluator reads only $|y_i| \leq |p| < m$.
3. Instead of storing $(a_0, \ldots, a_d)$, the evaluator may choose to store $d + 1$ arbitrary points $(x_0, \ldots, x_d)$, the corresponding evaluations $(f(x_0), \ldots, f(x_d))$, and the prime p. These pieces of information are enough to recover a via polynomial interpolation. As a result, if the expression of $(f(x_0), \ldots, f(x_d))$, the points $(x_0, \ldots, x_d)$ and the prime p could be effectively compressed, the evaluator will read fewer bits than expected when evaluating the polynomial.

To estimate the bits that an adversary/algorithm needs to read to evaluate $f(X)$ correctly, we built a bridge between the Kolmogorov complexity and polynomial evaluation. Our approach is based on two main observations.

First, any string a (of appropriate size) can be encoded into $f(X) = \sum_{i=0}^{d} a_i \cdot x^i$ by setting its coefficients to different sub-portions of a. Let p be a prime of size $\lambda+1$ bits. We can interpret a string $a \in \{0,1\}^{(d+1)\lambda}$ as $a = a_0 || \ldots || a_d$ where $a_i \in \mathbb{F}_p$ (i.e., $|a_i| \leq \lambda < |p|$) and use $(a_0, \ldots, a_d)$ as the coefficients of $f(X)$.

Second, if algorithm T is able to compute $(f(x_0), \ldots, f(x_d))$ taking in input a string α and the challenge d points $(x_0, \ldots, x_d)$, then $(T, \langle \alpha, x_0, \ldots, x_d \rangle)$ is a valid description of $(f(x_0), \ldots, f(x_d))$. As explained in Item 3, the tuples $(f(x_0), \ldots, f(x_d))$, $(x_0, \ldots, x_d)$, and the prime p, are enough to reconstruct $(a_0, \ldots, a_d)$ (i.e., the prime's size $\lambda + 1$ guarantees the encoding is injective).

By combining the above two observations, we can easily lower bound the size of α with the Kolmogorov complexity $C(a)$ of a. In more detail, consider a Turing machine T' that first executes $\mathsf{T}(\alpha, x_0, \ldots, x_d)$ to compute $f(x_0), \ldots, f(x_d)$, and then retrieves and return a via polynomial interpolation. This implies that $(\mathsf{T}', \langle p, \alpha, x_0, \ldots, x_d \rangle)$ is a description of a. As a consequence, the size of α (the string that T would read to compute $(f(x_0), \ldots, f(x_d)))$ cannot be too small and must be related to the complexity $C(a)$ of a. Below, we provide the formal result whose proof is included in the full version of this work.

Theorem 5 (Kolmogorov-bound for (adaptive) Polynomial Evaluation). *For any $\lambda \in \mathbb{N}$, let $a \in \{0,1\}^{(d+1)\lambda}$ be a binary string and p a prime of size $\lambda + 1$, respectively. Fix the polynomial $f(X) = \sum_{i=0}^{d} a_i \cdot x^i \in \mathbb{F}_p[x]$ of degree d with input space $\{0,1\}^{\ell_{in}}$ where $a = a_0 || \ldots || a_d$ and $a_i \in \mathbb{F}_p$ for $i \in [d]$. If a is (c', ℓ_{rnd})-RND-incompressible (Definition 3), then for every constant-size randomized unbounded Turing machine T with randomness space $\{0,1\}^{\ell_{rnd}}$, every $\alpha \in \{0,1\}^m$, every $r \in \{0,1\}^{\ell_{rnd}}$, and every tuple $(x_0, \ldots, x_d)$ such that $\underset{i \neq j}{\forall} i, j \in \{0, \ldots, d\}$, $x_i \neq x_j$ and $x_i \in \{0,1\}^{\ell_{in}}$, we have $Pr[(f(x_0), \ldots, f(x_d)) = \mathsf{T}(\alpha, x_0, \ldots, x_d; r)] = 0$ where $m = (d+1)(\lambda - \ell_{in} - 2\log(\ell_{in}) - 1) - c' - \lambda - 2\log((d+1)\lambda - c') - 2\log(\lambda+1) - 4$.*

An alternative way to interpret Theorem 5 is that any possible description (T, α) of $f(X)$ is bigger than the parameter m (defined in Theorem 5). Also, note that Theorem 5 presents a loss factor that is proportional to $(d+1)\ell_{in}$. This because each of the $d+1$ points may be correlated with the coefficients of $f(X)$ (i.e., each point x_i is equal to the first ℓ_{in} bits of a_i). The correlation may reduce the number of bits that must be read to compute the evaluations.

Lastly, we stress that Kolmogorov complexity permits us to prove Theorem 5 under the universal quantification of any $d+1$ evaluation points and any adversarial strategy (i.e., any memory α and evaluation strategy T) selected after the polynomial. This is essential in the adaptive space-based setting (Sect. 1.1) in which we want to estimate the size of information generated/read w.r.t. an arbitrary precomputation of the polynomial. Indeed, the precomputation adopted by an adversary may depend on both the polynomial and an arbitrary distribution of the evaluation points (e.g., dictionary attack). This aspect is fundamental to prove the *adaptive* security of our VCBF (see Sect. 4 and Sect. 5.1).

4   Definition of Verifiable Capacity-Bound Functions

A VCBF forces an evaluator to read at least m distinct bits from its main memory. Moreover, a VCBF does not permit to trade time for capacity, i.e., an evaluator is forced to read m distinct bits independently from its computational capabilities. As explained in [53], the number of off-chip memory accesses impacts the energy consumption of the machine. If the cache's size is significantly smaller than m, evaluating the function requires significant resources. However, on the (honest) receiver's side, the validity of the computation can be verified efficiently in terms of capacity.

Formally, a VCBF scheme Π with input space $\{0,1\}^{\ell_{in}}$ is composed of the following polynomial-time algorithms:

Setup($1^\lambda, 1^k$): Upon input the security parameter 1^λ and the capacity parameter 1^k (the *capacity parameter* 1^k regulates the actual capacity cost, i.e., the number of bits read by the evaluator), the randomized setup algorithm returns the evaluation key ek and the verification key vk.

Eval(ek, x): Upon input the evaluation key ek and an input $x \in \{0,1\}^{\ell_{in}}$, the deterministic evaluation algorithm returns the output y and a proof π. In the paper, we use the notation $y = $ Eval(ek, x) (or simply Eval(ek, x)) to denote solely the output y.

Verify(vk, x, y, π): Upon input the verification key vk, an input $x \in \{0,1\}^{\ell_{in}}$, an output y, and a proof π, the deterministic verification algorithm returns a decisional bit b.

Intuitively, a VCBF scheme is correct if the output of an honest execution of the evaluation algorithm is accepted by the verification algorithm. In addition, a VCBF scheme should satisfy the following three basic properties: *minimum capacity, soundness* and *capacity efficient verification*.

Adaptive Minimum Capacity. The name captures the scheme's lower-bound on the number of distinct bits m that must be fetched from the main memory to evaluate the function. In more detail, on input a random challenge $x \xleftarrow{\$} \{0,1\}^{\ell_{in}}$, the adversary A is asked to return the correct output $y = $ Eval(ek, x) while reading at most m bits from its main memory. We assume the main memory of A is bounded since there is a strict relationship between the memory available and A's advantage ϵ. Indeed, as discussed in Sect. 3, a viable adversarial strategy is to precompute a relatively large dictionary $\tau = ($Eval(ek, $x_1), \ldots,$ Eval(ek, $x_n))$ (stored in the main memory) and return Eval(ek, x), if x has been precomputed and included into τ. A larger memory would allow the adversary to store more precomputed values Eval(ek, x_i), thus increasing the probability of success.

More formally, let $\tau \in \{0,1\}^n$ and $x \in \{0,1\}^{\ell_{in}}$ be the binary string representing the memory of the adversary A and a challenge, respectively. We denote with $\mathcal{I}_{A(\tau,x;r)} = \{i_1, i_2, \ldots, i_{n'}\}_{n' \leq n}$ the ordered set of n' distinct indexes read by A during the computation of the output $y = $ A$(\tau, x; r)$ for the corresponding challenge x while having access to memory τ and randomness $r \in \{0,1\}^{\ell_{rnd}}$. Intuitively, on input the challenge x and randomness r, the adversary A fetches the binary string $\tau_{x,r} = b_{i_1} || \ldots || b_{i_{n'}}$ from τ (where b_i represents the i-th bit of τ and $\mathcal{I}_{A(\tau,x;r)} = \{i_1, i_2, \ldots, i_{n'}\}$) and then compute the output y using the knowledge of $\tau_{x,r}$, x, and r.[11] A VCBF scheme is secure in the *adaptive setting* if for

---

[11] Observe that $\tau_{x,r}$ can be fetched from τ in an adaptive fashion according to the challenge x and randomness r.

any unbounded adversary sampled after VCBF's instiantiation (i.e., execution of Setup) it is infeasible to compute the correct output $\mathsf{Eval}(\mathsf{ek}, x) \neq y = \mathsf{A}(\tau, x; r)$ when reading $|\mathcal{I}_{\mathsf{A}(\tau,x;r)}| = m$ bits.[12]

Definition 4 ((Adaptive) Minimum Capacity of VCBF). Fix the keys $(\mathsf{ek}, \mathsf{vk}) \leftarrow\!\!{\text{\tiny\$}}\, \mathsf{Setup}(1^\lambda, 1^k)$. A VCBF scheme Π with input space $\{0,1\}^{\ell_{in}}$ satisfies $(\epsilon, m, \ell_{rnd}, n)$-min-capacity with respect to keys $(\mathsf{ek}, \mathsf{vk})$ if for all constant-size unbounded randomized adversaries A with randomness space $\{0,1\}^{\ell_{rnd}}$ and for all $\tau \in \{0,1\}^n$, we have:

$$\Pr[\mathsf{Eval}(\mathsf{ek}, x) = y \wedge |\mathcal{I}_{\mathsf{A}(\tau,x;r)}| = m \,\big|\, x \leftarrow\!\!{\text{\tiny\$}}\, \{0,1\}^{\ell_{in}}, y = \mathsf{A}(\tau, x; r)] \leq \epsilon, \qquad (1)$$

where $r \leftarrow\!\!{\text{\tiny\$}}\, \{0,1\}^{\ell_{rnd}}$.

Informally, Definition 4 states that if a VCBF scheme Π satisfies $(\epsilon, m, \ell_{rnd}, n)$-min-capacity then the only way for an (exponential time) adversary A to increase its advantage ϵ is to either read more than m distinct bits or have access to a memory larger than n bits (e.g., by storing in the memory $\tau \in \{0,1\}^n$ more pre-computed values). This guarantees the impossibility of trading time for capacity.

Note that the evaluator must return the correct output $y = \mathsf{Eval}(\mathsf{ek}, x)$ and not a verifying proof π. The infeasibility of computing a verifying proof for a false output is defined by the soundness property (see next Definition 6). The choice of defining these two properties independently allows us to define them with respect to different settings, i.e., unbounded vs. computational adversaries. As mentioned above, defining adaptive minimum capacity in the unbounded setting is necessary to properly capture the absence of time/bits read trade-offs. See Remark 2 for more details.

Moreover, the definition captures the adaptive space-based setting described in Sect. 1.1. This is because the quantifiers of the security definition states that the VCBF remains secure for any memory τ and adversary A both selected after the VCBF's instantiation (i.e., Setup algorithm). Intuitively, each τ (resp. A) represents an arbitrary precomputed memory (resp. arbitrary evaluation/reading strategy) that can depend on ek and vk (e.g., polynomial's coefficients).

Relation between the memory size n and the advantage ϵ. Definition 4 is optimal in the sense that it does not put any constraint on the indexes $\mathcal{I}_{\mathsf{A}(\tau,x;r)}$ read by the adversary A. This means that A can arbitrarily access its memory. For example, it may perform multiple random accesses to the memory τ, i.e., perform one or more conditional jumps into specific memory indexes to read different portions of the memory). Hence, one (or more) couple of progressive indexes $\{i_j, i_{j+i}\} \subset \mathcal{I}_{\mathsf{A}(\tau,x;r)}$ may be not consecutive (i.e., $|i_j - i_{j+1}| > 1$).

The optimality of Definition 4 appears to be the primary (apparently insurmountable) obstacle when trying to relate the memory size n and the advantage ϵ. To retain an advantage ϵ, an adversary A may choose to store (in the

---

[12] Without loss of generality, we assume the adversary reads exactly m bits since the higher the number of bits read, the higher the probability to compute the correct output $y = \mathsf{Eval}(\mathsf{ek}, x)$.

memory) a precomputed data structure which contains (possibly partial) pre-computed values, e.g., some evaluations $y = \mathsf{Eval}(ek, x_i)$ of a subset of inputs $\mathcal{X} \subset \{0, 1\}^{\ell_{in}}$ (precomputed dictionary). However, the estimation of the memory size n (required to store the data structure) highly depends on what type of precomputation is performed (e.g., the entropy of the precomputed values, the algorithm used, etc.) and on the type of encoding and memory access strategy used by A when fetching the data from memory τ to answer to an incoming challenge x. Unfortunately, this turned out to be a primary challenge when having block-box access to A and working in the standard setting (i.e., no oracles, no idealized functionalities, no ROM).

As a foundation paper of VCBF, we initiate a fine-grained study regarding the level of minimum capacity that can be achieved according to specific classes of adversaries. In particular, we provide a feasibility result showing (in the concrete setting) the meaningful relation between parameters ϵ and n (using an information-theoretic approach) when dealing with the smaller class of adversaries $\mathcal{A}^{1\text{-access}}$. Such a class is composed by all the adversaries that perform exactly one (adaptive) random access to the memory τ, i.e., on input the memory $\tau \in \{0, 1\}^n$, the challenge $x \in \{0, 1\}^{\ell_{in}}$, and randomness $r \in \{0, 1\}^n$, an adversary $\mathsf{A} \in \mathcal{A}^{1\text{-access}}$ adaptively jumps to an index $i \in [n - m + 1]$ (memory location) and reads m consecutive indexes. Formally, when dealing with $\mathsf{A} \in \mathcal{A}^{1\text{-access}}$, the indexes $\mathcal{I}_{\mathsf{A}(\tau, x; r)} = \{i_1, \ldots, i_m\}$ read by A are consecutive, i.e., $i_j + 1 = i_{j+1}$ for $j \in [m - 1]$.[13] Observe that in $\mathcal{A}^{1\text{-access}}$ we can identify several adversarial strategies used mainly in practice, e.g., precomputed dictionary attacks or any rainbow table technique that leverages a single adaptive random access.

As we will see during the security analysis of our construction (Sect. 5.1), by restricting the adversaries to the ones of the class $\mathcal{A}^{1\text{-access}}$, we can use a counting argument to concretely estimate the memory size n that an adversary $\mathsf{A} \in \mathcal{A}^{1\text{-access}}$ requires in order to retain a fixed advantage ϵ. For completeness, we also include the results regarding the class $\mathcal{A}^{v\text{-access}}$ for $1 \le v \le m$, i.e., adversaries that perform exactly v (adaptive) random access to the memory (observe that Definition 4 coincides with Definition 5 when $\mathcal{A} = \bigcup_{i=1}^m \mathcal{A}^{i\text{-access}}$). However, due to the limited power of counting arguments, the memory size estimation n presents an exponential loss proportional to the number v of random accesses that $\mathsf{A} \in \mathcal{A}^{v\text{-access}}$ performs. In any case, this is enough to show that there exists a VCBF that satisfies $(\mathsf{negl}, O((d+1)\lambda), o((d+1)\lambda), \omega(\lambda^s))$-min-capacity (in the asymptotic setting) with respect to the class of adversaries $\mathcal{A}^{O(1)\text{-access}}$ for every positive constant s. Regarding $\mathcal{A}^{\omega(1)\text{-access}}$, the minimum capacity of our construction remains unclear. What we know is that the evaluation of a polynomial can not satisfy minimum capacity for $\epsilon \in \mathsf{negl}$ and $m \in \omega(\log(d)^{s_1}\lambda^{s_2})$ (for some positive $s_1, s_2 \in O(1)$) when n is close to or greater than $d^{1+\delta}\lambda^{1+o(1)}$ (for a constant $\delta > 0$) because of the efficient data structure for polynomial evaluation

---

[13] Without loss of generality, we assume that reading the first m bits of τ requires the adversary to perform a random access to the first index of τ.

of Kedlaya and Umans [39] (see Sect. 5.1). We now provide the formal security definition of minimum capacity with respect to a specific class of adversaries $\mathcal{A}$.

Definition 5 ($\mathcal{A}$-class (adaptive) minimum capacity of VCBF). A VCBF scheme Π with input space $\{0,1\}^{\ell_{in}}$ satisfies $(\epsilon, m, \ell_{rnd}, n)$-min-capacity with respect to the class of adversaries $\mathcal{A}$ if Π satisfies $(\epsilon, m, \ell_{rnd}, n)$-min-capacity of Definition 4 where A is sampled from $\mathcal{A}$.

Remark 1. The Definitions 4 and 5 give robust guarantees in terms of capacity (according to the corresponding class of adversaries). For example, they consider unbounded adversaries and the minimum capacity must hold for every possible adversary A and memory τ after the instantiation of the scheme (execution of the setup algorithm). This corresponds to the adaptive space-based security setting described in Sect. 1.1. Also, there is a more fundamental aspect to consider regarding Definitions 4 and 5: They do not rely on any heuristic assumptions, such as the Random Oracle (RO) or the Ideal Cipher [21], to measure the number of read bits. In fact, previous definitions of bandwidth-hard or memory-hard functions [2–6,15,19,21,54] do not directly measure the bits read by the evaluator. Instead, those models only calculate the number of the random oracle queries for each step. Therefore, the gap between RO queries and the actual number of bits read by the evaluator is artificially ignored in previous models. Finally, we stress that both RO and Ideal Cipher definitions neglect (and do not take into account) the adversary's strategy in organizing and accessing specific portions of the memory: A fundamental aspect that needs to be considered when proving specific concrete memory bounds (in the standard model) for VCBFs.

Soundness. Soundness captures the infeasibility of convincing the verifier that $y^* \neq \mathsf{Eval}(\mathsf{ek}, x)$ is the correct output of the computation. In more detail, it is infeasible for a malicious evaluator to compute a triple (x^*, y^*, π^*) that verifies successfully, but y^* is not the correct output of the computation. Soundness is also fundamental to enforce the $(\epsilon, m, \ell_{rnd}, n)$-min-capacity (Definitions 4 and 5) of a VCBF scheme. For example, if soundness does not hold, a malicious evaluator can deceive the verifier by returning a proof π^* and an output $y^* \neq \mathsf{Eval}(\mathsf{ek}, x)$ such that $\mathsf{Verify}(\mathsf{vk}, x, y^*, \pi^*) = 1$. In this case, the energy consumption is not guaranteed since the value y^* is incorrect and may have been computed without fetching any bit from the main memory.

Definition 6 (Soundness of VCBF). A VCBF scheme Π with input space $\{0,1\}^{\ell_{in}}$ is (ϵ)-sound if for all PPT adversary A we have:

$$\Pr\left[\begin{matrix} \mathsf{Verify}(\mathsf{vk}, x, y, \pi) = 1 \text{ and} \\ \mathsf{Eval}(\mathsf{ek}, x) \neq y \end{matrix} \middle| \begin{matrix} (\mathsf{ek}, \mathsf{vk}) \leftarrow_\$ \mathsf{Setup}(1^\lambda, 1^k) \\ (x, y, \pi) \leftarrow_\$ \mathsf{A}(1^\lambda, \mathsf{ek}, \mathsf{vk}) \end{matrix}\right] \leq \epsilon.$$

Remark 2 (On the combination of minimum capacity and soundness). Formalizing adaptive minimum capacity (Definitions 4 and 5) and soundness (Definition 6) separately allows us to define these notions with respect to two distinct settings, i.e., unbounded adversaries vs. computational bounded adversaries. In turn, minimum capacity with respect to unbounded adversaries is fundamental to capturing the (concrete) strict lower bound on the number of distinct bits guaranteed by a VCBF. This is because the unbounded setting guarantees that the lower bound must be satisfied independently of the running time of the adversary, i.e., trading time for bits read is infeasible. Observe that the computational bounded version of minimum capacity does not guarantee the absence of a time/bits read trade-off. For example, a VCBF presenting an exponential trade-off (e.g., a PPT adversary can choose not to read a few bits at the cost of doubling its running time) may satisfy, asymptotically speaking, computational minimum capacity. However, the concrete lower bound would not be strict since the adversary can play with the gap allowed by the trade-off (this is not allowed when considering minimum capacity w.r.t unbounded adversaries as in our results). This is problematic when the VCBF is instantiated in practice since it makes the capacity bound less clear. For this reason, we chose to formalize these notions separately instead of being combined into a single one with respect to computational bounded adversaries. Naturally, since we consider computational soundness, the final security of the VCBF holds only against computationally bounded adversaries (unless we drop the VCBF's efficient verification). Still, we emphasize once again that unbounded minimum capacity is fundamental since it guarantees the absence of a trade-off with which the (computationally bounded) adversary could play with. Lastly, it may seem that another natural approach is to combine minimum capacity and soundness into a single definition that considers unbounded adversaries. Unfortunately, this is not possible since a VCBF that has a capacity efficient verification (see next Definition 7) cannot satisfy, at the same time, both minimum capacity and soundness with respect to unbounded adversaries (soundness with respect to unbounded adversaries is also known as perfect soundness, i.e., it does not exist a valid proof for a false statement/output). This is because an exponential adversary always exists that brute-forces all pairs of proofs and outputs until it finds the one that verifies. By leveraging perfect soundness, the adversary is guaranteed that the corresponding output is the correct VCBF's evaluation. This attack only requires reading the VCBF's verification key vk, whose size must be sublinear in the VCBF's minimum capacity m. This is required to satisfy capacity efficient verification (see next Definition 7).

Capacity Efficient Verification. The resource considered by VCBFs is the capacity since an evaluator is forced to read m distinct bits from its main memory. The verifier, on the other hand, should not have the same workload. For this reason, we require a VCBF scheme Π to be efficiently verifiable:

Definition 7 (Capacity Efficient Verification of VCBF). If Π satisfies $(\epsilon, m, \ell_{rnd}, n)$-min-capacity (either Definition 4 or Definition 5) then an honest execution of the verification algorithm requires at most fetching $o(m)$ bits from the memory (i.e., sublinear in m).[14]

In particular, in this work, the capacity parameter is of the form $m \in O((d+1)\lambda)$ where d is the degree of a polynomial $f(X) = \sum_{i=0}^{d} a_i \cdot x^i \in \mathbb{F}_p[x]$ and $\lambda + 1$ is the size of the prime p. As we will see, to reach high capacities (such as GB or even TB), for a fixed λ we will have to set $d \in O(\lambda^c)$ for a constant $c \geq 1$. Nevertheless, the verification will be independent of d by leveraging the publicly VC scheme of Elkhiyaoui et al. [30]. Hence, we will obtain at least $O(\lambda^{c+1})$ of min-capacity for the evaluation, and at most $O(\lambda)$ of min-capacity for the verification (see Sect. 5.1).[15]

On Energy Consumption. A motivation for VCBFs is ASIC resistance. State-of-the-art hash engines [14,54] could be $200,000\times$ faster and $40,000\times$ more energy efficient than multi-core CPUs. However, the energy consumption for off-chip memory accesses is similar for CPUs and ASICs [54]. If we assume the ASIC can hardcode only s bits, min-capacity guarantees that the ASIC will transfer at least $m - s$ bits from the external memory during the evaluation. If the energy cost is u nJ per bit for external memory accesses, the evaluation of the VCBF costs at least $u(m - s)$ nJ.

5   VCBF from VC for Polynomial Evaluation

In this section we show how to build a VCBF from VC for polynomial evaluation.

Construction 1. *Let $\mathcal{F}_{\lambda,d,p} = \{f_a(X) = \sum_{i=0}^{d} a_i \cdot x^i \mod p\}_{a \in \{0,1\}^{(d+1)\lambda}}$ be an ensemble of polynomials where $a = a_0||\ldots||a_d$, $\lambda \in \mathbb{N}$, $d \in \mathbb{N}$, and p is a prime of $\lambda + 1$ bits. Let $\mathsf{VC} = (\mathsf{Setup}_{\mathsf{VC}}, \mathsf{ProbGen}_{\mathsf{VC}}, \mathsf{Compute}_{\mathsf{VC}}, \mathsf{Verify}_{\mathsf{VC}})$ be a publicly VC scheme for the class $\mathcal{F}_{\lambda,d,p}$. We build a VCBF scheme with input space $\{0,1\}^{\ell_{in}}$ in the following way:*

$\mathsf{Setup}(1^\lambda, 1^k)$: *Without loss of generality, we assume $k = (d+1)\lambda$. On input the security parameter 1^λ and the capacity parameter 1^k, the setup algorithm samples $a_0||\ldots||a_d = a \leftarrow_\$ \{0,1\}^{(d+1)\lambda}$ where $|a_i| = \lambda$ for $i \in \{0,\ldots,d\}$. Then, it outputs the evaluation key $\mathsf{ek} = (\mathsf{ek}_{f_a}, \mathsf{vk}_{f_a})$ and the verification key $\mathsf{vk} = \mathsf{vk}_{f_a}$ where $(\mathsf{ek}_{f_a}, \mathsf{vk}_{f_a}) \leftarrow_\$ \mathsf{Setup}_{\mathsf{VC}}(1^\lambda, f_a)$ and $f_a \in \mathcal{F}_{\lambda,d,p}$.*

$\mathsf{Eval}(\mathsf{ek}, x)$: *On input the evaluation key $\mathsf{ek} = (\mathsf{ek}_{f_a}, \mathsf{vk}_{f_a})$ and an input $x \in \{0,1\}^{\ell_{in}}$, the evaluation algorithm returns $(y, \pi) = \mathsf{Compute}_{\mathsf{VC}}(\mathsf{ek}_{f_a}, \sigma_x)$ where $(\sigma_x, \mathsf{vk}_x) = \mathsf{ProbGen}_{\mathsf{VC}}(\mathsf{vk}_{f_a}, x)$.*

---

[14] Observe that $|\mathsf{vk}| + |x| + |y| + |\pi| \in o(m)$ (i.e., vk, π, y, x are "succinct") is necessary to obtain a capacity-efficient verification of $o(m)$. This is because vk, π, y, x are part of the verification algorithm Verify of VCBF.

[15] In the verification, $O(\lambda)$ is for reading a constant number of group elements of order p of size at most $\lambda+1$. In the evaluation, $O((d+1)\lambda) = O(\lambda^{c+1})$ is for the d coefficients $(a_0, \ldots, a_d) \in \mathbb{F}_p^{d+1}$ of the polynomial $f(X) \in \mathbb{F}_p[x]$.

Verify(vk, x, y, π): *On input the verification key* vk $=$ vk$_{f_a}$, *an input* $x \in \{0,1\}^{\ell_{in}}$, *an output* $y \in \mathcal{Y}$, *and a proof* π, *the verification algorithm returns* $b =$ Verify$_{VC}$(vk$_x$, y, π) *where* $(\sigma_x, vk_x) =$ ProbGen$_{VC}$(vk$_{f_a}$, x).

In this scheme, honest evaluators need to read at least $k = (d+1)\lambda$ bits to load all the coefficients of the polynomial regardless of the cost of generating the proof π. Correctness follows directly from the correctness of the underlying schemes. For security and verification complexity, we establish the following results.

5.1   Security Analysis

The soundness is trivial. It simply follows from the (ϵ)-soundness of VC (see [30] for the formal definition of soundness for VC).

Theorem 6 (Soundness). *If* VC *is* (ϵ)*-sound, then the VCBF scheme* Π *of Construction 1 with input space* $\{0,1\}^{\ell_{in}}$ *is* (ϵ)*-sound (Definition 6).*

Next, we show the level of minimum capacity that our VCBF scheme Π of Construction 1 satisfies with respect to the class of adversaries $\mathcal{A}^{v\text{-access}}$ (Definition 5) for $1 \leq v \leq m$. This is formalized by Corollary 7 whose proof is deferred to full version. At high level, the proof is divided into two parts.

First, we prove that Construction 1 satisfies an alternative definition of minimum capacity dubbed *decomposed minimum capacity*. This definition is identical to Definition 4 except that the memory τ is decomposed into n distinct strings $(\tau_1, \dots, \tau_n)$ such that $\tau_i \in \{0,1\}^m$ for $i \in [n]$ (intuitively, each τ_i represents one possible string of length m that the adversary can read and interpret from its main memory, i.e., $(\tau_1, \dots, \tau_n)$ is the *decomposition* of the main memory). Then, the adversary succeeds if there exists $i \in [n]$ such that $y = \mathsf{A}(\tau_i, x; r_i)$ where $r_i \leftarrow_\$ \{0,1\}^{\ell_{rnd}}$ and $x \leftarrow_\$ \{0,1\}^{\ell_{in}}$. By leveraging Theorem 5, for each string $\tau_i \in \{0,1\}^m$, the adversary can compute at most d distinct points $x \in \{0,1\}^{\ell_{in}}$ under the condition that the coefficients $(a_0, \dots, a_d)$ of the polynomial $f_a(X) \in \mathcal{F}_{\lambda, d, p}$ are RND-incompressible.[16]

Second, we show that any VCBF that satisfies decomposed minimum capacity w.r.t. $n - m + 1$ strings $(\tau_1, \dots, \tau_{n-m+1})$ (each of length m), also satisfies ($\epsilon, m, \ell_{rnd}, n$)-min-capacity (the standard definition) with respect to the class of adversaries $\mathcal{A}^{1\text{-access}}$ (Definition 5). The result follows by using a counting argument: An adversary $\mathsf{A} \in \mathcal{A}^{1\text{-access}}$ with access to memory τ of length n can read at most $n - m + 1$ different strings each of length m. This argument can be generalized for each class $\mathcal{A}^{v\text{-access}}$ for $1 \leq v \leq m$. Unfortunately, due to the limited power of counting arguments, the memory size n presents an exponential loss proportional to v.

Theorem 7 ($\mathcal{A}^{v\text{-access}}$-class (adaptive) minimum capacity). *Let* $v \in \mathbb{N}$ *and* Π *be a* VCBF *scheme with input space* $\{0,1\}^{\ell_{in}}$. *Fix the keys*

---

[16] Note that the polynomial $f_a(X)$ is RND-incompressible with overwhelming probability since it is sampled at random. This follows by leveraging Theorems 3 and 4.

(ek, vk) $\leftarrow_s$ Setup$(1^\lambda, 1^k)$. *The VCBF scheme Π of Construction 1 with input space $\{0,1\}^{\ell_{in}}$ satisfies $(\epsilon, m, \ell_{rnd}, n)$-min-capacity with respect to the class of adversaries $\mathcal{A}^{v\text{-}access}$ and keys* (ek, vk) *(Definition 5) where $\lambda \in \mathbb{N}, d \in \mathbb{N}, c \in \mathbb{N}, \epsilon_1 \in [0,1]$,*

$$m = (d+1)(\lambda - \ell_{in} - 2\log(\ell_{in}) - 1) - c'$$
$$- \lambda - 2\log((d+1)\lambda - c') - 2\log(\lambda+1) - 4,$$
$$c' = c + \ell_{rnd} + 2\log(\ell_{rnd}) + 1 + O(1),$$
$$\epsilon = \epsilon_1 + \frac{d+1}{2^{\ell_{in}}} + \frac{1}{2^c} - \frac{1}{2^{(d+1)\lambda}},$$
$$n = \begin{cases} m + \frac{\epsilon_1 \cdot 2^{\ell_{in}}}{d} & \text{if } v = 1 \\ \sqrt[v]{\left(\frac{\epsilon_1 \cdot 2^{\ell_{in}}}{d} + 1\right) / \left(v! \left(\frac{m-1}{v-1}\right)^{v-1}\right)} \cdot v & \text{if } 1 < v \le m. \end{cases}$$

Recall that in the class of adversaries $\mathcal{A}^{1\text{-}access}$ we find common adversarial strategies (primarily used in practice) such as precomputed dictionary attacks (e.g., ordered dictionary in which the x-th evaluation $f(x)$ is stored at the x-th offset) or limited devices that are hindered from performing non-constant random accesses (e.g., for energy efficiency). Also, we stress that, if we consider memories of size $n = m$, our Construction 1 satisfies $(\epsilon, m, \ell_{rnd}, m)$-min-capacity with respect to the *optimal* Definition 4 (i.e., security against adversaries that arbitrarly access its memory) where $\epsilon = \frac{d+1}{2^{\ell_{in}}} + \frac{1}{2^c} - \frac{1}{2^{(d+1)\lambda}}$. This because $\tau \in \{0,1\}^m$ only allows an adversary to answer to at most d points (Theorem 5).

The following asymptotic Corollary 1 shows that a secure VCBF exists (in the standard model) with respect to the class of adversary $\mathcal{A}^{O(1)\text{-}access}$. We stress that this must be interpreted as a purely theoretical result showing the feasibility of VCBF since the constants hidden by the asymptotic notation are large.

Corollary 1. *For any $\lambda \in \mathbb{N}$ and $k = (d+1)\lambda \in \mathbb{N}$ such that $d \in \mathbb{N}$, there exists a VCBF that satisfies $(\text{negl}, O((d+1)\lambda), o((d+1)\lambda), \omega(\lambda^s))$-min-capacity with respect to the class of adversaries $\mathcal{A}^{O(1)\text{-}access}$ for every constant $s \ge 1$.*[17]

Verification Complexity. Corollary 1 shows that an evaluator needs to read at least $O((d+1)\lambda)$ distinct bits from its main memory. We now analyze the verifier capacity complexity. By inspecting Construction 1, we observe that the capacity complexity of Verify coincides with the ones of algorithms ProbGen$_{VC}$ and Verify$_{VC}$ of the underlying VC scheme. Therefore, we must consider a concrete instantiation of the VC scheme. For this reason, we measured the efficiency of our VCBF with respect to the VC scheme of Elkhiyaoui et

---

[17] We stress that the memory size n does not need to be super-polynomial (in the security parameter) in order to consider a VCBF secure. Indeed, in a scenario in which a machine has at most $n = \lambda^s \in$ poly bits of free memory (for a positive constant s), it is enough to show that the VCBF satisfies $(\epsilon, m, \ell_{rnd}, \lambda^s)$-min-capacity where ϵ is the target advantage.

al. [30] that uses an asymmetric bilinear pairing $e : \mathbb{G}_1 \times \mathbb{G}_2 \to \mathbb{G}_T$ in which the $(d/2)$-SDH assumption holds. The execution of $\mathsf{ProbGen_{VC}}(\mathsf{vk}_f, x)$ computes and returns $\mathsf{vk}_x = (\mathsf{vk}_x^0, \mathsf{vk}_x^1) = (g_{b_0} \cdot g^{x^2}, h_{r_1}^x \cdot h_{r_0})$ and $\sigma_x = x$, where $\mathsf{vk}_f = (g_{b_0}, h_{r_1}, h_{r_0}) \in \mathbb{G}_1 \times \mathbb{G}_2 \times \mathbb{G}_2$, $x \in \mathbb{F}_p$, and g the generator of $\mathbb{G}_1$ (observe that the size of the verification key vk_f is $O(\lambda)$, i.e., does not depend on the degree d of the polynomial). Moreover, $\mathsf{Verify_{VC}}(\mathsf{vk}_x, y, \pi_y)$ verifies the correctness of the computation by checking the equality $e(g, h^y) \stackrel{?}{=} e(\mathsf{vk}_x^0, \pi_y) \cdot e(g, \mathsf{vk}_x^1)$, where $\mathsf{vk}_x = (\mathsf{vk}_x^0, \mathsf{vk}_x^1)$ and h is a generator of $\mathbb{G}_2$. Hence, in the worst case, the verification capacity complexity of our VCBF is $O(\lambda) \in o((d+1)\lambda)$, while the verification time is $O(1)$ in the number of group operations. This is because the executions of $\mathsf{ProbGen_{VC}}$, $\mathsf{Verify_{VC}}$, and the sizes of $(\mathsf{vk}_f, x, y, \pi_y)$ (that compose the inputs of $\mathsf{ProbGen_{VC}}$ and $\mathsf{Verify_{VC}}$), are independent of the polynomial degree d in terms of both capacity and time.

Improve the Memory Size Bound. For $v \in \omega(1)$, our VCBF construction needs to face the efficient data structure for polynomial evaluation of Kedlaya and Umans [39]. In particular, they show that, for any constant $\delta > 0$, there exists a data structure D of size $d^{1+\delta}\lambda^{1+o(1)}$ that can be computed by preprocessing only the coefficients of $f(X) \in \mathbb{F}_p[X]$. An evaluator in $\mathcal{A}^{\omega(1)\text{-access}}$ can correctly evaluate $f(x)$ on every $x \in \{0,1\}^{\ell_{in}}$ in time $\mathsf{polylog}(d) \cdot \lambda^{1+o(1)}$, performing a non-constant number of random accesses and reading at most $\mathsf{polylog}(d)\lambda^{1+o(1)} \cdot w$ bits from D (with $w \in O(\lambda)$ we denote bit size of the elements contained in D). Hence, our VCBF construction can not achieve $(\epsilon, m, \ell_{rnd}, n)$ for $\epsilon \in \mathsf{negl}$ and $m \in \omega(\log(d)^{s_1}\lambda^{s_2})$ (for some positive $s_1, s_2 \in O(1)$) when n is close to or greater than $d^{1+\delta}\lambda^{1+o(1)}$. The above observation poses the natural question of whether an asymptotic VCBF (in the $\mathcal{A}^{\omega(1)\text{-access}}$ setting) that satisfies min-capacity for reasonably large m and n super-polynomial in λ as in Corollary 1 (i.e., n asymptotically larger than the size $d^{1+\delta} \cdot \lambda^{1+o(1)}$ of the data structure of Kedlaya and Umans [39]). The answer to the important question requires a non-trivial and precise study that can be undertake in future works.

Acknowledgments. We thank Irene Giacomelli and Luca Nizzardo for helpful discussions.

The authors were partially supported by Protocol Labs under the RFP-009 on Proof of Space and Useful Space. In addition, the second author was supported by the National Key R&D Program of China 2021YFB3100100 and CAS Project for Young Scientists in Basic Research Grant YSBR-035, the third author was supported by the Carlsberg Foundation under the Semper Ardens Research Project CF18-112 (BCM), and the fourth author was supported by Hong Kong Research Grants Council under grant GRF-16200721.

References

1. Abadi, M., Burrows, M., Manasse, M., Wobber, T.: Moderately hard, memory-bound functions. ACM Trans. Internet Technol. (TOIT) 5(2), 299–327 (2005)

2. Alwen, J., Blocki, J.: Efficiently computing data-independent memory-hard functions. In: Robshaw, M., Katz, J. (eds.) CRYPTO 2016. LNCS, vol. 9815, pp. 241–271. Springer, Heidelberg (2016). https://doi.org/10.1007/978-3-662-53008-5_9

3. Alwen, J., Blocki, J., Harsha, B.: Practical graphs for optimal side-channel resistant memory-hard functions. In: Proceedings of the 2017 ACM SIGSAC Conference on Computer and Communications Security, pp. 1001–1017 (2017)

4. Alwen, J., Blocki, J., Pietrzak, K.: Sustained space complexity. In: Nielsen, J.B., Rijmen, V. (eds.) EUROCRYPT 2018. LNCS, vol. 10821, pp. 99–130. Springer, Cham (2018). https://doi.org/10.1007/978-3-319-78375-8_4

5. Alwen, J., Chen, B., Pietrzak, K., Reyzin, L., Tessaro, S.: Scrypt is maximally memory-hard. In: Coron, J.-S., Nielsen, J.B. (eds.) EUROCRYPT 2017. LNCS, vol. 10212, pp. 33–62. Springer, Cham (2017). https://doi.org/10.1007/978-3-319-56617-7_2

6. Alwen, J., Serbinenko, V.: High parallel complexity graphs and memory-hard functions. In: Proceedings of the Forty-seventh Annual ACM Symposium on Theory of Computing, pp. 595–603 (2015)

7. Ateniese, G., Bonacina, I., Faonio, A., Galesi, N.: Proofs of space: when space is of the essence. In: Abdalla, M., De Prisco, R. (eds.) SCN 2014. LNCS, vol. 8642, pp. 538–557. Springer, Cham (2014). https://doi.org/10.1007/978-3-319-10879-7_31

8. Aura, T.: DOS-resistant authentication with client puzzles. In: Christianson, B., Malcolm, J.A., Crispo, B., Roe, M. (eds.) Security Protocols 2000. LNCS, vol. 2133, pp. 178–181. Springer, Heidelberg (2001). https://doi.org/10.1007/3-540-44810-1_23

9. Back, A.: Hashcash-a denial of service counter-measure (2002)

10. Bellare, M., Kane, D., Rogaway, P.: Big-key symmetric encryption: resisting key exfiltration. In: Robshaw, M., Katz, J. (eds.) CRYPTO 2016. LNCS, vol. 9814, pp. 373–402. Springer, Heidelberg (2016). https://doi.org/10.1007/978-3-662-53018-4_14

11. Biryukov, A., Bouillaguet, C., Khovratovich, D.: Cryptographic schemes based on the ASASA structure: Black-Box, White-Box, and Public-Key (Extended Abstract). In: Sarkar, P., Iwata, T. (eds.) ASIACRYPT 2014. LNCS, vol. 8873, pp. 63–84. Springer, Heidelberg (2014). https://doi.org/10.1007/978-3-662-45611-8_4

12. Biryukov, A., Khovratovich, D.: Egalitarian computing. In: Holz, T., Savage, S. (eds.) USENIX Security 2016, pp. 315–326. USENIX Association, August 2016

13. Biryukov, A., Perrin, L.: Symmetrically and asymmetrically hard cryptography. In: Takagi, T., Peyrin, T. (eds.) ASIACRYPT 2017. LNCS, vol. 10626, pp. 417–445. Springer, Cham (2017). https://doi.org/10.1007/978-3-319-70700-6_15

14. Bitmain: Antminer s9 (2020). https://shop.bitmain.com/product/detail?pid=00020200306153650096S2W5mY1i0661

15. Blocki, J., Ren, L., Zhou, S.: Bandwidth-hard functions: reductions and lower bounds. In: Proceedings of the 2018 ACM SIGSAC Conference on Computer and Communications Security, pp. 1820–1836 (2018)

16. Bogdanov, A., Isobe, T.: White-box cryptography revisited: space-hard ciphers. In: Proceedings of the 22nd ACM SIGSAC Conference on Computer and Communications Security, pp. 1058–1069 (2015)

17. Bogdanov, A., Isobe, T., Tischhauser, E.: Towards practical whitebox cryptography: optimizing efficiency and space hardness. In: Cheon, J.H., Takagi, T. (eds.) ASIACRYPT 2016, Part I. LNCS, vol. 10031, pp. 126–158. Springer, Heidelberg (2016). https://doi.org/10.1007/978-3-662-53887-6_5

18. Boneh, D., Bonneau, J., Bünz, B., Fisch, B.: Verifiable delay functions. In: Shacham, H., Boldyreva, A. (eds.) CRYPTO 2018. LNCS, vol. 10991, pp. 757–788. Springer, Cham (2018). https://doi.org/10.1007/978-3-319-96884-1_25

19. Boneh, D., Corrigan-Gibbs, H., Schechter, S.E.: Balloon hashing: a memory-hard function providing provable protection against sequential attacks. In: Cheon, J.H., Takagi, T. (eds.) ASIACRYPT 2016, Part I. LNCS, vol. 10031, pp. 220–248. Springer, Heidelberg (2016). https://doi.org/10.1007/978-3-662-53887-6_8

20. Canetti, R., Halevi, S., Steiner, M.: Hardness amplification of weakly verifiable puzzles. In: Kilian, J. (ed.) TCC 2005. LNCS, vol. 3378, pp. 17–33. Springer, Heidelberg (2005). https://doi.org/10.1007/978-3-540-30576-7_2

21. Chen, B., Tessaro, S.: Memory-hard functions from cryptographic primitives. In: Boldyreva, A., Micciancio, D. (eds.) CRYPTO 2019. LNCS, vol. 11693, pp. 543–572. Springer, Cham (2019). https://doi.org/10.1007/978-3-030-26951-7_19

22. Chen, L., Morrissey, P., Smart, N.P., Warinschi, B.: Security notions and generic constructions for client puzzles. In: Matsui, M. (ed.) ASIACRYPT 2009. LNCS, vol. 5912, pp. 505–523. Springer, Heidelberg (2009). https://doi.org/10.1007/978-3-642-10366-7_30

23. Cohen, B., Pietrzak, K.: Simple proofs of sequential work. In: Nielsen, J.B., Rijmen, V. (eds.) EUROCRYPT 2018. LNCS, vol. 10821, pp. 451–467. Springer, Cham (2018). https://doi.org/10.1007/978-3-319-78375-8_15

24. Dean, D., Stubblefield, A.: Using client puzzles to protect TLS. In: USENIX Security Symposium, vol. 42 (2001)

25. Döttling, N., Lai, R.W.F., Malavolta, G.: Incremental proofs of sequential work. In: Ishai, Y., Rijmen, V. (eds.) EUROCRYPT 2019. LNCS, vol. 11477, pp. 292–323. Springer, Cham (2019). https://doi.org/10.1007/978-3-030-17656-3_11

26. Dwork, C., Goldberg, A., Naor, M.: On memory-bound functions for fighting spam. In: Boneh, D. (ed.) CRYPTO 2003. LNCS, vol. 2729, pp. 426–444. Springer, Heidelberg (2003). https://doi.org/10.1007/978-3-540-45146-4_25

27. Dwork, C., Naor, M.: Pricing via processing or combatting junk mail. In: Brickell, E.F. (ed.) CRYPTO 1992. LNCS, vol. 740, pp. 139–147. Springer, Heidelberg (1993). https://doi.org/10.1007/3-540-48071-4_10

28. Dwork, C., Naor, M., Wee, H.: Pebbling and proofs of work. In: Shoup, V. (ed.) CRYPTO 2005. LNCS, vol. 3621, pp. 37–54. Springer, Heidelberg (2005). https://doi.org/10.1007/11535218_3

29. Dziembowski, S., Faust, S., Kolmogorov, V., Pietrzak, K.: Proofs of space. In: Gennaro, R., Robshaw, M. (eds.) CRYPTO 2015. LNCS, vol. 9216, pp. 585–605. Springer, Heidelberg (2015). https://doi.org/10.1007/978-3-662-48000-7_29

30. Elkhiyaoui, K., Önen, M., Azraoui, M., Molva, R.: Efficient techniques for publicly verifiable delegation of computation. In: Proceedings of the 11th ACM on Asia Conference on Computer and Communications Security, pp. 119–128. ACM (2016)

31. Ephraim, N., Freitag, C., Komargodski, I., Pass, R.: SPARKs: succinct parallelizable arguments of knowledge. In: Canteaut, A., Ishai, Y. (eds.) EUROCRYPT 2020, Part I. LNCS, vol. 12105, pp. 707–737. Springer, Heidelberg (2020). https://doi.org/10.1007/978-3-030-45721-1_25

32. Fiore, D., Gennaro, R.: Publicly verifiable delegation of large polynomials and matrix computations, with applications. In: Yu, T., Danezis, G., Gligor, V.D. (eds.) ACM CCS 2012, pp. 501–512. ACM Press, October 2012

33. Fisch, B.: Tight proofs of space and replication. In: Ishai, Y., Rijmen, V. (eds.) EUROCRYPT 2019, Part II. LNCS, vol. 11477, pp. 324–348. Springer, Heidelberg (May (2019)

34. Fouque, P.-A., Karpman, P., Kirchner, P., Minaud, B.: Efficient and provable white-box primitives. In: Cheon, J.H., Takagi, T. (eds.) ASIACRYPT 2016. LNCS, vol. 10031, pp. 159–188. Springer, Heidelberg (2016). https://doi.org/10.1007/978-3-662-53887-6_6

35. Grunwald, P., Vitányi, P.: Shannon information and Kolmogorov complexity. arXiv preprint cs/0410002 (2004)

36. Jaeger, J., Tessaro, S.: Tight time-memory trade-offs for symmetric encryption. In: Ishai, Y., Rijmen, V. (eds.) EUROCRYPT 2019. LNCS, vol. 11476, pp. 467–497. Springer, Cham (2019). https://doi.org/10.1007/978-3-030-17653-2_16

37. Juels, A.: Client puzzles: a cryptographic countermeasure against connection depletion attacks. In: Proceedings of Networks and Distributed System Security Symposium (NDSS) (1999)

38. Kaliski, B.: Password-based cryptography specification. RFC 2898 (2000)

39. Kedlaya, K.S., Umans, C.: Fast modular composition in any characteristic. In: 2008 49th Annual IEEE Symposium on Foundations of Computer Science, pp. 146–155. IEEE (2008)

40. Li, M., Vitányi, P.: An Introduction to Kolmogorov Complexity and Its Applications. TCS. Springer, New York (2008). https://doi.org/10.1007/978-0-387-49820-1

41. Liu, Y., Pass, R.: On one-way functions and Kolmogorov complexity. In: FOCS 2020, 61st Annual IEEE Symposium on Foundations of Computer Science (2020)

42. Mahmoody, M., Moran, T., Vadhan, S.: Publicly verifiable proofs of sequential work. In: Proceedings of the 4th Conference on Innovations in Theoretical Computer Science, pp. 373–388 (2013)

43. Merkle, R.C.: Secure communications over insecure channels. Commun. ACM **21**(4), 294–299 (1978)

44. Moran, T., Orlov, I.: Simple proofs of space-time and rational proofs of storage. In: Boldyreva, A., Micciancio, D. (eds.) CRYPTO 2019. LNCS, vol. 11692, pp. 381–409. Springer, Cham (2019). https://doi.org/10.1007/978-3-030-26948-7_14

45. Muchnik, A.A.: Kolmogorov complexity and cryptography. Proc. Steklov Inst. Math. **274**(1), 193 (2011)

46. Nakamoto, S.: Bitcoin: a peer-to-peer electronic cash system (2008)

47. Neary, T., Woods, D.: Four small universal Turing machines. Fundamenta Informaticae **91**(1), 123–144 (2009)

48. Papamanthou, C., Shi, E., Tamassia, R.: Signatures of correct computation. In: Sahai, A. (ed.) TCC 2013. LNCS, vol. 7785, pp. 222–242. Springer, Heidelberg (2013). https://doi.org/10.1007/978-3-642-36594-2_13

49. Percival, C.: Stronger key derivation via sequential memory-hard functions (2009)

50. Pietrzak, K.: Simple verifiable delay functions. In: 10th Innovations in Theoretical Computer Science Conference (ITCS 2019). Schloss Dagstuhl-Leibniz-Zentrum fuer Informatik (2018)

51. Protocol Labs: Filecoin: a decentralized storage network (2017). https://filecoin.io/filecoin.pdf. Accessed 8 Apr 2023

52. Provos, N., Mazieres, D.: A future-adaptable password scheme. In: USENIX Annual Technical Conference, FREENIX Track, pp. 81–91 (1999)

53. Ren, L., Devadas, S.: Proof of space from stacked expanders. In: Hirt, M., Smith, A. (eds.) TCC 2016. LNCS, vol. 9985, pp. 262–285. Springer, Heidelberg (2016). https://doi.org/10.1007/978-3-662-53641-4_11

54. Ren, L., Devadas, S.: Bandwidth hard functions for ASIC resistance. In: Kalai, Y., Reyzin, L. (eds.) TCC 2017. LNCS, vol. 10677, pp. 466–492. Springer, Cham (2017). https://doi.org/10.1007/978-3-319-70500-2_16

55. Rivest, R.L., Shamir, A., Wagner, D.A.: Time-lock puzzles and timed-release crypto (1996)
56. Souto, A., Teixeira, A., Pinto, A.: One-way functions using Kolmogorov complexity. In: Proceedings of the Computability in Europe, pp. 346–356 (2010)
57. Stebila, D., Kuppusamy, L., Rangasamy, J., Boyd, C., Gonzalez Nieto, J.: Stronger difficulty notions for client puzzles and denial-of-service-resistant protocols. In: Kiayias, A. (ed.) CT-RSA 2011. LNCS, vol. 6558, pp. 284–301. Springer, Heidelberg (2011). https://doi.org/10.1007/978-3-642-19074-2_19
58. Vitányi, P.: Personal webpage. https://homepages.cwi.nl/paulv/kolmogorov.html
59. Wesolowski, B.: Efficient verifiable delay functions. J. Cryptol. 1–35 (2020)
60. Woods, D., Neary, T.: The complexity of small universal Turing machines: a survey. Theor. Comput. Sci. **410**(4–5), 443–450 (2009)
61. Zhang, Y., Genkin, D., Katz, J., Papadopoulos, D., Papamanthou, C.: vSQL: verifying arbitrary SQL queries over dynamic outsourced databases. In: 2017 IEEE Symposium on Security and Privacy, pp. 863–880. IEEE Computer Society Press, May 2017

A Holistic Approach Towards Side-Channel Secure Fixed-Weight Polynomial Sampling

Markus Krausz[1], Georg Land[1,2(✉)], Jan Richter-Brockmann[1], and Tim Güneysu[1,2]

[1] Horst Görtz Institute for IT Security, Ruhr University Bochum, Bochum, Germany
{markus.krausz,georg.land,jan.richter-brockmann,tim.guneysu}@rub.de
[2] Cyber-Physical Systems, DFKI GmbH, Bremen, Germany

Abstract. The sampling of polynomials with fixed weight is a procedure required by round-4 Key Encapsulation Mechanisms (KEMs) for Post-Quantum Cryptography (PQC) standardization (BIKE, HQC, McEliece) as well as NTRU, Streamlined NTRU Prime, and NTRU LPRrime. Recent attacks have shown in this context that side-channel leakage of sampling methods can be exploited for key recoveries. While countermeasures regarding such timing attacks have already been presented, still, there is no comprehensive work covering solutions that are also secure against power side channels.

To close this gap, the contribution of this work is threefold: First, we analyze requirements for the different use cases of fixed weight sampling. Second, we demonstrate how *all* known sampling methods can be implemented securely against timing and power/EM side channels and propose performance-enhancing modifications. Furthermore, we propose a new, comparison-based methodology that outperforms existing methods in the masked setting for the three round-4 KEMs BIKE, HQC, and McEliece. Third, we present bitsliced and arbitrary-order masked software implementations and benchmarked them for all relevant cryptographic schemes to be able to infer recommendations for each use case. Additionally, we provide a hardware implementation of our new method as a case study and analyze the feasibility of implementing the other approaches in hardware.

Keywords: PQC · Fixed Weight Polynomial Sampling · Higher-order Masking · Cortex-M4

1 Introduction

With the potential advent of large-scale quantum computers, rendering "classic" asymmetric cryptosystems like Elliptic Curve Cryptography (ECC) insecure, wide deployment of Post-Quantum Cryptography (PQC) has become inevitable. After three rounds of thorough analysis and many broken cryptosystems, a first set of algorithms has been selected for standardization. To enable further diversification

A. Boldyreva and V. Kolesnikov (Eds.): PKC 2023, LNCS 13941, pp. 94–124, 2023.
https://doi.org/10.1007/978-3-031-31371-4_4

of security assumptions, a fourth round of standardization has been launched, consisting of the three code-based schemes BIKE, HQC, and McEliece.

One building block for all round-four candidates is fixed-weight polynomial sampling. Additionally, this is also required in the three lattice-based schemes NTRU, which may replace Kyber if potential patent issues are not resolved, Streamlined NTRU Prime, which is currently the default algorithm in OpenSSH 9, and NTRU LPRrime. The output of this sampling is a uniform random binary or ternary polynomial of a specific size with a fixed number of non-zero coefficients. Multiple algorithmic approaches have been proposed [5,9,10,15,18] for this.

Karabulut et al. presented the first power side-channel attack on fixed weight sampling [14], targeting NTRU, Streamlined NTRU Prime, and Dilithium. Recently, Guo et al. [12] introduced an attack on HQC and BIKE utilizing the fixed weight polynomial sampling with variable timing depending on the seed. Sendrier [18] seized their approach and presented suitable countermeasures for BIKE. While this attack exploits timing differences, there is no reason to believe that a power side channel cannot be exploited analogously.

On the defense end, however, there is no comprehensive analysis of effective countermeasures against this type of attack. In particular, given these recent attacks, it becomes urgent to develop also power side-channel secure methodologies for fixed-weight polynomial sampling.

Hence, we present a holistic examination of the fixed-weight polynomial sampling problem with different attacker models, parameters, sampling methods, and implementation variants. We show how power side-channel secure variants of all suitable algorithms can be realized, propose performance-enhancing modifications, and provide bitsliced masked software implementations for arbitrary masking order which we make publicly available[1]. Additionally, we develop a new probabilistic sampling method accompanied by a hardware implementation and a new methodology for Boolean masked comparison which is a core component for multiple algorithms. We benchmark and evaluate our implementations for all relevant PQC schemes.

2   Preliminaries

The two most important parameters for the fixed-weight polynomial sampling problem are the length of the polynomial and the weight (number of non-zero coefficients) denoted by N and W throughout the paper.

Binomial Distribution. For the Binomial probability distribution, we denote the probability mass function as

$$\mathcal{B}(k, n, p) = \binom{n}{k} p^k (1 - p)^{n-k} \qquad (1)$$

where k is the number of successes in n independent Bernoulli trials, each with probability p. We know that $\mathcal{B}(k, n, p)^{-1}$ is the expected number of repetitions of the overall experiment until *exactly* k out of n successes are reached.

---

[1] https://github.com/Chair-for-Security-Engineering/maskedFWPS.

2.1 Side-Channel Analysis

In this work, we consider timing behavior and power consumption of a target implementation of a cryptographic algorithm as possible side channels that could be exploited by an attacker. For timing attacks, we consider runtime differences caused by memory or cache accesses, branching on sensitive data, or secret-dependent arithmetic operations.

For power side-channel attacks, we distinguish between single-trace and multi-trace attacks. In the single-trace scenario, the attacker has given only one single trace of the cryptographic operation, i.e., the attacker cannot invoke the system multiple times with the same secret key. However, we additionally assume that an attacker can mount template attacks. In this case, the attack profiles a target device to create a power template which is used to match a single trace to the correct key.

For multi-trace attacks, we assume that an attacker can collect as many traces as possible. These traces are used for Differential Power Analysis (DPA) including statistical analyses like Correlation Power Analysis (CPA).

2.2 Masking

Masking is a well-established countermeasure against physical Side-Channel Analysis (SCA) and is based on the strong theoretic foundation of secret sharing. A secret value x is split into $d + 1$ shares x_i with $0 \leq i \leq d$. To provide the desired security, $d - 1$ shares are chosen uniformly at random while the remaining share is determined such that $x = x_0 \circ x_1 \circ \cdots \circ x_d$ holds. The group operator $\circ$ is usually addition, either in $\mathbb{F}_2$ (Boolean masking) or a larger field (additive masking). The parameter d defines the security order based on the d-probing model [13], where an attacker is assumed to obtain the exact values of up to d intermediate values of the target design. Hence, if the adversary does not learn anything about the secret values using d probes, the implementation is assumed to be secure against d-order attacks.

Functions that can be applied share-wise such that $f(x) = f(x_0) \circ f(x_1) \circ \cdots \circ f(x_d)$ are easy and efficient to mask. One of these linear functions is for example a XOR in the Boolean masking domain. Non-linear functions, for example, an AND, cannot be applied share-wise and need to be expressed differently. The challenge in masking cryptographic implementations relies upon avoiding or efficiently implementing non-linear functions.

2.3 Bitslicing

An important method for efficient Boolean-masked software implementations is bitslicing. Bitslicing changes the representation of values. Instead of storing n values in n distinct n-bit registers (32-bit in our case), we aggregate the i-th bit of each value in one register. This corresponds to a matrix transposition. If the maximum bit-length of the values is below the register width, bitslicing allows a condensed representation and simultaneously fewer Boolean instructions. Bitslicing is especially useful for algorithms that operate on single bits at a time because it allows doing single-bit operations on n values simultaneously with one instruction, comparable to Single Instruction Multiple Data (SIMD) instructions. For masked implementations, bitslicing helps to reduce the number of costly non-linear operations.

2.4 Random Integer Sampling from Range

Sampling a uniform random integer from a given range is not always as simple as it seems. Both in software and hardware we can obtain uniform random bits from e.g., a Pseudorandom Number Generator (PRNG). By concatenating l random bits, we get a random value in the range of $[0, 2^l)$.

If we need a random value r in the range of $[0, x)$ (which we denote with $\mathsf{rand}(x)$ in the following), where x is not a power of two, we can sample r from $[0, 2^l)$, with the smallest l such that $x < 2^l$, and reject r if it is not smaller than x. The closer x is to 2^l, the fewer rejections occur, in the worst case, however, the chance for rejection is almost 50%.

Instead of rejecting values, one can alternatively use a function that maps the values from $[0, 2^l)$ to $[0, x)$. An obvious function for this is computing $r \bmod x$. Given l random bits stored in r and a bit width of t for the target range x one can alternatively compute an $(l + t)$-bit multiplication rx and take the upper t bits of the result, which again will be a value between 0 and $x - 1$.

The drawback of both of these mapping methods is that they introduce a bias. When x is not a power of two, 2^l will not divide x, therefore some values in the output range $[0, x)$ will be more likely than others. With increasing 2^l compared to x, the bias becomes neglectable and the output becomes close to uniform random.

If we want to sample an integer from a range $[i, x)$ that is not starting at 0, we can use the previous methods and compute $i + \mathsf{rand}(x - i)$.

2.5 Applications

Fixed weight polynomial sampling is a part of many PQC schemes, and many of them can potentially become (or already are) a standard determined by the National Institute of Standards and Technology (NIST).

BIKE. Bit Flipping Key Encapsulation (BIKE) has among three other KEMs advanced to the fourth round of NIST's standardization process and is a code-based scheme relying on Quasi-Cyclic Moderate-Density Parity-Check (QC-MDPC) codes. Polynomials live in the cyclic polynomial ring $\mathcal{R} := \mathbb{F}_2[X]/(X^r - 1)$, thus coefficients are either 0 or 1 and the number of coefficients is determined by the parameter r of the reduction polynomial. During key generation, two random fixed-weight polynomials are sampled: (h_0, h_1) with $|h_0| = |h_1| = W/2$. Moreover, during encapsulation and decapsulation, two fixed weight polynomials e_0, e_1 are sampled with $|e_0| + |e_1| = t$ where t is a publicly known and fixed parameter.

HQC. HQC also advanced to the fourth round of standardization. HQC also deploys fixed-weight sampling in key generation, encapsulation, and decapsulation. Analogously, polynomials in HQC have the polynomial ring $\mathcal{R} := \mathbb{F}_2[X]/(X^r - 1)$. Apart from parameters, the only difference then is that the polynomial e_0, e_1 are sampled separately rather than with a joint fixed weight.

McEliece. The third remaining fourth-round candidate also uses fixed-weight sampling, but only during encapsulation to sample the "message". McEliece is deemed to be the most conservative candidate during the whole standardization, being based on the more than 40 years old original McEliece cryptosystem.

NTRU. NTRU is a lattice-based Key Encapsulation Mechanism (KEM) and comes in two "flavors": HRSS and HPS. For both, four polynomial rings are deployed. Fixed-weight sampling is used only during key generation of the HPS parameter sets. Furthermore, NTRU-HPS imposes the special requirement of having *exactly* $W/2$ coefficients $+1$ and $W/2$ to be -1.

Streamlined NTRU Prime and NTRU LPRrime. Streamlined NTRU Prime is a lattice-based KEM and is, together with X25519, currently the default algorithm for OpenSSH 9. NTRU LPRrime is a merger with Streamlined NTRU Prime during the second round of NIST standardization. Both require fixed-weight sampling in their respective key generations, similar to NTRU with a ternary target space. However, no requirement is set on the number of $+1$ and -1.

Dilithium. Dilithium is the designated PQC digital signature standard. It is based on the Module-Learning With Errors problem and operates on polynomials in the ring $\mathbb{Z}_q[X]/(X^{256} + 1)$ with $q = 8\,380\,417$. Security is scaled through the matrix parameters. Being constructed with the help of the Fiat-Shamir with aborts technique, it simulates the verifier by querying a random oracle to sample a challenge during signature generation. This challenge has the specific form of a fixed-weight polynomial with ternary coefficients and no special restrictions on the number of coefficients with value -1. Based on several abort checks, a signature candidate may get rejected, starting over the whole signature generation including computing a new challenge c. Thus, it is not directly clear that c from rejected iterations is public information, even though the final c is part of the signature.

Previous work on the GLP signature scheme, which is a predecessor of Dilithium, has found that if the rejected challenges are viewed as public information together with their respective commitment, either one has to live with an additional heuristic security assumption or add a statistically hiding commitment scheme, tolerating the additional communication cost [3]. This is also stated regarding Dilithium in a recent preprint [1], where they state that rejected challenges are public and the commitment as well, but based on the Learning with Rounding assumption. To avoid this additional assumption, in our opinion it would be also feasible to perform the rounding masked, hashing w_1 in masked domain, obtaining a masked bit-string $\tilde{c}$, which is already a representation of the challenge. This can then be unmasked (since we know that also rejected challenges are non-sensitive) and used to perform fixed-weight sampling.

3   Conceptual Considerations

Although the fixed weight polynomial sampling problem at is core is simple, its application comes with multiple problem dimensions depending on the algorithmic scheme, and implementation target.

Attacker Model. Sampling can be used in different parts of a KEM. If it is part of the key generation that is only executed once for one key, only single-trace side-channel attacks are applicable. The profiled Simple Power Analysis (SPA) is assumed as the strongest attacker model in our case.

Since in encapsulation, no secret key is used at all, usually no multi-trace attacks are eligible. In the current setting and applications, fixed weight sampling is used once during encapsulation to sample the message or an error. For decapsulation, multi-trace attacks are possible if the KEM key is non-ephemeral.

Target Space. Some use cases require binary polynomials while others sample ternary polynomials. For the ternary polynomials, it then can vary how the weight must be split between the ones and the minus ones.

Target Representation. The classic representation for a polynomial is an array of length N with one element for each coefficient (coefficient representation). However, polynomials can also be expressed by a list of non-zero indices (index representation). The cryptographic scheme may require different representations and the sampling methods output different representations. It is possible to convert one representation into the other.

Determinism. If the sampling is used in the encapsulation and decapsulation, it is usually required to provide the same output when given the same input seed. This can be achieved for all algorithmic approaches by using a PRNG as the source of randomness that is initialized with the seed. Determinism is usually not required in the key generation.

Secret Seed. In some use cases, the input seed for the PRNG is a secret value, thus the sampling algorithm must be constant-time not only with respect to the sampled polynomial but also with respect to the input seed. Concrete attacks have been presented recently in [12,18].

Parameters N and W. The most important parameters that determine the performance of the sampling methods are the number of coefficients N and the number of non-zero coefficients W or the weight of the polynomial. In particular, N can vary distinctly from values between 256 to 81 194.

Target Platform. Implementing hardware or software influences the performance of an algorithm. Parallelism is important in either case, in software it can sometimes be achieved with bitslicing as introduced in Sect. 2.3, while in hardware, more fine-grained parallelism and trade-offs are possible.

3.1   Requirement Analysis

In Table 1 we give an overview of the most important parameters and requirements of each relevant scheme for the fixed-weight polynomial sampling.

The parameter sets of BIKE and HQC include relatively large N and small to medium W, and therefore a small W/N ratio which are all important factors for the sampling algorithms. Both schemes are also the only ones, that require

Table 1. Requirements for all potential applications

Scheme	Param.	Where?	N	W	W/N	Target Space	Det.	Sec. Seed
BIKE	L1	en/decaps	24646	134	0.005	binary	yes	yes
BIKE	L1	keygen	12323	71	0.006	binary	no	no
BIKE	L3	en/decaps	49318	199	0.004	binary	yes	yes
BIKE	L3	keygen	24659	103	0.004	binary	no	no
BIKE	L5	en/decaps	81194	264	0.003	binary	yes	yes
BIKE	L5	keygen	40973	137	0.003	binary	no	no
HQC	128	en/decaps	17669	75	0.004	binary	yes	yes
HQC	128	keygen	17669	66	0.004	binary	no	no
HQC	192	en/decaps	35851	114	0.003	binary	yes	yes
HQC	192	keygen	35851	100	0.003	binary	no	no
HQC	256	en/decaps	57637	149	0.003	binary	yes	yes
HQC	256	keygen	57637	131	0.003	binary	no	no
McEliece	348864	encaps	3488	64	0.018	binary	no	no
McEliece	460896	encaps	4608	96	0.021	binary	no	no
McEliece	6688128	encaps	6688	128	0.019	binary	no	no
McEliece	6960119	encaps	6960	119	0.017	binary	no	no
McEliece	8192128	encaps	8192	128	0.016	binary	no	no
NTRU	hps2048509	keygen	509	254	0.499	$W/2$ ternary	no	no
NTRU	hps2048677	keygen	677	254	0.375	$W/2$ ternary	no	no
NTRU	hps4096821	keygen	821	510	0.379	$W/2$ ternary	no	no
sNTRU Prime	653	keygen	653	288	0.441	uni. ternary	no	no
NTRU LPRrime	653	keygen	653	252	0.386	uni. ternary	no	no
sNTRU Prime	761	keygen	761	286	0.376	uni. ternary	no	no
NTRU LPRrime	761	keygen	761	250	0.329	uni. ternary	no	no
sNTRU Prime	857	keygen	857	322	0.376	uni. ternary	no	no
NTRU LPRrime	857	keygen	857	329	0.384	uni. ternary	no	no
sNTRU Prime	953	keygen	953	396	0.416	uni. ternary	no	no
NTRU LPRrime	953	keygen	953	345	0.362	uni. ternary	no	no
sNTRU Prime	1013	keygen	1013	448	0.442	uni. ternary	no	no
NTRU LPRrime	1013	keygen	1013	392	0.387	uni. ternary	no	no
sNTRU Prime	1277	keygen	1277	492	0.385	uni. ternary	no	no
NTRU LPRrime	1277	keygen	1277	429	0.336	uni. ternary	no	no

seed security and a deterministic sampling algorithm for their encapsulation and decapsulation. Their polynomials have coefficients that are either 0 or 1, this is also the case for McEliece. NTRU on the other hand has ternary coefficients that are either 0, 1 or -1 and the fixed number of nonzero coefficients W must be equally split between the 1s and -1s. For the ternary coefficients in Streamlined NTRU Prime and NTRU LPRrime, this relation is uniformly random. The schemes with ternary coefficients also have in common that the sampling is only used during the key generation, security against single-trace side-channel attacks is therefore sufficient.

4 Designing Masked Fixed Weight Sampling

In the following sections, we present multiple side-channel secure approaches for fixed-weight polynomial sampling. The different approaches can be categorized into three different groups. The rejection method in Sect. 4.4 and its bounded variant in Sect. 4.5 solve the problem by sampling W distinct values in the range $[0, N)$, which represent the indices of the non-zero coefficients. The methods based on Fisher-Yates in Sect. 4.2 and sorting in Sect. 4.3 utilize shuffling of fixed input polynomials. ANDing in Sect. 4.7 and our comparison method in Sect. 4.6 both sample fixed-weight polynomials by randomly setting bits.

For each approach, we start by explaining the fundamental idea, then we clarify how to achieve a timing side-channel secure (constant-time) variant that is a necessity for a power side-channel secure implementation. Based on this, we explain how to realize a masked and efficient variant. In Sect. 5, we provide more details about our implementations. We present the algorithms only for the binary use case, in most cases they can easily be adapted for the ternary use case. If this adoption is not obvious, we explain how it can be achieved. Some of the algorithms have a small bias, so their output is only close to uniform random. Before actually deploying a scheme with one of the biased methods one needs to diligently prove that the bias does not impair the security.

Masked Sampling by Coron et al. In recent work [9], Coron et al. present an approach of side-channel-secure fixed-weight sampling for NTRU, which proposes the following strategy:

1. Initialize an empty polynomial with the first $W/2$ coefficients set to -1, the subsequent $W/2$ coefficients to $+1$, and the remaining coefficients set to 0.
2. Generate a fresh arithmetic masking of this polynomial.
3. Shuffle each share with the same permutation.
4. Re-share the arithmetic sharing.
5. Repeat the last two steps a total of $d + 1$ times, every time using a new permutation.

This high-level procedure is proven to be secure in the d-probing model. For their proof, however, the applied permutation is assumed to be a black box. Thus, we believe that it will be very hard, if not impossible, to instantiate securely in practice. Moreover, Karabulut et *al.* show a single-trace attack that targets the permutation itself [14] and there is no reason to believe that an attacker is not able to attack multiple subsequent executions of different permutations successfully. Hence, it is reasonable to assume that this countermeasure does not protect against SPA attackers comprehensively.

4.1 Core Operations

The masked algorithmic approaches for fixed-weight polynomial sampling that we present in the following sections, share a small set of operations that are repeatedly used and contribute distinctly to the overall performance. In this section, we explain how to perform a masked conditional move and different integer comparisons in the Boolean domain with little non-linear operations.

Conditional Move in Boolean Domain. A very important building block for our masked algorithms is the conditional move. The semantic of $\mathsf{cmov}(d, s, c)$ is that d is overwritten by s, if the condition flag c is set and d remains unchanged if c is 0.

For non-masked, but constant-time implementations, a conditional move is most efficiently expressed in software with a dedicated instruction, but can generally be expressed with a short sequence of arithmetic or Boolean instructions to avoid branching on the secret condition c and thus leak c via timing differences. A straightforward sequence would be $d = (d \wedge \neg c) \vee (s \wedge c)$.

This solution is, however, costly to mask, because it includes three non-linear operations, two ANDs, and one OR. It is possible to reduce the number of non-linear operations to one by using XOR operations: $d = d \oplus ((d \oplus s) \wedge c)$ evaluates to $d = d \oplus d \oplus s = s$, if c is true and to $d = d \oplus 0 = d$, if c is false.

Integer Comparison in Boolean Domain. Let $a[l-1:0], b[l-1:0]$ be bit vector variables representing integers in the range $[0, 2^l)$. To check whether $a < b$, we can simply compute $a - b$ and then check whether the result is negative, in which case we know that $a < b$, and else, $a \geq b$. Thus, in Boolean domain, we can employ a Ripple-Carry subtractor which computes $r[l:0] = a[l-1:0] - b[l-1:0]$. Then, $r[l]$ is the uppermost carry-out bit, which decides whether or not the result is negative. The Ripple-Carry subtractor performs the following computations:

$$r[0] = a[0] \oplus b[0] \tag{2}$$

$$c[0] = \overline{a[0]} \wedge b[0] \tag{3}$$

$$r[i] = a[i] \oplus b[i] \oplus c[i-1] \quad \forall 1 \leq i < l \tag{4}$$

$$c[i] = (c[i-1] \wedge (\overline{a[i]} \oplus b[i])) \oplus (\overline{a[i]} \wedge b[i]) \quad \forall 1 \leq i < l \tag{5}$$

$$r[l] = c[l-1] \tag{6}$$

This is usually done in Central Processing Units (CPUs), where the subtraction instruction is also used for integer comparison, but without writing the result back to the registers. In the masked case, however, we aim to achieve a very low number of secure AND gates. Thus, as we only want to recover $r[l]$ rather than the full subtraction result, we propose an alternative approach.

$t = a \oplus b$ gives us the bits, where a and b differ. The highest set bit of t determines the bit or rather the index g in a and b that determines which of the two variables is greater. Because we know that a and b differ at this bit, it is enough to look at one of them. E.g. if b_g is set, b is greater than a. To perform this concept in constant-time we iterate over all bits, starting from the lowest bit, and update our output with b_i if t_i is set, which ultimately results in b_g in our output. With our output initialized with 0, it will result in 0 if $a \geq b$ and 1 if $a < b$. Algorithm 1 describes this idea formally.

At first sight, Algorithm 1 does not need any expensive AND gadgets, but for implementing the conditional move securely we require one AND, as explained in the previous subsection. Compared to the traditional approach via subtraction, we can half the amount of expensive non-linear gadgets. The overall asymptotic runtime is determined by the bit length of the inputs. In the algorithms presented in the following, we compare values bounded by N, so the cost for one comparison is $\lceil \log_2(N) \rceil$.

Algorithm 1. Optimized Integer Comparison in Boolean Domain

Require: $a = \sum_{i=0}^{l} a_i 2^l$, $b = \sum_{i=0}^{l} b_i 2^l$
Ensure: $res \leftarrow a < b \,?\, 1 : 0$
  function CMPL(res, a, b)
    $t \leftarrow a \oplus b$
    $res \leftarrow 0$
    for $i \leftarrow 0$ **to** l **do**
      cmov(res, b_i, t_i) $\triangleright\ res := res \oplus ((res \oplus b_i) \wedge t_i)$
    end for
  end function

Comparison with Fixed Public Input. We can simplify this further when we have one fixed and public input b rather than two variable ones. Then, to compare whether or not $a < b$, we first employ the same procedure as in Algorithm 1. However, for each t_i, we now know publicly that it is either

- a_i in the case that $b_i = 0$, or
- $\neg a_i$ in the case that $b_i = 1$.

    Thus, we have

- for $b_i = 0$, $res := res \oplus ((res \oplus 0) \wedge a_i) = res \wedge \neg a_i$, and
- for $b_i = 1$, $res := res \oplus ((res \oplus 1) \wedge \neg a_i) = res \vee \neg a_i$.

This does not save non-linear gates, as we still need one per bit, but it saves several XOR operations, which are cheap, but not free. Moreover, we can completely omit all lower bits until the first $b_i = 1$, since we start with $res = 0$, which sets all subsequent intermediate res to zero.

Comparison on Equality. Evaluating whether two masked values are equal or not is even cheaper to realize in the Boolean domain. $c = a \oplus b$ is only zero if a is equal to b. Thus we can iterate over all bits in c and condense them to one bit with masked OR operations. After flipping the resulting bit, res will be one, if c is zero and thus a is equal to b and zero otherwise, denoted with cmpeq(res, a, b) in the following. The asymptotic runtime cost is again $\mathcal{O}(\log_2(N))$.

4.2 Fisher-Yates

The Fisher-Yates shuffle is an algorithm to get a uniform random permutation of a fixed input sequence in $\mathcal{O}(N)$ time. Similar to the sorting approach explained in Sect. 4.3 it can be directly applied to a fixed polynomial with the correct weight to get a random polynomial with the correct weight.

Alternatively, one can apply Fisher-Yates to an array with length N with distinct integers from 0 to N and treat the first W elements of the output as the indices respectively the coefficients of the polynomials which are non-zero. In this case, the permutation of the elements beyond the first W elements is irrelevant and the algorithm can be stopped after W iterations because the first W elements are not affected by further shuffling.

In its original version, Fisher-Yates is not timing side-channel-secure, because its memory accesses reveal the permutation and (only relevant for a secret seed) it requires uniform random numbers from a varying range, which requires a rejection step.

Sendrier [18] tackled these problems with two modifications. First of all, he showed for BIKE that the security of the cryptographic scheme is not necessarily impaired when the sampling is only close to uniform random if the parameters are correctly chosen. This eliminates the need for the rejection step by allowing a slightly biased constant-time approach as explained in Sect. 2.4. The secret dependent memory accesses can also be circumvented, but this comes with quadratic runtime instead of the original linear runtime. The solution for the index sampling method is depicted in Algorithm 2.

Algorithm 2. Constant-Time Fisher-Yates [18]

Require: N, W
Ensure: W distinct elements of $0, ..., N - 1$
  function FISHER-YATES(N, W)
    for $i \leftarrow 0$ **to** $W - 1$ **do**
      $p[i] \leftarrow i + $ rand($N - i$)
    end for
    for $i \leftarrow W - 1$ **to** 0 **do**
      for $j \leftarrow i + 1$ **to** $W - 1$ **do**
        cmpeq($cond, p[j], p[i]$)
        cmov($p[j], i, cond$)
      end for
    end for
  end function

For masking the constant-time Fisher-Yates algorithm two components need to be protected. The first component is sampling a random integer in the range of $[0, N - i)$. Sendrier [18] proposed to compute a random value $r \mod N - i$, but the implied division is a costly operation. Furthermore, in most CPUs, a division is an instruction with a variable cycle count depending on the input and thus not constant time. A modulo reduction with a constant modulo might be translated by a compiler to a constant-time Barrett reduction, but there is no guarantee for this.

We propose to use the faster multiplication approach as explained in Sect. 2.4 instead. Multiplication instructions are constant-time for most CPUs. In the additive masking domain, the multiplication with the public range value and the addition of the public index i can be efficiently performed sharewise.

The second component is the comparison of equality and the following conditional move, both can the done in Boolean domain, therefore a transformation from arithmetic to Boolean domain between the two components is necessary. The inner loop in Algorithm 2 containing the comparison and conditional move can be computed in parallel for multiple j, because the iterations are independent of each other.

A masked implementation of this Fisher-Yates algorithm results in an asymptotic runtime of $\mathcal{O}(W^2 \log_2(N))$, for sampling a close-to-uniform polynomial in the index representation without leaking a secret seed.

4.3 Sorting

An alternative approach to obtain a uniformly random permutation of a set is to attach distinct random values to each element and sort the pairs according to the random value. Bernstein [5] suggested applying this principle to sampling fixed-weight polynomials by starting with a polynomial with the desired weight and then getting a random permutation by sorting.

Algorithm 3. Sort based Sampling [5]

Require: $N, W, l, p[N]$
Ensure: random bitpolynomial in $p[N]$ with weight W
   function SORTSAMPLING(N, W)
      for $i \leftarrow 0$ **to** $N - 1$ **do**
         if $i < W$ **then**
            $t \leftarrow 1$
         else
            $t \leftarrow 0$
         end if
         $r \leftarrow \mathsf{rand}(2^l)$
         $p[i] \leftarrow (r << 1) + t$
      end for
      $\mathsf{sort}(p)$
      for $i \leftarrow 0$ **to** $N - 1$ **do**
         $p[i] \leftarrow p[i] \wedge 1$
      end for
   end function

To get *distinct* random values one can use rejection sampling, e.g., for each new randomly sampled value one checks if it collides with one of the values sampled before. If yes, the new value gets rejected and one continues until enough distinct values are sampled. Bernstein showed that the rejection step can be skipped if the size of the random value is big enough compared to the number of elements such that the chance of a collision becomes neglectable. With a constant-time sorting algorithm, the entire procedure is constant-time with respect to the sampled polynomial and the seed for the PRNG. The runtime depends on the implementation of the sorting algorithm and the polynomial size N as a parameter. This approach can be directly applied to sampling binary and ternary polynomials.

Sorting algorithms can have at lowest linear asymptotic runtime, but then usually no efficient constant-time implementation exists. A group of sorting algorithms that can be very efficiently implemented in constant-time is sorting networks, they consist only of a fixed number of comparisons and swaps. Comparison-based sorting algorithms have at best an asymptotic runtime of $\mathcal{O}(N \log(N))$. A naive masked implementation of a sorting network mainly consists of a comparison and a conditional move depending on the comparison, both can be masked efficiently in software and in hardware.

The sorting approach is deployed in NTRU and Streamlined NTRU Prime [6] with an implementation based on Batcher's Odd-Even mergesort [4]. For our implementation, we opted for Batchers's Bitonic mergesort [4], because it is easier to parallelize in the bitsliced domain, which is critical for our efficient masked software implementation. Both sorting algorithms have an asymptotic runtime of $\mathcal{O}(N \log^2(N))$. Although we use our improved comparison approach explained in Sect. 4.1 instead of a costly subtraction, the masked comparison and the conditional move are still the overwhelming driver in cycle costs.

A major drawback of this sampling method besides its high runtime costs for large polynomial size N is the high amount of randomness required upfront resulting also in high memory usage, compared to other methods. This can be circumvented by using radixsort. Radixsort utilizes an arbitrary, stable sorting algorithm to sort numbers e.g., bit by bit, starting from the lowest bit. The stableness of the sorting algorithm ensures that the order according to the lower bits is maintained when sorting according to the higher bits[2]. As radixsort only works on one bit per sorting iteration, only one random bit per element needs to be sampled and stored at a time because we are not interested in the sorted random values, but only in the permutation the sorting provides. Stable sorting networks exist, but they have a quadratic asymptotic runtime, which makes this approach more costly. Radixsort combined with an unstable sorting network does not result in correct sorting universally and coherently also not in uniform random permutations, which we confirmed for small parameters by exhaustive testing.

---

[2] Stable sorting in ascending manner according to the MSB of $(10, 11, 01)$ results in $(01, 10, 11)$ and not $(01, 11, 10)$.

4.4   Rejection Sampling

Probably the most obvious solution for fixed-weight polynomial sampling is the rejection method. One samples a uniform random value r below N by rejecting values from the range $[0, 2^l)$, with the smallest l such that $x < 2^l$. Then one iterates over the already sampled indices and checks for a collision, if a collision is found, r gets rejected. The rejection sampling continues until W distinct indices are sampled as presented in Algorithm 4.

The runtime of this probabilistic algorithm varies and depends on the randomness, therefore it is not suitable for cryptographic schemes, where the seed for the PRNG is secret. This restriction in application allows early termination of loops, as soon as the rejection becomes evident. Although the result of the comparisons for equality for the collision check is public, we cannot XOR both arguments and then simply unmask the result and check if it is zero or not. In this case, we would leak the bits in which r differs from $p[c]$. So the comparisons themselves must be side-channel secure to protect the non-rejected values. This can be done with the core operations presented in Sect. 4.1.

Algorithm 4. Rejection Sampling - Index

Require: $N, W, 2^l > N, p[W]$
Ensure: W distinct elements of $0, ..., N - 1$
  function REJECTION-INDEX(N, W)
    $i \leftarrow 0$
    while $i < W$ **do**
      $r \leftarrow \mathsf{rand}(2^l)$
      $\mathsf{cmpl}(t, r, N)$
      if $\neg t$ **then**
        continue
      end if
      $collision \leftarrow 0$
      for $c \leftarrow 0$ **to** $i - 1$ **do**
        $\mathsf{cmpeq}(t, p[c], r)$
        if t **then**
          $collision \leftarrow 1$ **break**
        end if
      end for
      if $collision = 1$ **then**
        continue
      end if
      $p[i] \leftarrow r$
      $i \leftarrow i + 1$
    end while
  end function

For this algorithm, N determines the probability for the first rejection step, with an N only slightly greater than the closest power of two this probability can be close to 50%. W/N determines the probability of the second rejection when checking for collisions. With a W/N close to 0.5, the chance for a collision for a single value gets close to 50% for the last iterations when i reaches W, so on average the probability for rejection due to a collision for a single value can be up to 25%. Drucker et al. [10] already pointed out that the fixed weight polynomial sampling problem is symmetric such that for $W/N > 0.5$, one can solve it for $(N - W)/N$ and invert the result.

4.5 Bounded Rejection Sampling

The idea of a bounded rejection sampling algorithm as presented by Drucker et al. [15] for the BIKE use case, is to transform the rejection sampling method as presented in Sect. 4.4 such that it is constant-time also with respect to the PRNG seed. This idea has also been implemented similarly by Guo et al. [12] for HQC.

For this, the rejections must not influence the path taken in the algorithm and therefore branches in a software implementation and the memory access pattern must be independent of the randomness. This is done by keeping track of the number of valid samples with a secret counter that indicates where to input the next valid index into the array and does not get incremented if a sample gets rejected so that the next sample can overwrite the rejected one. Early termination of loops is not possible anymore, so with every sampled value one has to iterate over the entire array of indices and securely check for a collision. These comparisons can however be performed in parallel. Also, the comparison of the current index with the counter and the conditional move can be parallelized, as the comparison only outputs 1 for a single index for one complete iteration

---

Algorithm 5. Bounded Rejection Sampling - Index [15]

Require: $N, W, B, 2^l > N, p[W]$
Ensure: W distinct elements of $0, ..., N - 1$
  function BOUND-REJECTION-INDEX(N, W, B)
    $cntr \leftarrow 0$
    for $i \leftarrow 0$ **to** $B - 1$ **do**
      $r \leftarrow \mathsf{rand}(2^l)$
      $dup \leftarrow 0$
      for $c \leftarrow 0$ **to** $W - 1$ **do**
        $\mathsf{cmpeq}(t, p[c], r)$
        $dup \leftarrow dup \vee t$
        $\mathsf{cmpeq}(f, c, cntr)$
        $\mathsf{cmov}(p[c], r, f)$
      end for
      $\mathsf{cmpl}(t, r, N)$
      $t \leftarrow !dup \wedge t$
      $cntr \leftarrow cntr + t$
    end for
  end function

---

over the array. Thus the counter can be conditionally incremented only once after iterating over the array and remains constant during the loop.

The second challenge for any seed-independent timing is the number of random values that need to be sampled which can not be determined exactly upfront, but they can be estimated. Depending on the parameters N and W one can compute a loose upper bound B of iterations or rather samples, within with overwhelming probability at least W valid indices are found.

The majority of the algorithm can be masked with Boolean components that we already discussed in previous algorithms. The incrementation of the secret counter is most efficient in the additive masking domain, however, the counter is also required in the Boolean domain for the comparison. To avoid the costly transformations between the domains, we propose performing the addition with a single bit in the Boolean domain with half-adders implying $\lceil \log_2(N) \rceil$ masked ANDs.

Algorithm 5 demonstrates this approach, since B is a multiple of W the runtime is $\mathcal{O}(W^2 \log_2(N))$. The asymptotic view indicates a similar performance to the Fisher-Yates algorithm, but a closer inspection reveals that first, bounded rejection takes more than W^2 iterations compared to $\frac{1}{2}W^2$ for Fisher-Yates and the rejection method requires two masked comparisons for each iteration compared to one comparison for Fisher-Yates. When the sampling $\mathsf{rand}(N - i)$ of W values in Fisher-Yates does not contribute significant costs, the bounded rejection is probably less performant when masked.

Algorithm 6. Bounded Rejection Sampling - Coefficient

Require: N, W, B, $2^l > N$, $p[N]$ initialized with zeros
Ensure: W random coefficients in p are set to 1
    function BOUND-REJECTION-COEFF(N, W, B)
        $cntr \leftarrow 0$
        for $i \leftarrow 0$ **to** $B - 1$ **do**
            $t \leftarrow 0$
            $r \leftarrow \mathsf{rand}(2^l)$
            $\mathsf{cmpeq}(f0, cntr, W)$
            for $c \leftarrow 0$ **to** $N - 1$ **do**
                $\mathsf{cmpeq}(f1, c, r)$
                $\mathsf{cmpeq}(f2, p[c], 0)$
                $f \leftarrow \neg f0 \wedge f1 \wedge f2$
                $\mathsf{cmov}(p[c], 1, f)$
                $t \leftarrow t \vee f$
            end for
            $cntr \leftarrow cntr + t$
        end for
    end function

Alternatively, the sampling of values less than N can be realized with the biased multiplication method as we use it for Fisher-Yates. For some parameter sets of HQC, this might be faster, because N is close to the next lower power of two, thus the chance of rejection when $r \geq N$ is high and the upper bound B is higher. In this case, however, the runtime comparison to Fisher-Yates is even more clear and indicates that Fisher-Yates is the faster solution.

In Algorithm 6 we show how the bounded rejection method can be adapted to output polynomials in the coefficient representation instead of the index representation with asymptotic runtime $\mathcal{O}(WN \log_2 N)$.

The bounded rejection sampling is only relevant for cryptographic schemes, where the PRNG input needs to be protected as the protection comes with a performance overhead compared to the simple rejection method.

4.6   Comparison Sampling

The idea of this novel approach is to sample each coefficient of the polynomial individually with an approximation of the probability W/N. This can be implemented efficiently by comparing a uniform random bit string of length ℓ with a fixed threshold t such that $t/2^\ell \approx W/N$. If t is smaller than the random ℓ-bit value, the coefficient is set to 1.

After performing this for each coefficient, a masked weight check of the polynomial is carried out and the polynomial is accepted only if the correct weight W is hit. Else, the whole procedure is repeated, which renders this approach infeasible for use cases that require runtime independent of the input seed. This method can be considered somewhat of a generalization of the RepeatedAND method by Drucker and Gueron that we cover in Sect. 4.7.

Table 2. BIKE Comparison sampling, for number of expected repetitions and expected random bits, see Eqs. 7 and 8

ℓ	BIKE-L1			BIKE-L3			BIKE-L5		
	t	rep.	rnd.	t	rep.	rnd.	t	rep.	rnd.
8	1	2439.74	240 518 881	1	31.88	6 289 754	1	169.06	55 415 054
9	3	21.30	2 362 385	2	31.88	7 075 973	2	169.06	62 341 935
10	6	21.30	2 624 872	4	31.88	7 862 192	3	92.48	37 892 643
11	12	21.30	2 887 359	9	29.10	7 892 628	7	30.30	13 658 519
12	24	21.30	3 149 847	17	25.46	7 533 925	14	30.30	14 900 203
13	47	21.10	3 379 948	34	25.46	8 161 752	27	29.73	15 833 552
14	94	21.10	3 639 944	68	25.46	8 789 579	55	29.34	16 829 906

For efficiency, the choice of ℓ, t is decisive and the expected number of repetitions of the overall procedure is determined by

$$\mathcal{B}(W, N, t/2^\ell)^{-1} \qquad (7)$$

Therefore, these parameters must be chosen carefully for each potential use case.

Let $p = W/N$ be the target probability. Then, for ℓ random bits, the best comparison threshold t is $\lfloor p2^\ell \rceil$. Intuitively, the larger we choose ℓ, the better we approximate p at cost of more randomness and more secure operations. Interestingly, for all applications, there exists a threshold for ℓ, from which increasing does not improve the success probability significantly.

Apart from minimizing the number of non-linear operations, we also want to minimize the number of fresh random bits that are required. For a given (N, W, ℓ, t), we know that

$$\mathcal{B}(W, N, t/2^\ell)^{-1} \cdot N\ell \tag{8}$$

is the expected number of fresh random bits for this method, which will help us choose ℓ, t for each use case. On the lower layer, we can employ our efficient comparison from Algorithm 1 and the optimizations for comparison with one fixed operand, resulting in $\ell - 1$ non-linear operations per coefficient and $\mathcal{B}(W, N, t/2^\ell)^{-1} \cdot N(\ell - 1)$ expected non-linear operations overall for a given (N, W, ℓ, t).

Note that these numbers refer to the *unprotected* instantiation. When masking this approach, we require $d + 1$ times as much randomness and in addition, fresh randomness for each non-linear operation.

In the following, we give details on each potential application.

BIKE and HQC Key Generation. For BIKE and HQC, we cannot deploy this method for encapsulation and decapsulation, due to the attack by [12,18]. Still, it is eligible for key generation in both cases. Table 2 and Table 3 give details on the choice of ℓ, t for both algorithms. As can be seen there, for BIKE-L1 $\ell = 9, t = 3$ is the obvious choice, as well as $\ell = 8, t = 1$ for BIKE-L3 and $\ell = 11, t = 7$ for BIKE-L5.

For HQC, $\ell = 8, t = 1$ is the best choice for HQC-128, $\ell = 10, t = 3$ for HQC-196, and $\ell = 12, t = 9$ for HQC-256. Moreover, the randomness numbers indicate that BIKE performs better with this approach.

Table 3. HQC Comparison Sampling, for number of expected repetitions and expected random bits, see Eqs. 7 and 8

ℓ	HQC-128			HQC-196			HQC-256		
	t	rep.	rnd.	t	rep.	rnd.	t	rep.	rnd.
8	1	21.77	3 076 984	1	1.5e4	4 270 634 825	1	3.7e11	1.7e17
9	2	21.77	3 461 607	1	7272.20	2 346 440 182	1	120.43	62 473 484
10	4	21.77	3 846 230	3	28.33	10 155 736	2	120.43	69 414 983
11	8	21.77	4 230 853	6	28.33	11 171 310	5	40.46	25 649 983
12	15	20.62	4 371 146	11	26.90	11 572 734	9	30.89	21 361 556
13	31	20.47	4 700 992	23	25.11	11 700 990	19	29.46	22 076 057
14	61	20.36	5 036 069	46	25.11	12 601 066	37	28.75	23 201 162

Table 4. McEliece Comparison Sampling, for number of expected repetitions and expected random bits, see Eqs. 7 and 8

ℓ	Parameter Set														
	348864			460896			6688128			6960119			8192128		
	t	rep.	rnd.	t	rep.	rnd.	t	rep.	rnd.	t	rep.	rnd.	t	rep.	rnd.
6	1	44.13	923655	1	965.40	26691249	1	344.42	13820908	1	43.68	1823905	1	28.16	1383882
7	2	44.13	1077597	3	49.42	1593954	2	344.42	16124392	2	43.68	2127889	2	28.16	1614530
8	5	22.66	632174	5	29.70	1094851	5	28.88	1544999	4	43.68	2431873	4	28.16	1845177
9	9	21.11	662545	11	25.49	1057213	10	28.88	1738124	9	28.43	1780973	8	28.16	2075824
10	19	19.98	696744	21	24.62	1134475	20	28.88	1931249	18	28.43	1978859	16	28.16	2306471

Table 5. NTRU HPS Comparison Sampling, for number of expected repetitions and expected random bits, see Eqs. 7 and 8. Note that these are the numbers for generating a masked *binary* polynomial. In Sect. 4.6 we explain the transformation into a ternary.

ℓ	Parameter Set								
	2048509			2048677			4096821		
	t	rep.	rnd.	t	rep.	rnd.	t	rep.	rnd.
1	1	28.32	14414	1	5.73e+10	3.878e+13	1	1.32e+12	1.086e+15
2	2	28.32	28827	2	5.73e+10	7.757e+13	2	1.32e+12	2.172e+15
3	4	28.32	43241	3	31.59	64164	5	35.75	88043
4	8	28.32	57655	6	31.59	85551	10	35.75	117391
5	16	28.32	72069	12	31.59	106939	20	35.75	146739
6	32	28.32	86482	24	31.59	128327	40	35.75	176087
7	64	28.32	100896	48	31.59	149715	80	35.75	205435
8	128	28.32	115310	96	31.59	171103	159	34.85	228911

Table 6. Streamlined NTRU Prime Comparison Sampling, for number of expected repetitions and expected random bits, see Eqs. 7 and 8

ℓ	Parameter Set											
	653		761		857		953		1013		1277	
	t	rnd.	t	rnd.	t	rnd.	t	rnd.	t	rnd.	t	rnd.
1	1	1966846	1	5.1e+14	1	1.3e+16	1	3.1e+10	1	3.5e+07	1	3.0e+19
2	2	3933692	2	1.0e+15	2	2.5e+16	2	6.3e+10	2	7.0e+07	2	6.0e+19
3	4	5900538	3	76571	3	91488	3	2945795	4	1.1e+08	3	222512
4	7	84497	6	102095	6	121985	7	371651	7	168223	6	296683
5	14	105621	12	127618	12	152481	13	215382	14	210278	12	370853
6	28	126745	24	153142	24	182977	27	235987	28	252334	25	360750
7	56	147869	48	178666	48	213473	53	255543	57	286495	49	396206

BIKE-L1 Optimization. We have $\ell = 9, t = 3$ and thus want to have $a = 2^9 - 4$ in Algorithm 1 to obtain a 1 output bit in $3/2^9$ cases for a random input b. Then, we apply the above-described optimizations for a fixed input comparison:

Table 7. NTRU LPRrime Comparison Sampling, for number of expected repetitions and expected random bits, see Eqs. 7 and 8

ℓ	Parameter Set											
	653		761		857		953		1013		1277	
	t	rnd.	t	rnd.	t	rnd.	t	rnd.	t	rnd.	t	rnd.
1	1	5.7e+11	1	1.7e+24	1	4.1e+14	1	3.3e+20	1	8.6e+15	1	1.4e+35
2	2	1.1e+12	1	6.4e+09	2	8.2e+14	1	4.1e+17	2	1.7e+16	1	1.8e+15
3	3	72090	3	2643045	3	106026	3	150085	3	160778	3	11021700
4	6	96120	5	155129	6	141368	6	200113	6	214370	5	1083789
5	12	120150	11	183384	12	176711	12	250142	12	267963	11	321266
6	25	126010	21	148387	25	199178	23	215790	25	243060	22	385519
7	49	144495	42	173118	49	214613	46	251755	50	283570	43	378276
8	99	163109	84	197849	98	245272	93	284544	99	315026	86	432315

$$r = ((0 \vee b_0) \vee b_1) \wedge b_2 \wedge b_3 \wedge b_4 \wedge b_5 \wedge b_6 \wedge b_7 \wedge b_8$$

$$= (b_0 \vee b_1) \wedge \bigwedge_{i=2}^{8} b_i = \neg(\neg b_0 \wedge \neg b_1) \wedge \bigwedge_{i=2}^{8} b_i$$

Note that we convert the logical OR into a logical AND by De Morgan's law since this is how it is implemented with masked gadgets. Inversion is $\mathcal{O}(1)$, while SecAnd is $\mathcal{O}(d^2)$, so this does not increase asymptotic complexity. Still, we can save two inversions, since b_0, b_1 are random input bits, which we can assume to be inverted already. It follows that for BIKE-L1, the following Boolean formula can be used to obtain a random bit with approximately the correct probability of being one, using random input bits $b_0, \ldots, b_8$.

$$r = \neg(b_0 \wedge b_1) \wedge \bigwedge_{i=2}^{8} b_i \tag{9}$$

BIKE-L3 and HQC-128 Optimization. With $\ell = 8, t = 1$, we fall back to the repeated AND method and can just compute $r = \bigwedge_{i=0}^{7} b_i$ for uniform random bits $b_0, \ldots, b_7$. Notably, we can use this approach both for BIKE-L3 and HQC-128.

BIKE-L5 Optimization. With $\ell = 11, t = 7$, we have $a = 2^{11} - 8$ in Algorithm 1 with random bits $b_0, \ldots, b_{10}$. Then, applying the analog optimizations as above, including not inverting random input bits:

$$r = \left(\bigvee_{i=0}^{2} b_i \right) \wedge \bigwedge_{i=3}^{10} b_i = \neg \left(\bigwedge_{i=0}^{2} \neg b_i \right) \wedge \bigwedge_{i=3}^{10} b_i$$

$$\sim \neg \left(\bigwedge_{i=0}^{2} b_i \right) \wedge \bigwedge_{i=3}^{10} b_i \tag{10}$$

HQC-196 Optimization. Using $\ell = 10, t = 3$, we set $a = 2^{10} - 4$ in Algorithm 1 with random bits $b_0, \ldots, b_9$. Applying the aforementioned optimizations, we obtain

$$r = (b_0 \lor b_1) \land \bigwedge_{i=2}^{9} b_i = \neg(\neg b_0 \land \neg b_1) \land \bigwedge_{i=2}^{9}$$

$$\sim \neg(b_0 \land b_1) \land \bigwedge_{i=2}^{9} b_i \tag{11}$$

HQC-256 Optimization. $\ell = 12, t = 9$ implies setting $a = 2^{12} - 10$ in Algorithm 1 with random bits $b_0, \ldots, b_{11}$.

$$r = \left(\left(\bigwedge_{i=0}^{2} b_i \right) \lor b_3 \right) \land \bigwedge_{i=4}^{11} b_i = \neg \left(\neg \left(\bigwedge_{i=0}^{2} b_i \right) \land \neg b_3 \right) \land \bigwedge_{i=4}^{11} b_i$$

$$\sim \neg \left(\neg \left(\bigwedge_{i=0}^{2} b_i \right) \land b_3 \right) \land \bigwedge_{i=4}^{11} b_i \tag{12}$$

McEliece Encapsulation. For this application, we have no special restrictions, which renders the Comparison approach possible. As can be seen from Table 4, there are feasible choices of ℓ, t for each parameter set. Notably, the highest parameter set has both N and W set to a power of two, which implies that the Comparison method falls back effectively to the RepeatedAND method.

NTRU, Streamlined NTRU Prime, and NTRU LPRrime Key Generation. For NTRU, Streamlined NTRU Prime and NTRU LPRrime, we have an interesting different case, since the target space is not binary, but ternary. Additionally, NTRU imposes the condition that *exactly* $W/2$ coefficients need to be $+1$ and the remaining -1. To convert a binary polynomial to a ternary one, we employ the following strategy, assuming that we already have sampled a Boolean masked, weight-W polynomial:

1. Sample a uniform random, masked bit r_i for each coefficient a_i with $0 \leq i < N$.
2. Compute securely the masked sign $s_i := r_i \land a_i$ for each masked coefficient.
3. If there is a weight restriction on the number of -1 and $+1$, accumulate all s_i securely, unmask the result and check whether the correct number of -1 is hit. If not so, start over from Step 1.

Note that for NTRU, the initially sampled binary weight-W polynomial is not rejected, but only the vector of signs. This adds $\mathcal{B}(127, 254, 0.5)^{-1} \approx 20$ expected repetitions of the above procedure for NTRU-HPS2048{509, 677}, and for NTRU-HPS4096821 $\mathcal{B}(255, 510, 0.5)^{-1} \approx 28.3$.

The numbers for sampling binary polynomials with correct weight are presented in Table 5, Table 6, and Table 7. It stands out that compared to the code-based schemes, a notably lower amount of randomness is required. This is due to the smaller polynomial degrees and the more favorable ratio between W and N. However, the very low numbers for NTRU are misleading, since they do not include the additional randomness required for sampling the correct sign weight.

4.7 RepeatedAND

In [10], Drucker and Gueron propose ANDing random bit strings repeatedly with subsequent dedicated correction of the weight as a method for sampling fixed weight vectors. Starting with a zero bit string A of length N, they compute a random bit string $\overline{A}$ of the same length by repeatedly ANDing random strings so that the expected weight of the string is halved with each AND, until the weight is below or equal to the target weight W. Then, A is set to $A \vee \overline{A}$, so that the new weight of A is less or equal the sum off the individual weights of A and $\overline{A}$. As long as the weight of A is not W, a new $\overline{A}$ is computed with a target weight of the difference between the weight of A and W and ORed with A to increase its weight towards W.

Just like the simple rejection and our comparison sampling, this method is not secure for the decapsulation in HQC and BIKE.

At first sight, this method can be masked in a straight-forward manner, by checking the weight of secret intermediate vectors being the only non-trivial component. However, it makes heavy use of computing the (secret) weight of intermediate vectors, which is cheap in unmasked domain, but a big cost factor for masking. Experimentally, we found that for BIKE, HQC and McEliece, the average number of required weight checks significantly exceeds the average for our Comparison method presented in Sect. 4.6, with the smallest difference being McEliece-348864 (31.02 vs. 22.66), and the biggest difference being BIKE-L5 (60.38 vs. 30.30). In software, this masked weight check would predominantly determine the performance, rendering RepeatedAND obsolete for BIKE, HQC and McEliece. In hardware, however, the weight check could be performed in parallel with the ANDing. For NTRU, Streamlined NTRU Prime and NTRU LPRrime the average number of comparisons are very similar, the RepeatedAND method, however, requires less randomness.

4.8 Conversions Between Polynomial Representations

Some implementations of the cryptographic schemes use the index representation for fast multiplications that follow the sampling process, but one can also transform this representation to the coefficient representation in a constant-time and masked way. For each of the W non-zero indices one iterates over all coefficients N that are initialized with 0, and if the current indices are hit one replaces the 0 with a 1. We therefore need NW iterations with a cmpeq and a cmov. A conversion in the other direction from coefficient to index representation can be done similarly with comparable costs.

5 Masked Implementation

5.1 Software

We implemented all methods presented in Sect. 4 in software generalized for arbitrary masking order and thus secure against multi-trace power side-channel attacks. Except for the comparison method, our implementations are parametrized for N and W. We based our software implementations on masked gadgets presented in [7]. These gadgets can be proven to be secure under the assumptions provided by the d-probing model. Additionally, they fulfill certain composability notions ensuring that a design constructed by these gadgets is still secure in the d-probing model.

For Boolean masked software implementations, bitslicing is often a very efficient methodology to improve performance. All of our implementations are bitsliced as far as the algorithms allow, we also bitsliced all core operations presented in Sect. 4.1.

Fisher-Yates. The first component of the Fisher-Yates algorithm is to sample a random value with a varying range $[0, N - i)$. We implemented this in the additive masking domain with the biased multiplication method. To be compatible with unmasked implementations we take 32-bit Boolean masked randomness (for example from a masked Keccak) as input and transform it bitsliced to the 48-bit additive domain (modulo 2^{48}). We unbitslice the randomness and perform the multiplication with the public value $N - i$ by a simple sharewise unmasked multiplication. The result is at most 48-bit wide, therefore the additive domain modulo 2^{48} and not e.g. 2^{64} which saves us some costly non-linear operations in the Boolean to arithmetic and arithmetic to Boolean conversions.

Taking the upper 16 bit from the results can be done in the Boolean domain, which we need anyway for the second component of the algorithm. But before transforming to the Boolean domain, we add i to the upper 16 bit, which is cheaper in the additive domain. The additive to Boolean transformation is again implemented bitsliced and we keep the data in the bitsliced domain for the comparisons and conditional moves of the second component. With W padded to the next multiple of 32, we can perform the inner loop with the comparison and condition move on 32 values at a time.

Sorting. To evaluate the sorting approach presented in Sect. 4.3 we implemented a masked bitonic sort in software. Bitonic sort for n elements performs $n/2$ comparisons operating on all n elements in each iteration and each pair of elements that are compared has the same distance during one iteration. For the cases where the distance is greater than our register width of 32, we thus can directly compare and conditionally swap a group of 32 consecutive values with their respective pairs in the bitsliced domain where 32 values share a register for each bit.

Comparisons of elements with a distance of less than 32 are also possible in the bitsliced domain but require a transformation. When the distance is halved from one iteration to the next as is the case for most iterations, we need to swap half of the bits of one group of 32 elements in one register with the respective other half of paired group. In the non-bitsliced domain, this would correspond to simple register swaps, in the bitsliced domain we need to swap bits by using rotations and Boolean operators. By implementing this transformation in the bitsliced domain, we are able to perform the entire sorting algorithm in the bitsliced domain and save transformations between the domains.

For distances below 32, our method works on 64 consecutive elements at a time, we therefore pad the polynomial width to the next multiple of 64 for a clear and efficient implementation. The additional coefficients appended by the padding get initialized with zero and not paired with random values, but with the highest value possible so that the nonzero lower coefficients will not be sorted to the additional indices and they can simply be cut off after sorting. Bitonic sort originally only works on power-of-two input sizes, but can be adapted to arbitrary sizes, as we did for our implementation.

Rejection. To be able to parallelize the comparison of r versus N we perform the outer loop on batches of 32 values. We then iterate over the batch, if the result of the comparison indicates that a value r is not less than N we directly continue with the next value. If not, we compare the value to the already sampled ones, again performing 32 bitsliced comparisons at a time. By performing 32 comparisons at a time we often perform comparisons with elements that are not yet set by the algorithm, but are initialized with a value e.g. zero. The result of these comparisons must not influence the rejection behavior, otherwise the initialization value can never be included in the output which would violate the uniform randomness requirement. We solve this by simply masking out the bits of these comparisons.

If no collision is found r is stored in the array, in contrast to the bounded rejection method, this condition is not a secret value, thus we do not need the masked cmov operation. But we implemented this move in the bitsliced domain, so that the array of indices can be kept in the bitsliced domain throughout the entire algorithm and only converted to the non-bitsliced domain at the end.

Bounded Rejection. Similar to the simple rejection method, the implementation of the bounded rejection method for the index representation has to deal with false collisions with the initialization values. Tracking which values are set and thus which comparisons are valid is cumbersome in this case because the amount of already correctly sampled values is secret. Instead, we implemented this by initializing the array with a value that is out of bound, e.g. N. This induces only a small overhead for the collision comparison, which now has to operate on $\lceil log_2(N) \rceil + 1$ bits instead of $\lceil log_2(N) \rceil$.

Again we parallelized the inner loop with bitslicing to significantly improve the performance.

We determined the bound according to the formulas provided by Drucker et al. [15]. Drucker et al. suggest bounds for BIKE Level 1 ($B = 327$) and Level 3

($B = 488$) which give a probability to fail of less than 2^{128}. If a sampling failure does not affect the security of the scheme, a lower bound can be chosen for better performance. We selected a bound of 704 for BIKE Level 5 and $364, 460$ and 267 for the three relevant parameter sets of HQC to reach the same probability.

Comparison. Generally, this approach can be parallelized very efficiently as each coefficient is sampled individually. For software, this means that bitslicing is eligible, and for hardware, an individual trade-off between area and latency can be found.

In software, the weight check is the bottleneck of this method. Since it is hard to accumulate single masked bits in Boolean sharing on software platforms, we first deploy a bitsliced Boolean-to-additive masking conversion, which converts 32 masked bits to 32 arithmetically masked values modulo 2^z for a sufficiently large chosen z. Then, we unbitslice these values and accumulate the additively masked values share-wise. Finally, when we iterated over the whole polynomial with this procedure, we can unmask the shared accumulation value to obtain the weight of the masked polynomial.

Optimized Masked Weight Check. To check whether the masked polynomial candidate has the correct weight or not, it is required to compute the weight of the polynomial. For this operation, the intermediate weight is a sensitive information as it could reveal the position of single coefficients. The masked weight computation itself is a secure accumulation of all masked coefficients to a value of size $\lceil \log_2 N \rceil$ bits, e.g., by means of a secure $\lceil \log_2 N \rceil$-plus-one-bit adder. It is worth noting that for all three code-based applications, though, W is *much smaller* than N. It follows that most of the upper bits of such a secure adder are not required with overwhelming probability.

Since we know the expected weight of our polynomial candidate (under the assumption that no biased randomness is used as input), we can decrease the secure accumulator size and accept the possibility of an overflow happening. An overflow of the accumulator is not critical as long as it does not lead to a false-positive result, i.e., approving a polynomial that has not the correct weight.

Let z be the bit length of the secure accumulator output. Then, for a given (N, W, ℓ, t) as explained in Sect. 4.6, we have probability p_{fp} of a false positive:

$$p_{\mathrm{fp}} = \sum_{\substack{i=-\lfloor \frac{W}{2^z} \rfloor \\ i \neq 0}}^{\lfloor \frac{N-W}{2^z} \rfloor} \mathcal{B}\left(W + i \cdot 2^z, N, \frac{t}{2^\ell}\right) \tag{13}$$

Obviously, it is desirable to have a negligible p_{fp}, but also a low z, since this affects the efficiency of the weight check. We find that for all use cases and parameter sets, choosing $z = 8$ (i.e., an 8-bit secure accumulator), yields $p_{\mathrm{fp}} < 2^{-200}$.

RepeatedAND. Using the same weight check module as above, we also implemented the RepeatedAND method presented in [10]. This time, however, we cannot use the optimization shown above, since we do not check for equality, but rather whether a weight is bigger or smaller. Thus, we use 10-bit secure accumulation, which is enough for nearly all parameter sets of NTRU, Streamlined NTRU Prime, and NTRU LPRrime. For Streamlined NTRU Prime- and NTRU LPRrime-1277, the probability that an intermediate weight is greater or equal than 2^{10} is negligible. This approach is not efficient for McEliece, BIKE and HQC, because compared to the Comparison approach, significantly more and bigger weight checks are required.

5.2   Hardware

As a case study, we implement the comparison sampling approach for BIKE in hardware. Additionally, we give some remarks on how hardware implementations of the other algorithms could be realized.

For hardware implementations, we generally have similar restrictions compared to embedded software platforms. Most importantly, only very limited memory is available, rendering sorting-based methods for high polynomial degrees infeasible. As an example, the smallest BIKE parameter set already would require $32 \cdot 12323 \cdot 2 = 788672$ bit storage for first-order masking assuming that 31 bit randomness per coefficient would be sufficient. On the other hand, comparison-based sorting networks can be implemented very efficiently for smaller N as in NTRU and its variants and parallelized in a more fine-grained manner than for software platforms. This allows for precise trade-offs between latency and area demand.

To reduce the latency of comparisons, a parallel-prefix subtractor could be deployed by optimizing it to only obtain the uppermost carry-out bit. In return, this would require more secure non-linear gadgets compared to our comparison method presented in Sect. 4.1.

For Fisher-Yates, the boolean to arithmetic and vice versa transformations could be implemented with secure Boolean adders, which is possible efficiently and pipelined [17]. Then, the relatively big integer multiplications are a major cost factor in hardware, as they involve many bit operations.

For the RepeatedAND method, we certainly expect a higher control overhead due to the more complex algorithm compared to the comparison approach. Also, an intermediate masked vector must be stored in addition to the output vector, which results in a higher memory requirement. On the other hand, in contrast to software implementations, where the weight check is the bottleneck, we can execute the weight check in parallel to the secure AND operations. This could make this method efficient for the BIKE and HQC key generations and McEliece encapsulation.

Comparison Method. Since we aim for a masked implementation, we store each share of the target sampled polynomial in a separate memory (for BIKE level 1, we instantiate one 18 KB memory for each share). Each of these memory modules can be accessed via a 32-bit interface. As explained in Sect. 4.6, the approach requires ℓ bits of randomness to sample one bit. Due to the 32-bit interface of the memory modules, our hardware design samples 32bit in parallel which leads to $\ell \cdot d \cdot 32$ bits of randomness required as input to the fixed input comparison. Since our target is to implement a side-channel resistant design, we replace all non-linear gates by secure gadgets (in our case study, we used Domain-Oriented Masking (DOM) gadgets [11]). As shown in Sect. 4.6, the comparison for BIKE level 1 consists of eight secure multiplication gadgets where each gadget requires $\frac{d \cdot (d+1)}{2}$ bit of fresh randomness.

To track the Hamming weight of the sampled masked polynomial, we instantiate a masked Hamming weight computation unit. The design follows the implementation concept of the unmasked Hamming weight unit from [16]. However, we realize each adder stage by masked Ripple-Carry Adder (RCA) generated from HPC2 gadgets [8]. Eventually, we obtain a masked six-bit result for each 32-bit block which is fed into an accumulation stage. The accumulator is implemented by a fully pipelined masked 8-bit Sklansky adder as proposed in [2]. Since the adder consists of eight register stages, we obtain eight masked intermediate results that need to be accumulated to a final result. For this, we utilize the same adder and cleverly feed in the intermediate results from the adder to its input to add up all intermediate results. The final result is not secret and can be unmasked in order to compare it to the desired weight W. The procedure needs to be repeated in case the weight is not met.

6   Evaluation

6.1   Software

The target of our software implementations is the 32-bit Cortex-M4 microcontroller on the STM32F4 discovery board. To measure the cycle counts we set the frequency to 24MHz to make the cycle counts independent of the memory speed. We used the `arm-none-eabigcc-10.3.1` compiler with optimization-level O3 and report average cycle counts of 10 runs for algorithms without data-dependent branching and average counts of 1000 runs otherwise. For comparison sampling, we measure the non-branching execution of one iteration and report this value multiplied by the expected number of repetitions.

We excluded the generation of randomness required by calls to rand in our measurements so that only the performance of the fixed weight polynomial sampling algorithm is measured and not the performance of the PRNG. The generation of randomness required by masked operations is however included.

Tables 8 show our measurements in kilo cycle counts for first-order masking on the Cortex-M4.

From our measurements, we can first of all conclude that masked fixed-weight polynomial sampling is expensive in software.

For masked sampling of fixed-weight polynomials in the index representation, the simple rejection method is the fastest and can always be applied when there is no need for seed security. If seed security is required, one could alternatively use the bounded method, which is always slower compared to the simple rejection. We thus only benchmarked the bounded rejection for the use cases in BIKE and HQC. Fisher-Yates also provides seed security, and outputs in the index representation and is faster than the bounded rejection for all parameter sets that we measured.

Table 8. Performance on the Cortex-M4 in kilo cycles for first order masking. Entries marked with – are irrelevant combinations that we did not implement/measure.

Scheme	N	W	Sort	Fisher-Y.	Reject	B. Reject	RepAND	Comp.	I2C Trans.
BIKE	24646	134	–	7128	–	34077	–	–	770708
BIKE	12323	71	–	2854	647	–	101629[a]	45838	195945
BIKE	49318	199	–	13206	–	69140	–	–	2394245
BIKE	24659	103	–	4901	1255	–	156631[a]	129050	592411
BIKE	81194	264	–	21680	–	131135	–	–	5497931
BIKE	40973	137	–	7514	2176	–	320522[a]	234007	1372560
HQC	17669	75	–	3063	–	25803	–	–	309894
HQC	17669	66	–	2852	620	–	185348[a]	63242	272707
HQC	35851	114	–	5377	–	41500	–	–	999526
HQC	35851	100	–	5034	1282	–	391503[a]	183833	876778
HQC	57637	149	–	7808	–	28930	–	–	2094589
HQC	57637	131	–	7367	2132	–	837777[a]	348099	1841552
McEliece	3488	64	108596	1847	462	–	19519[b]	12948	32246
McEliece	4608	96	160777	3326	972	–	31778[b]	20392	68236
McEliece	6688	128	240949	5044	1555	–	63766[b]	31652	131539
McEliece	6960	119	249618	4848	1386	–	59875[b]	34571	127568
McEliece	8192	128	300713	4591	1527	–	62867[b]	34609	161312
NTRU	509	254	9699	11532	4709	–	2141	1666	15342
NTRU	677	254	14958	12445	4833	–	3559	2935	22674
NTRU	821	510	18338	17737	7022	–	4140	3921	32655
sNTRU Prime	653	288	14958	15086	6345	–	3023	3033	24650
NTRU LPRrime	653	252	14958	12390	4806	–	3177	3299	21515
sNTRU Prime	761	286	16464	15063	6005	–	3699	3336	27828
NTRU LPRrime	761	250	16464	12350	4570	–	3457	3773	24264
sNTRU Prime	857	322	19848	20249	7461	–	4125	4012	34948
NTRU LPRrime	857	329	19848	20569	7805	–	4482	4650	35825
sNTRU Prime	953	396	21564	27494	11253	–	4403	6266	47664
NTRU LPRrime	953	345	21564	20867	8404	–	4496	6617	41385
sNTRU Prime	1013	448	23405	31680	14421	–	4836	5763	57395
NTRU LPRrime	1013	392	23405	27380	10843	–	5428	7015	50228
sNTRU Prime	1277	492	32361	42388	18445	–	6861	9612	85013
NTRU LPRrime	1277	429	32361	33673	13822	–	7285	9245	74318

[a] average over 3 executions   [b] average over 10 executions

The sorting method required too much stack to fit into the 192-KB SRAM of our board for the large N of BIKE and HQC, but the results of McEliece with medium sized N already indicate high costs for large N. As the runtime for sorting grows sub-quadratic in N, but Fisher-Yates performance is mainly determined by its $\mathcal{O}(W^2)$ loop iterations, the sorting method is faster for the higher parameter sets of Streamlined NTRU Prime and NTRU LPRrime which have medium sized N and relatively high W.

However, sorting is always outperformed by the two other coefficient representation methods, the RepeatedAND and our comparison method. For BIKE, HQC and McEliece the comparison method is superior to the RepeatedAND in runtime costs. For NTRU the performance of both methods is very similar, for Streamlined NTRU Prime and NTRU LPRrime, RepeatedAND is mostly faster.

In the last column of Table 8 we present the cycle counts for a masked transformation from index to coefficient representation. In general, it depends on the implementation of the scheme which representation is required for further operations, the index representation of sparse polynomials can for example be used for efficient multiplications. The high costs for a masked transformation indicate, that if only a single representation is required, a method that directly outputs the correct representation is usually preferable.

To summarize the recommendations for masked software implementations derived from our performance measurements: if no seed security is required, the simple rejection method is the fastest index sampling method and either RepeatedAND or our comparison method is preferable for an output in coefficient representation. For the scenarios in BIKE and HQC, where the seed must be kept secret, Fisher-Yates yields the best performance with an output in index representation, and one could use a masked transformation to get the coefficient representation, or implement a less memory-consuming variant of the sorting method, by utilizing radixsort, as explained in Sect. 4.3.

Two schemes have parameter sets that lead to a special case for some algorithms. When N is a power of two which is the case for one parameter set of McEliece, then Fisher-Yates and rejection sampling become easier because checking if $r < N$ is not necessary. We adopted our code accordingly when benchmarking this parameter set and the effect shows clearly in the cycle numbers of Fisher-Yates that are lower compared to the next smaller parameter set of McEliece. The second special case is the highest parameter set for NTRU where $W > N/2$. In this case, the symmetry of fixed weight sampling allows to sample with $W' = N - W$ instead.

6.2   Hardware

Table 9 shows the hardware implementation results for the comparison approach presented in Sect. 4.6 for BIKE level 1. Therefore, we implement our design for a Xilinx Artix-7 xc7a200 Field-Programmable Gate Array (FPGA) and report the required resources and performance numbers. As a baseline, we first implement an unprotected design that consumes just 100 slices and finishes on average one sampling process in 33.4 µs. Note, the number of required Block-RAMs (BRAMs) is reported in 36 KB memory modules. Therefore, the unprotected design requires only one 18 KB memory to store the final polynomial.

Table 9. Implementation results for the comparison sampling approach for BIKE level 1 on an Artix-7 FPGA.

d	Resources				Performance		
	Logic	Memory		Area	Cycles	Frequency	Latency
	LUT	FF	BRAM	Slices	Cycles	MHz	μs
0	194	115	0.5	100	8 350	250	33.400
1	1 957	2 721	1	627	9 756	250	39.024
2	5 075	5 815	1.5	1 548	9 756	250	39.024
3	9 038	10 085	2	2 584	9 756	250	39.024

The next three lines in Table 9 show the implementation results for a first, second, and third-order protected design. The first-order protected implementation consumes 627 slices compared to 100 slices of the unprotected design. However, all protected implementations of the sampler can be executed with the same frequency, but have a slightly higher latency due to additional register stages introduced by the masking approach.

7 Conclusion

In this work, we demonstrated how all fixed-weight polynomial sampling methods in the literature can be masked at arbitrary order. Our implementations indicate that despite bitslicing and optimized subcomponents, the existing algorithms are costly for masked software. Drucker and Gueron [10] benchmarked a subset of our algorithms and schemes without power side-channel countermeasures, their numbers indicate that the relative performance of the sampling algorithms for a given scheme is equal for masked and nonmasked software implementations.

The flexibility of hardware implementations allows faster solutions, further implementations would be an interesting target for future work. Additionally, we identified that shuffling should be investigated for the sampling algorithms as an efficient countermeasure against single-trace attacks.

Acknowledgments. The work described in this paper has been supported by the German Federal Ministry of Education and Research BMBF through the project QuantumRISC (16KIS1038) and PQC4Med (16KIS1044), the German Research Foundation DFG under Germany's Excellence Strategy - EXC 2092 CASA - 390781972 and the European Commission under the grant agreement number 101070374. We thank Eike Kiltz and Gregor Leander for their valuable comments.

References

1. Azouaoui, M., et al.: Leveling Dilithium against leakage: revisited sensitivity analysis and improved implementations. Cryptology ePrint Archive, Paper 2022/1406 (2022). https://eprint.iacr.org/2022/1406

2. Bache, F., Güneysu, T.: Boolean masking for arithmetic additions at arbitrary order in hardware. Appl. Sci. **12**(5), 2274 (2022)

3. Barthe, G., et al.: Masking the GLP lattice-based signature scheme at any order. In: Nielsen, J.B., Rijmen, V. (eds.) EUROCRYPT 2018. LNCS, vol. 10821, pp. 354–384. Springer, Cham (2018). https://doi.org/10.1007/978-3-319-78375-8_12

4. Batcher, K.E.: Sorting networks and their applications. In: AFIPS Conference, vol. 32, pp. 307–314. Thomson Book Company, Washington D.C. (1968)

5. Bernstein, D.J.: Divergence bounds for random fixed-weight vectors obtained by sorting (2020)

6. Bernstein, D.J., Chuengsatiansup, C., Lange, T., van Vredendaal, C.: NTRU prime: reducing attack surface at low cost. In: Adams, C., Camenisch, J. (eds.) SAC 2017. LNCS, vol. 10719, pp. 235–260. Springer, Cham (2018). https://doi.org/10.1007/978-3-319-72565-9_12

7. Bronchain, O., Cassiers, G.: Bitslicing Arithmetic/Boolean masking conversions for fun and profit with application to lattice-based KEMs. IACR Trans. Crypt. Hardware Embed. Syst. **2022**(4), 553–588 (2022)

8. Cassiers, G., Grégoire, B., Levi, I., Standaert, F.-X.: Hardware private circuits: from trivial composition to full verification. IEEE Trans. Comput. **70**(10), 1677–1690 (2021)

9. Coron, J.-S., Gérard, F., Trannoy, M., Zeitoun, R.: High-order masking of NTRU. Cryptology ePrint Archive, Report 2022/1188 (2022). https://eprint.iacr.org/2022/1188

10. Drucker, N., Gueron, S.: Generating a random string with a fixed weight. In: Dolev, S., Hendler, D., Lodha, S., Yung, M. (eds.) CSCML 2019. LNCS, vol. 11527, pp. 141–155. Springer, Cham (2019). https://doi.org/10.1007/978-3-030-20951-3_13

11. Groß, H., Mangard, S., Korak, T.: Domain-oriented masking: compact masked hardware implementations with arbitrary protection order. In: TIS@CCS, p. 3. ACM (2016)

12. Guo, Q., Hlauschek, C., Johansson, T., Lahr, N., Nilsson, A., Schröder, R.L.: Don't reject this: key-recovery timing attacks due to rejection-sampling in HQC and BIKE. IACR Trans. Crypt. Hardware Embed. Syst. **2022**(3), 223–263 (2022)

13. Ishai, Y., Sahai, A., Wagner, D.: Private circuits: securing hardware against probing attacks. In: Boneh, D. (ed.) CRYPTO 2003. LNCS, vol. 2729, pp. 463–481. Springer, Heidelberg (2003). https://doi.org/10.1007/978-3-540-45146-4_27

14. Karabulut, E., Alkim, E., Aysu, A.: Single-trace side-channel attacks on ω-small polynomial sampling: with applications to NTRU, NTRU prime, and CRYSTALS-DILITHIUM. In: IEEE HOST, pp. 35–45. IEEE (2021)

15. Kostic, D., Drucker, N., Gueron, S.: Isochronous implementation of the errors-vector generation of BIKE (2022). https://github.com/awslabs/bike-kem. Accessed 25 Oct 2022

16. Richter-Brockmann, J., Mono, J., Güneysu, T.: Folding BIKE: scalable hardware implementation for reconfigurable devices. IEEE Trans. Comput. **71**(5), 1204–1215 (2022)

17. Schneider, T., Moradi, A., Güneysu, T.: Arithmetic addition over boolean masking. In: Malkin, T., Kolesnikov, V., Lewko, A.B., Polychronakis, M. (eds.) ACNS 2015. LNCS, vol. 9092, pp. 559–578. Springer, Cham (2015). https://doi.org/10.1007/978-3-319-28166-7_27

18. Sendrier, N.: Secure sampling of constant-weight words - application to BIKE. Cryptology ePrint Archive, Report 2021/1631 (2021). https://eprint.iacr.org/2021/1631

MPC

Private Polynomial Commitments and Applications to MPC

Rishabh Bhadauria[1]([⊠]), Carmit Hazay[1,3],
Muthuramakrishnan Venkitasubramaniam[2,3], Wenxuan Wu[4],
and Yupeng Zhang[4]

[1] Bar Ilan University, Ramat Gan, Israel
rishabh.bhadauria@biu.ac.il
[2] Georgetown University, Washington, DC, USA
[3] Ligero Inc., Rochester, USA
[4] Texas A&M University, College Station, USA

Abstract. Polynomial commitment schemes allow a prover to commit to a polynomial and later reveal the evaluation of the polynomial on an arbitrary point along with proof of validity. This object is central in the design of many cryptographic schemes such as zero-knowledge proofs and verifiable secret sharing. In the standard definition, the polynomial is known to the prover whereas the evaluation points are not private. In this paper, we put forward the notion of *private polynomial commitments* that capture additional privacy guarantees, where the evaluation points are hidden from the verifier while the polynomial is hidden from both.

We provide concretely efficient constructions that allow simultaneously batch the verification of many evaluations with a small additive overhead. As an application, we design a new concretely efficient multi-party private set-intersection with malicious security and improved asymptotic communication and space complexities.

We demonstrate the concrete efficiency of our construction via an implementation. Our scheme can prove 2^{10} evaluations of a private polynomial of degree 2^{10} in 157 s. The proof size is only 169 KB and the verification time is 11.8 s. Moreover, we also implemented the multi-party private set intersection protocol and scale it to 1000 parties (which has not been shown before). The total running time for 2^{14} elements per party is 2,410 s. While existing protocols offer better computational complexity, our scheme offers significantly smaller communication and better scalability (in the number of parties) owing to better memory usage.

1 Introduction

A polynomial commitment is a cryptographic building block that allows a prover to commit to a polynomial, which can later be opened at any evaluation point with proof that the evaluation is correctly computed. Polynomial commitments, which serve as an important building block in constructing cryptographic protocols, were introduced by Kate et al. [46] for the construction of verifiable secret sharing in the synchronous and asynchronous setting [6].

© International Association for Cryptologic Research 2023
A. Boldyreva and V. Kolesnikov (Eds.): PKC 2023, LNCS 13941, pp. 127–158, 2023.
https://doi.org/10.1007/978-3-031-31371-4_5

The scheme was generalized to multivariate polynomials by Papamanthou et al. [51], and to zero-knowledge proofs of knowledge by Zhang et al. [69]. In recent years, they are extensively used to build efficient zero-knowledge proof systems [23,32,59,62,65,68], where recent new schemes without a trusted setup were proposed in [15,47,61,62,67]. Subsequent works considered batched openings for multiple evaluations [60] and multiple polynomials [37]. Another application where polynomial commitments are utilized is "Proof of retrievability" [45,66]. In this problem, the server wishes to prove to a verifier that all of the client's data is stored correctly. The polynomial commitment allow the prover to prove the integrity of the data storage. Logarithmic and constant size polynomial commitments are also used in constructing vector commitments [17,18,22].

To date, all concretely efficient polynomial commitments require the verifier to know the evaluation point and the prover to know the polynomial. While such a notion is sufficient to design succinct zero-knowledge arguments, secure multiparty computation (MPC) requires additional privacy guarantees. In this paper, we consider a different setting where the polynomial is unknown to the prover and is encrypted. Moreover, the evaluation points are committed by the prover and may not be publicly known to the verifier. This setting is very common in MPC where both the polynomial and the evaluation points must remain private as they are defined based on the parties' inputs. We denote this primitive by *private polynomial commitment* and show that it can be used as a building block in many applications that arise in the secure multi-party setting; see Sects. 1.1 and 4. Our scheme is particularly useful in batch scenarios when there are multiple evaluation points. In this case, the proof size and verifier's complexity grow additively with the number of points.

1.1   Our Contributions

Our contribution is threefold. (1) abstracting the new notion of private polynomial commitments and providing two constructions. (2) demonstrating its applicability for MPC and (3) implementing our commitment schemes and presenting a new multi-party private set-intersection (MPSI) protocol.

Private Polynomial Commitments. Our contribution includes two flavors of private polynomial commitments with a hidden (encrypted) polynomial; one where the evaluation points are public and the other where they are private. Our schemes are built on the recent scheme of an inner product argument [16], which generalizes the inner product argument from [14] to bilinear groups. Specifically, we embed the ciphertexts encrypting the coefficients in the base group using an Additively Homomorphic Encryption (AHE) scheme introduced in [13]. Working with bilinear maps allow to publicly verify a single multiplication in the exponent which allows any party to verify the proof. More specifically, for a polynomial of degree d, the overhead is dominated by $O(d)$ bilinear pairings whereas the proof size is $O(\log d)$ and the verifier time is $O(d)$ exponentiations. Our construction supports batched evaluations efficiently. To open at m evaluation points, the proof size is $O(m + \log d)$ and the verifier time is only $O(m + d)$. The polynomial is hidden from all parties and only an encrypted form is available to the prover.

Our constructions rely on two different commitment schemes for committing to the encrypted polynomial (using the pairing-based scheme from [4]) and the evaluation points (using Pedersen commitment [52]). We further rely on the Boneh et al. pairing-based encryption scheme [13] to be compatible with our pairing-based commitment scheme, both of which rely on the Decisional Linear Assumption (DLIN) and Double Pairing Problem (DPP).

Our commitment scheme uses an inner product argument [14] as a building block (denoted by BBB-IPA) and is the first polynomial commitment scheme where the prover does not know the actual polynomial and only has access to its encryption. The main challenge in constructing this commitment scheme was the integration of encrypted polynomials into the polynomial commitment scheme. Secondly, directly constructing a scheme would not provide batching. To ensure batching and overall small proof size, we reduce the proving of the polynomial evaluation to multiple inner products. First, we provide a new inner product argument that allows the prover to verify inner products on encrypted ciphertext with the evaluation vector. Second, we prove the correct structure of multiple evaluation vectors by verifying the linear and quadratic constraints. Both our linear and quadratic tests reduce the multiple constraints on all different evaluation vectors to verify a single inner product argument, thereby ensuring the batching feature is effective. An additional feature is that the proof can be made non-interactive using Fiat-Shamir.

Applications. Private polynomial commitment schemes are useful for private computations based on polynomials. We list four such applications that can benefit from the scalability and batching of the evaluations as inherent in our commitment scheme. Firstly, we use our new private polynomial commitment as a building block to present a new scalable multi-party PSI protocol that is secure against malicious adversaries. We also discuss three other applications - Oblivious Polynomial Evaluation, Verifiable Polynomial Evaluation, and Non-Interactive two-party PSI; for more details see Sect. 4.

Scalable Multi-party Private Set-Intersection (MPSI). PSI is a fundamental problem in secure computation that has been widely studied in the past decade. In this problem a set of parties $P_1, \ldots, P_n$, holding input sets $X_1, \ldots, X_n$ of sizes $m_1, \ldots, m_n$, respectively, wish to compute $X_1 \cap X_2 \cap \ldots \cap X_n$. The two-party setting has been studied extensively and continues to be a hot topic of research owing to numerous applications such as contact discovery, dating services, data mining, recommendation systems, and law enforcement. In a long line of works, highly efficient two-party protocols have been designed with almost linear overhead in the set sizes (see some recent works at [21,53–55] and references therein). Furthermore, Google has recently leveraged this technology to match login credentials against an encrypted database.

While considerable progress has been made in the two-party setting, very few works have explored the concrete efficiency of PSI in the multi-party setting and the existing works have mostly considered only the semi-honest setting. Furthermore, current approaches fail to achieve overheads as in the two-party setting and do not scale well due to communication and space bottlenecks. Multiparty PSI is a fundamental cryptographic primitive with a richer set of applications beyond the two-party ones such as distributed intrusion detection, identifying the most visited sites or watched movies, contact tracing and more.

Our starting point is the work of Freedman et al. [31] who designed a simple two-party PSI protocol based on polynomials. Roughly speaking, P_1 creates a polynomial $Q(\cdot)$ whose roots correspond to its input data set and sends this polynomial to P_2, encrypted under an additively homomorphic encryption scheme. P_2 homomorphically evaluates a "masked" variant of the encrypted polynomial on its data set. In more detail, for each element x in P_2's input set, P_2 generates fresh randomness r and sends an encryption of $r \cdot Q(x) + x$ to P_1. P_1 decrypts and identifies the elements in the set intersection. Namely, if the decrypted value x is in P_1's set, then x is extracted from the decryption of the ciphertext. Whereas if the item x is not in the intersection, with very low probability, there exists an element z for which $r \cdot Q(z) + z$ is a false positive.

More recently, Hazay and Venkitasubramaniam [43] extended [31] to the multi-party setting by reducing the multi-party PSI (MPSI) task among n parties to n instances of two-party PSI. In this work we explore the practicality of [43] in the malicious setting where up to $n - 1$ parties can be corrupted. On a high level, in [43], parties $P_2, \ldots, P_n$ create a polynomial whose roots correspond to their respective inputs and send their encrypted coefficients to P_1. P_1 then aggregates the polynomials and homomorphically evaluates the resulting encrypted polynomial on its input set. To make the protocol secure against malicious adversaries, [43] introduced a simple mechanism for P_1 to prove and the parties to verify that P_1 aggregated the polynomials correctly, and relied on zero-knowledge proofs for the remaining steps.

The protocol presented in [43] implies an overall communication complexity of $O(n^2 + n \cdot m_{\max} + n \cdot m_{\min} \cdot \log m_{\max})$ where $m_{\max}$ (resp. $m_{\min}$) is the size of the largest (resp. smallest) input set. The threshold key generation incurs a communication cost of $O(n^2)$. The central party aggregates the input polynomials of all the parties and returns the encrypted coefficients of the aggregated polynomial. This yields a communication overhead of $O(n \cdot m_{\max})$. The main source of overhead is due to the zero-knowledge proof applied by the central party for proving correct evaluation, which implies an overhead of $O(n \cdot m_{\min} \cdot \log m_{\max})$. This phase is captured in our protocol by private polynomial commitments.

More precisely, in this work, we introduce a variant of [43] where we rely on a new abstraction that is based on private polynomial commitments. By leveraging the efficiency and batching features of our commitment schemes, we manage to improve the communication and computation complexities of [43]. We further provide an implementation of our PSI protocol and explore its concrete efficiency. This is in contrast to [43] that had the potential of being concretely efficient but did not provide an implementation.

THE COMPLEXITY OF OUR PROTOCOL. In addition to our new abstraction, we further improve the asymptotic complexity of [43] to $O(n^2 + \sum_{i=1}^{n} m_i + n \cdot (m_{\min} +$

$\log m_{\max}))$. Introducing private polynomial commitments (PPC) as a building block, the central party in our protocol does not send the encrypted aggregated polynomial. Instead, a commitment of encrypted aggregated polynomials is sent to the parties. This allows us to remove the $O(n \cdot m_{\max})$ factor. To further reduce the communication complexity, we leverage the batching feature of PPC which allows the central party to prove the correctness of multiple evaluations on the aggregated polynomial. The proof size, in this case, is $O(m_{\min} + \log m_{\max})$ which contributes an additive factor of $O(n \cdot (m_{\min} + \log m_{\max}))$ to the communication complexity of our MPSI protocol. A detailed analysis is provided in Table 3 where the communication complexity is broken according to the central party overhead and the other parties and is presented for each phase separately.

COMPARISON WITH RECENT WORK. Three recent works that design PSI protocols with malicious security are [9,33,38]. Similarly to our work, these works also achieve linear communication complexity in the number of parties by relying on a star topology. The main advantage of these protocols is that they rely on oblivious transfer (OT), oblivious linear evaluation (OLE) (used in [38]) and symmetric-key primitives for which we have very efficient instantiations. In comparison to previous work [9,33,38], our protocol achieves the best communication and space complexities. Specifically, our communication complexity is dominated by the term $O(n^2\kappa + nm\kappa)$ where the gain compared to previous work is due to an aggregation of the encrypted input polynomials and the small batched proof size. We compare the communication complexity in Table 1. In the typical parameter regime, the computational security parameter κ is greater than the statistical parameter λ satisfying the inequality $\lambda + \log m < \kappa$ where m is the input set size. Applying this inequality to the asymptotic communication complexity of [33] yields communication complexity that matches ours.

Most MPSI protocols (including ours) are designed for a star topology, where a central party aggregates the other parties' messages and therefore requires larger space. In prior works, the space complexity of the central party is inflated with a factor that depends both on the input and the number of parties, whereas our space complexity only grows with $O(m\kappa)$. The space complexity of the other, "non-central" parties, is independent of the number of parties. We compare the space complexity in Table 2.

Our paper realizes a standard MPSI functionality where a single party (typically the central party) receives the output, but can be extended to guarantee security even when all parties receive the output. Both [38] and our protocol achieve this standard security whereas the works of [9,33] provide a weaker security guarantee that allows the party that first receives the output (if controlled by the adversary) to unnoticeably remove certain elements from the output when broadcasting it to all parties. Note that these protocols can achieve full security, but this will require applying general-purpose zero-knowledge proofs.

On the other hand, the computational cost of [9,33,38] grows with $\Omega(mn\kappa)$ field multiplications, while the dominating cost of our computation is $O(m^2)$ exponentiations. This can be further reduced into $O(m\frac{\log m}{\log\log m})$ using hashing. While for a small number of parties, our protocol is slower, the total running

Table 1. The communication complexity analysis of MPSI *in bits* where κ is the computational security parameter, λ is the statistical security parameter, n is the number of parties, m is an upper bound on the inputs set sizes and P_1 is the central party.

	P_1	P_i	Total
[9]	$O(nm\kappa^2 + nm\kappa \log m\kappa)$	$O(m\kappa^2 + m\kappa \log m\kappa)$	$O(nm\kappa^2 + nm\kappa \log m\kappa)$
[33]	$O(n\kappa + nm(\kappa + \lambda + \log m))$	$O(n\kappa + m(\kappa + \lambda + \log m))$	$O(n^2\kappa + nm(\kappa + \lambda + \log m))$
[38]	$O(nm\kappa + n\lambda\kappa \log m)$	$O((n+m)\kappa + \lambda\kappa \log m)$	$O(n^2\kappa + nm\kappa + n\lambda\kappa \log m)$
Theorem 2	$O(nm\kappa)$	$O((n+m)\kappa)$	$O(n^2\kappa + nm\kappa)$

time essentially remains the same when the number of parties increases. For instance, our experiments show that our scheme takes 9,141 s for 1000 parties and 2^{16} elements per party. Prior works cannot run at this scale.

We highlight some applications which require PSI for a large number of parties and large input sizes: (1) Cache-sharing [50] involves multiple network providers who wish to cache common elements with high access frequency in a shared cache and require privacy of their local cache. (2) Another application is to generate statistics over the Tor network. Prior literature e.g., [26,63] has relied on MPC, secure aggregation and differential privacy to generate statistics on Tor servers in a privacy-preserving manner. Large-scale MPSI can be useful here where common features need to be extracted among the relay servers without compromising the users' privacy. (3) Hospitals and healthcare providers can collaborate to analyze common features between databases which include a large number of medical records. (4) Finally, MPSI can be applied for contact tracing. A large group of patients can execute an MPSI protocol to find common locations they have been to without leaking each individual's travel history. The result can help the actions of testing or quarantine in these areas.

Table 2. The space complexity analysis of MPSI *in bits* where κ is the computational security parameter, n is the number of parties, m is an upper bound on the inputs set sizes and P_1 is the central party.

	P_1	P_i
[9]	$O(nm\kappa^2 + m\kappa \log m\kappa)$	$O(m\kappa^2)$
[33]	$O(nm\kappa + m(\kappa + \lambda + \log m))$	$O(m(\kappa + \lambda + \log m))$
[38]	$O(nm\kappa)$	$O(m\kappa)$
Theorem 2	$O(m\kappa)$	$O(m\kappa)$

Private polynomial commitments are also useful for reusable non-interactive two-party PSI. Non-interactive secure computation introduced in [44], considers a "receiver" that publicly broadcasts a single message and any "sender" can interact in a two-party secure computation protocol with the receiver by sending a single message to the receiver. The receiver only needs to broadcast once and any number of interactions with the receiver can be performed. Specializing the setting to PSI, our protocol enables non-interactive PSI which can be applied to dating services, ride-share matching, and contact tracing. While such a protocol may introduce high computational cost compared to existing works e.g., [57], its communication cost is competitive as it benefits from our batching feature, which is extremely useful in a client-server setting; see more details in Sect. 4.3.

Oblivious Polynomial Evaluation. The oblivious polynomial evaluation (OPE) functionality is an important functionality in the field of secure two-party computation. It considers a setting where party P_2 holds a d-degree polynomial $Q(\cdot)$ and party P_1 holds an element t, and the goal is that P_1 obtains $Q(t)$ and nothing else while P_2 learns nothing. OPE has proven to be a useful building block and can be used to solve numerous cryptographic problems; e.g., secure equality of strings, set-intersection, approximation of a Taylor series, RSA key generation, oblivious keyword search, set membership, blacklisting anonymous users, data entanglement and more [8,30,31,35,40,49].

In this work, we consider a distributed variant of OPE, where the input polynomial is additively secret shared amongst the parties, and the goal of the parties is to evaluate (in the exponent) the aggregated polynomial privately and correctly. The scenario where the polynomial is distributed naturally arises in settings where the data cannot be stored on a single memory device due to privacy considerations. Secret-sharing sensitive data protects it against leakage attacks and eliminates the risk of breaching the stored memory. In some cases, the data is distributed in order to avoid a single point of failure and to ensure continuous access to the data.

Private polynomial commitments are useful in this context and enable secure evaluation of the combined polynomial in the presence of $n-1$ malicious corruptions, similar to our PSI protocol. The ingoing communication complexity of P_1 is linear in the size of shares, whereas the outgoing communication only grows logarithmically in the polynomial degree plus P_1's input size (and hence sublinear in d). The bulk of the computational overhead is attributed to P_1, which evaluates the aggregated polynomial on its input. An interesting feature of our protocol is its usage for multi-point evaluations. Here P_1 evaluates $Q(\cdot)$ on multiple points $t_1, t_2, \ldots$ where the accumulated overhead per evaluation point for ensuring malicious security vanishes away due to our batching property.

Verifiable Polynomial Evaluations. In this setting, computationally weak devices (or clients) wish to outsource their computation and data to an *untrusted* server in the cloud. The ultimate goal in this setting is to design efficient protocols that minimize the computational overhead of the clients and instead rely on the extended resources of the server. Of course, the amount of work invested by the client for verifying the correctness of the computation is *substantially* smaller than running the computation by itself. Another ambitious challenge of verifiable computation is to minimize the *communication* from the cloud.

The problem of delegating a single polynomial was studied by Benabbas et al. [10], who introduced a new cryptographic primitive of algebraic PRFs, which enables the generation of short authentication message to verify the server's reply. Followup works [7,19,20,27] improved different aspects of [10]. Nevertheless, all prior constructions considered a setting where a single client communicates with the server. Extending these solutions to the multi-client setting is not immediate (even in the non-private setting) since the server needs to aggregate the shares of the polynomials and provide proof for validating the aggregation, which is highly non-trivial. We observe that polynomial commitment schemes directly imply a verifiable evaluation of distributed polynomials where correctness is established via the proof provided by the server.

When considering verifiable computation, one can consider a setting where the function is either public or private. Verifiable computation with function privacy is often harder to achieve. We note that our construction follows even if the polynomials are encrypted while the evaluation points are given in the clear. This can capture scenarios where the polynomial represents a database with secret payloads yet the queries are not private.

Implementation Details. To validate the concrete efficiency of our construction, we implemented our private polynomial commitment scheme and multi-party PSI protocol. Our implementation of the private polynomial commitment scheme demonstrates the advantage of the batch opening. For a polynomial of degree 2^{16}, the proof size is 18.6 KB and the verifier time is 53.7 s to open one evaluation, while they are only 6.1 MB and 757 s for 2^{16} evaluations respectively, which are significantly better than repeating the single opening 2^{16} times. Our multi-party PSI protocol with malicious security can scale to 1000 parties with 2^{16} elements per party. The majority of the time is spent on the computation of the proofs of our private polynomial commitment, which can be further accelerated through multi-threading and hashing. The communication and the memory usage of our protocol is an order of magnitude better than existing schemes, and thus our protocol performs better for a large number of parties and networks with limited bandwidth; see Sect. 5 for further details. We plan to open-source our implementation and the source code is available at https://anonymous.4open. science/r/PCOM-CCF4.

2   Private Polynomial Commitment Schemes

In this section, we introduce a new polynomial commitment scheme with privacy features. Loosely speaking, such a protocol is carried out between a committer C and a receiver R where C commits to an encrypted polynomial $\mathbf{C}$, denoted by a sequence of ciphertexts $\mathbf{C} = (c_0, c_1, \ldots, c_d)$ where c_i is a ciphertext that encrypts the ith coefficient of the underlying plaintext polynomial. In these schemes, upon committing to the encrypted polynomial, C sends $\mathbf{C}$ to R and later evaluates it at an evaluation point t. Following that, C proves that a ciphertext c_y is a correct evaluation of the encrypted polynomial at some private evaluation point t.

2.1 Security Definitions

We continue with the security definition of our new polynomial commitments.

Definition 1. *(Private Polynomial Commitments with Hidden Evaluation Points) Let* $\mathsf{E} = (\mathsf{KeyGen}, \mathsf{Enc}, \mathsf{Dec}, \mathsf{Eval}, \mathsf{Rerand})$ *be an AHE scheme with groups* $\mathcal{M}$ *and* $\mathcal{C}$. *Let PK be the public key of the underlying AHE scheme and generated by* $\mathsf{E.KeyGen}$. *A private commitment scheme* PCOM *w.r.t* E *is a tuple of algorithms* $(\mathsf{Setup}, \mathsf{Commit}, \mathsf{CommitPt})$ *and a protocol* (C, R) *defined as follows:*

- $\mathsf{pp} \leftarrow \mathsf{Setup}(1^\kappa, d)$: *takes an input* κ, d *where* κ *is the security parameter and* d *is the degree of the polynomial, and outputs public parameters* pp.
- $\mathsf{com}_\mathsf{C} \leftarrow \mathsf{Commit}(\mathsf{pp}, \mathbf{C}; r_\mathbf{C})$: *takes as input a public parameters* pp, *a vector of ciphertexts (representing an encrypted polynomial)* $\mathbf{C} = (c_0, c_1, \ldots, c_d)$ *where* $c_i \in \mathcal{C}$ *for all* i *and randomness* $r_\mathbf{C}$, *and outputs a commitment* com_C.
- $\mathsf{com}_T \leftarrow \mathsf{CommitPt}(\mathsf{pp}, t, d; r_T)$: *takes as input public parameters* pp, *an evaluation point* t, *a randomness* r_T *and* d *is the degree of the polynomial and outputs a commitment* com_T.
- (C, R) *is a public-coin interactive protocol between* C *and* R. *Both* C *and* R *have common inputs, public parameters* pp, *a public-key PK for the underlying AHE scheme, a commitment* com_C, *another commitment* com_T *and an evaluation ciphertext* $c_y, \in \mathcal{C}$. C *additionally receives as input an encrypted polynomial* $\mathbf{C}$, *an evaluation point* t *and randomness* $r_\mathbf{C}, r_{c_y}, r_t$. *At the end of the protocol execution,* R *either outputs accept or reject. We denote by* $\big(\mathsf{C}(\mathbf{C}, t, r_\mathbf{C}, r_{c_y}, r_T), \mathsf{R}\big)$ $(\mathsf{pp}, PK, \mathsf{ck}, \mathsf{com}_\mathsf{C}, \mathsf{com}_T, c_y)$ *the random variable representing an execution and given an instance of the execution* e, *we denote by* $\mathsf{view}_1(e)$ *(resp.* $\mathsf{view}_2(e)$*) the view of the* C *(resp.,* R*) and* $\mathsf{out}_1(e)$ *(resp.,* $\mathsf{out}_2(e)$*) the output of* C *(resp.,* R*).*

We require the following security properties to be satisfied:

Completeness: *For any vector of ciphertexts* $\mathbf{C} = (c_0, c_1, \ldots, c_d)$ *generated using* $PK \leftarrow \mathsf{E.KeyGen}(1^\kappa)$ *and an evaluation point* t, *we have that:*

$$\Pr\Big[\mathsf{pp} \leftarrow \mathsf{PCOM.Setup}(1^\kappa, d);$$
$$\mathsf{com}_\mathsf{C} \leftarrow \mathsf{PCOM.Commit}(\mathsf{pp}, \mathbf{C}; r_\mathbf{C});$$
$$\mathsf{com}_T \leftarrow \mathsf{PCOM.CommitPt}(\mathsf{pp}, t, d; r_T);$$
$$c_y = \mathsf{Eval}(PK, \mathbf{C}, t; r_{c_y}) :$$
$$\mathsf{out}_2(\mathsf{C}(\mathbf{C}, t, r_\mathbf{C}, r_{c_y}, r_T), \mathsf{R})$$
$$(\mathsf{pp}, PK, \mathsf{com}_\mathsf{C}, \mathsf{com}_T, c_y) = 1\Big] = 1$$

Binding: *For all PPT adversaries* $\mathcal{A}$, *there exists a negligible function* $\epsilon(\cdot)$ *such that:*

$$\Pr \Big[\mathsf{pp} \leftarrow \mathsf{PCOM.Setup}(1^\kappa, d);$$

$$PK \leftarrow \mathsf{E.KeyGen}(1^\kappa);$$

$$(\mathbf{C}_0, r_{\mathbf{C}_0}, \mathbf{C}_1, r_{\mathbf{C}_1}, t_0, r_{T_0}, t_1, r_{T_1}) \leftarrow \mathcal{A}(1^\kappa, n, \mathsf{pp}, PK; r_{\mathcal{A}});$$

$$\mathsf{com}_{\mathbf{C}_0} = \mathsf{PCOM.Commit}(\mathsf{pp}, \mathbf{C}_0; r_{\mathbf{C}_0})$$

$$\mathsf{com}_{\mathbf{C}_1} = \mathsf{PCOM.Commit}(\mathsf{pp}, \mathbf{C}_1; r_{\mathbf{C}_1})$$

$$\mathsf{com}_{T_0} = \mathsf{PCOM.CommitPt}(\mathsf{pp}, t_0, d; r_{T_0})$$

$$\mathsf{com}_{T_1} = \mathsf{PCOM.CommitPt}(\mathsf{pp}, t_1, d; r_{T_1})$$

$$(\mathsf{com}_{\mathbf{C}_0} = \mathsf{com}_{\mathbf{C}_1} \wedge \mathbf{C}_0 \neq \mathbf{C}_1)$$

$$\vee (\mathsf{com}_{T_0} = \mathsf{com}_{T_1} \wedge t_0 \neq t_1) \Big] \leq \epsilon(\kappa)$$

Witness-Extended Emulation: *For all PPT adversaries $\mathcal{A}$, there exists an expected polynomial time emulator $\mathcal{E}$ and negligible function $\epsilon(\cdot)$ such that:*

$$\Pr \Big[pp \leftarrow \mathsf{PCOM.Setup}(1^\kappa, d);$$

$$PK \leftarrow \mathsf{E.KeyGen}(1^\kappa);$$

$$(\mathsf{com}_{\mathbf{C}}, \mathsf{com}_T, c_y) \leftarrow \mathcal{A}(1^\kappa, n, \mathsf{pp}, PK; r_{\mathcal{A}});$$

$$e \leftarrow (\mathcal{A}(r_{\mathcal{A}}), \mathsf{R})(pp, PK, \mathsf{com}_{\mathbf{C}}, \mathsf{com}_T, c_y);$$

$$(\mathbf{C}, t, r_{\mathbf{C}}, r_{c_y}, r_T) \leftarrow \mathcal{E}^{\mathcal{A}(\mathsf{pp}, PK, \mathsf{com}_{\mathbf{C}}, \mathsf{com}_T, c_y; r_{\mathcal{A}})}$$

$$(pp, PK, \mathsf{com}_{\mathbf{C}}, \mathsf{com}_T, c_y, e) :$$

$$(\mathsf{out}_2(e) = 1) \Rightarrow$$

$$(\mathsf{com}_{\mathbf{C}} = \mathsf{PCOM.Commit}(\mathsf{pp}, \mathbf{C}; r_{\mathbf{C}})$$

$$\wedge \, \mathsf{com}_T = \mathsf{PCOM.CommitPt}(\mathsf{pp}, t, d; r_T)$$

$$\wedge \, c_y = \mathsf{Eval}_{PK}(\mathbf{C}, t; r_{c_y})) \Big] \geq 1 - \epsilon(\kappa)$$

Honest Verifier Privacy: *There exists a tuple of expected PPT algorithms $\mathcal{S}$, given any vector of coefficient of polynomial $(p_0, \ldots, p_d)$ and an evaluation point t, such that the following distributions are indistinguishable:*

$$-\left\{ \begin{array}{c} \mathsf{pp} \leftarrow \mathsf{PCOM.Setup}(1^\kappa, d); \\ PK \leftarrow \mathsf{E.KeyGen}(1^\kappa); \\ \mathbf{C} \leftarrow (c_0, \ldots, c_d) = (\mathsf{Enc}_{PK}(p_0; r_0), \ldots, \mathsf{Enc}_{PK}(p_d; r_d)) : \\ \mathsf{com}_{\mathbf{C}} \leftarrow \mathsf{PCOM.Commit}(\mathsf{pp}, \mathbf{C}; r_{\mathbf{C}}); \\ \mathsf{com}_T \leftarrow \mathsf{PCOM.CommitPt}(\mathsf{pp}, t, d; r_t); \\ c_y \leftarrow \mathsf{Eval}_{PK}(\mathbf{C}, t; r_{c_y}); \\ e \leftarrow (\mathsf{C}(\mathbf{C}, t, r_{\mathbf{C}}, r_{c_y}, r_T, r_{\mathcal{A}}), \mathsf{R}) \\ (\mathsf{pp}, PK, \mathsf{com}_{\mathbf{C}}, \mathsf{com}_T, c_y) : \\ \mathsf{view}_2(e) \end{array} \right\}$$

$$-\left\{ \begin{array}{c} pp \leftarrow \mathsf{PCOM.Setup}(1^\kappa, d); \\ PK \leftarrow \mathsf{E.KeyGen}(1^\kappa); \\ \mathcal{S}(\mathsf{pp}, PK, d; r_{\mathcal{S}}) \end{array} \right\}$$

2.2   Our Protocols

In this section, we present the construction of our private polynomial commitment. Our construction is based on the additive homomorphic encryption (AHE) scheme from [13] and the inner-pairing product argument from [16]. As a warm-up, we start by considering a single point where the idea is that the evaluation of a polynomial $f(x) = \sum_{i=0}^{d} a_i x^i$ at point t can be viewed as the inner product between the coefficients vector $(a_0, a_1, \ldots, a_d)$ and the evaluation vector $T = (1, t, t^2, \ldots, t^d)$. Therefore, given the ciphertexts encrypting the coefficients and the commitments of the evaluation vector T, the committer proves in Phase 1 that the polynomial evaluation on the ciphertext is indeed the inner product between the two vectors using the techniques in [16]. Next, it remains to show that the committed evaluation vector is well-formed, i.e., it is indeed the powers of the evaluation point t. To prove this property, denoting the i-th element in a vector T as $T[i]$, it suffices to show that (1) the 0-th element $T[0]$ is 1; (2) $T[i+1] = T[i] \cdot T[1]$ for $i = 0, \ldots, d-1$. These two conditions can further be translated into two types of constraints: linear constraints and quadratic constraints. The first condition is equivalent to the inner product between T and a public vector $(1, 0, \ldots, 0)$ is 1. For the second condition, we define three selector matrices $A, B, C \in \mathbb{F}^{d \times (d+1)}$ such that

$$
\begin{aligned}
X &= A \times T = (T[0], T[1], \ldots, T[d-1]), \\
Y &= B \times T = (T[1], T[1], \ldots, T[1]), \\
Z &= C \times T = (T[1], T[2], \ldots, T[d]). \quad (1)
\end{aligned}
$$

Finally, the committer proves that $X \odot Y = Z$, where $\odot$ denotes the Hadamard (element-wise) product. It is not hard to see that T is the correct evaluation vector if and only if it satisfies these constraints.

We use standard techniques such as [14] to reduce the linear constraints and the quadratic constraints to inner product arguments in Phases 2 and 3. Note that the protocols in these two phases are independent of the ciphertexts encrypting the coefficients. The formal protocol of our private polynomial commitment is presented in Fig. 1. This protocol uses the encryption scheme from [13], the pairing-based commitment from [4] and the Pedersen commitment [52] as building blocks. The protocol also involves private inner product argument, linear constraints test and quadratic constraints test, as described above in the three phases. We present these protocols later in Figs. 3, 4 and 5 together with our scheme for multiple evaluations.

Multiple Evaluations. The major advantage of our construction is that it supports batched evaluations on multiple points efficiently, where the proof size and the receiver's time do not increase by much compared to a single evaluation. We describe our scheme for multiple evaluations in Figs. 2. The differences from the single evaluation variant are highlighted in purple. In particular, in Phase 1 (Steps 1 and 2 in Fig. 2), C and R check the inner products between the coefficient vector in the ciphertext and all the evaluation vectors in the commitments using a single private inner product argument protocol via a random linear combination.

Setup($1^\kappa, d$): Generate the public parameters of the bilinear map and the commitment scheme Ped and AFG. $(\mathbb{G}_1, \mathbb{G}_2, \mathbb{G}_t, p, e, w, g) \leftarrow \mathcal{G}(1^\kappa)$, $\mathsf{ck}_1 = (w_r, w_0, \ldots, w_d), a, b) \leftarrow \mathsf{AFG}.KeyGen(S, 3d + 8)$. $\mathsf{ck}_2 = (v_r, v_0, \ldots, v_d) \leftarrow \mathsf{Ped}.\mathsf{KeyGen}(1^\kappa, d + 2)$, $\mathsf{ck}_3 \leftarrow \mathsf{Ped}.\mathsf{KeyGen}(1^\kappa, 2)$, $\mathsf{ck}_4 = (x_r, x_0, \ldots, x_d) \leftarrow \mathsf{Ped}.\mathsf{KeyGen}(1^\kappa, d + 2)$. Output $pp = (\mathsf{ck}_1, \mathsf{ck}_2, \mathsf{ck}_3, \mathsf{ck}_4, a, b)$.

Commit($pp, \mathbf{C}, r_C$): Given the ciphertext of the coefficients $\mathbf{C} = (c_0, \ldots, c_d)$, output $\mathsf{AFG}.\mathsf{Commit}_{\mathsf{ck}_1}(\mathbf{C}, g^{r_C}) = e(g^{r_C}, w_r) \cdot \prod_{i=0}^{d} e(c_i, w_i)$, where $r_C \in \mathbb{Z}_p$.
CommitPt(pp, t, r_T, d): Given an evaluation point t, generate $T = (1, t, \ldots, t^d)$ and output $\mathsf{Ped}.\mathsf{Commit}_{\mathsf{ck}_2}(T, r_T)$ where $r_T \in \mathbb{Z}_p$.

Protocol $\Pi_{priv}(\mathbf{C}(\mathbf{C}, r_C, t, r_T), \mathsf{R})(pp, \mathsf{com}_C, \mathsf{com}_T, c_y)$:

1. C and R execute **Private inner Product Argument** specified in (Figs. 3) with common input $pp, \mathsf{com}_C, \mathsf{com}_T, c_y$ and $\mathbf{C}, T$ as private inputs to C.
2. C → R: Let A, B, C be public selector matrices defined in Eq. 1. C computes $X = A \times T = (1, t, \ldots, t^{d-1})$, $Y = B \times T = (t, \ldots, t)$, $Z = C \times T = (t, \ldots, t^d)$. C commits to X, Y, Z by $\mathsf{com}_X = \mathsf{Ped}.\mathsf{Commit}_{\mathsf{ck}_2}(X, r_X), \mathsf{com}_Y = \mathsf{Ped}.\mathsf{Commit}_{\mathsf{ck}_2}(Y, r_Y), \mathsf{com}_Z = \mathsf{Ped}.\mathsf{Commit}_{\mathsf{ck}_2}(Z, r_Z)$, where $r_X, r_Y, r_Z \in \mathbb{Z}_p$. C sends $\mathsf{com}_X, \mathsf{com}_Y, \mathsf{com}_Z$ to R.
3. C ↔ R : C and R execute **Linear Constraints Test** specified in Fig. 4 with common input $\mathsf{com}_T, \mathsf{com}_X$ and T, X as private inputs to C. Repeat the same for Y and Z. Let D be public selector matrix defined as $D \times T = [1]$, C and R execute **Linear Constraints Test** specified in Fig. 4 with common input com_T, D and T as private inputs to C.
4. C ↔ R : C and R execute **Quadratic Constraint Test** specified in Fig. 5 with common input $\mathsf{com}_X, \mathsf{com}_Y, \mathsf{com}_Z$ and X, Y, Z as private inputs to C.
5. R outputs 1 if all checks pass.

Fig. 1. Private Polynomial Commitments (Single Evaluation).

In Phase 2 (Step 4 in Fig. 2), the product between a selector matrix (i.e., A, B or C) and all the evaluation vectors can be reduced to a single inner product via two random linear combinations, as shown in Fig. 4. In Phase 3 (Step 5 in Fig. 2), the protocol of the quadratic constraint test is more complicated. We are not able to reduce the Hadamard product of matrices $X \odot Y = Z$ to a single inner product. Instead, we reduce the Hadamard product to the sum of m inner products via a random linear combination in Step 1 of Fig. 5. Then we propose a protocol (Step 3 of Fig. 5) to prove the sum of the inner products with a proof size of only $O(\log d)$. The protocol is an extension of the scheme for the Hadamard product in [14] in a non-black-box way.

Protocol $\Pi_{priv}^{batched}(\mathsf{C}(\mathbf{C}, r_{\mathbf{C}}, \{t_i\}_{i\in[m]}, \{r_{T_i}\}_{i\in[m]}), \mathsf{R})(pp, \quad \mathsf{com}_{\mathbf{C}}, \{\mathsf{com}_{T_i}\}_{i\in[m]},$ $\{c_{y_i}\}_{i\in[m]})$:

1. $\mathsf{R} \to \mathsf{C}$: R sends $S = (s_1, s_2, \cdots, s_m) \in \mathbb{Z}_p^m$.

2. $\mathsf{C} \leftrightarrow \mathsf{R}$: Let $F = \sum_{i=1}^m s_i \cdot T_i$, $\mathsf{com}_F = \prod_{i=1}^m \mathsf{com}_{T_i}^{s_i}$ and $c_y = \prod_{i=1}^m c_{y_i}^{s_i}$.
   C and R execute **Private inner Product Argument** specified in (Figs. 3) with common input $pp, \mathsf{com}_{\mathbf{C}}, \mathsf{com}_F, c_y$ and $\mathbf{C}, F$ as private inputs to C

3. $\mathsf{C} \to \mathsf{R}$: Let A, B, C be public selector matrices defined in Eq. 1. C computes $X_i = (1, t_i, \ldots, t_i^{d-1})$, $Y_i = (t_i, \ldots, t_i)$ and $Z_i = (t_i, \ldots, t_i^d)$. Let $T \in \mathbb{Z}_p^{(d+1)\times m}$ be the matrix with the i-th column as T_i. C commits to each column of X, Y, Z, namely, $\mathsf{com}_{X_i} = \mathsf{Ped.Commit}_{\mathsf{ck}_2}(X_i, r_{X_i}), \mathsf{com}_{Y_i} = \mathsf{Ped.Commit}_{\mathsf{ck}_2}(Y_i, r_{Y_i}), \mathsf{com}_{Z_i} = \mathsf{Ped.Commit}_{\mathsf{ck}_2}(Z_i, r_{Z_i})$ where $r_{X_i}, r_{Y_i}, r_{Z_i} \in \mathbb{Z}_p$ and sends $\{\mathsf{com}_{X_i}, \mathsf{com}_{Y_i}, \mathsf{com}_{Z_i}\}_{i\in[m]}$ to the R.

4. $\mathsf{C} \leftrightarrow \mathsf{R}$: C and R execute **Linear Constraints Test** specified in Fig. 4 with common input $pp, \{\mathsf{com}_{T_i}\}_{i\in[m]}, \{\mathsf{com}_{X_i}\}_{i\in[m]}$ and T, X as private inputs to C. Repeat the same for Y and Z. Let D be public selector matrix defined as $D \times T = [1]^m$, C and R execute **Linear Constraints Test** specified in Fig. 4 with common input com_T, D and T as private inputs to C.

5. $\mathsf{C} \leftrightarrow \mathsf{R}$: C and R execute **Quadratic Constraint Test** specified in Fig. 5 with common input $pp, \{\mathsf{com}_{X_i}\}_{i\in[m]}, \{\mathsf{com}_{Y_i}\}_{i\in[m]}, \{\mathsf{com}_{Z_i}\}_{i\in[m]}$ and X, Y, Z as private inputs to C.

6. R outputs 1 if all checks pass.

Fig. 2. Batched proof for Private Polynomial Commitments. (Color figure online)

Theorem 1. *Protocol* PCOM *(Fig. 2) is a private polynomial commitment scheme as in Definition 1, under the Decisional Linear (DLIN) and the Double Pairing Problem (DPP) hardness assumptions.*

Proof Sketch: To show PCOM is a private polynomial commitment scheme (Definition 1), we show that the protocol satisfies completeness, binding, witness-extended emulation and honest verifier privacy.

Completeness: In the private inner product argument test, there are two phases - the masking phase and the inner product phase. In the end, R accepts if the combined commitment of the private polynomial, evaluation vector and evaluation ciphertext is decommitted correctly. This essentially follows from showing that the commitment of the private polynomial, the commitment of evaluation vector and evaluation ciphertext are updated correctly in each round. The rest of the protocol involving the linear constraint test, quadratic test and the BBB-IPA follow essentially observing that the corresponding constraints are satisfied.

Private inner Product Argument

Private Inputs: C : $\mathbf{C} = (c_0, \ldots, c_d) \in \mathbb{G}_E^{d+1}, F = (f_0, \ldots, f_d) \in \mathbb{Z}_p^{d+1}$.
Public Inputs: $pp = (\mathsf{ck}_1, \mathsf{ck}_2, \mathsf{ck}_3, a, b, \mathsf{PK}), \mathsf{com}_{\mathbf{C}}, \mathsf{com}_F, c_y$.

1. **Masking Phase:**
   (a) C → R: C generates a random encrypted polynomial $\mathbf{E} = (e_0, \ldots, e_d) \in \mathbb{G}_E^{d+1}$ where $e_i = \mathsf{Eval}_{\mathsf{PK}}(r_i)$ and $r_i \in \mathbb{Z}_p$. A random vector $M = (M_0, \ldots, M_d) \in \mathbb{Z}_p^{d+1}$ is also sampled and generates commitment $\mathsf{com}_{\mathbf{E}} = \mathsf{AFG.Commit}_{\mathsf{ck}_1}(\mathbf{E}, r_{\mathbf{E}})$ and $\mathsf{com}_M = \mathsf{Ped.Commit}_{\mathsf{ck}_2}(M, r_M)$ where $r_{\mathbf{E}}, r_M \in \mathbb{Z}_p$. C also computes: $c_l = \langle \mathbf{E}, F \rangle$, $c_r = \langle \mathbf{C}, M \rangle$, $c_m = \langle \mathbf{E}, M \rangle$ and sends $\mathsf{com}_{\mathbf{E}}, \mathsf{com}_M, c_l, c_r, c_m$ to R.
   (b) R → C: R sends a random challenge $x \in \mathbb{Z}_p$.
   (c) Both parties set com' where: $\mathsf{com} = \mathsf{com}_{\mathbf{C}} \cdot e(\mathsf{com}_F, a) \cdot e(c_y, b)$, $\mathsf{com}' = \mathsf{com} \cdot \mathsf{com}_{\mathbf{E}}^x \cdot e(\mathsf{com}_M, a)^{x^{-1}} \cdot e(c_l^x \cdot c_m \cdot c_r^{x^{-1}}, b)$, and C sets $\mathbf{C}' = \mathbf{C} \odot \mathbf{E}^x$ and $F' = F + x^{-1} \cdot M$ where $\odot$ denotes element-wise multiplication of two vectors.
   (d) Both parties update $\mathsf{com} = \mathsf{com}'$, $\mathbf{C} = \mathbf{C}'$, $F = F'$.
2. **Inner Product Phase:** For round $rnd = 1$ to $\log d - 1$:
   (a) Set $d' = (d+1)/2$. C sets $\mathbf{C}_L = \mathbf{C}[: d']$, $\mathbf{C}_R = \mathbf{C}[d' :]$, $F_L = F[: d']$ and $F_R = F[d' :]$ while both C and R sets $\mathsf{ck}_{1L} = \mathsf{ck}_1[: d']$, $\mathsf{ck}_{1R} = \mathsf{ck}_1[d' :]$, $\mathsf{ck}_{2L} = \mathsf{ck}_2[: d']$, and $\mathsf{ck}_{2R} = \mathsf{ck}_2[d' :]$.
   (b) C generates intermediate cross-commitments:
   $\mathsf{com}_{\mathbf{C}_L} = \mathsf{AFG.Commit}_{\mathsf{ck}_{1R}}(\mathbf{C}_L, r_{\mathbf{C}_L})$, $\mathsf{com}_{\mathbf{C}_R} = \mathsf{AFG.Commit}_{\mathsf{ck}_{1L}}(\mathbf{C}_R, r_{\mathbf{C}_R})$, $\mathsf{com}_{F_L} = \mathsf{Ped.Commit}_{\mathsf{ck}_{2R}}(F_L, r_{F_L})$, $\mathsf{com}_{F_R} = \mathsf{Ped.Commit}_{\mathsf{ck}_{2L}}(F_R, r_{F_R})$, where $r_{\mathbf{C}_L}, r_{\mathbf{C}_R}, r_{F_L}, r_{F_R} \in \mathbb{Z}_p$.
   (c) C → R: C generated L and R: $c_l = \langle \mathbf{C}_R, F_L \rangle$, $c_r = \langle \mathbf{C}_L, F_R \rangle$ $L = \mathsf{com}_{\mathbf{C}_R} \cdot e(\mathsf{com}_{F_L}, a) \cdot e(c_l, b)$, $R = \mathsf{com}_{\mathbf{C}_L} \cdot e(\mathsf{com}_{F_R}, a) \cdot e(c_r, b)$, where $a, b \in pp$ and sends L, R to C.
   (d) R → C: R sends a random challenge $x \in \mathbb{Z}_p$.
   (e) C sets $\mathbf{C}' = \mathbf{C}_L \odot \mathbf{C}_R^x$ and $F' = F_L + x^{-1} \cdot F_R$ where $\odot$ denotes element-wise multiplication of two vectors while C and R both locally compute the new keys $\mathsf{ck}_1' = \mathsf{ck}_{1L} \odot \mathsf{ck}_{1R}^{x^{-1}}$ and $\mathsf{ck}_2' = ck_{2L} \odot \mathsf{ck}_{2R}^x$
   (f) R computes new commitment $\mathsf{com}' = L^x \cdot \mathsf{com} \cdot R^{x^{-1}}$
   (g) C and R will update $\mathbf{C} = \mathbf{C}'$, $F = F'$, $\mathsf{com} = \mathsf{com}'$, and $\mathsf{ck}_i = \mathsf{ck}_i' \forall i \in [2]$
   In round $\log d$:
   (h) In the last round, C opens com to $\mathbf{C}', F'$ and c_y' and R accepts if $c_y = \langle \mathbf{C}', F \rangle$.
   (i) If all checks pass, R outputs $b = 1$ else output $b = 0$.

Fig. 3. Private Inner Product Argument.

Binding: To argue the binding property of PCOM, it can be trivially reduced to the binding property of the Ped and AFG commitment scheme.

Witness-Extended Emulation: To argue witness-extended emulation of PCOM, as shown in [14], it is enough to show that given $(n_1, \ldots, n_r)$-tree of

---

Linear constraint Test (Prove $A \times T = X$)

- Private Inputs: C has private inputs: $X \in \mathbb{Z}_p^{d \times m}, T \in \mathbb{Z}_p^{d+1 \times m}$.
- Public Inputs: $pp = (\mathsf{ck}_1, \mathsf{ck}_2, \mathsf{ck}_3, a, b, \mathrm{PK}), \{\mathsf{com}_{T_i}\}_{i \in [m]}, \{\mathsf{com}_{X_i}\}_{i \in [m]}$ where $\mathsf{com}_{T_i}, \mathsf{com}_{X_i} \in \mathbb{G}_1$.
  1. $\mathsf{R} \to \mathsf{C}$:   R sends random vectors $S \in \mathbb{Z}_p^d$ and $U \in \mathbb{Z}_p^m$. Let $S_A = S \times A$, $T_U = T \times U$, $X_U = X \times U$. We observe that if $A \times T = X$ then for any $S \in \mathbb{Z}_p^d$ and $U \in \mathbb{Z}_p^m$ we have:

$$S \times A \times T \times U = S \times X \times U, \text{ i.e., } \langle S_A, T_U \rangle - \langle S, X_U \rangle = 0.$$

  2. $\mathsf{C} \to \mathsf{R}$:   C computes two cross terms inner product l and r and sends their respective commitments $\mathsf{com}_l, \mathsf{com}_r$ to R: $l = \langle S_A, -X_U \rangle, r = \langle S, T_U \rangle$, $\mathsf{com}_l = \mathsf{Ped.Commit}_{\mathsf{ck}_3}(l, r_l), \mathsf{com}_r = \mathsf{Ped.Commit}_{\mathsf{ck}_3}(r, r_r)$, where $r_l, r_r \in \mathbb{Z}_p$.
  3. $\mathsf{R} \to \mathsf{C}$:   R sends a random challenge $x \in \mathbb{Z}_p$.
  4. $\mathsf{R} \leftrightarrow \mathsf{C}$: C computes $L = S_A + x^{-1} \cdot S$ and $R = T_U - x \cdot X_U$. C and R both compute $\mathsf{com}_L = \mathsf{Ped.Commit}_{\mathsf{ck}_4}(S_A + x^{-1} \cdot S; 0)$ and $\mathsf{com}_R = \prod_{i=1}^m \mathsf{com}_{T_i}^{U[i-1]} \cdot \mathsf{com}_{X_i}^{U[i-1] \cdot x}$ .C and R execute BBB-IPA on common inputs is $\mathsf{ck}_4, \mathsf{ck}_2, \mathsf{ck}_3, \mathsf{com}_L, \mathsf{com}_R, \mathsf{com}_l^x \cdot \mathsf{com}_r^{x^{-1}}$ and private inputs of C are , $L, R, x \cdot l + x^{-1} \cdot r$.
  5. If all checks pass, R outputs $b = 1$ else output $b = 0$.
- A special case is when $D \times T = X$ where X is a known vector of dimensions $1 \times m$. The above test can be simplified where R sends a random vector $U \in \mathbb{Z}_p^m$ and the check is reduced from $D \times T = X$ to $\langle D, T_U \rangle = d$ where $T_U = T \times U$ and $d = \sum_{i=0}^{m-1} U[i]$. C and R compute $\mathsf{com}_D = \mathsf{Ped.Commit}_{\mathsf{ck}_4}(D, 0), \mathsf{com}_{T_U} = \prod_{i=1}^m \mathsf{com}_{T_i}^{U[i-1]}, \mathsf{com}_d = \mathsf{Ped.Commit}(d, 0)$ .C and R execute BBB-IPA on common inputs is $\mathsf{ck}_4, \mathsf{ck}_2, \mathsf{ck}_3, \mathsf{com}_D, \mathsf{com}_{T_U}, \mathsf{com}_d$ and private inputs of C are D, T_U, d . If all checks pass, R outputs $b = 1$ else output $b = 0$.

Fig. 4. Linear Constraint Test.

accepting transcripts, there exist a PPT extractor $\mathcal{X}$ which extracts the witness for PCOM. To construct $\mathcal{X}$, we first construct a witness-extraction algorithm $\mathcal{X}_1$ that succeeds in extracting the witness of Private Inner Product Argument given $(n_1, \ldots, n_r)$-tree of accepting transcripts. Using the rewinding property of the extractor and choosing different randomness in each rewinding, the extractor $\mathcal{X}_1$ can extract the witness. Here, the witness is the encrypted polynomial, evaluation vector, encrypted evaluation and the randomness used to generate the commitments. Next $\mathcal{X}$ extracts the evaluation vector from Linear Test and Quadratic test to verify if the evaluation used in all three tests is the same. We use the witness-extended emulation extractor of BBB-IPA as a subprotocol in extracting the evaluation vector from the Linear and Quadratic tests.

Honest Verifier Privacy: To show honest verifier privacy, we construct a simulator $\mathcal{S}$. Indistinguishability of the simulation essentially follows from semantic security of the underlying encryption scheme, hiding of the commitment scheme,

---

Quadratic Constraint Test (Prove $X \odot Y = Z$)

Private Inputs: $C : X, Y, Z \in \mathbb{Z}_p^{d \times m}$.

Public Inputs: $pp = (\mathsf{ck}_1, \mathsf{ck}_2, \mathsf{ck}_3, \mathsf{ck}_4, a, b, \mathsf{PK}), \{\mathsf{com}_{X_i}\}_{i \in [m]}, \{\mathsf{com}_{Y_i}\}_{i \in [m]}, \{\mathsf{com}_{Z_i}\}_{i \in [m]}$ where $\mathsf{com}_{X_i}, \mathsf{com}_{Y_i}, \mathsf{com}_{Z_i} \in \mathbb{G}_1$.

1. $R \to C$: R sends a random vector $S \in \mathbb{Z}_p^m$ and a random value w. Now if $X \odot Y = Z$, then $\sum_{i \in m} w^i (\langle X_i, Y_i \odot S \rangle - \langle Z_i, S \rangle) = 0$.

2. Let $L_i = w^i \cdot X_i$, $L_{i+m} = w^i \cdot Z_i$, $R_i = Y_i \odot S$, $R_{i+m} = -S$ C and R compute a new key ck_5 where $\mathsf{ck}_5[j] = \mathsf{ck}_2^{S[j]^{-1}}[j]$ for all $j \in [0, d]$ and compute the commitments as follows: $\mathsf{com}_{L_i} = \mathsf{com}_{X_i}^{w^i}, \mathsf{com}_{L_{i+m}} = \mathsf{com}_{Z_i}^{w^i}, \mathsf{com}_{R_i} = \mathsf{com}_{Y_i}, \mathsf{com}_{R_{i+m}} = \mathsf{Ped.Commit}_{\mathsf{ck}_5}(-S)$.

3. C sets $d = 0$ while R sets $\mathsf{com}_d = 1$. Also set $m' = 2m$.

   For round 1 to $\log m$:

   (a) $C \to R$: Set $m' = m'/2$. C computes two cross terms inner product $l = \sum_{i=1}^{m'} \langle L_i, R_{i+m'} \rangle$ and $r = \sum_{i=1}^{m'} \langle L_{i+m'}, R_i \rangle$ and sends a Ped commitment of these two (com_l and com_r) to R.
   where $r_l, r_r \in \mathbb{Z}_p$.

   (b) $R \to C$: R sends a random challenge $x \in \mathbb{Z}_p$.

   (c) C computes $\{L'_i = L_i + x^{-1} \cdot L_{i+m}\}_{i \in [m']}$ and $\{R'_i = R_i + x \cdot R_{i+m}\}_{i \in [m']}$ while R updates the commitments $\mathsf{com}_{L'_i} = \mathsf{com}_{L_i} \cdot \mathsf{com}_{L_{i+m}}^{x^{-1}}$ and $\mathsf{com}_{R'_i} = \mathsf{com}_{R_i} \cdot \mathsf{com}_{R_{i+m}}^{x}$.

   (d) C computes $d' = d + x \cdot l + x^{-1} \cdot r$ while R computes $\mathsf{com}_{d'} = \mathsf{com}_d \cdot \mathsf{com}_l^x \cdot \mathsf{com}_r^{x^{-1}}$.

   (e) C updates $L_i = L'_i$, $R_i = R'_i$, $d = d'$ while R updates $\mathsf{com}_d = \mathsf{com}_{d'}$.

   In round $\log m + 1$:

   (f) C sets $L = L_1$ and $R = R_1$ while R sets $\mathsf{com}_L = \mathsf{com}_{L_1}$ and $\mathsf{com}_R = \mathsf{com}_{R_1}$ C and R execute BBB-IPA on instance with common input $\mathsf{ck}_2, \mathsf{ck}_5, \mathsf{ck}_3, \mathsf{com}_L, \mathsf{com}_R, \mathsf{com}_d$ and L, R, d as private inputs of C.

Fig. 5. Quadratic Constraint Test.

honest-verifier zero-knowledge property of the underlying BBB-IPA and standard masking techniques.

Complexity. The communication complexity of our polynomial commitments is $O(\log d)$ for a single evaluation and $O(m + \log d)$ for m points where d is the degree of the polynomial. Their round complexity is $O(\log m + \log d)$ rounds.

The computational complexity of the committer is $O(m \cdot d)$ modular exponentiations and $O(d)$ bilinear pairings, while the complexity of the receiver is $O(m + d)$ exponentiations. The space complexity of our private polynomial commitment scheme is $O(m + d)$ for the committer as it needs to store the encrypted polynomial and the evaluation points. The space complexity of the receiver is $O(m)$ (resp. $O(m + \log d)$) in the interactive (resp. non-interactive setting). This difference is due to the fact that in the non-interactive setting, the entire proof is stored for validation.

3   Scalable Multi-party PSI

Our first application is a new scalable PSI protocol that follows the blueprint of [43]. This protocol is carried out in a star topology network with P_1 being the central party. In this work, we show that the actions of P_1 can be captured by the abstraction of a private polynomial commitment.

We broadly split our protocol description into four main phases. In the first phase (Key Generation), the parties jointly generate a public key without disclosing their corresponding secret key shares, as well as the public parameters for the two polynomial commitments. The second phase (Commitment Phase) is executed by the central party P_1 that broadcasts commitments of its input together with a proof of knowledge. In the third phase (Aggregation), all parties (except P_1) send it an encrypted polynomial whose roots correspond to their inputs. P_1 combines these polynomials for each party and provides a commitment of the encrypted aggregated polynomial while proving the correctness of aggregation. The last phase (Intersection) concludes the protocol by extracting the intersection, where P_1 evaluates the aggregated polynomial on its input and provides proof of correct evaluation. Once the proof is validated, the parties decrypt each evaluation to get the intersection.

Our polynomial commitments will be useful in [43] for two purposes; proving the correctness of aggregation by evaluating on a public point and proving the correctness of evaluations on P_1's input finally to reveal the intersection.

We use the following primitives in our construction:

- A threshold additively homomorphic encryption scheme with protocols (Π_{GEN} and Π_{DecZero}) to respectively sample a public-key together with the secret key shares, and a protocol to determine if a target ciphertext decrypts to 0. We instantiate our scheme with BBS encryption scheme [13] which relies on DLIN assumption.
- Our polynomial commitment scheme PCOM, (that is compatible with the threshold encryption scheme), and is instantiated with non-interactive publicly verifiable proofs of evaluation of hidden points (in the batched setting) and public points (in the single instance setting). We respectively denote the committer and receiver algorithms for the corresponding (non-interactive) proof systems by (PCOM.C$_{hid}^{batch}$, PCOM.R$_{hid}^{batch}$) and (PCOM.C$_{pub}$, PCOM.R$_{pub}$). To construct PCOM, we require two commitment schemes: Pederson Commitment scheme [52] which relies on the DL assumption and the AFG Commitment scheme [4] which is based on bilinear pairing and relies on the DPP assumption.
- An n-party protocol Π_{COIN} to sample random coins.
- A simulation extractable non-interactive publicly verifiable proof system Π_{EXP} to prove knowledge of exponent. We instantiate this with the non-interactive variant of the classic protocol due to [58] via the Fiat-Shamir transform. We denote the prover and verifier algorithms by (DL.P$_{pub}$, DL.V$_{pub}$).

Protocol π_{MPSI} with Malicious Security (Part 1)

Input: Party P_i is given a set $X_i = \{x_i^1, \ldots, x_i^{m_i}\}$ of size m_i for all $i \in [n]$. All parties are given a security parameter 1^κ and a description of a group $\mathbb{G}$.

The protocol:

1. **Key Generation.** The parties mutually generate a public key PK and the corresponding secret key shares $(\mathrm{SK}_1, \ldots, \mathrm{SK}_n)$ by running π_{GEN}. P_1 also runs the setup for the polynomial commitment scheme by running $\mathsf{PCOM}.Setup(1^\kappa, m_{\max})$.

2. **Commitment phase.** P_1 creates commitments to its inputs $\{com_{T_1}, \ldots, com_{T_n}\}$ where $com_{T_i} = \mathsf{PCOM.CommitPt}(\mathsf{pp}, x_1^i, r_{T_i}, m_{\max})$ and $r_{T_i} \in \mathbb{Z}_p$ is randomly chosen and generates a proof using $\mathsf{DL}.P$ proving knowledge of the committed message and broadcasts the commitment and proof to all parties.

3. **Aggregation**

   (a) For all $i \in [2, n]$, party P_i computes the coefficients of a polynomial $A_i(\cdot) = (a_0^i, \ldots, a_{m_i}^i)$ of degree m_i, with roots set to the m_i elements of X_i. In addition, P_i chooses a random element $\lambda_i \leftarrow \mathbb{G}$ and computes the product $\lambda_i \cdot a_j^i$ for every coefficient within A_i. P_i sends P_1 the sets of ciphertexts $\mathbf{C}_i = (c_0^i, \ldots, c_{m_i}^i)$, encrypting the coefficients of $\lambda_i \cdot A_i(\cdot)$.

   (b) Upon receiving the ciphertexts from all parties, party P_1 combines the following ciphertexts

   $$c_0 = \prod_{i=2}^n c_0^i, \ldots, c_{m_{\max}} = \prod_{i=2}^n c_{m_{\max}}^i$$

   where $m_{\max} = \max(m_2, \ldots, m_n)$. Note that P_1 generates the ciphertexts by encrypting the coefficients of the combined polynomial $A(\cdot) = \lambda_2 \cdot A_2(\cdot) + \cdots + \lambda_n \cdot A_n(\cdot)$. P_1 then generates and broadcasts $com_\mathbf{C}$ which is a commitment of the encrypted polynomial $\mathbf{C}(\cdot) = (c_0, \ldots, c_{m_{\max}})$ using $\mathsf{PCOM.Commit}(pp, \mathbf{C}, r_\mathbf{C})$ where $r_\mathbf{C}$ is generated randomly.

   (c) Next, the parties verify whether the polynomials aggregation was done correctly. Specifically, the parties first agree on a random element u from the appropriate plaintext domain using the coin tossing protocol π_{COIN}. P_1 broadcasts the encrypted evaluation $\tilde{\lambda} = \mathsf{Eval}(\mathsf{PK}, \mathbf{C}, u)$ along with a proof of correct evaluation by using $\mathsf{PCOM}.C_{pub}$ on public inputs $\mathsf{pp}, com_C, u, \tilde{\lambda}$ and private inputs $\mathbf{C}, r_\mathbf{C}$.

   (d) Then, each party broadcasts the ciphertext $\tilde{\lambda}_i = \mathsf{Eval}(\mathsf{PK}, \mathbf{C}_i, u)$, together with a ZK proof of knowledge generated using $\mathsf{DL}.P$ for proving the knowledge of the plaintext. If all the proofs are verified correctly, then the parties check that $\tilde{\lambda} - \prod_{i=2}^n \tilde{\lambda}_i$ encodes a 0-message using π_{DecZero}.

Fig. 6. Multi-party PSI protocol (Part 1).

The protocol is split into two parts and presented in Figs. 6 and 7. The first three phases of the protocol: Key Generation, Commitment Phase and Aggregation are covered in Fig. 6 whereas the Intersection is contained in Fig. 7.

Theorem 2. *The protocol π_{MPSI} described in Figure 6 and Fig. 7 securely realizes $\mathcal{F}_{MPSI}$ in the presence of malicious adversaries and dishonest majority*

Protocol π_{MPSI} with Malicious Security (Part 2)

The protocol (continued):

4. **Intersection.**
   (a) If the above verification is completed correctly, P_1 evaluates the aggregated polynomial that is encrypted within ciphertexts $\mathbf{C} = (c_1, \ldots, c_{m_{\max}})$, on its input elements $\{x_1^j\}_{j=1}^{m_1}$, and proves consistency with the commitment $\text{com}_{\mathbf{C}}$. P_1 forwards the encrypted evaluations $c_y = \text{Eval}(PK, \mathbf{C}, t)$ along with a proof generated using $\text{PCOM.C}_{hid}^{batch}$ on public inputs $\text{pp}, \text{com}_{\mathbf{C}}, \{\text{com}_{T_i}\}_{i \in [m]}, \{c_{y_i}\}_{i \in [m_1]}$ and private inputs $\mathbf{C}, r_{\mathbf{C}}, X_1, \{r_{T_i}\}_{i \in [m_1]}$
   (b) All parties verify the evaluations and then decrypt the evaluations using protocol π_{DecZero} to reveal the intersection.

Fig. 7. Multi-party PSI protocol (Part 2).

Table 3. MPSI Communication Complexity.

	P_1	P_i	Total
KeyGen	$O(n)$	$O(n)$	$O(n^2)$
Commit	$O(n \cdot m_{\min})$	—	$O(n \cdot m_{\min})$
Aggregate	$O(n \cdot \log m_{\max})$	$O(m_i + n)$	$O(n^2 + \sum_{i=2}^{n} m_i + n \cdot \log m_{\max})$
Intersection	$O(n \cdot (m_{\min} + \log m_{\max}))$	$O(m_{\min})$	$O(n \cdot (m_{\min} + \log m_{\max}))$
MPSI	$O(n \cdot (m_{\min} + \log m_{\max}))$	$O(n + m_{\min} + m_i)$	$O(n^2 + \sum_{i=1}^{n} m_i + n \cdot (m_{\min} + \log m_{\max}))$

under Decisional Linear (DLIN) and Double Pairing Problem (DPP) hardness assumptions.

Proof Sketch: We split the analysis into two cases based on whether the set of corrupted parties includes the central party P_1 or not. Consider an adversary $\mathcal{A}$ that corrupts a set of parties that includes P_1. We define a simulator $\mathcal{S}$ and prove that the real and simulated executions are computationally indistinguishable. The indistinguishability between the real and simulated execution is reduced to the privacy property of the encryption scheme, the hiding property of the commitment schemes, and the privacy property of the polynomial commitment. In the first case, the central party P_1 is corrupted, and the input of P_1 can be extracted from P_1's input commitment in the commit phase. The input of other corrupted parties can be extracted by rewinding the aggregation phase. This is achieved by extracting $d+1$ evaluation points of every corrupted party's polynomial as shown in [43]. In the second case, the simulation is the same as the previous case with the exception that it does not need to extract P_1's input.

Complexity. The communication complexity of our protocol is linear in the input sizes and the number of parties, where the smallest input size can be given to P_1. Naively, the communication complexity of our protocol is $O(n^2 + \sum_{i=1}^n m_i + n \cdot m_{\min} \cdot \log m_{\max})$ when the polynomial commitment is separately used for each evaluation point. The batching feature of our scheme reduces the communication cost of our protocol to $O(n^2 + \sum_{i=1}^n m_i + n \cdot (m_{\min} + \log m_{\max}))$. For the central party P_1, the communication cost is $O(n(m_{\min} + \log m_{\max})$. P_1 generates a batched evaluation proof of size $O(m_{\min} + \log m)$. The dominating cost for P_1 is sending the evaluation proof to all other parties. For all other parties, the communication cost is $O(n + m_{\min} + m_i)$ where $O(n)$ is sent during the Key Generation phase as well as verifying the aggregation. Additionally, the communication cost in sending the encrypted polynomial to P_1 and generating the intersection is $O(m_i)$ and $O(m_{\min})$ respectively. We provide a detailed analysis in Table 3, providing the communication complexity of the parties individually as well as together along every phase of the MPSI protocol. The round complexity of our protocol is dominated by the round complexity of the underlying polynomial commitments. In the random oracle model, the round complexity is 4.

Computationally, the dominating part of the protocol is evaluating the aggregated polynomial and executing the private polynomial commitment from Sect. 2. The complexity of our protocol is $O(m_{\max} \cdot m_{\min})$ exponentiations. We further reduce the polynomial degrees and the overall workload using hashing techniques; see below for more details. The space complexity of our protocol in the interactive setting is $O(m_{\max})$ for P_1 and $O(m_i)$ for every other party P_i, while in the non-interactive setting the complexity is $O(m_{\max})$ for P_1 and $O(m_i + \log m_{\max})$ for party P_i. We note that the space complexity of P_1 is independent of the number of parties. In particular, the polynomials received by the parties can be aggregated on-the-fly and do not require any extra space. Regarding the polynomial commitments, the non-interactive variant requires P_i to store the entire proof in the memory which increases the space complexity by an additive factor of $O(\log m_{\max})$.

Hashing. A notable optimization in PSI protocols is using simple hashing to map the input into smaller sets (buckets), and running a different instance per bucket. In our context, this enables us to reduce the workload of P_1 from quadratic to quasilinear. The idea behind simple hashing lies in splitting the input set into bins where based on a hash function, each element is assigned to a bin. Next, the parties sort their input into bins and run an MPSI protocol separately on each bin. Splitting the input into bins reduces the size of the degree of the polynomials and improves the computation cost of the parties for the computationally heavy tasks of polynomials interpolations and evaluations.

Simple hashing can be directly used in the malicious setting where each bin induces a separated polynomial. Note that the adversary can only attempt to put an item in a wrong bin but this item can be ignored by the simulator. Let h be a hash function, $m_{\max}$ be the maximum number of items in an input set, $\mathcal{B}$ be the number of bins and M is the maximum of items in a bin. It is known that if a hash function maps $m_{\max}$ items into $\mathcal{B}$ bins and $m_{\max} \geq \mathcal{B} \log \mathcal{B}$ then with very high probability, $M = \frac{m_{\max}}{\mathcal{B}} + \sqrt{\frac{m_{\max} \log \mathcal{B}}{\mathcal{B}}}$ [56,64]. Setting $\mathcal{B} = \frac{m_{\max} \log \log m_{\max}}{\log m_{\max}}$ and applying the Chernoff bound implies that $M = O(\frac{\log m_{\max}}{\log \log m_{\max}})$ with negligible error in $m_{\max}$. Simple hashing can be used to reduce the number of exponentiations, thereby reducing the computational cost. Namely, for each bin, the number of required exponentiations is $O(M^2)$ and the overall number of exponentiations will be $O(\mathcal{B}M^2)$. Substituting the values of $\mathcal{B}$ and M using the above analysis will result in $O(m_{\max} \frac{\log m}{\log \log m})$ exponentiations. We refer to Sect. 5 for more details regarding the concrete improvement.

The hashing techniques are not useful for improving [9] as they cannot be broken into small instances. While the improvement for [33] will potentially be smaller since its computational complexity is quasilinear in the input size.

4 Other Applications

In this section, we consider a list of distributed tasks in different settings, whose realization can make use of private polynomial commitments. All applications can benefit from the batching of our scheme while achieving malicious security.

4.1 Oblivious Polynomial Evaluation

Following the discussion from Sect. 1, in this work, we consider a distributed variant of the oblivious polynomial evaluation functionality denoted by DOPE, where the polynomial $Q_i(\cdot)$ is linearly shared amongst a set of $n - 1$ parties. More formally, we define the DOPE functionality as follows. The input of party P_i for $i \in [2, n]$ is a polynomial $Q_i(\cdot)$ of degree at most d whereas the input of P_1 is an element t, and the goal is that P_1 learns $\sum_{i \in [2,n]} Q_i(t)$.

Table 4. Comparison between different DOPE protocols where comm refers to the communication complexity and comp refers to the computational complexity (stated as the number of exponentiations), κ is the computational security parameter, λ is the statistical security parameter, n is the number of parties and d is the degree of the polynomial.

	P_1 comm	P_i comm	Total comm	P_1 comp	P_i comp
[42]	$O(n(d\kappa) + n\lambda)$	$O(d\lambda\kappa)$	$O((n + \lambda)d\kappa)$	$O(nd\lambda)$	$O(d\lambda)$
[40]	$O(n\kappa \log d)$	$O(d\kappa)$	$O(nd\kappa)$	$O(nd)$	$O(d)$
Our Work	$O(n\kappa \log d)$	$O(d\kappa)$	$O(nd\kappa)$	$O(d)$	$O(d)$

We can realize our DOPE functionality in the presence of $n - 1$ malicious corruptions based on our polynomial commitment scheme following the blueprint of our PSI protocol. Namely, the parties send their encrypted coefficients to P_1 that aggregates the ciphertexts and evaluates $Q(\cdot)$ on its input t. P_1 further attaches proofs of correct aggregation and evaluation. Finally, the parties run a distributed decryption protocol for P_1 to learn $Q(t)$. Note that, while in PSI the inputs of the parties are extracted from the polynomials' roots, here the inputs are the polynomial's shares that form $Q(\cdot)$.

Our scheme is further flexible regarding the level of threshold introduced by the underlying secret sharing scheme. In particular, one may use any threshold linear secret sharing for splitting the polynomial into shares (rather than simple additive sharing), where the threshold parameter can be smaller than $n - 1$. We also have a simple aggregation mechanism which allows the DOPE to be reduced to a single OPE execution where $n - 1$ parties play the role of P_2.

Two prior OPE constructions with malicious security [40, 42] can be extended to the distributed setting, where each party P_i for $i \in [2, n]$ carries out an individual OPE with P_1. Compared to previous work; see Table 4, our construction achieves better computational complexity for the central party P_1 due to the fact that the aggregation mechanism allows P_1 to combine the polynomials cheaply and then run the protocol with almost the same cost as running a two-party instance of OPE. The overall communication complexity of our protocol is similar to [40] and is better than [42].

Finally, we note that we can further extend our protocol to support multivariate polynomials to cover a broader class of functionalities.

4.2   Verifiable Polynomial Evaluations

In this setting, we focus on verifying the evaluations of a polynomial $Q(\cdot)$, linearly shared across a set of $n - 1$ clients, that are aggregated and stored by a cloud server. Specifically, a set of clients outsource their shares of a d-degree polynomial (potentially in the clear), to an untrusted server while storing a short state. The server stores the aggregated polynomials and prepares a proof for this computation. Next, whenever the clients provide an input x, the server computes $Q(x)$ and a short proof that allows the clients to verify this computation in sublinear time in d. We require the verification process to be *public*. Finally, the clients output $Q(x)$.

Employing our polynomial commitment by the server, the clients can non-interactively verify the proofs it provides. Furthermore, our solution supports the feature that the polynomial may also be kept private since the shares can be stored on the server while encrypted, where only the evaluation points are public. In more details, each party P_i sends the server its polynomial share $Q_i(\cdot)$. The server aggregates the shares and computes a proof of correct aggregation (that can be made non-interactive by using the random oracle to choose the random evaluated point for this test). Upon receiving an input x, the parties forward it to the server that computes (the encryption of) $Q(x)$ together with a proof of correctness. Our protocol is secure in the presence of $n - 2$ corrupted clients, and a colluding server. Note that the degree of $Q(\cdot)$ may be huge, yet uploading it is a one time phase whose complexity amortizes away over multiple evaluation points. Moreover, the proofs of correct evaluations can be batched.

A related modeling is multi-clients verifiable computation where a set of clients wish to compute some function f on their joint inputs while non-interactively communicating only with the server over a sequence of evaluations [11,24,39]. Such constructions have only been demonstrated in a setting where the clients and the server do not collude [39]. Our protocol achieves full security but requires an additional round of communication at the end due to decryption.

Verifiable Polynomial Evaluations on Encrypted Data. The second application in this area is verifiable computation on encrypted data. The notion was proposed by Gennaro et al. in [34] and follow-up works [12,28,29,36] proposed constructions for computations such as linear functions and polynomial evaluations. These schemes provide both privacy of the outsourced data to the untrusted server and the integrity of the results computed by the server. However, these constructions rely on fully or somewhat homomorphic encryptions based on lattice and zero-knowledge proofs over polynomial rings, thus their overhead is high and they have not been realized in practice. Also these protocols cannot be directly extended to multi-clients.

Our scheme yields a more efficient verifiable computation on encrypted data for polynomial evaluations. The prover's computation only involves operations on bilinear maps, making it one step closer to being practical. In the amortized setting, the verifier's time is faster than evaluating the polynomial locally for multiple evaluations. In particular, to compute m evaluations on a degree-d polynomial, the proof size is $O(m + \log d)$ and the verifier's time is $O(d + m)$.

Our model requires a setup phase for the clients prior to communicating with the server. This setup phase is independent of the input and is only carried out once, regardless of the number of polynomial evaluations computed later. The clients store a short state upon concluding this phase, which is later used to extract $Q(x)$. In our protocol, the parties run the key generation protocol for the underlying threshold encryption scheme, store the secret key share, and use it to partially decrypt the ciphertext returned from the server.

4.3 Non-interactive Two-party PSI (NISI)

Ishai et al. [44] introduced the Non-interactive Secure computation (NISC) model where, a Receiver first posts an "encryption" of its input publicly and then a Sender can compute a function over the encrypted input along with its input and obtain an "encryption" of the output that the Receiver can decrypt. The classic Yao's garbled circuit based two-party protocol in the semi-honest setting when combined with a 2-round OT is an example of such a protocol. Several works have explored the feasibility and concrete efficiency of such protocols in the malicious Boolean setting [3,5,41,44,48]. Private polynomial commitments can be used directly to implement a non-interactive secure private set-intersection protocol by relying on a variant of the [31] protocol. Such a scheme will additionally have the feature of reusability where the receiver only needs to post its encrypted input once and any number of senders can transmit the result of the set intersection to the receiver. An important application of reusable NISI is applicable is contact discovery in messaging services such as Signal and Telegram.

Concretely to PSI in the malicious setting, Cristofaro et al. [25] design a two-round PSI protocol with linear communication complexity. More recently, the work by Rosulek and Trieu [57] showed how to obtain a 2-round PSI by relying on a variant of the Diffie-Hellman Key Agreement and an ideal permutation oracle. This work has highly competitive communication and computation costs for small set sizes (between 2^7 and 2^{16} elements). We provide a comparison of the communication costs in Table 5. We can see that our work is competitive in communication because the proofs are succinct in the batch setting. Additionally we rely on more standard assumptions. Even though our computation costs are higher our protocol could be useful in a client-server setting where the receiver is a lightweight client device and the sender is the server with significantly bigger computational resources. We further point out that the reported computational costs could be improved by further parallelizing our implementation. We leave this as future work to explore.

5   Implementation

We implemented our encrypted polynomial commitment scheme and the multi-party PSI scheme, and we present the experimental results in this section.

Software and Hardware. The system is implemented in C++. We use the ate-pairing library [1] for bilinear maps and the GMP library [2] for field arithmetic. Our experiments are executed on a BN-curve over a 254-bit prime, which offers 128-bit of security. There are 3200 lines of code for the encrypted polynomial commitment and 1000 lines for the other building blocks in the MPSI protocol. We ran all experiments on an AWS c5.9xlarge instance with an Intel Xeon Platinum 8000 processor and 72 GB of RAM. We report the average running time over 5 executions, except for the largest instances due to the long running time.

5.1   Private Polynomial Commitments

Single Evaluation. We first present the performance of our encrypted polynomial commitment scheme as a stand-alone primitive. Figure 8 shows the prover and verifier times (left y-axis) and proof size (right $y - axis$) of one evaluation

Table 5. Communication cost of two-party PSI with set size m.

n	2^8	2^{16}	2^{20}
[25]	62.74 (KB)	13.33 (MB)	213 (MB)
[57]	16.38 (KB)	4.19 (MB)	67.11 (MB)
Here (est.)	49.7 (KB)	5.86 (MB)	68 (MB)

of the variant with committed points (Sect. 2.2). We vary the degree of the polynomial from 2^4 to 2^{16}. As shown in the figure, the prover time grows linearly with the polynomial degree. It takes 11 s to generate the proof for $d = 2^{10}$ and 701 s to generate the proof for $d = 2^{16}$. The verifier time also grows linearly with the degree, as it has to update the commitment key together with the prover in our scheme. It takes 0.93 s to verify the proof for $d = 2^{10}$ and 53.7 s for $d = 2^{16}$, which roughly matches the time on reducing the commitment key in the prover's time. The proof size is only logarithmic on the degree of the polynomial and is very small in practice. It is 11.9 KB for $d = 2^{10}$ and 18.6 KB for $d = 2^{16}$.

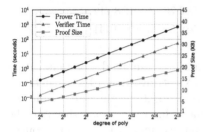

Fig. 8. Performance of single evaluation of our encrypted polynomial commitment with point hiding.

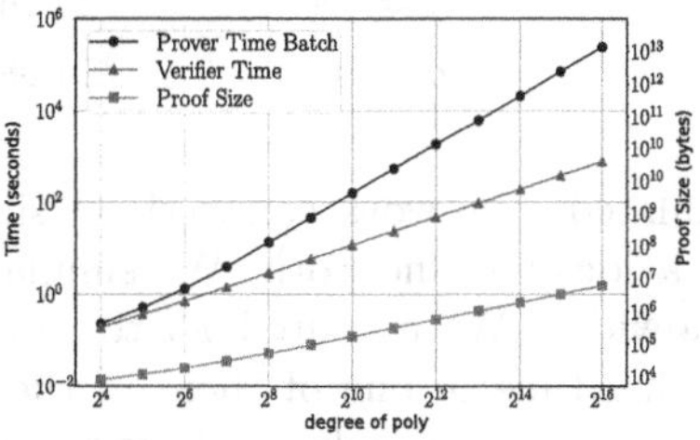

Fig. 9. Performance of multiple evaluations of our encrypted polynomial commitment with point hiding. $m = d$.

Multiple Evaluations. The major advantage of our scheme is the batched proofs for multiple evaluations and we further present the performance of evaluating multiple points in Fig. 9. In the figure, we set the number of evaluations the same as the degree of the polynomial, but our implementation supports both a larger degree and a larger number of evaluations. As shown in the figure, the prover time grows quadratically. It takes 0.225 s to generate a proof for $m = d = 2^4$ and 242,395 s for $m = d = 2^{16}$.

The proof size and the verifier time are particularly good for multiple evaluations. The proof size is only 7.9 KB for $m = d = 2^4$ evaluations and 6.1 MB for $m = d = 2^{16}$ evaluations, which is significantly smaller than repeating the single evaluation protocol the same number of times. The experimental result matches the logarithmic complexity in d and the linear complexity in m.

The verifier time only grows quasi-linearly now. It only takes 757s to verify 2^{16} proofs of evaluations of a degree-2^{16} polynomial, which is merely 14× larger than verifying a single proof. The experimental result justifies that the verifier time is amortized to $O(\log d)$ for multiple evaluations and is particularly efficient in our application of multiparty PSI.

5.2   Performance of Multi-party PSI

In this section, we report the performance of our multiparty PSI protocol with malicious security. We executed all parties on the single AWS instance and we

Table 6. Total running time of our multiparty PSI scheme in seconds.

# of elements m	2^8	2^{10}	2^{12}	2^{14}	2^{16}
Size of bin M	2^8	2^6	2^6	2^6	2^6
# of bins B	1	81	334	1,366	5,487
$n = 2$	13.94	130.01	536.1	2,192	8,264
$n = 8$	13.96	130.1	536.66	2,194	8,270
$n = 32$	13.97	130.4	538.4	2,199	8,292
$n = 128$	14.02	131.7	545.56	2,220	8,376
$n = 500$	14.26	136.4	562.76	2,301	8,712
$n = 1000$	14.58	142.9	589.5	2,410	9,141

simulated a network connection using the Linux tc command, communicating via a localhost network. We simulated a LAN setting with 10 Gbps network bandwidth. We executed P_2 to P_n on the same machine but only count the running time of one of them in the total time. This is to better simulate the scheme in practice where all the parties can run the computation simultaneously.

We tested our MPSI protocol for 2–1000 parties and 2^8–2^{16} elements per party (here we set $m_{max} = m_{min}$) and the total running time are shown in Table 6. We applied the hashing technique described in Sect. 3 and the parameters achieving 40-bit of statistical security are included in the table.

As shown in the table, our protocol is slow for a small number of parties where it takes 13.94 s to compute a two-party intersection with 2^8 elements per party. This is 55× slower than the malicious MPSI scheme based on symmetric key primitives from [9, Table 5]. The gap is even larger on larger sets, which is expected as our protocol relies on public-key primitives. However, our running time hardly grew with the number of parties where it still takes 14.02 s for 128 parties with 2^8 elements each, and 14.58 s for 1000 parties. This is because most of the running time is due to evaluating the aggregated polynomial and generating the proofs using our commitment scheme, which only depends on the maximum size of the set m_{max} and the size of P_1's set m_{min}. In contrast, the running time of PSimple [9] grows linearly with the number of parties and is 0.8 s for 32 parties with 2^8 elements each, which is 17× faster than ours. We expect that our protocol is faster than PSimple for 500 parties with 2^8 elements per party.

Our protocol is also efficient in communication. The total communication is shown in Fig. 10. As shown in the figure, the communication size for 2 parties with 2^8 elements per party is 279 KB, whereas the total communication for 1000 parties with 2^8 elements per party is 278MB, which is not the bottleneck of our protocol. Compared with [9], the communication size is 7.5MB for 2 parties and 7.5GB for 1000 parties respectively, which is around 27× larger than ours. The jump in Fig. 10 for $m = 2^{10}$ is due to using the hashing technique for $m \geq 2^{10}$.

We further show the breakdown of our total running time in Fig. 11. We fix the size of the set per party at 2^{12} and vary the number of parties from 2 to 1000.

As shown in the figure, our protocol is clearly computation-heavy and most of the time is on the evaluations of the aggregated polynomial, the proof generation and the verification of our private polynomial commitment. Even with 1000 parties, they contribute to 97.5% of the total running time. Due to this observation, we could improve the total running time significantly through parallelization. Both the polynomial evaluations and the private polynomial commitment are trivially parallelizable. Moreover, the total running time of our scheme is not sensitive to the bandwidth of the network. On a WAN network with 100Mbps bandwidth, our scheme would become around two times slower for 1000 parties. By contrast, the performance of symmetric-key-based schemes such as PSimple is limited by the communication overhead. It cannot be improved through parallelization and will become worse on a network with lower bandwidth.

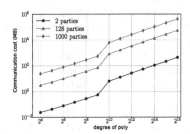

Fig. 10. Communication of our multiparty PSI protocol.

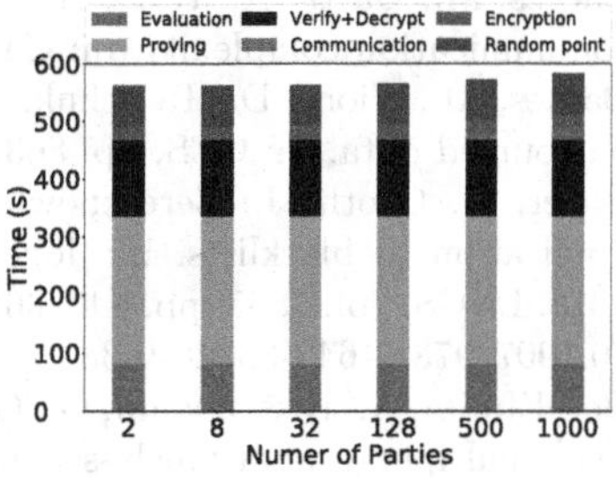

Fig. 11. Breakdown of the running time in our multiparty PSI protocol. $m = 2^{12}$ elements per party.

Finally, another major advantage of our protocol is memory usage and scalability. As the memory usage of P_1 is only $O(m_{max})$, we are able to scale up to 1000 parties and 2^{16} elements per party. The memory usage of P_1 on this largest instance is only 1GB. We did not test more elements per party due to the long running time, but not have high memory usage. To compare, the PSimple scheme [9] runs out of memory for 12 parties and 2^{20} elements per party. This is because P_1 has to store random OTs for the garbled bloom filter with each party, which leads to a high overhead on the memory.

Overall, the experimental results show that our scheme has good scalability and communication in practice, and is particularly efficient for applications with a large number of parties or limited bandwidth networks.

Acknowledgements. We thank the anonymous PKC'23 reviewers for their helpful comments. The first and second authors are supported by ISF grant No. 1316/18. The second, third and fifth authors are supported by DARPA under Contract No. HR001120C0087. The third author was supported by Technology and Humanity Fund from Georgetown University's McCourt School of Public Policy. Any opinions, findings and conclusions or recommendations expressed in this material are those of the author(s) and do not necessarily reflect the views of the United States Government or DARPA.

References

1. Ate pairing. https://github.com/herumi/ate-pairing
2. The GNU multiple precision arithmetic library. https://gmplib.org/
3. Abascal, J., Sereshgi, M.H.F., Hazay, C., Ishai, Y., Venkitasubramaniam, M.: Is the classical GMW paradigm practical? the case of non-interactive actively secure 2pc. In: CCS, pp. 1591–1605 (2020)
4. Abe, M., Fuchsbauer, G., Groth, J., Haralambiev, K., Ohkubo, M.: Structure-preserving signatures and commitments to group elements. J. Cryptol. **29**, 363–421 (2016)
5. Afshar, A., Mohassel, P., Pinkas, B., Riva, B.: Non-interactive secure computation based on cut-and-choose. In: Nguyen, P.Q., Oswald, E. (eds.) EUROCRYPT 2014. LNCS, vol. 8441, pp. 387–404. Springer, Heidelberg (2014). https://doi.org/10.1007/978-3-642-55220-5_22
6. Backes, M., Datta, A., Kate, A.: Asynchronous computational VSS with reduced communication complexity. In: CT-RSA, vol. 7779, pp. 259–276 (2013)
7. Backes, M., Fiore, D., Reischuk, R.M.: Verifiable delegation of computation on outsourced data. In: CCS, pp. 863–874 (2013)
8. Bayer, S., Groth, J.: Zero-knowledge argument for polynomial evaluation with application to blacklists. In: Johansson, T., Nguyen, P.Q. (eds.) EUROCRYPT 2013. LNCS, vol. 7881, pp. 646–663. Springer, Heidelberg (2013). https://doi.org/10.1007/978-3-642-38348-9_38
9. Ben-Efraim, A., Nissenbaum, O., Omri, E., Paskin-Cherniavsky, A.: Psimple: practical multiparty maliciously-secure private set intersection. In: ASIA CCS, pp. 1098–1112 (2022)
10. Benabbas, S., Gennaro, R., Vahlis, Y.: Verifiable delegation of computation over large datasets. In: Rogaway, P. (ed.) CRYPTO 2011. LNCS, vol. 6841, pp. 111–131. Springer, Heidelberg (2011). https://doi.org/10.1007/978-3-642-22792-9_7
11. Bhadauria, R., Hazay, C.: Multi-clients verifiable computation via conditional disclosure of secrets. In: SCN, pp. 150–171 (2020)
12. Bois, A., Cascudo, I., Fiore, D., Kim, D.: Flexible and efficient verifiable computation on encrypted data. In: Garay, J.A. (ed.) PKC 2021. LNCS, vol. 12711, pp. 528–558. Springer, Cham (2021). https://doi.org/10.1007/978-3-030-75248-4_19
13. Boneh, D., Boyen, X., Shacham, H.: Short group signatures. In: Franklin, M. (ed.) CRYPTO 2004. LNCS, vol. 3152, pp. 41–55. Springer, Heidelberg (2004). https://doi.org/10.1007/978-3-540-28628-8_3
14. Bünz, B., Bootle, J., Boneh, D., Poelstra, A., Wuille, P., Maxwell, G.: Bulletproofs: short proofs for confidential transactions and more. In: IEEE S&P, pp. 315–334 (2018)
15. Bünz, B., Fisch, B., Szepieniec, A.: Transparent SNARKs from DARK compilers. In: Canteaut, A., Ishai, Y. (eds.) EUROCRYPT 2020. LNCS, vol. 12105, pp. 677–706. Springer, Cham (2020). https://doi.org/10.1007/978-3-030-45721-1_24
16. Bünz, B., Maller, M., Mishra, P., Tyagi, N., Vesely, P.: Proofs for inner pairing products and applications. In: Tibouchi, M., Wang, H. (eds.) ASIACRYPT 2021. LNCS, vol. 13092, pp. 65–97. Springer, Cham (2021). https://doi.org/10.1007/978-3-030-92078-4_3
17. Camenisch, J., Dubovitskaya, M., Haralambiev, K., Kohlweiss, M.: Composable and modular anonymous credentials: definitions and practical constructions. In: Iwata, T., Cheon, J.H. (eds.) ASIACRYPT 2015. LNCS, vol. 9453, pp. 262–288. Springer, Heidelberg (2015). https://doi.org/10.1007/978-3-662-48800-3_11

18. Catalano, D., Fiore, D.: Vector commitments and their applications. In: Kurosawa, K., Hanaoka, G. (eds.) PKC 2013. LNCS, vol. 7778, pp. 55–72. Springer, Heidelberg (2013). https://doi.org/10.1007/978-3-642-36362-7_5

19. Catalano, D., Fiore, D., Gennaro, R., Vamvourellis, K.: Algebraic (Trapdoor) one-way functions and their applications. In: Sahai, A. (ed.) TCC 2013. LNCS, vol. 7785, pp. 680–699. Springer, Heidelberg (2013). https://doi.org/10.1007/978-3-642-36594-2_38

20. Catalano, D., Fiore, D., Warinschi, B.: Homomorphic signatures with efficient verification for polynomial functions. In: Garay, J.A., Gennaro, R. (eds.) CRYPTO 2014. LNCS, vol. 8616, pp. 371–389. Springer, Heidelberg (2014). https://doi.org/10.1007/978-3-662-44371-2_21

21. Chase, M., Miao, P.: Private set intersection in the internet setting from lightweight oblivious PRF. In: Micciancio, D., Ristenpart, T. (eds.) CRYPTO 2020. LNCS, vol. 12172, pp. 34–63. Springer, Cham (2020). https://doi.org/10.1007/978-3-030-56877-1_2

22. Chepurnoy, A., Papamanthou, C., Zhang, Y.: Edrax: a cryptocurrency with stateless transaction validation. IACR Cryptol. ePrint Arch., p. 968 (2018)

23. Chiesa, A., Hu, Y., Maller, M., Mishra, P., Vesely, N., Ward, N.: Marlin: preprocessing zkSNARKs with universal and updatable SRS. In: Canteaut, A., Ishai, Y. (eds.) EUROCRYPT 2020. LNCS, vol. 12105, pp. 738–768. Springer, Cham (2020). https://doi.org/10.1007/978-3-030-45721-1_26

24. Choi, S.G., Katz, J., Kumaresan, R., Cid, C.: Multi-client non-interactive verifiable computation. In: Sahai, A. (ed.) TCC 2013. LNCS, vol. 7785, pp. 499–518. Springer, Heidelberg (2013). https://doi.org/10.1007/978-3-642-36594-2_28

25. De Cristofaro, E., Kim, J., Tsudik, G.: Linear-complexity private set intersection protocols secure in malicious model. In: Abe, M. (ed.) ASIACRYPT 2010. LNCS, vol. 6477, pp. 213–231. Springer, Heidelberg (2010). https://doi.org/10.1007/978-3-642-17373-8_13

26. Fenske, E., Mani, A., Johnson, A., Sherr, M.: Distributed measurement with private set-union cardinality. In: CCS, pp. 2295–2312 (2017)

27. Fiore, D., Gennaro, R.: Publicly verifiable delegation of large polynomials and matrix computations, with applications. In: CCS, pp. 501–512 (2012)

28. Fiore, D., Gennaro, R., Pastro, V.: Efficiently encrypted data. In: ACM SIGSAC, pp. 844–855 (2014)

29. Fiore, D., Nitulescu, A., Pointcheval, D.: Boosting verifiable computation on encrypted data. In: Kiayias, A., Kohlweiss, M., Wallden, P., Zikas, V. (eds.) PKC 2020. LNCS, vol. 12111, pp. 124–154. Springer, Cham (2020). https://doi.org/10.1007/978-3-030-45388-6_5

30. Freedman, M.J., Ishai, Y., Pinkas, B., Reingold, O.: Keyword search and oblivious pseudorandom functions. In: Kilian, J. (ed.) TCC 2005. LNCS, vol. 3378, pp. 303–324. Springer, Heidelberg (2005). https://doi.org/10.1007/978-3-540-30576-7_17

31. Freedman, M.J., Nissim, K., Pinkas, B.: Efficient private matching and set intersection. In: Cachin, C., Camenisch, J.L. (eds.) EUROCRYPT 2004. LNCS, vol. 3027, pp. 1–19. Springer, Heidelberg (2004). https://doi.org/10.1007/978-3-540-24676-3_1

32. Gabizon, A., Williamson, Z.J., Ciobotaru, O.: Plonk: permutations over lagrange-bases for oecumenical noninteractive arguments of knowledge. IACR Cryptol. ePrint Arch. **2019**, 953 (2019)

33. Garimella, G., Pinkas, B., Rosulek, M., Trieu, N., Yanai, A.: Oblivious key-value stores and amplification for private set intersection. In: Malkin, T., Peikert, C. (eds.) CRYPTO 2021. LNCS, vol. 12826, pp. 395–425. Springer, Cham (2021). https://doi.org/10.1007/978-3-030-84245-1_14

34. Gennaro, R., Gentry, C., Parno, B.: Non-interactive verifiable computing: outsourcing computation to untrusted workers. In: Rabin, T. (ed.) CRYPTO 2010. LNCS, vol. 6223, pp. 465–482. Springer, Heidelberg (2010). https://doi.org/10.1007/978-3-642-14623-7_25

35. Ghosh, S., Nielsen, J.B., Nilges, T.: Maliciously secure oblivious linear function evaluation with constant overhead. In: Takagi, T., Peyrin, T. (eds.) ASIACRYPT 2017. LNCS, vol. 10624, pp. 629–659. Springer, Cham (2017). https://doi.org/10.1007/978-3-319-70694-8_22

36. Goldwasser, S., Kalai, Y.T., Popa, R.A., Vaikuntanathan, V., Zeldovich, N.: How to run turing machines on encrypted data. In: Canetti, R., Garay, J.A. (eds.) CRYPTO 2013. LNCS, vol. 8043, pp. 536–553. Springer, Heidelberg (2013). https://doi.org/10.1007/978-3-642-40084-1_30

37. Gorbunov, S., Reyzin, L., Wee, H., Zhang, Z.: Pointproofs: aggregating proofs for multiple vector commitments. In: ACM SIGSAC, pp. 2007–2023 (2020)

38. Gordon, S.D., Hazay, C., Le, P.H.: Fully secure PSI via mpc-in-the-head. PoPETS 2022(3), 291–313 (2022)

39. Gordon, S.D., Katz, J., Liu, F.-H., Shi, E., Zhou, H.-S.: Multi-Client verifiable computation with stronger security guarantees. In: Dodis, Y., Nielsen, J.B. (eds.) TCC 2015. LNCS, vol. 9015, pp. 144–168. Springer, Heidelberg (2015). https://doi.org/10.1007/978-3-662-46497-7_6

40. Hazay, C.: Oblivious polynomial evaluation and secure set-intersection from algebraic PRFs. In: Dodis, Y., Nielsen, J.B. (eds.) TCC 2015. LNCS, vol. 9015, pp. 90–120. Springer, Heidelberg (2015). https://doi.org/10.1007/978-3-662-46497-7_4

41. Hazay, C., Ishai, Y., Venkitasubramaniam, M.: Actively secure garbled circuits with constant communication overhead in the plain model. In: Kalai, Y., Reyzin, L. (eds.) TCC 2017. LNCS, vol. 10678, pp. 3–39. Springer, Cham (2017). https://doi.org/10.1007/978-3-319-70503-3_1

42. Hazay, C., Lindell, Y.: Efficient oblivious polynomial evaluation with simulation-based security. IACR Cryptol. ePrint Arch., p. 459 (2009)

43. Hazay, C., Venkitasubramaniam, M.: Scalable multi-party private set-intersection. In: Fehr, S. (ed.) PKC 2017. LNCS, vol. 10174, pp. 175–203. Springer, Heidelberg (2017). https://doi.org/10.1007/978-3-662-54365-8_8

44. Ishai, Y., Kushilevitz, E., Ostrovsky, R., Prabhakaran, M., Sahai, A.: Efficient non-interactive secure computation. In: Paterson, K.G. (ed.) EUROCRYPT 2011. LNCS, vol. 6632, pp. 406–425. Springer, Heidelberg (2011). https://doi.org/10.1007/978-3-642-20465-4_23

45. Juels, A., Jr., B.S.K.: Pors: proofs of retrievability for large files. In: CCS, pp. 584–597 (2007)

46. Kate, A., Zaverucha, G.M., Goldberg, I.: Constant-size commitments to polynomials and their applications. In: Abe, M. (ed.) ASIACRYPT 2010. LNCS, vol. 6477, pp. 177–194. Springer, Heidelberg (2010). https://doi.org/10.1007/978-3-642-17373-8_11

47. Lee, J.: Dory: efficient, transparent arguments for generalised inner products and polynomial commitments. IACR Cryptol. ePrint Arch. 2020, 1274 (2020)

48. Mohassel, P., Rosulek, M.: Non-interactive secure 2PC in the offline/online and batch settings. In: Coron, J.-S., Nielsen, J.B. (eds.) EUROCRYPT 2017. LNCS, vol. 10212, pp. 425–455. Springer, Cham (2017). https://doi.org/10.1007/978-3-319-56617-7_15

49. Naor, M., Pinkas, B.: Oblivious polynomial evaluation. SIAM J. Comput. 35, 1254–1281 (2006)

50. Nguyen, D.T., Trieu, N.: Mpccache: privacy-preserving multi-party cooperative cache sharing at the edge. IACR Cryptol. ePrint Arch. (2021). https://eprint.iacr.org/2021/317
51. Papamanthou, C., Shi, E., Tamassia, R.: Signatures of correct computation. In: Sahai, A. (ed.) TCC 2013. LNCS, vol. 7785, pp. 222–242. Springer, Heidelberg (2013). https://doi.org/10.1007/978-3-642-36594-2_13
52. Pedersen, T.P.: Non-interactive and information-theoretic secure verifiable secret sharing. In: Feigenbaum, J. (ed.) CRYPTO 1991. LNCS, vol. 576, pp. 129–140. Springer, Heidelberg (1992). https://doi.org/10.1007/3-540-46766-1_9
53. Pinkas, B., Rosulek, M., Trieu, N., Yanai, A.: SpOT-light: lightweight private set intersection from sparse OT extension. In: Boldyreva, A., Micciancio, D. (eds.) CRYPTO 2019. LNCS, vol. 11694, pp. 401–431. Springer, Cham (2019). https://doi.org/10.1007/978-3-030-26954-8_13
54. Pinkas, B., Rosulek, M., Trieu, N., Yanai, A.: PSI from PaXoS: fast, malicious private set intersection. In: Canteaut, A., Ishai, Y. (eds.) EUROCRYPT 2020. LNCS, vol. 12106, pp. 739–767. Springer, Cham (2020). https://doi.org/10.1007/978-3-030-45724-2_25
55. Pinkas, B., Schneider, T., Tkachenko, O., Yanai, A.: Efficient circuit-based PSI with linear communication. In: Ishai, Y., Rijmen, V. (eds.) EUROCRYPT 2019. LNCS, vol. 11478, pp. 122–153. Springer, Cham (2019). https://doi.org/10.1007/978-3-030-17659-4_5
56. Raab, M., Steger, A.: "balls into bins" - a simple and tight analysis. In: Randomization and Approximation Techniques in Computer Science, pp. 159–170 (1998)
57. Rosulek, M., Trieu, N.: Compact and malicious private set intersection for small sets. IACR Cryptol. ePrint Arch., p. 1159 (2021)
58. Schnorr, C.P.: Efficient signature generation by smart cards. J. Cryptol. 4(3), 161–174 (1991). https://doi.org/10.1007/BF00196725
59. Setty, S.: Spartan: efficient and general-purpose zkSNARKs without trusted setup. In: Micciancio, D., Ristenpart, T. (eds.) CRYPTO 2020. LNCS, vol. 12172, pp. 704–737. Springer, Cham (2020). https://doi.org/10.1007/978-3-030-56877-1_25
60. Tomescu, A., et al.: Towards scalable threshold cryptosystems. In: IEEE S&P, pp. 877–893 (2020)
61. Vlasov, A., Panarin, K.: Transparent polynomial commitment scheme with polylogarithmic communication complexity. IACR Cryptol. ePrint Arch. 2019, 1020 (2019)
62. Wahby, R.S., Tzialla, I., Shelat, A., Thaler, J., Walfish, M.: Doubly-efficient zkSNARKs without trusted setup. In: IEEE S&P, pp. 926–943 (2018)
63. Wails, R., Johnson, A., Starin, D., Yerukhimovich, A., Gordon, S.D.: Stormy: statistics in tor by measuring securely. In: CCS, pp. 615–632 (2019)
64. Wieder, U.: Balanced allocations with heterogenous bins. In: SPAA, pp. 188–193 (2007)
65. Xie, T., Zhang, J., Zhang, Y., Papamanthou, C., Song, D.: Libra: succinct zero-knowledge proofs with optimal prover computation. In: Boldyreva, A., Micciancio, D. (eds.) CRYPTO 2019. LNCS, vol. 11694, pp. 733–764. Springer, Cham (2019). https://doi.org/10.1007/978-3-030-26954-8_24
66. Yuan, J., Yu, S.: Proofs of retrievability with public verifiability and constant communication cost in cloud. In: SCC@ASIACCS, pp. 19–26. ACM (2013)
67. Zhang, J., Xie, T., Zhang, Y., Song, D.: Transparent polynomial delegation and its applications to zero knowledge proof. In: IEEE S&P (2020)

68. Zhang, Y., Genkin, D., Katz, J., Papadopoulos, D., Papamanthou, C.: VSQL: verifying arbitrary SQL queries over dynamic outsourced databases. In: IEEE S&P, pp. 863–880 (2017)

69. Zhang, Y., Genkin, D., Katz, J., Papadopoulos, D., Papamanthou, C.: A zero-knowledge version of VSQL. IACR Cryptol. ePrint Arch. **2017**, 1146 (2017)

Credibility in Private Set Membership

Sanjam Garg[1,2], Mohammad Hajiabadi[3], Abhishek Jain[4], Zhengzhong Jin[5],
Omkant Pandey[6], and Sina Shiehian[7(✉)]

[1] University of California, Berkeley, USA
[2] NTT Research, Sunnyvale, USA
[3] University of Waterloo, Waterloo, Canada
[4] Johns Hopkins University, Baltimore, USA
[5] MIT, Cambridge, USA
[6] Stony Brook University, Stony Brook, USA
[7] Snap Inc., Santa Monica, USA
shiayan@umich.edu

Abstract. A private set membership (PSM) protocol allows a "receiver" to learn whether its input x is contained in a large database DB held by a "sender". In this work, we define and construct *credible private set membership (C-PSM)* protocols: in addition to the conventional notions of privacy, C-PSM provides a soundness guarantee that it is hard for a sender (that does not know x) to convince the receiver that $x \in$ DB. Furthermore, the communication complexity must be logarithmic in the size of DB.

We provide 2-round (i.e., round-optimal) C-PSM constructions based on standard assumptions:

- We present a black-box construction in the plain model based on DDH or LWE.
- Next, we consider protocols that support predicates f beyond string equality, i.e., the receiver can learn if there exists $w \in$ DB such that $f(x, w) = 1$. We present two results with transparent setups: (1) A black-box protocol, based on DDH or LWE, for the class of NC^1 functions f which are efficiently searchable. (2) An LWE-based construction for all bounded-depth circuits. The only non-black-box use of cryptography in this construction is through the bootstrapping procedure in fully homomorphic encryption.

As an application, our protocols can be used to build enhanced round-optimal leaked password notification services, where unlike existing solutions, a dubious sender *cannot* fool a receiver into changing its password.

1 Introduction

A two-party private set membership (PSM) protocol is an interactive protocol between a receiver holding an input x and a sender holding a database DB. The goal is that at the end of the interaction, the receiver only learns whether $x \in$ DB while the sender learns nothing about x. Similar to private information retrieval [8], a desirable feature for PSM is efficiency of the receiver, which states

© International Association for Cryptologic Research 2023
A. Boldyreva and V. Kolesnikov (Eds.): PKC 2023, LNCS 13941, pp. 159–189, 2023.
https://doi.org/10.1007/978-3-031-31371-4_6

that the communication complexity and also the computational complexity of the receiver is sublinear (or more preferably logarithmic) in the size of DB. PSM and its closely related variant private set intersection (PSI) have found numerous applications such as contact discovery [17] and exposed password notification [2, 11,16].

In the exposed password notification use-case, a user and a service provider run a PSM protocol to determine whether the user's password is exposed in any leaked database. An often neglected aspect in this setting is whether the protocol provides a *credible* guarantee to the user that its password was actually leaked. In fact, a dubious sender might potentially keep falsely suggesting to the user that its password was exposed, causing the user to go through the process of updating its password.

A potential approach to enforce credibility might be requiring the sender to send its whole database in an encrypted format. It is plausible that such an approach, specially when implemented through protocols based on oblivious pseudorandom functions (OPRF) [2,11], can provide credibility. However, sending the whole database would obviously make the protocol's communication and the receiver's computational complexity linear in the size of the database, and thus violates efficiency. Another approach may be using generic cryptographic succinct zero-knowledge arguments of knowledge. Such solutions incur an unsatisfactory computational overhead due to the use of *non-black-box* techniques. Therefore, we ask

Can we construct asymptotically efficient black-box credible PSM protocols?

1.1   Our Contributions

Defining C-PSM. In this work we initiate the study of *credibility* in PSM protocols. We define the notion of *credible private set membership* (C-PSM). Informally, a C-PSM for a relation $\mathcal{R}$ is a two party protocol between a receiver and a sender where both the receiver and the sender have access to a common reference string (CRS). The receiver has an input x and the sender has a large database DB. The sender wants to convince the receiver that the database contains a witness w such that $(x, w) \in \mathcal{R}$. We require the following properties:

– The protocol consists of only two rounds.
– The communication and also the receiver's computational complexity is at most logarithmic in the size of DB.
– The receiver's input x remains hidden from the sender.
– The sender's database remains private, i.e., a (malicious) receiver does not learn anything more than the fact that the database contains a valid witness.
– The protocol is sound, i.e., if the sender does not have a witness in the database, then, it is computationally hard for it to make the receiver accept.

We focus on black-box protocols, i.e., protocols which only make black-box use of their underlying cryptographic tools. For the soundness property to be meaningful and achievable in 2 rounds, we require the input x to have high entropy. Otherwise, if x is predictable, the sender can always include a valid witness for x in its database and convince the receiver. For the same reason we consider relations $\mathcal{R}$ which are *instance entropic*. Roughly speaking, this means that any witness only satisfies a negligible fraction of instances. For example, the string equality relation is instance entropic.

C-PSM for String Equality. We start by considering the basic string equality relation, where the receiver wants to check if $x \in \mathsf{DB}$. For this relation we construct a black-box 2-round C-PSM protocol in the plain model from either of the DDH or LWE assumption.

Theorem 1 (Informal). *Assuming the hardness of either of DDH or LWE, there exists a black-box 2-round C-PSM protocol in the plain model for the string equality relation.*

C-PSM for Efficiently Searchable Relations. We then turn to instance entropic relations beyond string equality. Specifically, we will consider the scenario where for some function f, the receiver wants to check whether DB contains c entries $w_1, \cdots, w_c$ such that $f(x, \{w_i\}_{i \in [c]}) = 1$. We first consider the class of *efficiently searchable* functions, i.e., functions which are in NC^1, and, for any input x, searching DB for witnesses can be implemented by a branching program of length logarithmic in DB. We construct a fully black-box 2-round C-PSM protocol for the class of *efficiently searchable* functions assuming either of DDH or LWE.

Theorem 2 (Informal). *Assuming the hardness of either of DDH or LWE, for every searchable function there exists a black-box 2-round C-PSM protocol with transparent setup.*

Next, we construct a C-PSM from LWE which is not restricted to efficiently searchable functions and supports all bounded-depth circuits. While this construction is not fully black-box, however, its non-black-use of cryptography is limited to the bootstrapping procedure in its underlying homomorphic encryption.

Theorem 3 (Informal). *Assuming the hardness of LWE, there exists a 2-round C-PSM protocol with transparent setup for every (bounded-depth) circuit. The only non-black-box use of cryptography in this C-PSM protocol is through bootstrapping in homomorphic encryption.*

We mention that all of our C-PSM protocols satisfy *statistical sender privacy*. This means that, our constructions guarantee the privacy of the sender even against computationally unbounded malicious receivers. Additionally, in our constructions which need a setup, receiver privacy is guaranteed even if the CRS is maliciously generated.

Applications. Our construction for string equality immediately gives a credible protocol for password exposure notification. In fact, since the C-PSM protocol in this construction only consists of two rounds, the receiver can publish its first message and wait for senders to inform him/her of a password exposure via C-PSM second message.

With our black-box construction for efficiently searchable relations, we can have protocols that perform more complicated tasks. For instance, consider a situation where the sender's database consists of pairs of usernames and candidate passwords. A receiver wants to learn whether the database has an entry consisting of its username paired with a closely matching password (closely matching can for example mean having an edit distance no bigger than half the length of the password). We observe that our black-box construction supports this functionality. This is because given a username and password pair, the following branching program whose length is logarithmic in the size of the database can implement the corresponding search functionality:

1. First, search the database for an entry with a matching username. Note that this step can be implemented by a logarithmic length branching program through using the trie data structure.
2. Next, given an entry with a matching username, check whether the candidate password in the entry closely matches the input password. This step is independent of the size of the database and can be implemented by an NC^1 circuit, and consequently by a polynomial sized branching program.

1.2   Related Work

The notion of zero-knowledge sets [19] allows a sender to convince a receiver whether an element exist in its database or not by sending a short proof. Our work differs from zero-knowledge sets in two aspects. First, we consider 2-round protocols whereas zero-knowledge sets consist of protocols having 3 rounds, where, in the first round the sender commits to its database and publishes a digest of this commitments. Second, there is no receiver privacy in zero-knowledge sets, i.e., the receiver sends its input in the clear.

A line of work [6,7,9] constructed concretely efficient *unbalanced* PSI protocols, i.e., PSI protocols where the sender's set is considerably larger than the receiver's set, from FHE. The PSI protocols constructed in these works provide sender privacy, receiver privacy and and communication sub-linear in the size of the sender's set. While exposed password notification seems to be one of the main applications of the PSI protocols constructed in these works, however, they do not provide credibility. In fact [6] considers a heuristic approach to make it more difficult for a dubious sender to cheat. Roughly speaking, the proposal in [6] requires a sender to include the hash of the receiver's input in the FHE ciphertext that it outputs. Then, it sets the FHE parameters such that it does not support computing this hash function. Our construction for string equality in Sect. 4 can be seen as a dual of this idea, where, we use the output of a one-way function as the input and treat the original input as the *label*. Unlike [6], we are able to formally prove the credibility of our construction.

Another work [15] considers oblivious polynomial evaluation (OPE). In this setting, the receiver wants to learn the image of its private input under a secret high-degree polynomial that is held by the sender. Notice that an instance of PSM can be converted into an instance of OPE where the degree of the polynomial is equal to the size of the database. The protocol in [15] provides receiver privacy, sender privacy and communication sub-linear in the degree of the polynomial. Additionally, this construction ensures that the evaluated value that receiver obtains truly corresponds to the polynomial that is held by the sender. While the latter property can be viewed as credibility, however, the way [15] enforces this property is by requiring the sender to send a commitment to its polynomial to the receiver. Consequently, this protocol needs three rounds.

1.3 Techniques

C-PSM for String Equality. We start by providing an overview of our C-PSM construction for the basic string equality functionality. Since we are aiming to keep the receiver's complexity independent of the size of the database, it is natural to consider using homomorphic encryption (HE). However, a naive scheme where the receiver sends its input x encrypted under FHE, and the sender homomorphically searches its database, does not satisfy the properties of C-PSM:

- First and foremost, this construction is not credible because the sender can simply send a homomorphically encrypted positive answer regardless of its database.
- Furthermore, this construction does not provide sender privacy because homomorphic evaluation might reveal extra information about the sender's database.

Our insight to solve the first issue is noticing that the receiver's input has high entropy and therefore it is hard to invert its image under a one-way function. Specifically, the receiver, instead of sending an encryption of its input, sends an encryption of the image $y = f(x)$ of its input under a one-way function f. The sender computes the images of all entries in its database under f and proceeds to homomorphically search these images for y. If found, the sender can homomorphically include the pre-image x in the ciphertext it sends to the receiver.

To add sender privacy, we will use a homomorphic encryption scheme with a property known in the literature as *malicious function privacy* [21]. Informally, this notion states that the evaluated ciphertexts reveal nothing beyond the value they are encrypting, and in particular they hide the function that was homomorphically evaluated. While the malicious function private HE construction in [21] makes extensive non-black-box use of cryptography, however, fortunately, we can instantiate the OT-based black-box HE construction in [14] with the recent rate-1 statistical sender private OT [1], which can be based on either LWE or DDH, to get a black-box malicious function private HE for branching programs.

Beyond String Equality. We now describe how we build a C-PSM supporting predicates beyond string equality. For the ease of exposition, we present a 4-round protocol and then briefly sketch how we compress it to 2 rounds. Recall that in this setting, the receiver holds an input x and the sender wants to convince the receiver that its database contains a witness w such that $f(x, w) = 1$ for a specific predicate f. Our starting idea is to use homomorphic encryption for encrypting the receiver's input, a black-box commit-and-prove system for committing to the sender's database and generating zero-knowledge proofs, and Merkle trees [18] for creating a digest of this database. In more detail, similar to the string quality construction, the receiver encrypts its input under HE and sends the ciphertext to the sender. The sender then works as follows:

- First, it commits to the database using the commit and prove system, i.e., it secret shares each entry in the database and commits to these shares.
- Next, it hashes these commitments using a Merkle tree.
- Then, it homomorphically searches the database to find a valid witness w along with a Merkle hash opening for its corresponding commitment (or $\perp$ if the database does not contain such a witness). Note that this does not involve any hash computations under the hood of HE. All hashes can be computed "outside," and then moved to under the hood of HE.
- Next, the sender homomorphically generates the first prover message in the commit-and-prove system and sends it to the receiver.
- Finally, upon receiving a challenge from the receiver, the sender homomorphically opens a subset of the commitments produced in the first message and sends them to the receiver.

While this approach has succinct communication complexity, keeps the receiver's input private, and is black-box thanks to the MPC-in-the-head [13] paradigm, however, it fails to protect against a malicious sender. In fact, a malicious sender whose database does not contain a valid witness can homomorphically cook up a database containing a witness and proceed to deceive the receiver. A straightforward approach to provide security against malicious senders is to require the sender to attach (in plain) a succinct non-interactive argument of knowledge (SNARK), showing that the evaluated ciphertext is the result of an honest evaluation using an actual database known by the sender. However, in addition to relying on unfalsifiable assumptions, this approach results in a very prohibitive solution and involves expensive non-black-box use of cryptography. For string equality we were able to overcome this issue by using deterministic encryption, but for richer functionalities this idea does not seem to be applicable. In summary, with the goal of avoiding expensive cryptography, the main challenge we face is "how do we tie the hands of a malicious sender to prevent it from cooking up a database under the hood of homomorphic encryption?"

First Attempt: Attaching the Hash Root "Outside." Our first starting idea for tying the hands of the malicious sender is to have it send something "outside" the homomorphic encryption wrapper. The sender could cook up stuff under homomorphic encryption but cannot do so outside! The receiver could then compare the information obtained under the hood of HE and check if it is consistent with the information provided "outside." The hope is that given that a malicious sender cannot cook up stuff depending on receiver's input "outside," consistency is only possible if a valid witness exists in the database.

In particular, if we require the sender to include the root of the Merkle tree *in clear*, then, the homomorphic database cooking up attack that we described in the previous paragraph does not seem to work. Intuitively, the hash root seems to *bind* the prover to a database in clear, and if this database (and consequently the hash root) depends on the receiver's input, then, a cheating prover has to somehow break the security of HE.

However, unfortunately, it is unclear how to prove security of this strategy. In other words, it is unclear how we could reduce the ability of the sender to break soundness to breaking the security of HE or the Merkle hash. A key issue is that the hash root does not have any *extractable information* to help with breaking the security of HE.

Using SSB Hashing to Make a Random Point Extractable. In order to fix the above issue, while avoiding expensive tools, we try for a very simple approach. In particular, we replace the generic Merkle Hash with a somewhere statistically binding (SSB) hash [12]. At a high level, SSB hash is a Merkle tree with an additional binding property. In more detail, in a SSB hash, the hashing key can be generated for binding to a specific position i in the input. The guarantee is that, the hash root now *statistically binds* to commitments to the value of the database at position i, which remains computationally hidden by the *index hiding* property. We assume a stronger *extractability* guarantee from our SSB hash. Namely, we assume that it is possible to *extract* the ith value given only the hash root and a *extraction trapdoor* which is generated along with the hashing key. Fortunately, these objects can be built based on any rate-1 OT using previous known techniques [12,20].

Somewhat surprising, though with a subtle argument, this simple change allows us to reduce a malicious sender's ability to cheat to break the security of HE or violate the index-hiding property of the SSB hash. We now sketch how using extractable SSB hashing we can reduce the security of HE to the soundness of C-PSM. Our reduction simply generates a SSB hash key binding to a *uniformally random* position and puts it in the CRS. First, observe that the index hiding property of SSB hash ensures that, during the execution, with noticeable probability, this random position is the same position that the cheating sender opens under the hood of HE. Clearly, if the adversary can somehow always avoid the random position encoded in the SSB hash key then that adversary can be used to break the index hiding property of SSB with probability better than a random guess. In the final step, we show a reduction that uses the value extracted from the SSB hash root — which from the prior step we know is correlated with the encrypted value under HE with a small probability — to directly break the security of HE.

Instantiating HE. Similar to our construction for string equality, we can use the malicious circuit private HE for branching programs that can be instantiated by combining [1] and [14]. For achieving compact communication complexity when using this instantiation of HE, searching the database for a witness should be implementable with a branching program whose length is logarithmic in the size of the database. That is, the predicate should be *efficiently searchable*. This is because in the [14] HE construction, the size of evaluated ciphertexts grow linearly in the length of the evaluated branching programs.

Another option is to use the LWE-based malicious circuit private HE in [10]. With this HE, our C-PSM construction can support every instance entropic predicate that can be implemented by a (bounded-depth) circuit. However, the HE in [10] is not fully black-box as it performs bootstrapping for every evaluation.

Black-Box Commitment Generation. A delicate issue is that, the sender algorithm, as currently described, would be non-black-box, because, generating the first prover message for the commit-and-prove system involves generating new commitments. We avoid this non-black-box step via the following trick: the sender generates many fresh commitments to 0 and 1 in the clear and then, obliviously brings these fresh commitments under HE based on the message the prover commits to.

4-Round to 2-Round. Finally, we describe how to compress the described 4-round C-PSM to a 2-round protocol. To do this, the receiver sends its challenge via OT in the first round. In the second round, the sender prepares a C-PSM sender's message for each possible challenge and sends them to the receiver through OT response.

2   Preliminaries

We denote the security parameter by λ. For any $\ell \in \mathbb{N}$, we denote the set of the first ℓ positive integers by $[\ell]$. For a set S, $x \leftarrow S$ denotes sampling a uniformly random element x from S. For a distribution D, $x \leftarrow D$ denotes sampling an element x from D.

2.1   Oblivious Transfer

We review the definition of rate-1 statistical sender private oblivious transfer.

Definition 1 (Rate-1 Statistical Sender Private Oblivious Transfer).
A (string) 1-out-of-2 OT consists of three algorithms: $(\mathsf{OT}_1, \mathsf{OT}_2, \mathsf{OT}_3)$.

- $\mathsf{OT}_1(1^\lambda, b)$, *on input a security parameter* $\lambda \in \mathbb{N}$ *and a choice bit* $b \in \{0, 1\}$, *outputs a protocol message* ot_1 *and a state* st.
- $\mathsf{OT}_2(ot_1, (m_0, m_1))$, *on input* ot_1, *and two sender inputs* (m_0, m_1) *of the same length, outputs a response* ot_2.

- $OT_3(st, ot_2)$, *on input a state st and ot_2, outputs a message m.*

  We require the following properties:

1. Correctness, *for all security parameters λ, bits $b \in \{0,1\}$, and sender inputs $m_0, m_1 \in \{0,1\}^*$:*

$$\Pr\left[y = m_b \,\middle|\, \begin{array}{l}(ot_1, st) \leftarrow OT_1(1^\lambda, b) \\ ot_2 \leftarrow OT_2(ot_1, (m_0, m_1)) \\ y \leftarrow OT_3(st, ot_2)\end{array}\right] = 1.$$

2. Receiver Security, $ot \overset{c}{\approx} ot'$, *where* $(ot, *) \leftarrow OT_1(1^\lambda, 0)$ *and* $(ot', *) \leftarrow OT_1(1^\lambda, 1)$.

3. Statistical Sender Privacy, *there exists an unbounded simulator S such that for all (not necessarily honestly generated) ot_1 there exists a bit b, such that for all sender inputs $m_0, m_1 \in \{0,1\}^*$:*

$$OT_2(ot_1, (m_0, m_1)) \overset{s}{\approx} Sim(1^\lambda, ot_1, m_b).$$

4. Rate-1*: There exists a fixed polynomial* poly *such that for all polynomials $n := n(\lambda)$, for all first-round messages ot_1 and for all $(m_0, m_1) \in \{0,1\}^n \times \{0,1\}^n$, $|ot_2| = n + poly(\lambda)$, where $ot_2 \leftarrow OT_2(ot_1, (m_0, m_1))$.*

Theorem 4 ([1])**.** *Assuming either DDH or LWE, there exists a black-box construction of rate-1 statistical sender private OT.*

We also consider the following dual-mode variation of OT. Notice that this variation is not rate-1.

Definition 2 (Dual-mode OT). *Let C be a constant. A 1-out-of-C dual mode OT is a tuple of algorithms* (Setup, FakeSetup, Extract, OT_1, OT_2, OT_3), *with the following syntax:*

- Setup(1^λ), *takes as input a security parameter, and outputs a crs.*
- FakeSetup(1^λ), *takes as input a security parameter, and outputs a crs_S and a trapdoor td that can be used to extract the sender's input.*
- Extract(td, ot_2), *takes as input the trapdoor td, and any OT_2 message ot_2, outputs the sender's input $\{m_c\}_{c \in C}$.*
- OT_1, OT_2, OT_3 *have the same syntax as in Definition 1, except that they also take crs as input.*

The correctness, receiver security and statistical sender privacy properties are the same as Definition 1. We additionally require the following properties:

1. *CRS Indistinguishability*, we have

$$crs \overset{c}{\approx} crs_S,$$

where crs is generated by Setup, and crs_S is generated by FakeSetup.

2. *Extraction Correctness*, for any receiver's input $b \in [C]$ and any unbounded adversary $\mathcal{A}$, we have

$$\Pr_{\substack{(crs_S, td) \leftarrow \mathsf{FakeSetup}(1^\lambda), \\ (ot_1, st) \leftarrow \mathsf{OT}_1(crs, b) \\ ot_2^* \leftarrow \mathcal{A}(crs, ot_1)}} \left[y \leftarrow \mathsf{OT}_3(crs, st, ot_2^*), \{m_c^*\}_{c \in [C]} \leftarrow \mathsf{Extract}(td, ot_2^*) : y = m_b^* \right] = 1.$$

Theorem 5 ([22]). *Assuming hardness of either LWE or DDH, there exists a black-box construction of dual-mode oblivious transfer.*

2.2   Dual-Mode Commitments

We recall the definition of a dual-mode public key encryption system [22]. Since in our application the default mode these crypto systems are instantiated in is the *lossy* mode, we refer to them by *dual-mode commitments*.

Definition 3. *A dual-mode commitment is a tuple of PPT algorithms* $\mathsf{Com} = (\mathsf{Gen}, \mathsf{FakeGen}, \mathsf{Commit}, \mathsf{Extract})$ *having the following interface*

- $\mathsf{Gen}(1^\lambda)$, *on input a security parameter* λ, *outputs a common reference string* crs.
- $\mathsf{FakeGen}(1^\lambda)$, *on input a security parameter* λ, *outputs a common reference string* crs *and an* extraction trapdoor td.
- $\mathsf{Commit}(crs, b)$, *on input a bit* $b \in \{0, 1\}$, *outputs a commitment* com.
- $\mathsf{Extract}(td, \tilde{t})$, *on input an extraction trapdoor* td, *and a commitment* com, *outputs a bit* $b \in \{0, 1\}$.

We require the scheme to satisfy the following properties

1. Extraction Correctness, *for any* $\lambda \in \mathbb{N}$ *and* $b \in \{0, 1\}$,

$$\Pr[\mathsf{Extract}(td, \tilde{t}) = b] = 1,$$

where, $(crs, td) \leftarrow \mathsf{Gen}(1^\lambda)$ *and* $\tilde{t} \leftarrow \mathsf{Commit}(crs, b)$.
2. Indistinguishable CRS Modes, *we have*

$$\{crs : crs \leftarrow \mathsf{Gen}(1^\lambda)\}_{\lambda \in \mathbb{N}} \overset{c}{\approx} \{crs : (crs, td) \leftarrow \mathsf{FakeGen}(1^\lambda)\}_{\lambda \in \mathbb{N}}$$

3. Statistical Hiding, *the following two distributions are statistically indistinguishable*

$$\{\mathsf{Commit}(crs, 0) : crs \leftarrow \mathsf{Gen}(1^\lambda)\}_{\lambda \in \mathbb{N}} \overset{s}{\approx} \{\mathsf{Commit}(crs, 1) : crs \leftarrow \mathsf{Gen}(1^\lambda)\}_{\lambda \in \mathbb{N}}$$

Theorem 6 ([22]). *Assuming hardness of either LWE or DDH, there exists a black-box construction of dual-mode commitments.*

2.3   Commit-and-Prove

We formulate the properties and the interface that we need from a commit-and-prove system. Then, we observe that the MPC-in-the-head paradigm can be used to build a commit-and-prove system with these properties.

Definition 4. *A commit-and-prove system with challenge space $\mathcal{C}$ for a language $L \in$ NP, is a tuple of algorithms $\Pi = (\mathsf{Setup}, \mathsf{FakeSetup}, \mathsf{Com}, \mathsf{GenFresh}, \mathsf{P1}, \mathsf{P2}, \mathsf{Verify}, \mathsf{Extract})$ having the following interface*

- $\mathsf{Setup}(1^\lambda)$, *on input a security parameter λ, outputs a common reference string crs.*
- $\mathsf{FakeSetup}(1^\lambda)$, *on input a security parameter λ, outputs a common reference string crs and an* extraction trapdoor td.
- $\mathsf{Com}(crs, w; r)$ *on input a bitstring $w \in \{0,1\}^W$ outputs a commitment $\tilde{w}$.*
- $\mathsf{GenFresh}(crs)$, *on input a common reference string crs, outputs a sequence of* fresh commitments *along with their corresponding randomness Γ.*
- $\mathsf{P1}(crs, x, \mathbf{w}, \mathbf{r}, \Gamma; r_P)$, *on input a common reference string crs, an instance $x \in \{0,1\}^\ell$, a witness $\mathbf{w} = \{w_i \in \{0,1\}^W\}_{i \in [c]}$, initial commitment randomness $\mathbf{r} = \{r_i\}_{i \in [c]}$, fresh commitments and their randomness Γ, and the random coins r_P, outputs the first part of proof string π_1.*
- $\mathsf{P2}(crs, x, \mathbf{w}, \mathbf{r}, \Gamma, r_P, ch)$, *on input the same parameters of $\mathsf{P1}$, the random coins used by $\mathsf{P1}$, and the challenge ch, outputs the second part of the proof string π_2.*
- $\mathsf{Verify}(crs, x, \{\tilde{w}_i\}_{i \in [c]}, ch, \pi_1, \pi_2)$, *on input a common reference string crs, an instance $x \in \{0,1\}^\ell$, a sequence of commitments $\{\tilde{w}_i\}_{i \in [c]}$, a challenge $ch \in \mathcal{C}$, and a proof string (π_1, π_2), either accepts or rejects.*
- $\mathsf{Extract}(td, \tilde{t})$, *on input an extraction trapdoor td, and a commitment $\tilde{t}$, outputs a plaintext $t \in \{0,1\}^W$.*

We further require the commit and proof system to satisfy the following properties.

- *Completeness,* for any instance $x \in L$, and any tuple of strings $(w_1, w_2, \ldots, w_c) \in \{0,1\}^{c \times W}$ which is a witness for x, let $\tilde{w}_i \leftarrow \mathsf{Com}(crs, w_i)$ be commitments to w_i, we have

$$\Pr_{\substack{crs \leftarrow \mathsf{Setup}(1^\lambda) \\ \mathsf{P1}(crs, x, \mathbf{w}, \mathbf{r}, \Gamma) \\ ch \leftarrow \mathcal{C} \\ \pi_2 \leftarrow \mathsf{P2}(ch, \mathsf{st})}} \left[\mathsf{Verify}(crs, x, \{\tilde{w}_i\}_{i \in [c]}, ch, \pi_1, \pi_2) \text{ accepts}\right] = 1.$$

- *Indistinguishable CRS modes,* we have

$$crs \stackrel{c}{\approx} crs',$$

where crs is generated by the genuine setup $\mathsf{Setup}(1^\lambda)$, and crs' is generated by the fake setup $\mathsf{FakeSetup}(1^\lambda)$.

- *Statistical Hiding*, for any two sequences of bitstrings $w^0 = \{w^0\}_{\lambda \in \mathbb{N}}, w^1 = \{w^1\}_{\lambda \in \mathbb{N}}$, the commitments are statistically indistinguishable under the *genuine setup*, namely,

$$\{\mathsf{Com}(crs, w_\lambda^0) : crs \leftarrow \mathsf{Setup}(1^\lambda)\}_{\lambda \in \mathbb{N}} \overset{s}{\approx} \{\mathsf{Com}(crs, w_\lambda^1) : crs \leftarrow \mathsf{Setup}(1^\lambda)\}_{\lambda \in \mathbb{N}}.$$

- ϵ-*Soundness*, let $\mathcal{R}$ be the NP-relation for the language L. For any unbounded adversary $(\mathsf{P1}^*, \mathsf{P2}^*)$, after the following procedure,
  - Generate the fake CRS with trapdoor $(crs, td) \leftarrow \mathsf{FakeSetup}(1^\lambda)$
  - $(x, \{\tilde{w}_i\}_{i \in [c]}, \pi_1, \mathsf{st}) \leftarrow \mathsf{P1}^*(crs)$
  - Sample a random challenge $ch \leftarrow \mathcal{C}$
  - $\pi_2 \leftarrow \mathsf{P2}^*(ch, \mathsf{st})$
  we have

$$\Pr\left[\mathcal{R}(x, \{\mathsf{Extract}(td, \tilde{w}_i)\}_{i \in [c]}) \neq 1 \wedge \mathsf{Verify}(crs, x, \{\tilde{w}_i\}_{i \in [c]}, ch, \pi_1, \pi_2) \text{ accepts}\right] < \epsilon.$$

- *Special Statistical Zero-Knowledge*, there exists a simulator algorithm Sim, such that, under any crs sampled by the genuine Setup algorithm, for any family of instances $\{x_\lambda\}$ with $x_\lambda \in L$, any witness $\{w_{\lambda,i}\}_{i \in [c]}$ for x_λ, any challenge $ch \in \mathcal{C}$, we have

$$(\mathsf{Com}(crs, \{w_{\lambda,i}\}_{i \in [c]}; \mathbf{r}), \pi_1, \pi_2) \overset{s}{\approx} (c', \pi_1', \pi_2'),$$

where π_1, π_2 are the outputs of the honest prover's algorithm for the instance x_λ, witness $\{w_{\lambda,i}\}_{i \in [c]}$, initial commitment randomness $\mathbf{r}$, and challenge ch, and $(c', \pi_1', \pi_2') \leftarrow \mathsf{Sim}(x_\lambda, ch)$ is output by the simulator.

Theorem 7 (Black-Box Commit-and-Prove from MPC-in-the-Head).
There exists a commit-and-prove protocol with constant soundness error. Furthermore, the honest prover's algorithms $(\mathsf{P1}, \mathsf{P2})$ only use information-theoretic building-blocks. Moreover, if the NP-relation of L can be verified by a circuit of depth d, then the algorithms $\mathsf{P1}, \mathsf{P2}$ can also be computed by a circuit of depth $O(d)$.

Proof (Proof Sketch). The work [13] constructed zero-knowledge from secure multiparty computation protocols. We use their zero-knowledge protocol to build a commit-and-prove system, and prove that it only makes black-box use of cryptography. We now describe the main algorithms.

- $\mathsf{Com}(crs, w; r)$: Let $n = O(1)$ be a constant. First, it secret shares the witness $w = w_1 \oplus w_2 \oplus \ldots w_n$ to n shares, and then commits to each share separately using a dual-mode commitment scheme.
- $\mathsf{P1}(crs, x, \mathbf{w}, \mathbf{r}, \Gamma; r_P)$: Let $R(\cdot, \cdot)$ be the relation circuit of the language L. It uses a semi-honest information theoretic multiparty computation scheme (MPC) in the dishonest majority setting [4] for n parties. For every $i \in [n]$, the ith party holds w_i as its input. The prover runs the MPC "in its head" to jointly compute $R(x, w_1 \oplus w_2 \oplus \ldots \oplus w_n) = 1$, and obtains the view of each party $\mathsf{View}_1, \mathsf{View}_2, \ldots, \mathsf{View}_n$. Then, it outputs commitments to the views.

- $ch \leftarrow \mathcal{C}$: The challenge ch represent two random parties $ch \leftarrow [n] \times [n]$.
- $\mathsf{P2}(crs, x, \mathbf{w}, \mathbf{r}, \Gamma, r_P, ch)$: The prover does the same computation as $\mathsf{P1}$, and then opens the commitment of the views specified by ch, and also opens the commitments to the shares specified by ch.
- Verify: The verifier checks
  - The openings of the commitments are correct.
  - The views are consistent. Namely, the messages sent and received have the same values.

The zero-knowledge and the soundness property follow from the security and the correctness of the underlying MPC scheme. Now, we show that the construction only makes black-box use of cryptography. Since the MPC is information theoretic, the only part that uses cryptography is the commitments in $\mathsf{P1}$. To make $\mathsf{P1}$ information theoretic, we provide it a series of fresh commitments to 0 and 1 and their randomness in Γ. Then we have the prover choose which commitment it needs to use. This makes $\mathsf{P1}$ information theoretic.

Now we analyze the depth of $\mathsf{P1}$. Let the depth of the circuit R be d. Since we only have a constant number of parties, the secret sharing of $\mathbf{w}$ needs a constant depth circuit. For each gate in R, we only need a constant depth circuit to compute the corresponding messages in the MPC. Hence, the computation of the views $\mathsf{View}_1, \mathsf{View}_2, \cdots, \mathsf{View}_n$ can be done in depth $O(d)$.

The depth of $\mathsf{P2}$ can also be bounded by $O(d)$. This is because it does the same computation as $\mathsf{P1}$, and an additional commitment opening in the end. The commitment opening is selecting the commitment randomness specified by ch. Hence, it can be computed by a constant depth circuit.

2.4 Maliciously Function Private Homomorphic Encryption

We review the definition of maliciously function private homomorphic encryption. Notice that in our abstraction of homomorphic encryption, secret keys are generated corresponding to fresh ciphertexts, and can only decrypt the evaluated versions of their corresponding fresh ciphertexts. The reason we choose this abstraction is that we want it to be consistent with the construction in [14]. We mention that this abstraction is sufficient for our use-case.

Definition 5 ([21]). *Let $\mathcal{F} = \{\mathcal{F}_{\lambda,L}\}_{\lambda, L \in \mathbb{N}}$ be a family of boolean functions, where for each $\lambda, L \in \mathbb{N}$, the functions in $\mathcal{F}_{\lambda,L}$ have input size $\ell(\lambda, L)$. A maliciously function private homomorphic encryption (HE) scheme for $\mathcal{F}$ is a tuple of algorithms*
$\mathsf{HE} = (\mathsf{Enc}, \mathsf{Eval}, \mathsf{Dec}, \mathsf{Sim})$, *where, except for Sim the rest of the algorithms are PPT, having the following interfaces*

- $\mathsf{Enc}(1^\lambda, 1^L, m)$, *given a security parameter $\lambda \in \mathbb{N}$, a function family index $L \in \mathbb{N}$, and a message $m \in \{0,1\}^\ell$, outputs a ciphertext $ct \in \{0,1\}^{\ell_{ct}(\lambda, L)}$ and a private key sk.*
- $\mathsf{Eval}(ct, f)$, *given a ciphertext ct, and a boolean function $f : \{0,1\}^\ell \to \{0,1\}$, outputs an evaluated ciphertext $ct_{eval} \in \{0,1\}^{\ell_{eval}}$.*

- Dec(sk, ct), given a secret key sk and a ciphertext ct, outputs a bit $b \in \{0,1\}$.
- Sim(ct^*, b), on input a ciphertext $ct^* \in \{0,1\}^{\ell_{ct}(\lambda, L)}$, and a bit b, outputs a simulated ciphertext ct_{sim}.

We consider HE schemes that satisfy the following properties:

1. Completeness, for every $\lambda, L \in \mathbb{N}$, every function $f \in \mathcal{F}_{\lambda, L}$ and every input $m \in \{0,1\}^{\ell}$,

$$\Pr[\mathsf{Dec}(sk, ct_{eval}) = f(m)] = 1,$$

where,$(ct, sk) \leftarrow \mathsf{Enc}(1^{\lambda}, 1^{L}, m)$, and $ct_{eval} \leftarrow \mathsf{Eval}(ct, f)$.
2. Compactness, there exists a fixed polynomial $\ell_{eval} = \ell_{eval}(\lambda, L)$ such that evaluated ciphertexts have size $\ell_{eval}(\lambda, L)$, i.e., the size of evaluated ciphertexts only depend on the index of the family of functions being evaluated.
3. Semantic Security, for every non-uniform polynomial-size adversary $\mathcal{A}$, every $L \in \mathbb{N}$, and every two sequence of message $m^0 = \{m_{\lambda}^0 \in \{0,1\}^{\ell(\lambda, L)}\}_{\lambda \in \mathbb{N}}$ and $m^1 = \{m_{\lambda}^1 \in \{0,1\}^{\ell(\lambda, L)}\}_{\lambda \in \mathbb{N}}$ the probabilities

$$\Pr[\mathcal{A}(ct) = 1], \tag{1}$$

in the following two experiments differ by only negl(λ):
   - in experiment 0, $(ct, sk) \leftarrow \mathsf{Enc}(1^{\lambda}, 1^{L}, m_{\lambda}^0)$
   - in experiment 1, $(ct, sk) \leftarrow \mathsf{Enc}(1^{\lambda}, 1^{L}, m_{\lambda}^1)$
4. Malicious Function Privacy, for every $L \in \mathbb{N}$, and every ciphertext $ct^* \in \{0,1\}^{\ell_{ct}(\lambda, L)}$, there exists a $m^* \in \{0,1\}^{\ell(\lambda, L)}$ such that, for every function $f \in \mathcal{F}_{\lambda, L}$,

$$\mathsf{Eval}(ct^*, f) \overset{s}{\approx} \mathsf{Sim}(ct^*, f(m^*))$$

.

If we instantiate the rate-1 OT-based HE construction of [14] with the recent rate-1 statistical sender private OT of [1] we get a malicious function private HE for branching programs.

Theorem 8 ([1,14]). *Assuming either DDH or LWE, there exists a* black-box *construction of maliciously function private homomorphic encryption scheme for the function family* $\mathcal{B} = \{\mathcal{B}_L\}_{L \in \mathbb{N}}$, *where for each* $L \in \mathbb{N}$, $\mathcal{B}_L$ *is the set of branching programs of length* L.

If we slightly relax the black-box requirement, we can have a lattice-based leveled maliciously function private FHE scheme, i.e., a maliciously function private HE scheme supporting all bounded-depth polynomial circuits.

Theorem 9 ([10]). *Assuming LWE, there exists a leveled maliciously function private homomorphic encryption scheme. The non-black-box use of cryptography in this scheme is restricted to bootstrapping (which is needed for every evaluation).*

2.5   Somewhere Statistically Binding Hash

Here we define a variant of somewhere statistically binding hashes [12].

Definition 6. *Fix a word size $W = W(\lambda)$. A somewhere statistical binding hash scheme is a tuple of PPT algorithms* SSB = (Gen, Hash, Verify, Extract) *with the following syntax.*

- Gen$(1^\lambda, N, S)$, *on input a security parameter λ, a database size N, and a subset of indices $S \subseteq [N]$, outputs a hash key hk along with a trapdoor td.*
- Hash(hk, DB), *on input a hash key hk and a database* DB *of N words of size W, outputs a hash value h along with N openings $\{\tau_i\}_{i \in [N]}$.*
- Verify(hk, h, i, x, τ), *on input a hash key hk, a hash value h, an index i, a word x, and an opening ρ, either accepts or rejects.*
- Extract(td, h), *on input a hash value h , and a trapdoor td, outputs entries $\{x_i\}_{i \in S}$.*

We require the scheme to satisfy the following properties:

1. Correctness, *for all $\lambda, N \in \mathbb{N}$, any subset of indices $S \subseteq [N]$, any index $i \in [N]$, and any database* DB *of size N, we have*

$$\Pr[\text{Verify}(hk, h, i, DB_i, \tau_i) \; accepts] = 1,$$

   where, $(hk, td) \leftarrow$ Gen$(1^\lambda, N, S)$ and $(h, \{\tau_i\}_{i \in [N]}) :=$ Hash(hk, DB).
2. Index Hiding, *for any two sets S_1, S_2 of the same size, we have*

$$crs_1 \overset{c}{\approx} crs_2,$$

   where crs_1 is generated by Gen$(1^\lambda, N, S_1)$, *and crs_2 is generated by* Gen$(1^\lambda, N, S_2)$.
3. Extraction Correctness, *for all $\lambda, N \in \mathbb{N}$, any subset of indices $S \subseteq [N]$, any index $i \in [N]$, any database* DB *of size N, and any hash h, we have*

$$\Pr[\text{Verify}(hk, h, i, DB_i, \tau_i) \; accepts \wedge x_i \neq DB_i] = 0,$$

   where, $(hk, td) \leftarrow$ Gen$(1^\lambda, N, S)$ and $\{x_i\}_{i \in [S]} :=$ Extract(td, h).
4. Efficiency: *any hash key* hk *and opening τ corresponding to size N databases and index sets of size $|S|$, are of size $|S| \cdot \log(N) \cdot \text{poly}(\lambda)$. Further,* Verify *can be implemented by a circuit of size $|S| \cdot \log(N) \cdot \text{poly}(\lambda)$.*

Our definition is slightly stronger than the one in [12] in that (i) our hashing key is binding to a subset of indices instead of binding to a single index and, (ii) we need perfect extractable binding instead of just statistical binding, i.e., there is a trapdoor that allows extracting the ith value for each binding index i. We can get the former property by repeating any single-index binding scheme multiple times in parallel. For the latter property, we notice that the HE-based construction in [12] already achieves this property, however, it is non-black-box due to the use of bootstrapping in the underlying HE. We observe that if we use a rate-1 OT scheme instead of HE, then, we have a black-box construction satisfying all the requirements in Definition 6. Please refer to the full version for a sketch of the construction.

Theorem 10. *Assuming hardness of either DDH or LWE, there exists a black-box construction of somewhere statistically binding hash satisfying the properties listed in Definition 6.*

3 Defining C-PSM

First, we formally define the relations we consider in our protocols.

Definition 7 (H-Instance Entropic Relations). *Let X and Y be two sets. Let $\mathcal{R} \subseteq X \times Y$ be a relation. For any distribution D on X, we say $\mathcal{R}$ is H-instance entropic with respect to D, if, for every $w \in Y$,*

$$\Pr_{x \leftarrow D}[(x, w) \in \mathcal{R}] \leq 2^{-H}.$$

Next, we define the search functionality.

Definition 8 (Search function). *Fix parameters $\ell, c, W, N \in \mathbb{N}$. The procedure Search takes as input a boolean function $f : \{0,1\}^\ell \times \{0,1\}^{c \cdot W} \to \{0,1\}$, a bitstring $x \in \{0,1\}^\ell$, and a database DB consisting of N words of size W. It either outputs the lexicographically first c indices $i_1, \cdots, i_c \in [N]$ such that $f(x, \mathsf{DB}_{i_1}, \cdots, \mathsf{DB}_{i_c}) = 1$ or $\perp$ if no such c indices exist.*

We are now ready to define C-PSM.

Definition 9 (2-Round C-PSM). *Let $\ell = \ell(\lambda), c = c(\lambda), W = W(\lambda)$ and $H = H(\lambda)$ be integer parameters. Let D be a distribution on $\{0,1\}^\ell$. Fix a family of H-instance entropic boolean functions $f = \{f_\lambda : \{0,1\}^{\ell(\lambda)} \times \{0,1\}^{c(\lambda) \cdot W(\lambda)} \to \{0,1\}\}$ with respect to D. A credible private set membership protocol for f, denoted by C-PSM, is a protocol between a sender and a receiver described by a tuple of PPT algorithms (Setup, R, S, Verify), with the following syntax:*

- Setup($1^\lambda, N$), *on input a security parameter λ and database size N, outputs a CRS crs.*
- R(crs, x), *given a CRS crs and an input x, outputs a receiver message α and an internal state st.*
- S(crs, α, DB), *on input a CRS crs, receiver message α, and database DB, outputs a sender message β.*
- Verify(β, st), *on input a sender message β and internal state st, either accepts or rejects.*

We require the protocol to satisfy the following properties

1. *Correctness, for every $\lambda, N \in \mathbb{N}$, every input $x \in \{0,1\}^\ell$, and every database DB of size N such that $\mathsf{Search}(f, x, \mathsf{DB}) \neq \perp$, we have*

$$\Pr_{\substack{crs \leftarrow \mathsf{Setup}(1^\lambda, N) \\ (\alpha, st) \leftarrow \mathsf{R}(crs, x) \\ \beta \leftarrow \mathsf{S}(crs, \alpha, \mathsf{DB})}}[\mathsf{Verify}(\beta, st) \ accepts] = 1.$$

2. δ-Soundness, *for every non-uniform malicious sender* $S^* = \{S^*_\lambda\}_{\lambda \in \mathbb{N}}$, *and every* $\lambda, N \in \mathbb{N}$,

$$\Pr_{\substack{crs \leftarrow \text{Setup}(1^\lambda, N) \\ x \leftarrow D \\ (\alpha, st) \leftarrow R(crs, x) \\ \beta \leftarrow S^*(crs, \alpha)}} [\text{Verify}(\beta, st) \ accepts] \le \delta(\lambda) + 2^{-H(\lambda)}$$

3. Receiver Privacy, *for any sequence of CRS strings* $crs = \{crs_\lambda\}_{\lambda \in \mathbb{N}}$, *and for any two sequence of input strings* $x^0 = \{x^0_\lambda\}_{\lambda \in \mathbb{N}}$, $x^1 = \{x^1_\lambda\}_{\lambda \in \mathbb{N}}$,

$$\{crs_\lambda, \alpha : (\alpha, st) \leftarrow R(crs_\lambda, x^0_\lambda)\}_{\lambda \in \mathbb{N}} \overset{c}{\approx} \{crs_\lambda, \alpha : (\alpha, st) \leftarrow R(crs_\lambda, x^1_\lambda)\}_{\lambda \in \mathbb{N}}.$$

4. Statistical Malicious Sender Privacy, *there is a (possibly unbounded) simulator algorithm* Sim, *such that, for every sequence of first message strings* $\alpha = \{\alpha_\lambda\}_{\lambda \in \mathbb{N}}$, *there exists a sequence of inputs* $x^* = \{x^*_\lambda\}$, *such that for any* $N \in \mathbb{N}$, *and for every database* DB *of* N *records, the following two distributions are statistically indistinguishable,*
   – *first, generate* $crs \leftarrow$ Setup$(1^\lambda, N)$, *output* Sim$(crs_\lambda, \alpha_\lambda, x^*_\lambda, \text{Search}(f, x^*_\lambda, \text{DB}))$,
   – *first, generate* $crs \leftarrow$ Setup$(1^\lambda, N)$, *output* S$(crs, \alpha_\lambda, \text{DB})$.
5. Efficiency, *both* R *and* Verify *have runtime* poly$(\lambda, \ell, c, W, \log(N))$.

Remark 1. Notice that the notion of sender privacy in in Definition 9 does not prevent leaking the indices for the witness in the database. This is W.L.O.G and merely for the ease of exposition. To prevent this leakage, the sender can simply randomly shuffle the entries in its database.

4   Construction for String Equality

Here we present the simplest version of our construction where the predicate is simply string equality, that is, the receiver wants to learn whether its input is in the sender's database. The resulting protocol has 2 rounds, achieves negl(λ)-soundness in a single repetition, and, does not depend on a CRS. For this construction, let the input size and the database word size be equal, i.e., $\ell(\lambda) = W(\lambda) \ge \lambda$. Also, define D to be the uniform distribution on $\{0,1\}^\ell$. Observe that for strings of length ℓ, the string equality relation is an ℓ-instance entropic relation with respect to D.

We new describe the ingredients in our construction.

- The first ingredient is a one-way function $f : \{0,1\}^* \rightarrow \{0,1\}^*$. We assume f maps $\ell(\lambda)$-bit inputs to $m(\lambda)$-bit outputs.
- The second ingredient is a maliciously circuit private homomorphic encryption scheme HE = (Enc, Eval, Dec, Sim) for the class of branching programs $\mathcal{B} = \{\mathcal{B}_L\}_{\lambda, L \in \mathbb{N}}$. Where, for each $L \in N$, $\mathcal{B}_L$ consists of all branching programs of length L.

Construction 1. Let $L := L(\lambda, N)$ be the length of the branching program computing the function Find described in Fig. 1. The construction is as follows:

– R(x):
  • Compute the image of x under f to obtain $y := f(x)$.
  • Encrypt y under HE to produce $(ct, sk) \leftarrow$ HE.Enc$(1^\lambda, 1^L, y)$.
  • Output $\alpha := ct$ and store internal state $st := sk$.
– S(α, DB):
  • Parse $\alpha := ct$.
  • Apply f to every entry in DB to obtain $\widetilde{\text{DB}} = \{\widetilde{\text{DB}}_i := f(\text{DB}_i)\}_{i \in [N]}$.
  • Homomorphically evaluate the function $\text{Find}_{\widetilde{\text{DB}}, \text{DB}}$ on ct to obtain
    $ct_{eval} \leftarrow$ HE.Eval$(ct, \text{Find}_{\widetilde{\text{DB}}, \text{DB}},)$.
  • Output $\beta := ct_{eval}$.
– Verify(β, st):
  • Parse β and st as $\beta = ct_{eval}$ and $st = sk$ respectively.
  • Decrypt ct_{eval} to obtain $\tilde{x} :=$ HE.Dec(sk, ct_{eval}).
  • Accept iff $f(\tilde{x})$ equals $f(x)$.

---

procedure $\text{Find}_{\widetilde{\text{DB}}, \text{DB}}(y)$
  if $y \notin \widetilde{\text{DB}}$ **then**
    Output $\perp$
  else
    Find the smallest index i such that $\widetilde{\text{DB}}_i = y$.
    Output DB_i.

Fig. 1. Description of the labeled-PSM functionality Find

Correctness and receiver privacy of Construction 1 immediately follows from the correctness and semantic security of HE. For efficiency, we have to argue that the length of the branching program computing Find is logarithmic in N. To do this, as shown in [5], we can convert the database DB to a trie, and essentially implement Find by a branching program of length ℓ.

We now prove the soundness of Construction 1.

Theorem 11. *Assuming f is one-way, Construction 1 is* negl(λ)-*sound.*

Proof. Let S^* be a malicious sender. Denote the success probability of S^* by p. In more detail, p is defined as

$$p := \Pr_{\substack{x \leftarrow D \\ (ct,sk) \leftarrow \text{HE.Enc}(1^\lambda, 1^L, f(x)) \\ \beta \leftarrow S^*(ct) \\ \tilde{x} := \text{HE.Dec}(sk, \beta)}} [f(\tilde{x}) = f(x)].$$

We use S^* to build a PPT adversary $\mathcal{A}$ which breaks the one-wayness of f with probability p. $\mathcal{A}$ works as follows, on input an image y, it first encrypts y by HE to obtain $(ct, sk) \leftarrow$ HE.Enc$(1^\lambda, 1^L, y)$. It then runs S^* on input ct to get $ct_{eval} \leftarrow S^*(ct)$. Finally, $\mathcal{A}$ decrypts ct_{eval} using sk and outputs $\tilde{x} :=$ HE.Dec(sk, ct_{eval}) as the preimage of y. Now observe that as long as y is an image of an input chosen from the distribution D, the view of S^* when interacting with $\mathcal{A}$ is identical to its view in the soundness game. Therefore,

$$\Pr_{\substack{x \leftarrow D \\ y := f(x) \\ \tilde{x} \leftarrow \mathcal{A}(y)}} [f(\tilde{x}) = f(x)] = p.$$

This completes the proof.

Theorem 12. *Assuming* HE *is maliciously circuit private, Construction 1 satisfies statistical malicious sender privacy.*

Proof. Let α be an arbitrary first message and DB be any database of size $N \in \mathbb{N}$. We only describe the simulator algorithm Sim, the theorem follows instantly from the malicious function privacy of HE.

- Sim receives as input a first message $\alpha := ct$, and a bitstring x^*.
- Using the HE simulator it computes $ct_{eval} \leftarrow$ HE.Sim(ct, x^*).
- It outputs ct_{eval}.

5 Construction for Predicates Beyond String Equality

Now we consider richer families of predicates. Fix input length $\ell = \ell(\lambda)$, word size $W = W(\lambda)$, function arity $c = c(\lambda)$, distribution D on $\{0,1\}^\ell$, and entropy parameter $H = H(\lambda)$. Let $f : \{0,1\}^\ell \times \{0,1\}^{c \cdot W} \to \{0,1\}$ be an H-instance entropic function with respect to D.

In the rest of the paper, we construct a 2-round C-PSM protocol in three steps.

- First, we construct a 4-round protocol satisfying a weaker notion of soundness, where, it is only required that an adversary cannot convince a verifier for any *fixed* set of indices.
- Then, using dual-mode 2-round OT, we show how to compress the 4-round protocol to a 2-round protocol which still has weak soundness.
- Finally, we amplify the soundness of the 2-round protocol by parallel repetition to achieve a (strongly) sound 2-round protocol.

5.1 Weakly-Sound 4-Round Protocol

We first construct a *weakly-sound* 4-round protocol with constant soundness. Where a weakly-sound 4-round C-PSM protocol is defined as follows:

Definition 10 (Weakly-Sound 4-Round C-PSM). *A credible private set membership protocol with challenge space $\mathcal{C}$ for f is a protocol between a sender and a receiver described by a tuple of PPT algorithms* (Setup, R, S1, S2, Verify), *with the following syntax:*

- Setup$(1^\lambda, N)$, *on input a security parameter λ and database size N, outputs a CRS crs.*

- R(crs, x), *given a CRS crs and an input x, outputs a receiver message α and an internal state st_R.*
- S1(crs, α, DB), *on input a CRS crs, a receiver message α, and a database DB, outputs a sender message β_1 and an internal state st_S.*
- S2(crs, ch, st_S), *on input a CRS crs, a challenge ch, and an internal state st_S, outputs a sender message β_2.*
- Verify($\beta_1, ch, \beta_2, st_R$) *on input sender messages β_1, β_2, challenge ch, and internal state st_R, either accepts and outputs a sequence $S = \{i_k\}_{k\in[c]}$ of indices, or, rejects.*

We require the protocol to satisfy the following properties

1. Correctness, *for every $\lambda, N \in \mathbb{N}$, every input $x \in \{0,1\}^\ell$, every database DB of size N such that $\mathsf{Search}(f, x, \mathsf{DB}) \neq \bot$, and every challenge $ch \in \mathcal{C}$, we have*

$$\Pr_{\substack{crs\leftarrow\mathsf{Setup}(1^\lambda,N) \\ (\alpha,st_R)\leftarrow\mathsf{R}(crs,x) \\ (\beta_1,st_S)\leftarrow\mathsf{S1}(crs,\alpha,\mathsf{DB}) \\ \beta_2\leftarrow\mathsf{S2}(crs,ch,st_S)}} [\mathsf{Verify}(\beta_1, ch, \beta_2, st_R) \ accepts] = 1.$$

2. Weak δ-Soundness, *for every non-uniform malicious sender $\mathsf{S}^* = \{(\mathsf{S1}_\lambda^*, \mathsf{S2}_\lambda^*)\}_{\lambda\in\mathbb{N}}$, every $\lambda, N \in \mathbb{N}$, and every sequence of indices $I^* = \{i_k^*\}_{k\in[c]}$ of size c,*

$$\Pr_{\substack{crs\leftarrow\mathsf{Setup}(1^\lambda,N) \\ x\leftarrow D \\ (\alpha,st_R)\leftarrow\mathsf{R}(crs,x) \\ (\beta_1,st_S)\leftarrow\mathsf{S1}^*(crs,\alpha) \\ ch\leftarrow\mathcal{C} \\ \beta_2\leftarrow\mathsf{S2}^*(crs,ch,st_S)}} [\mathsf{Verify}(\beta_1, ch, \beta_2, st_R) = I^*] \leq \delta(\lambda) + 2^{-H(\lambda)}$$

3. Receiver Privacy, *for any sequence of CRS strings $crs = \{crs_\lambda\}_{\lambda\in\mathbb{N}}$, and for any two sequence of input strings $x^0 = \{x_\lambda^0\}_{\lambda\in\mathbb{N}}$, $x^1 = \{x_\lambda^1\}_{\lambda\in\mathbb{N}}$,*

$$\{crs_\lambda, \alpha : (\alpha, st) \leftarrow \mathsf{R}(crs_\lambda, x_\lambda^0)\}_{\lambda\in\mathbb{N}} \stackrel{c}{\approx} \{crs_\lambda, \alpha : (\alpha, st) \leftarrow \mathsf{R}(crs_\lambda, x_\lambda^1)\}_{\lambda\in\mathbb{N}}.$$

4. Special Statistical Malicious Sender Privacy, *there is a simulator algorithm Sim, such that, for every sequence of first message strings $\alpha = \{\alpha_\lambda\}_{\lambda\in\mathbb{N}}$, there exists a sequence of inputs $x^* = \{x_\lambda^*\}$, such that for every database DB, and for every $ch \in \mathcal{C}$, the following two distributions are statistically indistinguishable*
   - *sample $crs \leftarrow \mathsf{Setup}(1^\lambda, N)$, then, output $\mathsf{Sim}(crs, x_\lambda^*, ch, \mathsf{Search}(f, x_\lambda^*, \mathsf{DB}))$*
   - *sample $crs \leftarrow \mathsf{Setup}(1^\lambda, N)$, then, generate $(\beta_1, st) \leftarrow \mathsf{S1}(crs, \alpha_\lambda)$, next, compute $\beta_2 \leftarrow \mathsf{S2}(crs, ch, st)$, finally, output (β_1, β_2).*
5. Efficiency, *both R and Verify have runtime $\mathrm{poly}(\lambda, \ell, c, W, \log(N))$.*

Our construction uses the following ingredients:

- A commit-and-prove system $\Pi = (\mathsf{Setup}, \mathsf{FakeSetup}, \mathsf{Com}, \mathsf{GenFresh}, \mathsf{P}, \mathsf{Verify}, \mathsf{Extract})$ for the language specified by f.

- A maliciously circuit private homomorphic encryption scheme $\mathsf{HE} =$ ($\mathsf{Enc}, \mathsf{Eval}, \mathsf{Dec}, \mathsf{Sim}$) for a class of functions $\mathcal{F} = \{\mathcal{F}_L\}_{L \in \mathbb{N}}$.
- A somewhere statistically binding hash $\mathsf{SSB} = (\mathsf{Gen}, \mathsf{Hash}, \mathsf{Verify}, \mathsf{Extract})$ satisfying the properties in Definition 6.

Construction 2 (Weakly-Sound 4-Round C-PSM). Let $L := L(\lambda, N)$ be a function family index such that $\mathcal{F}_L$ includes both G^1 and G^2 (Figs. 2 and 3) for databases DB of size N. The construction is as follows:

- $\mathsf{Setup}(1^\lambda, N)$:
  - Generate a CRS for Π, $crs_\Pi \leftarrow \Pi.\mathsf{Setup}(1^\lambda)$.
  - Generate an SSB hash key binding to the first c indices (or any other arbitrary sequence of c indices), $(hk, td) \leftarrow \mathsf{SSB}.\mathsf{Gen}(1^\lambda, N, \{i\}_{i \in [c]})$.
  - Output $crs := (crs_\Pi, hk)$.
- $\mathsf{R}(crs, x)$:
  - Encrypt x under HE to produce $(ct, sk) \leftarrow \mathsf{HE}.\mathsf{Enc}(1^\lambda, 1^L, x)$.
  - Output $\alpha := ct$ and store internal state $st := sk$.
- $\mathsf{S1}(crs, \alpha, \mathsf{DB})$:
  - Parse crs and α as (crs_Π, hk) and ct respectively.
  - Commit to every entry in DB to produce $\widetilde{\mathsf{DB}} = \{\widetilde{\mathsf{DB}}_i \leftarrow \Pi.\mathsf{Com}$ $(crs_\Pi, \mathsf{DB}_i; r_i^{com})\}_{i \in [N]}$.
  - Hash $\widetilde{\mathsf{DB}}$ using SSB to obtain $(h, \{\tau_i\}_{i \in [N]}) := \mathsf{SSB}.\mathsf{Hash}(hk, \widetilde{\mathsf{DB}})$.
  - Produce fresh commitments and their randomness $\Gamma \leftarrow \Pi.\mathsf{GenFresh}(crs_\Pi)$.
  - Sample random coins r_P for $\Pi.\mathsf{P1}$.
  - Homomorphically evaluate the function G^1 on ct to obtain
    $ct_{eval,1} \leftarrow \mathsf{HE}.\mathsf{Eval}(crs_\Pi, ct, G^1_{\mathsf{DB}, \widetilde{\mathsf{DB}}, \{\tau_i\}_{i \in [N]}, \{r_i^{com}\}_{i \in [N]}, \Gamma, r_P})$.
  - Output $\beta_1 := (h, ct_{eval,1})$ and store internal state $st := (x, \mathsf{DB}, \{r_i^{com}\}_{i \in [N]}, \Gamma, r_P)$.
- $\mathsf{S2}(crs, ch, st)$:
  - Parse crs and st as (crs_Π, hk) and $(x, \mathsf{DB}, \{r_i^{com}\}_{i \in [N]}, \Gamma, r_P)$ respectively.
  - Homomorphically evaluate the function G^2 on ct to obtain
    $ct_{eval,2} \leftarrow \mathsf{HE}.\mathsf{Eval}(crs_\Pi, ct, G^2_{crs_\Pi, \mathsf{DB}, \{r_i^{com}\}_{i \in [N]}, \Gamma, r_P, ch})$.
  - Output $\beta_2 := ct_{eval,2}$.
- $\mathsf{Verify}(crs, \beta_1, ch, \beta_2, st)$:
  - Parse crs, β_1, β_2 and st as (crs_Π, hk), $(h, ct_{eval,1})$, $ct_{eval,2}$ and sk respectively.
  - Decrypt $ct_{eval,1}$ to obtain $(\{i_k\}_{k \in [c]}, \{\tilde{w}_k\}_{k \in [c]}, \pi_1, \{\tau_k\}_{k \in [c]}) := \mathsf{HE}.\mathsf{Dec}(sk, ct_{eval,1})$.
  - Decrypt $ct_{eval,2}$ to obtain $\pi_2 := \mathsf{HE}.\mathsf{Dec}(sk, ct_{eval,2})$.
  - Accept and output $\{i_k\}_{k \in [c]}$ iff $\Pi.\mathsf{Verify}(crs_\Pi, x, \{\tilde{w}_k\}_{k \in [c]}, ch, \pi_1, \pi_2)$ accepts and
    $\forall k \in [c] : \mathsf{SSB}.\mathsf{Verify}(hk, h, i_k, \tilde{w}_k, \tau_k)$ accepts.

We first prove δ-soundness and special statistical malicious sender privacy of Construction 2.

procedure $G^1_{crs_\Pi,\mathsf{DB},\widetilde{\mathsf{DB}},\{\tau_i\}_{i\in[N]},\Gamma,r_P}(x)$

    Let $out := \mathsf{Search}(x, f, \mathsf{DB})$
    if $out == \bot$ **then**
        Output $\bot$
    else
        Parse out as $out = (i_1, \cdots, i_c)$.
        Generate the first prover message:

$$\pi_1 \leftarrow \mathsf{P1}(crs_\Pi, x, \{\mathsf{DB}_{i_k}\}_{k\in[c]}, \{r_{i_k}\}_{k\in[c]}, \Gamma; r_P).$$

    Output $(\{i_k\}_{k\in[c]}, \{\widetilde{\mathsf{DB}}_{i_k}\}_{k\in[c]}, \pi_1, \{\tau_{i_k}\}_{k\in[c]})$.

Fig. 2. Description of G^1

procedure $G^2_{crs_\Pi,\mathsf{DB},\{r_i^{com}\}_{i\in[N]},\Gamma,r_P,ch}(x)$

    Let $out := \mathsf{Search}(x, f, \mathsf{DB})$
    if $out == \bot$ **then**
        Output $\bot$
    else
        Parse out as $out = (i_1, \cdots, i_c)$.
        Generate the second prover message:

$$\pi_2 \leftarrow \mathsf{P2}(crs_\Pi, x, \{\mathsf{DB}_{i_k}\}_{k\in[c]}, \{r_{i_k}\}_{k\in[c]}, \Gamma, r_P, ch).$$

    Output the second prover message π_2.

Fig. 3. Description of G^2

Theorem 13. *Assuming* SSB *is index-hiding,* Π *has indistinguishable CRS modes,* HE *has semantic security, and* Π *is* δ*-sound, Construction 2 is weakly* $(\delta + \gamma)$*-sound for any positive constant (or any non-negligible function)* γ .

Proof. Let $\mathsf{S}^* = (\mathsf{S1}^*, \mathsf{S2}^*)$ be a malicious sender and let $I^* = \{i_k^*\}_{k\in[c]}$ be any sequence of indices of size c. For each hybrid H_j, define the probability p_j as follows:

$$p_j := \Pr[\Pi.\mathsf{Verify}(crs_\Pi, x, \{\tilde{w}_k\}_{k\in[c]}, \pi_1, ch, \pi_2) \text{ accepts } \wedge \forall k \in [c] : \mathsf{SSB.Verify}(hk, h, i_k^*, \tilde{w}_k, \tau_k) \text{ accepts}].$$

where in each hybrid we describe how crs_Π, x, $\{\tilde{w}_k\}_{k\in[c]}$, π_1, ch, π_2, hk, h, and $\{\tau_k\}_{k\in[c]}$ are defined.

Hybrid H_0: This is the soundness experiment. In more detail, here,

- $crs_\Pi \leftarrow \Pi.\mathsf{Setup}(1^\lambda)$,
- $(hk, td_{SSB}) \leftarrow \mathsf{SSB.Gen}(1^\lambda, N, \{k\}_{k\in[c]})$,
- $x \leftarrow D$,
- $(ct, sk) \leftarrow \mathsf{HE.Enc}(1^\lambda, 1^L, x)$,
- $((h, ct_{eval,1}), st) \leftarrow \mathsf{S1}^*((crs_\pi, hk), ct)$,

- $ch \leftarrow \mathcal{C}$,
- $ct_{eval,2} \leftarrow \mathsf{S2}^*(crs, ch, st)$,
- $(\{i_k\}_{k \in [c]}, \{\tilde{w}_k\}_{k \in [c]}, \pi_1, \{\tau_k\}_{k \in [c]}) := \mathsf{HE.Dec}(sk, ct_{1,eval})$,
- and $\pi_2 := \mathsf{HE.Dec}(sk, ct_{eval,2})$.

Hybrid H_1: This is identical to H_0 except that here hk is generated binding to indices $i_1^*, \cdots, i_c^*$, i.e., $(hk, td_{ssb}) \leftarrow \mathsf{SSB.Gen}(1^\lambda, N, \{i_k^*\}_{k \in [c]})$. The index hiding property of SSB implies that $H_0 \overset{c}{\approx} H_1$. Consequently, $|p_0 - p_1| = \mathsf{negl}(\lambda)$.

Hybrid H_2: The only difference between this hybrid and H_1 is that here, crs_Π is generated along with a trapdoor td_Π via $(crs_\Pi, td_\Pi) \leftarrow \Pi.\mathsf{FakeSetup}(1^\lambda)$. Since Π has indistinguishable CRS modes, $H_1 \overset{c}{\approx} H_2$. Therefore, $|p_1 - p_2| = \mathsf{negl}(\lambda)$.

Lemma 1. *Assuming* HE *is semantically secure,* $p_2 - (\delta + 2^{-H}) = \mathsf{negl}(\lambda)$.

Proof. Using S^* we build an adversary $\mathcal{A}$ against the semantic security of HE. $\mathcal{A}$ works as follows:

- It generates crs_Π, hk, and td_{ssb} exactly as in H_2.
- It samples two elements $x_0 \leftarrow D, x_1 \leftarrow D$.
- $\mathcal{A}$ sends x_0, x_1 to the semantic security challenger of HE.
- It receives as response an HE ciphertext ct from the HE semantic security challenger. The ciphertext ct either encrypts x_0 or x_1 under an honestly generated HE key sk.
- $\mathcal{A}$ runs $\mathsf{S1}^*$ to obtain $((h, ct_{eval,1}), st) \leftarrow \mathsf{S1}^*((crs_\Pi, hk), ct)$
- $\mathcal{A}$ receives a random challenge $ch \leftarrow \mathcal{C}$.
- $\mathcal{A}$ runs $\mathsf{S2}^*$ to obtain $ct_{eval,2} \leftarrow \mathsf{S2}^*((crs_\Pi, hk), st)$.
- Using td_{ssb} it recovers commitments $\{\tilde{w}_k^*\}_{k \in [c]} := \mathsf{SSB.Extract}(td_{ssb}, h)$. Using td_{com}, for each $k \in [c]$ it recovers $w_k^* := \mathsf{Com.Extract}(td_{com}, \tilde{w}_k^*)$.
- If $f(x_0, \{w_k^*\}_{k \in [c]}) = 1$, it outputs 1. Otherwise, it outputs 0.

Now we analyze the success probability of $\mathcal{A}$ in breaking the semantic security of HE. Let

$$(\{i_k\}_{k \in [c]}, \{\tilde{w}_k\}_{k \in [c]}, \pi_1, \{\tau_k\}_{k \in [c]}) := \mathsf{HE.Dec}(sk, ct_{eval,1}).$$

First, we consider the case where ct encrypts x_0. In this case with probability at least p_2,

$$\forall k \in [c] : \mathsf{SSB.Verify}(hk, h, i_k^*, \tilde{w}_k, \tau_k) \text{ accepts}, \tag{2}$$

and

$$\Pi.\mathsf{Verify}(crs_\Pi, x_0, \{\tilde{w}_k\}_{k \in [c]}, \pi_1, ch, \pi_2) \text{ accepts}. \tag{3}$$

By extractability of SSB, the former implies that $\forall k \in [c] : \tilde{w}_k = \tilde{w}_k^*$. Consequently, by δ-soundness of Π, with probability at least $p_2 - \delta$, $f(x_0, \{w_k^*\}_{k \in [c]}) = 1$. We conclude that in this case $\mathcal{A}$ outputs 1 with probability at least $p_2 - \delta$. Now we turn to the other case where ct encrypts x_1. In this case, x_0 maintains all of its entropy , therefore, since f is H-instance entropic,

$$\Pr[f(x_0, \{w_k^*\}_{k \in [c]}) = 1] = 2^{-H},$$

i.e., $\mathcal{A}$ outputs 1 with probability 2^{-H}. We showed that $\mathcal{A}$ breaks the semantic security of HE with probability at least $p_2 - \delta - 2^{-H}$.

This concludes the proof.

Theorem 14. *Assuming* HE *is maliciously circuit private,* Π *satisfies special statistical zero-knowledge, and* Π *has statistically hiding commitments, Construction 2 satisfies special statistical malicious sender privacy.*

Proof. Let α be an arbitrary first message, $ch \in \mathcal{C}$ be any challenge, DB be any database of size $N \in \mathbb{N}$, and let $crs \leftarrow \mathsf{Setup}(1^\lambda, N)$ be a crs generated through Setup. First, we describe the simulator algorithm Sim.

- Sim receives as input a CRS parsed as $crs := (crs_\Pi, hk)$, a first message $\alpha := ct$, a bitstring x^*, and indices $\{i_k^*\}_{k \in [c]}$ (W.L.O.G assume that the indices are not $\perp$).
- Using the zero-knowledge simulator for Π, it computes $(\{\tilde{w}_k^*\}_{k\in[c]}, \pi_1^*, \pi_2^*) \leftarrow \Pi.\mathsf{Sim}(crs_\Pi, x, ch)$.
- For each $i \in [N]/\{i_k^*\}_{k\in[c]}$, Sim computes a commitment $\widetilde{\mathsf{DB}}_i \leftarrow \Pi.\mathsf{Commit}(crs_{com}, \mathbf{0})$. For each $k \in [c]$ it sets the i_k^*th commitment to be equal to $\widetilde{\mathsf{DB}}_{i_{k^*}} := \tilde{w}_k^*$.
- It hashes $\widetilde{\mathsf{DB}}$ to obtain $(h, \{\tau_i\}_{i\in[N]}) := \mathsf{SSB.Hash}(hk, \widetilde{\mathsf{DB}})$.
- Using the HE simulator it computes

$$ct_{eval,1} \leftarrow \mathsf{HE.Sim}(ct, (\{i_k^*\}_{k\in[c]}, \{\tilde{w}_k^*\}_{k\in[c]}, \pi_1^*, \{\tau_{i_k^*}\}_{k\in[c]})).$$

- Using the HE simulator it computes

$$ct_{eval,2} \leftarrow \mathsf{HE.Sim}(ct, \pi_2^*)$$

- It outputs $(h, ct_{eval,1}, ct_{eval,2})$.

We now proceed via a series of hybrids to show that the output of Sim is statistically indistinguishable from an honestly generated sender message.

Hybrid H_0: This hybrid corresponds to generating the sender messages β_1, β_2 honestly through $(\beta_1, st) := (h, ct_{eval}) \leftarrow \mathsf{S1}(crs, \alpha, \mathsf{DB})$ and $\beta_2 := ct_{eval} \leftarrow \mathsf{S2}(crs, ch, st)$.

Hybrid H_1: This hybrid uses HE.Sim to produce $ct_{eval,1}$ and $ct_{eval,2}$. In more detail, given ct, we know that there exists an x^* such that,

$$\mathsf{HE.Eval}(ct, G^1_{crs_\Pi, \mathsf{DB}, \widetilde{\mathsf{DB}}, \{\tau_i\}_{i\in[N]}, \Gamma, r_P}) \overset{s}{\approx} \mathsf{HE.Sim}(ct, G^1_{crs_\Pi, \mathsf{DB}, \widetilde{\mathsf{DB}}, \{\tau_i\}_{i\in[N]}, \Gamma, r_P}(x^*)),$$

and

$$\mathsf{HE.Eval}(ct, G^2_{crs_\Pi, \mathsf{DB}, \{r_i^{com}\}_{i\in[N]}, \Gamma, r_P, ch}) \overset{s}{\approx} \mathsf{HE.Sim}(ct, G^2_{crs_\Pi, \mathsf{DB}, \{r_i^{com}\}_{i\in[N]}, \Gamma, r_P, ch}(x^*)).$$

In this hybrid, $ct_{eval,1}$ and $ct_{eval,2}$ are generated as

$$ct_{eval,1} \leftarrow \mathsf{HE.Sim}(ct, G^1_{crs_\Pi, \mathsf{DB}, \widetilde{\mathsf{DB}}, \{\tau_i\}_{i\in[N]}, \Gamma, r_P}(x^*)),$$

and

$$ct_{eval,2} \leftarrow \mathsf{HE.Sim}(ct, G^2_{crs_\Pi, \mathsf{DB}, \{r_i^{com}\}_{i\in[N]}, \Gamma, r_P, ch}(x^*)).$$

It follows from the malicious circuit privacy of HE that $H_0 \overset{s}{\approx} H_1$.

Hybrid H_2: The difference between this hybrid and the previous hybrid is only syntactical. In this hybrid, to generate $ct_{eval,1}$ and $ct_{eval,2}$, first, the (lexicographically) smallest indices $\{i_k^*\}_{k \in [c]}$ such that $f(x^*, \{DB_{i_k^*}\}_{k \in [c]}) = 1$ are computed. Next, π_1 and π_2 are computed as

$$\pi_1 \leftarrow P1(crs_\Pi, x, \{DB_{i_k^*}\}_{k \in [c]}, \{r_{i_k^*}\}_{k \in [c]}, \Gamma; r_P)$$

and

$$\pi_2 \leftarrow P2(crs_\Pi, x, \{DB_{i_k^*}\}_{k \in [c]}, \{r_{i_k}\}_{k \in [c]}, \Gamma, r_P, ch).$$

Finally, $ct_{eval,1}$ and $ct_{eval,2}$ are computed as

$$ct_{eval,1} \leftarrow \mathsf{HE.Sim}(ct, (\{i_k^*\}_{k \in [c]}, \{\widetilde{DB}_{i_k^*}\}_{k \in [c]}, \pi_1, \{\tau_{i_k^*}\}_{k \in [c]})),$$

and

$$ct_{eval,2} \leftarrow \mathsf{HE.Sim}(ct, \pi_2).$$

As already stated H_1 and H_2 are identical.

Hybrid H_3: In this hybrid we modify how $\widetilde{DB}$ is generated. Here, for each $k \in [c]$,

$$\widetilde{DB}_{i_k^*} \leftarrow \Pi.\mathsf{Commit}(crs_\Pi, DB_{i_k^*}; r_{i_k^*}^{com})$$

as before, but the rest of the commitments are generated as

$$\{\widetilde{DB}_i \leftarrow \Pi.\mathsf{Commit}(crs_\Pi, 0)\}_{i \in [N]/\{i_k^*\}_{k \in [c]}}.$$

Notice that we don't modify the commitments whose randomness are used in the HE.Sim algorithm. Therefore, by the statistical hiding property of the commitments in Π, $H_2 \overset{s}{\approx} H_3$.

Hybrid H_4: The difference between this hybrid and the previous hybrid is that here $\{\widetilde{DB}_{i_k^*}\}_{k \in [c]}, \pi_1$, and π_2 are generated using the simulator for Π, i.e.,

$$(\{\widetilde{DB}_{i_k^*}\}_{k \in [c]}, \pi_1, \pi_2) \leftarrow \Pi.\mathsf{Sim}(x^*, ch).$$

The special zero-knowledge property of Π directly implies that $H_3 \overset{s}{\approx} H_4$. Observe that, H_4 corresponds to generating the sender messages via Sim.

Depending on how HE is instantiated, Construction 2 can support different classes of predicates with different trade-offs in terms of black-box usage of underlying cryptographic primitives. If we instantiate HE with Theorem 8, we can have a black-box construction supporting NC^1 predicates f where $\mathsf{Search}(\cdot, f, DB)$ can be implemented in by a branching program whose length is logarithmic in $|DB|$.

Theorem 15. *Assuming hardness of either of DDH or LWE, there exists a family of weakly-sound 4-round C-PSM protocols with the following properties:*

1. *It supports all predicates f such that f can be implemented by an NC^1 circuit and also for every database DB of size N, Search$(\cdot, f, DB)$ can be implemented by a branching program of length logarithmic in N.*
2. *It only makes black-box use of the underlying cryptographic primitives.*
3. *It is receiver private.*
4. *It is weakly δ-sound.*
5. *It satisfies special statistical malicious sender privacy.*

Proof. We instantiate Construction 2 with the black-box maliciously circuit private homomorphic encryption scheme of Theorem 8 for the class of branching programs $\{\mathcal{B}_L\}_{L\in\mathbb{N}}$. We have already proven weak δ-soundness and special statistical malicious sender privacy of Construction 2. Correctness follows from the correctness of HE, correctness of Π, and correctness of SSB. Receiver privacy follows from the semantic security of HE. For efficiency, we need to show that both G^1 and G^2 can be evaluated by a branching program of length $L = \text{poly}(\lambda, \log N)$. Observe that both G^1 and G^2 access the whole database only through the Search functionality. Therefore, since the Search functionality for f can be implemented by a branching program of length logarithmic in N, L is also logarithmic in N. Furthermore, since f is in NC^1, by Theorem 7, both P1 and P2 are also in NC^1. Consequently, by Barrington's theorem [3], P1 and P2 can be implemented by a polynomial (in λ) length branching program. Therefore, $L = \text{poly}(\lambda, \log N)$.

Alternatively, we can instantiate HE with Theorem 9 to get a construction supporting all bounded depth circuits. While this construction only makes black-box use of HE, however, the homomorphic encryption scheme constructed in Theorem 9 is non-black-box due to relying on bootstrapping.

Theorem 16. *Assuming hardness of LWE, there exists a family of weakly-sound 4-round C-PSM protocols with the following properties:*

1. *It supports all predicates f such that f can be implemented by bounded-depth circuits, i.e., the C-PSM protocol is leveled.*
2. *Its only non-black-box use of the underlying cryptographic primitives happens through bootstrapping.*
3. *It is receiver private.*
4. *It is weakly δ-sound.*
5. *It satisfies special statistical malicious sender privacy.*

Proof. We instantiate Construction 2 with the maliciously circuit private homomorphic encryption scheme of Theorem 9 for the class of circuits $\{\mathcal{F}_L\}_{L\in\mathbb{N}}$, where for each $L \in \mathbb{N}$, $\mathcal{F}_L$ consists of all circuits of depth at most L. Establishing weak δ-soundness, special statistical malicious sender privacy, correctness and receiver privacy is identical to Theorem 15. For efficiency, it is straightforward to verify that G^1 and G^2 can be evaluated by circuits of depth $L = \text{poly}(\lambda, \log N)$.

5.2   4-Round to 2-Round Transformation

Here we provide a generic transformation that converts any weakly-sound 4-round C-PSM protocol to a weakly-sound 2-round protocol. Analogously to weakly-sound 4-round C-PSM, we define weakly-sound 2-round C-PSM as follows:

Definition 11 (Weakly Sound 2-Round C-PSM). *Let ℓ, c, W, f, H, D be the same as Definition 9. A weakly sound C-PSM for f, is a protocol between a sender and a receiver described by a tuple of PPT algorithms* (Setup, R, S, Verify), *where the interface of* Setup, R *and* S *is identical to their interface in Definition 9 and* Verify *has the following syntax:*

- Verify(β, st), *on input a sender message β and internal state st, either accepts and outputs a sequence $I = \{i_k\}_{k \in [c]}$ of indices, or rejects.*

Except for δ-soundness we require the protocol to satisfy all properties in Definition 9. Additionally, we consider the following weaker variant of soundness:

1. Weak δ-Soundness, *for every non-uniform malicious sender* $S^* = \{S^*_\lambda\}_{\lambda \in \mathbb{N}}$, *every $\lambda, N \in \mathbb{N}$, and every sequence of indices $I^* = \{i^*_k\}_{k \in [c]}$ of size c,*

$$\Pr_{\substack{crs \leftarrow \text{Setup}(1^\lambda, N) \\ x \leftarrow D \\ (\alpha, st) \leftarrow \text{R}(crs, x) \\ \beta \leftarrow S^*(crs, \alpha)}} [\text{Verify}(\beta, st) = I^*] \leq \delta(\lambda) + 2^{-H(\lambda)}$$

Our transformation uses the following ingredients:

- A 4-round weakly sound C-PSM protocol $\Sigma = $ (Setup, R, S1, S2, Verify).
- A dual-mode statistically sender private OT scheme
  OT = (Setup, FakeSetup, Extract, OT1, OT2, OT3).

Construction 3. The construction is as follows:

- Setup$(1^\lambda, N)$:
  - Generate a CRS for Σ, $crs_\Sigma \leftarrow \Sigma.\text{Setup}(1^\lambda, N)$.
  - Generate a CRS for dual-mode OT, $crs_{OT} \leftarrow \text{OT.Setup}(1^\lambda)$.
  - Output $crs := (crs_\Sigma, crs_{OT})$.
- R(crs, x):
  - Generate a Σ first message for x along with an internal state, $(\alpha_\Sigma, st_\Sigma) \leftarrow \Sigma.\text{R}(crs_\Sigma, x)$.
  - Sample a random challenge $ch \leftarrow \mathcal{C}$ from the challenge space of Σ.
  - Generate an OT first message for ch along with an internal state, $(ot_1, st_{OT}) \leftarrow \text{OT.OT1}(crs_{OT}, ch)$.
  - Output first message $\alpha := (\alpha_\Sigma, ot_1)$ and internal state $st = (x, ch, st_\Sigma, st_{OT})$.
- S(crs, α, DB):
  - Parse crs and α as (crs_Σ, crs_{OT}) and (α_Σ, ot_1) respectively.
  - Compute $(\beta_1, st) \leftarrow \Sigma.\text{S1}(crs_\Sigma, \alpha_\Sigma, \text{DB})$.

- For each $ch \in C$ compute $\beta_{2,ch} \leftarrow \Sigma.S2(crs_\Sigma, st, ch, \mathsf{DB})$.
- Compute OT second message $ot_2 \leftarrow \mathsf{OT.OT2}(ot_1, \{\beta_{2,ch}\}_{ch \in C})$.
- Output $\beta := (\beta_1, ot_2)$.
- Verify(β, st):
  - Parse β and st as (β_1, ot_2) and $(x, ch, st_\Sigma, st_{OT})$ respectively.
  - Recover $\beta_{2,ch}$ as $\beta_{2,ch} := \mathsf{OT.OT3}(ot_2, st_{OT})$.
  - Output whatever $\Sigma.\mathsf{Verify}(\beta_1, ch, \beta_{2,ch}, st_\Sigma)$ outputs.

The correctness immediately follows from the correctness of Σ and OT. If the size of the challenge space of C is a constant (or scales logarithmically with N) then, the efficiency also directly follows from the efficiency of Σ. In the full version of this paper we prove the following two theorems.

Theorem 17 (Weak δ-Soundness). *Assuming Σ satisfies weak δ-soundness, Construction 3 satisfies weak $(\delta + \gamma)$-soundness for every constant (or even non-negligible function) $\gamma > 0$.*

Theorem 18 (Statistical Malicious Sender Privacy). *Assuming OT is statistical sender private, and Σ satisfies special statistical malicious sender privacy, Construction 3 is statistically malicious circuit private.*

5.3   Weakly δ-Sound to negl(λ)-Sound Transformation

Here we present a generic transformation that for any constant $\delta > 0$ converts a weakly δ-sound 2-round C-PSM to a negl(λ)-sound 2-round C-PSM. The transformation is essentially parallel repetition of the weakly-sound protocol, but the verification algorithm also checks that all the repetitions return the same set of indices.

For the following construction, let $\Sigma = (\mathsf{Setup}, \mathsf{R}, \mathsf{S}, \mathsf{Verify})$ be any weakly sound 2-round C-PSM with δ-soundness.

Construction 4. Let $rep := rep(\lambda, N, c)$ be a parameter indicating the number of repetitions. The construction is as follows:

- Setup$(1^\lambda, N)$:
  - Generate and output rep independent CRSs for Σ, $crs := \{crs_\Sigma^i \leftarrow \Sigma.\mathsf{Setup}(1^\lambda, N)\}_{i \in [rep]}$.
- R(crs, x):
  - Generate rep first messages for Σ along with their internal state, $\{(\alpha_\Sigma^i, st_\Sigma^i) \leftarrow \Sigma.\mathsf{R}(crs_\Sigma^i, x)\}_{i \in [rep]}$.
  - Output the first messages $\alpha := \{\alpha_\Sigma^i\}_{i \in [rep]}$ and internal state $st = (x, \{st_\Sigma^i\}_{i \in [rep]})$.
- S$(crs, \alpha, \mathsf{DB})$:
  - Compute and output rep second messages for Σ, $\beta := \{\beta_\Sigma^i \leftarrow \Sigma.\mathsf{S}(crs_\Sigma^i, \alpha_\Sigma^i, \mathsf{DB})\}_{i \in [rep]}$.
- Verify(β, st):
  - Accept iff each repetition accepts and outputs a sequence of indices of size c $\{I_i := \Sigma.\mathsf{Verify}\beta_i, st_i\}_{i \in [rep]}$ and all the sequences I_i are equal.

The correctness and statistical malicious sender privacy of Construction 4 immediately follow because the same properties hold in Σ. This construction satisfies efficiency as long as rep grows at most logarithmically in N.

Theorem 19. *If Σ is weakly δ-sound, then, Construction 4 is $N^c \cdot \delta^{rep}$-sound.*

Proof. For each possible sequence I^*, the probability that all of the repetitions accept and output I^* is at most δ^{rep}. Since we have at most N^c different sequences, the theorem follows.

By setting $rep := (\lambda + c \cdot \log(N))/\log(1/\delta)$ we get $2^{-\lambda}$ soundness.

5.4   Putting Everything Together

In this section, we combine the constructions in Subsect. 5.1 with the transformations in Subsect. 5.2 and Subsect. 5.3, to obtain 2-round C-PSM constructions for richer classes of functionalities.

Theorem 20. *Assuming hardness of either of DDH or LWE, there exists a family of 2-round C-PSM protocols in the CRS model with the following properties:*

1. *It supports all predicates f such that f can be implemented by an NC^1 circuit and also for every database DB of size N, Search$(\cdot, f, \mathsf{DB})$ can be implemented by a branching program of length logarithmic in N.*
2. *It only makes black-box use of the underlying cryptographic primitives.*
3. *It is receiver private.*
4. *It is (strongly) sound.*
5. *It satisfies statistical malicious sender privacy.*
6. *It has transparent setup, i.e., the CRS is simply a random string.*

Theorem 21. *Assuming hardness of LWE, there exists a family of 2-round C-PSM protocols in the CRS model with the following properties:*

1. *It supports all predicates f such that f can be implemented by bounded-depth circuits, i.e., the C-PSM protocol is leveled.*
2. *Its only non-black-box use of the underlying cryptographic primitives happens through bootstrapping.*
3. *It is receiver private.*
4. *It is (strongly) sound.*
5. *It satisfies statistical malicious sender privacy.*
6. *It has transparent setup.*

Acknowledgments. Sanjam Garg is supported in part by DARPA under Agreement No. HR00112020026, AFOSR Award FA9550-19-1-0200, NSF CNS Award 1936826, and research grants by the Sloan Foundation, and Visa Inc. Omkant Pandey is supported in part by DARPA SIEVE Award HR00112020026, NSF CAREER Award 2144303, NSF grants 2028920, 2106263, and 2128187. Any opinions, findings and conclusions or recommendations expressed in this material are those of the author(s) and do not necessarily reflect the views of the United States Government, DARPA, Sloan Foundation, Visa Inc., or NSF.

References

1. Aggarwal, D., Döttling, N., Dujmovic, J., Hajiabadi, M., Malavolta, G., Obremski, M.: Algebraic restriction codes and their applications. In: ITC, pp. 2:1–2:15 (2022)
2. Apple Inc: Password monitoring - apple support (2021). https://support.apple.com/guide/security/password-monitoring-sec78e79fc3b/web
3. Barrington, D.A.M.: Bounded-width polynomial-size branching programs recognize exactly those languages in NC^1. In: STOC, pp. 1–5 (1986)
4. Ben-Or, M., Goldwasser, S., Wigderson, A.: Completeness theorems for non-cryptographic fault-tolerant distributed computation (extended abstract). In: STOC, pp. 1–10 (1988)
5. Chase, M., Garg, S., Hajiabadi, M., Li, J., Miao, P.: Amortizing rate-1 OT and applications to PIR and PSI. In: Nissim, K., Waters, B. (eds.) TCC 2021. LNCS, vol. 13044, pp. 126–156. Springer, Cham (2021). https://doi.org/10.1007/978-3-030-90456-2_5
6. Chen, H., Huang, Z., Laine, K., Rindal, P.: Labeled PSI from fully homomorphic encryption with malicious security. In: CCS, pp. 1223–1237 (2018)
7. Chen, H., Laine, K., Rindal, P.: Fast private set intersection from homomorphic encryption. In: CCS, pp. 1243–1255 (2017)
8. Chor, B., Kushilevitz, E., Goldreich, O., Sudan, M.: Private information retrieval. J. ACM **45**(6), 965–981 (1998)
9. Cong, K., et al.: Labeled PSI from homomorphic encryption with reduced computation and communication. In: CCS, pp. 1135–1150 (2021)
10. Döttling, N., Dujmovic, J.: Maliciously circuit-private FHE from information-theoretic principles. In: ITC (2022)
11. Google Inc: Protect your accounts from data breaches with password checkup (2019). https://security.googleblog.com/2019/02/protect-your-accounts-from-data.html
12. Hubácek, P., Wichs, D.: On the communication complexity of secure function evaluation with long output. In: ITCS, pp. 163–172 (2015)
13. Ishai, Y., Kushilevitz, E., Ostrovsky, R., Sahai, A.: Zero-knowledge from secure multiparty computation. In: STOC, pp. 21–30 (2007)
14. Ishai, Y., Paskin, A.: Evaluating branching programs on encrypted data. In: Vadhan, S.P. (ed.) TCC 2007. LNCS, vol. 4392, pp. 575–594. Springer, Heidelberg (2007). https://doi.org/10.1007/978-3-540-70936-7_31
15. Izabachène, M., Nitulescu, A., de Perthuis, P., Pointcheval, D.: Myope: malicious security for oblivious polynomial evaluation. In: SCN, pp. 663–686 (2022)
16. Kannepalli, S., Laine, K., Moreno, R.C.: Password monitor: Safeguarding passwords in microsoft edge (2021). https://www.microsoft.com/en-us/research/blog/password-monitor-safeguarding-passwords-in-microsoft-edge/
17. Marlinspike, M.: The difficulty of private contact discovery (2014). https://whispersystems.org/blog/contact-discovery/
18. Merkle, R.C.: A digital signature based on a conventional encryption function. In: Pomerance, C. (ed.) CRYPTO 1987. LNCS, vol. 293, pp. 369–378. Springer, Heidelberg (1988). https://doi.org/10.1007/3-540-48184-2_32
19. Micali, S., Rabin, M.O., Kilian, J.: Zero-knowledge sets. In: FOCS, pp. 80–91 (2003)
20. Okamoto, T., Pietrzak, K., Waters, B., Wichs, D.: New realizations of somewhere statistically binding hashing and positional accumulators. In: Iwata, T., Cheon, J.H. (eds.) ASIACRYPT 2015. LNCS, vol. 9452, pp. 121–145. Springer, Heidelberg (2015). https://doi.org/10.1007/978-3-662-48797-6_6

21. Ostrovsky, R., Paskin-Cherniavsky, A., Paskin-Cherniavsky, B.: Maliciously circuit-private FHE. In: Garay, J.A., Gennaro, R. (eds.) CRYPTO 2014. LNCS, vol. 8616, pp. 536–553. Springer, Heidelberg (2014). https://doi.org/10.1007/978-3-662-44371-2_30

22. Peikert, C., Vaikuntanathan, V., Waters, B.: A framework for efficient and composable oblivious transfer. In: Wagner, D. (ed.) CRYPTO 2008. LNCS, vol. 5157, pp. 554–571. Springer, Heidelberg (2008). https://doi.org/10.1007/978-3-540-85174-5_31

Improved Private Set Intersection for Sets with Small Entries

Dung Bui[1] and Geoffroy Couteau[2(✉)]

[1] IRIF, Université Paris Cité, Paris, France
`bui@irif.fr`
[2] CNRS, IRIF, Université Paris Cité, Paris, France
`couteau@irif.fr`

Abstract. We introduce new protocols for private set intersection (PSI), building upon recent constructions of pseudorandom correlation generators, such as vector-OLE and ring-OLE. Our new constructions improve over the state of the art on several aspects, and perform especially well in the setting where the parties have databases with small entries. We obtain three main contributions:

1. We introduce a new semi-honest PSI protocol that combines subfield vector-OLE with hash-based PSI. Our protocol is the first PSI protocol to achieve communication complexity *independent* of the computational security parameter κ, and has communication lower than all previous known protocols for input sizes ℓ below 70 bits.

2. We enhance the security of our protocol to the malicious setting, using two different approaches. In particular, we show that applying the *dual execution technique* yields a malicious PSI whose communication remains independent of κ, and improves over all known PSI protocols for small values of ℓ.

3. As most previous protocols, our above protocols are in the random oracle model. We introduce a third protocol which relies on subfield ring-OLE to achieve maliciously secure PSI in the *standard model*, under the ring-LPN assumption. Our protocol enjoys extremely low communication, reasonable computation, and standard model security. Furthermore, it is *batchable*: the message of a client can be reused to compute the intersection of their set with that of multiple servers, yielding further reduction in the overall amortized communication.

1 Introduction

Private Set Intersection (PSI) is a cryptographic primitive that allows parties to jointly compute the set of all common elements between their datasets, without leaking any value outside of the intersection. It is a special case of secure multi-party computation (MPC). PSI enjoys a wide array of real-life applications; it is perhaps the most actively researched concrete functionality in secure computation, and has been the target of a tremendous number of works, see [10,13,18–24,26–28] and references therein for a sample. As a consequence of this intense research effort, modern PSI protocols now achieve impressive efficiency features,

A. Boldyreva and V. Kolesnikov (Eds.): PKC 2023, LNCS 13941, pp. 190–220, 2023.
https://doi.org/10.1007/978-3-031-31371-4_7

communicating only a few hundred bits per database items, and processing millions of items in seconds.

Improving PSI with Pseudorandom Correlation Generators. Pseudorandom correlation generators (PCG) have been introduced in the works of [3, 5, 8] and have been the subject of a long and fruitful line of work [3–8, 11, 30, 32, 34]. At a high level, a PCG allows two parties to securely stretch long pseudorandom correlated strings from short, correlated seeds. Securely sharing correlated random strings is a crucial component in most modern secure computation protocols, which operate in the preprocessing model; PCG allows to realize this functionality with almost no communication. Among their many applications, PCGs allow to construct *silent oblivious transfer extension* protocols [4], which can realize (pseudorandom) OT extension with minimal (logarithmic) communication.

Since the top-performing PSI protocols rely on efficient OT extension, using PCG-based techniques to improve their efficiency is a natural idea. And indeed, this was done recently for OKVS-based PSI in [27], leading to the most efficient PSI protocol known to date (OKVS stands for oblivious key-value store [13]; the use of OKVS is the leading paradigm for the design of PSI protocols). To give a single datapoint, computing the intersection between two databases of size $n = 2^{20}$ with the protocol of [27] communicates as little as $426n$ bits in total. In addition, some of the tools used in [27] have been significantly improved since: replacing their OKVS (which is the PaXoS OKVS of [21]) by the more recent 3H-GCT OKVS of [13], and replacing their PCG (which is the one from [32]) by the recent PCG of [11], the cost goes down to an impressive $247n$ bits of total communication. In comparison, even the *insecure* approach of exchanging the hashes of all items in the databases already requires $160n$ bits of communication. OKVS-based PSI protocols are now firmly established as the leading paradigm in the field, and the use of PCGs to reduce their communication overhead even more seems to further widen the gap with the other paradigms.

1.1   Our Contributions

We thoroughly investigate how the use pseudorandom correlation generators can reduce communication in PSI protocols. We obtain several contributions:

- A new family of semi-honest hash-based PSI protocols. Our protocols can be instantiated using several hashing techniques, and achieve very low communication, especially for databases whose entries have a small bitlength.
- New maliciously secure hash-based PSI protocols. Here, interestingly, we revive the dual execution technique, which had been used previously to design malicious PSI protocols in [26], but was considered outdated. We show that, combined with our new approach, it leads to very competitive protocols, which achieve lower communication than all known alternatives for databases with small entries.
- Eventually, we design a new maliciously secure polynomial-based PSI protocol. Our protocol enjoys several powerful features: competitive communication, security in the standard model under the ring-LPN assumption (in contrast, other maliciously secure PSI use the ROM), and the possibility for

a client to publish a single encoding of its database, and later retrieve the intersection of its database with that of multiple servers independently, with a single server-to-client message, plus minimal (database-independent) additional communication.

Below, we elaborate on each of our contributions.

Low Communication PSI for Databases with Small Entries. Modern PSI protocols have communication $O(\kappa \cdot n)$, where n is the database size, and κ is a computational security parameter. More precisely, the receiver-to-sender communication is $O(\kappa \dot{n})$, while the sender-to-receiver communication is $O(\lambda \cdot n)$, where λ is a *statistical* security parameter (typically, $\kappa = 128$ and $\lambda = 40$). We introduce a new protocol, that combines hashing techniques (e.g. Cuckoo hashing or its variants, as initially used in [18]) with a new PCG-based oblivious pseudorandom function (OPRF). In contrast to all previous works, our work avoid the $O(\kappa \cdot n)$ overhead: it reduces the receiver-to-sender communication to be roughly $\ell \cdot n$ (where ℓ is the bitsize of the database items), leading to a significant reduction in the overall communication. To our knowledge, our protocol is the first to achieve communication independent of κ (up to low order terms). To give a datapoint, for $n = 2^{20}$, with 64-bit entries, our protocol communicates $210n$ bits, and with 32-bit entries, it communicates only $148n$ bits. For the same parameters, the leading OKVS-based PSI of [27] communicates $197n$ bits, even after improving it with all relevant optimization (such as using the 3H-GCT OKVS of [13], and the recent PCG of [11]). We provide further datapoints and comparisons to the state of the art on Table 1, when instantiating our protocols with various hashing methods.

Fast Maliciously-Secure PSI for Small Entries. We then turn our attention to maliciously secure PSI. We provide two alternative protocols which achieve malicious security; both use standard paradigms for upgrading PSI to malicious security. The first protocol combines our new PCG-based OPRF with simple hashing, and applies the standard paradigm used in most previous OKVS-based PSI to achieve malicious security (e.g. [27]). This requires to increase the sender-to-receiver message length, from $O(\lambda \cdot n)$ to $O(\kappa \cdot n)$ (λ is a statistical security parameter, κ is a computational security parameter; typically, $\lambda = 40$ and $\kappa = 128$) to allow for extraction of the sender input. Along the way, we also notice a small mistake in the parameter choices of [27]: they devise a new ROM-based extraction strategy in the malicious setting, and prove that a Q-query adversary will make extraction fail with probability bounded $Q \cdot n/2^\kappa$ (this is the probability that one of the Q queries of the malicious receiver collides with an element of the sender set). This implies that, to target 128 bits of computational security, one must set $\kappa = 128 + \log n$. However, the numbers reported in [27] correspond to choosing $\kappa = 128$ at the 128-bit security level. We took this minor inconsistency into account in our tables.

More interestingly, our second protocol applies *dual execution* [26] to our PCG-based protocol with simple hashing. We observe that, in our context, this

Table 1. Comparison of the communication cost of several PSI protocols in the semi-honest setting and in the malicious setting, for various choices of the database size n (we assume that both parties have a database of the same size). ℓ denote the bit-length of the inputs in the database; we set the computational security parameter κ to 128 and the statistical security parameter λ to 40 (for usual applications) or 30 (which can be suitable for lower risk applications). For all protocols, we take into account the optimization of [31] which reduces the costs of sending n elements of bitlength $\lambda + 2 \cdot \log n$ to $n \cdot (\lambda + \log n)$. GCH stands for Generalized Cuckoo hashing (here, with 2 hash functions and 3 items per bin), 2CH for 2-choice hashing, and SH for simple hashing (N is the number of bins).

	$n = 2^{14}$	$n = 2^{16}$	$n = 2^{20}$	$n = 2^{24}$
Semi-honest setting				
KKRT16 [18]	$930n$	$936n$	$948n$	$960n$
PRTY19 [20] low*	$491n$	$493n$	$493n$	$494n$
PRTY19 [20] fast*	$560n$	$571n$	$579n$	$587n$
CM20 [10]	$668n$	$662n$	$674n$	$676n$
PRTY20 [21]	$1244n$	$1192n$	$1248n$	$1278n$
RS21 [27]	$2024n$	$898n$	$406n$	$374n$
RS21 [27] enhanced**	$280n$	$260n$	$263n$	$275n$
Ours ($\ell = 64$, GCH)	$246n$	$220n$	$210n$	$209n$
Ours ($\ell = 48$, GCH)	$215n$	$189n$	$179n$	$178n$
Ours ($\ell = 32$, GCH)	$184n$	$158n$	$148n$	$147n$
Ours ($\ell = 64$, 2CH)	$214n$	$190n$	$183n$	$185n$
Ours ($\ell = 48$, 2CH)	$193n$	$169n$	$162n$	$164n$
Ours ($\ell = 32$, 2CH)	$171n$	$148n$	$141n$	$142n$
Ours ($\ell = 64$, SH, $N = n/10$)	$332n$	$302n$	$284n$	$276n$
Ours ($\ell = 48$, SH, $N = n/10$)	$261n$	$230n$	$209n$	$198n$
Ours ($\ell = 32$, SH, $N = n/10$)	$191n$	$158n$	$133n$	$120n$
Ours ($\ell = 64$, SH, $N = 1$) ***	$154n$	$131n$	$125n$	$128n$
Ours ($\ell = 48$, SH, $N = 1$) ***	$138n$	$115n$	$109n$	$112n$
Ours ($\ell = 32$, SH, $N = 1$) ***	$122n$	$99n$	$93n$	$96n$
Malicious setting				
RS21 [27] enhanced**	$343n$	$320n$	$315n$	$318n$
Ours ($\ell = 48$, SH, $N = n/10$)	$430n$	$393n$	$356n$	$332n$
Ours ($\ell = 40$, SH, $N = n/10$)	$359n$	$321n$	$281n$	$253n$
Ours ($\ell = 32$, SH, $N = n/10$)	$289n$	$249n$	$205n$	$175n$

* PRTY19 has two variants, SpOT-low (lowest communication, higher computation) and SpOT-fast (higher communication, better computation). Both use expensive polynomial interpolation and require significantly more computation compared to all other protocols in this table.

** Using the 3H-GCT OKVS of [13] instead of PaXoS, and the VOLE of [11] instead of the one from [32]. Setting κ_{RS21} to $\kappa + \log n$ to achieve κ bits of security.

*** Using $N = 1$ requires an expensive degree-n polynomial interpolation.

allows to achieve malicious security without having to increase the length of the sender-to-receiver message, at the cost of increasing the receiver-to-sender communication by a factor 2. Since our approach makes this communication as low as $O(\ell \cdot n)$, this turns out to be an excellent tradeoff whenever the database entries are not too large. Therefore, our results show that the landscape of maliciously secure PSI is more subtle than previously thought: for large entries, the standard approach still dominates, but for smaller entries (e.g. $\ell \leq 40$), the dual execution technique leads to better performances. This revives the dual execution technique, which was previously considered obsolete compared to the modern alternatives.

Efficient PSI in the Standard Model. Eventually, our last contribution is a new "polynomial-based" PSI protocol that does not rely on the random oracle model, following the high level structure of previous works [14,15,17]. To this end, we introduce the notion of PCG for the *subfield ring-OLE* correlation, and show how a simple variant of the recent PCG for ring-OLE of [7] leads to efficient instantiations of this primitive. Then, we describe a new PSI protocol built on top of this PCG, which enjoys a number of very interesting features.

Security Features. Our PSI protocol is in the standard model: unlike our first protocol, it does not require the random oracle model, or any tailor-made correlation-robustness assumptions. We rely solely on the (relatively well-established) ring-LPN assumption over polynomial rings with irreducible polynomials. To our knowledge, our protocol is the first standard model protocol which offers competitive performances compared to protocols using the random oracle heuristic or tailored assumptions. Furthermore, our PSI protocol enjoys full malicious security (for both parties) *almost for free*. This stems from the use of PCGs, which allows to confine the "price" of achieving malicious security to the distributed seed generation only, which has logarithmic communication and computation (in the set size n).

We note that, though malicious security comes for free communication- and computation-wise, the tweaks used to guarantee malicious security in our protocol are not straightforward. In fact, achieving malicious security efficiently in polynomial-based PSI protocols is known to be complex and error prone. For example, previous works [14] used a superficially similar approach and claimed malicious security, but their protocol was found to be insecure in a recent preprint, which described powerful concrete attacks on this proposal [1]. Leveraging the specific structure of our protocol, we manage to get around these nontrivial subtleties with careful structural checks, for a minimal cost (independent of the database size).

Efficiency Features. Our PSI protocol enjoys a very low communication, considerably lower than all previous PSI protocols in the standard model which we are aware of (excluding iO- or FHE-based protocol, which can have very low communication but poor concrete efficiency). In fact, communication-wise, our PSI protocol is even on par with the best *ROM-based* PSI protocols of previous works. Concretely, for sets of size n with ℓ-bit entries, our protocol communicates $(2\ell + 3\lambda + 3 \log n) \cdot n + o(n)$ bits. To give a single datapoint, for $\ell = 32$ and $n = 2^{20}$, we estimate the total communication to be $278n$ bits. This is on par with the best maliciously secure protocol [27], which communicates $279n$ bits in the same setting, with comparable computation (it also uses polynomial interpolation), but without standard model security.

On Table 2, we compare our protocol to the current fastest maliciously secure PSI protocols [21,27,29]. As the table shows, the communication of our protocol is almost on par with that of the best protocol (the protocol of [27], enhanced with the latest VOLE protocol) for small-ish input size, and large enough set sizes. Yet, our protocol is in the standard model under the ring-LPN assumption, while [27] is only proven secure in the ROM.

Table 2. Comparison of the communication cost of several PSI protocols in the malicious model, for various choices of the database size n (we assume that both parties have a database of the same size) and statistical security parameter $\lambda = 40$, using the encoding technique of [31]. ℓ denote the bit-length of the inputs in the database; we set the computational security parameter κ to 128. For fairness of comparison, since our standard model PSI uses interpolation, we compare it to RS21 with an interpolation-based OKVS (which has better communication), and we compare our other PSIs with RS21 instantiated with (computationally) efficient OKVS.

Protocol	Communication					Hardness Assumption	Standard Model
	$n = 2^{16}$	$n = 2^{18}$	$n = 2^{20}$	$n = 2^{22}$	$n = 2^{24}$		
Our Standard PSI						Ring-LPN	✓
$\ell = 64$	$724n$	$423n$	$342n$	$324n$	$323n$	+ OT	
$\ell = 48$	$692n$	$391n$	$310n$	$292n$	$291n$		
$\ell = 32$	$660n$	$359n$	$278n$	$260n$	$259n$		
RS21 [27] enhanced*	$318n$	$286n$	$279n$	$279n$	$280n$	LPN + OT	✗
Our Direct PSI						LPN + OT	✗
$\ell = 64$	$421n$	$385n$	$374n$	$369n$	$365n$		
$\ell = 48$	$348n$	$311n$	$298n$	$292n$	$286n$		
$\ell = 32$	$277n$	$237n$	$223n$	$215n$	$208n$		
Our Dual PSI							
$\ell = 64$	$609n$	$535n$	$511n$	$499n$	$489n$		
$\ell = 48$	$465n$	$388n$	$361n$	$345n$	$333n$		
$\ell = 32$	$321n$	$240n$	$210n$	$192n$	$176n$		
PRTY20 [21]	$1766n$					OT	✗
RT21 [29]	$512n$					DH	✗
RS21 [27] enhanced**	$320n$	$315n$	$315n$	$317n$	$318n$	LPN + OT	✗

* Using interpolation instead of PaXoS, and the VOLE of [11] instead of the one from [32]. Sets κ_{RS21} to $\kappa + \log n$ to achieve κ bits of security.

** Using the new OKVS of [13] instead of PaXoS, and the VOLE of [11] instead of the one from [32]. Sets κ_{RS21} to $\kappa + \log n$ to achieve κ bits of security.

Batch Non-interactive PSI. On top of these security and efficiency features, the structure of our protocol allows to obtain a powerful interaction pattern: it leads to a batch non-interactive PSI, where after a short interaction with each server, a client C with set X can broadcast a *single* encoding of its database, and receive afterwards at anytime a single message from each server S_i with set X_i (plus, in the malicious setting, a small database-size-independent 2-round structural check), from which they can decode $X \cap X_i$. To achieve this feature, we build upon the fact that the PCG for subfield ring-OLE correlations is *programmable*, which means that we can enforce that a target party will receive the same pseudorandom string across executions with many different parties. Concretely, we achieve the following form of *batch non-interactive PSI* between a client C with database X and multiple servers S_i with datasets X_i (all of size n):

1. In a preprocessing phase, C interacts with each of the servers, using $O(\log n)$ communication *and* computation in each interaction, in a small constant number of rounds.
2. Then, C performs a single $\tilde{O}(n)$ cost local computation, and broadcasts a single $2\ell n$-size *encoding E_X* of X.
3. Each server S_i can, at any time, send a single message $M_i = m(X_i, E_X)$, of length $3(\lambda + \log n)n$, using $\tilde{O}(n)$ computation.
4. Eventually, given X and M_i, the client C can run a $\tilde{O}(n)$ cost decoding procedure and recover $X \cap X_i$, without further interaction.

When the number of servers becomes large, our batch PSI protocol leads to strong savings for the client compared to executing a PSI protocol individually with each server. Furthermore, in this setting, the amortized communication (per PSI instance) is reduced to $(2\ell/N_S + 3\lambda + \log n) \cdot n + o(n)$, where N_S denotes the number of servers. Even for relatively small number of servers, the amortized communication quickly outperforms that of even the best ROM-based maliciously secure PSI protocols. For example, for $n = 2^{24}$ and $\ell = 32$, the amortized communication per secure set intersection approaches $195n$ bits with our protocol, versus $280n$ for [27].

1.2   Concurrent Work

In a concurrent and independent work, recently accepted at CCS'22, Rindal and Raghuraman [25] introduced a new PSI protocol, using an approach similar to ours: the authors also leveraged subfield-VOLE to achieve communication independent of the computational security parameter κ. Our results have been obtained independently of theirs, around the same time period. Although their main result bears similarities to our first two contributions, we highlight some important distinctions between our work and theirs:

– The work of [25] uses an OKVS-based construction, and achieves a receiver-to-sender communication of $(\lambda + 2 \log n) \cdot n$. In contrast, we use a hash-based protocol, and achieve an $(\ell - \log n) \cdot n$ receiver-to-sender communication. Therefore, we get smaller communication overall in the setting where the databases have small entries, but a slightly larger computation.

- For malicious security, the work of [25] only considers the standard paradigm of previous works (e.g. [27]), hence having a $O(\kappa \cdot n)$ receiver-to-sender (and overall) communication. In contrast, we give two protocols, including one based on dual execution which achieves communication independent of κ (and smaller concrete communication for databases with small entries).
- Eventually, our last contribution, a "batchable" ring-OLE-based malicious PSI in the standard model with low communication, is unique to our work.

1.3   Structure of the Paper

We provide preliminaries in Sect. 2, and a detailed technical overview of our contributions in Sect. 3. Section 4 covers our ROM-based semi-honest and malicious protocols. Due to space limitation, our second malicious protocol, based on dual execution, is presented in the full version [9]. Section 5 covers our standard model PSI. Note that the additional preliminaries and all the missing proofs appear in full version [9].

2   Preliminaries

Notation. Throughout the paper we use the following notations: we let κ, λ denote the computational and statistical security parameters, respectively. We write $[1, m]$ to denote a set $\{1, 2, \ldots, m\}$. For a vector $\mathbf{x}$ we define by x_i its i-th coordinate. Given distribution ensembles $\{X_n\}, \{Y_n\}$, we write $X_n \approx Y_n$ to denote that X_n is computationally indistinguishable to Y_n.

We typically write $\mathbb{F}_q$ to denote a field with and arbitrary subfield $\mathbb{F}_p$, where p is a prime power and $q = p^t$. We use $\mathcal{R}_{\mathsf{p}} = \mathbb{F}_{\mathsf{p}}[\mathsf{X}]/\mathsf{F}(\mathsf{X})$ for the ring over the field $\mathbb{F}_p$ where $F(x)$ is some polynomial, and also denote $\mathcal{R}_{\mathsf{q}} = \mathbb{F}_{\mathsf{p}^t}[\mathsf{X}]/\mathsf{F}(\mathsf{X})$. Note that all operations in our paper are field/ring operations not modular arithmetic.

PSI Functionality. A private set intersection (PSI) protocol allows two parties to compute the intersection of their input sets while concealing all other information. We typically denote by n the input set sizes. For completeness, the ideal functionalities for PSI (in the semi-honest and in the malicious settings) are given in Appendix of the full version [9].

Pseudorandom Correlation Generators (PCG). Pseudorandom correlations generators have been introduced in a recent line of work [3–5]. A PCG allows to compress long correlations into short, correlated seeds that can later be locally expanded into pseudorandom instances of the target correlation. Slightly more formally, a PCG for a target correlation C (which samples pairs of long correlated strings (y_0, y_1)) is a pair (Gen, Expand) of algorithms such that $\mathsf{Gen}(1^\lambda)$ outputs a pair of short, correlated keys $(\mathsf{k}_0, \mathsf{k}_1)$ and $\mathsf{Expand}(\sigma, \mathsf{k}_\sigma)$ outputs a long string $\tilde{y}_\sigma$. Correctness states that $(\tilde{y}_0, \tilde{y}_1)$ are indistinguishable from a random sample from C, while security states that given $\mathsf{k}_{1-\sigma}$, $\tilde{y}_\sigma$ looks like a random sample from C conditioned on satisfying the target correlation with $\mathsf{Expand}(1-\sigma, \mathsf{k}_{1-\sigma})$, for $\sigma = 0, 1$.

A PCG does not in itself provide a protocol to efficiently generate long pseudorandom correlations. To get the latter, one must combine a PCG with a *distributed key generation* protocol, which allows two parties to obliviously run $\mathsf{Gen}(1^\lambda)$ such that each party gets one of the keys. Fortunately, for most PCGs of interest (and in particular, for all PCGs we use in this work), there exists very efficient low-communication distributed setup protocols [4,7]. Combining a PCG with a distributed setup protocols allows to securely instantiate (with low communication) functionalities that distribute instances of the target correlation. In this work, we will directly rely in a black-box way on such functionalities, and use known protocols to instantiate them. We now expand on the two main functionalities we use in this work.

PARAMETERS:

- 2 parties, a sender and receiver, an integer n, the size of the output vector.
- A finite field $\mathbb{F}_q$ where $q = p^r$, p is a power of prime, r an integer.

FUNCTIONALITY:

- Depending on the parties:
  - If the sender is corrupted then wait for $\mathcal{A}$ to send 2 vectors $\mathbf{u} \in \mathbb{F}_p^n, \mathbf{v} \in \mathbb{F}_q^n$; samples $\Delta \leftarrow_r \mathbb{F}_q$ and computes $\mathbf{w} := \Delta \cdot \mathbf{u} + \mathbf{v}$.
  - If the receiver is corrupted then wait for $\mathcal{A}$ to send $\mathbf{w} \in \mathbb{F}_q^n$, $\Delta \in \mathbb{F}_q$; samples $\mathbf{u} \leftarrow_r \mathbb{F}_p^n$ and computes $\mathbf{v} := \mathbf{w} - \Delta \cdot \mathbf{u}$.
  - Otherwise, samples $\mathbf{u} \in \mathbb{F}_p^n, \mathbf{v} \in \mathbb{F}_q^n, \Delta \leftarrow_r \mathbb{F}_q$ and computes $\mathbf{w} := \Delta \cdot \mathbf{u} + \mathbf{v}$.
- The functionality sends $\mathbf{u} \in \mathbb{F}_p^n$, $\mathbf{v} \in \mathbb{F}_q^n$ to sender and $\Delta \in \mathbb{F}_q$, $\mathbf{w} := \Delta \cdot \mathbf{u} + \mathbf{v}$ to receiver.

Fig. 1. Ideal functionality $(n, p, q) - \mathcal{F}_{\mathsf{svole}}$ of subfield vector-OLE

Subfield Vector-OLE. We described the subfield vector-OLE correlation in the technical overview of [9]. We represent on Fig. 1 the ideal functionality that distributes a subfield VOLE correlation. In our concrete instantiations, we will instantiate this functionality using the efficient protocol of [4]. The latter provides a general template which can be instantiated under various flavors of the LPN assumption, and provides a conservative choice under LPN for quasi-cyclic choice. A variant of LPN that leads to a considerably more efficient protocol, when plugged in the template of [4], was recently put forth in the work [11] (we note that our communications estimate are oblivious to the underlying variant: only the computational costs depends on the LPN flavor).

Subfield Ring-OLE. Recently, a new PCG construction was described in [7] for the *ring-OLE* correlation. The ring-OLE correlation over a ring $\mathcal{R}_q$ is the following correlation: $\{((x_0, z_0), (x_1, z_1)) \mid x_0, x_1, z_0 \leftarrow_r \mathcal{R}_q, z_1 \leftarrow x_0.x_1 - z_0\}$. In this work, we rely on a slight variant of the ring-OLE correlation, where x_0 is instead sampled from a subring $\mathcal{R}_p$ of $\mathcal{R}_q$. We represent the corresponding variant of the ideal functionality in the full version [9]. We note that the protocol of [7] to instantiate the ring-OLE functionality can be adapted to handle the subfield ring-OLE functionality in a straightforward way.

3 Technical Overview

Our starting point is the classical KKRT protocol [18], which combines Cuckoo hashing with a batch related-key oblivious pseudorandom function (BaRK-OPRF). We assume some familiarity with the KKRT protocol in this technical overview. For completeness, we provide a high level overview of KKRT, the notion of BaRK-OPRF (batch related-key oblivious pseudorandom function), and its communication costs in Appendix of full version [9]. Our construction will also rely on a functionality that distributes *subfield vector-OLE* correlation (the sVOLE functionality): Alice gets $(\mathbf{u}, \mathbf{v})$, and Bob gets $(\Delta, \mathbf{w} = \Delta\mathbf{u}+\mathbf{v})$. Such correlation can be distributed with very low communication using pseudorandom correlation generators.

3.1 A New sVOLE-Based PSI for Databases with Small Entries

Subfield-VOLE leads to a simple and natural construction of BaRK-OPRF. Let ℓ be the bitlength of Alice's inputs, and let $\mathbf{x} = (x_1, \cdots, x_n)$ be the inputs of Alice, viewed as elements of $\mathbb{F}_{2^\ell}$. We assume for simplicity that ℓ divides κ, the computational security parameter. Alice and Bob use an sVOLE protocol (e.g. [11]) over the field $\mathbb{F}_{2^\kappa}$, with subfield $\mathbb{F}_{2^\ell}$; let $(\mathbf{u}, \mathbf{v})$ be the output of Alice, and $(\Delta, \mathbf{w})$ be the output of Bob. Recall that $\mathbf{w} = \Delta\cdot\mathbf{u}+\mathbf{v}$. Alice sends $\mathbf{z} = \mathbf{x}-\mathbf{u}$ to Bob, who defines the BaRK-OPRF keys to be Δ and $(K_1, \cdots, K_n) = \Delta\cdot\mathbf{z}+\mathbf{w}$. The BaRK-OPRF is defined as follows: $F_{\Delta,K_i}(y) = H(i, K_i - \Delta\cdot y)$ (all operations are over $\mathbb{F}_{2^\kappa}$). Eventually, Alice outputs $(H(i, v_i))_{i \le n}$. Observe that

$$H(i, v_i) = H(i, w_i - \Delta u_i) = H(i, K_i - \Delta(z_i + u_i))$$
$$= H(i, K_i - \Delta \cdot x_i) = F_{\Delta,K_i}(x_i)$$

The use of sVOLE, rather than OT extension as in the original KKRT BaRK-OPRF, has two main advantages: first, the bitwise AND is now replaced by a field multiplication. In particular, this means that we do not need anymore to use error-correcting codes, and that $y \cdot \Delta$ retains the entire entropy of Δ. In other words, it suffices for Δ to be κ-bit long to achieve κ bits of security for the construction (in contrast, KKRT had to use around 5κ bits). Second, and most importantly, the use of *subfield* VOLE allows us to completely decorrelate the size of $\mathbf{u}$ from that of Δ, something which can fundamentally not be achieved with the INKP OT extension. Concretely, this means that $\mathbf{u}$ only needs to mask the input vector $\mathbf{x}$ of Alice. If $\mathbf{x} \in \mathbb{F}_{2^\ell}^n$, then so do $\mathbf{u}$ and $\mathbf{z}$: the communication now depends solely on the input size.

In total, our BaRK-OPRF communicates $\ell\cdot n$ bits, plus the cost of distributing the seeds for the sVOLE generator. Using the protocol of [4] to distribute the seeds[1], the cost is logarithmic in n, hence its effect on the overall communication vanishes for large enough n.

Combining the New OPRF with Permutation-Based Hashing. Plugging our new BaRK-OPRF into KKRT, and using the same parameters for Cuckoo hashing, leads to a protocol with total communication $(1.3 \cdot \ell + 3 \cdot (\lambda + 2 \log n))n + o(n)$ bits (where the $o(n)$ terms capture the costs of distributing the PCG seeds). Concretely, for $n = 2^{20}$ and $\ell = 32$ (resp. 64), this already brings the cost down, from $1008n$ bits to $282n$ bits (resp. $324n$ bits). However, this can be further improved using the well-established notion of *permutation-based* hashing [22]. Concretely, in *permutation-based* hashing, an item x is written as $x_L \| x_R$, where x_L is $\log(1.3n)$-bit long. The item x is inserted by mapping x_R to the bin $x_L \oplus f(x_R)$, where f is a k-wise independent hash function, for some large enough k. This guarantees that no collision occurs, because if two items x, x' end up mapping the same value to the same bin, this means that $x_R = x'_R$ and $x_L \oplus f(x_R) = x'_L \oplus f'(x'_R)$, hence $x = x'$. When multiple hash functions are used, as in Cuckoo hashing, the index of the hash function must be appended to x_R.

Interestingly, our use of sVOLE is crucial to enabling a permutation-hashing-based optimization: the latter only provides savings when the communication involves a $O(\ell \cdot n)$ component (which neither KKRT nor any modern OKVS-based PSI has). In our protocol, however, it further reduces the communication to $(1.3 \cdot (\ell - \log(1.3n) + 1) + 3 \cdot (\lambda + 2 \log n))n + o(n)$ bits, which gives $275n$ bits for $n = 2^{20}$ and 32-bit items, or $317n$ bits for 64-bit items. In itself, this is a really small communication improvement. However, it has an important consequence: it implies that the Alice-to-Bob communication is now completely dominated by the Bob-to-Alice communication. Concretely, this means that we can easily afford to use a much higher number of bins (which is $1.3n$ currently) if it can allow us to reduce the number of hash functions (which is 3). This brings us to our last optimization.

Packing Multiple Items per Bin with Generalized Cuckoo Hashing. In this last optimization, our goal is to reduce the number of hash functions used in the Cuckoo hashing protocol, from 3 to 2, by increasing the number of bins to compensate. Unfortunately, this does not work directly with standard cuckoo hashing even while using a reasonably small stash since the cost of handling the stash is high, and nullifies all communication benefits of using two hash functions in the first place. Instead, we use a different approach: we add one degree of freedom to the Cuckoo hashing parameters, *by allowing bins to contain multiple items*. This generalization of Cuckoo hashing is not new: it has been studied in details in several works [12,33], because it comes with a much nicer cache-friendliness than standard Cuckoo hashing.

In (d, k)-Cuckoo hashing, n items are mapped to $(1 + \varepsilon) \cdot n$ bins using k hash functions, and each bin is allowed to contain up to d items. Allowing more items per bins significantly improves the efficiency; for example, $(3, 2)$-Cuckoo hashing is known to perform strictly better than standard $(1, 3)$-Cuckoo hashing

---

[1] This protocol uses a length-t reverse VOLE protocol as a blackbox, which we instantiate with the construction of [2].

in terms of occupancy (i.e., the total number of slots $N = d \cdot (1 + \varepsilon) \cdot n$ which must be used to guarantee a $o(1)$ failure probability). Based on existing analysis of this variant [33], it seems reasonable to expect that $(3,2)$-Cuckoo hashing already achieves a strictly smaller failure probability compared to $(1,3)$-Cuckoo hashing, with a smaller number of bins.

We relied on extensive computer simulations on small values of n (from 256 to 2048) to select parameters, and extrapolated from these results parameters for larger values of n. More precisely, we ran 10^7 experiments with $(3,2)$-Cuckoo hashing for $n \in \{2^8, 2^9, 2^{10}\}$ (we also experimented with 2^{11}, but with a smaller number of experiments) with $c \cdot n$ bins for various values of c. Even for a value as low as $c = 0.65$ and values of n as low as 2^9, our experiments never reported any insertion failure, indicating that the empirical failure probability should already be way below 2^{-20}. Since the theoretical failure probability is known to scale as $O(1/n^\delta)$ for some constant δ with reasonably small constant factors, we extrapolate that for large enough values of n, e.g. $n \geq 2^{18}$, the failure probability should be well below 2^{-40}.

Alternative Hashing Variants. Alternatively, when allowing multiple items per bins, we can consider other hashing variants. Two natural choices are two-choice hashing [20], where each bin can have up two d items and each item is placed in the least-full of two bins, and simple hashing, where a single hash function is used to map the items to bins (standard results show that, when hashing n items to $O(n)$ bins this way, the maximum load with be of the order of $\log n / \log \log n$ with high probability). As we will see, these choices of hashing lead to various communication versus computation tradeoffs in our protocols, and the optimal choice also depends on the database size.

A Membership BaRK-OPRF. There remains a non-trivial task: to use some of the above hashing variants, we need a protocol to handle hashing with up to d items per bins. Intuitively, denoting $\mathbf{x_i} = (x_i^{(1)}, \cdots, x_i^{(d)})$ the d entries of the bin i, we want to construct a new kind of *membership* OPRF (similar in spirit to the notion of multi-point OPRF in the literature), where Bob obtains $F_{\Delta,K_i}(y)$ and Alice obtains the set $F_{\Delta,K_i}(\mathbf{x_i}) = \{F_{\Delta,K_i}(x_i^{(j)})\}_{j \leq d}$. This implies that $F_{\Delta,K_i}(y) \in F_{\Delta,K_i}(\mathbf{x_i})$ if and only if y is equal to any entry of $\mathbf{x_i}$, and $F_{\Delta,K_i}(y)$ looks pseudorandom to Alice otherwise.

Going back to the BaRK-OPRF, recall that for a bin i where Alice placed x_i and Bob placed y_i, Alice computes $H(i, v_i)$ and Bob computes $H(i, K_i - \Delta y_i) = H(i, \Delta \cdot (x_i - y_i) + v_i)$. Here, we view the $x_i - y_i$ term as $P_{x_i}(y_i)$, where $P_{x_i} = X - x_i$ is a degree-1 polynomial with root x_i. This view suggests a natural generalization of this approach, where the P_{x_i} polynomials are replaced by higher degree polynomials. Define $P_{\mathbf{x_i}}$ to be the polynomial $\prod_{j=1}^d (X - x_i^{(j)})$, and let $(c_{j,i})_{0 \leq j \leq d-1}$ denote its coefficients: $P_{\mathbf{x_i}}(X) = X^d + \sum_{j=0}^{d-1} c_{j,i} \cdot X^j$. Our new *membership* BaRK-OPRF is a direct generalization of the BaRK-OPRF from Sect. 3.1, which we sketch below.

Our Construction. Let m be the bitlength of Alice's inputs inside the bins, and let $(\mathbf{x_1}, \cdots, \mathbf{x_N})$ be the inputs of Alice in each of the N bins, where the inputs in each bin are viewed as length-d vectors of elements of $\mathbb{F}_{2^m}$. We assume for simplicity that m divides κ, the computational security parameter. Alice and Bob use d sVOLE protocol (e.g. [11]) over the field $\mathbb{F}_{2^\kappa}$, with subfield $\mathbb{F}_{2^m}$, *with the same value Δ.*[2] Let $(\mathbf{u_j}, \mathbf{v_j})_{j \le d}$ be the outputs of Alice, and $(\Delta, (\mathbf{w_j})_{j \le d})$ be the output of Bob. Recall that $\mathbf{w_j} = \Delta \cdot \mathbf{u_j} + \mathbf{v_j}$.

For each $\mathbf{x_i}$, let $(c_{0,i}, \cdots, c_{d-1,i})$ be the coefficients of the polynomial $P_{\mathbf{x_i}}$ (omitting the coefficient of X^d, which is always 1). Let $\mathbf{c_j}$ denote the vector $(c_{j,i})_{i \le N}$ for $j = 0$ to $d-1$. Alice sends $\mathbf{z_j} = \mathbf{c_j} - \mathbf{u_j}$ for $j = 0$ to $d-1$ to Bob, who defines the membership BaRK-OPRF keys to be Δ and $K_i = (k_{j,i})_{0 \le j \le d-1} = (\Delta \cdot z_{j,i} + w_{j,i})_{0 \le j \le d-1}$ for $i = 1$ to N. Define the following degree-d polynomial P_{Δ, K_i} over $\mathbb{F}_q$: $P_{\Delta, K_i}(X) = \Delta \cdot X^d + \sum_{j=0}^{d-1} k_{j,i} \cdot X^j$. The OPRF is defined as follows: $F_{\Delta, K_i}(y) = H(i, P_{\Delta, K_i}(y))$ (all operations are over $\mathbb{F}_{2^\kappa}$). Eventually, for each bin i, Alice sets her d tuple of outputs to be $F_{\Delta, K_i}(\mathbf{x_i}) = \{H(i, \sum_{j=0}^{d-1} v_{j,i} \cdot (x_i^{(k)})^j)\}_{k \le d}$. Observe that, since $k_{j,i} = \Delta z_{j,i} + w_{j,i} = \Delta c_{j,i} + v_{j,i}$ for all i, j, we have $H(i, P_{\Delta, K_i}(y)) = H\left(i, \Delta \cdot \left(y^d + \sum_{j=0}^{d-1} c_{j,i} y^j\right) + \sum_{j=0}^{d-1} v_{j,i} y^j\right)$, which is equal to $H\left(i, \Delta \cdot P_{\mathbf{x_i}}(y) + \sum_{j=0}^{d-1} v_{j,i} y^j\right)$. Therefore, if there exists $k \in \{1, \cdots, d\}$ such that $y = x_i^{(k)}$, we have $P_{\mathbf{x_i}}(y) = 0$, and $H(i, P_{\Delta, K_i}(y)) = H(i, \sum_{j=0}^{d-1} v_{j,i} \cdot (x_i^{(k)})^j) \in F_{\Delta, K_i}(\mathbf{x_i})$. On the other hand, whenever $P_{\mathbf{x_i}}(y) \ne 0$, then the $\Delta \cdot P_{\mathbf{x_i}}(y)$ term in the hash makes the output pseudorandom from the viewpoint of Alice, under the correlation robustness of the hash function.

Tying Up Loose Ends. Using the new construction from the previous Section, together with $(3, 2)$-Cuckoo hashing, leads to a total communication of $(0.65 \cdot 3(\ell - \log(0.65n) + 1) + 2 \cdot (\lambda + 2 \log n))n + o(n)$ bits, where the $o(n)$ corresponds to the cost of setting up the PCG seeds. For $n = 2^{20}$ and 32 bits items, this gives $148n$ bits of communication. We mention a few remaining details. First, in the construction of membership BaRK-OPRF, Alice and Bob need to invoke $d = 3$ length-N sVOLE. In fact, it suffices to invoke a single length-$3N$ sVOLE, and to cut the output in three equal length parts, to obtain the necessary correlation. This means that the concrete cost of distributing the sVOLE seeds remains that of generating a single sVOLE (e.g. $\approx 0.7n$ bits for $n = 2^{20}$).

Second, in the above, we overlooked an important subtlety: a bin can possibly contain less than d items. In KKRT, this was handled by adding dummy items to empty bins. We use instead a more efficient approach with a negligible extra cost called a *variant* of our OPRF (details in Sect. 4).

3.2   Malicious Security

We then turn our attention to maliciously secure PSI. Here, it is well known that Cuckoo hashing and two-choice hashing are not usable. Consequently, we focus on simple hashing as our choice of the underlying hash technique. Using maliciously secure subfield-VOLE, which can be implemented very efficiently [4,11],

---

[2] Note that all known sVOLE protocols allow Bob to choose the value of Δ, hence Bob can enforce the use of the same Δ across all instances.

we enhance our membership BaRK-OPRF to the malicious setting, with a minimal overhead. Then, we apply two standard methods to achieve security against malicious adversaries in our PSI protocol:

First Method: Direct Approach. The first method increases the PRF output length to κ. Using the analysis of [27], this suffices to allow for extracting the input of a malicious sender. However, this makes the communication depend linearly on κ, which severely harms communication complexity.

Second Method: Dual Execution. To recover a κ-independent communication complexity, we then turn our attention to the dual execution technique [26]. Here, the idea is simple: the parties will invoke the malicious BaRK-OPRF twice, exchanging their roles. Then, the sender sends, for each entry x of his database, a value of the form $\mathsf{PRF}_A(x) \oplus \mathsf{PRF}_B(x)$, where $\mathsf{PRF}_A(x)$ is obtained by the sender when invoking the BaRK-OPRF functionality as sender, and $\mathsf{PRF}_B(x)$ is the PRF output obtained when invoking the functionality as receiver. Here, it becomes possible to extract the input set of each party simply from its call as receiver to the BaRK-OPRF functionality, which does not require to increase the output length of the OPRF. The price to pay is that the protocol now uses two calls to the BaRK-OPRF. Concretely, the total communication becomes $(2 \cdot N \cdot d(\ell - \log(N)) + (\lambda + \log n))n + o(n)$, where N is the number of bins, d the maximum load of a bin, and ℓ the input size (e.g. for $n = 2^{20}$, one can choose $N = n/10$ and $d = 47$, see [26, Fig. 5]). For small database entries, this outperforms all known malicious PSI protocols.

3.3 An Efficient PSI in the Standard Model

In our last construction, we use a different functionality: we rely on the subfield ring-OLE functionality (given on Appendix of full version [9]), that generates a subfield ring-OLE correlation over the rings $\mathcal{R}_\mathsf{p} = \mathbb{F}_\mathsf{p}[X]/F(X)$, $\mathcal{R}_\mathsf{q} = \mathbb{F}_{\mathsf{p}^t}[X]/F(X)$, and $F(X)$ is some polynomial of degree $2n + 1$ (more generally, when the two parties have sets of different size n and m, F will be of degree $n + m + 1$). At a high level, the functionality $\mathcal{F}_\mathsf{sole}$ distributes to Alice $(a, s_A) \in \mathcal{R}_\mathsf{p} \times \mathcal{R}_\mathsf{q}$ and $(b, s_B) \in (\mathcal{R}_\mathsf{q})^2$ to Bob such that $ab = s_A + s_B$. Our protocol makes a single black-box call to this functionality. Consider two parties, a sender Alice and a receiver Bob, where Alice has a set $A = \{x_1, x_2, \ldots, x_n\} \in \mathbb{F}_p^n$ and Bob has a set $B = \{y_1, y_2, \ldots, y_n\} \in \mathbb{F}_p^n$. Define $p_A := \prod_{i=1}^n (X - x_i) \in \mathcal{R}_\mathsf{p}$ and $p_B := \prod_{i=1}^n (X - y_i) \in \mathcal{R}_\mathsf{p}$. Let $I := A \cap B$ denote the target output. The protocol computes the common roots of p_A and p_B, i.e., $\gcd(p_A, p_B)$.

By revealing appropriate linear combination of their shares and their input polynomials, Alice and Bob will "derandomize" this correlation, allowing Alice to learn the polynomial $u = p_A b_0 + p_B b_0'$, where b_0, b_0' are two uniformly random degree-n polynomials known by Bob (this also requires revealing the high-order coefficients of b, to reduce the degree-$2n$ random polynomial b to a degree-n random polynomial b_0). Using some standard lemmas about polynomials, the polynomial u can be factored as $\gcd(p_A, p_B) \cdot p_R$, where with high probability, p_R has no common root with p_A. This allows Alice to compute the intersection $I = A \cap B$ as $I = \{x_i \in A : u(x_i) = 0\}$. Concretely:

- Alice computes and sends $t_A = a - p_A$ to Bob.
- Bob sets $s'_B \leftarrow s_B - t_A b$. Then, Bob decomposes b as $b = b_0 + b_1 \cdot X^n$ (where b_0, b_1 are degree-n polynomials), sets $s'_B \leftarrow s_B - t_A b$, and picks a random degree-n polynomial b'_0 over $\mathcal{R}_q$. He sends b_1 and $t_B \leftarrow s'_B + p_B b'_0$ to Alice.
- **(Output)** Alice sets $u \leftarrow t_B - p_A b_1 \cdot X^n + s_A$; note that $u = p_A b_0 + p_B b'_0$. Alice outputs the set $I = \{x \in A \mid u(x) = 0\}$.

We prove that this construction achieves "augmented semi-honest security", a strengthening of honest-but-curious corruption where the adversary is allowed to change the corrupted parties' inputs. Furthermore, we securely realize the functionality $\mathcal{F}_{\mathsf{sole}}$ using the PCG-based protocol of [7], which is secure under the ring-LPN assumption. Instantiating the subfield ring OLE this way allows to import a powerful feature of the PCG of [7], which is its *programmability*: when generating a ring-OLE correlation, the receiver can ensure that her output a remains *identical* across multiple instances of the protocol with different parties. Using this programmability feature, we show that our protocol can be *batched*: a single $O(\ell \cdot n)$-size client message encoding her database A can be reused with N different servers with databases B_i, allowing her to learn $A \cap B_i$ using a single message from each server afterwards.

Achieving Malicious Security. We then turn our attention to security against malicious adversaries. Our upgrade introduces only a minimal communication overhead to the protocol, independent of the set sizes n. At a high level, the main issues that can occur in the malicious setting is when Alice sets $p_A = 0$, or when Bob sets $p_B b'_0 = 0$. Indeed, since Alice gets $u = p_A b_0 + p_B b'_0$, if $p_A = 0$, she can learn Bob's entire input set p_B. On the other hand, if $p_B b'_0 = 0$, Bob forces the output to be A.

We handle both issues separately. The second issue is intuitively simpler to handle, since when Bob carries out this attack, Alice will notice that her output is exactly her set A. This suggests a simple way around: if Alice notice at the end of the protocol that the output is equal to A, she aborts the protocol. Of course, a honest Bob could have an input B with $A \subseteq B$, in which case this modification would harm correctness. But there is a simple way around: prior to the protocol, Alice and Bob can just agree on a reserved dummy item d (we will pick $d = 1$ in the protocol, but this choice is arbitrary), which is guaranteed to be in neither databases. If database entries are elements of a field $\mathbb{F}_{p'}$, this can simply be done by choosing any slightly larger field $\mathbb{F}_p$ of size $|\mathbb{F}_p| \geq |\mathbb{F}_{p'}| + 1$, reserving one element of $\mathbb{F}_p$ to encode d, and mapping the elements of $\mathbb{F}_{p'}$ to the remaining elements. Then, Alice and Bob execute the protocol on inputs $A \cup \{1\}$ and B, which guarantees that B does not contain A.

For the first issue, Bob must check before sending $t_B = s'_B + p_B b'_0$ that Alice did not set p_A to be 0 when computing $t_A = a - p_A$. Intuitively, this will be done by letting Bob check that $p_A(x) \neq 0$, for an appropriate input x. This, however, must be done with some care, since learning $p_A(x)$ could leak information to a corrupted Bob. We handle this issue by reserving a second element of $\mathbb{F}_p$ (hence we now need $|\mathbb{F}_p| \geq |\mathbb{F}_{p'}| + 2$), which we assume w.l.o.g. to be 0, which should again be in neither set. Then, Alice will define the encoding of her set to be the degree-n polynomial p_A such that $p_A(\text{map}(a)) = 0$ for every $a \in A$, and $p_A(0) = 1$. Then, we let Bob first send b_1, without sending t_B. Afterwards, Bob computes $s'_B \leftarrow s_B - t_A b$ and Alice computes $s'_A \leftarrow s_A - p_A b_1 \cdot X^n$. Observe that if both parties behave honestly, $s'_a + s'_b = ab - t_A b - p_A b_1 \cdot X^n = ab - ab + p_A b - p_A b_1 \cdot X^n = p_A b_0$. To enforce $p_A \neq 0$, we will check that the above equation holds for some nonzero p_A. Crucially, since both p_A and b_0 have degree at most n, no reduction modulo $F(X)$ occurs in the right hand side of the equation. This implies that we can simply check that the equation holds for the reserved input $x = 0$ (since a honest p_A is guaranteed to satisfy $p_A(0) = 1 \neq 0$). To check this, we let Alice send $s'_A(0)$ to Bob, who checks that $s'_A(0) = b_0(0) - s'_B(0)$; if the check fails, Bob aborts the protocol.

4   PSI from Subfield-VOLE

4.1   A New Membership Batched OPRF

Our BaRK-OPRF allows the sender to hold a set of keys $(\mathbf{k_i})_{i \leq N}$ such that each key is assigned with a tuple of d input elements of the receiver and then the receiver learns a PRF output on each element in this tuple corresponding with the same key. More formally, denoting $\mathbf{x_i} = (x_i^{(1)}, \cdots, x_i^{(d)})$ consisting of d entries, the sender gets $F(i, y)$ and the receiver obtains a set $\{F(i, x_i^{(j)})\}_{j \leq d}$ such that $F(i, y) \in \{F(i, x_i^{(j)})\}_{j \leq d}$ if and only if y is equal to any entry of $\mathbf{x_i}$, and $F(i, y)$ looks pseudorandom to the receiver otherwise.

PARAMETERS:

$\mathbb{F}_p$ is a finite field. There are 2 parties, a sender and a receiver with input set $X = \{\mathbf{x_1}, \mathbf{x_2}, \ldots, \mathbf{x_N}\} \subseteq \mathbb{F}_p$ where $\mathbf{x_i} = (x_i^{(1)}, \cdots, x_i^{(d)})$.

FUNCTIONALITY:

- Wait for input (sender, id) from the sender and (receiver, id, X) from the receiver. The functionality samples a PRF F then $\forall x \in \mathbf{x_i}$ outputs $F(i, x)$ to the receiver for $i \in [1, N]$.
- When the sender inputs any $(i, y) \in [1, N] \times \mathbb{F}_p$, functionality gives $F(i, y)$ to the sender.

Fig. 2. Ideal functionality $\mathcal{F}_{\text{oprf}}$

Main Construction. Assume that the receiver inputs the set of $n = Nd$ elements: $X = \{\mathbf{x_1}, \mathbf{x_2}, \ldots, \mathbf{x_N}\} \subseteq \mathbb{F}_p$ where $\mathbf{x_i} = (x_i^{(1)}, \cdots, x_i^{(d)})$. First, the sender and the receiver invoke the $\mathcal{F}_{\text{svole}}$ protocol of dimension n, with their roles reversed, to get a random sVOLE correlation. Specifically, the receiver learns a pair of vectors $(\mathbf{u}, \mathbf{v})$ where $\mathbf{u} \in \mathbb{F}_p^n$, $\mathbf{v} \in \mathbb{F}_q^n$, the sender gets $\Delta \in \mathbb{F}_q$ and $\mathbf{w} := \Delta \cdot \mathbf{u} + \mathbf{v}$. Denoting $\mathbf{u} = (\mathbf{u_1}, \mathbf{u_2}, \ldots, \mathbf{u_N})$ where $(u_{j,i})_{1 \leq j \leq d}$ are d entries of vector $\mathbf{u_i}$. This notation is the same for $\mathbf{v}, \mathbf{w}$. Consider $\mathbf{x_i}$ and its associated polynomial as $P_{\mathbf{x_i}}(X) = \prod_{j=1}^{d}(X - x_i^{(j)}) = X^d + \sum_{j=1}^{d} c_{j,i} \cdot X^{j-1}$ where $c_{j,i} \in \mathbb{F}_p$ for $i \in [1, N]$, $j \in [1, d]$.

Now, the receiver defines $c_i := (c_{j,i})_{j \leq d}$, $c := (c_1, c_2, \ldots, c_N)$, and then $\forall i \in [1, N]$ sends to the sender $z_i := c_i - u_i \in \mathbb{F}_p^d$. Above, the u_i are masks for the coefficients c_i of (the polynomial associated) x_i. Indeed, u_i are distributed uniformly at random in the subfield $\mathbb{F}_p$, then the vector z_i is a uniformly random over $\mathbb{F}_p^n$ from the viewpoint of the sender. The two parties will run a coin flipping protocol to get a random value $t \leftarrow \mathbb{F}_q$. For $i \in [1, N]$, the receiver defines the PRF output on each input $x \in x_i$ as $F(i, x) = \mathsf{H}\left(i|t|x, \sum_{j=1}^d v_{j,i} \cdot x^{j-1} \right)$.

On the other hand, after receiving the vectors z_i, for $i \in [1, N]$, the sender defines the vector $k_i := w_i + \Delta \cdot z_i$. As a consequence, for any input $(i, y) \in [1, N] \times \mathbb{F}_p$, its PRF output is computed as: $F(i, y) = \mathsf{H}\left(i|t|y, \Delta \cdot y^d + \sum_{j=1}^d k_{j,i} \cdot y^{j-1} \right)$.

Correctness and Security. To see why PRF output is defined as above. Observe that $k_i := w_i + \Delta \cdot z_i = v_i + \Delta \cdot c_i$. Then, we have

$$\Delta \cdot y^d + \sum_{j=1}^d k_{j,i} \cdot y^{j-1} = \Delta \cdot y^d + \sum_{j=1}^d (v_{j,i} + \Delta \cdot c_{j,i}) \cdot y^{j-1}$$

$$= \Delta \cdot \left(y^d + \sum_{j=1}^d c_{j,i} \cdot y^{j-1} \right) + \sum_{j=1}^d v_{j,i} \cdot y^{j-1} = \Delta \cdot P_{x_i}(y) + \sum_{j=1}^d v_{j,i} \cdot y^{j-1}$$

so if $y \in x_i$ then $P_{x_i}(y) = 0$ which leads to $F(i, y) \in \{F(i, x_i^{(j)})\}_{j \leq d}$.

Theorem 1. *The protocol Π_{oprf} (Fig. 3) instantiated with random oracles H, H', securely realizes the ideal functionality of $\mathcal{F}_{\mathsf{oprf}}$ (Fig. 2) against a malicious setting in the $\mathcal{F}_{\mathsf{svole}}$ hybrid model.*

Note that the output v of H is chosen depending on the concrete structure of PSI and the target setting (semi-honest or malicious). This parameter is detailed in the Sect. 4.2 for a semi-honest setting and the Sect. 4.3 for a malicious setting.

4.2   A New Semi-honest PSI from mOPRF

A Variant of BaRK-OPRF. We now propose a variant of our BaRK-OPRF to deal with the case when the size of each tuple input is not necessarily equal to d. This means that the receiver now can divide the input set to N tuples x_i and each tuple has less than or equal to d items. Meanwhile, the sender is not allowed to learn about how many exactly items are in each tuple. This functionality can be obtained from our BaRK-OPRF plus a small extra cost, i.e., a *subfield* VOLE of length N over the subfield $\mathbb{F}_2$.

The idea is as follows. The receiver's input set $X = \{x_1, x_2, \ldots, x_N\} \subseteq \mathbb{F}_p$ where $x_i = (x_i^{(1)}, \cdots, x_i^{(j_i)})$, $j_i \leq d$. The polynomial associated to $\{x_i\}_{i \leq N}$ will be expressed as a polynomial of degree d: $P_{x_i}(X) = \prod_{j=1}^{j_i} (X - x_i^{(j)}) = \sum_{j=1}^{d+1} c_{j,i} \cdot X^{j-1}$ where $c_{j,i} \in \mathbb{F}_p$.

As a result, the set of the coefficients of $P_{x_i}(X) = (c_{1,i}, c_{2,i}, \ldots, c_{d+1,i})$. We remark that, compared to the associated polynomial in our original BaRK-OPRF which has a constant coefficient of degree d of 1, in our variant version

PARAMETERS:

- Given $\mathbb{F}_p \subseteq \mathbb{F}_q$ where $\mathbb{F}_q \approx O(2^\kappa)$, $\mathsf{H} : \{0,1\}^* \times \mathbb{F}_q \rightarrow \{0,1\}^v$ and H' : $\mathbb{F}_q \rightarrow \mathbb{F}_q$ are random oracles.
- The sender has no input and the receiver inputs a set $X = \{\mathbf{x_1}, \mathbf{x_2}, \ldots, \mathbf{x_N}\} \subseteq \mathbb{F}_p$ where $\mathbf{x_i} = (x_i^{(1)}, \cdots, x_i^{(d)})$ and $n = Nd$.

PROTOCOL:

1. The sender and the receiver invoke to the $\mathcal{F}_{\mathsf{svole}}$ of dimension n in the $\mathbb{F}_q$ over the $\mathbb{F}_p$ with the inverse role. The receiver gets two random vectors $\mathbf{u} \in \mathbb{F}_p^n, \mathbf{v} \in \mathbb{F}_q^n$ and the sender receives $\Delta \in \mathbb{F}_q$, $\mathbf{w} := \Delta\mathbf{u} + \mathbf{v} \in \mathbb{F}_q^n$. Denoting $\mathbf{u} = (\mathbf{u_1}, \mathbf{u_2}, \ldots, \mathbf{u_N})$ where $\mathbf{u_i} = (c_{j,i})_{1 \leq j \leq d}$. This denotation is the same for $\mathbf{v}, \mathbf{w}$.
2. The receiver samples $t_r \leftarrow \mathbb{F}_q$ and sends $h_r := \mathsf{H}'(t_r)$ to the sender.
3. The sender samples $t_s \leftarrow \mathbb{F}_q$ and sends $h_s := \mathsf{H}'(t_s)$ to the receiver.
4. The receiver determines the associated polynomial for each $\mathbf{x_i}$ as

$$P_{\mathbf{x_i}}(X) = \prod_{j=1}^{d} (X - x_i^{(j)}) = X^d + \sum_{j=1}^{d} c_{j,i} \cdot X^{j-1}$$

where $c_{j,i} \in \mathbb{F}_p$ for $i \in [1, N]$, $j \in [1, d]$.
5. Denoting $\mathbf{c_i} := (c_{j,i})_{1 \leq j \leq d}$; $\mathbf{c} := (\mathbf{c_1}, \mathbf{c_2}, \ldots, \mathbf{c_N})$, the receiver computes $\mathbf{z_i} := \mathbf{c_i} - \mathbf{u_i} \in \mathbb{F}_p^d$, and then sends $\mathbf{z_i}$ and t_r to the sender.
6. The sender aborts if $\mathsf{H}'(t_r) \neq h_r$.
7. The sender sends t_s to the receiver, the receiver aborts if $\mathsf{H}'(t_s) \neq h_s$ and both parties define $t = t_s \oplus t_r$.
8. The receiver outputs the PRF values on the input $x \in \mathbf{x_i}$ for $i \in [1, N]$ as

$$F(i, x) = \mathsf{H}\left(i|t|x , \sum_{j=1}^{d} v_{j,i} \cdot x^{j-1} \right)$$

9. For $i \in [1, N]$, the sender defines $\mathbf{k_i} = \mathbf{w_i} + \Delta\mathbf{z_i}$. For any input $(i, y) \in [1, N] \times \mathbb{F}_p$, the sender computes the PRF output by below formula

$$F(i, y) = \mathsf{H}\left(i|t|y , \Delta \cdot y^d + \sum_{j=1}^{d} k_{j,i} \cdot y^{j-1} \right)$$

Fig. 3. Our batch BaRK-OPRF Π_{oprf} based on subVOLE

this coefficient will equal 0 or 1 since the degree of $P_{\mathbf{x_i}}(X)$ is *less* than or equal to d. So, it requires $(d+1)$ masks for this polynomial instead of d, but the mask for the coefficient of degree d only needs to be in $\mathbb{F}_2$. For each tuple, we require an additional value $u_i \in \mathbb{F}_2$, so in total we need an additional subfield VOLE of length N over the subfield $\mathbb{F}_2$.

More formally, the sender and receiver invoke a subfield VOLE of length n over the subfield $\mathbb{F}_p$ as before (all the notations in Fig. 3 are reused), and additionally invoke another subfield VOLE instance over the subfield $\mathbb{F}_2$ of length N with an inverse role, while the receiver gets $\mathbf{u}' \in \mathbb{F}_2^N$, and $\mathbf{v}' \in \mathbb{F}_q^N$ the sender holds $\Delta \in \mathbb{F}_q$ (Δ is the same for each time invoking *subfield* VOLE) and $\mathbf{w}' := \Delta \cdot \mathbf{u}' + \mathbf{v}'$. The receiver sends to the sender vectors $\mathbf{z_i}$ as before, and an extra vector $\mathbf{z}'$ defined as $z_i' := c_{d+1,i} - u_i'$ for $i \in [1, N]$. The receiver outputs on input $x \in \mathbf{x_i}$ are computed as $F(i, x) = \mathsf{H}(i|t|x \, , \, v_i' \cdot x^d + \sum_{j=1}^d v_{j,i} \cdot x^{j-1})$. On the other hand, the sender defines their PRF values on input (i, y) where $i \in [1, N]$, $y \in \mathbb{F}_p$ as $F(i, y) = \mathsf{H}(i|t|y \, , \, (w_i' + \Delta z_i') \cdot y^d + \sum_{j=1}^d k_{j,i} \cdot y^{j-1})$.

Main Construction of a New PSI. The sender and the receiver have two input sets $X = \{x_1, x_2, \ldots, x_n\}$ and $Y = \{y_1, y_2, \ldots, y_n\}$. Assume that all of these elements have the bit-length ℓ. Intuitively, our BaRK-OPRF is constructed from subVOLE to handle the case when having multiple items per bin. Then this specialized BaRK-OPRF can combine with some hashing techniques to form an efficient PSI protocol. In the next part 4.2, we discuss these types of hashing. Our PSI protocol is described in Fig. 4; it builds upon the protocol of [18] using GCH and BaRK-OPRF. For simplicity, we describe our protocol directly with generalized Cuckoo hashing; adapting the protocol to other variants is immediate. We elaborate on our protocol below. In our protocol, the receiver first uses (d, k)-Cuckoo hashing to map his input set Y to a table with N bins, note that the bit-length of the values stored in a bin is $\ell - \log N$ instead of ℓ. Depending on the size of n, we use one of two approaches to handle the bins which are not full (the threshold was chosen empirically to optimize communication).

- If $n \geq 2^{20}$, the variant of our BaRK-OPRF (using an additional subfield VOLE over $\mathbb{F}_2$) is used; for such sizes, the concrete cost of implementing the additional sVOLE vanishes.
- Otherwise, when $n < 2^{20}$, the receiver adds dummy items to bins such that each bin contains *exactly* d items. To avoid collisions between the dummy items and the elements in the same bin of the sender, we pad an extra bit to all items in the following way: $i|x|b$ where i is the index of hash function corresponding with the stored value x while $b = 1$ if x is a dummy item added and $b = 0$ otherwise.

In both case, the sender computes $k \cdot n$ PRF evaluations and sends (shuffled) to the receiver, who compares them with his OPRF outputs, and outputs the intersection set. To reduce the computational cost in this step, the sender can send separately each set H_i ($i \in [1, k]$) which contains the PRF outputs of each $x \in X$ with the related bin $h_i(x)$. Then for each element, the receiver only needs to search for one set (among k sets H_i) of n items instead of $k \cdot n$.

Alternative Hashing Methods. There are two hashing schemes that can be fit into our PSI structure.

2-choice hashing [20] is a variant of Cuckoo hashing where one item x is assigned to one of two bins $h_1(x)$ or $h_2(x)$. However, there is no restriction on the number of items per bin and an item is put in a bin which already has fewer items. [20] proposes both theoretical references and heuristic parameters

---

PARAMETERS:

- The sender and the receiver have respectively input sets $X = \{x_1, x_2, \ldots, x_n\}$ and $Y = \{y_1, y_2, \ldots, y_n\}$, all elements of bit-length ℓ.
- A (d, k)-generalized Cuckoo hashing (GCH) scheme mapping n items to N bins by k hash functions $h_1, h_2, \ldots, h_k : \{0,1\}^* \to [N]$ where $Nd > n$ and $d = O(1)$ (see Sect. 4.2).

PROTOCOL:

1. The receiver uses (d, k)-Cuckoo hashing with k hash functions to map the elements in Y to the table $\mathcal{B}$ consisting of N bins, where each bin i has $j_i \leq d$ items. Denote $y_{j,i}$ is an element in Y assigned to position j of bin i and its stored value in table $\mathcal{B}$ is $y'_{j,i}$.

2. Depending on the size of n, there are two alternatives:
   (a) $n \geq 2^{20}$, the sender and receiver invoke our variant of Π_{oprf} where the receiver uses the input set $Y_{\mathcal{B}} = \{\mathbf{y_1}, \mathbf{y_2}, \ldots, \mathbf{y_N}\}$ defined as follows:
       - $\mathbf{y_i} = \{r_{1,i}, r_{2,i}, \ldots, r_{j_i,i}\}$.
       - $r_{j,i} = t \parallel y'_{j,i}$ where t is index of a hash function such that $h_t(y_{j,i}) = i$.
   (b) $n < 2^{20}$, the sender and receiver directly invoke the Π_{oprf} where the receiver uses the input set $Y_{\mathcal{B}} = \{\mathbf{y_1}, \mathbf{y_2}, \ldots, \mathbf{y_N}\}$ defined as follows:
       - $\mathbf{y_i} = \{r_{1,i}, r_{2,i}, \ldots, r_{d,i}\}$.
         • For $j \leq j_i$: $r_{j,i} = t \parallel y'_{j,i} \parallel 1$ where t is index of hash function such that $h_t(y_{j,i}) = i$.
         • Otherwise, $r_{j,i} = t \parallel$ dummy value $\parallel 0$ where $t \leftarrow_r [1, k]$.

3. The receiver obtains n instances OPRF:

$$Y' = \{\mathsf{PRF}(i \, , \, r_{i,j}) \mid i \in [1, N] \, , \, j \leq j_i\}$$

4. The sender uses the k hash functions to map the n element in X to the N bins. Let x_t denote the value stored at bin $h_t(x)$ when mapping x for $t \in [1, k]$.

5. The sender computes the sets of $k \cdot n$ PRF outputs:
   (a) For $n \geq 2^{20}$: $H_t = \{\mathsf{PRF}(h_t(x) \, , \, t \parallel x_t) \mid x \in X\}$ for $t \in [1, k]$.
   (b) For $n < 2^{20}$: $H_t = \{\mathsf{PRF}(h_t(x) \, , \, t \parallel x_t \parallel 1) \mid x \in X\}$ for $t \in [1, k]$.
   Then the sender randomly permutes and sends each set to the receiver.

6. The receiver finds the intersection:
   - if $y \in Y$ is mapped to the position j of bin i by function h_t then check whether $\mathsf{PRF}(i, r_{i,j}) \in H_t$ ($r_{i,j}$ is defined depending on n).
   - Outputs the intersection set.

Fig. 4. Our new semi-honest PSI protocol from BaRK-OPRF

for 2-choice hashing, which require only a small number of dummy items. Let us assume we have n items and 2 hash functions; using 2-choice hashing allows to map n items to N bins in time $O(n \log n)$ where each bin contains at most $L = \lceil n/N \rceil + 1$ items with a probability $1 - O(1/N)^{L-1}$.

Simple hashing uses one hash function h to map an item x to bin $h(x)$. For security, the number of items per bin can leak some information then it requires padding each bin with dummy items until having an equal number of items per bin. With very high probability, for $N = O(n \log n)$ bins, the maximum possible items per bin is $O(\log n)$. The percentage of the occupation of dummy items is higher than others. However, simple hashing avoids ambiguities about where an item can be placed, a property which is crucial in the malicious setting.

Parameters. In this section, we discuss concrete parameters used in our new PSI semi-honest protocol. We use $\kappa = 128$ and $\lambda = 40$. The protocol contains several parameters:

The Length of OPRF Output. The output domain of PRF would be $\{0,1\}^v$ where $v = \lambda + 2 \log_2(n)$ guarantees a $2^{-\lambda}$ bound on the collision probability of PRF outputs among the two size-n sets. Furthermore, communicating the hashes can be reduced to communicating only $\approx \lambda + \log n$ bits per hash, using a heuristic technique of [31] that directly leads to an optimization of our PSI protocol.

The size of $\mathbb{F}_p$ and $\mathbb{F}_q$ in BaRK-OPRF. After using permutation-based hashing, each element is mapped to a bin with a stored value in this bin, the bit-length reduces from ℓ to $\ell - \log N$. The input set of BaRK-OPRF in PSI protocol constructs from stored values concatenating with some extra bits. Then the bit-length of an input element of BaRK-OPRF is computed as $\ell - \log N + 1$ if $n \geq 2^{20}$ or $\ell - \log N + 2$ otherwise, i.e., the size of $q = 2^{\ell - \log N + 1}$ or $q = 2^{\ell - \log N + 2}$ respectively.

Generalized Cuckoo Hashing. We use a (d, k)-general cuckoo hashing scheme without stash. The parameters are chosen such that the failure probability is $2^{-\lambda}$. When $d = 1, k = 3$ these parameters are identical with KKRT except for the number of bins increases slightly to $N = 1.3n$ which is a trade-off to obtain no stash. Even with the higher number of bins, our PSI protocol significantly outperforms KKRT.

To minimize the overall communication, we set $k = 2$ to reduce the cost of sending $k \cdot n$ PRF outputs. We used a Python script to simulate randomly assigning n values to $N = c \cdot n$ bins using $(d, 2)$-Cuckoo hashing, for several values of d and c, and for $n = 2^9, 2^{10}, 2^{11}, 2^{12}$. For a value of c as low as 0.65, we never observed any insertion failure over 10^7 trials for each values of n (for $n = 2^{12}$, we could only do 10^6 trials), when using $d = 3$ items per bins. For $d = 2$, the failure probability became noticeable already for $c \approx 1$. Based on known theoretical analysis of (d, k)-Cuckoo hashing, the failure probability is known to scale inverse polynomially with n. Therefore, we expect that for reasonably large values of n (e.g. $n \geq 2^{18}$), our parameters should guarantee a failure probability significantly below 2^{-40}.

2-Choice Hashing. Following the analysis of [20], we set the number N of bins to $n/3$, and the maximum load $d = L + 1$ to 4. This guarantees a failure probability which we empirically estimate to be $1/N^{L-1}$, which is below 2^{-40} for all values of n above 2^{14}.

Simple Hashing. Eventually, for simple hashing, we set arbitrarily the number of bins N to $n/10$, and derive the corresponding value of d from Fig. 5 in [26]. We note that the parameters for simple hashing are much less heuristic that the other two, in that concrete bound can actually be achieved which are relatively close to the heuristic (computer-estimated) bounds. For example, [20] experimentally observes that for a 2^{-40} failure probability, setting $d = 47$ suffices when using $N = n/10$ bins. Using a standard Chernoff bound, it is in fact straightforward to prove formally that $d = 49$ already suffices to reach this failure probability, which is very close to the experimental bound. In contrast, experimental bounds in more complex hashing variants are typically much more distant from provable bounds. The choice of $N = n/10$ is entirely arbitrary: any smaller N leads to better communication, but requires using higher values of d, leading to worse computation (due to the need to perform N polynomial interpolations with degree-d polynomial). This allows for a smooth tradeoff between communication and computation, where better computational power can be used to further reduce the communication. At the extreme end of the spectrum, using $N = 1$ and $d = n$ requires one expensive degree-n polynomial interpolation, but can achieve extremely low communications, e.g. $93n$ bits of communication for $\ell = 32$ and $n = 2^{20}$.

Efficiency. We compare the communication of our protocols, using three hashing methods, on Table 1. Regarding computation, we provide a breakdown of the computation costs of our protocols in the Appendix of full version [9]. Briefly, though, compared to the protocol of [27], and when using a standard choice of parameters for our protocol (e.g. $n = 2^{20}$, and using generalized Cuckoo hashing with $d = 3$ and $N = 0.65n$), our protocol requires essentially a length-$1.9n$ VOLE (with a small subfield), $0.65n$ degree-3 polynomial interpolations (roughly $3n$ multiplications over a small field), and computing n hashes. In contrast, the enhanced version of [27] (using the OKVS of [13] and the VOLE of [11]) will require solving a linear system to set up an OKVS (this requires on the order of $(1.3 \log n + \lambda)^3$ multiplications over $\mathbb{F}_{2^{128}}$, plus $O(\lambda n)$ operations), computing a length-$1.3n$ VOLE (over $\mathbb{F}_{2^{128}}$), and computing $2n$ hashes. The cost of the VOLE dominates that of performing n hashes, so for sufficiently large set sizes ($n \gg 2^{20}$), the protocol of [27] should become roughly 30% more efficient than our protocol computation-wise. For smaller sets (e.g. $n \approx 2^{16}$), the cost of setting up the OKVS becomes more significant, requiring around $20n$ field multiplications over $\mathbb{F}_{2^{128}}$, hence the computational efficiency of our protocol becomes roughly on par with that of [27]. Of course, real runtimes can vary due to e.g. cache misses, so these estimations should only be viewed as a first order approximation indicating that the computational efficiency of our protocols is close to that of [27] (but likely slightly larger).

In terms of computation, the main computational overhead comes from performing N polynomial interpolations of *only degree-d* polynomials. Based on our analysis, to achieve $2^{-\lambda} = 2^{-40}$ probability of insertion failure, the following parameters can be chosen:

- $N = 0.65n$ and $d = 3$ for generalized Cuckoo hashing (GCH),
- $N = 0.33n$ and $d = 4$ for two-choice hashing,
- $N = n/10$ and $d \approx 46$ for simple hashing.

As the above illustrates, the cost of performing N polynomial interpolations will be very small for GCH, two-choice hashing, but becomes higher for simple hashing (though performing $n/10$ degree-46 interpolations remains reasonably fast).

4.3   A Malicious PSI from mOPRF

In this section, we propose a maliciously secure PSI protocol based on our BaRK-OPRF (Sect. 4.1) and simple hashing combining a permutation-based hash function. The PSI protocol is shown in Fig. 5 and its security against a corrupted adversary is proven in Theorem 2. The estimated overhead communication cost of this PSI is $Nd(\ell - \log N) + (\kappa + \log n)n + o(n)$. Observe that the PSI protocol in Sect. 4.2 is insecure against malicious settings since the general hashing scheme does not allow the simulation in ideal world. To handle this we use simple hashing schemes with only one permutation-based hash function. This protocol is constructed from the natural approach used recently in [10,20,21,27], i.e., Alice (a sender) and Bob (a receiver) invoke the $\mathcal{F}_{\mathsf{oprf}}$ then Bob gets the PRF values on his input and Alice enables to compute the PRF on any input so Alice computes on her input after that she sends these PRF values to Bob; Bob compares and outputs the intersection.

PARAMETERS:

- Alice (sender) and Bob (receiver) have respectively input set $X = \{x_1, x_2, \ldots, x_n\} \in \mathbb{F}_p$ and $Y = \{y_1, y_2, \ldots, y_n\} \in \mathbb{F}_p$, all elements of bit-length ℓ.
- A random hash functions $h : \{0, 1\}^* \to [N]$.
- A Permutation-based hashing $\mathsf{Per}_{h,X}$ maps a set X to table $\mathcal{B}_X$ consisting of N bins such that each bin has d slots where $Nd > |X|$, and $d = O(1)$. Denote $\mathsf{Per}(x) := (i, x')$ where x' is the stored value of x in bin i which defined by h and x then $\mathsf{Per}^{-1}(i, x') = x$.

PROTOCOL:

1. Bob uses Per to map Y to $\mathcal{B}_Y$, for each empty slot in each bin $\mathcal{B}_Y[i]$, put here a dummy item of length $\ell - \log N$.
2. Alice sends $(\mathsf{sender}, \mathsf{id})$ and Bob sends $(\mathsf{receiver}, \mathsf{id}, \mathcal{B}_Y)$ to $\mathcal{F}_{\mathsf{oprf}}$ then
   - Bob receives the $Y' = \{F(i, y') \mid y' \in \mathcal{B}_Y[i]\}_{i \le N}$.
3. For each $x \in X$, Alice queries x to $\mathcal{F}_{\mathsf{oprf}}$ with corresponding input (i, x') such that $\mathsf{Per}(x) = (i, x')$, then Alice gets $F(i, x')$. Alice sends to Bob

$$U = \{F(i, x') \mid x \in X \wedge \mathsf{Per}(x) = (i, x')\}$$

4. Now for each $y \in Y$, $\mathsf{Per}(y) = (i, y')$, if $F(i, y') \in U$ then Bob outputs y as an element in the intersection.

Fig. 5. Our malicious PSI protocol based on $\mathcal{F}_{\mathsf{oprf}}$

Intuitively, in a malicious setting, when the sender is corrupted, the simulation needs to extract the sender's input set X from the queries to $\mathcal{F}_{\mathsf{oprf}}$ and the set U. Denote $F(y) := F(i, y')$ where $\mathsf{Per}(y) = (i, y')$ and the set of all elements queried to $\mathcal{F}_{\mathsf{oprf}}$ is X' where $n' = |X'|$. The extraction procedure is that $X = \{x \in \mathbb{F}_p \mid x \in X' \wedge F(x) \in U\}$. Observe that if there exist two distinct elements $x_1, x_2 \in X'$ such that $F(x_1) = F(x_2) \in U$ then more than one element is extracted to X. The probability of existing collision is $2^{-v+2\log n'}$ then one approach to avoid collision is choosing $v = 2\kappa$. However, when $v = 2\kappa$, the overhead communication cost significantly increases.

Therefore, another approach is that Sim only extracts elements $x \in X'$ if its PRF is distinct and appears in U, i.e., $x \in X'$ such that $F(x) \in U$ and $\nexists x' \in X'$ where $F(x) = F(x')$. [27] proposed this simulation and claimed that if the output domain of PRF $v = \kappa$ then this simulation is correct and can not be distinguishable from the real protocol. We point out the proof of [27] has a gap and show that the output of PRF should be $\kappa + \log n$.

Indeed, if there exist some $x_1, x_2 \in X'$ such that $F(x_1) = F(x_2)$ then Sim only needs to extract x_1, x_2 when one of them is in Y. Let assume $x_1 \in Y$, the probability of $F(x_2) = F(y)$ for some $y \in Y$ is $2^{-v+\log(n_Y)}$ since Y is first fixed before the function F is sampled. [27] shows $n_Y = O(\kappa)$ then the security can hold if $v = \kappa$. However, this should be $v = \kappa + \log n_Y$ since $n_Y = O(\mathrm{poly}(\kappa))$ instead of $O(\kappa)$. In particular, PSI protocols in [27] are targeted on large input set because of the usage of vector OLE.

Theorem 2. *The PSI protocol on Fig. 5 securely realizes the ideal functionality $\mathcal{F}_{\mathsf{psi}}$ over the field $\mathbb{F}_p$ for set size n and malicious set size $n_X = n$, $n_Y = Nd$ with statistical security against malicious adversaries in $\mathcal{F}_{\mathsf{oprf}}$ hybrid model.*

In general, the malicious PSI (Fig. 5) has a communication cost that depends on the security parameter κ and is dominated by κn. We now present a new PSI protocol that is secure in malicious setting via a dual execution while its communication cost only depends on the statistic parameter λ and the set size n. The idea of using a dual execution has been used in [26] but when combining this with our BaRK-OPRF it achieves efficient results, i.e., the total communication cost is only $2Nd(\ell - \log N) + n(\lambda + \log n) + o(n)$. The detailed construction of dual PSI is shown in the Appendix of full version [9].

5   A Standard PSI from Subfield-Ring OLE

In this section, we describe a new PSI protocol, which builds upon a (simple variant of) a pseudorandom correlation generator for the ring-OLE correlation [7]. Our protocol enjoys a number of important features: it is in the *standard model*, achieves *malicious security* at essentially no cost, has *low communication* (competitive even with the best maliciously secure PSI protocols in the random oracle model), and reasonable computation (albeit superlinear in n). Our protocol can also be generalized to a powerful notion of *batch non-interactive PSI*, where (after a small logarithmic-cost preprocessing step with each server) a client can broadcast a single encoding of his database, and then obtain the intersection with any of the server databases at any time after receiving a single message from this server. We believe that this functionality itself is of independent interest.

5.1 Semi-Honest Batch Non-Interactive PSI from Subfield Ring-OLE

We describe a new PSI scheme in the semi-honest model. Our protocol enjoys two interesting features: (1) it is in the standard model, and (2) it is a *batch non-interactive* protocol, a useful communication pattern which we describe afterwards. The full construction is represented on Fig. 6.

Theorem 3. *The PSI protocol on Fig. 6 securely realizes the ideal functionality $\mathcal{F}_{\mathsf{psi}}$ over the field $\mathbb{F}_{\mathsf{p}}$ with set size n and malicious set size $n' = n_X = n_Y = 2n$, with statistical security against augmented semi-honest adversaries in the $\mathcal{F}_{\mathsf{sole}}$ hybrid model.*

Above, "augmented semi-honest security" refers to a strengthening of honest-but-curious corruption where the adversary is allowed to change the corrupted parties' inputs. This is a standard strengthening of semi-honest security, which has been argued to better capture real-world security [16]. It will also facilitate upgrading security to the malicious setting later on.

Batch Non-interactivity. To securely realize the functionality $\mathcal{F}_{\mathsf{sole}}$, we rely on the PCG-based protocol of [7] (using a straightforward adaptation to the subfield setting), which is secure under the ring-LPN assumption. Interestingly, instantiating the subfield ring OLE this way allows to import a powerful feature of the PCG of [7], which is its *programmability*: when generating a ring-OLE correlation, the receiver can ensure that her output a remains *identical* across multiple instances of the protocol with different parties.

This feature enables the following communication structure: after a short (logarithmic-communication) interaction with N servers, a client, playing the role of Alice with input set A, can broadcast a single compact encoding of her dataset to all the servers (with input sets $B_1 \cdots B_N$). Afterwards, each server B_i can at any time send a single message m_i to Alice, from which she can recover $A \cap B_i$ without further interaction. To our knowledge, this batch non-interactive communication pattern was never achieved by any prior proposal; we believe that it can make our protocol appealing in realistic scenarios.

More concretely, after a logarithmic-communication preprocessing phase where Alice sets up PCG seeds with each of servers, Alice broadcasts the value $t_A = a - p_A$ to everyone, which communicates $2n \log p \approx 2\ell n$ bits. This message can be seen as a compact public encoding of her dataset (it is only twice as large as Alice's set). Afterwards, each server can complete the protocol of Fig. 6 by sending a single message (b_1, t_B) to the receiver, of length $3n \log q \approx 3(\lambda + 2 \log n)n$, from which the receiver can locally recover $X \cap X_i$.

Furthermore, using the encoding technique of [31], the $\lambda + 2\log n$ term can be reduced to $\lambda + \log n$ (the improvement is based on the observation that for an appropriate ordering, n random elements of a set of size $2^{\lambda+2\log n}$ are on average at distance $2^{\lambda+\log n}$ for each other, hence the cost of transmitting them can be reduced to essentially $\lambda + \log n$ per element by sending the distance between consecutive elements instead).

Efficiency. The communication cost of protocol (Fig. 6) is $n \cdot (2\log p + 3\log q) + o(n)$ bits of communication. Here, the size of the subfield $\mathbb{F}_p$ depends only on the bitsize ℓ of the items in the sets A and B, hence we can set $\log p = \ell$. As we will see in the analysis, $\log q$ must be set to $\log q \approx \lambda + 2\log n$ to guarantee λ bits of statistical security. This leads to a total communication of $n \cdot (2\ell + 3\lambda + 6\log n) + o(n)$ bits, which is reduced to $n \cdot (2\ell + 3\lambda + 3\log n) + o(n)$ with the encoding of [31]. The $o(n)$ term above captures the cost of distributing the PCG seeds of the subfield ring-OLE (we discuss the concrete value of $o(n)$ later on, for our maliciously secure version of the protocol).

Regarding computation, the computational cost scales as $O(n\log^2 n)$ due to the fast polynomial interpolations, or as $O(n\log n)$ when using cyclotomic rings. We provide a concrete analysis of the computational cost of the maliciously secure version of our protocol in Sect. 5.2.

PARAMETERS:

- Two rings $\mathcal{R}_p = \mathbb{F}_p[X]/F(X) \subseteq \mathcal{R}_q = \mathbb{F}_{p^t}[X]/F(X)$, where $F(X)$ has degree $2n + 1$.
- The sender (Alice) and receiver (Bob) have respective input sets $A = \{a_1, a_2, \ldots, a_n\} \subset \mathbb{F}_p$ and $B = \{b_1, b_2, \ldots, b_n\} \subset \mathbb{F}_p$.
- A subfield ring-OLE in the ring $\mathcal{R}_q$ over the subring $\mathcal{R}_p$.

PROTOCOL:

1. **(Setting up the correlation)** Alice and Bob encode their sets to $p_A = \prod_{i=1}^{n}(X - a_i)$, $p_B = \prod_{i=1}^{n}(X - b_i)$ respectively, and invoke $\mathcal{F}_{\text{sole}}$ to generate a subfield ring-OLE correlation over $\mathcal{R}_p, \mathcal{R}_q$: Alice receives $(a, s_A) \in \mathcal{R}_p \times \mathcal{R}_q$ and Bob receives $(b, s_B) \in \mathcal{R}_q^2$ such that $s_A + s_B = ab$.

2. **(Broadcasting the client set encoding)** Alice computes and sends $t_A = a - p_A$ to Bob.

3. **(Server-to-client message)** Bob sets $s'_B \leftarrow s_B - t_A b$. Then, Bob decomposes b as $b = b_0 + b_1 \cdot X^n$ (where b_0, b_1 are degree-n polynomials), sets $s'_B \leftarrow s_B - t_A b$, and picks a random degree-n polynomial b'_0 over $\mathcal{R}_q$. He sends b_1 and $t_B \leftarrow s'_B + p_B b'_0$ to Alice.

4. **(Output)** Alice sets $u \leftarrow t_B - p_A b_1 \cdot X^n + s_A$; note that $u = p_A b_0 + p_B b'_0$. Alice outputs the set $I = \{x \in A \mid u(x) = 0\}$.

Fig. 6. Augmented semi-honest PSI protocol based on ring-OLE

5.2 Maliciously Secure PSI in the Standard Model

In this section, we upgrade the security of our protocol to the malicious setting. Our upgrade introduces only a minimal communication overhead to the protocol, independent of the set sizes n. The full protocol is represented on Fig. 7.

Theorem 4. *The PSI protocol on Fig. 7 securely realizes the ideal functionality $\mathcal{F}_{psi}$ over the field $\mathbb{F}_p$ with set size n and malicious set size $n' = n_X = n_Y = 2n$, with statistical security against malicious adversaries in the $\mathcal{F}_{sole}$-hybrid model.*

PARAMETERS:

- A field $\mathbb{F}_{p'}$ and two rings $\mathcal{R}_p = \mathbb{F}_p[X]/F(X) \subseteq \mathcal{R}_q = \mathbb{F}_{p^t}[X]/F(X)$, where $F(X)$ has degree $2n + 1$ and $|\mathbb{F}_{p'}| \le |\mathbb{F}_p| - 2$. map is an efficient (and efficiently invertible) injective mapping, with $\mathsf{map}(\mathbb{F}_{p'}) \subseteq \mathbb{F}_p \setminus \{0,1\}$.
- The sender (Alice) and receiver (Bob) have respective input sets $A = \{a_1, a_2, \ldots, a_n\} \subset \mathbb{F}_{p'}$ and $B = \{b_1, b_2, \ldots, b_n\} \subset \mathbb{F}_{p'}$.
- A subfield ring-OLE in the ring $\mathcal{R}_q$ over the subring $\mathcal{R}_p$.

PROTOCOL:

1. **(Setting up the correlation)** Alice and Bob encode their sets to $p_A = c \cdot (X - 1) \cdot \prod_{i=1}^{n}(X - \mathsf{map}(a_i))$ with $c = -(\prod_{i=1}^{n}(-\mathsf{map}(a_i)))^{-1}$ (note that this guarantees $p_A(0) = 1$ and $p_A(1) = 0$) and $p_B = \prod_{i=1}^{n}(X - \mathsf{map}(b_i))$ respectively. Alice and Bob invoke $\mathcal{F}_{sole}$ to generate a subfield ring-OLE correlation over $\mathcal{R}_p, \mathcal{R}_q$: Alice receives $(a, s_A) \in \mathcal{R}_p \times \mathcal{R}_q$ and Bob receives $(b, s_B) \in \mathcal{R}_q^2$ such that $s_A + s_B = ab$.
2. **(Broadcasting the client set encoding)** Alice computes and sends $t_A = a - p_A$ to Bob.
3. **(Server-to-client message)** Bob sets $s'_B \leftarrow s_B - t_A b$. Then, Bob decomposes b as $b = b_0 + b_1 \cdot X^n$ (where b_0, b_1 are degree-n polynomials), and sets $s'_B \leftarrow s_B - t_A b$. He sends b_1 to Alice.
4. **(Checking p_A)** Alice computes $s'_A \leftarrow s_A - p_A b_1 \cdot X^n$. Alice sends $y \leftarrow s'_A(0)$ to Bob. If $y \ne b_0(0) - s'_B(0)$, Bob aborts. Else, Bob picks a random degree-n polynomial b'_0 over $\mathcal{R}_q$ and sends $t_B \leftarrow s'_B + p_B b'_0$ to Alice.
5. **(Output)** Alice sets $u \leftarrow t_B - p_A b_1 \cdot X^n + s_A$; note that $u = p_A b_0 + p_B b'_0$. If $u(1) = 0$, Alice aborts; otherwise, Alice computes the set $I = \{x \in A \mid u(\mathsf{map}(x)) = 0\}$ and outputs I.

Fig. 7. Maliciously secure PSI protocol in the $\mathcal{F}_{sole}$-hybrid model

Efficiency. Our malicious protocol has minimal communication overhead over our augmented semi-honest protocol. The main overhead stems from starting from a slightly larger field in which two elements can be "reserved elements". If p' is a prime power and $\ell \approx \log p'$, the price to pay is therefore increasing ℓ to $\log p$ where p is the smallest prime power above $p'+2$. While an exact expression would be rather tedious, for any reasonable input size this cost should be negligible (the simplest strategy is to pick $\mathsf{p}' = 2^\ell$ and $\mathsf{p} = 2^{\ell+1}$, in which case ℓ is increased by one bit, but much better encoding methods exist). Therefore, the communication remains $n \cdot (2\ell + 3\lambda + 6 \log n) + o(n)$ bits, or $n \cdot (2\ell + 3\lambda + 3 \log n) + o(n)$ with the encoding of [31]. We provide a more concrete analysis of the $o(n)$ term (setting up the ring-OLE) in the malicious setting in the Appendix of full version [9].

Computation Cost. Note that our standard model protocol shares with our other protocols the feature of having a communication independent of κ. Our protocol requires more computation compared to the best ROM-based protocols, due to its use of polynomial interpolation. However, it still allows for very fast PSI computation (we estimate a few seconds to compute the intersection between databases of size 2^{20}, on one core of a standard laptop). Concretely, the protocol requires only

- a single degree-n polynomial interpolation, one FFT over a polynomial ring with degree-$2n$ polynomials, and 3 multiplications of degree-n polynomials for the receiver, and
- a single degree-n polynomial interpolation, one FFT as above, 2 multiplications of degree-n polynomials, and a single n-multipoint polynomial evaluation for the sender.

Furthermore, both polynomial interpolations only have to be performed over a field $\mathbb{F}$, of size $|\mathbb{F}| \approx 2^\ell$ where ℓ is the bit size of the set items (e.g. 32 or 64 bits), and the multipoint evaluation is over a field of size $\lambda + 2 \log n$ bits. This stands in stark contrasts with previous state of the art protocols [20] that relied on polynomial interpolation (*on top* of using the ROM), where the interpolations and multipoint evaluations had to be performed over a very large field $\mathbb{F}$ of size $|\mathbb{F}| \approx 2^{400}$. By using a cyclotomic ring, the FFTs and polynomial multiplications are much faster than the interpolations. On Table 2, we compare our protocol to the current fastest maliciously secure PSI protocols [21,27,29].

On the attacks of [1]. We note that constructing maliciously secure PSI protocols using an algebraic approach, along the lines of our protocol, is known to be non-trivial and error prone. Indeed, previous works [14] used a similar approach based on polynomial manipulation, OLEs, and the lemmas about the polynomial (appear in the Appendix of full version [9]), to build a malicious PSI protocol. However, their protocol was found to be insecure in a recent preprint, which described powerful concrete attacks on this proposal [1]. Intuitively, the key technical difficulties revolve in both cases around how to handle null polynomials ($p_A = 0$ or $p_B = 0$). In our specific context, it turns out that our direct use of ring-OLE enables relatively elegant and simple (in hindsight) strategies to enforce nonzero polynomials. Our modification has almost no impact on the communication or the computation of our protocol, essentially giving us malicious security for free (though we note that we still require an additional round of communication). It is not, however, completely clear how to adapt our strategy to the setting of OLE-based algebraic PSI in [14]. We believe that this provides further support for the intuition that ring-OLE is the right primitive to build PSI protocols using this algebraic approach (beyond its direct advantage in terms of communication efficiency) (Fig. 7).

Acknowledgement. We thank all reviewers for their helpful comments. The first author is supported by Dim Math Innov funding from the Paris Mathematical Sciences Foundation (FSMP) funded by the Paris Ile-de-France Region, and the second author acknowledges the support of the French Agence Nationale de la Recherche (ANR), under grant ANR-20-CE39-0001 (project SCENE). This work was also supported by the France 2030 ANR Project ANR-22-PECY-003 SecureCompute.

References

1. Abadi, A., Murdoch, S.J., Zacharias, T.: Polynomial representation is tricky: Maliciously secure private set intersection revisited. Cryptology ePrint Archive, Report 2021/1009 (2021). https://ia.cr/2021/1009
2. Applebaum, B., Damgård, I., Ishai, Y., Nielsen, M., Zichron, L.: Secure Arithmetic Computation with Constant Computational Overhead. In: Katz, J., Shacham, H. (eds.) CRYPTO 2017. LNCS, vol. 10401, pp. 223–254. Springer, Cham (2017). https://doi.org/10.1007/978-3-319-63688-7_8
3. Boyle, E., Couteau, G., Gilboa, N., Ishai, Y.: Compressing vector OLE. In: Lie, D., Mannan, M., Backes, M., Wang, X. (eds.) ACM CCS 2018. pp. 896–912. ACM Press (Oct 2018)
4. Boyle, E., et al.: Efficient two-round OT extension and silent non-interactive secure computation. In: Cavallaro, L., Kinder, J., Wang, X., Katz, J. (eds.) ACM CCS 2019, pp. 291–308. ACM Press (Nov 2019)
5. Boyle, E., Couteau, G., Gilboa, N., Ishai, Y., Kohl, L., Scholl, P.: Efficient Pseudorandom Correlation Generators: Silent OT Extension and More. In: Boldyreva, A., Micciancio, D. (eds.) CRYPTO 2019. LNCS, vol. 11694, pp. 489–518. Springer, Cham (2019). https://doi.org/10.1007/978-3-030-26954-8_16
6. Boyle, E., Couteau, G., Gilboa, N., Ishai, Y., Kohl, L., Scholl, P.: Correlated pseudorandom functions from variable-density LPN. In: 61st FOCS, pp. 1069–1080. IEEE Computer Society Press (Nov 2020)
7. Boyle, E., Couteau, G., Gilboa, N., Ishai, Y., Kohl, L., Scholl, P.: Efficient pseudorandom correlation generators from ring-LPN. In: Micciancio, D., Ristenpart, T. (eds.) CRYPTO 2020, Part II. LNCS, vol. 12171, pp. 387–416. Springer, Heidelberg (Aug (2020)
8. Boyle, E., Couteau, G., Gilboa, N., Ishai, Y., Orrù, M.: Homomorphic secret sharing: Optimizations and applications. In: Thuraisingham, B.M., Evans, D., Malkin, T., Xu, D. (eds.) ACM CCS 2017, pp. 2105–2122. ACM Press (Oct / Nov 2017)
9. Bui, D., Couteau, G.: Improved private set intersection for sets with small entries. Cryptology ePrint Archive, Paper 2022/334 (2022). https://eprint.iacr.org/2022/334https://eprint.iacr.org/2022/334
10. Chase, M., Miao, P.: Private Set Intersection in the Internet Setting from Lightweight Oblivious PRF. In: Micciancio, D., Ristenpart, T. (eds.) CRYPTO 2020. LNCS, vol. 12172, pp. 34–63. Springer, Cham (2020). https://doi.org/10.1007/978-3-030-56877-1_2

11. Couteau, G., Rindal, P., Raghuraman, S.: Silver: silent VOLE and oblivious transfer from hardness of decoding structured LDPC codes. In: Malkin, T., Peikert, C. (eds.) CRYPTO 2021. LNCS, vol. 12827, pp. 502–534. Springer, Cham (2021). https://doi.org/10.1007/978-3-030-84252-9_17

12. Dietzfelbinger, M., Weidling, C.: Balanced allocation and dictionaries with tightly packed constant size bins. Theoret. Comput. Sci. **380**(1–2), 47–68 (2007)

13. Garimella, G., Pinkas, B., Rosulek, M., Trieu, N., Yanai, A.: Oblivious key-value stores and amplification for private set intersection. In: Malkin, T., Peikert, C. (eds.) CRYPTO 2021. LNCS, vol. 12826, pp. 395–425. Springer, Cham (2021). https://doi.org/10.1007/978-3-030-84245-1_14

14. Ghosh, S., Nilges, T.: An algebraic approach to maliciously secure private set intersection. In: Ishai, Y., Rijmen, V. (eds.) EUROCRYPT 2019. LNCS, vol. 11478, pp. 154–185. Springer, Cham (2019). https://doi.org/10.1007/978-3-030-17659-4_6

15. Ghosh, S., Simkin, M.: The communication complexity of threshold private set intersection. In: Boldyreva, A., Micciancio, D. (eds.) CRYPTO 2019. LNCS, vol. 11693, pp. 3–29. Springer, Cham (2019). https://doi.org/10.1007/978-3-030-26951-7_1

16. Hazay, C., Lindell, Y.: A note on the relation between the definitions of security for semi-honest and malicious adversaries. Cryptology ePrint Archive, Report 2010/551 (2010). https://eprint.iacr.org/2010/551

17. Kissner, L., Song, D.: Privacy-preserving set operations. In: Shoup, V. (ed.) CRYPTO 2005. LNCS, vol. 3621, pp. 241–257. Springer, Heidelberg (2005). https://doi.org/10.1007/11535218_15

18. Kolesnikov, V., Kumaresan, R., Rosulek, M., Trieu, N.: Efficient batched oblivious PRF with applications to private set intersection. In: Weippl, E.R., Katzenbeisser, S., Kruegel, C., Myers, A.C., Halevi, S. (eds.) ACM CCS 2016, pp. 818–829. ACM Press (Oct 2016)

19. Kolesnikov, V., Rosulek, M., Trieu, N., Wang, X.: Scalable private set union from symmetric-key techniques. In: Galbraith, S.D., Moriai, S. (eds.) ASIACRYPT 2019. LNCS, vol. 11922, pp. 636–666. Springer, Cham (2019). https://doi.org/10.1007/978-3-030-34621-8_23

20. Pinkas, B., Rosulek, M., Trieu, N., Yanai, A.: SpOT-light: lightweight private set intersection from sparse OT extension. In: Boldyreva, A., Micciancio, D. (eds.) CRYPTO 2019. LNCS, vol. 11694, pp. 401–431. Springer, Cham (2019). https://doi.org/10.1007/978-3-030-26954-8_13

21. Pinkas, B., Rosulek, M., Trieu, N., Yanai, A.: PSI from PaXoS: Fast, malicious private set intersection. In: Canteaut, A., Ishai, Y. (eds.) EUROCRYPT 2020. LNCS, vol. 12106, pp. 739–767. Springer, Cham (2020). https://doi.org/10.1007/978-3-030-45724-2_25

22. Pinkas, B., Schneider, T., Segev, G., Zohner, M.: Phasing: Private set intersection using permutation-based hashing. In: Jung, J., Holz, T. (eds.) USENIX Security 2015, pp. 515–530. USENIX Association (Aug 2015)

23. Pinkas, B., Schneider, T., Weinert, C., Wieder, U.: Efficient circuit-based PSI via Cuckoo Hashing. In: Nielsen, J.B., Rijmen, V. (eds.) EUROCRYPT 2018. LNCS, vol. 10822, pp. 125–157. Springer, Cham (2018). https://doi.org/10.1007/978-3-319-78372-7_5

24. Pinkas, B., Schneider, T., Zohner, M.: Faster private set intersection based on OT extension. In: Fu, K., Jung, J. (eds.) USENIX Security 2014, pp. 797–812. USENIX Association (Aug 2014)

25. Rindal, P., Raghuraman, S.: Blazing fast PSI from improved OKVS and subfield VOLE. IACR Cryptol. ePrint Arch. p. 320 (2022). https://eprint.iacr.org/2022/320

26. Rindal, P., Rosulek, M.: Malicious-secure private set intersection via dual execution. In: Thuraisingham, B.M., Evans, D., Malkin, T., Xu, D. (eds.) ACM CCS 2017, pp. 1229–1242. ACM Press (Oct/Nov 2017)

27. Rindal, P., Schoppmann, P.: VOLE-PSI: fast OPRF and circuit-PSI from vector-OLE. In: Canteaut, A., Standaert, F.-X. (eds.) EUROCRYPT 2021. LNCS, vol. 12697, pp. 901–930. Springer, Cham (2021). https://doi.org/10.1007/978-3-030-77886-6_31

28. Rosulek, M., Trieu, N.: Compact and malicious private set intersection for small sets. Cryptology ePrint Archive, Report 2021/1159 (2021). https://eprint.iacr.org/2021/1159

29. Rosulek, M., Trieu, N.: Compact and malicious private set intersection for small sets. Cryptology ePrint Archive, Report 2021/1159 (2021). https://ia.cr/2021/1159

30. Schoppmann, P., Gascón, A., Reichert, L., Raykova, M.: Distributed vector-OLE: Improved constructions and implementation. In: Cavallaro, L., Kinder, J., Wang, X., Katz, J. (eds.) ACM CCS 2019, pp. 1055–1072. ACM Press (Nov 2019)

31. Tamrakar, S., Liu, J., Paverd, A., Ekberg, J.E., Pinkas, B., Asokan, N.: The circle game: Scalable private membership test using trusted hardware. In: Karri, R., Sinanoglu, O., Sadeghi, A.R., Yi, X. (eds.) ASIACCS 17, pp. 31–44. ACM Press (Apr 2017)

32. Weng, C., Yang, K., Katz, J., Wang, X.: Wolverine: fast, scalable, and communication-efficient zero-knowledge proofs for boolean and arithmetic circuits. In: 2021 IEEE Symposium on Security and Privacy (SP), pp. 1074–1091. IEEE (2021)

33. Wieder, U., et al.: Hashing, load balancing and multiple choice. Foundations Trends® Theor. Comput. Sci. **12**(3–4), 275–379 (2017)

34. Yang, K., Weng, C., Lan, X., Zhang, J., Wang, X.: Ferret: Fast extension for correlated OT with small communication. In: Ligatti, J., Ou, X., Katz, J., Vigna, G. (eds.) ACM CCS 20, pp. 1607–1626. ACM Press (Nov 2020)

Pseudorandom Correlation Functions from Variable-Density LPN, Revisited

Geoffroy Couteau[1]([✉]) and Clément Ducros[2]

[1] CNRS, IRIF, Université de Paris, Paris, France
couteau@irif.fr
[2] IRIF, INRIA, Université de Paris, Paris, France

Abstract. Pseudorandom correlation functions (PCF), introduced in the work of (Boyle *et al.*, FOCS 2020), allow two parties to locally generate, from short correlated keys, a near-unbounded amount of pseudorandom samples from a target correlation. PCF is an extremely appealing primitive in secure computation, where they allow to confine all pre-processing phases of all future computations two parties could want to execute to a single short interaction with low communication and computation, followed solely by offline computations. Beyond introducing the notion, Boyle *et al.* gave a candidate construction, using a new *variable-density* variant of the learning parity with noise (LPN) assumption. Then, to provide support for this new assumption, the authors showed that it provably resists a large class of linear attacks, which captures in particular all known attacks on LPN.

In this work, we revisit the analysis of the VDLPN assumption. We make two key contributions:

– First, we observe that the analysis of Boyle *et al.* is purely asymptotic: they do not lead to any concrete and efficient PCF instantiation within the bounds that offer security guarantees. To improve this state of affairs, we combine a new variant of a VDLPN assumption with an entirely new, much tighter security analysis, which we further tighten using extensive computer simulations to optimize parameters. This way, we manage to obtain for the first time a set of *provable* usable parameters (under a simple combinatorial conjecture which is easy to verify experimentally), leading to a concretely efficient PCF resisting all linear tests.
– Second, we identify a flaw in the security analysis of Boyle *et al.*, which invalidates their proof that VDLPN resists linear attacks. Using several new non-trivial arguments, we repair the proof and fully demonstrate that VDLPN resists linear attack; our new analysis is more involved than the original (flawed) analysis.

Our parameters set leads to PCFs with keys around 3 MB allowing $\sim$ 500 evaluations per second on one core of a standard laptop for 110 bits of security; these numbers can be improved to 350 kB keys and $\sim$ 3950 evaluations/s using a more aggressive all-prefix variant. All numbers are quite tight: only within a factor 3 of the best bounds one could heuristically hope for.

© International Association for Cryptologic Research 2023
A. Boldyreva and V. Kolesnikov (Eds.): PKC 2023, LNCS 13941, pp. 221–250, 2023.
https://doi.org/10.1007/978-3-031-31371-4_8

1   Introduction

The generation of secret correlated random string is the cornerstone of secure computation (MPC). Given access to a trusted source of correlated randomness, any n-party functionality can be securely computed with information-theoretic security (against $n-1$ corrupted parties), and with very high concrete efficiency. For example, given $2m$ random oblivious transfers (in a random oblivious transfer, Alice gets two random bits (s_0, s_1), and Bob gets (b, s_b) for a random bit b), two parties can securely compute any boolean circuit C with up to m AND gates, with perfect security, while exchanging only four bits per AND gate.

The simplicity and efficiency of this paradigm is well known, and most modern MPC protocols take advantage of its features by sharing the same high level two-step structure: in the first step, the *preprocessing phase*, the parties interact to distributively and securely generate these correlated randomness. Since this phase is input-independent, it can be carried out ahead of time. Then, in the second step, the *online phase*, the parties "consume" this correlated randomness in a fast, information-theoretic protocol. The core challenge is this approach lies in step 1: designing a secure protocol to distributively generate long correlated random string.

Pseudorandom Correlations. Until recently, all state of the art protocols, such as SPDZ [DPSZ12], required $\Omega(s)$ communication to generate s bits of correlated randomness (ignoring terms depending on the security parameter and the number of parties), leading to communication-intensive preprocessing phases. This state of affair changed in a recent and exciting line of work [BCG+17, BCGI18, BCG+19b, BCG+19a, SGRR19, BCG+20b, CRR21] which introduced the notion of *pseudorandom correlation generators* (PCG), a new cryptographic primitive which allows parties to locally generate, from short correlated seeds, long instances of correlated *pseudorandom* strings. These PCGs enable secure computation with *silent preprocessing* where, after a short interaction to generate the short correlated seeds, the parties never need to interact anymore, and locally generate the long correlated strings. The latest results in this area further demonstrated that this primitive could be achieved with very high concrete efficiency, under appropriate LPN-like cryptographic assumptions.

Pseudorandom Correlated Functions. The aforementioned constructions of PCG, however, share a common limitation: the expansion of the short keys into long pseudorandom correlated strings is a one-time, monolithic procedure. That is, these PCGs are limited to a single generation of an a priori bounded amount of correlated pseudorandomness. If the parties want to possibly use these correlations across many protocols, then they carry the burden of having to either re-do the distributed generation of the short keys each time, or storing a very large amount of correlated randomness for a possibly long duration.

These limitations were overcome in a recent work [BCG+20a], where the authors introduced the notion of pseudorandom correlated *functions*

(PCFs). PCFs are to PCGs what pseudorandom functions are to pseudorandom generators: they allow to generate an arbitrary amount of correlated (pseudo)randomness in an incremental fashion. That is, given two short correlated keys (K_0, K_1), two parties can locally compute an arbitrary number of correlated strings $F_{K_0}(x), F_{K_1}(x))$, which are all indistinguishable from independent random samples from the target correlation. PCFs allow to confine *all future preprocessing phases* of any future MPC protocols that two parties may wish to run to a *one-time* short interaction, followed solely by local computation to generate the preprocessing material in all subsequent computations.

1.1 Constructions of Pseudorandom Correlated Functions

A PCF is an extremely powerful primitive, but also one which is highly non-trivial to construct. A generic construction of PCF under the LWE assumption can be obtained by letting the two parties homomorphically evaluate a well-chosen circuit using a threshold fully-homomorphic encryption scheme [DHRW16, BCG+20a]: the circuit takes as input a PRF key K, and computes pseudorandom instances of the correlation, using the output of the PRF to generate the pseudorandomness used in these correlations. However, this approach falls short of providing a concretely usable solution. To our knowledge, there are currently two competing approaches to construct usable PCFs:

PCFs from Variable-Density LPN. The work of [BCG+20a] gave a generic construction of PCF, by combining two primitives:

- A function secret sharing scheme (FSS) for a class of circuits $\mathcal{C}$. At a high level, an FSS for $\mathcal{C}$ allows to share any function $f \in \mathcal{C}$ in two functions f_0, f_1 such that each f_i computationally hides f, yet for any input x, it holds that $f_0(x) + f_1(x) = f(x)$.
- One weak pseudorandom function (WPRF) for some class $\mathcal{C}'$ related to $\mathcal{C}$. A WPRF is a PRF where the adversary in the pseudorandomness game is restricted to only querying random inputs.

Previous works [GI14, BGI15, BGI16] have shown how to construct extremely efficient FSS schemes for simple complexity classes, such as multi-point functions (i.e., a function $f_{\alpha,\beta}$ equal to 0 everywhere, except on n specific points $\alpha = (\alpha_1, \cdots, \alpha_n)$, where it takes a fixed value β), from minimal assumptions (namely, the existence of one-way functions). The shares of an n-point function $f_{\alpha,\beta}$ over a domain of size N consist of $n \log N$ PRG seeds, and evaluating f_i on the entire domain requires only N PRG evaluations. Given this, the authors of [BCG+20a] put forward a new WPRF in the (particularly low) complexity class of multi-point functions, which essentially boils down to a WPRF of the form $F_K(x) = F(x \oplus K)$, where F is a depth-two circuit with one bottom layer of high fan-in ANDs, and a single top high fan-in XOR gate. The security of this new candidate relies on the hardness of a new variant of the learning parity with noise (LPN) assumption, called *variable density* LPN assumption; we will overview this assumption later on. Given this new WPRF and the efficient FSS scheme of [BGI16], the authors of [BCG+20a] obtain a PCF candidate which can handle a wide variety of low-degree correlations, including (but not limited to) oblivious transfer correlations. The authors provide several variants and parameter choices; their most aggressive choices of parameters lead to a reasonably efficient construction, which (based on rough estimations) could generate hundreds to thousands of pseudorandom OT correlations per second on one core of a standard computer.

PCFs from Decisional Composite Residuosity. An alternative approach to building PCFs was recently put forward in [OSY21], using a Paillier-based construction of homomorphic secret sharing. In contrast to [BCG+20a], this work does not need to rely on new assumptions, and instead only requires the well-established decision composite residuosity assumption. However, this alternative construction has several downsides:

- *Expressivity.* The construction of [OSY21] is inherently limited to oblivious transfer correlations. In contrast, the VDLPN-based construction can generate arbitrary low-degree polynomial correlations, such as OLE, (authenticated) Beaver triples, and many more; these alternative correlations are crucial in many secure computation protocols.
- *Post-quantumness.* The DCR assumption can be broken by Shor's algorithm. In contrast, while VDLPN is a new and little studied assumption, there seems to be no reason to believe that it should be quantumly broken, being a relatively natural LPN-style assumption.
- *Efficiency.* Eventually, the construction of [OSY21] requires a few hundred exponentiations in an RSA group for every OT correlation produced. Using standard benchmark for exponentiations in 2048-bit RSA groups on a modern laptop[1], this translates to a cost of the order of one second *for each OT produced*, which is several orders of magnitude less efficient than what the VDLPN-based approach can plausibly provide, for suitable choices of parameters.

Given the above, the VDLPN approach seems to provide the best alternative to obtain efficient and expressive PCFs; however, its reliance on a new assumption calls for a very careful examination of its security. The work of [BCG+20a] provided an initial security analysis, proving a number of important results regarding the resistance of VDLPN against standard attacks. However, this analysis is purely asymptotic, and does not say much about what concrete choices of parameters can be expected to provide a sufficient security level. In addition, a close inspection of their analysis uncovers an important gap in one of the claim, invalidating part of the analysis (we will expand on this later on). Before we detail our contribution, we provide more context on the underlying new assumption and its analysis.

---

[1] E.g. A laptop equipped with an Intel i5 2540M processor can compute an RSA decryption in 1.4ms of amortized time.

1.2   The Variable-Density LPN Assumption

At a high level, the standard LPN assumption with dimension k and number of samples $n > k$ states the following: given a uniformly random matrix $A \xleftarrow{\$} \mathbb{F}_2^{n \times k}$, sample a vector $\mathbf{b}$ as $\mathbf{b} = A \cdot \mathbf{s} + \mathbf{e}$, where $\mathbf{s}$ is a random vector from $\mathbb{F}_2^k$, and $\mathbf{e}$ is a random *sparse* vector (the noise vector) over $\mathbb{F}_2^n$ (the exact distribution of $\mathbf{e}$ depends on the LPN flavor: it follows a Bernoulli distribution for standard LPN, it is uniform over all vectors of a given weight for exact LPN (XLPN), and it is a concatenation of unit vectors for regular LPN). Then, LPN states that it is hard to distinguish $\mathbf{b}$ from a uniformly random vector (put otherwise, it is hard to solve noisy systems of linear equations).

In coding theoretic terms, LPN therefore states that a noisy codeword from a random linear code looks random. LPN admits an equivalent, dual formulation: viewing A as the generating matrix of a linear code of dimension k, let $H \in F_2^{(n-k) \times n}$ be a *parity-check matrix* of A (which satisfies $H \cdot A = 0$; that is, H^T generates the dual of the code generated by A). Then distinguish $\mathbf{b} = A \cdot \mathbf{s} + \mathbf{e}$ from random is equivalent to distinguishing $H \cdot \mathbf{b} = H \cdot \mathbf{e}$ from random – that is, finding whether an undetermined system of linear equation admits a sparse solution. This is also known as the *syndrome decoding* problem.

The (dual) LPN assumption implies a natural construction of pseudorandom generators, which maps (a short description of) $\mathbf{e}$ to $H \cdot \mathbf{e}$. This PRG (and variants thereof) is at the heart of all known construction of pseudorandom *correlation* generators, due to its linear structure which allows to preserve some target correlations. To obtain a pseudorandom correlation *function*, the work of [BCG+20a] faced the following dilemma: intuitively, we would like to extend the PRG that maps (a representation of) $\mathbf{e}$ to $H \cdot \mathbf{e}$ into a PRF, but this means that we need $H \cdot \mathbf{e}$ to be an exponentially long vector whose entry can be generated incrementally (in this view, an input defines a row $\mathbf{h}$ of the matrix H, the key defines $\mathbf{e}$, and the corresponding output is $\mathbf{h}^\mathsf{T} \cdot \mathbf{e}$). We need a way to guarantee that $\mathbf{e}$ and the rows of H both admit a short (polynomial size) representation, and that $\mathbf{h}^\mathsf{T} \cdot \mathbf{e}$ can be computed in polynomial time. Unfortunately, defining H and $\mathbf{e}$ to be exponentially sparse does not work in general: $H \cdot \mathbf{e}$ would then become sparse as well, and therefore trivial to distinguish from random.

The key observation in [BCG+20a], and the central idea of their design, is that we can circumvent this issue by making H and $\mathbf{e}$ exponentially sparse, but with *variable density*. Concretely, fix a security parameter λ and consider sampling the rows of H as follows: a row $\mathbf{h}$ is divided into λ blocks $(\mathbf{h}_i)_{i \leq \lambda}$ (looking ahead, the maximum number of queries to the PRF will be bounded by a quantity smaller than 2^λ). Each block $\mathbf{h}_i$ is of length $\lambda \cdot 2^i$ and contains exactly λ 1's: this guarantees that the *density* of $\mathbf{h}_i$ is $1/2^i$. More precisely, $\mathbf{h}_i$ is a concatenation of λ length-2^i unit vectors. This means that $\mathbf{h}$ constructed this way is a *variable density* vector, where the density drops by a factor two when going from one block to the next. The noise vector $\mathbf{e}$ is simply sampled as a row vector. Intuitively, the dense portion of the inner products $\mathbf{h}^\mathsf{T} \cdot \mathbf{e}$ guarantees that the result will not be sparse (but the corresponding portions being narrow, many linear dependencies appear), while the sparse portions of the $\mathbf{h}^\mathsf{T} \cdot \mathbf{e}$ break linear dependencies (being exponentially wide, though very sparse). The VDLPN assumption states, informally, that this suffices to guarantee indistinguishability from random.

Definition 1 (VDLPN assumption, informal). *Sample a matrix H as H =* $H_1|| \cdots ||H_\lambda$ *over* $\mathbb{F}_2^{N \times \lambda \cdot (2^{\lambda+1}-1)}$ *where the rows are independently sampled as described above, and where* $N \ll 2^\lambda$ *is some bound on the maximum number of queries. Sample a noise vector* **e** *according to the same distribution as the rows of H. Then the VDLPN assumption states that, given H, H · e is indistinguishable from a random length-N vector.*

VDLPN directly implies a natural construction of WPRF: a random input x (a bitstring of length $\lambda^2 \cdot (\lambda+1)/2$) is parsed as λ blocks of length $\lambda \cdot i$, for $i = 1$ to λ, where each block is further parsed as λ sub-blocks of length i each. A length-i string defines a random unit vector of length 2^i (it encodes the position of the nonzero entry in the vector). The concatenation of these unit vectors forms a uniformly random row $\mathbf{h}_x$ for the matrix H. A similar mapping is applied to convert the bitstring K (the WPRF key) into a noise vector $\mathbf{e}_K$. Eventually, observe that the mapping $F_K : x \to \mathbf{h}_x^{\mathsf{T}} \cdot \mathbf{e}_K$ is efficient, because each of $\mathbf{h}_x, \mathbf{e}_K$ is exponentially sparse: computing their inner product amounts to computing $O(\lambda^2)$ equality tests between the sub-blocks of x and of K. To construct a pseudorandom *correlation* function, the authors of [BCG+20a] build upon the fact that this WPRF can further be written as a XOR of point functions (each point function takes a sub-block of x as input and returns 0 unless it is equal to the corresponding sub-block of K), which makes it *FSS-friendly.*

1.3   Security of VDLPN

Since VDLPN is a variant of the LPN assumption, the natural first step to analyze its security is to look at existing attacks on LPN. There have been, however, a tremendous number of attacks on LPN designed over the years, including attacks such as Gaussian elimination and the BKW algorithm [BKW00,Lyu05, LF06,EKM17] and variants based on covering codes [ZJW16,BV16,BTV16, GJL20], and attacks based on information set decoding techniques [Pra62, Ste88,FS09,BLP11,MMT11,BJMM12,MO15,EKM17,BM18]. This list is far from exhaustive; one could also mention statistical decoding attacks [AJ01, FKI06,Ove06,DAT17], generalized birthday attacks [Wag02,Kir11], linearization attacks [BM97,Saa07], attacks based on finding low weight code vectors [Zic17], and many more. A core observation of [BCG+20a] is that *all* these attacks fit in a common framework, called *linear tests*. Roughly, a linear test is an attack in which the adversary attempts to distinguish **b** from a random vector by finding a nonzero linear function L_H (which can depend on H in an arbitrary way) such that $L_H(\mathbf{b})$ is *biased* (i.e., far from uniform in statistical distance) when $\mathbf{b} = H \cdot \mathbf{e}$. Being secure against linear tests is a statistical property, which one can hope to prove unconditionally. To this end, the work of [BCG+20a] put forward the notion of *low bias* WPRF:

Definition 2 (low-bias WPRF, informal). *A family* $\{F_K\}_K$ *of WPRFs has* low bias *up to N samples if*

$$\Pr_{x_1, \cdots, x_N} [\text{bias}(\mathcal{D}) \geq \text{negl}(\lambda)] \leq \text{negl}'(\lambda),$$

where $\mathcal{D}$ is the distribution that samples a random key K for the WPRF, and outputs the vector $(F_K(x_1), \cdots, F_K(x_N))$. Above, the N inputs are sampled from the input space of the WPRF family, and $\text{negl}, \text{negl}'$ *denote two negligible functions.*

Above, the bias of a distribution $\mathcal{D}$ over $\mathbb{F}_2^N$ is defined as $\max_{\mathbf{u} \neq 0} |1/2 - \Pr_{\mathbf{v} \leftarrow \mathcal{D}}[\mathbf{u}^{\mathsf{T}} \cdot \mathbf{v} = 1]|$; that is, it is the distance from the uniform distribution over $\mathbb{F}_2$ induced by computing $L(\mathbf{v})$ with the "worst possible" nonzero linear function $L : \mathbb{F}_2^N \mapsto \mathbb{F}_2$. One of the core security claims of [BCG+20a] hinges upon the fact that the VDLPN-based WPRF is a low-bias WPRF; in particular, this means that the VDLPN assumption cannot be broken using essentially any of the known attacks on LPN.

Theorem 3 (Resistance to linear tests [BCG+20a], informal). *The WPRF built from the VDLPN assumption has a low bias up to $N = 2^{O(\lambda)}$ samples (the functions* $\text{negl}, \text{negl}'$ *are both equal to $2^{O(-\lambda)}$ as well).*

To show that the VDLPN assumption is secure, we will only consider resistance against linear tests - and all our proof of security will consists of showing this resistance. A simple variant of the VDLPN assumption achieves smaller input size ($O(\lambda^2)$ instead of $O(\lambda^3)$), but we ignore it in this simplified overview. Note that [BCG+20a] also considers various other attacks, such as algebraic attacks, linear cryptanalysis, and attacks by low depth (AC^0) circuits. These analyses make VDLPN a plausible assumption, from which [BCG+20a] derives several consequences: a pseudorandom correlation function, as we already discussed, but also the first candidate WPRF in the very low complexity class XOR-AND (one layer of ANDs followed by a single XOR gate), which indicates that this class is perhaps hard to learn in the uniform PAC model. Furthermore, VDLPN also implies a WPRF secure against XOR related-key attacks, something which was previously known only assuming very strong cryptographic primitives (namely, high degree multilinear maps).

1.4 Our Contributions

We revisit the security analysis of VDLPN against linear tests. Our main motivation is that the analysis in [BCG+20a] is purely asymptotic, and trying to extract concrete parameters within the range where the analysis applies gives terrible performances. Concretely, let D be the number of blocks, w be the number of ones in each block, and N be a bound on the maximum number of queries (in our simplified exposition above, we used $w = D = \lambda$ and $N \ll 2^\lambda$). The authors of [BCG+20a] suggested the following concrete parameters to instantiate VDLPN: set $w = 1.5\lambda$, $D = w/4$, and $N = 2^D$. They conjectured that this should achieve λ bits of security. However, this choice of parameters is purely heuristic, and described as a challenge to cryptanalysts: it is not backed up by any concrete cryptanalysis.

On the other hand, their analysis guarantees $2^{\Omega(w)}$ bits of security against linear tests whenever $w > \Gamma \cdot D$, for up to 2^D samples, where Γ is a constant from the proof. A quick back-of-the-envelope calculation reveals that Γ in their analysis is of the order of magnitude of 10^5, and it is far from obvious to improve the constants without significantly changing the analysis (while the proof is not tight, a straightforward "tightening" only saves a small factor). This means that, when instantiating the parameters within the range where the proof offers some security guarantees, the security parameters must be of the order of *several million bits long* – of course, this is entirely impractical.

Furthermore, upon revisiting their analysis, we uncovered one mistake (as well as a second, relatively minor mistake), that invalidates their proof of security against linear attacks. Fixing the mistake turns out to be non-trivial, and constitutes an important part of our contribution.

First Contribution: A Tighter VDLPN. The corrected analysis we present offers even worse concrete bounds than in the original (flawed) proof: the Γ value is of the order of 10^6, leading to a security parameter w in the millions. In other words, there is no realistically usable range of parameters within the bounds handled by the security analysis. Thus, one is left with a plausible assumption with purely asymptotic parameters on the one hand, and some concrete candidate choices of parameters that lead to a reasonably efficient PCF construction, but that are not supported by any security analysis. The goal of this first contribution is to bridge this (huge) gap between *secure in theory* and *usable in practice*. Since the task is highly non-trivial, we attack the problem simultaneously on three angles. Each angle in itself forms an orthogonal contribution to the overall analysis (in the sense that each of the three techniques leads to significant improvements by themselves).

- *An entirely new proof approach.* First, we step back from the original analysis and seek to understand the main source of slackness in the parameters. Then, we develop an alternative, much more direct approach which, in a sense, allows us to exploit the contribution to the bias of every component of the matrix H (while the previous analysis could only take into account the contribution of the "top contributors", for technical reasons). The new approach achieves much tighter bounds.
- *A proof-friendly VDLPN variant.* Second, we allow ourselves to (slightly) *change* the VDLPN assumption. Concretely, our variant is identical to VDLPN, except for the first block H_1: here, we set H_1 to be a uniformly random matrix instead. This choice stems from the fact that in the analysis, we need to use two different arguments to handle the low weight linear tests and the high weight linear tests; sampling H_1 uniformly at random allows to achieve much tighter bounds for the analysis against low weight tests. We

observe that this variant of VDLPN remains FSS-friendly: using this variant does not harm any of the cryptographic applications.

– *Better bounds through simulations.* Eventually, we rely on extensive computer simulations to achieve tighter bounds. Concretely, we need a bound on the expectation of some complex random variable X, which we obtained using a generalized Chernoff inequality in the previous analysis. While this bound suffices for the asymptotic analysis, its looseness severely impacts the bounds. Here, instead, we estimate $\mathbb{E}[X]$ through computer simulations. We empirically observe that the samples from X have very low variance, and derive a tight bound on $\mathbb{E}[X]$ with a very high confidence interval.

Putting everything together, we manage to prove that (our variant of) VDLPN has bias at most 2^{-80} with probability at least $1 - 2^{-80}$, for a value of w as low as $w = 380$ (with $D = 30$, and up to $N = 2^D$ samples – this is just a sample of candidate parameters, we do not have a closed-form formula).[2] This is a tremendous improvement compared to the previous analysis, and gives for the first time a set of parameters which are simultaneously backed by a thorough security analysis, yet are usable in practice. We stress that, in spite of our computer-verified component, our bounds are much better than purely heuristic bounds: they are provable bounds under a simple, concrete combinatorial conjecture, which is easy to verify through computer experiments. In contrasts, even ignoring the flaw in their asymptotic analysis, all "usable parameters" proposed in [BCG+20a] were purely heuristic, based on the intuition that they might be hard to attack and described as challenges for cryptanalysis, but not supported by any analysis whatsoever.

We believe that our work constitutes a strong step in the direction of showing that one can construct secure and concretely efficient pseudorandom correlation functions, an important and intriguing goal.

Second Contribution: Fixing the Original Analysis. In essence, the analysis of a central claim in the proof of resistance against linear tests turned out to be incorrect. The claim, on the other hand, remains essentially correct (up to some concrete choice of the constants involved): only its analysis is flawed, it did not lead to attacks. The mistake appears in a bound on the expectation $\mathbb{E}[Z]$ of a random variable Z, of the form $\mathbb{E}[Z] \in [a, b]$, for some values $0 < a < b$. The authors deduced from this bound a bound of the form $\mathbb{E}[|Z - b| \leq b - a$, but this is wrong in general (the error might stem from an application of the Jensen inequality in the wrong direction): intuitively, if the distribution of Z is "anti-concentrated" with respect to its expectation, then the inequality $\mathbb{E}[|Z - b| \leq b - a$ does not follow from $\mathbb{E}[Z] \in [a, b]$.[3]

---

[2] The choice of 80 bits of security is more conservative than it appears: it means that an adversary will have to compute 2^{80} inner products with a length-2^{30} vector to detect a 2^{-80} bias in the output. In terms of bit-security, this corresponds to at least 110 bits of security.

[3] E.g. if Z is 0 with probability $1/2$, and 10 else, then $\mathbb{E}[Z] = 5 \in [4, 5]$, but $\mathbb{E}[|Z - 5|] = 5 > 5 - 4$.

On the other hand, if Z follows a "nice" distribution, typically a Gaussian-style distribution (or any bell-shape distribution), and if the value b is sufficiently close to $\mathbb{E}[Z]$, then the claim becomes true. A quick simulation reveals that Z indeed appears to exhibit the right structure. Central to our first contribution is a formal proof that the claim holds for Z. Compared to the analysis of [BCG+20a], our new analysis cannot simply bound the expected value of Z: we have to prove strong *tail bounds* on Z, which is significantly more complex, because Z is a sum of *dependent* variables. Our analysis relies on a power-full bound about the balls and bins problem.

We then turn to integrating our new proof of the central claim to the full proof of resistance against linear tests. Along the way, we found (and fixed) another minor mistake in the analysis, which requires changing the concrete choices of constants in the proof. Due to this, and due to some slackness in our new proof of the central claim (which stems from the limitations of the inequality which we use), the general proof ends up failing on some corner cases. Essentially, the analysis studies separately the contribution of each block H_i of the matrix H to the overall bias; the analysis, however, fails whenever i is too small. Nevertheless, we show that the case of very small values of i can be treated separately with two simple arguments, which completes the proof.

We stress that while the repaired proof follows the high level structure of that of [BCG+20a], the core of correction was not straight forward. This security analysis against linear tests is central to the claim that VDLPN is a plausible assumption (since it resists all known attacks against LPN), and therefore provides a plausible candidate to construct powerful objects such as a PCF (for all low-degree correlations), a XOR-RKA secure WPRF, and a family of extremely simple functions (in the XOR-AND class) hard to learn in the uniform PAC model. We also mention that we notified the authors of [BCG+20a] of our findings, and they acknowledged the flaws in the analysis.

1.5   New Cost Estimations for PCFs, and Challenges

Using the parameters from above ($w = 380, D = 30$), we compute the seed size and estimate the evaluation time of the pseudorandom correlation function of [BCG+20a] instantiated using our new VDLPN variant. On top of the VDLPN variant, the construction uses a puncturable pseudorandom function, instantiated with the GGM construction [GGM86]. We set the security parameter of the PRG used in GGM to $\lambda = 128$. With these parameters, we get the following costs:

- Seed size: 2.94 MB
- PCF evaluation time: the evaluation cost is (largely) dominated by $\approx 1.81 \cdot 10^5$ calls to a length-doubling pseudorandom generator.

To give a rough runtime estimation, the PRG can be instantiated using two calls to fixed-key AES. According to [MSY21], using the AES-NI instructions of modern CPUs, one byte of AES-128 can be computed in ~ 1.3 cycles. Hence, computing $3.6 \cdot 10^5$ blocks of 16 bytes requires about $7.5 \cdot 10^6$ cycles. Concretely, using a 3.8 GHz processor, this amounts to roughly 500 PCF evaluations per second on a single core (note that the estimation should not be too far off, because the computation requires no random data access, hence cache misses are unlikely). Since all evaluations are fully parallelizable, using c cores increases this number to $500c$ evaluations per second.

The work of [BCG+20a] also suggested an improved *all prefix* variant, which has shorter seeds and better runtimes, using existing efficient constructions of all-prefix function secret sharing. While this construction lacks a security analysis, this is only because it makes the noise vectors $\mathbf{e}_i$ correlated (our analysis fundamentally uses their independence). However, it seems very reasonable to conjecture that this is just an artefact of the analysis, and that the optimized construction provides the same security level. Under the heuristic assumption that the correlated $\mathbf{e}_i$ behave essentially as well as independent $\mathbf{e}_i$ for resistance to linear tests, we can reuse our previous analysis and obtain the following improved bounds for the *all-prefix* PCF: seed size 0.35MB, and PCF evaluation time around 3950 evaluations per second on a single 3.8GHz processor.

These numbers demonstrate that, already within the range of our provable bounds, PCFs can achieve very promising parameters, with short seeds, and reasonably fast runtimes. Note that we believe that there remains some small gap between our analysis and the "true" security of VDLPN – namely, smaller parameters might plausibly lead to a secure instance (perhaps as small as $w = 120$ and $D = 30$). We view further tightening our analysis as an interesting open question. Since the cost is linear in w, reducing w to 120 would lead to a factor 3 improvement (on seed size and evaluations per second). Nonetheless, our provable parameters appear already quite tight, being at most a factor-3 off compared to the best parameters one could heuristically hope for.

2   Preliminaries

We use bold font for vectors, and capitals for matrices. For vectors $\mathbf{u}, \mathbf{v}$, $\mathsf{HW}(\mathbf{u})$ denotes the Hamming weight of $\mathbf{u}$, $d_{\mathsf{H}}(\mathbf{u}, \mathbf{v})$ denotes the Hamming distance between $\mathbf{u}, \mathbf{v}$. Below, we recall the definition of the bias of a distribution, and some standard technical lemmas.

Definition 4 (Bias of a Distribution). *Given a distribution $\mathcal{D}$ over $\mathbb{F}^n$ and a vector $\mathbf{u} \in \mathbb{F}^n$, the bias of $\mathcal{D}$ with respect to $\mathbf{u}$, denoted $\mathsf{bias}_{\mathbf{u}}(\mathcal{D})$, is equal to*

$$\mathsf{bias}_{\mathbf{u}}(\mathcal{D}) = |\mathbb{E}_{\mathbf{x} \sim \mathcal{D}}[\mathbf{u}^{\mathsf{T}} \cdot \mathbf{x}] - \mathbb{E}_{\mathbf{x} \sim \mathcal{U}_n}[\mathbf{u}^{\mathsf{T}} \cdot \mathbf{x}]| = \left| \mathbb{E}_{\mathbf{x} \sim \mathcal{D}}[\mathbf{u}^{\mathsf{T}} \cdot \mathbf{x}] - \frac{1}{|\mathbb{F}|} \right|,$$

where $\mathcal{U}_n$ denotes the uniform distribution over $\mathbb{F}^n$. The bias of $\mathcal{D}$, denoted $\mathsf{bias}(\mathcal{D})$, is the maximum bias of $\mathcal{D}$ with respect to any nonzero vector $\mathbf{u}$.

Standard Probability Lemmas. Given t distributions $(\mathcal{D}_1, \cdots, \mathcal{D}_t)$ over $\mathbb{F}_2^n$, we denote by $\bigoplus_{i \leq t} \mathcal{D}_i$ the distribution obtained by *independently* sampling $\mathbf{v}_i \xleftarrow{\$} \mathcal{D}_i$ for $i = 1$ to t and outputting $\mathbf{v} \leftarrow \mathbf{v}_1 \oplus \cdots \oplus \mathbf{v}_t$. We will use the following bias of the exclusive-or (cf. [Shp09]).

Lemma 5. *Let $t \in \mathbb{N}$ be an integer, and let $(\mathcal{D}_1, \cdots, \mathcal{D}_t)$ be t independent distributions over $\mathbb{F}_2^n$. Then $\mathsf{bias}(\bigoplus_{i \leq t} \mathcal{D}_i) \leq 2^{t-1} \cdot \prod_{i=1}^{t} \mathsf{bias}(\mathcal{D}_i) \leq \min_{i \leq t} \mathsf{bias}(\mathcal{D}_i)$.*

Let $\mathsf{Ber}_r(\mathbb{F}_2)$ denote the Bernoulli distribution that outputs 1 with probability r, and 0 otherwise. More generally, we denote by $\mathsf{Ber}_r(\mathbb{F})$ the distribution that outputs a uniformly random element of $\mathbb{F}$ with probability r, and 0 otherwise (this does not exactly match our definition of $\mathsf{Ber}(\mathbb{F}_2)$, but the slight discrepancy will not matter in our applications). We will use a standard simple lemma for computing the bias of a XOR of Bernoulli samples:

Lemma 6 (Piling-up lemma). *For any $0 < r < 1/2$ and any integer n, given n random variables $X_1, \cdots, X_n$ i.i.d. to $\mathsf{Ber}_r(\mathbb{F}_2)$, it holds that $\Pr[\bigoplus_{i=1}^{n} X_i = 0] = 1/2 + (1 - 2r)^n/2$.*

We will also need two concentration bounds. The bounded difference inequality [McD89] is an application of the more general Azuma inequality [Azu67]. Let $(n, m) \in \mathbb{N}^2$ be two integers. We say that a function $\Phi : [n]^m \mapsto \mathbb{R}$ satisfies the *Lipschitz property with constant d* if for every $\mathbf{x}, \mathbf{x}' \in [n]^m$ which differ in a single coordinate, it holds that $|\Phi(\mathbf{x}) - \Phi(\mathbf{x}')| \leq d$.

Lemma 7 (Bounded Difference Inequality). *Let $\Phi : [n]^m \mapsto \mathbb{R}$ be a function satisfying the Lipschitz property with constant d, and let $(X_1, \cdots, X_m)$ be independent random variables over $[n]$. Then*

$$\Pr[\Phi(X_1, \cdots, X_m) < \mathbb{E}[\Phi(X_1, \cdots, X_m)] - t] \leq \exp\left(-\frac{2t^2}{m \cdot d^2}\right).$$

Eventually we will rely on the Occupancy Bound from [KMPS94], which provides tight bounds for the balls and bins problem.

Lemma 8 (Occupancy Bound). *Let E be the number of empty bins when m balls are placed randomly into n bins, and define $r = m/n$. The expectation of E is given by $\mu = \mathbb{E}[E] = (1 - \frac{1}{n})^m \approx ne^{-r}$. For any $\theta > 0$,*

$$\Pr[|E - \mu| \geq \theta\mu] \leq 2\exp\left(-\frac{\theta^2\mu^2(n - \frac{1}{2})}{n^2 - \mu^2}\right) = \mathcal{B}$$

Note that we can derive the following two equations : $\Pr[E \geq \mu(\theta + 1)] < \mathcal{B}$ and $\Pr[E \leq \mu(1 - \theta)] < \mathcal{B}$.

2.1 Coding Theory

Definition 9. *Let n be a positive integer, $\mathcal{C}$ is a linear code if $\mathcal{C}$ is a vector subspace of $\mathbb{F}_q^n$. The integer n is called the length of $\mathcal{C}$. The dimension of $\mathcal{C}$ is its dimension as an $\mathbb{F}_q$-vector space. It is denoted by $k = \dim_{\mathbb{F}_q} \mathcal{C}$*

Definition 10. *(Minimum distance of a code) Let $\mathcal{C}$ be a linear code of length n. The minimum distance of $\mathcal{C}$, is the minimum distance $d_{\mathcal{C}}$ between two distinct codewords of $\mathcal{C}$.*

$$d_{\mathcal{C}} = \min_{\mathbf{x}, \mathbf{y} \in \mathcal{C}, \mathbf{x} \neq \mathbf{y}} \{d_H(\mathbf{u}, \mathbf{v})(\mathbf{x}, \mathbf{y})\}$$

Learning Parity with Noise. We define the LPN assumption over a ring $\mathcal{R}$ with dimension k, number of samples n, w.r.t. a code generation algorithm $\mathbf{C}$, and a noise distribution $\mathcal{D}$:

Definition 11 (Dual LPN). *Let* $\mathcal{D}(\mathcal{R}) = \{\mathcal{D}_{k,n}(\mathcal{R})\}_{k,n\in\mathbb{N}}$ *denote a family of efficiently sampleable distributions over a ring* $\mathcal{R}$, *such that for any* $k, n \in \mathbb{N}$, $\mathsf{Im}(\mathcal{D}_{k,n}(\mathcal{R})) \subseteq \mathcal{R}^n$. *Let* $\mathbf{C}$ *be a probabilistic code generation algorithm such that* $\mathbf{C}(k,n,\mathcal{R})$ *outputs a matrix* $H \in \mathcal{R}^{k\times n}$. *For dimension* $k = k(\lambda)$, *number of samples (or block length)* $n = n(\lambda)$, *and ring* $\mathcal{R} = \mathcal{R}(\lambda)$, *the (dual)* $(\mathcal{D}, \mathbf{C}, \mathcal{R})$-$\mathsf{LPN}(k, n)$ *assumption states that*

$$\{(H, \mathbf{b}) \mid H \xleftarrow{\$} \mathbf{C}(k, n, \mathcal{R}), \mathbf{e} \xleftarrow{\$} \mathcal{D}_{k,n}(\mathcal{R}), \mathbf{b} \leftarrow H \cdot \mathbf{s}\}$$

$$\overset{c}{\approx} \{(H, \mathbf{b}) \mid H \xleftarrow{\$} \mathbf{C}(k, n, \mathcal{R}), \mathbf{b} \xleftarrow{\$} \mathcal{R}^n\}.$$

The dual LPN assumption is also called the *syndrome decoding assumption* in the code-based cryptography literature. The dual LPN assumption as written above is equivalent to the *primal* LPN assumption with respect to G (a matrix $G \in \mathcal{R}^{n\times n-k}$ such that $H \cdot G = 0$), which states that $G \cdot \mathbf{s} + \mathbf{e}$ is indistinguishable from random, where $\mathbf{s} \xleftarrow{\$} \mathcal{R}^{n-k}$ and $\mathbf{e} \xleftarrow{\$} \mathcal{D}_{k,n}(\mathcal{R})$; the equivalence follows from the fact that $H(G \cdot \mathbf{s} + \mathbf{e}) = H \cdot \mathbf{e}$.

The standard LPN assumption refers to the case where H is a uniformly random matrix over $\mathbb{F}_2$, and $\mathbf{e}$ is sampled from $\mathsf{Ber}_r(\mathbb{F}_2)$, where r is called the *noise rate*. Other common noise distributions include exact noise (the noise vector $\mathbf{e}$ is a uniformly random weight-rn vector from $\mathbb{F}_2^n$; this is a common choice in concrete LPN-based constructions) and regular noise (the noise vector $\mathbf{e}$ is a concatenation of rn random unit vectors from $\mathbb{F}_2^{1/r}$, widely used in the PCG literature [BCGI18,BCG+19b,BCG+19a]).

2.2 The Variable Density LPN Assumption

We recall the *regular VDLPN* assumption from [BCG+20a]; other variants exist. Let λ be a security parameter. We fix three parameters: a *sparsity* parameter $w = w(\lambda)$ (controlling the number of ones per row of a block), a *block* parameter $D = D(\lambda)$ (controlling the number of blocks), and a bound $N = N(\lambda)$ on the number of samples. The reader can think of w, D as being $\Omega(\lambda)$, with $D < w$, and $N = 2^D$ for concreteness. We set par $\leftarrow (w, D, N)$.

Let $\mathcal{S}_{1,2^i}$ the distribution of unit vector of size 2^i. Let $\mathcal{R}_{w,i}$ be the distribution of random w-regular vectors over $\mathbb{F}_2^{w \cdot 2^i}$, i.e., the concatenation of w vector sampled from $\mathcal{S}_{1,2^i}$). Let $\mathcal{H}_{\mathsf{par}}^i$ denote the distribution over $N \times (w \cdot 2^i)$ matrices over $\mathbb{F}_2$, where each row of the matrix is sampled independently from $\mathcal{R}_{w,i}$, and let $\mathcal{H}_{\mathsf{par}}$ denote the distribution over $\mathbb{F}_2^{N\times 2N\cdot w}$, obtained by sampling $H_i \xleftarrow{\$} \mathcal{H}_{\mathsf{par}}^i$ for $i = 1$ to D and outputting $H = H_1||\cdots||H_D$, where $||$ is the horizontal concatenation. Eventually we denote $\mathcal{N}_{\mathsf{par}}$ the noise distribution obtained by sampling $\mathbf{e}_i^\top$ according $\mathcal{R}_{w,i}$ and outputting $\mathbf{e} \leftarrow (\mathbf{e}_1 /\!/ \cdots /\!/ \mathbf{e}_D) \in \mathbb{F}_2^{2N\cdot w}$ where $/\!/$ is this time the vertical concatenation. The matrix H_i sampled from $\mathcal{H}_{\mathsf{par}}^i$ is:

$$H_i = \begin{bmatrix} u^i_{1,1} & \cdots & \overbrace{u^i_{1,w}}^{2^i \text{ columns}} \\ \vdots & \vdots & \vdots \\ u^i_{N,1} & \cdots & u^i_{N,w} \end{bmatrix}$$

where $(u^i_{k,j})_{1 \leq k \leq N, 1 \leq j \leq w}$ are sampled from the distribution $\mathcal{S}_{1,2^i}$, and are unit vector over $\mathbb{F}_2^{2^i}$. Thus, there is w non-zero coordinates by rows. Eventually, the matrix H sampled from $\mathcal{H}_{\text{par}}$ is a horizontal concatenation of the H_i:

$$H = \underbrace{\begin{bmatrix} H_1 & \cdots & H_D \end{bmatrix}}_{w \cdot 2^{D+1} \text{ columns}}$$

The term *variable density* refers to the fact that the density of 1's in each block H_i is $1/2^i$ by construction. For any H sampled from the distribution $\mathcal{H}_{\text{par}}$ let $\mathcal{O}_{\text{par}}(H)$ be the distribution which samples $\mathbf{e} \xleftarrow{\$} \mathcal{N}_{\text{par}}$ and return $H \cdot \mathbf{e}$.

Definition 12 (rVDLPN(w, D, N)). *The regular VDPLN assumption, with parameters* par $= (w, D, N)$, *denoted* rVDLPN(w, D, N)), *states that:*

$$\{(H, \mathbf{b}) | H \xleftarrow{\$} \mathcal{H}_{\text{par}}, \mathbf{e} \xleftarrow{\$} \mathcal{N}_{\text{par}}, \mathbf{b} \leftarrow H \cdot \mathbf{e}\} \approx \{(H, \mathbf{b}) | H \xleftarrow{\$} \mathcal{H}_{\text{par}}, \mathbf{b} \xleftarrow{\$} \mathbb{F}_2^N\}$$

Note that this is exactly the dual LPN assumption where both the matrix and the noise are sampled from a specific distribution variable-density matrices and vectors.

A WPRF Candidate from the rVDLPN Assumption. Fix parameters par$(\lambda) = (w(\lambda), D(\lambda), N(\lambda) = 2^{D(\lambda)})$. Recall that a vector from the distribution $\mathcal{N}_{\text{par}}$ is in fact the vertical concatenation of D vectors from $\mathbf{e_i}$, where $\mathbf{e_i}$ is the transpose vector of the vector from the distribution $\mathcal{R}_{w,i}$. Moreover, $\mathcal{R}_{w,i}$ is the concatenation of w unit vector over $\mathbb{F}_2^{2^i}$, where each of them can be generated with i random bits (encoding the index of the nonzero entry). Therefore, sampling a vector $\mathcal{N}_{\text{par}}$ requires exactly $w \cdot \sum_{i=1}^{D} i = w \cdot D(D-1)/2$ random bits; we write $\mathcal{N}_{\text{par}}(r)$ to denote the vector $\mathbf{e}$ sampled from $\mathcal{N}_{\text{par}}$ using randomness r. We describe the WPRF candidate below.

- Key size: $K \in \{0,1\}^{\pi(\lambda)}$ with $\pi(\lambda) = \rho(\lambda) = w \cdot D(D-1)/2$
- Input size : $x \in \{0,1\}^{\rho(\lambda)}$ with $\rho(\lambda) = w \cdot D(D-1)/2$
- $F_K(x)$: on input $x \in \{0,1\}^\rho$, sample $\mathbf{h}^\top \leftarrow \mathcal{N}_{\text{par}}(x)$ and output $\langle \mathbf{h}, \mathcal{N}_{\text{par}}(K)\rangle$

Theorem 13 ([BCG+20a]). *Suppose that* rVDLPN(par) *holds. Then the above construction is an N-query WPRF, with input length and key length equal at* $w \cdot D(D-1)/2$.

2.3 Pseudorandom Correlation Functions

Pseudorandom correlation functions, introduced in [BCG+20a], allow to locally generate, from a pair of short correlated keys, an arbitrary polynomial amount of pseudorandom correlations, in an incremental way. A fundamental application of PCF is to secure computation in the preprocessing model: two parties can distributively generate PCF keys, and later use them every time they wish to engage in a secure computation protocol, to generate locally (without any interaction) all preprocessing material required for the protocol. Therefore, PCFs allow to confine *all* future preprocessing phases of all secure computation protocols two parties could want to execute, to a single, one time generation of short correlated keys, followed solely by local computations. Slightly more formally, a PCF is a pair (PCF.Setup, PCF.Eval) where PCF.Setup generates short correlated keys (k_0, k_1), and PCF.Eval(σ, k_σ, x) outputs a value y_σ such that for any input x, given $k_{1-\sigma}$, the value y_σ is indistinguishable from a random value sampled conditioned on satisfying the target correlation with PCF.Eval$(\sigma, k_{1-\sigma}, x)$ (for $\sigma = 0, 1$). Due to lack of space, we defer the definition of PCF in the full version.

2.4 Pseudorandom Correlation Function from VDLPN

A construction of PCF from VDLPN follows from the general template established in [BCG+20a], which combines a WPRF in a suitably low complexity class with a function secret sharing scheme for a related class. Instantiating this general template with the VDLPN-based WPRF and the FSS scheme of [BGI16], one gets a PCF for a general class of constant degree polynomial additive correlations. For the sake of concreteness, though, we focus here on PCFs for the random oblivious transfer (OT) correlation, one of the most fundamental and useful correlation in secure computation. A random OT correlation is a pair $(y_0, y_1) \in \{0,1\}^2 \times \{0,1\}^2$, where $y_0 = (u, v)$ for two random bits u, v, and $y_1 = (b, u \cdot (1 - b) \oplus v \cdot b)$ for a random bit b.

It is known that, to generate n pseudorandom OT correlations, it suffices to generate the following simpler correlation: Alice gets a (pseudo)random pair of length-n vectors $(\mathbf{u}, \mathbf{v})$, where $\mathbf{u} \xleftarrow{\$} \mathbb{F}_2^n$ and $\mathbf{v} \in \mathbb{F}_{2^\lambda}^n$, and Bob gets $x \xleftarrow{\$} \mathbb{F}_{2^\lambda}$ and $\mathbf{w} \leftarrow x \cdot \mathbf{u} + \mathbf{v}$. This correlation (known as the *subfied vector-OLE* correlation) can be locally converted by Alice and Bob into n pseudorandom OT correlations using a correlation-robust hash function; see [BCG+19b] for details. Therefore, we focus on building a PCF for the subfield VOLE correlation. Unlike the general case, this does not require the full power of function secret sharing: it suffices to rely on a simpler primitive, namely, a puncturable pseudorandom function.

Puncturable Pseudorandom Functions. A *puncturable pseudorandom function* (PPRF) is a PRF F such that given an input x, and a PRF key k, one can generate a *punctured* key, denoted $k\{x\}$, which allows evaluating F at every point except for x, and does not reveal any information about the value F.Eval(k, x). PPRFs have been introduced in [KPTZ13, BW13, BGI14].

Formally, a t-puncturable pseudorandom function (PPRF) with key space $\mathcal{K}$, domain $\mathcal{X}$, and range $\mathcal{Y}$, is a pseudorandom function F with an additional punctured key space $\mathcal{K}_p$ and three probabilistic polynomial-time algorithms $(F.\mathsf{KeyGen}, F.\mathsf{Puncture}, F.\mathsf{Eval})$ such that

- $F.\mathsf{KeyGen}(1^\lambda)$ outputs a random key $K \in \mathcal{K}$,
- $F.\mathsf{Puncture}(K, S)$, on input a ley $K \in \mathcal{K}$, and a subset $S \subset \mathcal{X}$ of size (at most) t, outputs a punctured key $K\{S\} \in \mathcal{K}_p$,
- $F.\mathsf{Eval}(K\{S\}, x)$, on input a key $K\{S\}$ punctured at all points in S, and a point x, outputs $F(K, x)$ if $x \notin S$, and $\bot$ otherwise.

The (static) security of a t-PPRF states is captured by the following game: the adversary $\mathcal{A}$ sends a size-t subset S of inputs. The challenger generates a key K, a punctured key $K\{S\}$, and a random bit b. He sends $K\{S\}$ to $\mathcal{A}$, together with either the values $F_K(x) = F.\mathsf{Eval}(K\{\emptyset\}, x)$ for all $x \in S$ if $b = 0$, or t random bits if $b = 1$. The PPRF is secure if any adversary has negligible advantage over the random guess for finding b in this game. A t-PPRF can be constructed from any one-way function, using the GGM construction [GGM86].

A PCF for SVOLE from VDLPN and a PPRF. We briefly sketch the construction, and refer to [BCG+20a] for a formal analysis. Fix VDLPN parameters $\mathsf{par} = (w, D, N)$ and set $t \leftarrow D \cdot w$. Let F be a t-PPRF with range $\mathbb{F}_{2^\lambda}$.

- $\mathsf{PCF.Setup}(1^\lambda)$: sample $r \xleftarrow{\$} \{0, 1\}^{t(D-1)/2}$ and set $\mathbf{e} \leftarrow \mathcal{N}_{\mathsf{par}}(r)$. Let $S \subseteq [w \cdot (2^{D+1} - 1)]$ be the size-t subset of nonzero entries of $\mathbf{e}$. Sample $K \leftarrow F.\mathsf{KeyGen}(1^\lambda)$ and set $K\{S\} \leftarrow F.\mathsf{Puncture}(K, S)$. Sample $x \xleftarrow{\$} \mathbb{F}_{2^\lambda}$ and let $(K_y)_{y \in S} \leftarrow (F_K(i) - x)_{i \in S}$. Set $\mathsf{k}_0 \leftarrow (K, x)$ and $\mathsf{k}_1 \leftarrow (r, K\{S\}, (K_i)_{i \in S})$.
- $\mathsf{PCF.Eval}(\sigma, \mathsf{k}_\sigma, z)$: parse z as a row $\mathbf{h}_z$ of the VDLPN matrix H (i.e., set $\mathbf{h}_z^\mathsf{T} \leftarrow \mathcal{N}(z)$). Let $S_z \subseteq [w \cdot (2^{D+1} - 1)]$ denote the index of the 1's in $\mathbf{h}_z$. If $\sigma = 0$, output x and $w = \sum_{i \in S_z} F_K(i)$. If $\sigma = 1$, output $u = h_z^\mathsf{T} \cdot \mathbf{e}$ and $v = \sum_{i \in S_z \setminus S} F.\mathsf{Eval}(K\{S\}, i) + \sum_{i \in S_z \cap S} K_i$.

For correctness, observe that for every $i \in S_z \setminus S$, $F_K(i) - F.\mathsf{Eval}(K\{S\}, i) = 0$, and for every i in $S_z \cap S$, $F_K(i) - K_i = x$. Since S_z denotes the 1 entries in $\mathbf{h}_z$ and S denotes the 1 entries in $\mathbf{e}$, we have $w - v = \sum_{i \in S_z} F_K(i) - \sum_{i \in S_z \setminus S} F.\mathsf{Eval}(K\{S\}, i) - \sum_{i \in S_z \cap S} K_i = x \cdot (\mathbf{h}_z^\mathsf{T} \cdot \mathbf{e}) = x \cdot u$; the pseudorandomness of u follows from the fact that $z \mapsto h_z^\mathsf{T} \cdot \mathbf{e})$ is a WPRF under the VDLPN assumption, and that of w follows from the pseudorandomness of the PPRF.

2.5 Outline of the Original Proof of Resistance Against Linear Test

We provide here an overview of the original security analysis in [BCG+20a], resistance against linear attacks. The two claims for which the analysis was flawed are the Eq. 1 and the Lemma 17 . We explain the errors and provide a correction in the Sect. 4.

As outlined in the introduction, the goal of this analysis is to show that the VDLPN assumption cannot be broken by any *linear test*, which captures in particular all known attacks against LPN. This is formalized in the following theorem:

Theorem 14. *(Resistance against linear tests) There exist constants (Γ, μ, ν), such that for any large enough w, any $\Gamma \cdot D \leq w$, $N \leftarrow 2^D$, par $\leftarrow (w, D, N)$, it holds that*

$$\Pr_{H \xleftarrow{\$} \mathcal{H}_{\mathsf{par}}} [\mathsf{bias}(\mathcal{O}_{\mathsf{par}}(H)) > \mu^w] \leq \nu^w.$$

This theorem states that with high probability (at least $1 - \nu^w$), over the choice of at most $N = 2^D$ random inputs $(x^{(1)}, \cdots, x^{(N)})$ any distinguisher that computes a linear function of the entire output string $\mathbf{y} = (F_K(x^{(1)}), \cdots, F_K(x^{(N)}))$ has an advantage of at most μ^w in distinguishing the string from uniform. Note that the choice of the linear function can depend arbitrarily on $(x^{(1)}, \cdots, x^{(N)})$.

To bound the bias of $\mathcal{O}_{\mathsf{par}}(H)$, the authors look at the sub-matrices of H, and introduce a notion of *good* and *bad* matrices:

Definition 15. *Given a matrix $M \in \mathbb{F}_2^{N \times 2^i}$, M is judged bad with respect to a vector $\mathbf{v} \in \mathbb{F}_2^N$ if*

$$\mathsf{HW}(\mathbf{v}^\top \cdot M) \notin \left[\frac{2^i}{5}, \frac{2^{i+2}}{5} \right].$$

Moreover, given w matrices $(M_1, \cdots, M_w)$ in $\mathbb{F}_2^{N \times 2^i}$, we denote by $N_\mathbf{v}(M_1, \cdots, M_w)$ the number of matrices which are bad against $\mathbf{v}$ among $M_1 \cdots M_w$.

A matrix is bad with respect to a vector $\mathbf{v}$ if the bias it induces against the test vector $\mathbf{v}$ is large. The goal of the proof is to guarantee that, with high probability, at least half of the matrices are good. This is stated in the following lemma.

Lemma 16. *There is a constant C, such that for any $1 \leq i \leq D$, and for any vector $\mathbf{v} \in \mathbb{F}_2^N$ such that $\mathsf{HW}(\mathbf{v}) \in [2^{i-1}, 2^i]$, it holds that*

$$\Pr_{M_1, \cdots, M_w \xleftarrow{\$} \mathcal{H}_{\mathsf{par}}^i} \left[N_\mathbf{v}(M_1, \cdots, M_w) \geq \frac{w}{2} \right] \leq 2^{-C \cdot 2^i \cdot w}.$$

The above lemma shows that for any fixed vector $\mathbf{v}$ of weight close to 2^i, the distribution induced by $\mathcal{H}_{\mathsf{par}}^i$ has a low bias against $\mathbf{v}$. The probability that this holds is so high that it remains overwhelming even after a union bound over *all* vectors $\mathbf{v}$ of weight in $[2^{i-1}, 2^i]$. Hence, this implies that in the output $H \cdot \mathbf{e} = \bigoplus_i H_i \cdot \mathbf{e}_i$, each component $H_i \cdot \mathbf{e}_i$ will guarantee low-bias against all vectors in this window of weight; the XOR of these independent samples will inherit the low-bias of all its components, and therefore resist all linear tests.

Bounding the Number of Bad Matrices. In [BCG+20a], the authors reformulate the event that a matrix M is *bad* as a balls and bins problem. Let $M \xleftarrow{\$} \mathcal{H}^i_{\mathsf{par}}$. Recall that by definition of $\mathcal{H}^i_{\mathsf{par}}$, the rows of M are generated independently from $\mathcal{S}_{1,2^i}$. We start with 2^i empty bins, each bin corresponding to a column of M. Sampling a row of M according to the $\mathcal{S}_{1,2^i}$ distribution amounts to throwing a ball randomly into one of the 2^i bins. For a vector $\mathbf{v}$ of weight $l \in [2^{i-1}, 2^i]$, the event $\mathsf{HW}(\mathbf{v}^\top \cdot M) \notin \left[\frac{2^i}{5}, \frac{2^{i+2}}{5}\right] = I_i$ is equivalent to the following event: after randomly throwing l balls into 2^i bins, the number T of bins that contain an odd number of balls satisfies $T \notin I_i$. We have therefore the following experiment: take 2^i bins and throw $l \cdot w$ balls into the bins in w consecutive phase. Each time that l balls have been thrown, we check that the proportion of the number of bins that contains an odd number of balls is between $1/5$ and $4/5$, and clear out the bins. At the end, we return *failure* if more than $w/2$ of the w checks have failed. To bound the probability of returning a failure, define the following *cost function* $\Phi(X_{1,1}, \cdots, X_{l,w}) = \sum_{k=1}^w \left(2^{i-1} - \left|\mathsf{HW}\left(\bigoplus_{j=1}^l X_{j,k}\right) - 2^{i-1}\right|\right)$, where each $X_{j,k}, 1 \le j \le l, 1 \le k \le w$, is the random variable corresponding to the bin in which the j-th balls of the k-th phase was thrown (seen as a length-2^i unit vector with a 1 at the bin position). The $X_{j,k}$ are independent. Bounding the number of bad matrices, the authors claimed, amounts to bounding Φ. Indeed:

$$\Pr_{M_1, \cdots, M_w \xleftarrow{\$} M^i_{par}} \left[N_\mathbf{v}(M_1, \cdots, M_w) \ge \frac{w}{2}\right] \le \Pr\left[\Phi(X_{1,1}, \cdots, X_{l,w}) < \frac{w \cdot 2^i}{10}\right].$$

$$(1)$$

Afterwards, it suffices to bound Φ to conclude. The claim is that the following bound holds:

$$\Pr\left[\Phi(X_{1,1}, \cdots, X_{l,w}) < \frac{w \cdot 2^i}{10}\right] \le 2^{-C \cdot 2^i \cdot w}.$$

$$(2)$$

The choice of Φ is of course not arbitrary: Φ is a well-behaved function, in the sense that it is 2-Lipschitz – i.e., changing any single input to Φ can only change its output by at most 2. Fortunately, strong concentration bounds are known on the probability that Lipschitz functions deviate too much from their mean. It therefore only remains to apply such a bound (which is here the McDiarmid inequality, a variant of the Azuma inequality), to get an estimate of the mean of Φ. This bound is stated in the following lemma:

Lemma 17.

$$\mathbb{E}[\Phi(X_{1,1}, \cdots, X_{l,w})] \ge \frac{w \cdot 2^i}{5}.$$

Given the proof of Lemma 17, the McDiarmid inequality provides a bound on Φ, which translates to a bound on $N_\mathbf{v}$ by Eq. 1. A union bound over all vectors of weight between $[2^{i-1}, 2^i]$ allows to conclude:

$$\Pr_{M_1,\cdots,M_w \xleftarrow{\$} \mathcal{H}_{\mathsf{par}}^i} \left[\exists \mathbf{v} \in \mathcal{S}_{i,N}, N_{\mathbf{v}}(M_1,\cdots,M_w) \geq \frac{w}{2} \right] \leq 2^{D \cdot 2^i} \cdot 2^{-C \cdot w \cdot 2^i} \leq 2^{-a \cdot w},$$

with $a = \frac{C}{2} > D$. The proof ends with a last union bound over all matrices H_i, for $1 \leq i \leq D$.

Some Notations. In the following, we will denote by $X_{j,k}$ indicates the bin into which the j-th ball of the k-th phase is thrown ($X_{j,k}$ is a unit vector). Given a test vector $\mathbf{v} \in \mathbb{F}_2^N$ of weight $\mathsf{HW}(\mathbf{v}) = l$, we define $R_{i,l,k} = \mathsf{HW}(\mathbf{v}^\top \cdot M) = \mathsf{HW}\left(\bigoplus_{j=1}^l X_{j,k}\right)$. That is, $R_{i,l,k}$ it is the number of bins that contains an odd number of 1 in the k-th phase; we usually write it $R_{l,k}$ when i is clear from the context. We further define $Z_{i,l,k}$ as $Z_{i,l,k} = |2^{i-1} - R_{l,k}|$ (also usually written $Z_{l,k}$). Eventually, we denote by $\mathcal{S}_{i,N}$ the set of vectors $\mathbf{v} \in \mathbb{F}_2^N$ with $\mathsf{HW}(\mathbf{v}) \in [2^{i-1}, 2^i]$.

3 Faster PCF from a VDLPN Variant

The original proof shows that for an appropriate choice of a constant Γ, if $w \geq \Gamma \cdot D$, then the bias of $\mathcal{O}_{\mathsf{par}}$ is $2^{-\Omega(w)}$ with probability $1 - 2^{-\Omega(w)}$. However, the concrete constants are utterly impractical (the correction of the flaw doesn't help as we will see in Sect. 4). With a quick back-of-the-envelope calculation, to guarantee $D \cdot 2^{-a \cdot w} < 2^{-80}$ we need $w > \frac{85}{a}$ (for $D = 30$). However, the value a in our analysis satisfies $a < \frac{1}{40000}$, leading to a necessary value of $w \approx 10^6$. These parameters are of course completely unusable. Therefore, in its current state, the proof only shows the asymptotic security of the construction in a parameter range which cannot be instantiated; any concrete instantiation is bound to rely only on heuristic parameters instead, not backed up by any security analysis. In this section, we aim at mitigating this unsatisfying situation, and provide a parameter set which is simultaneously usable in practice, and comes with provable security guarantees.

3.1 A Proof Friendly VDLPN Variant for Resistance Against Linear Attack

We put forth a simple tweak of the VDLPN assumption which allows for a much tighter proof of resistance against linear attack, yet enjoys the same applications as the original VDLPN assumption. The tweak is straightforward: recall that in the original construction, the matrix H is sampled as a concatenation of matrices $H_1 \cdots H_D$, where each H_i is a concatenation of w matrices whose rows are unit vectors of length 2^i. In the security analysis, the authors bound the bias of the $H_i \cdot \mathbf{e}_i$ terms against length-$\Theta(2^i)$ attack vectors. However, the bounds from the new correct analysis of Sect. 4 turned out to be much worse for small constant values of i (to the point that the bounds do not suffice anymore for very small i, and we have to handle them separately). Here, we suggest replacing

$H_1||\cdots||H_{i^*-1}$, where i^* is some fixed small constant (we will pick $i^* = 5$ in our concrete instantiation), by a uniformly random matrix R of appropriate dimensions. That is, H is now of the form $H = [R||H_{i^*}||\cdots||H_D]$. As before, the noise distribution will be identical to the row distribution of H. This means that we will have $H \cdot \mathbf{e} = R \cdot \mathbf{e}_r + \sum_{i=i^*}^{D} H_i \cdot \mathbf{e}_i$, where $\mathbf{e}_r$ is a uniformly random vector.

Let t be the width of R. We show that the $R \cdot \mathbf{e}_r$ term guarantees resistance against all low-weight tests. Then, saying that the distribution $\mathcal{D}_R = \{R \cdot \mathbf{e}_r : \mathbf{e}_r \xleftarrow{\$} \mathbb{F}_2^t\}$ has zero bias against all vectors of weight below d is equivalent to saying that $\mathcal{D}_R$ is a d-wise independent distribution. It is a well-known fact that this is equivalent to the following: the dual of the code generated by R, which is a random linear code of dimension $2^D - t$, has minimum distance at least d. Fortunately, the minimum distance of random linear codes is well-known. Let S be a random code of dimension $2^D - t$, and codeword length 2^D. Then,

$$\Pr[S \text{ has minimum distance } < d] \le 2^{-t - H_2(d/2^D) \cdot 2^D},$$

where $H_2(x) = -x \log x - (1 - x) \log(1 - x)$ is the binary entropy function. Concretely, suppose that we want to perfectly withstand all linear tests of weight at most $d = 15$, with probability at least $1 - 2^{-\lambda}$, given up to $2^D = 2^{30}$ samples. This means we need to pick t such that $t = H_2(15/2^{30}) * 2^{30} + \lambda$; using $\lambda = 128$, this gives $t = 541$. Hence, picking a uniformly random width-541 matrix guarantees that, with probability at least $1 - 2^{-128}$, we only have to worry about any linear test of weight at least $16 = 2^{i^*-1}$. Note that this variant can be used exactly in the same way as the original VDPLN one, as a building block to construct PCF, as long as we can prove its security against linear tests.

3.2 A New Tight Proof Strategy

For the rest of the analysis, we assume that we start with $i \ge i^* = 5$. The adversary chooses an attack vector $\mathbf{v}$ of hamming weight $l \in [2^{i-1}, 2^i]$. We use the following random variable:

$$Z_{i,l,k} = \left| \mathsf{HW}\left(\bigoplus_{j=1}^{l} X_{j,k}^{(i)} \right) - 2^{i-1} \right|.$$

Unlike the original proof (see Sect. 2.5), this time we aim at a much more direct strategy. Since we ultimately want to bound the probability that the bias of $\mathcal{O}_{\mathrm{par}}(H)$ is too high, we rewrite this bias directly in terms of the above random variable. For a fixed choice of H, let $\mathcal{O}_{\mathrm{par}}^i = \mathcal{O}_{\mathrm{par}}^i(H)$ be the distribution that samples $\mathbf{e}_i$ (a concatenation of w length-2^i unit vectors) and outputs $H_i \cdot \mathbf{e}_i$. Of course, we have $\mathcal{O}_{\mathrm{par}} = \bigoplus_{i \ge i^*} \mathcal{O}_{\mathrm{par}}^i \oplus \mathcal{O}_{\mathrm{par}}^R$ (where $\mathcal{O}_{\mathrm{par}}^R$ denotes the distribution that samples a uniformly random length-t vector $\mathbf{e}_r$ and outputs $R \cdot \mathbf{e}_r$, where t is a parameter which will be fixed afterwards). Furthermore, for any test vector

$\mathbf{v}$, we have $\mathsf{bias}_{\mathbf{v}}(\mathcal{O}_{\mathsf{par}}) \geq \mathsf{bias}_{\mathbf{v}}(\mathcal{O}_{\mathsf{par}}^i)$. We therefore focus on bounding the bias against a test vector $\mathbf{v}$ of $\mathcal{O}_{\mathsf{par}}^i$. We have

$$\mathsf{bias}_{\mathbf{v}}(\mathcal{O}_{\mathsf{par}}^i) = \left| \frac{1}{2} - \Pr[(\mathbf{v}^\top \cdot H_i) \cdot \mathbf{e_i} = 1] \right|.$$

$(\mathbf{v}^\top \cdot H_i) \cdot \mathbf{e_i}$ is the XOR of w independent terms $(\mathbf{v}^\top \cdot H_{i,j}) \cdot \mathbf{e_{i,j}}$ where each $\mathbf{e}_{i,j}$ is a length-2^i unit vector. Therefore, we further decompose $\mathcal{O}_{\mathsf{par}}^i$ as the XOR of w distributions $D_1, \cdots, D_w$ (we drop the parameters i, par, and H for now as we consider a fixed choice of them, to lighten the notations). To bound the bias of $\mathcal{O}_{\mathsf{par}}^i$, we must therefore bound

$$\Pr\left[\bigoplus_{k=1}^w D_k = 1 \right] = \frac{1}{2}\left(1 - \prod_{k=1}^w \left(1 - \frac{R_{i,l,k}}{2^{i-1}} \right) \right),$$

where you get the right hand side by applying the piling-up lemma. Hence, we obtain a direct expression of the bias of $\mathcal{O}_{\mathsf{par}}^i$ in terms of the $Z_{i,l,k}$ random variables:

$$\mathsf{bias}_{\mathbf{v}}(\mathcal{O}_{\mathsf{par}}^i) = \frac{1}{2} \cdot \prod_{k=1}^w \frac{Z_{i,l,k}}{2^{i-1}}.$$

Fix any bound B. Then by the above,

$$\Pr[\mathsf{bias}_{\mathbf{v}}(\mathcal{O}_{\mathsf{par}}^i) > B] = \Pr\left[\prod_{k=1}^w Z_{i,l,k} > 2^{(i-1)w} \times (2B) \right].$$

Now, the key to bounding the right hand side term is the following observation: independently of the exact behavior of the random variables $Z_{i,l,k}$, constrained on the product $\prod_k Z_{i,l,k}$ being at least $2^{(i-1)w} \cdot (2B)$, the sum $\sum_k Z_{i,l,k}$ is minimized when all the terms in the product are equal. This implies that whenever $\prod_{k=1}^w Z_{i,l,k} > 2^{(i-1)w} \times (2B)$, it necessarily further holds that

$$\sum_{k=1}^w Z_{i,l,k} > w \cdot \left(2^{(i-1)w} \times (2B) \right)^{1/w},$$

which allows to upper bound the probability of the bias being too large by

$$\Pr[\mathsf{bias}_{\mathbf{v}}(\mathcal{O}_{\mathsf{par}}^i) > B] \leq \Pr\left[\sum_{k=1}^w Z_{i,l,k} > w \cdot 2^{(i-1)} \cdot c \right],$$

where $c = (2B)^{\frac{1}{w}}$. As in the previous proof, we can now re-introduce the function $\Phi(X_{1,1}, \cdots, X_{l,w}) = 2^{i-1} \cdot w - \sum_{k=1}^w Z_{i,l,k}$:

$$\Pr[\Phi < \mathbb{E}[\phi] - t] = \Pr\left[\sum_{k=1}^w Z_{i,l,k} > w \cdot (\mathbb{E}[Z_{i,l}] + 2^i \cdot \varsigma) \right].$$

With $t = \zeta \cdot w \cdot 2^i$. Let β be a constant such that $\mathbb{E}[Z_{i,l}] \leq \beta \cdot 2^i$ (In the correction of the original proof, we will show that $\beta = 0.44$ works ; we will actually use a tighter constant here). This gives $c = 2(\beta + \zeta)$. As we did before, we can now apply McDiarmid's inequality 7 to get

$$\Pr\left[\sum_{k=1}^{w} Z_{i,l,k} > w \cdot 2^{i-1} \cdot c\right] < \exp\left(-w\frac{2^{2i-1}}{l} \cdot \zeta^2\right),$$

and obtain the bound

$$\Pr\left(\mathsf{bias_v}(\mathcal{O}_{\mathsf{par}}^i) > \frac{1}{2}(2(\beta + \zeta))^w\right) \leq \exp\left(-w\frac{2^{2i-1}}{l} \cdot \zeta^2\right).$$

While this might be obscured by the many variables involved, this last bound is tremendously tighter than what was achieved with the previous proof. In essence, this is because the previous proof relied on Lemma 5 to bound the bias of the XOR of independent distributions, but the latter introduces some exponential slackness in the *number* of distributions involved. To overcome this slackness, the strategy was to only "count" the distributions that contribute the most to the bias, by identifying *good* distributions, showing that, over the choice of H, a sufficient number of distributions will be good, and applying the lemma only to these good distributions. This guarantees that the slackness is compensated by the contribution of each distribution. If, instead, one tries to apply the lemmas to all distribution, the bound obtain is too loose and does not provide any usable guarantee.

Here, we manage to directly account for the contribution to the bias of *all* distributions, by carefully rewriting the bias formula in terms of the $Z_{i,l,k}$ random variables, and by using a standard "optimization trick" to bound the product of the $Z_{i,l,k}$ in terms of their sum. This turns out to be the key to get back to the function which we can bound with known tools (the function Φ, which is Lipschitz), without paying any slackness in the number of distributions involved.

In the following, we will numerically evaluate the constant β (this is an orthogonal optimization: In the correction of the mistake in Sect. 4, we prove that $\beta \leq 0.44$. Using this value for β would already lead to significant improvements, as we will see) and carefully tune the parameters to find out the smallest value of w for which we can achieve 80-bit security against all test vectors simultaneously, fixing the number of samples to a reasonable bound of $N = 2^{30}$.

3.3 Concrete Parameters

In our bound on the bias, the l in the denominator of the probability is one of the key factors for concrete efficiency. Our previous proof used $l \in [2^{i-1}, 2^i]$. In fact, we cannot expect l to be any smaller: $\mathbb{E}[Z_{i,l}]$ measures how, when one throws l balls at random in 2^i bins, the number of bins which end up containing an odd number of balls diverges from the middle value 2^{i-1}. When we throw less than 2^{i-1} balls in total, this number will of course be bounded away from 2^{i-1}; yet, as simulations reveal, it becomes tightly concentrated around 2^{i-1} as soon as l gets larger. We therefore fix $l \in [2^{i-1}, 2^i]$ and empirically estimate $\mathbb{E}[Z_{i,l}]$. Our script can be found in the full version. Table 1 shows the value of β obtained for different choices of $n = 2^i$ and l. For larger values of n and a fixed $l = l(n)$, note that our estimate value for β barely increase (for $l < n$) or decrease (for $l \geq n$).

Table 1. Estimated value of β for different values of n and l, in a confidence interval of 99% (rounded value ± 0.002)

	$n = 32$	$n = 64$	$n = 512$	$n = 1024$	$n = 2048$
$l = \frac{n}{2}$	0.178	0.181	0.184	0.184	0.184
$l = \frac{3 \cdot n}{4}$	0.111	0.111	0.111	0.111	0.112
$l = n$	0.084	0.073	0.067	0.067	0.067

Let us go back to our bound. For a given vector of Hamming weight l,

$$\Pr\left(\mathsf{bias}_\mathbf{v}(\mathcal{O}^i_{\mathsf{par}}) > \frac{1}{2}(2(\beta + \varsigma))^w \right) \leq \exp\left(-w\frac{2^{2i-1}}{l} \cdot \varsigma^2 \right),$$

hence, by a union bound over all vectors of Hamming weight l,

$$\Pr\left(\exists \mathbf{v}, \mathsf{HW}(\mathbf{v}) = l, \mathsf{bias}_\mathbf{v}(\mathcal{O}^i_{\mathsf{par}}) > \frac{1}{2}(2(\beta + \varsigma))^w \right) \leq \binom{N}{l} \exp\left(-w\frac{2^{2i-1}}{l} \cdot \varsigma^2 \right)$$

From the above inequality, we numerically look for a w such that, for all l such that $\mathsf{HW}(l) \in [2^{i-1}, 2^i]$, $(2 \cdot (\beta + \varsigma))^w / 2 \leq 2^{-80}$ and

$$\binom{N}{l} \cdot \exp\left(-w\frac{2^{2i-1}}{l} \cdot \varsigma^2 \right) \leq \exp\left(\ln(N) \cdot l - w \cdot \frac{2^{2i-1}}{l} \cdot \varsigma^2 \right) \leq 2^{-90}.$$

(The 2^{-90} bound is to anticipate the cost of the union bound.) In the following we set the number of samples $N = 2^D = 2^{30}$, which is a realistic value for target applications. To find a suitable w, we calculate the required w for different values of l. Let us first assume that $l = 2^{i-1}$. The second inequality can be rewritten as $\exp\left(2^{i-1} \cdot (\ln(2) \cdot 30 - 2 \cdot w \cdot \varsigma^2) \right) \leq 2^{-90}$. If $w \cdot \varsigma^2 \geq 12.35$, then the condition is met. Thus, we can now turn to the other inequality to satisfy; we therefore set w to $\varsigma^2/12.35$. Using Table 1, we set $\beta = 0.184$ and numerically solve $(2 \cdot (0.184 + \varsigma))^{12.35/\varsigma^2} \leq 2^{-80}$ to guarantee that the bias will be lower than 2^{-80}. This gives $\varsigma \leq 0.219$ and $w = 12.35/0.219^2 \approx 257$. At the other end of the interval, setting $l = 2^i$, the second inequality becomes $\exp\left(2^i \cdot (\ln(2) \cdot 30 - \frac{1}{2}w \cdot \varsigma^2) \right) \leq 2^{-90}$.

This time, we get $w \cdot \varsigma^2 \geq 45.5$ and set $\beta = 0.084$ using Table 1. Solving $(2 \cdot (0.084 + \varsigma))^{\frac{45.5}{\varsigma^2}} \leq 2^{-80}$ gives $\varsigma = 0.347$, and eventually $w = 45.5/0.347^2 \approx 380$. Generalizing this method, we numerically extrapolate how the value of w evolves when l varies from 2^{i-1} to 2^i. The calculations show that w is monotonously increasing, leading to an overall choice of $w \approx 380$ as a single parameter that suffices for the entire range of values. This is a major improvement compared to the previous proof.[4] From here, finishing the proof boils down to two union bounds, giving

$$\Pr(\exists \mathbf{v}, \mathsf{HW}(\mathbf{v}) \in [2^{i-1}, 2^i], \mathsf{bias}_{\mathbf{v}} > 2^{-80})$$

$$\leq \sum_{l=2^{i-1}}^{2^i} \binom{N}{l} \exp\left(-w\frac{2^{2i-1}}{l} \cdot \zeta^2\right) \leq 2^{i^*-1} \cdot 2^{-90} = 2^{-86},$$

where the last inequality comes from the fact that $2^{i^*} = 2^5$. For $i > i^*$, the bound in the probability decreases (exponentially) faster than the increase of 2^i, and the result remains valid. Eventually, by a union bound on all i, with $D = 30$, $\Pr(\exists \mathbf{v}, \mathsf{HW}(\mathbf{v}) \geq 2^4, \mathsf{bias}_{\mathbf{v}} > 2^{-80}) \leq (D-8) \cdot 2^{-86} < 2^{-80}$. Concrete cost estimations for the pseudorandom correlation function obtained by using the VDLPN parameters of our improved analysis are given in the introduction.

4   Security of VDLPN Against Linear Tests, Revisited

As pointed out, the analysis of [BCG+20a], while the proof strategy seems sound and appropriate, contains some errors which invalidate the proof. Fixing the errors turns out to be quite delicate. Below, we elaborate on the two issues; the first is a minor error, which can be fixed relatively easily, at the cost of changing the (arbitrary) choice of constants (in particular, the 1/5 and 1/10 constants): Claim 1 is incorrect as stated; the error in its analysis stems from a reversed inequality. However, a variant of Claim 1 with different constants can be easily shown to hold; this does not change the spirit of the proof, nor its conclusion. The second error is more delicate to fix, and will be the main focus of this Section.

Main Error. The main error appears in the proof of Eq. 2. The error is in the analysis of Lemma 17. As sketched in the introduction, after calculating an upper bound on the expectation $\mathbb{E}\left[\mathsf{HW}(\bigoplus_{j=1}^l X_{j,k})\right]$, the authors deduce a bound on $\mathbb{E}\left[\left|2^{i-1} - \mathsf{HW}(\bigoplus_{j=1}^l X_{j,k})\right|\right]$. However, a bound on $\mathbb{E}[Z]$ does not imply a bound on $\mathbb{E}[|Z - b|]$ in general (and typically when Z is "concentrated away" from b). Up to the choice of the constant 1/5 (the proof actually only requires any constant below 1/2), the lemma remains true; however, proving the lemma fundamentally requires characterizing the shape of the random variable $\mathsf{HW}(\bigoplus_{j=1}^l X_{j,k})$. This turns out to be non-trivial.

---

[4] The improvement comes from a better estimation of the β parameter on one hand, but also from the better inherent quality of the new proof. In fact, we can consider the same calculation as before, but with $l = 2^7$ and $\beta = 0.44$. This is a non-computer-optimized, provable value of β using $i^* = 7$. With this value, we get $w \approx 13000$, which is already a big gain from the previous method: this is already several orders of magnitudes better than the previous method, though still not practical.

4.1 Repairing the Proof

In this section, we put forward a corrected detailed analysis of the resistance of VDLPN against linear tests. Our proof fixes the two errors in [BCG+20a], at the cost of achieving worse constants, and being more involved. As before, we study individually the bias induced by the H_i components against vectors of weight close to 2^i. However, for now, we only consider large enough values of i, and assume that $n = 2^i \geq 2^7$. The missing cases are handled in the full version.

Definition 18 (δ-Bad Matrices).

Let $M \in \mathbb{F}_2^{N \times 2^i}$. We say that $M \in \mathsf{Bad}_{\delta,\mathbf{v}}$ with respect to a vector $\mathbf{v} \in \mathbb{F}_{2^N}$ if

$$\mathsf{HW}(\mathbf{v}^\top \cdot M) = R_{l,k} \notin \left[\delta \cdot 2^i, (1 - \delta) \cdot 2^i\right].$$

Stated in terms of $Z_{l,k}$, this condition rewrites to $Z_{l,k} \in \left[(1/2 - \delta) \cdot 2^i, 2^{i-1}\right]$. We let $\mathsf{Good}_{\delta,\mathbf{v}}$ denote the complement of $\mathsf{Bad}_{\delta,\mathbf{v}}$ Given vector $\mathbf{v}$, we also denote $B_{\delta,\mathbf{v}} = \#\mathsf{Bad}_{\delta,\mathbf{v}} = N_{\mathbf{v}}(M_1, \cdots, M_w)$ and $G_{\delta,\mathbf{v}} = \#\mathsf{Good}_{\delta,\mathbf{v}} = w - B_{\delta,\mathbf{v}}$.

The Proof. We now prove Theorem 14. Let $\mathcal{O}_{\mathsf{par}}^i(H)$ be the distribution induced by sampling $\mathbf{e}_i$ (as a concatenation of w length-2^i vectors) and outputting $H_i \cdot \mathbf{e}_i$. A sample from $\mathcal{O}_{\mathsf{par}}^i(H)$ can be further decomposed as $\bigoplus_{j \leq w} H_{i,j} \cdot \mathbf{e}_{i,j}$ where the $\mathbf{e}_{i,j}$ are unit vectors. Let D_i denote the distribution of $H_{i,j} \cdot \mathbf{e}_{i,j}$ (these terms are w samples from the same distribution). Let α be a constant. Then,

Lemma 19. If $B_{\delta,\mathbf{v}} \leq \alpha \cdot w$, then

$$\mathsf{bias}\left(\bigoplus_{i=1}^{w} D_i\right) \leq \frac{1}{2} \cdot \left((1 - 2\delta)^{(1-\alpha)}\right)^w.$$

Proof. By the piling-up lemma (Lemma 6),

$$\mathsf{bias}\left(\bigoplus_{i=1}^{w} D_i\right) \leq 2^{(1-\alpha)w-1} \cdot \left(\frac{1}{2} - \delta\right)^{(1-\alpha)\cdot w} \leq \frac{1}{2} \cdot \left((1 - 2\delta)^{(1-\alpha)}\right)^w$$

$\square$

Lemma 19 provides an upper bound of the bias, which depends on the number of good matrices and their quality. We now show that the condition $B_{\delta,\mathbf{v}} \leq \alpha \cdot w$ holds with very high probability:

Lemma 20. For any $\mathbf{v} \in S_{i,N}$, there is a constant C such that

$$\Pr\left[B_{\delta,\mathbf{v}} > \alpha \cdot w\right] \leq 2^{-C \cdot 2^i \cdot w}.$$

Proof. As in the original proof, we introduce the function Φ:

$$\Phi(X_{1,1}, \cdots, X_{l,w}) = \sum_{k=1}^{w} \left(2^{i-1} - \left|\mathsf{HW}\left(\bigoplus_{j=1}^{l} X_{j,k}\right) - 2^{i-1}\right|\right)$$

$$= 2^{i-1} \cdot w - \sum_{k=1}^{w} Z_{l,k}.$$

We want to bound the probability of large bias by a bound on Φ. This is where the first error appeared in the previous proof.

Lemma 21 (Correction of the first error).

$$\Pr\left[B_{\delta,\mathbf{v}} \geq \alpha \cdot w\right] \leq \Pr\left[\Phi(X_{1,1}, \cdots, X_{l,w}) < \gamma \cdot w \cdot 2^i\right],$$

with $\gamma = \frac{1}{2} - \alpha(\frac{1}{2} - \delta)$.

Due to lack of space, the proof of the above lemma will appear in the full version. It remains now to find an upper bound on the right hand side probability. As in the original proof, we used the bounded difference inequality. Since Φ is 2-Lipschitz, (this was proved in the original proof),

$$\Pr[\Phi(X_{1,1}, \cdots, X_{l,w}) \leq \mathbb{E}[\Phi(X_{1,1}, \cdots, X_{l,w})] - t] \leq \exp\left(-\frac{t^2}{2lw}\right).$$

We finally want to prove a lower bound on $\mathbb{E}[\phi(X_{1,1}, \cdots, X_{l,w})]$. Recall that $\Phi(X_{1,1}, \cdots, X_{l,w}) = 2^{i-1} \cdot w - \sum_{k=1}^{w} Z_{l,k}$, so this reduces to bounding $\mathbb{E}[Z_{l,k}]$. Our main contribution in this analysis is the proof of the following lemma:

Lemma 22 (Correction of the second error). *For all $n \in \mathbb{N}$, there exists $\beta < 1/2$ such that $\mathbb{E}[Z_{l,k}] < \beta \cdot n$.*

Proof (Sketch). We first provide a high level overview, and due to lack of space, we defer the full proof of Lemma 22 to the full version of the article. The proof consists in finding an upper bound on both $\Pr[R_{l,k} \geq p \cdot n]$ and $\Pr[R_{l,k} \leq (1-p) \cdot n]$ for $p \in [\frac{1}{2}, 1]$ and to use it to find the one on $\mathbb{E}[Z_{l,k}] = \sum_{j=0}^{2^{i-1}-1} \Pr\left(|R_{l,k} - 2^{i-1}| > j\right)$.

Lemma 23. *Let $n = 2^i > 2^7$, $l \in [2^{i-1}, 2^i]$ and $\mu = (1 - \frac{1}{n})^l$. There exists $0.5 \leq p \leq 1$ such that with $\theta = \frac{pn - l/2}{\mu} - 1$, it holds that*

$$\max\left(\Pr[R_{l,k} \geq pn], \Pr[R_{l,k} \leq (1-p)n]\right) \leq 2\exp\left(-\frac{\theta^2 \mu^2(n - \frac{1}{2})}{n^2 - \mu^2}\right).$$

To prove this lemma, we use the Occupancy Bound for balls and bins from Lemma 8. The occupancy bound is about the proportion of empty bins, but can shrewdly be transformed to bring it back to our specific problem which focuses on parity in bins. This concludes the sketch.   □

The end of the proof is the same as in the original proof, up to handling separately the case of small i's. The total number of vectors $\mathbf{v} \in S_{i,N}$ can be bounded by

$$\sum_{l=2^{i-1}}^{2^i} \binom{N}{l} \leq (2^i - 2^{i-1}) \cdot \frac{N^{2^i}}{(2^{i-1})!} \leq 2^{D \cdot 2^i}.$$

Hence, choosing constant such that $Cw/2 > D$, and setting $a = C/2$, by a union bound, we have

$$\Pr\left[\exists \mathbf{v} \in S_{i,N}, B_{\delta,\mathbf{v}} \geq \alpha \cdot w\right] \leq 2^{D \cdot 2^i} \cdot 2^{-C \cdot 2^i \cdot w} \leq 2^{-a \cdot w}.$$

We eventually use a union bound again on all values of $i \leq D$:

$$\Pr\left[\exists i \leq D, \mathbf{v} \in S_{i,N}, B_{\delta,\mathbf{v}} \geq \alpha \cdot w\right] \leq D \cdot 2^{-a \cdot w}.$$

which, using Lemma 19, rewrites to

$$\Pr\left[\exists i \leq D, \mathbf{v} \in S_{i,N}, \mathsf{bias}_{\mathbf{v}}\left(\bigoplus_{i=1}^{w} D_i\right) \geq \frac{1}{2} \cdot ((1 - 2\delta)^{(1-\alpha)})^w\right] \leq D \cdot 2^{-a \cdot w}.$$

The argument for small values of i is completely different. In essence, we show that the first block of H, H_1, does already suffice to withstand all even-weight test vectors. Then, with a "brute-force" union bound, we show that the second block H_2 allows to withstand all tests of *odd* weight, provided that $w = \Omega(2^i \cdot D)$. When i is a constant, this is already captured by the requirement that $w \geq \Gamma \cdot D$ for a suitable constant Γ, which suffices to handle all remaining corner cases. Refer to the full version for complete explanation   □

Acknowledgements. The first author acknowledges the support of the French Agence Nationale de la Recherche (ANR), under grant ANR-20-CE39-0001 (project SCENE), and of the France 2030 ANR Project ANR-22-PECY-003 SecureCompute. The second author was supported by the DIM RFSI grant LICENCED.

References

[AJ01] Al Jabri, A.A.: A statistical decoding algorithm for general linear block codes (2001)

[Azu67] Azuma, K.: Weighted sums of certain dependent random variables. Tohoku Math. J. Second Series **19**(3), 357–367 (1967)

[BCG+17] Boyle, E., Couteau, G., Gilboa, N., Ishai, Y., Orrù, M.: Homomorphic secret sharing: Optimizations and applications. In: Thuraisingham, B.M., Evans, D., Malkin, T., Xu, D., (eds.) ACM CCS 2017, pp. 2105–2122. ACM Press (October/November 2017)

[BCG+19a] Boyle, E., et al.: Efficient two-round OT extension and silent non-interactive secure computation. In: Cavallaro, L., Kinder, J., Wang, X., Katz, J., (eds.) ACM CCS 2019, pp. 291–308. ACM Press (November 2019)

[BCG+19b] Boyle, E., et al.: Efficient pseudorandom correlation generators: silent ot extension and more. In: Boldyreva, A., Micciancio, D. (eds.) CRYPTO 2019. LNCS, vol. 11694, pp. 489–518. Springer, Cham (2019). https://doi.org/10.1007/978-3-030-26954-8_16

[BCG+20a] Boyle, E., Couteau, G., Gilboa, N., Ishai, Y., Kohl, L., Scholl, P.: Correlated pseudorandom functions from variable-density LPN. In: 61st FOCS, pages 1069–1080. IEEE Computer Society Press (November 2020)

[BCG+20b] Boyle, E., Couteau, G., Gilboa, N., Ishai, Y., Kohl, L., Scholl, P.: Efficient pseudorandom correlation generators from ring-LPN. In: Micciancio, D., Ristenpart, T. (eds.) CRYPTO 2020. LNCS, vol. 12171, pp. 387–416. Springer, Cham (2020). https://doi.org/10.1007/978-3-030-56880-1_14

[BCGI18] Boyle, E., Couteau, G., Gilboa, N., Ishai, Y.: Compressing vector OLE. In: Lie, D., Mannan, M., Backes, M., Wang, X., (eds.) ACM CCS 2018, pp. 896–912. ACM Press (October 2018)

[BGI14] Boyle, E., Goldwasser, S., Ivan, I.: Functional signatures and pseudorandom functions. In: Krawczyk, H. (ed.) PKC 2014. LNCS, vol. 8383, pp. 501–519. Springer, Heidelberg (2014). https://doi.org/10.1007/978-3-642-54631-0_29

[BGI15] Boyle, E., Gilboa, N., Ishai, Y.: Function secret sharing. In: Oswald, E., Fischlin, M. (eds.) EUROCRYPT 2015. LNCS, vol. 9057, pp. 337–367. Springer, Heidelberg (2015). https://doi.org/10.1007/978-3-662-46803-6_12

[BGI16] Boyle, E., Gilboa, N., Ishai, Y.: Function secret sharing: Improvements and extensions. In: Weippl, E.R., Katzenbeisser, S., Kruegel, C., Myers, A.C., Halevi, S., (eds.) ACM CCS 2016, pp. 1292–1303. ACM Press (October 2016)

[BJMM12] Becker, A., Joux, A., May, A., Meurer, A.: Decoding random binary linear codes in $2^{n/20}$: How $1 + 0$ improves information set decoding. In: Pointcheval, D., Johansson, T. (eds.) EUROCRYPT 2012. LNCS, vol. 7237, pp. 520–536. Springer, Heidelberg (2012). https://doi.org/10.1007/978-3-642-29011-4_31

[BKW00] Blum, A., Kalai, A., Wasserman, H.: Noise-tolerant learning, the parity problem, and the statistical query model. In: 32nd ACM STOC, pp. 435–440. ACM Press (May 2000)

[BLP11] Bernstein, D.J., Lange, T., Peters, C.: Smaller decoding exponents: ball-collision decoding. In: Rogaway, P. (ed.) CRYPTO 2011. LNCS, vol. 6841, pp. 743–760. Springer, Heidelberg (2011). https://doi.org/10.1007/978-3-642-22792-9_42

[BM97] Bellare, M., Micciancio, D.: A new paradigm for collision-free hashing: incrementality at reduced cost. In: Fumy, W. (ed.) EUROCRYPT 1997. LNCS, vol. 1233, pp. 163–192. Springer, Heidelberg (1997). https://doi.org/10.1007/3-540-69053-0_13

[BM18] Both, L., May, A.: Decoding linear codes with high error rate and its impact for LPN security. In: Lange, T., Steinwandt, R. (eds.) PQCrypto 2018. LNCS, vol. 10786, pp. 25–46. Springer, Cham (2018). https://doi.org/10.1007/978-3-319-79063-3_2

[BTV16] Bogos, S., Tramer, F., Vaudenay, S.: On solving lpn using bkw and variants (2016)

[BV16] Bogos, S., Vaudenay, S.: Optimization of LPN solving algorithms. In: Cheon, J.H., Takagi, T. (eds.) ASIACRYPT 2016. LNCS, vol. 10031, pp. 703–728. Springer, Heidelberg (2016). https://doi.org/10.1007/978-3-662-53887-6_26

[BW13]   Boneh, D., Waters, B.: constrained pseudorandom functions and their
         applications. In: Sako, K., Sarkar, P. (eds.) ASIACRYPT 2013. LNCS,
         vol. 8270, pp. 280–300. Springer, Heidelberg (2013). https://doi.org/10.
         1007/978-3-642-42045-0_15
[CRR21] Couteau, G., Rindal, P., Raghuraman, S.: Silver: silent VOLE and obliv-
         ious transfer from hardness of decoding structured LDPC Codes. In:
         Malkin, T., Peikert, C. (eds.) CRYPTO 2021. LNCS, vol. 12827, pp. 502–
         534. Springer, Cham (2021). https://doi.org/10.1007/978-3-030-84252-
         9_17
[DAT17] Debris-Alazard, T., Tillich, J.-P.: Statistical decoding (2017)
[DHRW16] Dodis, Y., Halevi, S., Rothblum, R.D., Wichs, D.: Spooky encryption and
         its applications. In: Robshaw, M., Katz, J. (eds.) CRYPTO 2016. LNCS,
         vol. 9816, pp. 93–122. Springer, Heidelberg (2016). https://doi.org/10.
         1007/978-3-662-53015-3_4
[DPSZ12] Damgård, I., Pastro, V., Smart, N., Zakarias, S.: Multiparty computation
         from somewhat homomorphic encryption. In: Safavi-Naini, R., Canetti, R.
         (eds.) CRYPTO 2012. LNCS, vol. 7417, pp. 643–662. Springer, Heidelberg
         (2012). https://doi.org/10.1007/978-3-642-32009-5_38
[EKM17] Esser, A., Kübler, R., May, A.: LPN decoded. In: Katz, J., Shacham, H.
         (eds.) CRYPTO 2017. LNCS, vol. 10402, pp. 486–514. Springer, Cham
         (2017). https://doi.org/10.1007/978-3-319-63715-0_17
[FKI06] Fossorier, M.P.C., Kobara, K., Imai, H.: Modeling bit flipping decoding
         based on nonorthogonal check sums with application to iterative decoding
         attack of mceliece cryptosystem (2006)
[FS09]   Finiasz, M., Sendrier, N.: Security bounds for the design of code-based
         cryptosystems. In: Matsui, M. (ed.) ASIACRYPT 2009. LNCS, vol. 5912,
         pp. 88–105. Springer, Heidelberg (2009). https://doi.org/10.1007/978-3-
         642-10366-7_6
[GGM86] Goldreich, O., Goldwasser, S., Micali, S.: How to construct random func-
         tions. J. ACM 33(4), 792–807 (1986)
[GI14]   Gilboa, N., Ishai, Y.: Distributed point functions and their applications.
         In: Nguyen, P.Q., Oswald, E. (eds.) EUROCRYPT 2014. LNCS, vol. 8441,
         pp. 640–658. Springer, Heidelberg (2014). https://doi.org/10.1007/978-3-
         642-55220-5_35
[GJL20] Guo, Q., Johansson, T., Löndahl, C.: Solving LPN using covering codes.
         J. Cryptol. 33(1), 1–33 (2020)
[Kir11] Kirchner, P.: Improved generalized birthday attack. Cryptology ePrint
         Archive, Report 2011/377 (2011). https://eprint.iacr.org/2011/377
[KMPS94] Kamath, A., Motwani, R., Palem, K.V., Spirakis, P.G.: Tail bounds for
         occupancy and the satisfiability threshold conjecture. In: 35th FOCS, pp.
         592–603. IEEE Computer Society Press (November 1994)
[KPTZ13] Kiayias, A., Papadopoulos, S., Triandopoulos, N., Zacharias, T.: Delegat-
         able pseudorandom functions and applications. In: Sadeghi, A.-R., Gligor,
         V.D., Yung, M., (eds.) ACM CCS 2013, pp. 669–684. ACM Press (Novem-
         ber 2013)
[LF06]   Levieil, É., Fouque, P.-A.: An improved LPN algorithm. In: De Prisco,
         R., Yung, M. (eds.) SCN 2006. LNCS, vol. 4116, pp. 348–359. Springer,
         Heidelberg (2006). https://doi.org/10.1007/11832072_24
[Lyu05] Lyubashevsky, V.: The parity problem in the presence of noise, decoding
         random linear codes, and the subset sum problem (2005)

[McD89] McDiarmid. C.: On the method of bounded differences. In: Simons, J., (ed.)"Survey in Combinatorics," London Mathematical Society Lecture Notes, vol. 141 (1989)

[MMT11] May, A., Meurer, A., Thomae, E.: Decoding random linear codes in $\tilde{\mathcal{O}}(2^{0.054n})$. In: Lee, D.H., Wang, X. (eds.) ASIACRYPT 2011. LNCS, vol. 7073, pp. 107–124. Springer, Heidelberg (2011). https://doi.org/10.1007/978-3-642-25385-0_6

[MO15] May, A., Ozerov, I.: On computing nearest neighbors with applications to decoding of binary linear codes. In: Oswald, E., Fischlin, M. (eds.) EUROCRYPT 2015. LNCS, vol. 9056, pp. 203–228. Springer, Heidelberg (2015). https://doi.org/10.1007/978-3-662-46800-5_9

[MSY21] Münch, J.-P., Schneider, T., Yalame, H.: Vasa: Vector aes instructions for security applications. In: Annual Computer Security Applications Conference, pp. 131–145 (2021)

[OSY21] Orlandi, C., Scholl, P., Yakoubov, S.: The rise of paillier: homomorphic secret sharing and public-key silent OT. In: Canteaut, A., Standaert, F.-X. (eds.) EUROCRYPT 2021. LNCS, vol. 12696, pp. 678–708. Springer, Cham (2021). https://doi.org/10.1007/978-3-030-77870-5_24

[Ove06] Overbeck, R.: Statistical decoding revisited. In: Batten, L.M., Safavi-Naini, R. (eds.) ACISP 2006. LNCS, vol. 4058, pp. 283–294. Springer, Heidelberg (2006). https://doi.org/10.1007/11780656_24

[Pra62] Prange, E.: The use of information sets in decoding cyclic codes (1962)

[Saa07] Saarinen, M.-J.O.: Linearization attacks against syndrome based hashes. In: Srinathan, K., Rangan, C.P., Yung, M. (eds.) INDOCRYPT 2007. LNCS, vol. 4859, pp. 1–9. Springer, Heidelberg (2007). https://doi.org/10.1007/978-3-540-77026-8_1

[SGRR19] Schoppmann, P., Gascón, A., Reichert, L., Raykova, M.: Distributed vector-OLE: Improved constructions and implementation. In: Cavallaro, L., Kinder, J., Wang, X., Katz, J., (eds.) ACM CCS 2019, pp. 1055–1072. ACM Press (November 2019)

[Shp09] Shpilka, A.: Constructions of low-degree and error-correcting ε-biased generators (2009)

[Ste88] Stern, J.: A method for finding codewords of small weight (1988)

[Wag02] Wagner, D.: A generalized birthday problem. In: Yung, M. (ed.) CRYPTO 2002. LNCS, vol. 2442, pp. 288–303. Springer, Heidelberg (2002)

[Zic17] Zichron, L.: Locally computable arithmetic pseudorandom generators (2017)

[ZJW16] Zhang, B., Jiao, L., Wang, M.: Faster algorithms for solving LPN. In: Fischlin, M., Coron, J.-S. (eds.) EUROCRYPT 2016. Part I, volume 9665 of LNCS, pp. 168–195. Springer, Heidelberg (2016)

Threshold Private Set Intersection with Better Communication Complexity

Satrajit Ghosh[1] and Mark Simkin[2(✉)]

[1] Indian Institute of Technology Kharagpur, Kharagpur, India
[2] Ethereum Foundation, Aarhus, Denmark
mark.simkin@ethereum.org

Abstract. Given ℓ parties with sets $X_1, \ldots, X_\ell$ of size n, we would like to securely compute the intersection $\cap_{i=1}^{\ell} X_i$, if it is larger than $n-t$ for some threshold t, without revealing any other additional information. It has previously been shown (Ghosh and Simkin, Crypto 2019) that this function can be securely computed with a communication complexity that only depends on t and in particular does not depend on n. For small values of t, this results in protocols that have a communication complexity that is sublinear in the size of the inputs. Current protocols either rely on fully homomorphic encryption or have an at least quadratic dependency on the parameter t.

In this work, we construct protocols with a quasilinear dependency on t from simple assumptions like additively homomorphic encryption and oblivious transfer. All existing approaches, including ours, rely on protocols for computing a single bit, which indicates whether the intersection is larger than $n-t$ without actually computing it. Our key technical contribution, which may be of independent interest, takes any such protocol with secret shared outputs and communication complexity $\mathcal{O}(\lambda\ell\operatorname{poly}(t))$, where λ is the security parameter, and transforms it into a protocol with communication complexity $\mathcal{O}(\lambda^2\ell t\operatorname{polylog}(t))$.

1 Introduction

In the private set intersection (PSI) setting, ℓ parties with private input sets $X_1, \ldots, X_\ell$ would like to jointly compute $\cap_{i=1}^{\ell} X_i$ without revealing anything else about any of the sets to each other. PSI is a powerful tool with applications in various places, such as botnet detection [NMH+10], online advertising [PSSZ15], private contact discovery [Mar14], and contact tracing [DPT20]. Various works have shown how to design asymptotically and practically efficient protocols in both the two and multiparty setting with security against both passive and active adversaries [Mea86, FNP04, KS05, DCW13, PSSZ15, KKRT16, PRTY19, PRTY20]. Unfortunately, all these protocols have communication complexities that are at least linear in the size of the smallest input set and it was observed by Freedman, Nissim, and Pinkas [FNP04] that one cannot hope to do better in general.

Ghosh and Simkin [GS19] have recently shown that the communication complexity can be sublinear in the sizes of the input sets, when the intersection is

A. Boldyreva and V. Kolesnikov (Eds.): PKC 2023, LNCS 13941, pp. 251–272, 2023.
https://doi.org/10.1007/978-3-031-31371-4_9

very large. The authors considered the threshold private set intersection (TPSI) setting, where the parties would like to compute the intersection of their sets, if and only if it is larger than $n - t$, where n is the size of each set and t is some threshold. Based on simple assumptions, such as the existence of oblivious transfer and additively homomorphic encryption, Ghosh and Simkin construct protocols for TPSI with a communication complexity of $\mathcal{O}(\lambda t^2 \operatorname{polylog} t)$ bits, where λ is the computational security parameter, for the two-party case. The authors also show how to construct a close to optimal two-party protocol based on fully homomorphic encryption with $\mathcal{O}(\lambda t \operatorname{polylog} t)$ bits and outline how these protocols can be extended to the multiparty case. The authors show an $\Omega(t)$ lower bound on the communication complexity for the two-party case. Subsequently Branco, Döttling, and Pu [BDP21] present an ℓ-party protocol with a communication complexity of $\mathcal{O}(\lambda \ell t^2 \operatorname{polylog} t)$ bits based on threshold additively homomorphic encryption. Badrinarayanan et al. [BMRR21] propose a protocol for a setting similar to the TPSI setting above, namely for computing the intersection of ℓ sets with a communication complexity of $\mathcal{O}(\lambda \ell t \operatorname{polylog} t)$, when $\left|(\cup_{i=1}^{\ell} X_i) \setminus (\cap_{i=1}^{\ell} X_i)\right| \leq t$. For $\ell = 2$, the work of Badrinarayanan et al. is equivalent to two-party TPSI, but for $\ell > 2$ their work requires the set intersection to not only be large, but additionally they require that the parties have less than t distinct elements outside the intersection among all sets. Both Branco, Döttling, and Pu as well as Badrinarayanan et al. show that one cannot do better than $\Omega(\ell t)$ in their respective settings and provide, up to polylog factors, matching upper bounds based on fully homomorphic encryption.

All three works [GS19, BDP21, BMRR21] leave constructing asymptotically optimal multiparty protocols from other assumptions than the existence of fully homomorphic encryption as an open problem.

1.1 Applications of Threshold Private Set Intersection

As has been pointed out by the previous works, threshold private set intersection is not just an interesting theoretical object to study, but also has the potential to be useful in a variety of practical applications, where parties are only interested in the actual intersection if it is indeed large. In the biometric authentication setting, we have a biometric reading represented as a feature vector and a template. An authentication attempt can directly be discarded, if the reading has a small intersection with the template. In the setting of ride sharing or dating apps, users may not care to share their private data with each other, if they do not have a large intersection.

Even protocols for general private set intersection can benefit from more efficient TPSI protocols. Parties that would like to compute the intersection of their sets, can first execute a private intersection cardinality test protocol on thresholds $2, 2^2, 2^4, \ldots$ to determine the correct threshold and then compute the intersection using the TPSI protocol. Using this approach, leads to a general private set intersection protocol with a communication complexity that depends on the size of the output and not on the size of the inputs. This is in stark contrast to the majority of existing works on PSI that usuall have a communication complexity that is at least linear in the smallest set size.

1.2 Our Contribution

In this work, we present new protocols for computing the threshold private set intersection among ℓ parties with a quasilinear rather than quadratic dependency on t from simple assumptions. More concretely, we construct protocols with a communication complexity of $\mathcal{O}(\lambda^2 \ell t \operatorname{polylog} t)$ bits. We follow the blueprint of Ghosh and Simkin [GS19] and tackle the problem by splitting it into two smaller problems. We first execute a private intersection cardinality test (PICT) protocol $\Pi_{\ell\text{-pict}}^{n,t}(X_1, \ldots, X_\ell)$ that checks, whether the given sets $X_1, \ldots, X_\ell$ have an intersection of size at least $n - t$. If they do, we can execute another protocol for computing the actual intersection in a communication efficient manner.

Computing the intersection, when it has already been established that it is indeed large enough, can be done generically from assumptions, like the existence of oblivious transfer or additively homomorphic encryption, with a close to optimal communication complexity of $\tilde{\mathcal{O}}(\lambda \ell t)$ bits as has been shown by Ghosh and Simkin. Thus, the main challenge and the focus of this work is to construct communication efficient PICT protocols from simple assumptions, which output a single bit that indicates, whether the intersection is large enough.

Our main technical contribution is a transformation that takes any PICT protocol with secret shared outputs[1] and communication complexity $\mathcal{O}(\lambda \ell \operatorname{poly}(t))$ and transforms it into a new protocol that solves the same task, but has a communication complexity of only $\mathcal{O}(\lambda^2 \ell t \operatorname{polylog}(t))$. An implication of this compiler is the existence of multiparty protocols with the above stated communication complexity from effectively any assumption that implies secure computation. The efficiency of a protocol that is given as input to our transformation only affects the constant in the $\operatorname{polylog}(t)$ exponent.

Is This Stuff Practical? We stress that the main focus of this work is to construct asymptotically efficient protocols from simpler assumptions. We hope that our work will eventually lead to practically efficient protocols, but we think that our current results achieving a communication complexity of $\mathcal{O}(\lambda^2 \ell t \log^c t)$ bits for some $c \geq 2$ are still slightly too inefficient for most reasonable real-world parameters. We leave constructing protocols with $c \leq 1$ as an exciting open question for future work. Nonetheless, we view our work as a significant theoretical step towards more efficient protocols for threshold private set intersection.

1.3 Technical Overview

For the sake of this overview, let us focus on the two-party case. We would like to design a protocol that takes two sets $X, Y \subset U$ from some universe U as input

---

[1] All existing protocols can easily be adapted to output secret shares of the output instead of the output itself.

and outputs a bit that indicates, whether $|X \cap Y| \geq n-t$ or equivalently, whether the symmetric set difference $|X \triangle Y| := |X \setminus Y \cup Y \setminus X| \leq 2t$. Our main idea is to approach this problem via a divide and conquer strategy, i.e. to partition the sets X and Y into smaller sets $X_1, \ldots, X_t$ and $Y_1, \ldots, Y_t$ and then to perform a series of independent PICTs on each pair X_i and Y_i for $i \in [t] := \{1, \ldots, t\}$.

More precisely, imagine we have random functions[2] $H^i : U \to [t]$ for $i \in [\epsilon]$ for some value ϵ that take set elements as input and outputs values in $[t]$. Define $X_i^j = \{x \mid x \in X \wedge H^j(x) = i\}$ and $Y_i^j = \{y \mid y \in Y \wedge H^j(y) = i\}$ for $i \in [t]$ and $j \in [\epsilon]$ and observe that for all $j \in [\epsilon]$

$$|X \triangle Y| = \sum_{i=1}^{t} \left| X_i^j \triangle Y_i^j \right|.$$

Consider some fixed $j \in [\epsilon]$. If $|X \triangle Y| \leq 2t$, then in expectation each pair of sets X_i^j and Y_i^j contains at most two elements in their symmetric set difference and one can show that (for a fixed j) with a constant probability none of the pairs has a symmetric set difference that is larger than $\mathcal{O}(\ln t)$. It follows that when $|X \triangle Y| \leq 2t$, there must exist at least one j for which $\left| X_i^j \triangle Y_i^j \right| \in \mathcal{O}(\ln t)$ for all $i \in [t]$ with an overwhelming in ϵ probability.

So how is this helpful? Imagine we were given access to an auxiliary functionality $\mathcal{F}_\triangle^{n,\tilde{t},v}$ that takes two sets as input and either returns a secret sharing of the size of their *exact* symmetric set difference or a secret sharing of some default value v, if the symmetric set difference is larger than $\tilde{t} \approx \ln t$. We can use $\mathcal{F}_\triangle^{n,\tilde{t},v}$ on each of the ϵt many subset pairs to obtain equally many secret shared values and then add all the values together that belong to inputs, which were partitioned using the same random partitioning function to get a total of ϵ many secret shared sums. Each of those sums either equals the exact size of the symmetric set difference of X and Y or some value, which has v as a summand. By picking $v = t + 1$, we ensure that each sum containing v is larger than t. As the final step in our protocol, we run a generic secure computation protocol for checking, whether any of the ϵ sums is at most t in which case we conclude that the inputs X and Y have a large enough intersection.

To make our protocol work, we still need to instantiate $\mathcal{F}_\triangle^{n,\tilde{t},v}$. We show that this can be done from any PICT protocol with secret shared outputs for thresholds $\tilde{t}$. If the given protocol has a communication complexity of $\mathcal{O}(\lambda \operatorname{poly}(\tilde{t}))$ bits, then our instantiation of $\mathcal{F}_\triangle^{n,\tilde{t},v}$ has a communication complexity of $\mathcal{O}(\lambda \tilde{t} \operatorname{poly}(\tilde{t})) = \mathcal{O}(\lambda \ln t \operatorname{polylog} t) = \mathcal{O}(\lambda \operatorname{polylog} t)$. Since our approach only relies on generic secure computation and existing PICT protocols, it follows that we can instantiate our constructions from assumptions that imply both of these cryptographic objects. As we will see, this means that we can instantiate our results from oblivious transfer or generic additively homomorphic encryption.

---

[2] Throughout the paper we will use random functions for the sake of simplicity, but we stress that all of our constructions and arguments work equally well with pseudorandom functions, where the key is known to all parties.

Our multiparty PICT protocols follows the same blueprint as the protocol outlined above, but need to overcome several other challenges. In the the two-party case we got away with just talking about the symmetric set difference, since an upper bound on that quantity directly translates into a lower bound on the set intersection size. In the multiparty setting this is not the case any longer and we will need to directly talk about the set intersection sizes in all the buckets instead. While it may sounds like an irrelevant change, it does introduce some small technical challenges that we will highlight in Sect. 4.

Paper Outline. In Sect. 2 we recall some basic preliminaries and define all the required notation that will be needed throughout the paper. In Sect. 3, we present our protocol for the two-party case. We stress that this *does not* asymptotically improve upon the state-of-the-art, which has a communication complexity of $\mathcal{O}(\lambda t \operatorname{polylog} t)$ bits[3]. We do, however, believe that our two-party protocol highlights the main ideas of this work quite well, while avoiding some of the complexities that come from considering multiple parties. In Sect. 4 we present our multiparty protocol, which is the main technical contribution of this work.

2 Preliminaries

Notation. We write $[n] = \{1, 2, \ldots, n\}$. Let $\log x$ be the logarithm of x with base 2 and $\ln x$ the one with base e. For convenience, we assume the natural numbers start at one, i.e. $\mathbb{N} = \{1, 2, 3, \ldots\}$. Let λ be the computational and ϵ the statistical security parameter and we assume that $\epsilon/\lambda \in \mathcal{O}(1)$. We write $\mathbb{F}$ to denote a finite field of prime order and we assume that $|\mathbb{F}| \geq 2^\epsilon$. For parties $P_1, \ldots, P_\ell$ with inputs $X_1, \ldots, X_\ell$ that have oracle access to an ideal functionality $\mathcal{F}$, we write $(b_1, \ldots, b_\ell) \leftarrow \mathcal{F}(X_1, \ldots, X_\ell)$ as a shorthand notation for each party i sending X_i to the ideal functionality and, once all inputs are received, receiving back output b_i. For a protocol Π, we write $\mathsf{CC}(\Pi)$ to denote the communication complexity of Π, i.e. the number of bits exchanged in one execution of the protocol.[4]

Theorem 1 (Chernoff Bound). *Let* $I_1, \ldots, I_n$ *be random variables with* $0 \leq I_i \leq 1$ *for all* $i \in [n]$. *Define* $I = \sum_{i=1}^n I_i$ *and let* $\mu = \mathbb{E}[I]$. *For any* $\delta \geq 1$,

$$\Pr[I \geq (1 + \delta)\mu] \leq e^{-\frac{\delta\mu}{3}}.$$

---

[3] This communication complexity can be obtained, without using fully homomorphic encryption, by using the construction of Ghosh and Simkin [GS19] in combination with an observation due to Badrinarayanan et al. [BMRR21].

[4] We assume that the communication complexity is a deterministic function of the inputs and parameters of Π.

Set Gymnastics. Let U be the universe from which set elements will be sampled and let $Z = (z_1, z_2, \dots)$ be an auxiliary (sorted) universe such that $U \cap Z = \emptyset$. We will use upper case letter for sets and lower case letters for their elements, e.g. $S = \{s_1, \dots, s_n\}$. For $S \in U^n$ and function $H : U \to [t]$, we write $(S_1, \dots, S_t) \leftarrow H(S)$ as a shorthand notation to specify the sets $S_i = \{s \mid s \in S \land H(s) = i\}$.

Secret Sharing. Let $\mathsf{Share}_n : \mathbb{F} \to \mathbb{F}^\ell$ be an ℓ-out-of-ℓ secret sharing algorithm that takes $v \in \mathbb{F}$ as input and outputs uniformly random $v_1, \dots, v_\ell \in \mathbb{F}$, such that $v = \sum_{i=1}^{\ell} v_i$. When an algorithm or a functionality outputs $\mathsf{Share}_\ell(v)$, we mean that party i receives shares v_i.

2.1 Secure Multiparty Computation

We assume familiarity with standard secure computation notions in the standalone model (see [Lin17]). In this paper, we assume that all parties are pairwise connected via a synchronous network and authenticated private channels. Additionally the parties have access to a broadcast channel. We consider an adversary that can corrupt all but one parties passively.

2.2 Private Intersection Cardinality Testing

For the two-party case the functionality we are interested in is the $\mathcal{F}_{\mathsf{pict}}^{n,t}(X, Y)$ functionality shown in Fig. 1. It is helpful to note that for X and Y with $n = |X| = |Y|$, it holds that

$$|X \cap Y| \leq n - t \iff |X \triangle Y| > 2t,$$

which means that the functionality outputs a sharing of 1 for two sets of size n if and only if $|X \cap Y| > n - t$. The functionality $\mathcal{F}_{\mathsf{pict}}^{n,t}(X, Y)$ does allow for the input sets to be of unequal sizes smaller than n in which case the equivalence above does not hold. This is done for the sake of simplifying the presentation of our construction in the two-party case. The multiparty functionality will be introduced in Sect. 4 and it will require the input sets to be of the same size.

2.3 Some Auxiliary Functionalities

In the following, we define some helpful functionalities that will come in handy later on. They can be realized using any generic secure computation protocol and will not affect our communication complexities in any meaningful way.

The functionalities in Fig. 2 allow for comparing a secret shared input against a publicly known threshold and returning either the secret shared value or a default value. Both functionalities can be easily realized with communication complexities that are linear in their input length with standard secure computation tools.

Functionality $\mathcal{F}_{\text{pict}}^{n,t}(X, Y)$

---

if $|X| > n$ or $|Y| > n$

    return $\perp$

if $|X \triangle Y| > t$

    return $\text{Share}_2(0)$

else

    return $\text{Share}_2(1)$

Fig. 1. Functionality takes two sets X and Y of size at most n as input and checks whether $|X \triangle Y| \leq t$.

Functionality $\mathcal{F}_{\text{cmp}}^{t,v}(r_1, r_2)$

---

if $r_1 + r_2 = t$

    return $\text{Share}_2(v)$

else

    return $\text{Share}_2(r_1 + r_2)$

Functionality $\mathcal{F}_{\ell\text{-geq}}^{t,v}(r_1, \ldots, r_\ell)$

Compute $s := \displaystyle\sum_{i=1}^{\ell} r_i$

if $s \geq t$

    return $\text{Share}_\ell(s)$

else

    return $\text{Share}_\ell(v)$

Fig. 2. Some useful private comparison function of secret shared inputs.

Functionality $\mathcal{F}_{\ell\text{-vec-leq}}^{t,\epsilon}((s_1^1, \ldots s_1^\epsilon), \ldots, (s_\ell^1, \ldots s_\ell^\epsilon))$ in Fig. 3 takes ϵ many ℓ-out-of-ℓ secret shared field elements as input and returns 1 if any one of them is smaller than t and 0 otherwise. This functionality can be realized using generic secure computation with a communication complexity of $\mathcal{O}(\epsilon\ell\,|\mathbb{F}|)$ bits.

Functionality $\mathcal{F}_{\ell\text{-vec-leq}}^{t,\epsilon}((s_1^1, \ldots s_1^\epsilon), \ldots, (s_\ell^1, \ldots s_\ell^\epsilon))$

---

if $\exists\, j \in [\epsilon] : \displaystyle\sum_{i=1}^{\ell} s_i^j \leq t$

    return $\text{Share}_\ell(1)$

else

    return $\text{Share}_\ell(0)$

Fig. 3. Functionality for checking, whether one of the ϵ many secret shared inputs is at most t.

The functionality in Fig. 4 computes the minimum among a list of input values and returns that value in secret shared form.

Functionality $\mathcal{F}_{\ell\text{-min}}(d_1, \ldots, d_\ell)$

Compute $d_{\min} := \min\{d_1, \ldots, d_\ell\}$

return $\text{Share}_\ell(d_{\min})$

Fig. 4. Functionality for computing a secret sharing of the minimum among a set of inputs.

The functionality in Fig. 5 checks whether at least one of multiple secret shared values is within a given interval.

3   The Two-Party Divide-and-Conquer Approach

In this section, we will focus on the two-party case for the sake of presenting our main ideas in a simplified setting.

Let us begin with a simple lemma, which states that one can partition sets X and Y into smaller sets and compute the size of their symmetric set difference in a divide-and-conquer fashion.

Functionality $\mathcal{F}^{n,t,\epsilon}_{\ell\text{-vec-intrvl}}((s_1^1, \ldots s_1^\epsilon), \ldots, (s_\ell^1, \ldots s_\ell^\epsilon))$

---

if $\exists \, j \in [\epsilon] : n - t \leq \sum_{i=1}^{\ell} s_i^j \leq n$

   return $\text{Share}_\ell(1)$

else

   return $\text{Share}_\ell(0)$

Fig. 5. Functionality for checking, whether at least one of ϵ many secret shared input values is in between $n - t$ and n.

Lemma 1. *Let* $X, Y \subset U$, *let* $t \in \mathbb{N}$, *and let* $H : U \to [t]$ *be an arbitrary function. For* $(X_1, \ldots, X_t) \leftarrow H(X)$ *and* $(Y_1, \ldots, Y_t) \leftarrow H(Y)$, *it holds that*

$$|X \triangle Y| = \sum_{i=1}^{t} |X_i \triangle Y_i|.$$

Proof. Consider two arbitrary sets $X, Y \subset U$. We observe that $|X \triangle Y| = |X \setminus Y| + |Y \setminus X|$. If $v \in X \setminus Y$, then there exists an index $i \in [t]$ such that $v \in X_i \setminus Y_i$ and since $X_i \cap X_j = \emptyset$ for any $j \neq i$, it holds that i is unique. The other way round, for any $i \in [t]$ and any $v \in X_i \setminus Y_i$, it holds that $v \in X \setminus Y$. Thus

$$|X \setminus Y| = \sum_{i=1}^{t} |X_i \setminus Y_i|$$

and by symmetry of the above argument

$$
\begin{aligned}
|X \triangle Y| &= |X \setminus Y| + |Y \setminus X| \\
&= \sum_{i=1}^{t} |X_i \setminus Y_i| + \sum_{i=1}^{t} |Y_i \setminus X_i| \\
&= \sum_{i=1}^{t} |X_i \setminus Y_i| + |Y_i \setminus X_i| = \sum_{i=1}^{t} |X_i \triangle Y_i|.
\end{aligned}
$$

$\square$

Next, we observe that, if the symmetric set difference of X and Y is at most t, then the symmetric set difference of each pair of subsets X_i and Y_i for $i \in [t]$ is in $\mathcal{O}(\ln t)$ with a constant probability.

Lemma 2. *Let $n, t, \tilde{t} \in \mathbb{N}$ with $t < n$ and $\tilde{t} \geq 1 + 3 \ln 2t$. Let $H : U \to [t]$ be a random function, and let $X, Y \in U^n$. If $|X \triangle Y| \leq t$, then for $(X_1, \ldots, X_t) \leftarrow H(X)$ and $(Y_1, \ldots, Y_t) \leftarrow H(Y)$ it holds that*

$$\Pr \left[\exists i \in [t] : |X_i \triangle Y_i| \geq \tilde{t} \right] \leq 1/2,$$

where the probability is taken over the random choice of H.

Proof. Assume that $|X \triangle Y| \leq t$. For all $i \in [t]$, it holds that $X_i \triangle Y_i = \{v \mid v \in X \triangle Y \wedge H(v) = i\} \subset X \triangle Y$. Fix one bucket j and let I_v be the indicator variable for whether $v \in X \triangle Y$ landed in bucket j or not. For

$$\mathbb{E}[|X_j \triangle Y_j|] = \mathbb{E} \left[\sum_{v \in X \triangle Y} I_v \right] = \sum_{v \in X \triangle Y} 1/t \leq 1$$

we get by Chernoff bound that

$$\Pr \left[|X_j \triangle Y_j| \geq 1 + 3 \ln 2t \right] \leq e^{-\frac{3 \ln 2t}{3}} = 1/2t,$$

where the probability is taken over the random choice of the function H. The statement follows by union bounding over all t buckets. $\square$

Now, if $|X \triangle Y| \leq t$ and we partition sets X and Y not once, but ϵ many times, then we are guaranteed with overwhelming probability that at least one of those partitions has no bucket that contains more than $\mathcal{O}(\ln t)$ elements.

Theorem 2. *Let $n, t, \tilde{t} \in \mathbb{N}$ with $t < n$ and $\tilde{t} \geq 1 + 3 \ln 2t$. For each $i \in [\epsilon]$, let $H^i : U \to [t]$ be a random function. Let $X, Y \in U^n$ be two sets of size n and $(X_1^i, \ldots, X_t^i) \leftarrow H^i(X)$ and $(Y_1^i, \ldots, Y_t^i) \leftarrow H^i(Y)$ for $i \in [\epsilon]$. If $|X \triangle Y| \leq t$, then*

$$\Pr\left[\exists i_1, \ldots i_\epsilon \in [t] : \left| X_{i_j}^j \triangle Y_{i_j}^j \right| \geq \tilde{t} \; \forall j \in [\epsilon] \right] \leq 2^{-\epsilon},$$

where the probability is taken over the random choice of $H^1, \ldots, H^\epsilon$.

Proof. Assume $|X \triangle Y| \leq t$, then

$$\Pr\left[\exists i_1, \ldots i_\epsilon \in [t] : \left| X_{i_j}^j \triangle Y_{i_j}^j \right| \geq 1 + 3 \ln 2t \; \forall j \in [\epsilon] \right]$$

$$= \prod_{j=1}^{\epsilon} \Pr\left[\exists i_j \in [t] : \left| X_{i_j}^j \triangle Y_{i_j}^j \right| \geq 1 + 3 \ln 2t \right]$$

$$\leq \prod_{j=1}^{\epsilon} 1/2 = 2^{-\epsilon},$$

where the last inequality follows from Lemma 2.

$\square$

From the above it now follows that, if there exists at least a single bucket in each of the ϵ partitions, which contains more than $1 + 3 \ln 2t$ elements of the symmetric set difference, then we can conclude that $|X \triangle Y| > t$ with overwhelming probability.

Corollary 1. *Let $n, t, \tilde{t} \in \mathbb{N}$ with $t < n$ and $\tilde{t} \geq 1 + 3 \ln 2t$. For each $i \in [\epsilon]$, let $H^i : U \to [t]$ be a random function. Let $X, Y \in U^n$ be two sets of size n and $(X_1^i, \ldots, X_t^i) \leftarrow H^i(X)$ and $(Y_1^i, \ldots, Y_t^i) \leftarrow H^i(Y)$ for $i \in [\epsilon]$. If there exist indices $i_1, \ldots i_\epsilon \in [t]$, such that for all $j \in [\epsilon]$ it holds that $\left| X_{i_j}^j \triangle Y_{i_j}^j \right| \geq \tilde{t}$, then*

$$\Pr[|X \triangle Y| > t] \geq 1 - 2^{-\epsilon},$$

where the probability is taken over the random choices of $H^1, \ldots H^\epsilon$.

Functionality $\mathcal{F}_\triangle^{n,t,v}(X, Y)$

if $|X| > n$ or $|Y| > n$

    return $\perp$

if $|X \triangle Y| > t$

    return $\mathsf{Share}_2(v)$

else

    return $\mathsf{Share}_2(|X \triangle Y|)$

Fig. 6. Functionality for computing the exact symmetric set difference, if it is smaller than t, of sets X and Y with elements from U. The sets X and Y may be of different sizes, but neither of them is larger than n.

Armed with the above observations, we are now ready to present our construction. The description of our protocol makes use of an ideal functionality $\mathcal{F}_{\triangle}^{n,t,v}$ (see Fig. 6) that takes two sets as input and either returns a secret sharing of their symmetric set difference or returns a sharing of some value v. The sets may be of different sizes, but are both not larger than n. We want to highlight that allowing for input sets of unequal size is only possible, because we are currently talking about the symmetric set difference. Looking ahead, we will be directly talking about the size of the intersection in the multiparty protocols in Sect. 4 and therefore we will need to take care of making the sets be of the correct and same size. We show how to instantiate $\mathcal{F}_{\triangle}^{n,t,v}$ in Sect. 3.1

Theorem 3. *Let $n, t, \tilde{t} \in \mathbb{N}$ with $n > t$ and $\tilde{t} = 1 + 3\ln 2t$. The protocol Π_{pict} depicted in Fig. 7 securely realizes $\mathcal{F}_{\mathsf{pict}}^{n,t}$ using $\epsilon \cdot t$ calls to $\mathcal{F}_{\triangle}^{n,\tilde{t},t+1}$ and one call to $\mathcal{F}_{\mathsf{vec\text{-}cmp}}^{t,\epsilon}$.*

Proof. We prove correctness and privacy separately.

Correctness. If there exists indices $j_1, \ldots, j_\epsilon \in [t]$ such that $\left|X_{j_i}^i \triangle Y_{j_i}^i\right| > \tilde{t}$ for all $j \in [\epsilon]$, then by Corollary 1 we know that $|X \triangle Y| > t$ with overwhelming probability and thus the output of $\Pi_{\mathsf{pict}}^{n,t}(X, Y)$ should be a secret sharing of 0. We observe that for these indices it holds that $r_{j_i}^i + s_{j_i}^i = t + 1$ and thus for all $i \in [\epsilon]$ it holds that $r^i + s^i > t$. Therefore $r + s = 0$

Construction $\Pi_{\mathsf{pict}}^{n,t}(X, Y)$

1: **for** $i \in [\epsilon]$:

2:    **Alice:** $(X_1^i, \ldots, X_t^i) \leftarrow H^i(X)$

3:    **Bob:** $(Y_1^i, \ldots, Y_t^i) \leftarrow H^i(Y)$

4:    **for** $j \in [t]$:

5:       $(r_j^i, s_j^i) \leftarrow \mathcal{F}_{\triangle}^{n,\tilde{t},t+1}\left(X_j^i, Y_j^i\right)$

6:    **Alice:** $r^i := \sum_{j=1}^{t} r_j^i$

7:    **Bob:** $s^i := \sum_{j=1}^{t} s_j^i$

8: $(r, s) \leftarrow \mathcal{F}_{\mathsf{2\text{-}vec\text{-}leq}}^{t,\epsilon}\left((r^1, \ldots, r^\epsilon), (s^1, \ldots, s^\epsilon)\right)$

9: **return** (r, s)

Fig. 7. Protocol for private intersection cardinality testing.

If on the other hand there exists an $i \in [\epsilon]$, such that $\left| X_j^i \triangle Y_j^i \right| \leq \tilde{t}$ for all $j \in [t]$, then

$$r^i + s^i = \sum_{j=1}^{t} r_j^i + s_j^i = \sum_{j=1}^{t} \left| X_j^i \triangle Y_j^i \right| \stackrel{(Lemma\ 1)}{=} |X \triangle Y|$$

and thus the $\mathcal{F}_{\text{vec-cmp}}^{t,\epsilon}$ outputs a sharing of 1 if and only if $|X \triangle Y| \leq t$.

Privacy. Without loss of generality assume that Alice is corrupted. At each step of the protocol, she only sees one share of freshly independent secret shared values returned by the ideal functionalities. Her view can simply be simulated by providing her shares of independent secret sharings of 0 instead of the real values. The indistinguishability of Alice's simulated view follows from the indistinguishability of the secret sharing scheme.

□

3.1   Instantiating $\mathcal{F}_{\triangle}^{n,t,v}$

To instantiate $\mathcal{F}_{\triangle}^{n,t,v}$, we simply use $\mathcal{F}_{\text{pict}}^{n,i}$ once for each threshold $i \in [t]$ and then accumulate the result.

Theorem 4. *Let $n, t \in \mathbb{N}$ with $n > t$ and $v \in \mathbb{F}$. The protocol $\Pi_{\triangle}^{n,t,v}$ depicted in Fig. 8 securely implements $\mathcal{F}_{\triangle}^{n,t,v}$ using one call to $\mathcal{F}_{\text{pict}}^{n,i}$ for each $i \in [t]$.*

Construction $\Pi_{\triangle}^{n,t,v}(X, Y)$

1:   **for** $i \in [t]$:

2:       $(r_i, s_i) \leftarrow \mathcal{F}_{\text{pict}}^{n,i}(X, Y)$

3:   **Alice:** $r := t - \sum_{j=1}^{t} r_i$

4:   **Bob:** $s := -\sum_{j=1}^{t} s_j$

5:   $(d_1, d_2) \leftarrow \mathcal{F}_{\text{cmp}}^{t,v}(r, s)$

6:   **return** (d_1, d_2)

Fig. 8. Protocol $\Pi_{\triangle}^{n,t,v}$ realizing $\mathcal{F}_{\triangle}^{n,t,v}$.

Proof. For correctness, we observe that $\mathcal{F}_{\text{pict}}^{n,i}(X, Y)$ outputs a sharing of 1, when $|X \triangle Y|$ is at most i. Thus, for $|X \triangle Y| \leq t$, we have that (r, s) is a secret sharing of exactly $|X \triangle Y|$ and if $|X \triangle Y| > t$, then (r, s) is a secret sharing of t.

For seeing that the protocol is secure, assume that Alice is corrupted. To simulated the responses of $\mathcal{F}_{\text{pict}}^{n,i}(X, Y)$, we add shares of a secret sharing of 0 to her view. Given the output of the functionality, we secret share that value and add one share to Alice's view. It is straightforward to see that this perfectly simulates Alice's view in the real world, which completes the proof.

$\square$

To instantiate our overall protocol, we now need to instantiate the $\mathcal{F}_{\text{pict}}^{n,t}$ functionality that is being used inside of $\varPi_{\triangle}^{n,t,v}$. Formally, the two-party protocols of Ghosh and Simkin [GS19] require the input sets to be of the same size. Their protocols, however, work equally well for sets of different sizes and thus can be used to instantiate our functionality $\mathcal{F}_{\text{pict}}^{n,t}$. Internally, their work relies on a protocol for securely computing the determinant of a secret shared matrix. They instantiate that protocol with a communication complexity of $\mathcal{O}(\lambda t^2 \operatorname{polylog}(t))$ via additively homomorphic encryption, but using a protocol for computing that determinant by Cramer and Damgård [CD01], one can instantiate the protocol of Ghosh and Simkin with communication complexity $\mathcal{O}(\lambda \ln^3 t)$ from generic secure computation. It follows that our result can be instantiated from any assumption, such as the existence of additively homomorphic encryption or oblivious transfer, that implies secure computation.

In our instantiation, we have ϵt buckets and for each of them we execute the protocol of Ghosh and Simkin $\mathcal{O}(\ln t)$ times with a threshold of $\mathcal{O}(\ln t)$. Thus we get the following corollaries.

Corollary 2. *Assuming the existence of oblivious transfer (or additively homomorphic encryption), there exists a constant-round protocol for securely computing the two-party private intersection cardinality test for threshold t with communication complexity of $\mathcal{O}(\epsilon^2 t \operatorname{polylog} t)$ bits.*

Combining the results in our paper with the protocols for actually computing the intersection, once it is known that it is large enough, from by Ghosh and Simkin [GS19], we get the following result.

Corollary 3. *Assuming the existence of oblivious transfer (or additively homomorphic encryption), there exists a constant-round protocol for threshold private set intersection among two parties with threshold t with communication complexity of $\mathcal{O}(\epsilon^2 t \operatorname{polylog} t)$ bits.*

4   The Multiparty Case

We now proceed to present our protocol for the multiparty case, which follows the blueprint from Sect. 3, but needs to overcome several additional challenges. The functionality that we would like to realize in this section is depicted in Fig. 9.

$$\boxed{\begin{array}{l}
\textbf{Functionality } \mathcal{F}_{\ell\text{-pict}}^{n,t}(X_1,\ldots,X_\ell) \\[4pt]
\hline \\[-6pt]
\textbf{if } |X_1| \neq n \textbf{ or } \ldots \textbf{ or } |X_\ell| \neq n \\[2pt]
\quad \textbf{return } \bot \\[4pt]
\textbf{if } \left|\bigcap_{i=1}^{\ell} X_i\right| \geq n - t \\[6pt]
\quad \textbf{return } \text{Share}_\ell(1) \\[2pt]
\textbf{else} \\[2pt]
\quad \textbf{return } \text{Share}_\ell(0)
\end{array}}$$

Fig. 9. Functionality for multiparty private intersection cardinality testing among sets of *size exactly* n.

In the two-party case we got away with talking about the set difference as a surrogate for the size of the set intersection due to the equivalence of intersection size and size of the symmetric set difference that is pointed out in Sect. 2.2. In the multiparty case, we make no such assumption.

To call a protocol for computing the size of the intersection in each bucket among ℓ parties, we will now ensure that the sets in each bucket are of the same size. We achieve this by padding sets with elements from an (ordered) auxiliary universe $Z = \{z_1, z_2, \ldots\}$ with $Z \cap U = \emptyset$. For $n, b \in \mathbb{N}$ with $b > n$ and any set $X \in U^n$, we define $\text{Pad}(X, b) := X \cup \{z_i \mid i \in [n - b]\}$. Lemma 3 shows the relationship between the size of the intersection among padded sets and unpadded sets.

Lemma 3. *Let $b \in \mathbb{N}$ and let $X_1, \ldots, X_\ell \subset U$ with $|X_i| \leq b$ for all $i \in [\ell]$. Let $d_i := |\,|X_i| - b|$ for $i \in [\ell]$. Then*

$$\left|\bigcap_{i=1}^{\ell} X_i\right| = \left|\bigcap_{i=1}^{\ell} \text{Pad}(X_i, b)\right| - \min(d_1, \ldots, d_\ell)$$

Proof. Define $W_i = \text{Pad}(X_i, b) \setminus X_i$ for $i \in [\ell]$. We observe that

$$\left|\bigcap_{i=1}^{\ell} \text{Pad}(X_i, b)\right| = \left|\bigcap_{i=1}^{\ell}(X_i \cup W_i)\right| = \left|\bigcap_{i=1}^{\ell} X_i\right| + \left|\bigcap_{i=1}^{\ell} W_i\right| = \left|\bigcap_{i=1}^{\ell} X_i\right| + \min(d_1, \ldots, d_\ell),$$

where the second equality follows from the fact that $Z \cap U = \emptyset$ and thus the lemma statement follows. □

The following Lemma can be seen as a generalization of Lemma 1 to the multiparty case. On an intuitive level, it states that a lower bound on the size of the intersection of ℓ sets translates into a lower bound on the cumulative size of the intersections in each buckets

Lemma 4. *Let* $n, \ell, t \in \mathbb{N}$ *with* $t < n$, *let* $H : U \rightarrow [t]$ *be a random function, let* $X_1, \ldots, X_\ell \in U^n$, *and* $(X_{i,1}, \ldots, X_{i,t}) \leftarrow H(X_i)$ *for* $i \in [\ell]$. *It holds that*

$$\left| \bigcap_{i=1}^{\ell} X_i \right| \geq n - t$$

if and only if

$$\sum_{k=1}^{t} \left| X_{j,k} \setminus \bigcap_{i=1}^{\ell} X_{i,k} \right| \leq t, \forall j \in [\ell].$$

Proof. Let $W_{j,k} := X_{j,k} \setminus \bigcap_{i=1}^{\ell} X_{i,k}$ for $k \in [t]$ and $j \in [\ell]$. We observe that for each pair $k, k' \in [t]$, it holds that $W_{j,k} \cap W_{j,k'} = \emptyset$ and thus

$$\left| X_j \setminus \bigcap_{i=1}^{\ell} X_i \right| = \sum_{k=1}^{t} \left| X_{j,k} \setminus \bigcap_{i=1}^{\ell} X_{i,k} \right|.$$

The statement follows from the fact that

$$\left| \bigcap_{i=1}^{\ell} X_i \right| \geq n - t,$$

if and only if

$$\left| X_j \setminus \bigcap_{i=1}^{\ell} X_i \right| \leq t, \forall j \in [\ell].$$

$\square$

Similarly to Theorem 2, we will now show that, if the intersection is large enough, then there exists an index $j \in [\epsilon]$ such that the partitioning with H^j will not result in any one party having too many elements in a single bucket that do not belong to that buckets intersection.

Theorem 5. *Let* $n, \ell, t, \tilde{t} \in \mathbb{N}$ *with* $t < n$ *and* $\tilde{t} \geq 1 + 3\ln(2t\ell)$. *For each* $j \in [\epsilon]$, *let* $H^j : U \rightarrow [t]$ *be a random function. Let* $X_1, \ldots, X_\ell \in U^n$ *be sets of size* n *and* $(X_{i,1}^j, \ldots, X_{i,t}^j) \leftarrow H^j(X_i)$ *for* $j \in [\epsilon]$ *and* $i \in [\ell]$. *If*

$$\left| \bigcap_{i=1}^{\ell} X_i \right| \geq n - t,$$

then

$$\Pr\left[\exists \begin{array}{l} k_1, \ldots, k_\epsilon \in [t] \\ i_1, \ldots, i_\epsilon \in [\ell] \end{array} : \left| X_{i_j,k_j}^j \setminus \bigcap_{m=1}^{\ell} X_{m,k_j}^j \right| \geq \tilde{t} \ \forall j \in [\epsilon] \right] \leq 2^{-\epsilon},$$

where the probability is taken over the random choice of $H^1, \ldots, H^\epsilon$.

Proof. Let $W_i := X_i \setminus \left(\bigcap_{m=1}^{\ell} X_m \right)$ for $i \in [\ell]$. Assume $\left| \bigcap_{m=1}^{\ell} X_m \right| > n - t$, then for each $i \in [\ell]$, it holds that $|W_i| \leq t$. Fix some $i \in [\ell]$, $j \in [\epsilon]$, $k \in [t]$ and consider $X_{i,k}^j$, where $(X_{i,1}^j, \ldots, X_{i,t}^j) \leftarrow H^j(X_i)$. For $v \in W_i$, let I_v be the indicator variable for whether $v \in X_{i,k}^j$ or not. Then,

$$\mathbb{E}\left[\sum_{v \in W_i} I_v \right] = \sum_{v \in W_i} 1/t \leq 1$$

and thus by Chernoff bound

$$\Pr\left[\sum_{v \in W_i} I_v \geq 1 + 3\ln(2t\ell) \right] \leq e^{-\frac{3\ln(2t\ell)}{3}} = 1/2t\ell.$$

By union bound over all t buckets and all ℓ sets, we can thus conclude that

$$\Pr\left[\exists k \in [t], i \in [\ell] : \left| X_{i,k}^j \setminus \left(\bigcap_{m=1}^{\ell} X_{m,k}^j \right) \right| > 1 + 3\ln(2t\ell) \right] \leq 1/2.$$

It follows that

$$\Pr\left[\exists \begin{array}{c} k_1, \ldots k_\epsilon \in [t] \\ i_1, \ldots, i_\epsilon \in [\ell] \end{array} : \left| X_{i_j,k_j}^j \setminus \bigcap_{m=1}^{\ell} X_{m,k_j}^j \right| \geq 1 + 3\ln(2t\ell) \ \forall j \in [\epsilon] \right]$$

$$= \prod_{j=1}^{\epsilon} \Pr\left[\exists k_j \in [t], i_j \in [\ell] : \left| X_{i_j,k_j}^j \setminus \bigcap_{m=1}^{\ell} X_{m,k_j}^j \right| \geq 1 + 3\ln(2t\ell) \ \forall j \in [\epsilon] \right] \leq 2^{-\epsilon}.$$

$\square$

Corollary 4. *Let $n, t, \tilde{t} \in \mathbb{N}$ with $t < n$ and $\tilde{t} \geq 1 + 3\ln(2t\ell)$. For each $j \in [\epsilon]$, let $H^j : U \to [t]$ be a random function. Let $X_1, \ldots, X_\ell \in U^n$ be sets of size n and $(X_{i,1}^j, \ldots, X_{i,t}^j) \leftarrow H^j(X_i)$ for $j \in [\epsilon]$ and $i \in [\ell]$. If there exist indices $k_1, \ldots k_\epsilon \in [t]$ and $i_1, \ldots, i_\epsilon \in [\ell]$, such that for all $j \in [\epsilon]$ it holds that*

$$\left| X_{i_j,k_j}^j \setminus \bigcap_{m=1}^{\ell} X_{m,k_j}^j \right| \geq \tilde{t},$$

then

$$\Pr\left[\left| \bigcap_{i=1}^{\ell} X_i \right| < n - t \right] \geq 1 - 2^{-\epsilon}$$

where the probability is taken over the random choices of $H^1, \ldots H^\epsilon$.

When partitioning a set into several subsets randomly, one cannot guarantee that all subsets will be of the same size. This is problematic, since we would like to view each party's buckets as inputs to smaller instances of a private multi-party intersection cardinality testing problem. That is, if the different parties have inputs of different (secret) sizes, then it is not clear what it means for an intersection to be large enough. For this reason, each party will not directly input its subset, but rather a padded version of it. Since the communication complexities of our protocols never depend on the input sizes, we simply pad each bucket to its maximum size.

Lemma 5. *Let $n, \ell, t, \tilde{t}, b \in \mathbb{N}$ with $t \le \tilde{t} < n$ and $b := n$ and $H : U \to [t]$ be a random function. Let $X_1, \ldots, X_\ell \in U^n$ be sets of size n and $(X_{i,1}, \ldots, X_{i,t}) \leftarrow H(X_i)$ for $i \in [\ell]$.*
If

$$\left| X_{j,k} \setminus \bigcap_{i=1}^{\ell} X_{i,k} \right| < \tilde{t}, \forall j \in [\ell], k \in [t], \tilde{t} \in \mathbb{N}$$

then

$$\left| \mathsf{Pad}(X_{j,k}, b) \setminus \bigcap_{i=1}^{\ell} \mathsf{Pad}(X_{i,k}, b) \right| < \tilde{t}, \forall j \in [\ell], k \in [t].$$

Proof. Fix some $k \in [t]$ and define $t_j := \left| X_{j,k} \setminus \bigcap_{i=1}^{\ell} X_{i,k} \right|$ for $j \in [\ell]$. Observe that

$$t_j + \left| \bigcap_{i=1}^{\ell} X_{i,k} \right| + |\mathsf{Pad}(X_{j,k}, b) \setminus X_{j,k}| = b$$

and thus for $j, j' \in [\ell]$ we have

$$t_j + \left| \bigcap_{i=1}^{\ell} X_{i,k} \right| + |\mathsf{Pad}(X_{j,k}, b) \setminus X_{j,k}| = t_{j'} + \left| \bigcap_{i=1}^{\ell} X_{i,k} \right| + |\mathsf{Pad}(X_{j',k}, b) \setminus X_{j',k}|$$
$$\iff t_j + |\mathsf{Pad}(X_{j,k}, b) \setminus X_{j,k}| - |\mathsf{Pad}(X_{j',k}, b) \setminus X_{j',k}| = t_{j'}$$

Now consider index j' such that $|X_{j',k}| \ge |X_{j,k}|$ for any other $j \in [\ell]$. For that index j' it holds that $\mathsf{Pad}(X_{j',k}, b) \setminus X_{j',k} \subseteq \mathsf{Pad}(X_{j,k}, b) \setminus X_{j,k}$. In other words, this means that the elements that were used for padding the bucket belonging to party j' will be exactly the added elements in the intersection. Thus, for any other j the number of elements not in the intersection will be $t_j + |\mathsf{Pad}(X_{j,k}, b) \setminus X_{j,k}| - |\mathsf{Pad}(X_{j',k}, b) \setminus X_{j',k}|$. Now if by assumption $t_{j'} < \tilde{t}$, then $t_j + |\mathsf{Pad}(X_{j,k}, b) \setminus X_{j,k}| - |\mathsf{Pad}(X_{j',k}, b) \setminus X_{j',k}| < \tilde{t}$. □

Combining all of the above observations, we now get the following lemma.

Theorem 6. *Let $n, \ell, t, \tilde{t}, b \in \mathbb{N}$ with $t < n$, $\tilde{t} \ge 1 + 3\ln(2t\ell)$ and let $b = n$. For each $j \in [\epsilon]$, let $H^j : U \to [t]$ be a random function. Let $X_1, \ldots, X_\ell \in U^n$ be sets of size n and $(X_{i,1}^j, \ldots, X_{i,t}^j) \leftarrow H^j(X_i)$ for $j \in [\epsilon]$ and $i \in [\ell]$. If*

$$\left| \bigcap_{i=1}^{\ell} X_i \right| \ge n - t,$$

then

$$\Pr\left[\forall k \in [t], \forall i \in [\ell], \exists j \in [\epsilon] : \left| \mathsf{Pad}(X_{i,k}^j, b) \setminus \bigcap_{m=1}^{\ell} \mathsf{Pad}(X_{m,k}^j, b) \right| < \tilde{t} \right] \geq 1 - 2^{-\epsilon},$$

where the probability is taken over the random choice of $H^1, \ldots, H^\epsilon$.

Proof. By Theorem 5 we know that if $\left| \bigcap_{i=1}^{\ell} X_i \right| \geq n - t$, then for all $i \in [\ell]$ and $k \in [t]$, there exist $j \in [\epsilon]$, such that $\left| X_{i,k}^j \setminus \bigcap_{m=1}^{\ell} X_{m,k}^j \right| < \tilde{t}$ with overwhelming probability. Also from Lemma 5 we know $\left| \mathsf{Pad}(X_{i,k}^j, b) \setminus \bigcap_{m=1}^{\ell} \mathsf{Pad}(X_{m,k}^j, b) \right| < \tilde{t}$ in that case. The proof directly follows from these two observations.

□

Armed with the insights from above, we are now ready to present our multi-party construction. We will assume that we are given access to an ideal functionality $\mathcal{F}_{\ell-\cap}^{n,t,v}$ as depicted in Fig. 10 and we will show how to concretely instantiate it in Sect. 4.1. We also use two other simple functionalities $\mathcal{F}_{\ell\text{-min}}$ and $\mathcal{F}_{\ell\text{-vec-intrvl}}^{n,t,\epsilon}$ in our protocol, which is described in Fig. 4 and Fig. 5 respectively. Note that these functionalities can be implemented using any generic MPC protocol with communication complexities that are independent of the initial set size n or threshold t.

In Fig. 11 we instantiate the protocol for multiparty private cardinality testing. Similar to the two-party case, here all the parties throw their set elements into t buckets and then run separate instances of cardinality test protocol among those buckets with a threshold parameter $\tilde{t}$, as stated in Theorem 6.

Functionality $\mathcal{F}_{\ell-\cap}^{n,t,v}(X_1, \ldots, X_\ell)$

$u := \left| \bigcap_{i=1}^{\ell} X_i \right|$

if $u < n - t$

    return $\mathsf{Share}_n(v)$

else

    return $\mathsf{Share}_n(u)$

Fig. 10. Functionality for computing the number of elements in the intersection.

Construction $\Pi_{\ell\text{-pict}}^{n,t}(X_1, \ldots, X_\ell)$

---

1 : **for** $j \in [\epsilon]$:

2 :   **for** $i \in [\ell]$:

3 :   **Party** i :

4 : $(X_{i,1}^j, \ldots, X_{i,t}^j) \leftarrow H^j(X_i)$

5 :   **for** $k \in [t]$:

6 : $(s_{1,k}^j, \ldots, s_{\ell,k}^j) \leftarrow \mathcal{F}_{\ell\text{-}\cap}^{n,\tilde{t},n+1}\left(\text{Pad}(X_{1,k}^j, n+1), \ldots, \text{Pad}(X_{\ell,k}^j, n+1)\right)$

7 : $(d_{1,k}^j, \ldots, d_{\ell,k}^j) \leftarrow \mathcal{F}_{\ell\text{-min}}\left(\{\left|\text{Pad}(X_{i,k}^j, n+1)\right| - \left|X_{i,k}^j\right|\}_{i\in[\ell]}\right)$

8 :   **for** $i \in [\ell]$:

9 :   **Party** i : $s_i^j = \sum_{k=1}^{t}(s_{i,k}^j - d_{i,k}^j)$

10 : $(r_1, \ldots, r_\ell) \leftarrow \mathcal{F}_{\ell\text{-vec-intrvl}}^{n,t,\epsilon}((s_1^1, \ldots, s_1^\epsilon), \ldots, (s_\ell^1, \ldots, s_\ell^\epsilon))$

11 : **return** $(r_1, \ldots, r_\ell)$

Fig. 11. Protocol for multiparty private intersection cardinality testing.

Theorem 7. *Let* $n, t, \tilde{t} \in \mathbb{N}$ *with* $n > t$ *and* $\tilde{t} \geq 1 + 3\ln(2t\ell)$. *The protocol* $\Pi_{\ell\text{-pict}}$ *depicted in Fig. 11 securely realizes* $\mathcal{F}_{\ell\text{-pict}}^{n,t}$ *using* $\epsilon \cdot t$ *calls to* $\mathcal{F}_{\ell\text{-}\cap}^{b,\tilde{t},n+1}$ *and* $\mathcal{F}_{\ell\text{-min}}$ *and one call to* $\mathcal{F}_{\ell\text{-vec-intrvl}}^{n,t,\epsilon}$.

Proof. We prove correctness and privacy separately.

Correctness. If $\left|\bigcap_{i=1}^{\ell} X_i\right| < n - t$, then by Theorem 6, we know that no bucket will overflow with an overwhelming probability in which case the protocol computes the size of the intersection correctly. If $\left|\bigcap_{i=1}^{\ell} X_i\right| \geq n - t$, then two things can happen. Either there will exist indices $k_1, \ldots k_\epsilon \in [t]$ and $i_1, \ldots, i_\epsilon \in [\ell]$, such that for all $j \in [\epsilon]$ it holds that $\left|X_{i_j,k_j}^j \setminus \bigcap_{m=1}^{\ell} X_{m,k_j}^j\right| \geq \tilde{t}$. In this case, by Corollary 4, we know that the intersection was too small with an overwhelming probability. By construction, each sum of secret shared values per partitioning will contain a summand of $n + 1$ and thus the sums will always be larger than n in which case $\mathcal{F}_{\ell\text{-vec-intrvl}}^{n,t,\epsilon}$ returns 0 as desired.

Otherwise, the intersection is too small, but no bucket overflows. Since no bucket overflows, the parties correctly compute a secret sharing of the actual intersection and thus $\mathcal{F}_{\ell\text{-vec-intrvl}}^{n,t,\epsilon}$ will produce the correct output of the computation.

Privacy. Without loss of generality assume that $P_1, \ldots, P_{\ell-1}$ are corrupted. We observe that the only communication the parties have during a protocol execution is through oracle calls. Each oracle call returns a fresh secret sharing of some random value and the parties always receives a subset of shares that is insufficient to reconstruct. To simulate the corrupted parties' views, we simply return shares of fresh secret sharings of 0 for each oracle call.

$\square$

4.1   Instantiating $\mathcal{F}_{\ell\text{-}\cap}^{n,t,v}$

To instantiate $\mathcal{F}_{\ell\text{-}\cap}^{n,t,v}$, we use $\mathcal{F}_{\ell\text{-pict}}^{n,i}$ once for each threshold $i \in [t]$ and then accumulate the result. We also use $\mathcal{F}_{\ell\text{-geq}}^{n-t,v}$ functionality which is described in Sect. 2. $\mathcal{F}_{\ell\text{-geq}}^{n-t,v}$ checks whether the secret shared values obtained from $\mathcal{F}_{\ell\text{-pict}}^{n,i}$ indicates that the size of the intersection is greater than $n - t$. If that is the case $\mathcal{F}_{\ell\text{-geq}}$ returns the exact size of the intersection, otherwise it returns the default value v. The protocol $\Pi_{\ell\text{-}\cap}^{n,t,v}$ is described in Fig. 12.

Theorem 8. *Let $n, t \in \mathbb{N}$ with $n > t$ and $v \in \mathbb{F}$. The protocol $\Pi_{\ell\text{-}\cap}^{n,t,v}$ depicted in Fig. 12 securely implements $\mathcal{F}_{\ell\text{-}\cap}^{n,t,v}$ using one call to $\mathcal{F}_{\ell\text{-pict}}^{n,i}$ for each $i \in [t]$ and one call to $\mathcal{F}_{\ell\text{-geq}}^{n-t,v}$.*

Proof. For correctness, we observe that $\mathcal{F}_{\ell\text{-pict}}^{n,i}(X_1, \ldots, X_\ell)$ outputs sharing of 1, when the size of the intersection is greater than equal to $n - i$. Thus, if $\left| \bigcap_{j=1}^{\ell} X_j \right| \geq n - t$ then $\mathcal{F}_{\ell\text{-pict}}$ will return sharing of 1 exactly $t - t^* + 1$ times, where $n - t^*$ is the true intersection size. Consequently the protocol produces the correct output.

Construction $\Pi_{\ell\text{-}\cap}^{n,t,v}(X_1, \ldots, X_\ell)$

1 :   **for** $i \in [t]$

2 : $(r_{1,i}, \ldots, r_{\ell,i}) \leftarrow \mathcal{F}_{\ell\text{-pict}}^{n,i}(X_1, \ldots, X_\ell)$

3 :   **for** $i \in [\ell]$

4 :   **Party** $i : r_i := \sum_{j=1}^{t} r_{i,j}$

5 :   **Party** $1 : r_1 := n - t - 1 + r_1$

6 : $(d_1, \ldots, d_\ell) \leftarrow \mathcal{F}_{\ell\text{-geq}}^{n-t,v}(r_1, \ldots, r_\ell)$

7 :   **return** $(d_1, \ldots, d_\ell)$

Fig. 12. Protocol $\Pi_{\ell\text{-}\cap}^{n,t,v}$ realizing $\mathcal{F}_{\ell\text{-}\cap}^{n,t,v}$.

Privacy. Without loss of generality assume that $P_1, \ldots, P_{\ell-1}$ are corrupted. The view of the corrupted parties only contain received messages from the oracles. Each oracle query to $\mathcal{F}^{n,i}_{\ell\text{-pict}}$ returns a fresh secret sharing, which can be simulated by providing the corrupted parties with fresh shares of secret sharings of 0. The last query to $\mathcal{F}^{n-t,v}_{\ell\text{-geq}}(r_1, \ldots, r_\ell)$ can be simulated by returning the outputs given to the simulator. Indistinguishability of the simulated transcript from the real one directly follows from the security guarantees of additive secret sharing.

$\square$

We can use the protocol of Branco, Döttling, and Pu [BDP21] to instantiate $\mathcal{F}^{n,t}_{\ell\text{-pict}}$ in $\mathcal{F}^{n,t,v}_{\ell\text{-}\cap}$. They present an ℓ-party protocol with a communication complexity of $\mathcal{O}(\lambda \ell t^2 \operatorname{polylog} t)$ bits based on additively homomorphic encryption. Their protocol can easily be extended to use generic secure computation techniques in all places, where additively homomorphic encryption was used. With this change, their protocol provides a solution based on, for instance, oblivious transfer with a communication complexity of $\mathcal{O}(\lambda \ell \operatorname{poly}(t))$ bits.

In our instantiation, we have ϵt buckets and for each of them we execute the protocol of Branco et al. $\mathcal{O}(\ln t)$ times with a threshold of $\mathcal{O}(\ln t)$. Thus we get a total communication complexity of $\mathcal{O}(\epsilon \lambda \ell t \operatorname{polylog} t)$.

Corollary 5. *Assuming the existence of oblivious transfer and or additively homomorphic encryption, there exists a protocol for securely computing the ℓ-party private intersection cardinality test for threshold t with communication complexity of $\mathcal{O}(\epsilon^2 \ell t \operatorname{polylog} t)$ bits.*

Combining the results in our paper with the protocols for actually computing the intersection, once it is known that it is large enough, from by Ghosh and Simkin [GS19], we get the following result.

Corollary 6. *Assuming the existence of oblivious transfer or additively homomorphic encryption, there exists a passively secure protocol for threshold private set intersection among ℓ parties with threshold t with communication complexity of $\mathcal{O}(\epsilon^2 \ell t \operatorname{polylog} t)$ bits.*

References

[BDP21]   Branco, P., Döttling, N., Pu, S.: Multiparty cardinality testing for threshold private intersection. In: Garay, J.A. (ed.) PKC 2021. LNCS, vol. 12711, pp. 32–60. Springer, Cham (2021). https://doi.org/10.1007/978-3-030-75248-4_2

[BMRR21] Badrinarayanan, S., Miao, P., Raghuraman, S., Rindal, P.: Multi-party threshold private set intersection with sublinear communication. In: Garay, J.A. (ed.) PKC 2021. LNCS, vol. 12711, pp. 349–379. Springer, Cham (2021). https://doi.org/10.1007/978-3-030-75248-4_13

[CD01]   Cramer, R., Damgård, I.: Secure distributed linear algebra in a constant number of rounds. In: Kilian, J. (ed.) CRYPTO 2001. LNCS, vol. 2139, pp. 119–136. Springer, Heidelberg (2001). https://doi.org/10.1007/3-540-44647-8_7

[DCW13] Dong, C., Chen, L., Wen, Z.: When private set intersection meets big data: an efficient and scalable protocol. In: Sadeghi, A.-R., Gligor, V.D., Yung, M., (eds.) ACM CCS 2013: 20th Conference on Computer and Communications Security, Berlin, Germany, 4–8 November 2013, pp. 789–800. ACM Press (2013)

[DPT20] Duong, T., Phan, D.H., Trieu, N.: Catalic: delegated psi cardinality with applications to contact tracing. In: Moriai, S., Wang, H. (eds.) ASIACRYPT 2020. LNCS, vol. 12493, pp. 870–899. Springer, Cham (2020). https://doi.org/10.1007/978-3-030-64840-4_29

[FNP04] Freedman, M.J., Nissim, K., Pinkas, B.: Efficient private matching and set intersection. In: Cachin, C., Camenisch, J.L. (eds.) EUROCRYPT 2004. LNCS, vol. 3027, pp. 1–19. Springer, Heidelberg (2004). https://doi.org/10.1007/978-3-540-24676-3_1

[GS19] Ghosh, S., Simkin, M.: The communication complexity of threshold private set intersection. In: Boldyreva, A., Micciancio, D. (eds.) CRYPTO 2019. LNCS, vol. 11693, pp. 3–29. Springer, Cham (2019). https://doi.org/10.1007/978-3-030-26951-7_1

[KKRT16] Kolesnikov, V., Kumaresan, R., Rosulek, M., Trieu, N.: Efficient batched oblivious PRF with applications to private set intersection. In Weippl, E.R., Katzenbeisser, S., Kruegel, C., Myers, A.C., Halevi, S., (eds.) ACM CCS 2016: 23rd Conference on Computer and Communications Security, Vienna, Austria, 24–28 October 2016, pp. 818–829. ACM Press (2016)

[KS05] Kissner, L., Song, D.: Privacy-preserving set operations. In: Shoup, V. (ed.) CRYPTO 2005. LNCS, vol. 3621, pp. 241–257. Springer, Heidelberg (2005). https://doi.org/10.1007/11535218_15

[Lin17] Lindell, Y.: How to simulate it-a tutorial on the simulation proof technique. In: Tutorials on the Foundations of Cryptography, pp. 277–346 (2017)

[Mar14] Marlinspike, M.: The difficulty of private contact discovery (2014). https://www.whispersystems.org/blog/contact-discovery

[Mea86] Meadows., C.A.: A more efficient cryptographic matchmaking protocol for use in the absence of a continuously available third party. In: Proceedings of the 1986 IEEE Symposium on Security and Privacy, Oakland, California, USA, 7–9 April, pp. 134–137 (1986)

[NMH+10] Nagaraja, S., Mittal, P., Hong, C.-Y., Caesar, M., Borisov, N.: Botgrep: Finding P2P bots with structured graph analysis. In: 19th USENIX Security Symposium, Proceedings, Washington, DC, USA, 11–13 August 2010, pp. 95–110 (2010)

[PRTY19] Pinkas, B., Rosulek, M., Trieu, N., Yanai, A.: SpOT-light: lightweight private set intersection from sparse OT Extension. In: Boldyreva, A., Micciancio, D. (eds.) CRYPTO 2019. LNCS, vol. 11694, pp. 401–431. Springer, Cham (2019). https://doi.org/10.1007/978-3-030-26954-8_13

[PRTY20] Pinkas, B., Rosulek, M., Trieu, N., Yanai, A.: PSI from PaXoS: fast, malicious private set intersection. In: Canteaut, A., Ishai, Y. (eds.) EUROCRYPT 2020. LNCS, vol. 12106, pp. 739–767. Springer, Cham (2020). https://doi.org/10.1007/978-3-030-45724-2_25

[PSSZ15] Pinkas, B., Schneider, T., Segev, G., Zohner, M.: Phasing: Private set intersection using permutation-based hashing. In: 24th USENIX Security Symposium, USENIX Security 2015, Washington, D.C., USA, 12–14 August 2015, pp. 515–530 (2015)

Encryption

Encryption

Almost Tightly-Secure Re-randomizable and Replayable CCA-Secure Public Key Encryption

Antonio Faonio[1], Dennis Hofheinz[2], and Luigi Russo[1(✉)]

[1] EURECOM, Sophia Antipolis, France
{faonio,russol}@eurecom.fr
[2] ETH Zurich, Zurich, Switzerland
hofheinz@inf.ethz.ch

Abstract. Re-randomizable Replayable CCA-secure public key encryption (Rand-RCCA PKE) schemes guarantee security against chosen-ciphertext attacks while ensuring the useful property of re-randomizable ciphertexts. We introduce the notion of multi-user and multi-ciphertext Rand-RCCA PKE and we give the first construction of such a PKE scheme with an almost tight security reduction to a standard assumption. Our construction is structure preserving and can be instantiated over Type-1 pairing groups. Technically, our work borrows ideas from the state-of-the-art Rand-RCCA PKE scheme of Faonio *et al.* (ASIACRYPT'19) and the adaptive partitioning technique of Hofheinz (EUROCRYPT'17). Additionally, we show (1) how to turn our scheme into a publicly verifiable (pv) Rand-RCCA scheme and (2) that plugging our pv-Rand-RCCA PKE scheme into the MixNet protocol of Faonio *et al.* we can obtain the first *almost tightly-secure* MixNet protocol.

1 Introduction

Security against chosen-ciphertext attacks (CCA) is considered to be the standard notion of security for PKE schemes. This security definition, formulated by Rackoff and Simon [33], is elegant and easy to understand, and it has shown, by any means, to withstand the test of time.

Replayable and Re-randomizable CCA Security. Canetti, Krawczyk and Nielsen [7] pointed out that CCA security is not necessary for implementing secure channels. They showed that "replayable chosen-ciphertext" (RCCA) security suffices for secure channels, and might in fact allow for more efficient instantiations. Subsequently, Groth [20] showed that RCCA PKE schemes (called Rand-RCCA secure) can have re-randomizable ciphertexts. Specifically, Groth constructed a scheme with a ciphertext re-randomization procedure that, given a ciphertext as input, produces a fresh and unlinkable ciphertext that decrypts to the same message. Such a re-randomization procedure opens the door for applications that require secure communication *and* anonymity. For instance, Rand-RCCA secure PKE schemes enable anonymous and secure message transmissions (see Prabhakaran and Rosulek [32]), Mix-Nets (see Faonio *et al.* [13]

A. Boldyreva and V. Kolesnikov (Eds.): PKC 2023, LNCS 13941, pp. 275–305, 2023.
https://doi.org/10.1007/978-3-031-31371-4_10

and Pereira and Rivest [31]), Controlled Functional Encryption (see Naveed *et al.* [30]), and one-round message-transmission protocols with reverse firewalls (see Dodis, Mironov and Stephens-Davidowitz [10]).

Tight Security. Yet another criticism of the original definition of CCA security is that while the definition postulates that the message underlying *one single* ciphertext remains protected even under CCA attacks, in the real world, a PKE scheme is used to protect a large number of ciphertexts from possibly many users. Now, it is well-known that security for one single ciphertext implies, through a hybrid argument, security for many ciphertexts and many users. However, it is unclear how much *concrete* security a PKE scheme really offers when it is used in the wild. This question, initially posed by Bellare, Boldyreva and Micali [4] created a fruitful area of research that investigates how tight the security of an encryption scheme translates to the trust that we have with respect to the cryptographic assumption that it relies on. In more detail, a tight security reduction ensures that for any attack on the PKE scheme, there exists an attack on the assumption that is similar both in terms of complexity (i.e. the running time, the space required, etc.) and success probability. Thus, in the setting of tight security reductions, the number of ciphertexts considered by the security definition matters.

By now, many CCA-PKE schemes have been proven to have tight security in the multi-ciphertext and multi-user setting: some notable examples are the works of [17,18,21,22,25,26]. However, tight security in the context of Rand-RCCA security has not been studied.

1.1   Our Contributions

We initiate the study of tight security for Rand-RCCA secure PKE schemes in the multi-ciphertext and multi-user setting. Our main contributions are a new security definition for RCCA security in multi-ciphertext and multi-user setting (hereafter, mRCCA security), and a Rand-mRCCA PKE scheme whose mRCCA security (almost[1]) tightly reduces to the $\mathcal{D}_d$-MDDH assumption in symmetric (a.k.a. type-1) pairing groups.

Moreover, as an application, we revise the protocol for universally composable MixNet based on Rand-RCCA PKE from [13]. In the following paragraphs, we elaborate more about each of the contributions.

Multi-user Multi-ciphertext RCCA Security. In the security experiment of the (single-ciphertext) RCCA security notion, the decryption oracle, called "guarded decryption oracle", can be queried on any ciphertext, including the challenge ciphertext. However, when decryption leads to one of the challenge messages (M_0, M_1), the oracle answers with a special symbol $\diamond$ (meaning "same"). As a warm-up, consider a trivial extension to the case of (single-user) multi-ciphertext RCCA security where the attacker is given:

- an encryption oracle that, on input a pair of messages M_0, M_1, returns some valid encryption of M_b where b is the challenge bit,

---

[1] As most of the tightly-secure schemes, the security reduction suffers from a small multiplicative loss that is however independent of the number of uses of the scheme.

– and a guarded decryption oracle that, on input a ciphertext C, returns a message M, or the special indexed symbol $\diamond_j$ if C corresponds to an encryption of a message that was given as input to the encryption oracle as j-th query.

We notice that this trivial extension of RCCA security to multiple ciphertexts is impossible to achieve. Namely, consider the following generic attacker $\mathcal{A}$ that makes three queries to the encryption oracle: (i) $\mathcal{A}$ sends (M_1, M_2), and receives back C_A; (ii) sends (M_2, M_3), and receives back C_B; (iii) sends (M_3, M_1), and receives back C_C. $\mathcal{A}$ now queries the decryption oracle with C_C. If the bit b is 0, the decryption oracle returns $\diamond_2$; if b is 1, the decryption oracle returns $\diamond_1$.

Yet another natural extension of the single-ciphertext RCCA security notion to the multi-ciphertext setting is to consider a guarded decryption oracle that upon input a ciphertext C either returns a message or the special symbol $\diamond$, but without notifying the adversary of which index j triggered the special symbol. Even if this definition avoids the attack described above, it is not as convenient as we would like it to be. Roughly speaking, the guarded decryption oracle reveals to the adversary that the queried ciphertext is a replay attack, but it doesn't tell which ciphertext was replayed; therefore, the larger the number of challenge ciphertexts, the less informative the output of the guarded decryption oracle will be. In particular, this definition is not sufficient for our MixNet application.

"In medio stat virtus", as the saying goes: the definition we propose is weaker than the first attempted (yet impossible to achieve) definition, but stronger than the above-mentioned definition. To build some intuition, in an equivalent version of the single-ciphertext RCCA security definition, the guarded decryption oracle would output the minimal set of messages that the queried ciphertext could decrypt to and such that such set does not trivially break the RCCA security definition: namely, if the ciphertext is a replay attack then the oracle replies with the set of challenge messages $\{M_0, M_1\}$, otherwise with a message $M' \notin \{M_0, M_1\}$. We take a similar approach in our (multi-user) multi-ciphertext RCCA definition. The guarded decryption oracle outputs the minimal set of messages that the ciphertext could decrypt to without trivially breaking security. This set of messages includes all the pairs of challenge messages for which at least one of them is equal to the decryption of the queried ciphertext. To support the claim that our definition is indeed the most natural extension of RCCA to the multi-ciphertext setting, we prove that the simulation-based notion for RCCA security from [7] is tightly implied by our mRCCA security notion.

A Tightly-Secure Rand-mRCCA PKE Scheme. Our starting points are the recent work of Faonio *et al.* [13] (hereafter FFHR19), which is the state of art for Rand-RCCA PKE scheme, and the tightly-secure CCA PKE schemes based on the adaptive partitioning techniques of Hofheinz [22] and Gay *et al.* [19].

Very briefly, the main idea of our construction is to encrypt the message similarly to FFHR19, and append a non-interactive proof of consistency for (part of) the ciphertext; the latter proof needs to have a (weak) form of simulation soundness property that can be obtained information-theoretically. Namely, using the notation of [22], we append to the ciphertext a *benign proof* for the consistency of part of the ciphertext (which lies in a linear language) of a proof system that is statistically sound even when the adversary has oracle access to simulated proofs for a larger language that includes the disjunction of two linear spaces.

Some Technical Details. To go from the rough idea described above to the actual scheme, we need to overcome two technical problems. The first problem is that our benign proof system needs to be re-randomizable (or, to better say, "malleable" as it needs to be able to re-randomize proofs of re-randomized statements), as we are aiming to construct a Rand-PKE scheme. We notice that none of the benign proof systems or affine notions we are aware of (such as [2,18,19,22]) are re-randomizable. To solve this problem, we introduce a new malleable proof system based on the work of Abdalla, Benhamouda and Pointcheval [1].

The second (and more challenging) technical problem is that we need to reconcile the adaptive partitioning technique with the Rand-RCCA technique of [13]. In particular, at the core of the adaptive partitioning technique there is a complex argument that shows that the decryption oracle can safely reject *ill-formed* ciphertexts even when the adversary can observe (many) ill-formed challenge ciphertexts. In some sense, these challenge ciphertexts are the only ill-formed ciphertexts that correctly decrypt, while all other ill-formed ciphertexts produced by the adversary do not. However, in our security proof the adversary can easily produce ill-formed ciphertexts that correctly decrypt, simply by re-randomizing challenge ciphertexts.

In more detail, the adaptive partitioning technique moves the challenge ciphertexts back and forth between two different linear spaces (different from the linear space of honestly-generated ciphertexts). In our proof, differently than in previous works, we need to carefully define the relationship between these different linear spaces. In particular, it is necessary to make sure that re-randomizations of the challenge ciphertexts still lie in the prescribed linear space (and thus can be identified by our technique when answering ⋄). More technically, a ciphertext for our scheme can be parsed as a vector $[\mathbf{x}]$ in the source group (the CPA part of the ciphertext) plus two zero-knowledge proofs of consistency. The vector $[\mathbf{x}]$ for a well-formed ciphertext lies in the affine space defined by the encrypted message and the span of a matrix $[\mathbf{D}^*]$ which is part of the public key. Re-randomization works by summing up a random vector from the span of $\mathbf{D}^*$ to $\mathbf{x}$ (and updating the proofs accordingly). To apply the adaptive partitioning techniques, we move the challenge ciphertexts back and forth from two well-crafted distinct superspaces of $\mathbf{D}^*$. Thanks to this choice, we can recognize the challenge ciphertexts after re-randomization by multiplying the decrypted ciphertext by a matrix orthogonal to $\mathbf{D}^*$: this operation could be roughly interpreted as an "extended decryption" of the ciphertexts (since $\mathbf{D}^*$ encodes partial information of the secret key), however, we are not only interested to identify the encrypted message but also to uniquely link the decrypted (possibly re-randomized) ciphertext with one of the challenge ciphertexts. Thus, like previous adaptive partitioning approaches, we separate the randomness space of the PKE scheme into an honest part (the span of $\mathbf{D}^*$) and a normally unused part (spanned by the vectors in the mentioned super spaces, independent of $\mathbf{D}^*$) that is also used to hide the messages. In our view, the main technical insight is that the span of $\mathbf{D}^*$ is used for re-randomization, while the other space is kept fixed for the challenge ciphertexts. We highlight that in order for the aforementioned strategy to work smoothly, we preferred to follow a flavor of adaptive partitioning as in Gay *et al.* [19], where secret keys are randomized, instead of the original strategy of Hofheinz [22], where ciphertexts are randomized. Finally, the original adaptive partitioning strategy relies on the pairwise universality of a hash proof system [9] that guarantees simpler statements about linear languages. We adapt this proof system to re-randomizable statements by considering higher-dimensional languages and refining the "core lemma for Rand-RCCA" from [13]. We highlight that this lemma was designed for the single-ciphertext scenario, thus, some extra care is needed in our adaptive partitioning argument, more in detail, when defining the notion of *critical query*. In particular, a critical query is commonly defined as a decryption query for an ill-formed ciphertext that would decrypt without errors under one of the randomized secret keys; the usual goal is to show that an adversary cannot make such a query. In our case, we need to refine this notion by additionally specifying when (allegedly) re-randomizations of challenge ciphertexts are critical. Since each one of the challenge ciphertexts is an ill-formed ciphertext that decrypts correctly under one of the randomized keys, we cannot consider critical a re-randomization of such a challenge ciphertext when it decrypts correctly under the same randomized key. Thus, after having recognized a decryption query as a re-randomization, we make sure that this ciphertext is decrypted only using a specific (a univocally linked) secret key; on the other hand, other kinds of decryption queries can be safely decrypted with any of the secret keys. This rule allows eventually to use the lemma of [13] which provides security even given an interface for decryption of re-randomizations of one challenge ciphertext under one specific secret key.

Extensions and Applications. Following the strategy of [13] we show that our Rand-mRCCA PKE can be used to instantiate a PKE with the nice property of publicly verifiable ciphertexts (pv-Rand-mRCCA PKE). We propose two pv-Rand-mRCCA PKE schemes: one based on the Matrix Diffie-Hellman Assumption (MDDH), and a second more efficient scheme based on a new MDDH-like assumption (see Sect. 1.2 for the details) which we prove secure in the generic group model.

As an application of our framework, we show that we can plug a pv-Rand-mRCCA scheme into the MixNet protocol of [13]. Instantiating such protocol with our schemes, we obtain an (almost) *"tightly-secure"* MixNet protocol: namely a protocol, the first of its kind, whose security guarantees depend linearly on the number of mixer parties but only logarithmically on the number of mixed messages. To compare with the state of the art for MixNet protocols, we notice that the Bayer and Groth [3] proof of shuffle is based on the Fiat-Shamir transform applied to a multi-round Sigma protocol, thus the security reduction degrades with the number of rounds of the underlying Sigma protocol, while the proof of shuffle in the pairing setting of Fauzi *et al.* [16] relies on new kinds of $\mathcal{D}_n$-KerMDH assumptions (proved to hold generically in the same paper) where n is the number of shuffled ciphertexts.

1.2 Related Work

Prabhakaran and Rosulek [32] introduced the first Rand-RCCA PKE in the standard model. Abstracting the scheme of [32], and solving a long-standing open problem, recently Wang *et al.* [35] introduced the first receiver-anonymous Rand-RCCA PKE. Faonio and Fiore [12] introduced a practical Rand-RCCA PKE in the random oracle model. Considering the state of the art on pairing-based Rand-RCCA PKE schemes, the most relevant works are the Rand-RCCA PKE scheme of Chase *et al.* [8], the recent works of Libert, Peters and Qian [27], and of Faonio *et al.* [13]. In Table 1 we offer a comparison, in terms of security properties and functionalities, of our schemes of Sect. 5, i.e. $\mathcal{PKE}_1, \mathcal{PKE}_2$ and $\mathcal{PKE}_3$, and the previous schemes. From a technical point of view, our schemes inherit from the scheme of [13], however, we notice that our schemes are instantiated on type-1 pairing group, while FFHR19 is instantiated on type-3 pairing group (see the next section and [14] for more details). On the other hand, our schemes are the only ones that have (almost) tight-security reductions. In Table 2 we compare the most efficient Rand-RCCA PKE schemes with ours. In particular, we instantiate $\mathcal{PKE}_1$ and $\mathcal{PKE}_2$ under DLIN assumption for type-1 pairing group ($d = 2$ and, because of the security of the benign proof system, $n = 6$) while we instantiate $\mathcal{PKE}_3$ under $\mathcal{U}_{9,4}$-TMDDH assumption. We compare the number of operations required by the three algorithms (Enc, Rand and Dec) and the size of the ciphertext. In particular, we have considered the cost of exponentiations in the source and target groups, and the number of pairings. We give only a rough estimation of the costs of $\mathcal{PKE}_2$ and $\mathcal{PKE}_3$ to provide some intuition on the considerable efficiency gap between them: their cost is derived in terms of group elements and operations needed to instantiate the proof systems for $\mathcal{PKE}_2$ (resp. $\mathcal{PKE}_3$) under $\mathcal{D}_{6,2}$-MDDH (resp. $\mathcal{U}_{9,4}$-TMDDH) assumption from [11] and [13].

We note that $\mathcal{PKE}_2$ and $\mathcal{PKE}_3$ are far from being considered practical, while $\mathcal{PKE}_1$ is considerably less efficient than [13]. Indeed, our main goal is to prove feasibility. We view our work as a potential first towards a tightly secure practical solution. For instance, while the first tightly IND-CCA secure PKE schemes were highly impractical, state-of-the-art schemes (see [17,18]) have a realistic break-even point[2]. We hope for a similar development with Rand-RCCA PKE schemes.

Our benign proof system uses the "OR-Proof" technique from [1]. We notice that, in the context of tightly-secure reductions, the same technique from [1] has been used in [21] to instantiate their (Leakage-Resilient) Ardent Quasi-Adaptive Hash Proof System. We stress that in our work, in contrast with [21], the main reason to use the technique from [1] is because of its nice linear property that, in turn, allows for *malleable* proof system.

1.3 Open Problems

Our Rand-RCCA PKE schemes require type-1 pairing groups, which are less efficient than type-3. It is natural to ask whether we can instantiate our PKE

---

[2] For the same security parameter, the work of [17,18] outperforms state-of-the-art non-tightly secure schemes like Kurosawa-Desmedt [24] around 2^{30} ciphertexts.

Table 1. Comparison of the properties of a selection of Rand-RCCA-secure PKE schemes. The symbol * indicates that the structure-preserving property of the schemes is not strict since ciphertexts contain some elements in $\mathbb{G}_T$.

PKE	Group Setting	Assumption	Struc. Pres.	Pub. Ver.	Tight
[8] CKLM12, [27] LPQ17	Type-3	SXDH	✓	✓	
[13] FFHR19	Type-3	$\mathcal{D}_{d+1,d}$-MDDH	✓*	✓	
$\mathcal{PKE}_1$	Type-1	$\mathcal{D}_{n,d}$-MDDH	✓*		✓
$\mathcal{PKE}_2$	Type-1	$\mathcal{D}_{n,d}$-MDDH	✓*	✓	✓
$\mathcal{PKE}_3$	Type-1	$\mathcal{U}_{n,d}$-TMDDH	✓*	✓	✓

Table 2. Efficiency comparison among the best Rand-RCCA-secure PKE schemes. We denote as E_i the cost of 1 exponentiation in $\mathbb{G}_i$, P the cost of computing a bilinear pairing. In the third column, we consider the cost of Enc which is almost always comparable with the cost of Rand. The first two schemes are privately verifiable, while the last four are publicly verifiable. We consider the most efficient instantiations for $\mathcal{PKE}_1, \mathcal{PKE}_2$ (DLIN), for $\mathcal{PKE}_3$ ($\mathcal{U}_{9,4}$-TMDDH) and for [13] (SXDH).

PKE	|C|	Enc ≈ Rand	Dec
[13] FFHR19 (1)	$3\mathbb{G}_1+2\mathbb{G}_2+\mathbb{G}_T$	$4E_1+5E_2+2E_T+5P$	$8E_1+4E_2+4P$
$\mathcal{PKE}_1$	$7\mathbb{G}_1+2\mathbb{G}_T$	$14E_1+2E_T+14P$	$48E_1+36E_T+49P$
[27] LPQ17	$42\mathbb{G}_1+20\mathbb{G}_2$	$79E_1+64E_2$	$1E_1+142P$
[13] FFHR19 (2)	$14\mathbb{G}_1+15\mathbb{G}_2+4\mathbb{G}_T$	$36E_1+45E_2+6E_T+5P$	$2E_1+50P$
$\mathcal{PKE}_2$	$380\mathbb{G}_1+330\mathbb{G}_T$	$\approx 180E1+110E_T+38P$	$\approx 6E_1+400P$
$\mathcal{PKE}_3$	$105\mathbb{G}_1+9\mathbb{G}_T$	$\approx 261E_1+9E_T+16P$	$\approx 6E_1 + 11P$

schemes from type-3 pairings. Unfortunately, we do not know how to do so, because it is not clear how to reconcile the adaptive partitioning technique [22] with a Rand-RCCA construction in settings with type-3 pairings (such as the one from [13]). We elaborate more on the challenges to overcome for obtaining a type-3 instantiation in [14] and leave the construction of a tightly-secure type-3 Rand-RCCA PKE scheme as an interesting open problem.

Our approach is semi-generic, as we work with pairing-based cryptography. We leave as open problem to provide a generic framework to instantiate (almost) tightly-secure Rand-RCCA-secure PKE. Possible starting points are the HPS-based frameworks of [35] for Rand-RCCA schemes and [21] for tightly-secure (LR-)CCA-secure schemes. Recently, Faonio and Russo [15] improved over the mix-net protocol of [13], giving a more efficient instantiation based on non publicly-verifiable Rand-RCCA PKE schemes; however, their construction requires a leakage-resilient scheme. We leave as open problem the extension of our analysis to tightly-secure LR-RCCA PKE schemes to extend their approach.

2 Preliminaries

A function is negligible in λ if it vanishes faster than the inverse of any polynomial in λ. We write $f(\lambda) \in \texttt{negl}(\lambda)$ when f is negligible in λ. For any bit string $\tau \in \{0,1\}^*$, we denote by $\tau[i]$ the i-th bit of τ and by $\tau_{|i}$ the bit string comprising the first i bits of τ. A symmetric (type-1) bilinear group $\mathcal{G}$ is a tuple $(q, \mathbb{G}_1, \mathbb{G}_T, e, \mathcal{P}_1)$, where $\mathbb{G}_1$ and $\mathbb{G}_T$ are groups of prime order q, the element $\mathcal{P}_1$ is a generator of $\mathbb{G}_1$, $e : \mathbb{G}_1 \times \mathbb{G}_1 \rightarrow \mathbb{G}_T$ is an efficiently computable, non-degenerate bilinear map. Let GGen be a PPT algorithm which on input 1^λ, where λ is the security parameter, returns a description of a symmetric bilinear group $\mathcal{G}$. Elements in $\mathbb{G}_i$, are denoted in implicit notation as $[a]_i := a\mathcal{P}_i$, where $i \in \{1, T\}$ and $\mathcal{P}_T := e(\mathcal{P}_1, \mathcal{P}_1)$. Every element in $\mathbb{G}_i$ can be written as $[a]_i$ for some $a \in \mathbb{Z}_q$, but note that given $[a]_i$, $a \in \mathbb{Z}_q$ is in general hard to compute (discrete logarithm problem). Given $a, b \in \mathbb{Z}_q$ we distinguish between $[ab]_i$, namely the group element whose discrete logarithm base $\mathcal{P}_i$ is ab, and $[a]_i \cdot b$, namely the execution of the multiplication of $[a]_i$ and b, and $[a]_1 \cdot [b]_1 = [a \cdot b]_T$, namely the execution of a pairing between $[a]_1$ and $[b]_1$. Sometimes, to simplify the notation, we will write $[a]$ instead of $[a]_1$ for elements in the source group. Vectors and matrices are denoted in boldface. We extend the pairing operation to vectors and matrices as $e([\mathbf{A}]_1, [\mathbf{B}]_1) = [\mathbf{A}^\top \cdot \mathbf{B}]_T$ and $e([y]_1, [\mathbf{A}]_1) = [y \cdot \mathbf{A}]_T$. Let $span(\mathbf{A})$ denote the linear span of the columns of $\mathbf{A}$. $\mathcal{D}_{n,d}$ is a matrix distribution if outputs (in probabilistic polynomial time, with overwhelming probability) matrices in $\mathbb{Z}_q^{n \times d}$.

Definition 1 (Matrix Decisional Diffie-Hellman Assumption, [11]). *The $\mathcal{D}_{n,d}$-MDDH assumption holds if for all non-uniform PPT adversaries $\mathcal{A}$,*

$$|\Pr[\mathcal{A}(\mathcal{G}, [\mathbf{A}]_1, [\mathbf{Aw}]_1) = 1] - \Pr[\mathcal{A}(\mathcal{G}, [\mathbf{A}]_1, [\mathbf{z}]_1) = 1]| \in \mathtt{negl}(\lambda),$$

where the probability is taken over $\mathcal{G} = (q, \mathbb{G}_1, \mathbb{G}_T, e, \mathcal{P}_1) \leftarrow \mathsf{GGen}(1^\lambda)$, $\mathbf{A} \leftarrow \mathcal{D}_{n,d}, \mathbf{w} \leftarrow \mathbb{Z}_q^d, [\mathbf{z}]_1 \leftarrow \mathbb{G}_1^n$ and the coin tosses of adversary $\mathcal{A}$.

For $Q \in \mathbb{N}$, $\mathbf{W} \leftarrow_\$ \mathbb{Z}_q^{d \times Q}$ and $\mathbf{U} \leftarrow_\$ \mathbb{Z}_q^{n \times Q}$, the Q-fold $\mathcal{D}_{n,d}$-MDDH assumption states that distinguishing tuples of the form $([\mathbf{A}]_1, [\mathbf{AW}]_1)$ from $([\mathbf{A}]_1, [\mathbf{U}]_1)$ is hard. That is, a challenge for the Q-fold $\mathcal{D}_{n,d}$-MDDH assumption consists of Q independent challenges of the $\mathcal{D}_{n,d}$-MDDH Assumption (with the same $\mathbf{A}$ but different randomness $\mathbf{w}$). In [11] it is shown that the two problems are equivalent, where the reduction loses at most a factor $n - d$.

Tensor Product. Let $\mathbf{a} \in \mathbb{Z}_q^n$ and $\mathbf{b} \in \mathbb{Z}_q^{n'}$, we define $\mathbf{a} \otimes \mathbf{b} \in \mathbb{Z}_q^{nn'}$ to be the tensor product between the two vectors. We can show the following property:

$$(\mathbf{A} \cdot \mathbf{R}) \otimes (\mathbf{B} \cdot \mathbf{S}) = (\mathbf{A} \otimes \mathbf{B}) \cdot (\mathbf{R} \otimes \mathbf{S}) \tag{1}$$

Lemma for Rand-RCCA Security. The main technical tool employed by [13], to which they refer as their "core lemma", roughly speaking says that, for any $\mathbf{u} \in \mathbb{Z}_q^{d+1}$, the projective hash function with hash key $\mathbf{f}, \mathbf{F}$ that maps $\mathbf{v}$ to $(\mathbf{f} + \mathbf{Fv})^\top \mathbf{u}$ is pair-wise independent with respect to the quotient set $\mathbb{Z}_q^{d+2}/span(\mathbf{E})$ when given as side information the matrix $\mathbf{FE}$ where $\mathbf{E} \in \mathbb{Z}_q^{d+2 \times d}$. We generalize their result to $\mathbf{u} \in \mathbb{Z}_q^n$ and $\mathbf{E} \in \mathbb{Z}_q^{n' \times d}$ for any $n > d$ and $n' > d + 1$. The proof of the lemma follows by reduction to the original lemma from [13] and it can be found in [14]. For the sake of clarity, in this paper we prefer to call this lemma the "Rand-RCCA lemma", rather than "core lemma" (for Rand-RCCA) as in [13], because the core technical parts of our work and theirs are different.

Lemma 1 (Rand-RCCA Lemma). *Let d be a positive integer. For any matrix $\mathbf{D} \in \mathbb{Z}_q^{n \times d}$, $\mathbf{E} \in \mathbb{Z}_q^{n' \times d}$ where $n > d$ and $n' > d + 1$, and any (possibly unbounded) adversary A:*

$$\Pr\left[\begin{array}{c} \mathbf{u} \notin span(\mathbf{D}) \\ (\mathbf{v} - \mathbf{v}^*) \notin span(\mathbf{E}) \; : \\ z = (\mathbf{f} + \mathbf{Fv})^\top \mathbf{u} \end{array} \quad \begin{array}{c} \mathbf{f} \xleftarrow{\$} \mathbb{Z}_q^n, \mathbf{F} \xleftarrow{\$} \mathbb{Z}_q^{n \times n'}, \\ (z, \mathbf{u}, \mathbf{v}) \xleftarrow{\$} A^{\mathcal{O}}(\mathbf{D}, \mathbf{E}, \mathbf{f}^\top \mathbf{D}, \mathbf{F}^\top \mathbf{D}, \mathbf{FE}) \end{array} \right] \leq \frac{n \cdot n'}{q}.$$

where the adversary outputs a single query $\mathbf{v}^*$ to $\mathcal{O}$ that returns $\mathbf{f} + \mathbf{F} \cdot \mathbf{v}^*$.

3   Non-Interactive Proof Systems (NIPS)

Definition 2 (Proof system). *Let $\mathcal{L} = \{\mathcal{L}_{pars}\}$ be a family of languages with $\mathcal{L}_{pars} \subseteq \mathcal{X}_{pars}$, and with efficiently computable witness relation $\mathcal{R}$. A non-interactive proof system (NIPS) $\mathbf{PS} = (\mathsf{PGen}, \mathsf{PPrv}, \mathsf{PVer}, \mathsf{PSim})$ for $\mathcal{L}$ consists of the following PPT algorithms:*

- $\mathsf{PGen}(1^\lambda, pars)$ *outputs a proving key ppk, a verification key psk.*
- $\mathsf{PPrv}(ppk, x, w)$, $x \in \mathcal{L}$ *and* $\mathcal{R}(x, w) = 1$, *outputs a proof π.*
- $\mathsf{PVer}(psk, x, \pi)$, $x \in \mathcal{X}$ *and a proof π, outputs a verdict $b \in \{0, 1\}$.*
- $\mathsf{PSim}(psk, x)$, $x \in \mathcal{L}$, *outputs a proof π.*

Completeness: *For all pars, all (ppk, psk) in the range of $\mathsf{PGen}(1^\lambda, pars)$, all $x \in \mathcal{L}$, and all w with $\mathcal{R}(pars, x, w) = 1$, we have $\mathsf{PVer}(psk, x, \mathsf{PPrv}(ppk, x, w)) = 1$.*

When $ppk \neq psk$ we say that the proof system is *designated verifier*. In the definition above we let the verification and proving key depend on the parameters of the relation, namely, the proof systems are *quasi-adaptive* as defined by Jutla and Roy [23]. All the NIPSs of this paper are *structure-preserving*: i.e., all the public interfaces are vectors in the source groups, all the private material is in $\mathbb{Z}_q$ and all the algorithms can be described with pairing-product equations; also, as in [13] the proof π could lie in the target group.

Benign Proof Systems. All relevant security properties of a benign NIDVPS are condensed in the following definitions, taken verbatim from [22].

Definition 3 (Benign proof system). *Let $\mathbf{PS}$ be an NIDVPS for $\mathcal{L}$ as in Definition 2, and let $\mathcal{L}^{\mathrm{sim}} = \{\mathcal{L}_{pars}^{\mathrm{sim}}\}$, $\mathcal{L}^{\mathrm{ver}} = \{\mathcal{L}_{pars}^{\mathrm{ver}}\}$, and $\mathcal{L}^{\mathrm{snd}} = \{\mathcal{L}_{pars}^{\mathrm{snd}}\}$ be families of languages. We say that $\mathbf{PS}$ is $(\mathcal{L}^{\mathrm{sim}}, \mathcal{L}^{\mathrm{ver}}, \mathcal{L}^{\mathrm{snd}})$-benign if the following properties hold:*

(Perfect) zero-knowledge. *For all pars, all (ppk, psk) that lie in the range of $\mathsf{PGen}(1^\lambda, pars)$, and all $x \in \mathcal{L}$ and w with $\mathcal{R}(pars, x, w) = 1$, we have that the distribution $\mathsf{PPrv}(ppk, x, w)$ is equivalent to $\mathsf{PSim}(psk, x)$.*

(Statistical) $(\mathcal{L}^{\mathrm{sim}}, \mathcal{L}^{\mathrm{ver}}, \mathcal{L}^{\mathrm{snd}})$-soundness. *Let $\mathbf{Exp}_{A, \mathbf{PS}}^{\mathrm{snd}}$ be the game played by A in Fig. 1. Let $\mathbf{Adv}_{\mathbf{PS}, A}^{\mathrm{snd}}(\lambda)$ be the probability that $\mathbf{Exp}_{A, \mathbf{PS}}^{\mathrm{snd}}(\lambda) = 1$. We require that for all (possibly unbounded) A that only make a polynomial number of oracle queries, $\mathbf{Adv}_{\mathbf{PS}, A}^{\mathrm{snd}}(\lambda)$ is negligible.*

Non-Interactive Zero-Knowledge Proof Systems. We adapt Definition 2 for the case of publicly verifiable proof systems by requiring the prover key and the verification key to be identical, and we refer to such key as the *common reference string*. (Nontrivial) proof systems with this syntax are commonly called zero-knowledge proof systems (NIZKs).

Notice that in the syntax of proof system we give in Definition 3 both the simulator PSim and the verifier PVer receive as input the verification key, while in the usual definition of NIZK the simulator receives a simulation trapdoor. This difference is only syntactical. We say that a NIZK **PS** for $\mathcal{L}$ is *adaptively sound* if it is statistically $(\emptyset, \mathcal{L}, \emptyset)$-sound according to Definition 3.

Definition 4. *Let **PS** be a NIPS for $\mathcal{L}$ as in Definition 2, we say that **PS** is (ϵ, T)-composable zero-knowledge if there exists a PPT algorithm $\overline{\mathsf{PGen}}$ such that:*

- *For all pars, the distributions induced by the first output of $\mathsf{PGen}(1^\lambda, pars)$ and $\overline{\mathsf{PGen}}(1^\lambda, pars)$ are ϵ-close for any adversary with running time T.*
- *For all pars, all (ppk, psk) that lie in the range of $\overline{\mathsf{PGen}}(1^\lambda, pars)$, and all $x \in \mathcal{L}$ and w with $\mathcal{R}(pars, x, w) = 1$, we have that the distribution $\mathsf{PPrv}(ppk, x, w)$ is equivalent to $\mathsf{PSim}(psk, x)$.*

Malleable NIPS. We use the definitional framework of Chase *et al.* [8] for malleable proof systems. For simplicity of the exposition we consider only the unary case for transformations (see the aforementioned paper for more details). Moreover, we adapt their definition to the quasi-adaptive setting by having a transformation that depends on the *pars*. Let $T = (T_{\mathsf{el}}, T_{\mathsf{wit}})$ be a pair of efficiently computable functions, that we refer to as a *transformation*.

Definition 5 (Admissible transformation). *We say that an efficient relation $\mathcal{R}$ is closed under a transformation $T = (T_{\mathsf{el}}, T_{\mathsf{wit}})$ if for any $(pars, x, w) \in \mathcal{R}$ the pair $(pars, T_{\mathsf{el}}(pars, x), T_{\mathsf{wit}}(w)) \in \mathcal{R}$. If $\mathcal{R}$ is closed under T then we say that T is* admissible *for $\mathcal{R}$. Let $\mathcal{T}$ be a set of transformations, if for every $T \in \mathcal{T}$, T is admissible for $\mathcal{R}$, then $\mathcal{T}$ is an* allowable *set of transformations.*

Definition 6 (Malleable NIPS). *Let **PS** be an NIPS for $\mathcal{L}$ as in Definition 2, and let $\mathsf{PEvl}(ppk, x, \pi, T)$ be a PPT algorithm that takes as inputs ppk, an instance x, a proof π, and a transformation $T \in \mathcal{T}$, and it outputs a proof π'. We say that **PS** and PEvl form a* malleable proof system *for $\mathcal{L}$ with set $\mathcal{T}$ of allowable transformations for $\mathcal{R}$, if, for all pars, (ppk, psk) that lie in the range of $\mathsf{PGen}(1^\lambda, pars)$, all $T \in \mathcal{T}$, and all x, π we have $\mathsf{PVer}(psk, T_{\mathsf{el}}(pars, x), \pi') = 1$ if and only if $\mathsf{PVer}(psk, x, \pi) = 1$.*

Definition 7 (Derivation Privacy). *Let **PS** be a malleable NIPS for $\mathcal{L}$ with relation $\mathcal{R}$ and an allowable set of transformations $\mathcal{T}$ and corresponding PEvl. We say that **PS** is* derivation private *if for any PPT adversary $\mathcal{A}$:*

$$\mathbf{Adv}_{\mathcal{A},\mathbf{PS}}^{\mathtt{der-priv}}(\lambda) := \left| \Pr\left[\mathbf{Exp}_{\mathcal{A},\mathbf{PS}}^{\mathtt{der-priv}}(\lambda) = 1 \right] - \tfrac{1}{2} \right| \in \mathsf{negl}(\lambda)$$

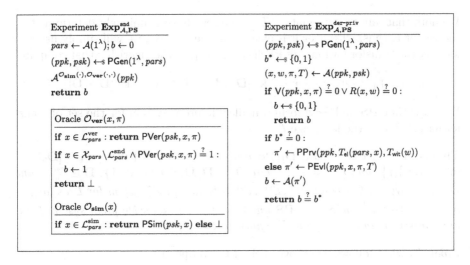

Fig. 1. Security experiments for benign soundness and derivation privacy of NIPS.

where **Exp**$^{\text{der-priv}}$ *is the game described in Fig. 1. Moreover we say that* **PS** *is* perfectly *(resp.* statistically*) derivation private when for any (possibly unbounded) adversary the advantage above is 0 (resp. negligible).*

Similarly to [13], we require a technical property to show re-randomizability of our encryption scheme that we call *tightness for proofs*, which roughly speaking says that it is hard to find a proof for a valid instance that does not lie in the set of the proofs created by the prover. For space reasons, we give more details in [14].

3.1 Our Malleable NIDVPS Based on Type-1 Pairing

Let $\mathbf{D} \in \mathbb{Z}_q^{n \times d}$. We show that the following **PS** is a NIPS for $\mathcal{L} = span([\mathbf{D}]_1)$:

- PGen(*pars*) parses *pars* as $\text{prm}_G, [\mathbf{D}]_1 \in \mathbb{G}_1^{n \times d}$ where $n, d \in \mathbb{N}$, samples $\mathbf{k} \leftarrow\!\!\$\ \mathbb{Z}_q^{n^2}$, let $\mathbf{I}_n$ be the identity matrix of dimension n, set:

$$psk \leftarrow \mathbf{k} \quad \text{and} \quad ppk \leftarrow (\mathbf{k}^\top [\mathbf{D} \otimes \mathbf{I}_n]_1, \mathbf{k}^\top [\mathbf{I}_n \otimes \mathbf{D}]_1, \mathbf{k}^\top [\mathbf{D} \otimes \mathbf{D}]_T)$$

- PPrv($ppk, [\mathbf{u}]_1, \mathbf{r}$) computes $\pi \leftarrow \mathbf{k}^\top [\mathbf{D} \otimes \mathbf{D}]_T \cdot (\mathbf{r} \otimes \mathbf{r})$ for $[\mathbf{u}]_1 = [\mathbf{D}]_1 \mathbf{r}$
- PSim($psk, [\mathbf{u}]_1$) computes $\pi \leftarrow \mathbf{k}^\top ([\mathbf{u}]_1 \otimes [\mathbf{u}]_1)$
- PVer($psk, [\mathbf{u}]_1, \pi$) returns 1 if and only if $\mathbf{k}^\top ([\mathbf{u}]_1 \otimes [\mathbf{u}]_1) \overset{?}{=} \pi$

The first two vectors in the *ppk* are necessary to enable for the malleability of the proof system. While the third element of the public key could be efficiently derived from the previous two, we decide to publish it to speed up re-randomization and proving time. Consider the set $\mathcal{T}$ of admissible transformations for $\mathbb{Z}_q^n$:

$$\mathcal{T} = \{T : T_{\text{el}}(pars, [\mathbf{u}]_1) = [\mathbf{u}]_1 + [\mathbf{D}]_1 \hat{\mathbf{r}}; \ T_{\text{wit}}(\mathbf{r}) = \mathbf{r} + \hat{\mathbf{r}}\} \tag{2}$$

We note that any transformation T in the set above is uniquely determined by the vector $\hat{\mathbf{r}}$, thus, whenever it is clear from the context, we will simply use $\hat{\mathbf{r}}$ to identify the transformation. Let $\mathsf{PEvl}(ppk, \hat{\mathbf{r}}, [\mathbf{u}]_1, \pi)$ the algorithm that computes

$$\hat{\pi} \leftarrow \pi + \mathbf{k}^\top [\mathbf{I}_n \otimes \mathbf{D}]_1 \cdot [\mathbf{u} \otimes \hat{\mathbf{r}}]_1 + \mathbf{k}^\top [\mathbf{D} \otimes \mathbf{I}_n]_1 \cdot [\hat{\mathbf{r}} \otimes \mathbf{u}]_1 + \mathbf{k}^\top [\mathbf{D} \otimes \mathbf{D}]_T \cdot \hat{\mathbf{r}} \otimes \hat{\mathbf{r}}.$$

We show that **PS** and PEvl form a malleable proof system for the set of transformation T and the language $\mathcal{L}$.

Theorem 1. *Let* $\mathcal{L} = span([\mathbf{D}]_1)$ *and let* $\mathcal{L}^{\mathrm{snd}} = \mathcal{L}^{\mathrm{sim}} = \{[\mathbf{u}]_1 : [\mathbf{u}]_1 = [\mathbf{D}_0]_1 \mathbf{r} \vee [\mathbf{u}]_1 = [\mathbf{D}_1]_1 \mathbf{r}\}$, *and* $\mathcal{L}^{\mathrm{ver}} = \mathbb{Z}_q^n$, *where* $\mathbf{D}_i = \mathbf{D}\|\bar{\mathbf{D}}_i$ *for* $i \in \{0,1\}$, $\mathbf{D} \in \mathbb{Z}_q^{n \times d}$ *and* $\bar{\mathbf{D}}_0, \bar{\mathbf{D}}_1 \in \mathbb{Z}_q^{n \times d'}$. **PS** *is a* $(\mathcal{L}^{\mathrm{sim}}, \mathcal{L}^{\mathrm{ver}}, \mathcal{L}^{\mathrm{snd}})$*-benign proof system for* $\mathcal{L}$ *as long as* $n^2 > 2n \cdot d + 2d'^2$, *moreover,* **PS** *and* PEvl *form a malleable proof system for* $\mathcal{L}$ *and the set of transformation* T *defined in Eq. (2).*

Proof. In what follows, we prove each of the properties.

Completeness and Malleability. Our benign proof system is complete, as by Eq. (1) for any $\mathbf{u} = \mathbf{D}\mathbf{r}$ we have $(\mathbf{u} \otimes \mathbf{u}) = (\mathbf{D} \otimes \mathbf{D}) \cdot (\mathbf{r} \otimes \mathbf{r})$. We prove that our scheme is *malleable* (Definition 6) with respect to set of transformation T defined in Eq. (2), i.e., we prove that for any $[\mathbf{u}]$ and any $\hat{\mathbf{r}}$, a proof π for $[\mathbf{u}]$ verifies if and only if the proof $\hat{\pi}$ obtained executing PEvl on π and the transformation $\hat{\mathbf{r}}$ verifies for $[\mathbf{u} + \mathbf{D}\hat{\mathbf{r}}]$. For the first direction of the implication:

$$\begin{aligned}
\hat{\pi} &= \pi + \mathbf{k}^\top (\mathbf{I}_n \otimes \mathbf{D}) \cdot (\mathbf{u} \otimes \hat{\mathbf{r}}) + \mathbf{k}^\top (\mathbf{D} \otimes \mathbf{I}_n) \cdot (\hat{\mathbf{r}} \otimes \mathbf{u}) + \mathbf{k}^\top (\mathbf{D} \otimes \mathbf{D}) \cdot (\hat{\mathbf{r}} \otimes \hat{\mathbf{r}}) \\
&= \mathbf{k}^\top (\mathbf{u} \otimes \mathbf{u}) + \mathbf{k}^\top ((\mathbf{I}_n \mathbf{u}) \otimes (\mathbf{D}\hat{\mathbf{r}})) + \mathbf{k}^\top ((\mathbf{D}\hat{\mathbf{r}}) \otimes (\mathbf{I}_n \mathbf{u})) + \mathbf{k}^\top ((\mathbf{D}\hat{\mathbf{r}}) \otimes (\mathbf{D}\hat{\mathbf{r}})) \\
&= \mathbf{k}^\top (\mathbf{u} \otimes \mathbf{u} + \mathbf{u} \otimes (\mathbf{D}\hat{\mathbf{r}}) + (\mathbf{D}\hat{\mathbf{r}}) \otimes \mathbf{u} + (\mathbf{D}\hat{\mathbf{r}}) \otimes (\mathbf{D}\hat{\mathbf{r}})) \\
&= \mathbf{k}^\top ((\mathbf{u} + \mathbf{D}\hat{\mathbf{r}}) \otimes (\mathbf{u} + \mathbf{D}\hat{\mathbf{r}}))
\end{aligned}$$

We highlight that the second equation holds because of the definition of π and (1), while the third equation is obtained by grouping the previous line by $\mathbf{k}^\top$. The sequence of equations above also proves the other direction; indeed, if $\pi \neq \mathbf{k}^\top \mathbf{u} \otimes \mathbf{u}$, then $\hat{\pi} \neq \mathbf{k}^\top (\mathbf{u} + \mathbf{D}\hat{\mathbf{r}}) \otimes (\mathbf{u} + \mathbf{D}\hat{\mathbf{r}})$.

Soundness. We recall that $\mathbf{D} \in \mathbb{Z}_q^{n \times d}, \bar{\mathbf{D}}_i \in \mathbb{Z}_q^{n \times d'}$. If we only consider the view of the adversary given the verification key and the outputs of the simulation oracle we have that the proving key is uniformly distributed over a set of cardinality $q^{n^2 - 2nd - 2d'^2}$. Therefore, we require that $n^2 > 2n \cdot d + 2d'^2$ holds.

To see this, think of $\mathbf{k}$ as a formal variable and notice that publishing $\mathbf{k}^\top (\mathbf{D} \otimes \mathbf{I}_n)$ counts for $n \cdot d$ equations; also, $\mathbf{k}^\top (\mathbf{I}_n \otimes \mathbf{D})$ counts for $n \cdot d$ equations which in total gives us $2n \cdot d$ equations. Moreover, in order to simulate proofs for $[\mathbf{u}]_1 \in span([\mathbf{D}_i])$ the oracle gives away, at the worst case, the equations $\mathbf{k}^\top (\bar{\mathbf{D}}_i \otimes \bar{\mathbf{D}}_i)$ which count for d'^2 equations for each $i \in \{0,1\}$ which sum up to $2d'^2$ equations in total. Indeed, expanding $\mathbf{k}^\top (\mathbf{D}_i \otimes \mathbf{D}_i)$, we obtain $\mathbf{k}^\top (\mathbf{D} \otimes \mathbf{D}|\bar{\mathbf{D}}_i \otimes \mathbf{D}|\mathbf{D} \otimes \bar{\mathbf{D}}_i|\bar{\mathbf{D}}_i \otimes \bar{\mathbf{D}}_i)$. Now $\mathbf{k}^\top (\bar{\mathbf{D}}_i \otimes \mathbf{D})$ and $\mathbf{k}^\top (\mathbf{D} \otimes \bar{\mathbf{D}}_i)$ can be computed given the proving key and $\mathbf{D}_0, \mathbf{D}_1$. In fact, when we compute

$\mathbf{k}^\top (\mathbf{D} \otimes \mathbf{I}) (\mathbf{I} \otimes \bar{\mathbf{D}}_i)$, we obtain $\mathbf{k}^\top (\mathbf{DI} \otimes \mathbf{I}\bar{\mathbf{D}}_i) = \mathbf{k}^\top (\mathbf{D} \otimes \bar{\mathbf{D}}_i)$. And in a similar way, we can compute $\mathbf{k}^\top (\bar{\mathbf{D}}_i \otimes \mathbf{D})$. In total, we are giving up $2n \cdot d + 2d'^2$ equations and the length of our key k is n^2.

Notice that the adversary can gather additional information about the proving key $\mathbf{k}$ through the verification oracle. Indeed, whenever it sends a query $([\mathbf{u}]_1, \pi)$ with $[\mathbf{u}]_1 \in \mathcal{L}^{\mathrm{ver}} \setminus \mathcal{L}^{\mathrm{snd}}$ either it wins the security game or the adversary learns that $\pi \neq \mathbf{k}^\top [\mathbf{u}]_1 \otimes [\mathbf{u}]_1$.

Consider the hybrid experiment $\mathbf{H}_j$ where the first j-th queries ($[\mathbf{u}]_1, \pi)$ to the verification oracle with $[\mathbf{u}]_1 \notin \mathcal{L}^{\mathrm{snd}}$ are answered with 0, in particular, the bit b is left unmodified, while the remaining queries are handled as in the soundness experiment. Clearly, $\mathbf{H}_0$ is the original experiment, while $\mathbf{H}_Q$ where Q is an upper bound on the number of verification oracle queries made by the adversary is a trivial experiment where the adversary cannot win (since the bit b will never be set to 1), thus $\Pr[\mathbf{H}_Q = 1] = 0$. The distinguishing event between two consecutive hybrids is the event that the adversary wins the soundness experiment at the j-th query, which happens with probability $1/q^{n^2-2nd+2d'^2} \leq 1/q$, as it is the same as the event of guessing a uniformly random vector from a subspace of dimension $n^2 - 2nd + 2d'^2$ of $\mathbb{Z}_q^{n^2}$, thus $\Pr[\mathbf{H}_j = 1] \leq \Pr[\mathbf{H}_{j+1} = 1] + 1/q$. Finally, by the triangular equation and noticing that Q is polynomial in the security parameter we can conclude our proof of soundness.

Derivation Privacy and Zero-Knowledge. The scheme is perfectly derivation private and zero-knowledge. For the former, notice that, for any $\hat{\mathbf{r}}$, we have that $\mathsf{PPrv}(ppk, [\mathbf{u}+\mathbf{D}\hat{\mathbf{r}}]_1, \mathbf{r}+\hat{\mathbf{r}}) = \mathbf{k}^\top [\mathbf{D}\otimes\mathbf{D}]_T \cdot ((\mathbf{r}+\hat{\mathbf{r}})\otimes(\mathbf{r}+\hat{\mathbf{r}})) = \mathsf{PEvl}(ppk, \pi, \hat{\mathbf{r}})$. For the latter, given an instance $[\mathbf{u}]_1$ such that $[\mathbf{u}]_1 = [\mathbf{D}]_1\mathbf{r}$, we have that $\mathsf{PSim}(psk, [\mathbf{u}]_1) = \mathbf{k}^\top ([\mathbf{u}]_1 \otimes [\mathbf{u}]_1) = \mathbf{k}^\top ([\mathbf{Dr}]_1 \otimes [\mathbf{Dr}]_1) = \mathsf{PPrv}(ppk, [\mathbf{u}]_1, \mathbf{r})$.

4 Rand RCCA PKE for Multi-users and Multi-Ciphertexts

A re-randomizable PKE (Rand-PKE) scheme $\mathcal{PKE}$ is a tuple of five algorithms: (i) The algorithm Setup upon input the security parameter 1^λ produces public parameters prm which include the description of the message and ciphertext space $\mathcal{M}, \mathcal{C}$; (ii) The algorithm KGen upon input prm, outputs a key pair (pk, sk); (iii) The algorithm Enc upon inputs pk and a message $\mathsf{M} \in \mathcal{M}$, outputs a ciphertext $\mathsf{C} \in \mathcal{C}$; (iv) The algorithm Dec upon input sk and a ciphertext C, outputs a message $\mathsf{M} \in \mathcal{M}$ or an error symbol $\perp$; (v) The algorithm Rand upon inputs pk and a ciphertext C, outputs another ciphertext C'.

Definition 8 (multi-user and multi-ciphertext Replayable CCA Security). *Consider the experiment $\mathbf{Exp}^{\mathrm{mRCCA}}$ in Fig. 2, with parameters λ, an adversary $\mathcal{A}$, and a PKE scheme $\mathcal{PKE}$. We say that $\mathcal{PKE}$ is indistinguishable secure under replayable chosen-ciphertext attacks in the multi-user and multi-ciphertext setting (mRCCA-secure) if for any PPT adversary $\mathcal{A}$:*

$$\mathbf{Adv}^{\mathrm{mRCCA}}_{\mathcal{A},\mathcal{PKE}}(\lambda) := \left| \Pr\left[\mathbf{Exp}^{\mathrm{mRCCA}}_{\mathcal{A},\mathcal{PKE}}(\lambda) = 1\right] - \frac{1}{2} \right| \in \mathtt{negl}(\lambda).$$

Experiment $\mathbf{Exp}_{\mathcal{A},\mathcal{PKE}}^{\text{mRCCA}}(\lambda)$

$\mathrm{prm} \leftarrow \mathsf{Setup}(1^\lambda); b^* \leftarrow_\$ \{0,1\}$

$b' \leftarrow \mathcal{A}^{\mathcal{O}_{\text{kgen}}(), \mathcal{O}_{\text{enc}}(\cdot,\cdot,\cdot), \mathcal{O}_{\text{dec}}(\cdot)}(\mathrm{prm})$

return $b' \stackrel{?}{=} b^*$

Oracle $\mathcal{O}_{\text{kgen}}()$	Oracle $\mathcal{O}_{\text{enc}}(j, M_0, M_1)$	Oracle $\mathcal{O}_{\text{dec}}(j, C)$
$z \leftarrow z+1$	**if** $j \notin [z]$:	$M \leftarrow \mathsf{Dec}(\mathsf{sk}_j, C)$
$\mathcal{Q}_z \leftarrow \mathsf{DisjointSet}()$	**return** $\perp$	$\mathcal{J} \leftarrow \mathcal{Q}_j.\mathsf{find}(M)$
$(\mathsf{pk}_z, \mathsf{sk}_z) \leftarrow \mathsf{KGen}(\mathrm{prm})$	$\mathcal{Q}_j.\mathsf{union}(\{M_0, M_1\})$	**if** $\mathcal{J} \neq \perp$:
return pk_z	$C \leftarrow_\$ \mathsf{Enc}(\mathsf{pk}_j, M_{b^*})$	**return** $\diamond_{\mathcal{J}}$
	return C	**return** M

Fig. 2. The multi-user and multi-ciphertext RCCA Security Experiment.

In Fig. 2, for each user j we define $\mathcal{Q}_j$ to be a partition of the set of the challenge messages sent to the encryption oracle for the user j. To do so we use the classical "*Disjoint-Set*" (also called "*Union-Find*") data structure from Tarjan [34]. Whenever two challenge messages are submitted to the encryption oracle, indeed, we merge the sets to which they belong so that a future call to the guarded decryption oracle behaves consistently. This allows us to express in Fig. 2 the syntax of the encryption and the guarded decryption oracle in terms of three operations: DisjointSet() that allows initializing the partition (initially empty), union(S) that adds to the partition the minimal subset of the challenge messages that contains the messages in S meanwhile maintaining invariant the partition property (i.e. a collection of disjoint sets), and find(M) that returns the set in the partition where M belongs to, or $\perp$ if M is not in the set of challenge messages of the user j. We confirm that our definition is indeed the right multi-user and multi-ciphertext extension of the IND-RCCA definition of [7] by showing that our definition tightly implies the UC-RCCA definition of the same paper[3]. For space reasons, we recall the definition of the ideal functionality $\mathcal{F}_{\text{RPKE}}$ which formalizes the notion of replay security for PKE scheme in the universal composability model in [14], where we also give the proof of the theorem below.

Theorem 2. *Let* $\mathcal{PKE}$ *be a PKE scheme with message space* $\mathcal{D}$. *There exists a simulator* S *such that for any static-corruption environment* $\mathcal{Z}$ *with running time* $T_{\mathcal{Z}}$ *there exists an adversary* $\mathcal{B}$ *whose running time is* $O(T_{\mathcal{Z}}(\lambda))$ *such that:*

$$\left| \Pr\left[\text{REAL}_{\mathcal{Z}, \Pi_{\mathcal{PKE}}}(\lambda) = 1\right] - \Pr\left[\text{IDEAL}_{\mathcal{Z}, \mathsf{S}}^{\mathcal{F}_{\text{RPKE}}}(\lambda) = 1\right] \right| \leq 2\mathbf{Adv}_{\mathcal{B}, \mathcal{PKE}}^{\text{mumc}-\text{RCCA}}(\lambda) + \frac{T_{\mathcal{Z}}}{|\mathcal{D}|}$$

For space reasons, we only informally introduce the notions of perfect re-randomizability and public verifiability, and give more details in [14]. For the notion of perfect re-randomizability, we consider the definition given in [13] which consists of three conditions: (i) the re-randomization of a valid ciphertext and a

---

[3] In [7], the IND-RCCA notion implies the UC-RCCA notion with a loss of security that is proportional to the running time of the environment.

fresh ciphertext (for the same message) are equivalently distributed; (ii) the re-randomization procedure maintains correctness, i.e., the randomized ciphertext and the original decrypt to the same value, and in particular, invalid ciphertexts keep being invalid; (iii) it is hard to find a valid ciphertext that is not in the support of the encryption scheme. A PKE scheme is publicly verifiable if the validity of the ciphertexts can be checked only using public material.

5 Our Rand-RCCA PKE Scheme

$\mathsf{Setup}(1^\lambda)$

$\mathrm{prm}_G = (q, \mathbb{G}_1, \mathbb{G}_T, e, \mathcal{P}_1) \leftarrow_\$ \mathsf{GGen}(1^\lambda)$

$\mathcal{M} \leftarrow \mathbb{G}_1; \ \mathcal{C} \leftarrow \mathbb{G}_1^{n+2} \times \mathbb{G}_T \times \mathcal{P}$

$\mathrm{prm} \leftarrow (\mathrm{prm}_G, \mathcal{M}, \mathcal{C})$

return prm

$\mathsf{KGen}(\mathrm{prm})$

$\mathbf{D} \leftarrow_\$ \mathcal{D}_{n,d}, \mathbf{a} \leftarrow_\$ \mathbb{Z}_q^n$

$\mathbf{D}^* \leftarrow (\mathbf{D}^\top, (\mathbf{a}^\top \mathbf{D})^\top)^\top$

$\mathbf{f} \leftarrow_\$ \mathbb{Z}_q^n, \mathbf{F} \leftarrow_\$ \mathbb{Z}_q^{n \times n+1}$

$pars \leftarrow (\mathrm{prm}_G, [\mathbf{D}]_1)$

$ppk, psk \leftarrow \mathsf{PGen}(pars)$

$pk \leftarrow ([\mathbf{D}^*]_1, [\mathbf{f}^\top \mathbf{D}]_T, [\mathbf{F}^\top \mathbf{D}]_1, [\mathbf{FD}^*]_1, ppk)$

$sk \leftarrow (\mathbf{a}, \mathbf{f}, \mathbf{F}, psk)$

return (pk, sk)

$\mathsf{Enc}(pk, [\mathsf{M}]_1)$

$\mathbf{r} \leftarrow_\$ \mathbb{Z}_q^d$

$[\mathbf{u}]_1 \leftarrow [\mathbf{D}]_1 \cdot \mathbf{r}, \pi \leftarrow \mathsf{PPrv}(ppk, [\mathbf{u}]_1, \mathbf{r})$

$[p]_1 \leftarrow [\mathbf{a}^\top \mathbf{D}]_1 \cdot \mathbf{r} + [\mathsf{M}]_1$

$[\mathbf{x}]_1 \leftarrow ([\mathbf{u}^\top]_1, [p]_1)^\top$

$[y]_T \leftarrow \left([\mathbf{f}^\top \mathbf{D}]_T + e([\mathbf{x}]_1^\top, [\mathbf{F}^\top \mathbf{D}]_1)\right) \cdot \mathbf{r}$

return $C := ([\mathbf{x}]_1, [y]_T, \pi)$

$\mathsf{Dec}(sk, C)$

parse C as $([\mathbf{x}]_1, [y]_T, \pi)$

parse $[\mathbf{x}^\top]_1$ as $([\mathbf{u}^\top]_1, [p]_1)$

$[\mathsf{M}]_1 \leftarrow [p]_1 - [\mathbf{a}^\top \mathbf{u}]_1$

$[y']_T \leftarrow \mathbf{f}^\top e([1]_1, [\mathbf{u}]_1) + e(\mathbf{F}[\mathbf{x}]_1, [\mathbf{u}]_1)$

$b_1 \leftarrow [y']_T \overset{?}{=} [y]_T, \ b_2 \leftarrow \mathsf{PVer}(psk, [\mathbf{u}]_1, \pi)$

if $b_1 \wedge b_2$ **return** $[\mathsf{M}]_1$ **else** $\perp$

$\mathsf{Rand}(pk, C)$

parse C as $([\mathbf{x}]_1, [y]_T, \pi),$ parse $[\mathbf{x}^\top]_1$ as $([\mathbf{u}^\top]_1, [p]_1)$

$\hat{\mathbf{r}} \leftarrow_\$ \mathbb{Z}_q^d, [\hat{\mathbf{x}}]_1 \leftarrow [\mathbf{x}]_1 + [\mathbf{D}^*]_1 \cdot \hat{\mathbf{r}}$

$[\hat{y}]_T \leftarrow [y]_T + [\mathbf{f}^\top \mathbf{D}]_T \cdot \hat{\mathbf{r}} + e([\mathbf{x}]_1, [\mathbf{F}^\top \mathbf{D}]_1 \cdot \hat{\mathbf{r}}) + e([\mathbf{FD}^*]_1 \cdot \hat{\mathbf{r}}, [\hat{\mathbf{u}}]_1)$

$\hat{\pi} \leftarrow \mathsf{PEvl}(ppk, [\mathbf{u}]_1, \pi, \hat{\mathbf{r}})$

return $\hat{C} := ([\hat{\mathbf{x}}]_1, [\hat{y}]_T, \hat{\pi})$

Fig. 3. Rand-RCCA PKE scheme $\mathcal{PKE}$ based on the $\mathcal{D}_{n,d}$-MDDH assumption in type-1 bilinear groups. $\mathcal{P}$ is the support of the proofs for **PS**.

We present our scheme in Fig. 3. With the goal of improving readability for developers, all the operations (and in particular the pairing operations) in the figure are described explicitly using e for the pairing and $\cdot$ for the exponentiations. The scheme can be summarized as a type-1 pairing group version of the scheme in [13] where we additionally append a benign proof to prove almost tight-security. The main technical component from [13] to obtain RCCA security is the *consistency check* at decryption time which checks that $[y]_T \overset{?}{=} \mathbf{f}^\top [\mathbf{u}]_T + [\mathbf{x}]_1^\top \mathbf{F}^\top [\mathbf{u}]_1$

Perfect Re-Randomizability. The proof of perfect re-randomizability follows from [13] and the derivation privacy of **PS**. Here we highlight the following lemma, whose proof is in [14].

Lemma 2. *For any* $[\mathbf{x}]_1$ *and* $\hat{\mathbf{r}}$, *let* $[\hat{\mathbf{x}}]_1 = [\mathbf{x}]_1 + [\mathbf{D}^*]_1\hat{\mathbf{r}}$, *we have that:*

$$(\mathbf{f}^\top + [\hat{\mathbf{x}}]_1^\top \mathbf{F}^\top)[\hat{\mathbf{u}}]_1 = (\mathbf{f}^\top + [\mathbf{x}]_1^\top \mathbf{F}^\top)[\mathbf{u}]_1 + [\mathbf{f}^\top \mathbf{D}]_T \cdot \hat{\mathbf{r}}$$
$$+ e([\mathbf{x}]_1, [\mathbf{F}^\top \mathbf{D}]_1 \cdot \hat{\mathbf{r}}) + e([\mathbf{F}\mathbf{D}^*]_1 \cdot \hat{\mathbf{r}}, [\hat{\mathbf{u}}]_1)$$

The correctness of $\mathcal{PKE}$ follows from the lemma above and the fact that **PS** and PEvl form a malleable proof system. More details are in [14].

Security. We prove that the security of the scheme reduces to the $\mathcal{D}_{n,d}$-MDDH assumption. Below we state the main theorem.

Theorem 3. *For every PPT adversary $\mathcal{A}$ that makes at most Q_{Enc} encryption and Q_{Dec} decryption queries, there exist adversaries $\mathcal{B}^{\mathrm{mddh}}$, $\mathcal{B}^{\mathrm{snd}}$ with similar running time $T(\mathcal{B}^{\mathrm{mddh}}) \approx T(\mathcal{B}^{\mathrm{snd}}) \approx T(\mathcal{A}) + (Q_{\mathsf{Enc}} + Q_{\mathsf{Dec}}) \cdot \mathrm{poly}(\lambda)$, where $\mathrm{poly}(\lambda)$ is a polynomial independent of $T(\mathcal{A})$, and such that*

$$\mathbf{Adv}_{\mathcal{A},\mathcal{PKE}}^{\mathrm{RCCA}}(\lambda) \leq O\left(d \log Q_{\mathsf{Enc}}\right) \cdot \mathbf{Adv}_{\mathbb{G}_1,\mathcal{D}_{n,d},\mathcal{B}^{\mathrm{mddh}}}^{\mathrm{MDDH}}(\lambda)$$
$$+ \log Q_{\mathsf{Enc}} \cdot \mathbf{Adv}_{\mathcal{B}^{\mathrm{snd}},\mathbf{PS}}^{\mathrm{snd}}(\lambda) + O\left(\frac{n^2 Q_{\mathsf{Dec}} Q_{\mathsf{Enc}} \log Q_{\mathsf{Enc}}}{q}\right).$$

Proof. We give a proof only for the single-user, multi-ciphertext case, i.e. when the adversary calls the key generation oracle only once. The proof can be easily generalized[4] to the multi-user case almost equivalently to [4,18].

To simplify the notation, since we are in the single-user setting, we omit the index j (which specifies the user) from both encryption and decryption queries. We let $\mathbf{G}_0$ be the $\mathbf{Exp}_{\mathcal{A},\mathcal{PKE}}^{\mathrm{mRCCA}}$ experiment, and we denote with ϵ_i the advantage of $\mathcal{A}$ to win $\mathbf{G}_i$, i.e. $\epsilon_i := |\Pr[\mathbf{G}_i = 1] - \frac{1}{2}|$.

The games keep track of the number of challenge ciphertexts produced. Specifically, let ctr be a variable that counts the number of challenge ciphertexts output by the encryption oracle: ctr is set to 0 at the beginning of the games and, whenever the adversary calls the encryption oracle, it is increased.

Game $\mathbf{G}_1$. This game is identical to the previous one, but the encryption oracle computes the values $[y]_T$ and $[p]$ using secret keys (instead of public keys). Specifically, upon the j-th query to the encryption oracle, the game computes the ciphertext $\mathsf{C}_j = ([\mathbf{x}_j], [y_j]_T, \pi_j)$ as described by the encryption procedure,

---

[4] We rely on the self-reducibility of the MDDH assumption: in particular, we can generate m different matrices $\mathbf{D}_j$ (one for each user) from one single challenge of the (many-fold) MDDH-assumption and adapt accordingly the ciphertexts, namely, by mapping the ciphertext for the j-th user through the same linear transformation that maps the MDDH-challenge matrix to the matrix $\mathbf{D}_j$.

but where we compute $[y_j]_T \leftarrow \mathbf{f}^\top[\mathbf{u}_j] + [\mathbf{x}_j]^\top \mathbf{F}^\top[\mathbf{u}_j]$ and $[p_j] \leftarrow \mathbf{a}^\top[\mathbf{u}_j] + [\mathsf{M}_{j,b^*}]$. By linearity, this game is perfectly equivalent to the previous one, thus $\epsilon_1 = \epsilon_0$.

Game $\mathbf{G}_2$. This game is identical to the previous one, but the encryption oracle simulates the benign proofs π. We rely on the perfect zero-knowledge of the benign proof system. The reduction is standard, therefore we omit it. Since the proof system satisfies perfect zero-knowledge we have $\epsilon_2 = \epsilon_1$.

Game $\mathbf{G}_3$. At the very beginning, the game additionally samples matrices $\bar{\mathbf{D}}_b \leftarrow_\$$ $\mathbb{Z}_q^{n \times d}$ for $b \in \{0, 1\}$, and sets $\mathbf{D}_b \leftarrow (\mathbf{D}|\bar{\mathbf{D}}_b)$. The encryption oracle in this game samples $[\mathbf{u}]$ from the span of $[\mathbf{D}_0]$. We apply a standard reduction to the Q_{Enc}-fold $\mathcal{D}_{n,d}$-MDDH assumption, twice, and we prove that no adversary can distinguish this game from the previous one: we first tightly switch the vectors in the challenge ciphertexts from the span of $[\mathbf{D}]$ to uniformly random vectors of $\mathbb{G}_1^n$; next, we use the Q_{Enc}-fold $\mathcal{D}_{n,2d}$-MDDH assumption to switch these vectors from random to the span of $[\mathbf{D}_0]$. The proof of this step is standard: in [14], we show how we can build adversaries $\mathcal{B}, \mathcal{B}'$ such that

$$|\epsilon_3 - \epsilon_2| \leq \mathbf{Adv}_{\mathbb{G}_1, \mathcal{D}_{n,d}, \mathcal{B}}^{Q_{\mathsf{Enc}} - \mathrm{MDDH}}(\lambda) + \mathbf{Adv}_{\mathbb{G}_1, \mathcal{D}_{n,2d}, \mathcal{B}'}^{Q_{\mathsf{Enc}} - \mathrm{MDDH}}(\lambda)$$

Game $\mathbf{G}_4$. In this experiment, we add an explicit check to the decryption oracle. First recall that $\mathbf{D}^*$ is defined in Fig. 3 as the matrix whose first n rows are equal to $\mathbf{D}$ and last row is equal to $\mathbf{a}^\top \mathbf{D}$. Upon query $\mathsf{C} := ([\mathbf{x}], [y]_T, \pi)$ to the decryption oracle, where $[\mathbf{x}]^\top := ([\mathbf{u}]^\top, [p])$, the oracle additionally checks that:

$$\mathbf{u} \in span(\mathbf{D}) \vee \exists j : \mathbf{D}^{*\perp}\mathbf{x}_j = \mathbf{D}^{*\perp}\mathbf{x} \tag{3}$$

where $\mathbf{D}^{*\perp}\mathbf{D}^* = 0$, and $\mathcal{Q}_{\mathsf{Enc}} = \{\mathsf{C}_j = ([\mathbf{x}_j], [y_j]_T, \pi_j) : j \leq [\mathrm{ctr}]\}$ is the set of challenge ciphertexts. If the condition holds, the decryption oracle proceeds by running the decryption procedure as usual, otherwise it returns $\perp$ to the adversary. We notice that the new condition can be checked efficiently since we know $\mathbf{D} \in \mathbb{Z}_q^{n \times d}$ and $\mathbf{a} \in \mathbb{Z}_q^n$.

The distinguishing event between $\mathbf{G}_4$ and $\mathbf{G}_3$ is that the adversary queries the decryption oracle with a ciphertext that would not decrypt to $\perp$ (according to the original decryption rules of $\mathbf{G}_3$), but where Eq. (3) holds. We call such query to the decryption oracle a "critical query", i.e. a decryption query where:

- $[\mathbf{u}] \notin span([\mathbf{D}])$ and $\forall j : \mathbf{D}^{*\perp}\mathbf{x}_j \neq \mathbf{D}^{*\perp}\mathbf{x}$ (the latter implies that $[\mathbf{u}]$ is not the result of an honest rerandomization of a previous challenge ciphertext)
- π is valid, and $[y]_T = \mathbf{f}^\top[\mathbf{u}]_T + [\mathbf{x}]^\top \mathbf{F}^\top[\mathbf{u}]$, i.e., the consistency check holds.

For this step, we refer to Lemma 3.

Game $\mathbf{G}_5$. This game is equivalent to $\mathbf{G}_4$, but we modify the rules of the decryption oracle once again. For any j, let $\mathsf{M}_{j,0}$ and $\mathsf{M}_{j,1}$ be the challenge messages queried by $\mathcal{A}$ at the j-th query to the encryption oracle. Upon decryption query $\mathsf{C} = ([\mathbf{x}], [y]_T, \pi)$, if $\exists j : \mathbf{D}^{*\perp}\mathbf{x}_j = \mathbf{D}^{*\perp}\mathbf{x}$ where recall $\mathcal{Q}_{\mathsf{Enc}} = \{([\mathbf{x}_j], [y_j], \pi_j) : j \leq \mathrm{ctr}\}$, and both the proof π verifies and the consistency check holds, then the decryption oracle immediately returns the symbol $\diamond_{\mathcal{J}}$ where $\mathcal{J} \leftarrow \mathcal{Q}.\mathsf{find}(\mathsf{M}_{j,0})$.

Notice that we can rewrite the decryption procedure as $M = (-a^\top, 1)[x]$. We observe that the vector $(-a^\top, 1)$ is in the span of $D^{*\perp}$, since it holds that $(-a^\top, 1)D^* = -a^\top D + a^\top D = 0$. Thus, at any decryption query, if $D^{*\perp}x_j = D^{*\perp}x_j$ for some challenge ciphertext C_j then $(-a^\top, 1)[x_j] = (-a^\top, 1)[x]$, and therefore the decryption oracle would compute the message M_{j,b^*} and output the symbol $\diamond_{\mathcal{J}}$, where $\mathcal{J} = \mathcal{Q}.\text{find}(M_{j,b^*})$. Moreover, notice that $\mathcal{Q}.\text{find}(M_{j,b^*}) = \mathcal{Q}.\text{find}(M_{j,0})$ by definition of the security experiment. This shows that $\epsilon_5 = \epsilon_4$.

Game G_6. In this last step, we encrypt random messages. Formally, at the j-th encryption query the oracle (on input messages $M_{j,0}, M_{j,1}$) encrypts the message $M_{j,b^*} + R_j$, where R_j is random. Clearly, it holds that $\epsilon_6 = 0$ as in fact, because of the change introduced in G_6, the ciphertexts are independent of the challenge bit b^*, and, by the changes introduced in G_4 and G_5, the decryption queries are independent of the challenge bit. We prove that G_5 and G_6 are indistinguishable, as this step is almost the same as in [18], we defer its proof to [14].

Lemma 3. *For any PPT adversary $\mathcal{A}$, we build PPT adversaries $\mathcal{B}, \mathcal{B}'$ with running times similar to $\mathcal{A}$ such that:*

$$|\epsilon_3 - \epsilon_4| \leq O(d \log Q_{\text{Enc}}) \mathbf{Adv}_{G_1, \mathcal{D}_{n,d}, \mathcal{B}}^{\text{MDDH}}(\lambda) + \log Q_{\text{Enc}} \mathbf{Adv}_{\mathcal{B}'}^{\text{snd}}(\lambda)$$
$$+ O\left(\frac{n^2 Q_{\text{Dec}} Q_{\text{Enc}} \log Q_{\text{Enc}}}{q}\right)$$

Proof. We denote the probability that the adversary $\mathcal{A}$ wins game H_x by ϵ_{H_x}. In the following, we will bound ϵ_{H_0} via a sequence of games.

Hybrid H_0. This hybrid is the same as G_3 but immediately outputs 1 if the adversary makes a "critical query". Specifically, the hybrid executes G_3 but the decryption oracle upon input C parses it as $([x], [y]_T, \pi)$ and checks that Eq. (3) holds; if it holds, the decryption oracle continues as before. Otherwise, returns the message "critical", and H_0 stops the interaction, immediately returning 1. Since the hybrid outputs 1 when the distinguishing event between G_3 and G_4 happens, we have that $|\epsilon_3 - \epsilon_4| \leq \epsilon_{H_0}$. Also notice that the checks in Eq. (3) can be efficiently performed given the knowledge of D.

Hybrid H_1. This hybrid is preparatory for the next one. We inject randomness into the encryption/decryption keys, adding a vector $(zD^\perp)$ to the secret key $f^\top$, common to all the encryption queries, where $z \in \mathbb{Z}_q^{n-d}$. Specifically, at the very beginning of the experiment we sample the vector $z \leftarrow_{\$} \mathbb{Z}_q^{n-d}$, we sample f and compute the public key material $[f^\top D]$ and moreover:

- The encryption oracle, at the j-th query, computes the values $[y_j]_T$ as follows:

$$[y_j]_T \leftarrow (f^\top \boxed{+zD^\perp})[u_j]_T + [x_j]^\top F^\top[u_j]$$

- Similarly, the decryption oracle, upon input the ciphertext $C = ([x], [y]_T, \pi)$ computes the bit b_1 (i.e. the bit of the consistency check) by computing the value $[y']_T$ and checking if $[y]_T \overset{?}{=} [y']_T$ where $[y']_T$ is computed as:

$$[y']_T \leftarrow (f^\top \boxed{+zD^\perp})[u]_T + [x]^\top F^\top[u]$$

These new rules do not change the view of the adversary since both $\mathbf{f}^\top$ and $\mathbf{f}^\top + \mathbf{z}\mathbf{D}^\perp$ are uniformly distributed over $\mathbb{Z}_q^{1 \times n}$ given the public key material $[\mathbf{f}^\top \mathbf{D}]$. Thus we obtain $\epsilon_{\mathbf{H}_1} = \epsilon_{\mathbf{H}_0}$.

Hybrid $\mathbf{H}_2$. Let $P : \{0,1\}^* \to \mathbb{Z}_q^{1 \times n-d}$ be an uniformly random function. In this hybrid we use the following rules for encryption and decryption:

- The encryption oracle, at the j-th query, computes the values $[y_j]_T$ as follows:

$$[y_j]_T \leftarrow (\mathbf{f}^\top + \boxed{P(j)}\, \mathbf{D}^\perp)[\mathbf{u}_j]_T + [\mathbf{x}_j]^\top \mathbf{F}^\top [\mathbf{u}_j]$$

- For each decryption oracle query, we first define a set $\mathcal{S}$ over which the decryption oracle iterates to test the consistency check. The definition of the set $\mathcal{S}$ is carefully crafted to define the behavior of the hybrid experiment in case of *replay attack* from the adversary
  Recall that ctr counts the number of challenge ciphertexts output by the encryption oracle and that $\mathcal{Q}_{\mathsf{Enc}} = \{\mathsf{C}_j = ([\mathbf{x}_j], [y_j]_T, \pi_j) : j \leq \mathrm{ctr}\}$. Upon input the ciphertext $\mathsf{C} = ([\mathbf{x}], [y]_T, \pi)$, the decryption oracle first sets:

$$\mathcal{S} := \{j\} \qquad\qquad \text{if } \exists j \leq \mathrm{ctr} : \mathbf{D}^{*\perp}[\mathbf{x}] = \mathbf{D}^{*\perp}[\mathbf{x}_j]$$
$$\mathcal{S} := \{j : j \leq \mathrm{ctr}\} \qquad\qquad \text{otherwise}$$

then it computes the bit b_1 (i.e. the bit of the consistency check for C, see Fig. 3) differently by checking that

$$\boxed{\exists j \in \mathcal{S}} : [y]_T \stackrel{?}{=} (\mathbf{f}^\top + \boxed{P(j)}\, \mathbf{D}^\perp)[\mathbf{u}]_T + [\mathbf{x}]^\top \mathbf{F}^\top [\mathbf{u}].$$

Moving from $\mathbf{H}_1$ to $\mathbf{H}_2$ requires a series of hybrids $\mathbf{H}_{1,i,i'}$, $i \in [\log(Q_{\mathsf{Enc}})]$, $i' \in [6]$. We give in [14] the formal definitions of all these hybrids, and we highlight their differences.

Hybrid $\mathbf{H}_{1,i,0}$. Let P_i be a random function that takes in input strings of length i (for $i = 0$, we can imagine this as a constant function defined on the empty string) and returns row vectors of length $n - d$.

- On input the j-th query, the encryption oracle samples $[\mathbf{u}_j]$ from the span of $[\mathbf{D}_0]$. The element $[y_j]_T$ is computed as

$$[y_j]_T \leftarrow (\mathbf{f} + \boxed{P_i(j_{|i})}\, \mathbf{D}^\perp)[\mathbf{u}_j] + [\mathbf{x}_j]^\top \mathbf{F}^\top [\mathbf{u}_j].$$

- Upon input the ciphertext $\mathsf{C} = ([\mathbf{x}], [y]_T, \pi)$, define:

$$\mathcal{S} := \boxed{\{j_{|i}\}} \qquad\qquad \text{if } \exists j \leq \mathrm{ctr} : \mathbf{D}^{*\perp}[\mathbf{x}] = \mathbf{D}^{*\perp}[\mathbf{x}_j]$$
$$\mathcal{S} := \boxed{\{j_{|i} : j \leq \mathrm{ctr}\}} \qquad\qquad \text{otherwise}$$

it then executes the same code of the previous hybrid.

When $i = 0$, for any value j the string $j_{|0}$ is equal to the empty string, thus, in $\mathbf{H}_{1,0,0}$, the random function P_0 is always called on input the empty string. In particular, either when $\mathbf{D}^{*\perp}[\mathbf{x}] = \mathbf{D}^{*\perp}[\mathbf{x}_j]$ holds or when it does not, the consistency check performed is exactly the same. Thus the difference between hybrid $\mathbf{H}_{1,0,0}$ and $\mathbf{H}_1$ is only syntactical.

Hybrid $\mathbf{H}_{1,i,1}$. This hybrid is equivalent to the previous one, but here the encryption oracle, on input the j-the query, generates $[\mathbf{u}_j]$ in the span of $[\mathbf{D}_{j[i+1]}]$. We rely on the MDDH assumption to prove indistinguishability between the two hybrids. We proceed in two steps:

- We first switch the j-th vector $[\mathbf{u}_j]$ computed by the encryption oracle to a vector in the span of $[(\mathbf{D}|\mathbf{U})]$, where $\mathbf{U}$ is uniform over $\mathbb{Z}_q^{n \times d}$, if the $(i+1)$-th bit of the binary representation of j is equal to 1. We call this intermediate hybrid $\mathbf{H}_{A_i}$.
- Finally, we switch the j-th vector $[\mathbf{u}_j]$ computed by the encryption oracle to a vector in the span of $[(\mathbf{D}|\bar{\mathbf{D}}_1)] = [\mathbf{D}_1]$, if the $(i+1)$-th bit of the binary representation of j is equal to 1.

First we show indistinguishability between $\mathbf{H}_{1,i,0}$ and $\mathbf{H}_{A_i}$. Let $\mathcal{B}_A$ be an MDDH-adversary receiving the Q_{Enc}-fold $\mathcal{D}_{n,d}$-MDDH challenge $([\bar{\mathbf{D}}_0], [\mathbf{h}_1], \ldots, [\mathbf{h}_{Q_{\mathsf{Enc}}}])$ as input. $\mathcal{B}_A$ can sample a random matrix $\mathbf{D} \leftarrow\!\!\$\ \mathcal{D}_{n,d}$, a random matrix $\bar{\mathbf{D}}_1 \in \mathbb{Z}_q^{n \times d}$, the secret material $\mathbf{a} \leftarrow\!\!\$\ \mathbb{Z}_q^n$, $\mathbf{f} \leftarrow\!\!\$\ \mathbb{Z}_q^d$, $\mathbf{F} \leftarrow\!\!\$\ \mathbb{Z}_q^{n \times n+1}$ and the secret material for the benign proof system (since $\mathcal{B}_A$ knows $\mathbf{D}$, this can be easily achieved running $\mathsf{PGen}([\mathbf{D}])$). Finally, $\mathcal{B}_A$ samples a challenge bit b and gives the public key of the scheme to $\mathcal{A}$. $\mathcal{B}_A$ simulates the encryption oracle as follows. On input the j-th pair of messages $(\mathsf{M}_0, \mathsf{M}_1)$:

- if the $(i+1)$-th bit of the binary representation of j is equal to 0, the adversary sets $[\mathbf{u}_j] \leftarrow [\mathbf{D}_0]\mathbf{r}_j$,
- else, samples a random vector $\tilde{\mathbf{r}} \in \mathbb{Z}_q^d$, and computes $[\mathbf{u}_j] \leftarrow [\mathbf{D}]\tilde{\mathbf{r}} + [\mathbf{h}_j]$.

Note that $\mathcal{B}_A$ can still simulate the decryption oracle, because of the knowledge of the secret material $\mathbf{a}, \mathbf{f}, \mathbf{F}$ and of the matrix $\mathbf{D}$. Since $\mathcal{B}_A$ knows both the matrix $\mathbf{D}$ and the vector $\mathbf{a}$, can always find a matrix $\mathbf{D}^{*\perp}$ such that $\mathbf{D}^{*\perp}\mathbf{D}^* = 0$. This allows $\mathcal{B}_A$ to catch critical queries. If the tuple is a real MDDH tuple, i.e. $[\mathbf{h}_j] = [\bar{\mathbf{D}}_0]\mathbf{r}_j$, the game described is perfectly equivalent to $\mathbf{H}_{1,i,0}$. Otherwise, if the challenge vectors are uniformly random, the game simulated is equivalent to $\mathbf{H}_{A,i}$. The next step is to switch the j-th vector $[\mathbf{u}_j]$ computed by the encryption oracle to a vector in the span of $[(\mathbf{D}|\bar{\mathbf{D}}_1)] = [\mathbf{D}_1]$ if the $(i+1)$-th bit of the binary representation of j is equal to 1. This transformation is similar to the previous one, therefore we omit the details. Altogether, combining the previous adversaries, we obtain an adversary $\mathcal{C}$ such that:
$$|\epsilon_{\mathbf{H}_{1,i,1}} - \epsilon_{\mathbf{H}_{1,i,0}}| \leq 2(n-d)\mathbf{Adv}_{\mathbb{G}_1, \mathcal{D}_{n,d}, \mathcal{C}}^{\mathrm{mddh}}(\lambda) + \frac{2}{q-1}.$$

Hybrid $\mathbf{H}_{1,i,2}$. We add an explicit check to the decryption oracle. Specifically, at each decryption oracle query the hybrid additionally checks if $\mathbf{u} \notin span(\mathbf{D}_0) \cup span(\mathbf{D}_1)$, and if it is the case the decryption oracle returns immediately $\perp$ to the adversary. We rely on the soundness of the underlying benign proof system. In particular, the only condition that would allow to distinguish between this hybrid and the previous one is to query the decryption oracle with a ciphertext $C = ([\mathbf{x}], [y]_T, \pi)$ where:

- $\mathbf{u} \notin span(\mathbf{D}_0) \cup span(\mathbf{D}_1)$
- the decryption oracle in the hybrid $\mathbf{H}_{1,i,1}$ would not return $\bot$.

For such query it holds that $\mathsf{PVer}(psk, [\mathbf{u}], \pi) = 1$. We build an adversary $\mathcal{B}$ against the $(\mathcal{L}^{sim}, \mathcal{L}^{ver}, \mathcal{L}^{snd})$-soundness of the proof system. (Recall that $\mathcal{L}^{snd} = \mathcal{L}^{sim} = span(\mathbf{D}_0) \cup span(\mathbf{D}_1)$, and $\mathcal{L}^{ver} = \mathbb{Z}_q^n$.)

The adversary $\mathcal{B}$ samples the secret material $\mathbf{a}, \mathbf{f}, \mathbf{F}$; then, it queries the challenger to obtain the public key of the benign proof system, associated with the matrix $\mathbf{D}$, and finally gives $\mathcal{A}$ all the public key material. The adversary $\mathcal{B}$ can easily simulate the encryption oracle since it knows all the necessary information. To compute the proof π_j associated with the j-th encryption oracle query, it queries the simulation oracle offered by the challenger: it holds that $\mathbf{u}_j \in \mathcal{L}^{sim}$, for all $j \in [Q_{\mathsf{Enc}}]$. When the adversary makes a decryption query, $\mathcal{B}$ needs to verify that the proof π is accepted by PVer; so, it forwards $(\mathbf{u}, \pi)$ to the challenger. Since $\mathcal{L}^{ver}$ is equal to $\mathbb{Z}_q^n$, the verification oracle always returns a verdict bit, and $\mathcal{B}$ can proceed in the natural way the simulation of the decryption oracle. At some point $\mathcal{B}$ queries the verification oracle with some $([\mathbf{u}], \pi)$ such that $\mathbf{u} \notin span(\mathbf{D}_0) \cup span(\mathbf{D}_1)$, i.e., $\mathbf{u} \notin \mathcal{L}^{snd}$, but $\mathsf{PVer}(psk, [\mathbf{u}], \pi) = 1$. This is the event that lets $\mathcal{B}$ win the soundness game. The adversary $\mathcal{B}$ runs in time $T(\mathcal{B}) \approx T(\mathcal{A}) + (Q_{\mathsf{Enc}} + Q_{\mathsf{Dec}}) \cdot \mathsf{poly}(\lambda)$, where poly is a polynomial independent of $T(\mathcal{A})$. Moreover, notice that when the distinguishing event happens the adversary $\mathcal{B}$ wins the soundness game, thus: $|\epsilon_{\mathbf{H}_{1,i,2}} - \epsilon_{\mathbf{H}_{1,i,1}}| \le \mathbf{Adv}_{\mathcal{B},\mathbf{PS}}^{snd}(\lambda)$.

Hybrid $\mathbf{H}_{1,i,3}$. In this hybrid, we increase the entropy of the secret keys during encryption queries.

- The encryption oracle, at the j-th query, computes the values $[y_j]_T$ as follows:

$$[y_j]_T \leftarrow (\mathbf{f}^\top + \boxed{P_{i+1}(j_{|i+1})} \mathbf{D}^\perp)[\mathbf{u}_j] + [\mathbf{x}_j]^\top \mathbf{F}^\top[\mathbf{u}_j].$$

- The decryption oracle, upon input the ciphertext $C = ([\mathbf{x}], [y]_T, \pi)$ additionally checks that $\exists d$ s.t. $\mathbf{u} \in span(\mathbf{D}_d)$ and in such a case it sets:

$$\mathcal{S} := \{j_{|i} \,\|d\, \} \qquad \text{if } \exists j \le \mathsf{ctr} : \mathbf{D}^{*\perp}[\mathbf{x}] = \mathbf{D}^{*\perp}[\mathbf{x}_j]$$

$$\mathcal{S} := \{j_{|i} \,\|d\, : j \le \mathsf{ctr}\} \qquad \text{otherwise}$$

and it continues executing the same code as the previous hybrid.

We prove that $|\epsilon_{\mathbf{H}_{1,i,2}} - \epsilon_{\mathbf{H}_{1,i,3}}|$ is negligible. We first transit to an intermediate hybrid $\mathbf{H}_i'$ where instead of using the function $P_i(\cdot)\mathbf{D}^\perp$, we use the function $P_i'(\cdot) := P_i^{(0)}(\cdot)\mathbf{D}_0^\perp + P_i^{(1)}(\cdot)\mathbf{D}_1^\perp$, where $P_i^{(0)}$ and $P_i^{(1)}$ are two uniformly random functions with domain $\{0,1\}^i$. Notice that $P_i'(\cdot)$ is an uniformly random function that maps strings in $\{0,1\}^i$ to vectors in $rowspan(\mathbf{D}_0^\perp) + rowspan(\mathbf{D}_1^\perp)$ while $P_i(\cdot)\mathbf{D}^\perp$ is an uniformly random function that maps string in $\{0,1\}^i$ to vectors in $rowspan(\mathbf{D}^\perp)$. Thus the distinguishing event between $\mathbf{H}_{i,j,2}$ and this intermediate hybrid is the event that $rowspan(\mathbf{D}_0^\perp) + rowspan(\mathbf{D}_1^\perp) \neq rowspan(\mathbf{D}^\perp)$. The latter event happens with probability at most $1/q$: in fact, the event happens if and only if the subspace $span(\bar{\mathbf{D}}_0|\bar{\mathbf{D}}_1)$ has dimension strictly less than $2d$ and recall that the columns of such matrices are sampled uniformly at random. Next, we define the function $P_{i+1}^{(b)} : \{0,1\}^{i+1} \to \mathbb{Z}_q^{1 \times (n-2d)}$, $\forall b \in \{0,1\}$:

$$P_{i+1}^{(b)}(\mathbf{x}) = \begin{cases} P_i^{(b)}(\mathbf{x}_{|i}), & \mathbf{x}[i+1] \neq b \\ \tilde{P}_i^{(b)}(\mathbf{x}_{|i}), & \text{else} \end{cases}$$

where $P_i, \tilde{P}_i$ are two uniformly (and independent) random functions. Notice that $P_{i+1}^{(b)}$ is an uniformly random function.

We define a second intermediate hybrid $\mathbf{H}_{i+1}'$ where for the encryption oracle queries instead of using the random function P_i' applied to the indexes $j_{|i}$ we use the function P_{i+1}' applied to the indexes $j_{|i+1}$, and for the decryption oracle queries we use P_{i+1}' applied to $(j_{|i}\|d)$, where d is such that $\mathbf{u}_j \in span(\mathbf{D}_d)$ (as described in the $\mathbf{H}_{1,i,3}$). We show that $\mathbf{H}_i'$ and $\mathbf{H}_{i+1}'$ are equivalently distributed. Indeed, in this second intermediate hybrid, at the j-th encryption oracle query we compute $[y_j]_T \leftarrow (\mathbf{f}^\top + P_{i+1}'(j_{|i+1}))[\mathbf{u}_j] + [\mathbf{x}_j]^\top \mathbf{F}^\top [\mathbf{u}_j]$. Moreover, we have that $P_{i+1}'(j_{|i+1})\mathbf{u}_j = P_i'(j_{|i})\mathbf{u}_j$, in fact:

$$P_{i+1}'(j_{|i+1})\mathbf{u}_j = \left(P_i^{(1-j[i+1])}(j_{|i})\mathbf{D}_{1-j[i+1]}^\perp + \tilde{P}_i^{(j[i+1])}(j_{|i})\mathbf{D}_{j[i+1]}^\perp \right) \mathbf{D}_{j[i+1]}\mathbf{r}_j$$

$$= \left(P_i^{(1-j[i+1])}(j_{|i})\mathbf{D}_{1-j[i+1]}^\perp \right) \mathbf{D}_{j[i+1]}\mathbf{r}_j$$

$$= \left(P_i^{(0)}(j_{|i})\mathbf{D}_0^\perp + P_i^{(1)}(j_{|i})\mathbf{D}_1^\perp \right) \mathbf{D}_{j[i+1]}\mathbf{r}_j$$

$$= P_i'(j_{|i})\mathbf{D}_{j[i+1]}\mathbf{r}_j = P_i'(j_{|i})\mathbf{u}_j$$

In the above derivation, we first applied the definitions of P_{i+1} and $\mathbf{u}_j$, then we simplified the second term by noticing that $\mathbf{D}_{j[i+1]}^\perp \mathbf{D}_{j[i+1]} = 0$, then for the same exact reason we can add the component $P_j^{(j[i+1])}(j_{|i})\mathbf{D}_{j[i+1]}$, and finally we have the definition of P_i'.

Similarly, for the decryption oracle queries with input $\mathsf{C} = ([\mathbf{x}], [y]_T, \pi)$ where $\exists d : \mathbf{u} \in span(\mathbf{D}_d)$, we have that $P_{i+1}'(j_{|i+1})\mathbf{u} = P_i'(j_{|i})\mathbf{u}$. The derivation is identical to before. Thus the two intermediate hybrids are equivalent.

Finally, we show that the second intermediate hybrid, $\mathbf{H}_{i+1}'$, is statistically close to $\mathbf{H}_{i,i,3}$; in fact, the only difference is that in the latter hybrid we use the function $P_{j+1}(\cdot)\mathbf{D}^\perp$. Equivalently as before, the two random functions are not equivalently distributed only when $span(\bar{\mathbf{D}}_0\|\bar{\mathbf{D}}_1)$ has rank less then $2d$, which happens with probability at most $1/q$. Thus $|\epsilon_{\mathbf{H}_{1,i,2}} - \epsilon_{\mathbf{H}_{1,i,3}}| \leq \frac{2}{q}$.

Hybrid $\mathbf{H}_{1,i,4}$. We remove the direct check $[\mathbf{u}]_1 \in span([\mathbf{D}_1]_1) \cup span([\mathbf{D}_0]_1)$ introduced in $\mathbf{H}_{1,i,2}$. This removal can only increase the winning probability of the adversary. Thus $\epsilon_{\mathbf{H}_{1,i,3}} \leq \epsilon_{\mathbf{H}_{1,i,4}}$.

Hybrid $H_{1,i,5}$. To decrypt, we increase the number of keys used by the decryption oracle to compute the bit b_1.

$$\mathcal{S} := \{j_{|i} \| b : b \in \{0,1\}\} \qquad\qquad \text{if } \exists j \le \text{ctr} : \mathbf{D}^{*\perp}[\mathbf{x}] = \mathbf{D}^{*\perp}[\mathbf{x}_j]$$

$$\mathcal{S} := \{j_{|i} \| b : b \in \{0,1\}, j \le \text{ctr}\} \qquad\qquad \text{otherwise}$$

This change can only increase the winning probability of the adversary since the set of the strings $\mathcal{S}$ used in $H_{1,i,5}$ contains the set of strings used in $H_{1,i,4}$.

As for non-critical queries, we need to show that the view of the adversary does not change: in particular, any non-critical query that decrypts to $\perp$ in $H_{1,i,4}$ should decrypt to $\perp$ in $H_{1,i,5}$ as well. This is easy to prove when the decryption query has $[\mathbf{u}] \in span([\mathbf{D}])$: indeed, even if we modify the set $\mathcal{S}$, this change does not affect the way we decrypt such queries (recall that any key $P_{i+1}(\cdot)$ is then multiplied by $\mathbf{D}^\perp$.) Also, a non-critical query could be a query for which it holds that there exists $j \in [Q_{\mathsf{Enc}}]$ such that $\mathbf{D}^{*\perp}\mathbf{x}_j$ is equal to $\mathbf{D}^{*\perp}\mathbf{x}$. If a query of this form succesfully decrypts in $H_{1,i,4}$, the same happens in $H_{1,i,5}$: again, this is because $\mathcal{S}$ in the latter hybrid is a superset of $\mathcal{S}$ in $H_{1,i,4}$. But, it is still possible that a query of this form decrypts to $\perp$ in $H_{1,i,4}$, but the 'augmented' $\mathcal{S}$ in this new hybrid makes the consistency bit b_1 be 1, for some new key: we bound the probability of a similar event since we know that the only way to learn the image of the random function $P_{i+1}(\cdot)$ is via oracle queries to $\mathcal{O}_{\mathbf{dec}}$ and $\mathcal{O}_{\mathbf{enc}}$. By union bound, we obtain a statistical distance of $O(Q_{\mathsf{Enc}}Q_{\mathsf{Dec}}/q)$.

$$\epsilon_{H_{1,i,4}} - O(Q_{\mathsf{Enc}}Q_{\mathsf{Dec}}/q) \le \epsilon_{H_{1,i,5}}.$$

Hybrid $H_{1,i,6}$. This hybrid is equivalent to the previous one, but the decryption oracle computes a different set $\mathcal{S}$, as follows:

$$\mathcal{S} := \boxed{\{j_{|i+1}\}} \qquad\qquad \text{if } \exists j \le \text{ctr} : \mathbf{D}^{*\perp}[\mathbf{x}] = \mathbf{D}^{*\perp}[\mathbf{x}_j]$$

$$\mathcal{S} := \boxed{\{j_{|i+1} : j \le \text{ctr}\}} \qquad\qquad \text{otherwise}$$

Notice that the set $\mathcal{S}$ as defined in $H_{1,i,6}$ might be a (strict) subset of the set $\mathcal{S}$ as defined in $H_{1,i,5}$. Thus the distinguishing event is that the consistency check would pass in $H_{1,i,5}$ but it would not pass in $H_{1,i,6}$. In particular, such consistency check passes for an index of the form $j_i\|1$, such that $j[i+1] = 0$ and $j \le \text{ctr}$, and by the definition of the distinguishing event the integer representation of $(j_i\|1) \cdot 2^{|\log Q_{\mathsf{Enc}}|-i-1}$ is bigger than ctr. Thus the key $\mathbf{f}^\top + P_i(j_i\|1)\mathbf{D}^\perp$ was never used for an encryption query. The only way an adversary can learn information about one of such keys is via decryption queries. In particular, each decryption query can at most decrease the set of possibilities (namely a valid y that matches the consistency check) by one. Moreover, the number of such keys is (very loosely) upper-bounded by Q_{Enc}, thus by union bound over all such keys and over all the decryption queries we obtain: $|\epsilon_{H_{1,i,6}} - \epsilon_{H_{1,i,5}}| \le \frac{Q_{\mathsf{Enc}} \cdot Q_{\mathsf{Dec}}}{q - Q_{\mathsf{Dec}}}$.

Hybrid $\mathbf{H}_{1,i+1,0}$. We then switch back the distribution of $[\mathbf{u}_j]$ to the span of $[\mathbf{D}_0]$. This transition is the reverse of what we have done to move from $\mathbf{H}_{1,i,0}$ to $\mathbf{H}_{1,i,1}$. We proceed in two steps:

- We first switch the j-th vector $[\mathbf{u}_j]$ computed by the encryption oracle to a vector in the span of $[(\mathbf{D}|\mathbf{U})]$, where $\mathbf{U}$ is uniform over $\mathbb{Z}_q^{n \times d}$, if the $(i+1)$-th bit of the binary representation of j is equal to 1.
- Then, we switch the j-th vector $[\mathbf{u}_j]$ computed by the encryption oracle to a vector in the span of $[\mathbf{D}_0]$.

Altogether we obtain and adversary $\mathcal{C}$ such that:

$$|\epsilon_{\mathbf{H}_{1,i+1,0}} - \epsilon_{\mathbf{H}_{1,i,6}}| \le 2(n-d)\mathbf{Adv}^{\mathrm{mddh}}_{\mathbb{G}_1, \mathcal{D}_{n,d}, \mathcal{C}}(\lambda) + \frac{2}{q-1}.$$

It is easy to see that $\epsilon_{\mathbf{H}_2} = \epsilon_{\mathbf{H}_{1,\lceil \log Q_{\mathsf{Enc}} \rceil, 6}}$. Next, we prove that $\epsilon_{\mathbf{H}_2} \le \frac{O(n^2) Q_{\mathsf{Enc}} Q_{\mathsf{Dec}}}{q}$. We reduce the adversary $\mathcal{A}$ playing in $\mathbf{H}_2$ to an (unbounded) adversary $\mathcal{B}$ upon which we can invoke the Lemma 1. We say that $\mathcal{B}$ *forged a valid tuple* if the output of $\mathcal{B}$ matches the event described in the lemma. For any assignments of the vector $\mathbf{a}$ and of the matrix $\mathbf{D}$ in the support of $\mathcal{D}_{n,d}$, we can consider in the Lemma 1 the matrix $\mathbf{E}$ to be set equal to $\mathbf{D}^*$.

Claim. $\Pr[\mathbf{H}_2 = 1] \le \frac{O(n^2) Q_{\mathsf{Enc}} Q_{\mathsf{Dec}}}{q}$.

Let $(\mathbf{D}, \mathbf{D}^*, \mathbf{D}^\top \mathbf{f}, \mathbf{D}^\top \mathbf{F}, \mathbf{F}\mathbf{D}^*)$ be the tuple received by $\mathcal{B}$ from the challenger. The adversary $\mathcal{B}$ samples uniformly random values $(\bar{\mathbf{f}}, \bar{\mathbf{F}})$ such that $\bar{\mathbf{f}}^\top \mathbf{D} = \mathbf{f}^\top \mathbf{D}$, $\bar{\mathbf{F}}^\top \mathbf{D} = \mathbf{F}^\top \mathbf{D}$ and $\bar{\mathbf{F}}\mathbf{D}^* = \mathbf{F}\mathbf{D}^*$. We can think of the tuple $(\bar{\mathbf{f}}, \bar{\mathbf{F}})$ as a "fake" proving key that matches the verification key given by the challenger. Given $\mathbf{D}$ and $\mathbf{a}$, the reduction $\mathcal{B}$ can sample all the secret material needed to simulate the hybrid $\mathbf{H}_2$. In particular, it can compute the proving key and verification key of the proof system $\mathbf{PS}$ and sample the challenge bit. The reduction $\mathcal{B}$ samples an index value $j^*_{\mathsf{Enc}} \in [Q_{\mathsf{Enc}}]$ and an index $j^*_{\mathsf{Dec}} \in [Q_{\mathsf{Dec}}]$. (Recall that Q_{Enc} and Q_{Dec} denote the number of encryption, resp. decryption queries made by $\mathcal{A}$.) At the j-th query to the encryption oracle:

- If $j \ne j^*_{\mathsf{Enc}}$, the reduction $\mathcal{B}$ generates $\mathbf{x}_j$ following the prescribed algorithms. Then, it computes $y_j \leftarrow \left((\bar{\mathbf{f}} + \bar{\mathbf{F}}\mathbf{x}_j)^\top + P(j)\mathbf{D}^\perp \right)\mathbf{u}_j$, where we recall that $P(\cdot)$ is a random function.
- Else, for $j = j^*_{\mathsf{Enc}}$, $\mathcal{B}$ computes $\mathbf{x}_j$ as prescribed, queries its own oracle with $\mathbf{x}_j$ and obtains a value $\mathbf{v} = \mathbf{f} + \mathbf{F} \cdot \mathbf{x}_j$, then, it uses $\mathbf{v} + P(j)\mathbf{D}^\perp$ to compute the proof y, associated with $\mathbf{u}_j$, namely: $y_j \leftarrow \left(\mathbf{v}^\top + P(j)\mathbf{D}^\perp \right)\mathbf{u}_j$.

At the j-th query to decryption oracle with ciphertext $\mathsf{C} = ([\mathbf{x}], [y]_T, \pi)$ there are three possible cases. The easiest case to handle is if $\mathbf{u} \in span(\mathbf{D})$ or $\exists j \ne j^*_{\mathsf{Enc}}$ such that $\mathbf{D}^{*\perp}\mathbf{x}_j = \mathbf{D}^{*\perp}\mathbf{x}$. The reduction $\mathcal{B}$ can compute the consistency check using the keys $\bar{\mathbf{f}}, \bar{\mathbf{F}}$ and the random function P.

The second case is when $\mathbf{D}^{*\perp}\mathbf{x}_{j_{\mathsf{Enc}}^*} = \mathbf{D}^{*\perp}\mathbf{x}$, in this case let $\mathbf{r}'$ be such that $\mathbf{x} - \mathbf{x}_{j_{\mathsf{Enc}}^*} = \mathbf{D}^*\mathbf{r}'$ and compute

$$y' \leftarrow y_{j_{\mathsf{Enc}}^*} + \mathbf{f}^\top \mathbf{D}\mathbf{r}' + \mathbf{x}_{j_{\mathsf{Enc}}^*}^\top \mathbf{F}^\top \mathbf{D}\mathbf{r}' + (\mathbf{F}\mathbf{D}^*\mathbf{r}')^\top(\mathbf{u}_{j_{\mathsf{Enc}}^*} + \mathbf{D}\mathbf{r}')$$

namely, compute the element $[y']_T$ as if it was computed in the re-randomization of the ciphertext $\mathsf{C}_{j_{\mathsf{Enc}}^*}$ using randomness $\mathbf{r}'$. Notice that, by definition of $\mathbf{H}_2$ the consistency check for $[y]_T$ would be computed by checking if

$$y \overset{?}{=} \left((\mathbf{f} + \mathbf{F}\mathbf{x})^\top + P(j_{\mathsf{Enc}}^*)\mathbf{D}^\perp\right)\mathbf{u}.$$

By Lemma 2 and by definition of $y_{j_{\mathsf{Enc}}^*}$, the two checks are equivalent. The last case is when $\mathbf{u} \notin span(\mathbf{D}) \wedge \forall j : \mathbf{D}^{*\perp}\mathbf{x}_j \neq \mathbf{D}^{*\perp}\mathbf{x}$, i.e., the query might be "critical":

- If $j < j_{\mathsf{Dec}}^*$ then return $\perp$ to the adversary $\mathcal{A}$, in this case we assume that the query was not critical and that the decryption would fail.
- If $j = j_{\mathsf{Dec}}^*$ then output the tuple $(y - P(j_{\mathsf{Enc}}^*)\mathbf{D}^\perp\mathbf{u}, \mathbf{u}, \mathbf{x})$ as the forgery of $\mathcal{B}$.

We condition on the event that j_{Dec}^* is the first critical query of $\mathcal{A}$ and that, let the ciphertext sent by $\mathcal{A}$ at the j_{Dec}^* query be $\mathsf{C} = ([\mathbf{x}], [y]_T, \pi)$ we have that the equation $[y]_T = (\mathbf{f} + P(j_{\mathsf{Enc}}^*)\mathbf{D}^\perp + \mathbf{F}\mathbf{x})^\top[\mathbf{u}]$ holds. Let Guess be such event. Conditioned on such a lucky event, $\mathcal{B}$ indeed produces a valid forgery, in fact by the definition of a critical query $(\mathbf{x}_{j_{\mathsf{Enc}}^*} - \mathbf{x}) \notin span(\mathbf{D}^*)$ and $\mathbf{u} \notin span(\mathbf{D})$.

We show that the view provided by $\mathcal{B}$ to the adversary $\mathcal{A}$ up to the j_{Dec}^*-th decryption query and conditioned on Guess is equivalent to the view of the adversary up to the j_{Dec}^*-th decryption query in the hybrid game $\mathbf{H}_2$. The intuition is that the values $P(j)\mathbf{D}^\perp$, for all j, mask the components of $(\mathbf{f}, \mathbf{F})$ and $(\bar{\mathbf{f}}, \bar{\mathbf{F}})$ that differ. Indeed, we know that for some row vectors $\mathbf{v}, \mathbf{w}, \mathbf{w}'$, it holds that $\mathbf{f} = \mathbf{D}\mathbf{v} + (\mathbf{w}\mathbf{D}^\perp)^\top$ and $\bar{\mathbf{f}} = \mathbf{D}\mathbf{v} + (\mathbf{w}'\mathbf{D}^\perp)^\top$. Similarly, for some $\mathbf{V}, \mathbf{W}$ and $\mathbf{W}'$, $\mathbf{F} = \mathbf{D}\mathbf{V} + (\mathbf{W}\mathbf{D}^\perp)^\top$, and $\bar{\mathbf{F}} = \mathbf{D}\mathbf{V} + (\mathbf{W}'\mathbf{D}^\perp)^\top$.

Let P' be a uniformly random function, and consider the following function:

$$P(j) = \begin{cases} P'(j), & j = j_{\mathsf{Enc}}^* \\ P'(j) + \Delta_j, & j \neq j_{\mathsf{Enc}}^* \end{cases}$$

where $\Delta_j = \mathbf{w} - \mathbf{w}' + \mathbf{x}_j^\top(\mathbf{W} - \mathbf{W}')$. It is not hard to see that P is a uniformly random function. Now consider the mental experiment where $\mathcal{B}$ runs the same but using the random function P defined above. Since P is uniformly random, the probability that $\mathcal{B}$ forges a valid tuple in this mental experiment is the same as the probability that $\mathcal{B}$ forges a valid tuple in the real experiment. Also, for any $j \neq j_{\mathsf{Enc}}^*$ the value y computed at the j-th encryption oracle query is:

$$y = \left((\bar{\mathbf{f}} + \bar{\mathbf{F}}\mathbf{x}_j)^\top + P(j)\mathbf{D}^\perp\right)[\mathbf{u}_j]\left((\bar{\mathbf{f}} + \bar{\mathbf{F}}\mathbf{x}_j)^\top + (P'(j) + \Delta_j)\mathbf{D}^\perp\right)[\mathbf{u}_j]$$

$$= \left((\bar{\mathbf{f}} + ((\mathbf{w} - \mathbf{w}')\mathbf{D}^\perp)^\top + (\bar{\mathbf{F}} + ((\mathbf{W} - \mathbf{W}')\mathbf{D}^\perp)^\top)\mathbf{x}_j)^\top + P'(j)\mathbf{D}^\perp\right)[\mathbf{u}_j]$$

$$= \left((\mathbf{f} + \mathbf{F}\mathbf{x}_j)^\top + P'(j)\mathbf{D}^\perp\right)[\mathbf{u}_j].$$

The probability that the reduction $\mathcal{B}$ creates a forgery is $\Pr[\mathbf{H}_2 = 1 \wedge \mathsf{Guess}]$, and the two events are independent. Moreover, since $\Pr[\mathsf{Guess}] = (Q_{\mathsf{Enc}}Q_{\mathsf{Dec}})^{-1}$, by the Rand-RCCA Lemma in [14] we have that $\Pr[\mathbf{H}_2 = 1] \leq \frac{n(n+1)Q_{\mathsf{Enc}}Q_{\mathsf{Dec}}}{q}$.

5.1   Publicly-Verifiable Rand-RCCA PKE

We show two publicly verifiable Rand-RCCA PKE schemes based on the scheme from Sect. 5. Following the ideas in [13], we append a malleable NIZK proof (essentially a Groth-Sahai proof) that $[y]_T$ and π are well-formed to the ciphertexts of $\mathcal{PKE}$ from the previous section. The decryption algorithm outputs the decrypted message only if the NIZK proofs are valid. Public verifiability follows because the NIZK proofs can be verified using the public parameters.

Let $\mathcal{PKE}_1 = (\mathsf{KGen}_1, \mathsf{Enc}_1, \mathsf{Dec}_1, \mathsf{Rand}_1)$ be the scheme of Sect. 5 instantiated using the benign proof system of Sect. 3.1, and let $\mathbf{PS}_2 = (\mathsf{PGen}_2, \mathsf{PPrv}_2, \mathsf{PVer}_2)$ and PEvl_2 form a malleable NIZK system for membership in the relation

$$\mathcal{R}_2 = \left\{ (\mathsf{pk}, [\mathbf{x}]), ([y]_T, \pi, \mathbf{r}) : \begin{array}{c} y = \mathbf{f}^\top\mathbf{u} + \mathbf{x}^\top\mathbf{F}\mathbf{u} \\ \mathsf{PPrv}_1(ppk, [\mathbf{u}], \mathbf{r}) = \pi \end{array} \right\},$$

and where the allowable set of transformations contains all the transformations $(T_{\mathsf{el}}, T_{\mathsf{wit}})$ such that it exists $\hat{\mathbf{r}}$ with $T_{\mathsf{el}}(\mathsf{pk}, [\mathbf{x}]) = \mathsf{pk}, [\hat{\mathbf{x}}]$, $T_{\mathsf{wit}}([y]_T, \pi, \mathbf{r}) = [\hat{y}]_T, \hat{\mathsf{pk}}, \mathbf{r} + \hat{\mathbf{r}}$ and $([\hat{\mathbf{x}}], [\hat{y}]_T, \hat{\pi}) = \mathsf{Rand}_1(\mathsf{pk}, ([\mathbf{x}], [y]_T, \pi); \hat{\mathbf{r}})$; each transformation in the set of allowable transformation is uniquely identified by a vector $\hat{\mathbf{r}}$.

The pv-Rand-PKE scheme $\mathcal{PKE}_2 = (\mathsf{Init}, \mathsf{KGen}_2, \mathsf{Enc}_2, \mathsf{Dec}_2, \mathsf{Rand}_2, \mathsf{Ver})$ is identical to $\mathcal{PKE}_1$, except that (i) KGen_2 additionally samples the common reference string for $\mathbf{PS}_2$, (ii) the encryption procedure computes a ciphertext as in $\mathcal{PKE}_1$ but additionally computes a proof π_2 for $\mathbf{PS}_2$ and outputs a ciphertext $\mathsf{C} = ([\mathbf{x}_1], \pi_2)$, (iii) the decryption procedure first checks the proof π_2 holds w.r.t. the instance $(\mathsf{pk}, [\mathbf{x}])$ and, if so, it outputs $\mathsf{M} = (-\mathbf{a}^\top, 1)[\mathbf{x}]$ (and $\perp$ otherwise), (iv) the re-randomization procedure randomizes $[\mathbf{x}]$ as in $\mathcal{PKE}_1$ and uses PEvl_2 for the remaining part of the ciphertext, and (v) Ver_2 simply checks π_2.

Theorem 4. *If $\mathbf{PS}_2$ is adaptively sound, $(\epsilon, O(T))$-composable zero-knowledge, and perfect derivation private, and $\mathcal{PKE}_1$ is mRCCA secure then $\mathcal{PKE}_2$ is publicly verifiable, perfectly re-randomizable, and mRCCA-secure. Specifically, for any PPT $\mathcal{A}$ making up to Q_{Enc} encryption queries and Q_{Dec} decryption queries and with running time T exist PPT $\mathcal{B}^{\mathrm{rcca}}$ making the same number of queries and adversaries $\mathcal{B}^{\mathrm{snd}}, \mathcal{B}^{\mathrm{zk}}$ with similar running times*

$$\mathbf{Adv}_{\mathcal{A}, \mathcal{PKE}_2}^{\mathrm{mRCCA}}(\lambda) \leq \mathbf{Adv}_{\mathcal{B}^{\mathrm{rcca}}, \mathcal{PKE}_1}^{\mathrm{mRCCA}}(\lambda) + \mathbf{Adv}_{\mathcal{B}^{\mathrm{snd}}, \mathbf{PS}_2}^{\mathrm{snd}}(\lambda) + \epsilon$$

The proof follows by inspection of the proof of Theorem 2 in [13]. In more detail, their proof proceeds in two steps. First, it reduces to the adaptive soundness of the NIZK proof system to claim that if a *publicly-verifiable* ciphertext decrypts correctly then its respective *non-publicly verifiable* ciphertext should decrypt correctly too. We notice that this step can be performed tightly relying either on statistical adaptive soundness of the proof system or relying on the computational soundness of the proof system when the language proved is witness samplable. The reason is that the reduction can check which one of the many NIZK-proofs from the adversary breaks adaptive soundness before submitting it as its forgery. The second step uses composable zero-knowledge to first tightly switch the way the public parameters are generated and then to switch (all together) the proofs for the ciphertexts from real to simulated.

To instantiate the malleable NIZK, we consider a construction along the same line of [13]. In more detail, [13] introduced an extension of the Groth-Sahai proof system that is zero-knowledge even for pairing product equations where the $\mathbb{G}_T$-elements are variables. Their idea is to commit the elements in $\mathbb{G}_T$ using a commitment scheme with nice bilinear properties. Groth-Sahai proofs can be instantiated under any $\mathcal{D}_k$-MDDH Assumption [11] and, given their nice algebraic properties they are malleable [8]. More details are given in [14].

A More Efficient Tight-Secure pv-Rand-RCCA PKE. To facilitate our more efficient scheme, we introduce a stronger variant of the MDDH assumption (cf. Definition 1) in which the adversary gets not only a matrix $[\mathbf{A}]$, but also the tensor product $[\mathbf{A} \otimes \mathbf{A}]$ to distinguish an element from $span([\mathbf{A}])$ and random:

Definition 9 (Tensor Matrix Diffie-Hellman assumption in $\mathbb{G}_\gamma$). *The* $\mathcal{D}_{\ell,k}$-*Tensor-Matrix-Decisional-Diffie-Hellman (TMDDH) assumption in group* $\mathbb{G}_\gamma$ *holds if for all non-uniform PPT adversaries* $\mathcal{A}$,

$$|\Pr\left[\mathcal{A}(\mathcal{G}, [\mathbf{A} \otimes \mathbf{A}]_\gamma, [\mathbf{A}]_\gamma, [\mathbf{A}\mathbf{w}]_\gamma) = 1\right] - \Pr\left[\mathcal{A}(\mathcal{G}, [\mathbf{A} \otimes \mathbf{A}]_\gamma, [\mathbf{A}]_\gamma, [\mathbf{z}]_\gamma) = 1\right]|$$

is negligible, where the probability is taken over $\mathcal{G} = (q, \mathbb{G}_1, \mathbb{G}_2, \mathbb{G}_T, e, \mathcal{P}_1, \mathcal{P}_2) \leftarrow$ GGen(1^λ), $\mathbf{A} \leftarrow \mathcal{D}_{\ell,k}, \mathbf{w} \leftarrow \mathbb{Z}_q^k$, $[\mathbf{z}]_\gamma \leftarrow \mathbb{G}_\gamma^\ell$, *and the coin tosses of adversary* $\mathcal{A}$.

The TMDDH assumption can be seen as a generalization of the "square-Diffie-Hellman" assumption [6,29], and as a special case of the "Uber assumption family" [5]. Since a TMDDH adversary gets quadratic terms $[\mathbf{A} \otimes \mathbf{A}]$ "in the exponent", it is not clear how this assumption relates to the more standard MDDH assumption. However, we remark that the TMDDH assumption holds generically for large enough dimensions, at least for uniformly random $\mathbf{A}$.

Lemma 4 (Generic security of TMDDH). *For* $k \geq 4$, *the* $\mathcal{U}_{k+1,k}$-*TMDDH assumption holds against generic adversaries in a symmetric pairing setting.*

In [14] we explain what we mean by "holds generically" according to the formulation of Maurer [28] and we sketch a proof of the lemma.

The idea of the second publicly-verifiable PKE scheme is to (1) add in the public key the values $\mathbf{k}^\top [\mathbf{D} \otimes \mathbf{D}]$ and (2) use a malleable proof system $\mathbf{PS}_3$ for membership in the relation

$$\mathcal{R}_3 = \left\{ (\mathsf{pk}, [\mathbf{x}]), ([y]_T, \pi, \mathbf{r}) : \begin{array}{c} y = \mathbf{f}^\top \mathbf{u} + \mathbf{x}^\top \mathbf{F}\mathbf{u} \\ \mathbf{k}^\top [\mathbf{D} \otimes \mathbf{D}]\mathbf{r} \otimes \mathbf{r} \cdot [1] = \pi \end{array} \right\},$$

with the same set of allowable transformations as in the previous publicly verifiable PKE scheme. The languages associated with the relation $\mathcal{R}_3$ and $\mathcal{R}_2$ are identical, but we can obtain a more efficient NIZK proof for $\mathcal{R}_3$.

Theorem 5. *The pv-Rand-PKE scheme $\mathcal{PKE}_3$ is publicly verifiable, perfectly re-randomizable and RCCA-secure. Specifically:*

$$\mathbf{Adv}_{\mathcal{A},\mathcal{PKE}}^{\mathrm{RCCA}}(\lambda) \leq \mathbf{Adv}_{\mathbb{G}_1,\mathcal{U}_{n,d},\mathcal{B}}^{\mathrm{TMDDH}}(\lambda) + O\left(d \log Q_{\mathsf{Enc}}\right) \cdot \mathbf{Adv}_{\mathbb{G}_1,\mathcal{U}_{n,d},\mathcal{B}'}^{\mathrm{MDDH}}(\lambda)$$
$$+ \log Q_{\mathsf{Enc}} \cdot \mathbf{Adv}_{\mathcal{B}'',\mathbf{PS}}^{\mathrm{snd}}(\lambda) + O\left(\frac{n^2 Q_{\mathsf{Dec}} Q_{\mathsf{Enc}} \log Q_{\mathsf{Enc}}}{q}\right)$$

We only sketch the proof, which is only a slight variation of the proof of Theorem 3. Notice that in the proof of Theorem 3 to move from $\mathbf{G}_3$ to $\mathbf{G}_4$ we use the $\mathcal{D}_{n,d}$-MDDH assumption. This step changes with our modified scheme, since we add $[\mathbf{D} \otimes \mathbf{D}]$ to the public key. We thus need to rely on the stronger TMDDH assumption. Also notice that this is the only step in the proof of Theorem 3 where the assumption over the matrix $[\mathbf{D}]$ is used. Finally, observe that we can prove both composable zero-knowledge and computational adaptive soundness of the NIZK proof system for $\mathcal{R}_3$ using the classical $\mathcal{D}_k$-MDDH assumption.

6   Application: Universally Composable MixNet

We can plug-and-play our pv-Rand-RCCA PKE schemes in the MixNet protocol of [13] because their protocol works for any pv-Rand RCCA scheme that has the property of being *linear* and a property that holds for both $\mathcal{PKE}_2$ and $\mathcal{PKE}_3$. For space reasons, we defer the details in [14].

The MixNet ideal functionality interacts with n sender parties and m mixer parties. The i-th sender sends the message M_i, while the mixer can decide to mix the messages. At the end, when all the mixer have sent their inputs, the functionality returns the list of sorted messages. For space reasons, the ideal functionality is formally defined in [14].

The protocol is divided into 3 phases: (i) at the input phase, the *sender parties* send pv-Rand-RCCA ciphertexts of their messages and a simulation-extractable[5] NIZK of knowledge; (ii) at the mixing phase, the mixers, one after the other, shuffle the ciphertexts and compute the so-called *check-sum* NIZK proofs that paired with the public-verifiability and the RCCA property are sufficient to prove the validity of the shuffles; (iii) at the output phase, the ciphertexts are decrypted. The nice feature of the protocol is that the statements proved by the *check-sum* proofs are of constant size, independent of the number of shuffled ciphertexts.

The NIZK proofs employed in the input-submission phase are needed only to make sure independence of the inputs. We notice that to obtain our "tightly-secure" MixNet we need only to make sure that the Rand-mRCCA PKE and the simulation-extractable NIZK proofs are tightly secure. Let $\mathbf{Adv}_{\mathcal{A},\mathbf{PS}}^{\mathrm{sim-ext}}(\lambda)$ be the advantage of an adversary $\mathcal{A}$ against the simulation extractability experiment for $\mathbf{PS}$, we are ready now to state the main contribution of this section.

---

[5] Actually, they need a weaker form of soundness called all-but-one soundness, however simulation extractability is sufficient.

Theorem 6. *Let $\mathcal{PKE}$ be a linear pv-Rand RCCA PKE, **PS** be a simulation-extractable NIZK, and let Π be the MixNet protocol from [13] instantiated with $\mathcal{PKE}$ and **PS**. The protocol Π realizes $\mathcal{F}_{\mathsf{Mix}}$ with setup assumptions a threshold decryption functionality $\mathcal{F}_{\mathsf{TDec}}[\mathcal{PKE}]$ and a common-reference string functionality $\mathcal{F}_{\mathsf{CRS}}$. More in detail, there exist a simulator S and negligible function $\mathtt{negl}(\lambda, m)$ such that for any static-corruption environment $\mathcal{Z}$ with running time $T_{\mathcal{Z}}$ there exist an adversaries $\mathcal{B}, \mathcal{B}'$ whose running time is $O(T_{\mathcal{Z}}(\lambda))$, such that:*

$$| \Pr\left[\mathrm{REAL}_{\mathcal{Z}, \Pi}(\lambda) = 1\right] - \Pr\left[\{\mathcal{F}_{\mathsf{CRS}}, \mathcal{F}_{\mathsf{TDec}}\}\text{-}\mathrm{HYBRID}_{\mathcal{Z}, \mathsf{S}}^{\mathcal{F}_{\mathsf{Mix}}}(\lambda) = 1\right] |$$

$$\leq 3\mathbf{Adv}_{\mathcal{B}, \mathcal{PKE}}^{\mathrm{mRCCA}}(\lambda) + \mathbf{Adv}_{\mathcal{B}', \mathbf{PS}'}^{\mathrm{sim-ext}}(\lambda) + \mathtt{negl}(\lambda, m)$$

We stress that the function $\mathtt{negl}(\lambda, m)$ in the statement of Theorem 6 is independent of $T_{\mathcal{Z}}$ and only depends on the number of mixers (which we can think as a small number). The proof of the theorem follows by inspection of the proof of Theorem 5 in [13] and observing that the three steps of the proof that reduce to the pv-Rand-RCCA security of $\mathcal{PKE}$ can be performed tightly by relying on the multi-ciphertext RCCA security definition (cf. Definition 8). In [14] we give more details and we show how to instantiate the necessary simulation-extractable NIZK using the tightly-secure QA-NIZK based on the MDDH assumption of Abe et al. [2]. Thus, instantiating the protocol with $\mathcal{PKE}_2$ (resp. $\mathcal{PKE}_3$) we obtain a MixNet protocol that reduces almost-tightly in the number of mixed messages to the MDDH (resp. TMDDH) Assumption.

References

1. Abdalla, M., Benhamouda, F., Pointcheval, D.: Disjunctions for hash proof systems: new constructions and applications. In: Oswald, E., Fischlin, M. (eds.) EUROCRYPT 2015. LNCS, vol. 9057, pp. 69–100. Springer, Heidelberg (2015). https://doi.org/10.1007/978-3-662-46803-6_3
2. Abe, M., Jutla, C.S., Ohkubo, M., Roy, A.: Improved (Almost) tightly-secure simulation-sound QA-NIZK with applications. In: Peyrin, T., Galbraith, S. (eds.) ASIACRYPT 2018. LNCS, vol. 11272, pp. 627–656. Springer, Cham (2018). https://doi.org/10.1007/978-3-030-03326-2_21
3. Bayer, S., Groth, J.: Efficient zero-knowledge argument for correctness of a shuffle. In: Pointcheval, D., Johansson, T. (eds.) EUROCRYPT 2012. LNCS, vol. 7237, pp. 263–280. Springer, Heidelberg (2012). https://doi.org/10.1007/978-3-642-29011-4_17
4. Bellare, M., Boldyreva, A., Micali, S.: Public-key encryption in a multi-user setting: security proofs and improvements. In: Preneel, B. (ed.) EUROCRYPT 2000. LNCS, vol. 1807, pp. 259–274. Springer, Heidelberg (2000). https://doi.org/10.1007/3-540-45539-6_18
5. Boyen, X.: The uber-assumption family (invited talk). In: Pairing 2008 (2008)
6. Burmester, M., Desmedt, Y., Seberry, J.: Equitable key escrow with limited time span (or, how to enforce time expiration cryptographically) extended abstract. In: Ohta, K., Pei, D. (eds.) ASIACRYPT 1998. LNCS, vol. 1514, pp. 380–391. Springer, Heidelberg (1998). https://doi.org/10.1007/3-540-49649-1_30

7. Canetti, R., Krawczyk, H., Nielsen, J.B.: Relaxing chosen-ciphertext security. In: Boneh, D. (ed.) CRYPTO 2003. LNCS, vol. 2729, pp. 565–582. Springer, Heidelberg (2003). https://doi.org/10.1007/978-3-540-45146-4_33

8. Chase, M., Kohlweiss, M., Lysyanskaya, A., Meiklejohn, S.: Malleable proof systems and applications. In: Pointcheval, D., Johansson, T. (eds.) EUROCRYPT 2012. LNCS, vol. 7237, pp. 281–300. Springer, Heidelberg (2012). https://doi.org/10.1007/978-3-642-29011-4_18

9. Cramer, R., Shoup, V.: A practical public key cryptosystem provably secure against adaptive chosen ciphertext attack. In: Krawczyk, H. (ed.) CRYPTO 1998. LNCS, vol. 1462, pp. 13–25. Springer, Heidelberg (1998). https://doi.org/10.1007/BFb0055717

10. Dodis, Y., Mironov, I., Stephens-Davidowitz, N.: Message transmission with reverse firewalls—secure communication on corrupted machines. In: Robshaw, M., Katz, J. (eds.) CRYPTO 2016. LNCS, vol. 9814, pp. 341–372. Springer, Heidelberg (2016). https://doi.org/10.1007/978-3-662-53018-4_13

11. Escala, A., Herold, G., Kiltz, E., Ràfols, C., Villar, J.: An algebraic framework for diffie-hellman assumptions. In: Canetti, R., Garay, J.A. (eds.) CRYPTO 2013. LNCS, vol. 8043, pp. 129–147. Springer, Heidelberg (2013). https://doi.org/10.1007/978-3-642-40084-1_8

12. Faonio, A., Fiore, D.: Improving the efficiency of re-randomizable and replayable CCA secure public key encryption. In: Conti, M., Zhou, J., Casalicchio, E., Spognardi, A. (eds.) ACNS 2020. LNCS, vol. 12146, pp. 271–291. Springer, Cham (2020). https://doi.org/10.1007/978-3-030-57808-4_14

13. Faonio, A., Fiore, D., Herranz, J., Ràfols, C.: Structure-preserving and re-randomizable RCCA-secure public key encryption and its applications. In: Galbraith, S.D., Moriai, S. (eds.) ASIACRYPT 2019. LNCS, vol. 11923, pp. 159–190. Springer, Cham (2019). https://doi.org/10.1007/978-3-030-34618-8_6

14. Faonio, A., Hofheinz, D., Russo, L. .: Almost tightly-secure re-randomizable and replayable CCA-secure public key encryption. Cryptology ePrint Archive, Paper 2023/152 (2023). https://eprint.iacr.org/2023/152

15. Faonio, A., Russo, L.: Mix-nets from re-randomizable and replayable CCA-secure public-key encryption. In: Security and Cryptography for Networks (2022). https://doi.org/10.1007/978-3-031-14791-3_8

16. Fauzi, P., Lipmaa, H., Siim, J., Zając, M.: An efficient pairing-based shuffle argument. In: Takagi, T., Peyrin, T. (eds.) ASIACRYPT 2017. LNCS, vol. 10625, pp. 97–127. Springer, Cham (2017). https://doi.org/10.1007/978-3-319-70697-9_4

17. Gay, R., Hofheinz, D., Kiltz, E., Wee, H.: Tightly CCA-secure encryption without pairings. In: Fischlin, M., Coron, J.-S. (eds.) EUROCRYPT 2016. LNCS, vol. 9665, pp. 1–27. Springer, Heidelberg (2016). https://doi.org/10.1007/978-3-662-49890-3_1

18. Gay, R., Hofheinz, D., Kohl, L.: Kurosawa-desmedt meets tight security. In: Katz, J., Shacham, H. (eds.) CRYPTO 2017. LNCS, vol. 10403, pp. 133–160. Springer, Cham (2017). https://doi.org/10.1007/978-3-319-63697-9_5

19. Gay, R., Hofheinz, D., Kohl, L., Pan, J.: More efficient (almost) tightly secure structure-preserving signatures. In: Nielsen, J.B., Rijmen, V. (eds.) EUROCRYPT 2018. LNCS, vol. 10821, pp. 230–258. Springer, Cham (2018). https://doi.org/10.1007/978-3-319-78375-8_8

20. Groth, J.: Rerandomizable and replayable adaptive chosen ciphertext attack secure cryptosystems. In: Naor, M. (ed.) TCC 2004. LNCS, vol. 2951, pp. 152–170. Springer, Heidelberg (2004). https://doi.org/10.1007/978-3-540-24638-1_9

21. Han, S., Liu, S., Lyu, L., Gu, D.: Tight leakage-resilient CCA-security from quasi-adaptive hash proof system. In: Boldyreva, A., Micciancio, D. (eds.) CRYPTO 2019. LNCS, vol. 11693, pp. 417–447. Springer, Cham (2019). https://doi.org/10.1007/978-3-030-26951-7_15

22. Hofheinz, D.: Adaptive partitioning. In: Coron, J.-S., Nielsen, J.B. (eds.) EURO-CRYPT 2017. LNCS, vol. 10212, pp. 489–518. Springer, Cham (2017). https://doi.org/10.1007/978-3-319-56617-7_17

23. Jutla, C.S., Roy, A.: Shorter quasi-adaptive NIZK proofs for linear subspaces. In: Sako, K., Sarkar, P. (eds.) ASIACRYPT 2013. LNCS, vol. 8269, pp. 1–20. Springer, Heidelberg (2013). https://doi.org/10.1007/978-3-642-42033-7_1

24. Kurosawa, K., Desmedt, Y.: A new paradigm of hybrid encryption scheme. In: Franklin, M. (ed.) CRYPTO 2004. LNCS, vol. 3152, pp. 426–442. Springer, Heidelberg (2004). https://doi.org/10.1007/978-3-540-28628-8_26

25. Libert, B., Joye, M., Yung, M., Peters, T.: Concise Multi-challenge CCA-secure encryption and signatures with almost tight security. In: Sarkar, P., Iwata, T. (eds.) ASIACRYPT 2014. LNCS, vol. 8874, pp. 1–21. Springer, Heidelberg (2014). https://doi.org/10.1007/978-3-662-45608-8_1

26. Libert, B., Peters, T., Joye, M., Yung, M.: Compactly hiding linear spans. In: Iwata, T., Cheon, J.H. (eds.) ASIACRYPT 2015. LNCS, vol. 9452, pp. 681–707. Springer, Heidelberg (2015). https://doi.org/10.1007/978-3-662-48797-6_28

27. Libert, B., Peters, T., Qian, C.: Structure-preserving chosen-ciphertext security with shorter verifiable ciphertexts. In: Fehr, S. (ed.) PKC 2017. LNCS, vol. 10174, pp. 247–276. Springer, Heidelberg (2017). https://doi.org/10.1007/978-3-662-54365-8_11

28. Maurer, U.M.: Abstract models of computation in cryptography (invited paper). In: 10th IMA International Conference on Cryptography and Coding (2005)

29. Maurer, U.M., Wolf, S.: Diffie-hellman oracles. In: Koblitz, N. (ed.) CRYPTO 1996. LNCS, vol. 1109, pp. 268–282. Springer, Heidelberg (1996). https://doi.org/10.1007/3-540-68697-5_21

30. Naveed, M., et al.: Controlled functional encryption. In: ACM CCS 2014 (2014)

31. Pereira, O., Rivest, R.L.: Marked mix-nets. In: Brenner, M., et al. (eds.) FC 2017. LNCS, vol. 10323, pp. 353–369. Springer, Cham (2017). https://doi.org/10.1007/978-3-319-70278-0_22

32. Prabhakaran, M., Rosulek, M.: Rerandomizable RCCA encryption. In: Menezes, A. (ed.) CRYPTO 2007. LNCS, vol. 4622, pp. 517–534. Springer, Heidelberg (2007). https://doi.org/10.1007/978-3-540-74143-5_29

33. Rackoff, C., Simon, D.R.: Non-interactive zero-knowledge proof of knowledge and chosen ciphertext attack. In: Feigenbaum, J. (ed.) CRYPTO 1991. LNCS, vol. 576, pp. 433–444. Springer, Heidelberg (1992). https://doi.org/10.1007/3-540-46766-1_35

34. Tarjan, R.E.: Efficiency of a good but not linear set union algorithm. J. ACM (1975)

35. Wang, Y., Chen, R., Yang, G., Huang, X., Wang, B., Yung, M.: Receiver-anonymity in rerandomizable RCCA-secure cryptosystems resolved. In: Malkin, T., Peikert, C. (eds.) CRYPTO 2021. LNCS, vol. 12828, pp. 270–300. Springer, Cham (2021). https://doi.org/10.1007/978-3-030-84259-8_10

Multi-authority ABE for Non-monotonic Access Structures

Miguel Ambrona[1] and Romain Gay[2(✉)]

[1] Nomadic Labs, Paris, France
[2] IBM Research Zurich, Zurich, Switzerland
romain.rgay@gmail.com

Abstract. Attribute-Based Encryption (ABE) is a cryptographic primitive which supports fine-grained access control on encrypted data, making it an appealing building block for many applications. Multi-Authority Attribute-Based Encryption (MA-ABE) is a generalization of ABE where the central authority is distributed across several independent parties.

We provide the first MA-ABE scheme from asymmetric prime-order pairings where no trusted setup is needed and where the attribute universe of each authority is unbounded. Moreover, it is the first to handle non-monotonic access structures. These features broaden the applicability and improve the efficiency of our scheme. Our construction makes a modular use of Functional Encryption schemes with fine-grained access control.

1 Introduction

Attribute-Based Encryption (ABE) [SW05, GPSW06] subsumes traditional public-key encryption by providing fine-grained access to the encrypted data. Namely, each ciphertext is associated with an access policy, and each user receives a so-called user secret key according to their credentials. If these credentials fulfill the policy, the user secret key can be used to successfully decrypt the ciphertext. Otherwise, the plaintext remains hidden, even if several non-authorized users collude.

Despite being a prominent topic in the research community, the notion of ABE suffers from several drawbacks. User secret keys are generated from a so-called master secret key, which can decrypt any ciphertext. Consequently, the generation of these keys must be performed by a trusted third party, who controls the master secret key and who must be online every time a key is requested (not only during the setup phase of the scheme). Such a third party is a single point of failure in the system and is likely to be a target for attacks. Copying the master secret and using redundant servers to alleviate this bottleneck only increases the chances of key exposure. Besides, the master secret key owner can impersonate any user of its choice, acting as an escrow (see [Rog15] for further details on this issue). To mitigate these shortcomings, a solution is to decentralize the key-generation so that no single party holds the master secret key in full. Furthermore, decentralization is encouraged given that in many scenarios

© International Association for Cryptologic Research 2023
A. Boldyreva and V. Kolesnikov (Eds.): PKC 2023, LNCS 13941, pp. 306–335, 2023.
https://doi.org/10.1007/978-3-031-31371-4_11

the access policy used to generate a ciphertext includes attributes coming from different organizations.

The work of [Cha07] and later [MKE08] considered a variation of ABE where any party can become an authority by publishing some public key; these authorities, created on the fly, handle different attributes, and no coordination is required among them. In these systems, a user equipped with a global identifier can collect different credentials associated with different attributes from each authority. However, the user must then interact with a trusted central authority that will process such credentials and provide the actual ABE user secret keys. The advantage of their approach is that this central authority is agnostic to the meaning of the attributes and credentials of the user, and does not need to communicate with the other authorities. However, most of the aforementioned shortcomings remain. Afterward, [LCLS08] removed the need for a central authority, but the set of authorities in their construction is fixed and they must interact during the setup phase. Another limitation is that the security of their scheme is only proven for an a priori bounded number of collusions. [CC09] also presented a scheme with no central authority relying on distributed PRFs. However, their scheme is still limited in terms of expressiveness (it can only express a strict AND policy) and only handles a pre-determined set of attributes. In [LW11], the authors gave the first construction where there is no central authority, authorities can join the system on the fly without communicating with each other and the ciphertexts can be associated with a rich class of expressive access policies (including Boolean formulas). Despite these impressive features, their construction still suffers from some limitations: it requires a trusted setup; it uses inefficient composite-order pairings; each authority can only handle a small (poly-size) set of attributes as, in fact, the public key of each authority grows with the number of attributes owned by the authority. Later on, in [OT13, RW15], the authors built MA-ABE where there is no trusted setup beyond the mere agreement of which groups and which hash function to use, and where the attribute set of each authority is of exponential size or unbounded. Moreover, these schemes have the advantage of using prime-order pairings, which are more efficient than their composite-order counterparts. However, the scheme from [OT13] is not shown to achieve security in the presence of corrupted authorities, an important requirement in the standard security definition for MA-ABE. The scheme from [RW15] inherits from [LW11] prohibitively large ciphertexts. Indeed, in these schemes, each ciphertext contains a number of *target* group elements that grows with the size of its associated access policy, which are significantly larger than source group elements. Another reason all existing schemes lack practical efficiency is their use of *symmetric* pairings, which are less efficient than their asymmetric counterparts. This is in contrast with state-of-the-art single-authority ABE schemes, defined over *asymmetric* pairings and without target group elements in the ciphertext.

Finally, existing MA-ABE can only handle monotonic access structures. Namely, policies that can be expressed by a Boolean formula with *positive literals* only, e.g. of the form: Role = *Reviewer* $\land$ Year = *2022*. Suppose the document to be encrypted is an audit of the security department of some company for the year 2022. In order to avoid conflict of interests, employees from the security department should not be able to access the document. This corresponds to the non-monotonic formula: $(\mathsf{Role} = \mathit{Reviewer} \wedge \mathsf{Year} = \mathit{2022}) \wedge \neg(\mathsf{Department} = \mathit{Security})$. A naive way to implement negative literals would be to give user secret keys associated with both the credential owned by the user and all the negative literals not owned by the user, e.g. $\neg(\mathsf{HumanResources})$, $\neg(\mathsf{IT})$, $\neg(\mathsf{Marketing})$, $\neg(\mathsf{R\&D})$, $\neg(\mathsf{Production})$, and so on, for all existing departments in the company where the user does not belong. This solution yields very large user secret keys, since they grow proportionally with the number of possible attributes. In fact, this becomes unfeasible for large attribute universe (where the number of attribute is super-polynomial), let alone unbounded universe (where there is no restriction on the number of possible attributes, i.e. any bit string can serve as an attribute). [OSW07] gave the first ABE for non-monotonic formulas, but their techniques do not seem to be directly applicable to the multi-authority setting. This prompts the question: *Can we achieve MA-ABE with similar features and efficiency than single-authority ABE?*

Our contribution. We provide the first MA-ABE scheme from asymmetric prime-order pairings, without trusted setup and where the attribute universe of each authority is of unbounded size. Furthermore, our scheme handles non-monotonic access structures. It makes a modular use of practical Functional Encryption (FE) schemes for simple functions, namely, inner-products (we refer to our technical overview for more details about the FE we use). We prove security from standard assumptions using pairings (namely, the SXDH assumption) in the random oracle model. Our construction achieves security against adversaries that can choose the access structure of the challenge ciphertext and the attributes of the user secret keys, but the access structure and the attributes chosen cannot depend on the cryptographic material received. That is, they must not depend on the challenge ciphertext or the user secret keys (although they can depend on the public key). We refer to this security notion as super-selective security—the selective security notion traditionally refers to the setting where the adversary is constrained to choose the access structure used in the challenge ciphertext before receiving any cryptographic material (either the public key or the user secret keys). We leave it as an open problem to obtain adaptive security. Table 1 compares our scheme with the state-of-the-art.

Technical overview. We consider an MA-ABE where access policies are represented by monotone span programs (MSP) (as per Definition 1), which capture monotonic Boolean formulas. We explain how to handle non-monotonic formulas later in this overview. In a nutshell, an MSP allows users to produce shares $s_1, \ldots, s_\ell$ of a secret s, where ℓ is the size of the MSP, and each share s_j is associated with an attribute $\rho(j)$. Akin to standard secret sharing schemes, the secret s can be recovered if and only if sufficiently many shares s_j are given. The ABE uses cyclic groups $\mathbb{G}_1, \mathbb{G}_2, \mathbb{G}_t$ of prime order p, equipped with a bilinear map $e : \mathbb{G}_1 \times \mathbb{G}_2 \to \mathbb{G}_t$. We use additive bracket notation for all three groups,

Table 1. Comparison among MA-ABE schemes. The attribute universe is said to be small when it is a-priori bounded by a polynomial in the security parameter. It is said to be large when it is of a-priori bounded exponential size in the security parameters, or not bounded at all. "Corrupted authorities" refers to whether or not the scheme is secure when the adversary can acquire the secret keys of some authorities of their choice, or even create authorities with a public key of their choice (this is the standard definition for MA-ABE). "q-type" refers to a family of parameterized computational assumptions in pairing groups. "s-selective" refers to the super-selective security notion (defined in Sect. 2.5).

Reference	[LW11]	[RW15]	[OT13]	This work
pairing type	comp. sym.	prime. sym.	prime sym.	prime asym.
assumption	composite	q-type	DLIN	SXDH
security	adaptive	selective	adaptive	s-selective
attribute universe	small	large	large	large
attributes per authority	bounded	unbounded	bounded	unbounded
non-monotonic access structures	no	no	no	yes
corrupted authorities	yes	yes	no	yes

that is, for $s \in \{1, 2, t\}$, and all scalars $x \in \mathbb{Z}_p$, we write $[\![x]\!]_s = xP_s$ where P_s is a generator of $\mathbb{G}_s$. Finally, we make use of Functional Encryption (FE) schemes, which are an advanced form of public-key encryption where the secret key can be used to derive functional secret keys sk_f for certain functions f. Decryption can use sk_f to extract from an encryption $\mathsf{Enc}(\mathsf{pk}, m)$ of the message m the value $f(m)$. Nothing else is revealed about the message m apart from the value $f(m)$. Many functional secret keys can be derived for different functions from the secret key (which is referred to as master secret key, just like in the ABE setting). In short, FE enables selective computations on encrypted data. We rely on practical FE schemes that handle a particular class of functions of interest.

For encryption, an exponent s is uniformly sampled from $\mathbb{Z}_p$ and the encapsulation key is defined as $[\![s]\!]_t$ (we consider the KEM variant of ABE). The MSP is used to create shares $\{s_j\}_{j \in [\ell]}$ of s and shares $\{u_j\}_{j \in [\ell]}$ of 0. The MA-ABE ciphertext consists of one FE ciphertext of the vector (s_j, u_j) per $j \in [\ell]$. The public key of the FE used for each $j \in [\ell]$ is published by the authority that owns the attribute $\rho(j)$. Note that in order to register into the system, each authority will run the FE setup algorithm to create its pair of keys (FE.pk, FE.msk).

The FE we are using is for identity-based inner-products. That is, each ciphertext encrypts a vector $\boldsymbol{x}$ (of some fixed dimension, say d, which is then set to 2 for our modular construction), and an identity id. Each functional secret key is associated with a vector $[\![\boldsymbol{y}]\!]_2 \in \mathbb{G}_2^d$ and an identity id$'$. The decryption of the ciphertext with the functional secret key succeeds if the identities match, in which case the inner-product $[\![\boldsymbol{x}^\top \boldsymbol{y}]\!]_t$ is recovered. Nothing else is revealed about the encrypted vector $\boldsymbol{x}$. However, we do not require that the identities id and id$'$

or the vector $[\![y]\!]_2$ remain hidden. These functional secret keys can be generated from the master secret key of the FE scheme.

As we explained, the MA-ABE ciphertext will contain the FE encryption of the vector (s_j, u_j) for the identity $\rho(j)$, under the FE.pk of the authority that owns attribute $\rho(j)$, for all $j \in [\ell]$.

The secret key of a user identified by a global identifier gid, for an attribute att, will contain the FE functional secret key for the vector $[\![(1, z_{\mathsf{gid}})]\!]_2$ and the identity att, where $[\![z_{\mathsf{gid}}]\!]_2$ is the output of the hash value $H(\mathsf{gid})$. This FE functional secret key is computed using the FE master secret key of the authority that owns the attribute att.

The user gid collects all the FE functional secret keys $\mathsf{sk}_{[\![(1,z_{\mathsf{gid}})]\!]_2,\mathsf{att}}$, by making a request (att, gid) to the relevant authorities. Each FE key $\mathsf{sk}_{[\![(1,z_{\mathsf{gid}})]\!]_2,\mathsf{att}}$ yields the value $[\![s_j + z_{\mathsf{gid}} u_j]\!]_t$ if j is such that $\rho(j) = \mathsf{att}$. If sufficiently many such values are revealed, then they can be combined to obtain $[\![s + z_{\mathsf{gid}} \cdot 0]\!]_t = [\![s]\!]_t$, the encapsulation key. Otherwise said, if the user gid possesses enough attributes to satisfy the MSP in the ciphertext, it recovers the encapsulation key. Here we rely on the fact that the share reconstruction for an MSP is linear.

To argue security, we could simply rely on the simulation security of the underlying FE scheme, which states that only the value $[\![s_j + z_{\mathsf{gid}} u_j]\!]_t$ is revealed by the ciphertext and the FE functional secret key for identity $\rho(j)$ and vector $[\![(1, z_{\mathsf{gid}})]\!]_2$ (together with the value $[\![z_{\mathsf{gid}}]\!]_2$, which is public). Note that the term $[\![z_{\mathsf{gid}} u_j]\!]_t$ prevent collusions across different gid. In fact it hides the share s_j, assuming the values $[\![z_{\mathsf{gid}}]\!]_2$ generated by the hash function are pseudo-random (this holds in the random oracle model). So, if for any given gid there are not enough attributes to satisfy the access structure associated to the ciphertext, then there are not enough values $[\![s_j + z_{\mathsf{gid}} u_j]\!]_t$ to recover $[\![s]\!]_t$, which remains hidden.

This approach works, but it requires an FE scheme that is simulation-secure with many challenge ciphertexts. Unfortunately, such primitive cannot be built from standard assumptions (this can be proved by an incompressibility argument, similar to [BSW11], see Remark 1). We use an FE with indistiguishability-based security instead, which means that our MA-ABE requires a more sophisticated security proof relying on some prime-order variant of the dual vector pairing space methodology [OT09, Lew12]. Our modular construction can be instantiated with any FE with indistinguishability-based security for the appropriate functionality, such as the scheme from [ACGU20].

We now explain how to handle non-monotonic access structures, represented by span programs where each share is associated with either a normal or negated attribute (as per Definition 2). For negated attributes, we simply replace the identity-based FE for inner-products (which we call $\mathcal{FE}_1$ here) in our modular construction with an FE with revocations (called $\mathcal{FE}_2$). That is, the ciphertext of $\mathcal{FE}_2$ encrypts a vector x together with an identity id, as before, but now each functional secret key is associated with a vector $[\![y]\!]_2$ and a set of identities $\mathcal{S}$. If id $\notin \mathcal{S}$, then the decryption recovers $[\![x^\top y]\!]_t$. Else, no information is revealed about x (although the identity id, the vector $[\![y]\!]_2$ and the set $\mathcal{S}$ are not hidden).

We present a new construction for such an FE scheme whose selective security is proven under standard pairing assumptions (SXDH). Our modular MA-ABE for non-monotonic access structures uses $\mathcal{FE}_1$ and $\mathcal{FE}_2$ as follows. The encryption creates shares $\{s_j\}_{j\in[\ell]}$ of a random value s and shares $\{u_j\}_{j\in[\ell]}$ of 0 according to the span program that represents the access structure, as before. The novelty here is that each share $j \in [\ell]$ is mapped to $\rho(j)$ which is either a normal attribute, in which case the encryption encrypts the vector (s_j, u_j) with the identity $\rho(j)$ using $\mathcal{FE}_1$; or it is mapped to $\rho(j)$ which is a negated attribute, in which case the encryption encrypts (s_j, u_j) with the identity $\rho(j)$ but this time using $\mathcal{FE}_2$. Let gid be the global identifier of a user that possesses different sets of attributes $\mathcal{S}_{\mathsf{aut}} = \{\mathsf{att}_1^{\mathsf{aut}}, \dots, \mathsf{att}_{n_{\mathsf{aut}}}^{\mathsf{aut}}\}$ each owned by a different authority aut. For each authority aut, the user collects the $\mathcal{FE}_2$ functional secret key for the vector $[\![(1, z_{\mathsf{gid}})]\!]_2$ and the set $\mathcal{S}_{\mathsf{aut}}$, together with a set of n_{aut} $\mathcal{FE}_1$ functional secret keys for the vector $[\![(1, z_{\mathsf{gid}})]\!]_2$ and the identity $\mathsf{att}_i^{\mathsf{aut}}$ for $i = 1, \dots, n_{\mathsf{aut}}$. Thanks to these keys, a user can recover the values $[\![s_j + z_{\mathsf{gid}} u_j]\!]_{\mathsf{t}}$ for the shares j associated with $\rho(j)$ which is either a normal attribute owned by the user gid, or a negated attributed that is not part of the set of attributes owned by gid. As a result, decryption succeeds if and only if the attributes of the user gid satisfy the non-monotonic access structure. The security of the MA-ABE boils down to the security of the underlying FE schemes.

To build the FE for inner-products with revocations, we start with a one-time statistically secure scheme where the encryption of a vector $\boldsymbol{x} \in \mathbb{Z}_p^n$ for an identity $\mathsf{id}^\star \in \mathbb{Z}_p$ is of the form $\mathsf{ct} = (\boldsymbol{x} + \boldsymbol{v}, P(\mathsf{id}^\star))$ where $\boldsymbol{v} \in \mathbb{Z}_p^n$ is a random vector and P is a random polynomial evaluated on $\mathsf{id}^\star \in \mathbb{Z}_p$. The functional secret key for a vector $\boldsymbol{y} \in \mathbb{Z}_p^n$ and a set of identities $\mathcal{S} \subset \mathbb{Z}_p$ is of the form $\mathsf{sk}_{\boldsymbol{y},\mathcal{S}} = (\boldsymbol{y}^\top \boldsymbol{v} + P(0), \{P(\mathsf{id})\}_{\mathsf{id}\in\mathcal{S}})$. We assume the identity space is $\mathbb{Z}_p^*$, excluding 0 as a valid identity. Polynomial P is of degree d, and we assume the set $\mathcal{S}$ associated with each functional secret key is of size exactly d. We explain later how to remove this restriction. If $\mathsf{id}^\star \notin \mathcal{S}$, we have the evaluation of the polynomial P on $d+1$ distinct points, so we can recover $P(0)$ using Lagrange interpolation and get $\boldsymbol{y}^\top \boldsymbol{v}$, thanks to which we can obtain $\boldsymbol{x}^\top \boldsymbol{y}$. On the other hand, if $\mathsf{id}^\star \in \mathcal{S}$, we only have the evaluation of P on d distinct points, which reveals no information about $P(0)$, which completely masks $\boldsymbol{v}^\top \boldsymbol{y}$. Therefore, $\boldsymbol{v}$ masks $\boldsymbol{x}$ perfectly. To obtain an FE scheme with public-key encryption and security for many functional secret keys, we use standard techniques from pairing groups:

- instead of using the vector $\boldsymbol{v}$ and the polynomial P, the encryption uses $[\![\boldsymbol{v}]\!]_1$ and the coefficients of P in $\mathbb{G}_1$ that are part of pk to compute:

$$\mathsf{ct} = ([\![\boldsymbol{x} + \boldsymbol{v}r]\!]_1, [\![rP(\mathsf{id}^\star)]\!]_1) , \text{ for } r \leftarrow_R \mathbb{Z}_p .$$

- to obtain security against collusions, we randomize the functional secret keys:

$$\mathsf{sk}_{\boldsymbol{y},\mathcal{S}} = ([\![\boldsymbol{y}^\top \boldsymbol{v} + sP(0)]\!]_2, \{[\![sP(\mathsf{id})]\!]_2\}_{\mathsf{id}\in\mathcal{S}}) , \text{ for } s \leftarrow_R \mathbb{Z}_p .$$

The scheme describe here would be secure in the generic group model. To accommodate for a security proof using the SXDH assumption (i.e. the assumption that

DDH holds both in $\mathbb{G}_1$ and $\mathbb{G}_2$), we modify slightly the scheme using techniques reminiscent from the hash proof system from [CS02], similarly to [ALS16] in the context of functional encryption for inner-products.

Remark 1 (Impossibility of simulation secure FE). We consider an adversary playing against the many-ciphertexts simulation security of an identity-based FE scheme for inner-products, which makes q_1 functional secret key queries for random vectors $[\![\boldsymbol{y}_1]\!]_2, \dots, [\![\boldsymbol{y}_{q_1}]\!]_2$ and identities $\mathsf{id}_1, \dots, \mathsf{id}_{q_1}$. The adversary also chooses random vectors $\boldsymbol{x}_1, \dots, \boldsymbol{x}_{q_2}$ and identities $\mathsf{id}_1^\star, \dots, \mathsf{id}_{q_2}^\star$ for the challenge ciphertexts. The adversary chooses $\mathsf{id}_1 = \mathsf{id}_2 = \dots = \mathsf{id}_{q_1} = \mathsf{id}_1^\star = \dots = \mathsf{id}_{q_2}^\star$. The simulator must produce the challenge ciphertexts and the functional secret keys using only the values $[\![\boldsymbol{x}_i^\top \boldsymbol{y}_j]\!]_t$ and $[\![\boldsymbol{y}_j]\!]_2$ for $i = 1, \dots, q_2$ and $j = 1, \dots, q_1$, plus the identities. By the SXDH assumption (which we require for our MA-ABE), the $q_1 \cdot q_2$ values $[\![\boldsymbol{x}_i^\top \boldsymbol{y}_j]\!]_t$ are pseudo-random. The ciphertexts and functional secret keys, which are of total size $(q_1 + q_2) \cdot \mathsf{poly}(\lambda)$ must encode these values of total size $q_1 \cdot q_2 \cdot \mathsf{poly}'(\lambda)$ where $\mathsf{poly}, \mathsf{poly}'$ are polynomials, which is a contradiction. It is not clear how to bypass this impossibility result even in the random oracle model. In fact [AKW18] presents similar impossibility results for FE even in the random oracle model.

Related Works. [Kim19] builds a multi-authority ABE for all circuits from LWE for a slightly different notion that the GID model presented here (it can be seen as a relaxation of the GID model). In a recent work, [DKW21a] builds an MA-ABE for DNF formula from LWE, followed by [WWW22] that removed the use of random oracles. In [MJ18], the authors present a decentralized ABE, which is similar to an MA-ABE except the number of authorities of the system is fixed ahead of time, and each authority requires the public keys of the other authorities to generate its share of the user secret key. They realized this notion for the orthogonality-testing predicate (a.k.a. inner-product), which captures NC_0 circuits. Later on, [AYY22] extended their construction to partially hide the predicate in the user secret keys. In the same paper, they also presented a distributed ciphertext-policy ABE for NC_1, based on the LWE assumption and the bilinear generic group model. A distributed ABE is like an MA-ABE except the number of authorities is fixed ahead of time, and the adversary cannot create corrupted authorities with arbitrary public keys, but is instead restricted to (statically) recover the secret keys of honestly generated authorities. In [OT13], the authors build decentralized attribute-based signatures, which generalize the notion of ring signatures, by allowing a user whose attributes satisfy a predicate to sign a message with respect to the predicate. The validity of the signature implies that the signer has valid credentials, but the identity of the signer (or its attributes) remain hidden. As a side result, they also build a multi-authority ABE whose adaptive security is proven under the DLIN assumption in prime-order symmetric pairing groups in the random oracle model. Their scheme supports non-monotone access structures combined with inner-products. However, the security they prove does not handle corruptions of authorities. That is, in the security game, the adversary cannot get the secret key of a set of selected authorities, as is the case for others multi-authority ABE. In a paper concurrent to our work [DKW21b], the authors give the first MA-ABE for monotone span programs from the *search* variant of the Bilinear Diffie Hellman assumption. In their scheme, the size of the MSP, the number of attribute re-use and the size of the attribute universe of each authorities are all a-priori bounded. Their construction also inherits some of the practical deficiencies from prior schemes, namely, it uses symmetric pairings and the ciphertexts contain many target group elements. In [WFL19], the authors build an MA-ABE for bounded collusions (that is, where the number of possible user secret keys that can be corrupted is a priori bounded). Their construction also relies on inner-product FE but which are not identity-based nor handle revocation. They can be built from DDH (without pairing). The main different with our work lies in the unbounded-collusion security feature we achieve, which requires different techniques.

2 Preliminaries

2.1 Notations

We say a function $f : \mathbb{N} \to \mathbb{R}$ is negligible if f is asymptotically dominated by the inverse of any polynomial, i.e. for every polynomial $p \in \mathbb{R}[X]$, there exists $\lambda_p \in \mathbb{N}$ such that $|f(\lambda)| \leq |1/p(\lambda)|$ for all $\lambda \geq \lambda_p$. We denote by $|v|$ the length or dimension of vector v and by v_i its i-th component. For any $n \in \mathbb{N}$, we denote $\{1, \ldots, n\}$ by $[n]$. For any column vector $u \in \mathbb{Z}^n$ and $v \in \mathbb{Z}^m$, we denote by $(v, u) \in \mathbb{Z}^{n+m}$ the column vector obtained by concatenating them. Given two matrices (or vectors) $A \in \mathbb{Z}^{m_1 \times n_1}$ and $B \in \mathbb{Z}^{m_2 \times n_2}$, we denote by $A \otimes B \in \mathbb{Z}^{m_1 m_2 \times n_1 n_2}$ their Kronecker product, aka. tensor product defined as follows. For all $i \in [m_1 m_2]$ and $j \in [n_1 n_2]$ which we can write $i = m_1 i_1 + i_2$ with $i_1 \in [m_2]$, $i_2 \in [m_2]$, $j = n_1 j_1 + j_2$ with $j_1 \in [n_2]$, $j_2 \in [n_2]$, the (i,j)'th coordinate of $A \otimes B$ is $a_{i_1,j_1} \cdot b_{i_2,j_2}$.

2.2 Lagrange Interpolation

Let p be a prime and $\mathbb{Z}_p[X]$ denotes the mono-variate polynomials over $\mathbb{Z}_p$. There exists an efficient deterministic algorithm Lagr such that for all $P \in \mathbb{Z}_p[X]$ of degree d, given as input $d + 1$ distinct values $x_1, \ldots, x_{d+1} \in \mathbb{Z}_p \setminus \{0\}$, outputs $(\alpha_1, \ldots, \alpha_{d+1}) = \mathsf{Lagr}(x_1, \ldots, \ldots, x_{d+1})$ such that $\alpha_i \in \mathbb{Z}_p$ for all $i \in [d+1]$ and $P(0) = \sum_{i=1}^{d+1} \alpha_i P(x_i)$. The following fact states that when the evaluations of a polynomial P of degree d at only d or less distinct points (different from 0) are given, it is impossible to recover the value $P(0)$, because it is statistically independent from the values at the other points.

Fact 1. Let $d \in \mathbb{N}$, p be a prime, $x_1, \ldots, x_d \in \mathbb{Z}_p \setminus \{0\}$ be d distinct values and P be a uniformly random polynomial over $\mathbb{Z}_p[X]$ of degree d. The value $P(0)$ is statistically independent from $\{P(x_1), \ldots, P(x_d)\}$.

2.3   Access Structure

We recall the definition of monotonic access structures using the language of monotonic span programs [KW93], which capture Boolean formulas. The set of all possible attributes used by an access structure is referred to as the attribute universe. Most of the prior works consider attribute universes of polynomial size (aka small universe) or at least attribute universe of finite size (aka large universe). Here we focus on unbounded attribute universe, where any bit string can serve as an attribute. This is the most advantageous setting in term of flexibility. We denote the set of all possible bit strings by $\{0,1\}^*$.

Definition 1 (Monotonic access structure [Bei96,KW93]). *A monotonic access structure is a pair (M, ρ) where $M \in \mathbb{Z}_p^{n \times \ell}$ and $\rho : [\ell] \to \{0,1\}^*$. The matrix M is used to generate shares as described in Fig. 1, and ρ maps each share to its associated attribute. Given a set of attributes $S \subseteq \{0,1\}^*$, we say that*

$$S \ satisfies \ (M, \rho) \ iff \ \mathbf{1} \in \mathsf{Span}(M_S),$$

where $\mathbf{1} := (1, 0, \dots, 0) \in \mathbb{Z}^n$; M_S denotes the collection of vectors $\{M_j : \rho(j) \in S\}$ where M_j denotes the j'th column of M; and Span refers to linear span of collection of vectors over $\mathbb{Z}_p$.

That is, S satisfies (M, ρ) iff there exists constants $\omega_1, \dots, \omega_\ell \in \mathbb{Z}_p$ such that

$$\sum_{\rho(j) \in S} \omega_j M_j = \mathbf{1} \tag{1}$$

Observe that the constants $\{\omega_i\}$ can be computed in time polynomial in the size of the matrix M via Gaussian elimination.

Share($M \in \mathbb{Z}_p^{n \times \ell}, a \in \mathbb{Z}_p^d$):

Sample $U \leftarrow_R \mathbb{Z}_p^{d \times (n-1)}$, and for all $j \in [\ell]$, set $a_j := (a|U)M_j \in \mathbb{Z}_p^d$.

Return $\{a_j\}_{j \in [\ell]}$.

Fig. 1. Share generation algorithm. Here, M_j denotes the j-th column of M. For each $j \in [\ell]$, a_j is a share of the secret $a \in \mathbb{Z}_p^d$.

Now we consider non-monotonic access structures, where ρ maps each share to either an attribute or a *negated* attribute. A set of attribute S satisfies the non-monotonic access structure (M, ρ) if given all the shares that correspond to an attribute in S or a negated attribute of the form ¬att where att is not in S, it is possible to recover the secret. For any set $S \subseteq \{0,1\}^*$, we denote by $\{\neg\} \cdot S$ the set defined as $\{\neg \mathrm{att}\}_{\mathrm{att} \in S}$. The formal definition of a non-monotonic access structure is given below.

Definition 2 (Non-monotonic access structure [OSW07]). *A non-monotonic access structure is a pair (M, ρ) where $M \in \mathbb{Z}_p^{n \times \ell}$ and $\rho : [\ell] \to \{0,1\}^* \cup (\{\neg\} \cdot \{0,1\}^*)$. The matrix M is used to generate shares as described in Fig. 1,* and ρ maps each share to its associated attribute in $\{0,1\}^*$ or negated attribute in $\{\neg\} \cdot \{0,1\}^*$. Given a set of attributes $\mathcal{S} \subseteq \{0,1\}^*$, we say that

$$\mathcal{S} \, satisfies\, (M, \rho) \, iff\, \mathbf{1} \in \mathsf{Span}(M_{\mathcal{S}}),$$

where $\mathbf{1} := (1, 0, \ldots, 0) \in \mathbb{Z}^n$; $M_{\mathcal{S}}$ denotes the collection of vectors $\{M_j : \rho(j) \in \mathcal{S}$ or $\rho(j) = \neg att$ with $att \in \{0,1\}^* \setminus \mathcal{S}\}$, M_j denotes the j'th column of M, and Span refers to the linear span of a collection of (column) vectors over $\mathbb{Z}_p$.

For any set of attributes $\mathcal{S}_{\mathsf{corr}} \subset \{0,1\}^*$, we say

$$\mathcal{S} \, satisfies\, (M, \rho) \, with\, corruptions\, \mathcal{S}_{\mathsf{corr}} \, iff\, \mathbf{1} \in \mathsf{Span}(M_{\mathcal{S}, \mathcal{S}_{\mathsf{corr}}}),$$

where $\mathbf{1} := (1, 0, \ldots, 0) \in \mathbb{Z}^n$; $M_{\mathcal{S}}$ denotes the collection of vectors $\{M_j : \rho(j) \in \mathcal{S} \cup \mathcal{S}_{\mathsf{corr}}$ or $\rho(j) = \neg att$ with $att \in \{0,1\}^* \setminus \mathcal{S}\}$, M_j denotes the j'th column of M, and Span refers to the linear span of a collection of (column) vectors over $\mathbb{Z}_p$.

That is, $\mathcal{S}$ satisfies (M, ρ) iff there exists constants $\omega_1, \ldots, \omega_\ell, \omega'_1, \ldots, \omega'_\ell \in \mathbb{Z}_p$ such that

$$\sum\nolimits_{\rho(j) \in \mathcal{S} \cup \mathcal{S}_{\mathsf{corr}}} \omega_j M_j + \sum\nolimits_{\rho(j) = \neg att, att \notin \mathcal{S}} \omega'_j M_j = \mathbf{1} \tag{2}$$

Observe that the constants $\{\omega_i, \omega'_i\}$ can be computed in time polynomial in the size of the matrix M via Gaussian elimination. Now we recall a useful fact about access structures represented by span programs.

Lemma 1 ([KW93]). *Let (M, ρ) be a non-monotonic access structure where $M \in \mathbb{Z}_p^{n \times \ell}$. For all sets $\mathcal{S}, \mathcal{S}_{\mathsf{corr}} \subseteq \{0,1\}^*$ such that $\mathcal{S}$ does do not satisfy (M, ρ) with corruptions $\mathcal{S}_{\mathsf{corr}}$, there exists a vector $w_{\mathcal{S}} \in \mathbb{Z}_p^{\ell-1}$ such that $(1, w)^\top M_j = 0$ for all $j \in [\ell]$ such that $\rho(j) \in \mathcal{S} \cup \mathcal{S}_{\mathsf{corr}}$ or $\rho(j) = \neg att$ with $att \in \{0,1\}^* \setminus \mathcal{S}$.*

2.4 Pairing Groups

Let GGen be a PPT algorithm that on input the security parameter 1^λ, outputs a description $\mathcal{PG} = (p, \mathbb{G}_1, \mathbb{G}_2, P_1, P_2, \mathbb{G}_t, e)$ of pairing groups where $\mathbb{G}_1, \mathbb{G}_2$ and $\mathbb{G}_t$ are cyclic groups of order p for a 2λ-bit prime p; P_1 and P_2 are generators of $\mathbb{G}_1$ and $\mathbb{G}_2$ respectively and $e : \mathbb{G}_1 \times \mathbb{G}_2 \to \mathbb{G}_t$ is an efficiently computable (non-degenerate) bilinear map, thus $P_t := e(P_1, P_2)$ generates $\mathbb{G}_t$.

We use implicit representation of group elements. For $s \in \{1, 2, t\}$ and $a \in \mathbb{Z}_p$, define $[\![a]\!]_s = a \cdot P_s \in \mathbb{G}_s$ as the implicit representation of a in $\mathbb{G}_s$. More generally, for a matrix $A = (a_{ij}) \in \mathbb{Z}_p^{n \times m}$ we define $[\![A]\!]_s$ as the implicit representation of A in $\mathbb{G}_s$:

$$[\![A]\!]_s := \begin{pmatrix} a_{11} \cdot P_s & \ldots & a_{1m} \cdot P_s \\ & & \\ a_{n1} \cdot P_s & \ldots & a_{nm} \cdot P_s \end{pmatrix} \in \mathbb{G}_s^{n \times m}.$$

Given $[\![a]\!]_1$ and $[\![b]\!]_2$, one can efficiently compute $[\![a \cdot b]\!]_t$ using the pairing e. For matrices A and B of matching dimensions, define $e([\![A]\!]_1, [\![B]\!]_2) := [\![AB]\!]_t$. For any matrix $A, B \in \mathbb{Z}_p^{n \times m}$, any group $s \in \{1, 2, t\}$, we denote by $[\![A]\!]_s + [\![B]\!]_s = [\![A + B]\!]_s$.

Definition 3 (DDH assumption). *For any adversary $\mathcal{A}$, any group $s \in \{1, 2, t\}$ and any security parameter λ, let*

$$\mathsf{Adv}_{\mathbb{G}_s, \mathcal{A}}^{\mathsf{DDH}}(\lambda) := |\Pr[1 \leftarrow \mathcal{A}(\mathcal{PG}, [\![a]\!]_s, [\![ar]\!]_s)] - \Pr[1 \leftarrow \mathcal{A}(\mathcal{PG}, [\![a]\!]_s, [\![u]\!]_s)]|,$$

where the probabilities are taken over $\mathcal{PG} \leftarrow_R \mathsf{GGen}(1^\lambda, d)$, $a \leftarrow_R \mathbb{Z}_p^2$, $r \leftarrow_R \mathbb{Z}_p$, $u \leftarrow_R \mathbb{Z}_p^2$, and the random coins of $\mathcal{A}$. We say DDH holds in $\mathbb{G}_s$ if for all PPT adversaries $\mathcal{A}$, $\mathsf{Adv}_{\mathbb{G}_s, \mathcal{A}}^{\mathsf{DDH}}(\lambda)$ is a negligible function of λ.

Definition 4 (SXDH assumption). *For any security parameter λ and any pairing group $\mathcal{PG} = (\mathbb{G}_1, \mathbb{G}_2, \mathbb{G}_T, p, P_1, P_2, e) \leftarrow_R \mathsf{GGen}(1^\lambda)$, we say SXDH holds in $\mathcal{PG}$ if DDH holds in $\mathbb{G}_1$ and $\mathbb{G}_2$.*

It is well known that the DDH and SXDH assumptions are equivalent when the dimensions of the vectors are larger than 2 (for any polynomially large dimensions).

2.5 Functional Encryption

We recall the notion of functional encryption originally given in [BSW11]. Let $\mathcal{F} = \{\mathcal{F}_\lambda\}_{\lambda \in \mathbb{N}}$ be a family of sets, where for each $\lambda \in \mathbb{N}$, $\mathcal{F}_\lambda$ is a set of functions from the message space $\mathcal{X}_\lambda$ to the output space $\mathcal{Y}_\lambda$. A functional encryption scheme for $\mathcal{F}$ consists of the following PPT algorithms.

- $\mathsf{Setup}(1^\lambda) \rightarrow (\mathsf{msk}, \mathsf{pk})$. On input the global parameters gp, it outputs a master secret key msk and a public key pk. The public key is (sometimes implicitly) input to all other algorithms.
- $\mathsf{Enc}(\mathsf{pk}, m) \rightarrow \mathsf{ct}$. On input the public key pk and a message $m \in \mathcal{X}_\lambda$, it outputs a ciphertext ct.
- $\mathsf{KeyGen}(\mathsf{msk}, f) \rightarrow \mathsf{sk}_f$. On input the master secret key msk and a function $f \in \mathcal{F}_\lambda$, it outputs a functional secret key sk_f, which includes the description of the function f.
- $\mathsf{Dec}(\mathsf{pk}, \mathsf{ct}, \mathsf{sk}_f) \rightarrow m$. On input the public key pk, a ciphertext ct and a functional secret key sk_f, the decryption algorithm deterministically outputs a value $\mu \in \mathcal{Y}_\lambda$ (or a special rejection symbol if it fails to decrypt).

Correctness. For all $\lambda \in \mathbb{N}$, all $(\mathsf{pk}, \mathsf{msk})$ in the support of $\mathsf{Setup}(1^\lambda)$, all messages $m \in \mathcal{X}_\lambda$ and all functions $f \in \mathcal{F}_\lambda$, we have

$$\Pr[\mathsf{Dec}(\mathsf{pk}, \mathsf{Enc}(\mathsf{pk}, m), \mathsf{KeyGen}(\mathsf{msk}, f)) = f(m)] = 1,$$

where the probability is taken over the random coins of Enc and KeyGen.

We now describe the indistinguishability-based security notion for FE.

Adaptive Security. Given an FE scheme denoted by FE for $\mathcal{F}$, for any adversary $\mathcal{A}$ and security parameter λ, we define the advantage function:

$$\mathsf{Adv}^{\mathsf{FE}}_{\mathcal{A}}(\lambda) := \left| \Pr \left[\begin{array}{c} (\mathsf{pk}, \mathsf{msk}) \leftarrow \mathsf{Setup}(1^\lambda) \\ (m_0, m_1, \mathsf{st}) \leftarrow \mathcal{A}^{\mathcal{O}_{\mathsf{KeyGen}}(\cdot)}(\mathsf{pk}) \\ \beta \leftarrow_R \{0,1\} \\ \mathsf{ct}^\star \leftarrow \mathsf{Enc}(\mathsf{pk}, m_\beta) \\ \beta' \leftarrow \mathcal{A}^{\mathcal{O}_{\mathsf{KeyGen}}(\cdot)}(\mathsf{ct}^\star, \mathsf{st}) \end{array} : \beta' = \beta \right] - \frac{1}{2} \right| ,$$

where the oracle $\mathcal{O}_{\mathsf{KeyGen}}$, when given as input a function $f \in \mathcal{F}_\lambda$, returns $\mathsf{KeyGen}(\mathsf{msk}, f)$ and st denotes the state of the adversary $\mathcal{A}$. We say the adversary $\mathcal{A}$ is admissible if for all functions $f \in \mathcal{F}_\lambda$ queried to $\mathcal{O}_{\mathsf{KeyGen}}$, it holds that $f(m_0) = f(m_1)$. An FE scheme FE is said to be IND-secure if for all PPT admissible adversaries $\mathcal{A}$, $\mathsf{Adv}^{\mathsf{FE}}_{\mathcal{A}}$ is negligible.

Selective, Super-Selective Security. In the security game above, we say an adversary is selective if it chooses a pair of messages (m_0, m_1) before querying any functional secret key to $\mathcal{O}_{\mathsf{KeyGen}}$. An adversary is said to be super-selective if it is selective and it chooses the queries to $\mathcal{O}_{\mathsf{KeyGen}}$ independently of the challenge ciphertext $\mathsf{ct}^\star$. That is, an FE scheme FE is said to be super-selective if for all admissible PPT adversaries $\mathcal{A}$, the function $\mathsf{Adv}^{\mathsf{ssel\text{-}FE}}_{\mathcal{A}}$ is negligible, where $\mathsf{Adv}^{\mathsf{ssel\text{-}FE}}_{\mathcal{A}}$ is defined for all $\lambda \in \mathbb{N}$ as follows:

$$\mathsf{Adv}^{\mathsf{ssel\text{-}FE}}_{\mathcal{A}}(\lambda) := \left| \Pr \left[\begin{array}{c} (\mathsf{pk}, \mathsf{msk}) \leftarrow \mathsf{Setup}(1^\lambda) \\ (m_0, m_1, \mathsf{st}) \leftarrow \mathcal{A}(\mathsf{pk}) \\ \mathsf{st}' \leftarrow \mathcal{A}(\mathsf{st})^{\mathcal{O}_{\mathsf{KeyGen}}(\cdot)} \\ \beta \leftarrow_R \{0,1\} \\ \mathsf{ct}^\star \leftarrow \mathsf{Enc}(\mathsf{pk}, m_\beta) \\ \beta' \leftarrow \mathcal{A}(\mathsf{ct}^\star, \mathsf{st}') \end{array} : \beta' = \beta \right] - \frac{1}{2} \right| ,$$

where the oracle $\mathcal{O}_{\mathsf{KeyGen}}$, when given as input a function $f \in \mathcal{F}_\lambda$, returns $\mathsf{KeyGen}(\mathsf{msk}, f)$ and $\mathsf{st}, \mathsf{st}'\mathsf{s}$ denote the states of the adversary $\mathcal{A}$. As for the IND-security above, we say the adversary $\mathcal{A}$ is admissible if for all functions $f \in \mathcal{F}_\lambda$ queried to $\mathcal{O}_{\mathsf{KeyGen}}$, it holds that $f(m_0) = f(m_1)$.

2.6 Definition of Multi-authority ABE

We recall the definition of multi-authority ABE from [LW11]. We assume every authority is identified by a public key. For every authority pk, we denote by $\mathcal{U}_{\mathsf{pk}}$ the associated attribute universe. Without loss of generality, we assume that attribute universes are disjoint for different authorities.

We consider access structures $(\boldsymbol{M}, \rho)$ where $\boldsymbol{M} \in \mathbb{Z}_p^{n \times \ell}$, and ρ maps each row $j \in [\ell]$ to an attribute in $\mathcal{U}_{\theta(j)}$, where θ maps a row $j \in [\ell]$ to the authority who owns the attribute $\rho(j)$. To keep notations simple, we assume the map θ is implicitly part of the description of the access structure.

Definition. A MA-ABE scheme consists of the following PPT algorithms:

- GlobalSetup$(1^\lambda) \to$ gp. On input the security parameter, it outputs global parameters, which are input to all other algorithms (usually implicitly).
- AuthSetup(gp) $\to$ (pk, sk). Each authority runs a setup procedure to generate its own pair of keys. The public key serves as a univocal identifier for the authority, which is associated with an attribute universe denoted by $\mathcal{U}_{\mathsf{pk}}$.
- Enc$(\boldsymbol{M}, \rho, \Pi) \to$ (ct, κ). On input an access structure $\boldsymbol{M} \in \mathbb{Z}_p^{n \times \ell}$, $\rho : [\ell] \to \{0,1\}^*$ and a set of authorities Π such that for all columns $j \in [\ell]$, we have $\theta(j) \in \Pi$, the encryption algorithm outputs a ciphertext ct and a symmetric encryption key $\kappa \in \mathcal{K}$. The ciphertext implicitly contains a description of the access structure $(\boldsymbol{M}, \rho)$.
- KeyGen(pk, sk, gid, $\mathcal{S}$) $\to$ sk$_{\mathsf{gid},\mathcal{S}}$. On input an authority's public key pk and the corresponding secret key sk, a global identifier gid and a set of attribute $\mathcal{S} \subset \mathcal{U}_{\mathsf{pk}}$, the key generation algorithm outputs a user secret key sk$_{\mathsf{gid},\mathcal{S}}$, which implicitly contains a description of gid and $\mathcal{S}$.
- Dec(ct, $\{\mathsf{sk}_{\mathsf{gid},\mathcal{S}_i}\}_i$) $\to \kappa/\bot$. On input a ciphertext ct and a set of user secret keys $\{\mathsf{sk}_{\mathsf{gid},\mathcal{S}_i}\}_i$ created for the same global identifier, the decryption algorithm deterministically outputs a symmetric key κ or $\bot$.

Correctness. For all $\lambda \in \mathbb{N}$, all gp in the support of GlobalSetup(1^λ), all $\nu \in \mathbb{N}$, all $(\mathsf{pk}_1, \mathsf{sk}_1), \cdots, (\mathsf{pk}_\nu, \mathsf{sk}_\nu)$ in the support of Setup(gp), all access structures $(\boldsymbol{M}, \rho)$ associated with the set of authorities $\Pi = \{\mathsf{pk}_1, \ldots, \mathsf{pk}_\nu\}$, all pairs (ct, κ) in the support of Enc$(\boldsymbol{M}, \rho, \Pi)$, all sets of attributes $\mathcal{S}_i \subset \mathcal{U}_{\mathsf{pk}_i}$ for all $i \in [\nu]$ such that $\mathcal{S} = \cup_{i \in [\nu]} \mathcal{S}_i$ satisfies $(\boldsymbol{M}, \rho)$ and all global identifiers gid $\in \{0,1\}^*$:

$$\Pr\left[\mathsf{Dec}(\mathsf{ct}, \{\mathsf{sk}_{\mathsf{gid},\mathcal{S}_i}\}_{i \in [\nu]}) = \kappa\right] = 1 \ ,$$

where the probability is taken over sk$_{\mathsf{gid},\mathcal{S}_i} \leftarrow$ KeyGen$(\mathsf{pk}_i, \mathsf{sk}_i, \mathsf{gid}, \mathcal{S}_i)$ for all $i \in [\nu]$.

Adaptive Security. Given a multi-authority ABE denoted by ABE, for any stateful adversary $\mathcal{A}$ and security parameter λ, we define the advantage function:

$$\mathsf{Adv}_{\mathcal{A}}^{\mathsf{ABE}}(\lambda) :=$$

$$\left| \Pr \left[\begin{array}{c} \mathsf{gp} \leftarrow \mathsf{GlobalSetup}(1^\lambda) \\ (\boldsymbol{M}, \rho, \Pi_{\mathsf{hon}}, \Pi_{\mathsf{corr}}) \leftarrow \mathcal{A}^{\mathcal{O}_{\mathsf{create}}, \mathcal{O}_{\mathsf{corr}}(\cdot), \mathcal{O}_{\mathsf{KeyGen}}(\cdot,\cdot,\cdot)}(\mathsf{gp}) \\ (\mathsf{ct}^\star, \kappa) \leftarrow \mathsf{Enc}(\boldsymbol{M}, \rho, \Pi) \\ \beta \leftarrow_R \{0,1\}; \ K_0 := \kappa; \ K_1 \leftarrow_R \mathcal{K} \\ \beta' \leftarrow \mathcal{A}^{\mathcal{O}_{\mathsf{corr}}(\cdot), \mathcal{O}_{\mathsf{KeyGen}}(\cdot,\cdot,\cdot)}(\mathsf{ct}^\star, K_\beta) \end{array} : \beta' = \beta \right] - \frac{1}{2} \right| .$$

The oracles are defined as follows:

- $\mathcal{O}_{\mathsf{create}}$: runs $(\mathsf{pk}, \mathsf{sk}) \leftarrow \mathsf{AuthSetup}(\mathsf{gp})$, adds pk to the sets of honest authorities denoted by $\mathcal{S}_{\mathsf{hon}}$ (initially empty) and returns pk.
- $\mathcal{O}_{\mathsf{corr}}(\mathsf{pk})$: if $\mathsf{pk} \in \mathcal{S}_{\mathsf{hon}}$, it returns the associated secret key sk and removes pk from $\mathcal{S}_{\mathsf{hon}}$.
- $\mathcal{O}_{\mathsf{KeyGen}}(\mathsf{pk}, \mathsf{gid}, \mathcal{S})$: if $\mathsf{pk} \in \mathcal{S}_{\mathsf{hon}}$ and $\mathcal{S} \subset \mathcal{U}_{\mathsf{pk}}$, it returns $\mathsf{KeyGen}(\mathsf{pk}, \mathsf{sk}, \mathsf{gid}, \mathcal{S})$ where sk is the secret key associated with pk; otherwise, it returns $\perp$. This oracle can be queried at most once per $(\mathsf{pk}, \mathsf{gid})$ pair. That is, there cannot be two queries of the form $(\mathsf{pk}, \mathsf{gid}, \mathcal{S})$ and $(\mathsf{pk}, \mathsf{gid}, \mathcal{S}')$ for different $\mathcal{S} \neq \mathcal{S}'$ to $\mathcal{O}_{\mathsf{KeyGen}}$. This restriction is necessary for non-monotonic access structure (see Remark 2).

The adversary $\mathcal{A}$ outputs an access structure $(\boldsymbol{M}, \rho)$ with respect to the authorities $\Pi = \Pi_{\mathsf{hon}} \cup \Pi_{\mathsf{corr}}$, where Π_{hon} denotes the set of honest authorities, that is, which have been created via $\mathcal{O}_{\mathsf{create}}$, and which have not been queried to $\mathcal{O}_{\mathsf{corr}}$ (they can still be queried to $\mathcal{O}_{\mathsf{corr}}$ later on), whereas Π_{corr} denotes the set of corrupted authorities, that is, authorities created via $\mathcal{O}_{\mathsf{create}}$ that have been subsequently queried to $\mathcal{O}_{\mathsf{corr}}$, or authorities whose public keys were maliciously created by the adversary $\mathcal{A}$ himself. We require that Π_{corr} contains not only the public keys of the corrupted authorities, but also their associated secret keys[1].

We denote by $\mathcal{Q}_{\mathsf{KeyGen}}$ the set of queries to $\mathcal{O}_{\mathsf{KeyGen}}$, $\mathcal{S}_{\mathsf{hon}} \subseteq \Pi_{\mathsf{hon}}$ the set of authorities in Π_{hon} that are still honest at the end of the experiment, $\mathcal{S}_{\mathsf{corr}} = \Pi_{\mathsf{corr}} \cup \Pi_{\mathsf{hon}} \setminus \mathcal{S}_{\mathsf{hon}}$, $\Sigma_{\mathsf{corr}} = \cup_{\mathsf{pk} \in \mathcal{S}_{\mathsf{corr}}} \mathcal{U}_{\mathsf{pk}}$, and for every global identifier $\mathsf{gid} \in \{0,1\}^*$, $\mathcal{S}_{\mathsf{gid}} = \cup_{\mathsf{pk} \in \mathcal{S}_{\mathsf{hon}}, (\mathsf{pk}, \mathsf{gid}, \mathcal{S}) \in \mathcal{Q}_{\mathsf{KeyGen}}} \mathcal{S}$. We say the adversary $\mathcal{A}$ is admissible if for all $\mathsf{gid} \in \{0,1\}^*$, $\mathcal{S}_{\mathsf{gid}}$ does not satisfy $(\boldsymbol{M}, \rho)$ with corruptions Σ_{corr} (as per Definition 1). We say ABE is adaptively secure if for all PPT admissible adversaries $\mathcal{A}$, there exists a negligible function ν such that for all $\lambda \in \mathbb{N}$, $\mathsf{Adv}_{\mathcal{A}}^{\mathsf{ABE}}(\lambda) \leq \nu(\lambda)$.

Static Corruptions. We say an ABE is secure with static corruptions if the adversary does not have access to the oracle $\mathcal{O}_{\mathsf{corr}}$. He can still create authorities maliciously as part of Π_{corr}, but all authorities created by $\mathcal{O}_{\mathsf{create}}$ remain honest throughout the experiment.

---

[1] The restriction which requires that the adversary provide the secret keys of the corrupted authorities in Π_{corr} can be lifted via a generic use of Zero-Knowledge Argument of Knowledge. See Remark 3 for further details.

Selective, Super-Selective Security. In the security game above, we say an adversary is selective if it chooses the tuple $(M, \rho, \Pi_{\text{corr}}, \Pi_{\text{hon}})$ before querying any user secret key to $\mathcal{O}_{\text{KeyGen}}$. An adversary is said to be super-selective if it is selective and it chooses the queries to $\mathcal{O}_{\text{KeyGen}}$ independently of the challenge ciphertext $\text{ct}^\star$. That is, an MA-ABE scheme ABE is said to be super-selective if for all admissible PPT adversaries $\mathcal{A}$, the function $\text{Adv}_{\mathcal{A}}^{\text{ssel-ABE}}$ is negligible, where $\text{Adv}_{\mathcal{A}}^{\text{ssel-ABE}}$ is defined for all $\lambda \in \mathbb{N}$ as follows:

$$
\text{Adv}_{\mathcal{A}}^{\text{ABE}}(\lambda) :=
\left| \Pr \left[
\begin{array}{c}
\text{gp} \leftarrow \text{GlobalSetup}(1^\lambda) \\
(M, \rho, \Pi_{\text{hon}}, \Pi_{\text{corr}}, \text{st}) \leftarrow \mathcal{A}^{\mathcal{O}_{\text{create}}, \mathcal{O}_{\text{corr}}(\cdot)}(\text{gp}) \\
\text{st}' \leftarrow \mathcal{A}^{\mathcal{O}_{\text{corr}}(\cdot), \mathcal{O}_{\text{KeyGen}}(\cdot,\cdot,\cdot)}(\text{st}) \\
(\text{ct}^\star, \kappa) \leftarrow \text{Enc}(M, \rho, \Pi) \\
\beta \leftarrow_R \{0,1\}; K_0 := \kappa; K_1 \leftarrow_R \mathcal{K} \\
\beta' \leftarrow \mathcal{A}^{\mathcal{O}_{\text{corr}}(\cdot)}(\text{ct}^\star, K_\beta, \text{st}')
\end{array}
: \beta' = \beta
\right] - \frac{1}{2} \right| .
$$

where the oracles are defined as above, and st, st' denote the states of the adversary $\mathcal{A}$.

Remark 2 (At most one user secret key query per gid). In the definitions above, we restrict the adversary to query the oracle $\mathcal{O}_{\text{KeyGen}}$ at most once per (pk, gid) pair . This restriction is necessary when considering non-monotone access structure. In fact, security relies on the fact that users only obtain user secret keys associated to the set of *all* attributes they possess. Giving the adversary access to at most one query to $\mathcal{O}_{\text{KeyGen}}$ per (pk, gid) is one way to ensure this is the case.

For instance, suppose a user Alice possesses the attributes att_1 and att_2 that are owned by an authority. Alice should not be able to obtain user secret keys associated to strict subsets of $\{\text{att}_1, \text{att}_2\}$. If for example she obtains a user secret key for $\{\text{att}_1\}$, she would be able to decrypt a ciphertext associated with an access structure excluding users possessing att_2.

Remark 3 (Stronger security via ZK-AoK). In the security definition above, we require the adversary to provide not only the public keys, but also the secret keys of all the authorities in Π_{corr}. It is possible to lift this restriction, and thereby strengthen the security definition, using standard techniques involving Zero-Knowledge Argument of Knowledge (ZK-AoK). Any authority must publish not only a public key, but also an argument of knowledge of the associated secret key. The zero-knowledge property ensures that nothing is revealed about the secret key, and the argument of knowledge property forces the issuer to know the associated secret key. This way, the adversary must know the secret key associated to any authority it creates maliciously, since it has to provide an argument of knowledge. Note that in our ABE constructions we use a ZK-AoK for a very simple language that admits an efficient sigma protocol, that can be made non-interactive with the Fiat-Shamir heuristic. Consequently, strengthening the security comes at a modest efficiency cost. In the rest of this paper, we focus on the weaker security definition, which is easier to prove.

3 Inner-Product FE

3.1 Identity-Based Inner-product FE

We recall the definition of Identity-Based Inner-Product Functional Encryption (ID-IPFE) which is a particular case of Functional Encryption where the family $\mathcal{F} = \{\mathcal{F}_\lambda\}_{\lambda \in \mathbb{N}}$ is as follows. Let d be a polynomial and GGen a pairing group generator. For every $\lambda \in \mathbb{N}$, the set of functions $\mathcal{F}_\lambda$ is associated with a pairing group $(p, \mathbb{G}_1, \mathbb{G}_2, P_1, P_2, \mathbb{G}_t, e) = \mathsf{GGen}(1^\lambda)$, where p is a prime which denotes the order of the groups $\mathbb{G}_1, \mathbb{G}_2$, and $\mathbb{G}_t$. We assume the pairing group $\mathcal{PG}$ is given as input of the setup algorithm. The message space $\mathcal{X}_\lambda = \mathbb{Z}_p^{d(\lambda)} \times \mathbb{Z}_p$. That is, every message is of the form $(\boldsymbol{x}, \mathsf{id})$, where $\boldsymbol{x} \in \mathbb{Z}_p^{d(\lambda)}$ is referred to as the message vector, and $\mathsf{id} \in \mathbb{Z}_p$ is referred to as the identity. The function space $\mathcal{F}_\lambda = \mathbb{G}_2^{d(\lambda)} \times \mathbb{Z}_p$. Every function is of the form $([\![\boldsymbol{y}]\!]_2, \mathsf{id}')$ where $[\![\boldsymbol{y}]\!]_2 \in \mathbb{G}_2^{d(\lambda)}$ and $\mathsf{id}' \in \mathbb{Z}_p$. Decryption recovers the inner product $[\![\boldsymbol{x}^\top \boldsymbol{y}]\!]_t \in \mathbb{G}_t$ when $\mathsf{id} = \mathsf{id}'$. When $\mathsf{id}' \neq \mathsf{id}$, the vector $\boldsymbol{x}$ remains hidden. In both cases, the vector $[\![\boldsymbol{y}]\!]_2$ and the identities id and id' are revealed.

In [DP19, TT18], the authors give an unbounded variant of the related family where functions are of the form $(\boldsymbol{y}, \mathsf{id}) \in \mathbb{Z}_p^{d(\lambda)} \times \mathbb{Z}_p$, that is, the vector $\boldsymbol{y}$ needs to be known in $\mathbb{Z}_p^{d(\lambda)}$ instead of $\mathbb{G}_2^{d(\lambda)}$. In our MA-ABE that uses the ID-IPFE as a building block, the party generating the functional secret keys only know the value $[\![\boldsymbol{y}]\!]_2 \in \mathbb{G}_2^{d(\lambda)}$, which prevents us from using their scheme. In [ACGU20], the authors present an ID-IPFE for the functions described above (where $\mathcal{F}_\lambda = \mathbb{G}_2^{d(\lambda)} \times \mathbb{Z}_p$) which is selectively secure under the SXDH assumption. They also present an adaptively secure construction but only for the messages $(\boldsymbol{x}, \mathsf{id})$ and functions $([\![\boldsymbol{y}]\!]_2, \mathsf{id}')$ such that $\boldsymbol{x}^\top \boldsymbol{y}$ is small (i.e. lies in a set of polynomial size), which is not the case for our application. Indeed the value of the inner product $[\![\boldsymbol{x}^\top \boldsymbol{y}]\!]_t$ in our case will be well-spread in the full group $\mathbb{G}_t$. This prevents from using the adaptively secure scheme from [ACGU20]. It is an open problem to build an adaptively secure ID-IPFE for large values.

3.2 Inner-Product FE with Revocations

Here we consider a Functional Encryption scheme for the family $\mathcal{F} = \{\mathcal{F}_\lambda\}_{\lambda \in \mathbb{N}}$ where for all $\lambda \in \mathbb{N}$, $\mathcal{X}_\lambda = \mathbb{Z}_p^{d(\lambda)} \times \mathbb{Z}_p$, $\mathcal{F}_\lambda = \mathbb{G}_2^{d(\lambda)} \times \mathcal{S}_t$, $\mathcal{S}_t$ denotes all the sets of size t included in $\mathbb{Z}_p$, and p is a prime which denotes the order of a pairing group $\mathcal{PG} = (p, \mathbb{G}_1, \mathbb{G}_2, P_1, P_2, \mathbb{G}_t, e)$. We assume the pairing group $\mathcal{PG}$ is given as input of the setup algorithm. For every message of the form $(\boldsymbol{x}, \mathsf{id})$ where $\boldsymbol{x} \in \mathbb{Z}_p^{d(\lambda)}$ and $\mathsf{id} \in \mathbb{Z}_p$, and every function of the form $([\![\boldsymbol{y}]\!]_2, \mathcal{S})$ where $\mathcal{S} \subset \mathbb{Z}_p$ is of size t, decryption recovers $[\![\boldsymbol{x}^\top \boldsymbol{y}]\!]_t$ when $\mathsf{id} \notin \mathcal{S}$. When $\mathsf{id} \in \mathcal{S}$, then the vector $\boldsymbol{x}$ remains hidden. In both cases, the identity id, the set $\mathcal{S}$ and the vector $[\![\boldsymbol{y}]\!]_2$ are revealed. Note that the set $\mathcal{S}$ associated to each functional secret key is required to be of size *exactly* t. We argue in Sect. 3.3 how to remove this restriction and have sets of size at most t. We now give the first construction of such an FE scheme, whose selective security we prove under SXDH. It is described in Fig. 2. It makes use of Lagrange interpolation, described in Sect. 2.2.

Setup($1^\lambda, \mathcal{PG}$) :

Given as input the security parameter $\lambda \in \mathbb{N}$ and a pairing group $\mathcal{PG} := (p, \mathbb{G}_1, \mathbb{G}_2, P_1, P_2, \mathbb{G}_t, e)$, it samples $\boldsymbol{U}_0, \ldots, \boldsymbol{U}_t \leftarrow_R \mathbb{Z}_p^{2\times 2}$, $\boldsymbol{a}, \boldsymbol{b} \leftarrow_R \mathbb{Z}_p^2$, $\boldsymbol{V} \leftarrow_R \mathbb{Z}_p^{d\times 2}$.

For all $x \in \mathbb{Z}_p$, we define $\boldsymbol{P}(x) = \boldsymbol{U}_0 + \boldsymbol{U}_1 x + \cdots + \boldsymbol{U}_t x^t \in \mathbb{Z}_p^{2\times 2}$.

Set $\mathsf{msk} = \left(\boldsymbol{V}, [\![\boldsymbol{b}]\!]_2, ([\![\boldsymbol{U}_i^\top \boldsymbol{b}]\!]_2)_{i\in\{0,\ldots,t\}} \right)$, $\mathsf{pk} = \left([\![\boldsymbol{a}]\!]_1, ([\![\boldsymbol{U}_i\boldsymbol{a}]\!]_1)_{i\in\{0,\ldots,t\}}, [\![\boldsymbol{V}\boldsymbol{a}]\!]_1 \right)$ and output $(\mathsf{msk}, \mathsf{pk})$.

Enc($\mathsf{pk}, \boldsymbol{x}, \mathsf{id}$) :

Given pk, $\boldsymbol{x} \in \mathbb{Z}_p^d$, $\mathsf{id} \in \mathbb{Z}_p$, it samples $r \leftarrow_R \mathbb{Z}_p$ and returns $\mathsf{ct} = \left([\![\boldsymbol{a}r]\!]_1, [\![\boldsymbol{x} + \boldsymbol{V}\boldsymbol{a}r]\!]_1, [\![\boldsymbol{P}(\mathsf{id})\boldsymbol{a}r]\!]_1 \right) \in \mathbb{G}_1^{2+d+2}$.

KeyGen($\mathsf{msk}, [\![\boldsymbol{y}]\!]_2, \mathcal{S}$):

Given msk, $[\![\boldsymbol{y}]\!]_2 \in \mathbb{G}_2^d$ and a set $\mathcal{S} \subset \mathbb{Z}_p$ of size t, it samples $s \leftarrow_R \mathbb{Z}_p$, and returns $\mathsf{sk} = \left([\![\boldsymbol{b}s]\!]_2, [\![\boldsymbol{V}^\top\boldsymbol{y} + \boldsymbol{P}(0)^\top\boldsymbol{b}s]\!]_2, ([\![\boldsymbol{P}(\mathsf{id}_j)^\top\boldsymbol{b}s]\!]_2)_{\mathsf{id}_j \in \mathcal{S}} \right) \in \mathbb{G}_2^{2+2+2t}$.

Dec($\mathsf{ct}, \mathsf{id}, \mathsf{sk}, [\![\boldsymbol{y}]\!]_2, \mathcal{S}$):

Parse ct as $([\![\boldsymbol{c}_1]\!]_1, [\![\boldsymbol{c}_2]\!]_1, [\![\boldsymbol{c}_3]\!]_1) \in \mathbb{G}_1^2 \times \mathbb{G}_1^d \times \mathbb{G}_1^2$, sk as $([\![\boldsymbol{k}_1]\!]_2, [\![\boldsymbol{k}_2]\!]_2, ([\![\boldsymbol{k}_{j,3}]\!]_2)_{j\in[t]}) \in \mathbb{G}_2^2 \times \mathbb{G}_2^2 \times (\mathbb{G}_1^2)^t$, and $\mathcal{S}$ as $\mathcal{S} = \{\mathsf{id}_1, \ldots, \mathsf{id}_t\}$.

For all $j \in [t]$, compute $[\![\gamma_j]\!]_t = e([\![\boldsymbol{c}_1^\top]\!]_1, [\![\boldsymbol{k}_{j,3}]\!]_2)$ and $[\![\gamma_{t+1}]\!]_t = e([\![\boldsymbol{c}_3^\top]\!]_1, [\![\boldsymbol{k}_1]\!]_2)$.

Compute $(\alpha_1, \ldots, \alpha_{t+1}) = \mathsf{Lagr}(\mathsf{id}_1, \ldots, \mathsf{id}_t, \mathsf{id})$. Return $e([\![\boldsymbol{c}_2^\top]\!]_1, [\![\boldsymbol{y}]\!]_2) \cdot \prod_{j\in[t+1]} [\![\gamma_j]\!]_t^{\alpha_j} / e([\![\boldsymbol{c}_1]\!]_1, [\![\boldsymbol{k}_2]\!]_2)$.

Fig. 2. Inner-product FE with revocations for d-dimensional vectors and sets of size t. Its selective security is proven under SXDH. The algorithm Lagr is described in Sect. 2.2.

Correctness. Since $\mathsf{id} \notin \mathcal{S}$, we can use the correctness of the algorithm Lagr, which states that: $\prod_{j\in[t+1]}[\![\gamma_j]\!]_t^{\alpha_j} = [\![s\boldsymbol{b}^\top\boldsymbol{P}(0)\boldsymbol{a}r]\!]_t$. Thus, the decryption computes:

$$e([\![\boldsymbol{c}_2^\top]\!]_1, [\![\boldsymbol{y}]\!]_2) \cdot \prod_{j\in[t+1]} [\![\gamma_j]\!]_t^{\alpha_j} / e([\![\boldsymbol{c}_1]\!]_1, [\![\boldsymbol{k}_2]\!]_2)$$

$$= [\![(\boldsymbol{x} + \boldsymbol{V}\boldsymbol{a}r)^\top\boldsymbol{y} + s\boldsymbol{b}^\top\boldsymbol{P}(0)\boldsymbol{a}r - r\boldsymbol{a}^\top(\boldsymbol{V}^\top\boldsymbol{y} + \boldsymbol{P}(0)^\top\boldsymbol{b}s)]\!]_t$$

$$= [\![\boldsymbol{x}^\top\boldsymbol{y}]\!]_t.$$

Theorem 1 (Selective security). *The scheme presented in Fig. 2 is selectively secure under the SXDH assumption.*

Proof. We proceed via a series of hybrid games described bellow (the differences from one game to the next are highlighted in red).

Game_0 : is the game from the selective security definition in Sect. 2.5. Recall that the adversary $\mathcal{A}$ first receives $\mathsf{pk} = \left([\![a]\!]_1, ([\![U_i a]\!]_1)_{i \in \{0,\dots,t\}}, [\![Va]\!]_1 \right)$. Then, it chooses a pair of messages $((x_0, \mathsf{id}_0), (x_1, \mathsf{id}_1))$, upon which it receives $\mathsf{ct}^\star = ([\![ar]\!]_1, [\![x_\beta + Var]\!]_1, [\![P(\mathsf{id}_\beta)ar]\!]_1)$, where $\beta \leftarrow_R \{0,1\}$. Afterwards, it can query its oracle $\mathcal{O}_{\mathsf{KeyGen}}$ on inputs of the form $([\![y]\!]_2, \mathcal{S})$, upon which it gets $\mathsf{sk} = ([\![bs]\!]_2, [\![V^\top y + P(0)^\top bs]\!]_2, ([\![P(\mathsf{id}_j)^\top bs]\!]_2)_{\mathsf{id}_j \in \mathcal{S}})$. The adversary $\mathcal{A}$ is admissible, which means that $\mathsf{id}_0 = \mathsf{id}_1$, which we denote by $\mathsf{id}^\star = \mathsf{id}_0 = \mathsf{id}_1$, and that for all queries $([\![y]\!]_2, \mathcal{S})$ to $\mathcal{O}_{\mathsf{KeyGen}}$, we have $\mathsf{id}^\star \in \mathcal{S}$ or $(\mathsf{id}^\star \notin \mathcal{S}$ and $x_0^\top y = x_1^\top y)$. At the end, the adversary $\mathcal{A}$ outputs a guess β'.

Game_1 : we change the way the challenge ciphertext is computed. Namely, we have now

$$\mathsf{ct}^\star = \left([\![z]\!]_1, [\![x_\beta + Vz]\!]_1, [\![P(\mathsf{id}^\star)z]\!]_1 \right) \ ,$$

where $z \leftarrow_R \mathbb{Z}_p^2$. We prove that $\mathsf{Game}_0 \approx_c \mathsf{Game}_1$ by the DDH assumption in $\mathbb{G}_1$. Namely, we have $([\![a]\!]_1, [\![ar]\!]_1) \approx_c ([\![a]\!]_1, [\![z]\!]_1)$ where the leftmost distribution corresponds to Game_0, whereas the rightmost distribution corresponds to Game_1.

Game_2 : we change the way the challenge ciphertext is computed. Namely, we have now

$$\mathsf{ct}^\star = \left([\![z]\!]_1, [\![x_\beta + Vz]\!]_1, [\![P(\mathsf{id}^\star)z]\!]_1 \right) \ ,$$

where $z \leftarrow_R \mathbb{Z}_p^2 \setminus \mathsf{Span}(a)$. Here $\mathsf{Span}(a)$ denotes the set of vectors proportional to a. The cardinal of $\mathsf{Span}(a)$ is p, thus, the statistical distance between the uniform distribution over $\mathbb{Z}_p^2 \setminus \mathsf{Span}(a)$ and uniform over $\mathbb{Z}_p^2$ is $1/p$, and $\mathsf{Game}_1 \approx_s \mathsf{Game}_2$.

Game_3 : we change the way the functional keys and the challenge ciphertext are computed. Namely, the ciphertext is now of the form:

$$\mathsf{ct}^\star = \left([\![z]\!]_1, [\![Vz]\!]_1, [\![P(\mathsf{id}^\star)z]\!]_1 \right) \ .$$

Note that the ciphertext does not depend on the message x_β anymore. Each query $([\![y]\!]_2, \mathcal{S})$ to $\mathcal{O}_{\mathsf{KeyGen}}$ is now answered with

$$\left([\![bs]\!]_2, [\![V^\top y - a^\perp \cdot x_\beta^\top y + P(0)^\top bs]\!]_2, ([\![P(\mathsf{id}_j)^\top bs]\!]_2)_{\mathsf{id}_j \in \mathcal{S}} \right) \ ,$$

where $\boldsymbol{a}^\perp \in \mathbb{Z}_p^2$ is the vector such that $\boldsymbol{a}^\top \boldsymbol{a}^\perp = 0$ and $\boldsymbol{z}^\top \boldsymbol{a}^\perp = 1$. Game_2 and Game_3 are identically distributed, since for all $\boldsymbol{x}_\beta \in \mathbb{Z}_p^d$, all $\boldsymbol{a}^\perp \in \mathbb{Z}_p^2$, the following are identically distributed: $\{\boldsymbol{V} \leftarrow_R \mathbb{Z}_p^{d\times2} : \boldsymbol{V}\}$ and $\{\boldsymbol{V} \leftarrow_R \mathbb{Z}_p^{d\times2} : \boldsymbol{V} - \boldsymbol{x}_\beta(\boldsymbol{a}^\perp)^\top\}$. The former distribution corresponds to Game_2 with some pre and post-processing, whereas the latter corresponds to Game_3 with the same pre and post-processing. Note that Game_3 crucially relies on the fact that the adversary is selective, since the vector $\boldsymbol{x}_\beta$ needs to be known to generate all functional secret keys.

$\underline{\mathsf{Game}_4}$: we change the way the functional keys are computed. Namely, each query $(\llbracket\boldsymbol{y}\rrbracket_2, \mathcal{S})$ to $\mathcal{O}_{\mathsf{KeyGen}}$ is now answered with

$$\left(\llbracket\boldsymbol{bs}\rrbracket_2, \llbracket\boldsymbol{V}^\top\boldsymbol{y} - 1_{\mathsf{id}^\star \notin \mathcal{S}}\boldsymbol{a}^\perp\boldsymbol{x}_\beta^\top\boldsymbol{y} + \boldsymbol{P}(0)^\top\boldsymbol{bs}\rrbracket_2, (\llbracket\boldsymbol{P}(\mathsf{id}_j)^\top\boldsymbol{bs}\rrbracket_2)_{\mathsf{id}_j \in \mathcal{S}}\right) .$$

That is, now we only have the term $\boldsymbol{a}^\perp\boldsymbol{x}_\beta^\top\boldsymbol{y}$ for functional key queries $(\boldsymbol{y}, \mathcal{S})$ where $\mathsf{id}^\star \notin \mathcal{S}$. To transition from Game_3 to Game_4, we use the following hybrid games.

$\underline{\mathsf{Game}_{3.i}}$: for all $i \in \{0, \dots, Q\}$, where Q denotes the number of functional key queries, $\mathsf{Game}_{3.i}$ is defined as Game_4 for the first i'th key queries and as Game_3 for the last $Q - i$ queries. By definition we have $\mathsf{Game}_3 = \mathsf{Game}_{3.0}$ and $\mathsf{Game}_4 = \mathsf{Game}_{3.Q}$. It suffices to show that for all $i \in [Q]$, $\mathsf{Game}_{3.i-1} \approx_c \mathsf{Game}_{3.i}$. To do so, we introduce new intermediate games, defined as follows.

$\underline{\mathsf{Game}_{3.i-1.1}}$: is defined as $\mathsf{Game}_{3.i-1}$, except the i'th query to $\mathcal{O}_{\mathsf{KeyGen}}$, denoted by $(\llbracket\boldsymbol{y}_i\rrbracket_2, \mathcal{S}_i)$, is now answered with

$$\left(\llbracket\boldsymbol{d}\rrbracket_2, \llbracket\boldsymbol{V}^\top\boldsymbol{y}_i - \boldsymbol{a}^\perp \cdot \boldsymbol{x}_\beta^\top\boldsymbol{y}_i + \boldsymbol{P}(0)^\top\boldsymbol{d}\rrbracket_2, (\llbracket\boldsymbol{P}(\mathsf{id}_j)^\top\boldsymbol{d}\rrbracket_2)_{\mathsf{id}_j \in \mathcal{S}_i}\right) ,$$

where $\boldsymbol{d} \leftarrow_R \mathbb{Z}_p^2$. We have $\mathsf{Game}_{3.i-1} \approx_c \mathsf{Game}_{3.i-1.1}$ by the DDH assumption in $\mathbb{G}_2$, which states that $(\llbracket\boldsymbol{b}\rrbracket_2, \llbracket\boldsymbol{bs}_i\rrbracket_2) \approx_c (\llbracket\boldsymbol{b}\rrbracket_2, \llbracket\boldsymbol{d}\rrbracket_2)$ where $\boldsymbol{b}, \boldsymbol{d} \leftarrow_R \mathbb{Z}_p^2, s_i \leftarrow_R \mathbb{Z}_p$. The former distribution corresponds to $\mathsf{Game}_{3.i-1}$ with some efficient post-processing, whereas the latter corresponds to $\mathsf{Game}_{3.i-1.1}$ with the same post-processing.

$\underline{\mathsf{Game}_{3.i-1.2}}$: is defined as $\mathsf{Game}_{3.i-1.1}$, except the vector $\boldsymbol{d}$ used to compute the i'th queried functional secret key is sampled as $\boldsymbol{d} \leftarrow_R \mathbb{Z}_p^2 \setminus \mathsf{Span}(\boldsymbol{b})$, instead of uniformly random over $\mathbb{Z}_p^2$. Since the cardinal of $\mathsf{Span}(\boldsymbol{b})$ is at most p, the uniform distribution over $\mathbb{Z}_p^2 \setminus \mathsf{Span}(\boldsymbol{b})$ has statistical distance at most $1/p$ with the uniform distribution over $\mathbb{Z}_p^2$. Thus, $\mathsf{Game}_{3.i-1.1} \approx_s \mathsf{Game}_{3.i-1.2}$.

$\underline{\mathsf{Game}_{3.i-1.3}}$: is defined as $\mathsf{Game}_{3.i-1.2}$, except the i'th query to $\mathcal{O}_{\mathsf{KeyGen}}$ is now answered with

$$\left(\llbracket\boldsymbol{d}\rrbracket_2, \llbracket\boldsymbol{V}^\top\boldsymbol{y}_i - 1_{\mathsf{id}^\star \notin \mathcal{S}_i}\boldsymbol{a}^\perp\boldsymbol{x}_\beta^\top\boldsymbol{y}_i + \boldsymbol{P}(0)^\top\boldsymbol{d}\rrbracket_2, (\llbracket\boldsymbol{P}(\mathsf{id}_j)^\top\boldsymbol{d}\rrbracket_2)_{\mathsf{id}_j \in \mathcal{S}_i}\right) ,$$

where $d \leftarrow_R \mathbb{Z}_p^2 \setminus \mathsf{Span}(b)$. Note that if $\mathsf{id}^\star \notin \mathcal{S}_i$, then the two games $\mathsf{Game}_{3.i-1.2}$ and $\mathsf{Game}_{3.i-1.3}$ are identical. Thus we focus on the case $\mathsf{id}^\star \in \mathcal{S}_i$. In that case we show that $\mathsf{Game}_{3.i-1.3}$ is also identically distributed to $\mathsf{Game}_{3.i-1.2}$ using a statistical argument, which relies on the fact that vectors $P(\mathsf{id}_j)^\top b$ and $P(\mathsf{id}_j)^\top d$ are statistically independent since b and d are linearly independent. The same holds with respect to the matrix $P(0)$. Moreover, since $\mathsf{id}^\star \in \mathcal{S}_i$, the set of values $\{(P(\mathsf{id}_j))_{\mathsf{id}_j \in \mathcal{S}_i}, P(\mathsf{id}^\star)\}$ are statistically independent from the value $P(0)$—recall that the polynomial P is of degree t; we are using Fact 1 from Sect. 2.2. Combining these two facts, we know that the vector $P(0)^\top d$ is uniformly random, independent from everything else (challenge ciphertext, public key and other functional secret keys). Thus, it can act as a one-time pad on the value $a^\perp x_\beta^\top y$ that we wish to remove.

$\mathsf{Game}_{3.i-1.4}$: is defined as $\mathsf{Game}_{3.i-1.3}$, except the vector d used to compute the i'th queried functional secret key is sampled $d \leftarrow_R \mathbb{Z}_p^2$, instead of uniformly random over $\mathbb{Z}_p^2 \setminus \mathsf{Span}(b)$. This is the reverse to the transition from $\mathsf{Game}_{3.i-1.1}$ to $\mathsf{Game}_{3.i-1.2}$. By the same statistical argument, we obtain $\mathsf{Game}_{3.i-1.3} \approx_s \mathsf{Game}_{3.i-1.4}$.

Finally, note that $\mathsf{Game}_{3.i-1.4}$ is the same as $\mathsf{Game}_{3.i}$ except the i'th queried key is computed using $[\![d]\!]_2 \leftarrow_R \mathbb{G}_2^2$ in the former, and $[\![bs_i]\!]_2 \in \mathbb{G}_2^2$ with $s_i \leftarrow_R \mathbb{Z}_p$ in the latter. Therefore, we have $\mathsf{Game}_{3.i-1.4} \approx_c \mathsf{Game}_{3.i}$ by the DDH assumption, which states that $([\![b]\!]_2, [\![d]\!]_2) \approx_c ([\![b]\!]_2, [\![bs_i]\!]_2)$ where $b, d \leftarrow_R \mathbb{Z}_p^2, s_i \leftarrow_R \mathbb{Z}_p$. The former distribution corresponds to $\mathsf{Game}_{3.i-1.4}$, whereas the latter distribution corresponds to $\mathsf{Game}_{3.i}$. Note that this transition is exactly reverse to the transition from $\mathsf{Game}_{3.i-1}$ to $\mathsf{Game}_{3.i-1.1}$. This concludes the proof that $\mathsf{Game}_{3.i-1} \approx_c \mathsf{Game}_{3.i}$ and consequently, that $\mathsf{Game}_3 \approx_c \mathsf{Game}_4$.

Note that in Game_4, the only values that possibly reveal some information about the bit β is the set $\{x_\beta^\top y_i\}$ for all queries $([\![y_i]\!]_2, \mathcal{S}_i)$ such that $\mathsf{id}^\star \notin \mathcal{S}_i$. Since the adversary $\mathcal{A}$ is admissible, we know that for all such values, $x_\beta^\top y_i = x_0^\top y_i = x_1^\top y_i$. In other words, these values do not depend on β and the advantage of $\mathcal{A}$ is 0. $\qquad\square$

3.3 Revocations with Arbitrary-Size Identity Sets

Our previous construction requires that the size of any identities set $\mathcal{S}$ be exactly t (a pre-established system parameter).

A possible way to relax this limitation is to introduce dummy identities and use them as "fillers", to extend an identity set until it reaches size t. Furthermore, in order to make the secret-key size proportional to the identity set $\mathcal{S}$, we could run different instances of the IPFE for different set-size bounds $t_1, \ldots, t_n$. A secret-key for set $\mathcal{S}$ would then be issued only with respect to the i-th IPFE instance, where t_i is the smallest such that $|\mathcal{S}| \leq t_i$. (Ciphertexts would need to be provided with respect to all IPFE instances). A natural and effective choice for the values of t_i is the set of powers of 2. That way, the ciphertext-size would be increased by a factor of $\log_2$ of the global maximum identity set size. Note that such factor is logairthmic in the security parameter. This technique has already been used in the literature and in particular in the context of ABE, e.g. by Ostrovsky et al. [OSW07, Section 3.3].

4 Generic Construction of MA-ABE from IPFE

We present a modular construction of MA-ABE for non-monotone access structures based on inner-product FE schemes. We show that the resulting MA-ABE is super selectively secure for static corruptions, provided the underlying FE are super selectively secure. The security is proven in the random oracle model.

$\mathsf{GlobalSetup}(1^\lambda)$:

Generate a pairing group $\mathcal{PG} = (p, \mathbb{G}_1, \mathbb{G}_2, P_1, P_2, \mathbb{G}_t, e) \leftarrow \mathsf{GGen}(1^\lambda)$ and a hash functions $H : \{0,1\}^* \to \mathbb{G}_2^3$ and return $\mathsf{gp} := (\mathcal{PG}, H)$.

$\mathsf{AuthSetup}(\mathsf{gp})$:

Compute $(\mathsf{pk}_\Gamma, \mathsf{msk}_\Gamma) \leftarrow \Gamma.\mathsf{Setup}(1^\lambda, \mathcal{PG})$ and $(\mathsf{pk}_\Sigma, \mathsf{msk}_\Sigma) \leftarrow \Sigma.\mathsf{Setup}(1^\lambda, \mathcal{PG})$. return $\mathsf{pk} = (\mathsf{pk}_\Gamma, \mathsf{pk}_\Sigma)$ and $\mathsf{sk} = (\mathsf{msk}_\Gamma, \mathsf{msk}_\Sigma)$.

$\mathsf{Enc}\big((M \in \mathbb{Z}_p^{n \times \ell}, \rho : [\ell] \to \{0,1\}^* \cup (\{\neg\} \cdot \{0,1\}^*)), \{\mathsf{pk}_i\}_{i \in [\nu]}\big)$:

Sample $s \leftarrow_R \mathbb{Z}_p$, and $\{s_j\}_{j \in [\ell]} \leftarrow \mathsf{Share}(M, s)$, $\{u_j\}_{j \in [\ell]} \leftarrow \mathsf{Share}(M, 0)$, $a \leftarrow_R \mathbb{Z}_p^3$. For all $j \in [\ell]$, parse $\mathsf{pk}_{\theta(j)} = (\mathsf{pk}_{\Gamma,\theta(j)}, \mathsf{pk}_{\Sigma,\theta(j)})$, set $x_j = (s_j, u_j \cdot a) \in \mathbb{Z}_p^4$, then

- if $\rho(j) = \mathsf{att}_j$ where $\mathsf{att}_j \in \{0,1\}^*$, then $\mathsf{ct}_j \leftarrow \Gamma.\mathsf{Enc}(\mathsf{pk}_{\Gamma,\theta(j)}, x_j, \mathsf{att}_j)$.

- if $\rho(j) = \neg\mathsf{att}_j$ where $\mathsf{att}_j \in \{0,1\}^*$, then $\mathsf{ct}_j \leftarrow \Sigma.\mathsf{Enc}(\mathsf{pk}_{\Sigma,\theta(j)}, x_j, \mathsf{att}_j)$.

Return $(\{\mathsf{ct}_j\}_{j \in [\ell]}, \kappa := [\![s]\!]_t)$.

$\mathsf{KeyGen}(\mathsf{pk}, \mathsf{sk}, \mathsf{gid}, \mathcal{S})$:

Parse $\mathsf{sk} = (\mathsf{msk}_\Gamma, \mathsf{msk}_\Sigma)$. Compute $H(\mathsf{gid}) = [\![z_\mathsf{gid}]\!]_2$, $\mathsf{sk}_\Sigma \leftarrow \Sigma.\mathsf{KeyGen}(\mathsf{msk}_\Sigma, [\![1, z_\mathsf{gid}]\!]_2, \mathcal{S})$, for all $\mathsf{att}_j \in \mathcal{S}$, $\mathsf{sk}_{\Gamma,j} \leftarrow \Gamma.\mathsf{KeyGen}(\mathsf{msk}_\Gamma, [\![1, z_\mathsf{gid}]\!]_2, \mathsf{att}_j)$. Return $\mathsf{sk}_{\mathsf{gid},\mathcal{S}} = (\mathsf{sk}_\Sigma, (\mathsf{sk}_{\Gamma,j})_{\mathsf{att}_j \in \mathcal{S}})$.

$\mathsf{Dec}\,(\mathsf{ct}, \{\mathsf{sk}_{\mathsf{gid},\mathcal{S}_i}\}_i)$:

Parse the ciphertext $\mathsf{ct} = \{\mathsf{ct}_j\}_{j \in [\ell]}$ which contains the description of an access structure (M, ρ). Let $\mathcal{S} = \cup_{i \in [\nu]} \mathcal{S}_i$. Compute $\{\omega_j, \omega'_j\}_{j \in [\ell]}$ such that $\sum_{\rho(j) \in \mathcal{S}} \omega_j M_j + \sum_{\rho(j) = \neg\mathsf{att}, \mathsf{att} \notin \mathcal{S}} \omega'_j M_j = 1$. Return $\sum_{\rho(j) \in \mathcal{S}} \omega_j \Gamma.\mathsf{Dec}(\mathsf{pk}_{\theta(j)}, \mathsf{ct}_j, \mathsf{sk}_{\mathsf{gid},\mathcal{S}_{\theta(j)}}, [\![1, z_\mathsf{gid}]\!]_2) + \sum_{\rho(j) = \neg\mathsf{att}, \mathsf{att} \notin \mathcal{S}} \omega'_j \Sigma.\mathsf{Dec}(\mathsf{pk}_{\theta(j)}, \mathsf{ct}_j, \mathsf{sk}_{\mathsf{gid},\mathcal{S}_{\theta(j)}}, [\![1, z_\mathsf{gid}]\!]_2)$, where $[\![z_\mathsf{gid}]\!]_2 = H(\mathsf{gid})$.

Fig. 3. Construction of Multi-Authority ABE from an ID-IPFE scheme Γ and an IPFE with revocations Σ (for vectors of dimension 4). Recall that θ maps a row $j \in [\ell]$ to the authority that owns the attribute associated to that row.

Correctness. Let $[\![z_{\text{gid}}]\!]_2 := H(\text{gid})$. Observe that, by the correctness of Γ and Σ, we have:

$$\sum_{\rho(j) \in S} \omega_j \Gamma.\text{Dec}(\text{pk}_{\theta(j)}, \text{ct}_j, \text{sk}_{\text{gid}, S_{\theta(j)}}, [\![1, z_{\text{gid}}]\!]_2)$$

$$+ \sum_{\rho(j) = \neg\text{att}, \text{att} \notin S} \omega'_j \Sigma.\text{Dec}(\text{pk}_{\theta(j)}, \text{ct}_j, \text{sk}_{\text{gid}, S_{\theta(j)}}, [\![1, z_{\text{gid}}]\!]_2)$$

$$= \sum_{\rho(j) \in S} \omega_j [\![s_j + a^\top z_{\text{gid}} u_j]\!]_t + \sum_{\rho(j) = \neg\text{att}, \text{att} \notin S} \omega'_j [\![s_j + a^\top z_{\text{gid}} u_j]\!]_t$$

$$= [\![s + a^\top z_{\text{gid}} \cdot 0]\!]_t = \kappa .$$

Theorem 2 (Super-selective security). *The scheme from Fig. 3, is a super-selectively secure MA-ABE with static corruption in the random oracle model, assuming the schemes Γ and Σ are super-selectively secure and the DDH assumption holds in $\mathbb{G}_2$.*

Combining with the existence of an ID-IPFE selectively secure under SXDH (from [ACGU20]) and Theorem 1 (the existence of selectively secure IPFE with revocations from SXDH) and noting that selective security implies super-selective security, we obtain the following corollary.

Corollary 1. *There exists a super-selectively secure MA-ABE with static corruptions from SXDH.*

We now proceed to prove the theorem.

Proof. We prove security via a sequence of hybrid games. We highlight in red the changes from one hybrid to the next when relevant.

Game$_0$: The first game corresponds to the super-selective security game for MA-ABE with static corruptions, defined in Sect. 2.6. We recall it here for completeness. We call $\mathcal{A}$ the admissible adversary. First, $\mathcal{A}$ receives the global parameters $\text{gp} = (\Gamma.\text{gp}, H)$. Then, it can query its oracle $\mathcal{O}_{\text{create}}$ that creates a new (honest) authority with an associated (pk, sk) pair when invoked, adds pk to the set of honest authorities denoted by S_{hon} and returns pk to $\mathcal{A}$. Then, $\mathcal{A}$ sends $(M, \rho, \Pi_{\text{hon}}, \Pi_{\text{corr}})$ to its challenger, where $M \in \mathbb{Z}_p^{n \times \ell}$, $\rho : [\ell] \to \mathbb{Z}_p$ is an access structure with attributes owned by the authorities in the set $\Pi = \Pi_{\text{hon}} \cup \Pi_{\text{corr}}$. Here, Π_{hon} is a set of honest authorities' public keys, that is, $\Pi_{\text{hon}} \subseteq S_{\text{hon}}$, and Π_{corr} is a set of authorities' public key created by $\mathcal{A}$ itself (and not via $\mathcal{O}_{\text{create}}$). Because $\mathcal{A}$ is free to create these public keys however it wants (potentially maliciously), these are referred to as corrupted authorities. Note that $\mathcal{A}$ cannot query its oracle $\mathcal{O}_{\text{corr}}$, since we assume only static corruptions here. We write $\Pi = \{\text{pk}_1, \ldots, \text{pk}_\nu\}$, and we define $\theta : [\ell] \to [\nu]$, which maps each column $j \in [\ell]$ to the authority that owns the attribute associated with that column.

Afterwards, the adversary can query its oracle $\mathcal{O}_{\text{KeyGen}}$ on inputs $\text{pk} \in S_{\text{hon}}$ associated with the secret key $\text{sk} = (\text{msk}_\Sigma, \text{msk}_\Gamma)$ and $S \subset \mathcal{U}_{\text{pk}}$, which computes $\text{sk}_\Sigma \leftarrow \Sigma.\text{KeyGen}(\text{msk}_\Sigma, [\![1, z_{\text{gid}}]\!]_2, S)$ and for all attributes $\text{att}_j \in S$, it computes $\mathsf{sk}_{\Gamma,j} \leftarrow \Gamma.\mathsf{KeyGen}(\mathsf{msk}_\Gamma, [\![1, z_\mathsf{gid}]\!]_2, \mathsf{att}_j)$, where $[\![z_\mathsf{gid}]\!]_2 = H(\mathsf{gid})$. It returns $\mathsf{sk}_{\mathsf{gid},\mathcal{S}} = (\mathsf{sk}_\Sigma, (\mathsf{sk}_{\Gamma,j})_{\mathsf{att}_j \in \mathcal{S}})$ to the adversary $\mathcal{A}$.

At this point, the challenger samples $s \leftarrow_R \mathbb{Z}_p$ and computes $(s_1, \ldots, s_\ell) \leftarrow \mathsf{Share}(M, s)$, $(u_1, \ldots, u_\ell) \leftarrow \mathsf{Share}(M, 0)^2$, $a \leftarrow_R \mathbb{Z}_p^3$, $\kappa_0 = [\![s]\!]_t$, $\kappa_1 \leftarrow_R \mathbb{G}_t$, $\beta \leftarrow_R \{0,1\}$, for all $j \in [\ell]$, $x_j = (s_j, u_j \cdot a) \in \mathbb{Z}_p^4$, and

- if $\rho(j) = \mathsf{att}_j$ where $\mathsf{att}_j \in \{0,1\}^*$, then $\mathsf{ct}_j \leftarrow \Gamma.\mathsf{Enc}(\mathsf{pk}_{\Gamma,\theta(j)}, x_i, \rho(j))$,

- if $\rho(j) = \neg\mathsf{att}_j$ where $\mathsf{att}_j \in \{0,1\}^*$, then $\mathsf{ct}_j \leftarrow \Sigma.\mathsf{Enc}(\mathsf{pk}_{\Sigma,\theta(j)}, x_i, \rho(j))$.

It sets $\mathsf{ct}^* = \{\mathsf{ct}_j\}_{j \in [\ell]}$ and returns $(\mathsf{ct}^*, \kappa_\beta)$ to $\mathcal{A}$. Finally, $\mathcal{A}$ outputs a guess $\beta' \in \{0,1\}$. Recall that $\mathcal{A}$ is admissible, which means it cannot compute κ_0 from ct^* simply by correctness of the scheme with the user secret keys it queried and the secret key of the corrupted authorities (see Sect. 2.6 for more details). The experiment outputs 1 if $\beta = \beta'$, 0 otherwise.

In the following hybrids, we use the following dual basis: first, we choose a random basis $(a_1|a_2|a_3) \in \mathbb{Z}_p^{3\times3}$ of $\mathbb{Z}_p^3$ such that $a = r_1 a_1$ for $r_1 \leftarrow_R \mathbb{Z}_p^*$ (recall that the vector a is sampled to produce the challenge ciphertext). Strictly speaking, such a basis exists only when $a \neq 0$. Since a is sampled uniformly at random over $\mathbb{Z}_p^3$, it is different from 0 with overwhelming probability. Thus, we implicitly assume a is sampled uniformly over $\mathbb{Z}_p^3 \setminus \{0\}$ in the proof (this only changes the distribution by a negligible statistical distance). Then, we denote by $(a_1^*|a_2^*|a_3^*) \in \mathbb{Z}_p^{3\times3}$ its dual basis, that is, such that for all $i, j \in \{1,2,3\}$, $a_i^\top a_j^* = 0$ if $i \neq j$ and $a_i^\top a_j^* = 1$ if $i = j$. We make use of the following assumptions relative to the pairing groups $(\mathbb{G}_1, \mathbb{G}_2, \mathbb{G}_T)$ and the random dual basis $(a_1|a_2|a_3)$ and $(a_1^*|a_2^*|a_3^*)$.

Assumption 1. $\{v \leftarrow_R \mathbb{Z}_p^3 : ([\![a_1]\!]_1, [\![v]\!]_2)\} \approx_c \{v \leftarrow_R \mathsf{Span}(a_1^*) : ([\![a_1]\!]_1, [\![v]\!]_2)\}$.

This assumption is known to be implied by the DDH assumption in $\mathbb{G}_2$ (see for instance [Lew12]).

$\underline{\mathsf{Game}_1}$: is the same as Game_0 except that the outputs of the hash function are computed as follows: for all gid, $H(\mathsf{gid}) = [\![z_\mathsf{gid}]\!]_2$ where $z_\mathsf{gid} \leftarrow_R \mathsf{Span}(a_1^*)$. We have $\mathsf{Game}_0 \approx_c \mathsf{Game}_1$ by **Assumption 1**. Technically, we need to use this assumption for each query of $\mathcal{A}$ to the hash function H (modeled as a random oracle) using a hybrid argument.

$\underline{\mathsf{Game}_2}$: is the same as Game_1, except that the challenge ciphertext uses the vectors $x_j = (s_j, u_j r_1 a_1 + v_j a_3), \rho(j))$, for all $j \in [\ell]$ such that $\theta(j) \in \mathcal{S}_\mathsf{hon}$, where $v_j = (\gamma, v)^\top M_j$, $v \leftarrow_R \mathbb{Z}_p^{n-1}$, and $\gamma \leftarrow_R \mathbb{Z}_p$. That is, the v_j are shares of a random value γ. Recall that $a_1, a_3 \in \mathbb{Z}_p^3$ are vectors part of the basis $(a_1|a_2|a_3)$

---

[2] See Fig. 1 for the definition of the algorithm Share.

and $\boldsymbol{a} = r_1 \boldsymbol{a}_1$ where $r_1 \leftarrow_R \mathbb{Z}_p^*$. The shares s_j and u_j are computed as before. For all $j \in [\ell]$ such that $\theta(j) \in \Pi_{\text{corr}}$, the vector $\boldsymbol{x}_j$ are as before. The challenge ciphertext is set to be $(\{\text{ct}_j\}_{j \in [\ell]}, \kappa_\beta)$, where κ_β is computed as before. We argue that $\mathsf{Game}_1 \approx_c \mathsf{Game}_2$ using the super-selective security of Γ and Σ, since the extra red vector $(0, v_j \boldsymbol{a}_3)$ is orthogonal to the vectors $[\![1, \boldsymbol{z}_{\text{gid}}]\!]_2$ from the user secret keys. This is because for all queried gid, $\boldsymbol{z}_{\text{gid}} \in \mathsf{Span}(\boldsymbol{a}_1^*)$ and $\boldsymbol{a}_3^\top \boldsymbol{a}_1^* = 0$.

$\underline{\mathsf{Game}_3}$: is the same as Game_2, except that the outputs of the hash function are computed as follows: for all gid, $H(\text{gid}) = [\![\boldsymbol{a}_1^* r_{\text{gid}} + \boldsymbol{a}_3^*]\!]_2$, where $r_{\text{gid}} \leftarrow_R \mathbb{Z}_p$. We prove that $\mathsf{Game}_2 \approx_c \mathsf{Game}_3$ in Lemma 2.

$\underline{\mathsf{Game}_4}$: is the same as Game_3, except that the challenge ciphertext uses the vectors $\boldsymbol{x}_j = (s_j', u_j r_1 \boldsymbol{a}_1 + v_j' \boldsymbol{a}_3)$ for all $j \in [\ell]$ such that $\theta(j) \in \mathcal{S}_{\text{hon}}$, where $s_j' = (s + \gamma, \boldsymbol{w})^\top \boldsymbol{M}_j$ and $v_j' = (0, \boldsymbol{v})^\top \boldsymbol{M}_j$. That is, the s_j' are now shares of $s + \gamma$ instead of s and the v_j' are now shares of 0 instead of γ. The shares u_j are computed as before. We argue that $\mathsf{Game}_3 \approx_c \mathsf{Game}_4$ thanks to the super-selective security of Γ and Σ. Indeed, for all $j \in [\ell]$ and all queried gid, we have $(s_j', u_j r_1 \boldsymbol{a}_1 + v_j' \boldsymbol{a}_3)^\top (1, \boldsymbol{a}_1^* r_{\text{gid}} + \boldsymbol{a}_3^*) = (s + \gamma, \boldsymbol{w})^\top \boldsymbol{M}_j + r_1 r_{\text{gid}} (0, \boldsymbol{u})^\top \boldsymbol{M}_j + (0, \boldsymbol{v})^\top \boldsymbol{M}_j = (s, \boldsymbol{w})^\top \boldsymbol{M}_j + r_1 r_{\text{gid}} (0, \boldsymbol{u})^\top \boldsymbol{M}_j + (\gamma, \boldsymbol{v})^\top \boldsymbol{M}_j = s_j + r_1 r_{\text{gid}} u_j + v_j = (s_j, u_j r_1 \boldsymbol{a}_1 + v_j \boldsymbol{a}_3)^\top (1, \boldsymbol{a}_1^* r_{\text{gid}} + \boldsymbol{a}_3^*)$, just as in Game_3. That is, the change of the vectors encrypted under Γ from Game_3 to Game_4 preserves the value of the inner product.

Finally, to conclude the proof, we show that in Game_4, the advantage of $\mathcal{A}$ is 0. This comes from the fact that the value $\kappa_0 = [\![s]\!]_t$ is uniformly random, independent of the rest of the adversary's view. Indeed, the only place where the value s appears is in the challenge ciphertext, in the vectors $\boldsymbol{x}_j$ encrypted under Γ or Σ. For all $j \in [\ell]$ such that $\theta(j) \in \mathcal{S}_{\text{hon}}$, the vector $\boldsymbol{x}_j$ is of the form $\boldsymbol{x}_j = (s_j', u_j r_1 \boldsymbol{a}_1 + v_j' \boldsymbol{a}_3))$ where s_j' is of the form $s_j' = (s + \gamma, \boldsymbol{w})^\top \boldsymbol{M}_j$ for all $j \in [\ell]$. That is, the values s_j' are shares of the secret $s + \gamma$. But the value $\gamma \leftarrow_R \mathbb{Z}_p$ is independent of the rest of the adversary's view, thus it acts as a one-time pad on s. Consequently, $\boldsymbol{x}_j$ is independent of the value s. For all $j \in [\ell]$ such that $\theta(j) \in \Pi_{\text{corr}}$, we have $\boldsymbol{x}_j = (s_j, u_j r_1 \boldsymbol{a}_1 + v_j \boldsymbol{a}_3))$, where the values s_j are shares of the secret s. But because the adversary $\mathcal{A}$ is admissible, we know that the shares $\{s_j\}_{j \in [\ell], \theta(j) \in \Pi_{\text{corr}}}$ are independent of s, by security of the MSP. Thus, both κ_0 and κ_1 are uniformly random independent of everything else, the view of the adversary does not depend on the bit β; its advantage is 0. $\qquad\square$

Now we state and prove the lemma used in the proof above. Its proof relies on the assumptions below, which are known to be implied by DDH in $\mathbb{G}_2$ (see for instance [Lew12]).

Lemma 2. *We have* $\mathsf{Game}_2 \approx_c \mathsf{Game}_3$ *assuming the super-selective security of* Γ *and* Σ, *and the SXDH assumption.*

To prove the lemma, we rely on the following assumptions, which are known to be implied by DDH in $\mathbb{G}_2$ (see for instance [Lew12]).

Assumption 2.

$$\{v \leftarrow_R \mathsf{Span}(a_1^*), r_1, r_2 \leftarrow_R \mathbb{Z}_p^* : (\llbracket r_1 a_1 + r_2 a_2 \rrbracket_1, \llbracket a_1 \rrbracket_1, \llbracket a_3 \rrbracket_1, \llbracket a_1^* \rrbracket_2, \llbracket a_3^* \rrbracket_2, \llbracket v \rrbracket_2)\}$$
$$\approx_c \{v \leftarrow_R \mathsf{Span}(a_1^*, a_2^*), r_1, r_2 \leftarrow_R \mathbb{Z}_p^* : (\llbracket r_1 a_1 + r_2 a_2 \rrbracket_1, \llbracket a_1 \rrbracket_1, \llbracket a_3 \rrbracket_1, \llbracket a_1^* \rrbracket_2, \llbracket a_3^* \rrbracket_2, \llbracket v \rrbracket_2)\}.$$

Assumption 3.

$$\{v \leftarrow_R \mathsf{Span}(a_1^*, a_2^*), r \leftarrow_R \mathbb{Z}_p : (\llbracket a_1 \rrbracket_1, \llbracket r a_2 + a_3 \rrbracket_1, \llbracket a_1^* \rrbracket_2, \llbracket a_3^* \rrbracket_2, \llbracket v \rrbracket_2)\}$$
$$\approx_c \{v \leftarrow_R \mathsf{Span}(a_1^*, a_2^*, a_3^*), r \leftarrow_R \mathbb{Z}_p : (\llbracket a_1 \rrbracket_1, \llbracket r a_2 + a_3 \rrbracket_1, \llbracket a_1^* \rrbracket_2, \llbracket a_3^* \rrbracket_2, \llbracket v \rrbracket_2)\}.$$

Proof. To prove the lemma, we introduce the following hybrid games for all $i \in \{0, \ldots, q\}$ where $q \in \mathbb{N}$ denotes the number of distinct gid queried via $\mathcal{O}_{\mathsf{KeyGen}}$: Game$_{2.i}$ is like Game$_2$, except that for the first i'th gid, $\mathcal{O}_{\mathsf{KeyGen}}$ behaves like in Game$_3$. Namely, for the first i'th gid queried to $\mathcal{O}_{\mathsf{KeyGen}}$, the oracle uses $H(\mathsf{gid}) = \llbracket a_1^* r_{\mathsf{gid}} + a_3^* \rrbracket_2$, whereas it uses $H(\mathsf{gid}) = \llbracket a_1^* r_{\mathsf{gid}} \rrbracket_2$ for the last $q - i$ queries. It is clear by definition of the games that Game$_{2.0}$ = Game$_2$ and Game$_{2.q}$ = Game$_3$. We prove that for all $i \in [q]$, Game$_{2.i-1} \approx_c$ Game$_{2.i}$. To do so, we use the following hybrid games.

Game$_{2.i-1.1}$: is the same as Game$_{2.i-1}$, except that the challenge ciphertext uses the vectors $x_j = (s_j, u_j r_1 a_1 + u_j r_2 a_2 + v_j a_3)$ for all $j \in [\ell]$ such that $\theta(j) \in \mathcal{S}_{\mathsf{hon}}$, where $r_2 \leftarrow_R \mathbb{Z}_p^*$. We argue that Game$_{2.i-1} \approx_c$ Game$_{2.i-1.1}$ thanks to the super-selective security of Γ and Σ. Indeed, for all $j \in [\ell]$ and all queried gid, we have $z_{\mathsf{gid}} \in \mathsf{Span}(a_1^*, a_3^*)$, thus $(s_j, u_j r_1 a_1 + u_j r_2 a_2 + v_j \cdot a_3)^\top (1, z_{\mathsf{gid}}) = (s_j, u_j r_1 a_1 + v_j \cdot a_3)^\top (1, z_{\mathsf{gid}})$, just as in game Game$_{2.i-1}$, since $a_2^\top a_1^* = a_2^\top a_3^* = 0$.

Game$_{2.i-1.2}$: is the same as Game$_{2.i-1.1}$ except that the output of the hash function on the i'th queried global identifier, which we denote by gid$_i$, is computed as follows: $H(\mathsf{gid}_i) = \llbracket z_{\mathsf{gid}_i} \rrbracket_2$ where $z_{\mathsf{gid}_i} \leftarrow_R \mathsf{Span}(a_1^*, a_2^*)$, as opposed to uniformly random over $\mathsf{Span}(a_1^*)$ in Game$_{2.i-1.1}$. We have Game$_{2.i-1.1} \approx_c$ Game$_{2.i-1.2}$ by **Assumption 2**.

Game$_{2.i-1.3}$: is the same as Game$_{2.i-1.2}$ except that the challenge ciphertext uses the vectors $x_j = (s_j, u_j r_1 a_1 + r_j a_2 + v_j a_3)$ for all $j \in [\ell]$ such that $\theta(j) \in \mathcal{S}_{\mathsf{hon}}$, where $r_j = (0, r)^\top M_j$, and $r \leftarrow_R \mathbb{Z}_p^{n-1}$. We have that Game$_{2.i-1.2} \approx_c$ Game$_{2.i-1.3}$ from the DDH assumption in $\mathbb{G}_1$, which implies that $\{r_2 \leftarrow_R \mathbb{Z}_p^*, u \leftarrow_R \mathbb{Z}_p^{n-1} : (\llbracket u \rrbracket_1, \llbracket r_2 u \rrbracket_1)\} \approx_c \{u, r \leftarrow_R \mathbb{Z}_p^{n-1} : (\llbracket u \rrbracket_1, \llbracket r \rrbracket_1)\}$[3].

Game$_{2.i-1.4}$: is the same as Game$_{2.i-1.3}$ except that the challenge ciphertext uses the vectors $x_j = (s_j, u_j r_1 a_1 + r_j a_2 + \eta_j a_2 + v_j a_3)$ for all $j \in [\ell]$ such that $\theta(j) \in \mathcal{S}_{\mathsf{hon}}$, where the value η_j is defined as $\eta(1, w_{\mathsf{gid}_i})^\top M_j$, where $\eta \leftarrow_R \mathbb{Z}_p$ and w_{gid_i} is a vector such that $(1, w_{\mathsf{gid}_i})^\top M_j = 0$ for all $j \in [\ell]$ such that

---

[3] Strictly speaking, the DDH as per Definition 3 is stated with $r_2 \leftarrow_R \mathbb{Z}_p$, not $r_2 \leftarrow_R \mathbb{Z}_p^*$ used here. This makes no difference, however, since the two distributions are within negligible statistical distance.

$\rho(j) \in \mathcal{S}_{\text{gid}_i}$ or ($\rho(j) = \neg\text{att}_j$ and $\text{att}_j \in \{0,1\}^* \setminus \mathcal{S}_{\text{gid}_i}$). The set $\mathcal{S}_{\text{gid}_i}$ is defined as $\mathcal{S}_{\text{gid}_i} = \cup_{\text{pk}\in\mathcal{S}_{\text{hon}},(\text{pk},\text{gid}_i,S)\in\mathcal{Q}_{\text{KeyGen}}}S$. We know that $\mathcal{S}_{\text{gid}_i}$ does not satisfy the access structure $(\boldsymbol{M},\rho)$ of the challenge ciphertext, because the adversary is admissible. Thus, by security of the access structure (Lemma 1), we know that such a vector $\boldsymbol{w}_{\text{gid}_i} \in \mathbb{Z}_p^{n-1}$ exists. Note that we crucially rely on the selectivity here, since the vector $\boldsymbol{w}_{\text{gid}_i}$ used in the challenge ciphertext depends on attributes queried to $\mathcal{O}_{\text{KeyGen}}$. The fact that $\text{Game}_{2.i-1.4} \approx_c \text{Game}_{2.i-1.3}$ follows from the super-selective security of Γ and Σ. Indeed, the extra red component $\eta_j a_2$ encrypted under Γ or Σ never interacts with the vectors used to produce user secret keys. Namely, for all $\text{gid} \neq \text{gid}_i$, we have $H(\text{gid}) = [\![z_{\text{gid}}]\!]_2$ with $z_{\text{gid}} \in \text{Span}(a_1^*, a_3^*)$ so $(0, \eta_j a_2)^\top (1, z_{\text{gid}}) = 0$. For $\text{gid} = \text{gid}_i$, we argue that for all $j \in [\ell]$ such that $\theta(j) \in \mathcal{S}_{\text{hon}}$, either $\eta_j = 0$, or the extra $\eta_j a_2$ can be added thanks to the super-selective security of Γ and Σ. When $\rho(j) \in \mathcal{S}_{\text{gid}_i}$ or $\rho(j) = \neg\text{att}$ with $\text{att} \in \{0,1\}^* \setminus \mathcal{S}_{\text{gid}_i}$, we know that $\eta_j = 0$. When $\rho(j)$ is not of this form, then we know that none of the functional secret keys generated by $\mathcal{O}_{\text{KeyGen}}$ on gid_i decrypt the ciphertext ct_j. Thus, we can conclude using the super-selective security of Σ and Γ.

$\underline{\text{Game}_{2.i-1.5}}$: is the same as $\text{Game}_{2.i-1.4}$ except that the challenge ciphertext uses the vectors $\boldsymbol{x}_j = (s_j, u_j r_1 \boldsymbol{a}_1 + \eta_j' \boldsymbol{a}_2 + v_j \boldsymbol{a}_3)$ where $\eta_j' = (\eta, \boldsymbol{r})^\top \boldsymbol{M}_j$, for all $j \in [\ell]$ such that $\theta(j) \in \mathcal{S}_{\text{hon}}$. The fact that $\text{Game}_{2.i-1.5} = \text{Game}_{2.i-1.4}$ follows from the fact a uniformly random vector $\boldsymbol{r} \leftarrow_R \mathbb{Z}_p^{n-1}$ is distributed identically to an offset $\boldsymbol{x} \in \mathbb{Z}_p^{n-1}$ plus a uniformly random vector $\boldsymbol{r} \leftarrow_R \mathbb{Z}_p^{n-1}$. This is true no matter the value of $\boldsymbol{x}$, as long as $\boldsymbol{r}$ is sampled independently of $\boldsymbol{x}$. So, the following distributions are equals: $\{r_j + \eta_j\}_{j\in[\ell]} = \{(0, \boldsymbol{r})^\top \boldsymbol{M}_j + \eta(1, \boldsymbol{w}_{\text{gid}_i})^\top \boldsymbol{M}_j\}_{j\in[\ell]} = \{(\eta, \boldsymbol{r} + \eta\boldsymbol{w}_{\text{gid}_i})^\top \boldsymbol{M}_j\}_{j\in[\ell]} \equiv \{(\eta, \boldsymbol{r})^\top \boldsymbol{M}_j\}_{j\in[\ell]} = \{\eta_j'\}_{j\in[\ell]}$. This first distribution corresponds to $\text{Game}_{2.i-1.4}$, whereas the last distribution corresponds to $\text{Game}_{2.i-1.5}$.

$\underline{\text{Game}_{2.i-1.6}}$: is the same as $\text{Game}_{2.i-1.5}$ except that the challenge ciphertext uses the vectors $\boldsymbol{x}_j = (s_j, u_j r_1 \boldsymbol{a}_1 + r_j' \boldsymbol{a}_2 + v_j \boldsymbol{a}_3)$ or all $j \in [\ell]$ such that $\theta(j) \in \mathcal{S}_{\text{hon}}$, where $r_j' = r(\gamma, \boldsymbol{v})^\top \boldsymbol{M}_j$, $r \leftarrow_R \mathbb{Z}_p$. Recall that $\gamma \in \mathbb{Z}_p$ and $\boldsymbol{v} \in \mathbb{Z}_p^{n-1}$ are used to compute the shares v_j, namely $v_j = (\gamma, \boldsymbol{v})^\top \boldsymbol{M}_j$. We argue that $\text{Game}_{2.i-1.5} \approx_c \text{Game}_{2.i-1.6}$ using the DDH assumption in $\mathbb{G}_1$, which implies that $\{\boldsymbol{r}, \boldsymbol{v} \leftarrow_R \mathbb{Z}_p^{n-1}, \eta, \gamma \leftarrow_R \mathbb{Z}_p : ([\![\eta]\!]_1, [\![\boldsymbol{r}]\!]_1, [\![\gamma]\!]_1, [\![\boldsymbol{v}]\!]_1)\} \approx_c \{\boldsymbol{v} \leftarrow_R \mathbb{Z}_p^{n-1}, r, \gamma \leftarrow_R \mathbb{Z}_p : ([\![r\gamma]\!]_1, [\![rv]\!]_1, [\![\gamma]\!]_1, [\![\boldsymbol{v}]\!]_1)\}$.

$\underline{\text{Game}_{2.i-1.7}}$: is the same as $\text{Game}_{2.i-1.6}$ except that the output of the hash function on the i'th queried global identifier, which we denote by gid_i, is computed as follows: $H(\text{gid}_i) = [\![z_{\text{gid}_i} + a_3^*]\!]_2$ where $z_{\text{gid}_i} \leftarrow_R \text{Span}(a_1^*, a_2^*)$. We have $\text{Game}_{2.i-1.6} \approx_c \text{Game}_{2.i-1.7}$ by **Assumption 3**. Indeed, we have $\{z_{\text{gid}_i} \leftarrow_R \text{Span}(a_1^*, a_2^*) : [\![z_{\text{gid}_i}]\!]_2\} \approx_c \{z_{\text{gid}_i} \leftarrow_R \text{Span}(a_1^*, a_2^*, a_3^*) : [\![z_{\text{gid}_i}]\!]_2\} \equiv \{z_{\text{gid}_i} \leftarrow_R \text{Span}(a_1^*, a_2^*, a_3^*) : [\![z_{\text{gid}_i} + a_3^*]\!]_2\} \approx_c \{z_{\text{gid}_i} \leftarrow_R \text{Span}(a_1^*, a_2^*) : [\![z_{\text{gid}_i} + a_3^*]\!]_2\}$, where the $\approx_c$ follows from **Assumption 3**. The first distribution corresponds to $\text{Game}_{2.i-1.6}$, whereas the last distribution corresponds to $\text{Game}_{2.i-1.7}$. Note that for readability we omit the other values ($[\![a_1]\!]_1, [\![ra_2 + a_3]\!]_1, [\![a_1^*]\!]_2, [\![a_3^*]\!]_2$) present in the output of all distributions. These values are sufficient to generate the entire adversary's view.

$\mathsf{Game}_{2.i-1.8}$: is the same as $\mathsf{Game}_{2.i-1.7}$ except that the challenge ciphertext uses the vectors $\boldsymbol{x}_j = (s_j, u_j r_1 \boldsymbol{a}_1 + \eta'_j \boldsymbol{a}_2 + v_j \boldsymbol{a}_3)$ for all $j \in [\ell]$ such that $\theta(j) \in \mathcal{S}_{\mathsf{hon}}$, where $\eta'_j = (\eta, \boldsymbol{r})^\top M_j$, $\eta \leftarrow_R \mathbb{Z}_p$, $\boldsymbol{r} \leftarrow_R \mathbb{Z}_p^{n-1}$. This is the reverse of the transition from $\mathsf{Game}_{2.i-1.5}$ and $\mathsf{Game}_{2.i-1.6}$. We have $\mathsf{Game}_{2.i-1.7} \approx_c \mathsf{Game}_{2.i-1.8}$ using the DDH assumption in $\mathbb{G}_1$, which implies that $\{r, \gamma \leftarrow_R \mathbb{Z}_p, \boldsymbol{v} \leftarrow_R \mathbb{Z}_p^{n-1} : ([\![r\gamma]\!]_1, [\![r\boldsymbol{v}]\!]_1, [\![\gamma]\!]_1, [\![\boldsymbol{v}]\!]_1)\} \approx_c \{\eta, \gamma \leftarrow_R \mathbb{Z}_p, \boldsymbol{r}, \boldsymbol{v} \leftarrow_R \mathbb{Z}_p^{n-1} : ([\![\eta]\!]_1, [\![\boldsymbol{r}]\!]_1, [\![\gamma]\!]_1, [\![\boldsymbol{v}]\!]_1)\}$.

$\mathsf{Game}_{2.i-1.9}$: is the same as $\mathsf{Game}_{2.i-1.8}$ except that the challenge ciphertext uses the vectors $\boldsymbol{x}_j = (s_j, u_j r_1 \boldsymbol{a}_1 + r_j \boldsymbol{a}_2 + \eta_j + v_j \boldsymbol{a}_3)$ for all $j \in [\ell]$ such that $\theta(j) \in \mathcal{S}_{\mathsf{hon}}$, where $r_j = (0, \boldsymbol{r})^\top M_j$, $\eta_j = \eta(1, \boldsymbol{w}_{\mathsf{gid}_i})^\top M_j$, $\eta \leftarrow_R \mathbb{Z}_p$ and $\boldsymbol{w}_{\mathsf{gid}_i}$ is defined as before. This is the reverse of the transition from $\mathsf{Game}_{2.i-1.4}$ and $\mathsf{Game}_{2.i-1.5}$. The fact that $\mathsf{Game}_{2.i-1.8} = \mathsf{Game}_{2.i-1.9}$ follows from the fact a uniformly random vector $\boldsymbol{r} \leftarrow_R \mathbb{Z}_p^{n-1}$ is distributed identically to an offset $\boldsymbol{x} \in \mathbb{Z}_p^{n-1}$ plus a uniformly random vector $\boldsymbol{r} \leftarrow_R \mathbb{Z}_p^{n-1}$, as long as $\boldsymbol{r}$ is sampled independently of $\boldsymbol{x}$. So, the following distributions are equals: $\{\eta'_j\}_{j \in [\ell]} = \{(\eta, \boldsymbol{r})^\top M_j\}_{j \in [\ell]} \equiv \{(\eta, \boldsymbol{r} + \eta \boldsymbol{w}_{\mathsf{gid}_i})^\top M_j\}_{j \in [\ell]} = \{(0, \boldsymbol{r})^\top M_j + \eta(1, \boldsymbol{w}_{\mathsf{gid}_i})^\top M_j\}_{j \in [\ell]} = \{r_j + \eta_j\}_{j \in [\ell]}$. This first distribution corresponds to $\mathsf{Game}_{2.i-1.8}$, whereas the last distribution corresponds to $\mathsf{Game}_{2.i-1.9}$.

$\mathsf{Game}_{2.i-1.10}$: is the same as $\mathsf{Game}_{2.i-1.9}$ except that the challenge ciphertext uses the vectors $\boldsymbol{x}_j = (s_j, u_j r_1 \boldsymbol{a}_1 + r_j \boldsymbol{a}_2 + v_j \boldsymbol{a}_3)$ for all $j \in [\ell]$ such that $\theta(j) \in \mathcal{S}_{\mathsf{hon}}$, where $r_j = (0, \boldsymbol{r})^\top M_j$, $\boldsymbol{r} \leftarrow_R \mathbb{Z}_p^{n-1}$. This is the reverse of the transition from $\mathsf{Game}_{2.i-1.3}$ and $\mathsf{Game}_{2.i-1.4}$. The fact that $\mathsf{Game}_{2.i-1.9} \approx_c \mathsf{Game}_{2.i-1.10}$ follows from the super-selective security of Γ and Σ. Indeed, the component $\eta_j \boldsymbol{a}_2$ encrypted under Γ and Σ in $\mathsf{Game}_{2.i-1.9}$ never interacts with the vectors used to produce user secret keys. Namely, for all $\mathsf{gid} \neq \mathsf{gid}_i$, we have $H(\mathsf{gid}) = [\![\boldsymbol{z}_{\mathsf{gid}}]\!]_2$ with $\boldsymbol{z}_{\mathsf{gid}} \in \mathsf{Span}(\boldsymbol{a}_1^*, \boldsymbol{a}_3^*)$ so $(0, \eta_j \boldsymbol{a}_2)^\top (1, \boldsymbol{z}_{\mathsf{gid}}) = 0$. For $\mathsf{gid} = \mathsf{gid}_i$, we know that all queries $(\mathsf{pk}, \mathsf{gid}_i, S)$ to $\mathcal{O}_{\mathsf{KeyGen}}$ are such that $S \in \mathcal{S}_{\mathsf{gid}_i}$ (by definition of the set $\mathcal{S}_{\mathsf{gid}_i}$), and, as argued before, we know that for all $j \in [\ell]$ such that $\theta(j) \in \mathcal{S}_{\mathsf{hon}}$, either $\eta_j = 0$ or ct_j cannot be decrypted by the functional secret keys generated by $\mathcal{O}_{\mathsf{KeyGen}}$ on gid_i.

$\mathsf{Game}_{2.i-1.11}$: is the same as $\mathsf{Game}_{2.i-1.10}$ except that the challenge ciphertext uses the vectors $\boldsymbol{x}_j = (s_j, u_j r_1 \boldsymbol{a}_1 + u_j r_2 \boldsymbol{a}_2 + v_j \cdot \boldsymbol{a}_3)$ for all $j \in [\ell]$ such that $\theta(j) \in \mathcal{S}_{\mathsf{hon}}$, where $r_2 \leftarrow_R \mathbb{Z}_p^*$. This is the reverse of the transition from $\mathsf{Game}_{2.i-1.2}$ and $\mathsf{Game}_{2.i-1.3}$. We have that $\mathsf{Game}_{2.i-1.10} \approx_c \mathsf{Game}_{2.i-1.11}$ from the DDH assumption in $\mathbb{G}_1$, which implies that $\{\boldsymbol{u}, \boldsymbol{r} \leftarrow_R \mathbb{Z}_p^{n-1} : ([\![\boldsymbol{u}]\!]_1, [\![\boldsymbol{r}]\!]_1)\} \approx_c$

$\{r_2 \leftarrow_R \mathbb{Z}_p^*, \boldsymbol{u} \leftarrow_R \mathbb{Z}_p^{n-1} : (\llbracket\boldsymbol{u}\rrbracket_1, \llbracket r_2 \cdot \boldsymbol{u}\rrbracket_1)\}^4$. This first distribution corresponds to $\mathsf{Game}_{2.i-1.10}$, whereas the last distribution corresponds to $\mathsf{Game}_{2.i-1.11}$.

$\mathsf{Game}_{2.i-1.12}$: is the same as $\mathsf{Game}_{2.i-1.11}$ except that the output of the hash function on the i'th queried global identifier, which we denote by gid_i, is computed as follows: $H(\mathsf{gid}_i) = \llbracket z_{\mathsf{gid}_i} + \boldsymbol{a}_3^*\rrbracket_2$ where $z_{\mathsf{gid}_i} \leftarrow_R \mathsf{Span}(\boldsymbol{a}_1^*)$, as opposed to uniformly random over $\mathsf{Span}(\boldsymbol{a}_1^*, \boldsymbol{a}_2^*)$ in $\mathsf{Game}_{2.i-1.11}$. This is the reverse of the transition from $\mathsf{Game}_{2.i-1.1}$ and $\mathsf{Game}_{2.i-1.2}$. We have $\mathsf{Game}_{2.i-1.1} \approx_c \mathsf{Game}_{2.i-1.2}$ by **Assumption 2**.

$\mathsf{Game}_{2.i}$: is the same as $\mathsf{Game}_{2.i-1.12}$, except that the challenge ciphertext uses the vectors $\boldsymbol{x}_j = (s_j, u_j r_1 \boldsymbol{a}_1 + v_j \boldsymbol{a}_3)$ for all $j \in [\ell]$ such that $\theta(j) \in \mathcal{S}_{\mathsf{hon}}$. That is, we remove the component $u_j r_2 \boldsymbol{a}_2$. We argue that $\mathsf{Game}_{2.i-1.12} \approx_c \mathsf{Game}_{2.i}$ thanks to the super-selective security of Γ and Σ. Indeed, for all $j \in [\ell]$ such that $\theta(j) \in \mathcal{S}_{\mathsf{hon}}$ and all queried gid, we have $z_{\mathsf{gid}} \in \mathsf{Span}(\boldsymbol{a}_1^*, \boldsymbol{a}_3^*)$, thus $(s_j, u_j r_1 \boldsymbol{a}_1 + u_j r_2 \boldsymbol{a}_2 + v_j \cdot \boldsymbol{a}_3)^\top (1, z_{\mathsf{gid}}) = (s_j, u_j r_1 \boldsymbol{a}_1 + v_j \cdot \boldsymbol{a}_3)^\top (1, z_{\mathsf{gid}})$, just as in game $\mathsf{Game}_{2.i}$, since $\boldsymbol{a}_2^\top \boldsymbol{a}_1^* = \boldsymbol{a}_2^\top \boldsymbol{a}_3^* = 0$. $\square$

References

[ACGU20] Abdalla, M., Catalano, D., Gay, R., Ursu, B.: Inner-product functional encryption with fine-grained access control. In: Moriai, S., Wang, H. (eds.) ASIACRYPT 2020. LNCS, vol. 12493, pp. 467–497. Springer, Cham (2020). https://doi.org/10.1007/978-3-030-64840-4_16

[AKW18] Agrawal, S., Koppula, V., Waters, B.: Impossibility of simulation secure functional encryption even with random oracles. In: Beimel, A., Dziembowski, S. (eds.) TCC 2018. LNCS, vol. 11239, pp. 659–688. Springer, Cham (2018). https://doi.org/10.1007/978-3-030-03807-6_24

[ALS16] Agrawal, S., Libert, B., Stehlé, D.: Fully secure functional encryption for inner products, from standard assumptions. In: Robshaw, M., Katz, J. (eds.) CRYPTO 2016. LNCS, vol. 9816, pp. 333–362. Springer, Heidelberg (2016). https://doi.org/10.1007/978-3-662-53015-3_12

[AYY22] Agrawal, S., Yadav, A., Yamada, S.: Multi-input attribute based encryption and predicate encryption. In: Dodis, Y., Shrimpton, T. (eds) Advances in Cryptology – CRYPTO 2022. CRYPTO 2022. LNCS, vol. 13507, pp. 590–621. Springer, Cham (2022). https://doi.org/10.1007/978-3-031-15802-5_21

[Bei96] Beimel, A.: Secure Schemes for Secret Sharing and Key Distribution. Ph.D, Technion - Israel Institute of Technology (1996)

[BSW11] Boneh, D., Sahai, A., Waters, B.: Functional encryption: definitions and challenges. In: Ishai, Y. (ed.) TCC 2011. LNCS, vol. 6597, pp. 253–273. Springer, Heidelberg (2011). https://doi.org/10.1007/978-3-642-19571-6_16

---

[4] Again, strictly speaking, the DDH as per Definition 3 is stated with $r_2 \leftarrow_R \mathbb{Z}_p$, not $r_2 \leftarrow_R \mathbb{Z}_p^*$ but as we argued above, this makes no difference since the two distributions are within negligible statistical distance.

[CC09]   Chase, M., Chow, S.S.M.: Improving privacy and security in multi-authority attribute-based encryption. In: Al-Shaer, E., Jha, S., Keromytis, A.D. (eds.) ACM CCS 2009, pp. 121–130. ACM Press, November 2009

[Cha07]   Chase, M.: Multi-authority attribute based encryption. In: Vadhan, S.P. (ed.) TCC 2007. LNCS, vol. 4392, pp. 515–534. Springer, Heidelberg (2007). https://doi.org/10.1007/978-3-540-70936-7_28

[CS02]   Cramer, R., Shoup, V.: Universal hash proofs and a paradigm for adaptive chosen ciphertext secure public-key encryption. In: Knudsen, L.R. (ed.) EUROCRYPT 2002. LNCS, vol. 2332, pp. 45–64. Springer, Heidelberg (2002). https://doi.org/10.1007/3-540-46035-7_4

[DKW21a]   Datta, P., Komargodski, I., Waters, B.: Decentralized multi-authority ABE for DNFs from LWE. In: Canteaut, A., Standaert, F.-X. (eds.) EUROCRYPT 2021. LNCS, vol. 12696, pp. 177–209. Springer, Cham (2021). https://doi.org/10.1007/978-3-030-77870-5_7

[DKW21b]   Datta, P., Komargodski, I., Waters, B.: Decentralized multi-authority ABE for NC^1 from computational-BDH. Cryptology ePrint Archive (2021)

[DP19]   Dufour-Sans, E., Pointcheval, D.: Unbounded inner-product functional encryption with succinct keys. In: Deng, R.H., Gauthier-Umaña, V., Ochoa, M., Yung, M. (eds.) ACNS 2019. LNCS, vol. 11464, pp. 426–441. Springer, Cham (2019). https://doi.org/10.1007/978-3-030-21568-2_21

[GPSW06]   Goyal, V., Pandey, O., Sahai, A., Waters, B.: Attribute-based encryption for fine-grained access control of encrypted data. In: Juels, A., Wright, R.N., De Capitani di Vimercati, S. (eds.) ACM CCS 2006, pp. 89–98. ACM Press (2006). Available as Cryptology ePrint Archive Report 2006/309

[Kim19]   Kim, S.: Multi-authority attribute-based encryption from LWE in the OT model. IACR Cryptology ePrint Archive 2019:280 (2019)

[KW93]   Karchmer, M., Wigderson, A.: On span programs. In: Structure in Complexity Theory Conference, 1993, Proceedings of the Eighth Annual, pp. 102–111, May 1993

[LCLS08]   Lin, H., Cao, Z., Liang, X., Shao, J.: Secure threshold multi authority attribute based encryption without a central authority. In: Chowdhury, D.R., Rijmen, V., Das, A. (eds.) INDOCRYPT 2008. LNCS, vol. 5365, pp. 426–436. Springer, Heidelberg (2008). https://doi.org/10.1007/978-3-540-89754-5_33

[Lew12]   Lewko, A.: Tools for simulating features of composite order bilinear groups in the prime order setting. In: Pointcheval, D., Johansson, T. (eds.) EUROCRYPT 2012. LNCS, vol. 7237, pp. 318–335. Springer, Heidelberg (2012). https://doi.org/10.1007/978-3-642-29011-4_20

[LW11]   Lewko, A., Waters, B.: Decentralizing attribute-based encryption. In: Paterson, K.G. (ed.) EUROCRYPT 2011. LNCS, vol. 6632, pp. 568–588. Springer, Heidelberg (2011). https://doi.org/10.1007/978-3-642-20465-4_31

[MJ18]   Michalevsky, Y., Joye, M.: Decentralized policy-hiding ABE with receiver privacy. In: Lopez, J., Zhou, J., Soriano, M. (eds.) ESORICS 2018. LNCS, vol. 11099, pp. 548–567. Springer, Cham (2018). https://doi.org/10.1007/978-3-319-98989-1_27

[MKE08]   Müller, S., Katzenbeisser, S., Eckert, C.: Distributed attribute-based encryption. In: Lee, P.J., Cheon, J.H. (eds.) ICISC 2008. LNCS, vol. 5461, pp. 20–36. Springer, Heidelberg (2009). https://doi.org/10.1007/978-3-642-00730-9_2

[OSW07] Ostrovsky, R., Sahai, A., Waters, B.: Attribute-based encryption with non-monotonic access structures. In: Ning, P., De Capitani di Vimercati, S., Syverson, P.F. (eds.) ACM CCS 2007, pp. 195–203. ACM Press, October 2007

[OT09] Okamoto, T., Takashima, K.: Hierarchical predicate encryption for inner-products. In: Matsui, M. (ed.) ASIACRYPT 2009. LNCS, vol. 5912, pp. 214–231. Springer, Heidelberg (2009). https://doi.org/10.1007/978-3-642-10366-7_13

[OT13] Okamoto, T., Takashima, K.: Decentralized attribute-based signatures. In: Kurosawa, K., Hanaoka, G. (eds.) PKC 2013. LNCS, vol. 7778, pp. 125–142. Springer, Heidelberg (2013). https://doi.org/10.1007/978-3-642-36362-7_9

[Rog15] Rogaway, P.: The moral character of cryptographic work. IACR Cryptology ePrint Archive 2015:1162 (2015)

[RW15] Rouselakis, Y., Waters, B.: Efficient statically-secure large-universe multi-authority attribute-based encryption. In: Böhme, R., Okamoto, T. (eds.) FC 2015. LNCS, vol. 8975, pp. 315–332. Springer, Heidelberg (2015). https://doi.org/10.1007/978-3-662-47854-7_19

[SW05] Sahai, A., Waters, B.: Fuzzy identity-based encryption. In: Cramer, R. (ed.) EUROCRYPT 2005. LNCS, vol. 3494, pp. 457–473. Springer, Heidelberg (2005). https://doi.org/10.1007/11426639_27

[TT18] Tomida, J., Takashima, K.: Unbounded inner product functional encryption from bilinear maps. In: Peyrin, T., Galbraith, S. (eds.) ASIACRYPT 2018. LNCS, vol. 11273, pp. 609–639. Springer, Cham (2018). https://doi.org/10.1007/978-3-030-03329-3_21

[WFL19] Wang, Z., Fan, X., Liu, F.-H.: FE for inner products and its application to decentralized ABE. In: Lin, D., Sako, K. (eds.) PKC 2019. LNCS, vol. 11443, pp. 97–127. Springer, Cham (2019). https://doi.org/10.1007/978-3-030-17259-6_4

[WWW22] Waters, B., Wee, H., Wu, D.J.: Multi-authority ABE from lattices without random oracles. In: Kiltz, E., Vaikuntanathan, V. (eds.) Theory of Cryptography Conference. Springer, Cham (2022). https://doi.org/10.1007/978-3-031-22318-1_23

Multi-instance Secure Public-Key Encryption

Carlo Brunetta[1] , Hans Heum[2] , and Martijn Stam[1]

[1] Simula UiB, Bergen, Norway
{carlob,martijn}@simula.no
[2] Department of Mathematical Sciences, NTNU - Norwegian University of Science and Technology, Trondheim, Norway
hans.heum@ntnu.no

Abstract. Mass surveillance targets many users at the same time with the goal of learning as much as possible. Intuitively, breaking many users' cryptography simultaneously should be at least as hard as that of only breaking a single one, but ideally security degradation is gradual: an adversary ought to work harder to break more. Bellare, Ristenpart and Tessaro (Crypto'12) introduced the notion of multi-instance security to capture the related concept for password hashing with salts. Auerbach, Giacon and Kiltz (Eurocrypt'20) motivated the study of public key encryption (PKE) in the multi-instance setting, yet their technical results are exclusively stated in terms of key encapsulation mechanisms (KEMs), leaving a considerable gap.

We investigate the multi-instance security of public key encryption. Our contributions are twofold. Firstly, we define and compare possible security notions for multi-instance PKE, where we include PKE schemes whose correctness is not perfect. Secondly, we observe that, in general, a hybrid encryption scheme of a multi-instance secure KEM and an arbitrary data encapsulation mechanism (DEM) is unlikely to inherit the KEM's multi-instance security. Yet, we show how with a suitable information-theoretic DEM, and a computationally secure key derivation function if need be, inheritance is possible. As far as we are aware, ours is the first inheritance result in the challenging multi-bit scenario.

Keywords: Multi-Instance Security · Hybrid Encryption · Property Inheritance · Mass Surveillance

1 Introduction

Security of cryptographic schemes is increasingly studied concretely. The question changes from whether a scheme is secure or not, to how secure it is. The change in emphasis also results in increased importance in more realistic security notions that model a world where an adversary might have many potential targets. If an adversary simply tries to learn something about one of its κ targets, then intuitively the more targets there are, the easier the adversary's job

---

Work by Hans Heum performed as part of his PhD studies at Simula UiB.

A. Boldyreva and V. Kolesnikov (Eds.): PKC 2023, LNCS 13941, pp. 336–367, 2023.
https://doi.org/10.1007/978-3-031-31371-4_12

becomes. Indeed, using simple hybrid arguments results in a security degradation that is linear in κ. But what happens if the adversary is greedy and wants to learn more, maybe even targets everyone? On the one hand, one could argue that if breaking one instance is hard, then so is breaking many. Yet, on the other hand, one would hope that breaking multiple instances, say n, is strictly harder than breaking just a single one.

This second perspective made Bellare, Ristenpart and Tessaro [12], henceforth BRT, realize that new security notions are needed to reason about such greedy adversaries. They were motivated by how salts in password hashing protect against attackers re-using precomputation to retrieve multiple passwords. For their study into probabilistic symmetric schemes, they identified left-or-right indistinguishability under xor as the strongest notion. Roughly speaking, there are κ keys in the system each associated with its own left-or-right challenge bit b_i and the goal of the adversary is to guess the xor of all those bits.

Recently, Auerbach, Giacon and Kiltz [4], henceforth AGK, argued the importance of BRT's concept to protect against mass surveillance. They introduced the (n, κ) scaling factor as the effort to break n out of κ instances relative to the effort needed to break a single instance. After recalling several well-known greedy attacks against public key schemes with dubious scaling factors, they set out to provide an encryption scheme with good, non-trivial scaling factor.

They discussed various versions of Hashed ElGamal that differed in whether users shared group parameters and/or generators, plus whether the underlying group was elliptic curve or finite field based. In the programmable random oracle model, they showed that the multi-instance security of Hashed ElGamal tightly relates to a novel multi-instance Gap Computational Diffie–Hellman (MI-GapCDH) assumption, whose validity was further supported by an analysis in the generic group model.

There was, or rather is, just one small problem: Hashed ElGamal is a key encapsulation mechanism (KEM), not a public key encryption (PKE) scheme. Indeed, although AGK use PKE as their motivation, their formalization is entirely centred around KEMs. Of course, Cramer and Shoup [18] already showed how a secure KEM can be combined with a secure data encapsulation mechanism (DEM) to create a secure PKE (for various notions of security). This so-called hybrid encryption paradigm is widely deployed in the real world, yet, can its composition theorem be easily lifted to the multi-instance setting?

For key unrecoverability, all seems fine, but for indistinguishability one quickly uncovers various challenges. Consider an adversary $\mathbb{A}$ that wants to recover n out of κ challenge bits b_i: it can attempt to recover roughly half of its b_i by somehow breaking the DEM, and recovering the remaining half by breaking the KEM. Intuitively, such a divide-and-conquer strategy essentially rules out inheriting full multi-instance security of both KEM and DEM simultaneously. Instead, perhaps we should aim to bound an adversary's multi-instance advantage against the hybrid encryption in terms of either breaking the full multi-instance security of the KEM or breaking only one of many instances of the DEM.

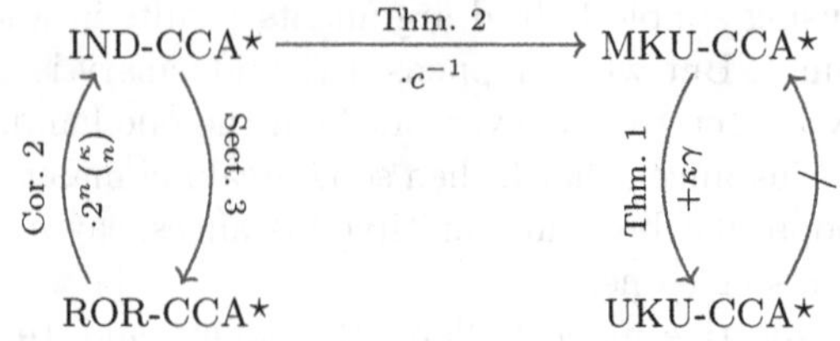

$$\text{IND-CCA}\star \xrightarrow[\cdot c^{-1}]{\text{Thm. 2}} \text{MKU-CCA}\star$$

$$\text{ROR-CCA}\star \qquad\qquad \text{UKU-CCA}\star$$

Fig. 1. An overview of multi-instance security notions for public-key encryption, where γ relates to imperfect correctness (Definition 1), and the loss factor c is explained in Theorem 2.

Special care would have to be taken to ensure that the corresponding multi-user DEM advantage is not overwhelming the multi-instance KEM advantage. After all, already when showing multi-user security of hybrid encryption, ensuring the DEM advantage does not overshadow the multi-user KEM advantage is challenging [23]. Furthermore, the study of multi-user KEMs highlights a second, more technical problem.

For multi-user security, there are essentially two different formalizations possible: one where each user comes with its own challenge bit and one where the users share a global challenge bit. Jager et al. [29] recently observed that only the latter lends itself to an easy adaptation of composition theorems using KEMs, as it allows a simple game-hop where all KEM-derived ephemeral keys are replaced by randomly selected keys (decoupled from the KEM encapsulations). That proof technique fails when there are multiple challenge bits. Unfortunately, for multi-instance security, the only option available is a notion with multiple challenge bits. In such a setting, inheritance of security properties of the KEM to any construction based on the KEM is an open problem.

Our Contribution. As mentioned above, multi-instance security was introduced by BRT in the context of probabilistic symmetric primitives and later adapted to key encapsulation mechanisms by AGK, who provide an excellent motivation for the study of multi-instance security in a public key setting. We adapt those notions to multi-instance security for PKE schemes, but make a number of non-trivial changes in the process. Firstly, we observe that the mechanisms used by BRT and AGK to model multi-instance games differ, which seems to have gone unnoticed hitherto. BRT's mechanism is stronger as it allows for corruptions (denoted by $\star$), yet AGK's mechanism is more expressive by making explicit how many instances an adversary should break. We use elements of both in our notions, incorporating both BRT's corruptions and AGK's explicit expression of the number of targeted instances. Secondly, we allow for correctness to be imperfect, which has ramifications for how to deal with decryption oracles (for chosen-ciphertext attacks) and corruptions. We delve into the differences between the various mechanisms in Sect. 3.3, furthermore we use our revised mechanism to study a number of related notions, as summarized in Fig. 1.

In more detail, we start out by porting BRT's notion of key unrecoverability to the public-key setting. In fact, we consider two distinct versions of key unrecoverability: "Universal Key Unrecoverability" (UKU), where the adversary is tasked to recover the exact challenge private key(s) and "Matching Key Unrecoverability" (MKU), where it suffices to recover suitably equivalent private keys, where we leverage our imperfect correctness notion to define "suitably equivalent". As one would expect, this relaxed key unrecoverability notion implies the stronger, exact notion up to a small loss related to how we model imperfect correctness (Theorem 1).

For our main notion of multi-instance security, we follow BRT's identification of left-or-right xor-indistinguishability as the strongest notion and adapt it to the public key setting. As for the symmetric encryption setting studied by BRT, this indistinguishability notion implies the above key unrecoverability notions (Theorem 2); however, the differences between perfect symmetric encryption and imperfect PKE affect the corresponding implications and their proofs.

Finally, we explore an alternative notion, namely real-or-random xor-indistinguishability (ROR). Trivially, left-or-right tightly implies real-or-random and in the multi-instance setting BRT showed that the usual factor-2 loss from the single instance implication between real-or-random to left-or right, becomes an exponential factor-2^κ loss. A similar loss is possible in our setting, however, we can also achieve a typically preferable bound of $\binom{\kappa}{n}2^n$ (Corollary 2).

With suitable notions for multi-instance PKE available, we focus on how to turn a suitably multi-instance secure KEM into a multi-instance secure PKE scheme using hybrid encryption. For key unrecoverability, inheritance is immediate, yet we would like to guarantee good multi-instance indistinguishability (the left-hand branch of Fig. 1). We summarize our findings in Fig. 2.

Our first observation is that we can expand the length of the ephemeral key to any desired length using a pseudorandom extendable output function (XOF). The resulting extendable KEM, or XEM, inherits the multi-instance security of the underlying KEM, provided the XOF is secure against multi-challenge adversaries (Theorem 5). To ensure that the XOF does not become the weakest link, its seed will need to be long enough, which in turn implies that the underlying KEM already needs to output a sufficiently long ephemeral key.

The XOF above of course plays the role of key derivation function, but it is more common that it is modelled as part of any key expansion done by the DEM. Moving it into the KEM allows us to use an information-theoretic DEM, read one-time pad (OTP), irrespective of the message length. The OTP's properties enable a simplified proof for the security of hybrid encryption (Theorem 6), where the PKE does indeed inherit the multi-instance security of the XEM, with two important caveats. Firstly, the OTP is only passively secure, so the PKE only achieves CPA not CCA security, and secondly, standard KEM indistinguishability only tightly provides real-or-random indistinguishability for the PKE (see the top line of Fig. 2).

Switching to the TagKEM framework [2], or in our case TagXEM, takes care of the first shortcoming and tightly achieves multi-instance ROR-CCA secure

PKE, or IND-CCA non-tightly (Theorem 7). For the PKE to inherit multi-instance IND-CCA security tightly, we introduce a novel KEM indistinguishability notion that more closely matches PKE's left-or-right idea, namely real-or-permuted (ROP). Finally, we can show tight multi-instance inheritance for the most desirable PKE notion, based on a ROP-secure TagXEM (Theorem 8).

One small hiccough remains, as our KEM-to-XEM result unfortunately only works for classical KEM indistinguishability, not for ROP indistinguishability, nor does it look feasible to convert a KEM or XEM to a TagKEM or TagXEM, respectively, inheriting multi-instance security using standard reductions. Here, the random oracle, as used by AGK to prove their construction secure, comes to the rescue, although rather than looking at Hashed ElGamal under the MI-GapCDH assumption, we consider more general KEMs that are multi-instance one-way under plaintext checking attacks (unfortunately, also at this point we need to restrict to perfect correctness), which we combine with Abe et al.'s TagKEM construction from a KEM and a MAC (message authentication code).

Recalling that the original random oracle [14] was in fact a XOF, we can bake the extendability into the random oracle, including the key needed for an information-theoretic secure MAC. Moreover, the power of the ROM allows proving the stronger ROP indistinguishability just as easily as classical KEM indistinguishability. All in all, with Theorem 9 we achieve a suitably multi-instance secure TagXEM based on a KEM that can be instantiated by Hashed ElGamal. In that case, the security relies on the MI-GapCDH* assumption, i.e. with corruptions. As an added benefit of using the random oracle, the resulting multi-instance bounds no longer rely on sufficiently long XOF inputs, thus for determining a suitable group size (when instantiating by Hashed ElGamal) the MI-GapCDH* advantage is leading.

For low granularity, which corresponds to a setting where every user generates its own group as part of its public key, AGK's technique can easily be extended to include corruptions and in the generic group model we arrive at the same bound for the hardness of MI-GapCDH*, so with corruptions, as AGK did without corruptions. Unfortunately, for the more realistic high granularity setting, where users share the same (standardized) group, AGK's proof strategy does not easily allow incorporating corruptions. We provide details in the full version [17].

Thus, we can conclude that XOF-based Hashed ElGamal combined with a suitable information-theoretically secure MAC and the one-time-pad, provides good multi-instance security in the programmable random oracle model and generic group model, provided that users each select their own independent group. We briefly touch upon a concrete interpretation in the full version, where we also informally address AGK's scaling factor.

Related Work. Farshim and Tessaro [20] recently followed up BRT's line of work on the multi-instance security of password hashing by combining it with the related preprocessing setting. AGK [4] motivated their investigation into multi-instance security by the threat of mass surveillance. The latter had previously motivated Bellare et al. [11] to consider subversion, namely the ease with

$$\text{IND-CCA}^{\star}_{\text{KEM}} \xrightarrow[+\text{ XOF}]{\text{Thm. 5}} \text{IND-CCA}^{\star}_{\text{XEM}} \xrightarrow[+\text{ OTP}]{\text{Thm. 6}} \text{ROR-CPA}^{\star}_{\text{PKE}}$$

AGK [4]   + RO

$$\text{MI-GapCDH}^{\star} \qquad\qquad \text{IND-CCA}^{\star}_{\text{TXEM}} \xrightarrow[+\text{ OTP}]{\text{Thm. 7}} \text{ROR-CCA}^{\star}_{\text{PKE}}$$

Lemma 4 (full version)

$$\text{OW-PCA}^{\star}_{\text{KEM}} \xrightarrow[+\text{ MAC} + \text{RO}]{\text{Thm. 9}} \text{ROP-CCA}^{\star}_{\text{TXEM}} \xrightarrow[+\text{ OTP}]{\text{Thm. 8}} \text{IND-CCA}^{\star}_{\text{PKE}}$$

Fig. 2. An overview of our constructions achieving various flavours of multi-instance security. The left upwards arrow is dotted, as AGK did not consider corruptions.

which a "big brother" might subvert an encryption algorithm by replacing it surreptitiously with a trapdoored one with otherwise identical behaviour.

The multi-instance setting is closely related to the multi-user setting, in which the adversary is tasked with breaking only one rather than n out of κ possible instances. Multi-user security was introduced by Bellare et al. [7] in the public-key setting, with the goal of deriving concrete security parameters in a more realistic setting. There have been many recent follow-up works, including how the hybrid paradigm generalizes to the setting without corruptions [23], and later with corruptions [33], as well as the construction of tightly-secure authenticated key exchange (AKE) from multi-user KEMs [29]. Various versions of the multi-user GapCDH problem with corruptions were recently proposed and analysed in that context [30].

One definitional subtlety of multi-user security is the number of challenge bits: either a single one, as originally conceived, or many, as typical for the multi-instance setting. The various definitions do not appear to imply each other tightly [26], which slightly hinders regarding the multi-user setting as a special case of the multi-instance setting (due to potential tightness losses).

2   Preliminaries

2.1   Notation

For a positive integer n, we write $[n]$ for the set $\{1, \ldots, n\}$. We use code-based experiments, where $\leftarrow$ denotes deterministic assignment and $\leftarrow$\$ denotes probabilistic assignment. By convention, all sets and lists are initialized empty. For a set X, we use the shorthand $X \xleftarrow{\cup} x$ for the operation $X \leftarrow X \cup \{x\}$. If X is a list, then $X \xleftarrow{\frown} x$ denotes appending the element x to X; to retrieve the ith element of the list, we write $X[i]$ where by convention $X[i] = \emptyset$ for out-of-bounds i.

We use $\Pr[Code : Event \mid Condition]$ to denote the conditional probability of $Event$ occurring when $Code$ is executed, conditioned on $Condition$. We omit $Code$ when it is clear from the context and $Condition$ when it is not needed.

For Boolean values, we use {true, false} and {0, 1} interchangeably, where by convention 1 corresponds to true.

When proving relations between notions and security of constructions, we will often refer to simple fully black box (SFBB) reductions. A reduction is fully black box iff it works for all schemes and adversaries, and only accesses them in a black box manner [6, 38] (we leave the black box dependence implicit in our notation). Moreover, if the reduction only runs its adversary once and without rewinding, then the reduction is simple [34].

Finally, the respective games that the adversary and the reduction are playing often have matching (though not identical) oracles; for instance, both may have access to a decryption oracle or a key corruption oracle. We call a reduction type-preserving with respect to, say, a decryption oracle iff the reduction will make decryption queries iff its black-box adversary makes decryption queries. Type-preservation, without explicit mention of any oracles, is implicitly meant to imply for all meaningfully matching oracles (unless otherwise specified).

Type-preservation of reductions appears folklore and can easily be established by inspection. Intuitively, a type-preserving reduction can be used to show simultaneously that CCA security of some kind implies CCA security of another kind and that CPA security of the same kind implies CPA security of the other kind. In Sect. 3.3 we will encounter several reductions that are only partially type-preserving.

2.2 PKE Syntax

A public-key encryption scheme PKE consists of four algorithms: the probabilistic key generation algorithm PKE.Kg, which takes as input some system parameter pm (see also Remark 1) and outputs a public/private key pair (pk, sk); the deterministic key validation algorithm PKE.Check, which takes as input the system parameters pm as well as a purported public/private key pair (pk, sk) and returns true or false (see Remark 2 below), the probabilistic encryption algorithm PKE.Enc, which on input a public key pk and a message $m \in \mathcal{M}$ (see Remark 3), outputs a ciphertext c; and the deterministic decryption algorithm PKE.Dec, which on input of a secret key sk and a ciphertext c, outputs either a message m, or a special symbol $\perp$ denoting failure.

Remark 1. The system parameters pm are implicitly input to PKE.Enc and PKE.Dec as well; for concreteness, they can for instance be the description of an elliptic curve group with generator for an ECDLP-based system or the dimensions and noise sampling algorithm for an LWE-based system. When one is interested in re-phrasing our results in an asymptotic setting, the parameters pm will be generated by a probabilistic, polynomial-time algorithm that only takes the security parameter as input.

Remark 2. For various modern cryptosystems, especially schemes targeting post-quantum security or tight multi-user security, the relationship between public and private keys is not one-to-one. For instance, a single public key can have various private keys [23] or a single private key can lead to various public keys [16].

Naively, one could check whether a public key and private key belong together by simply verifying whether encrypting and then decrypting a number of random messages always returns the original messages. With imperfect correctness, such a canonical checking algorithm can produce both false positives and false negatives. Yet, it is usually still possible to ckeck whether a private–public key pair matches more directly, which we model by the key validation algorithm PKE.Check. We will define both correctness and key unrecoverability in terms of this key validation algorithm.

Remark 3. The message space $\mathcal{M}$ may depend on the parameters pm, but for simplicity we assume it independent of the public key pk. Often $\mathcal{M}$ consists of arbitrary length bitstrings, or at least all bitstrings up to some large length (e.g. 2^{64}) and messages of the same length are deemed equivalent as they are expected to yield ciphertexts of identical lengths. We will model these equivalences more abstractly by assuming that pm implicitly defines a number $\mathfrak{m}$ of equivalence classes, together with an efficient method $[\![\cdot]\!] : \mathcal{M} \to [\mathfrak{m}]$ to determine the class (e.g. length) of a message and an efficient algorithm to sample uniformly from a given equivalence class. We write $\sim$ for the equivalence, so for $m \in \mathcal{M}$, $m \sim m'$ iff $[\![m]\!] = [\![m']\!]$.

Correctness. Perfect correctness states that for all parameters pm, all key pairs (pk, sk) that can be output by PKE.Kg(pm), and all messages $m \in \mathcal{M}$, we always have that $\mathsf{PKE.Dec_{sk}(PKE.Enc_{pk}}(m)) = m$. Yet modern schemes, especially lattice-based ones, often allow a small decryption error, where occasionally decryption will fail or it will return a wrong message.

Various relaxations of correctness have appeared in the literature in order to argue about such schemes as it turns out that some classical results implicitly or subtly relied on perfect correctness. In order for our work to be meaningful for a large range of both classical and modern schemes, we introduce a stronger version of imperfect correctness based on the key validation algorithm.

Definition 1 ((γ, δ)-**Correctness**). *Let* $\gamma, \delta \in [0, 1]$. *Then a public-key encryption scheme* PKE *is called* (γ, δ)-*correct iff for all* pm,

1. $\Pr[(\mathsf{pk, sk}) \leftarrow_{\$} \mathsf{PKE.Kg(pm)} : \mathsf{PKE.Check(pm, pk, sk)} = \mathsf{false}] \leq \gamma$;
2. *for all* (pk, sk) *and all* $m \in \mathcal{M}$, *if* PKE.Check(pm, pk, sk) = true *then*

$$\Pr[\mathsf{PKE.Dec_{sk}(PKE.Enc_{pk}}(m)) \neq m] \leq \delta .$$

Perfect correctness corresponds to $(0, 0)$-correctness and any scheme is trivially both $(1, 0)$-correct and $(0, 1)$-correct. For good schemes γ and δ can simultaneously be chosen small, where typically increasing γ allows for decreasing δ. As we will see, both γ and δ will appear in various bounds, thus allowing larger γ to enable smaller δ (or vice versa) might give preferable bounds.

3   Multi-instance Security of Public-Key Encryption

3.1   Two Flavours of Key Recovery

The minimal requirement for public-key encryption schemes is that, given a public key, it should be difficult to recover the private key. Although key unrecoverability is a very weak notion theoretically, its study has two main motivations: firstly, many multi-instance attacks target key recovery, and secondly, conceptually the notion is relatively simple, allowing both an instructive introduction of formalizing multi-instance security and an initial comparison between BRT's perfect symmetric encryption and our imperfect public key encryption.

At first sight, the generalization to the multi-instance setting appears immediate: an adversary tries to recover the respective private keys for a number of public keys. BRT introduced universal key unrecoverability (UKU) as a suitable notion for multi-instance security of symmetric encryption. We provide an analogue for public-key encryption, but there are some crucial changes in the game's mechanics (see also Sect. 3.3).

Let $0 < n \leq \kappa$ be integer parameters, then the universal key unrecoverability experiment $\mathsf{Exp}_{\mathrm{PKE}}^{(n,\kappa)\text{-uku-cca}\star}(\mathbb{A})$ for public-key encryption scheme PKE and adversary $\mathbb{A}$ is described in Fig. 3. It generates κ key pairs and provides the public keys to $\mathbb{A}$, who is then tasked with recovering exactly n of the corresponding private keys.

The adversary has access to both a decryption oracle $\mathcal{D}$ and a key corruption oracle $\mathcal{K}$, giving rise to chosen ciphertexts attacks with corruptions (CCA$\star$; the $\star$ denotes corruptions). The decryption oracle $\mathcal{D}(i, c)$ takes as input an index i and a ciphertext c, and returns the output of the decryption algorithm PKE.Dec on input sk_i and c. The corruption oracle $\mathcal{K}(i)$ simply takes as input a key index i, and returns the corresponding private key sk_i. The game notes that the key pair with index i has been corrupted by adding it to the global set K.

Eventually, $\mathbb{A}$ outputs a set of key indices I and a list $(\mathsf{sk}_i)_{i \in \mathrm{I}}$ of guesses of the private keys corresponding to those indices. In order for I to be eligible, it needs to have cardinality n without containing any corrupted key pairs, that is, the sets of guessed keys I and corrupted keys K should be disjoint. If I is eligible and every guessed private key matches the corresponding sampled one, the adversary wins the game. In that case, the game halts with output 1; otherwise, it halts with output 0. The advantage is the probability that the game outputs 1.

Definition 2. *Let* PKE *be a public-key encryption scheme. Then the universal key unrecoverability advantage of an adversary* $\mathbb{A}$ *is*

$$\mathsf{Adv}_{\mathrm{PKE}}^{(n,\kappa)\text{-uku-cca}\star}(\mathbb{A}) = \Pr\left[\mathsf{Exp}_{\mathrm{PKE}}^{(n,\kappa)\text{-uku-cca}\star}(\mathbb{A}) = 1\right],$$

where the experiment is defined in Fig. 3.

Weaker notions emerge by dropping either or both of the two oracles. Without key corruption, standard CCA security results. Without decryption oracle, chosen plaintext security (CPA$\star$ resp. CPA) emerges. As usual, an encryption oracle is superfluous in the PKE setting.

$$\underline{\text{Experiment } \mathsf{Exp}_{\mathrm{PKE}}^{(n,\kappa)\text{-}(\mathrm{u/m})\mathrm{ku\text{-}cca}\star}(\mathbb{A})} \qquad \underline{\text{Oracle } \mathcal{D}(i,c)}$$

$(\mathsf{pk}_1,\mathsf{sk}_1),\dots,(\mathsf{pk}_\kappa,\mathsf{sk}_\kappa) \leftarrow\!\!\$ \, \mathsf{PKE.Kg} \qquad\quad m \leftarrow \mathsf{PKE.Dec}_{\mathsf{sk}_i}(c)$

$(\mathtt{I},(\hat{\mathsf{sk}}_i)_{i\in\mathtt{I}}) \leftarrow\!\!\$ \, \mathbb{A}^{\mathcal{D},\mathcal{K}}(\mathsf{pk}_1,\dots,\mathsf{pk}_\kappa) \qquad \textbf{return } m$

$\textbf{if } |\mathtt{I}| \neq n \lor \mathtt{I} \cap \mathtt{K} \neq \emptyset \textbf{ then return } 0$

$\text{UKU} : \textbf{return } \bigwedge_{i\in\mathtt{I}} \mathsf{sk}_i = \hat{\mathsf{sk}}_i \qquad\qquad \underline{\text{Oracle } \mathcal{K}(i)}$

$\qquad\qquad\qquad\qquad\qquad\qquad\qquad\qquad \mathtt{K} \xleftarrow{\cup} i$

$\text{MKU} : \textbf{return } \bigwedge_{i\in\mathtt{I}} \mathsf{PKE.Check}(\mathsf{pk}_i,\hat{\mathsf{sk}}_i,) \qquad \textbf{return } \mathsf{sk}_i$

Fig. 3. The key recovery experiments $\mathsf{Exp}_{\mathrm{PKE}}^{(n,\kappa)\text{-}\mathrm{uku\text{-}cca}\star}(\mathbb{A})$ and $\mathsf{Exp}_{\mathrm{PKE}}^{(n,\kappa)\text{-}\mathrm{mku\text{-}cca}\star}(\mathbb{A})$; they only differ in their win condition.

For cryptosystems where a single public key may have many matching private keys (such as Cramer–Shoup [19]), universal key unrecoverability is rather weak. Hence, we consider a second, slightly stronger notion of key recovery, in which the recovered private keys are no longer required to be identical to those sampled in the game. Instead, it suffices that each passes the keypair checking algorithm PKE.Check; here we leverage our correctness definition (Definition 1). We call the resulting notion *matching key unrecoverability* (MKU), whose game is included in Fig. 3. That MKU security indeed implies UKU security is captured by Theorem 1 below, where the error term $\kappa\gamma$ results from the unique correct keys as output by the key generation not always passing the PKE.Check algorithm (see the full version for the proof).

Theorem 1 (MKU $\longrightarrow$ UKU). *Let $0 < n \leq \kappa$ be integer parameters and let PKE be a (γ,δ)-correct encryption scheme. Then, there is a type-preserving SFBB reduction $\mathbb{B}_{\mathrm{mku}}$, such that for every adversary $\mathbb{A}_{\mathrm{uku}}$,*

$$\mathsf{Adv}_{\mathrm{PKE}}^{(n,\kappa)\text{-}\mathrm{uku\text{-}cca}\star}(\mathbb{A}_{\mathrm{uku}}) \leq \mathsf{Adv}_{\mathrm{PKE}}^{(n,\kappa)\text{-}\mathrm{mku\text{-}cca}\star}(\mathbb{B}_{\mathrm{mku}}) + \kappa\gamma.$$

3.2 Left-or-Right XOR Indistinguishability

To capture a stronger notion of security than simply hardness of key recovery, BRT considered various generalizations of indistinguishability to the multi-instance setting. For perfect probabilistic symmetric encryption, they concluded that left-or-right xor-indistinguishability is the strongest notion. Here each key comes with its own challenge bit that determines the left-or-right nature of the corresponding challenge encryption oracle; the adversary is tasked to retrieve the xor of all the challenge bits. In Definition 3, we use our modified game mechanics to adapt left-or-right xor-indistinguishability for potentially non-perfect public-key encryption.

Definition 3. *Let PKE be a public-key encryption scheme. Then the xor-indistinguishability advantage of an adversary $\mathbb{A}$ is*

$$\mathsf{Adv}_{\mathrm{PKE}}^{(n,\kappa)\text{-}\mathrm{ind\text{-}cca}\star}(\mathbb{A}) = 2 \cdot \Pr\left[\mathsf{Exp}_{\mathrm{PKE}}^{(n,\kappa)\text{-}\mathrm{ind\text{-}cca}\star}(\mathbb{A}) = 1\right] - 1,$$

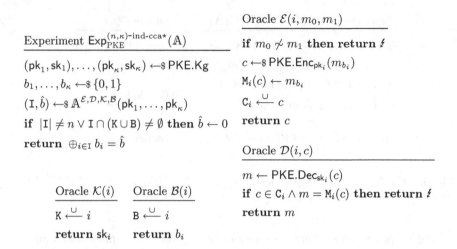

Fig. 4. Our main notion of multi-instance indistinguishability. In blue the slightly non-standard strengthening of the decryption oracle in case of imperfect correctness. (Colour figure online)

where the experiment is defined in Fig. 4.

In the experiment $\mathsf{Exp}_{\mathrm{PKE}}^{(n,\kappa)\text{-ind-cca}\star}(\mathbb{A})$, the adversary gets access to κ independently drawn public keys and helper oracles $\mathcal{D}$ and $\mathcal{K}$ (as described in Sect. 3.1). Furthermore, $\mathbb{A}$ gets access to a challenge encryption oracle $\mathcal{E}$ and a separate bit corruption oracle $\mathcal{B}$.

On input two equivalent messages m_0 and m_1 and a public key index i, the challenge encryption oracle returns $\mathsf{PKE.Enc}_{\mathsf{pk}_i}(m_{b_i})$ where b_i is the challenge bit associated with the public key indexed by i. As usual for IND-CCA notions, challenge ciphertexts cannot be queried to the decryption oracle, which we catch on-the-fly [9]. Owing to the imperfect decryption, we allow a slight relaxation: if a challenge ciphertext decrypts incorrectly, we do not suppress the output and essentially allow the query. This relaxation strengthens the notion, but as challenge ciphertexts are honestly generated, the advantage gained by an adversary can be bound by the correctness parameters of the PKE using an identical-until-bad argument; however such a generic approach might not give bounds appropriate for the multi-instance setting.

Eventually, the adversary* returns a set $\mathtt{I}$ of targets and a guess $\hat{b}$ of the xor of the corresponding challenge bits b_i. If $\mathtt{I}$ is a set of n uncorrupted indices, then intuitively an adversary's uncertainty about any of the n challenge bits will be affected in the final guess $\hat{b}$, so in that sense $\hat{b}$ neatly captures an adversary's need to break n instances in order to win. If $\mathtt{I}$ is not a set of n uncorrupted indices, the game resets $\mathbb{A}$'s guess $\hat{b}$ to 0, ensuring an adversary gains zero advantage from such a bad $\mathtt{I}$.

The Relationship with Key Recovery. BRT showed that in their perfect symmetric setting, multi-instance indistinguishability implies multi-instance universal key unrecoverability. While that may sound like a triviality, their proof [13,

App. C] was not entirely straightforward and, to ensure that the advantages carried over neatly, the distinguishing reduction receiving recovered keys needed to amplify its success probability by repeated random challenge encryptions. Their bound ends up with an additive term that corresponds to the likelihood that decrypting using an incorrect key results in the opposite message from the decrypted one.

Our imperfect public key setting is slightly different. On the one hand, the reduction can check the recovered keys with the PKE.Check algorithm, yet on the other hand correct keys can still cause incorrect decryptions. As a result, our amplification based on multiple challenge encryptions differs from BRT's, as we move from unanimity to a plurality vote. Furthermore, our reduction can use fixed messages (to match how correctness is defined), which reduces a dependency (in the bound) on the size of the message space. We suspect that our amplification can be tightened further by a combination of exploiting randomness and more fine-tuned voting, coupled with more fine-grained bounding of probabilities.

As is, the complexity of the bound makes its behaviour somewhat opaque and for some parameter choices vacuous (when $c < 0$). The main idea is that $\mathbb{B}_{\mathrm{ind}}$ can increase q, the number of challenge encryptions per user, to counteract the losses inferred by large n and/or large δ, with a small penalty to its running time. For $\delta = 2^{-64}$, $q = 1$ already suffices for $c > 1/2$ for $n < 2^{25}$. In case of perfect correctness for keys that check out, corresponding to $\delta = 0$, the bound is completely tight.

Theorem 2 (IND $\longrightarrow$ MKU). *Let* PKE *be a* (γ, δ)-*correct encryption scheme with* $\delta < 1/2$. *Then there is a type-preserving SFBB reduction* $\mathbb{B}_{\mathrm{ind}}$ *such that, for every* $\mathbb{A}_{\mathrm{mku}}$,

$$\mathsf{Adv}_{\mathrm{PKE}}^{(n,\kappa)\text{-ind-cca}\star}(\mathbb{B}_{\mathrm{ind}}) \geq c \cdot \mathsf{Adv}_{\mathrm{PKE}}^{(n,\kappa)\text{-mku-cca}\star}(\mathbb{A}_{\mathrm{mku}}),$$

with $c = 2\left(1 - 2^q(\delta(1-\delta))^{\frac{q}{2}}\right)^n - 1$ *where* $q \in \mathbb{Z}_{>0}$ *is an amplification parameter of the reduction;* $\mathbb{B}_{\mathrm{ind}}$'s *overhead consists of* $q \cdot n$ *calls to* $\mathcal{E}$, n *offline key checks, and* $q \cdot n$ *offline decryptions.*

Proof. Let $\mathbb{B}_{\mathrm{ind}}$ run adversary $\mathbb{A}_{\mathrm{mku}}$ on the same κ public keys as it received itself. Whenever $\mathbb{A}_{\mathrm{mku}}$ makes a decryption or corruption query, $\mathbb{B}_{\mathrm{ind}}$ simply forwards the queries to its own oracle, relaying the response back to $\mathbb{A}_{\mathrm{mku}}$. Eventually, $\mathbb{A}_{\mathrm{mku}}$ terminates with output $(\mathtt{I}, (\hat{\mathsf{sk}}_i)_{i \in \mathtt{I}})$ and $\mathbb{B}_{\mathrm{ind}}$ first confirms whether $\mathbb{A}_{\mathrm{mku}}$ won, by checking, for all the returned private keys, whether PKE.Check$(\mathsf{pk}_i, \hat{\mathsf{sk}}_i)$ holds. If any check fails, $\mathbb{B}_{\mathrm{ind}}$ halts with output 0.

Let m_0 and m_1 be two distinct yet equivalent messages. Then for all $i \in \mathtt{I}$, $\mathbb{B}_{\mathrm{ind}}$ creates a guess $\hat{b}_i$ by querying its challenge encryption oracle q times on those two messages, so q queries $\mathcal{E}(i, m_0, m_1)$ resulting in c_{ij}, for $j \in [q]$. It then decrypts those ciphertexts using the private key $\hat{\mathsf{sk}}_i$ it obtained from $\mathbb{A}_{\mathrm{mku}}$, resulting in purported messages $m_{ij} \leftarrow$ PKE.Dec$_{\hat{\mathsf{sk}}_i}(c_{ij})$. If, for a fixed i, there are strictly more than $q/2$ appearances of m_0 amongst the m_{ij}, it sets $\hat{b}_i$ to 0;

if there are strictly more than $q/2$ appearances of m_1, then it sets $\hat{b}_i$ to 1. If neither message appears more than $q/2$ times, $\mathbb{B}_{\text{ind}}$ halts with output 0. Once $\mathbb{B}_{\text{ind}}$ has created a guess $\hat{b}_i$ for all $i \in I$, it terminates on output $(I, \bigoplus_{i \in I} \hat{b}_i)$.

For $i \in I$, let Check_i be the event that $\mathbb{A}_{\text{mku}}$ outputs a key sk_i that passes the test and let Good_i be the event that $\mathbb{B}_{\text{ind}}$'s guess $\hat{b}_i$ actually equals b_i. Let Check_I be the event that all Check_i hold (for $i \in I$) and define Good_I analogously.

As $\mathbb{B}_{\text{ind}}$'s simulation of $\text{Exp}_{\text{PKE}}^{(n,\kappa)\text{-mku-cca}\star}$ is perfect, we know that

$$\text{Adv}^{(n,\kappa)\text{-mku-cca}\star}(\mathbb{A}_{\text{mku}}) = \Pr[\text{Check}_I] ,$$

moreover,

$$\Pr\left[\text{Exp}_{\text{PKE}}^{(n,\kappa)\text{-ind-cca}\star}(\mathbb{B}_{\text{ind}}) = 1\right] \geq \Pr[\text{Check}_I \wedge \text{Good}_I] + \Pr[\neg\text{Check}_I \wedge b = 0]$$

$$= \Pr[\text{Good}_I \mid \text{Check}_I]\Pr[\text{Check}_I] + \frac{1}{2}\left(1 - \Pr[\text{Check}_I]\right)$$

which implies that

$$\text{Adv}_{\text{PKE}}^{(n,\kappa)\text{-ind-cca}\star}(\mathbb{B}_{\text{ind}}) \geq (2\Pr[\text{Good}_I \mid \text{Check}_I] - 1)\,\text{Adv}^{(n,\kappa)\text{-mku-cca}\star}(\mathbb{A}_{\text{mku}}) .$$

To bound $\Pr[\text{Good}_I \mid \text{Check}_I]$ we exploit the correctness definition, specifically that its quantification (Definition 1) ensures that whenever Check_i holds, we have that $\Pr\left[\text{PKE.Dec}_{\text{sk}_i}(\text{PKE.Enc}_{\text{pk}_i}(m)) = m\right] \geq 1 - \delta$, irrespective of m and where the probability is only over the randomness of PKE.Enc.

If, for a given i, decryption is correct strictly more than $q/2$ times, then we are guaranteed that Good_i occurs. If we let $B(q, p)$ be the binomial distribution over q trials and with probability p, then

$$\Pr[\text{Good}_i \mid \text{Check}_i] \geq \Pr\left[B(q, (1 - \delta)) > \frac{q}{2}\right]$$

and, as this bound only relies on the randomness of the challenge encryption oracle, guaranteed independent for differing i, we may conclude that

$$\Pr[\text{Good}_I \mid \text{Check}_I] \geq \left(\Pr\left[B(q, (1 - \delta)) > \frac{q}{2}\right]\right)^n .$$

Finally, we note that

$$\Pr\left[B(q, (1 - \delta)) > \frac{q}{2}\right] \geq 1 - 2^q\,(\delta(1 - \delta))^{\frac{q}{2}}$$

by a standard application of known bounds on binomial tails, requiring $\delta \leq 1/2$ (see details below). Plugging in all the various bounds recovers the theorem statement.

For the binomial tail bound, we use the Chernoff–Hoeffding bound [27], which states that, for a binomial distribution $B(q, p)$ over q trials and with probability p, and any k satisfying $p < \frac{k}{q} < 1$ the tail bound

$$\Pr[B(q, p) \geq k] \leq \exp\left[-qD\left(\frac{k}{q} \bigg\| p\right)\right]$$

holds, where $D(a\|b)$ is the Kullback–Leibler divergence defined as $D(a\|b) = a \ln\left(\frac{a}{b}\right) + (1-a)\ln\left(\frac{1-a}{1-b}\right)$.

We further use the trick that $\Pr\left[B(q,(1-\delta)) > \frac{q}{2}\right] = 1 - \Pr\left[B(q,\delta) \leq \frac{q}{2}\right]$, so the relevant Kullback–Leibler divergence becomes

$$
\begin{aligned}
D\left(\frac{1}{2} \,\middle\|\, \delta\right) &= \frac{1}{2}\ln\left(\frac{\frac{1}{2}}{\delta}\right) + \left(1 - \frac{1}{2}\right)\ln\left(\frac{(1-\frac{1}{2})}{1-\delta}\right) \\
&= \frac{1}{2}\ln\left(\frac{1}{2\delta}\right) + \frac{1}{2}\ln\left(\frac{1}{2(1-\delta)}\right) \\
&= \ln\left[\left(\frac{1}{4\delta(1-\delta)}\right)^{\frac{1}{2}}\right],
\end{aligned}
$$

which allows us to compute the bound

$$
\begin{aligned}
\Pr\left[B(q,(1-\delta)) > \frac{q}{2}\right] &\geq 1 - \exp\left[-qD\left(\frac{1}{2}\,\middle\|\,\delta\right)\right] \\
&= 1 - \exp\left[-q\ln\left[\left(\frac{1}{4\delta(1-\delta)}\right)^{\frac{1}{2}}\right]\right] \\
&= 1 - 2^q\left(\delta(1-\delta)\right)^{\frac{q}{2}}.
\end{aligned}
$$

$\square$

Corollary 1 (IND $\longrightarrow$ UKU). *Let* PKE *be a (γ,δ)-correct encryption scheme with $\delta < 1/2$. Then there is a type-preserving SFBB reduction $\mathbb{B}_{\mathrm{ind}}$ such that, for every $\mathbb{A}_{\mathrm{uku}}$,*

$$
\mathsf{Adv}_{\mathrm{PKE}}^{(n,\kappa)\text{-ind-cca}\star}(\mathbb{B}_{\mathrm{ind}}) \geq c \cdot \mathsf{Adv}_{\mathrm{PKE}}^{(n,\kappa)\text{-uku-cca}\star}(\mathbb{A}_{\mathrm{uku}}) - \kappa\gamma,
$$

with c, q, and $\mathbb{B}_{\mathrm{ind}}$'s overhead as above (Theorem 2).

3.3 Alternative Mechanisms

As we mentioned before, our mechanism to capture multi-instance security differs slightly from those used by BRT and AGK, respectively, even when accounting for changes in primitive and correctness. At first sight, the differences might appear mostly cosmetic, though there are some subtleties involved.

The BRT Notion: Requiring $n = \kappa$, Possibly Corrupted, Targets. BRT require an adversary to return the xor of all bits, but allow those bits or corresponding users to be corrupted. Figure 5 reflects the small change needed in the code of our security experiment to match BRT's mechanism (ignoring a minor, inconsequential difference, as BRT have a single, merged corruption oracle that returns both key and bit). As motivation for including corruptions, BRT discuss the scenario that, say, half of the keys generated are hopelessly insecure: an adversary breaks the insecure half and corrupts the rest, thus being successful.

Experiment $\mathsf{Exp}_{\mathrm{PKE}}^{(\leq \kappa, \kappa)\text{-ind-cca}\star}(\mathbb{A})$	Experiment $\mathsf{Exp}_{\mathrm{PKE}}^{(\geq n, \kappa)\text{-ind-cca}\star}(\mathbb{A})$
4 : **if** $|\mathrm{I}| \neq \kappa$ **then** $\hat{b} \leftarrow 0$	4 : **if** $|\mathrm{I}| < n \vee \mathrm{I} \cap (\mathrm{K} \cup \mathrm{B}) \neq \emptyset$ **then** $\hat{b} \leftarrow 0$

Fig. 5. The main differences between our mechanism for multi-instance indistinguishability (Fig. 4) and prior art revolve around line 4: BRT's experiment $\mathsf{Exp}_{\mathrm{PKE}}^{(\leq \kappa, \kappa)\text{-ind-cca}\star}(\mathbb{A})$ (left) and AGK's experiment $\mathsf{Exp}_{\mathrm{PKE}}^{(\geq n, \kappa)\text{-ind-cca}\star}(\mathbb{A})$ (right). The differences are highlighted in blue. (Colour figure online)

Moreover, they mention that their choice implies security under a corruptionless notion with dynamically chosen I.

Although the implication is of course true, and something can be said to target the strongest possible notion, corruptions have a habit of creating complications for reductions and provable security in general. Yet, we believe the inclusion of corruptions, or not, should reflect the threat model of the adversary and that choice should be orthogonal to the number of users being targeted. BRT, instead of having an explicit hardness parameter n, restrict an adversary to make at most q_c corruption queries to avoid trivial wins when $q_c = \kappa$. Yet, whether the resulting, intuitive hardness will or should then match $n = \kappa - q_c$, is unclear.

We address the equivalence between BRT's mechanism and our general mechanism (with corruptions) in Lemmas 1 and 2. Both lemmas have in common that the respective reductions may make up to $\kappa - n$ additional bit corruptions. In other words, the reductions are not type-preserving, making the equivalence somewhat sloppy. As an aside, using techniques similar to those to prove Theorem 2, the key corruption oracle could be used (at a loss) to simulate the bit corruption oracle instead (see the full version for the proofs).

Lemma 1 (main notion $\implies$ BRT). *Let $n \leq \kappa$ and $q_c \leq \kappa - n$. Then there is an SFBB reduction $\mathbb{B}$ such that, for every adversary $\mathbb{A}$ making at most q_c corruption oracle calls,*

$$\mathsf{Adv}_{\mathrm{PKE}}^{(\leq \kappa, \kappa)\text{-ind-cca}\star}(\mathbb{A}) \leq \mathsf{Adv}_{\mathrm{PKE}}^{(n, \kappa)\text{-ind-cca}\star}(\mathbb{B}),$$

where $\mathbb{B}$ makes at most $\kappa - n$ additional bit corruption oracle calls.

Lemma 2 (BRT $\implies$ main notion). *Let $n \leq \kappa$. Then there is an SFBB reduction $\mathbb{B}$ such that, for every adversary $\mathbb{A}$,*

$$\mathsf{Adv}_{\mathrm{PKE}}^{(n, \kappa)\text{-ind-cca}\star}(\mathbb{A}) \leq \mathsf{Adv}_{\mathrm{PKE}}^{(\leq \kappa, \kappa)\text{-ind-cca}\star}(\mathbb{B}),$$

where $\mathbb{B}$ makes at most $\kappa - n$ additional bit corruption oracle calls.

The AGK Notion: Allowing More than n Targets without Corruptions. When AGK studied KEMs in the multi-instance setting, they used a xor notion with the n as the *minimum* number of targets to attack (out of κ possible) as an explicit parameter; moreover, an adversary would not have access to any corruption oracles. Figure 5 reflects the small change needed in the code of our security experiment to match AGK's mechanism with corruptions added (where we fixed a minor bug in their code; rather than setting $\hat{b} \leftarrow 0$ their experiment would immediately return 0 instead, inadvertently granting an adversary that deliberately returns a compromised handle the significant advantage of -1).

Absent corruptions, AGK indicated that for some pathological schemes, breaking more targets might paradoxically be easier than breaking fewer [3, App. C]. In those cases, the freedom to return a set I of cardinality greater than n would make life easier for an adversary, leading to a stronger notion.

In the presence of corruptions, requiring the adversary to target exactly n users as we do is without loss of generality. As an example, if an adversary can figure out the xor of $n + 1$ honest bits, it can bit-corrupt any single one of these $n + 1$, and xor the resulting bit out of the initial guess to obtain a final one on n bits instead. We formalize this intuition below.

Lemma 3 (main notion $\implies$ AGK⋆). *There is an SFBB adversary* $\mathbb{B}$ *such that, for every* $\mathbb{A}$,

$$\mathsf{Adv}_{\mathrm{PKE}}^{(\geq n, \kappa)\text{-ind-cca}\star}(\mathbb{A}) \leq \mathsf{Adv}_{\mathrm{PKE}}^{(n, \kappa)\text{-ind-cca}\star}(\mathbb{B}).$$

If $\mathbb{A}$ *returns a list of* n' *targets,* $\mathbb{B}$ *makes* $n' - n$ *additional calls to its bit corruption oracle.*

3.4   Real-or-Random XOR Indistinguishability

An alternative notion of indistinguishability, known as real-or-random indistinguishability (ROR), sees the adversary tasked with figuring out whether a challenge ciphertext contains the adversarially chosen message m or an unknown, randomly chosen message. The game $\mathsf{Exp}_{\mathrm{PKE}}^{(n, \kappa)\text{-ror-cca}\star}$ is exactly as in Fig. 4, apart from the challenge encryption oracle $\mathcal{E}_{\mathrm{ROR}}(i, m)$, which sets $m_0 \leftarrow m$ and $m_1 \leftarrow\!\!\$\ [m]$ to then call (left-or-right) $\mathcal{E}(i, m_0, m_1)$.

By construction, left-or-right indistinguishability easily implies real-or-random indistinguishability. That statement is as true in the multi-instance setting as it is in the classical single-user setting. Conversely, in the single-user setting, it has long been established that the reduction from ROR to IND loses a factor 2 [8]. However, BRT showed that in the multi-instance setting, the factor 2 blows up exponentially to, in their case, 2^κ. Yet, BRT argue that this exponential loss is not as bad as it might seem, given that the multi-instance advantages are supposed to be exponentially smaller than their single-user counterparts. Thus, reductions incurring losses exponential in κ or n can still be valuable.

To adapt BRT's reduction to our setting, we require $n = \kappa$, implying that $\mathbb{A}$ cannot access its corruption oracles. Otherwise, corruptions would make the reduction noticeable once at least one b_i is set to 1, potentially influencing an adversary's behaviour in unpredictable ways (see the full version for the proof).

Theorem 3. *There is an SFBB reduction* $\mathbb{B}$ *such that, for every adversary* $\mathbb{A}$,

$$\mathsf{Adv}_{\mathrm{PKE}}^{(\kappa,\kappa)\text{-ind-cca}}(\mathbb{A}) \leq 2^{\kappa} \cdot \mathsf{Adv}_{\mathrm{PKE}}^{(\kappa,\kappa)\text{-ror-cca}}(\mathbb{B}),$$

where $\mathbb{B}$ *additionally draws* κ *bits uniformly at random.*

Furthermore, a reduction playing an (n, n) game can exploit an adversary playing a (n, κ) game by guessing in advance the set I of targets that the adversary will return. A correct guess allows the reduction to simulate the remaining keys without being noticed (see the full version for the proof).

Theorem 4. *There is an SFBB reduction* $\mathbb{B}$ *such that, for every adversary* $\mathbb{A}$,

$$\mathsf{Adv}_{\mathrm{PKE}}^{(n,\kappa)\text{-ind-cca}\star}(\mathbb{A}) \leq \binom{\kappa}{n} \cdot \mathsf{Adv}_{\mathrm{PKE}}^{(n,n)\text{-ind-cca}}(\mathbb{B}).$$

$\mathbb{B}$ *'s overhead consists of generating* $\kappa - n$ *fresh keypairs, sampling* $\kappa - n$ *bits, and choosing a subset of* $[\kappa]$ *of cardinality* n *uniformly at random.*

Composing Theorem 3 and 4, we obtain the following bound.

Corollary 2. (ROR $\implies$ IND). *There is an SFBB reduction* $\mathbb{B}$ *such that, for any adversary* $\mathbb{B}$,

$$\mathsf{Adv}_{\mathrm{PKE}}^{(n,\kappa)\text{-ind-cca}\star}(\mathbb{A}) \leq \binom{\kappa}{n} \cdot 2^{n} \cdot \mathsf{Adv}_{\mathrm{PKE}}^{(n,n)\text{-ror-cca}}(\mathbb{B}).$$

$\mathbb{B}$ *'s overhead consists of generating* $\kappa - n$ *fresh keypairs, sampling* κ *bits, and choosing a subset of* $[\kappa]$ *of cardinality* n *uniformly at random.*

An alternative bound losing a factor 2^{κ} is possible by combining Theorem 3 with Lemma 2, however a simple analysis shows that whenever $n < \kappa/5$ the corollary above is preferable.

At first glance, an exponential-looking loss of 2^{κ} might seem severe, potentially rendering the resulting bound vacuous. Yet, as BRT already highlighted, the multi-instance advantages themselves might vanish exponentially in n, making the bounds relevant for the notions being compared. Nonetheless, tigher bounds still matter; unfortunately achieving even tighter bounds in the general case seems challenging [5, 12].

4   Inheriting Multi-instance Security

4.1   TagKEM: Definition and Notion of Security

Our goal is to turn the AGK multi-instance secure KEM into a PKE. Yet, for the construction of hybrid encryption, the more general TagKEMs, where encapsulation is split into two algorithms (TKEM.Key and TKEM.Enc) have proven more powerful [2]: intuitively speaking, splitting the algorithm allows the tag and consequently the key encapsulation to depend on the data encapsulation, making

Experiment $\mathsf{Exp}_{\text{TXEM}}^{(n,\kappa)\text{-ind-cca}\star}(\mathbb{A})$	Oracle $\mathcal{C}(i,\ell)$
$(\mathsf{pk}_1,\mathsf{sk}_1),\ldots,(\mathsf{pk}_\kappa,\mathsf{sk}_\kappa) \leftarrow\!\!\$\ \mathsf{TXEM.Kg}$	$(K_0,\sigma) \leftarrow\!\!\$\ \mathsf{TXEM.Key}_{\mathsf{pk}_i}(\ell)$
$b_1,\ldots,b_\kappa \leftarrow\!\!\$\ \{0,1\}$	$\mathsf{E}_i \overset{\frown}{\leftarrow} \langle \sigma, K_0 \rangle$
$(\mathtt{I},\hat{b}) \leftarrow\!\!\$\ \mathbb{A}^{\mathcal{C},\mathcal{E},\mathcal{D},\mathcal{K},\mathcal{B}}(\mathsf{pk}_1,\ldots,\mathsf{pk}_\kappa)$	$K_1 \leftarrow\!\!\$\ \{0,1\}^\ell$
if $|\mathtt{I}| \neq n \vee \mathtt{I} \cap (\mathtt{K} \cup \mathtt{B}) \neq \emptyset$ then $\hat{b} \leftarrow 0$	return K_{b_i}
return $\oplus_{i \in \mathtt{I}}\, b_i = \hat{b}$	

Oracle $\mathcal{D}(i, \langle c, \tau \rangle, \ell)$

Oracle $\mathcal{E}(i,j,\tau)$

$K \leftarrow \mathsf{TXEM.Dec}_{\mathsf{sk}_i}(c, \tau, \ell)$

if $\mathsf{E}_i[j] = \emptyset$ then return $\mathit{\frac{4}{}}$

if $\mathsf{P}_i(c,\tau) \neq \emptyset$

$\langle \sigma, K \rangle \leftarrow \mathsf{E}_i[j], \mathsf{E}_i[j] \leftarrow \emptyset$

  $K' \leftarrow \mathsf{P}_i(c,\tau), \ell' \leftarrow \min\{\ell, |K'|\}$

$c \leftarrow\!\!\$\ \mathsf{TXEM.Enc}(\sigma, \tau)$

else

$\mathsf{P}_i(c,\tau) \leftarrow K$

  $K' \leftarrow \varepsilon, \ell' \leftarrow 0$

$\mathsf{C}_i \overset{\cup}{\leftarrow} \langle c, \tau \rangle$

if $\langle c, \tau \rangle \in \mathsf{C}_i \wedge K[\![\ell']\!] = K'[\![\ell']\!]$

return c

  return $\mathit{\frac{4}{}}$

return K

Oracle $\mathcal{K}(i)$	Oracle $\mathcal{B}(i)$
$\mathsf{K} \overset{\cup}{\leftarrow} i$	$\mathsf{B} \overset{\cup}{\leftarrow} i$
return sk_i	return b_i

Fig. 6. Multi-instance indistinguishability notion for TXEM. In blue the same strengthening as in Fig. 4 in the case of imperfect correctness, with a slightly more complex admin to accomodate tags and length extension. We take $K[\![\ell]\!]$ to mean the first ℓ bits of K and ε as the empty string. (Colour figure online)

CCA security of the hybrid construction easier to achieve (cf. the Kurosawa–Desmedt scheme [31]). In Definition 4 we introduce a further generalization, called TagXEM, by allowing extendable output lengths for the ephemeral keys produced by the TagXEM.

Definition 4 (TagXEM). *A TagXEM is a tuple of algorithms* (TXEM.Kg, TXEM.Key, TXEM.Enc, TXEM.Dec, TXEM.Check), *where long-term key generation* TXEM.Kg *on input* pm *outputs a random keypair* (pk, sk); *ephemeral key generation* TXEM.Key *on input* pk *and* $\ell \in \mathbb{Z}_{>0}$, *outputs a random ephemeral key* $K \in \{0,1\}^\ell$ *and an internal state* σ, *subsequently encapsulation* TXEM.Enc *on input a state* σ *and a tag* $\tau \in \mathcal{T}$, *deterministically outputs an encapsulation* c, *or a special symbol* $\bot$ *denoting failure. The deterministic decapsulation algorithm* TXEM.Dec *takes input a private key* sk, *an encapsulation* c, *a tag* τ, *and a length* ℓ, *and outputs either a key* $K \in \{0,1\}^\ell$ *or* $\bot$ *to denote failure. Finally, the deterministic* TXEM.Check *takes as input the system parameters* pm *as well as a purported public/private key pair* (pk, sk) *and returns* true *or* false.

If we restrict to a single value ℓ, the usual notion of TagKEMs appears; moreover if we restrict to a single value of τ, the TXEM.Key and TXEM.Enc algorithms can be merged into a single key encapsulation mechanism, leading to normal KEMs (or XEMs if the variable output length is still incorporated). Consequently, the correctness and security definitions for the more general TagXEMs, as discussed throughout this section, imply corresponding definitions for KEM, XEM, and TagKEM.

For correctness, we allow the effective tag space $\mathcal{T}_\ell$ to depend on the length ℓ of the ephemeral key. Similarly to Definition 1, we define (γ, δ)-correctness for TagXEM. To ensure correctness for all τ, including those that depend on K, τ's quantifier sits inside the probability statement.

Definition 5 ((γ, δ)-Correctness TagXEM). *Let* $\gamma, \delta \in [0, 1]$. *Then a tag extendable-output key encapsulation mechanism* TXEM *is called* (γ, δ)-*correct iff*

1. $\Pr\left[(\mathsf{pk}, \mathsf{sk}) \leftarrow_\$ \mathsf{TXEM.Kg(pm)} : \mathsf{TXEM.Check(pm, pk, sk)} = \mathsf{false}\right] \leq \gamma$;
2. *if* $\mathsf{TXEM.Check(pm, pk, sk)} = \mathsf{true}$ *then for all* $\ell \in \mathbb{Z}_{>0}$ *it holds that*

$$\Pr\left[(K, \sigma) \leftarrow_\$ \mathsf{TXEM.Key_{pk}}(\ell) : \exists \tau \in \mathcal{T}_\ell \text{ s.th. } \begin{array}{c} c \leftarrow \mathsf{TXEM.Enc}(\sigma, \tau) \\ \mathsf{TXEM.Dec_{sk}}(c, \tau, \ell) \neq K \end{array}\right] \leq \delta .$$

For security, Abe et al.'s notion of TagKEM indistinguishability [2] transfers easily to the multi-instance setting. The relevant game is given in Fig. 6, where we also made the necessary changes to deal with the variable output length of TagXEMs, plus the strengthening of $\mathcal{D}$ in the case of imperfect correctness (cf. Sect. 3.2).

Definition 6. *Let* TXEM *be a* TagXEM. *Then the xor-indistinguishability advantage of an adversary* $\mathbb{A}$ *is*

$$\mathsf{Adv}_{\mathsf{TXEM}}^{(n, \kappa)\text{-ind-cca}\star}(\mathbb{A}) = 2 \cdot \Pr\left[\mathsf{Exp}_{\mathsf{TXEM}}^{(n, \kappa)\text{-ind-cca}\star}(\mathbb{A}) = 1\right] - 1 ,$$

where the experiment is defined in Fig. 6.

If we fix ℓ and set $\mathcal{T}_\ell$ to a single element, the notion captures multi-instance security for standard KEMs, which is near equivalent (see Sect. 3.3) the notion that AGK used. In other words, provided MI-gapCDH is hard, their construction achieves (n, κ)-IND-CCA security in the random oracle model, but only for fixed ℓ and trivial $\mathcal{T}_\ell$ [4, Thm. 2].

4.2 Extending the Output of a TagKEM

First, we show how combining a TagKEM with a fixed output length and a suitable pseudorandom extendable output function (XOF), yields a TagXEM that inherits the MI security of the underlying KEM. Recall that a XOF, for instance SHAKE128 and SHAKE256 as standardized by NIST [35], is a function $F : \mathcal{X} \times \mathbb{Z}_{>0} \to \{0, 1\}^*$ for some finite domain $\mathcal{X}$ that on input a seed $s \in \mathcal{X}$ and a desired output length ℓ, outputs a value $y \in \{0, 1\}^\ell$. Moreover, if $\ell < \ell'$, then $F(s, \ell)$ is a prefix of $F(s, \ell')$ for all s. This prefix preservation is not a requirement

$\mathsf{TXEM.Key}_{\mathsf{pk}}(\ell)$	$\mathsf{TXEM.Enc}(\sigma', \tau)$	$\mathsf{TXEM.Dec}(c, \tau, \ell)$
$(K^{\mathrm{kem}}, \sigma) \leftarrow\!\!\$ \, \mathsf{TKEM.Key}_{\mathsf{pk}}$	$\langle \sigma, \ell \rangle \leftarrow \sigma'$	if $\tau \notin \mathcal{T}_\ell$:
$K^{\mathrm{xem}} \leftarrow F(K^{\mathrm{kem}}, \ell)$	if $\tau \notin \mathcal{T}_\ell$:	$\quad$ return $\perp_{\mathrm{TAG}}$
$\sigma' \leftarrow \langle \sigma, \ell \rangle$	$\quad$ return $\perp$	$K^{\mathrm{kem}} \leftarrow \mathsf{TKEM.Dec}(c, \tau)$
return $(K^{\mathrm{xem}}, \sigma')$	$c \leftarrow \mathsf{TKEM.Enc}(\sigma, \tau)$	if $K^{\mathrm{kem}} = \perp$:
	return c	$\quad$ return $\perp_{\mathrm{KEM}}$
		$K^{\mathrm{xem}} \leftarrow F(K^{\mathrm{kem}}, \ell)$
		return K^{xem}

Fig. 7. A TagXEM TXEM from a TagKEM TKEM with keyspace $\{0,1\}^k$ and a XOF with seed space $\mathcal{X} = \{0,1\}^k$. The key generation algorithm TXEM.Kg is unchanged from TKEM.Kg.

of our constructions; rather we model the property to ensure SHAKE128 and SHAKE256 are suitable real-world instantiations.

As security notion for a XOF F we use its multi-challenge pseudorandomness, which is a standard distinguishing advantage $\mathsf{Adv}_F^{\mathrm{psrnd}}(\mathbb{A})$: an adversary needs to distinguish between either a real oracle that, on input a desired length ℓ, samples a seed $s \leftarrow\!\!\$ \, \mathcal{X}$ uniformly at random and returns $F(s, \ell)$, or an ideal oracle that, on input said ℓ, simply returns a uniformly sampled string of length ℓ.

The construction of the TagXEM is given in Fig. 7 and the security claim follows in Theorem 5 (see the full version for the proof). If the PsRND advantage of F is sufficiently small, then TXEM inherits the multi-instance security of TKEM; moreover, as the result holds for arbitrary $\mathcal{T}$ and $\mathcal{T}_\ell$, it holds for the trivial spaces, yielding a slightly simpler XEM from KEM result.

Theorem 5. *Let* TKEM *be a* (γ, δ)-*correct TagKEM sampling keys from* $\{0,1\}^k$ *and with tagspace* $\mathcal{T}$, *let* $F : \{0,1\}^k \times \mathbb{Z}_{>0} \rightarrow \{0,1\}^*$ *be a XOF, and let* TXEM *be a TagXEM as given in Fig. 7 for arbitrary* $\mathcal{T}_\ell \subseteq \mathcal{T}$. *Then* TXEM *is* (γ, δ)-*correct, and there are SFBB reductions* $\mathbb{B}$ *and* $\mathbb{C}$ *such that, for every adversary* $\mathbb{A}$,

$$\mathsf{Adv}_{\mathrm{TXEM}}^{(n,\kappa)\text{-ind-cca}\star}(\mathbb{A}) \leq \mathsf{Adv}_{\mathrm{TKEM}}^{(n,\kappa)\text{-ind-cca}\star}(\mathbb{B}) + 2 \cdot \mathsf{Adv}_F^{\mathrm{psrnd}}(\mathbb{C}).$$

If $\mathbb{A}$ *calls* $\mathcal{C}$ q_c *times and* $\mathcal{D}$ q_d *times, then* $\mathbb{B}$'s *overhead consists of at most* $q_c + q_d$ *evaluations of* F, *while* $\mathbb{C}$'s *overhead consists of doing* κ *executions of* TKEM.Kg, *at most* q_c *executions of* TKEM.Key *and* TKEM.Enc, *and at most* q_d *executions of* TKEM.Dec.

One concern is whether the PsRND advantage of F will be sufficiently small. Suppose k is the output length of the underlying TagKEM. A generic attacker would always be able to fix $\ell > k$ and evaluate F for, say, N seeds offline in the hope of colliding with any of the challenge evaluations. The PsRND distinguishing advantage of such an adversary is of order $(q_c + q_d)N/2^k$, indicating that the underlying TagKEM already needs to provide keys long enough for Theorem 5 to yield meaningful multi-instance security.

$PKE.Enc_{pk}(m)$	$PKE.Dec_{sk}(\langle c_1, c_2 \rangle)$
$(K, c_1) \leftarrow\!\!\$\ XEM.Enc_{pk}(|m|)$	$K \leftarrow XEM.Dec_{sk}(c_1, |c_2|)$
$c_2 \leftarrow K \oplus m$	**if** $K = \bot$ **then return** $\bot$
return $\langle c_1, c_2 \rangle$	$m \leftarrow K \oplus c_2$
	return m

$PKE'.Enc_{pk}(m)$	$PKE'.Dec_{sk}(\langle c_1, c_2 \rangle)$
$(K, \sigma) \leftarrow\!\!\$\ TXEM.Key_{pk}(|m|)$	$K \leftarrow TXEM.Dec_{sk}(c_1, c_2, |c_2|)$
$c_2 \leftarrow K \oplus m$	**if** $K = \bot$ **then return** $\bot$
$c_1 \leftarrow TXEM.Enc(\sigma, c_2)$	$m \leftarrow K \oplus c_2$
return $\langle c_1, c_2 \rangle$	**return** m

Fig. 8. Two hybrid encryption schemes: PKE (top row) is a conventional hybrid scheme combining a XEM with the OTP to yield a CPA-secure PKE, while PKE' (bottom row) combines a TagXEM with the OTP to yield a CCA-secure PKE. The key generation and checking algorithms are equivalent to their XEM resp. TXEM counterparts.

4.3   A PKE Inheriting (Tag)XEM Security

As a multi-instance secure XEM provides us with ephemeral keys of any desired length, we can combine it with an information-theoretic DEM in order to achieve PKE. Here we opt for the one-time-pad (OTP), as it is the simplest and best-known primitive providing perfect secrecy. The beauty of the OTP is that whether you switch out the ephemeral key for a uniform random one, or the message for a uniform random one, the resulting ciphertext distribution is the same. It allows the PKE to tightly inherit the MI-security of the XEM, albeit yielding only real-or-random security under chosen-plaintext attacks. The construction is provided in full in Fig. 8 (top row); the security claim is captured in Theorem 6 (see the full version for the proof).

Theorem 6 (ROR-CPA PKE). *Let* XEM *be a* (γ, δ)-*correct XEM, and let* PKE *be a hybrid encryption scheme as given in Fig. 8. Then* PKE *is* (γ, δ)-*correct, and there is a type-preserving SFBB reduction* $\mathbb{B}$ *such that for every adversary* $\mathbb{A}$,

$$\mathsf{Adv}_{\mathsf{PKE}}^{(n,\kappa)\text{-ror-cpa}\star}(\mathbb{A}) \leq \mathsf{Adv}_{\mathsf{XEM}}^{(n,\kappa)\text{-ind-cpa}\star}(\mathbb{B}).$$

One might hope that adding information-theoretic MACs to the DEM would result in the inheritance of CCA security, but that is easier said than shown. For instance, the usual proof technique of a game hop where all decryption queries are disallowed does not work: after breaking only a single KEM private key,

Oracle $\mathcal{C}_{\mathrm{ROP}}(i, \ell, \Pi)$

$(K_0, \sigma) \leftarrow\!\!\$ \, \mathsf{TXEM.Key}_{\mathsf{pk}_i}(\ell)$

$\mathsf{E}_i \xleftarrow{\frown} \sigma$

$K_1 \leftarrow \Pi(K_0)$

return K_{b_i}

Fig. 9. Fig. 6 is upgraded to $\mathsf{Exp}_{\mathrm{TXEM}}^{(n,\kappa)\text{-rop-cca}\star}$ by letting $\mathcal{C}_{\mathrm{ROP}}$ replace $\mathcal{C}$.

the reduction will be found out as not being faithful. Sadly, a single-instance break (of the reduction) suffices to show that reduction cannot demonstrate multi-instance security.

Luckily, TagKEMs allow for a modified hybrid scheme for which the DEM no longer needs to satisfy CCA security for the resulting PKE to be guaranteed CCA-secure: in the single-instance setting, if the TagKEM is CCA-secure, then so is the PKE [2]. We upgrade the construction to use TagXEMs and the OTP in Fig. 8 (bottom row) and show its multi-instance inheritance in Theorem 7 (see the full version for the proof).

Theorem 7 (ROR-CCA PKE). *Let* TXEM *be a* (γ, δ)*-correct TagXEM, and let* PKE$'$ *be a hybrid encryption scheme as given in Fig. 8. Then* PKE$'$ *is* (γ, δ)*-correct, and there is a type-preserving SFBB reduction* $\mathbb{B}$ *such that for every adversary* $\mathbb{A}$,

$$\mathsf{Adv}_{\mathrm{PKE}'}^{(n,\kappa)\text{-ror-cca}\star}(\mathbb{A}) \leq \mathsf{Adv}_{\mathrm{TXEM}}^{(n,\kappa)\text{-ind-cca}\star}(\mathbb{B}).$$

While encouraging, the claim that the constructed PKE inherits the multi-instance security of the TagXEM is dampened by the exponential separation between the ROR security notion and IND, as argued in Sect. 3.4. Indeed, extrapolating to the latter notion by combining Theorem 7 with Corollary 2, we have only achieved the following bound.

Corollary 3. *Let* TXEM *be a* (γ, δ)*-correct TagXEM, and let* PKE$'$ *be a hybrid encryption scheme as given in Fig. 8. Then* PKE$'$ *is* (γ, δ)*-correct, and there is a type-preserving SFBB reduction* $\mathbb{B}$ *such that for every adversary* $\mathbb{A}$,

$$\mathsf{Adv}_{\mathrm{PKE}'}^{(n,\kappa)\text{-ind-cca}\star}(\mathbb{A}) \leq \binom{\kappa}{n} \cdot 2^n \cdot \mathsf{Adv}_{\mathrm{TXEM}}^{(n,n)\text{-ind-cca}}(\mathbb{B}),$$

where $\mathbb{B}$*'s overhead is dominated by generating* $\kappa - n$ *fresh keypairs, sampling* κ *bits, and choosing a subset of* $[\kappa]$ *of cardinality* n *uniformly at random.*

4.4 Real-or-Permuted: A Strengthened Notion for KEM Security

If we want to achieve an IND-CCA PKE more tightly, we seem to need a different notion of security for our TagXEMs. What could such a notion look like?

Our solution is a novel, stronger KEM notion, which we will refer to as "real-or-permuted", or ROP for short. Figure 9 provides the crucial new challenge oracle. The adversary has to guess whether a tentative K is the one encapsulated under c, or whether an adaptively chosen permutation has been applied to it. As permutations preserve the distribution of the sampling space, there are no choices of Π that make the game generically and trivially winnable.

Technically, we need to specify how the adversary provides Π such that it is guaranteed, or can be checked, to be a permutation. Hence, formally we define ROP with respect to a class of permutations $\mathcal{P}$, reminiscent of for instance key-dependent message [24] or related-key attack [10] definitions. We require that membership $\Pi \in \mathcal{P}$ is easy to check (e.g. ROP can simply index an element in $\mathcal{P}$) and that, by definition, $\mathcal{P}$ can be verified to indeed only contain permutations. For our main results, it suffices if $\mathcal{P}$ is the class of one-time pads, in the sense that Π specifies the key (or pad) of the one-time pad enciphering. Henceforth, we will assume that ROP is defined with respect to that class, unless explicitly stated otherwise.

The new notion ROP and IND relate to each other much the same way as IND and ROR for PKE. It is not hard to see that ROP tightly implies IND, whereas the other direction seems to incur the same loss as the ROR-to-IND implication for PKE (see the full version). For completeness, ROP lends itself equally well to XEMs and KEMs, or notions without corruptions or a decryption oracle. Finally, if any of the above primitives are constructed using an IND-secure PKE (e.g. using a Fujisaki–Okamoto style transform [21,22,28]), then achieving ROP is as easy as achieving IND: simply let K be the "left" message, and $\Pi(K)$ be the "right"!

4.5 PKE' Tightly Inherits IND-CCA Security

Using ROP in place of IND, we are able to show directly that the PKE constructions of Fig. 8 are IND-CPA resp. IND-CCA secure, by (as before) giving a (Tag)XEM reduction that provides a perfect simulation for the PKE adversary.

The crucial observation is that for any pair of messages $m_0, m_1 \in \{0,1\}^\ell$, there exist a permutation $\Pi_{m_0 \to m_1}$ on $\{0,1\}^\ell$ such that the message encapsulations are related as $K \oplus m_1 = \Pi_{m_0 \to m_1}(K) \oplus m_0$. Namely, the permutation that on input K, outputs $m_0 \oplus m_1 \oplus K$ (see the full version for the proof).

Theorem 8 (IND-CCA PKE). *Let* TXEM *be a* (γ, δ)-*correct TagXEM, and let* PKE' *be a hybrid encryption scheme as given in Fig. 8. Then* PKE' *is* (γ, δ)-*correct, and there is a type-preserving SFBB reduction* $\mathbb{B}$ *such that for every adversary* $\mathbb{A}$,

$$\mathsf{Adv}_{\mathrm{PKE}'}^{(n,\kappa)\text{-ind-cca}\star}(\mathbb{A}) \leq \mathsf{Adv}_{\mathrm{TXEM}}^{(n,\kappa)\text{-rop-cca}\star}(\mathbb{B}).$$

We leave it to the reader to verify that as before, employing a ROP-CPA XEM in place of the TagXEM yields IND-CPA security for the PKE of Fig. 8 (top row), by adapting the proof of Theorem 6 to the above. We again stress that using an information-theoretically CCA-secure DEM together with a CCA XEM does not seem to yield a proof of CCA inheritance to the PKE (see Sect. 4.3).

TXEM.Kg	TXEM.Key$_{\mathsf{pk}}(\ell)$
$(\mathsf{pk}', \mathsf{sk}') \leftarrow\!\!\$\ \mathsf{KEM.Kg}$	$(K^{\mathrm{kem}}, c) \leftarrow\!\!\$\ \mathsf{KEM.Enc}_{\mathsf{pk}}$
$\mathsf{pk} \leftarrow \mathsf{pk}'$	$\ell' \leftarrow \ell + \ell_{\mathrm{mackey}}$
$\mathsf{sk} \leftarrow \langle \mathsf{pk}', \mathsf{sk}' \rangle$	$K^{\mathrm{mac}} \| K^{\mathrm{xem}} \leftarrow F(\mathsf{pk}, c, K^{\mathrm{kem}}, \ell')$
return $(\mathsf{pk}, \mathsf{sk})$	$\sigma \leftarrow \langle c, K^{\mathrm{mac}} \rangle$
	return K^{xem}

TXEM.Check(pk, sk)

$\langle \mathsf{pk}', \mathsf{sk}' \rangle \leftarrow \mathsf{sk}$

TXEM.Dec$_{\mathsf{sk}}(\langle c, \mathsf{mac} \rangle, \tau, \ell)$

if $\mathsf{pk} \neq \mathsf{pk}'$ then return 0

return KEM.Check$(\mathsf{pk}', \mathsf{sk}')$ $\langle \mathsf{pk}', \mathsf{sk}' \rangle \leftarrow \mathsf{sk}$

$K^{\mathrm{kem}} \leftarrow \mathsf{KEM.Dec}_{\mathsf{sk}'}(c)$

TXEM.Enc(σ, τ)   if $K^{\mathrm{kem}} = \perp$ then return $\perp$

$\ell' \leftarrow \ell + \ell_{\mathrm{mackey}}$

$\langle c, K^{\mathrm{mac}} \rangle \leftarrow \sigma$ $K^{\mathrm{mac}} \| K^{\mathrm{xem}} \leftarrow F(\mathsf{pk}', c, K^{\mathrm{kem}}, \ell')$

$\mathsf{mac} \leftarrow \mathsf{MAC}_{K^{\mathrm{mac}}}(\tau)$ if $\mathsf{MAC}_{K^{\mathrm{mac}}}(\tau) \neq \mathsf{mac}$ then return $\perp$

return $\langle c, \mathsf{mac} \rangle$ return K^{xem}

Fig. 10. A TagXEM from a KEM, a MAC, and an XOF F.

4.6 TagXEM from a KEM, a MAC, and a Random Oracle

With Theorem 8, we achieved what we set out to do: demonstrating tight MI inheritance from a TagXEM to an IND-CCA PKE. However, AGK only showed how to construct an IND-CCA KEM, providing a reduction to the MI-GapCDH assumption in the programmable random oracle model. Without the crucial support of tags, our construction only achieves CPA security. Furthermore, Theorem 5 does *not* easily transfer to the ROP setting: it is not clear how to combine a ROP-CCA KEM with a XOF to yield a ROP-CCA XEM.

We complete the picture by providing a TagXEM construction from a KEM, a MAC, and a XOF. Our construction (Fig. 10) is inspired by Abe et al.'s TagKEM construction [2] and we show that with an information-theoretic MAC, if the KEM is perfectly correct, has unique encapsulations [25] and is multi-instance one-way secure under plaintext-checking attacks (OW-PCA), then the TagXEM is ROP-CCA secure in the programmable random oracle model (to model the XOF). Before stating our concrete security result (Theorem 9), we will define the relevant concepts and advantages below.

Preliminaries. One-wayness for KEMs tasks an adversary to retrieve the ephemeral key that has been encapsulated, given the public key and the encapsulation. In the multi-instance setting, an adversary has access to many public keys and various encapsulations per public key and endeavours to find ephemeral keys for encapsulations for as many different public keys as possible (no reward for breaking multiple encapsulations under the same public key).

$$
\begin{array}{ll}
\mathsf{Exp}_{\mathrm{KEM}}^{(n,\kappa)\text{-ow-pca}\star}(\mathbb{A}) & \mathcal{E}(i) \\
\hline
(\mathsf{pk}_1,\mathsf{sk}_1),\ldots,(\mathsf{pk}_\kappa,\mathsf{sk}_\kappa) \leftarrow\!\$\ \mathsf{KEM.Kg} & (K,c) \leftarrow\!\$\ \mathsf{KEM.Enc}_{\mathsf{pk}_i} \\
(\mathtt{I},(j_i,\hat{K}_i)_{i\in\mathtt{I}}) \leftarrow\!\$\ \mathbb{A}^{\mathcal{E},\mathcal{P},\mathcal{K}}(\mathsf{pk}_1,\ldots,\mathsf{pk}_\kappa) & \mathsf{P}_i \overset{\frown}{\leftarrow} K \\
\textbf{if } |\mathtt{I}| \neq n \vee \mathtt{I}\cap\mathtt{K} \neq \emptyset \textbf{ then return } 0 & \textbf{return } c \\
\textbf{return } \bigwedge_{i\in\mathtt{I}} \mathsf{P}_i[j_i] = \hat{K}_i & \\
 & \mathcal{K}(i) \\
\mathcal{P}(i,c,K) & \hline \\
\hline & \mathtt{K}\overset{\cup}{\leftarrow} i \\
K' \leftarrow \mathsf{KEM.Dec}_{\mathsf{sk}_i}(c) & \textbf{return } \mathsf{sk}_i \\
\textbf{return } K = K' &
\end{array}
$$

Fig. 11. Multi-instance one-way security in the presence of plaintext checking attacks.

Plaintext-checking attacks (PCA) were introduced by Okamoto and Pointcheval [36, Definition 8] in a single-user public key encryption setting. Intuitively, PCA provides the adversary access to an oracle that, on input a pair (m,c) determines whether c encrypts m or not; more formally [1], the oracle checks whether c decrypts to m or not. In the context of KEMs, the PCA oracle takes a pair (K^{kem},c) as input and determines whether c decapsulates to K^{kem} or not. The multi-user or multi-instance generalization is straightforward and the definition (in its modern decryption incarnation) inherently deals with imperfect correctness in the decryption.

Definition 7 considers one-wayness under plaintext checking attacks. For standard ElGamal KEM, where a (multiplicative) discrete-log group with generator g and of prime order q is given as part of the parameters, a public key consists of $h = g^x$ with $x \leftarrow\!\$\ \mathbb{Z}_q$ the private key, and an encapsulation outputs $(K^{\mathrm{kem}},c) = (h^r,g^r)$ for random $r \leftarrow\!\$\ \mathbb{Z}_q$, the one-wayness problem (in the single-user case) is equivalent to the computational Diffie–Hellman (CDH) problem. The plaintext checking oracle allows an adversary to learn, for group elements (k,c) of its choice, whether $k = c^x$ or not. The corresponding hardness assumption for OW-PCA is known as the Strong CDH assumption. An even stronger assumption is the GapCDH assumption, where an adversary instead can use an oracle that determines whether a quadruple of group elements is a Diffie–Hellman tuple or not.

Definition 7 (OW-PCA). *Let KEM be a key encapsulation mechanism. Then the one-way advantage under plaintext-checking attacks of an adversary $\mathbb{A}$ is*

$$
\mathsf{Adv}_{\mathrm{KEM}}^{(n,\kappa)\text{-ow-pca}\star}(\mathbb{A}) = \Pr\left[\mathsf{Exp}_{\mathrm{KEM}}^{(n,\kappa)\text{-ow-pca}\star}(\mathbb{A}) = 1\right],
$$

where the experiment is defined in Fig. 11.

In addition to perfect correctness and OW-PCA security, the security reduction for our construction (Theorem 9) relies on two further properties of the underlying KEM. Unique encapsulation captures that for a fixed public key and ephemeral key, the encapsulation corresponding to that ephemeral key is unique (without saying anything about how to compute it). Unique encapsulations have been used before, for instance by Heuer et al. [25] (see also Remark 4 below).

Definition 8 (Unique Encapsulation). *Let* KEM *be a perfectly correct* KEM. *Then it has unique encapsulations iff*

$$\Pr\left[\begin{array}{l}(\mathsf{pk},\mathsf{sk}) \leftarrow\!\!\$\ \mathsf{KEM.Kg}\\ (K_0^{kem}, c_0) \leftarrow\!\!\$\ \mathsf{KEM.Enc}_{\mathsf{pk}}\ :\ K_0^{kem} = K_1^{kem} \wedge c_0 \neq c_1\\ (K_1^{kem}, c_1) \leftarrow\!\!\$\ \mathsf{KEM.Enc}_{\mathsf{pk}}\end{array}\right] = 0\ .$$

The second additional property we require from the KEM is that collisions amongst encapsulations (under a single randomly drawn public key) are suitably rare. Definition 9 captures the relevant probability of a k-way encapsulation collision. If a KEM is perfectly correct with unique encapsulations, then colliding encapsulations are equivalent to colliding ephemeral keys; if, as is usually the case, these ephemeral keys are furthermore chosen uniformly at random from a finite set $\mathcal{X}$, we can upper bound $\epsilon_k(q)$ by $q^k/|\mathcal{X}|^{k-1}$ using a standard bound on k-way collisions (see e.g. [37, Appendix B]).

Definition 9 (Encapsulation Multi-Collisions). *Let* KEM *be a KEM, and let* $q, k \in \mathbb{Z}_{>1}$ *be parameters. Then the k-out-of-q encapsulation multi-collision probability is*

$$\epsilon_k(q) = \Pr\left[\begin{array}{l}(\mathsf{pk}, \mathsf{sk}) \leftarrow\!\!\$\ \mathsf{KEM.Kg}\\ \forall_{i \in [q]} (K_i^{kem}, c_i) \leftarrow\!\!\$\ \mathsf{KEM.Enc}_{\mathsf{pk}}\end{array}\ :\ \exists_{\mathsf{J} \subseteq [q], |\mathsf{J}| = k} \forall_{i,j \in \mathsf{J}} c_i = c_j\right]\ .$$

For completeness, we also present definitions of a deterministic message authentication code, so we dispense with an explicit verification algorithm in Definition 10 (for concreteness, we restrict to bitstrings for both keys and tags, of length ℓ_{mackey} and ℓ_{mac} respectively), and an information-theoretic notion of forgeries (Definition 11) where we use the same parameter k as above (or rather $k - 1$ in Theorem 9), but this time to denote the number of valid message–tag pairs available to an adversary. The usual choice is $k = 1$, e.g. when considering strongly universal$_2$ hash functions, but Wegman and Carter [40] already investigated $k > 1$. Provided ℓ_{mackey} is large enough (at least $k \cdot \ell_{\mathsf{mac}}$), one can achieve $\hat{\epsilon}_k = 2^{-\ell_{\mathsf{mac}}}$, which is optimal.

Definition 10 (Message Authentication Code (MAC)). *A message authentication code* MAC *is a pair of algorithms* MAC.Kg *and* MAC.Mac, *where* MAC.Kg *randomly generates a* $K^{mac} \in \{0,1\}^{\ell_{\mathsf{mackey}}}$, *and the deterministic* MAC.Mac *takes a key* K^{mac} *and a message* $m \in \mathcal{M}$ *to output tag* $\mathsf{mac} \leftarrow$ MAC.Mac$_{K^{mac}}(m) \in \{0,1\}^{\ell_{\mathsf{mac}}}$.

Definition 11 (Information-Theoretic MAC Forgeries). *Let* MAC *be given and let* $k \in \mathbb{Z}_{\geq 0}$ *be a parameter, then the forging advantage after observing* k *valid message–tag pairs is defined as*

$$\hat{\epsilon}_k = \max_{\substack{\forall i \in \{0\} \cup [k]\\(m_i, \mathsf{mac}_i)}} \Pr\left[\mathsf{MAC.Mac}_{K^{mac}}(m_0) = \mathsf{mac}_0\ \middle|\ \forall_{i \in [k]} \mathsf{MAC.Mac}_{K^{mac}}(m_i) = \mathsf{mac}_i\right].$$

Security Claim. With all elements in place, we can state the security of Fig. 10's TXEM, in Theorem 9 (see the full version for the proof). The security bound depends on a tuning parameter k that feeds into both the collision probability of the underlying KEM and the forgery advantage of the MAC, with opposite effects. The ability to tune the bound therefore allows some flexibility when instantiating the three underlying primitives KEM, MAC, and XOF: for fixed q_c, increasing k will result in a smaller upper bound on $\epsilon_k(q_c)$, but to ensure that $\hat{\epsilon}_{k-1}$ does not dominate, it might then be necessary to increase the key size ℓ_{mackey} (and possibly tag size ℓ_{mac}) of the information-theoretic MAC (see Corollary 5 for a concrete instantiation) . Otherwise, instantiating the information-theoretic MAC and the XOF is relatively straightforward (with the usual ROM caveats for the latter).

Theorem 9. *Let* TXEM *be as in Fig. 10, let* KEM *be a perfectly correct KEM with unique encapsulations, and let* $k \in \mathbb{Z}_{>1}$. *Then there is an SFBB reduction* $\mathbb{B}$ *such that, for all* $\mathbb{A}$ *that makes* q_c *challenge and* q_d *decryption oracle queries,*

$$\mathsf{Adv}_{\mathrm{TXEM}}^{(n,\kappa)\text{-rop-cca}\star}(\mathbb{A}) \leq \mathsf{Adv}_{\mathrm{KEM}}^{(n,\kappa)\text{-ow-pca}\star}(\mathbb{B}) + 2\big(q_d\hat{\epsilon}_{k-1} + \epsilon_k(q_c)\big)$$

in the programmable random oracle model, where $\hat{\epsilon}_{k-1}$ *is the forging advantage after observing* $k - 1$ *valid message–tag pairs (Definition 11) and* $\epsilon_k(q_c)$ *is the* k-*out-of-*q_c *encapsulation multi-collision probability of KEM (Definition 9). If* $\mathbb{A}$ *makes* q_f *queries to the random oracle, then* $\mathbb{B}$ *makes at most* q_f *queries to its plaintext checking oracle.*

The proof borrows some ideas already used to prove AGK's Theorem 2. In fact, it is relatively straightforward to recast AGK's Theorem 2 as the multi-instance version of a OW-PCA KEM plus a programmable random oracle yielding an IND-CCA KEM, although the presence of the error terms $\hat{\epsilon}_{k-1}$ and especially $\epsilon_k(q_c)$ render recovery of AGK's Theorem 2 as a special case of our Theorem 9 not immediate.

Combining Theorem 8 and 9 in Corollary 4, we can finally conclude that our construction yields a PKE inheriting the multi-instance security of the underlying KEM (for parameter regimes where the loss term does not dominate).

Corollary 4. *Let* PKE' *be as in Fig. 8, let the underlying TagXEM be as in Fig 10, let* KEM *be a perfectly correct KEM with unique encapsulations, and let* $k \in \mathbb{Z}_{>1}$. *Then, there is an SFBB reduction* $\mathbb{B}$ *such that, for all* $\mathbb{A}$ *that makes* q_c *challenge and* q_d *decryption oracle queries,*

$$\mathsf{Adv}_{\mathrm{PKE'}}^{(n,\kappa)\text{-ind-cca}\star}(\mathbb{A}) \leq \mathsf{Adv}_{\mathrm{KEM}}^{(n,\kappa)\text{-ow-pca}\star}(\mathbb{B}) + 2\big(q_d\hat{\epsilon}_{k-1} + \epsilon_k(q_c)\big)$$

in the programmable random oracle model, where $\hat{\epsilon}_{k-1}$ *is the forging advantage after observing* $k - 1$ *valid message–tag pairs (Definition 11) and* $\epsilon_k(q_c)$ *is the* k-*out-of-*q_c *encapsulation multi-collision probability of KEM (Definition 9). If* $\mathbb{A}$ *makes* q_f *queries to the random oracle, then* $\mathbb{B}$ *makes at most* q_f *queries to its plaintext checking oracle.*

Remark 4. The resulting construction is remarkably similar to the PKE studied by Heuer et al. [25] in the context of selective opening attacks (and to a lesser extent its predecessor by Steinfeld et al. [39] and successor by Lai et al. [32]). They too use a random oracle to derive a MAC key and a one-time pad from an ephemeral KEM key. The only two differences are that Heuer et al. do not consider arbitrary length messages and that their random oracle outputs $K^{\mathrm{xem}} \| K^{\mathrm{mac}}$, i.e. the opposite order from what we do.

For fixed length messages, the order in which those two keys are output does not matter. However, when moving to arbitrary length-messages, the order of the XOF output does matter. Outputting $K^{\mathrm{xem}} \| K^{\mathrm{mac}}$ instead would allow a length extension attack enabling the adversary to recover the MAC key, at which point producing forgeries would be trivial.

In a way, the construction is quite brittle that these small details matter. Another example of brittleness is that our reduction for Theorem 9 requires $\perp$ produced from a KEM decryption error to be indistinguishable from a failed MAC verification. In implementations, a timing attack might well break this requirement.

Remark 5. The proof of Theorem 9 does rely on perfect correctness of the underlying KEM, thus excluding many popular post-quantum KEMs based on the hardness of LWE. Having said that, establishing the post-quantum security of TXEM would require a proof in the quantum random oracle model [15]. We leave the construction of a post-quantum TagXEM as an enticing open problem.

A Concrete Instantiation. We conclude by providing a concrete bound for the construction when instantiating with low granularity ElGamal KEM on groups of size $\geq p$. ElGamal KEM satisfies perfect correctness and unique encapsulation (ensuring compatibility with Theorem 9) and produces uniformly random group elements as ephemeral keys, so $\epsilon_k(q_c) \leq q^k/p^{k-1}$. Furthermore, the relevant multi-instance OW-PCA security can be linked to the low granularity MI-GapCDH problem with corruptions (Theorem 12 of the full version). By extending AGK's low granularity bound [4, Thm. 6] to include corruptions (Thm. 11 of the full version) and combining with Corollary 4, we arrive at a clean information-theoretic bound (Corollary 5) in the generic group and programmable random oracle model. To keep the bound easier to interpret, we assume that the adversary makes at most $\sqrt{p}$ queries to the encryption and decryption oracles; realistically, an adversary will be able to make far more offline queries q to its generic group and for $q \approx \sqrt{p}$ a single discrete logarithm instance can already be broken. In a similar vein, the requirement that each group instance receive at least $\max\{60 \log_2 p, \sqrt{q_f}/2\}$ group operation calls (allowing some simplifications in the MI-GapCDH bound) is a reasonable one, as already argued by AGK, given that the number of group operations performed by an ElGamal adversary is "typically large".

Corollary 5. *Let* PKE′ *be as in Fig. 8, let the underlying TagXEM be as in Fig 10, let KEM be instantiated as low granularity ElGamal (see the full version* *for details) and let p be a lower bound on the generated groups. Let $k \in \mathbb{Z}_{>1}$, let MAC be an information-theoretic MAC with key length ℓ_{mackey} and output length ℓ_{mac} and satisfying $\hat{\epsilon}_{k-1} = 2^{-\ell_{\mathsf{mac}}}$. Then, for any information-theoretic $\mathbb{A}$ that makes at most $\sqrt{p}$ challenge oracle queries, at most $\sqrt{p}$ decryption oracle queries, q_f queries to the random oracle, and a total of q queries to the group-operation oracles with at least $\max\{60 \log_2 p, \sqrt{q_f}/2\}$ queries per group instance, it holds that*

$$\mathsf{Adv}_{\mathsf{PKE}'}^{(n,\kappa)\text{-ind-cca}\star}(\mathbb{A}) \leq \left(\frac{4 \cdot e \cdot q^2}{n^2 \cdot p} \right)^n + 2 \left(\frac{\sqrt{p}}{2^{\ell_{\mathsf{mac}}}} + \frac{1}{p^{\frac{k}{2}-1}} \right)$$

in the programmable random oracle and generic group model.

For the construction to exhibit meaningful multi-instance security, we want the upper bound on the adversary's advantage to diminish with increasing n. Since the second term on the right hand side of Corollary 5 is independent of n, the first term has to dominate for advantages of interest. Thus, for a fixed p, we want to set ℓ_{mac} and k so that, irrespective of n, we do not really care about the other two terms, where ℓ_{mac} directly corresponds to the PKE's ciphertext expansion and increasing k will require longer ephemeral keys as output by the XOF to ensure that $\ell_{\mathsf{mackey}} \geq k \cdot \ell_{\mathsf{mac}}$. To minimize overhead, having both terms equal is optimal, corresponding to $2\ell_{\mathsf{mac}} = (k-1) \log_2 p$. Some reasonable options are then $(\ell_{\mathsf{mac}}, k) = (\log_2 p, 3)$ or $(\ell_{\mathsf{mac}}, k) = (3/2 \log_2 p, 4)$.

Alternatively, the bound can be interpreted in terms of the scaling factor, which focuses on the minimum resources needed to achieve an overwhelming advantage (see the full version for details). In that case, the second term, being independent of n, is manifestly of little interest for either of our suggested parameter choices.

References

1. Abdalla, M., Benhamouda, F., Pointcheval, D.: Public-key encryption indistinguishable under plaintext-checkable attacks. In: Katz, J. (ed.) PKC 2015. LNCS, vol. 9020, pp. 332–352. Springer, Heidelberg (2015). https://doi.org/10.1007/978-3-662-46447-2_15

2. Abe, M., Gennaro, R., Kurosawa, K.: Tag-KEM/DEM: a new framework for hybrid encryption. J. Cryptol. 21(1), 97–130 (2007). https://doi.org/10.1007/s00145-007-9010-x

3. Auerbach, B., Giacon, F., Kiltz, E.: Everybody's a target: scalability in public-key encryption. Cryptology ePrint Archive, Report 2019/364 (2019). https://eprint.iacr.org/2019/364

4. Auerbach, B., Giacon, F., Kiltz, E.: Everybody's a target: scalability in public-key encryption. In: Canteaut, A., Ishai, Y. (eds.) EUROCRYPT 2020. LNCS, vol. 12107, pp. 475–506. Springer, Cham (2020). https://doi.org/10.1007/978-3-030-45727-3_16

5. Bader, C., Jager, T., Li, Y., Schäge, S.: On the impossibility of tight cryptographic reductions. In: Fischlin, M., Coron, J.-S. (eds.) EUROCRYPT 2016. LNCS, vol. 9666, pp. 273–304. Springer, Heidelberg (2016). https://doi.org/10.1007/978-3-662-49896-5_10

6. Baecher, P., Brzuska, C., Fischlin, M.: Notions of black-box reductions, revisited. In: Sako, K., Sarkar, P. (eds.) ASIACRYPT 2013. LNCS, vol. 8269, pp. 296–315. Springer, Heidelberg (2013). https://doi.org/10.1007/978-3-642-42033-7_16

7. Bellare, M., Boldyreva, A., Micali, S.: Public-key encryption in a multi-user setting: security proofs and improvements. In: Preneel, B. (ed.) EUROCRYPT 2000. LNCS, vol. 1807, pp. 259–274. Springer, Heidelberg (2000). https://doi.org/10.1007/3-540-45539-6_18

8. Bellare, M., Desai, A., Pointcheval, D., Rogaway, P.: Relations among notions of security for public-key encryption schemes. In: Krawczyk, H. (ed.) CRYPTO 1998. LNCS, vol. 1462, pp. 26–45. Springer, Heidelberg (1998). https://doi.org/10.1007/BFb0055718

9. Bellare, M., Hofheinz, D., Kiltz, E.: Subtleties in the definition of IND-CCA: when and how should challenge decryption be disallowed? J. Cryptol. 28(1), 29–48 (2013). https://doi.org/10.1007/s00145-013-9167-4

10. Bellare, M., Kohno, T.: A theoretical treatment of related-key attacks: RKA-PRPs, RKA-PRFs, and applications. In: Biham, E. (ed.) EUROCRYPT 2003. LNCS, vol. 2656, pp. 491–506. Springer, Heidelberg (2003). https://doi.org/10.1007/3-540-39200-9_31

11. Bellare, M., Paterson, K.G., Rogaway, P.: Security of symmetric encryption against mass surveillance. In: Garay, J.A., Gennaro, R. (eds.) CRYPTO 2014. LNCS, vol. 8616, pp. 1–19. Springer, Heidelberg (2014). https://doi.org/10.1007/978-3-662-44371-2_1

12. Bellare, M., Ristenpart, T., Tessaro, S.: Multi-instance security and its application to password-based cryptography. In: Safavi-Naini, R., Canetti, R. (eds.) CRYPTO 2012. LNCS, vol. 7417, pp. 312–329. Springer, Heidelberg (2012). https://doi.org/10.1007/978-3-642-32009-5_19

13. Bellare, M., Ristenpart, T., Tessaro, S.: Multi-instance security and its application to password-based cryptography. Cryptology ePrint Archive, Report 2012/196 (2012). https://eprint.iacr.org/2012/196

14. Bellare, M., Rogaway, P.: Random oracles are practical: a paradigm for designing efficient protocols. In: Denning, D.E., Pyle, R., Ganesan, R., Sandhu, R.S., Ashby, V. (eds.) ACM CCS 93, pp. 62–73. ACM Press, November 1993. https://doi.org/10.1145/168588.168596

15. Boneh, D., Dagdelen, Ö., Fischlin, M., Lehmann, A., Schaffner, C., Zhandry, M.: Random oracles in a quantum world. In: Lee, D.H., Wang, X. (eds.) ASIACRYPT 2011. LNCS, vol. 7073, pp. 41–69. Springer, Heidelberg (2011). https://doi.org/10.1007/978-3-642-25385-0_3

16. Bos, J., et al.: Crystals - Kyber: a CCA-secure module-lattice-based KEM. In: 2018 IEEE European Symposium on Security and Privacy (EuroS P), pp. 353–367 (2018). https://doi.org/10.1109/EuroSP.2018.00032

17. Brunetta, C., Heum, H., Stam, M.: Multi-instance secure public-key encryption. Cryptology ePrint Archive, Report 2022/909 (2022). https://eprint.iacr.org/2022/909

18. Cramer, R., Shoup, V.: Design and analysis of practical public-key encryption schemes secure against adaptive chosen ciphertext attack. SIAM J. Comput. 33(1), 167–226 (2003)

19. Cramer, R., Shoup, V.: A practical public key cryptosystem provably secure against adaptive chosen ciphertext attack. In: Krawczyk, H. (ed.) CRYPTO 1998. LNCS, vol. 1462, pp. 13–25. Springer, Heidelberg (1998). https://doi.org/10.1007/BFb0055717

366   C. Brunetta et al.

20. Farshim, P., Tessaro, S.: Password hashing and preprocessing. In: Canteaut, A., Standaert, F.-X. (eds.) EUROCRYPT 2021. LNCS, vol. 12697, pp. 64–91. Springer, Cham (2021). https://doi.org/10.1007/978-3-030-77886-6_3
21. Fujisaki, E., Okamoto, T.: Secure integration of asymmetric and symmetric encryption schemes. In: Wiener, M. (ed.) CRYPTO 1999. LNCS, vol. 1666, pp. 537–554. Springer, Heidelberg (1999). https://doi.org/10.1007/3-540-48405-1_34
22. Fujisaki, E., Okamoto, T.: Secure integration of asymmetric and symmetric encryption schemes. J. Cryptol. 26(1), 80–101 (2011). https://doi.org/10.1007/s00145-011-9114-1
23. Giacon, F., Kiltz, E., Poettering, B.: Hybrid encryption in a multi-user setting, revisited. In: Abdalla, M., Dahab, R. (eds.) PKC 2018. LNCS, vol. 10769, pp. 159–189. Springer, Cham (2018). https://doi.org/10.1007/978-3-319-76578-5_6
24. Halevi, S., Krawczyk, H.: Security under key-dependent inputs. In: Ning, P., De Capitani di Vimercati, S., Syverson, P.F. (eds.) ACM CCS 2007, pp. 466–475. ACM Press, October 2007. https://doi.org/10.1145/1315245.1315303
25. Heuer, F., Jager, T., Kiltz, E., Schäge, S.: On the selective opening security of practical public-key encryption schemes. In: Katz, J. (ed.) PKC 2015. LNCS, vol. 9020, pp. 27–51. Springer, Heidelberg (2015). https://doi.org/10.1007/978-3-662-46447-2_2
26. Heum, H., Stam, M.: Tightness subtleties for multi-user PKE notions. In: Paterson, M.B. (ed.) IMACC 2021. LNCS, vol. 13129, pp. 75–104. Springer, Cham (2021). https://doi.org/10.1007/978-3-030-92641-0_5
27. Hoeffding, W.: Probability inequalities for sums of bounded random variables. J. Am. Stat. Assoc. 58, 13–30 (1963)
28. Hofheinz, D., Hövelmanns, K., Kiltz, E.: A modular analysis of the Fujisaki-Okamoto transformation. In: Kalai, Y., Reyzin, L. (eds.) TCC 2017. LNCS, vol. 10677, pp. 341–371. Springer, Cham (2017). https://doi.org/10.1007/978-3-319-70500-2_12
29. Jager, T., Kiltz, E., Riepel, D., Schäge, S.: Tightly-secure authenticated key exchange, revisited. In: Canteaut, A., Standaert, F.-X. (eds.) EUROCRYPT 2021. LNCS, vol. 12696, pp. 117–146. Springer, Cham (2021). https://doi.org/10.1007/978-3-030-77870-5_5
30. Kiltz, E., Pan, J., Riepel, D., Ringerud, M.: Multi-user CDH problems and the concrete security of NAXOS and HMQV. In: Rosulek, M. (ed.) CT-RSA 2023. Springer, Heidelberg (2023, to appear). https://eprint.iacr.org/2023/115
31. Kurosawa, K., Desmedt, Y.: A new paradigm of hybrid encryption scheme. In: Franklin, M. (ed.) CRYPTO 2004. LNCS, vol. 3152, pp. 426–442. Springer, Heidelberg (2004). https://doi.org/10.1007/978-3-540-28628-8_26
32. Lai, J., Yang, R., Huang, Z., Weng, J.: Simulation-based bi-selective opening security for public key encryption. In: Tibouchi, M., Wang, H. (eds.) ASIACRYPT 2021. LNCS, vol. 13091, pp. 456–482. Springer, Cham (2021). https://doi.org/10.1007/978-3-030-92075-3_16
33. Lee, Y., Lee, D.H., Park, J.H.: Tightly CCA-secure encryption scheme in a multi-user setting with corruptions. Des. Codes Cryptogr. 88(11), 2433–2452 (2020)
34. Lewko, A., Waters, B.: Why proving HIBE systems secure is difficult. In: Nguyen, P.Q., Oswald, E. (eds.) EUROCRYPT 2014. LNCS, vol. 8441, pp. 58–76. Springer, Heidelberg (2014). https://doi.org/10.1007/978-3-642-55220-5_4
35. NIST: SHA-3 standard: Permutation-based hash and extendable-output functions. Federal Information Processing Standards Publication 202, NIST, August 2015

36. Okamoto, T., Pointcheval, D.: REACT: rapid enhanced-security asymmetric cryptosystem transform. In: Naccache, D. (ed.) CT-RSA 2001. LNCS, vol. 2020, pp. 159–174. Springer, Heidelberg (2000). https://doi.org/10.1007/3-540-45353-9_13
37. Preneel, B.: Analysis and design of cryptographic hash functions. Ph.D. thesis, KU Leuven, February 1993
38. Reingold, O., Trevisan, L., Vadhan, S.: Notions of reducibility between cryptographic primitives. In: Naor, M. (ed.) TCC 2004. LNCS, vol. 2951, pp. 1–20. Springer, Heidelberg (2004). https://doi.org/10.1007/978-3-540-24638-1_1
39. Steinfeld, R., Baek, J., Zheng, Y.: On the necessity of strong assumptions for the security of a class of asymmetric encryption schemes. In: Batten, L., Seberry, J. (eds.) ACISP 2002. LNCS, vol. 2384, pp. 241–256. Springer, Heidelberg (2002). https://doi.org/10.1007/3-540-45450-0_20
40. Wegman, M.N., Carter, L.: New hash functions and their use in authentication and set equality. J. Comput. Syst. Sci. **22**, 265–279 (1981)

Unidirectional Updatable Encryption and Proxy Re-encryption from DDH

Peihan Miao[1], Sikhar Patranabis[2]($\boxtimes$), and Gaven Watson[3]

[1] Brown University, Providence, USA
peihan_miao@brown.edu
[2] IBM Research India, Bangalore, India
sikhar.patranabis@ibm.com,sikharpatranabis@gmail.com
[3] Meta, Menlo Park, USA
gavenwatson@meta.com

Abstract. Updatable Encryption (UE) and Proxy Re-encryption (PRE) allow *re-encrypting* a ciphertext from one key to another in the symmetric-key and public-key settings, respectively, without decryption. A longstanding open question has been the following: do *unidirectional* UE and PRE schemes (where ciphertext re-encryption is permitted in only one direction) necessarily require stronger/more structured assumptions as compared to their bidirectional counterparts? Known constructions of UE and PRE seem to exemplify this "gap" – while bidirectional schemes can be realized as relatively simple extensions of public-key encryption from standard assumptions such as DDH or LWE, unidirectional schemes typically rely on stronger assumptions such as FHE or indistinguishability obfuscation (iO), or highly structured cryptographic tools such as bilinear maps or lattice trapdoors.

In this paper, we bridge this gap by showing the first feasibility results for realizing unidirectional UE and PRE from a new generic primitive that we call Key and Plaintext Homomorphic Encryption (KPHE) – a public-key encryption scheme that supports additive homomorphisms on its plaintext and key spaces simultaneously. We show that KPHE can be instantiated from DDH. This yields the first constructions of unidirectional UE and PRE from DDH.

Our constructions achieve the strongest notions of *post-compromise security* in the standard model. Our UE schemes also achieve "backwards-leak directionality" of key updates (a notion we discuss is equivalent, from a security perspective, to that of unidirectionality with no-key updates). Our results establish (somewhat surprisingly) that unidirectional UE and PRE schemes satisfying such strong security notions *do not*, in fact, require stronger/more structured cryptographic assumptions as compared to bidirectional schemes.

1 Introduction

Cryptographic encryption is a powerful tool for ensuring data confidentiality. A common security guarantee offered by any encryption scheme (either symmetric-key or public-key) is the following: encrypted data can only be decrypted using a

© International Association for Cryptologic Research 2023
A. Boldyreva and V. Kolesnikov (Eds.): PKC 2023, LNCS 13941, pp. 368–398, 2023.
https://doi.org/10.1007/978-3-031-31371-4_13

certain secret key. However, a limitation of traditional encryption schemes is that once data is encrypted, it is generally hard to allow a third party to transform the ciphertext so that it can be decrypted with a different key, without sharing either the original or the new secret key with the third party.

Re-encryption schemes such as Proxy Re-encryption (PRE) [BBS98] and Updatable Encryption (UE) [BLMR13] circumvent this limitation by enabling a public transformation of ciphertexts from encryption under one key to that of another, while protecting the underlying secret keys. Classic applications for such schemes include key rotation for secure outsourced storage [BBB+12, Pay18], access control, the delegation of email access, and many more.

Proxy Re-encryption (PRE). PRE is a public-key encryption scheme which enables a party Alice, with the help of a proxy, to re-encrypt her ciphertexts for decryption by an alternate party Bob. To facilitate re-encryption, Alice and Bob, with key pairs $(\mathsf{pk}_A, \mathsf{sk}_A)$ and $(\mathsf{pk}_B, \mathsf{sk}_B)$ respectively, will together compute a re-encryption key rk_{AB} and then provide this to the proxy. Whenever the proxy needs to perform re-encryption, it can use rk_{AB} to transform a ciphertext encrypted under pk_A into a ciphertext encrypted under pk_B. Security of the PRE scheme guarantees that the proxy learns nothing about the underlying plaintext during the re-encryption process.

Updatable Encryption (UE). UE was introduced by Boneh et al. [BLMR13] to address the problem of key rotation for secure outsourced storage. UE addresses re-encryption by using similar techniques to those of PRE, with two main differences: (1) UE is a symmetric-key encryption scheme, and (2) UE typically only allows sequential updates. More specifically, in UE we divide time into a series of epochs. In the first epoch a fresh symmetric key k_0 is chosen and used to encrypt all data. When we rotate a key from k_{e-1} to k_e, we transition to the next epoch by calculating an update token Δ_e. All new ciphertexts are encrypted under the new key k_e and all existing ciphertexts ct_{e-1} are re-encrypted using the update token Δ_e so that they can be decrypted by k_e. The benefit of this approach is that the storage server can perform the re-encryption of data using the update token without the risk of exposing any plaintext data.

There are two variants of UE schemes, *ciphertext-dependent* schemes [EPRS17, BEKS20] and *ciphertext-independent* schemes [LT18, KLR19, BDGJ20, Jia20]. In ciphertext-dependent UE schemes, the update token $\Delta_{e, \mathsf{ctx}_{e-1}}$ depends on the ciphertext ctx_{e-1} to be updated, while in ciphertext-independent schemes, the update token Δ_e is generated independent of the updated ciphertext, hence a single token can be used to update all ciphertexts on the storage server. In the rest of the paper, when we refer to UE, we mean a ciphertext-independent scheme unless otherwise specified.

Directionality of PRE and UE. Re-encryption schemes are either *bidirectional* or *unidirectional*. A scheme is said to be bidirectional if a re-encryption key/update token can be used to re-encrypt a ciphertext to either the next party/epoch or the previous party/epoch. In contrast, the re-encryption key/update token of a unidirectional scheme can only be used to re-encrypt a ciphertext to the next party/epoch and *not* the previous. So far we have only discussed the directionality within the context of ciphertext updates. The (uni)directionality with regards to keys differs slightly between PRE and UE, as we discuss next.

Bidirectionality vs. Unidirectionality in PRE. In bidirectional PRE schemes, the re-encryption key rk_{AB} from Alice to Bob is generated from Alice's key-pair $(\mathsf{pk}_A, \mathsf{sk}_A)$ and Bob's key-pair $(\mathsf{pk}_B, \mathsf{sk}_B)$. Given rk_{AB} along with sk_A (resp. sk_B), it is usually possible to derive sk_B (resp. sk_A). In unidirectional PRE schemes, the re-encryption key rk_{AB} is derived from $((\mathsf{pk}_A, \mathsf{sk}_A), \mathsf{pk}_B)$; Bob's secret key sk_B is not used. In fact, given the re-encryption key rk_{AB} and Alice's secret key sk_A, it should be impossible to derive any knowledge of Bob's secret key sk_B.

Unidirectionality in UE. For UE schemes, there is an extra level of subtlety regarding the *directionality of keys* in addition to ciphertexts. A recent work of Jiang [Jia20] extensively studied the question: given an update token Δ_e along with either k_{e-1} or k_e, is it possible to derive the other key? A scheme has bidirectional key updates if Δ_e can be used to derive keys in both directions, and has unidirectional key updates if Δ_e can be used in one direction, to derive k_e from k_{e-1}. Jiang [Jia20] showed that UE with bidirectional key and ciphertext updates implies UE with unidirectional key and ciphertext updates.

In the same work, Jiang postulated that to capture the same security level as the unidirectional PRE schemes, one requires even stronger UE schemes with *no-directional key updates*, where k_e cannot be derived from k_{e-1} and Δ_e. In Jiang [Jia20], the definition of no-directional key updates intuitively requires that it is *also* impossible to derive k_{e-1} from Δ_e and k_e. The recent work of Nishimaki [Nis21] proposed a seemingly weaker notion called *backward-leak unidirectional key updates* where Δ_e can only be used in one direction to derive k_{e-1} from k_e. However, we observe that this new notion is essentially equivalent to no-directional key updates because derivation of k_{e-1} does not increase the adversary's advantage in breaking the scheme. In particular, if the adversary obtains a ciphertext ct_{e-1} and corrupts Δ_e and k_e, then it can first update the ciphertext to ct_e and decrypt it using k_e. Jiang emphasized that UE with no-directional key updates is the ideal security model, which by our argument above, extends to backwards-leak key updates. Henceforth, when we refer to unidirectional UE, we mean unidirectional UE with backwards-leak directional key updates unless otherwise specified.

Gap between Unidirectionality and Bidirectionality. In general, unidirectional UE and PRE schemes are more ideally suited to real-world applications as compared to their bidirectional counterparts due to their superior security guarantees. For example, unlike bidirectional UE schemes, unidirectional UE schemes guarantee security of data as if "freshly encrypted" in epoch e (i.e., not re-encrypted from epoch $(e-1)$) even if the adversary gains access to the secret key k_{e-1} and the update token Δ_e. Unidirectional PRE schemes also offer similarly superior security guarantees over their bidirectional counterparts.

Another natural point of comparison between unidirectional and bidirectional UE and PRE schemes is the nature of cryptographic assumptions from which such schemes can be realized. Known constructions of UE and PRE seemingly exemplify an apparent "gap" in terms of the assumptions required – unidirectional schemes have historically relied on stronger/more structured cryptographic assumptions as compared to their bidirectional counterparts.

Blaze et al. [BBS98] showed how to construct bidirectional PRE schemes from the Decisional Diffie-Hellman (DDH) assumption by suitably extending the well-known ElGamal encryption scheme [Gam85]. Similarly, a long line of works [BLMR13, LT18, KLR19, BDGJ20, Jia20] have shown how to realize bidirectional UE schemes as relatively simple extensions of public-key encryption from standard assumptions such as DDH and Learning With Errors (LWE).

On the other hand, unidirectional UE and PRE schemes typically rely on a stronger set of assumptions such as FHE [Gen09] and indistinguishability obfuscation (iO) [BGI+12], or highly structured cryptographic tools such as bilinear maps [BF03] and "hard" lattice trapdoors [GPV08]. Examples of constructions of unidirectional PRE from FHE and/or structured lattice trapdoors can be found in [NX15, CCL+14, Kir14, NAL15, PWA+16, FL17, PRSV17]. Constructions of unidirectional PRE schemes have also been shown to exist from bilinear maps [AFGH06, LV11]; however, these constructions are restricted to the *single-hop* setting in the sense that they only permit a single re-encryption of a ciphertext. Known constructions of unidirectional UE include the construction in [SS21] (which relies on bilinear maps), and two constructions in [Nis21] (one which achieves backward-leak key updates from lattice-specific techniques, and one which achieves no-directional key updates from iO). Sehrawat and Desmedt show a construction of UE from bi-homomorphic lattice-based pseudorandom functions [SD19]; however, their construction only achieves unidirectional ciphertext updates while still incurring bidirectional key updates (and is hence effectively bidirectional as per the recent findings in [Jia20]). To date, there exist no constructions of unidirectional PRE or UE from the plain DDH assumption (to our knowledge).

In this paper, we are motivated by the following longstanding open question in the study of UE and PRE:

> *Do unidirectional UE and PRE schemes necessarily require stronger/more structured assumptions as compared to their bidirectional counterparts?*

More concretely, we ask the following question:

> *Can we construct unidirectional UE/PRE schemes from DDH?*

1.1 Our Results

In this paper, we bridge this gap between the assumptions for unidirectional and bidirectional UE/PRE. We establish (somewhat surprisingly) that unidirectional UE and PRE schemes *do not*, in fact, require stronger/more structured cryptographic assumptions as compared to their bidirectional counterparts.

More concretely, we present generic constructions of unidirectional UE and PRE from a new primitive that we call Key and Plaintext Homomorphic Encryption (KPHE). We also show that such a KPHE scheme can be instantiated from the BHHO encryption scheme [BHHO08] based on the DDH assumption. This yields the first constructions of unidirectional UE and PRE from the plain DDH assumption.

Our main result is summarized by the following (informal) theorem:

Theorem 1 (Informal). *Assuming the existence of a Key and Plaintext Homomorphic Encryption (KPHE) scheme that satisfies certain special properties, there exist post-compromise secure unidirectional UE and PRE schemes.*

On KPHE. The KPHE scheme with special properties required in our constructions can be viewed as a generalization of the BHHO public-key encryption scheme due to Boneh et al. [BHHO08]. It is a public key encryption scheme where the secret key is a bit-string $sk \in \{0,1\}^{\ell}$ and the plaintext is also a bit-string $m \in \{0,1\}^{\ell'}$ (in our constructions we use $\ell = \ell' = 2n$). The specialized KPHE scheme satisfies the following three properties:

- **Distributional Semantic Security:** We require a KPHE scheme to achieve semantic security even when the secret keys are sampled from a specific distribution. In particular, we use KPHE schemes with $2n$-bit secret keys where the secret key is uniformly random subject to the constraint that it has equally many 0 and 1 bits (i,e., n bits of 0 and n bits of 1).
- **Additive Key and Plaintext Homomorphisms:** We require a KPHE scheme to satisfy the following property: let T, T' be two arbitrary affine transformations that map 0–1 vectors to 0–1 vectors of the same length (in our constructions we use permutation maps over the bits of a $2n$-bit string). Then, given a public key pk corresponding to some secret key sk and a ciphertext $ct \xleftarrow{\$} Enc(pk, m)$, one can generate a public key pk' corresponding to the secret key $T(sk)$ and a ciphertext $ct' \xleftarrow{\$} Enc(pk', T'(m))$, without the knowledge of the original secret key sk or the original message m.
- **Blinding:** We also require the KPHE scheme to satisfy an associated security property called "blinding", that (informally) argues that the public key and ciphertext generated via the aforementioned homomorphic transformations are indistinguishable from freshly generated public keys and ciphertexts (we make this more formal in Sect. 2).

For our PRE constructions, we also require that the KPHE scheme satisfies a notion of distributional circular security (i.e., circular security when the secret keys are sampled from a specific distribution). This is not required for our UE constructions.

Instantiating KPHE. We show how to concretely instantiate a KPHE scheme satisfying all of the aforementioned properties from DDH (based on the BHHO scheme [BHHO08]).

Lemma 1 (Informal). *Assuming DDH, there exists a secure construction of KPHE that satisfies the aforementioned properties.*

Table 1. Summary of bi/unidirectional UE and PRE schemes. We focus on ciphertext-independent UE and multi-hop PRE. In this table, "bi, uni, bwd-uni, no" stand for bidirectional, unidirectional, backward-leak unidirectional, no-directional, respectively. We note that the notion of *key-directionality* differs for UE and PRE; in the case of UE, unidirectionality of key updates implies that, given the source (secret) key and the update token, the destination (secret) key can be computed. This is not the case for PRE, where unidirectional key update simply denotes that the re-key generation algorithm takes as input the source secret key and the destination public key (as opposed to bidirectional key update, where the re-key generation algorithm takes as input both secret keys).

	scheme	dir. (ctx)	dir. (key)	security	assumption
UE	[BLMR13]	bi	bi	IND-ENC	DDH/LWE
UE	[LT18, KLR19, BDGJ20]	bi	bi	IND-UE	DDH
UE	[Jia20]	bi	bi	IND-UE	DLWE
UE	[SD19]	uni	bi	IND-UE	LWE
UE	[Nis21]	uni	bwd-uni	IND-UE	LWE
UE	[Nis21]	uni	no	IND-UE	iO
UE	[SS21]	uni	no	IND-UE	SXDH
UE	Ours	uni	bwd-uni	IND-UE	DDH
PRE	[BBS98]	bi	bi	IND-CPA	DDH
PRE	[CCL+14]	uni	uni	IND-CPA	DLWE
PRE	[PWA+16]	uni	uni	IND-CCA	LWE
PRE	[PRSV17]	uni	uni	IND-CPA	RLWE
PRE	Ours	uni	uni	IND-HRA	DDH

Corollary 1 (Informal). *Assuming DDH, there exist post-compromise secure unidirectional UE and PRE schemes.*

Security of Our Constructions. Our constructions of unidirectional UE and PRE achieve the strongest notions of *post-compromise security* in the standard model. Our construction of unidirectional UE achieves the state-of-the-art post-compromise security definition due to Boyd et al. [BDGJ20], while also ensuring backward-leak unidirectional key updates [Nis21]. Our unidirectional PRE construction achieves the post-compromise security definition recently proposed by Davidson et al. [DDLM19], which is, to our knowledge, the only notion of post-compromise PRE security to be proposed to date. We present a more detailed discussion on post-compromise security (and other related security notions) of UE and PRE in the next subsection. Table 1 presents a comparison of our results with those in the existing literature.

1.2   Background and Related Work

There has been extensive research on both UE and PRE, including various settings, definitions, and constructions. Below we only mention works that are the most directly relevant. For both UE and PRE, we focus on the CPA-type definitions, which are by far the most well-studied notions.

Security Notions for UE. Since the introduction of UE in [BLMR13], several works have explored its security notions [EPRS17, LT18, AMP19, KLR19, BDGJ20, Jia20]. Most notable is the work of Lehmann and Tackmann [LT18], which improved the model and studied the notion of post-compromise security for UE. Their Indistinguishability of Update notion (IND-UPD) returns a challenge ciphertext ct^* which is either the re-encryption of a ciphertext ct_0 or ct_1. A scheme is IND-UPD secure if an adversary is unable to determine which of the ciphertexts was re-encrypted.

In subsequent works a stronger combined notion of IND-UE security has been used, first defined by Boyd et al. [BDGJ20]. The IND-UE notion requires an adversary be unable to distinguish between a fresh encryption of a plaintext m and the re-encryption of a ciphertext ct. As a result this notion captures both CPA (specifically IND-ENC) and IND-UPD security.

Security Notions for PRE. In the context of PRE, the traditional notion of IND-CPA security [ID03, AFGH06] have been shown to be insufficient in practice. To address this, Cohen [Coh19] introduced the notion of Honest Re-Encryption Attack (HRA) security where an adversary is additionally permitted to re-encrypt (from honest to corrupt users) ciphertexts previously output by the encryption oracle. While only recently considered in the analysis of PRE, the essence of this notion is also fundamental in formalizing security for UE.

More recently, Davidson et al. [DDLM19] have investigated achieving post-compromise secure PRE schemes. They introduced a notion of IND-PCS security for PRE, which can be viewed as the analogue of IND-UPD security of UE in the context of PRE, albeit for more complex re-encryption graphs. To date this is the only paper that studies the PCS security of PRE schemes. Their work again demonstrates the challenges in constructing such schemes in the unidirectional setting. They discuss two PCS-secure constructions which are based on a prior unidirectional PRE scheme, Construction 7b of Fuchsbauer et al. [FKKP19] and an extension of BV-PRE [PRSV17].

Updatable Public Key Encryption. In order to achieve forward security in public key encryption (PKE), a notion called *updatable PKE (UPKE)* has recently been proposed and studied [JMM19, ACDT20, DKW21], where any sender (encryptor) can initiate a key update by sending a special update ciphertext to the receiver (decryptor). This ciphertext updates the public key and also, once processed by the receiver, will update its secret key. These are PKE schemes that encrypt messages under different public keys and aim to achieve forward security. In contrast, UE and PRE schemes studied in this paper aim to update ciphertexts encrypted under an old key to a new key without leaking the message content. The notions of UE/PRE as well as our techniques are very different from UPKE despite the partial naming collision.

Comparison with Umbral. There exists a practically deployed construction of unidirectional PRE, namely Umbral [Nun18], from the DDH Assumption, albeit in the random oracle model. It turns out that the Umbral construction is only single-hop, and focuses on achieving threshold PRE rather than multi-hop PRE. In particular, the Umbral construction crucially relies on the Diffie-Hellman key change, and it is unclear how to extend the construction to multiple hops. On the other hand, our primary aim is to achieve multi-hop unidirectional PRE in the traditional non-threshold setting. We note additionally that Umbral would not achieve post-compromise security, which is an important property provided by our constructions. Fundamentally, this is due to the fact that Umbral adopts a KEM-DEM style approach where only the KEM is re-encrypted.

Concurrent Work. A concurrent work by Galteland and Pan [GP23] constructs unidirectional UE with backward-leak unidirectional key update from public key encryption (PKE) schemes with certain properties, which can be realized from the DDH or LWE assumption. Their techniques are significantly different from ours and do not trivially extend to the PRE setting. The authors of [GP23] also demonstrate a formal proof that the security definition for unidirectional UE with backward-leak unidirectional key updates is equivalent to the one with no-directional key updates, which confirms our observation discussed earlier.

1.3 Technical Overview

In this section, we provide a high-level overview of our techniques for constructing unidirectional UE and PRE from any generic KPHE scheme satisfying the special properties described earlier.

IND-ENC Secure UE. Our first attempt is to build a unidirectional IND-ENC secure UE scheme, and we start with a naïve idea. Take an arbitrary symmetric-key encryption scheme and each epoch key is a freshly generated key of this encryption scheme. The update token Δ_e from k_{e-1} to k_e is an encryption of k_{e-1} under k_e, namely $\Delta_e = \mathsf{Enc}_{k_e}(k_{e-1})$. When we update a ciphertext from epoch $(e-1)$ to epoch e, we just attach the update token Δ_e to the end of the ciphertext. For a message m first encrypted in epoch e and then updated through epoch e', the resulting ciphertext is of the form:

$$\mathsf{ct}_{e'} = \left(\mathsf{Enc}_{k_e}(m), \mathsf{Enc}_{k_{e+1}}(k_e), \ldots, \mathsf{Enc}_{k_{e'}}(k_{e'-1})\right).$$

Given $k_{e'}$, one can easily decrypt $\mathsf{ct}_{e'}$ layer by layer to recover m.

   This naïve approach does not achieve IND-ENC security. We show a concrete attack in the following. Let e^* be the challenge epoch and m^* be the challenge message queried by the adversary. Let $\mathsf{ct}_{e^*} = \mathsf{Enc}_{k_{e^*}}(m^*)$ be the challenge ciphertext. To extract the secret key k_{e^*}, the adversary proceeds as follows. It first queries for an encryption of an arbitrary message m in epoch 0 and then updates it to epoch e (for some $e > e^*$) via a sequence of update queries. This way the adversary obtains a ciphertext of m of the form:

$$\mathsf{ct}_e = \left(\mathsf{Enc}_{k_0}(m), \mathsf{Enc}_{k_1}(k_0), \ldots, \mathsf{Enc}_{k_e}(k_{e-1})\right).$$

Now the adversary corrupts the secret key k_e. Then it can recover all the previous keys from k_0 to k_{e-1} (including k_{e^*}) during decryption of the ciphertext ct_e.

Nonetheless, this simple approach demonstrates some nice properties of uni-directionality. For key updates, it is impossible to derive k_e from k_{e-1} and Δ_e. For ciphertext updates, given a *fresh* ciphertext ct_e in epoch e and the previous update token Δ_e (from epoch $(e-1)$ to e), it is impossible to transition the ciphertext ct_e to the previous epoch ct_{e-1} (i.e. the epoch prior to its existence). In fact, Cohen [Coh19] applied this idea to PRE and showed a CPA-secure but not HRA-secure PRE scheme (HRA security is inherently required in IND-ENC UE schemes).

Re-randomizing the Secret Keys. The problem with these chained cipher-texts is that during decryption of a single ciphertext, all the previous secret keys are also leaked. To resolve this problem, our hope is to somehow re-randomize all the previous secret keys in the chain, in a consistent and homomorphic manner. In particular, we want the ciphertext to be of the form

$$ct_e = \left(Enc_{\overline{k}_0}(m), Enc_{\overline{k}_1}(\overline{k}_0), \ldots, Enc_{\overline{k}_{e-1}}(\overline{k}_{e-2}), Enc_{k_e}(\overline{k}_{e-1}) \right),$$

where $\overline{k}_0, \overline{k}_1, \ldots, \overline{k}_{e-1}$ are all re-randomized secret keys that are different for each ciphertext. During the decryption of ct_e, only these re-randomized secret keys are leaked, which does not affect the security of other ciphertexts.

To enable such re-randomization, our idea is inspired by the re-randomizable Yao's garbled circuits [GHV10]. We propose a new primitive called Key and Plaintext Homomorphic Encryption (KPHE), which can be seen as a gener-alization of the circular secure encryption scheme of Boneh et al. [BHHO08]. Instead of using an arbitrary symmetric-key encryption scheme, we use the KPHE scheme for encryption, where the UE secret key k_e is a key pair (pk_e, sk_e) of the KPHE scheme. The update token is a KPHE encryption of the previous epoch's secret key under the current epoch's public key, namely $\Delta_e = KPHE.Enc_{pk_e}(sk_{e-1})$.

To update a ciphertext we exploit the two homomorphism properties of the KPHE scheme, in both the message space and the key space. Given an update token Δ_e and a ciphertext of the form

$$ct_{e-1} = \left(KPHE.Enc_{\overline{pk}_0}(m), KPHE.Enc_{\overline{pk}_1}(\overline{sk}_0), \ldots, KPHE.Enc_{pk_{e-1}}(\overline{sk}_{e-2}) \right),$$

we focus on the last component $ctx = KPHE.Enc_{pk_{e-1}}(\overline{sk}_{e-2})$ and the update token $\Delta_e = KPHE.Enc_{pk_e}(sk_{e-1})$, In our update operation we first generate a random permutation π and then perform two important steps:

- Use the KPHE key-space homomorphism to transform ctx from an encryption under sk_{e-1} to an encryption under $\pi(sk_{e-1})$.
- Use the KPHE message-space homomorphism to transform Δ_e from an encryption of sk_{e-1} to an encryption of $\pi(sk_{e-1})$.

The updated ciphertext becomes

$$\mathsf{ct}_e = \Big(\mathsf{KPHE.Enc}_{\overline{\mathsf{pk}}_0}(\mathsf{m}), \mathsf{KPHE.Enc}_{\overline{\mathsf{pk}}_1}(\overline{\mathsf{sk}}_0), \ldots, \mathsf{KPHE.Enc}_{\overline{\mathsf{pk}}_{e-1}}(\overline{\mathsf{sk}}_{e-2}), \mathsf{KPHE.Enc}_{\mathsf{pk}_e}(\overline{\mathsf{sk}}_{e-1})\Big),$$

where $\overline{\mathsf{sk}}_{e-1} = \pi(\mathsf{sk}_{e-1})$ (with corresponding public key $\overline{\mathsf{pk}}_{e-1}$). In our construction, the KPHE secret key is a $2n$-bit string, which is randomly sampled with exactly n bits of 0 and n bits of 1. The affine transformation π is a random permutation on the $2n$ bits of the string. By transforming from sk_{e-1} to $\overline{\mathsf{sk}}_{e-1}$ we ensure that a fresh secret key is used for each update operation and hence there is appropriate isolation between all ciphertexts updated in a given epoch. The blinding property of KPHE ensures that re-randomization can be done without knowledge of the underlying secret keys, and that the re-randomized ciphertexts are computationally indistinguishable from freshly generated ciphertexts.

Use of Balanced KPHE Keys. The astute reader might have noticed that we use "balanced" secret keys for our KPHE scheme, wherein each secret key is a randomly sampled $2n$-bit string with exactly n bits of 0 and n bits of 1. The restriction is required to offset some leakage that our scheme incurs during the honest re-encryption query phase in the security proofs. Informally, the adversary can use a sequence of honest re-encryption queries to learn some information about the intermediate (re-randomized) secret keys; in particular, it learns the number of 0 and 1 bits in each secret key. Intuitively, we offset this leakage by specifying at setup that all secret keys have an equal number of 0 and 1 entries. As a result, the adversary learns no additional information about these intermediate keys, irrespective of the number of honest re-encryption queries that it issues. We defer a formal treatment to the detailed proofs of security for our constructions.

Achieving Post-Compromise Secure UE. We can extend the IND-ENC secure UE construction to achieve post-compromise security. To achieve IND-UPD security, we can modify the update operation to ensure that all the chained ciphertexts are updated (rather than just the last one). In effect what our enhanced construction does is again exploit properties of the KPHE scheme to re-randomize each of the ciphertext components. This ensures that two updated ciphertexts of the same length are computationally indistinguishable. To further achieve the combined IND-UE security, we need to additionally guarantee that a freshly generated ciphertext has the same length as an updated ciphertext in a certain epoch. More details on our UE constructions are given in Sect. 3.

Achieving Unidirectional PRE. We can use the same high-level approach to construct a unidirectional PRE scheme, where a ciphertext consists of a chain of KPHE ciphertexts, and re-encryption exploits the two KPHE homomorphisms to transform each new KPHE ciphertext to a fresh secret key. The crucial subtlety in the PRE case, which makes proving security slightly more involved, is that we no longer consider sequential ciphertext updates but must consider re-encryption between all possible key pairs. As a result we need to further exploit the circular security properties of the KPHE scheme to prove security. This is further detailed in Sect. 4.

Connections between UE and PRE. Generally speaking, unidirectional PRE can be viewed as a stronger primitive than unidirectional UE because UE only allows for sequential updates while PRE allows for re-encryption between every pair of keys. In fact, we observe that if we treat the public-secret key pair of PRE as a secret key for UE, and the PRE re-encryption key as an update token for UE, then IND-HRA secure PRE implies IND-ENC secure UE, and IND-PCS secure PRE implies IND-UPD secure UE. This is also why our constructions for unidirectional UE and PRE follow a very similar framework. On the other hand, since PRE supports re-encryption between (potentially) every pair of keys, our constructions of PRE require stronger security guarantees (in particular, circular security) from the underlying KPHE scheme.

Efficiency and Feasibility. We acknowledge that the ciphertext length in our UE/PRE constructions grows linearly with the number of epochs/re-encryption hops, unlike certain existing constructions (e.g. in [Nis21, PWA+16, PRSV17]) where the ciphertext size remains the same. In this context, we emphasize that our paper is the first to achieve backward-leak unidirectional UE and unidirectional PRE from standard assumptions, specifically DDH. It has been a long-standing open problem for over a decade whether obfuscation/FHE is necessary for unidirectional UE/(multi-hop) PRE, and our work closes this assumption gap. As a result, we believe that our results should be viewed with emphasis on the new theoretical insights/understanding into unidirectional-UE/PRE that they enable as opposed to concrete efficiency. Our work opens up the discussion of whether obfuscation/FHE is necessary for achieving unidirectional UE/PRE with "succinctness" in the ciphertext length.

We note that in the UE setting, key rotation may only happen a small number of times in practice. For example, once a year for the lifetime of the ciphertext (say 10years). Thus, taking a similar approach to [BEKS20] (from the ciphertext-dependent setting) we could bound the number of updates and have fixed-length ciphertexts through some form of padding. We also point out that while the size of ciphertexts in our general constructions grow linearly, the secret keys and update tokens/re-encryption keys remain constant-sized. We also note that for the basic versions of our UE/PRE construction (IND-CPA unidirectional UE and IND-HRA secure unidirectional PRE), the work done per update/re-encryption operation is also constant (independent of the number of epochs/update hops).

We note here that a naïve approach to achieving unidirectional UE is the so called "download–decrypt–re-encrypt–upload" approach, where the client downloads the encrypted data (e.g. from the server storing the encrypted data), locally decrypts it, re-encrypts it using the new key, and re-uploads the newly encrypted data to the server. Our UE constructions are non-trivial in the sense that we achieve significantly better properties as compared to this naïve approach. In particular, for applications of UE (e.g. key rotation) where the client outsources encrypted data to the server, this entails constant computational/ communication/storage overheads at the client during key rotation (the client simply generates and sends the update token to the server); the corresponding client-overheads are linear (in database size) in the naïve solution.

Using Random Oracles. A possible approach towards achieving practical efficiency is to use random oracles (such as in the single-hop unidirectional threshold PRE scheme Umbral [Nun18]). Our focus is primarily on feasibility results for unidirectional UE/PRE in the standard model, and we consciously avoid the use of random oracles. We also point out that a previous result [AMP19] showed that, even in the symmetric-key setting, unidirectional UE/PRE implies public-key encryption, and so a construction from just a random oracle is unlikely. However, it might be possible to achieve efficiency gains using a random oracle. We leave investigating such a random oracle-based construction of unidirectional UE/PRE as an interesting direction of future research.

1.4 Paper Outline

The rest of the paper is organized as follows. Section 2 formally defines a KPHE scheme and its associated security properties. Section 3 presents our constructions of IND-CPA and IND-UPD secure UE from any KPHE scheme. Section 4 presents our construction of IND-HRA secure PRE from any KPHE scheme. We defer detailed proofs of security for these schemes, our constructions of IND-UE secure UE and IND-PCS secure PRE from any KPHE scheme, and the instantiation of KPHE from DDH to the full version of our paper [MPW22].

For readers not familiar with the formal definitions of UE and PRE, we present relatively self-contained background material on UE and PRE in Sects. 3.1 and 4.1, respectively. Due to lack of space, the formal security notions of PRE are deferred to the full version of our paper [MPW22].

1.5 Notations

We summarize here the notations used in the rest of the paper. We write $x \xleftarrow{\$} \chi$ to represent that an element x is sampled randomly from a set/distribution $\mathcal{X}$. The output x of a deterministic (resp. randomized) algorithm $\mathcal{A}$ is denoted by $x = \mathcal{A}$ (resp. $x \xleftarrow{\$} \mathcal{A}$). For $a \in \mathbb{N}$ such that $a \geq 1$, we denote by $[a]$ the set of integers lying between 1 and a (both inclusive). We refer to $\lambda \in \mathbb{N}$ as the security parameter, and denote by $\text{poly}(\lambda)$ and $\text{negl}(\lambda)$ any generic (unspecified) polynomial function and negligible function in λ, respectively.

2 Key and Plaintext Homomorphic Encryption

In this section, we present the definitions for the core building block for our constructions, namely key and plaintext homomorphic encryption (KPHE). Informally, a KPHE scheme has the following features:

- **Keys and Plaintexts:** Each secret key sk is an ℓ-bit string for some $\ell = \text{poly}(\lambda)$ (λ being the security parameter). Additionally, each plaintext message m is an ℓ'-bit string for some $\ell' = \text{poly}(\lambda)$.
- **Key Distribution:** Each secret key is sampled according to some distribution $\mathcal{D}$ over $\{0,1\}^\ell$. In particular, for our applications, we assume KPHE schemes where each secret key sk is a $2n$-bit string with equally many 0 and 1 entries.
- **Key Homomorphism:** Let T be any linear transformation that maps ℓ-bit strings to ℓ-bit strings. Then, it is possible to efficiently evaluate the following:
  - Given a public key pk corresponding to some secret key $\text{sk} \in \{0,1\}^\ell$, it is possible to efficiently compute a valid public key pk' corresponding to the transformed secret key $\text{sk}' = T(\text{sk})$, without the knowledge of sk.
  - Given a ciphertext ct encrypting a message m under some secret key $\text{sk} \in \{0,1\}^\ell$, it is possible to efficiently compute a ciphertext ct' encrypting the same message m under the transformed secret key $\text{sk}' = T(\text{sk})$, without the knowledge of sk.
- **Plaintext Homomorphism:** Let T' be any linear transformation that maps ℓ'-bit strings to ℓ'-bit strings. Then, given a ciphertext ct encrypting a message $\text{m} \in \{0,1\}^{\ell'}$ under some secret key sk, it is possible to efficiently compute a ciphertext ct'' encrypting the transformed message $\text{m}' = T'(\text{m})$ under the same secret key sk.

We now summarize these features of KPHE formally below.

Definition 1 (KPHE). *A KPHE scheme is a tuple of PPT algorithms of the form* KPHE = (Setup, SKGen, PKGen, Enc, Dec, Eval) *that are defined as follows:*

- pp $\xleftarrow{\$}$ Setup(1^λ): *On input the security parameter λ, the setup algorithm outputs a public parameter* pp.
- sk $\xleftarrow{\$}$ SKGen(pp, $\mathcal{D}$): *On input the public parameter* pp *and a distribution $\mathcal{D}$ over $\{0,1\}^\ell$ (for $\ell = \text{poly}(\lambda)$), the secret key generation algorithm outputs a secret key* sk $\xleftarrow{\$} \mathcal{D}$.
- pk $\xleftarrow{\$}$ PKGen(pp, sk): *On input the public parameter* pp *and a secret key* sk $\in \{0,1\}^\ell$, *the public key generation algorithm outputs a public key* pk.
- ct $\xleftarrow{\$}$ Enc(pk, m): *On input a public key* pk *and a message* $\text{m} \in \{0,1\}^{\ell'}$ (for $\ell' = \text{poly}(\lambda)$), *the encryption algorithm outputs a ciphertext* ct.
- m/$\perp$ $\xleftarrow{\$}$ Dec(sk, ct): *On input a secret key* sk $\in \{0,1\}^\ell$ *and a ciphertext* ct, *the decryption algorithm outputs a plaintext message string* m *or an error symbol* $\perp$.
- (pk', ct') $\xleftarrow{\$}$ Eval(pk, ct, T, T'): *On input a public key* pk, *a ciphertext* ct, *and a pair of (linear) transformations $T : \{0,1\}^\ell \rightarrow \{0,1\}^\ell$ and $T' : \{0,1\}^{\ell'} \rightarrow \{0,1\}^{\ell'}$, the homomorphic evaluation algorithm outputs a tuple consisting of a transformed public key and a transformed ciphertext* (pk', ct').

Correctness. A KPHE scheme (Setup, SKGen, PKGen, Enc, Dec, Eval) is said to be correct with respect to a distribution $\mathcal{D}$ over $\{0,1\}^\ell$ if for any pp $\xleftarrow{\$}$ Setup(1^λ), any sk $\xleftarrow{\$}$ SKGen(pp, $\mathcal{D}$), any pk $\xleftarrow{\$}$ PKGen(pp, sk), any m $\in \{0,1\}^{\ell'}$, and any pair of (linear) transformations $T : \{0,1\}^\ell \to \{0,1\}^\ell$ and $T' : \{0,1\}^{\ell'} \to \{0,1\}^{\ell'}$, letting sk$' = T(\text{sk})$, m$' = T'(\text{m})$ and

$$\text{ct} \xleftarrow{\$} \text{Enc}(\text{pk}, \text{m}), \quad (\text{pk}', \text{ct}') \xleftarrow{\$} \text{Eval}(\text{pk}, \text{ct}, T, T'),$$

both of the following hold with overwhelmingly large probability:

- pk$'$ is a valid public key with respect to sk$' = T(\text{sk})$, i.e., for any $\bar{\text{m}} \in \{0,1\}^{\ell'}$, it holds that $\text{Dec}(\text{sk}', \text{Enc}(\text{pk}', \bar{\text{m}})) = \bar{\text{m}}$.
- ct$'$ is a valid encryption of m$'$ under (pk', sk'), i.e., $\text{Dec}(\text{sk}', \text{ct}') = \text{m}'$.

Distributional Semantic Security. We (informally) say that a KPHE satisfies distributional semantic security with respect to some distribution $\mathcal{D}$ over $\{0,1\}^\ell$ if it remains semantically secure even when the secret key sk is sampled according to the distribution $\mathcal{D}$. Formally, this is modeled using a semantic security game where the secret key is sampled by the challenger as per the distribution $\mathcal{D}$.

Definition 2 ($\mathcal{D}$-Semantic Security). *A KPHE scheme with ℓ-bit secret keys is said to be $\mathcal{D}$-semantically secure with respect to a distribution $\mathcal{D}$ over $\{0,1\}^\ell$ if for any security parameter $\lambda \in \mathbb{N}$ and any PPT adversary $\mathcal{A}$, the following holds with overwhelmingly large probability:*

$$| \Pr[\text{Expt}_{\mathcal{D}}^{\text{DSS-KPHE}}(\lambda, \mathcal{A}) = 1] - 1/2 | < \text{negl}(\lambda),$$

where the experiment $\text{Expt}_{\mathcal{D}}^{\text{DSS-KPHE}}(\lambda, \mathcal{A})$ is as defined in Fig. 1.

Distributional Circular Security. We (informally) say that a KPHE satisfies distributional circular security with respect to some distribution $\mathcal{D}$ over $\{0,1\}^\ell$ if it satisfies the standard notion of circular security [CL01, BRS02, BHHO08, ACPS09] even when each secret key is sampled from the distribution $\mathcal{D}$. Formally, this is modeled using a circular security game where the secret keys are sampled by the challenger as per the distribution $\mathcal{D}$.

Definition 3 ($\mathcal{D}$-Circular Security). *A KPHE scheme with ℓ-bit secret keys and ℓ-bit messages is said to be $\mathcal{D}$-circular secure with respect to a distribution $\mathcal{D}$ over $\{0,1\}^\ell$ if for any security parameter $\lambda \in \mathbb{N}$ and any PPT adversary $\mathcal{A}$, the following holds with overwhelmingly large probability:*

$$| \Pr[\text{Expt}_{\mathcal{D}}^{\text{DCC-KPHE}}(\lambda, \mathcal{A}) = 1] - 1/2 | < \text{negl}(\lambda),$$

where the experiment $\text{Expt}_{\mathcal{D}}^{\text{DCC-KPHE}}(\lambda, \mathcal{A})$ is as defined in Fig. 2.

Experiment $\mathsf{Expt}_{\mathcal{D}}^{\mathsf{DSS-KPHE}}(\lambda, \mathcal{A})$:

1. The challenger generates $\mathsf{pp} \xleftarrow{\$} \mathsf{Setup}(1^\lambda)$, $\mathsf{sk} \xleftarrow{\$} \mathsf{SKGen}(\mathsf{pp}, \mathcal{D})$, and $\mathsf{pk} \xleftarrow{\$}$ $\mathsf{PKGen}(\mathsf{pp}, \mathsf{sk})$, and provides the adversary $\mathcal{A}$ with $(\mathsf{pp}, \mathsf{pk})$.
2. The adversary $\mathcal{A}$ issues a challenge encryption query for a pair of messages $(\mathsf{m}_0, \mathsf{m}_1)$.
3. The challenger samples $b \xleftarrow{\$} \{0, 1\}$, creates the challenge ciphertext

$$\mathsf{ct}^* \xleftarrow{\$} \mathsf{Enc}(\mathsf{pk}, \mathsf{m}_b),$$

   and sends ct^* to the adversary $\mathcal{A}$.
4. The adversary $\mathcal{A}$ outputs a bit $b' \in \{0, 1\}$.
5. Output 1 if $b = b'$ and 0 otherwise.

Fig. 1. The $\mathcal{D}$-Semantic Security Experiment for KPHE

Experiment $\mathsf{Expt}_{\mathcal{D}}^{\mathsf{DCC-KPHE}}(\lambda, \mathcal{A})$:

1. The challenger generates $\mathsf{pp} \xleftarrow{\$} \mathsf{Setup}(1^\lambda)$ and provides it to the adversary.
2. The adversary $\mathcal{A}$ outputs $n = \mathrm{poly}(\lambda)$.
3. The challenger samples $\mathsf{sk}_1, \ldots, \mathsf{sk}_n \xleftarrow{\$} \mathsf{SKGen}(\mathsf{pp}, \mathcal{D})$, sets

$$\mathsf{pk}_1 \xleftarrow{\$} \mathsf{PKGen}(\mathsf{pp}, \mathsf{sk}_1), \ldots, \mathsf{pk}_n \xleftarrow{\$} \mathsf{PKGen}(\mathsf{pp}, \mathsf{sk}_n),$$

   and provides $(\mathsf{pk}_1, \ldots, \mathsf{pk}_n)$ to the adversary $\mathcal{A}$.
4. The challenger also sets the following for each $i, j \in [n]$:

$$\mathsf{ct}_{i,j,0} \xleftarrow{\$} \mathsf{Enc}(\mathsf{pk}_i, \mathsf{sk}_j), \quad \mathsf{ct}_{i,j,1} \xleftarrow{\$} \mathsf{Enc}(\mathsf{pk}_i, 0^{|\mathsf{sk}_j|}).$$

5. The challenger finally samples a bit $b \xleftarrow{\$} \{0, 1\}$ and provides the adversary $\mathcal{A}$ with the ensemble $\{\mathsf{ct}_{i,j,b}\}_{i,j\in[n]}$.
6. The adversary $\mathcal{A}$ outputs a bit $b' \in \{0, 1\}$.
7. Output 1 if $b = b'$ and 0 otherwise.

Fig. 2. The $\mathcal{D}$-Circular Security Experiment for KPHE

Blinding. We (informally) say that a KPHE scheme satisfies public key and ciphertext blinding if the homomorphic evaluation algorithm outputs a public key-ciphertext pair $(\mathsf{pk}', \mathsf{ct}')$ corresponding to the transformed secret key sk' and the transformed message m' such that:

- The transformed public key pk' is computationally indistinguishable from a public key sampled uniformly at random from the set of all valid public keys corresponding to the secret key sk'.
- The transformed ciphertext ct' is computationally indistinguishable from a ciphertext sampled uniformly at random from the set of all valid ciphertexts corresponding to the transformed message m' under pk'.

Experiment $\mathsf{Expt}_{\mathcal{D}}^{\mathsf{Blind-KPHE}}(\lambda, \mathcal{A})$:

1. The challenger generates $\mathsf{pp} \overset{\$}{\leftarrow} \mathsf{Setup}(1^{\lambda})$, $\mathsf{sk} \overset{\$}{\leftarrow} \mathcal{D}$, and $\mathsf{pk} \overset{\$}{\leftarrow} \mathsf{PKGen}(\mathsf{pp}, \mathsf{sk})$, and provides the adversary $\mathcal{A}$ with $(\mathsf{pp}, \mathsf{sk}, \mathsf{pk})$.
2. The adversary $\mathcal{A}$ sends a message $\mathsf{m} \in \{0, 1\}^{\ell'}$ to the challenger.
3. The challenger responds to $\mathcal{A}$ with a ciphertext $\mathsf{ct} \overset{\$}{\leftarrow} \mathsf{Enc}(\mathsf{pk}, \mathsf{m})$.
4. The adversary $\mathcal{A}$ then sends a pair of (linear) transformations

$$T : \{0, 1\}^{\ell} \to \{0, 1\}^{\ell}, \quad T' : \{0, 1\}^{\ell'} \to \{0, 1\}^{\ell'}.$$

5. The challenger sets
$$\mathsf{sk}' = T(\mathsf{sk}), \quad \mathsf{m}' = T'(\mathsf{m}),$$
and computes the following:

$$(\mathsf{pk}_0, \mathsf{ct}_0) \overset{\$}{\leftarrow} \mathsf{Eval}(\mathsf{pk}, \mathsf{ct}, T, T'), \quad \mathsf{pk}_1 \overset{\$}{\leftarrow} \mathsf{PKGen}(\mathsf{pp}, \mathsf{sk}'), \quad \mathsf{ct}_1 \overset{\$}{\leftarrow} \mathsf{Enc}(\mathsf{pk}_1, \mathsf{m}'),$$

6. The challenger finally samples a bit $b \overset{\$}{\leftarrow} \{0, 1\}$ and provides the adversary $\mathcal{A}$ with $(\mathsf{pk}_b, \mathsf{ct}_b)$.
7. The adversary $\mathcal{A}$ outputs a bit $b' \in \{0, 1\}$.
8. Output 1 if $b = b'$ and 0 otherwise.

Fig. 3. The Blinding Experiment for KPHE

More formally, we define this blinding property as follows.

Definition 4 (Blinding). *A KPHE scheme with ℓ-bit secret keys and ℓ'-bit messages is said to satisfy blinding security with respect to a distribution $\mathcal{D}$ over $\{0, 1\}^{\ell}$ if for any security parameter $\lambda \in \mathbb{N}$ and any PPT adversary $\mathcal{A}$, the following holds with overwhelmingly large probability:*

$$| \Pr[\mathsf{Expt}_{\mathcal{D}}^{\mathsf{Blind-KPHE}}(\lambda, \mathcal{A}) = 1] - 1/2 | < \mathrm{negl}(\lambda),$$

where the experiment $\mathsf{Expt}_{\mathcal{D}}^{\mathsf{Blind-KPHE}}(\lambda, \mathcal{A})$ is as defined in Fig. 3.

KPHE from DDH. In full version of our paper [MPW22], we prove the following (informal) theorem:

Theorem 2 (Informal). *Assuming DDH, there exists a KPHE scheme with $2n$-bit secret keys that satisfies distributional semantic security with respect to the distribution $\mathcal{U}_n$, distributional circular security with respect to the distribution $\mathcal{U}_n$, and blinding, as defined above.*

In particular, we rely on known results from [BHHO08, NS12, GHV10] for the DDH-based instantiation of KPHE. See [MPW22] for details.

KPHE from LWE. In this paper, we do not explicitly describe a construction of KPHE from LWE since there already exist constructions of unidirectional

UE/PRE from LWE [CCL+14, PWA+16, PRSV17, Nis21]. Our aim in this work is to close the gap between bidirectional and unidirectional constructions of UE/PRE in terms of assumptions, and so we choose to focus on the feasibility results from the DDH assumption.

We note, however, that constructing KPHE from LWE is a very interesting direction of future work. In particular, one needs to be careful during re-encryption, which potentially increases the level of noise in the ciphertext of the LWE-based encryption scheme and could leak extra information. For example, due to increase in the noise level during re-encryption, it is not straightforward to prove the ciphertext blinding property, which requires that a freshly created ciphertext and a re-encrypted ciphertext are distributed in an indistinguishable manner. This issue can be handled using noise flooding techniques, albeit at the cost of a larger ciphertext size.

KPHE from Other Assumptions. We also leave it as an interesting open question to construct KPHE from concrete hardness assumptions other than DDH or LWE (e.g., factorization-based assumptions or LPN). Given our results on achieving unidirectional UE/PRE from KPHE, such realizations of KPHE would immediately yield new constructions of unidirectional UE/PRE from these assumptions.

3   Unidirectional UE from KPHE

In this section, we show how to construct unidirectional UE satisfying various security notions (IND-ENC, IND-UPD and IND-UE) from any KPHE scheme.

3.1   Definition

Definition 5. *An updatable encryption (UE) scheme for message space $\mathcal{M}$ is a tuple of PPT algorithms* UE = (UE.setup, UE.next, UE.enc, UE.upd, UE.dec) *with the following syntax:*

- $k_0 \xleftarrow{\$} $ UE.setup(1^λ): *On input a security parameter 1^λ, it returns a secret key k_e for epoch $e = 0$.*
- $(k_{e+1}, \Delta_{e+1}) \xleftarrow{\$} $ UE.next(k_e): *On input a secret key k_e for epoch e, it outputs a new secret key k_{e+1} and an update token Δ_{e+1} for epoch $e + 1$.*
- $ct_e \xleftarrow{\$} $ UE.enc(k_e, m): *On input a secret key k_e for epoch e and a message $m \in \mathcal{M}$, it outputs a ciphertext ct_e.*
- $ct_{e+1} \xleftarrow{\$} $ UE.upd(Δ_{e+1}, ct_e): *On input a ciphertext ct_e from epoch e and the update token Δ_{e+1}, it returns the updated ciphertext ct_{e+1}.*
- $m'/\perp \leftarrow $ UE.dec(k_e, ct_e): *On input a ciphertext ct_e and a secret key k_e of some epoch e, it returns a message m' or $\perp$.*

Setup(1^λ):

  $k_0 \xleftarrow{\$} \text{UE.setup}(1^\lambda)$
  $e := 0; \text{phase} := 0$
  $\mathcal{L}, \widetilde{\mathcal{L}}, \mathcal{K}, \mathcal{T}, \mathcal{C} \xleftarrow{\$} \emptyset$

$\mathcal{O}.\text{enc}(m)$:

  $ct \xleftarrow{\$} \text{UE.enc}(k_e, m)$
  $\mathcal{L} := \mathcal{L} \cup \{(e, ct)\}$
  return ct

$\mathcal{O}.\text{next}$:

  $e := e + 1$
  $(k_e, \Delta_e) \xleftarrow{\$} \text{UE.next}(k_{e-1})$
  if phase $= 1$ **then**
    $\widetilde{ct}_e \xleftarrow{\$} \text{UE.upd}(\Delta_e, \widetilde{ct}_{e-1})$
    $\widetilde{\mathcal{L}} := \widetilde{\mathcal{L}} \cup \{(e, \widetilde{ct}_e)\}$

$\mathcal{O}.\text{upd}(ct_{e-1})$:

  if $(e - 1, ct_{e-1}) \notin \mathcal{L}$ **then**
    return $\bot$
  $ct_e \xleftarrow{\$} \text{UE.upd}(\Delta_e, ct_{e-1})$
  $\mathcal{L} := \mathcal{L} \cup \{(e, ct_e)\}$
  return ct_e

$\mathcal{O}.\text{corr}(inp, \hat{e})$:

  if $\hat{e} > e$ **then**
    return $\bot$
  if $inp = \text{key}$ **then**
    $\mathcal{K} := \mathcal{K} \cup \{\hat{e}\}$
    return $k_{\hat{e}}$
  if $inp = \text{token}$ **then**
    $\mathcal{T} := \mathcal{T} \cup \{\hat{e}\}$
    return $\Delta_{\hat{e}}$

$\mathcal{O}.\text{chall-IND-ENC}(\overline{m}_0, \overline{m}_1)$:

  if $|\overline{m}_0| \neq |\overline{m}_1|$ **then**
    return $\bot$
  phase $:= 1; \tilde{e} := e$
  $\widetilde{ct}_{\tilde{e}} \xleftarrow{\$} \text{UE.enc}(k_{\tilde{e}}, \overline{m}_b)$
  $\mathcal{C} := \mathcal{C} \cup \{\tilde{e}\}$
  $\widetilde{\mathcal{L}} := \widetilde{\mathcal{L}} \cup \{(\tilde{e}, \widetilde{ct}_{\tilde{e}})\}$
  return $\widetilde{ct}_{\tilde{e}}$

$\mathcal{O}.\text{chall-IND-UPD}(\overline{ct}_0, \overline{ct}_1)$:

  if $(e - 1, \overline{ct}_0) \notin \mathcal{L}$ **or** $(e - 1, \overline{ct}_1) \notin \mathcal{L}$ **or** $|\overline{ct}_0| \neq$
  $|\overline{ct}_1|$ **then**
    return $\bot$
  phase $:= 1; \tilde{e} := e$
  $\widetilde{ct}_{\tilde{e}} \xleftarrow{\$} \text{UE.upd}(\Delta_{\tilde{e}}, \overline{ct}_b)$
  $\mathcal{C} := \mathcal{C} \cup \{\tilde{e}\}$
  $\widetilde{\mathcal{L}} := \widetilde{\mathcal{L}} \cup \{(\tilde{e}, \widetilde{ct}_{\tilde{e}})\}$
  return $\widetilde{ct}_{\tilde{e}}$

$\mathcal{O}.\text{chall-IND-UE}(\overline{m}, \overline{ct})$:

  if $(e - 1, \overline{ct}) \notin \mathcal{L}$ **then**
    return $\bot$
  phase $:= 1; \tilde{e} := e$
  if $b = 0$ **then**
    $\widetilde{ct}_{\tilde{e}} \xleftarrow{\$} \text{UE.enc}(k_{\tilde{e}}, \overline{m})$
  else
    $\widetilde{ct}_{\tilde{e}} \xleftarrow{\$} \text{UE.upd}(\Delta_{\tilde{e}}, \overline{ct})$
  $\mathcal{C} := \mathcal{C} \cup \{\tilde{e}\}$
  $\widetilde{\mathcal{L}} := \widetilde{\mathcal{L}} \cup \{(\tilde{e}, \widetilde{ct}_{\tilde{e}})\}$
  return $\widetilde{ct}_{\tilde{e}}$

$\mathcal{O}.\text{upd}\widetilde{\mathcal{C}}$:

  if phase $= 0$ **then**
    return $\bot$
  $\mathcal{C} := \mathcal{C} \cup \{e\}$
  return $\widetilde{ct}_e$

Fig. 4. Oracles in security games for updatable encryption.

We stress that UE.next *generates a new key along with an update token, which follows from the definition in the work of Lehmann and Tackmann [LT18]. In our constructions, the update token* Δ_{e+1} *can also be generated from* k_e *and* k_{e+1}.

Definition 6 (Correctness). *Let* UE $=$ (UE.setup, UE.next, UE.enc, UE.upd, UE.dec) *be an updatable encryption scheme. We say* UE *is* correct *if for any* $m \in \mathcal{M}$, *any* $k_0 \xleftarrow{\$} \text{UE.setup}(1^\lambda)$, *any sequence of* $(k_1, \Delta_1), \ldots, (k_e, \Delta_e)$ *gener-*

ated as $(k_i, \Delta_i) \xleftarrow{\$} \mathsf{UE.next}(k_{i-1})$ for all $i \in [e]$, and for any $0 \leq \hat{e} \leq e$, let $\mathsf{ct}_{\hat{e}} \xleftarrow{\$} \mathsf{UE.enc}(k_{\hat{e}}, m)$ and $\mathsf{ct}_j \xleftarrow{\$} \mathsf{UE.upd}(\Delta_j, \mathsf{ct}_{j-1})$ for all $j = \hat{e} + 1, \ldots, e$, then $\mathsf{UE.dec}(k_e, \mathsf{ct}_e) = m$.

Confidentiality. The adversary $\mathcal{A}$ has access to the oracles defined in Fig. 4. We follow the bookkeeping techniques of [LT18, KLR19, BDGJ20, Jia20], using the following sets to keep track of the generated and updated ciphertexts, and the epochs in which the adversary corrupted a key or a token, or learned a version of the challenge-ciphertext.

- $\mathcal{L}$: Set of non-challenge ciphertexts (e, ct_e) produced by calls to the $\mathcal{O}.\mathsf{enc}$ or $\mathcal{O}.\mathsf{upd}$ oracle. $\mathcal{O}.\mathsf{upd}$ only updates ciphertexts obtained in $\mathcal{L}$.
- $\tilde{\mathcal{L}}$: Set of updated versions of the challenge ciphertexts $(e, \tilde{\mathsf{ct}}_e)$. $\tilde{\mathcal{L}}$ is initiated with the challenge ciphertext $(\tilde{e}, \tilde{\mathsf{ct}}_{\tilde{e}})$. Any call to the $\mathcal{O}.\mathsf{next}$ oracle automatically updates the challenge ciphertext to the new epoch, which the adversary can fetch via a call to $\mathcal{O}.\mathsf{updC}$.
- $\mathcal{K}$: Set of epochs e in which the adversary corrupted the secret key k_e (from $\mathcal{O}.\mathsf{corr}$).
- $\mathcal{T}$: Set of epochs e in which the adversary corrupted the update token Δ_e (from $\mathcal{O}.\mathsf{corr}$).
- $\mathcal{C}$: Set of epochs e in which the adversary learned a version of the challenge ciphertext (from $\mathcal{O}.\mathsf{chall}$ or $\mathcal{O}.\mathsf{updC}$).

We further define the epoch identification sets $\mathcal{C}^*, \mathcal{K}^*, \mathcal{T}^*$ as the extended sets of $\mathcal{C}, \mathcal{K}, \mathcal{T}$ in which the adversary learned or inferred information. We focus on *no-directional* key updates and *uni-directional* ciphertext updates.

$$\mathcal{K}^* := \mathcal{K}$$
$$\mathcal{T}^* := \{e \in \{0, \ldots, e_{\mathsf{end}}\} | (e \in \mathcal{T}) \vee (e - 1 \in \mathcal{K}^* \wedge e \in \mathcal{K}^*)\}$$
$$\mathcal{C}^* := \{e \in \{0, \ldots, e_{\mathsf{end}}\} | \mathsf{ChallEq}(e) = \mathsf{true}\}$$
$$\text{where } \mathsf{true} \leftarrow \mathsf{ChallEq}(e) \iff (e \in \mathcal{C}) \vee (\mathsf{ChallEq}(e - 1) \wedge e \in \mathcal{T}^*)$$

Remark 1. The constructions we present later will in fact permit *backward-leak key updates*. At first glance the *backward-leak key updates* notion proposed by Nishimaki [Nis21] is seemingly weaker than *no-directionality key updates*. However, as mentioned in the introduction, this notion is essentially equivalent to no-directional key updates because backward-leak derivation of k_{e-1} does not increase the adversary's advantage in breaking the scheme. In particular, if the adversary obtains a challenge ciphertext $\tilde{\mathsf{ct}}_{e-1}$ and corrupts Δ_e and k_e, then it does *not* matter if the adversary can derive k_{e-1} or not, as it can always update the ciphertext to $\tilde{\mathsf{ct}}_e$ and decrypt it using k_e.

Definition 7 (IND-ENC, IND-UPD, IND-UE security). *Let* $\mathsf{UE} = (\mathsf{UE.setup}, \mathsf{UE.next}, \mathsf{UE.enc}, \mathsf{UE.upd}, \mathsf{UE.dec})$ *be an updatable encryption scheme. We say* UE

is notion-secure for notion $\in \{\mathsf{IND\text{-}ENC}, \mathsf{IND\text{-}UPD}, \mathsf{IND\text{-}UE}\}$ *if for all PPT adversary $\mathcal{A}$ it holds that*

$$\left| \Pr\left[\mathsf{Exp}_{\mathcal{A},\mathsf{UE}}^{\mathsf{notion}}(1^\lambda) = 1 \right] - \frac{1}{2} \right| \le \mathrm{negl}(\lambda)$$

for some negligible function $\mathrm{negl}(\cdot)$.

Experiment $\mathsf{Exp}_{\mathcal{A},\mathsf{UE}}^{\mathsf{notion}}(1^\lambda)$:

Run Setup(1^λ)

$(\mathsf{state}, \mathsf{Chall}_0, \mathsf{Chall}_1) \overset{\$}{\leftarrow} \mathcal{A}^{\mathcal{O}.\mathsf{enc}, \mathcal{O}.\mathsf{next}, \mathcal{O}.\mathsf{upd}, \mathcal{O}.\mathsf{corr}}(1^\lambda)$

$b \overset{\$}{\leftarrow} \{0,1\}$

$\widetilde{\mathsf{ct}} \overset{\$}{\leftarrow} \mathcal{O}.\mathsf{chall\text{-}notion}(\mathsf{Chall}_0, \mathsf{Chall}_1)$

Proceed only if $\widetilde{\mathsf{ct}} \ne \bot$

$b' \overset{\$}{\leftarrow} \mathcal{A}^{\mathcal{O}.\mathsf{enc}, \mathcal{O}.\mathsf{next}, \mathcal{O}.\mathsf{upd}, \mathcal{O}.\mathsf{corr}, \mathcal{O}.\mathsf{upd}\widetilde{\mathsf{C}}}(\mathsf{state}, \widetilde{\mathsf{ct}})$

return 1 if $b = b'$ and $\mathcal{C}^* \cap \mathcal{K}^* = \emptyset$

3.2   IND-ENC Secure Unidirectional UE

We begin by showing that any KPHE scheme with $2n$-bit secret keys that satisfies distributional semantic security with respect to the distribution $\mathcal{U}_n$, as well as public key and ciphertext blinding as described in Sect. 2 implies an IND-ENC secure unidirectional UE scheme.

Construction. Given a KHPE scheme of the form

$$\mathsf{KPHE} = (\mathsf{KPHE.Setup}, \mathsf{KPHE.SKGen}, \mathsf{KPHE.PKGen}, \mathsf{KPHE.Enc}, \mathsf{KPHE.Dec}, \mathsf{KPHE.Eval}),$$

with $2n$-bit secret keys, we construct a unidirectional UE scheme

$$\mathsf{UE} = (\mathsf{UE.setup}, \mathsf{UE.next}, \mathsf{UE.enc}, \mathsf{UE.upd}, \mathsf{UE.dec}),$$

with message space $\mathcal{M} = \{0,1\}^{2n}$ as follows:

- $\mathsf{UE.setup}(1^\lambda)$: Generate $\mathsf{pp} \overset{\$}{\leftarrow} \mathsf{KPHE.Setup}(1^\lambda)$, $\mathsf{sk}_0 \overset{\$}{\leftarrow} \mathsf{KPHE.SKGen}(\mathsf{pp}, \mathcal{U}_n)$, and output
$$\mathsf{k}_0 = (\mathsf{pp}, \mathsf{sk}_0).$$

- $\mathsf{UE.next}(\mathsf{k}_e)$: Parse $\mathsf{k}_e = (\mathsf{pp}, \mathsf{sk}_e)$. Generate $\mathsf{sk}_{e+1} \overset{\$}{\leftarrow} \mathsf{KPHE.SKGen}(\mathsf{pp}, \mathcal{U}_n)$ and $\mathsf{pk}_{e+1} \overset{\$}{\leftarrow} \mathsf{KPHE.PKGen}(\mathsf{pp}, \mathsf{sk}_{e+1})$. Output
$$\mathsf{k}_{e+1} = (\mathsf{pp}, \mathsf{sk}_{e+1}), \quad \Delta_{e+1} = (\mathsf{pk}_{e+1}, \mathsf{KPHE.Enc}(\mathsf{pk}_{e+1}, \mathsf{sk}_e)).$$

- $\mathsf{UE.enc}(\mathsf{k}_e, m)$: Parse $\mathsf{k}_e = (\mathsf{pp}, \mathsf{sk}_e)$. Generate $\mathsf{pk}_e \overset{\$}{\leftarrow} \mathsf{KPHE.PKGen}(\mathsf{pp}, \mathsf{sk}_e)$ and compute $\mathsf{ctx}_e \overset{\$}{\leftarrow} \mathsf{KPHE.Enc}(\mathsf{pk}_e, m)$. Output
$$\mathsf{ct}_e = (0(\mathsf{pk}_e, \mathsf{ctx}_e)).$$

- UE.upd(Δ_{e+1}, ct$_e$): Parse the update token and the ciphertext as

$$\Delta_{e+1} = (\mathsf{pk}_\Delta, \mathsf{ctx}_\Delta), \quad \mathsf{ct}_e = (t, (\overline{\mathsf{pk}}_{e-t}, \overline{\mathsf{ctx}}_{e-t}), \ldots, (\overline{\mathsf{pk}}_{e-1}, \overline{\mathsf{ctx}}_{e-1}), (\mathsf{pk}_e, \mathsf{ctx}_e))$$

Sample a uniform random permutation $\pi : [2n] \to [2n]$. Also, let $\pi_{\mathsf{id}} : [2n] \to [2n]$ denote the *identity* permutation. Compute

$$(\overline{\mathsf{pk}}_e, \overline{\mathsf{ctx}}_e) \overset{\$}{\leftarrow} \mathsf{KPHE.Eval}(\mathsf{pk}_e, \mathsf{ctx}_e, \pi, \pi_{\mathsf{id}}), \quad (\mathsf{pk}_{e+1}, \mathsf{ctx}_{e+1}) \overset{\$}{\leftarrow} \mathsf{KPHE.Eval}(\mathsf{pk}_\Delta, \mathsf{ctx}_\Delta, \pi_{\mathsf{id}}, \pi).$$

and output the updated ciphertext as:

$$\mathsf{ct}_{e+1} = (t + 1, (\overline{\mathsf{pk}}_{e-t}, \overline{\mathsf{ctx}}_{e-t}), \ldots, (\overline{\mathsf{pk}}_e, \overline{\mathsf{ctx}}_e), (\mathsf{pk}_{e+1}, \mathsf{ctx}_{e+1})).$$

- UE.dec(k_e, ct$_e$): Parse $\mathsf{k}_e = (\mathsf{pp}, \mathsf{sk}_e)$ and the ciphertext as

$$\mathsf{ct}_e = (t, (\overline{\mathsf{pk}}_{e-t}, \overline{\mathsf{ctx}}_{e-t}), \ldots, (\overline{\mathsf{pk}}_{e-1}, \overline{\mathsf{ctx}}_{e-1}), (\mathsf{pk}_e, \mathsf{ctx}_e)).$$

If $t = 0$, then output $\mathsf{m} \leftarrow \mathsf{KPHE.Dec}(\mathsf{sk}_e, \mathsf{ctx}_e)$.
Otherwise, compute $\overline{\mathsf{sk}}_{e-1} \leftarrow \mathsf{KPHE.Dec}(\mathsf{sk}_e, \mathsf{ctx}_e)$. Then for each j from $(e-1)$ downto $(e - t + 1)$, compute

$$\overline{\mathsf{sk}}_{j-1} \leftarrow \mathsf{KPHE.Dec}(\overline{\mathsf{sk}}_j, \overline{\mathsf{ctx}}_j).$$

Finally, output the message $\mathsf{m} \leftarrow \mathsf{KPHE.Dec}(\overline{\mathsf{sk}}_{e-t}, \overline{\mathsf{ctx}}_{e-t})$.

Correctness. We first prove the correctness of the UE scheme. For any $\mathsf{m} \in \mathcal{M}$, any $\mathsf{k}_0 \leftarrow \mathsf{UE.setup}(1^\lambda)$, any sequence of $(\mathsf{k}_1, \Delta_1), \ldots, (\mathsf{k}_e, \Delta_e)$ generated as $(\mathsf{k}_i, \Delta_i) \leftarrow \mathsf{UE.next}(\mathsf{k}_{i-1})$ for all $i \in [e]$, let $\mathsf{ct}_0 \leftarrow \mathsf{UE.enc}(\mathsf{k}_0, \mathsf{m})$ and $\mathsf{ct}_i \leftarrow \mathsf{UE.upd}(\Delta_i, \mathsf{ct}_{i-1})$ for all $j \in [e]$, then the final ciphertext is of the form $\mathsf{ct}_e = (e, (\overline{\mathsf{pk}}_0, \overline{\mathsf{ctx}}_0), \ldots, (\overline{\mathsf{pk}}_{e-1}, \overline{\mathsf{ctx}}_{e-1}), (\mathsf{pk}_e, \mathsf{ctx}_e))$. All the secret keys are of the form $\mathsf{k}_0 = (\mathsf{pp}, \mathsf{sk}_0), \ldots, \mathsf{k}_e = (\mathsf{pp}, \mathsf{sk}_e)$. Let π_j be the random permutation sampled in $\mathsf{UE.upd}(\Delta_{j+1}, \mathsf{ct}_j)$ and let $\overline{\mathsf{sk}}_j = \pi_j(\mathsf{sk}_j)$ for all $j = 0, 1, \ldots, e - 1$. We can prove by induction that $\mathsf{KPHE.Dec}(\overline{\mathsf{sk}}_0, \overline{\mathsf{ctx}}_0) = \mathsf{m}, \mathsf{KPHE.Dec}(\overline{\mathsf{sk}}_1, \overline{\mathsf{ctx}}_1) = \overline{\mathsf{sk}}_0, \ldots, \mathsf{KPHE.Dec}(\overline{\mathsf{sk}}_{e-1}, \overline{\mathsf{ctx}}_{e-1}) = \overline{\mathsf{sk}}_{e-2}, \mathsf{KPHE.Dec}(\mathsf{sk}_e, \mathsf{ctx}_e) = \overline{\mathsf{sk}}_{e-1}$. Therefore, $\mathsf{UE.dec}(\mathsf{k}_e, \mathsf{ct}_e)$ outputs m. This argument is for any ciphertext starting from epoch 0. The same argument holds for any ciphertext starting from any epoch $\hat{e}$ where $0 \le \hat{e} \le e$.

Confidentiality. Next we prove the IND-ENC security of our UE scheme. More formally, we state and prove the following theorem:

Theorem 3 (IND-ENC Security). *Assuming that* KPHE *satisfies distributional security with respect to the distribution* $\mathcal{U}_n$, *as well as public key and ciphertext blinding as described in Sect. 2, the above* UE *construction is an IND-ENC secure unidirectional* UE *scheme.*

Proof. The proof proceeds via a hybrid argument.

Hyb$_0$ The challenger plays the real game with the adversary.

Hyb_1 Same as Hyb_0 but for $\mathsf{UE.upd}(\Delta_e, \mathsf{ct}_{e-1})$ in $\mathcal{O}.\mathsf{upd}$ and $\mathsf{UE.upd}(\Delta_e, \widetilde{\mathsf{ct}}_{e-1})$ in $\mathcal{O}.\mathsf{next}$, do the following:

- Let $\mathsf{k}_{e-1} = (\mathsf{pp}, \mathsf{sk}_{e-1})$ and $\mathsf{k}_e = (\mathsf{pp}, \mathsf{sk}_e)$.
- Parse the ciphertext ct_{e-1} or $\widetilde{\mathsf{ct}}_{e-1}$ as

$$(t, (\overline{\mathsf{pk}}_{e-1-t}, \overline{\mathsf{ctx}}_{e-1-t}), \ldots, (\overline{\mathsf{pk}}_{e-2}, \overline{\mathsf{ctx}}_{e-2}), (\mathsf{pk}_{e-1}, \mathsf{ctx}_{e-1})),$$

where $\mathsf{ctx}_{e-1} = \mathsf{KPHE.Enc}(\mathsf{pk}_{e-1}, x)$. Note that if $t = 0$, then $x = \mathsf{m}$ for some message, otherwise $x = \overline{\mathsf{sk}}_{e-2}$ that is the KPHE secret key corresponding to $\overline{\mathsf{pk}}_{e-2}$.

- Sample a uniform random permutation $\pi : [2n] \to [2n]$, let $\overline{\mathsf{sk}}_{e-1} = \pi(\mathsf{sk}_{e-1})$, and sample $\overline{\mathsf{pk}}_{e-1} \xleftarrow{\$} \mathsf{KPHE.PKGen}(\mathsf{pp}, \overline{\mathsf{sk}}_{e-1})$. Compute $\overline{\mathsf{ctx}}_{e-1} \xleftarrow{\$} \mathsf{KPHE.Enc}(\overline{\mathsf{pk}}_{e-1}, x)$.

- Sample $\mathsf{pk}_e \xleftarrow{\$} \mathsf{KPHE.PKGen}(\mathsf{pp}, \mathsf{sk}_e)$ and compute $\mathsf{ctx}_e \xleftarrow{\$} \mathsf{KPHE.Enc}(\mathsf{pk}_e, \overline{\mathsf{sk}}_{e-1})$.

- Let ct_e or $\widetilde{\mathsf{ct}}_e$ be

$$(t + 1, (\overline{\mathsf{pk}}_{e-1-t}, \overline{\mathsf{ctx}}_{e-1-t}), \ldots, (\overline{\mathsf{pk}}_{e-1}, \overline{\mathsf{ctx}}_{e-1}), (\mathsf{pk}_e, \mathsf{ctx}_e)).$$

We prove in Lemma 2 that this hybrid is computationally indistinguishable from Hyb_0 to any PPT adversary by the blinding property of KPHE.

Hyb_2 Same as Hyb_1 but for $\mathsf{UE.upd}(\Delta_e, \mathsf{ct}_{e-1})$ in $\mathcal{O}.\mathsf{upd}$ and $\mathsf{UE.upd}(\Delta_e, \widetilde{\mathsf{ct}}_{e-1})$ in $\mathcal{O}.\mathsf{next}$, instead of letting $\overline{\mathsf{sk}}_{e-1} = \pi(\mathsf{sk}_{e-1})$, sample $\overline{\mathsf{sk}}_{e-1}$ from the distribution $\mathcal{U}_n$. This hybrid is statistically identical to Hyb_1.

Hyb_3 Let $\widetilde{e}$ be the challenge epoch, and let $\overline{e}$ be the last epoch where the adversary corrupts continuous update tokens from $\widetilde{e}$, namely the adversary corrupts $\Delta_{\widetilde{e}+1}, \Delta_{\widetilde{e}+2}, \ldots, \Delta_{\overline{e}}$ but not $\Delta_{\overline{e}+1}$. This hybrid is the same as Hyb_2 except that the challenger guesses $\widetilde{e}^*$ and $\overline{e}^*$ at the beginning of the game and aborts the game if guessing incorrectly. Let E be the upper bound on the number of epochs during the game. If the challenger does not abort, then this hybrid is identical to Hyb_2, which happens with probability at least $\frac{1}{E^2}$. In the remaining hybrids, we assume for simplicity that the challenger guesses $\widetilde{e}$ and $\overline{e}$ correctly.

Hyb_4 Same as Hyb_3 except that for each $\mathsf{k}_e = (\mathsf{pp}, \mathsf{sk}_e)$, generate a single public key $\widehat{\mathsf{pk}}_e \xleftarrow{\$} \mathsf{KPHE.PKGen}(\mathsf{pp}, \mathsf{sk}_e)$. Then whenever $\mathsf{KPHE.Enc}(\mathsf{pk}_e, x)$ is computed for a freshly generated pk_e and some x, compute it as $\mathsf{KPHE.Eval}(\widehat{\mathsf{pk}}_e, \mathsf{KPHE.Enc}(\widehat{\mathsf{pk}}_e, x), \pi_{\mathsf{id}}, \pi_{\mathsf{id}})$. That is, instead of generating a fresh pk_e from sk_e every time, use the same $\widehat{\mathsf{pk}}_e$ to encrypt x and use then KPHE.Eval to re-randomize it.

This hybrid is computationally indistinguishable from Hyb_3 by the blinding property of KPHE. We omit the detailed reduction here, but it is similar to the reduction in the proof of Lemma 2.

Hyb_5 Same as Hyb_4 except that for all $\widetilde{e} + 1 \leq e \leq \overline{e}$, $\mathsf{UE.next}(\mathsf{k}_{e-1})$ is computed as follows. Generate $\mathsf{sk}_e \xleftarrow{\$} \mathsf{KPHE.SKGen}(\mathsf{pp}, \mathcal{U}_n)$ and let $\widehat{\mathsf{pk}}_e \xleftarrow{\$}$

KPHE.PKGen(pp, sk_e) be the single public key for k_e (that will be used for every KPHE.Enc). Output

$$k_e = (pp, sk_e), \quad \Delta_e = (\widehat{pk_e}, \text{KPHE.Enc}(\widehat{pk_e}, 0^{2n})).$$

We prove in Lemma 3 that this hybrid is computationally indistinguishable from Hyb_4 to any PPT adversary based on the distributional semantic security of KPHE.

Hyb_6 Same as Hyb_5 except that for each $k_e = (pp, sk_e)$, generate a single public key $\widehat{pk_e} \xleftarrow{\$} \text{KPHE.PKGen}(pp, sk_e)$ and use $\text{KPHE.Eval}(\widehat{pk_e}, \text{KPHE.Enc}(\widehat{pk_e}, \cdot),$ $\pi_{id}, \pi_{id})$ for all the computation of $\text{KPHE.Enc}(k_e, \cdot)$ (including the computation of Δ_e). The only exception is the challenge ciphertext $\widetilde{ct_{\widetilde{e}}}$, which is computed using $\widehat{pk_{\widetilde{e}}}$ without re-randomization, namely

$$\widetilde{ct_{\widetilde{e}}} = (0, (\widehat{pk_{\widetilde{e}}}, \text{KPHE.Enc}(\widehat{pk_{\widetilde{e}}}, \overline{m}_b))).$$

This hybrid is computationally indistinguishable from Hyb_5 by the blinding property of KPHE. We omit the detailed reduction here, but it is similar to the reduction in the proof of Lemma 2.

Finally, we argue that in the final hybrid Hyb_6, any PPT adversary cannot distinguish an encryption of $\overline{m}_0$ or $\overline{m}_1$ in the challenge epoch $\widetilde{e}$, which relies on the distributional semantic security of KPHE, which will conclude our proof.

Assume for the purpose of contradiction that there exists a PPT adversary $\mathcal{A}$ that can distinguish an encryption of $\overline{m}_0$ or $\overline{m}_1$ in the challenge epoch. Then we construct a PPT adversary $\mathcal{B}$ that breaks the distributional semantic security of KPHE. The adversary $\mathcal{B}$ first receives (pp, pk) from the challenger in the semantic security security game. Then $\mathcal{B}$ plays the UE game with $\mathcal{A}$ as a challenger in Hyb_6. $\mathcal{B}$ uses pp to generate UE keys and update tokens as in Hyb_6 except that for epoch $\widetilde{e}$, the UE key $k_{\widetilde{e}}$ is unknown. When $\mathcal{B}$ receives the challenge messages $(\overline{m}_0, \overline{m}_1)$ from $\mathcal{A}$ in the UE game, it forwards the two messages to the KPHE challenger and gets back ctx, and then responds to $\mathcal{A}$ with $ct = (0, (pp, ctx))$. Note that $\mathcal{B}$ doesn't need to know $k_{\widetilde{e}}$ because it is never used. In particular, $\mathcal{B}$ can use pk to compute all the $\text{UE.enc}(k_{\widetilde{e}}, \cdot)$. Finally, $\mathcal{B}$ outputs whatever $\mathcal{A}$ outputs.

If $\mathcal{A}$ can distinguish between encryptions of $\overline{m}_0$ and $\overline{m}_1$ with non-negligible probability, then $\mathcal{B}$ can break the distributional semantic security of KPHE with non-negligible probability, which leads to contradiction.

Lemma 2. $\text{Hyb}_0 \overset{c}{\approx} \text{Hyb}_1$ *in the proof of Theorem 3.*

Lemma 3. $\text{Hyb}_4 \overset{c}{\approx} \text{Hyb}_5$ *in the proof of Theorem 3.*

We defer the formal proofs of Lemmas 2 and 3 to the full version of our paper [MPW22]. These proofs complete the overall proof of Theorem 3. □

Remark 2. In our construction one can derive k_{e-1} from Δ_e and k_e. It is for this reason that our construction permits *backward-leak unidirectional key updates* proposed by Nishimaki [Nis21] where secret keys can be derived in the backward direction but not forward direction. However, as discussed earlier, this notion is essentially equivalent to no-directional key updates (the optimal case) and has no bearing on our security analysis.

3.3 Post-Compromise Secure Unidirectional UE

In this section, we show that any KPHE scheme with $2n$-bit secret keys that satisfies distributional security with respect to the distribution $\mathcal{U}_n$, as well as public key and ciphertext blinding as described in Sect. 2 implies a post-compromise secure unidirectional UE scheme.

3.3.1 IND-UPD Secure Unidirectional UE

We first show how to construct an UE scheme that satisfies the IND-UPD security definition as proposed in [LT18]. Given a KHPE scheme of the form

$$\mathsf{KPHE} = (\mathsf{KPHE.Setup}, \mathsf{KPHE.KeyGen}, \mathsf{KPHE.Enc}, \mathsf{KPHE.Dec}, \mathsf{KPHE.TransPK}, \mathsf{KPHE.Eval}),$$

with $2n$-bit secret keys, we construct a unidirectional UE scheme

$$\mathsf{UE} = (\mathsf{UE.setup}, \mathsf{UE.next}, \mathsf{UE.enc}, \mathsf{UE.upd}, \mathsf{UE.dec}),$$

that only differs from the IND-ENC construction in UE.upd:

- UE.upd$(\Delta_{e+1}, \mathsf{ct}_e)$: Parse the update token and the ciphertext as

$$\Delta_{e+1} = (\mathsf{pk}_\Delta, \mathsf{ctx}_\Delta), \quad \mathsf{ct}_e = (t, (\overline{\mathsf{pk}}_{e-t}, \overline{\mathsf{ctx}}_{e-t}), \dots, (\overline{\mathsf{pk}}_{e-1}, \overline{\mathsf{ctx}}_{e-1}), (\mathsf{pk}_e, \mathsf{ctx}_e))$$

Sample $(t+1)$ uniform random permutations $\pi_{e-t}, \dots, \pi_e : [2n] \to [2n]$. Also, let $\pi_{\mathsf{id}} : [2n] \to [2n]$ denote the identity permutation. For each $i \in \{e-t+1, \dots, e-1\}$, compute

$$(\widetilde{\mathsf{pk}}_i, \widetilde{\mathsf{ctx}}_i) \xleftarrow{\$} \mathsf{KPHE.Eval}(\overline{\mathsf{pk}}_i, \overline{\mathsf{ctx}}_i, \pi_i, \pi_{i-1}).$$

Additionally, compute

$$(\widetilde{\mathsf{pk}}_{e-t}, \widetilde{\mathsf{ctx}}_{e-t}) \xleftarrow{\$} \mathsf{KPHE.Eval}(\overline{\mathsf{pk}}_{e-t}, \overline{\mathsf{ctx}}_{e-t}, \pi_{e-t}, \pi_{\mathsf{id}}),$$

$$(\overline{\mathsf{pk}}_e, \overline{\mathsf{ctx}}_e) \xleftarrow{\$} \mathsf{KPHE.Eval}(\mathsf{pk}_e, \mathsf{ctx}_e, \pi_e, \pi_{e-1}),$$

$$(\mathsf{pk}_{e+1}, \mathsf{ctx}_{e+1}) \xleftarrow{\$} \mathsf{KPHE.Eval}(\mathsf{pk}_\Delta, \mathsf{ctx}_\Delta, \pi_{\mathsf{id}}, \pi_e).$$

Output the updated ciphertext as:

$$\mathsf{ct}_{e+1} = (t+1, (\widetilde{\mathsf{pk}}_{e-t}, \widetilde{\mathsf{ctx}}_{e-t}), \dots, (\widetilde{\mathsf{pk}}_{e-1}, \widetilde{\mathsf{ctx}}_{e-1}), (\overline{\mathsf{pk}}_e, \overline{\mathsf{ctx}}_e), (\mathsf{pk}_{e+1}, \mathsf{ctx}_{e+1})).$$

Correctness. We first prove the correctness of the UE scheme. For any $m \in \mathcal{M}$, any $k_0 \leftarrow$ UE.setup(1^λ), any sequence of $(k_1, \Delta_1), \ldots, (k_e, \Delta_e)$ generated as $(k_i, \Delta_i) \leftarrow$ UE.next(k_{i-1}) for all $i \in [e]$, let $ct_0 \leftarrow$ UE.enc(k_0, m) and $ct_i \leftarrow$ UE.upd(Δ_i, ct_{i-1}) for all $j \in [e]$, then the final ciphertext is of the form $ct_e = (e, (\overline{pk}_0, \overline{ctx}_0), \ldots, (\overline{pk}_{e-1}, \overline{ctx}_{e-1}), (pk_e, ctx_e))$. All the UE secret keys are of the form $k_0 = (pp, sk_0), \ldots, k_e = (pp, sk_e)$. We can prove by induction that there exist permutations $\pi_0, \pi_1 \ldots, \pi_{e-1} : [2n] \rightarrow [2n]$ such that $\overline{sk}_i = \pi_i(sk_i)$ for all $i = 0, 1, \ldots, e-1$, and that KPHE.Dec($\overline{sk}_0, \overline{ctx}_0$) = m, KPHE.Dec($\overline{sk}_1, \overline{ctx}_1$) = $\overline{sk}_0, \ldots,$ KPHE.Dec($\overline{sk}_{e-1}, \overline{ctx}_{e-1}$) = $\overline{sk}_{e-2}$, KPHE.Dec(sk_e, ctx_e) = $\overline{sk}_{e-1}$. Therefore, UE.dec(k_e, ct_e) outputs m. This argument is for any ciphertext starting from epoch 0. The same argument holds for any ciphertext starting from any epoch $\hat{e}$ where $0 \leq \hat{e} \leq e$.

Confidentiality. Next we prove the IND-UPD security the UE scheme. More formally, we state and prove the following theorem (the proof is provided in the full version of our paper [MPW22]):

Theorem 4 (IND-UPD Security). *Assuming that KPHE satisfies distributional security with respect to the distribution $\mathcal{U}_n$, as well as public key and ciphertext blinding as described in Sect. 2, the above UE construction is an IND-UPD secure unidirectional UE scheme.*

3.3.2 IND-UE Secure Unidirectional UE

The basic IND-UPD construction allows ciphertexts from the same epoch e to have different sizes. In particular, a freshly created ciphertext in epoch e can be trivially distinguished from a ciphertext that was created as an update of a ciphertext from epoch (e − 1). So it cannot satisfy the combined security definition of post-compromise security for UE due to Boyd et al. [BDGJ20].

In the full version of our paper [MPW22], we showcase a simple extension of the basic construction wherein we ensure that the size for any ciphertext in epoch e is the same, irrespective of whether it was freshly created, or created as an update of a ciphertext from epoch (e − 1). The overall construction remains exactly the same; the key alteration is in how we generate fresh ciphertexts. At a high level, a freshly created ciphertext in epoch e is made to look exactly like a ciphertext that has undergone e update operations. We do this by having e "dummy wrapper" layers over and above the core ciphertext generated by the basic construction. We defer the detailed construction and security proof to the full version of our paper [MPW22].

4 Unidirectional PRE from Circular-Secure KPHE

In this section, we show how to construct unidirectional PRE from any KPHE scheme that satisfies distributional circular security. We present the simpler construction of IND-HRA unidirectional PRE in Sect. 4.2. In the full version of our paper [MPW22], we show how to augment it to achieve the stronger notion of strong post-compromise security (PCS) as introduced in a recent work by Davidson et al. [DDLM19].

4.1   Definition of Unidirectional PRE

Definition 8 (Unidirectional Proxy Re-Encryption (PRE)). *A unidirectional PRE scheme is a tuple of PPT algorithms of the form*

$$PRE = (Setup, KeyGen, Enc, ReKeyGen, ReEnc, Dec),$$

described as follows:

- pp $\overset{\$}{\leftarrow}$ Setup(1^λ): *On input the security parameter* λ, *the setup algorithm outputs some public parameters* pp *(these parameters are implicit to all other algorithms).*
- (sk, pk) $\overset{\$}{\leftarrow}$ KeyGen(pp): *On input the public parameters* pp, *the key-generation algorithm outputs a secret key-public key pair,* (sk, pk).
- ct $\overset{\$}{\leftarrow}$ Enc(pk, m): *On input a public key* pk *and a message* m, *the encryption algorithm outputs a ciphertext* ct.
- $rk_{i,j}$ $\overset{\$}{\leftarrow}$ ReKeyGen((sk_i, pk_i), pk_j): *The re-key generation algorithm returns a re-encryption key* $rk_{i,j}$ *for translation of a ciphertext from a key-pair* (sk_i, pk_i) *to a key-pair* (sk_j, pk_j). *It takes as input* (sk_i, pk_i) *and* pk_j, *and outputs the re-encryption key* $rk_{i,j}$.[1]
- ct_j $\overset{\$}{\leftarrow}$ ReEnc($rk_{i,j}, ct_i$): *On input a re-encryption key* $rk_{i,j}$ *and a ciphertext* ct_i, *the re-encryption algorithm outputs an updated ciphertext* ct_j.[2]
- m/$\perp$ $\leftarrow$ Dec(sk, ct): *On input a secret key* sk *and a ciphertext* ct, *the decryption algorithm outputs either a plaintext message or an error symbol.*

Definition 9 (Correctness). *A PRE scheme* PRE = (Setup, KeyGen, Enc, ReKeyGen, ReEnc, Dec) *is said to be correct if for any* pp $\overset{\$}{\leftarrow}$ Setup(1^λ), *for any* $\ell \geq 0$, *for any* ($\ell + 1$) *key-pairs* (pk_0, sk_0), ..., (pk_ℓ, sk_ℓ) $\overset{\$}{\leftarrow}$ KeyGen(pp), *and for any plaintext message* m, *letting* ct_0 $\overset{\$}{\leftarrow}$ Enc(pk_0, m), *and letting for each* $j \in [\ell]$

$$rk_j \overset{\$}{\leftarrow} ReKeyGen(sk_{j-1}, pk_{j-1}, pk_j), \quad ct_j \overset{\$}{\leftarrow} ReEnc(rk_j, ct_{j-1}),$$

we have Dec(sk_ℓ, ct_ℓ) = m *(with all but negligible probability).*

Confidentiality. We defer the confidentiality definitions to the full version of our paper [MPW22].

---

[1] In a bidirectional PRE scheme, the re-key generation algorithm additionally takes as input the destination secret key sk_j, i.e., it takes as input (sk_i, pk_i) and (sk_j, pk_j), and outputs the re-encryption key $rk_{i,j}$.

[2] The re-encryption algorithm could be either deterministic or randomized; in this work, we assume throughout that the re-encryption algorithm is randomized.

4.2 HRA-Secure Unidirectional PRE

We show that any KPHE scheme with $2n$-bit secret keys and plaintext messages that satisfies: (a) distributional semantic and *circular* security with respect to the distribution $\mathcal{U}_n$, and (b) blinding, implies the existence of a multi-hop IND-HRA secure unidirectional PRE scheme.

Construction. Given a KHPE scheme of the form

$$\mathsf{KPHE} = (\mathsf{KPHE.Setup}, \mathsf{KPHE.SKGen}, \mathsf{KPHE.PKGen}, \mathsf{KPHE.Enc}, \mathsf{KPHE.Dec}, \mathsf{KPHE.Eval}),$$

with $2n$-bit secret keys, we construct a unidirectional PRE scheme

$$\mathsf{PRE} = (\mathsf{PRE.Setup}, \mathsf{PRE.KeyGen}, \mathsf{PRE.Enc}, \mathsf{PRE.ReKeyGen}, \mathsf{PRE.ReEnc}, \mathsf{PRE.Dec}),$$

with message space $\mathcal{M} = \{0,1\}^{2n}$ as follows:

- $\mathsf{PRE.Setup}(1^\lambda)$: Sample $\mathsf{pp} \xleftarrow{\$} \mathsf{KPHE.Setup}(1^\lambda)$ and output pp.
- $\mathsf{PRE.KeyGen}(\mathsf{pp})$: Sample and output $(\mathsf{pk}, \mathsf{sk})$ where

$$\mathsf{sk} \xleftarrow{\$} \mathsf{KPHE.SKGen}(\mathsf{pp}, \mathcal{U}_n), \quad \mathsf{pk} \xleftarrow{\$} \mathsf{KPHE.PKGen}(\mathsf{pp}, \mathsf{sk}).$$

- $\mathsf{PRE.Enc}(\mathsf{pk}, \mathsf{m})$: Compute $\mathsf{ctx}_0 \xleftarrow{\$} \mathsf{KPHE.Enc}(\mathsf{pk}, \mathsf{m})$ and output

$$\mathsf{ct} = (0, (\mathsf{pk}, \mathsf{ctx}_0)).$$

- $\mathsf{PRE.ReKeyGen}(\mathsf{sk}_i, \mathsf{pk}_i, \mathsf{pk}_j)$: Output $\mathsf{rk}_{i,j} = (\mathsf{pk}_j, \mathsf{ctx}_\Delta)$, where

$$\mathsf{ctx}_\Delta \xleftarrow{\$} \mathsf{KPHE.Enc}(\mathsf{pk}_j, \mathsf{sk}_i).$$

- $\mathsf{PRE.ReEnc}(\mathsf{rk}_{i,j}, \mathsf{ct})$: Parse the reencryption key and the ciphertext as

$$\mathsf{rk}_{i,j} = (\mathsf{pk}_j, \mathsf{ctx}_\Delta), \quad \mathsf{ct} = (t, (\overline{\mathsf{pk}}_0, \overline{\mathsf{ctx}}_0), \dots, (\overline{\mathsf{pk}}_{t-1}, \overline{\mathsf{ctx}}_{t-1}), (\widehat{\mathsf{pk}}_t, \widehat{\mathsf{ctx}}_t)),$$

for some $t \geq 0$. Sample a uniformly random permutation $\pi : [2n] \to [2n]$. Also, let $\pi_{\mathsf{id}} : [2n] \to [2n]$ denote the *identity* permutation. Compute

$$(\overline{\mathsf{pk}}_t, \overline{\mathsf{ctx}}_t) \xleftarrow{\$} \mathsf{KPHE.Eval}(\widehat{\mathsf{pk}}_t, \widehat{\mathsf{ctx}}_t, \pi, \pi_{\mathsf{id}}),$$

$$(\widehat{\mathsf{pk}}_{t+1}, \widehat{\mathsf{ctx}}_{t+1}) \xleftarrow{\$} \mathsf{KPHE.Eval}(\mathsf{pk}_j, \mathsf{ctx}_\Delta, \pi_{\mathsf{id}}, \pi),$$

and output the updated ciphertext as:

$$\mathsf{ct}' = (t+1, (\overline{\mathsf{pk}}_0, \overline{\mathsf{ctx}}_0), \dots, (\overline{\mathsf{pk}}_t, \overline{\mathsf{ctx}}_t), (\widehat{\mathsf{pk}}_{t+1}, \widehat{\mathsf{ctx}}_{t+1})).$$

- PRE.Dec(sk, ct): Parse the ciphertext as

$$ct = (t, (\overline{\mathsf{pk}}_0, \overline{\mathsf{ctx}}_0), \ldots, (\overline{\mathsf{pk}}_{t-1}, \overline{\mathsf{ctx}}_{t-1}), (\widehat{\mathsf{pk}}_t, \widehat{\mathsf{ctx}}_t)),$$

for some $t \geq 0$. Compute $\overline{\mathsf{sk}}_{t-1} = \mathsf{KPHE.Dec}(\mathsf{sk}, \widehat{\mathsf{ctx}}_t)$. Next, compute the following for each ℓ from $(t-1)$ to 1 in decreasing order:

$$\overline{\mathsf{sk}}_{\ell-1} = \mathsf{KPHE.Dec}(\overline{\mathsf{sk}}_\ell, \overline{\mathsf{ctx}}_\ell).$$

Finally, output the message $\mathsf{m} = \mathsf{KPHE.Dec}(\overline{\mathsf{sk}}_0, \overline{\mathsf{ctx}}_0)$.

Correctness. We defer the detailed proof of correctness to the full version of our paper [MPW22]. At a high level, the correctness argument is very similar to that for our unidirectional UE scheme in Sect. 3.2.

Theorem 5 (IND-HRA Security). *Assuming that* KPHE *satisfies blinding and distributional semantic+circular security with respect to the distribution* $\mathcal{U}_n$, PRE *is a multi-hop IND-HRA secure unidirectional PRE scheme.*

We defer the detailed proofs of correctness and IND-HRA security to the full version of our paper [MPW22]. Also, see [MPW22] for our construction of IND-PCS secure unidirectional PRE from any circular-secure KPHE scheme.

Acknowledgements. The authors thank the anonymous reviewers of IACR PKC 2023 for their helpful comments and suggestions. The authors did part of the work while at VISA Research. P. Miao is supported in part by the NSF CNS Award 2055358, a 2020 DPI Science Team Seed Grant, and a Meta award.

References

[ACDT20] Alwen, J., Coretti, S., Dodis, Y., Tselekounis, Y.: Security analysis and improvements for the IETF MLS standard for group messaging. In: Micciancio, D., Ristenpart, T. (eds.) CRYPTO 2020. LNCS, vol. 12170, pp. 248–277. Springer, Cham (2020). https://doi.org/10.1007/978-3-030-56784-2_9

[ACPS09] Applebaum, B., Cash, D., Peikert, C., Sahai, A.: Fast cryptographic primitives and circular-secure encryption based on hard learning problems. In: Halevi, S. (ed.) CRYPTO 2009. LNCS, vol. 5677, pp. 595–618. Springer, Heidelberg (2009). https://doi.org/10.1007/978-3-642-03356-8_35

[AFGH06] Ateniese, G., Kevin, F., Green, M., Hohenberger, S.: Improved proxy re-encryption schemes with applications to secure distributed storage. ACM Trans. Inf. Syst. Secur. 9(1), 1–30 (2006)

[AMP19] Alamati, N., Montgomery, H., Patranabis, S.: Symmetric primitives with structured secrets. In: Boldyreva, A., Micciancio, D. (eds.) CRYPTO 2019. LNCS, vol. 11692, pp. 650–679. Springer, Cham (2019). https://doi.org/10.1007/978-3-030-26948-7_23

[BBB+12] Barker, E., Barker, W., Burr, W., Polk, W., Smid, M., Gallagher, P.D., Under Secretary For.: NIST Special Publication 800–57 Recommendation for Key Management - Part 1: General (2012)

[BBS98]   Blaze, M., Bleumer, G., Strauss, M.: Divertible protocols and atomic proxy cryptography. In: Nyberg, K. (ed.) EUROCRYPT 1998. LNCS, vol. 1403, pp. 127–144. Springer, Heidelberg (1998). https://doi.org/10.1007/BFb0054122

[BDGJ20]   Boyd, C., Davies, G.T., Gjøsteen, K., Jiang, Y.: Fast and secure updatable encryption. In: Micciancio, D., Ristenpart, T. (eds.) CRYPTO 2020. LNCS, vol. 12170, pp. 464–493. Springer, Cham (2020). https://doi.org/10.1007/978-3-030-56784-2_16

[BEKS20]   Boneh, D., Eskandarian, S., Kim, S., Shih, M.: Improving speed and security in updatable encryption schemes. In: Moriai, S., Wang, H. (eds.) ASIACRYPT 2020. LNCS, vol. 12493, pp. 559–589. Springer, Cham (2020). https://doi.org/10.1007/978-3-030-64840-4_19

[BF03]   Boneh, D., Franklin, M.K.: Identity-based encryption from the weil pairing. SIAM J. Comput. 32(3), 586–615 (2003)

[BGI+12]   Barak, B., et al.: On the (im)possibility of obfuscating programs. J. ACM 59(2), 6:1–6:48 (2012)

[BHHO08]   Boneh, D., Halevi, S., Hamburg, M., Ostrovsky, R.: Circular-secure encryption from decision Diffie-Hellman. In: Wagner, D. (ed.) CRYPTO 2008. LNCS, vol. 5157, pp. 108–125. Springer, Heidelberg (2008). https://doi.org/10.1007/978-3-540-85174-5_7

[BLMR13]   Boneh, D., Lewi, K., Montgomery, H., Raghunathan, A.: Key homomorphic PRFs and their applications. In: Canetti, R., Garay, J.A. (eds.) CRYPTO 2013. LNCS, vol. 8042, pp. 410–428. Springer, Heidelberg (2013). https://doi.org/10.1007/978-3-642-40041-4_23

[BRS02]   Black, J., Rogaway, P., Shrimpton, T.: Encryption-scheme security in the presence of key-dependent messages. In: Nyberg, K., Heys, H. (eds.) SAC 2002. LNCS, vol. 2595, pp. 62–75. Springer, Heidelberg (2003). https://doi.org/10.1007/3-540-36492-7_6

[CCL+14]   Chandran, N., Chase, M., Liu, F.-H., Nishimaki, R., Xagawa, K.: Re-encryption, functional re-encryption, and multi-hop re-encryption: a framework for achieving obfuscation-based security and instantiations from lattices. In: Krawczyk, H. (ed.) PKC 2014. LNCS, vol. 8383, pp. 95–112. Springer, Heidelberg (2014). https://doi.org/10.1007/978-3-642-54631-0_6

[CL01]   Camenisch, J., Lysyanskaya, A.: An efficient system for non-transferable anonymous credentials with optional anonymity revocation. In: Pfitzmann, B. (ed.) EUROCRYPT 2001. LNCS, vol. 2045, pp. 93–118. Springer, Heidelberg (2001). https://doi.org/10.1007/3-540-44987-6_7

[Coh19]   Cohen, A.: What about bob? the inadequacy of CPA security for proxy reencryption. In: Lin, D., Sako, K. (eds.) PKC 2019. LNCS, vol. 11443, pp. 287–316. Springer, Cham (2019). https://doi.org/10.1007/978-3-030-17259-6_10

[DDLM19]   Davidson, A., Deo, A., Lee, E., Martin, K.: Strong post-compromise secure proxy re-encryption. In: Jang-Jaccard, J., Guo, F. (eds.) ACISP 2019. LNCS, vol. 11547, pp. 58–77. Springer, Cham (2019). https://doi.org/10.1007/978-3-030-21548-4_4

[DKW21]   Dodis, Y., Karthikeyan, H., Wichs, D.: Updatable public key encryption in the standard model. In: Nissim, K., Waters, B. (eds.) TCC 2021. LNCS, vol. 13044, pp. 254–285. Springer, Cham (2021). https://doi.org/10.1007/978-3-030-90456-2_9

[EPRS17] Everspaugh, A., Paterson, K., Ristenpart, T., Scott, S.: Key rotation for authenticated encryption. In: Katz, J., Shacham, H. (eds.) CRYPTO 2017. LNCS, vol. 10403, pp. 98–129. Springer, Cham (2017). https://doi.org/10.1007/978-3-319-63697-9_4

[FKKP19] Fuchsbauer, G., Kamath, C., Klein, K., Pietrzak, K.: Adaptively secure proxy re-encryption. In: Lin, D., Sako, K. (eds.) PKC 2019. LNCS, vol. 11443, pp. 317–346. Springer, Cham (2019). https://doi.org/10.1007/978-3-030-17259-6_11

[FL17] Fan, X., Liu, F.-H.: Proxy re-encryption and re-signatures from lattices. Cryptology ePrint Archive, Report 2017/456, 2017. https://eprint.iacr.org/2017/456

[Gam85] El Gamal, T.: A public key cryptosystem and a signature scheme based on discrete logarithms. IEEE Trans. Inf. Theor. **31**(4), 469–472 (1985)

[Gen09] Gentry, C.: Fully homomorphic encryption using ideal lattices. In ACM STOC **2009**, 169–178 (2009)

[GHV10] Gentry, C., Halevi, S., Vaikuntanathan, V.: i-Hop homomorphic encryption and rerandomizable Yao circuits. In: Rabin, T. (ed.) CRYPTO 2010. LNCS, vol. 6223, pp. 155–172. Springer, Heidelberg (2010). https://doi.org/10.1007/978-3-642-14623-7_9

[GP23] Galteland, Y.J., Pan, J.: Backward-leak uni-directional updatable encryption from public key encryption. In: PKC 2023 (to appear) 2023. https://eprint.iacr.org/2022/324

[GPV08] Gentry, C., Peikert, C., Vaikuntanathan, V.: Trapdoors for hard lattices and new cryptographic constructions. In: ACM STOC 2008, pp. 197–206. ACM (2008)

[ID03] Ivan, A.-A., Dodis, Y.: Proxy cryptography revisited. In NDSS 2003. The Internet Society (2003)

[Jia20] Jiang, Y.: The direction of updatable encryption does not matter much. In: Moriai, S., Wang, H. (eds.) ASIACRYPT 2020. LNCS, vol. 12493, pp. 529–558. Springer, Cham (2020). https://doi.org/10.1007/978-3-030-64840-4_18

[JMM19] Jost, D., Maurer, U., Mularczyk, M.: Efficient ratcheting: almost-optimal guarantees for secure messaging. In: Ishai, Y., Rijmen, V. (eds.) EUROCRYPT 2019. LNCS, vol. 11476, pp. 159–188. Springer, Cham (2019). https://doi.org/10.1007/978-3-030-17653-2_6

[Kir14] Kirshanova, E.: Proxy re-encryption from lattices. In: Krawczyk, H. (ed.) PKC 2014. LNCS, vol. 8383, pp. 77–94. Springer, Heidelberg (2014). https://doi.org/10.1007/978-3-642-54631-0_5

[KLR19] Klooß, Michael, Lehmann, Anja, Rupp, Andy: (R)CCA Secure Updatable Encryption with Integrity Protection. In: Ishai, Yuval, Rijmen, Vincent (eds.) EUROCRYPT 2019. LNCS, vol. 11476, pp. 68–99. Springer, Cham (2019). https://doi.org/10.1007/978-3-030-17653-2_3

[LT18] Lehmann, Anja, Tackmann, Björn.: Updatable encryption with post-compromise security. In: Nielsen, Jesper Buus, Rijmen, Vincent (eds.) EUROCRYPT 2018. LNCS, vol. 10822, pp. 685–716. Springer, Cham (2018). https://doi.org/10.1007/978-3-319-78372-7_22

[LV11] Libert, B., Vergnaud, D.: Unidirectional chosen-ciphertext secure proxy re-encryption. IEEE Trans. Inf. Theor. **57**(3), 1786–1802 (2011)

[MPW22] Miao, P., Patranabis, S., Watson, G.: Unidirectional updatable encryption and proxy re-encryption from DDH. In: IACR Cryptol. ePrint Arch., p. 311 (2022)

[NAL15] Nuñez, D., Agudo, I., López, J.: Ntrureencrypt: An efficient proxy re-encryption scheme based on NTRU. In: ACM ASIA CCS 2015 (2015)

[Nis21] Nishimaki, R.: The direction of updatable encryption does matter. Cryptology ePrint Archive, Report 2021/221 (2021). https://eprint.iacr.org/2021/221

[NS12] Naor, M., Segev, G.: Public-key cryptosystems resilient to key leakage. SIAM J. Comput. **41**(4), 772–814 (2012)

[Nun18] Nunez, D.: Umbral: a threshold proxy re-encryption scheme. NuCypher Inc and NICS Lab, University of Malaga, Spain (2018)

[NX15] Nishimaki, R., Xagawa, K.: Key-private proxy re-encryption from lattices, revisited. IEICE Trans. **98**-A(1), 100–116 (2015)

[Pay18] Payment Card Industry (PCI). Data Security Standard - Version 3.2.1, May (2018)

[PRSV17] Polyakov, Y., Rohloff, K., Sahu, G., Vaikuntanathan, V.: Fast proxy re-encryption for publish/subscribe systems. ACM Trans. Priv. Secur., **20**(4):14:1–14:31 (2017)

[PWA+16] Phong, L.T., Wang, L., Aono, Y., Nguyen, M.H., Boyen, X.: Proxy re-encryption schemes with key privacy from LWE. Cryptology ePrint Archive, Report 2016/327 (2016) https://eprint.iacr.org/2016/327

[SD19] Sehrawat, V.S., Desmedt, Y.: Bi-homomorphic lattice-based PRFs and uni-directional updatable encryption. In: Mu, Y., Deng, R.H., Huang, X. (eds.) CANS 2019. LNCS, vol. 11829, pp. 3–23. Springer, Cham (2019). https://doi.org/10.1007/978-3-030-31578-8_1

[SS21] Slamanig, D., Striecks, C.: Puncture 'em all: Stronger updatable encryption with no-directional key updates. Cryptology ePrint Archive, Report 2021/268 (2021) https://eprint.iacr.org/2021/268

Backward-Leak Uni-Directional Updatable Encryption from (Homomorphic) Public Key Encryption

Yao Jiang Galteland[1]([⊠]) [iD] and Jiaxin Pan[2] [iD]

[1] Department of Information Security and Communication Technology, NTNU – Norwegian University of Science and Technology, Gjøvik, Norway
yao.jiang@ntnu.no
[2] Department of Mathematical Sciences, NTNU – Norwegian University of Science and Technology, Trondheim, Norway
jiaxin.pan@ntnu.no

Abstract. The understanding of directionality for updatable encryption (UE) schemes is important, but not yet completed in the literature. We show that security in the backward-leak uni-directional key updates setting is equivalent to the no-directional one. Combining with the work of Jiang (ASIACRYPT 2020) and Nishimaki (PKC 2022), it is showed that the backward-leak notion is the strongest one among all known key update notions and more relevant in practice. We propose two novel generic constructions of UE schemes that are secure in the backward-leak uni-directional key update setting from public key encryption (PKE) schemes: the first one requires a key and message homomorphic PKE scheme and the second one requires a bootstrappable PKE scheme. These PKE can be constructed based on standard assumptions (such as the Decisional Diffie-Hellman and Learning With Errors assumptions).

Keywords: Updatable Encryption · Public Key Encryption · Backward-leak Uni-Directional Key Update · No-Directional Key Update · Standard Assumption

1 Introduction

To mitigate key compromise over time, a data subject wishes to periodically update her outsourced data on a data host. The outsourced data is expected to be refreshed from the old key to the new key without changing the underlying

Y. Jiang Galteland—Her work has been co-funded by the IKTPLUSS program of the Research Council of Norway under the scope of and as part of the outcome from the research project Reinforcing the Health Data Infrastructure in Mobility and Assurance through Data Democratization (Health Democratization, 2019–2024, Project No. 288856.
J. Pan—His work is supported by the Research Council of Norway under Project No. 324235.

A. Boldyreva and V. Kolesnikov (Eds.): PKC 2023, LNCS 13941, pp. 399–428, 2023.
https://doi.org/10.1007/978-3-031-31371-4_14

message. During this process, it is also reasonable to expect that no information of plaintexts are leaked while updating.

Updatable encryption (UE) schemes [2–4,6,11,12,14,16] are a special kind of encryption schemes that allow the data host to update ciphertexts with the help of a data subject generated updating material, namely update token. Update tokens can rotate ciphertexts or keys, which makes UE schemes particularly interesting for outsourced data storage. However, leaked tokens together with key corruption an adversary may break confidentiality of the future or past epoch by upgrading or downgrading keys or ciphertexts, which is captured by the directionality of UE schemes. The study of UE mainly focuses on the security notions and efficient constructions. Directionality for UE schemes is important to study since it plays a central role in influencing the security result. The challenge is that there are two types of ciphertext update settings and four types of key update settings in the literature, and a combination of these settings results in eight different types of update settings for UE schemes to analyze.

Directionality of Ciphertext Updates. If an update token can only update a ciphertext under a key in the past to a ciphertext under a new key without changing the encrypted message, it is in the forward direction, then we call that such a UE scheme has uni-directional ciphertext updates; and if an update token can additionally update a ciphertext to another ciphertext under a key in the past, we call such a UE scheme with bi-directional ciphertext updates.

Directionality of Key Updates. Secret key leakage is a serious security threat to encryption. For instance, there is no security guarantee for standard encryption schemes if their secret keys are leaked. However, for UE schemes, the update token offers a potential to preserve confidentiality, since the update token allows us to update a secret key and the corresponding ciphertexts. Realizing this fully is very challenging and requires careful treatments, since the update token may also leak information about the key.

Directionality of key update is used to capture which information adversaries can learn about the secret keys given the update token. Roughly speaking, there are four key update settings given by the literature [9,12,14]. For a precise description, let e be an epoch, namely, the index of a time period. In the *forward-leak* uni-directional key update setting[1] [12], given a key k_e and an update token Δ_{e+1} adversaries can only learn a key k_{e+1} in the forward direction. Similarly, in the *backward-leak* uni-directional key update setting [14], adversaries can only learn a key k_e in the backward direction, given k_{e+1} and Δ_{e+1}. If both forward-leak and backward-leak are satisfied in a setting, then it is called *bi-directional key update*. In contrary, if an update token leaks nothing about any secret key, then this setting is called *no-directional key update* [9].

Security Implications Among Different Key Update Settings. Security of a UE scheme is defined with respect to the aforementioned key update settings.

---

[1] This was called uni-directional key updates in [12], but here we follow the more precise terminology of Nishimaki [14] and call it forward-leak uni-directional key updates.

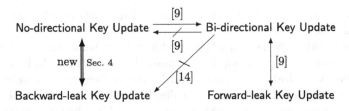

Fig. 1. Security implications among different key update settings assuming unidirectional ciphertext updates. $X \rightarrow Y$ means that security in the X setting implies that in the Y setting, and $X \nrightarrow Y$ means that security in the X setting does not imply that in the Y setting, and $X \leftrightarrow Y = (X \rightarrow Y) \wedge (Y \rightarrow X)$. Contribution in this paper is marked with a double arrow '$\leftrightarrow$'.

Roughly speaking, UE security guarantees confidentiality if the trivial win conditions are not triggered. The trivial win conditions are defined differently in each key update setting, and more information leaked about keys leads to more trivial win conditions in the confidentiality game for UE schemes. With more trivial win conditions, it seems harder for an adversary to win the confidentiality, since it is easier for it to trigger the trivial win conditions. Thus, intuitively, a setting with less key leakage seems to give stronger security.

This intuition partially holds true, according to the work of Jiang [9] and Nishimaki [14]. More precisely, in [9] it has been showed that security in the no-directional setting is strictly stronger than that in the bi-directional setting, and security in the bi-directional key update setting is equivalent to that in the forward-leak setting. To further complete the work of Jiang, Nishimaki [14] proposed the backward-leak uni-directional setting and showed that UE schemes in prior works [4,9,12] are secure in the bi-directional setting but insecure in the backward-leak uni-directional setting. Here we consider that an update token can only update a ciphertext in the forward direction, since if the ciphertext updates are bi-directional then all four settings are equivalent as shown in [9]. The implications among these four key update settings are shown figuratively in Fig. 1.

To sum up the discussions above, it is currently unclear that the relation between the no-directional and backward-leak uni-directional key update settings, although they both are stronger than the bi-directional and forward-leak setting.

Our Goal: UE schemes with Strong Security from Weak Assumptions. We aim at constructing UE schemes with strong security from weak assumptions. In achieving our goal, we first need to decide which notion is the strongest among the above four settings. Jumping ahead, our first contribution is proving the no-directional and backward-leak settings are equivalent. Given our equivalence result, we claim it is more desirable to construct a UE scheme that is secure in the backward-leak uni-directional key update setting for the following reasons.

Firstly, UE schemes secure in the backward-leak setting are technically more promising to construct based on weak assumptions, since the existing UE scheme [14] with no-directional key updates are based on strong assumptions. Namely,

the scheme in [14] requires a rather strong and impractical primitive, indistinguishability obfuscation.

Secondly, although there is a backward-leak UE scheme based on the Learning With Errors (LWE) assumption proposed by Nishimaki [14], it is unknown
whether backward-leak UE schemes can be constructed from a wider class of
weak assumptions, for instance, the Diffie-Hellman assumption without pairings. We are particularly interested in constructing UE schemes generically from
public-key encryption (PKE), since this not only is theoretically interesting, but
also can give us UE schemes from rather weak assumptions. Recently, Alamati,
Montgomery, and Patranabis [1] have proved that ciphertext-independent UE
implies PKE, but the implication in the other direction is unknown.

Finally, we stress that the backward-leak setting is relevant for practice, as
discussed in [14]. In practice, the purpose of updating our keys is mostly because
the current key and those in the past may be leaked. In such a scenario, UE
schemes in the backward-leak uni-directional key update setting are required,
since they can provide confidentiality in an epoch, even though all previous keys
and tokens are corrupted. Moreover, backward-leak UE schemes remain secure
even if the data host forgets to delete older keys and tokens, while this is not the
case for forward-leak UE schemes, since with the older keys an adversary can
learn the keys in the future.

1.1 Our Contributions

Intuition Behind Security Definitions. Our first contribution is providing an
intuitive understanding of trivial win conditions, firewalls, directionality and
security notions. Explanations of all these topics exists in [3,4,9,11,12,14],
however, we aim to provide a simple description to show the relations among
these definitions. We consider two classes of UE schemes (discussed in Sect. 3.2
and 3.3): the first class of UE schemes have update settings such that keys cannot upgrade and ciphertexts cannot downgrade, the second class of UE schemes
have update settings where keys and ciphertexts both can leak information in the
forward direction. We observe that the first class of UE schemes (including UE
schemes with backward-leak uni-directional key updates and no-directional key
updates) can achieve the strongest confidentiality notion (with post-compromise
security). Thus, it is only necessary to analyze two classes of UE schemes, and
these two classes of UE schemes matches with the equivalence result in the literature [9,14] and our work. That is, the eight variants of confidentiality notions
can be seen as only two classes of confidentiality notions. We will show that
notions in the same class are equivalent and one class is strictly stronger that
the other.

Equivalence Result. Our second contribution is proving that security in the
backward-leak uni-directional key update and uni-directional ciphertext update
setting is equivalent to that in the no-directional key update and uni-directional
ciphertext update setting. All our UE schemes have uni-directional ciphertext
updates, and for simplicity, we do not mention it explicitly in the remaining of
this section. This means that UE schemes with no-directional key updates do not

provide stronger security than UE schemes with backward-leak uni-directional key update. Our result suggests that constructing UE schemes with backward-leak uni-directional key update is equivalent to constructing UE schemes with no-directional key update.

Generic Constructions of UE from PKE. Our third contribution is constructing two generic constructions of UE schemes with backward-leak uni-directional key update from PKE schemes. Our constructions require additional properties of the underlying PKE schemes. Our first construction requires key and message homomorphism for PKE schemes. Such PKE schemes can be instantiated under the Decisional Diffie-Hellman (using the ElGamal encryption) and LWE (using the Regev encryption [15]) assumptions. Combining with our equivalence result, the aforementioned two schemes provide us with the *first* no-directional secure UE schemes without pairings in the Diffie-Hellman setting and based on a post-quantum assumption, respectively. We note that the uni-directional schemes from FHE or IO or lattice trapdoors [14] usually do not have this increased key-size or ciphertext-size. But without these assumptions and technique, uni-directional schemes relying on standard assumptions (namely, ours and the work in [13]) are constructed with growing key and cipehrtextext. It remains an open problem to construct uni-directional schemes relying on standard assumptions where the key and cipehrtextext size keeps the same.

Our second generic construction uses a bootstrappable PKE [8] that can be implemented using the LWE assumption, which again gives us a post-quantum UE scheme with security in the no-directional key update setting.

Of independent interest, we propose a generic construction of bi-directional UE scheme from a key homomorphic PKE scheme. Our generic construction abstracts the constructions of RISE [12] and LWEUE [9]. We stress that our notion of key homomorphic PKE is inspired by the key homomorphic PRF of Boneh et al. [3] but different to theirs. More precisely, our key homomorphic property is defined with respect to a public key and a secret key, while theirs is with respect to two secret keys.

Technical Overview. Here we provide a brief technical overview of our generic backward-leak UE constructions from PKEs. The full descriptions of our schemes can be found in Sects. 5.3 and 6. The update token plays an important role in a UE scheme, and therefore we mostly focus on it in the following.

In our first construction, its key contains a pair of secret and public keys from the PKE scheme. The update token contains the difference between the old and new secret keys. In addition, the token includes an independently generated public key, which will play a central role for the confidentiality in the next epoch. To update a ciphertext, we have two steps: Firstly, by the key homomorphic property of the PKE, the difference between the old and new secret keys can be used to modify the ciphertext under the old key to one under the new key. Secondly, we randomize this ciphertext so that it is indistinguishable to a freshly generated ciphertext under the new key. In doing this, we use the aforementioned independent public key to encrypt a randomness to homomorphically randomize the ciphertext, since our PKE is further message homomorphic. In the security proof, we can show that message is hidden by the randomness and confidentiality in the new epoch is preserved.

In our second construction, the update token is an encryption of the old secret key under the new public key. This token will not reveal any information about the new secret key even with the knowledge of the old secret key. To update a ciphertext, we evaluate the decryption circuit on the encryption of the old key (that is the token) and the encryption of the old ciphertext. The bootstrapping property states that this output is statistically close to a fresh ciphertext under the new key.

Concurrent Work. We note a recent work from Miao, Patranabis, and Watson [13] which has a construction of backward-leak uni-directional UE similar to ours, while our work contains a formal proof about the equivalence between backward-leak and no-directional UE.

1.2   More Discussion

Ciphertext-Dependent v.s. Ciphertext-Independent. We call an updatable encryption scheme is ciphertext-dependent [2,3,5,6] if the token generation process depends on the old ciphertext. If the token generation process is independent of the ciphertext to be updated, then the UE scheme is called ciphertext-independent [4,9,11,12,14,16]. A ciphertext-independent UE scheme is usually more efficient in terms of bandwidth cost, and, thus, we focus on such schemes in this paper.

Deterministic Update. The update algorithm in UE schemes can be deterministic or randomized. UE schemes with randomized update algorithm provide stronger security, in which the updated ciphertext can be in the same distribution of a fresh encryption. However, the work of Klooß et al. [11] shows that such UE schemes with randomized update cannot achieve ciphertext integrity and security against chosen-cipertext attacks (CCA), but replayable CCA security. For instance, SHINE [4] and E&M [11] are UE schemes with deterministic update that have ciphertext integrity and CCA security. Klooß et al.'s result also means that our constructions cannot be CCA secure, but it is promising to make it RCCA secure. We leave constructing this as an open problem.

Security Notions. Boneh et al. [3] presented the first security notion for UE schemes. After that, the works in [4,9,11,12] proposed more realistic security notion by providing more capability to an adversary. For instance, it can adaptively corrupt epoch keys or update tokens at any point within the security game. Jiang [9] first discussed the directionality of security notions and showed that security notions with forward-leak uni- and bi-directional updates are equivalent in the current state-of-the-art UE security notion of Boyd et al. [4]. In addition, Jiang [9] proved that confidentiality notions with no-directional key updates are strictly stronger than uni- and bi-directional update variants of the corresponding notions. Nishimaki [14] defined a new type of key update, backward-leak uni-directional key update, which is not covered in the work of [9]. We will prove the relation between the backward-leak uni-directional key update variant of a confidentiality notion with other update variants of the same confidentiality notion. We will show that confidentiality notions with backward-leak uni-directional key update is equivalent to no-directional key updates variants of the corresponding notions. Which means the backward-leak uni-directional key update variant of notions are the strongest notions.

Slamanig and Striecks [16] introduced a stronger model for UE schemes, where they consider an "expiry epoch", e_{exp}. If a ciphertext is updated to an epoch e, where $e \geq e_{exp}$ and e_{exp} is this ciphertext's expiry epoch, then this ciphertext can no longer be decryptable. Their model allows the adversary knows "all"[2] tokens. Forward security is guaranteed if the key updates are at most in the forward-direction and leaked keys are in epochs after the expiry epoch of a ciphertext. Post compromise security is guaranteed if the key updates are at most in the backward-direction. Realizing such strong security strictly requires no-directional UE schemes where keys must not be updatable in any direction. Note that Jiang's equivalence theorem [9] holds in the setting where there is no expiry date for ciphertexts, i.e., $e_{exp} = \infty$. We consider the case for $e_{exp} = \infty$ in this paper. We do not compare the efficiency of our construction with the UE construction in [16], due to schemes are in different UE models.

2 Preliminaries

In this section we describe the notation used in this paper and present the necessary background material of updatable encryption. Due to space limitations, we provide the preliminaries for public key encryption in the full version [7]. y parameter and negl denotes a negligible function. For distributions X and Y, $X \overset{s}{\approx} Y$ means X is statistically indistinguishable from Y.

2.1 Updatable Encryption and Confidentiality Notions

Updatable encryption (UE) schemes [3,4,11,12] are a special kind of encryption schemes with an additional functionality where ciphertexts under one key can be transferred to ciphertexts under another key by an update token.

Definition 1 (UE). *An updatable encryption scheme* UE *is parameterized by a tuple of algorithms* (Setup, Next, Enc, Dec, Upd) *that operates over epochs such that*

- *The setup algorithm* Setup(λ) *takes a security parameter λ as input, and outputs an initial epoch key k_1.*
- *The next algorithm* Next(k_e) *takes an epoch key k_e as input, and outputs a new key k_{e+1} and an update token Δ_{e+1}, the update token can be used to update ciphertexts from epoch e to $e + 1$.*

---

[2] except for some end epoch e_{end}, if $e_{exp} \leq e_{end}$.

– *The encryption algorithm* $\mathsf{Enc}(k_e, m)$ *takes an epoch key* k_e *and a message* m *as input, and outputs a ciphertext* c_e.
– *The decryption algorithm* $\mathsf{Dec}(k_e, c_e)$ *takes an epoch key* k_e *and a ciphertext* c_e *as input, and outputs a message* m.
– *The update algorithm* $\mathsf{Upd}(\Delta_{e+1}, c_e)$ *takes an update token* Δ_{e+1} *and a ciphertext* c_e *as input, and outputs an updated ciphertext* c_{e+1}.

UE *is* correct *if for any message* m, *any* $k_1 \leftarrow \mathsf{Setup}(\lambda)$, *any* $(k_j, \Delta_j) \leftarrow \mathsf{Next}(k_{j-1})$ *for* $j = 2, ..., e$, *and any* $c_i \leftarrow \mathsf{Enc}(k_i, m)$ *with* $i \in \{1, ..., e\}$, *we have* $m = \mathsf{Dec}(k_e, c_e)$ *where* $c_j \leftarrow \mathsf{Upd}(\Delta_j, c_{j-1})$ *for* $j = i + 1, ..., e$.

Security notions for UE schemes include confidentiality and integrity. We do not consider integrity notions in this paper, see the paper by Jiang [9] for details. We review the confidentiality notion for UE schemes in Definition 2 and extend the six variants of security notions for UE schemes given by [9], in which the backward-leak uni-directional key update [14] variants are not included.

The confidentiality game is played between a challenger and an adversary, the adversary aims to distinguish a fresh encryption from an updated ciphertext. It is allowed for the adversary to adaptively corrupt keys and tokens, if any trivial win condition is triggered during the game the adversary will always lose. We will provide technical and high level understanding of trivial win conditions in Sect. 2.2 and 3.

Definition 2 ([4,9]). *Let* $\mathsf{UE} = (\mathsf{Setup}, \mathsf{Next}, \mathsf{Enc}, \mathsf{Dec}, \mathsf{Upd})$ *be an updatable encryption scheme. Then the* $(\mathsf{kk}, \mathsf{cc})\text{-xxIND-UE-atk}$ *advantage, for* $\mathsf{kk} \in \{\mathsf{no}, \mathsf{f\text{-}uni}, \mathsf{b\text{-}uni}, \mathsf{bi}\}$, $\mathsf{cc} \in \{\mathsf{uni}, \mathsf{bi}\}$, $\mathsf{xx} \in \{\mathsf{det}, \mathsf{rand}\}$ *and* $\mathsf{atk} \in \{\mathsf{CPA}, \mathsf{CCA}\}$, *of an adversary* $\mathcal{A}$ *against* UE *is defined as*

$$\mathbf{Adv}_{\mathsf{UE}, \mathcal{A}}^{(\mathsf{kk},\mathsf{cc})\text{-xxIND-UE-atk}}(\lambda)$$
$$= \left| \mathbf{Pr}[\mathbf{Exp}_{\mathsf{UE}, \mathcal{A}}^{(\mathsf{kk},\mathsf{cc})\text{-xxIND-UE-atk-1}} = 1] - \mathbf{Pr}[\mathbf{Exp}_{\mathsf{UE}, \mathcal{A}}^{(\mathsf{kk},\mathsf{cc})\text{-xxIND-UE-atk-0}} = 1] \right|,$$

where the experiment $\mathbf{Exp}_{\mathsf{UE}, \mathcal{A}}^{(\mathsf{kk},\mathsf{cc})\text{-xxIND-UE-atk-b}}$ *is given in Fig. 2.*

2.2 Leakage Sets and Trivial Win Conditions

In this section, we review the definition of leakage sets and trivial win discussions [4,9,11,12], the leaked information can be used to help an adversary trivially win the confidentiality game.

Trivial Win via Key and Ciphertext Leakage. If an adversary knows both the key and the challenge-equal ciphertext in the same epoch period e, then the adversary can use this key to decrypt the challenge-equal ciphertext and obtain the underlying plaintext to win the confidentiality game. We use leakage sets to identify if this trivial win condition ("$\mathcal{K}^* \cap \mathcal{C}^* \neq \emptyset$") is triggered.

Leakage sets [9,11,12] are defined to track epochs in which the adversary knows a key, a token, or learned a version of challenge ciphertext. The direct

$\mathbf{Exp}_{\mathsf{UE},\,\mathcal{A}}^{\mathsf{xxIND\text{-}UE\text{-}atk\text{-}b}}$:

do Setup; phase $\leftarrow 0$
  $b' \leftarrow \mathcal{A}^{oracles}(\lambda)$
  if $\Big((\mathcal{K}_{\mathsf{kk}}^* \cap \mathcal{C}_{\mathsf{kk,cc}}^* \neq \emptyset)$ **or** $\big(\mathsf{xx} = \mathsf{det}$ **and**
  $(\tilde{e} \in \mathcal{T}_{\mathsf{kk}}^*$ **or** $\mathcal{O}.\mathsf{Upd}(\bar{c})$ is queried$)\big)\Big)$ **then**
    $\mathsf{twf} \leftarrow 1$

  if $\mathsf{twf} = 1$ **then**
    $b' \xleftarrow{\$} \{0, 1\}$
  return b'

$\underline{\mathbf{Setup}(\lambda)}$
  $k_1 \xleftarrow{\$} \mathsf{Setup}(\lambda)$
  $\Delta_1 \leftarrow \perp;\, \mathsf{e}, \mathsf{c}, \mathsf{twf} \leftarrow 0$
  $\mathcal{L}, \tilde{\mathcal{L}}, \mathcal{C}, \mathcal{K}, \mathcal{T} \leftarrow \emptyset$

$\underline{\mathcal{O}.\mathsf{Enc}(m)}$:
  $\mathsf{c} \leftarrow \mathsf{c} + 1$
  $c_{\mathsf{e}} \xleftarrow{\$} \mathsf{Enc}(k_{\mathsf{e}}, m)$
  $\mathcal{L} \leftarrow \mathcal{L} \cup \{(\mathsf{c}, c_{\mathsf{e}}, \mathsf{e}; m)\}$
  return c_{e}

$\underline{\mathcal{O}.\mathsf{Dec}(c)}$:
  m' **or** $\perp \leftarrow \mathsf{Dec}(k_{\mathsf{e}}, c)$
  if $\Big((\mathsf{xx} = \mathsf{det}$ **and** $(c, \mathsf{e}) \in \tilde{\mathcal{L}}_{\mathsf{kk,cc}}^*)$ **or**
  $(\mathsf{xx} = \mathsf{rand}$ **and** $(m', \mathsf{e}) \in \tilde{\mathcal{Q}}_{\mathsf{kk,cc}}^*)\Big)$ **then**
    $\mathsf{twf} \leftarrow 1$
  return m' **or** $\perp$

$\underline{\mathcal{O}.\mathsf{Next}()}$:
  $(\Delta_{\mathsf{e}+1}, k_{\mathsf{e}+1}) \leftarrow \mathsf{Next}(k_{\mathsf{e}})$
  if $\mathsf{phase} = 1$ **then**
    $\tilde{c}_{\mathsf{e}+1} \leftarrow \mathsf{Upd}(\Delta_{\mathsf{e}+1}, \tilde{c}_{\mathsf{e}})$
  $\mathsf{e} \leftarrow \mathsf{e} + 1$

$\underline{\mathcal{O}.\mathsf{Upd}(c_{\mathsf{e}-1})}$:
  if $(j, c_{\mathsf{e}-1}, \mathsf{e} - 1; m) \notin \mathcal{L}$ **then**
    return $\perp$
  $c_{\mathsf{e}} \leftarrow \mathsf{Upd}(\Delta_{\mathsf{e}}, c_{\mathsf{e}-1})$
  $\mathcal{L} \leftarrow \mathcal{L} \cup \{(j, c_{\mathsf{e}}, \mathsf{e}; m)\}$
  return c_{e}

$\underline{\mathcal{O}.\mathsf{Corr}(\mathsf{inp}, \hat{e})}$:
  if $\hat{e} > \mathsf{e}$ **then**
    return $\perp$
  if $\mathsf{inp} = \mathsf{key}$ **then**
    $\mathcal{K} \leftarrow \mathcal{K} \cup \{\hat{e}\}$
    return $k_{\hat{e}}$
  if $\mathsf{inp} = \mathsf{token}$ **then**
    $\mathcal{T} \leftarrow \mathcal{T} \cup \{\hat{e}\}$
    return $\Delta_{\hat{e}}$

$\underline{\mathcal{O}.\mathsf{Chall}(\bar{m}, \bar{c})}$:
  if $\mathsf{phase} = 1$ **then**
    return $\perp$
  $\mathsf{phase} \leftarrow 1;\, \tilde{e} \leftarrow \mathsf{e}$
  if $(\cdot, \bar{c}, \tilde{e} - 1; \cdot) \notin \mathcal{L}$ **then**
    return $\perp$
  if $b = 0$ **then**
    $\tilde{c}_{\tilde{e}} \leftarrow \mathsf{Enc}(k_{\tilde{e}}, \bar{m})$
  else
    $\tilde{c}_{\tilde{e}} \leftarrow \mathsf{Upd}(\Delta_{\tilde{e}}, \bar{c})$
  $\mathcal{C} \leftarrow \mathcal{C} \cup \{\tilde{e}\}$
  $\tilde{\mathcal{L}} \leftarrow \tilde{\mathcal{L}} \cup \{(\tilde{c}_{\tilde{e}}, \tilde{e})\}$
  return $\tilde{c}_{\tilde{e}}$

$\underline{\mathcal{O}.\mathsf{Upd}\tilde{\mathsf{C}}}$:
  if $\mathsf{phase} \neq 1$ **then**
    return $\perp$
  $\mathcal{C} \leftarrow \mathcal{C} \cup \{\mathsf{e}\}$
  $\tilde{\mathcal{L}} \leftarrow \tilde{\mathcal{L}} \cup \{(\tilde{c}_{\mathsf{e}}, \mathsf{e})\}$
  return $\tilde{c}_{\mathsf{e}}$

Fig. 2. The confidentiality experiment $\mathbf{Exp}_{\mathsf{UE},\,\mathcal{A}}^{(\mathsf{kk,cc})\text{-}\mathsf{xxIND\text{-}UE\text{-}atk\text{-}b}}$ for updatable encryption scheme UE and adversary $\mathcal{A}$, for $\mathsf{kk} \in \{\mathsf{no}, \mathsf{f\text{-}uni}, \mathsf{b\text{-}uni}, \mathsf{bi}\}$, $\mathsf{cc} \in \{\mathsf{uni}, \mathsf{bi}\}$, $\mathsf{xx} \in \{\mathsf{det}, \mathsf{rand}\}$ and $\mathsf{atk} \in \{\mathsf{CPA}, \mathsf{CCA}\}$. The flag phase tracks whether or not $\mathcal{A}$ has queried the $\mathcal{O}.\mathsf{Chall}$ oracle, $\tilde{e}$ denotes the epoch in which the $\mathcal{O}.\mathsf{Chall}$ oracle happens, and twf tracks if the trivial win conditions are triggered. Oracles an adversary can query are $\mathcal{O}.\mathsf{Enc}$, $\mathcal{O}.\mathsf{Next}$, $\mathcal{O}.\mathsf{Upd}$, $\mathcal{O}.\mathsf{Corr}$, $\mathcal{O}.\mathsf{Chall}$ and $\mathcal{O}.\mathsf{Upd}\tilde{\mathsf{C}}$ if $\mathsf{atk} = \mathsf{CPA}$. If $\mathsf{atk} = \mathsf{CCA}$, $\mathcal{O}.\mathsf{Dec}$ is included in the oracles. Leakage sets $\mathcal{C}, \mathcal{K}, \mathcal{T}, \mathcal{K}_{\mathsf{kk}}^*, \mathcal{T}_{\mathsf{kk}}^*, \mathcal{C}_{\mathsf{kk,cc}}^*, \tilde{\mathcal{L}}_{\mathsf{kk,cc}}^*, \tilde{\mathcal{Q}}_{\mathsf{kk,cc}}^*$ are discussed in Sect. 2.2.

leakage sets $\mathcal{K}, \mathcal{T}, \mathcal{C}$ are describe as follows. Furthermore, $\mathcal{K}^*, \mathcal{T}^*$ and $\mathcal{C}^*$ are defined as the extended sets of $\mathcal{K}, \mathcal{T}$ and $\mathcal{C}$ to track the indirect leakage.

- $\mathcal{K}$: Set of epochs in which the adversary corrupted the key (from $\mathcal{O}.\mathsf{Corr}$).
- $\mathcal{T}$: Set of epochs in which the adversary corrupted the token (from $\mathcal{O}.\mathsf{Corr}$).
- $\mathcal{C}$: Set of epochs in which the adversary learned a challenge-equal ciphertext[3] (from $\mathcal{O}.\mathsf{Chall}$ or $\mathcal{O}.\mathsf{Upd\tilde{C}}$).

Key Leakage. The size of the key leakage set $\mathcal{K}^*$ can be influenced by the key update direction of UE schemes. In the no-directional key update setting [9], the adversary does not have more information about keys except for set $\mathcal{K}$. In the forward-leak uni-directional key update setting, if the adversary knows a key k_e and an update token Δ_{e+1} then it can infer the next key k_{e+1}. In the backward-leak [14] uni-directional key update setting, if the adversary knows a key k_{e+1} and an update token Δ_{e+1} then it can infer the previous key k_e.

The notations f-uni and b-uni denote forward-leak uni and backward-leak uni, resp.. In the kk-directional key update setting, for $\mathsf{kk} \in \{\mathsf{no}, \mathsf{f\text{-}uni}, \mathsf{b\text{-}uni}, \mathsf{bi}\}$, denote the set $\mathcal{K}^*_{\mathsf{kk}}$ as the extended set of corrupted key epochs. We compute these sets as follows, where the boxed part is only computed for $\mathsf{kk} \in \{\mathsf{b\text{-}uni}, \mathsf{bi}\}$, the gray boxed part is only computed for $\mathsf{kk} \in \{\mathsf{f\text{-}uni}, \mathsf{bi}\}$

$$\mathcal{K}^*_{\mathsf{kk}} \leftarrow \{e \in \{0, ..., l\} | \mathsf{CorrK}(e) = \mathsf{true}\}$$
$$\mathsf{true} \leftarrow \mathsf{CorrK}(e) \iff$$
$$(e \in \mathcal{K}) \vee \boxed{\mathsf{CorrK}(e+1) \wedge e+1 \in \mathcal{T}} \vee \boxed{\mathsf{CorrK}(e\text{-}1) \wedge e \in \mathcal{T}}. \tag{1}$$

Token Leakage. The adversary directly learns all corrupted tokens, it can also compute a token from two consecutive epoch keys. We follow the assumption (an update token can be computed via two consecutive epoch keys) in the page 7 of [10], this assumption is essential to formulate the known knowledge to the adversary. Hence, for $\mathsf{kk} \in \{\mathsf{no}, \mathsf{f\text{-}uni}, \mathsf{b\text{-}uni}, \mathsf{bi}\}$, denote $\mathcal{T}^*_{\mathsf{kk}}$ as the extended set of corrupted token epochs.

$$\mathcal{T}^*_{\mathsf{kk}} \leftarrow \{e \in \{0, ..., l\} | (e \in \mathcal{T}) \vee (e \in \mathcal{K}^*_{\mathsf{kk}} \wedge e\text{-}1 \in \mathcal{K}^*_{\mathsf{kk}})\}. \tag{2}$$

Challenge-Equal Ciphertext Leakage. The adversary learned all versions of challenge ciphertexts in epochs in $\mathcal{C}$. Additionally, the adversary can compute challenge-equal ciphertexts via tokens. In the uni-directional ciphertext update setting, the adversary can upgrade ciphertexts. In the bi-directional ciphertext update setting, the adversary can additionally downgrade ciphertexts.

For $\mathsf{kk} \in \{\mathsf{no}, \mathsf{f\text{-}uni}, \mathsf{b\text{-}uni}, \mathsf{bi}\}$ and $\mathsf{cc} \in \{\mathsf{uni}, \mathsf{bi}\}$, denote the set $\mathcal{C}^*_{\mathsf{kk}, \mathsf{cc}}$ as the extended set of challenge-equal epochs. We compute these sets as follows, where the boxed part is only computed for $\mathsf{cc} = \mathsf{bi}$.

$$\mathcal{C}^*_{\mathsf{kk}, \mathsf{cc}} \leftarrow \{e \in \{0, ..., l\} | \mathsf{ChallEq}(e) = \mathsf{true}\}$$
$$\mathsf{true} \leftarrow \mathsf{ChallEq}(e) \iff$$
$$(e \in \mathcal{C}) \vee (\mathsf{ChallEq}(e\text{-}1) \wedge e \in \mathcal{T}^*_{\mathsf{kk}}) \vee \boxed{\mathsf{ChallEq}(e+1) \wedge e+1 \in \mathcal{T}^*_{\mathsf{kk}}}. \tag{3}$$

---

[3] A challenge-equal ciphertext is either a challenge ciphertext or an updated ciphertext of the challenge ciphertext.

Trivial Win Due to Deterministic Update. In a confidentiality game with deterministic update setting. If the adversary knows the updated version (by either knowing the update token $\Delta_{\tilde{e}}$ or asking for an update oracle $\mathcal{O}.\mathsf{Upd}$ on $\bar{c}$) of the challenge input ciphertext $\bar{c}$, it can compare the updated ciphertext with the challenge ciphertext to win the confidentiality game. This trivial win condition is "$\tilde{e} \in \mathcal{T}^*$ or $\mathcal{O}.\mathsf{Upd}(\bar{c})$ is queried".

Trivial Wins via Decryption. If the adversary submits a challenge-equal ciphertext to the decryption oracle, it can trivially win the confidentiality game by comparing the challenge plaintexts with the decryption output. Hence, the adversary is not allowed to ask for a decryption oracle on such ciphertexts. We use the following sets to track challenge ciphertexts, challenge plaintexts and their updated versions that can be known to the adversary. These sets can be used to identify the above trivial win condition. More precisely, "$(c, \mathsf{e}) \in \tilde{\mathcal{L}}^*$" is a trivial win condition that is checked by the decryption oracle in the detIND-UE-CCA game, "$(m', \mathsf{e}) \in \tilde{\mathcal{Q}}^*$" is a trivial win condition that is checked by the decryption oracle in the randIND-UE-CCA game.

- $\tilde{\mathcal{L}}^*$: Set of challenge-equal ciphertexts $(\tilde{c}_\mathsf{e}, \mathsf{e})$. The adversary learned these ciphertexts from $\mathcal{O}.\mathsf{Chall}$ or $\mathcal{O}.\mathsf{Upd}\tilde{\mathsf{C}}$, or derived these ciphertexts from tokens.
- $\tilde{\mathcal{Q}}^*$: Set of challenge plaintexts $\{(\bar{m}, \mathsf{e}), (\bar{m}_1, \mathsf{e})\}$, where $(\bar{m}, \bar{c})$ is the input of challenge query $\mathcal{O}.\mathsf{Chall}$ and $\bar{m}_1$ is the underlying message of $\bar{c}$. The adversary learned or was able to compute a challenge-equal ciphertext in epoch e with the underlying message $\bar{m}$ or $\bar{m}_1$.

3 Intuitions Behind Security Definitions

In this section, we propose some high level intuitions behind the security notions for UE.

We aim to clarify the relations among trivial win conditions, directionality and security results. If a UE scheme potentially leaks more information (which can be influenced by directionality), then there exists more vulnerabilities (trivial win conditions) for such scheme. Forward security in prior work of UE are achieved under the limitation that no trivial win condition is triggered, namely, there may exist some token after the challenge epoch cannot be corrupted. In our work, we define a relaxed version of forward security that, after the challenge epoch, any keys and tokens can be corrupted and the confidentiality of the challenge epoch remains. Similarly, we discussed post-compromise security. In the end, we provide some observations about what types of UE schemes can achieve forward or post-compromise security.

3.1   Intuition of Trivial Wins Conditions

The more information that get leaked in a confidentiality game the more chances the adversary gains to win that game, and trivial win conditions are defined to exclude such winning conditions. Generally speaking, the more update directions a UE scheme has the more information the adversary can infer. That is, the directionality of the update setting influences how much information gets leaked.

Trivial win conditions can be seen as a way of limiting the adversary's attacking power and this can be used to compare two notions, where two notions for UE schemes are equivalent if they have the same winning probability. Consider a modified confidentiality game where the adversary is not allowed to perform certain actions that will trigger trivial win conditions. If such action happens, the game aborts. The winning probability of the original confidentiality game is the same as this modified confidentiality game. In other words, trivial win conditions are equivalent to an attacking model. Such attacking model defines the restriction to the adversary, for example, the adaptive corruption ability is restricted by not triggering the trivial win conditions. Only when the adversary's attack actions does not trigger the trivial win conditions it is possible to win the game. Informally, a security notion for a system can be seen as stronger if the system remains secure even if the adversary has more attacking ability.

Combining this with the discussion above, we see that the more update direction a UE scheme has the more key and ciphertext leakage there will be and more trivial win conditions to evaluate. This means that the adversary will be limited more in such a confidentiality game. From a security point of view, the less attacking ability the adversary has the weaker we can regard a security notion.

3.2   Intuition of Firewalls

The observation of firewalls was introduced in the work of Lehmann and Tackmann [12], Klooß et al. [11] provided an extended description of this *key insulation* technique, and Boyd et al. [4] formally defined it as *firewall technique*. Furthermore, Nishimaki [14] proposed a *relaxed firewall*, where the token on the left side of the insulated region (Δ_{fwl}) can be corrupted. In any security game, if the adversary never triggers the trivial win conditions, a cryptographic separation (firewalls) exists, for a detailed discussion of the existence of firewalls see [4,11,12,14].

Definition 3 (Firewalls [4,11,12]). *An* insulated region *with* firewalls fwl *and* fwr *is a consecutive sequence of epochs* (fwl, . . . , fwr) *for which:*

- *no key in the sequence of epochs* (fwl, . . . , fwr) *is corrupted;*
- *the tokens* Δ_{fwl} *and* $\Delta_{\mathsf{fwr}+1}$ *are not corrupted (if they exist);*
- *all tokens* $(\Delta_{\mathsf{fwl}+1}, \dots, \Delta_{\mathsf{fwr}})$ *are corrupted (if any exist).*

Definition 4 (Relaxed Firewalls [14]). *A* relaxed insulated region *with* relaxed firewalls fwl *and* fwr *is a consecutive sequence of epochs* (fwl, ..., fwr) *for which:*

- *no key in the sequence of epochs* (fwl, ..., fwr) *is corrupted;*
- *the token* $\Delta_{\mathsf{fwr}+1}$ *is not corrupted (if it exists);*
- *all tokens* $(\Delta_{\mathsf{fwl}+1}, ..., \Delta_{\mathsf{fwr}})$ *are corrupted (if any exist).*

The firewall technique is used when proving the security for UE schemes, it provides a method of describing a cryptographic separation, which is required in the epoch based model to simulate where keys and ciphertexts are known or unknown to the adversary. Firewalls, and relaxed firewalls, define a "safe" or insulated region for keys, where no key within the region can be inferred from keys outside of this region. We can regard the tokens Δ_{fwl} and $\Delta_{\mathsf{fwr}+1}$ as the left and right firewalls, the cryptographic separation is created when these two tokens are unknown to the adversary. In some UE settings, the token Δ_{fwl} can be corrupted and the cryptographic separation still holds, which means that the insulated region can be relaxed even without the left firewall.

The relaxed insulated region is suitable for analyzing security for UE schemes with update settings such that keys cannot upgrade and ciphertexts cannot downgrade, namely ciphertext and key will not leak information in the same direction. In UE schemes with uni-directional ciphertext update setting and key update settings without forward-leak direction, we have that the token Δ_{fwl} cannot upgrade early epoch keys to learn keys inside the insulated region, it cannot downgrade challenge-equal ciphertexts to learn early challenge-equal ciphertexts outside of the insulated region as well. Hence, keys and ciphertexts inside and outside of the insulated region are separated even when Δ_{fwl} is known to the adversary, the insulated region can be relaxed to allow the token Δ_{fwl} to be corrupted.

The (original) insulated region is suitable for analyze UE schemes with update settings such that keys and ciphertexts can both leak information in the forward direction, namely ciphertext and key will leak information in the same direction. In UE schemes with ciphertext and key update settings that both have at least forward-leak direction, we have that the token Δ_{fwl} can upgrade early corrupted keys to learn keys inside the insulated region. For these UE schemes we have that the token Δ_{fwr} can upgrade challenge-equal ciphertexts to an epoch outside the insulated region where the adversary knows a corrupted key. Hence, both tokens Δ_{fwl} and $\Delta_{\mathsf{fwr}+1}$ are required to be unknown to the adversary to make a cryptographic separation.

3.3 Forward Security and Post-compromise Security

Forward and post-compromise security for UE schemes were discussed by Lehmann and Tackmann [12]. However, all confidentiality games in their work are restricted by not triggering trivial win conditions, which means there exists a cryptographic separation between the leaked key region and the "safe" region (see the discussion of cryptographic separation in Sect. 3.2). That is, there exists two tokens one before and one after the epoch where the adversary aims to break the confidentiality such that these tokens cannot be corrupted.

We consider the standard definitions for forward and post-compromise security, in which we do not have the restrictions of tokens which cannot be corrupted. We say a UE scheme have

- *forward security* if the confidentiality in early epochs are not broken even if an adversary compromises keys and tokens in some later epochs.
- *post-compromise security* if the confidentiality in later epochs are not broken even if an adversary compromises keys and tokens in some early epochs.

We observe that only some specific UE schemes can achieve post-compromise security. No UE scheme can achieve forward security.

The first class of UE schemes, discussed in Sect. 3.2, have update settings such that keys cannot upgrade and ciphertexts cannot downgrade. Since the ciphertext update is forward direction, an adversary can upgrade challenge-equal ciphertexts by the help of tokens to an epoch where the adversary knows a key to break the confidentiality in early epochs. Therefore, such UE schemes cannot achieve forward security. However, an adversary compromises keys and tokens in some early epochs cannot learn keys to break the confidentiality in later epochs. Additionally, the adversary cannot downgrade a challenge-equal ciphertext to an early epoch where the adversary knows a key to break the confidentiality in later epochs. Hence, such UE schemes can have post-compromise security.

The second class of UE schemes, discussed in Sect. 3.2, have update settings where keys and ciphertexts both can leak information in the forward direction. An adversary can infer keys by tokens in the forward direction to break the confidentiality in later epochs, therefore, such UE schemes cannot achieve post-compromise security. Moreover, since the ciphertext update is forward direction, similar to the discussion in above paragraph, such UE schemes cannot achieve forward security either.

The above discussion matches with the equivalence results of confidentiality notions (see Sect. 4). It implies that the first class of UE schemes (including UE schemes with backward-leak uni-directional key updates and no-directional key updates) can achieve the strongest confidentiality notion (with post-compromise security).

3.4   Directionality for UE Schemes and Confidentiality Notions

We specify that directionality for UE schemes and directionality for confidentiality notions are two different concepts. The update directionality for UE schemes was defined to measure how much keys and ciphertexts are leaked because of update tokens. However, such leakage can be the whole information leakage or just partial information leakage. The partial leakage is not captured in the directionality for UE schemes, there is no definition for partial information leakage. Under current definitions, we consider update direction for UE schemes to be without partial information leakage. However, partial information leakage may be used to break the confidentiality. An adversary may be able to decrypt ciphertexts where it only knows partial information about the corresponding key. Such partial information leakage is considered in the security notion and it can be seen as equivalent to the whole information leakage. For example, suppose tokens in a UE scheme can be used to infer partial key information in both update direction, such UE schemes are considered as a no-directional key update UE scheme. However, if an adversary can use this partially leaked key to break confidentiality, then such UE scheme is not secure in the no-directional update variant of confidentiality, it can at most be secure in the bi-directional update variant of confidentiality. Overall, UE schemes with one kind of update setting do not immediately have the same update direction variant of security.

A specific update variant of security notion is suitable for examining UE schemes with the same update setting. But we stress that our security definitions are not restricted to UE schemes with some particular update setting, such UE schemes are simply insecure in a less updating (or leakage) variant of notion.

4 Relations Among Confidentiality Notions

In the work of [10], Jiang showed that all variants of the same integrity notions are equivalent, hence, we do not consider integrity notions in this work and focus on discussing the relations among confidentiality notions in this section. We prove that the backward-leak uni- and no directional key update variant of the same confidentiality notion are equivalent. As a result, UE schemes with backward-leak uni-directional key updates is as strong as UE schemes with no directional key update. It implies that we can construct a less hard (backward-leak uni-directional key updates) UE scheme to achieve the same security result.

4.1 Equivalence for Trivial Win Conditions

We prove four equivalence of the trivial win conditions. The proofs of these equivalence lemmas follow the proof strategy in [9], and they are provided in the full version [7]. The trivial win conditions considered in this section are checked in a confidentiality game. In conclusion, if the trivial win conditions in the backward-leak uni-directional key update setting are triggered then the same trivial win conditions in the no directional key update setting would be triggered. We will use these trivial win equivalences to prove the relation in Theorem 1.

Lemma 1 (Equivalence for Trivial Win Condition "$\mathcal{K}^* \cap \mathcal{C}^* \neq \emptyset$"). *For any sets* $\mathcal{K}, \mathcal{T}, \mathcal{C} \subseteq \{0, ..., l\}$, *we have* $\mathcal{K}^*_{\text{b-uni}} \cap \mathcal{C}^*_{\text{b-uni,uni}} \neq \emptyset \iff \mathcal{K}^*_{\text{no}} \cap \mathcal{C}^*_{\text{no,uni}} \neq \emptyset$.

Lemma 2 (Equivalence for Trivial Win Condition "$\tilde{e} \in \mathcal{T}^*$ or $\mathcal{O}.\text{Upd}(\bar{c})$ is queried"). *For any* $\mathcal{K}, \mathcal{T}, \mathcal{C}$. *Suppose* $\mathcal{K}^*_{\text{kk}} \cap \mathcal{C}^*_{\text{kk,cc}} = \emptyset$, *where* $\text{kk} \in \{\text{b-uni}, \text{no}\}$, $\text{cc} = \text{uni}$, *then*

$$\tilde{e} \in \mathcal{T}^*_{\text{no}} \text{ or } \mathcal{O}.\text{Upd}(\bar{c}) \text{ is queried} \iff \tilde{e} \in \mathcal{T}^*_{\text{b-uni}} \text{ or } \mathcal{O}.\text{Upd}(\bar{c}) \text{ is queried}.$$

Lemma 3 (Equivalence for Trivial Win Condition "$(c, e) \in \tilde{\mathcal{L}}^{*}$"). *For any sets* $\mathcal{K}, \mathcal{T}, \mathcal{C} \subseteq \{0, ..., e\}$. *Suppose* $\mathcal{K}^{*}_{\text{b-uni}} \cap \mathcal{C}^{*}_{\text{b-uni,uni}} = \emptyset$, *then*

$$(c, e) \in \tilde{\mathcal{L}}^{*}_{\text{b-uni,uni}} \iff (c, e) \in \tilde{\mathcal{L}}^{*}_{\text{no,uni}}.$$

Lemma 4 (Equivalence for Trivial Win Condition "$(m', e) \in \tilde{\mathcal{Q}}^{*}$"). *For any sets* $\mathcal{K}, \mathcal{T}, \mathcal{C} \subseteq \{0, ..., e\}$. $\mathcal{K}^{*}_{\text{b-uni}} \cap \mathcal{C}^{*}_{\text{b-uni,uni}} = \emptyset$, *then* $(m', e) \in \tilde{\mathcal{Q}}^{*}_{\text{b-uni,uni}} \iff (m', e) \in \tilde{\mathcal{Q}}^{*}_{\text{no,uni}}$.

4.2   Relations Among Confidentiality Notions

Jiang [10] showed that the bi-directional key update and the forward-leak uni-directional key update variants of the same confidentiality notions are equivalent, and confidentiality in the no-directional key update is strictly stronger than that in the above mentioned two key update settings. However, the relation between the backward-leak uni-directional key update and the no-directional key update variants of the same confidentiality notion is missing in the previous work. We complete the relations among the eight variants of the same confidentiality notion, they are described as in Fig. 3. This is proven via Theorem 1, given below, and results in [10].

Recall discussions in Sect. 3.2 and 3.3, where we consider update settings in $\{(\text{b-uni}, \text{uni}), (\text{no}, \text{uni})\}$ are in one class and the rest update settings are in another class. Intuitive observation shows notions in the same class are equivalent and the prior class is strictly stronger than the latter. Interestingly, the result showed in Fig. 3 matches with this intuition and provides a rigorous proof.

$$(\text{b-uni}, \text{uni})\text{-notion} \xLeftrightarrow{\text{Theorem 1}} (\text{no}, \text{uni})\text{-notion} \underset{*}{\overset{*}{\rightleftharpoons}} (\text{kk}, \text{cc})\text{-notion}$$

Fig. 3. Relations among the eight variants of the same confidentiality notion, where notion $\in \{\text{detIND-UE-CPA}, \text{randIND-UE-CPA}, \text{detIND-UE-CCA}, \text{randIND-UE-CCA}\}$, kk $\in \{\text{no}, \text{b-uni}, \text{f-uni}, \text{bi}\}$ and cc $\in \{\text{uni}, \text{bi}\}$, the notation of (kk, cc) are except for values in $\{(\text{b-uni}, \text{uni}), (\text{no}, \text{uni})\}$. Results in work of [10] are marked with $*$.

In Theorem 1, we compare two types of UE notions: the no-directional key update setting and the backward-leak uni-directional setting. To illustrate the intuition for our equivalence between these two settings we have two scenarios: the first is where the adversary has corrupted a key located in an epoch earlier that the challenge epoch, and the second is where the adversary has corrupted a key located in an epoch later that the challenge epoch. In the first scenario, the adversary cannot update the key even if she had all update token because in both update settings forward key update is impossible. Similarly, the challenge ciphertext cannot be downgraded. Thus, in the first scenario, both update settings are equivalent. For the second scenario, we have that the adversary will win the game in both update settings if she has access to enough tokens, because now the key can either be downgraded, using the tokens, or the challenge ciphertext can be upgraded, using the same tokens. So, in the second scenario, both update settings are equivalent.

Theorem 1. *Let* $\mathsf{UE} = (\mathsf{Setup}, \mathsf{Next}, \mathsf{Enc}, \mathsf{Dec}, \mathsf{Upd})$ *be an updatable encryption scheme and* notion $\in \{\mathsf{detIND\text{-}UE\text{-}CPA}, \mathsf{randIND\text{-}UE\text{-}CPA}, \mathsf{detIND\text{-}UE\text{-}CCA}, \mathsf{randIND\text{-}UE\text{-}CCA}\}$. *For any* (b-uni, uni)*-notion adversary* $\mathcal{A}$ *against* UE, *there exists a* (no, uni)*-notion adversary* $\mathcal{B}_1$ *against* UE *such that*

$$\mathbf{Adv}_{\mathsf{UE},\ \mathcal{A}}^{(\text{b-uni,uni})\text{-notion}}(\lambda) = \mathbf{Adv}_{\mathsf{UE},\ \mathcal{B}_1}^{(\text{no,uni})\text{-notion}}(\lambda).$$

Proof. The proof follows the same method as the proof of Theorem 3.1 in [10]. We construct a reduction $\mathcal{B}_1$ running the (no, uni)-notion experiment which will simulate the responses of queries made by the (b-uni, uni)-notion adversary $\mathcal{A}$. The reduction will send all queries received from $\mathcal{A}$ to its (no, uni)-notion challenger, and forwarding the responses to $\mathcal{A}$. Eventually, the reduction receives a guess from $\mathcal{A}$ and forwards it to its own challenger. In the end, the (no, uni)-notion challenger evaluates whether or not the reduction wins, if a trivial win condition was triggered the reduction is considered as losing the game. This final win evaluation will be passed to the adversary $\mathcal{A}$.

By the equivalences of trivial win conditions in Sect. 4.1 (Lemma 1 to 4), if $\mathcal{A}$ does not trigger the trivial win conditions in the (b-uni, uni)-notion game, then the reduction will not trigger the trivial win conditions in the (no, uni)-notion game either. If $\mathcal{A}$ triggers the trivial win conditions in the (b-uni, uni)-notion game, then the reduction will also trigger the trivial win conditions in the (no, uni)-notion game. Therefore, the reduction perfectly simulates the responses to adversary $\mathcal{A}$. And we have $\mathbf{Adv}_{\mathsf{UE},\ \mathcal{B}_1}^{(\text{no,uni})\text{-notion}}(\lambda) = \mathbf{Adv}_{\mathsf{UE},\ \mathcal{A}}^{(\text{b-uni,uni})\text{-notion}}(\lambda).$

5   UE from Key Homomorphic PKE

We use key homomorphic PKE schemes to construct UE schemes in this section. The idea of key homomorphic by Boneh et al. [3] inspired this construction idea. Our key homomorphic is more general than the key homomorphic construction presented by Boneh et al. [3], where we can rotate information based on a public value and a secret value instead of two secret values.

5.1   Key Homomorphic PKE

We define key homomorphic PKE in this section, which will be used to build updatable encryption schemes in the later two sections.

Definition 5 (Key Homomorphic PKE). *We say public key encryption* $\mathsf{PKE} = (\mathsf{KG}, \mathsf{Enc}, \mathsf{Dec})$ *is* key homomorphic *if:*

1. *there exists an efficiently computable secret key to public key algorithm* $[\cdot]$:
   $\mathcal{SK} \rightarrow \mathcal{PK}$ *such that for any* $(sk, pk) \leftarrow \mathsf{KG}(\lambda)$, *the following two pairs of distributions are statistically close:*

$$(sk, [sk]) \stackrel{s}{\approx} (sk, pk). \tag{4}$$

$$\{(sk_1 \otimes sk_2, [sk_1 \otimes sk_2]) \mid sk_1, sk_2 \stackrel{\$}{\leftarrow} \mathcal{SK}\} \stackrel{s}{\approx} \{(sk, [sk]) \mid sk \stackrel{\$}{\leftarrow} \mathcal{SK}\}. \tag{5}$$

   where $\otimes$ *is an operation (which can be addition, multiplication, etc.) over the secret key space.*

2. *there exists an efficiently computable key homomorphic to key algorithm defined as:*
   $\mathsf{KHK} : \mathcal{SK} \times \mathcal{PK} \rightarrow \mathcal{PK}$ *takes a secret key and a public key as input and outputs a public key, such that for any secret key* $sk_2 \in \mathcal{SK}$ *and public key* $pk_1 \in \mathcal{PK}$, *the following two distributions are statistically close:*

$$\mathsf{KHK}(sk_2, pk_1) \stackrel{s}{\approx} [sk_1 \otimes sk_2], \tag{6}$$

   where sk_1 *is the secret key of* pk_1.

3. *there exists an efficiently commutable key homomorphic to ciphertext algorithm* KHC, *defined as:*
   $\mathsf{KHC} : \mathcal{SK} \times \mathcal{CS} \rightarrow \mathcal{CS}$ *takes a secret value and a ciphertext as input and outputs a ciphertext, such that for any keys* $(sk_1, pk_1) \leftarrow \mathsf{KG}$, *secret value* $sk_2 \stackrel{\$}{\leftarrow} \mathcal{SK}$, *and any message* m, *the following two distributions are statistically close:*

$$(c, \mathsf{KHC}(sk_2, c)) \stackrel{s}{\approx} (c, \mathsf{Enc}([sk_1 \otimes sk_2], m)), \tag{7}$$

   where $c = \mathsf{Enc}(pk_1, m)$.

Remark 1. Equation (4) guarantees that we can compute a public key from a secret key. Equation (5) makes sure the distribution generated from the homomorphism of keys is statistically close to the original key distribution. Equation (6) allows us to compute a new public key from a secret key (assume sk_2) and an old public key (assume $pk_1 = [sk_1]$), the underlying secret key of the newly generated public key matches the output of the homomorphic operation applied to the input secret keys (sk_1 and sk_2). It is essential for our security proof of Theorem 2. We need an algorithm to simulate new public keys from the corresponding old public keys and some secret values. In the proof of Theorem 2, when we use a reduction to simulate the game to an adversary within the firewall, the reduction has no knowledge of any secret keys, but it can simulate public keys with KHK from its own challenge public key and simulated secrets (cf. Fig. 11 in the full version [7]). Without these simulated public keys, the reduction cannot simulate valid ciphertexts within the firewall region. Additionally, we require the two distributions to be statistically close to make sure any adversary cannot distinguish simulated public keys from the real ones. All the PKE considered here satisfy this property. This statistical property is crucial, since the correctness of our scheme requires Equation (7) to hold statistically. This, in turn, requires the two public keys are statistically indistinguishable, since otherwise Equation (7) cannot hold for an unbounded adversary. Equation (7) enables us to compute a new ciphertext from one public key to another public key without changing the underlying message.

Examples of key homomorphic public key encryption schemes are ElGamal encryption and LWE-based PKE (for some parameter choice) schemes. The security of such PKE schemes are based on DDH and LWE problems, resp..

- ElGamal encryption: Let $\mathbb{G}$ be a cyclic group of order q with generator g. For any secret key $x \in \mathbb{Z}_q$, the corresponding public key is $[x] = g^x$. Given any public value $[y]$ and any secret value x, we can compute $\mathsf{KHK}(x, [y]) = [y]^x = g^{xy} = [x \otimes y]$. Here, $\otimes$ is multiplication of integers and function KHK is computed as $\mathsf{KHK}(x, y) = y^x$. For any ciphertext $c = ([rx], [r] \cdot m)$, any $(y, [y]) \xleftarrow{\$} \mathsf{KG}$ and a random value $r' \xleftarrow{\$} \mathbb{Z}_q^*$, note that $[xy] = \mathsf{KHK}(y, [x]) = [x]^y$, then $\mathsf{KHC}(y, c) = (c_1^y \cdot [xy]^{r'}, [r'] \cdot c_2) = ([(r + r')xy], [r + r'] \cdot m)$ is a ciphertext encrypted under public key $[xy]$ with the same underlying message m of the original ciphertext c.
- Lattice based PKE: Denote $[s] = as + e$, then we can compute $\mathsf{KHK}(s, [t]) = [s] + [t] \overset{s}{\approx} [s \otimes t]$, the right side public key has a bigger error. Here, $\otimes$ is group addition. For any ciphertext $c = (ar, [s]r + e' + m)$ and any $(t, [t]) \xleftarrow{\$} \mathsf{KG}$, note that $[s \otimes t] \overset{s}{\approx} [s] + [t]$, then $\mathsf{KHC}(t, c) = (c_1 + ar', c_2 + c_1 t + [s \otimes t]r' + e'') \overset{s}{\approx} (a(r + r'), [s \otimes t](r + r') + (e' + e'') + m)$ is a ciphertext encrypted under public key $[s \otimes t]$.

5.2   Bi-directional UE from Key Homomorphic PKE

We construct a UE scheme PKEUE, which is constructed from a key homomorphic PKE scheme PKE, the construction is described in Fig. 4. Note that the next key pair (sk_{e+1}, pk_{e+1}) is statistically close to a real key pair generated from $\mathsf{PKE.KG}(\lambda)$ by Eq. (4) and (5). Note that RISE [12] and LWEUE [9] are constructed by this method, they are built from ElGamal encryption and LWE-based PKE.

Correctness. The correctness of PKEUE follows from the correctness of PKE. It is sufficient to prove that the updated ciphertext is a valid ciphertext which keeps the same underlying message as the original ciphertext. Since PKE is key homomorphic (see Definition 5), we have that $c_{e+1} = \mathsf{PKE.KHC}(\Delta_{e+1}, c_e) \overset{s}{\underset{Equation\ (7)}{\approx}}$

$\mathsf{PKE.Enc}([sk_e \otimes \Delta_{e+1}], m) = \mathsf{PKE.Enc}(pk_{e+1}, m)$.

Next, we prove that the UE scheme constructed above satisfies the weaker variant of rand-IND-UE security, namely the (bi, bi)-rand-IND-UE security.

Setup(λ) :
  $(sk_1, pk_1) \leftarrow$ PKE.KG(λ)
  return (sk_1, pk_1)

Next(sk_e) :
  $(\Delta_{e+1}, [\Delta_{e+1}]) \leftarrow$ PKE.KG(λ)
  $sk_{e+1} \leftarrow sk_e \otimes \Delta_{e+1}$
  $pk_{e+1} \leftarrow [sk_{e+1}]$
  return $\Delta_{e+1}, (sk_{e+1}, pk_{e+1})$

Enc(pk_e, m) :
  $c_e \leftarrow$ PKE.Enc(pk_e, m)
  return c_e

Dec(sk_e, c_e) :
  $m' \leftarrow$ PKE.Dec(sk_e, c_e)
  return m'

Upd(Δ_{e+1}, c_e) :
  $c_{e+1} \leftarrow$ PKE.KHC(Δ_{e+1}, c_e)
  return c_{e+1}

Fig. 4. PKEUE = (Setup, Next, Enc, Dec, Upd) is a UE scheme constructed from a key homomorphic PKE PKE.

Theorem 2. *Let* PKEUE *be the updatable encryption scheme described in Fig. 4. For any* (bi, bi)-rand-IND-UE *adversary* $\mathcal{A}$ *against* PKEUE, *there exists an* IND-CPA *adversary* $\mathcal{B}_2$ *against* PKE *such that*

$$\mathbf{Adv}_{\mathsf{PKEUE},\,\mathcal{A}}^{\text{(bi,bi)-randIND-UE-CPA}}(\lambda) \leq l^3 \cdot \mathbf{Adv}_{\mathsf{PKE},\mathcal{B}_2}^{\text{IND-CPA}} + \mathsf{negl}(\lambda),$$

where l *is the upper bound on the last epoch.*

Proof. In this proof, we use three steps to reach our desired goal. In the first step, we play a hybrid game over epochs, where the reduction constructs one hybrid for each epoch. In hybrid i, to the left of epoch i the game returns an updated ciphertext as the challenge output, to the right of epoch i it gives an encryption of the challenge input message as output. Therefore, we can move the (bi, bi)-randIND-UE-CPA game from left to right across the epoch space. In the second step, we apply the firewall technique [4,11,12] (recall the discussion in Sect. 3.2) so that we can construct a reduction (in step 3) playing the IND-CPA game by simulating the hybrid game to the adversary. Due to space limitations, the detailed security proof is shown in the full version [7].

5.3 Uni-Directional UE from Key and Message Homomorphic PKE

In this section, we construct a UE scheme with backward-leak uni-directional key update, which is called UNIUE. The UNIUE scheme is built from a key and message homomorphic PKE scheme. Recall that key homomorphic PKE is defined in Definition 5. The message homomorphic PKE is defined as the standard homomorphic encryption, we name it message homomorphic to distinguish two types of homomorphism (key homomorphism and message homomorphism) in this paper.

Definition 6 (Message Homomorphic PKE). *We say public key encryption* PKE = (KG, Enc, Dec) *is message homomorphic if for any message* $m_1, m_2 \in \mathcal{M}$ *and any public key* pk, Enc(pk, m_1) $\otimes$ Enc(pk, m_2) = Enc($pk, m_1 \oplus m_2$), *where* $\otimes$ *is an operation over the ciphertext space and* $\oplus$ *is an operation over the message space.*

Notation. For a vector $\mathbf{A} = (a_1, ..., a_n)$, we define $[\mathbf{A}] = ([a_1], ..., [a_n])$. For vectors $\mathbf{A}, \mathbf{B}$ and function f, we define $f(\mathbf{A}, \mathbf{B}) = (f(a_1, b_1), ..., f(a_n, b_n))$.

Constructing Uni-Directional UE. We construct a backward-leak uni-directional key update and uni-directional ciphertext update UE scheme UNIUE from a key and message homomorphic PKE scheme. The construction is described in Fig. 5. The idea of this construction is that only the public value $pk_{e+1,e+1}$ is included in the update token $\mathbf{\Delta}_{e+1}$, secret key $sk_{e+1,e+1}$ is not included, in other words, no information of this secret key can be revealed from the token. We can deploy this key pair to protect the confidentiality in the new epoch. The detailed construction is shown in Fig. 5. When epoch period turns into the next epoch period, the new epoch key will increase one key element. That is, epoch key $\mathbf{k}_e$ has e pairs of secret key and public key, epoch key $\mathbf{k}_{e+1}$ has $e + 1$ pairs of secret key and public key. To update a ciphertext, we use the difference of $\mathbf{sk}_e$ and $\mathbf{sk}_{e+1}$ (except for the last element) to move encryption of random elements from epoch e to epoch $e + 1$. Due to PKE is message homomorphic, we can perform a re-randomization to refresh the underlying random values. Then, we add an encryption of a new random value, which is encrypted under $pk_{e+1,e+1}$, into the updated ciphertext. This new random value can be used to hide the message. Note that if we do not include this additional randomness, the above construction is bi-directional.

Correctness. It is sufficient to prove that the updpated ciphertext is a ciphertext in epoch $e+1$, with underlying message m. We compute the updpated ciphertext as follows. $\mathbf{c}^1 = \mathsf{PKE.KHC}(\mathbf{\Delta}^{sk}_{e+1}, \mathbf{c}_{e,1}) \overset{s}{\underset{Equation\ (7)}{\approx}} \mathsf{PKE.Enc}([\mathbf{sk}_e \otimes \mathbf{\Delta}^{sk}_{e+1}], \mathbf{R}_e)$ and $\mathbf{c}_{e+1,1} \leftarrow (\mathbf{c}^1, 0) + \mathsf{PKE.Enc}(\mathbf{pk}_{e+1}, \mathbf{R}) = \mathsf{PKE.Enc}(\mathbf{pk}_{e+1}, (\mathbf{R}_e, 0) + \mathbf{R})$. Denote $\mathbf{R}_{e+1} = (r_{e+1,1}, ..., r_{e+1,e+1}) = (\mathbf{R}_e, 0) + \mathbf{R}$, due to the randomness of $\mathbf{R}$ we know $\mathbf{R}_{e+1}$ is a random vector. Furthermore, $c_{e+1,2} \leftarrow c_{e,2} \oplus r_1 \oplus \cdots \oplus r_{e+1} = r_{e+1,1} \oplus \cdots \oplus r_{e+1,e+1} \oplus m$. Therefore, the updated ciphertext $\mathbf{c}_{e+1}$ is a valid ciphertext in epoch $e + 1$. Note that we consider epoch bounded UE, which implies that the noise in lattice-based constructions will not grow too large.

Backward-Leak Uni-Directional Key Updates. Any new key $\mathbf{sk}_{e+1}$ has a random key element $sk_{e+1,e+1}$ which is independent from the update token $\mathbf{\Delta}_{e+1}$ and the previous key $\mathbf{sk}_e$, hence, any adversary cannot upgrade keys.

Uni-Directional Ciphertext Updates. If there exists an adversary $\mathcal{A}$ which can infer a valid previous ciphertext $\mathbf{c}_e$ from token $\mathbf{\Delta}_{e+1}$ and ciphertext $\mathbf{c}_{e+1}$. Then we claim that $\mathcal{A}$ can use this ability to win the IND\$-CPA game for PKE. Initially, $\mathcal{A}$ receives a public key $pk_{e+1,e+1}$ from its IND\$-CPA challenger. $\mathcal{A}$ generates a secret key $\mathbf{sk}_e$ and a token $\mathbf{\Delta}^{sk}_{e+1}$ as algorithms of UNIUE specify. $\mathcal{A}$ computes the public key $\mathbf{pk}_{e+1}$ and token $\mathbf{\Delta}_{e+1}$ by embedding the public key $pk_{e+1,e+1}$. Suppose $\mathcal{A}$ asks for a challenge query with input $r_{e+1,e+1}$, it gets the challenge ciphertext $\tilde{c}$. Then $\mathcal{A}$ uses $r_{e+1,e+1}$ and $\tilde{c}$ to create a ciphertext in epoch $e + 1$, say $\tilde{\mathbf{c}}_{e+1}$. $\mathcal{A}$ can move the ciphertext $\tilde{\mathbf{c}}_{e+1}$ to a ciphertext $\tilde{\mathbf{c}}_e$ by the token $\mathbf{\Delta}_{e+1}$

$\text{Setup}(\lambda):$
$\quad (sk_{1,1}, pk_{1,1}) \leftarrow \text{PKE.KG}(\lambda)$
$\quad \textbf{return } (sk_{1,1}, pk_{1,1})$

$\text{Next}(\textbf{sk}_e):$
$\quad \text{parse } \textbf{sk}_e = (sk_{e,1}, ..., sk_{e,e})$
$\quad \textbf{for } i \in \{1, ..., e\} \textbf{ do}$
$\qquad (\Delta_i, [\Delta_i]) \leftarrow \text{PKE.KG}(\lambda)$
$\qquad sk_{e+1,i} \leftarrow sk_{e,i} \otimes \Delta_i$
$\qquad pk_{e+1,i} \leftarrow [sk_{e+1,i}]$
$\quad (sk_{e+1,e+1}, pk_{e+1,e+1}) \leftarrow \text{PKE.KG}(\lambda)$
$\quad \textbf{sk}_{e+1} \leftarrow (sk_{e+1,1}, ..., sk_{e+1,e+1})$
$\quad \textbf{pk}_{e+1} \leftarrow (pk_{e+1,1}, ..., pk_{e+1,e+1})$
$\quad \Delta_{e+1}^{sk} \leftarrow (\Delta_1, ..., \Delta_e)$
$\quad \Delta_{e+1} \leftarrow (\Delta_{e+1}^{sk}, pk_{e+1,e+1})$
$\quad \textbf{return } \Delta_{e+1}, (\textbf{sk}_{e+1}, \textbf{pk}_{e+1})$

$\text{Enc}(\textbf{pk}_e, m):$

$\quad \textbf{R}_e \xleftarrow{\$} \mathcal{M}^{e \times 1}$
$\quad \text{parse } \textbf{R}_e = (r_{e,1}, ..., r_{e,e})$
$\quad c_{e,1} \leftarrow \text{PKE.Enc}(\textbf{pk}_e, \textbf{R}_e)$
$\quad c_{e,2} \leftarrow r_{e,1} \oplus \cdots \oplus r_{e,e} \oplus m$
$\quad \textbf{return } \textbf{c}_e = (c_{e,1}, c_{e,2})$

$\text{Dec}(\textbf{sk}_e, \textbf{c}_e):$
$\quad \text{parse } \textbf{c}_e = (c_{e,1}, c_{e,2})$
$\quad \textbf{R}_e \leftarrow \text{PKE.Dec}(\textbf{sk}_e, c_{e,1})$
$\quad \text{parse } \textbf{R}_e = (r_{e,1}, ..., r_{e,e})$
$\quad m' \leftarrow c_{e,2} \oplus^{-1} (r_{e,1} \oplus \cdots \oplus r_{e,e})$
$\quad \textbf{return } m'$

$\text{Upd}(\Delta_{e+1}, \textbf{c}_e):$
$\quad \text{parse } \Delta_{e+1} = (\Delta_{e+1}^{sk}, pk_{e+1})$
$\quad \text{parse } \textbf{c}_e = (c_{e,1}, c_{e,2})$
$\quad \textbf{R} \xleftarrow{\$} \mathcal{M}^{(e+1) \times 1}$
$\quad \textbf{c}^1 \leftarrow \text{PKE.KHC}(\Delta_{e+1}^{sk}, c_{e,1})$
$\quad c_{e+1,1} \leftarrow (\textbf{c}^1, 0) + \text{PKE.Enc}(pk_{e+1}, \textbf{R})$
$\quad \text{parse } \textbf{R} = (r_1, ..., r_{e+1})$
$\quad c_{e+1,2} \leftarrow c_{e,2} \oplus r_1 \oplus \cdots \oplus r_{e+1}$
$\quad \textbf{c}_{e+1} \leftarrow (c_{e+1,1}, c_{e+1,2})$
$\quad \textbf{return } \textbf{c}_{e+1}$

Fig. 5. UNIUE $= (\text{Setup}, \text{Next}, \text{Enc}, \text{Dec}, \text{Upd})$ is a UE scheme built from a key and message homomorphic PKE scheme PKE. $\oplus$ is an operation on the message space and assume its inverse operation exists.

and then decrypt $\tilde{\textbf{c}}_e$ by the secret key $\textbf{sk}_e$. Eventually, $\mathcal{A}$ compares the message with the message used when it creates $\tilde{\textbf{c}}_{e+1}$. If they are the same then $\mathcal{A}$ guesses it received a real encryption from its IND\$-CPA challenger, otherwise, it guesses it received a random ciphertext from its IND\$-CPA challenger. The advantage of $\mathcal{A}$ winning the IND\$-CPA game is equal to the probability of $\mathcal{A}$ successfully downgrades the ciphertext $\textbf{c}_{e+1}$ to a ciphertext $\textbf{c}_e$ by the token Δ_{e+1}.

Next, we prove that the UE scheme constructed in Fig. 5 satisfies the stronger variant of rand-IND-UE security, namely the (b-uni, uni)-rand-IND-UE security.

Theorem 3. *Let* UNIUE *be the updatable encryption scheme described in Fig. 5. For any* (b-uni, uni)-rand-IND-UE *adversary* $\mathcal{A}$ *against* UNIUE, *there exists an* IND\$-CPA *adversary* $\mathcal{B}_3$ *against* PKE *such that*

$$\textbf{Adv}_{\text{UNIUE}, \mathcal{A}}^{\text{(b-uni,uni)-randIND-UE-CPA}}(\lambda) \leq 2l^2 \cdot \textbf{Adv}_{\text{PKE}, \mathcal{B}_3}^{\text{IND\$-CPA}} + \text{negl}(\lambda),$$

where l *is the upper bound on the last epoch.*

Remark 2. The difference between proving a UE scheme is (b-uni, uni)-rand-IND-UE secure and (bi, bi)-rand-IND-UE secure are trivial win conditions, and how the reduction runs the simulation.

Consider the backward-leak uni-directional key updates variant of a confidentiality notion, there will exist a the relaxed insulated region (recall the discussion in Sect. 3.2). Assume $\tilde{e}$ is the challenge epoch, where key in this epoch should not be corrupted. Hence, there exists an epoch after $\tilde{e}$, say fwr, such that keys in epoch $\{\tilde{e}, ..., \mathsf{fwr}\}$ and token in epoch $\mathsf{fwr} + 1$ are not corrupted, in addition, tokens in epoch $\{\tilde{e} + 1, ..., \mathsf{fwr}\}$ are corrupted. By Definition 4, we know that epoch region $\{\tilde{e}, ..., \mathsf{fwr}\}$ is a relaxed insulated region. Tokens and keys before $\tilde{e}$ can be corrupted, which will not trigger the trivial win condition. Because knowing any token and any key before epoch $\tilde{e}$ will not break the confidentiality in epoch $\tilde{e}$, the key element $sk_{\tilde{e},\tilde{e}}$ in $\mathbf{sk}_{\tilde{e}}$ is an independent and random value compared to all previous update tokens and keys, hence, ciphertexts in epoch $\tilde{e}$ are random looking without the knowledge of the key element $sk_{\tilde{e},\tilde{e}}$.

Proof. The proof is similar to the proof in Theorem 2. We construct hybrid games and apply the firewall technique on relaxed insulated regions.

Step 1. In the initial hybrid games, we move challenges from real to random over epochs. We construct a sequence of hybrid games $H_1, ..., H_l$. For $b \in \{0, 1\}$, experiment H_i^b is defined as follows, if the adversary asks for a challenge-equal ciphertext by the $\mathcal{O}.\mathsf{Chall}$ query or a $\mathcal{O}.\mathsf{Upd\tilde{C}}$ query, with challenge input $(\bar{m}, \bar{c})$, in epoch j:

- if $j \leq i$, for $b = 1$ return an updated ciphertext of $\bar{c}$, for $b = 0$ return (an updated ciphertext which is updated from) an encrypted ciphertext of $\bar{m}$.
- if $j > i$, return a random ciphertext.

Thus H_l^1 is $\mathbf{Exp}_{\mathsf{UNIUE}, \mathcal{A}}^{\mathsf{(b\text{-}uni,uni)\text{-}randIND\text{-}UE\text{-}CPA\text{-}1}}$, i.e. all challenge responses are challenge-equal ciphertexts of $\mathsf{Upd}(\bar{c})$. And H_l^0 is $\mathbf{Exp}_{\mathsf{UNIUE}, \mathcal{A}}^{\mathsf{(b\text{-}uni,uni)\text{-}randIND\text{-}UE\text{-}CPA\text{-}0}}$, i.e. all challenge responses are challenge-equal ciphertexts of $\mathsf{Enc}(\bar{m})$. Notice that $H_0^0 = H_0^1$, in which all challenge ciphertexts are random ciphertexts. We have

$$\mathbf{Adv}_{\mathsf{UNIUE}, \mathcal{A}}^{\mathsf{(b\text{-}uni,uni)\text{-}randIND\text{-}UE\text{-}CPA}} = \left| \mathbf{Pr}[H_l^1 = 1] - \mathbf{Pr}[H_l^0 = 1] \right|$$

$$\leq \sum_{i=1}^{l} \left| \mathbf{Pr}[H_i^1 = 1] - \mathbf{Pr}[H_{i-1}^1 = 1] \right|$$

$$+ \sum_{i=1}^{l} \left| \mathbf{Pr}[H_i^0 = 1] - \mathbf{Pr}[H_{i-1}^0 = 1] \right|.$$

Step 2. We define a new game $\mathcal{G}_i$ that is the same as game H_i, except for the game randomly picks a number $\mathsf{fwr} \xleftarrow{\$} \{0, ..., l\}$. If the adversary corrupts a key in the sequence of epochs $(i, ..., \mathsf{fwr})$ or a token in epoch $\mathsf{fwr}+1$, the game aborts. This loss is upper bounded by l.
Then we have $\left| \mathbf{Pr}[H_i^b = 1] - \mathbf{Pr}[H_{i-1}^b = 1] \right| \leq l \left| \mathbf{Pr}[\mathcal{G}_i^b = 1] - \mathbf{Pr}[\mathcal{G}_{i-1}^b = 1] \right|$.

Step 3. In this step, we prove that $|\mathbf{Pr}[\mathcal{G}_i^b = 1] - \mathbf{Pr}[\mathcal{G}_{i-1}^b = 1]| = \mathbf{Adv}_{\mathsf{PKE}, \mathcal{B}_3}^{\mathsf{IND\$-CPA}} +$ $\mathsf{negl}(\lambda)$. Assume $\mathcal{A}_i$ is an adversary attempting to distinguish $\mathcal{G}_i^b$ from $\mathcal{G}_{i-1}^b$. We construct a reduction $\mathcal{B}_3$, detailed in Fig. 6, playing the IND\$-CPA game by simulating the responses to adversary $\mathcal{A}_i$.

Initially, the reduction guesses a number fwr. If $\mathcal{A}_i$ corrupts $\mathbf{k}_i, ..., \mathbf{k}_{\mathsf{fwr}}$, or $\Delta_{\mathsf{fwr}+1}$ the reduction aborts the game.

A summary of the technical simulations are as follows.

- In the setup phrase, $\mathcal{B}_3$ generates all keys and tokens, except for $\mathbf{k}_i, ..., \mathbf{k}_{\mathsf{fwr}}$, $\Delta_{\mathsf{fwr}+1}$, as follows.
  - The key pairs and tokens outside of the relaxed insulated regions are generated as in $\mathcal{G}_i$.
  - The public keys within relaxed firewalls are generated by embedding public key pk to the i-th term of $\mathbf{pk}_i$, where pk is the public key received from its IND\$-CPA game.
- To simulate non-challenge ciphertexts: $\mathcal{B}_3$ uses public keys to simulate encrypted ciphertexts and updated ciphertexts.
- To simulate challenge-equal ciphertexts in an epoch that is:
  - $j < i$: $\mathcal{B}_3$ uses public keys to simulate encryption and updating.
  - $j = i$: $\mathcal{B}_3$ embeds the challenge ciphertext $\tilde{c}$ received from its IND\$-CPA challenger to the challenge-equal ciphertext in epoch i. More precisely, suppose $\mathcal{B}_3$ receives a challenge query $\mathcal{O}.\mathsf{Chall}$ with input $(\bar{m}_0, \bar{\mathbf{c}})$ in challenge epoch $\tilde{\mathsf{e}}$, where the underlying message of $\bar{\mathbf{c}}$ is $\bar{m}_1$. $\mathcal{B}_3$ sends a random value r_i to its IND\$-CPA challenger and obtains $\tilde{c}_\beta$. $\mathcal{B}_3$ embeds $\tilde{c}_\beta$ to the i-th term of the challenge ciphertext and uses r_i and m_b to compute the last term of the challenge ciphertext. Afterwards, $\mathcal{B}_3$ returns $\tilde{\mathbf{c}}_i$ to the adversary $\mathcal{A}$. Again, by Eq. (7), $\mathcal{B}_3$ perfectly simulate the challenge ciphertexts in game $\mathcal{G}_{i-1+\beta}$ except for a negligible probability $\mathsf{negl}(\lambda)$.
  - $j > i$: $\mathcal{B}_3$ outputs random ciphertext as challenge ciphertext.

Eventually, $\mathcal{B}_3$ receives the output bit from $\mathcal{A}_i$ and if $\mathcal{A}_i$ guesses it is playing $\mathcal{G}_i$ (suppose it represents the guess response of $\mathcal{A}_i$ is 1), then $\mathcal{B}_3$ guesses it received a real encryption and sends 1 to its IND\$-CPA challenger. Otherwise, sends 0 to its IND\$-CPA challenger. We have $|\mathbf{Pr}[\mathcal{G}_i^b = 1] - \mathbf{Pr}[\mathcal{G}_{i-1}^b = 1]| = \mathbf{Adv}_{\mathsf{PKE}}^{\mathsf{IND\$-CPA}} + \mathsf{negl}(\lambda)$.

6   UE from Bootstrappable PKE

Bootstrappability can be used to refresh ciphertexts without revealing the underlying message, which implies updatable encryption.

Definition 7 (Bootstrappable PKE). *We say a public key encryption* BPKE $=$ (KG, Enc, Dec) *is bootstrappable if it can evaluate its own decryption circuit D. More precisely, there exists a re-encryption algorithm* Recrypt *that takes a public key, the decryption circuit D, an encryption of a secret key and a ciphertext as input and outputs a new ciphertext, such that for any keys*

For $b \in \{0,1\}$ $\mathcal{B}_3$ plays
IND\$-CPA game by running $\mathcal{A}_i$:
  receive pk
  do Setup
  $b' \leftarrow \mathcal{A}_i^{oracles}(\lambda)$
  if ABORT occurred or $\mathcal{C}^* \cap \mathcal{K}^* \neq \emptyset$
  or $i > $ fwr **then**
    $b' \xleftarrow{\$} \{0,1\}$
  return b'

Setup(λ)

$\Delta_1 \leftarrow \perp$; $e \leftarrow 1$; phase, twf $\leftarrow 0$;
$\mathcal{L}, \tilde{\mathcal{L}}, \mathcal{C}, \mathcal{K}, \mathcal{T} \leftarrow \emptyset$
fwr $\xleftarrow{\$} \{0, ..., l\}$
$(sk_{1,1}, pk_{1,1}) \leftarrow$ PKE.KG(λ)
for $j \in \{2, ..., i\text{-}1\}$ **do**
  $\Delta_j, (\mathbf{sk}_j, \mathbf{pk}_j) \leftarrow$ UNIUE.Next$(\mathbf{sk}_{j\text{-}1})$

for $j \in \{i, ..., \text{fwr}\}$ **do**
  parse $\mathbf{pk}_{j\text{-}1} = (pk_{j\text{-}1,1}, ..., pk_{j\text{-}1,j\text{-}1})$
  for $t \in \{1, ..., j\text{-}1\}$ **do**
    $(\Delta_t, \cdot) \leftarrow$ PKE.KG(λ)
    $pk_{j,t} \leftarrow$ KHK$(\Delta_t, pk_{j\text{-}1,t})$
  if $j = i$ **then**
    $pk_{i,i} \leftarrow pk$
  else
    $(\cdot, pk_{j,j}) \leftarrow$ PKE.KG(λ)
  $\Delta_j^{sk} \leftarrow (\Delta_1, ..., \Delta_{j\text{-}1})$
  $\mathbf{pk}_j = (pk_{j,1}, ..., pk_{j,j})$
for $j = $ fwr+1 **do**
  for $t \in \{1, ..., \text{fwr+1}\}$ **do**
    $(sk_{\text{fwr+1},t}, pk_{\text{fwr+1},t}) \leftarrow$ PKE.KG(λ)
  $\mathbf{sk}_{\text{fwr+1}} = (sk_{\text{fwr+1},1}, ..., sk_{\text{fwr+1},\text{fwr+1}})$
  $\mathbf{pk}_{\text{fwr+1}} = (pk_{\text{fwr+1},1}, ..., pk_{\text{fwr+1},\text{fwr+1}})$
for $j \in \{\text{fwr+2}, ..., l\}$ **do**
  $\Delta_j, (\mathbf{sk}_j, \mathbf{pk}_j) \leftarrow$ UNIUE.Next$(\mathbf{sk}_{j\text{-}1})$

$\mathcal{O}.\mathsf{Enc}(m)$:
  $\mathbf{c}_e \leftarrow$ UNIUE.Enc$(\mathbf{pk}_e, m)$
  $\mathcal{L} \leftarrow \mathcal{L} \cup \{(\cdot, \mathbf{c}_e, e; m)\}$
  return $\mathbf{c}_e$

$\mathcal{O}.\mathsf{Next}$:
  $e \leftarrow e\text{+}1$

$\mathcal{O}.\mathsf{Upd}(\mathbf{c}_{e\text{-}1})$:
  if $(\cdot, \mathbf{c}_{e\text{-}1}, e\text{-}1; m) \notin \mathcal{L}$ **then**
    return $\perp$

  $\mathbf{c}_e \leftarrow$ UNIUE.Enc$(\mathbf{pk}_e, m)$
  $\mathcal{L} \leftarrow \mathcal{L} \cup \{(\cdot, \mathbf{c}_e, e; m)\}$
  return $\mathbf{c}_e$

$\mathcal{O}.\mathsf{Corr}(\mathsf{inp}, \hat{e})$:
  if $(\mathsf{inp} = \mathsf{key}$ and $\hat{e} \in \{i, ..., \text{fwr}\})$
  or $(\mathsf{inp} = \mathsf{token}$ and $\hat{e} = \text{fwr+1})$ **then**
    ABORT
  else
    do as $\mathcal{O}.\mathsf{Corr}(\mathsf{inp}, \hat{e})$ specifies

$\mathcal{O}.\mathsf{Chall}(\bar{m}_0, \bar{c})$:
  if phase $= 1$ **then**
    return $\perp$
  phase $\leftarrow 1$; $\tilde{e} \leftarrow e$
  if $(\cdot, \bar{c}, \tilde{e}\text{-}1; \bar{m}_1) \notin \mathcal{L}$ **then**
    return $\perp$
  for $j \in \{1, ..., i\text{-}1\}$ **do**
    $\tilde{\mathbf{c}}_j \leftarrow$ UNIUE.Enc$(\mathbf{pk}_j, m_b)$
  for $j = i$ **do**
    $r_i \xleftarrow{\$} \mathcal{M}$
    Send r_i to the IND\$-CPA challenger,
    get $\tilde{c}_\beta$
    parse $\tilde{\mathbf{pk}}_i = (pk_{i,1}, ..., pk_{i,i\text{-}1})^{\mathsf{T}}$
    $(\tilde{\mathbf{c}}'_{i,1}, c_{i,2}) \leftarrow$ UNIUE.Enc$(\tilde{\mathbf{pk}}_i, m_b)$
    $\tilde{c}_{i,1} \leftarrow (\tilde{\mathbf{c}}'_{i,1}, \tilde{c}_\beta)$
    $\tilde{c}_{i,2} \leftarrow c_{i,2} \oplus r_i$
    $\tilde{\mathbf{c}}_i \leftarrow (\tilde{c}_{i,1}, \tilde{c}_{i,2})$
  for $j \in \{i\text{+}1, ..., l\}$ **do**
    $\tilde{\mathbf{c}}_j \xleftarrow{\$} \mathcal{CS}$
    $\mathcal{C} \leftarrow \mathcal{C} \cup \{j\}$
    $\tilde{\mathcal{L}} \leftarrow \tilde{\mathcal{L}} \cup \{(\tilde{\mathbf{c}}_j, j)\}$
  return $\tilde{\mathbf{c}}_{\tilde{e}}$

$\mathcal{O}.\mathsf{Upd}\tilde{\mathsf{C}}$:
  if phase $\neq 1$ **then**
    return $\perp$
  $\mathcal{C} \leftarrow \mathcal{C} \cup \{e\}$
  $\tilde{\mathcal{L}} \leftarrow \tilde{\mathcal{L}} \cup \{(\tilde{\mathbf{c}}_e, e)\}$
  return $\tilde{\mathbf{c}}_{\tilde{e}}$

Fig. 6. Reduction $\mathcal{B}_3$ for proof of Theorem 3.

$(sk_1, pk_1), (sk_2, pk_2) \leftarrow \mathsf{KG}(\lambda)$ and any message m, the following two distributions are statistically close:

$$(c, \mathsf{Recrypt}(pk_2, D, \mathsf{Enc}(pk_2, sk_1), c)) \stackrel{s}{\approx} (c, \mathsf{Enc}(pk_2, m)), \qquad (8)$$

where $c = \mathsf{Enc}(pk_1, m)$.

Note that bootstrappable PKE is simpler than a FHE scheme. Most FHE scheme requires bootstrappability, while only bootstrappability is not enough for FHE. Gentry [8, Chapter 4] constructed a re-encryption algorithm Recrypt (see Fig. 7), which allows us to update a ciphertext under pk_1 to a ciphertext under pk_2.

$\mathsf{Recrypt}(pk_2, D, \langle \overline{sk_{1,j}} \rangle, c_1) :$
$\quad \overline{c_{1,j}} \stackrel{\$}{\leftarrow} \mathsf{BPKE.Enc}(pk_2, c_{1,j})$
$\quad c_2 \leftarrow \mathsf{BPKE.Evaluate}(pk_2, D, \langle\langle \overline{sk_{1,j}} \rangle, \langle \overline{c_{1,j}} \rangle\rangle)$
$\quad \mathbf{return}\ c_2$

Fig. 7. Recrypt algorithm. For any key pairs $(sk_1, pk_1), (sk_2, pk_2) \leftarrow \mathsf{KG}(\lambda)$. Let $sk_{1,j}$ be the j-th bit of sk_1 and $\overline{sk_{1,j}} = \mathsf{Enc}(pk_2, sk_{1,j})$. For any plaintext $m \in \mathcal{M}$, let $c_1 = \mathsf{Enc}(pk_1, m)$, and $c_{1,j}$ denote the j-th bit of c_1. The output c_2 is an encryption of $\mathsf{Dec}(sk_1, c_1) = m$ under pk_2.

The Recrypt algorithm can be used to update ciphertext, where the update token is the encryption of the current secret key sk_e under the next public key pk_{e+1}. We construct an updatable encryption scheme BPKEUE from BPKE, which is shown in Fig. 8.

$\mathsf{Setup}(\lambda) :$
$\quad \overline{(sk_1, pk_1)} \leftarrow \mathsf{BPKE.KG}(\lambda)$
$\quad \mathbf{return}\ (sk_1, pk_1)$

$\mathsf{Next}(sk_e) :$
$\quad \overline{(sk_{e+1}, pk_{e+1})} \leftarrow \mathsf{BPKE.KG}(\lambda)$
$\quad \Delta_{e+1} \leftarrow \mathsf{BPKE.Enc}(pk_{e+1}, sk_e)$
$\quad \mathbf{return}\ \Delta_{e+1}, (sk_{e+1}, pk_{e+1})$

$\mathsf{Enc}(pk_e, m) :$
$\quad \overline{c_e \leftarrow \mathsf{BPKE.Enc}(pk_e, m)}$
$\quad \mathbf{return}\ c_e$

$\mathsf{Dec}(sk_e, c_e) :$
$\quad \overline{m' \leftarrow \mathsf{BPKE.Dec}(sk_e, c_e)}$
$\quad \mathbf{return}\ m'$

$\mathsf{Upd}(\Delta_{e+1}, c_e) :$
$\quad \overline{c_{e+1} \leftarrow \mathsf{BPKE.Recrypt}(pk_{e+1}, D, \Delta_{e+1}, c_e)}$
$\quad \mathbf{return}\ c_{e+1}$

Fig. 8. BPKEUE $=$ (Setup, Next, Enc, Dec, Upd) is a UE scheme constructed from a bootstrappable PKE scheme BPKE.

Correctness. The correctness of encrypting then decrypting follows the correctness of the underlying PKE scheme. The correctness of encrypting then updating then decrypting is because of the bootstrappability of BPKE scheme, the re-encrypted ciphertext is a new ciphertext encrypted under the new public key with the same message. Note that we consider epoch bounded UE, which implies that the noise will not grow too large.

Backward-Leak Uni-Directional Key Updates. We can see the earlier key sk_e and token Δ_{e+1} as a plaintext and the corresponding ciphertext under public key pk_{e+1}. Hence, any adversary can not obtain the secret key sk_{e+1}.

Uni-Directional Ciphertext Updates. If there exists an adversary which can infer a valid previous ciphertext c_e from token Δ_{e+1} and ciphertext c_{e+1}. Then we claim that the adversary can use this ability to win the IND-CPA game for BPKE. Initially, the adversary receives a public key pk_{e+1} from its IND-CPA challenger. The adversary generates a secret key sk_e and computes the token Δ_{e+1} by the knowledge of the public key pk_{e+1} and the secret key sk_e. Then the adversary can move the challenge ciphertext $\tilde{c}_{e+1}$ (encrypted under pk_{e+1}) to a ciphertext $\tilde{c}_e$ by the token Δ_{e+1}. Note that $\tilde{c}_{e+1}$ and $\tilde{c}_e$ have the same underlying message. Therefore, the adversary can decrypt $\tilde{c}_e$ by sk_e and then compare the output with the challenge messages to win the IND-CPA game.

Remark 3. Nishimaki [14] observed that if the update token Δ_{e+1} is generated by the old secret key sk_e and the new public key pk_{e+1}, such UE schemes may have backward-leak uni-directional key updates. The reason is that it will be difficult to break the confidentiality in epoch $e + 1$ with only the knowledge of pk_{e+1}, Δ_{e+1} and sk_e, no information about sk_{e+1} is revealed.

We observed that such UE schemes may have uni-directional ciphertext updates as well. The proof idea is similar to the proof of BPKEUE has uni-directional ciphertext updates. We claim that if such UE schemes do not have uni-directional ciphertext updates, then any adversary can break the confidentiality of such UE schemes without the knowledge of any epoch key. If an adversary aims to attack the confidentiality in epoch $e+1$, it can generate a new secret key in epoch e. Then the adversary computes the token Δ_{e+1} by the generated secret key sk_e and the public key pk_{e+1}. It can move ciphertexts from epoch $e+1$ to epoch e by token Δ_{e+1} and then decrypt it by sk_e to win the confidentiality in epoch $e+1$.

Next, we prove that the UE scheme constructed in Fig. 8 is secure under the (b-uni, uni)-rand-IND-UE notion.

Theorem 4. *Let* BPKEUE *be the UE scheme described in Fig. 8. For any* (b-uni, uni)-rand-IND-UE *adversary* $\mathcal{A}$ *against* BPKEUE, *there exists an* IND-CPA *adversary* $\mathcal{B}_4$ *against* BPKE *such that*

$$\mathbf{Adv}_{\mathsf{BPKEUE},\,\mathcal{A}}^{(\text{b-uni,uni})\text{-randIND-UE-CPA}}(\lambda) \leq 2l^3 \cdot \mathbf{Adv}_{\mathsf{BPKE},\mathcal{B}_4}^{\mathsf{IND\text{-}CPA}} + \mathsf{negl}(l),$$

where l *is the upper bound on the last epoch.*

Before proving the above theorem, we prove a lemma first. In the IND game, any adversary can only ask for tokens and encryption oracles.

Lemma 5. *Let* BPKEUE *be the UE scheme described in Fig. 8. For any* IND *adversary* $\mathcal{A}$ *against* BPKEUE, *there exists an* IND-CPA *adversary* $\mathcal{B}_5$ *against* BPKE *such that*

$$\mathbf{Adv}^{\mathsf{IND}}_{\mathsf{BPKEUE},\ \mathcal{A}}(\lambda) \leq 2l \cdot \mathbf{Adv}^{\mathsf{IND\text{-}CPA}}_{\mathsf{BPKE},\mathcal{B}_5},$$

where l *is the upper bound on the last epoch.*

Proof (of Lemma 5). The proof is similar to the proof of Theorem 4.2.3 in [8]. We use a hybrid games to move tokens from real to random. In hybrid i, the last $l - i$ tokens are random from the real keys. More precisely, for $i \in \{1, ..., l\}$ let $\mathcal{G}_i$ be a game that is identical to the IND game against BPKEUE, except for all $j > i$:

$$(sk'_j, pk'_j) \overset{\$}{\leftarrow} \mathsf{KG}(\lambda), \Delta_j \overset{\$}{\leftarrow} \mathsf{Enc}(pk_j, sk'_{j-1}).$$

Note that the last $l - i$ tokens are not related to the real keys.

We have that $\mathcal{G}_l$ is the IND game and the advantage of any adversary winning $\mathcal{G}_0$ is upper bounded by $l \cdot \mathbf{Adv}^{\mathsf{IND\text{-}CPA}}_{\mathsf{BPKE}}$. Next, we claim that for any $i \in \{1, ..., l\}$, $|\mathbf{Pr}[\mathcal{G}_i = 1] - \mathbf{Pr}[\mathcal{G}_{i-1} = 1]| = \mathbf{Adv}^{\mathsf{IND\text{-}CPA}}_{\mathsf{BPKE}}$.

Suppose $\mathcal{A}$ is an adversary aiming to distinguish $\mathcal{G}_i$ from $\mathcal{G}_{i-1}$. We construct a reduction $\mathcal{B}_5$ playing the IND-CPA game (against BPKE) and simulating the response to $\mathcal{A}$. Initially, $\mathcal{B}_5$ receives a public key pk from its IND-CPA challenger. $\mathcal{B}_5$ generates key pairs as in $\mathcal{G}_i$ except for it embeds pk to pk_i. It generates a random key pair $(sk'_{i-1}, pk'_{i-1}) \overset{\$}{\leftarrow} \mathsf{KG}(\lambda)$, sets $(m_0, m_1) = (sk'_{i-1}, sk_{i-1})$ and sends (m_0, m_1) to its challenger. The challenger flips a coin $\beta \overset{\$}{\leftarrow} \{0, 1\}$ and returns the encryption of m_β. $\mathcal{B}_5$ sets the received challenge ciphertext as Δ_i. Note that $\mathcal{B}_5$ perfectly simulates public keys and tokens in $\mathcal{G}_{i-1+\beta}$ to $\mathcal{A}$. When $\mathcal{A}$ asks for a challenge query on $(\bar{m}_0, \bar{m}_1)$, $\mathcal{B}_5$ flips a coin $\mathsf{b} \overset{\$}{\leftarrow} \{0, 1\}$ and sends the encryptions of $\bar{m}_\mathsf{b}$ to $\mathcal{A}$. Eventually, $\mathcal{A}$ submit a guess, if $\mathcal{A}$ guesses it is $\mathcal{G}_i$ then $\mathcal{B}_5$ returns 1 to its challenger, otherwise, $\mathcal{B}_5$ returns 0.

Since $\mathcal{B}_5$ perfectly simulate $\mathcal{G}_{i-1+\beta}$ to $\mathcal{A}$. The probability of $\mathcal{A}$ is able to distinguish which game it is playing is equal to $\mathbf{Adv}^{\mathsf{IND\text{-}CPA}}_{\mathsf{BPKE},\mathcal{B}_5}$.

Proof (of Theorem 4). We use firewall technique and construct a sequence of hybrid games to move challenges from left to right over the relaxed insulated regions. Define game $\mathcal{G}_i$ as (b-uni, uni)-randIND-UE-CPA game, except for

- The game randomly choose a number fwr $\overset{\$}{\leftarrow} \{0, ..., l\}$. If fwr is not the i-th right firewall, returns a random bit for b'. This loss is upper bounded by l.
- To the left side of epoch fwr, the game returns a ciphertext with respect to $\bar{c}$, to the right side of epoch fwr returns a encryption of $\bar{m}$.

If fwr is guessed correct, then $\mathcal{G}_0$ is $\mathbf{Exp}^{\mathsf{(b\text{-}uni,uni)\text{-}randIND\text{-}UE\text{-}CPA\text{-}0}}_{\mathsf{BPKEUE}}$ and $\mathcal{G}_l$ is $\mathbf{Exp}^{\mathsf{(b\text{-}uni,uni)\text{-}randIND\text{-}UE\text{-}CPA\text{-}1}}_{\mathsf{BPKEUE}}$. So we can bound the (b-uni, uni)-randIND-UE-CPA advantage by the advantage of distinguishing $\mathcal{G}_0$ and $\mathcal{G}_l$.

$$\mathbf{Adv}^{\mathsf{(b\text{-}uni,uni)\text{-}randIND\text{-}UE\text{-}CPA}}_{\mathsf{BPKEUE},\ \mathcal{A}}(\lambda) \leq \sum_{i=1}^{l} |\mathbf{Pr}[\mathcal{G}_i = 1] - \mathbf{Pr}[\mathcal{G}_{i-1} = 1]|,$$

Notice that if $\mathcal{G}_{i-1}$ and $\mathcal{G}_i$ have the same right firewall fwr, then they are the same game, hence, we assume $\mathcal{G}_{i-1}$ and $\mathcal{G}_i$ have different right firewall. Suppose $\mathcal{A}_i$ is an adversary attempting to distinguish $\mathcal{G}_{i-1}$ from $\mathcal{G}_i$. For all queries concerning epochs outside of the i-th relaxed insulated region ($\{i,...,\text{fwr}\}$) the responses will be equal in either game, We construct a reduction $\mathcal{B}_4$ playing the IND game (within the epoch region $\{i,...,\text{fwr}\}$) for BPKEUE and will simulate the responses of queries made by $\mathcal{A}_i$. Initially, the reduction guesses a numbers fwr. If $\mathcal{A}_i$ corrupts $k_i, ..., k_{\text{fwr}}$, or $\Delta_{\text{fwr}+1}$ the reduction aborts the game. A summary of the technical simulations are as follows.

- In the setup phrase, $\mathcal{B}_4$ generates all keys and tokens, except for $k_i, ..., k_{\text{fwr}}$, $\Delta_{\text{fwr}+1}$, as follows.
  - The key pairs and tokens outside of the relaxed insulated regions are generated as in $\mathcal{G}_i$.
  - The public key within firewalls are generated by embedding public keys $(pk_i, ..., pk_{\text{fwr}})$ and tokens $(\Delta_{i+1}, ..., \Delta_{\text{fwr}})$, which are received from the IND challenger.
- To simulate non-challenge ciphertexts: $\mathcal{B}_4$ uses public keys to simulate encrypted ciphertexts and updated ciphertexts. Due to updated ciphertext is statistically close to the fresh encryption of the same underlying message, the adversary notice this change with negligible probability.
- To simulate challenge-equal ciphertexts in an epoch that is:
  - $j < i$ or $j > \text{fwr}$: $\mathcal{B}_4$ uses public keys to simulate encryption and updating.
  - $j \in \{i, ..., \text{fwr}\}$: $\mathcal{B}_4$ sends $(\bar{m}_0, \bar{m}_1)$ to its IND challenger and forwards the response to $\mathcal{A}_i$, where $\bar{m}_1$ is the underlying message of $\bar{c}$.

Eventually, $\mathcal{A}_i$ sends a guess. If $\mathcal{A}_i$ guesses it is playing $\mathcal{G}_{i-1}$ then $\mathcal{B}_4$ guesses 0 to its IND challenger. Otherwise, $\mathcal{B}_4$ sends 1 to its IND challenger. Note that $\mathcal{B}_4$ perfectly simulates $\mathcal{G}_{i-1}$ to $\mathcal{A}_i$ when its challenger encrypts $\bar{m}_0$ and perfectly simulates $\mathcal{G}_i$ to $\mathcal{A}_i$ when its challenger encrypts $\bar{m}_1$.

$$\mathbf{Adv}_{\text{BPKEUE, }\mathcal{A}_i}^{(\text{b-uni,uni})\text{-randIND-UE-CPA}}(\lambda) \leq l^2 \cdot \mathbf{Adv}_{\text{BPKEUE,}\mathcal{B}_4}^{\text{IND}} + \text{negl}(l),$$

Combing the result of Lemma 5, we have the desired result.

Acknowledgements. We thank the anonymous reviewers of Eurocrypt 2022, Crypto 2022, and PKC 2023 for their useful comments. We also thank Christoph Striecks and Daniel Slamanig for their valuable suggestions to improve the previous version of our paper.

References

1. Alamati, N., Montgomery, H., Patranabis, S.: Symmetric primitives with structured secrets. In: Boldyreva, A., Micciancio, D. (eds.) CRYPTO 2019. LNCS, vol. 11692, pp. 650–679. Springer, Cham (2019). https://doi.org/10.1007/978-3-030-26948-7_23

2. Boneh, D., Eskandarian, S., Kim, S., Shih, M.: Improving speed and security in updatable encryption schemes. In: Moriai, S., Wang, H. (eds.) ASIACRYPT 2020. LNCS, vol. 12493, pp. 559–589. Springer, Cham (2020). https://doi.org/10.1007/978-3-030-64840-4_19

3. Boneh, D., Lewi, K., Montgomery, H., Raghunathan, A.: Key homomorphic PRFs and their applications. In: Canetti, R., Garay, J.A. (eds.) CRYPTO 2013. LNCS, vol. 8042, pp. 410–428. Springer, Heidelberg (2013). https://doi.org/10.1007/978-3-642-40041-4_23

4. Boyd, C., Davies, G.T., Gjøsteen, K., Jiang, Y.: Fast and Secure updatable encryption. In: Micciancio, D., Ristenpart, T. (eds.) CRYPTO 2020. LNCS, vol. 12170, pp. 464–493. Springer, Cham (2020). https://doi.org/10.1007/978-3-030-56784-2_16

5. Chen, L., Li, Y., Tang, Q.: CCA updatable encryption against malicious re-encryption attacks. In: Moriai, S., Wang, H. (eds.) ASIACRYPT 2020. LNCS, vol. 12493, pp. 590–620. Springer, Cham (2020). https://doi.org/10.1007/978-3-030-64840-4_20

6. Everspaugh, A., Paterson, K., Ristenpart, T., Scott, S.: Key rotation for authenticated encryption. In: Katz, J., Shacham, H. (eds.) CRYPTO 2017. LNCS, vol. 10403, pp. 98–129. Springer, Cham (2017). https://doi.org/10.1007/978-3-319-63697-9_4

7. Galteland, Y.J., Pan, J.: Backward-leak UNI-directional updatable encryption from (homomorphic) public key encryption. Cryptology ePrint Archive, Paper 2022/324 (2022). https://eprint.iacr.org/2022/324

8. Gentry, C.: A fully homomorphic encryption scheme. Ph.D. thesis, Stanford, CA, USA (2009)

9. Jiang, Y.: The direction of updatable encryption does not matter much. In: Moriai, S., Wang, H. (eds.) ASIACRYPT 2020. LNCS, vol. 12493, pp. 529–558. Springer, Cham (2020). https://doi.org/10.1007/978-3-030-64840-4_18

10. Jiang, Y.: The direction of updatable encryption does not matter much. Cryptology ePrint Archive, Report 2020/622 (2020). https://ia.cr/2020/622

11. Klooß, M., Lehmann, A., Rupp, A.: (R)CCA secure updatable encryption with integrity protection. In: Ishai, Y., Rijmen, V. (eds.) EUROCRYPT 2019. LNCS, vol. 11476, pp. 68–99. Springer, Cham (2019). https://doi.org/10.1007/978-3-030-17653-2_3

12. Lehmann, A., Tackmann, B.: Updatable encryption with post-compromise security. In: Nielsen, J.B., Rijmen, V. (eds.) EUROCRYPT 2018. LNCS, vol. 10822, pp. 685–716. Springer, Cham (2018). https://doi.org/10.1007/978-3-319-78372-7_22

13. Miao, P., Patranabis, S., Watson, G.: Unidirectional updatable encryption and proxy re-encryption from DDH or LWE. Cryptology ePrint Archive, Report 2022/311 (2022). https://ia.cr/2022/311

14. Nishimaki, R.: The direction of updatable encryption does matter. In: Hanaoka, G., Shikata, J., Watanabe, Y. (eds.) PKC 2022. LNCS, vol. 13178, pp. 194–224. Springer, Cham (2022). https://doi.org/10.1007/978-3-030-97131-1_7

15. Regev, O.: On lattices, learning with errors, random linear codes, and cryptography. In: Gabow, H.N., Fagin, R. (eds.) 2005 Proceedings of the 37th Annual ACM Symposium on Theory of Computing, pp. 84–93. ACM (2005). https://doi.org/10.1145/1060590.1060603

16. Slamanig, D., Striecks, C.: Puncture 'em all: Stronger updatable encryption with no-directional key updates. IACR Cryptol. ePrint Arch. 268 (2021). https://eprint.iacr.org/2021/268

Functional Encryption Against Probabilistic Queries: Definition, Construction and Applications

Geng Wang, Shi-Feng Sun, Zhedong Wang, and Dawu Gu$^{(\boxtimes)}$

School of Electronic Information and Electrical Engineering,
Shanghai Jiao Tong University, 200240 Shanghai, P. R. China
{wanggxx,shifeng.sun,wzdstill,dwgu}@sjtu.edu.cn

Abstract. Functional encryption (FE for short) can be used to calculate a function output of a message, without revealing other information about the message. There are mainly two types of security definitions for FE, exactly simulation-based security (SIM-security) and indistinguishability-based security (IND-security). Both of them have some limitations: FE with SIM-security supporting all circuits cannot be constructed for unbounded number of ciphertext and/or key queries, while IND-security is sometimes not enough: there are examples where an FE scheme is IND-secure but not intuitively secure. In this paper, we present a new security definition which can avoid the drawbacks of both SIM-security and IND-security, called indistinguishability-based security against probabilistic queries (pIND-security for short), and we give an FE construction for all circuits which is secure for unbounded key/ciphertext queries under this new security definition. We prove that this new security definition is strictly between SIM-security and IND-security, and provide new applications for FE which were not known to be constructed from IND-secure or SIM-secure FE.

Keywords: functional encryption · probabilistic queries · indistinguishability-based security · provable security

1 Introduction

Functional encryption (FE) was first introduced by Boneh et al. in 2011 [BSW11], which can calculate the function output $f(m)$ given the encrypted message $\mathsf{Enc}(m)$, and leaks nothing else about the message m. Functional encryption is a mighty cryptographic primitive, and can be considered as a generalization of attribute-based encryption, predicate encryption and inner product encryption.

Functional encryption is also an important method for computing on encrypted data, especially for cloud computing [KLM+18, RSG+19, MSH+19]. Using functional encryption, the cloud server can take ciphertexts as input, and outputs the required computation result as plaintext. This is different from homomorphic encryption, where the result is a ciphertext that requires additional decryption procedure and may not be suitable for some applications.

© International Association for Cryptologic Research 2023
A. Boldyreva and V. Kolesnikov (Eds.): PKC 2023, LNCS 13941, pp. 429–458, 2023.
https://doi.org/10.1007/978-3-031-31371-4_15

Informally, a functional encryption scheme consists of four algorithms: despite the normally defined algorithms Setup, Enc, Dec as in public key encryption, there is another algorithm KeyGen in functional encryption, which takes the master secret key and a function $f \in \mathcal{F}$ as input, and outputs a function key sk_f. In the decryption algorithm, function key sk_f instead of the master secret key is used, and the function value $f(m)$ instead of the message m itself is returned. (See Sect. 2 for the formal definition.)

There are mainly two types of security definitions for functional encryption: indistinguishability-based security (IND-security) and simulation-based security (SIM-security). However, both of them have their own drawbacks. We first briefly introduce the two types of security notions, then show why it is necessary to define a new type of security notions between them.

1.1   Overview of Security Notions for FE

The standard IND-security is equivalent to the natural notion of semantic security in public key encryption, and is also defined for many other cryptographic primitives, such as identity-based and attribute-based encryption. But for functional encryption, it has been pointed out that IND-security is not the strongest security definition. We first informally recall the definition of IND-security for FE:

An adversary $\mathcal{A}$ cannot distinguish between a ciphertext for m_0 and a ciphertext for m_1, even if allowed to query secret keys $\{sk_f\}$ for polynomial many different functions $\{f \in \mathcal{F}\}$, providing that $f(m_0) = f(m_1)$. (We say that $\mathcal{A}$ is "admissible" if it only makes queries such that $f(m_0) = f(m_1)$.)

It seems to be natural for the restriction $f(m_0) = f(m_1)$, since $\mathcal{A}$ can trivially determine whether the ciphertext is for m_0 or m_1 otherwise. However, such a restriction leads to the counter-intuitive example given in [O'N10, BSW11] and refined in [AGVW13]:

Example 1.1 ([BSW11, AGVW13]*).* Let $\mathcal{F}$ be a family of one-way permutations. Suppose that PKE = (PKE.KeyGen, PKE.Enc, PKE.Dec) is a secure public-key encryption scheme. Then the following FE construction for $\mathcal{F}$ is IND-secure:

- Setup(1^λ): Let (PKE.pk, PKE.sk) ← PKE.KeyGen(1^λ), and return PK = PKE.pk, MSK = PKE.sk.
- Enc(PK, m): Return PKE.Enc(PK, m).
- KeyGen(MSK, f): Return (MSK, f).
- Dec(sk_f, ct_m): Let sk_f = (MSK, f), return f(PKE.Dec(MSK, ct_m)).

However, each sk_f totally leaks m, while $f(m)$ does not leak m (since f is one-way).

It is not difficult to understand why such a counter-example exists: since the adversary is only allowed to query on f such that $f(m_0) = f(m_1)$, it is not allowed to make any single key query if $\mathcal{F}$ is a family of one-way permutations.

In [BSW11], the authors defined a stronger security notion, called simulation-based security to handle such cases. Informally speaking, SIM-security implies that there exists a simulator that, given only the length of m and the function outputs $\{f(m)\}$, but not m itself, can simulate the role of the challenger in the real game. However, SIM-security is so strong that it suffers from the following impossible results:

(1) [BSW11]: SIM-secure FE for P/poly cannot be constructed for unbounded ciphertext queries before a single key query;
(2) [AGVW13]: SIM-secure FE for P/poly cannot be constructed for unbounded key queries before a single ciphertext query.

These impossible results hold even under the random oracle model [AKW18]. Indeed, there are already some constructions for simulation-based FE schemes, but they only work for either bounded ciphertext queries or bounded key queries (which means that the number of ciphertext/key queries must be pre-determined at the Setup phase) [GVW12, GJKS15, ALMT20]. However, for applications in the real world, we need to know how an FE scheme already proven to be SIM-secure performs when handling unbounded ciphertext and key queries. Therefore, a natural question is that: is there a new security notion between IND-security and SIM-security that overcomes the above drawbacks? Intuitively, the new security notion should satisfy the following properties:

- The new security notion must avoid the counter-intuitive example in Example 1.1;
- There must be a construction of FE for P/poly under the new security notion that supports both unbounded ciphertext and key queries;
- Any SIM-secure FE scheme should satisfy the new security notion, so that we are able to discuss the unbounded ciphertext/key security for existing SIM-secure schemes;
- The new security notion should be stronger than IND-security, so that the properties for IND-security also hold for this new security notion.

Next, we show how to define this new security notion by modifying the existing IND-security definition. We note that, the problem in the counter-example can be handled for IND-security, if we loose the restriction on the adversary, such that $\mathcal{A}$ is still allowed to make query f even if f is a one-way permutation. We start from the distributional indistinguishable security (DI-security), first introduced in [AM18], by letting the input of ciphertext queries be a pair of message distributions M_0, M_1, instead of a pair of messages m_0, m_1. For example, let M_0 be the uniform distribution of messages such that the first bit is 0, and M_1 be the uniform distribution of messages such that the first bit is 1. When the adversary submits M_0, M_1 to the challenger, the challenger first randomly chooses a bit b, and then samples $m \leftarrow M_b$.

Now we show that why the counter-example can no longer satisfy the DI-security definition which allows probabilistic ciphertexts. We only need to construct an adversary $\mathcal{A}$ which queries the challenger with a pair of message distributions, instead of a pair of messages, such that $\mathcal{A}$ can break the scheme in Example 1.1.

- Let b be a hardcore predicate of f, we let $\mathcal{A}$ submit two distributions: M_0 is uniform on all strings with $b(m) = 0$, M_1 is uniform on all strings with $b(m) = 1$. (More details can be found in Sect. 5.)
- Now $\mathcal{A}$ can make queries on f for the one-way permutation f, since $f(M_0)$ and $f(M_1)$ are computationally indistinguishable by the property of hard core predicate.
- $\mathcal{A}$ can calculate $\mathsf{PKE.Dec}(sk_f, ct_{m_b})$ and check its first bit to successfully recover b.

On computational indistinguishability and queries with trapdoors. However, DI-security is not enough, mainly because the usage of computational indistinguishability in its security definition. We point out that it is not easy to include computational indistinguishability *inside* a security game. Below we show the difficulties we discovered while attempting to define a new security notion through probabilistic queries, and that how we solved them. We first give an example, where distributional indistinguishability fails to handle.

Example 1.2. Let PKE be a public key encryption scheme. We explicitly write the randomness used in the encryption algorithm: $\mathsf{PKE.Enc}(pk, m; r)$, let $\mathcal{R}$ be the space of random seeds where $r \leftarrow \mathcal{R}$. We define function class $\mathcal{F}$ as follows:

$$f_{pk}(m, r) \in \mathcal{F} \Leftrightarrow \exists (pk, sk) \leftarrow \mathsf{PKE.KeyGen}, f_{pk}(m, r) = \mathsf{PKE.Enc}(pk, m; r).$$

Let FE be a functional encryption scheme for $\mathcal{F}$, and we consider the security notion which allows message distributions instead of messages.

We construct an adversary $\mathcal{A}$ which makes following queries:

- $\mathcal{A}$ runs $\mathsf{PKE.KeyGen}$ to get (pk, sk).
- Then, $\mathcal{A}$ submits f_{pk} as a key query.
- $\mathcal{A}$ chooses random m_0, m_1, and submits M_0, M_1 which are uniform distributions on $\{m_0\} \times \mathcal{R}$ and $\{m_1\} \times \mathcal{R}$.

Now we have that $f_{pk}(M_0) \leftarrow \mathsf{PKE.Enc}(pk, m_0)$ and $f_{pk}(M_1) \leftarrow \mathsf{PKE.Enc}(pk, m_1)$, hence the two distributions: $f(M_0)$ and $f(M_1)$ are computationally indistinguishable according to the IND-CPA security of PKE. However, the adversary $\mathcal{A}$ can easily distinguish between a ciphertext in $f(M_0)$ and $f(M_1)$ since it holds the secret key sk.

Although in [AM18], the authors constructed DI-secure FE for all polynomial-sized circuits, we show here that DI-security cannot be satisfied for a function family with trapdoors[1], which makes a contradictory. The main reason for this problem is that the notion of computational indistinguishability was

---

[1] We also note that a trapdoor may not only be hidden in the function, but also in the messages. We slightly modify the function in Example 1.2, and let f be defined as: $f(pk, m, r) = \mathsf{PKE.Enc}(pk, m; r)$, and $M_b = \{pk\} \times \{m_b\} \times \mathcal{R}$, so $f(M_0)$ and $f(M_1)$ are distributions with trapdoor, and the trapdoor is hidden in the message distribution, not the function.

not well-defined as in [AM18]: it must be made clear for which party it is to distinguish between the two distributions, and how much information it has. In Example 1.2, since an adversary may cheat, we cannot let $\mathcal{A}$ be the distinguisher. However, $\mathcal{A}$ is the only one who has the secret key sk, and for any other party, $f(M_0)$ and $f(M_1)$ are indistinguishable, which meets the same difficulties.

This is why we must extend computational indistinguishability into a stronger notion for such a security notion of FE to be well-defined. We informally state what it means by saying that two distributions are strictly computationally indistinguishable even considering trapdoors.

Definition 1.1. *(informal) Let $\mathcal{D}$ be a p.p.t. algorithm that outputs a pair of distributions D_0, D_1, we say that distributions from $\mathcal{D}$ are strictly computationally indistinguishable, if there is no auxiliary string aux corresponding with D_0, D_1 such that (D_0, aux) and (D_1, aux) are computational distinguishable.*

Note that the auxiliary string aux can be viewed as the trapdoor in distributions D_0, D_1.

Now, we revisit Example 1.2. We consider $\mathcal{A}$ as the algorithm which outputs $f_{pk}(M_0)$ and $f_{pk}(M_1)$ as a pair of distributions, and we let sk be the auxiliary string aux. So we can easily construct $\mathcal{B}$ that distinguish between $sk, f_{pk}(M_0)$ and $sk, f_{pk}(M_1)$, thus $f_{pk}(M_0)$ and $f_{pk}(M_1)$ cannot satisfy the condition of strict computational indistinguishability.

This additional auxiliary string has no affect on function families without trapdoors. Just consider PKE, for $(pk, sk) \leftarrow$ PKE.KeyGen, sk can be the auxiliary string if pk is fixed, but if we choose random pk, then there is no such aux as long as PKE has semantic security (we note that aux is not a variable, hence cannot be sk). Otherwise, aux becomes a "master trapdoor" which is unrelated to the randomness used in PKE.KeyGen. Let $\mathcal{A}$ be an adversary which distinguishes between (D_0, aux) and (D_1, aux), then $\mathcal{A}^{aux}(.) = \mathcal{A}(., aux)$ (with aux hardwired in the adversary) can break the semantic security of PKE. We shall give a formal explanation for this case in Sect. 6.

The need for probabilistic function queries. It seems that everything is right with a new definition for computational indistinguishability. However, since we consider trapdoor functions, we extend Example 1.2 to construct another example just like Example 1.1:

Example 1.3. Let $\mathcal{F}$ be defined as in Example 1.2, and PKE′ be a semantic secure public key encryption scheme, then the following FE construction for $\mathcal{F}$ is IND-secure even if we consider probabilistic ciphertext queries:

- Setup(1^λ): Let (PKE′.pk^*, PKE′.sk^*) $\leftarrow$ PKE′.Setup(1^λ), and returns PK = PKE′.pk^*, MSK = PKE′.sk^*.
- Enc(PK, (m, r)): Return PKE′.Enc(PK, $m\|r$).
- KeyGen(MSK, f): Return (MSK, f).
- Dec(sk_f, ct_m): Parse sk_f = (MSK, f), decrypt $m\|r$ = PKE′.Dec(MSK, ct_m), and return $f(m, r)$.

However, each sk_f totally leaks m, while $f(m, r)$ does not leak m (since f is the encryption of a semantic secure PKE).

The counter-example above holds, since if we allow the adversary to make even a single query, it can first use PKE.Setup to generate a pair pk, sk, and then query the function key for $f_{pk} = \mathsf{PKE.Enc}(pk, .; .) \in \mathcal{F}$, hence having the ability to trivially distinguish between $f_{pk}(M_0)$ and $f_{pk}(M_1)$. (To match Definition 1.1 above, we can trivially construct a distinguisher $\mathcal{B}$ with sk as the auxiliary string.) Since the adversary cannot make any queries, the same problem in Example 1.1 also occurs.

In order to avoid such counter-examples, we must allow probabilistic queries not only in the ciphertext query, but also in key queries. Each time the adversary makes a probabilistic key query F, the challenger first samples $f \leftarrow F$, then returns both f and sk_f to the adversary. We construct an adversary $\mathcal{A}$ which makes following queries (including probabilistic key queries):

- We let $\mathcal{A}$ submit two distributions: M_0 is uniform on all strings which first bit is 0, M_1 is uniform on all strings which first bit is 1.
- $\mathcal{A}$ makes a single key query by submitting a distribution F which is uniform on $\mathcal{F}$, and gets $f_{pk} \in \mathcal{F}$.
- $\mathcal{A}$ can calculate $\mathsf{PKE'.Dec}(MSK, ct_{m_b})$ and check its first bit to successfully recover b.

Since f_{pk} is randomly chosen by the challenger, the adversary $\mathcal{A}$ cannot get the corresponding sk. Here, instead of $f(M_0)$ and $f(M_1)$, we only require that the distributions $F, F(M_0)$ and $F, F(M_1)$ be strictly computationally indistinguishable (sampling from $F, F(M_b)$ means sampling $f \leftarrow F$, $m \leftarrow M_b$ and returning $f, f(m)$.) By our definition, the auxiliary string aux is only related to the distribution $F, F(M_b)$ but independent from how the challenger chooses $f_{pk} \leftarrow F$ (thus independent with either pk or sk).

Now we finished the discussion of rationality for probabilistic queries. We can see that such a security notion can be well-defined, and also avoids the counter-intuitive examples in Example 1.1, 1.2 and 1.3. We call the new security notion *indistinguishability-based security against probabilistic queries* (pIND-security), and show that it is weaker than SIM-security but stronger than IND-security.

Construction of pIND*-secure FE for* P/poly. In this paper, we also give a construction of pIND-secure FE for P/poly, which allows unbounded number of both ciphertext and key queries. Concretely, we show that a fully pIND-secure FE scheme for P/poly can be constructed from a selective IND-secure FE scheme, while the latter can be constructed from both indistinguishability obfuscation [GGH+13] and well-founded assumptions [JLS21, GP21, WW21]. We note that, although the existence of $i\mathcal{O}$ is a strong assumption, unbounded IND-secure FE for P/poly is more than sufficient in constructing $i\mathcal{O}$ [AJ15]. So the FE scheme we construct has stronger security without stronger assumptions.

1.2   Related Works

FE for randomized functionalities. Functional encryption for randomized functionalities (rFE) was introduced in [GJKS15]. The authors gave both SIM-based and IND-based security notions for rFE. We note that, since the authors also used computational indistinguishability to define IND-based security for rFE, the same problems occur as we pointed out in Example 1.2, so that the IND-security of rFE given by [GJKS15] cannot handle trapdoors or public-key encryption. By moving our definition (and construction, using the generic transformation of [AW17]) into the randomized case, these problems can be solved to get a well-defined pIND-based security for rFE.

Distributional Indistinguishability for FE. In [AM18], the authors gave the definition of distributional indistinguishability (DI) for FE, which is previously discussed on garbled circuit and randomized encodings [GHRW14,LPST16], and also gave a construction for DI-secure FE from standard IND-secure FE. Our security definition shares some similarities with theirs, such as allowing the adversary to submit two message distributions, rather than two messages, in the ciphertext query. However, since the DI definition does not allow probabilistic key queries, it still suffers from Example 1.2 and 1.3 which we pointed out above (see also the discussion in Sect. 6). Moreover, we also give a pIND-secure FE construction for P/poly with adaptive security, while the construction in [AM18] only satisfies selective security.

Function-private public key FE. Probabilistic key queries are also considered in the function-privacy of public key FE [BRS13,PMR19,BCJ+19] as in our work. However, we do not consider function-privacy: In our definition, the function chosen by the challenger is always known to the adversary. It is interesting that whether we can extend our security definition to handle function-privacy.

Other security definitions for FE. There are some other security definitions in early works of functional encryption. In [BO13], the authors gave some new security definitions compared with IND-security, but without a general construction. In [BF13], the authors considered the cases where a trapdoor is hidden in the function family $\mathcal{F}$ supported by FE (instead of function-key queries, which we consider in this paper), and made new security definitions that are even stronger than SIM-security. However, in this paper, we mainly focus on the case where the function family $\mathcal{F}$ is P/poly, so we will not consider this problem.

2   Preliminaries

Notations . $x \leftarrow \chi$ for a distribution χ means that x is sampled from χ. $x \leftarrow X$ for a set X means that x is uniformly random chosen from X. $x \leftarrow \mathcal{X}$ for a p.p.t. algorithm $\mathcal{X}$ means that x is a random output of $\mathcal{X}$, where the abbreviation p.p.t. stands for probabilistic polynomial time. We say that ϵ is negligible in λ, if $\epsilon < 1/\Omega(\lambda^c)$ for any $c > 0$ with sufficiently large λ. $[n]$ for $n \in \mathbb{Z}_+$ is the set $\{1, ..., n\}$.

2.1   Functional Encryption and Security Definitions

Definition 2.1. *A functional encryption scheme* FE *for a function family* $\mathcal{F}$ *consists of the following four algorithms (let* $\mathcal{M}$ *be the message space):*

- Setup(1^λ): *output a pair* (PK, MSK).
- KeyGen(MSK, f): *for $f \in \mathcal{F}$, output a function key* SK$_f$.
- Enc(PK, m): *for $m \in \mathcal{M}$, output a ciphertext* CT$_m$.
- Dec(SK$_f$, CT$_m$): *output the function value* $f(m)$.

FE *is correct if for any* (PK, MSK) $\leftarrow$ Setup(1^λ), SK$_f$ $\leftarrow$ KeyGen(MSK, f), CT$_m$ $\leftarrow$ Enc(PK, m), *the probability that* Dec(SK$_f$, CT$_m$) $\neq f(m)$ *is negligible.*

Now we give the definition for both IND-security and SIM-security of functional encryption.

Definition 2.2. *An 1-CT adaptive IND-CPA-security game for an FE scheme is defined as follows:*

- Setup: *The challenger runs* Setup(1^λ) *and returns* PK *to the adversary.*
- Phase 1: *The adversary chooses $f \in \mathcal{F}$ and gives it to the challenger. The challenger generates $sk_f \leftarrow$ KeyGen(MSK, f) and returns sk_f to the adversary. This can be repeated adaptively for any polynomial times.*
- Challenge: *The adversary chooses two messages of identical length m_0, m_1 and gives it to the challenger. The challenger randomly chooses $b \leftarrow \{0,1\}$, generates $ct \leftarrow$ Enc(PK, m_b) and returns ct to the adversary.*
- Phase 2: *Same as Phase 1.*
- Output: *The adversary outputs a bit b', and the winning advantage for the adversary is defined by* Adv$^{\text{IND}}(\mathcal{A}) = |\Pr(b' = b) - 1/2|$.

An adversary $\mathcal{A}$ is said to be admissible, if for any query f in Phase 1 or Phase 2, $f(m_0) = f(m_1)$. FE *is said to be ad-IND-secure if for any p.p.t. admissible adversary $\mathcal{A}$,* Adv$^{\text{IND}}(\mathcal{A})$ *is negligible.*

For the selective IND-security (sel-IND-security), we require that $\mathcal{A}$ submits m_0, m_1 to the challenger at the beginning of the game.

For the many-CT version of the game, we let the adversary submits any polynomial number of pairs of messages in the challenge phase, say $(m_0^1, m_1^1), ..., (m_0^q, m_1^q)$, such that $f(m_0^i) = f(m_1^i)$ for any query f and $i \in [q]$. In the challenge phase, the challenger samples $b \leftarrow \{0,1\}$ and returns $(\text{Enc}(\text{PK}, m_b^i))_{i \in [q]}$.

It is not hard to show that 1-CT IND-security implies many-CT IND-security through hybrid arguments. In [ABSV15], the authors showed that any sel-IND secure FE scheme which is sufficiently expressive can be turned into an ad-IND secure FE scheme. Even if the FE scheme is not expressive enough, we can still use the standard complexity leverage method [BB04] to prove the ad-IND-security, if we assume the sub-exponential hardness of the underlying hardness assumptions.

Next, we give the simulation-based security definition.

Definition 2.3. *Let FE be a functional encryption scheme for a function family $\mathcal{F}$. Consider a p.p.t. adversary $\mathcal{A} = (\mathcal{A}_1, \mathcal{A}_2)$ and a stateful p.p.t. simulator Sim. Let $U_m(.)$ denote a universal oracle, such that $U_m(f) = f(m)$. Consider the following two experiments:*

$\mathrm{Exp}_{\mathsf{FE},\mathcal{A}}^{\mathrm{real}}(1^\lambda)$	$\mathrm{Exp}_{\mathsf{FE},\mathcal{A}}^{\mathrm{ideal}}(1^\lambda)$
1. $(\mathsf{PK}, \mathsf{MSK}) \leftarrow \mathsf{FE.Setup}(1^\lambda);$	1. $\mathsf{PK} \leftarrow \mathrm{Sim}(1^\lambda);$
2. $(m, st) \leftarrow \mathcal{A}_1^{\mathsf{FE.KeyGen}(\mathsf{MSK},\cdot)}(\mathsf{PK});$	2. $(m, st) \leftarrow \mathcal{A}_1^{\mathrm{Sim}(\cdot)}(\mathsf{PK});$
3. $\mathsf{CT} \leftarrow \mathsf{FE.Enc}(\mathsf{PK}, m);$	3. $\mathsf{CT} \leftarrow \mathrm{Sim}^{U_m(\cdot)}(1^\lambda, 1^{|m|});$
4. $\alpha \leftarrow \mathcal{A}_2^{\mathsf{FE.KeyGen}(\mathsf{MSK},\cdot)}(\mathsf{PK}, \mathsf{CT}, st);$	4. $\alpha \leftarrow \mathcal{A}_2^{\mathrm{Sim}^{U_m(\cdot)}(\cdot)}(\mathsf{PK}, \mathsf{CT}, st);$
5. Output m, α	5. Output m, α

We call a stateful simulator algorithm Sim *admissible* if, on each input f, Sim makes just a single query to its oracle $U_m(\cdot)$ on f itself. The functional encryption scheme FE is then said to be *adaptive simulation-based secure (*ad-SIM-*security)* if there is an admissible stateful p.p.t. simulator Sim such that for every p.p.t. adversary $\mathcal{A} = (\mathcal{A}_1, \mathcal{A}_2)$, the two experiments are computationally indistinguishable.

For the selective SIM-security (sel-SIM-*security*), we require that $\mathcal{A}$ submits m to the challenger at the beginning of the game.

3 Indistinguishability-Based Security Against Probabilistic Queries

3.1 Definition for pIND Security

First, we give a formal definition for the idea of strict computational indistinguishability introduced in Sect. 1. We say that a distribution F is efficiently samplable, if there exists a p.p.t. algorithm $\mathcal{F}$ which output follows F. Moreover, sampling from F means to run $\mathcal{F}$ with random seed and fetch its output, so we can use $\mathcal{F}$ to represent F if there is no confusion.

Definition 3.1. *Let $\mathcal{D}$ be a p.p.t. algorithm that outputs a pair of efficiently samplable distributions D_0, D_1. We say that distributions from $\mathcal{D}$ are strictly computationally indistinguishable, if for any p.p.t. algorithm $\mathcal{S}$ which outputs a pair of efficiently samplable distributions S_0, S_1 and an auxiliary string aux, either:*

(1) there exists a p.p.t. algorithm $\mathcal{P}$ which distinguishes between the output of $\mathcal{D}$ and $\mathcal{S}$ (without aux), which means that $\Pr(\mathcal{P}(D_0, D_1) = 1|(D_0, D_1) \leftarrow \mathcal{D}) - \Pr(\mathcal{P}(S_0, S_1) = 1|(S_0, S_1, aux) \leftarrow \mathcal{S})$ is non-negligible; or

(2) there is no p.p.t. algorithm $\mathcal{B}$ which distinguishes between aux, S_0 and aux, S_1, which means that $\Pr(\mathcal{B}(aux, s_0) = 1|s_0 \leftarrow S_0) - \Pr(\mathcal{B}(aux, s_1) = 1|s_1 \leftarrow S_1)$ must be negligible.

Without loss of generality, we let the auxiliary string *aux* contains the two distributions S_0, S_1 (in the form of sampling algorithms), so the distinguisher $\mathcal{B}$ knows exactly the two distributions.

Since there must be no restriction on how $\mathcal{D}$ works, we cannot suppose that aux is output by $\mathcal{D}$, hence we introduce another algorithm $\mathcal{S}$ which outputs both the pair of distributions and the auxiliary string aux. In most cases, we can simply suppose that $\mathcal{S}$ acts similar as $\mathcal{D}$. However, since no p.p.t. algorithm can determine whether two distributions are equal or even statistical indistinguishable, in order to get a formal definition, we simply let the outputs of $\mathcal{D}$ and $\mathcal{S}$ be computationally indistinguishable.

Next, we use the idea of strict computational indistinguishability to define our new definition for functional encryption.

Definition 3.2. *Given message space $\mathcal{M}$ and function space $\mathcal{F}$, an 1-CT adaptive* pIND-*CPA-security game for an FE scheme is defined as the following:*

- Setup: *The challenger runs* Setup(1^λ) *and returns* PK *to the adversary.*
- Phase 1: *The adversary chooses an efficiently samplable distribution F on the function space $\mathcal{F}$, and gives the sampling algorithm to the challenger. The challenger samples $f \leftarrow F$, generates $sk_f =$ KeyGen(MSK, f) and returns f, sk_f to the adversary. This can be repeated adaptively for any polynomial times.*
- Challenge: *The adversary chooses two efficiently samplable distributions M_0, M_1 on the message space $\mathcal{M}$ which contain messages of same length, and gives the sampling algorithms to the challenger. The challenger randomly chooses $b \leftarrow \{0,1\}$, $m \leftarrow M_b$, generates $ct_m \leftarrow$ Enc(PK, m) and returns ct_m to the adversary.*
- Phase 2: *Same as Phase 1.*
- Output: *The adversary outputs b', and the winning advantage for the adversary is defined by* Adv$^{\text{pIND}}(\mathcal{A}) = |\Pr(b' = b) - 1/2|$.

An adversary $\mathcal{A}$ is said to be admissible, if the two distributions $(F_i, F_i(M_0))_{i \in [Q]}$ and $(F_i, F_i(M_1))_{i \in [Q]}$ are strictly computationally indistinguishable, Q is the number of KeyGen queries. FE *is said to be* ad-pIND-*secure if for any p.p.t. admissible adversary $\mathcal{A}$,* Adv$^{\text{pIND}}(\mathcal{A})$ *is negligible.*

For the selective pIND-*security (*sel-pIND-*security), we require that $\mathcal{A}$ submits M_0, M_1 to the challenger at the beginning of the game.*

For the many-CT version of the game, we let the adversary submits any polynomial number of pairs of messages in the challenge phase, say (M_0^1, M_1^1), ..., (M_0^q, M_1^q), and the admissability is changed to: $(F_i, F_i(M_0^1), ..., F_i(M_0^q))_{i \in [Q]}$ and $(F_i, F_i(M_1^1), ..., F_i(M_1^q))_{i \in [Q]}$ are strictly computationally indistinguishable. In the challenge phase, the challenger samples $b \leftarrow \{0,1\}$ and returns $($Enc$(PK, m_b^i))_{i \in [q]}$.

We note that when sampling from the distribution $(F_i, F_i(M_b))_{i \in [Q]}$, we only sample once from each F_i and M_b, so the elements from the distribution are in fact dependent with each other.

Now we present a lemma by applying the contrapositive of strict computational indistinguishability onto pIND-security definition. This lemma is useful in the following proofs.

Lemma 3.1. *For an adversary $\mathcal{A}$ in the* pIND-*CPA-security game, we define the trace of $\mathcal{A}$ as:*

$$tr_{\mathcal{A}} = (M_0, M_1, (F_i, f_i, f_i(m))_{i \in [Q]}).$$

Then FE *is* pIND-*secure, if and only if for every p.p.t. $\mathcal{A}$ such that* $\mathrm{Adv}^{\mathsf{pIND}}(\mathcal{A})$ *is non-negligible (not necessarily admissible), there exists a p.p.t. sampling algorithm $\mathcal{T}$ which outputs the distribution:*

$$(aux, \bar{b} \leftarrow \{0,1\}, \bar{m} \leftarrow \bar{M}_{\bar{b}}, \overline{tr} = (\bar{M}_0, \bar{M}_1, (\bar{F}_i, \bar{f}_i, \bar{f}_i(\bar{m}))_{i \in [Q]})),$$

and a p.p.t. algorithm $\mathcal{B}$ where:

- *(1) For any p.p.t. algorithm $\mathcal{P}$, $\Pr(\mathcal{P}(tr_{\mathcal{A}}) = 1) - \Pr(\mathcal{P}(\overline{tr}) = 1)$ is negligible;*
- *(2) aux is independent with the following conditional distributions: $\bar{m}|\bar{M}_0, \bar{M}_1$; $\bar{f}_1|\bar{F}_1; \dots; \bar{f}_Q|\bar{F}_Q$ (which can be considered as the randomness used in the choice of $\bar{m}, \bar{f}_1, \dots, \bar{f}_Q$);*
- *(3) $\Pr(\mathcal{B}(aux, \overline{tr}) = \bar{b}) - 1/2$ is non-negligible.*

Proof. If FE is pIND-secure, then $\mathcal{A}$ with non-negligible advantage must be non-admissible, which means that $(F_i, F_i(M_0))_{i \in [Q]}$ and $(F_i, F_i(M_1))_{i \in [Q]}$ are not strictly computationally indistinguishable.

By the definition of strict computational indistinguishability, there is a sampling algorithm $\mathcal{S}$ which outputs $(\bar{F}_i, \bar{F}_i(\bar{M}_0))_{i \in [Q]}, (\bar{F}_i, \bar{F}_i(\bar{M}_1))_{i \in [Q]}, aux$, such that:

(1) The output of $\mathcal{S}$ except aux are computationally indistinguishable with $(F_i, F_i(M_0))_{i \in [Q]}, (F_i, F_i(M_1))_{i \in [Q]}$;
(2) There exists $\mathcal{B}$ which distinguishes between $aux, (\bar{F}_i, \bar{F}_i(\bar{M}_0))_{i \in [Q]}$ and $aux, (\bar{F}_i, \bar{F}_i(\bar{M}_1))_{i \in [Q]}$.

Let $\mathcal{T}$ do the following: first sample S_0, S_1, aux from $\mathcal{S}$, then sample $\bar{b} \leftarrow \{0,1\}$, $\bar{f}_i \leftarrow \bar{F}_i$, $\bar{m} \leftarrow \bar{M}_{\bar{b}}$, and return $(aux, \bar{b}, \bar{m}, \overline{tr} = (\bar{M}_0, \bar{M}_1, (\bar{F}_i, \bar{f}_i, \bar{f}_i(\bar{m}))_{i \in [Q]}))$. Since in the pIND-CPA-security game, the challenger samples from F_i and M_b honestly, we can see that $\overline{tr}$ is computationally indistinguishable with $tr_{\mathcal{A}}$, and aux is independent with the choice of $\bar{f}_i$ and $\bar{m}$, which means that aux is independent with $\bar{m}|\bar{M}_0, \bar{M}_1$; $\bar{f}_1|\bar{F}_1; \dots; \bar{f}_Q|\bar{F}_Q$, hence satisfies all three conditions.

Now, suppose that there exists $\mathcal{T}, \mathcal{B}$ satisfies all three conditions. Let $\mathcal{S}$ runs $\mathcal{T}$ and outputs aux and the two distributions $(\bar{F}_i, \bar{F}_i(\bar{M}_0))_{i \in [Q]}$, $(\bar{F}_i, \bar{F}_i(\bar{M}_1))_{i \in [Q]}$, which are computationally indistinguishable with $(F_i, F_i(M_0))_{i \in [Q]}$, $(F_i, F_i(M_1))_{i \in [Q]}$.

Then, we sample random $\bar{b} \leftarrow \{0,1\}$, $\bar{m} \leftarrow \bar{M}_{\bar{b}}$, $\bar{f}_i \leftarrow \bar{F}_i$, $i \in [Q]$, and let $(aux, (\bar{M}_0, \bar{M}_1, (\bar{F}_i, \bar{f}_i, \bar{f}_i(\bar{m}))_{i \in [Q]}))$ be the input of $\mathcal{B}$, then $\mathcal{B}$ distinguishes the two distributions $(\bar{F}_i, \bar{F}_i(\bar{M}_0))_{i \in [Q]}$, $(\bar{F}_i, \bar{F}_i(\bar{M}_1))_{i \in [Q]}$. By the definition of strict computational indistinguishability, $(F_i, F_i(M_0))_{i \in [Q]}$ and $(F_i, F_i(M_1))_{i \in [Q]}$ cannot be strictly computationally indistinguishable, which means that any adversary $\mathcal{A}$ with non-negligible advantage cannot be admissible. $\square$

For the many-CT version of the game, we define the trace $tr_\mathcal{A}$ as:

$$((M_0^i, M_1^i)_{i \in [q]}, (F_k, f_k, f_k(m_1), ..., f_k(m_q))_{k \in [Q]}).$$

It is not hard to show that the result is the same as the 1-CT case.

In a general case, it seems to be hard to determine whether two distributions are strictly computationally indistinguishable, especially with the auxiliary string. But if the function class is a cryptographic primitive such as hash family or public key encryption, we can use its security definition to prove the indistinguishability. We give more details in Sect. 5 and Sect. 6.

3.2   Relationship Between Different Security Definitions

In this section, we show that pIND-security satisfies the four properties we discussed in Sect. 1.1, which means that pIND-security can be used to avoid the drawbacks for both SIM-security and IND-security.

Theorem 3.1. *If FE is* SIM*-secure, then FE is* pIND*-secure.*

Proof. Let $\mathcal{A}$ be any pIND adversary, we can construct a SIM adversary $\mathcal{E}^\mathcal{A}$ as follows (for the real experiment):

- When $\mathcal{A}$ outputs a key query F, $\mathcal{E}$ chooses $f \leftarrow F$ and gives f to the challenger $\mathcal{C}$. When the challenger returns sk_f, $\mathcal{E}$ returns f, sk_f to $\mathcal{A}$.
- When $\mathcal{A}$ outputs the ciphertext query M_0, M_1, $\mathcal{E}$ first chooses $b \leftarrow \{0, 1\}$ and gives $m \leftarrow M_b$ to the challenger $\mathcal{C}$.
- When $\mathcal{C}$ returns a ciphertext CT, CT is returned to $\mathcal{A}$ directly.
- When $\mathcal{A}$ outputs the guess b', $\mathcal{E}$ outputs b' along with the trace: $tr_\mathcal{A} = (M_0, M_1, (F_1, f_1, f_1(m)), ..., (F_Q, f_Q, f_Q(m)))$.

Since b' is the same as the output of $\mathcal{A}$ in the sel-pIND game, $\Pr(b' = b) - 1/2$ is non-negligible iff $\mathrm{Adv}^{\mathsf{pIND}}(\mathcal{A})$ is non-negligible.

Now consider the ideal experiment with simulator $\mathcal{S}$. Differ from the real experiment, we let the random bit and sampled message be $\tilde{b}, \tilde{m}$, output be $\tilde{b}'$, the trace by $\tilde{tr}_\mathcal{A}$, and $\tilde{tr}_\mathcal{A}$ is computationally indistinguishable with $tr_\mathcal{A}$ by the SIM-based security of the FE scheme. So $\Pr(\tilde{b}' = \tilde{b}) - 1/2$ is non-negligible iff $\mathrm{Adv}^{\mathsf{pIND}}(\mathcal{A})$ is non-negligible.

Using Lemma 3.1, we only need to construct the algorithm $\mathcal{B}$ and a sampling algorithm $\mathcal{T}$ which samples $(aux, \bar{b}, \bar{m}, \overline{tr})$.

Let $\mathcal{T}$ run the ideal experiment with adversary $\mathcal{E}^\mathcal{A}$ and simulator $\mathcal{S}^{U_{\tilde{m}}(\cdot)}$. When $\mathcal{S}$ queries $U_{\tilde{m}}(f)$, it directly returns $f(\tilde{m})$ to $\mathcal{S}$ (since $\tilde{m}$ is chosen by $\mathcal{E}^\mathcal{A}$), and let $\bar{b} = \tilde{b}, \bar{m} = \tilde{m}, \overline{tr} = \tilde{tr}_\mathcal{A}$. Finally, let $aux = (r_\mathcal{A}, r_\mathcal{S})$, where $r_\mathcal{A}, r_\mathcal{S}$ are the randomness used in $\mathcal{A}, \mathcal{S}$.

$\mathcal{B}(aux = (r_\mathcal{A}, r_\mathcal{S}), \overline{tr} = (\bar{M}_0, \bar{M}_1, (\bar{F}_i, \bar{f}_i, \bar{f}_i(\tilde{m}))_{i \in [Q]}))$ is constructed from $\mathcal{A}, \mathcal{S}$ with $r_\mathcal{A}, r_\mathcal{S}$ as their randomness:

- $\mathcal{B}$ first runs $\mathcal{A}$ with randomness $r_\mathcal{A}$. When $\mathcal{A}$ outputs the ciphertext query $\tilde{M}_0, \tilde{M}_1$, first check $\tilde{M}_0 = \bar{M}_0, \tilde{M}_1 = \bar{M}_1$, otherwise abort. $\mathcal{S}$ is run with randomness $r_\mathcal{S}$.

- When $\mathcal{A}$ outputs the i-th key query $\tilde{F}_i$, first check $\tilde{F}_i = \bar{F}_i$, otherwise abort. Send $\bar{f}_i$ to $\mathcal{S}$, and when $\mathcal{S}$ queries $U_{\tilde{m}}$, return $\bar{f}_i(\tilde{m})$ to $\mathcal{S}$. Return $\bar{f}_i$ and $sk_{\bar{f}_i}$ generated by $\mathcal{S}$ to $\mathcal{A}$.
- When $\mathcal{S}$ returns a ciphertext CT, CT is returned to $\mathcal{A}$ directly.
- When $\mathcal{A}$ outputs the guess $\tilde{b}'$, return $\bar{b}' = \tilde{b}'$.

It is easy to see that if $\mathcal{B}$ never aborts, the output distribution is the same as $\mathcal{E}^{\mathcal{A}}$ in the ideal game, which means that $\Pr(\mathcal{B}(aux, \overline{tr}) = b) - 1/2$ is non-negligible iff $\mathrm{Adv}^{\mathsf{pIND}}(\mathcal{A})$ is non-negligible, hence FE satisfies pIND-security. The non-abortness directly follows from the fact that the queries from $\mathcal{A}$ in both $\mathcal{B}$ and $\mathcal{T}$ are uniquely determined by the same randomness used by $\mathcal{A}, \mathcal{E}, \mathcal{S}$, so that $\tilde{M}_0, \tilde{M}_1, \tilde{F}_1, ..., \tilde{F}_Q$ in $\mathcal{B}$ are exactly the same as $\bar{M}_0, \bar{M}_1, \bar{F}_1, ..., \bar{F}_Q$ contained in $\overline{tr}$ generated from $\mathcal{T}$. Thus we finish the proof. $\square$

Theorem 3.2. *If FE is* pIND-*secure, then FE is* IND-*secure.*

Proof. For any admissible IND adversary $\mathcal{A}$, we construct a pIND adversary $\mathcal{A}'$ as follows:

- When $\mathcal{A}$ submits m_0, m_1, $\mathcal{A}'$ submits M_0, M_1 such that $M_b(m_b) = 1$, $M_b(m') = 0$ for $m' \neq m_b$, $b \in \{0, 1\}$.
- When $\mathcal{A}$ submits f, $\mathcal{A}'$ submits F such that $F(f) = 1$, $F(f') = 0$ for $f' \neq f$, $f(m_0) = f(m_1)$.
- When $\mathcal{A}$ outputs a bit b', $\mathcal{A}'$ also outputs b'.

If $\mathrm{Adv}^{\mathsf{pIND}}(\mathcal{A}')$ is non-negligible, then there exists $\mathcal{B}$, aux and $\overline{tr} = (\bar{M}_0, \bar{M}_1, (\bar{F}_i, \bar{f}_i, \bar{f}_i(\tilde{m}))_{i \in [Q]})$, such that $\Pr(\mathcal{B}(aux, \overline{tr}) = \bar{b}) - 1/2$ is non-negligible. Also, $\overline{tr}$ is indistinguishable from $tr_{\mathcal{A}}$, which means that sampling from $\bar{M}_0, \bar{M}_1$ and $\bar{F}_i$ always outputs fixed values $\bar{m}_0, \bar{m}_1, \bar{f}_i$, where $\bar{f}_i(\bar{m}_0) = \bar{f}_i(\bar{m}_1)$ for $i \in [Q]$ (otherwise $tr_{\mathcal{A}}$ and $\overline{tr}$ can easily be distinguished). So $\overline{tr}$ is independent from $\bar{b}$, also aux is independent from $\bar{b}$ by Lemma 3.1. Thus $\Pr(\mathcal{B}(aux, \overline{tr}) = \bar{b}) - 1/2 = 0$, which makes a contradiction.

So for every $\mathcal{A}'$ defined above, $\mathrm{Adv}^{\mathsf{pIND}}(\mathcal{A}')$ is negligible, which means that $\mathrm{Adv}^{\mathsf{IND}}(\mathcal{A})$ is negligible. $\square$

Now we show that 1-CT pIND-security implies many-CT pIND-security, so that our new definition can really bypass the impossible result in [BSW11].

Theorem 3.3. *If FE is* 1-CT pIND-*secure, then FE is* many-CT pIND-*secure.*

Proof. We define a sequence of games:

G_i: the first i ciphertext queries always choose $m_i \leftarrow M_0$ despite whether b is. Suppose that $\mathcal{A}$ makes a total of q ciphertext queries, then G_0 is the original game, and the advantage for $\mathcal{A}$ in G_q is always 0.

If the advantage for $\mathcal{A}$ in G_0 is non-negligible, then there exists $i \in [q]$ such that the advantage of $\mathcal{A}$ to distinguish between G_{i-1} and G_i is non-negligible. Then we construct an 1-CT pIND adversary $\mathcal{A}_i$ as follows:

- For $(M_0^j, M_1^j)_{j \in [q]}$, we define $M_0(x), M_1(x)$ be two sampling algorithms with a single input $x \in [q]$, which sample from M_0^x and M_1^x. Thus $M_0(x), M_1(x)$ contains all information about $(M_0^j, M_1^j)_{j \in [q]}$.
- When $\mathcal{A}$ submits $(M_0^j, M_1^j)_{j \in [q]}$, submit $M_0(i), M_1(i)$ to the challenger and get the ciphertext CT; sample $m_j \leftarrow M_0^j$ for $j < i$, $m_j \leftarrow M_1^j$ for $j > i$, let $CT_j \leftarrow \mathsf{Enc}(\mathsf{PK}, m_j)$ for $j \neq i$ and $CT_i = CT$, return $(CT_1, ..., CT_q)$ to $\mathcal{A}$.
- When $\mathcal{A}$ submits a key query F, directly pass it to the challenger and return (f, sk_f) to $\mathcal{A}$.
- When $\mathcal{A}$ outputs b', output b'.

So $\mathsf{Adv}^{\mathsf{pIND}}(\mathcal{A}_i)$ is non-negligible. By the 1-CT pIND security, there exist $\mathcal{T}_i$ and $\mathcal{B}_i$ satisfying Lemma 3.1, let $(aux, \overline{tr}_i)$ be sampled by $\mathcal{T}_i$, we write $\overline{tr}_i = (\bar{M}_0(i), \bar{M}_1(i), (\bar{F}_k, \bar{f}_k, \bar{f}_k(\bar{m}_i))_{k \in [Q]})$, and since $\bar{M}_0(i), \bar{M}_1(i)$ are indistinguishable from $M_0(i), M_1(i)$, we write the q pairs of distributions extracted from $\bar{M}_0(i), \bar{M}_1(i)$ as $(\bar{M}_0^j, \bar{M}_1^j)_{j \in [q]}$.

We first sample $(\bar{m}_j \leftarrow \bar{M}_b^j)_{j \neq i}$ and calculate $(\bar{f}_k(\bar{m}_j))_{j \neq i, k \in [Q]}$. Let $\mathcal{B}$ proceed the same as $\mathcal{B}_i$ except that we let the input $\overline{tr} = ((\bar{M}_0^j, \bar{M}_1^j)_{j \in [q]}, (\bar{F}_k, \bar{f}_k, \bar{f}_k(\bar{m}_1), ..., \bar{f}_k(\bar{m}_q))_{k \in [Q]})$. So $(aux, \bar{b}, (\bar{m}_i)_{i \in [q]}, \overline{tr})$ can be sampled by $\mathcal{T}_i$ with slight modification, aux is independent from the choices of $(\bar{m}_j)_{j \in [q]}$ and $(\bar{f}_k)_{k \in [Q]}$, and $\Pr(\mathcal{B}(aux, \overline{tr}) = \bar{b}) - 1/2$ is non-negligible, since the outputs of $\mathcal{B}$ and $\mathcal{B}_i$ are the same. Thus we finish the proof.   □

4   Fully pIND-secure FE from IND-based FE Schemes

We already show that pIND-secure FE can support unbounded ciphertext. The problem remaining is to show the existence of adaptive pIND-secure FE scheme for P/poly which supports unbounded key, so that our new security definition can avoid the [AGVW13] impossibility result. We show that the [ABSV15] generic transformation, which transforms selective IND-secure FE schemes into adaptive IND-secure ones, can be extended into pIND-security. In fact, we prove a result stronger than expected: we can transform any selective IND-secure FE scheme into an adaptive pIND-secure FE scheme.

Technical Overview. In [ABSV15], the authors constructed an adaptive IND-secure FE scheme for any function class $\mathcal{F}$ (even if $\mathcal{F} = \mathsf{P}/\mathsf{poly}$) from an IND-secure private-key FE scheme for $\mathcal{F}$ with 1-CT query and unbounded key queries, and a "sufficiently expressive" selective IND-secure FE scheme, here private-key FE means that the encryption algorithm uses master secret key instead of master public key.

To prove the existence of IND-secure private-key FE with 1-CT and unbounded key queries, [ABSV15] relies on several results in the literature. First, in [GVW12], the authors constructed a 1-key, unbounded-CT SIM-secure private-key FE scheme for P/poly, which is also a 1-key, unbounded-CT IND-secure private-key FE scheme. In [BS15], the authors gave the generic transformation from private-key FE to function-private private-key FE, here function-private means that the function f is hidden from the adversary even given the function key sk_f. (A private-key FE without function-privacy is also called message-private.) Then, one can swap KeyGen and Enc in a function-private private-key FE with 1-key and unbounded-CT, to obtain a private-key FE with unbounded-key and 1-CT.

The same method can easily be extended to pIND-security. Similar with [ABSV15], we can construct an adaptive pIND-secure FE scheme from pIND-secure private-key FE scheme and IND-secure (public-key) FE scheme, and by Theorem 3.1 in this paper (extended to private-key settings), we can show the existence of a 1-key, unbounded-CT message-private pIND-secure private-key FE scheme for P/poly. What left for us is to transform a pIND-secure message-private private-key FE scheme into a pIND-secure function-private private-key FE scheme.

The idea of this construction is similar to the one in [BS15], but more complicated since we consider probabilistic queries. The [BS15] construction used two symmetric keys k, k' to hide the two functions f_0, f_1 correspondingly in both the message-private and function-private game. However, in our pIND-secure settings, in message-private game, the adversary learns an exact function f, while in function-private game, the adversary learns only two distributions F_0 and F_1 (see the formal definition below). So we need three keys k, k', k'' to encrypt f, F_0, F_1 correspondingly, and an additional game to switch between them, while the other parts of the proof is similar to [BS15].

Finally, combining all components together, we can construct an adaptive pIND-secure FE scheme for P/poly.

Before further discussions, first we give formal definitions for both message-private and function-private private-key functional encryption with pIND-security.

Definition 4.1. *A private-key functional encryption scheme* skFE *for a function family $\mathcal{F}$ consists of the following four algorithms (let $\mathcal{M}$ be the message space):*

- Setup(1^λ): *output the master secret key* MSK.
- KeyGen(MSK, f): *for $f \in \mathcal{F}$, output a function key* SK$_f$.
- Enc(MSK, m): *for $m \in \mathcal{M}$, output a ciphertext* CT$_m$.
- Dec(SK$_f$, CT$_m$): *output the function value $f(m)$.*

FE *is correct if for any* MSK $\leftarrow$ Setup(1^λ), SK$_f \leftarrow$ KeyGen(MSK,f), CT$_m \leftarrow$ Enc(MSK,m), *the probability of* Dec(SK$_f$, CT$_m$) $\neq f(m)$ *is negligible.*

Next, we define the (message-private) pIND-based security and function-private pIND-based security for private-key FE schemes.

Definition 4.2. *Given message space $\mathcal{M}$ and function space $\mathcal{F}$, a q-CT (or unbounded-CT), Q-key (or unbounded-key) adaptive (message-private) pIND-CPA-security game for a private-key FE scheme is defined as the following:*

- *Setup: The challenger runs* Setup(1^λ) *to get* MSK, *and randomly samples a bit $b \leftarrow \{0, 1\}$.*

– *Query Phase: The adversary can adaptively makes the following two types of queries:*
   • *Key Query: The adversary chooses a p.p.t. sampling algorithm F which output is in $\mathcal{F}$, and gives it to the challenger. The challenger samples $f \leftarrow F$, generates $sk_f = \mathsf{KeyGen}(\mathsf{MSK}, f)$ and returns f, sk_f to the adversary. This can be repeated adaptively for any polynomial times.*
   • *Ciphertext Query: The adversary chooses two p.p.t. sampling algorithms M_0, M_1 which outputs are in $\mathcal{M}$ and gives them to the challenger. The challenger randomly chooses $m \leftarrow M_b$, generates $ct_m \leftarrow \mathsf{Enc}(\mathsf{PK}, m)$ and returns ct_m to the adversary.*
   The number of key queries is bounded by Q or unbounded; the number of ciphertext queries is bounded by q or unbounded.
– *Output: The adversary outputs b', and the winning advantage for the adversary is defined by $Adv^{\mathsf{pIND}}(\mathcal{A}) = |\Pr(b' = b) - 1/2|$.*

Let q, Q be the number of ciphertext queries and key queries, we write the i-th key query and the chosen function by F^i, f^i, the j-th ciphertext query and the chosen message by M_0^j, M_1^j, m^j.

An adversary $\mathcal{A}$ is said to be admissible, if the two distributions $(F^i, F^i(M_0^1), ..., F^i(M_0^q))_{i \in [Q]}$ and $(F^i, F^i(M_1^1), ..., F^i(M_1^q))_{i \in [Q]}$ are strictly computationally indistinguishable. We say that skFE is a (message-private) pIND-secure private-key FE if for any p.p.t. admissible adversary $\mathcal{A}$, $\mathrm{Adv}^{\mathsf{pIND}}(\mathcal{A})$ is negligible.

Lemma 4.1. *For a (message-private) pIND adversary $\mathcal{A}$ for a secret key FE scheme, define the trace of $\mathcal{A}$ as:*

$$tr_{\mathcal{A}} = ((M_0^j, M_1^j)_{j \in [q]}, (F^i, f^i, f^i(m^1), ..., f^i(m^q))_{i \in [Q]}).$$

Then skFE is a (message-private) pIND-secure private-key FE, if and only if for every p.p.t. $\mathcal{A}$ such that $Adv^{\mathsf{pIND}}(\mathcal{A})$ is non-negligible, there exists a p.p.t. algorithm $\mathcal{T}$ which outputs the following distribution:

$$(aux, \bar{b}, (\bar{m}_j)_{j \in [q]}, \overline{tr} = ((\bar{M}_0^j, \bar{M}_1^j,)_{j \in [q]}, (\bar{F}^i; \bar{f}^i, \bar{f}^i(\bar{m}^1), ..., \bar{f}^i(\bar{m}^q))_{i \in [Q]})),$$

where $\bar{b} \leftarrow \{0, 1\}, \bar{m}^j \leftarrow \bar{M}_{\bar{b}}^j$ for $j \in [q]$, $\bar{f}^i \leftarrow \bar{F}^i$ for $i \in [Q]$, and a p.p.t. algorithm $\mathcal{B}$, which satisfies:

– *(1) For any p.p.t. algorithm $\mathcal{P}$, $\Pr(\mathcal{P}(tr_{\mathcal{A}}) = 1) - \Pr(\mathcal{S}(\overline{tr}) = 1)$ is negligible;*
– *(2) aux is independent with the following conditional distributions: $\bar{m}^j | \bar{M}_0^j, \bar{M}_1^j, j \in [q]$; $\bar{f}^i | \bar{F}^i, i \in [Q]$;*
– *(3) $\Pr(\mathcal{B}(aux, \overline{tr}) = \bar{b}) - 1/2$ is non-negligible.*

Proof. The proof is similar to Lemma 3.1 and we omit the details. □

Definition 4.3. *Given message space $\mathcal{M}$ and function space $\mathcal{F}$, a q-CT (or unbounded-CT), Q-key (or unbounded-key) adaptive function-private pIND-CPA-security game for a private-key FE scheme is defined as the following:*

- *Setup: The challenger runs* $\mathsf{Setup}(1^\lambda)$ *to get* MSK, *and randomly samples a bit* $b \leftarrow \{0, 1\}$.
- *Query Phase: The adversary can adaptively makes the following two types of queries:*
  - *Key Query: The adversary chooses two p.p.t. sampling algorithms* F_0, F_1 *which output is in* $\mathcal{F}$, *and gives it to the challenger. The challenger samples* $f \leftarrow F_b$, *generates* $sk_f = \mathsf{KeyGen}(\mathsf{MSK}, f)$ *and returns* sk_f *to the adversary. This can be repeated adaptively for any polynomial times.*
  - *Ciphertext Query: The adversary chooses two p.p.t. sampling algorithms* M_0, M_1 *which outputs are in* $\mathcal{M}$ *and gives them to the challenger. The challenger randomly chooses* $m \leftarrow M_b$, *generates* $ct_m \leftarrow \mathsf{Enc}(\mathsf{PK}, m)$ *and returns* ct_m *to the adversary.*

  The number of key queries is bounded by Q *or unbounded; the number of ciphertext queries is bounded by* q *or unbounded.*
- *Output: The adversary outputs* b', *and the winning advantage for the adversary is defined by* $Adv^{\mathsf{pIND}}(\mathcal{A}) = |\Pr(b' = b) - 1/2|$.

Let q, Q *be the number of ciphertext queries and key queries, we write the i-th key query and the chosen function by* F_0^i, F_1^i, f^i, *the j-th ciphertext query and the chosen message by* M_0^j, M_1^j, m^j.

An adversary $\mathcal{A}$ *is said to be admissible, if the two distributions* $(F_0^i(M_0^1), ..., F_0^i(M_0^q))_{i \in [Q]}$ *and* $(F_1^i(M_1^1), ..., F_1^i(M_1^q))_{i \in [Q]}$ *are strictly computationally indistinguishable. We say that* skFE *is a function-private pIND-secure private-key FE if for any p.p.t. admissible adversary* $\mathcal{A}$, $\mathrm{Adv}^{\mathsf{pIND}}(\mathcal{A})$ *is negligible.*

Lemma 4.2. *For a function-private pIND adversary* $\mathcal{A}$ *for a secret key FE scheme, define the trace of* $\mathcal{A}$ *as:*

$$tr_\mathcal{A} = ((M_0^j, M_1^j)_{j \in [q]}, (F_0^i, F_1^i, f^i(m^1), ..., f^i(m^q))_{i \in [Q]}).$$

Then skFE *is a function-private pIND-secure private-key FE, if and only if for every p.p.t.* $\mathcal{A}$ *such that* $Adv^{\mathsf{pIND}}(\mathcal{A})$ *is non-negligible, there exists a p.p.t. algorithm* $\mathcal{T}$ *which outputs the following distribution:*

$$(aux, \bar{b}, (\bar{m}^j)_{j \in [q]}, \overline{tr} = ((\bar{M}_0^j, \bar{M}_1^j)_{j \in [q]}, (\bar{F}_0^i, \bar{F}_1^i, \bar{f}^i(\bar{m}^1), ..., \bar{f}^i(\bar{m}^q))_{i \in [Q]})),$$

where $\bar{b} \leftarrow \{0, 1\}, \bar{m}^j \leftarrow \bar{M}_{\bar{b}}^j$ *for* $j \in [q]$, $\bar{f}^i \leftarrow \bar{F}_{\bar{b}}^i$ *for* $i \in [Q]$, *and a p.p.t. algorithm* $\mathcal{B}$, *which satisfies:*

- *(1) For any p.p.t. algorithm* $\mathcal{S}$, $\Pr(\mathcal{S}(tr_\mathcal{A}) = 1) - \Pr(\mathcal{S}(\overline{tr}) = 1)$ *is negligible;*
- *(2)* aux *is independent with the following conditional distributions:* $\bar{m}^j | \bar{M}_0^j, \bar{M}_1^j, j \in [q]$; $\bar{f}^i | \bar{F}_0^i, \bar{F}_1^i, i \in [Q]$;
- *(3)* $\Pr(\mathcal{B}(aux, \overline{tr}) = \bar{b}) - 1/2$ *is non-negligible.*

Proof. The proof is similar to Lemma 3.1 and we omit the details. $\square$

We give a lemma on the existence of private-key pIND-secure FE.

Lemma 4.3. *There exists a private-key pIND-secure FE with 1-CT and unbounded key for P/poly, assuming the existence of one-way functions.*

Proof. By Theorem 3.1 (which can also be applied to private-key FE schemes), we can show that the SIM-secure private-key FE scheme for P/poly with 1-key and unbounded-CT queries in [GVW12] is also pIND-secure. If we can lift this scheme into a function-private pIND-secure private-key FE scheme, we can simply swap the KeyGen and Enc algorithms to obtain a private-key pIND-secure FE with unbounded-key and 1-CT for P/poly.

The lifting is similar to the one in [BS15]. Let skFE be the pIND-secure message-private private-key FE scheme, Sym be a symmetric encryption scheme, PRF be a pseudo-random function family. We construct the pIND-secure function-private private-key FE as follows:

- Setup(1^λ): Generate three symmetric encryption keys $k, k', k'' \leftarrow$ Sym.KeyGen(1^λ), let skFE.MSK $\leftarrow$ skFE.Setup(1^λ). Return MSK $= (k, k', k'', \text{skFE.MSK})$.
- KeyGen(MSK, f): Let $\tilde{f}$ be defined as: $\tilde{f}(m, r) = f(m)$. Let $c = $ Sym.Enc($k, \tilde{f}$), $c' = $ Sym.Enc($k', \tilde{f}$), $c'' = $ Sym.Enc($k'', \tilde{f}$). Return skFE.KeyGen (skFE.MSK, $g_{c,c',c''}$, where for any c_1, c_2, c_3, $g_{c_1,c_2,c_3}(m, k_1, k_2, k_3, r)$ is defined as follows:
  - If $k_1 \neq \perp$, let $f \leftarrow$ Sym.Dec(k_1, c_1), return $f(m; r)$.
  - Else if $k_2 \neq \perp$, let $f \leftarrow$ Sym.Dec(k_2, c_2), return $f(m; r)$.
  - Else if $k_3 \neq \perp$, let $f \leftarrow$ Sym.Dec(k_3, c_3), return $f(m; r)$.
  - Else return $\perp$.
- Enc(MSK, m): Sample a random seed r and return $ct \leftarrow$ skFE.Enc(skFE.MSK, $(m, k, \perp, \perp, r)$).
- Dec(sk, ct): return skFE.Dec(sk, ct).

Now we prove the security of the construction above through a hybrid of games.

Game 0 is the original game.

In Game 1, the challenger first samples a uniform random seed r^*, and for each ciphertext query, returns skFE.Enc(MSK, $(m, k, \perp, \perp, r^*)$) instead of skFE.Enc(MSK, $(m, k, \perp, \perp, r)$) for a freshly sampled r. Game 0 and Game 1 are indistinguishable from the pIND-security of skFE. (Note that the distribution of messages in different ciphertext queries share the same r^*.)

In Game 2, when the adversary makes a key query, instead of sampling $f \leftarrow F_b$ using a random seed, the challenger samples two seeds s_0, s_1, and uses PRF(r^*, s_b) as the seed to sample $f \leftarrow F_b$. Game 1 and Game 2 are indistinguishable from the pseudorandomness of PRF.

In Game 3, for each key query, let $\tilde{c}' = $ Sym.Enc(k', G_{F_0,s_0}), $\tilde{c}'' = $ Sym.Enc(k'', G_{F_1,s_1}), returns skFE.KeyGen(MSK, $g_{c,\tilde{c}',\tilde{c}''}$) instead of skFE.KeyGen(MSK, $g_{c,c',c''}$), where $G_{F_b,s_b}(m, r)$ is defined as:

- Sample $f \leftarrow F_b$ using the seed PRF(r, s_b);
- Return $f(m)$.

Game 2 and Game 3 are indistinguishable from the security of Sym.

In Game 4, we change the ciphertext into $\mathsf{skFE.Enc}(\mathsf{MSK}, m, \bot, k', \bot, r^*)$ for $b = 0$ and $\mathsf{skFE.Enc}(\mathsf{MSK}, m, \bot, \bot, k'', r^*)$ for $b = 1$. Since $f_b(m) = G_{F_b}(m, r^*)$, we can see that the trace for skFE is the same in Game 3 and Game 4, so Game 3 and Game 4 are indistinguishable from the security of skFE.

In Game 5, for each key query, let $\tilde{c} = \mathsf{Sym.Enc}(k, \bot)$, returns $\mathsf{skFE.KeyGen}(\mathsf{MSK}, g_{\tilde{c},\tilde{c}',\tilde{c}''})$ instead of $\mathsf{skFE.KeyGen}(\mathsf{MSK}, g_{c,\tilde{c}',\tilde{c}''})$. Game 4 and Game 5 are indistinguishable from the security of Sym. Note that the function $g_{\tilde{c},\tilde{c}',\tilde{c}''}$ is the same for $b = 0$ and $b = 1$ in Game 5.

Now in Game 5, if $\mathcal{A}$ is an adversary for the function-private scheme with non-negligible advantage, there is an adversary $\mathcal{A}'$ which is an adversary for skFE with non-negligible advantage. By the pIND-based security of skFE, there exist a sampling algorithm $\mathcal{T}'$ and an algorithm $\mathcal{B}'$ with non-negligible advantage which satisfy Lemma 4.1. We write the output of $\mathcal{T}'$ as:

$$(aux, \bar{b}', (\bar{m}'^j)_{j\in[q]}, \overline{tr}' = ((\bar{M}'^j_0, \bar{M}'^j_1)_{j\in[q]}, (\bar{F}'^i, \bar{f}'^i, \bar{f}'^i(\bar{m}'^1), ..., \bar{f}'^i(\bar{m}'^q))_{i\in[Q]})).$$

Since $\overline{tr}'$ is indistinguishable with $tr_{\mathcal{A}'}$, so elements in both $\overline{tr}'$ and $tr_{\mathcal{A}'}$ has the same structure, so we can write $\bar{m}'^j = (\bar{m}^j, \bot, \bar{k}', \bot, \bar{r}^*)$ for $\bar{b}' = 0$ and $\bar{m}'^j = (\bar{m}^j, \bot, \bot, \bar{k}'', \bar{r}^*)$ for $\bar{b}' = 1$, $\bar{f}'^i = g_{\tilde{c},\tilde{c}',\tilde{c}''}$ where $\bar{c}, \bar{c}', \bar{c}''$ are Sym ciphertexts of $\bot, G_{\bar{F}_0, \bar{s}_0}, G_{\bar{F}_1, \bar{s}_1}$ defined as above.

Without loss of generalization, we suppose that $\bar{k}', \bar{k}''$ are contained in aux, since $\bar{k}', \bar{k}''$ are predetermined and independent with the choice of either queried message or function.

Now we construct $\mathcal{T}$ and $\mathcal{B}$ from $\mathcal{T}'$ and $\mathcal{B}'$.

$\mathcal{T}$ does the following:

- Call $\mathcal{T}'$ to get $\bar{h}', aux, \bar{b}', (\bar{m}'^j)_{j\in[q]}, \overline{tr}'$;
- Extract $\bar{M}^j_0, \bar{M}^j_1, \bar{m}^j$ from $\bar{M}'^j_0, \bar{M}'^j_1, \bar{m}'^j$, $\bar{F}^i_0, \bar{F}^i_1$ from $\bar{f}'^i$;
- Sample $\bar{f}^i \leftarrow \bar{F}^i_{\bar{b}'}$;
- Return
  $aux, \bar{b}', (\bar{m}^j)_{j\in[q]}, \overline{tr} = ((\bar{M}^j_0, \bar{M}^j_1)_{j\in[q]}, (\bar{F}^i_0, \bar{F}^i_1, \bar{f}^i(\bar{m}^1), ..., \bar{f}^i(\bar{m}^q))_{i\in[Q]})).$

$\mathcal{B}(aux, \overline{tr})$ does the following:

- For each $\bar{M}^j_b$, $j \in [q]$, $b \in \{0,1\}$, sampling from $\bar{M}'^j_b$ does the following:
  - Sample $\bar{m} \leftarrow \bar{M}^j_b$;
  - If $j = 1$, sample a random seed $\bar{r}^*$, otherwise use the same $\bar{r}^*$ as in $j' < j$[2];
  - If $b = 0$, return $\bar{m}'^j = (\bar{m}, \bot, \bar{k}', \bot, \bar{r}^*)$, otherwise return $\bar{m}'^j = (\bar{m}, \bot, \bot, \bar{k}'', \bar{r}^*)$.
- For each $\bar{F}^i_0$ and $\bar{F}^i_1$, sampling from $\bar{F}'^i$ does the following:

---

[2] Here we allows different distributions $\bar{M}'^j_b$ to include the same randomness $\bar{r}^*$, which means that there is a shared inner state between these sampling algorithms. We note that SIM-secure FE implies pIND-secure FE even considering stateful ciphertext queries like this, so it will not affect the validity of the proof.

- Sample two random seeds $\bar{s}_0, \bar{s}_1$;
- Let $G_{\bar{F}_0, \bar{s}_0}$ and $G_{\bar{F}_1, \bar{s}_1}$ be defined as above, and $\bar{c}' = \mathsf{Sym.Enc}(\bar{k}', G_{\bar{F}_0, \bar{s}_0})$, $\bar{c}'' = \mathsf{Sym.Enc}(\bar{k}'', G_{\bar{F}_1, \bar{s}_1})$;
- Return $\bar{f}'^{\,i} = g_{\bar{c}, \bar{c}', \bar{c}''}$.
- Call $\mathcal{B}'(aux, ((\bar{M}'^j_0, \bar{M}'^j_1)_{j \in [q]}, (\bar{F}'^i; \bar{f}'^i, \bar{f}'^i(\bar{m}'^1), ..., \bar{f}'^i(\bar{m}'^q))_{i \in [Q]}))$ to get the output.

It is not hard to see that $\mathcal{B}$ calls $\mathcal{B}'$ exactly with $(aux, \overline{tr}')$, where $\overline{tr}'$ is defined as above, and we already know that $\Pr(\mathcal{B}'(aux, \overline{tr}') = \bar{b}) - 1/2$ is non-negligible. So we successfully construct $\mathcal{T}$ and $\mathcal{B}$ satisfies Lemma 4.2. Thus the new scheme is a function-private pIND-secure private-key FE scheme. □

Theorem 4.1. *There exists a construction for* ad-pIND-*secure FE for* P/poly *from* sel-IND-*secure FE for* P/poly *assuming the existence of one-way functions.*

Proof. We simply write down the [ABSV15] construction here, and give a high level proof. The details are similar to the ad-IND-security proof in [ABSV15]. Given the following primitives:

- A sel-IND secure public-key FE scheme for P/poly Sel;
- An ad-pIND secure 1-CT private-key FE scheme for P/poly OneCT;
- A symmetric encryption scheme with pseudorandom ciphertexts Sym;
- A pseudorandom function family PRF.

The adaptive scheme Ad is constructed as follows:

- Setup(1^λ): Sample (Sel.PK, Sel.MSK) ← Sel.Setup(1^λ), and return PK = Sel.PK, MSK = Sel.MSK.
- KeyGen(MSK, f): Sample $C_E \leftarrow \{0,1\}^{l_1(\lambda)}$, $\tau \leftarrow \{0,1\}^{l_2(\lambda)}$, return $sk_f \leftarrow$ Sel.KeyGen(Sel.MSK, $G_{f, C_E, r}$), $G_{f, C_E, r}$(OneCT.MSK, K, Sym.K, β) defined as follows:
  - If $\beta = 1$, output Sym.Dec(Sym.K, C_E);
  - Otherwise, output OneCT.KeyGen(OneCT.MSK, f; $\mathsf{PRF}_K(\tau)$).
- Enc(PK, m): Output CT = (CT$_0$ ← OneCT.Enc(OneCT.MSK, m), CT$_1$ ← Sel.Enc(Sel.MPK, (OneCT.MSK, K, 0^λ, 0))).
- Dec(sk_f, CT): Output OneCT.Dec(Sel.Dec(sk_f, CT$_1$), CT$_0$).

The ad-pIND-security of this construction can be proved by a hybrid of games. Let Game 0 be the original pIND-CPA game.

In Game 1, C_E is replaced by Sym.Enc(Sym.K*, sk_f ← OneCT.KeyGen(OneCT.MSK, f; $\mathsf{PRF}_K(\tau)$)) for random Sym.K*. Game 0 and Game 1 are indistinguishable from the security of Sym.

In Game 2, CT_1 is replaced by Sel.Enc(Sel.MPK, (0^λ, 0^λ, Sym.K*, 1)). Since any adversary $\mathcal{A}$ distinguishing Game 1 and Game 2 makes only deterministic ciphertext queries to Sel, we can see that Game 1 and Game 2 are indistinguishable from the IND-security of Sel.

In Game 3, $\mathsf{PRF}_\mathsf{K}(\tau)$ is replaced by a truly random R. Game 2 and Game 3 are indistinguishable by the pseudorandomness of PRF.

We see that any adversary $\mathcal{A}$ which has non-negligible advantage in Game 3 has also a non-negligible advantage in the ad-pIND-CPA game of OneCT. Then if OneCT is ad-pIND-secure, we can construct $\mathcal{B}$ and the input distribution $(h', aux, tr_\mathcal{B})$ for $\mathcal{A}$ which satisfies Lemma 3.1, hence Ad is ad-pIND-secure. $\quad\square$

5   Application of pIND-secure FE: Hashing a Secret Value

Next, we introduce a specific application scenario, which can be constructed from pIND-secure FE. This application is inspired by Example 1.1, the counter-example for IND-based security. We show that how we can use pIND-secure FE to output the hash of a secret value. Like blind signature [Cha82], we name this new primitive "blind hash". We first give its syntax, which is similar to the syntax of functional encryption.

Definition 5.1. *A* blind hash system *consists of the following algorithms:*

- Setup($1^\lambda, 1^n, 1^k$): *output the public key pk and the main secret key msk. We require that $n \geq k$.*
- HashGen(msk, h): *for a hash function $h : \{0,1\}^n \to \{0,1\}^k$, output its blinded version H.*
- Enc(pk, m): *output the encrypted message c.*

The blind hash system is called correct, if for $(pk, msk) \leftarrow$ Setup(λ), $H \leftarrow$ HashGen(msk, h), $c \leftarrow$ Enc(pk, m), the probability of $H(c) \neq h(m)$ is negligible.

In this definition, we restrict the input length of the hash function to be n instead of arbitrary length, in order for Enc to be well-defined. We can choose large enough n, and pad any string with length $n' < n$ into a string of length n.

We require the one-wayness of a blind hash system.

Definition 5.2. *A* blind hash system (Setup, HashGen, Enc) *is called* one-way, *if for any p.p.t. adversary $\mathcal{A}$ and a set $\mathcal{S}$ of (polynomial number of) universal one-way hash families, the winning advantage of the following game is negligible:*

- *Setup: The challenger runs* Setup(1^λ) *and returns pk to the adversary.*
- *Phase 1: Each time the adversary submits a universal one-way hash family $\mathcal{H} \in \mathcal{S}$, the challenger samples $h \leftarrow \mathcal{H}$, and returns $(h, H \leftarrow$ HashGen(msk, h)) to the adversary. This can be repeated for any polynomial numbers of times.*
- *Challenge: The challenger chooses $m \leftarrow \mathcal{M}$, and returns* Enc(pk, m) *to the adversary.*
- *Phase 2: Same as Phase 1.*
- *Guess: The adversary outputs m'. The winning advantage of $\mathcal{A}$ is defined by $\Pr(m' = m)$.*

In this definition, we give a set of universal one-way hash families outside the game instead of letting them to be chosen by the adversary, since both the adversary and the challenger are p.p.t., hence cannot have the ability to determine whether a hash family is universal one-way.

Before we give our construction for the blind hash system, we first introduce the Goldreich-Levin hardcore predicate for one-way functions.

Definition 5.3. *A polynomial time computable predicate b is a hardcore predicate of a function $f : \{0,1\}^n \to \{0,1\}^k$, if for any p.p.t. algorithm $\mathcal{P}$, $|\Pr_{m \leftarrow \{0,1\}^n}(\mathcal{P}(f(m)) = b(m)) - 1/2|$ is negligible.*

Lemma 5.1 (Goldreich-Levin Theorem). *If $f : \{0,1\}^n \to \{0,1\}^n$ is a one-way function, then $b(m,r) = \langle m, r \rangle$ is a predicate of the function $g : \{0,1\}^{2n} \to \{0,1\}^{2n}$, $g(m\|r) = f(m)\|r$.*

Now we are ready to construct our blind hash system. Given a functional encryption scheme FE, the blind hash system is constructed as follows:

- Setup(1^λ): Run FE.Setup(1^λ) and output the public key pk and the main secret key msk.
- HashGen(msk, h): Let $\bar{h}$ be the function which pads the output of h from k bits into n bits (by filling 0s). Let function g_h be defined as: $g_h(m\|r) = \bar{h}(m)\|r$. Calculate $sk_{g_h} \leftarrow$ FE.KeyGen(msk, g_h). Let the blinded hash $H(c)$ be defined as:
  - Let $t \leftarrow$ FE.Dec(sk_{g_h}, c);
  - Output the first k bits of t.
- Enc(pk, m): Let $r \leftarrow \{0,1\}^n$, output FE.Enc($pk, m\|r$).

Theorem 5.1. *Let FE be pIND-based secure, then the construction above is a one-way blind hash system.*

Proof. Let $\mathcal{G}_\mathcal{H}$ be the p.p.t. algorithm that first samples $h \leftarrow \mathcal{H}$ and then outputs g_h (as define above), and M_0 (resp. M_1) be a p.p.t. algorithm that outputs a random string $m\|r \in \{0,1\}^{2n}$ where $\langle m, r \rangle = 0$ (resp. $\langle m, r \rangle = 1$). For each adversary $\mathcal{A}'$ attacks the one-wayness of the blind hash system, we consider any pIND adversary $\mathcal{A}$ for FE which makes specific queries as follows:

- When $\mathcal{A}'$ submits a query $\mathcal{H}_j$ in Phase 1 or Phase 2, $\mathcal{A}$ submits $\mathcal{G}_{\mathcal{H}_j}$, and gets sk_{g_h} from inside the blinded hash function H.
- At the challenge phase, $\mathcal{A}$ submits (M_0, M_1) to the challenger, and gets the challenge ciphertext of $\mathcal{A}'$.

We do not restrict the way that $\mathcal{A}$ gives its outputs b'.

By the definition of pIND-based security, if $Adv(\mathcal{A})$ is non-negligible, there exists a sampling algorithm $\mathcal{T}$ and an algorithm $\mathcal{B}$, where $(aux, \bar{b}, \bar{m}, \overline{tr}) \leftarrow \mathcal{T}$, $\overline{tr}$ is computationally indistinguishable from $tr_\mathcal{A}$, and $\Pr(\mathcal{B}(aux, \overline{tr}) = \bar{b}) - 1/2$ is non-negligible, where $\overline{tr}$ takes the form as:

$$\overline{tr} = (\bar{M}_0, \bar{M}_1, (\bar{F}_i, \bar{f}_i, \bar{f}_i(\bar{m}))_{i \in [Q]}).$$

Since M_0, M_1 are fixed and each F_i in tr_A is chosen only from a pre-determined polynomial size set $\{\mathcal{G}_\mathcal{H}\}_{\mathcal{H} \in \mathcal{S}}$, we can see that the computational indistinguishability between tr_A and $\overline{tr}$ implies that $\bar{M}_0 = M_0$, $\bar{M}_1 = M_1$, and $\bar{F}_i = \mathcal{G}_\mathcal{H}$ for some $\mathcal{H} \in \mathcal{S}$. We also write $\bar{f}_i$ as $g_{\bar{h}_i}$ where $\bar{h}_i \in \mathcal{H}$, thus $\bar{f}_i(\bar{m}) = g_{\bar{h}_i}(m\|r)$ for some m, r, and $\bar{b} = \langle m, r \rangle$.

Since aux is independent with the choice of $\bar{f}_i$ and $\bar{m}$, we define $\mathcal{B}_i(g_{\bar{h}_i}(m\|r)) := \mathcal{B}_i(aux, \overline{tr})$, so by a standard hybrid argument, $\Pr(\mathcal{B}(aux, \overline{tr}) = \bar{b}) - 1/2$ is non-negligible, only if there exists $\mathcal{B}_i$, such that $\Pr(\mathcal{B}_i(\{g_{\bar{h}_i}(m\|r)\}_{i \in [q]}) = \langle m, r \rangle) - 1/2$ is non-negligible. However, from Goldreich-Levin Theorem, $\langle m, r \rangle$ is a hardcore predicate for $g_{\bar{h}_i}(m\|r)$, and since each $\bar{h}_i$ is independently chosen from universal hash families, we have that $\{g_{\bar{h}_i}(m\|r)\}_{i \in [q]}$ are independent, so $\langle m, r \rangle$ is also a hardcore predicate for $g(m\|r) := g_{\bar{h}_1}(m\|r)\|...\|g_{\bar{h}_q}(m\|r)$, which means that $\Pr(\mathcal{B}'(\{g_{\bar{h}_i}(m\|r)\}_{i \in [q]}) = \langle m, r \rangle) - 1/2$ must be negligible. So we have that $\Pr(\mathcal{B}(aux, \overline{tr}) = \bar{b}) - 1/2$ is also negligible, hence $Adv(\mathcal{A})$ is negligible.

We know that if a function is one-one, then having a hardcore predicate implies one-wayness. Since the advantage of $\mathcal{A}$ is negligible, if we consider the function $f(m\|r) = sk_{h_1}\|...\|sk_{h_q}\|ct$, $ct \leftarrow \mathsf{FE.Enc}(pk, m\|r)$, which is a one-one function, we see that $\langle m, r \rangle$ is also its hardcore predicate, so $f(m\|r)$ is one-way. Since r can be directly generated from $\mathsf{FE.Dec}(sk_i, ct)$ given any sk_i, we can see that $f(m\|r)$ is one-way according to the input m, hence the advantage for $\mathcal{A}'$ is also negligible. Thus we finish the proof.   □

The construction from pIND-secure FE to blind hash systems are quite straightforward. Since pIND-secure FE can be constructed from IND-secure FE schemes, blind hash systems can be constructed from IND-secure FE schemes.

However, we show that the same method in this section cannot be used to directly construct blind hash systems from IND-secure FE: let h be a collision-resistant hash function, and construct the hash family $\mathcal{H}$ be: $\{h_k : h_k(m) := h(k\|m)\}$. So if $\mathcal{A}$ make an admissible query, which means that $h_{k_1}(m) = h_{k_2}(m)$, it finds a collision for h, which contradicts the security of h, so $\mathcal{A}$ cannot make any queries. So if the construction above uses an IND-based FE scheme, the one-way property cannot be satisfied, like what we showed in Example 1.1.

Also, For SIM-based secure FE schemes, as it was proven in [AGVW13], there is no unbound-key SIM-based secure FE schemes supporting one-way functions, so SIM-based FE schemes for $\mathcal{H}$ cannot be constructed, hence it is impossible to directly construct blind hash systems from SIM-based FE schemes.

6   Application of pIND-secure FE: Semi-universal Proxy Re-encryption

Now we give another application scenario which can be constructed from pIND-secure FE but not other security definitions. We consider proxy re-encryption (PRE) schemes [BBS98], which can be used to transform a ciphertext encrypted under a delegator key into one encrypted under a delegatee key, without leaking the plaintext. However, in most existing PRE constructions, the delegator encryption scheme and the delegatee encryption scheme must be the same:

they cannot re-encrypt a given ciphertext into another ciphertext under another public-key encryption scheme.

In [DN21], the authors introduced universal proxy re-encryption, and gave their construction from probabilistic $i\mathcal{O}$, where both the delegator and the delegatee can be arbitrary PKE schemes. Here, we discuss a weaker version of universal PRE, where only the delegatee ciphertext can be encrypted by arbitrary PKE schemes, and we call it semi-universal PRE. We now show that semi-universal PRE can be constructed by pIND-secure FE for P/poly. We note that pIND-secure FE for P/poly can be constructed from IND-secure FE for P/poly as we proved in Sect. 4, thus our construction of semi-universal PRE also has a weaker requirement than the existence of $pi\mathcal{O}$ in the construction of universal PRE [DN21] (we note that even constructing $i\mathcal{O}$ requires sub-exponential hardness IND-secure FE for P/poly).

We first give the syntax definition of semi-universal PRE.

Definition 6.1. *A semi-universal PRE consists of the following algorithms:*

- KeyGen(1^λ): *Output a public-key/secret-key pair* (pk, sk).
- Enc(pk, m): *For a public key generated from* KeyGen(1^λ), *output a ciphertext* ct *for* m.
- ReKeyGen(sk_f, PKE, pk_t): *Let* sk_f *be generated from* KeyGen(1^λ) *and* pk_t *be a public key of the PKE scheme PKE. This algorithm outputs a re-encryption key* $rk_{f \to t}$.
- ReEnc($rk_{f \to t}, ct$): *Let* ct *be a ciphertext encrypted by* pk_f, *output a new ciphertext encrypted by* pk_t.
- Dec(sk_f, ct): *For a ciphertext* $ct \leftarrow$ Enc(pk_f, m), *output the corresponding message* m.

Let PKE = PKE.KeyGen, PKE.Enc, PKE.Dec *be any public key encryption scheme. A semi-universal PRE scheme is correct, if for* $(pk_f, sk_f) \leftarrow$ KeyGen(1^λ), $ct_f \leftarrow$ Enc(pk_f, m), *both: (1)* Dec(sk_f, ct_f) = m *except for a negligible probability; (2)* $(pk_t, sk, t) \leftarrow$ PKE.KeyGen(1^λ), $rk_{f \to t} \leftarrow$ ReKeyGen(sk_f, PKE, pk_t), *the ciphertext* $ct_t \leftarrow$ ReEnc($rk_{f \to t}, ct_f$) *satisfies:* PKE.Dec(sk_t, ct_t) = m *except for a negligible probability.*

We only define a weaker version of the single-hop security of PRE, where each delegator key must be generated at the setup phase, and allows only static corruption. For simplicity reason, we assume that the delegatee PKE scheme is always different from the delegator PKE scheme (which is a pIND-secure FE scheme as in our construction).

Definition 6.2. *For a semi-universal PRE* (Setup, Enc, ReKeyGen, ReEnc), *let* $\mathcal{P}$ *be a set of semantic secure PKE scheme, and for any* PKE $\in \mathcal{P}$, Enc $\neq$ PKE.Enc. *The weak-CRA security of the semi-functional PRE is satisfied if for every adversary* $\mathcal{A}$, *the winning advantage of the following game is negligible:*

- *Setup: The adversary asks the challenger to run* $\mathsf{Setup}(1^\lambda)$ *for any polynomial numbers of times to get* $(\widehat{pk_i}, \widehat{sk_i})_{i \in [q]}$. *The challenger returns* $(\widehat{pk_i})_{i \in [q]}$ *to the adversary. Let L be an empty list.*
- *Phase 1: The adversary can make one of the following types of queries in arbitrary sequence:*
    - *Type 1: The adversary submits* $\mathsf{PKE} \in \mathcal{P}$. *The challenger generates* $(pk_{|L|+1}, sk_{|L|+1}) \leftarrow \mathsf{PKE.KeyGen}(1^\lambda)$, *adds the pair* $(\mathsf{PKE}; pk_{|L|+1})$ *into L, and returns* $pk_{|L|+1}$ *to the adversary.*
    - *Type 2: The adversary submits* $\mathsf{PKE} \in \mathcal{P}$. *The challenger generates* $(pk_{|L|+1}, sk_{|L|+1}) \leftarrow \mathsf{PKE.KeyGen}(1^\lambda)$, *adds the pair* $(\mathsf{PKE}; pk_{|L|+1})$ *into L, and returns* $(pk_{|L|+1}, sk_{|L|+1})$ *to the adversary.*
    - *Type 3: The adversary submits* $\widehat{pk_i}, i \in [q]$, *and* $(\mathsf{PKE}, pk_j) \in L$. *The challenger runs* $\mathsf{ReKeyGen}(\widehat{sk_i}, \mathsf{PKE}, pk_j)$ *and returns* $rk_{i \to j}$ *to the adversary if* $rk_{i \to j}$ *has not been generated before.*

    These queries can be repeated adaptively.
- *Challenge: The adversary submits* $\widehat{pk_{i^*}}, i^* \in [q]$ *and a pair of messages* (m_0, m_1), *providing that for each Type 3 query which returns* $rk_{i^* \to j}$ *for some j,* pk_j *is generated from a Type 1 query. The challenger chooses* $b \leftarrow \{0, 1\}$, *and returns* $\mathsf{Enc}(\widehat{pk_{i^*}}, m_b)$ *to the adversary.*
- *Phase 2: Same as Phase 1, under the restriction that for all Type 3 queries* $(\widehat{pk_{i^*}}, \mathsf{PKE}, pk_j)$, pk_j *is generated from a Type 1 query.*
- *Guess: The adversary outputs* b'. *The winning advantage of* $\mathcal{A}$ *is defined by* $|Pr(b' = b) - 1/2|$.

Now we construct a weak-CRA secure semi-universal PRE from a pIND-secure functional encryption scheme FE. Let PRF be a pseudorandom function.

- $\mathsf{KeyGen}(1^\lambda)$: Output $(pk, sk) \leftarrow \mathsf{FE.Setup}(1^\lambda)$.
- $\mathsf{Enc}(pk, m)$: Sample a random seed r, and output $ct \leftarrow \mathsf{FE.Enc}(pk, m\|r)$.
- $\mathsf{ReKeyGen}(sk_f, \mathsf{PKE}, pk_t)$: Sample a random key K, and let $F(m\|r) := \mathsf{PKE.Enc}(pk_t, m; PRF(K, r))$. Return $\mathsf{FE.KeyGen}(sk_f, F)$.
- $\mathsf{ReEnc}(rk_{f \to t}, ct)$: Output $\mathsf{FE.Dec}(rk_{f \to t}, ct)$.
- $\mathsf{Dec}(sk, ct)$: Let $sk_{ID} \leftarrow \mathsf{FE.KeyGen}(sk, ID)$ where $ID(m) = m$, then output $\mathsf{FE.Dec}(sk_{ID}, ct)$.

Before we prove the security of the PRE scheme, we first give a lemma to show that the auxiliary string has no effect in distinguishing a PKE ciphertext with random key.

Lemma 6.1. *Let* PKE *be a public key encryption scheme with semantic security. For a pair of messages* m_0, m_1, *any p.p.t. algorithm* $\mathcal{B}$ *and auxiliary string* aux, *let* $(pk, sk) \leftarrow \mathsf{PKE.KeyGen}(1^\lambda)$, $c_0 \leftarrow \mathsf{PKE.Enc}(pk, m_0)$, $c_1 \leftarrow \mathsf{PKE.Enc}(pk, m_1)$. *Then* $\Pr(\mathcal{B}(aux, pk, c_0) = 1) - \Pr(\mathcal{B}(aux, pk, c_1) = 1)$ *is negligible.*

Proof. Let $\mathcal{B}_{aux}(.,.)$ be the algorithm $\mathcal{B}(aux, ., .)$. We construct a IND-CPA adversary $\mathcal{A}$ for PKE, which submits m_0, m_1 as the challenge messages, and runs

$\mathcal{B}_{aux}(pk, c)$ to get the output, then by the semantic security of PKE, the advantage of $\mathcal{A}$ is negligible, hence $\Pr(\mathcal{B}(aux, pk, c_0) = 1) - \Pr(\mathcal{B}(aux, pk, c_1) = 1)$ is negligible.   □

We note that the adversary $\mathcal{A}$ in the proof above is non-uniform, so the scheme PKE must be secure against non-uniform adversaries, which is a rather standard assumption.

Theorem 6.1. *Let* FE *be pIND-based secure, then the construction above satisfies weak-CRA security.*

Proof. Given an adversary $\mathcal{A}'$ for the semi-universal PRE game. We construct a pIND adversary $\mathcal{A}$ for FE as follows:

In the setup phase, suppose that the adversary asks the challenger to run Setup(1^λ) for q times. $\mathcal{A}$ randomly choose $i' \leftarrow [q]$, and asks for the FE public key pk. Let $\widehat{pk_{i'}} := pk$. For $i \neq i'$, the challenger runs FE.Setup(1^λ) to get $(\widehat{pk_i}, \widehat{sk_i})$. $\mathcal{A}$ returns $(\widehat{pk_i})_{i \in [q]}$.

When $\mathcal{A}'$ generates a Type 1 query PKE, let F_{PKE} be the following algorithm:

- Run (PKE.pk, PKE.sk) $\leftarrow$ PKE.KeyGen(1^λ);
- Sample a random key K and return the function f where $f(m\|r) :=$ PKE.Enc(PKE.pk, m; PRF(K, r)).

$\mathcal{A}$ submits a KeyGen query F_{PKE}, and gets (f, sk_f), where f contains PKE.pk. Let $pk_{|L|+1} = $ PKE.pk, store $sk_{f_{|L|+1}} := sk_f$. Return $pk_{|L|+1}$ and add (PKE, $pk_{|L|+1}$) into L.

For a Type 2 query PKE, return $(pk_{|L|+1}, sk_{|L|+1}) \leftarrow$ PKE.KeyGen(1^λ) directly while adding (PKE, $pk_{|L|+1}$) into L.

For a Type 3 query $(\widehat{pk_i}, \mathsf{PKE}, pk_j)$, if $i = i'$ and pk_j is generated from Type 2 queries, then return a random guess $b' \leftarrow \{0, 1\}$ and abort. If $i = i'$ and pk_j is generated from Type 1 queries, return $rk_{i \to j} := sk_{f_j}$ (generated in Type 1 queries). If $i \neq i'$, return $rk_{i \to j} \leftarrow$ FE.KeyGen($\widehat{sk_i}, f_j$).

In the challenge phase, if $\mathcal{A}'$ queries for $i^* \neq i'$, then return a random guess $b' \leftarrow \{0, 1\}$ and abort. Otherwise, let $M_b, b \in \{0, 1\}$ be the algorithm that first randomly samples r and returns $m_b\|r$. Submit (M_0, M_1) and get the ciphertext ct, return ct to $\mathcal{A}'$.

Finally, return the guess b' from $\mathcal{A}'$.

We can see that $\mathcal{A}$ does not abort if and only if $i^* = i'$. Since q is polynomial, the non-aborting probability $1/q$ is non-negligible, so if the advantage of $\mathcal{A}'$ is non-negligible, the advantage of $\mathcal{A}$ is also non-negligible. By the definition of pIND-based security, there exists a sampling algorithm $\mathcal{T}$ and an algorithm $\mathcal{B}$ satisfies the definition. We write the output of $\mathcal{T}$ as $aux, \bar{b}, \bar{m}, \overline{tr} = (\bar{M}_0, \bar{M}_1, (\bar{F}_i, \bar{f}_i, \bar{f}_i(\bar{m}))_{i \in [Q]})$.

Since each key query of $\mathcal{A}$ is from a polynomial size set $\{F_{\mathsf{PKE}} : \mathsf{PKE} \in \mathcal{S}\}$ and a ciphertext query M_b samples $m_b\|r$, $b \leftarrow \{0, 1\}$, we can see that as long as $\overline{tr}$ is computationally indistinguishable from $tr_{\mathcal{A}}$, $\bar{F}_i \in \{F_{\mathsf{PKE}} : \mathsf{PKE} \in \mathcal{S}\}$

and $\bar{M}_0, \bar{M}_1$ samples $\bar{m}_0 \| r, \bar{m}_1 \| r$ for fixed $\bar{m}_0, \bar{m}_1$ and random r. So we rewrite $\bar{f}_i(\bar{m})$ as $\bar{f}_i(\bar{m}_{\bar{b}} \| r) = \mathsf{PKE.Enc}(pk, \bar{m}_{\bar{b}}; \mathsf{PRF}(K, r))$, which is indistinguishable from $\mathsf{PKE.Enc}(pk, \bar{m}_{\bar{b}})$ by the pseudorandomness of PRF.

Since aux is independent from the choice of $\bar{f}_i$, it is also independent from the choice of pk, by Lemma 6.1, we have that $\Pr(\mathcal{B}(aux, (..., \bar{F}_i, \bar{f}_i, \bar{f}_i(\bar{m}_0 \| r), ...)) = 1) - \Pr(\mathcal{B}(aux, (..., \bar{F}_i, \bar{f}_i, \bar{f}_i(\bar{m}_1 \| r), ...)) = 1)$ is negligible. By a standard hybrid argument, we have that $\Pr(\mathcal{B}(aux, \overline{tr}) = 1 | \bar{b} = 0) - \Pr(\mathcal{B}(aux, \overline{tr}) = 1 | \bar{b} = 1)$ is negligible, hence $\Pr(\mathcal{B}(aux, \overline{tr}) = \bar{b}) - 1/2$ is negligible, which makes a contradiction. So the advantage of $\mathcal{A}'$ is negligible, thus we finish the proof. $\square$

By a discussion similar to Sect. 5, we can see that SIM-based and IND-based FE schemes cannot be used to construct semi-universal PRE schemes directly. We also point out that why semi-universal PRE cannot be directly constructed from rFE [GJKS15]. The SIM-based secure rFE in [GJKS15] supports only selective security, hence cannot satisfy our security definition. (We note that adaptively SIM-based secure rFE also suffers from the impossible result of [AGVW13].) For IND-based secure rFE, the authors require that each post-challenge key query f, where f is a probabilistic function, satisfies that $f(m_0)$ and $f(m_1)$ are statically indistinguishable, rather than computationally indistinguishable, hence cannot be satisfied if $m_0 \neq m_1$ and f is $\mathsf{PKE.Enc}(pk, .)$ for a PKE scheme PKE. Even if we consider only pre-challenge key queries, where the authors only require that $f(m_0)$ and $f(m_1)$ are computationally indistinguishable, it still cannot handle the case where f is $\mathsf{PKE.Enc}(pk, .)$ since the adversary may hold the secret key sk corresponding to pk. The same thing happens for the distributional indistinguishability definition [AM18], which also requires $f(m_0)$ and $f(m_1)$ to be computationally indistinguishable.

7 Conclusion and Future Works

In this paper, we define a new security notion for FE: indistinguishability-based security against probabilistic queries (pIND-security). We justify our security notion from the following four points: (1) Our pIND-security is strictly between the classical SIM-security and IND-security; (2) Our pIND-security has both 1-CT to many-CT and selective to adaptive reductions; (3) We give a construction of fully secure FE for P/poly which satisfies pIND-security; (4) We give applications that can be directly constructed from pIND-secure FE schemes, but cannot be constructed from SIM-secure or IND-secure FE schemes in a same way.

We believe that our new definition has more potential applications than what we showed in this paper. We also hope that this new security notion can be used to simplify the construction from FE to $i\mathcal{O}$, hence pushing $i\mathcal{O}$ further into practical.

Acknowledgement. This work is partially supported by the National Key R&D Program of China (No. 2020YFA0712300) and the National Natural Science Foundation of China (No. 62202294, No. 62272294).

References

[ABSV15] Ananth, P., Brakerski, Z., Segev, G., Vaikuntanathan, V.: From selective to adaptive security in functional encryption. In: Gennaro, R., Robshaw, M. (eds.) CRYPTO 2015. LNCS, vol. 9216, pp. 657–677. Springer, Heidelberg (2015). https://doi.org/10.1007/978-3-662-48000-7_32

[AGVW13] Agrawal, S., Gorbunov, S., Vaikuntanathan, V., Wee, H.: Functional encryption: new perspectives and lower bounds. In: Canetti, R., Garay, J.A. (eds.) CRYPTO 2013. LNCS, vol. 8043, pp. 500–518. Springer, Heidelberg (2013). https://doi.org/10.1007/978-3-642-40084-1_28

[AJ15] Ananth, P., Jain, A.: Indistinguishability obfuscation from compact functional encryption. In: Gennaro, R., Robshaw, M. (eds.) CRYPTO 2015. LNCS, vol. 9215, pp. 308–326. Springer, Heidelberg (2015). https://doi.org/10.1007/978-3-662-47989-6_15

[AKW18] Agrawal, S., Koppula, V., Waters, B.: Impossibility of simulation secure functional encryption even with random oracles. In: Beimel, A., Dziembowski, S. (eds.) TCC 2018. LNCS, vol. 11239, pp. 659–688. Springer, Cham (2018). https://doi.org/10.1007/978-3-030-03807-6_24

[ALMT20] Agrawal, S., Libert, B., Maitra, M., Titiu, R.: Adaptive simulation security for inner product functional encryption. In: Kiayias, A., Kohlweiss, M., Wallden, P., Zikas, V. (eds.) PKC 2020. LNCS, vol. 12110, pp. 34–64. Springer, Cham (2020). https://doi.org/10.1007/978-3-030-45374-9_2

[AM18] Agrawal, S., Maitra, M.: FE and iO for turing machines from minimal assumptions. In: Beimel, A., Dziembowski, S. (eds.) TCC 2018. LNCS, vol. 11240, pp. 473–512. Springer, Cham (2018). https://doi.org/10.1007/978-3-030-03810-6_18

[AW17] Agrawal, S., Wu, D.J.: Functional encryption: deterministic to randomized functions from simple assumptions. In: Coron, J.-S., Nielsen, J.B. (eds.) EUROCRYPT 2017. LNCS, vol. 10211, pp. 30–61. Springer, Cham (2017). https://doi.org/10.1007/978-3-319-56614-6_2

[BB04] Boneh, D., Boyen, X.: Efficient selective-ID secure identity-based encryption without random oracles. In: Cachin, C., Camenisch, J.L. (eds.) EUROCRYPT 2004. LNCS, vol. 3027, pp. 223–238. Springer, Heidelberg (2004). https://doi.org/10.1007/978-3-540-24676-3_14

[BCJ+19] Bartusek, J., et al.: Public-key function-private hidden vector encryption (and more). In: Galbraith, S.D., Moriai, S. (eds.) ASIACRYPT 2019. LNCS, vol. 11923, pp. 489–519. Springer, Cham (2019). https://doi.org/10.1007/978-3-030-34618-8_17

[BF13] Barbosa, M., Farshim, P.: On the semantic security of functional encryption schemes. In: Kurosawa, K., Hanaoka, G. (eds.) PKC 2013. LNCS, vol. 7778, pp. 143–161. Springer, Heidelberg (2013). https://doi.org/10.1007/978-3-642-36362-7_10

[BO13] Bellare, M., O'Neill, A.: Semantically-secure functional encryption: possibility results, impossibility results and the quest for a general definition. In: Abdalla, M., Nita-Rotaru, C., Dahab, R. (eds.) CANS 2013. LNCS, vol. 8257, pp. 218–234. Springer, Cham (2013). https://doi.org/10.1007/978-3-319-02937-5_12

[BRS13] Boneh, D., Raghunathan, A., Segev, G.: Function-private identity-based encryption: hiding the function in functional encryption. In: Canetti, R., Garay, J.A. (eds.) CRYPTO 2013. LNCS, vol. 8043, pp. 461–478. Springer, Heidelberg (2013). https://doi.org/10.1007/978-3-642-40084-1_26

[BS15] Brakerski, Z., Segev, G.: Function-private functional encryption in the private-key setting. In: Dodis, Y., Nielsen, J.B. (eds.) TCC 2015. LNCS, vol. 9015, pp. 306–324. Springer, Heidelberg (2015). https://doi.org/10.1007/978-3-662-46497-7_12

[BSW11] Boneh, D., Sahai, A., Waters, B.: Functional encryption: definitions and challenges. In: Ishai, Y. (ed.) TCC 2011. LNCS, vol. 6597, pp. 253–273. Springer, Heidelberg (2011). https://doi.org/10.1007/978-3-642-19571-6_16

[Cha82] Chaum, D.: Blind signatures for untraceable payments. In: Chaum, D., Rivest, R.L., Sherman, A.T., eds., Advances in Cryptology: Proceedings of CRYPTO '82, Santa Barbara, California, USA, August 23–25, 1982, pp. 199–203. Plenum Press, New York (1982)

[DN21] Döttling, N., Nishimaki, R.: Universal proxy re-encryption. In: Garay, J.A. (ed.) PKC 2021. LNCS, vol. 12710, pp. 512–542. Springer, Cham (2021). https://doi.org/10.1007/978-3-030-75245-3_19

[GGH+13] Garg, S., Gentry, C., Halevi, S., Raykova, M., Sahai, A., Waters, B.: Candidate indistinguishability obfuscation and functional encryption for all circuits. In: 54th Annual IEEE Symposium on Foundations of Computer Science, FOCS 2013, 26–29 October, 2013, Berkeley, CA, USA, pp. 40–49. IEEE Computer Society (2013)

[GHRW14] Gentry, C., Halevi, S., Raykova, M., Wichs, D.: Outsourcing private RAM computation. In: 55th IEEE Annual Symposium on Foundations of Computer Science, FOCS 2014, Philadelphia, PA, USA, October 18–21, 2014, pp. 404–413. IEEE Computer Society (2014)

[GJKS15] Goyal, V., Jain, A., Koppula, V., Sahai, A.: Functional encryption for randomized functionalities. In: Dodis, Y., Nielsen, J.B. (eds.) TCC 2015. LNCS, vol. 9015, pp. 325–351. Springer, Heidelberg (2015). https://doi.org/10.1007/978-3-662-46497-7_13

[GP21] Gay, R., Pass, R.: Indistinguishability obfuscation from circular security. In: Samir Khuller and Virginia Vassilevska Williams, editors, STOC '21: 53rd Annual ACM SIGACT Symposium on Theory of Computing, Virtual Event, Italy, June 21–25, 2021, pp. 736–749. ACM (2021)

[GVW12] Gorbunov, S., Vaikuntanathan, V., Wee, H.: Functional encryption with bounded collusions via multi-party computation. In: Safavi-Naini, R., Canetti, R. (eds.) CRYPTO 2012. LNCS, vol. 7417, pp. 162–179. Springer, Heidelberg (2012). https://doi.org/10.1007/978-3-642-32009-5_11

[JLS21] Jain, A., Lin, H., Sahai, A.: Indistinguishability obfuscation from well-founded assumptions. In: Khuller, S., Williams, V.V., editors, STOC '21: 53rd Annual ACM SIGACT Symposium on Theory of Computing, Virtual Event, Italy, June 21–25, 2021, pp. 60–73. ACM (2021)

[KLM+18] Kim, S., Lewi, K., Mandal, A., Montgomery, H., Roy, A., Wu, D.J.: Function-hiding inner product encryption is practical. In: Catalano, D., De Prisco, R. (eds.) SCN 2018. LNCS, vol. 11035, pp. 544–562. Springer, Cham (2018). https://doi.org/10.1007/978-3-319-98113-0_29

[LPST16] Lin, H., Pass, R., Seth, K., Telang, S.: Output-compressing randomized encodings and applications. In: Kushilevitz, E., Malkin, T. (eds.) TCC 2016. LNCS, vol. 9562, pp. 96–124. Springer, Heidelberg (2016). https:// doi.org/10.1007/978-3-662-49096-9_5

[MSH+19] Marc, T., Stopar, M., Hartman, J., Bizjak, M., Modic, J.: Privacy-enhanced machine learning with functional encryption. In: Sako, K., Schneider, S., Ryan, P.Y.A. (eds.) ESORICS 2019. LNCS, vol. 11735, pp. 3–21. Springer, Cham (2019). https://doi.org/10.1007/978-3-030-29959-0_1

[O'N10] O'Neill, A.: Definitional issues in functional encryption. In: IACR Cryptol. ePrint Arch., p. 556 (2010)

[PMR19] Patranabis, S., Mukhopadhyay, D., Ramanna, S.C.: Function private predicate encryption for low min-entropy predicates. In: Lin, D., Sako, K. (eds.) PKC 2019. LNCS, vol. 11443, pp. 189–219. Springer, Cham (2019). https://doi.org/10.1007/978-3-030-17259-6_7

[RSG+19] Ryffel, T., Sans, E.D., Gay, R., Bach, F.R., Pointcheval, D.: Partially encrypted machine learning using functional encryption. CoRR, abs/1905.10214 (2019)

[WW21] Wee, H., Wichs, D.: Candidate obfuscation via oblivious LWE sampling. In: Canteaut, A., Standaert, F.-X. (eds.) EUROCRYPT 2021. LNCS, vol. 12698, pp. 127–156. Springer, Cham (2021). https://doi.org/10.1007/978-3-030-77883-5_5

ZK I

A Generic Transform from Multi-round Interactive Proof to NIZK

Pierre-Alain Fouque[1], Adela Georgescu[2], Chen Qian[3,4](✉),
Adeline Roux-Langlois[5], and Weiqiang Wen[6](✉)

[1] Rennes University, CNRS, INRIA, Rennes, France
[2] Department of Computer Science, University of Bucharest, Bucharest, Romania
[3] Key Laboratory of Cryptologic Technology and Information Security of Ministry of
Education, Shandong University, Qingdao, Shandong, China
chen.qian@sdu.edu.cn
[4] School of Cyber Science and Technology, Shandong University, Qingdao, Shandong, China
[5] Normandie Univ, UNICAEN, ENSICAEN, CNRS, GREYC, 14000 Caen, France
[6] LTCI, Telecom Paris, Institut Polytechnique de Paris, Palaiseau, France
weiqiang.wen@telecom-paris.fr

Abstract. We present a new generic transform that takes a multi-round interactive proof for the membership of a language $\mathcal{L}$ and outputs a non-interactive zero-knowledge proof (not of knowledge) in the common reference string model. Similar to the Fiat-Shamir transform, it requires a hash function H. However, in our transform the zero-knowledge property is in the standard model, and the adaptive soundness is in the non-programmable random oracle model (NPROM). Behind this new generic transform, we build a new generic OR-composition of two multi-round interactive proofs. Note that the two common techniques for building OR-proofs (parallel OR-proof and sequential OR-proof) cannot be naturally extended to the multi-round setting. We also give a proof of security for our OR-proof in the quantum oracle model (QROM), surprisingly the security loss in QROM is independent from the number of rounds.

1 Introduction

Non-interactive zero-knowledge (NIZK) proofs [18,25] can prove a statement without leaking any additional information about the witness. Since its first introduction, NIZK plays an important role in constructing almost every primitive from the basic ones like chosen-ciphertext encryption [33], signature [22] to complex cryptographic protocols like e-voting [17], and e-cash system [12].

Fiat-Shamir and Random Oracle Model. The most common and efficient way to construct a non-interactive zero-knowledge proof in the random oracle model (ROM) is via the Fiat-Shamir transform [22]. One first constructs a Σ-protocol (1-round interactive proof), then turns it into non-interactive by simulating the random challenge using a hash function modeled as a random oracle.

Since its first introduction [2], the random oracle model (ROM) has been controversial. The advantage of ROM is that, it is generally easier to build cryptographic

© International Association for Cryptologic Research 2023
A. Boldyreva and V. Kolesnikov (Eds.): PKC 2023, LNCS 13941, pp. 461–481, 2023.
https://doi.org/10.1007/978-3-031-31371-4_16

primitives with it, and the resulting primitives are usually more efficient than their standard model version (without random oracle). However, a decade after its introduction Canetti, Goldreich and Halevi [10] discovered that the instantiation of RO is theoretically impossible. More precisely, there exist cryptosystems that are secure in the random oracle model, but for which replacing the random oracle by any implementation leads to an insecure cryptosystem. Therefore, standard model constructions are usually considered as more secure than the constructions in ROM.

Beside of theoretical impossibility, ROM also suffers from some security concerns in real world applications. For example, a common way to instantiate the random oracle is with hash functions (like MD5, SHA-1, SHA-2, SHA-3 etc.). Therefore, any progress in cryptanalysis of hash functions could potentially make the ROM-based schemes insecure. As a concrete example, the work of [35,38] have shown that standard hash functions like MD5 or SHA-1 are far from behaving like random oracles. Based on these attacks, Stevens *et al.* [36] showed an attack on constructing two colliding X.509 certificates for different identities and public keys, while the system is still secure in the ROM.

NIZK Without Random Oracle. Efficient NIZK in the standard model is considered as a challenging problem. In the ' NIZK in the standard model has been proposed by [26]. However, the situation of the efficient standard model NIZK in the post-quantum setting is less clear. Several works have constructed efficient post-quantum NIZK schemes by relaxing the soundness definition (only average-case soundness [14] against classical worst-case soundness) or the syntax of NIZK itself (Designated-Verifier NIZK [31], NIZK in the preprocessing model [28]). The full-fledged post-quantum NIZK in the standard model is only due to a new framework in the recent breakthrough results [8, 9], which gives the first lattice-based NIZK without RO [34]. As another instantiation of this framework, a new NIZK based on Learning Parity with Noise assumption and Trapdoor Hash Functions has also been proposed [6]. However, the efficiency of all these constructions in the standard model is still far from that of post-quantum NIZK in ROM [7,21,32].

Non-Programmable Random Oracle. In recent years, there is another research direction of NIZK consists of replacing the ROM by its weaker variant non-programmable random oracle model NPROM, while preserving the efficiency [15,29]. These constructions are both generic transforms from Σ-protocols to NIZK. Interestingly, they both have zero-knowledge property in the standard model, and soundness property in the non-programmable random oracle model (NPROM).

Another interesting point about these two constructions is that, their zero-knowledge property is independent of the random oracle model. Therefore, in many applications, such as e-voting or authenticated encryptions, it guarantees that even the hash function is broken in the future, the privacy is still preserved.

Limits of NIZK in NPROM. One big problem of both transforms [15,29] is that, they only work for Σ protocols but not the more generic multi-round public-coin interactive proofs (PCIP). As several recent results of interactive proofs are exploiting the multi-round property of PCIP to gain efficiency, such as bullet proofs [7], exact proofs [21] or amortized exact proofs [4], an interesting question would be to extend the [15,29] transforms to multi-round interactive protocols. Moreover, between these two transforms, [15] not only requires less properties of the starting Σ-protocol than [29] (optimal soundness against special soundness) but it is also more efficient. Therefore, we have chosen to focus on extending [15] in this paper. Unfortunately, it cannot be easily extended, as its principal building block is an OR-composition of two Σ-protocol, and the existing OR-composition techniques do not apply to multi-round PCIP. We will give below a quick overview of the existing OR-proofs.

OR-Proof. The OR-composition of Σ-protocols has been initially used to construct ring-signature schemes by [16] based on the programmable random oracle. Another OR-composition technique has been proposed by [1] to weaken the model, they only require the NPROM, and [1] has a shorter proof than [16] (one hash value less in the proof.) However, neither of them can be extended to the OR-composition of multiround public-coin interactive proofs. Note that, for multi-round interactive proofs, we can firstly use Fiat-Shamir transform to reduce the number of rounds, then apply [16] or [1] to construct NIZK. But, the Fiat-Shamir transform requires programmability of the random oracle for the zero-knowledge property. As our goal is to keep the zeroknowledge property in the standard model, this approach does not work. This raises a natural question:

Can we build a generic OR-composition of multi-round PCIP, with zero-knowledge in the standard model and soundness in NPROM?

We will answer this question positively by giving a new technique for OR-composition.

Security in the Quantum Random Oracle Model (QROM). Security of random oracle model in the quantum setting is not a trivial problem. Intuitively, a quantum adversary can build the hash function and run the primitive himself by querying quantum states. Therefore, the adversary can get a superposition of exponentially many samples of the random oracle, which gives him more advantage than a classical adversary. Many recent works address this issue [19,20,30], and they give detailed analysis for the Fiat-Shamir transform in this setting. As we claim that we have a post-quantum zero-knowledge proof, we also give an analysis of our transform in the QROM.

1.1 Our Contributions

In this paper, we bring several contributions. Firstly, we propose a new generic transform from multi-round PCIP to NIZK, with zero-knowledge property in the standard model and soundness in NPROM. The principal new technique behind this transform is a new OR-proof of two different PCIPs. Surprisingly, the soundness in QROM of both multi-round PCIP to NIZK and OR-proof of PCIPs has a security loss of $O(Q_H^4)$ which is independent from the number of rounds.

More precisely:

- We propose in this paper a new generic transform from multi-round public-coin interactive proofs (PCIP) to a non-interactive zero-knowledge proof system (NIZK). Compared to Fiat-Shamir transform, the zero-knowledge property of our transform is in the *standard model*, and soundness property is in the *non-programmable random oracle model* (NPROM) (RO without programmability). While comparing with similar type of transforms [15,29], ours additionally supports multi-round PCIP.
- Behind our generic transform, we have developed a new technique to generate an OR-proof from two optimal sound PCIP: $PCIP_0$, $PCIP_1$. The direct approach consists of using Fiat-Shamir transform to turn both $PCIP_0$ and $PCIP_1$ into Σ-protocols, then apply either [16] or [1] transform to get an OR-proof. Compared to the direct approach, the zero-knowledge property of our transform is in the *standard model*, and our adaptive soundness property is in the NPROM. We believe that this new OR-composition has other applications and independent interests.
- Finally, we analyze the soundness property of our OR-proof in the QROM. Note that the zero-knowledge property of our OR-proof is in the standard model, therefore it is naturally secure in the QROM. Moreover, our transform from PCIP to NIZK has the same security loss as our OR-proof. Surprisingly, the security loss of the soundness is $O(Q_H^4)$ which is independent of the number of rounds.

1.2 Technical Overview

Our main technique consists in constructing the OR-proof for multi-round PCIPs. We dedicate this section to explain the intuition behind our OR-proof. Firstly, we will give a quick overview of the existing parallel OR-proof [16] and sequential OR-proof [1,24] as we will borrow ideas from both transforms. Then, we explain why they can not be extended to n-round PCIPs, and our new techniques of OR-proof.

Why [16] Does Not Work for n-round PCIPs? Given Σ_0 and Σ_1 two Σ-protocols with transcripts $\{R_0, h_0, s_0\}$ and $\{R_1, h_1, s_1\}$, the intuition behind the parallel [16] transform is that, after generating the first round commitments (R_0, R_1), the corresponding challenges are chosen such that $h_0 \oplus h_1 = H(R_0, R_1)$. Therefore any adversary can freely choose one (and only one) between h_0 and h_1 even before seeing (R_0, R_1). By using the HVZK property of the Σ-protocol, once h_0 (or h_1) chosen, the adversary can simulate the proof (R_0, s_0) or (R_1, s_1) without knowing any witness.

Let us now see why this approach can not be extended to n-round interactive protocols when $n > 1$. The natural extension of [16] would be to define the i-th round challenges $(i \in [n])$ such that $h_{i,0} \oplus h_{i,1} = H(\{R_{j,0}, R_{j,1}\}_{j=1}^i)$. This transform is not secure. To show this, we construct below an example of two 2-round protocols that are secure individually, but once combined, the resulting OR-proof is not secure anymore.

Counter-Example of [16] Applying on 2-round PCIPs. Given two Σ-protocols Σ_0 and Σ_1, we will construct two 2-round protocols $PCIP_0$, $PCIP_1$ by adding one unused round into each of Σ_0, Σ_1 but in different order. Namely, valid transcripts of $PCIP_0$ and $PCIP_1$ are of the form $(\bar{R}_0, \bar{h}_0, R_0, h_0, s_0)$ and $(R_1, h_1, \bar{R}_1, \bar{h}_1, s_1)$, where $(\bar{R}_0, \bar{h}_0, \bar{R}_1, \bar{h}_1)$ are just random strings and ignored in the verification process. If we apply the naive extension of [16] transform to PCIP_0 and PCIP_1, an adversary $\mathcal{A}$ can randomly choose h_0, h_1, then use HVZK to simulate (R_0, h_0, s_0) and (R_1, h_1, s_1). As $(\bar{R}_0, \bar{h}_0, \bar{R}_1, \bar{h}_1)$ are ignored by the individual verification of PCIP_0 and PCIP_1, $\mathcal{A}$ can define $\bar{R}_0, \bar{R}_1$ to be random strings and

$$\bar{h}_0 := h_1 \oplus H(\bar{R}_0, R_1), \qquad\qquad \bar{h}_1 := h_0 \oplus H(R_0, \bar{R}_1).$$

By the correctness of PCIP_0 and PCIP_1, $(\bar{R}_0, \bar{h}_0, R_0, h_0, s_0, R_1, h_1, \bar{R}_1, \bar{h}_1, s_1)$ is a valid proof for which $\mathcal{A}$ does not need to know any witness in order to produce it, so he can easily break soundness of the OR-proof composition.

The above attack works because we have given too much "freedom" to $\mathcal{A}$. He can freely chose one challenge per round. Therefore, we need to limit $\mathcal{A}$ to only be able to freely choose the challenges from the same interactive protocol.

Overview of Sequential OR-Proof [1,24]. Given two Σ-protocols Σ_0 and Σ_1, together with two statements x_0, x_1 and a witness w_0. (w.l.o.g. we can assume that we know w_0.) The intuition of the sequential OR-proof is that $H(R_0)$ is used as the challenge h_1 for Σ_1 and $H(R_1)$ is used as the challenge h_0 for Σ_0. The honest generation of the proof is given as in Fig. 1.

```
Prove(x₀, x₁, w₀):
01  (R₀, st₀) ⇐$ Σ₀.Prove₁(x₀, w₀)
02  h₁ := H(R₀)
03  (R₁, s₁) ⇐$ Σ₁.Sim(x₁, h₁)
04  h₀ := H(R₁)
05  s₀ ⇐$ Σ₀.Prove₂(x₀, w₀, h₀, st₀)
06  return (R₀, R₁, h₀, h₁, s₀, s₁)
```

Fig. 1. Prove algorithm of sequential OR-proof

The intuition behind the sequential OR-proof is that, one can freely choose to generate R_0 or R_1 first. However, once chosen to generate R_b and h_{1-b} first, then h_b will be chosen independently from the value R_b. By the soundness of Σ_b without w_b, no PPT adversary can generate a valid transcript $\mathsf{Trans}_b = (R_b, h_b, s_b)$.

For n-round PCIPs, we can notice that before the honest side (b) has been executed until the $(n-1)th$ round, the simulation side ($1-b$) doesn't have all the challenges, therefore even an honest prover with w_b cannot generate a valid proof when $n > 1$.

Intuition Behind Our Approach. Let us consider two n-round public-coin interactive proofs PCIP_0 and PCIP_1 for proving the membership of two languages $\mathcal{L}_0$ and $\mathcal{L}_1$. For simplicity, we assume PCIP_0 and PCIP_1 have same number of rounds in this section. We will prove that $x_0 \in \mathcal{L}_0$ or $x_1 \in \mathcal{L}_1$ without revealing exactly which witness is used. Let $\mathsf{Trans}_0 = (\{R_{i,0}, h_{i,0}\}_{i=1}^n, s_0)$ and $\mathsf{Trans}_1 = (\{R_{i,1}, h_{i,1}\}_{i=1}^n, s_1)$ be two transcripts of PCIP_0 and PCIP_1 respectively.

Our starting point is the parallel OR-proof. To prevent the above attack against multi-round parallel OR-proof, our idea is to combine all the challenges of the same side together by an offset. Therefore, once the offset and the first i rounds commitments are fixed, the challenges are fixed. More precisely, for $b \in \{0,1\}$, we denote by $A_b = \{a_{1,b}, \ldots, a_{n,b}\}$ two offsets, we could compute the challenges of the i-th round as follows,

$$h_{i,0} = H(\{R_{j,0}\}_{j=1}^{i}) + a_{i,0}, \qquad h_{i,1} = H(\{R_{j,1}\}_{j=1}^{i}) + a_{i,1}. \qquad (1)$$

Now, the challenges are all related. We emphasize the fact that the adversary can freely choose A_b, where $b \in \{0,1\}$, is equivalent to be able to choose every challenge of b side.

The second step is to only allow the adversary to freely choose one and only one offset between A_0 and A_1. To do this, we borrow the idea from the sequential or-proof by putting A_0 and A_1 into the hash of the opposite side. More precisely, we have

$$h_{i,0} = H(\{R_{j,0}\}_{j=1}^{i}, A_1) + a_{i,0}, \qquad h_{i,1} = H(\{R_{j,1}\}_{j=1}^{i}, A_0) + a_{i,1}. \qquad (2)$$

As in sequential OR-proof, the order of query A_0 and A_1 is crucial in our case. Namely, at least one of the two cases must happen:

- Before the RO query on $(\{R_{j,0}\}_{j=1}^{i}, A_1)$, there exists a query of the form $(\cdot, A_0)$.
- Before the RO query on $(\{R_{j,1}\}_{j=1}^{i}, A_0)$, there exists a query of the form $(\cdot, A_1)$.

This forces the adversary to choose A_0 before having seen $H(\{R_{j,0}\}_{j=1}^{i}, A_1)$ or A_1 before having seen $H(\{R_{j,1}\}_{j=1}^{i}, A_0)$. We can use this property to reduce the adaptive soundness of our OR-proof to the optimal soundness of the underlying PCIPs.

Security in the QROM. In our QROM security proof, we apply the Measure-then-Reprogram 2.0 technique [19]. There is a price to pay for proving our transform in the QROM, that is we need the programmability of the random oracle. Moreover, if we want to prove our transform for round-by-round, we need to program the random oracle in every round, this will introduce an exponential security loss in the number of rounds. Therefore, we restrict our transform to only optimal-sound PCIPs, then we can prove our transform with only $O(Q_H^4)$ security loss.

Note that, despite the fact that our OR-proof is a composition of two multi-round PCIPs, we only need to apply the Measure-then-Reprogram 2.0 technique on 2 entries. This is due to the fact that our OR-proof is not a proof of knowledge, but only a proof of membership, which is already useful in many applications such as voting schemes etc.

Therefore, we do not need all the entries to be able to extract the witness. This observation makes our security loss of the adaptive soundness as low as $O(Q_H^4)$ in QROM, which is independent from the number of rounds n. Different from our result, [19] has considered the soundness with proof of knowledge (stronger than our adaptive soundness) of Fiat-Shamir transform and their security loss is $O(Q_H^{2n})$.

Very recently, there is a new semi-generic transformation [27] from PCIPs to non-interactive proofs in the QROM while achieving proof of knowledge. However it requires the prover's response to be in linear form. As a comparison, our transformation is generic and does not impose any restriction on the prover's response.

In comparison, Unruh's transform [37] works for any Σ-protocol, but introduces a noticeable overhead depending on the size of the challenge set. In [13], Chen et al. extend Unruh's framework for a 3-round protocol where the second challenge is binary.

2 Preliminaries

2.1 Notations

For $n \in \mathbb{N}$, let $[n] = \{1, \ldots, n\}$. For a finite set $\mathcal{S}$, we denote the sampling of a uniform random element $\times$ by $\times \xleftarrow{\$} \mathcal{S}$. For simplicity of the notations, we omit that every algorithm takes as input the public parameter par. For an algorithm A which takes $\times$ as input, we denote its computation by $y \xleftarrow{\$} A(\times)$. We assume all the algorithms (including adversaries) in this paper to be probabilistic unless stated otherwise. We denote an algorithm A with access to an oracle $\mathcal{O}$ by $A^{\mathcal{O}}$.

For an NP language $\mathcal{L}$, we denote by $\times \in_{\mathbf{w}} \mathcal{L}$ the fact that the statement $\times$ is in the language $\mathcal{L}$ with the witness $\mathbf{w}$.

We use code-based games [3] to present our definitions and proofs. We implicitly assume all Boolean flags to be initialized to 0 (**false**), numerical variables to 0, sets to $\varnothing$ and strings to $\bot$. We make the convention that a procedure terminates once it has returned an output. $\mathrm{Exp}_{\Sigma,A}^{G}(1^{\lambda}) = b$ denotes the final (Boolean) output b of the adversary A running the security experiment G on the scheme Σ with security parameter λ, and if $b = 1$ we say A wins G. The randomness in $\Pr[\mathrm{Exp}_{\Sigma,A}^{G}(1^{\lambda}) = 1]$ is over all the random coins in experiment G. Within a procedure, "**abort** " means that we terminate the run of an adversary A.

2.2 n-Round Public Coin Interactive Proof (PCIP)

The general structure of an n-round Public-Coin Interactive Proof of the form depicted in Fig. 2 is defined as follows.[1] Notice that for $n = 1$, PCIP is a Σ-protocol, and PCIP is also named as identification scheme in some literatures.

Definition 1 (n-round Public-Coin Interactive Proof). *Let $\mathcal{L}$ be an NP language. To prove a statement $\times \in_{\mathbf{w}} \mathcal{L}$, an n-round public-coin interactive proof consists of $n + 2$ PPT stateful algorithms* PCIP $= (\{\mathrm{Prove}_i\}_{i=1}^{n+1}, \mathrm{Verif})$ *with the following syntax:*

- $\mathrm{Prove}_i(h_{i-1}, \mathsf{st}_{i-1})$ *takes a challenge h_{i-1} and a state st_{i-1} as input, and returns a commitment R_i and a new state st_i, where $\mathsf{st}_0 = (\times, \mathbf{w})$, and $R_{n+1} = \mathsf{s}$.*
- $\mathrm{Verif}(\times, (\{R_i, h_i\}_{i=1}^{n}, \mathsf{s}))$: *The verification* Verif *takes as input a statement $\times$ and a transcript $(\{R_i, h_i\}_{i=1}^{n}, \mathsf{s})$ and returns a decision 0 or 1.*

We introduce the following definitions for a PCIP scheme:

---

[1] In this paper, we use the convention that n-round PCIP has $2n + 1$ moves.

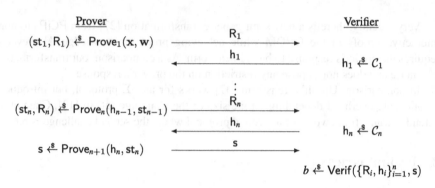

Fig. 2. An n-round Interactive Protocol

- **Transcript:** *We define a **transcript** as all messages between the prover and the verifier of the form* $\text{Trans} = (\{R_i, h_i\}_{i=1}^n, s)$. *Moreover, we define a partial transcript* Trans' *as prefix of another transcript of the form* $(\{R_i, h_i\}_{i=1}^j)$ *with* $j \le n$.

We require the following properties for an n-round PCIP:

- **Correctness:** *For all* $(\mathbf{x}, \mathbf{w})$ *such that* $\mathbf{x} \in_{\mathbf{w}} \mathcal{L}$ *and for all honestly generated transcripts* $\text{Trans} = (\{R_i, h_i\}_{i=1}^n, s)$ *using* $(\mathbf{x}, \mathbf{w})$, *we say that* PCIP *is ρ-correct if we have:*

$$\Pr[\text{Verif}(\mathbf{x}, (\{R_i, h_i\}_{i=1}^n, s)) = 0] \le \rho.$$

- **Honest-Verifier Zero-Knowledge:** *For all* $(\mathbf{x}, \mathbf{w})$ *such that* $\mathbf{x} \in_{\mathbf{w}} \mathcal{L}$, *we say that* PCIP *is Δ-HVZK, if there exists a* PPT *simulator* Sim *that takes* $\mathbf{x}$ *as input, and returns a transcript* Trans, *such that the distribution of* Trans *is at statistical distance at most Δ from the distribution of an honestly generated transcript. In particular, if $\Delta = 0$, we say that* PCIP *has perfect* HVZK.
- **Round-by-Round Soundness:** *Let* PCIP *be an interactive-proof with i-th round challenge space* $\mathbb{Z}_{\ell_i}$. *We say that* PCIP *is round-by-round sound if, there exists a "doomed set"* $\mathcal{D} \in \{0, 1\}^*$ *such that,*
  - *If* $\mathbf{x} \notin \mathcal{L}$, *then* $(\mathbf{x}, \varnothing) \in \mathcal{D}$, *where* $\varnothing$ *denotes the empty transcript.*
  - *For all partial transcript* Trans, *such that* $(\mathbf{x}, \text{Trans}) \in \mathcal{D}$, *for all next message* R_i *given by the prover, there exists a negligible function* $\text{negl}(\cdot)$ *such that*

$$\Pr[(\mathbf{x}, \text{Trans}\|R_i\|h_i) \notin \mathcal{L} \mid h_i \xleftarrow{\$} \mathbb{Z}_{\ell_i}] \le \text{negl}(\lambda).$$

  - *For any complete transcript* Trans, *if* $(\mathbf{x}, \text{Trans}) \in \mathcal{D}$ *then* Verifier$(\mathbf{x}, \text{Trans}) =$ *false.*

Notice that the round-by-round soundness originally proposed by [8] is a very weak security notion. Since we only consider the constant rounds interactive proofs, by [8, Proposition 5.3 and 5.4] round-by-round soundness and negligible soundness are equivalent. On the other hand, optimal soundness (c.f. Definition 9 which is a multi-round version of special soundness) is a commonly used term for many protocols. If a protocol is ε-optimal sound then it can be seen as no transcript can escape the doomed set except in one specific round with probability ε. Therefore, optimal soundness tightly implies round-by-round soundness. This provides us an alternative way to use our transform.

2.3 Non-Interactive Proof NIP

For the sake of completeness, we define two different types of non-interactive proofs NIP: Non-Interactive Zero-Knowledge proofs (NIZK) and Non-Interactive Witness Indistinguishable proofs (NIWI). Notice that we don't consider the proof of knowledge in this paper, and we use the adaptive soundness for NIPs.

Definition 2 (Non-Interactive Proof NIP**).** *Let $\mathcal{L}$ be an* NP *language. To prove a statement* $\mathbf{x} \in_{\mathbf{w}} \mathcal{L}$, *a non-interactive proof consists of four* PPT *algorithms* $\Pi = $ (Setup, Prove, Verif, Sim $= (\mathsf{Sim}_0, \mathsf{Sim}_1))$ *defined as follows:*

- Setup$(1^\lambda) \to$ CRS : *The setup algorithm* Setup *returns a common reference string* CRS.
- Prove(CRS, $\mathbf{x}, \mathbf{w}) \to \pi$: *The prove algorithm* Prove *returns a proof π that* $\mathbf{x} \in_{\mathbf{w}} \mathcal{L}$ *using* $\mathbf{w}$ *as witness.*
- Verif(CRS, $\mathbf{x}, \pi) \to \{0, 1\}$: *The verification algorithm* Verif *returns a decision,* 1 *(acceptance) or* 0 *(rejection).*
- Sim$_0(1^\lambda) \to$ (CRS, τ) : *The first part of the simulation algorithm* Sim$_0$ *outputs a common reference string* CRS *and a simulation trapdoor* τ.
- Sim$_1(\tau, \mathbf{x}) \to \pi$: *The second part of the simulation algorithm* Sim$_1$ *outputs a simulated proof π.*

We will also define the completeness, adaptive soundness, zero-knowledge, witness-indistinguishability of NIP as follows.

Definition 3 (ρ-Completeness). *A NIP is ρ-complete if, for all* $\mathbf{x} \in_{\mathbf{w}} \mathcal{L}$ *we have:*

$$\Pr\left[\mathsf{Verif}(\mathsf{CRS}, \mathbf{x}, \pi) = 0 \,\middle|\, \begin{array}{l} \mathsf{CRS} \xleftarrow{\$} \mathsf{Setup}(1^\lambda) \\ \pi \xleftarrow{\$} \mathsf{Prove}(\mathsf{CRS}, \mathbf{x}, \mathbf{w}) \end{array}\right] \le \rho.$$

Definition 4 ((ε, Q$_\mathsf{H}$)-Adaptive Soundness). *A NIP is $(\varepsilon, \mathsf{Q_H})$-adaptively sound in the non-programmable random oracle model* NPROM, *if for all* PPT *adversaries $\mathcal{A}$ requiring at most* Q$_\mathsf{H}$ *hash queries we have:*

$$\Pr\left[\mathbf{x}^\star \in \{0, 1\}^n \setminus \mathcal{L} \wedge \mathsf{Verif}(\mathsf{CRS}, \mathbf{x}^\star, \pi^\star) = 1 \,\middle|\, \begin{array}{l} \mathsf{CRS} \xleftarrow{\$} \mathsf{Setup}(1^\lambda) \\ (\mathbf{x}^\star, \pi^\star) \xleftarrow{\$} \mathcal{A}^{\mathcal{O}_{Hash}}(\mathsf{CRS}) \end{array}\right] \le \varepsilon.$$

We consider the hash function as an NPRO *in the soundness proof.*

Definition 5 (Zero-Knowledge). *A NIP is Δ-Zero-Knowledge, if there exists a simulator* Sim $= (\mathsf{Sim}_0, \mathsf{Sim}_1)$ *such that, the statistical distance between the output distributions of **Game** Sim and **Game** Real as defined in Fig. 3 is at most Δ.*
Moreover, if $\Delta = 0$, NIP is perfectly zero-knowledge.

Game Sim:		Game Real:	
01 $(\mathrm{CRS}, \tau) \xleftarrow{\$} \mathrm{Sim}_0(1^\lambda)$		05 $\mathrm{CRS} \xleftarrow{\$} \mathrm{Setup}(1^\lambda)$	
02 $(\mathbf{x}, \mathbf{w}) \xleftarrow{\$} \mathcal{A}(\mathrm{CRS})$	$/\!/ \mathbf{x} \in_{\mathbf{w}} \mathcal{L}$	06 $(\mathbf{x}, \mathbf{w}) \xleftarrow{\$} \mathcal{A}(\mathrm{CRS})$	$/\!/ \mathbf{x} \in_{\mathbf{w}} \mathcal{L}$
03 $\pi \xleftarrow{\$} \mathrm{Sim}_1(\mathbf{x}, \tau)$		07 $\pi \xleftarrow{\$} \mathrm{Prove}(\mathrm{CRS}, \mathbf{x}, \mathbf{w})$	
04 **return** (CRS, π)		08 **return** (CRS, π)	

Fig. 3. Real and Sim experiments for the zero-knowledge property

Definition 6 (Witness Indistinguishable for OR-Composition). *Let* $\mathcal{L}_\vee = \mathcal{L}_0 \vee \mathcal{L}_1$ *be an OR-relation. A NIP is* Δ-*Witness Indistinguishable for* $\mathcal{L}_\vee$, *if for the statement* $\mathbf{x} = (\mathbf{x}_0, \mathbf{x}_1)$ *and the witness* $(\mathbf{w}_0, \mathbf{w}_1)$ *such that* $\mathbf{x}_0 \in_{\mathbf{w}_0} \mathcal{L}_0 \vee \mathbf{x}_1 \in_{\mathbf{w}_1} \mathcal{L}_1$, *the statistical distance between the output distributions of the* **Game** 0 *and the* **Game** 1 *as defined in Fig. 4 is at most* Δ.

Game 0:	Game 1:
01 $\mathrm{CRS} \xleftarrow{\$} \mathrm{Setup}(1^\lambda)$	04 $\mathrm{CRS} \xleftarrow{\$} \mathrm{Setup}(1^\lambda)$
02 $\pi \xleftarrow{\$} \mathrm{Prove}(\mathrm{CRS}, \mathbf{x}, \mathbf{w}_0)$	05 $\pi \xleftarrow{\$} \mathrm{Prove}(\mathrm{CRS}, \mathbf{x}, \mathbf{w}_1)$
03 **return** π	06 **return** π

Fig. 4. Real and Sim experiments for the witness-indistinguishability

Moreover, if $\Delta = 0$, *NIP is perfectly witness indistinguishable.*

We define NIZK as NIP that satisfy completeness, adaptive soundness and zero-knowledge property while for NIWI, the zero-knowledge property is replaced with witness-indistinguishability.

3   From Interactive to Non-interactive

One of the most common way to construct a non-interactive zero-knowledge proof is via the Fiat-Shamir [23] transform. However, we additionally require the zero-knowledge property to be ROM-free, which is not the case using this transform. The two existing variants available for Σ-protocols (1-round protocols) are [29] and its more efficient and more generic improvement [15].

Lindell's Transform. [29] In Lindell's transform, the challenge of Σ-protocol is of the form $\mathrm{H}(\mathbf{x}, \mathrm{Com}(R))$, where R is the first round message of the Σ-protocol and Com is a dual-mode commitment [29] (*aka.* hybrid trapdoor commitment [11]). However, if we want to generalize this transform to multi-round PCIP, this approach is not very efficient. That is because, we need to include the commitments and the decommitments of every round of PCIP into the final proof. Moreover, following the generic construction of dual-mode commitment from PCIP schemes in [29], the size of one commitment and one decommitment is equal to the size of one PCIP proof. Therefore, if we directly apply the Lindell's transform, we will have a proof size blow-up of factor $O(n)$, where n is the number of rounds. Consequently, it may loose the efficiency gain of multi-round PCIP schemes over Σ-protocols.

Ciampi et al. Transform [15] The transform in [15] requires only computational optimal soundness (weaker than special soundness) and computational HVZK of the underlying interactive protocols, and it is more efficient than [29]. However, the [15] transform relies heavily on the existence of an OR-composition of interactive protocols. Unfortunately, the most efficient interactive lattice-based proof systems are all 2-round protocols [4,5,21], and the previous OR-compositions of interactive proof systems [1,16,24] cannot be applied to multi-round PCIPs.

In this section, we further improve the [15] transform by extending it to support OR-composition of an n_0-round computational HVZK and round-by-round sound PCIP$_0$ and an n_1-round computational HVZK and round-by-round sound PCIP$_1$. Notice that if we apply our transform to two 1-round PCIPs (Σ-protocols), the resulting NIZK scheme is almost as efficient as in [15]. More precisely, in the case of Σ-protocol, we only have two more elements $(a_0, a_1) \in \mathbb{Z}_{\ell_{1,0}} \times \mathbb{Z}_{\ell_{1,1}}$ than [15], where $\ell_{1,0}, \ell_{1,1}$ are the size of the challenge spaces of PCIP$_0$ and PCIP$_1$. In Sect. 2.3 we recall the definitions of two different types of non-interactive proofs NIP: NIZK proofs and Non-Interactive Witness Indistinguishable (NIWI) proofs.

3.1 Construction of Our OR-Proof

We recall that the intuition behind our OR-proof is explained in Sect. 1.2. We then directly give the construction of our OR-proof in this section.

Let PCIP$_0$ (*resp.* PCIP$_1$) be an n_0-round (*resp.* n_1-round) public coin interactive proof for proving the membership of two languages $\mathcal{L}_0$ and $\mathcal{L}_1$, and we denote the size of challenge spaces by $(\ell_{1,0}, \ldots, \ell_{n_0,0}, \ell_{1,1}, \ldots, \ell_{n_1,1})$. The goal is to prove that $\mathbf{x}_0 \in \mathcal{L}_0$ or $\mathbf{x}_1 \in \mathcal{L}_1$ without revealing exactly which witness is used. The idea behind this proof, using $\mathbf{w}_b$, is to first sample a random offset $A_b = (a_{1,b}, \ldots, a_{n_b,b})$. Then, we simulate the proof PCIP$_{1-b}$ for which we don't have a witness to build the second offset $(a_{1,1-b}, \ldots, a_{n_{1-b},1-b})$, which depends on A_b and on the commitments $\{R_{i,1-b}\}_{j=1}^{n_{1-b}}$. Finally, we can use A_{1-b} to build the proof PCIP$_b$ for which we know the witness. To verify the proof, we first verify that all the $\{h_{i,b}\}$ have been correctly generated, then that both proofs pass their verification algorithm.

We give our transform in pseudo-code in Fig. 5. We define $\mathcal{C}_{i,b}$ as the challenge space of i-th round of PCIP$_b$, we assume that $\mathcal{C}_{i,b}$ is isomorphic to the additive group $(\mathbb{Z}_{\ell_{i,b}}, +)$.

Properties of Our NIP. We will prove in the remaining part of this section that the non-interactive proof NIP constructed as in Fig. 5 is correct (Theorem 1), witness-indistinguishable (Theorem 2), and adaptively sound (Theorem 3), if the underlying protocols PCIP$_0$, PCIP$_1$ are both correct, HVZK and round-by-roudn sound. Moreover, if PCIP$_0$ and PCIP$_1$ are both perfectly HVZK, then the resulting NIP is a NIWI proof with perfect witness-indistinguishability.

```
Prove(x₀, x₁, w_b):
01  A_b := (a_{1,b}, ..., a_{n_b,b}) ⇐$ Z_{ℓ_{1,b}} × ... × Z_{ℓ_{n_b,b}}
02  Trans_{1-b} ⇐$ PCIP_{1-b}.Sim(1^λ, x_{1-b})
03  ({R_{i,1-b}, h_{i,1-b}}^{n_{1-b}}_{i=1}, s_{1-b}) =: Trans_{1-b}
04  for i = 1..n_{1-b} do
05     a_{i,1-b} ← h_{i,1-b} − H({R_{j,1-b}}^{i}_{j=1}, A_b)
06  A_{1-b} ← (a_{1,1-b}, ..., a_{n_{1-b},1-b})
07  st_{0,b} = ∅; h_{0,b} = ⊥
08  for i = 1..n_b do
09     (R_{i,b}, st_{i,b}) ⇐$ PCIP_b.Prove_i(st_{i-1,b}, h_{i-1,b}, x_b, w_b)
10     h_{i,b} := H({R_{j,b}}^{i}_{j=1}, A_{1-b}) + a_{i,b}
11  s_b ⇐$ PCIP_b.Prove_{n_b}(st_{n_b-1,b}, h_{n_b-1,b}, x_b, w_b)
12  return π := ({R_{i,0}}^{n_0}_{i=1}, {R_{i,1}}^{n_1}_{i=1}, A_0, A_1, s_0, s_1)
Verif(x₀, x₁, π):
13  for i = 1..n_0 do
14     h_{i,0} := H({R_{j,0}}^{i}_{j=1}, A_1) + a_{i,0}
15  for i = 1..n_1 do
16     h_{i,1} := H({R_{j,1}}^{i}_{j=1}, A_0) + a_{i,1}
17  Trans_0 := ({R_{i,0}, h_{i,0}}^{n_0}_{i=1}, s_0)
18  Trans_1 := ({R_{i,1}, h_{i,1}}^{n_1}_{i=1}, s_1)
19  if PCIP_0.Verify(x₀, Trans_0) = 1 ∧ PCIP_1.Verify(x₁, Trans_1) = 1 then
20     return 1
21  else return 0
```

Fig. 5. In this figure, we construct an NIP system $\Pi = (\text{Setup}, \text{Prove}, \text{Verif})$, which is an OR-composition to prove that $x_0 \in \mathcal{L}_0 \vee x_1 \in \mathcal{L}_1$. We recall that all challenge spaces are considered as an additive group. Namely, for all operations in the i-th round of PCIP_b are modulo $Z_{\ell_i,b}$.

Theorem 1 (Correctness). *If PCIP_0 and PCIP_1 are both ρ-correct and Δ-HVZK, then Π is $2\rho + \Delta$-correct.*

Proof. We can observe that in the resulting proof π, we have randomly chosen a bit b, and the proof π can be divided into two parts (π_0, π_1), where $\pi_b = (\{R_{i,b}\}^{n_b}_{i=1}, A_b, s_b)$ is an honestly generated proof of PCIP_b with correctness error at most ρ, and π_{1-b} is a simulated transcript of PCIP_{1-b} with correctness error at most $\rho + \Delta$. Therefore, by the union bound over the correctness of π_0 and π_1, we have π has correctness error at most $2\rho + \Delta$.   □

Theorem 2 (Witness-Indistinguishability). *If PCIP_0 and PCIP_1 are two Δ-HVZK (n_0, n_1)-rounds public-coin interactive proofs for the language $\mathcal{L}_0$ and $\mathcal{L}_1$ respectively, then Π is 2Δ-Witness-Indistinguishable. Namely, given a statement $x = (x_0, x_1)$ such that $x_0 \in_{w_0} \mathcal{L}_0 \wedge x_1 \in_{w_1} \mathcal{L}_1$, the statistical distance between the proof generated using w_0 and the one generated using w_1 is at most 2Δ.*

Theorem 3 (Adaptive Soundness). *For $b \in \{0, 1\}$, let PCIP_b be an n_b-round round-by-round ε'-sound interactive protocol, then Π is $(t, \varepsilon, \mathsf{Q_H})$-adaptively sound, where*

$$t = \mathsf{poly}(\lambda), \qquad \varepsilon \le (\mathsf{Q_H} + 2n)^2 \cdot n \cdot \varepsilon',$$

with $n = max(n_0, n_1)$.

Proof. Assuming $\mathcal{A}$ a PPT adversary, running in polynomial time t, wins the adaptive soundness game within probability ε by generating a valid OR-proof π for $(\mathbf{x}_0, \mathbf{x}_1)$ where $\mathbf{x}_0 \notin \mathcal{L}_0$ and $\mathbf{x}_1 \notin \mathcal{L}_1$,

$$\pi = (\{\mathsf{R}_{i,0}\}_{i=1}^{n_0}, \{\mathsf{R}_{i,1}\}_{i=1}^{n_1}, \mathsf{A}_0, \mathsf{A}_1, \mathsf{s}_0, \mathsf{s}_1).$$

Moreover, we can compute $\mathsf{A}_0 = (a_{1,0}, \ldots, a_{n_0,0})$, $\mathsf{A}_1 = (a_{1,1}, \ldots, a_{n_1,1})$, and $h_{i,b} = \mathsf{H}(\{\mathsf{R}_{j,b}\}_{j=1}^{i}, \mathsf{A}_{1-b}) + a_{i,b}$. We give the security proof via a sequence of games:

- **Game$_0$** : The **Game$_0$** is the original adaptive soundness game.
- **Game$_1$** : In this game, we assume that for $i_0 \in [n_0], i_1 \in [n_1]$, all the queries of the form $(\{\mathsf{R}_{i,0}\}_{j=1}^{i_0}, \mathsf{A}_1)$ and $(\{\mathsf{R}_{i,1}\}_{j=1}^{i_1}, \mathsf{A}_0)$ have been queried to the random oracle. Remind that if the adversary $\mathcal{A}$ does not fulfil this condition, we can construct a new adversary $\mathcal{B}$ that additionally makes the above two queries with the same running time and winning probability against the adaptive soundness game. Therefore, we have $\mathsf{Adv}_0 = \mathsf{Adv}_1$, but the number of queries has slightly increased $\mathsf{Q}'_\mathsf{H} = \mathsf{Q_H} + n_0 + n_1$.

Analysis of the Winning Probability Adv_1 *of* $\mathcal{A}$ *in* **Game$_1$**. We define the bit $b \in \{0, 1\}$ such that there is a random oracle query of the form $(\cdot, \mathsf{A}_b)$ happens before any query of the form $(\cdot, \mathsf{A}_{1-b})$.

Since π is a valid proof, we have for $i \in [n_b]$ that $h_{i,b} = \mathsf{H}(\{\mathsf{R}_{j,b}\}_{j=1}^{j}, \mathsf{A}_{1-b}) + a_{i,b}$. Note that in the proof given by the adversary is of the form $\pi = (\pi_0, \pi_1)$ where any query of the form $(\cdot, \mathsf{A}_{1-b})$ happens after a query of the form $(\cdot, \mathsf{A}_b)$. Therefore, the adversary $\mathcal{A}$ can only choose at most $\mathsf{Q_H} + 2n$ different offsets as A_b. Moreover, for all $i \in [n_b]$, given $\{\mathsf{R}_{j,b}\}_{j=1}^{i}$ and $\mathsf{A}_b = (\{a_{j,b}\}_{j=1}^{n_b})$, there are at most $\mathsf{Q_H} + 2n$ different challenge values $h_{i,b} := \mathsf{H}(\{\mathsf{R}_{j,b}\}_{j=1}^{i}, \mathsf{A}_{1-b}) + a_{i,b}$ depending on the choice of A_{1-b}. Thus, the adversary has in total at most $(\mathsf{Q_H} + 2n)^2$ choices of $h_{i,b}$

We emphasize that the output distribution of the random oracle is uniformly random. Therefore, the distribution of $h_{i_b,b}$ conditioned on the choice of $\mathsf{A}_b, \mathsf{A}_{1-b}$ is still uniformly random by using the One-Time Pad argument.

We recall that, for the round-by-round ε-soundness, for all $j \in [n_b]$, given the prover's messages $(\{\mathsf{R}_{i,0}\}_{i=1}^{j})$, if the challenge is selected uniformly, the partial transcript has probability $1 - \varepsilon$ to be "doomed". The adversary has $(\mathsf{Q_H} + 2n)^2$ choices over $(\mathsf{A}_b, \mathsf{A}_{1-b})$. On the other hand, the total transcript is in the "doomed set" with probability $1 - (1 - \varepsilon')^n \le n \cdot \varepsilon'$. Therefore, we have that the success probability for the adversary in finding a pair of $(\mathsf{A}_b, \mathsf{A}_{1-b})$ such that the transcript of the side b is not doomed is at most $(\mathsf{Q_H} + 2n)^2 \cdot n \cdot \varepsilon'$.

Summarizing all the hybrid games, we have

$$t = \mathsf{poly}(\lambda), \qquad \varepsilon \le (\mathsf{Q_H} + 2n)^2 \cdot n \cdot \varepsilon'.$$

$\square$

3.2   Adaptively Sound Non-Interactive Zero-Knowledge Proof

We follow the same framework of [15] for defining a transform from n-round interactive proof systems to NIZK: we use our OR-composition in Sect. 3.1 to let the prover combine the interactive proof system with a proof of hard membership problem.

Since the transform of [15] (and ours) makes use of a membership-hard language $\mathcal{L}$, let us first define it in Definition 7.

Definition 7 (NP **membership problem**[29])**.** *A language $\mathcal{L}$ is a $(t, \varepsilon_{\mathcal{L}})$-hard NP membership language if there exists a PPT sampler $\mathcal{S} = (\mathcal{S}_0, \mathcal{S}_1)$ such that for every PPT distinguisher $\mathcal{D}$, running in polynomial time t, we have*

$$\left| \Pr\left[\mathcal{D}(\mathcal{S}_0(1^\lambda), 1^\lambda) = 1 \right] - \Pr\left[\mathcal{D}(\mathcal{S}_1(1^\lambda), 1^\lambda) = 1 \right] \right| \le \varepsilon_{\mathcal{L}},$$

where $\mathcal{S}$ behaves as follows

- *$\mathcal{S}_0(1^\lambda)$ samples $(\mathbf{x}_0, \mathbf{w}_0) \xleftarrow{\$} \mathcal{L}$, and returns $\mathbf{x}_0$.*
- *$\mathcal{S}_1(1^\lambda)$ samples $\mathbf{x}_1 \xleftarrow{\$} \{0,1\}^\lambda \setminus \mathcal{L}$, and returns $\mathbf{x}_1$.*

Transform from Interactive to Non-Interactive. Given a language $\mathcal{L}_0$ and an instance $\mathbf{x}_0 \in_{\mathbf{w}_0} \mathcal{L}_0$, our goal is to prove that $\mathbf{x}_0 \in \mathcal{L}_0$ without leaking any additional information about $\mathbf{w}_0$. We follow the same overall framework as [15] by adding a membership-hard langage $\mathcal{L}_1$ together with an instance $\mathbf{x}_1 \in \mathcal{L}_1$, then the NIZK proof consists of a proof that $\mathbf{x}_0 \in \mathcal{L}_0 \vee \mathbf{x}_1 \in \mathcal{L}_1$, and $(\mathbf{x}_1, \mathcal{L}_1)$ is the CRS of the NIZK proof system. We give below some intuitions behind the soundness and the zero-knowledge property of this general construction.

- **Soundness:** As $\mathcal{L}_1$ is a membership-hard problem, we can switch $\mathbf{x}_1 \in_{\mathbf{w}_1} \mathcal{L}_1$ into $\mathbf{x}_1' \in \{0,1\}^\lambda \setminus \mathcal{L}_1$ without the adversary noticing it. Since $\mathbf{x}_1' \in \{0,1\}^\lambda \setminus \mathcal{L}_1$, a valid proof π for the fact that $\mathbf{x}_0 \in \mathcal{L}_0 \vee \mathbf{x}_1' \in \mathcal{L}_1$ directly implies that $\mathbf{x}_0 \in \mathcal{L}_0$.
- **Zero-Knowledge:** We can simulate every proof using $\mathbf{w}_1$ instead of $\mathbf{w}_0$. By the witness-indistinguishability of the OR-proof, this change is oblivious for the adversary. This proves the zero-knowledge property of the NIZK proof system.

Formally, let PCIP_0 be a (k, ℓ)-sound n_0-round interactive proof system for the NP language $\mathcal{L}_0$. We will consider a $(t, \varepsilon_{\mathcal{L}})$-hard NP membership $\mathcal{L}_1$ and its associated interactive proof system PCIP_1. Let Π denote the NIWI scheme obtained by applying the OR-composition from Sect. 3.1 to PCIP_0 and PCIP_1. We give the explicit transform from an IP protocol PCIP_0 to a NIZK scheme Σ in Fig. 6.

The correctness of Σ is straightforward from Theorem 1:

Theorem 4 (Correctness). *If PCIP_0 and PCIP_1 are both at least ρ-correct and Δ-HVZK, then Σ is $2\rho + \Delta$-correct.*

Theorem 5 (Zero-Knowledge). *If PCIP_0 and PCIP_1 are both Δ-HVZK multi-round (n_0, n_1 rounds respectively) interactive protocols, then Σ is 2Δ-Zero-Knowledge.*

Proof. Since we have $\mathbf{x}_1 \in_{\mathbf{w}_1} \mathcal{L}_1$, we can use $\mathbf{w}_1$ to compute the NIWI proof, which simulates an honestly generated proof with statistical distance at most 2Δ by Theorem 2. $\qquad \square$

Setup(1^λ):	Prove(CRS, $\mathbf{x}_0$, $\mathbf{w}_0$):
01 $(\mathbf{x}_1, \mathbf{w}_1) \xleftarrow{\$} \mathcal{L}_1$	04 $\pi \xleftarrow{\$} \Pi.\text{Prove}((\mathbf{x}_0, \text{CRS}), \mathbf{w}_0)$
02 CRS := $\mathbf{x}_1$	05 return π
03 return CRS	Verif(CRS, $\mathbf{x}$, π):
	06 return $\Pi.\text{Verif}((\mathbf{x}, \text{CRS}), \pi)$

Fig. 6. Transform from an optimal-sound interactive protocol PCIP_0 into adaptively sound NIZK scheme Σ.

Theorem 6 (Adaptive Soundness). *For $b \in \{0,1\}$, let PCIP_b be a ε_b-Round-By-Round sound n_b-round interactive protocol such that PCIP_1 is the interactive proof associated to a $(t', \varepsilon'_\mathcal{L})$-hard NP membership language $\mathcal{L}_1$, then Σ is (t, ε, Q_H)-adaptively sound, where*

$$t \approx t', \qquad\qquad \varepsilon \leq (Q_H + 2n)^2 \cdot n \cdot \varepsilon' + \varepsilon'_\mathcal{L},$$

with $\varepsilon' = max(\varepsilon_0, \varepsilon_1)$ and $n = max(n_0, n_1)$.

Proof. We will give a simple game-based proof of this theorem. There are only 2 hybrids described as in Fig. 7.

$\text{Exp}_{\text{AdSnd}}(1^\lambda)$:		$\mathcal{O}_{Hash}(R)$:
01 $(\mathbf{x}_1, \mathbf{w}_1) \xleftarrow{\$} \mathcal{L}_1$	//**Game**$_0$	08 $h \xleftarrow{\$} \mathcal{C}$
02 $\mathbf{x}_1 \xleftarrow{\$} \{0,1\}^\lambda \setminus \mathcal{L}_1$	//**Game**$_1$	09 return h
03 CRS := $\mathbf{x}_1$		
04 $(\mathbf{x}^\star, \pi^\star) \xleftarrow{\$} \mathcal{A}^{\mathcal{O}_{Hash}}(\text{CRS})$		
05 if $\mathbf{x}^\star \in \{0,1\}^n \setminus \mathcal{L}_0 \wedge \text{Verif}(\text{CRS}, \mathbf{x}^\star, \pi^\star) = 1$ then		
06 return 1		
07 else return 0		

Fig. 7. The security games for proving the adaptive soundness of Σ. The line commented with **Game**$_i$ is the pseudo-code that only exists in i-th hybrid.

The **Game**$_0$ is the original security game for the adaptive soundness of Σ. In game **Game**$_1$, the only difference is that $\mathbf{x}_1$ in CRS is chosen from the set $\{0,1\}^\lambda \setminus \mathcal{L}_1$. Therefore, we have

$$\text{Adv}_0 = \varepsilon, \qquad\qquad |\text{Adv}_1 - \text{Adv}_0| \leq \varepsilon'_\mathcal{L}.$$

where Adv_0 (respectively Adv_1) is the advantage of $\mathcal{A}$ in game **Game**$_0$ (respectively **Game**$_1$). Moreover, in **Game**$_1$, since $\mathbf{x}_1$ is not in $\mathcal{L}_1$ and $\mathbf{x}_0$ is neither in $\mathcal{L}_0$, π is a valid attack for the underlying NIWI scheme. Therefore, we have $\text{Adv}_1 \leq (Q_H + 2n)^2 \cdot n \cdot \varepsilon'$ from Theorem 3. Combining hybrids together we have $t \approx t'$ and

$$\varepsilon \leq (Q_H + 2n)^2 \cdot n \cdot \varepsilon' + \varepsilon'_\mathcal{L}.$$

$\square$

4   Security of Our Transform in the Quantum Random Oracle Model

In this section, we give a security proof of our OR-composition from two public-coin interactive proofs (n_0-round and n_1-round respectively) into one NIZK in the quantum random oracle model. Note that we can straightforwardly extend our proof in the QROM to our transform from PCIP to NIZK as described in Sect. 3.2.

While it is an important achievement to prove security in the QROM for post-quantum primitives, there is a price that one has to pay. One drawback is that there is a significant loss in the security argument. The second one is related to the programmability of the random oracle: proofs that were in the NPROM in the classical setting now need the quantum random oracle to be programmable in the security reduction. The last one is that we cannot prove our transform for round-by-round sound PCIP with acceptable security loss (polynomial in the number of rounds), due to the fact that we need to reprogram every round to fulfill a reduction, which introduces a exponential security loss in the number of rounds. Therefore, we limit our transform to optimal-sound PCIP protocols. Firstly, we introduce the notion of answerable challenge and provide the formal definition of optimal-soundness.

Definition 8 (Answerable Challenges). *Let* $\mathsf{Ans}(\mathsf{Trans}_i, \mathsf{h}_i)$ *be a function that takes a partial transcript until i-th round* $\mathsf{Trans}_i = (\{\mathsf{R}_j, \mathsf{h}_j\}_{j=1}^{i-1}, \mathsf{R}_i)$ *and a challenge* h_i *as input, and returns 1 if there exists* $\mathsf{Trans}' = (\{\mathsf{R}_j, \mathsf{h}_j\}_{j=i+1}^{n}, \mathsf{s})$ *such that* $(\mathsf{Trans}_i, \mathsf{h}_i, \mathsf{Trans}')$ *is a valid transcript and 0 otherwise. We say that a challenge h_i is an **answerable challenge** for round i if* $\mathsf{Ans}(\mathsf{Trans}_i, \mathsf{h}_i) = 1$.

We emphasize that the function Ans *can be a non-efficiently computable function here.*

Definition 9 (Optimal Soundness). *Let $\mathcal{L}$ be an NP language, we say that PCIP is (k, ℓ, i)-optimal sound if, for all statement not in the language* $\mathbf{x} \notin \mathcal{L}$, *and for all partial transcripts* $\mathsf{Trans}_i = (\{\mathsf{R}_j, \mathsf{h}_j\}_{j=1}^{i-1}, \mathsf{R}_i)$ *there exist at most k answerable challenges* $\{\mathsf{h}_i^{(j)}\}_{j\in[\mathsf{k}]}$ *such that* $\mathsf{Ans}(\mathsf{Trans}_i, \mathsf{h}_i^{(j)}) = 1$ *for all* $j \in [\mathsf{k}]$ *and the size of the i-th challenge space is at least 2^{ℓ}.*

We note that, the optimal soundness is implied by the special soundness which is the case for most PCIP protocols. Moreover optimal soundness straightforwardly imply the negligible soundness, while the latter one is equivalent to the round-by-round soundness in our case. Thus, limiting our transform to the PCIPs with optimal soundness is indeed a restriction.

We will use the measure-and-reprogram 2.0 technique proposed in [19] and we apply it to our NIZK transform in the same way that [19] apply it for proving sequential-OR proof. Firstly, we give a quick overview of the measure-and-reprogram 2.0 technique proposed in [19].

Measure-and-Reprogram 2.0, Multiple Input [19]. Let $\mathcal{A}$ be a quantum adversary that has Q_H quantum queries to a random oracle $H : \mathcal{X} \to \mathcal{Y}$, where $\mathcal{X}, \mathcal{Y}$ are both finite non-empty sets. Assuming that for a predicate (possibly quantum and not efficiently computable) Γ, the adversary $\mathcal{A}$ can output in polynomial time t a transcript $\text{Trans} = (X_0, \ldots, X_{n-1}, z)$ such that $\Gamma(\text{Trans}, H(X_0), \ldots, H(X_{n-1})) = \text{True}$.

The goal is to build a multi-stage simulator $\mathcal{R}^{\mathcal{A}}$ such that stage by stage it outputs X_i's and takes the corresponding Θ_i's as input and finally outputs a (possibly quantum) z such that for the same predicate we have $\Gamma(X_0, \ldots, X_{n-1}, z, \Theta_0, \ldots, \Theta_{n-1}) = \text{True}$.

Don et al. [19] showed the existence of a quantum adversary $\mathcal{R}^{\mathcal{A}}$ that proceeds as follows: Firstly, it outputs a permutation σ together with a hash input $\mathbf{x}_{\sigma(0)}$ and it takes as input $\Theta_{\sigma(0)}$ from a third party $\mathcal{V}$. Then for every stage $0 < i \leq n - 1$, $\mathcal{R}^{\mathcal{A}}$ outputs a hash input $\mathbf{x}_{\sigma(i)}$ and it takes as input $\Theta_{\sigma(i)}$ from $\mathcal{V}$. Finally, it outputs a possibly quantum z. We denote this procedure as $(\sigma, \sigma(X), z) \xleftarrow{\$} \langle \mathcal{R}^{\mathcal{A}}, \sigma(\Theta) \rangle$, where $X = (X_0, \ldots, X_{n-1})$ and $\Theta = (\Theta_0, \ldots, \Theta_{n-1})$. In the special case of PCIP protocols, $\mathcal{V}$ refers to the verifier.

More precisely, we have the following theorem:

Theorem 7 ([19, **Theorem 6**]). *Let $\mathcal{X}$ and $\mathcal{Y}$ be the input and output sets of the hash function $H : \mathcal{X} \to \mathcal{Y}$. Let $\mathcal{A}$ be a polynomial time oracle quantum algorithm that makes Q_H random oracle queries to H and outputs an n-dimensional vector $X = (X_0, \ldots, X_{n-1})$ and a possibly quantum z. There exists a $(n + 1)$-stage quantum algorithm $\mathcal{R}^{\mathcal{A}}$ that behaves as described above, satisfying the following property: For any $X^{\star} \in \mathcal{X}^n$ without duplicate entries and for any predicate (possibly quantum and not efficiently computable) Γ, and a third party $\mathcal{V}$, we have:*

$$\Pr\left[\begin{matrix} X = X^{\star} \wedge \\ \Gamma(X, \Theta, z) \end{matrix} \;\middle|\; (\sigma, \sigma(X), z) \xleftarrow{\$} \langle \mathcal{R}^{\mathcal{A}}, \sigma(\Theta) \rangle \right]$$
$$\geq \frac{1}{(2Q_H + 1)^{2n}} \cdot \Pr\left[\begin{matrix} X = X^{\star} \wedge \\ \Gamma(X, H(X), z) \end{matrix} \;\middle|\; (X, z) \xleftarrow{\$} \mathcal{A}(1^{\lambda}) \right] \quad (3)$$

Application to Our Zero-Knowledge Proof. Formally, given a n_0-round PCIP_0 and a n_1-round PCIP_1, for languages $\mathcal{L}_0$ and $\mathcal{L}_1$ respectively. We proposed a non-interactive proof of the form $\pi_{\mathsf{V}} = (A_0, A_1, \{R_{i,0}\}_{i=0}^{n_0}, \{R_{i,1}\}_{i=1}^{n_1}, s_0, s_1)$ for the language $\mathcal{L}_{\mathsf{V}} = \{(\mathbf{x}_0, \mathbf{x}_1) : \mathbf{x}_0 \in \mathcal{L}_0 \vee \mathbf{x}_1 \in \mathcal{L}_1\}$.

We assume that for $b \in \{0, 1\}$, the interactive protocol PCIP_b is (k_b, ℓ_b, i_b)-optimal sound, and we have $i_b^{\star}$ such that given the first $i_b^{\star}$ elements $R_{1,b}, \ldots, R_{i_b^{\star}, b}$, there are only k_b answerable challenges. This property is captured by the answerable predicates given in the optimal soundness $\text{Ans}_b(R_{1,b}, \ldots, R_{i_b^{\star}, b}, h_{i_b^{\star}, b})$.

Theorem 8. *For $b \in \{0, 1\}$, let PCIP_b be a (k, ℓ, i_b)-optimal sound n_b-round interactive protocol Let Π_{V} be the non-interactive zero-knowledge proof given by applying our transform in Sect. 3.1. Any quantum adversary $\mathcal{A}$ running in time t, making Q_H quantum random oracle, breaks the adaptive soundness of Π_{V} with probability at most $\frac{k}{2^{\ell}} \cdot (2Q_H + 1)^4$.*

Proof. Assuming $\mathcal{A}$ is a quantum adversary making Q_H quantum random oracle queries against the adaptive soundness of Π_V. By the definition of adaptive soundness, given two false statements $x_0 \notin \mathcal{L}_0$ and $x_1 \notin \mathcal{L}_1$, $\mathcal{A}$ can generate a valid proof $\pi_V = (A_0, A_1, \{R_{i,0}\}_{i=1}^{n_0}, \{R_{i,1}\}_{i=1}^{n_1}, s_0, s_1)$ with non-negligible advantage. For simplicity, we denote the challenge by,

$$h_{i,b} := H(\{R_{j,b}\}_{j=1}^i, A_{1-b}) + a_{i,b}. \tag{4}$$

Note that, in our non-interactive proof construction $h_{i,b}$ is used as the challenges in the underlying interactive protocols. Since π_V is a valid proof, for $b \in \{0,1\}$, and $i \in [n_b]$, we have $\mathsf{Ans}_b(\{R_{j,b}\}_{j=1}^i, h_{j,b}) = \mathsf{True}$.

For our convenience, we will consider an adversary $\mathcal{A}'$ that proceeds exactly like $\mathcal{A}$, except that it only outputs a partial proof $\pi' = (\{R_{i,0}\}_{i=1}^{i_0^*}, A_1, \{R_{i,1}\}_{i=1}^{i_1^*}, A_0)$. For more compact notation, we denote $X_b = (\{R_{i,b}\}_{i=1}^{i_b^*}, A_{1-b})$ for $b \in \{0,1\}$. We also define a predicate Γ as follows:

$$\Gamma((X_0, X_1), (H(X_0), H(X_1))) = \mathsf{Ans}_0(\{R_{i,0}\}_{i=1}^{i_0^*}, h_{i_0^*,0}) \wedge \mathsf{Ans}_1(\{R_{i,1}\}_{i=1}^{i_1^*}, h_{i_1^*,1}).$$

Here, we recall that $h_{i_b^*,b}$ can be computed by using $\pi', H(X_0), H(X_1)$ as in Equation (4). By the definition of the answerable challenge predicate, assuming a valid proof π_V, the corresponding partial proof $\pi' = (X_0, X_1)$ verifies that $\Gamma((X_0, X_1), (H(X_0), H(X_1))) = \mathsf{True}$.

Now, it is easy to see that $(\mathcal{A}', \Gamma)$ fits into the requirement of Theorem 7. By simply applying Theorem 7, for all (X_0^*, X_1^*), two uniformly chosen Θ_0, Θ_1 and two instances (x_0, x_1), we have an adversary $\mathcal{B}$ such that:

$$\Pr\begin{bmatrix} X_0 = X_0^* \wedge \\ X_1 = X_1^* \wedge \\ \Gamma((X_0, X_1), (\Theta_0, \Theta_1)) \end{bmatrix} (\sigma, \sigma(X_0, X_1), \bot) \xleftarrow{\$} \langle \mathcal{B}(x_0, x_1), \sigma(\Theta_0, \Theta_1) \rangle \end{bmatrix}$$

$$\geq \frac{1}{(2Q_H + 1)^4} \cdot \Pr\begin{bmatrix} X_0 = X_0^* \wedge \\ X_1 = X_1^* \wedge \\ \Gamma((X_0, X_1), (H(X_0), H(X_1))) \end{bmatrix} (X_0, X_1, \bot) \xleftarrow{\$} \mathcal{A}'^H(x_0, x_1) \end{bmatrix}. \tag{5}$$

In the final step, we will construct an adversary $\mathcal{C}$ that helps us to choose (Θ_0, Θ_1). More precisely, we describe the behavior of $\mathcal{C}$ as in Fig. 8.

Note that the left side of Equation (5) can be bounded by $\frac{k}{2^\ell}$. More precisely, since we have $\Gamma((X_0, X_1), (\Theta_0, \Theta_1)) = \mathsf{True}$, we have also $\mathsf{Ans}_b(X_b, h_b) = \mathsf{True}$. But, the challenge h_b is chosen uniformly random by an honest verifier $\mathsf{Verifier}_b$ in line 09 Fig. 8. Therefore $\Pr[\mathsf{Ans}_b(X_b, h_b)] \leq \frac{k}{2^\ell}$ by the optimal soundness. Combining this upper bound with Eq. 5, we have the probability of $\mathcal{A}$ breaking the adaptive soundness of Π_V is at most $\frac{k}{2^\ell} \cdot (2Q_H + 1)^4$. □

$$\underline{\mathcal{C}(\mathbf{x} \notin \mathcal{L})}:$$

```
01  (σ, X_{σ(0)}, st) ←$ B₁(x₀, x₁)
02  b ← σ(1)
03  x_b := x;  L_b := L;  Verifier_b := Verifier
04  x_{1-b} ←$ {0,1}*;  L_{1-b} ←$ {0,1}*
05  Θ_{σ(0)} ←$ Y
06  (X_{σ(1)}, st) ←$ B₂(Θ_{σ(0)}, st)
07  parse (R_{1,σ(1)}, ..., R_{i_{σ(1)},σ(1)}, A_{σ(1)}) =: X_{σ(1)}
08  parse (a_{1,σ(1)}, ..., a_{n_{σ(1)},σ(1)}) =: A_{σ(1)}
09  h_{σ(1)} ←$ Verifier_{σ(1)}(X_{σ(1)})
10  Θ_{σ(1)} := h_{σ(1)} − a_{i_{σ(1)},σ(1)}
11  ⊥ ←$ B₃(Θ_{σ(1)}, st)
12  return (X_{σ(1)}, h_{σ(1)}, Θ₀, Θ₁)
```

Fig. 8. Assuming PCIP_0 and PCIP_1 are (k, ℓ, i)-optimal sound, we give the description of the adversary $\mathcal{C}$ which interacts with the verifier Verifier of the underlying PCIP. Note that $\mathcal{B} = (\mathcal{B}_1, \mathcal{B}_2, \mathcal{B}_3)$ is a 3-stage algorithm with an internal state st.

Acknowledgement. We thank the anonymous reviewers of Asiacrypt 2022 and PKC 2023 for their many insightful suggestions to improve our paper.

This work is supported by the National Key Research and Development Program of China (Grant No. 2018YFA0704702), the Major Basic Research Project of Natural Science Foundation of Shandong Province, China (Grant No. ZR202010220025). This work is also supported by the PEPR quantique France 2030 programme (ANR-22-PETQ-0008),and by the ANR ASTRID project AMIRAL (ANR-21-ASTR-0016). This work was carried out in the context of Beyond5G, a project funded by the French government as part of the economic recovery plan, namely "France Relance", and the investments for the future program. Adela Georgescu was partly funded by the Direction Générale de l'Armement (Pôle de Recherche CYBER), with the support of Région Bretagne.

References

1. Abe, M., Ohkubo, M., Suzuki, K.: 1-out-of-n signatures from a variety of keys. In: Zheng, Y. (ed.) ASIACRYPT 2002. LNCS, vol. 2501, pp. 415–432. Springer, Heidelberg (2002)

2. Bellare, M., Rogaway, P.: Random oracles are practical: A paradigm for designing efficient protocols. In: Denning, D.E., Pyle, R., Ganesan, R., Sandhu, R.S., Ashby, V. editors, ACM CCS 93, pp. 62–73. ACM Press, November (1993)

3. Bellare, M., Rogaway, P.: The security of triple encryption and a framework for code-based game-playing proofs. In: Vaudenay, S. (ed.) EUROCRYPT 2006. LNCS, vol. 4004, pp. 409–426. Springer, Heidelberg (2006). https://doi.org/10.1007/11761679_25

4. Bootle, J., Lyubashevsky, V.: Ngoc Khanh Nguyen, and Gregor Seiler. More efficient amortization of exact zero-knowledge proofs for LWE. In: Bertino, E., Shulman, H., Waidner, M. (eds.) ESORICS 2021. Part II, volume 12973 of LNCS, pp. 608–627. Springer, Heidelberg (2021)

5. Bootle, J., Lyubashevsky, V., Seiler, G.: Algebraic techniques for short(er) exact lattice-based zero-knowledge proofs. In: Boldyreva, A., Micciancio, D. (eds.) CRYPTO 2019. Part I, volume 11692 of LNCS, pp. 176–202. Springer, Heidelberg (2019)

6. Brakerski, Z., Koppula, V., Mour, T.: NIZK from LPN and trapdoor hash via correlation intractability for approximable relations. In: Micciancio, D., Ristenpart, T. (eds.) CRYPTO 2020. Part III, volume 12172 of LNCS, pp. 738–767. Springer, Heidelberg (2020)
7. Bünz, B., Bootle, J., Boneh, D., Poelstra, A., Wuille, P., Maxwell, G.: Bulletproofs: Short proofs for confidential transactions and more. In: 2018 IEEE Symposium on Security and Privacy, pp. 315–334. IEEE Computer Society Press, May (2018)
8. Canetti, R., et al.: Fiat-Shamir: from practice to theory. In: Moses Charikar and Edith Cohen, editors, 51st ACM STOC, pp. 1082–1090. ACM Press June (2019)
9. Canetti, R., Chen, Y., Reyzin, L., Rothblum, R.D.: Fiat-shamir and correlation intractability from strong KDM-secure encryption. In: Nielsen, J.B., Rijmen, V. (eds.) EUROCRYPT 2018. LNCS, vol. 10820, pp. 91–122. Springer, Cham (2018)
10. Canetti, R., Goldreich, O., Halevi, S.: On the random-oracle methodology as applied to length-restricted signature schemes. In: Naor, M. (ed.) TCC 2004. LNCS, vol. 2951, pp. 40–57. Springer, Heidelberg (2004)
11. Catalano, D., Visconti, I.: Hybrid commitments and their applications to zero-knowledge proof systems. Theor. Comput. Sci. **374**(1–3), 229–260 (2007)
12. Chaum, D.: Blind signature system. In: Chaum, D. (ed.) CRYPTO'83, page 153. Plenum Press, New York, USA (1983)
13. Chen, M.-S., Hülsing, A., Rijneveld, J., Samardjiska, S., Schwabe, P.: SOFIA: $\mathcal{MQ}$-based signatures in the QROM. In: Abdalla, M., Dahab, R. (eds.) PKC 2018. Part II, volume 10770 of LNCS, pp. 3–33. Springer, Heidelberg (2018)
14. Chen, Y., Lombardi, A., Ma, F., Quach, W.: Does fiat-shamir require a cryptographic hash function? In: Malkin, T., Peikert, C. (eds.) CRYPTO 2021. LNCS, vol. 12828, pp. 334–363. Springer, Cham (2021)
15. Ciampi, M., Persiano, G., Siniscalchi, L., Visconti, I.: A transform for NIZK almost as efficient and general as the Fiat-Shamir transform without programmable random oracles. In: Kushilevitz, E., Malkin, T. (eds.) TCC 2016-A. Part II, volume 9563 of LNCS, pp. 83–111. Springer, Heidelberg (2016)
16. Cramer, R., Damgård, I., Schoenmakers, B.: Proofs of partial knowledge and simplified design of witness hiding protocols. In: Desmedt, Y. (ed.) CRYPTO'94. LNCS, vol. 839, pp. 174–187. Springer, Heidelberg (1994)
17. Cramer, R., Gennaro, R., Schoenmakers, B.: A secure and optimally efficient multi-authority election scheme. In: Fumy, W. (ed.) EUROCRYPT'97. LNCS, vol. 1233, pp. 103–118. Springer, Heidelberg (1997)
18. De Santis, A., Micali, S., Persiano, G.: Non-interactive zero-knowledge proof systems. In: Pomerance, C. (ed.) CRYPTO'87. LNCS, vol. 293, pp. 52–72. Springer, Heidelberg (1988)
19. Don, J., Fehr, S., Majenz, C.: The measure-and-reprogram technique 2.0: Multi-round fiat-shamir and more. In: Micciancio, D., Ristenpart, T. (eds.) CRYPTO 2020. Part III, volume 12172 of LNCS, pp. 602–631. Springer, Heidelberg (2020)
20. Don, J., Fehr, S., Majenz, C., Schaffner, C.: Security of the Fiat-Shamir transformation in the quantum random-oracle model. In: Boldyreva, A., Micciancio, D. (eds.) CRYPTO 2019. Part II, volume 11693 of LNCS, pp. 356–383. Springer, Heidelberg (2019)
21. Esgin, M.F., Nguyen, N.K., Seiler, G.: Practical exact proofs from lattices: New techniques to exploit fully-splitting rings. In: Moriai, S., Wang, H. (eds.) ASIACRYPT 2020. Part II, volume 12492 of LNCS, pp. 259–288. Springer, Heidelberg (2020). https://doi.org/10.1007/978-3-030-64834-3_9
22. Feige,U., Fiat, A., Shamir, A.: Zero knowledge proofs of identity. In: Aho, A., editor, 19th ACM STOC, pp. 210–217. ACM Press, May (1987)
23. Fiat, A., Shamir, A.: How to prove yourself: practical solutions to identification and signature problems. In: Odlyzko, A.M. (ed.) CRYPTO'86. LNCS, vol. 263, pp. 186–194. Springer, Heidelberg (1987)

24. Fischlin, M., Harasser, P., Janson, C.: Signatures from sequential-OR proofs. In: Canteaut, A., Ishai, Y. (eds.) EUROCRYPT 2020. Part III, volume 12107 of LNCS, pp. 212–244. Springer, Heidelberg (2020)

25. Goldreich, O., Micali, S., Wigderson, A.: How to play any mental game or A completeness theorem for protocols with honest majority. In: Aho, A., editor, 19th ACM STOC, pp. 218–229. ACM Press, May (1987)

26. Groth, J., Sahai, A.: Efficient non-interactive proof systems for bilinear groups. In: Smart, N.P. (ed.) EUROCRYPT 2008. LNCS, vol. 4965, pp. 415–432. Springer, Heidelberg (2008)

27. Katsumata, S.: A new simple technique to bootstrap various lattice zero-knowledge proofs to QROM secure NIZKs. In: Malkin, T., Peikert, C. (eds.) CRYPTO 2021. LNCS, vol. 12826, pp. 580–610. Springer, Cham (2021). https://doi.org/10.1007/978-3-030-84245-1_20

28. Kim, S., David, J.W.: Multi-theorem preprocessing NIZKs from lattices. In: Shacham, H., Boldyreva, A. (eds.) CRYPTO 2018. Part II, volume 10992 of LNCS, pp. 733–765. Springer, Heidelberg (2018)

29. Lindell, Y.: An efficient transform from sigma protocols to NIZK with a CRS and non-programmable random oracle. In: Dodis, Y., Nielsen, J.B. (eds.) TCC 2015. LNCS, vol. 9014, pp. 93–109. Springer, Heidelberg (2015)

30. Liu, Q., Zhandry, M.: Revisiting post-quantum Fiat-Shamir. In: Boldyreva, A., Micciancio, D. (eds.) CRYPTO 2019. Part II, volume 11693 of LNCS, pp. 326–355. Springer, Heidelberg (2019)

31. Lombardi, A., Quach, W., Rothblum, R.D., Wichs, D., David, J.W.: New constructions of reusable designated-verifier NIZKs. In: Boldyreva, A., Micciancio, D. (eds.) CRYPTO 2019. Part III, volume 11694 of LNCS, pp. 670–700. Springer, Heidelberg (2019)

32. Lyubashevsky, V.: Fiat-Shamir with aborts: applications to lattice and factoring-based signatures. In: Matsui, M. (ed.) ASIACRYPT 2009. LNCS, vol. 5912, pp. 598–616. Springer, Heidelberg (2009)

33. Naor, M., Yung, M.: Public-key cryptosystems provably secure against chosen ciphertext attacks. In: 22nd ACM STOC, pp. 427–437. ACM Press, May (1990)

34. Peikert, C., Shiehian, S.: Noninteractive zero knowledge for NP from (plain) learning with errors. In: Boldyreva, A., Micciancio, D. (eds.) CRYPTO 2019. Part I, volume 11692 of LNCS, pp. 89–114. Springer, Heidelberg (2019)

35. Stevens, M., Bursztein, E., Karpman, P., Albertini, A., Markov, Y.: The first collision for full SHA-1. In: Katz, J., Shacham, H. (eds.) CRYPTO 2017. Part I, volume 10401 of LNCS, pp. 570–596. Springer, Heidelberg (2017)

36. Stevens, M., Lenstra, A.K., de Weger, B.: Chosen-prefix collisions for MD5 and colliding X.509 certificates for different identities. In: Naor, M. (ed.) EUROCRYPT 2007. LNCS, vol. 4515, pp. 1–22. Springer, Heidelberg (2007)

37. Unruh, D.: Non-interactive zero-knowledge proofs in the quantum random oracle model. In: Oswald, E., Fischlin, M. (eds.) EUROCRYPT 2015. Part II, volume 9057 of LNCS, pp. 755–784. Springer, Heidelberg (2015)

38. Wang, X., Hongbo, Yu.: How to break MD5 and other hash functions. In: Cramer, R. (ed.) EUROCRYPT 2005. LNCS, vol. 3494, pp. 19–35. Springer, Heidelberg (2005)

Fine-Grained Verifier NIZK and Its Applications

Xiangyu Liu[1,2], Shengli Liu[1,2,3(✉)], Shuai Han[1,2(✉)], and Dawu Gu[1]

[1] School of Electronic Information and Electrical Engineering,
Shanghai Jiao Tong University, Shanghai 200240, China
{xiangyu_liu,slliu,dalen17,dwgu}@sjtu.edu.cn
[2] State Key Laboratory of Cryptology, P.O. Box 5159, Beijing 100878, China
[3] Westone Cryptologic Research Center, Beijing 100070, China

Abstract. In this paper, we propose a new type of non-interactive zero-knowledge (NIZK), called *Fine-grained Verifier NIZK (FV-NIZK)*, which provides more flexible and more fine-grained verifiability of proofs than standard NIZK that supports public verifiability and designated-verifier NIZK (DV-NIZK) that supports private verifiability. FV-NIZK has two statistically equivalent verification approaches:

- a master verification using the master secret key msk;
- a fine-grained verification using a derived secret key sk_d, which is derived from msk w.r.t. d (which may stand for user identity, email address, vector, etc.).

We require *unbounded simulation soundness (USS)* of FV-NIZK to hold, even if an adversary obtains derived secret keys sk_d with d of its choices, and define *proof pseudorandomness* which stipulates the pseudorandomness of proofs for adversaries that are not given any secret key.

We present two instantiations of FV-NIZK for linear subspace languages, based on the matrix decisional Diffie-Hellman (MDDH) assumption. One of the FV-NIZK instantiations is *pairing-free* and achieves almost tight USS and proof pseudorandomness.

We illustrate the usefulness of FV-NIZK by showing two applications and obtain the following pairing-free schemes:

- the *first* almost tightly multi-challenge CCA (mCCA)-secure inner-product functional encryption (IPFE) scheme *without pairings*;
- the *first* public-key encryption (PKE) scheme that reconciles the inherent contradictions between public verifiability and anonymity. We formalize such PKE as *Fine-grained Verifiable PKE (FV-PKE)*, which derives a special key from the decryption secret key, such that for those who obtain the derived key, they can check the validity of ciphertexts but the anonymity is lost from their views (CCA-security still holds for them), while for others who do not get the derived key, they cannot do the validity check but the anonymity holds for them. Our FV-PKE scheme achieves almost tight mCCA-security for adversaries who obtain the derived keys, and achieves almost tight ciphertext pseudorandomness (thus anonymity) for others who do not get any derived key.

© International Association for Cryptologic Research 2023
A. Boldyreva and V. Kolesnikov (Eds.): PKC 2023, LNCS 13941, pp. 482–511, 2023.
https://doi.org/10.1007/978-3-031-31371-4_17

1   Introduction

NIZK with Unbounded Simulation Soundness (USS). Over decades, non-interactive zero-knowledge (NIZK) proofs have shown great power in constructing a variety of cryptographic primitives, e.g., public-key encryption (PKE) [14,27], digital signatures [7], etc. Towards better efficiency and shorter proofs, Jutla and Roy [23] defined a weaker notion called *quasi-adaptive* NIZK (QA-NIZK), where the common reference string (CRS) might depend on the specific language. In this paper, we will focus on quasi-adaptive NIZK and omit the term "quasi-adaptive" for simplicity.

One important security property for NIZK is *unbounded simulation soundness* (USS) [25,30], which plays an important role in many applications of NIZK, e.g., CCA-secure PKE [16,21], publicly verifiable CCA identity-based encryption (IBE) [22], structure preserving signatures [4,5], etc. Loosely speaking, USS requires the computational hardness for an adversary to generate a valid proof for an instance outside the language, even if the adversary has access to an oracle that outputs simulated proofs for instances (not necessarily in the language) of its choices.

Tight Security and NIZK with Tight USS. The security of a cryptographic primitive is usually proved via a reduction, which turns an adversary $\mathcal{A}$ that breaks the security of the primitive with running time t and advantage ϵ into an algorithm $\mathcal{B}$ that solves some hard problem with running time $t' \approx t$ and advantage ϵ'. Intuitively, we would desire ϵ' to be as large as ϵ. To reflect this, we define $L := \epsilon/\epsilon'$ as the security loss factor, which is the smaller the better. We call the reduction *tight* if L is a small constant or *almost tight* if L is linear (or even better, logarithmic) in the security parameter λ. For a loose reduction, L usually depends on $\mathcal{A}$'s behaviours, e.g., the number of $\mathcal{A}$'s queries, which can be as large as 2^{50} in practical settings.

Pursuing (almost) tight security has both theoretical and practical significance. For a scheme with a loose security reduction, the deployer has to choose larger security parameters to compensate the security loss, resulting in larger elements and lower efficiency. In contrast, schemes with (almost) tight security enjoy many advantages like universal key recommendations and more flexible choices of parameters. Recently, (almost) tight security has been explored in many areas, including PKE [16,17,20,21], signatures [8,19,21,24], IBE [9,11], etc.

In the scenario of NIZK, Libert et al. [25] proposed the first scheme with (almost) tight USS, and Gay et al. [16] gave a more efficient construction later. In both schemes, the size of the CRS (in terms of the number of group elements) is linear in λ. The first (almost) tightly secure NIZK with constant-size CRS was designed by Abe et al. [5]. Recently in [4], Abe et al. proposed a shorter NIZK with both constant-size CRS and proofs.

Designated-Verifier NIZK (DV-NIZK). Standard NIZK allows *public verification*, so that anyone who gets the CRS can verify the validity of proofs. Such a property is useful in certain applications, e.g., when constructing signature schemes [4,7], the public verifiability of signatures requires the public verifiability of NIZK proofs. However, in some other applications such as constructing CCA-secure PKE [12,16], public verification is not necessary, and in fact, a *designated-verifier* NIZK (DV-NIZK) [16] that supports only private verification of proofs is sufficient. Roughly speaking, DV-NIZK is the same as NIZK except that, the verification algorithm additionally takes a secret key sk as input, so that only the designated verifier can check the validity of proofs. Moreover, the secret key should be kept private, since otherwise the (simulation) soundness might not hold any more.

Compared to NIZK, DV-NIZK usually has more succinct and more efficient constructions, since it is only required to support private verification. For example, the efficient hash proof systems (HPS) in [12] can be viewed as DV-NIZKs. As another example, to the best of our knowledge, all NIZK schemes with tight USS (constructed in discrete-logarithm setting) relies on bilinear pairings to support public verification [4,5,16,25], while DV-NIZK with tight USS can be constructed without pairings [16].

However, both NIZK (that supports public verification) and DV-NIZK (that supports private verification) have their limitations on the flexibility of verification in certain applications. We demonstrate with two examples below.

Fine-grained Verification Setting in IPFE. Inner-product functional encryption (IPFE) [1] is a special subclass of functional encryption [10,28] for inner-product functions. In an IPFE scheme, a ciphertext is an encryption of a vector $\mathbf{x} \in \mathbb{Z}^m$, a secret key $\widetilde{sk}_{\mathbf{y}}$ (delegated from the master secret key $\widetilde{msk}$) is related with a vector $\mathbf{y} \in \mathbb{Z}^m$, and the decryption just returns their inner product $\langle \mathbf{x}, \mathbf{y} \rangle$. The inner-product function supports a large set of computation formulas, ranging from conjunctions and disjunctions to descriptive statistics and polynomial evaluations.

There are many explorations of CPA-secure IPFE schemes over the past years, e.g., [2,6,31]. All ciphertexts in these constructions fall into the HPS paradigm [12] with a pattern (c, v), where c is an instance in a language specified by the public key and v masks the message m.

To lift these CPA-secure IPFE schemes to CCA-secure IPFE schemes, one may want to resort to NIZK or DV-NIZK to reject ill-formed ciphertexts (i.e., ciphertexts with c outside the language) in decryption, thus making the decryption oracle useless to the adversary. This can be done by adding a NIZK/DV-NIZK proof in the ciphertext to prove that c belongs to the language. However, here comes the dilemma when choosing a suitable NIZK argument:

- DV-NIZK does not work in this setting with the following reason. To verify the well-formedness of ciphertexts, the decryption algorithm of IPFE has to know the secret key sk of DV-NIZK to verify the DV-NIZK proofs in ciphertexts. Thus all secret keys $\widetilde{sk}_{\mathbf{y}}$ of IPFE should contain the secret key sk. However, note that an adversary in the CPA/CCA-security experiment of IPFE is free to ask $\widetilde{sk}_{\mathbf{y}}$ for vectors $\mathbf{y}$ of its choices. Consequently, the adversary only needs to ask a single $\widetilde{sk}_{\mathbf{y}}$ to know the secret key sk of DV-

NIZK, in which case the (simulation) soundness of DV-NIZK might not hold any more, and consequently, the CCA-security of IPFE might not hold.

- In contrast, NIZK with public verification is sufficient, but seems to be overqualified in this setting. In fact, it is not necessary for everyone, but only those who hold secret keys $\widetilde{sk}_\mathbf{y}$, to be able to check the well-formedness of ciphertexts in decryption.

In summary, DV-NIZK does not work in converting CPA-secure IPFE schemes into CCA-secure ones but it has more efficient constructions (e.g., pairing-free constructions), while NIZK is sufficient but at the price of heavy constructions (especially, the pairing operations) and it seems to be overqualified.

Actually, what we need is a NIZK with *fine-grained verifiability*, lying between public verifiability and private verifiability. More precisely, there is a master secret key msk for verification, and the ability of verification can be delegated via deriving different secret keys sk_d from msk w.r.t. different d (which stands for, e.g., user identity, email address, vector, etc.), so that one can use sk_d to do the verification of NIZK proofs (hence execute decryptions of IPFE). On the one hand, all these verification approaches, no matter using msk or using sk_d w.r.t. any d, are statistically equivalent. On the other hand, (simulation) soundness is guaranteed even if the adversary obtains several sk_d with d chosen by itself, as long as msk is not leaked to the adversary.

In this work, we will formalize such NIZK as *Fine-grained Verifier NIZK (FV-NIZK)*, and show that it is sufficient for lifting CPA-secure IPFE schemes to CCA-secure ones. FV-NIZK has pairing-free constructions, and hence solves the aforementioned dilemma.

Fine-grained Verification Setting in PKE. In traditional PKE setting, only the owner of the secret key sk can check the validity of a ciphertext (i.e., whether a ciphertext decrypts to some plaintext or the decryption fails). In some applications, it is desirable to outsource this validity check to others. For example, a manager may ask an assistant to filter out invalid ciphertexts for her/him so that the manager can decrypt only the valid ciphertexts herself/himself, but the manager does not want to reveal the secret key to the assistant. To solve such problems, the concept of *publicly verifiable* PKE (PV-PKE) [3,21] is developed, in which anyone can check the validity of a ciphertext with only the public key of the owner.

Though public verifiability is desirable in some scenarios, it also brings the disadvantage of *losing anonymity*. Namely, anyone can identify the intended receiver of a ciphertext, by just doing a verification under someone's public key.

In order to reconcile the inherent contradictions between public verifiability and anonymity, we put forward a new primitive called *Fine-grained Verifiable PKE (FV-PKE)*, which can derive a special key (for validity check of ciphertexts) from the secret key (for decryption). Roughly speaking, with the derived key, one can check the validity of ciphertexts but cannot decrypt the ciphertexts, while without the key, the anonymity of ciphertexts holds. Let us move back to the above example. Now the manager can safely give this derived key to the assistant to filter out invalid ciphertexts. For the assistant, the anonymity is lost but the CCA-security of the PKE still holds. For others who only obtain the public key of the manager, the anonymity of ciphertexts holds. Furthermore, we allow that different keys (for validity check) can be derived from the secret key (for decryption), to achieve fine-grained verifiability.

Now we consider how to construct FV-PKE. Let us start from any CPA-secure PKE scheme. To lift it to CCA-secure FV-PKE, one may want to resort to NIZK (as in [14,27]) or DV-NIZK (as in [12,16]) to reject ill-formed ciphertexts. However, neither NIZK nor DV-NIZK leads to FV-PKE:

- DV-NIZK does not support the delegation of verifiability. Thus to check the validity of ciphertexts, the derived key of PKE should contain the secret key of DV-NIZK. Then for anyone with the derived key (e.g., the assistant in the above example), the (simulation) soundness of DV-NIZK might not hold, and consequently, the CCA-security of PKE might not hold.
- NIZK allows public verification of proofs. Thus anyone (who obtains the CRS of NIZK from the public key of PKE[1]) can check the validity of ciphertexts, and consequently the anonymity of PKE is sacrificed. Even in the setting that all users of a group (e.g., a company or a college) share the same CRS, the identity of the group is still leaked.

In fact, our new *Fine-grained Verifier NIZK (FV-NIZK)* is suitable in this setting and can successfully convert a CPA-secure PKE into a CCA-secure FV-PKE. More precisely, the owner can derive an sk_d from the master secret key msk of FV-NIZK, so that sk_d can be used to do validity check of ciphertexts. Meanwhile, obtaining sk_d does not compromise the (simulation) soundness of FV-NIZK, and hence CCA-security of PKE holds, even for those who have the derived key. Furthermore, for others who do not obtain the derived key, the anonymity of PKE holds, as long as the underlying CPA-secure PKE is anonymous and FV-NIZK has pseudorandom proofs.

Our Contributions. Now we summarize our contributions in this paper. We introduce a new primitive called *Fine-grained Verifier NIZK (FV-NIZK)*, which provides more flexible and more fine-grained verifiability than standard NIZK (with public verifiability) and DV-NIZK (with private verifiability). Intuitively, FV-NIZK has two main verification approaches:

- a master verification (MVer) using the master secret key msk;
- a fine-grained verification (FVer) using a derived secret key sk_d, which is derived from msk w.r.t. $d \in \mathcal{D}$. Here d belongs to a delegation space $\mathcal{D}$, and may stand for user identity, email address, vector, etc.

We equip FV-NIZK with a set of useful security properties. The statistical *verification equivalence* property requires that the two verification approaches, no matter using msk or using sk_d w.r.t. any $d \in \mathcal{D}$, are statistically equivalent. Besides, we adapt *unbounded simulation soundness (USS)* to FV-NIZK, by additionally allowing the adversary to obtain derived secret keys sk_d with d of its

---

[1] Note that the CRS of NIZK is contained in the public key of PKE, since the encryption algorithm of PKE involves NIZK proof generation which requires the CRS.

choices. We also define *proof pseudorandomness* which stipulates the pseudorandomness of proofs for adversaries that are not given any secret key.

Then we propose two instantiations of FV-NIZK with almost tight USS for linear subspace languages, based on the matrix decisional Diffie-Hellman (MDDH) assumption [15] (which covers the standard DDH and k-Linear assumptions).

- Our first instantiation is inspired by the DV-NIZK scheme constructed in [16]. The resulting FV-NIZK is *pairing-free*, and achieves almost tight USS and proof pseudorandomness, with a linear loss factor $L = O(\lambda)$.
- Our second instantiation is inspired by the DV-NIZK and NIZK schemes in [4]. The resulting FV-NIZK is pairing-based, but involves *less pairing operations* than the NIZK scheme in [4]. It achieves almost tight USS with a loss factor $L = O(\log \lambda)$, logarithmic in the security parameter λ.

Finally, we illustrate the usefulness of FV-NIZK by showing two applications.

- The first application is in constructing CCA-secure IPFE. Using our FV-NIZK with almost tight USS as the core technique tool, we construct a tightly multi-challenge CCA (mCCA)-secure IPFE scheme from the almost tightly multi-challenge CPA (mCPA)-secure IPFE proposed in [31].
  By instantiating FV-NIZK, we obtain the first almost tightly mCCA-secure IPFE scheme *without pairings*, where the loss factor is $L = O(\lambda)$. We also obtain another almost tightly mCCA-secure IPFE scheme that uses less pairing operations than the only known scheme [26] (12 *vs.* $2m + 16$ pairings, with m the vector dimension of IPFE), where the loss factor is $L = O(\log \lambda)$, the same as [26].
- The second application is in constructing *Fine-grained Verifiable PKE (FV-PKE)*. This is a new primitive formalized in this paper to reconcile the inherent contradictions between public verifiability and anonymity of PKE. Loosely speaking, FV-PKE derives a special key from the decryption secret key, such that for those who obtain the derived key, they can check the validity of ciphertexts but the anonymity is lost from their views (CCA-security still holds for them), while for others who do not get the derived key, they cannot do the validity check but the anonymity holds for them.
  By using our first FV-NIZK instantiation with almost tight USS and proof pseudorandomness as the core building block, we construct the first FV-PKE scheme that achieves both almost tight mCCA-security and almost tight ciphertext pseudorandomness (thus anonymity). Moreover, the FV-PKE scheme is pairing-free.

Technical Overview of Our FV-NIZK Instantiations. Below we give a high-level overview of our FV-NIZK instantiations from the MDDH assumption. Let $\mathbb{G}$ be a cyclic group of order q with generator g. For a matrix $\mathbf{A} := (a_{ij}) \in \mathbb{Z}_q^{n_1 \times n_2}$, we define $[\mathbf{A}] := (g^{a_{ij}}) \in \mathbb{G}^{n_1 \times n_2}$ as the implicit representation of $\mathbf{A}$ in $\mathbb{G}$ [15]. Our FV-NIZK instantiations are for linear subspace language $\mathscr{L}_{[\mathbf{A}]} := \mathsf{Span}([\mathbf{A}]) := \{[\mathbf{c}] \in \mathbb{G}^{n_1} \mid \exists \mathbf{s} \ s.t. \ \mathbf{c} = \mathbf{As}\}$ and the delegation space is $\mathcal{D} := \mathbb{Z}_q^m$.

Our starting point is the tag-based DV-NIZK scheme proposed by Gay et al. [16], which is pairing-free and has almost tight USS, as recalled below. The CRS is $\mathsf{crs} := ([\mathbf{k}^\top\mathbf{A}], [\mathbf{B}], \{[\widehat{\mathbf{k}}_{\ell,b}^\top\mathbf{B}]\}_{\ell,b})$, and the secret key msk for verification is $msk := (\mathbf{k}, \{\widehat{\mathbf{k}}_{\ell,b}\}_{\ell,b})$, where $\mathbf{k}\xleftarrow{\$}\mathbb{Z}_q^{n_1}$, $\mathbf{B}\xleftarrow{\$}\mathbb{Z}_q^{3k\times k}$ and $\widehat{\mathbf{k}}_{\ell,b}\xleftarrow{\$}\mathbb{Z}_q^{3k}$ for $1 \leq \ell \leq \lambda, b \in \{0,1\}$. With respect to a tag $\tau \in \{0,1\}^\lambda$, the proof of $[\mathbf{c}] = [\mathbf{A}]\mathbf{s} \in \mathscr{L}_{[\mathbf{A}]}$ is $\pi := ([\mathbf{t}], [u])$, where $[\mathbf{t}] := [\mathbf{B}]\mathbf{r}$ for $\mathbf{r}\xleftarrow{\$}\mathbb{Z}_q^k$ and

$$[u] := [\mathbf{k}^\top\mathbf{A}]\mathbf{s} + [\widehat{\mathbf{k}}_\tau^\top\mathbf{B}]\mathbf{r}, \quad \text{with } \widehat{\mathbf{k}}_\tau := \textstyle\sum_{\ell=1}^\lambda \widehat{\mathbf{k}}_{\ell,\tau_\ell},$$

which can be verified via $[u] \overset{?}{=} \mathbf{k}^\top[\mathbf{c}] + \widehat{\mathbf{k}}_\tau^\top[\mathbf{t}]$ using msk.

How to derive keys for fine-grained verification? To support deriving keys for different delegations $\mathbf{d} \in \mathcal{D} = \mathbb{Z}_q^m$, a natural idea is to extend the master secret key in the DV-NIZK above from a set of vectors to a sets of matrices, i.e., $\mathsf{crs} := ([\mathbf{KA}], [\mathbf{B}], \{[\widehat{\mathbf{K}}_{\ell,b}\mathbf{B}]\}_{\ell,b})$ and $msk := (\mathbf{K}, \{\widehat{\mathbf{K}}_{\ell,b}\}_{\ell,b})$ with $\mathbf{K}\xleftarrow{\$}\mathbb{Z}_q^{m\times n_1}$ and $\widehat{\mathbf{K}}_{\ell,b}\xleftarrow{\$}\mathbb{Z}_q^{m\times 3k}$. Accordingly, the proof is $\pi := ([\mathbf{t}], [\mathbf{u}])$ with

$$[\mathbf{u}] := [\mathbf{KA}]\mathbf{s} + [\widehat{\mathbf{K}}_\tau\mathbf{B}]\mathbf{r}, \quad \text{with } \widehat{\mathbf{K}}_\tau := \textstyle\sum_{\ell=1}^\lambda \widehat{\mathbf{K}}_{\ell,\tau_\ell},$$

and the *master* verification checks $[\mathbf{u}] \overset{?}{=} \mathbf{K}[\mathbf{c}] + \widehat{\mathbf{K}}_\tau[\mathbf{t}]$ using msk. One can view it as m-parallel DV-NIZKs in [16].

Now we can derive a key $sk_{\mathbf{d}}$ w.r.t. a delegation $\mathbf{d} \in \mathcal{D} = \mathbb{Z}_q^m$ as follows

$$sk_{\mathbf{d}} := (\mathbf{d}, \mathbf{d}^\top\mathbf{K}, \{\mathbf{d}^\top\widehat{\mathbf{K}}_{\ell,b}\}_{\ell,b}),$$

and the *fine-grained* verification using $sk_{\mathbf{d}}$ checks

$$\mathbf{d}^\top[\mathbf{u}] \overset{?}{=} \mathbf{d}^\top\mathbf{K}[\mathbf{c}] + \mathbf{d}^\top\widehat{\mathbf{K}}_\tau[\mathbf{t}].$$

Intuitively, delegation algorithm for $\mathbf{d}$ derives a "projection" of msk on $\mathbf{d}$, so that this derived secret key can be used to check the proof on $\mathbf{d}$'s projection.

However, here come two problems. Firstly, the two verification approaches are not statistically equivalent. In fact, given only crs, an adversary $\mathcal{A}$ can easily produce a proof $\pi^* = ([\mathbf{t}^*], [\mathbf{u}^*])$ for $[\mathbf{c}]$ such that it passes the fine-grained verification w.r.t. $sk_{\mathbf{d}}$, but does not pass the master verification, i.e.,

$$\mathbf{d}^\top[\mathbf{u}^*] = \mathbf{d}^\top\mathbf{K}[\mathbf{c}] + \mathbf{d}^\top\widehat{\mathbf{K}}_\tau[\mathbf{t}^*], \quad \text{but } [\mathbf{u}^*] \neq \mathbf{K}[\mathbf{c}] + \widehat{\mathbf{K}}_\tau[\mathbf{t}^*].$$

This can be done as follows. $\mathcal{A}$ first generates a proof $\pi = ([\mathbf{t}], [\mathbf{u}])$ for an instance $[\mathbf{c}] \in \mathscr{L}_{[\mathbf{A}]}$ honestly using crs, and then chooses a pair of non-zero orthogonal vectors $\mathbf{d}, \mathbf{e} \in \mathbb{Z}_q^m$ s.t. $\mathbf{d}^\top\mathbf{e} = 0$, and sets $\pi^* = ([\mathbf{t}^*], [\mathbf{u}^*]) := ([\mathbf{t}], [\mathbf{u}+\mathbf{e}])$. Clearly $[\mathbf{u}^*] - \mathbf{K}[\mathbf{c}] - \widehat{\mathbf{K}}_\tau[\mathbf{t}^*] = [\mathbf{u}^*] - [\mathbf{u}] = [\mathbf{e}] \neq [\mathbf{0}]$, but $\mathbf{d}^\top([\mathbf{u}^*] - \mathbf{K}[\mathbf{c}] - \widehat{\mathbf{K}}_\tau[\mathbf{t}^*]) = \mathbf{d}^\top[\mathbf{e}] = [0]$.

Moreover, USS cannot hold if an adversary $\mathcal{A}$ is allowed to obtain derived keys. Due to the linearity of $sk_\mathbf{d}$ in $\mathbf{d}$, each derived key $sk_\mathbf{d}$ leaks a part of information about msk. If $\mathcal{A}$ asks derived keys for m linearly independent vectors $\mathbf{d}$, then the whole msk is exposed to $\mathcal{A}$, and consequently, $\mathcal{A}$ can easily generate a valid proof for an instance $[\mathbf{c}] \notin \mathcal{L}_{[\mathbf{A}]}$ via computing $[\mathbf{u}] := \mathbf{K}[\mathbf{c}] + \widehat{\mathbf{K}}_\tau[\mathbf{t}]$.

First Idea. Introducing a Random Matrix as a Secret Permutation. In order to solve the aforementioned problems, we introduce a uniformly random matrix $\mathbf{M} \in \mathbb{Z}_q^{m \times m}$ in msk, i.e., $msk := (\mathbf{K}, \{\widehat{\mathbf{K}}_{\ell,b}\}_{\ell,b},\ \mathbf{M})$ with $\mathbf{M} \xleftarrow{\$} \mathbb{Z}_q^{m \times m}$. The crs, the proof generation and the master verification approach are the same as before, while the key deriving process and fine-grained verification are changed as follows. Now the derived key $sk_\mathbf{d}$ w.r.t. $\mathbf{d} \in \mathbb{Z}_q^m$ is

$$sk_\mathbf{d} := (\ \mathbf{d}^\top \mathbf{M}, \mathbf{d}^\top \mathbf{M}\mathbf{K}, \{\mathbf{d}^\top \mathbf{M}\widehat{\mathbf{K}}_{\ell,b}\}_{\ell,b}\ ),$$

and the *fine-grained* verification using $sk_\mathbf{d}$ checks

$$\mathbf{d}^\top \mathbf{M}[\mathbf{u}] \overset{?}{=} \mathbf{d}^\top \mathbf{M}\mathbf{K}[\mathbf{c}] + \mathbf{d}^\top \mathbf{M}\widehat{\mathbf{K}}_\tau[\mathbf{t}].$$

Intuitively, now the $sk_\mathbf{d}$ no longer projects msk on vector $\mathbf{d}$, but on a random vector $\mathbf{d}^\top \mathbf{M}$ which secretly rotates $\mathbf{d}$ by the matrix $\mathbf{M}$ in msk. As long as $\mathbf{d}^\top \mathbf{M}$ contains enough entropy from an adversary $\mathcal{A}$'s view[2], it is impossible for $\mathcal{A}$ to output a proof $\pi^* = ([\mathbf{t}^*], [\mathbf{u}^*])$ for $[\mathbf{c}]$ such that

$$\mathbf{d}^\top \mathbf{M}[\mathbf{u}^*] = \mathbf{d}^\top \mathbf{M}\mathbf{K}[\mathbf{c}] + \mathbf{d}^\top \mathbf{M}\widehat{\mathbf{K}}_\tau[\mathbf{t}^*], \text{ but } [\mathbf{u}^*] \neq \mathbf{K}[\mathbf{c}] + \widehat{\mathbf{K}}_\tau[\mathbf{t}^*],$$

except with negligible probability, since otherwise $[\mathbf{u}^*] - \mathbf{K}[\mathbf{c}] - \widehat{\mathbf{K}}_\tau[\mathbf{t}^*]$ constitutes a non-zero vector in the right kernel space of $\mathbf{d}^\top \mathbf{M}$. As a result, verification equivalence is guaranteed.

However, USS still cannot hold, since the whole msk is still exposed to $\mathcal{A}$ if $\mathcal{A}$ asks derived keys for m linearly independent vectors $\mathbf{d}$.

Second Idea. Enlarging the Random Matrix as an Entropy Filter. To rescue USS, we enlarge $\mathbf{M}$ to be a matrix in $\mathbb{Z}_q^{m \times (m+1)}$. Now even if $\mathcal{A}$ queries derived keys $sk_\mathbf{d}$ for m linearly independent vectors $\mathbf{d}$, the information about msk leaked to $\mathcal{A}$ is limited in

$$(\mathbf{M}, \mathbf{M}\mathbf{K}, \{\mathbf{M}\widehat{\mathbf{K}}_{\ell,b}\}_{\ell,b}),$$

and there is still entropy left. More precisely, let $\mathbf{m}^\perp \in \mathbb{Z}_q^{m+1}$ be a vector s.t. $\mathbf{M}\mathbf{m}^\perp = \mathbf{0}$, and let $(\mathbf{K}, \{\widehat{\mathbf{K}}_{\ell,b}\}_{\ell,b}) := (\mathbf{K}' + \mathbf{m}^\perp \boxed{\widetilde{\mathbf{k}}}, \{\widehat{\mathbf{K}}'_{\ell,b} + \mathbf{m}^\perp \boxed{\widetilde{\mathbf{k}}_{\ell,b}}\}_{\ell,b})$, where

---

[2] This entropy requirement is necessary to achieve verification equivalence, see Remark 1 in Sect. 3 for more discussions.

$\mathbf{K}' \overset{\$}{\leftarrow} \mathbb{Z}_q^{m \times n_1}$, $\widehat{\mathbf{K}}'_{\ell,b} \overset{\$}{\leftarrow} \mathbb{Z}_q^{m \times 3k}$ and $\boxed{\widetilde{\mathbf{k}} \overset{\$}{\leftarrow} \mathbb{Z}_q^{1 \times n_1}, \widetilde{\mathbf{k}}_{\ell,b} \overset{\$}{\leftarrow} \mathbb{Z}_q^{1 \times 3k}}$. Then the entropy of

$\boxed{(\widetilde{\mathbf{k}}, \{\widetilde{\mathbf{k}}_{\ell,b}\}_{\ell,b})}$ is reserved from the derived key queries, by observing that

$$(\mathbf{M}, \mathbf{MK}, \{\mathbf{M}\widehat{\mathbf{K}}_{\ell,b}\}_{\ell,b}) = (\mathbf{M}, \mathbf{MK}', \{\mathbf{M}\widehat{\mathbf{K}}'_{\ell,b}\}_{\ell,b}).$$

Consequently, the enlarged matrix $\mathbf{M}$ also works as an entropy filter in our FV-NIZK instantiation.

Finally, by using the reserved $\boxed{(\widetilde{\mathbf{k}}, \{\widetilde{\mathbf{k}}_{\ell,b}\}_{\ell,b})}$ (which in turn corresponds to the msk of the DV-NIZK in [16]), we can prove the almost tight USS of our FV-NIZK following the proof strategy in [16].

Others. By using the MDDH assumption, we further prove the almost tight pseudorandomness of the proofs $\pi = ([\mathbf{t}], [\mathbf{u}])$ for adversaries that are not given any derived secret key. This property serves as the core technical tool to achieve anonymity in the fine-grained verifiable PKE application.

Moreover, we note that our aforementioned ideas seem to be general ideas to lift a DV-NIZK scheme with good linearity to an FV-NIZK. Following the similar ideas, we also extend the DV-NIZK scheme proposed by Abe et al. [4] to an FV-NIZK, as our second instantiation.

Roadmap. In Sect. 2 we present notations and recall the MDDH assumptions. The definition and security properties of FV-NIZK are formally described in Sect. 3. Then in Sect. 4, we propose two instantiations of FV-NIZK with almost tight USS for linear subspace languages. In Sect. 5, we illustrate two applications of FV-NIZK in IPFE and FV-PKE, respectively.

2   Preliminaries

Let $\lambda \in \mathbb{N}$ denote the security parameter and $\emptyset$ the empty set. For $\mu \in \mathbb{N}$, define $[\mu] := \{1, 2, ..., \mu\}$. For $a, b \in \mathbb{Z}$ with $a < b$, define $[a, b] := \{a, a+1, ..., b\}$. Denote by $x := y$ the operation of assigning y to x. Denote by $x \overset{\$}{\leftarrow} \mathcal{Q}$ the operation of sampling x uniformly at random from a set $\mathcal{Q}$. For a distribution $\mathcal{D}$, denote by $x \leftarrow \mathcal{D}$ the operation of sampling x according to $\mathcal{D}$. For an algorithm $\mathcal{A}$, denote by $y \leftarrow \mathcal{A}(x; r)$, or simply $y \leftarrow \mathcal{A}(x)$, the operation of running $\mathcal{A}$ with input x and randomness r and assigning the output to y. "PPT" is short for probabilistic polynomial-time. $\mathsf{poly}(\lambda)$ and $\mathsf{negl}(\lambda)$ denote polynomial and negligible functions in λ, respectively.

We use bold lower-case letters to denote vectors (e.g., $\mathbf{x}$), and bold upper-case letters to denote matrices (e.g., $\mathbf{A}$). Unless specific description, all vectors are column vectors in this paper. For matrices $\mathbf{A}$ and $\mathbf{B}$, we use $\mathbf{A} \otimes \mathbf{B}$ for their tensor (or Kronecker) product $(a_{i,j}\mathbf{B})_{i,j}$. For vectors $\mathbf{x}, \mathbf{y} \in \mathbb{Z}^m$, let $\langle \mathbf{x}, \mathbf{y} \rangle$ denote their inner product $\mathbf{x}^\top \mathbf{y} \in \mathbb{Z}$. Let $\mathbf{I}_n$ and $\mathbf{0}_{n_1 \times n_2}$ denote the identity and zero matrices respectively.

For random variables X and Y, the min-entropy of X is defined as $\mathbf{H}_\infty(X) := -\log(\max_x \Pr[X = x])$, and the average min-entropy of X conditioned on Y is defined as $\widetilde{\mathbf{H}}_\infty(X|Y) := -\log(\mathbb{E}_{y \leftarrow Y}[\max_x \Pr[X = x|Y = y]])$, following [13].

Definition 1 (Collision Resistant Hash Families). *Let $\mathcal{X}, \mathcal{Y}$ be two finite sets. A family of hash functions $\mathcal{H} = \{H : \mathcal{X} \to \mathcal{Y}\}$ is collision resistant, if for any PPT adversary $\mathcal{A}$, it holds that*

$$\mathsf{Adv}^{cr}_{\mathcal{H},\mathcal{A}}(\lambda) := \Pr[H \xleftarrow{\$} \mathcal{H}, (x, x') \leftarrow \mathcal{A}(H) : x \neq x' \wedge H(x) = H(x')] \leq \mathsf{negl}(\lambda).$$

2.1 Group Assumptions

Let $\mathcal{G} = (\mathbb{G}, g, q) \leftarrow \mathsf{GGen}$ be a group generation algorithm that inputs 1^λ and returns a cyclic group $\mathbb{G}$ of order q with generator g. For matrix $\mathbf{A} := (a_{ij})_{n_1 \times n_2}$ with $a_{ij} \in \mathbb{Z}_q$, we define $[\mathbf{A}] := (g^{a_{ij}})_{n_1 \times n_2}$ as the implicit representation of $\mathbf{A}$ in $\mathbb{G}$ [15]. For $\mathbf{A} \in \mathbb{Z}_q^{n_1 \times n_2}$, the linear subspace spanned by $\mathbf{A}$ is $\mathsf{Span}(\mathbf{A}) := \{\mathbf{c} \mid \exists \mathbf{s} \ s.t. \ \mathbf{c} = \mathbf{As}\}$, and similarly, $\mathsf{Span}([\mathbf{A}]) := \{[\mathbf{c}] \mid \exists \mathbf{s} \ s.t. \ \mathbf{c} = \mathbf{As}\}$. Given $\mathbf{A} \in \mathbb{Z}_q^{n_1 \times n_2}$, it is efficient to sample an $\mathbf{A}^\perp \in \mathbb{Z}_q^{(n_1 - n_2) \times n_1}$ s.t. $\mathbf{A}^\perp \mathbf{A} = \mathbf{0}$.

Let $\ell, k \in \mathbb{N}$ and $\ell > k$. A matrix distribution $\mathcal{D}_{\ell,k}$ is a probabilistic distribution that outputs matrices in $\mathbb{Z}_q^{\ell \times k}$ of full rank k in polynomial time. Especially, if $\mathcal{D}_{\ell,k}$ is a uniform distribution, then we denote it by $\mathcal{U}_{\ell,k}$. In the case $\ell = k+1$, we simply denote it as $\mathcal{D}_k$ or $\mathcal{U}_k$.

Definition 2 ($\mathcal{D}_{\ell,k}$-MDDH Assumption). *Let $\mathcal{D}_{\ell,k}$ be a matrix distribution. The $\mathcal{D}_{\ell,k}$-$\underline{M}$atrix $\underline{D}$ecisional $\underline{D}$iffie-$\underline{H}$ellman ($\mathcal{D}_{\ell,k}$-MDDH) assumption holds in $\mathbb{G}$, if for any PPT adversary $\mathcal{A}$, it holds that*

$$\mathsf{Adv}^{mddh}_{\mathcal{D}_{\ell,k},\mathbb{G},\mathcal{A}}(\lambda) := |\Pr[\mathcal{A}(\mathcal{G}, [\mathbf{A}], [\mathbf{As}]) = 1] - \Pr[\mathcal{A}(\mathcal{G}, [\mathbf{A}], [\mathbf{u}]) = 1]| \leq \mathsf{negl}(\lambda),$$

where $\mathcal{G} \leftarrow \mathsf{GGen}(1^\lambda)$, $\mathbf{A} \leftarrow \mathcal{D}_{\ell,k}$, $\mathbf{s} \xleftarrow{\$} \mathbb{Z}_q^k$, and $\mathbf{u} \xleftarrow{\$} \mathbb{Z}_q^\ell$.

Definition 3 (n-fold $\mathcal{D}_{\ell,k}$-MDDH Assumption). *Let $n \geq 1$ and let $\mathcal{D}_{\ell,k}$ be a matrix distribution. The n-fold $\mathcal{D}_{\ell,k}$-MDDH assumption holds in $\mathbb{G}$, if for any PPT adversary $\mathcal{A}$, it holds that*

$$\mathsf{Adv}^{n\text{-}mddh}_{\mathcal{D}_{\ell,k},\mathbb{G},\mathcal{A}} := |\Pr[\mathcal{A}(\mathcal{G}, [\mathbf{A}], [\mathbf{AS}]) = 1] - \Pr[\mathcal{A}(\mathcal{G}, [\mathbf{A}], [\mathbf{U}]) = 1]| \leq \mathsf{negl}(\lambda),$$

where $\mathcal{G} \leftarrow \mathsf{GGen}(1^\lambda)$, $\mathbf{A} \leftarrow \mathcal{D}_{\ell,k}$, $\mathbf{S} \xleftarrow{\$} \mathbb{Z}_q^{k \times n}$, and $\mathbf{U} \xleftarrow{\$} \mathbb{Z}_q^{\ell \times n}$.

Lemma 1 (Random Self-Reducibility [15,16]). *Let $n \geq 1$. For any adversary $\mathcal{A}$, there exists an algorithm $\mathcal{B}$ s.t. $Time(\mathcal{B}) \approx Time(\mathcal{A}) + n \cdot \mathsf{poly}(\lambda)$, and $\mathsf{Adv}^{n\text{-}mddh}_{\mathcal{D}_{\ell,k},\mathbb{G},\mathcal{A}}(\lambda) \leq (\ell - k)\mathsf{Adv}^{mddh}_{\mathcal{D}_{\ell,k},\mathbb{G},\mathcal{B}}(\lambda) + \frac{1}{q-1}$.*

For any adversary $\mathcal{A}$, there exists an algorithm $\mathcal{B}$ s.t. $Time(\mathcal{B}) \approx Time(\mathcal{A}) + n \cdot \mathsf{poly}(\lambda)$, and $\mathsf{Adv}^{n\text{-}mddh}_{\mathcal{U}_{\ell,k},\mathbb{G},\mathcal{A}}(\lambda) \leq \mathsf{Adv}^{mddh}_{\mathcal{U}_{\ell,k},\mathbb{G},\mathcal{B}}(\lambda) + \frac{1}{q-1}$.

Lemma 2 ($\mathcal{D}_{\ell,k}$-MDDH $\Rightarrow \mathcal{U}_k$-MDDH $\Leftrightarrow \mathcal{U}_{\ell,k}$-MDDH [15,16]). *Let $\ell, k \in \mathbb{N}$ and $\ell > k$. For any adversary $\mathcal{A}$, there exists an algorithm $\mathcal{B}$ s.t. $Time(\mathcal{B}) \approx Time(\mathcal{A})$, and $\mathsf{Adv}^{mddh}_{\mathcal{U}_k,\mathbb{G},\mathcal{B}}(\lambda) \leq \mathsf{Adv}^{mddh}_{\mathcal{D}_{\ell,k},\mathbb{G},\mathcal{A}}(\lambda)$.*

For any adversary $\mathcal{A}$, there exists an algorithm $\mathcal{B}$ (and vice versa) s.t. $Time(\mathcal{B}) \approx Time(\mathcal{A})$, and $\mathsf{Adv}^{mddh}_{\mathcal{U}_k,\mathbb{G},\mathcal{A}}(\lambda) = \mathsf{Adv}^{mddh}_{\mathcal{U}_{\ell,k},\mathbb{G},\mathcal{B}}(\lambda)$.

3   Fine-Grained Verifier NIZK: Definition and Security

In this section, we give the formal definition of *Fine-grained Verifier NIZK (FV-NIZK)*, and propose a set of useful security properties for it.

Let $\mathscr{L} = \{\mathscr{L}_\rho\}$ be a collection of NP-languages indexed by parameter ρ. Each language $\mathscr{L}_\rho$ is determined by a binary relation R_ρ, such that an instance c belongs to $\mathscr{L}_\rho$ iff there exists a witness w s.t. $R_\rho(c,w) = 1$. We consider $\mathscr{L}_\rho$ with a trapdoor td_ρ, which can be used to decide the membership of $\mathscr{L}_\rho$ efficiently.

Definition 4 (Tag-Based FV-NIZK). *A tag-based $\underline{F}$ine-grained $\underline{V}$erifier quasi-adaptive $\underline{N}$on-$\underline{I}$nteractive $\underline{Z}$ero-$\underline{K}$nowledge (FV-NIZK) argument consists of seven PPT algorithms, namely* $\Pi = (\mathsf{Par}, \mathsf{Gen}, \mathsf{Prove}, \mathsf{MVer}, \mathsf{Sim}, \mathsf{Delegate}, \mathsf{FVer})$.

- $\mathsf{pp} \leftarrow \mathsf{Par}(1^\lambda, \mathscr{L}_\rho)$. *Initialization algorithm takes the security parameter λ and a language $\mathscr{L}_\rho$ as inputs, and outputs a public parameter* pp, *which defines the tag space $\mathcal{T}$ and the delegation space $\mathcal{D}$.*
- $(\mathsf{crs}, \mathsf{td}, msk) \leftarrow \mathsf{Gen}(\mathsf{pp})$. *Generation algorithm takes* pp *as input, and outputs a common reference string* crs, *a trapdoor* td, *and a master secret key* msk. *Without loss of generality, we assume* crs *contains* pp, *and it serves as an implicit input of* MVer, Sim, $\mathsf{Delegate}$, *and* FVer.
- $\pi \leftarrow \mathsf{Prove}(\mathsf{crs}, c, w, \tau)$. *Proof algorithm takes* crs, *an instance* $c \in \mathscr{L}_\rho$ *along with a witness w, and a tag $\tau \in \mathcal{T}$ as inputs, and outputs a proof π.*
- $0/1 \leftarrow \mathsf{MVer}(msk, c, \tau, \pi)$. *Master verification algorithm takes* msk, *an instance c, a tag $\tau \in \mathcal{T}$ and a proof π as inputs, and outputs a decision bit.*
- $\pi \leftarrow \mathsf{Sim}(\mathsf{td}, c, \tau)$. *Simulation algorithm takes* td, *an instance c and a tag $\tau \in \mathcal{T}$ as inputs, and outputs a simulated proof π.*
- $sk_d \leftarrow \mathsf{Delegate}(msk, d)$. *Delegation algorithm takes* msk *and a delegation $d \in \mathcal{D}$ as inputs, and outputs a delegated secret key sk_d.*
- $0/1 \leftarrow \mathsf{FVer}(sk_d, c, \tau, \pi)$. *Fine-grained verification algorithm takes sk_d, an instance c, a tag $\tau \in \mathcal{T}$ and a proof π as inputs, and outputs a decision bit.*

If the tag space $\mathcal{T}$ is the empty set $\emptyset$ or contains only one element (e.g., $\{0\}$), we call Π an FV-NIZK argument.

We require Π to have completeness and (perfect) zero-knowledge.

Completeness. *For all* $\mathsf{pp} \leftarrow \mathsf{Par}(1^\lambda, \mathscr{L}_\rho)$, $(\mathsf{crs}, \mathsf{td}, msk) \leftarrow \mathsf{Gen}(\mathsf{pp})$, (c, w) *s.t.* $R_\rho(c, w) = 1$, $\tau \in \mathcal{T}$ *and* $\pi \leftarrow \mathsf{Prove}(\mathsf{crs}, c, w, \tau)$, *it holds that*

(1) $\mathsf{MVer}(msk, c, \tau, \pi) = 1$, *and*

(2) $\mathsf{FVer}(sk_d, c, \tau, \pi) = 1$ *for all* $sk_d \leftarrow \mathsf{Delegate}(msk, d)$ *of all* $d \in \mathcal{D}$.

Perfect Zero-Knowledge. *For all* $\mathsf{pp} \leftarrow \mathsf{Par}(1^\lambda, \mathscr{L}_\rho)$, $(\mathsf{crs}, \mathsf{td}, msk) \leftarrow \mathsf{Gen}(\mathsf{pp})$, (c, w) *s.t.* $R_\rho(c, w) = 1$ *and* $\tau \in \mathcal{T}$, *the following two distributions are identical:*

$$\mathsf{Prove}(\mathsf{crs}, c, w, \tau) \quad \equiv \quad \mathsf{Sim}(\mathsf{td}, c, \tau).$$

Note that the first five algorithms (Par, Gen, Prove, MVer, Sim) of FV-NIZK basically constitute a DV-NIZK scheme as defined in [16]. Moreover, the two additional algorithms (Delegate, FVer) provide the fine-grained verification ability, by allowing different users owning different secret keys sk_d ($d \in \mathcal{D}$) to verify proofs in different ways by invoking $\mathsf{FVer}(sk_d, \cdot, \cdot, \cdot)$.

Now, we define a statistical property called *verification equivalence* for FV-NIZK. Intuitively, it requires that all proofs passing the master verification algorithm MVer using msk also pass the fine-grained verification algorithm FVer using any secret key sk_d of any d, and (with high probability) vice versa.

Definition 5 (Verification Equivalence). *Let $\delta, \epsilon > 0$. A tag-based FV-NIZK Π has (δ, ϵ)-verification equivalence, if the following two properties hold.*

1. $\mathsf{MVer} \Longrightarrow \mathsf{FVer}$: *For all* $pp \leftarrow \mathsf{Par}(1^\lambda, \mathscr{L}_\rho)$, $(crs, td, msk) \leftarrow \mathsf{Gen}(pp)$, *instances c, proofs π and tags $\tau \in \mathcal{T}$, if $\mathsf{MVer}(msk, c, \tau, \pi) = 1$ holds, then $\mathsf{FVer}(sk_d, c, \tau, \pi) = 1$ holds for all $sk_d \leftarrow \mathsf{Delegate}(msk, d)$ of all $d \in \mathcal{D}$.*

2. $\mathsf{MVer} \overset{w.h.p.}{\Longleftarrow} \mathsf{FVer}$: *For any (even unbounded) adversary $\mathcal{A}$, it holds that*

$$\mathsf{Adv}_{\Pi, \mathcal{A}, \delta}^{ver\text{-}equ}(\lambda) := \Pr[\mathsf{Exp}_{\Pi, \mathcal{A}, \delta}^{ver\text{-}equ}(\lambda) \Rightarrow 1] \leq \epsilon,$$

where the experiment $\mathsf{Exp}_{\Pi, \mathcal{A}, \delta}^{ver\text{-}equ}(\lambda)$ is defined in Fig. 1.

$\mathsf{Exp}_{\Pi, \mathcal{A}, \delta}^{ver\text{-}equ}(\lambda)$:

$pp \leftarrow \mathsf{Par}(1^\lambda, \mathscr{L}_\rho)$, $(crs, td, msk) \leftarrow \mathsf{Gen}(pp)$
$\mathcal{Q}_{sim} := \emptyset$, $\mathcal{Q}_{sk} := \emptyset$
$(c^*, \tau^*, \pi^*, d^*) \leftarrow \mathcal{A}^{\textsc{Sim}(\cdot, \cdot), \textsc{Delegate}(\cdot)}(pp, crs)$
$sk_{d^*} \leftarrow \mathsf{Delegate}(msk, d^*)$

If $\widetilde{\mathbf{H}}_\infty(sk_{d^*} | crs, \mathcal{Q}_{sim}, \mathcal{Q}_{sk}, d^*) > \delta$
$\quad \wedge\ \mathsf{FVer}(sk_{d^*}, c^*, \tau^*, \pi^*) = 1$
$\quad \wedge\ \mathsf{MVer}(msk, c^*, \tau^*, \pi^*) = 0$: output 1
Otherwise: output 0

$\textsc{Sim}(c, \tau)$:
$\pi \leftarrow \mathsf{Sim}(td, c, \tau)$
$\mathcal{Q}_{sim} := \mathcal{Q}_{sim} \cup \{(c, \tau, \pi)\}$
Return π

$\textsc{Delegate}(d)$:
$sk_d \leftarrow \mathsf{Delegate}(msk, d)$
$\mathcal{Q}_{sk} := \mathcal{Q}_{sk} \cup \{(d, sk_d)\}$
Return sk_d

Fig. 1. The verification equivalence experiment $\mathsf{Exp}_{\Pi, \mathcal{A}, \delta}^{ver\text{-}equ}(\lambda)$ for tag-based FV-NIZK. In the condition "$\widetilde{\mathbf{H}}_\infty(sk_{d^*} | crs, \mathcal{Q}_{sim}, \mathcal{Q}_{sk}, d^*)$", sk_{d^*} means the distribution $\mathsf{Delegate}(msk, d^*; r)$ with uniformly chosen randomness r, rather than a fixed value.

Remark 1 (On the formalization of "$\mathsf{MVer} \overset{w.h.p.}{\Longleftarrow} \mathsf{FVer}$"). We stress that we do not require MVer and FVer perform identically on all inputs. In other words, there might exist (c, τ, π) such that $\mathsf{FVer}(sk_d, c, \tau, \pi) = 1$ for some sk_d but $\mathsf{MVer}(msk, c, \tau, \pi) = 0$. Similarly, for different d_1, d_2, FVer using sk_{d_1} and FVer using sk_{d_2} might perform differently on some inputs, i.e., there might exist (c, τ, π) such that $\mathsf{FVer}(sk_{d_1}, c, \tau, \pi) = 1$ but $\mathsf{FVer}(sk_{d_2}, c, \tau, \pi) = 0$.

In fact, what our "MVer $\overset{w.h.p.}{\Longleftrightarrow}$ FVer" property tries to characterize is that for any (unbounded) adversary $\mathcal{A}$ who does not get enough information about sk_{d^*} (and thus msk), it is hard to find a (c^*, τ^*, π^*) that makes MVer and FVer perform differently. This also explains the condition "$\widetilde{\mathbf{H}}_\infty(sk_{d^*}|\mathsf{crs}, \mathcal{Q}_{sim}, \mathcal{Q}_{sk}, d^*) > \delta$" in Fig. 1 for $\mathcal{A}$ to win. Otherwise, if the min-entropy of sk_{d^*} is lower than some threshold (say δ), $\mathcal{A}$ can guess sk_{d^*} correctly with a noticeable probability. Meanwhile, it can obtain sk_d for some $d \neq d^*$ by querying $\mathrm{DELEGATE}(d)$. With the knowledge of sk_{d^*} and sk_d, it is feasible for $\mathcal{A}$ to find (c^*, τ^*, π^*) such that $\mathsf{FVer}(sk_{d^*}, c^*, \tau^*, \pi^*) = 1$ but $\mathsf{FVer}(sk_d, c^*, \tau^*, \pi^*) = 0$ (e.g., via brute-force search). According to the first property "MVer $\Longrightarrow$ FVer", $\mathsf{FVer}(sk_d, c^*, \tau^*, \pi^*) = 0$ implies $\mathsf{MVer}(msk, c^*, \tau^*, \pi^*) = 0$, and consequently $\mathcal{A}$ wins in $\mathsf{Exp}_{\Pi, \mathcal{A}, \delta}^{ver\text{-}equ}(\lambda)$. To prevent such trivial attacks, we require $\widetilde{\mathbf{H}}_\infty(sk_{d^*}|\mathsf{crs}, \mathcal{Q}_{sim}, \mathcal{Q}_{sk}, d^*) > \delta$.

Remark 2 (On the parameter δ). Jumping ahead, both our FV-NIZK constructions in Sect. 4 has (δ, ϵ)-verification equivalence with $\delta = 0$. It seems that the only way to achieve verification equivalence is if the parameter δ is either exactly 0 (as in our case) or large, but nothing in between.

Next, we adapt the *unbounded simulation soundness (USS)* of NIZK to our FV-NIZK. Recall that USS for NIZK and DV-NIZK ensures that a PPT adversary cannot generate a valid proof for a fresh and false statement $c \notin \mathscr{L}_\rho$, even if it can obtain multiple simulated proofs for instances not necessarily in $\mathscr{L}_\rho$ [16,30]. For FV-NIZK, we also allow the adversary to obtain many secret keys sk_d with d of its choices. Moreover, we consider a *strong* USS by giving the adversary multiple chances to win, following [16].

Definition 6 (Strong USS). *A tag-based FV-NIZK Π has strong USS, if for any PPT adversary $\mathcal{A}$, it holds that*

$$\mathsf{Adv}_{\Pi, \mathcal{A}}^{uss}(\lambda) := \Pr[\mathsf{Exp}_{\Pi, \mathcal{A}}^{uss}(\lambda) \Rightarrow 1] \leq \mathsf{negl}(\lambda),$$

where the experiment $\mathsf{Exp}_{\Pi, \mathcal{A}}^{uss}(\lambda)$ is defined in Fig. 2.

Remark 3 (On the formalization of strong USS). Note that in the strong USS experiment in Fig. 2, $\mathrm{SIM}(c, \tau)$ returns $\perp$ directly if τ was queried to $\mathrm{SIM}(\cdot, \cdot)$ before, following the definition of strong USS for DV-NIZK in [16]. Similar to [16], such a requirement is not an obstacle in many applications. For example, as we will see, in all our applications in Sect. 5, τ is a hash of some random values. Thus τ is different with overwhelming probability each time $\mathrm{SIM}(\cdot, \cdot)$ is invoked when the security of applications is reduced to the strong USS.

Moreover, we note that in the strong USS defined in [16], $\mathrm{VER}(\cdot, \tau, \cdot)$ also returns $\perp$ if τ was queried to $\mathrm{SIM}(\cdot, \tau)$ before, while ours does not have such a requirement. This relaxation seems reasonable when considering the security of NIZK, and it helps us to construct other cryptographic algorithms in a more straightforward way (e.g., constructing CCA-secure PKE without resorting to one-time signatures or authenticated encryption, as shown in Subsect. 5.2).

$\mathrm{Exp}_{\Pi,\mathcal{A}}^{uss}(\lambda)$:	$\mathrm{SIM}(c,\tau)$:
$\mathsf{pp} \leftarrow \mathsf{Par}(1^\lambda, \mathscr{L}_\rho)$, $(\mathsf{crs},\mathsf{td},msk) \leftarrow \mathsf{Gen}(\mathsf{pp})$	If $(\cdot,\tau,\cdot) \in \mathcal{Q}_{sim}$: return $\perp$
$\mathcal{Q}_{sim} := \emptyset$, $\mathcal{Q}_{sk} := \emptyset$	$\pi \leftarrow \mathsf{Sim}(\mathsf{td},c,\tau)$
win $:= 0$ // A flag indicating whether $\mathcal{A}$ wins	$\mathcal{Q}_{sim} := \mathcal{Q}_{sim} \cup \{(c,\tau,\pi)\}$
$\perp \leftarrow \mathcal{A}^{\mathrm{SIM}(\cdot,\cdot),\mathrm{DELEGATE}(\cdot),\mathrm{VER}(\cdot,\cdot,\cdot)}(\mathsf{pp},\mathsf{crs})$	Return π
Output win	
	$\mathrm{VER}(c,\tau,\pi)$:
$\mathrm{DELEGATE}(d)$:	If $(c,\tau,\pi) \in \mathcal{Q}_{sim}$: return $\perp$
$sk_d \leftarrow \mathsf{Delegate}(msk,d)$	If $\mathsf{MVer}(msk,c,\tau,\pi) = 1 \ \wedge \ c \notin \mathscr{L}_\rho$:
$\mathcal{Q}_{sk} := \mathcal{Q}_{sk} \cup \{(d,sk_d)\}$	win $:= 1$
Return sk_d	Return $\mathsf{MVer}(msk,c,\tau,\pi)$

Fig. 2. The strong USS experiment $\mathrm{Exp}_{\Pi,\mathcal{A}}^{uss}(\lambda)$ for tag-based FV-NIZK.

Finally, we define *proof pseudorandomness* for FV-NIZK, which stipulates the pseudorandomness of proofs for PPT adversaries that are not given any secret key but allowed to access the verification oracle. Jumping ahead, this property serves as the core technical tool for the ciphertext pseudorandomness (thus anonymity) of our fine-grained verifiable PKE in Subsect. 5.2.

Definition 7 (Proof Pseudorandomness). *A tag-based FV-NIZK Π has proof pseudorandomness, if for any PPT adversary $\mathcal{A}$, it holds that*

$$\mathsf{Adv}_{\Pi,\mathcal{A}}^{pp}(\lambda) := |\Pr[\mathrm{Exp}_{\Pi,\mathcal{A},0}^{pp}(\lambda) \Rightarrow 1] - \Pr[\mathrm{Exp}_{\Pi,\mathcal{A},1}^{pp}(\lambda) \Rightarrow 1]| \leq \mathsf{negl}(\lambda),$$

where the experiments $\mathrm{Exp}_{\Pi,\mathcal{A},\beta}^{pp}(\lambda)$ ($\beta \in \{0,1\}$) are defined in Fig. 3.

$\mathrm{Exp}_{\Pi,\mathcal{A},\beta}^{pp}(\lambda)$: // $\beta \in \{0,1\}$	$\mathrm{SAM}(\cdot)$:	$\mathrm{SIM}(c,\tau)$:
$\mathsf{pp} \leftarrow \mathsf{Par}(1^\lambda, \mathscr{L}_\rho)$, $(\mathsf{crs},\mathsf{td},msk) \leftarrow \mathsf{Gen}(\mathsf{pp})$	If $\beta = 0$: $c \xleftarrow{\$} \mathscr{L}_\rho$	If $c \notin \mathcal{Q}_c$: return $\perp$
$\mathcal{Q}_c := \emptyset$, $\mathcal{Q}_{sim} := \emptyset$	If $\beta = 1$: $c \xleftarrow{\$} \mathcal{X}$	If $(\cdot,\tau,\cdot) \in \mathcal{Q}_{sim}$: return $\perp$
$\beta' \leftarrow \mathcal{A}^{\mathrm{SAM}(\cdot),\mathrm{SIM}(\cdot,\cdot),\mathrm{VER}(\cdot,\cdot,\cdot)}(\mathsf{pp},\mathsf{crs})$	$\mathcal{Q}_c := \mathcal{Q}_c \cup \{c\}$	If $\beta = 0$: $\pi \leftarrow \mathsf{Sim}(\mathsf{td},c,\tau)$
Output β'	Return c	If $\beta = 1$: $\pi \xleftarrow{\$} \mathcal{P}$
		$\mathcal{Q}_c := \mathcal{Q}_c \backslash \{c\}$
$\mathrm{VER}(c,\tau,\pi)$:		$\mathcal{Q}_{sim} := \mathcal{Q}_{sim} \cup \{(c,\tau,\pi)\}$
If $(c,\tau,\pi) \in \mathcal{Q}_{sim}$: return $\perp$		Return π
Return $\mathsf{MVer}(msk,c,\tau,\pi)$		

Fig. 3. The proof pseudorandomness experiments $\mathrm{Exp}_{\Pi,\mathcal{A},\beta}^{pp}(\lambda)$ for tag-based FV-NIZK, where $\mathcal{X}$ denotes the instance space, and $\mathcal{P}$ denotes the proof space of Π.

Remark 4 (On the formalization of proof pseudorandomness). In fact, the proof pseudorandomness asks the pseudorandomness of proofs for instances *uniformly sampled* from the language $\mathscr{L}_\rho$. Moreover, the adversary $\mathcal{A}$ in Fig. 3 has access to two oracles, $\mathrm{SAM}(\cdot)$ and $\mathrm{SIM}(\cdot,\cdot)$, to obtain instances and simulated proofs, respectively. In particular, the oracle $\text{SIM}(c, \tau)$ returns proofs only for instances c output by $\text{SAM}(\cdot)$, but τ can be determined by $\mathcal{A}$. Indeed, in certain applications of tag-based NIZK, the tag τ may depend on the instance c. For example, in our application in PKE (cf. Subsect. 5.2), τ is a hash of c. Our formalization captures such dependency between c and τ.

Remark 5 (Extension to the multi-user setting). We can naturally extend the definitions of strong USS and proof pseudorandomness (i.e., Definitions 6 and 7) to the multi-user setting, and define strong μ-USS and μ-proof pseudorandomness in the setting of $\mu \in \mathbb{N}$ users. The formal definitions can be found in the full version. More precisely, all μ users share the same pp and each user $i \in [\mu]$ invokes $\text{Gen}(\text{pp})$ independently to get its own $(\text{crs}^{(i)}, \text{td}^{(i)}, msk^{(i)})$. Accordingly, the adversary $\mathcal{A}$ has access to $\text{SIM}(i, \cdot, \cdot), \text{DELEGATE}(i, \cdot), \text{VER}(i, \cdot, \cdot, \cdot)$ which additionally take a user index $i \in [\mu]$ as input and prepare the responses using $(\text{crs}^{(i)}, \text{td}^{(i)}, msk^{(i)})$.

Jumping ahead, both the two schemes in Sect. 4 have almost tight strong USS (and the first one also have almost tight proof pseudorandomness) in the multi-user setting.

4 FV-NIZK for Linear Subspace Languages

In this section, we propose two tightly secure FV-NIZK schemes for linear subspace languages, based on the MDDH assumption. The first scheme is pairing-free and the second one relies on pairings.

Let $\mathcal{G} = (\mathbb{G}, g, q)$ be a cyclic group $\mathbb{G}$ of order q with generator g. Let $\mathbf{A} \in \mathbb{Z}_q^{n_1 \times n_2}$ with $n_1 > n_2$. The linear subspace language is $\mathscr{L}_{[\mathbf{A}]} := \text{Span}([\mathbf{A}]) := \{[\mathbf{c}] \mid \exists \mathbf{s} \in \mathbb{Z}_q^{n_2} \text{ s.t. } \mathbf{c} = \mathbf{As}\}$ with $\mathbf{A}$ the trapdoor of $\mathscr{L}_{[\mathbf{A}]}$.

4.1 The First Construction without Pairings

Let $m, k, n_1, n_2 \in \mathbb{N}$ and $\mathcal{D}_{3k,k}$ be a matrix distribution. Let $\mathcal{H} : \{0,1\}^* \to \mathbb{Z}_q$ be a family of collision resistant hash functions. Our first construction of tag-based FV-NIZK Π is shown in Fig. 4, where the tag space is $\mathcal{T} = \{0,1\}^\lambda$ and the delegation space is $\mathcal{D} = \mathbb{Z}_q^m$. Note that this construction is pairing-free.

Completeness and perfect zero-knowledge follow directly from the fact that

$$\mathbf{u} = (\mathbf{K}_0 + \theta\mathbf{K}_1)\mathbf{As} + \widehat{\mathbf{K}}_\tau\mathbf{Br} = (\mathbf{K}_0 + \theta\mathbf{K}_1)\mathbf{c} + \widehat{\mathbf{K}}_\tau\mathbf{t} \quad \text{// completeness (1)}$$

$$= (\mathbf{K}_0 + \theta\mathbf{K}_1)\mathbf{c} + \widehat{\mathbf{K}}_\tau\mathbf{Br}, \qquad\qquad \text{// perfect zero-knowledge}$$

which implies $\mathbf{d}^\top\mathbf{Mu} = \mathbf{d}^\top\mathbf{M}(\mathbf{K}_0 + \theta\mathbf{K}_1)\mathbf{c} + \mathbf{d}^\top\mathbf{M}\widehat{\mathbf{K}}_\tau\mathbf{t}$. // completeness (2)

Next, we show the verification equivalence of Π.

Theorem 1 (Verification Equivalence). *The tag-based FV-NIZK scheme Π in Fig. 4 has $(0, 1/q)$-verification equivalence.*

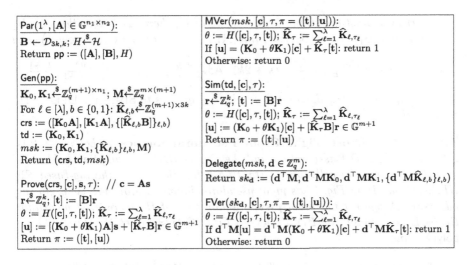

Fig. 4. The pairing-free construction of tag-based FV-NIZK Π.

Proof. The first property (MVer $\Longrightarrow$ FVer) is straightforward, since $[\mathbf{u}] = (\mathbf{K}_0 + \theta\mathbf{K}_1)[\mathbf{c}] + \widehat{\mathbf{K}}_\tau[\mathbf{t}]$ directly implies $\mathbf{d}^\top\mathbf{M}[\mathbf{u}] = \mathbf{d}^\top\mathbf{M}(\mathbf{K}_0 + \theta\mathbf{K}_1)[\mathbf{c}] + \mathbf{d}^\top\mathbf{M}\widehat{\mathbf{K}}_\tau[\mathbf{t}]$.

To show the second property (MVer $\overset{w.h.p.}{\Longleftarrow}$ FVer), we consider an (unbounded) adversary $\mathcal{A}$ that finally outputs $([\mathbf{c}^*], \tau^*, \pi^* = ([\mathbf{t}^*], [\mathbf{u}^*]), \mathbf{d}^*)$ in the experiment $\mathsf{Exp}_{\Pi,\mathcal{A},0}^{ver\text{-}equ}(\lambda)$ (cf. Fig. 1). Let $\mathbf{D}$ denote the matrix consisting of all vectors $\mathbf{d}$ that $\mathcal{A}$ queried DELEGATE$(\cdot)$. We analyze $\mathcal{A}$'s advantage as follows.

Note that the algorithm Delegate is deterministic and linear in $\mathbf{d}$. That is, if $\mathbf{d}^* \in \mathsf{Span}(\mathbf{D})$, then $sk_{\mathbf{d}^*}$ is totally determined by $\mathcal{Q}_{sk} = \{(\mathbf{d}, sk_{\mathbf{d}})\}$ and $\mathbf{d}^*$, and hence has no entropy left at all. Therefore, for $\mathcal{A}$ to win, $\widetilde{\mathbf{H}}_\infty(sk_{\mathbf{d}^*}|\mathsf{crs}, \mathcal{Q}_{sim}, \mathcal{Q}_{sk}, \mathbf{d}^*) > 0$ holds, and we must have $\mathbf{d}^* \notin \mathsf{Span}(\mathbf{D})$. Moreover, since the algorithm Sim does not involve $\mathbf{M}$ at all, $\mathcal{A}$ obtains nothing about $\mathbf{M}$ from SIM$(\cdot, \cdot)$. Thus, $\mathbf{d}^* \notin \mathsf{Span}(\mathbf{D})$ implies that $\mathbf{d}^{*\top}\mathbf{M}$ is uniformly random over $\mathbb{Z}_q^{1\times(m+1)}$ from $\mathcal{A}$'s view. And consequently, the event FVer$(sk_{\mathbf{d}^*}, [\mathbf{c}^*], \tau^*, \pi^*) = 1 \wedge$ MVer$(msk, [\mathbf{c}^*], \tau^*, \pi^*) = 0$, i.e.,

$$\mathbf{d}^{*\top}\mathbf{M}\underbrace{\left(\mathbf{u}^* - (\mathbf{K}_0 + \theta^*\mathbf{K}_1)\mathbf{c}^* - \widehat{\mathbf{K}}_{\tau^*}\mathbf{t}^*\right)}_{\neq 0} = 0,$$

occurs with probability at most $1/q$. This shows $\mathsf{Adv}_{\Pi,\mathcal{A},0}^{ver\text{-}equ}(\lambda) \leq 1/q$. $\square$

Now we show that Π has almost tight strong USS and almost tight proof pseudorandomness via the following two theorems.

Theorem 2 (Almost Tight Strong USS). *If the $\mathcal{D}_{3k,k}$-MDDH assumption holds in $\mathbb{G}$ and $\mathcal{H}$ is a family of collision resistant hash functions, then the tag-based FV-NIZK scheme Π in Fig. 4 has strong USS. More precisely, for any*

adversary $\mathcal{A}$ *against the strong USS security of* Π, *there exist algorithms* $\mathcal{B}_1, \mathcal{B}_2$
s.t. $\max(Time(\mathcal{B}_1), Time(\mathcal{B}_2)) \approx Time(\mathcal{A}) + (Q_{sim} + Q_{ver} + Q_{del}) \cdot \mathsf{poly}(\lambda)$, *and*

$$\mathsf{Adv}_{\Pi,\mathcal{A}}^{uss}(\lambda) \leq \mathsf{Adv}_{\mathcal{H},\mathcal{B}_1}^{cr}(\lambda) + (8\lambda k + 2k) \cdot \mathsf{Adv}_{\mathcal{D}_{3k,k},\mathbb{G},\mathcal{B}_2}^{mddh}(\lambda) + \frac{(2\lambda+2)Q_{ver}+4\lambda+1}{q-1},$$

where $Q_{sim}, Q_{ver}, Q_{del}$ *denote the numbers of queries to* SIM, VER, DELEGATE,
respectively.

Theorem 3 (Almost Tight Proof Pseudorandomness). *Let* $n_1 \geq 2n_2$.
If the $\mathcal{D}_{n_1,n_2}$-*MDDH assumption and the* $\mathcal{D}_{3k,k}$-*MDDH assumption hold in* $\mathbb{G}$,
and $\mathcal{H}$ *is a family of collision resistant hash functions, then the tag-based FV-
NIZK scheme* Π *in Fig. 4 has proof pseudorandomness. More precisely, for any
adversary* $\mathcal{A}$ *against the proof pseudorandomness of* Π, *there exist algorithms*
$\mathcal{B}_1, \mathcal{B}_2, \mathcal{B}_3$ *s.t.* $\max(Time(\mathcal{B}_1), Time(\mathcal{B}_2)\, Time(\mathcal{B}_3)) \approx Time(\mathcal{A}) + (Q_{sim} + Q_{ver}) \cdot$
$\mathsf{poly}(\lambda)$, *and*

$$\mathsf{Adv}_{\Pi,\mathcal{A}}^{pp}(\lambda) \leq (n_1 - n_2 + 2)\mathsf{Adv}_{\mathcal{D}_{n_1,n_2},\mathbb{G},\mathcal{B}_1}^{mddh}(\lambda) + (16\lambda k + 6k)\mathsf{Adv}_{\mathcal{D}_{3k,k},\mathbb{G},\mathcal{B}_2}^{mddh}(\lambda)$$
$$+ 2\mathsf{Adv}_{\mathcal{H},\mathcal{B}_3}^{cr}(\lambda) + \frac{(4\lambda+4)Q_{ver}+8\lambda+6}{q-1},$$

where Q_{sim} *and* Q_{ver} *denote the numbers of queries to* SIM *and* VER,
respectively.

We prove Theorems 2 and 3 in our full version due to space limitations. See
Sect. 1 for a high-level proof sketch.

Remark 6 (On the almost tightness of strong USS and proof pseudorandomness).
The terms $\frac{(2\lambda+2)Q_{ver}+4\lambda+1}{q-1}$ and $\frac{(4\lambda+4)Q_{ver}+8\lambda+6}{q-1}$ in Theorem 2 and Theorem 3
do not affect the tightness of the reductions since they are statistically small.
Moreover, n_1, n_2, k are parameters of the MDDH assumptions and are constants
(e.g., $n_1 = 2, n_2 = 1, k = 1$). Consequently, the strong USS and proof pseudorandomness have security loss factors $O(\lambda)$, and thus are almost tight.

4.2   The Second Construction with Pairings

Let $m, k, n_1, n_2 \in \mathbb{N}$ and $\mathcal{D}_{2k,k}$ be a matrix distribution. Let $\mathcal{H} : \{0,1\}^* \to \mathbb{Z}_q$
be a family of collision resistant hash functions. Similar to [4], we use a NIZK
proof $\Pi_{or} = (\Pi_{or}.\mathsf{Gen}, \Pi_{or}.\mathsf{TGen}, \Pi_{or}.\mathsf{Prove}, \Pi_{or}.\mathsf{Sim}, \Pi_{or}.\mathsf{Ver})$ for OR-language
$\mathscr{L}_{[\mathbf{B}_0],[\mathbf{B}_1]}^{\vee} := \mathsf{Span}([\mathbf{B}_0]) \cup \mathsf{Span}([\mathbf{B}_1]) := \{[\mathbf{t}] \mid \exists \mathbf{r} \in \mathbb{Z}_q^k \text{ s.t. } \mathbf{t} = \mathbf{B}_0\mathbf{r} \vee \mathbf{t} = \mathbf{B}_1\mathbf{r}\}$
as a building block, where $\mathbf{B}_0, \mathbf{B}_1 \in \mathbb{Z}_q^{2k \times k}$. We refer our full version for the
syntax of NIZK proofs and a concrete MDDH-based scheme of Π_{or} proposed
in [18,29]. Our second construction of tag-based FV-NIZK Π is shown in Fig. 5,
where the tag space is $\mathcal{T} = \{0,1\}^*$ and the delegation space is $\mathcal{D} = \mathbb{Z}_q^m$. Note
that compared to the QA-NIZK scheme proposed in [4], our FV-NIZK scheme
uses less pairing operations, since only $\Pi_{or}.\mathsf{Ver}$ involves pairings.

$\mathsf{Par}(1^\lambda, [\mathbf{A}] \in \mathbb{G}^{n_1 \times n_2})$: $\mathbf{B}_0, \mathbf{B}_1 \leftarrow \mathcal{D}_{2k,k}; H \xleftarrow{\$} \mathcal{H}$ $\mathsf{crs}_{or} \leftarrow \Pi_{or}.\mathsf{Gen}(1^\lambda, [\mathbf{B}_0], [\mathbf{B}_1])$ Return $\mathsf{pp} := ([\mathbf{A}], [\mathbf{B}_0], \mathsf{crs}_{or}, H)$	$\mathsf{MVer}(msk, [\mathbf{c}], \tau, \pi = ([\mathbf{t}], [\mathbf{u}], \pi_{or}))$: If $\Pi_{or}.\mathsf{Ver}(\mathsf{crs}_{or}, [\mathbf{t}], \pi_{or}) = 0$: return 0 $\theta := H([\mathbf{c}], \tau, [\mathbf{t}], \pi_{or})$ If $[\mathbf{u}] = (\mathbf{K}_0 + \theta\mathbf{K}_1)[\mathbf{c}] + \widehat{\mathbf{K}}[\mathbf{t}]$: return 1 Otherwise: return 0
$\mathsf{Gen}(\mathsf{pp})$: $\mathbf{K}_0, \mathbf{K}_1 \xleftarrow{\$} \mathbb{Z}_q^{(m+1) \times n_1}$ $\widehat{\mathbf{K}} \xleftarrow{\$} \mathbb{Z}_q^{(m+1) \times 2k}; \mathbf{M} \xleftarrow{\$} \mathbb{Z}_q^{m \times (m+1)}$ $\mathsf{crs} := ([\mathbf{K}_0\mathbf{A}], [\mathbf{K}_1\mathbf{A}], [\widehat{\mathbf{K}}\mathbf{B}_0])$ $\mathsf{td} := (\mathbf{K}_0, \mathbf{K}_1)$ $msk := (\mathbf{K}_0, \mathbf{K}_1, \widehat{\mathbf{K}}, \mathbf{M})$ Return $(\mathsf{crs}, \mathsf{td}, msk)$	$\mathsf{Sim}(\mathsf{td}, [\mathbf{c}], \tau)$: $\mathbf{r} \xleftarrow{\$} \mathbb{Z}_q^k; [\mathbf{t}] := [\mathbf{B}_0]\mathbf{r}$ $\pi_{or} \leftarrow \Pi_{or}.\mathsf{Prove}(\mathsf{crs}_{or}, [\mathbf{t}], \mathbf{r})$ $\theta := H([\mathbf{c}], \tau, [\mathbf{t}], \pi_{or})$ $[\mathbf{u}] := (\mathbf{K}_0 + \theta\mathbf{K}_1)[\mathbf{c}] + [\widehat{\mathbf{K}}\mathbf{B}_0]\mathbf{r} \in \mathbb{G}^{m+1}$ Return $\pi := ([\mathbf{t}], [\mathbf{u}], \pi_{or})$
	$\mathsf{Delegate}(msk, \mathbf{d} \in \mathbb{Z}_q^m)$: Return $sk_\mathbf{d} := (\mathbf{d}^\top\mathbf{M}, \mathbf{d}^\top\mathbf{M}\mathbf{K}_0, \mathbf{d}^\top\mathbf{M}\mathbf{K}_1, \mathbf{d}^\top\mathbf{M}\widehat{\mathbf{K}})$
$\mathsf{Prove}(\mathsf{crs}, [\mathbf{c}], \mathbf{s}, \tau)$: // $\mathbf{c} = \mathbf{A}\mathbf{s}$ $\mathbf{r} \xleftarrow{\$} \mathbb{Z}_q^k; [\mathbf{t}] := [\mathbf{B}_0]\mathbf{r}$ $\pi_{or} \leftarrow \Pi_{or}.\mathsf{Prove}(\mathsf{crs}_{or}, [\mathbf{t}], \mathbf{r})$ $\theta := H([\mathbf{c}], \tau, [\mathbf{t}], \pi_{or})$ $[\mathbf{u}] := [(\mathbf{K}_0 + \theta\mathbf{K}_1)\mathbf{A}]\mathbf{s} + [\widehat{\mathbf{K}}\mathbf{B}_0]\mathbf{r} \in \mathbb{G}^{m+1}$ Return $\pi := ([\mathbf{t}], [\mathbf{u}], \pi_{or})$	$\mathsf{FVer}(sk_\mathbf{d}, [\mathbf{c}], \tau, \pi = ([\mathbf{t}], [\mathbf{u}], \pi_{or}))$: If $\Pi_{or}.\mathsf{Ver}(\mathsf{crs}_{or}, [\mathbf{t}], \pi_{or}) = 0$: return 0 $\theta := H([\mathbf{c}], \tau, [\mathbf{t}], \pi_{or})$ If $\mathbf{d}^\top\mathbf{M}[\mathbf{u}] = \mathbf{d}^\top\mathbf{M}(\mathbf{K}_0 + \theta\mathbf{K}_1)[\mathbf{c}] + \mathbf{d}^\top\mathbf{M}\widehat{\mathbf{K}}[\mathbf{t}]$: return 1 Otherwise: return 0

Fig. 5. The pairing-based construction of tag-based FV-NIZK Π, where $\Pi_{or} = (\Pi_{or}.\mathsf{Gen}, \Pi_{or}.\mathsf{TGen}, \Pi_{or}.\mathsf{Prove}, \Pi_{or}.\mathsf{Sim}, \Pi_{or}.\mathsf{Ver})$ is a NIZK proof for OR-language $\mathscr{L}^\vee_{[\mathbf{B}_0], [\mathbf{B}_1]}$.

Completeness and perfect zero-knowledge follow directly from the fact that

$$\mathbf{u} = (\mathbf{K}_0 + \theta\mathbf{K}_1)\mathbf{A}\mathbf{s} + \widehat{\mathbf{K}}\mathbf{B}_0\mathbf{r} = (\mathbf{K}_0 + \theta\mathbf{K}_1)\mathbf{c} + \widehat{\mathbf{K}}\mathbf{t} \quad // \text{ completeness (1)}$$

$$= (\mathbf{K}_0 + \theta\mathbf{K}_1)\mathbf{c} + \widehat{\mathbf{K}}\mathbf{B}_0\mathbf{r}, \quad // \text{ perfect zero-knowledge}$$

which implies $\mathbf{d}^\top\mathbf{M}\mathbf{u} = \mathbf{d}^\top\mathbf{M}(\mathbf{K}_0 + \theta\mathbf{K}_1)\mathbf{c} + \mathbf{d}^\top\mathbf{M}\widehat{\mathbf{K}}\mathbf{t}$. // completeness (2)

Next, we show the verification equivalence and almost tight strong USS of Π.

Theorem 4 (Verification Equivalence). *The tag-based FV-NIZK scheme Π in Fig. 5 has $(0, 1/q)$-verification equivalence.*

The proof is very similar to that of Theorem 1 and we show it in the full version.

Theorem 5 (Almost Tight Strong USS). *If the $\mathcal{D}_{2k,k}$-MDDH assumption holds in $\mathbb{G}$, $\mathcal{H}$ is a family of collision resistant hash functions, and Π_{or} is a NIZK proof for $\mathscr{L}^\vee_{[\mathbf{B}_0], [\mathbf{B}_1]}$ with completeness, perfect soundness and zero-knowledge, then the tag-based FV-NIZK scheme Π in Fig. 5 has strong USS. More precisely, for any adversary $\mathcal{A}$ against the strong USS security of Π, there exist algorithms $\mathcal{B}_1, \mathcal{B}_2, \mathcal{B}_3$ s.t. $\max(Time(\mathcal{B}_1), Time(\mathcal{B}_2), Time(\mathcal{B}_3)) \approx Time(\mathcal{A}) + (Q_{sim} + Q_{ver} + Q_{del}) \cdot \mathsf{poly}(\lambda)$, and*

$$\mathsf{Adv}_{\Pi,\mathcal{A}}^{uss}(\lambda) \leq \mathsf{Adv}_{\mathcal{H},\mathcal{B}_1}^{cr}(\lambda) + (2\mathfrak{n}+2)\cdot\mathsf{Adv}_{\Pi_{or},\mathcal{B}_2}^{zk}(\lambda)$$
$$+ (4k\mathfrak{n}+2k)\cdot\mathsf{Adv}_{\mathcal{D}_{2k,k},\mathsf{G},\mathcal{B}_3}^{mddh}(\lambda) + \tfrac{(\mathfrak{n}+1)(Q_{sim}Q_{ver}+4)}{q-1}.$$

where $Q_{sim}, Q_{ver}, Q_{del}$ denote the numbers of queries to SIM, VER, DELEGATE, respectively, and $\mathfrak{n} := \lceil \log Q_{sim} \rceil$.

The proof is provided in the full version due to space limitations.

Remark 7 (On the almost tightness of strong USS). Similar to Remark 6, the term $\frac{(\mathfrak{n}+1)(Q_{sim}Q_{ver}+4)}{q-1}$ in Theorem 5 does not affect the tightness of the reduction since it is statistically small. Moreover, k is the parameter of the MDDH assumption (e.g., $k = 1$ corresponds to the standard DDH assumption). Consequently, the strong USS has security loss factor $O(\mathfrak{n}) = O(\lceil \log Q_{sim} \rceil)$, which is $O(\log \lambda)$ for PPT adversaries due to $Q_{sim} = \mathsf{poly}(\lambda)$, and thus is almost tight.

Remark 8 We note that our tag-based FV-NIZK scheme Π in Fig. 5 does not achieve proof pseudorandomness, since its proof π contains a proof π_{or} of the underlying NIZK scheme Π_{or} which supports public verification, so that anyone who obtains crs_{or} from pp can check the validity of π_{or}.

5   Applications of FV-NIZK

In this section, we illustrate the usefulness of tag-based FV-NIZK by showing two applications, including CCA-secure IPFE in Subsect. 5.1 and CCA-secure fine-grained verifiable PKE (FV-PKE) in Subsect. 5.2.

By instantiating with the almost tightly secure FV-NIZK schemes constructed in Sect. 4, we immediately obtain IPFE and FV-PKE schemes that achieve almost tight mCCA (multi-challenge CCA) security. Moreover, the resulting schemes are either pairing-free (when using the FV-NIZK scheme in Subsect. 4.1), or use less pairing operations than existing works (when using the FV-NIZK scheme in Subsect. 4.2).

5.1   Almost Tightly mCCA-Secure IPFE Schemes

In [26], Liu et al. proposed the first almost tightly mCCA secure IPFE scheme, based on a tightly mCPA secure scheme [31] and an almost tightly secure QA-NIZK argument for linear subspace languages [4]. However, the QA-NIZK argument in [4] involves pairings, so does Liu et al.'s IPFE.

To reduce the number of pairing operations or even get rid of pairings, we replace the QA-NIZK with our tag-based FV-NIZK for linear subspace languages in the IPFE construction. When the tag-based FV-NIZK is instantiated with the construction in Subsect. 4.1, we obtain the first pairing-free IPFE scheme with almost tight mCCA security. When it is instantiated with the construction in Subsect. 4.2, we obtain a pairing-based IPFE scheme that uses less pairing operations than [26].

Formally, we present the syntax of IPFE and its mCCA security in the full version and describe our IPFE construction as follows. Let $m, k, X, Y \in \mathbb{N}$, and let $\mathcal{D}_k$ be a matrix distribution. Let $\Pi = (\Pi.\mathsf{Par}, \Pi.\mathsf{Gen}, \Pi.\mathsf{Prove}, \Pi.\mathsf{MVer}, \Pi.\mathsf{Sim}, \Pi.\mathsf{Delegate}, \Pi.\mathsf{FVer})$ be a tag-based FV-NIZK for linear subspace language $\mathscr{L}_{[\mathbf{A}]}$ with tag space $\mathcal{T}$ and delegation space $\mathcal{D} = \mathbb{Z}_q^m$. Let $\mathcal{H} : \{0,1\}^* \to \mathcal{T}$ be a family of collision resistant hash functions. Our IPFE construction $\mathsf{IPFE}_{\mathsf{mcca}} = (\mathsf{Par}, \mathsf{Setup}, \mathsf{Enc}, \mathsf{KeyGen}, \mathsf{Dec})$ is described in Fig. 6, where the message space is $[-X, X]^m \subseteq \mathbb{Z}_q^m$ and the inner product function is defined by $\mathbf{y} \in [-Y, Y]^m \subseteq \mathbb{Z}_q^m$. Similar to [26, 31], we require mXY to be a polynomial in λ.

The correctness of $\mathsf{IPFE}_{\mathsf{mcca}}$ follows from the completeness of Π and the fact that for $\mathbf{x} \in [-X, X]^m$ and $\mathbf{y} \in [-Y, Y]^m$, it holds

$$d = \mathbf{y}^\top (\mathbf{WAs} + \mathbf{x}) - \mathbf{y}^\top \mathbf{W}(\mathbf{As}) = \mathbf{y}^\top \mathbf{x} \in [-mXY, mXY].$$

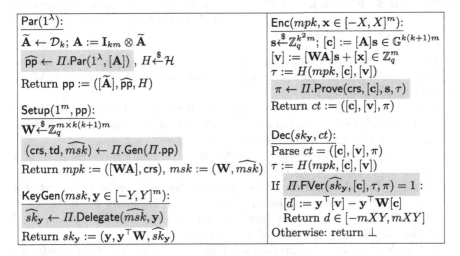

Fig. 6. Construction of $\mathsf{IPFE}_{\mathsf{mcca}}$ from tag-based FV-NIZK Π. For the ease of reading, we emphasize different parts with [26] in gray boxes.

Theorem 6 (Almost Tight mCCA Security of $\mathsf{IPFE}_{\mathsf{mcca}}$). *If the $\mathcal{D}_k$-MDDH assumption holds in $\mathbb{G}$, $\mathcal{H}$ is a family of collision resistant hash functions, and Π is a tag-based FV-NIZK with $(0, \epsilon)$-verification equivalence and strong USS, then $\mathsf{IPFE}_{\mathsf{mcca}}$ shown in Fig. 6 is mCCA-secure. Concretely, for any PPT adversary $\mathcal{A}$, there exist PPT algorithms $\mathcal{B}_1, \mathcal{B}_2, \mathcal{B}_3$ s.t. $\max(Time(\mathcal{B}_1), Time(\mathcal{B}_2), Time(\mathcal{B}_3)) \approx Time(\mathcal{A}) + (Q_{enc} + Q_{sk} + Q_{dec}) \cdot \mathsf{poly}(\lambda, m)$ with $\mathsf{poly}(\lambda, m)$ independent of $\mathcal{A}$, and*

$$\mathsf{Adv}_{\mathsf{IPFE}_{\mathsf{mcca}}, \mathcal{A}}^{mcca}(\lambda) \le 2\mathsf{Adv}_{\mathcal{H}, \mathcal{B}_1}^{cr}(\lambda) + 4\mathsf{Adv}_{\mathcal{D}_k, \mathbb{G}, \mathcal{B}_2}^{mddh}(\lambda) + 2\mathsf{Adv}_{\Pi, \mathcal{B}_3}^{uss}(\lambda) + 2Q_{dec} \cdot \epsilon + \frac{2}{q-1},$$

where Q_{enc}, Q_{sk} *and* Q_{dec} *denote the total numbers of encryption, key generation and decryption queries, respectively.*

The proof is shown in the full version due to space limitations.

5.2 Almost Tightly mCCA-Secure FV-PKE Schemes

In this subsection, we formalize the new primitive called *Fine-grained Verifiable PKE (FV-PKE)*, and define verification soundness, mCCA security, and ciphertext pseudorandomness for it. Then we show how to construct FV-PKE based on our tag-based FV-NIZK. By instantiating with the almost tightly secure FV-NIZK scheme proposed in Subsect. 4.1, we obtain the first FV-PKE scheme with almost tight mCCA security and ciphertext pseudorandomness.

We first present the syntax of FV-PKE.

Definition 8 (FV-PKE). *A Fine-grained Verifiable Public-Key Encryption (FV-PKE) scheme consists of six PPT algorithms, namely* FPKE = (Par, Gen, Enc, Dec, Delegate, Ver).

- pp ← Par(1^λ): *Initialization algorithm takes the security parameter λ as input and outputs a public parameter* pp, *which defines the message space $\mathcal{M}$ and the delegation space $\mathcal{D}$.*
- (pk, sk) ← Gen(pp): *Generation algorithm takes* pp *as inputs, and outputs a public key pk and a secret key sk. We assume pk contains* pp, *and it serves as an implicit input of* Enc, Dec, Delegate, *and* Ver.
- ct ← Enc(pk, M): *Encryption algorithm takes pk and a message $M \in \mathcal{M}$ as inputs, and outputs a ciphertext ct.*
- $M'/\perp$ ← Dec(sk, ct): *Decryption algorithm takes sk and a ciphertext ct as inputs, and outputs a message $M' \in \mathcal{M}$ or a special failure symbol $\perp$.*
- sk_d ← Delegate(sk, d): *Delegation algorithm takes sk and a delegation $d \in \mathcal{D}$ as inputs, and outputs a delegated secret key sk_d.*
- $0/1$ ← Ver(sk_d, ct): *Verification algorithm takes sk_d and ct as inputs, and outputs a bit indicating whether ct is a valid ciphertext or not.*

We require FPKE *to have decryption correctness and verification correctness.*

Decryption Correctness. *For all* pp, (pk, sk) ← Gen(pp), $M \in \mathcal{M}$ *and* ct ← Enc(pk, M), *it holds that* Dec(sk, ct) = M.

Verification Correctness. *For all* pp, (pk, sk) ← Gen(pp), $M \in \mathcal{M}$ *and* ct ← Enc(pk, M), *it holds* Ver(sk_d, ct) = 1 *for all* sk_d ← Delegate(sk, d) *of all $d \in \mathcal{D}$.*

Note that the first four algorithms (Par, Gen, Enc, Dec) of FV-PKE basically constitute a standard PKE scheme. Moreover, the two additional algorithms (Delegate, Ver) provide the fine-grained ability for verifying ciphertext validity.

Next, we define a statistical property called *verification soundness* for FV-PKE. Loosely speaking, it essentially requires that for any ciphertext ct and any sk_d, Ver(sk_d, ct) outputs 1 if and only if ct is a valid ciphertext, i.e., Dec(sk, ct) succeeds, except for a negligible probability.

Definition 9 (Verification Soundness of FV-PKE). *Let $\delta, \epsilon > 0$. An FV-PKE scheme* FPKE *has (δ, ϵ)-verification soundness, if for any (even unbounded) adversary $\mathcal{A}$, it holds that*

$$\mathsf{Adv}^{ver\text{-}snd}_{\mathsf{FPKE},\mathcal{A},\delta}(\lambda) := \Pr[\mathsf{Exp}^{ver\text{-}snd}_{\mathsf{FPKE},\mathcal{A},\delta}(\lambda) \Rightarrow 1] \leq \epsilon,$$

where the experiment $\mathsf{Exp}^{ver\text{-}snd}_{\mathsf{FPKE},\mathcal{A},\delta}(\lambda)$ *is defined in Fig. 7.*

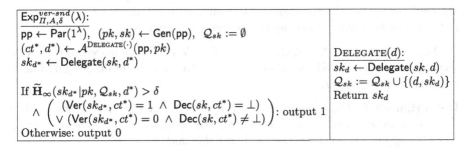

Fig. 7. The verification soundness experiment $\mathsf{Exp}^{ver\text{-}snd}_{\mathsf{FPKE},\mathcal{A},\delta}(\lambda)$ for FV-PKE.

Remark 9 (On the formalization of verification soundness). We stress that we do not require Ver can always correctly decide whether a ciphertext is valid or not. That is, there might exist a ciphertext ct and a pair (d, sk_d) s.t., $\mathsf{Dec}(sk, ct) = \perp$ but $\mathsf{Ver}(sk_d, ct) = 1$, or $\mathsf{Dec}(sk, ct) \neq \perp$ but $\mathsf{Ver}(sk_d, ct) = 0$. Nevertheless, verification soundness of FV-PKE ensures that even for an (unbounded) adversary $\mathcal{A}$, if it does not get enough information about sk_{d^*} (and thus sk), it is hard for $\mathcal{A}$ to find a ct^* that makes $\mathsf{Dec}(sk, \cdot)$ and $\mathsf{Ver}(sk_{d^*}, \cdot)$ perform inconsistently. Similar to Remark 1, we require "$\widetilde{\mathbf{H}}_\infty(sk_{d^*}|pk, \mathcal{Q}_{sk}, d^*) > \delta$" in Fig. 7 to prevent trivial attacks, since for those who get sk_{d^*}, it might be easy for them to produce such a ct^*.

Remark 10 (On the motivation for defining FV-PKE with the delegation space $\mathcal{D}$). The main motivation for defining FV-PKE with the delegation d is to provide the flexibility of verification, which can be used to make the verification result closer to the validity of ciphertexts, as explained below. Let us go back to the motivating example described in the introduction, where a manager asks an assistant to filter out invalid ciphertexts. By using FV-PKE, the manager can give a delegated key sk_d to the assistant, and the property of verification soundness guarantees that verification using sk_d can correctly decide the validity for ciphertexts generated by the outsider (i.e., anyone other than the manager and the assistant). However, since the assistant has sk_d, it does not exclude the possibility that the assistant itself produces ill-formed ciphertexts which are invalid but pass the verification, or are valid but do not pass the verification. We refer to this as an "insider" attack.

Thanks to the fact that FV-PKE supports delegation d, such "insider" attacks can be easily prevented: the manager can ask several assistants, give them different delegated keys $(sk_{d_1}, sk_{d_2}, ...)$, and regard a ciphertext valid only if it passes all the verifications. As long as not all the assistants collude, it is hard for them to produce ill-formed ciphertexts which are invalid but pass all the verifications, or are valid but do not pass all the verifications. Of course, the manager can also set a threshold, and regard a ciphertext valid if the number of verifications that it passes is above the threshold, in order to tolerate inadvertent errors. This reflects the flexibility of verification. Stepping back, even if an "insider" attack occurs, the manager can identify which assistant produced the ill-formed ciphertexts, by tracing the delegation d from sk_d.

Then we formalize the mCCA security for FV-PKE. Compared to the CCA security for standard PKE, we also allow the adversary to obtain delegated keys sk_d with d of its choices.

Definition 10 (mCCA Security of FV-PKE). *An FV-PKE scheme* FPKE *is indistinguishable under chosen ciphertext attacks in the multi-challenge setting (mCCA), if for any PPT adversary* $\mathcal{A}$, *it holds that*

$$\mathsf{Adv}^{mcca}_{\mathsf{FPKE},\mathcal{A}}(\lambda) := \left| \Pr[\mathsf{Exp}^{mcca}_{\mathsf{FPKE},\mathcal{A},0}(\lambda) \Rightarrow 1] - \Pr[\mathsf{Exp}^{mcca}_{\mathsf{FPKE},\mathcal{A},1}(\lambda) \Rightarrow 1] \right| \leq \mathsf{negl}(\lambda),$$

where the experiments $\mathsf{Exp}^{mcca}_{\mathsf{FPKE},\mathcal{A},\beta}(\lambda)$ *($\beta \in \{0,1\}$) are defined in Fig. 8.*

$\mathsf{Exp}^{mcca}_{\mathsf{FPKE},\mathcal{A},\beta}(\lambda)$: // $\beta \in \{0,1\}$	$\mathrm{ENC}(M^0, M^1)$:
$\mathsf{pp} \leftarrow \mathsf{Par}(1^\lambda)$, $(pk, sk) \leftarrow \mathsf{Gen}(\mathsf{pp})$ $\mathcal{Q}_{enc} := \emptyset; \mathcal{Q}_{sk} := \emptyset$ $\beta' \leftarrow \mathcal{A}^{\mathrm{ENC}(\cdot,\cdot),\mathrm{DEC}(\cdot),\mathrm{DELEGATE}(\cdot)}(\mathsf{pp}, pk)$ Output β'	$ct \leftarrow \mathsf{Enc}(pk, M^\beta)$ $\mathcal{Q}_{enc} := \mathcal{Q}_{enc} \cup \{ct\}$ Return ct
$\mathrm{DELEGATE}(d)$:	$\mathrm{DEC}(ct)$:
$sk_d \leftarrow \mathsf{Delegate}(sk, d)$ $\mathcal{Q}_{sk} := \mathcal{Q}_{sk} \cup \{(d, sk_d)\}$ Return sk_d	If $ct \in \mathcal{Q}_{enc}$: return $\bot$ Return $\mathsf{Dec}(sk, ct)$

Fig. 8. The IND-mCCA security experiments $\mathsf{Exp}^{mcca}_{\mathsf{FPKE},\mathcal{A},\beta}(\lambda)$ for FV-PKE.

Finally, we define *ciphertext pseudorandomness* for FV-PKE, which requires the pseudorandomness of ciphertexts for PPT adversaries that are not given any secret key but allowed to access the decryption oracle. This clearly implies anonymity.

Definition 11 (Ciphertext Pseudorandomness of FV-PKE). *An FV-PKE scheme* FPKE *has ciphertext pseudorandomness in the multi-challenge setting, if for any PPT adversary* $\mathcal{A}$, *it holds that*

$$\mathsf{Adv}^{cp}_{\mathsf{FPKE},\mathcal{A}}(\lambda) := |\Pr[\mathsf{Exp}^{cp}_{\mathsf{FPKE},\mathcal{A},0}(\lambda) \Rightarrow 1] - \Pr[\mathsf{Exp}^{cp}_{\mathsf{FPKE},\mathcal{A},1}(\lambda) \Rightarrow 1]| \leq \mathsf{negl}(\lambda),$$

$\mathsf{Exp}^{cp}_{\mathsf{FPKE},\mathcal{A},\beta}(\lambda)$: // $\beta \in \{0,1\}$	
$\mathsf{pp} \leftarrow \mathsf{Par}(1^\lambda),\ (pk, sk) \leftarrow \mathsf{Gen}(\mathsf{pp}),\ \mathcal{Q}_{enc} := \emptyset$	$\textsc{Enc}(M):$
$\beta' \leftarrow \mathcal{A}^{\textsc{Enc}(\cdot),\textsc{Dec}(\cdot)}(\mathsf{pp}, pk)$	If $\beta = 0$: $ct \leftarrow \mathsf{Enc}(pk, M)$
Output β'	If $\beta = 1$: $ct \xleftarrow{\$} \mathcal{CT}$
	$\mathcal{Q}_{enc} := \mathcal{Q}_{enc} \cup \{ct\}$
$\textsc{Dec}(ct):$	Return ct
If $ct \in \mathcal{Q}_{enc}$: return $\bot$	
Return $\mathsf{Dec}(sk, ct)$	

Fig. 9. The ciphertext pseudorandomness experiments $\mathsf{Exp}^{cp}_{\mathsf{FPKE},\mathcal{A},\beta}(\lambda)$ for FV-PKE, where $\mathcal{CT}$ denotes the ciphertext space.

where the experiments $\mathsf{Exp}^{cp}_{\mathsf{FPKE},\mathcal{A},\beta}(\lambda)$ *($\beta \in \{0,1\}$) are defined in Fig. 9.*

Construction of FV-PKE. Now we describe our FV-PKE construction as follows. Let $\Pi = (\Pi.\mathsf{Par}, \Pi.\mathsf{Gen}, \Pi.\mathsf{Prove}, \Pi.\mathsf{MVer}, \Pi.\mathsf{Sim}, \Pi.\mathsf{Delegate}, \Pi.\mathsf{FVer})$ be a tag-based FV-NIZK for linear subspace language $\mathscr{L}_{[\mathbf{A}]}$ with tag space $\mathcal{T}$ and delegation space $\mathcal{D}$. Let $\mathcal{H} : \{0,1\}^* \to \mathcal{T}$ be a family of collision resistant hash functions. Our FV-PKE construction $\mathsf{FPKE}_{\mathsf{mcca}} = (\mathsf{Par}, \mathsf{Gen}, \mathsf{Enc}, \mathsf{Dec}, \mathsf{Delegate}, \mathsf{Ver})$ is described in Fig. 10, where the message space is $\mathbb{G}$ and the delegation space is $\mathcal{D}$.

The decryption correctness follows from the completeness (1) of Π and the fact that

$$[v] - \mathbf{w}^\top[\mathbf{c}] = ([\mathbf{w}^\top \mathbf{A}]\mathbf{s} + M) - \mathbf{w}^\top[\mathbf{As}] = M,$$

and the verification correctness follows from the completeness (2) of Π.

Theorem 7 (Verification Soundness of $\mathsf{FPKE}_{\mathsf{mcca}}$). *If Π is a tag-based FV-NIZK with (δ, ϵ)-verification equivalence, then FPKE shown in Fig. 10 has (δ, ϵ)-verification soundness.*

Proof. The proof is straightforward. Since Π has (δ, ϵ)-verification equivalence, the algorithms $\Pi.\mathsf{MVer}$ and $\Pi.\mathsf{FVer}$ perform identically, except with probability at most ϵ. Consequently, it is hard for an (even unbounded) adversary to find (ct^*, d^*) that passes the verification algorithm Ver of FPKE (i.e., passing $\Pi.\mathsf{FVer}$) but fails the decryption of ct^* (i.e., not passing $\Pi.\mathsf{MVer}$), or fails to pass Ver (i.e., not passing $\Pi.\mathsf{FVer}$) but decrypts successfully (i.e., passing $\Pi.\mathsf{MVer}$). $\square$

Now we show that $\mathsf{FPKE}_{\mathsf{mcca}}$ has almost tight mCCA security and almost tight ciphertext pseudorandomness via the following two theorems.

Theorem 8 (Almost Tight mCCA Security of $\mathsf{FPKE}_{\mathsf{mcca}}$). *If the $\mathcal{D}_{2k,k}$-MDDH assumption holds in $\mathbb{G}$, $\mathcal{H}$ is a family of collision resistant hash functions, and Π is a tag-based FV-NIZK with strong USS, then $\mathsf{FPKE}_{\mathsf{mcca}}$ shown in Fig. 10 is mCCA-secure. Concretely, for any PPT adversary $\mathcal{A}$, there exist PPT algorithms $\mathcal{B}_1, \mathcal{B}_3, \mathcal{B}_3$ s.t. $\max(Time(\mathcal{B}_1), Time(\mathcal{B}_2), Time(\mathcal{B}_3)) \approx Time(\mathcal{A}) + (Q_{enc} + Q_{sk} + Q_{dec}) \cdot \mathsf{poly}(\lambda)$ with $\mathsf{poly}(\lambda)$ independent of $\mathcal{A}$, and*

$$\mathsf{Adv}^{mcca}_{\mathsf{FPKE}_{\mathsf{mcca}},\mathcal{A}}(\lambda) \leq 2\mathsf{Adv}^{cr}_{\mathcal{H},\mathcal{B}_1}(\lambda) + (2k+4)\mathsf{Adv}^{mddh}_{\mathcal{D}_{2k,k},\mathbb{G},\mathcal{B}_2}(\lambda) + 2\mathsf{Adv}^{uss}_{\Pi,\mathcal{B}_3}(\lambda) + \tfrac{6}{q-1},$$

Par(1^λ):	
$\mathbf{A} \leftarrow \mathcal{D}_{2k,k}$; $H \xleftarrow{\$} \mathcal{H}$	Dec($sk, ct = ([\mathbf{c}], [v], \pi)$):
$\widehat{pp} \leftarrow \Pi.\mathsf{Par}(1^\lambda, [\mathbf{A}])$	$\tau := H(pk, [\mathbf{c}], [v])$
Return pp := $([\mathbf{A}], \widehat{pp}, H)$	If $\Pi.\mathsf{MVer}(\widehat{msk}, [\mathbf{c}], \tau, \pi) = 1$:
Gen(pp):	Return $M' := [v] - \mathbf{w}^\top[\mathbf{c}]$
$\mathbf{w} \leftarrow \mathbb{Z}_q^{2k}$	Otherwise: return $\bot$
$(\mathrm{crs}, \mathrm{td}, \widehat{msk}) \leftarrow \Pi.\mathsf{Gen}(\widehat{pp})$	Delegate(sk, d):
Return $pk := ([\mathbf{w}^\top \mathbf{A}], \mathrm{crs})$, $sk := (\mathbf{w}, \widehat{msk})$	$sk_d \leftarrow \Pi.\mathsf{Delegate}(\widehat{msk}, d)$
Enc($pk, M \in \mathbb{G}$):	Return sk_d
$\mathbf{s} \xleftarrow{\$} \mathbb{Z}_q^k$; $[\mathbf{c}] := [\mathbf{A}]\mathbf{s} \in \mathbb{G}^{2k}$	
$[v] := [\mathbf{w}^\top \mathbf{A}]\mathbf{s} + M \in \mathbb{G}$	Ver($sk_d, ct = ([\mathbf{c}], [v], \pi)$):
$\tau := H(pk, [\mathbf{c}], [v])$	$\tau := H(pk, [\mathbf{c}], [v])$
$\pi \leftarrow \Pi.\mathsf{Prove}(\mathrm{crs}, [\mathbf{c}], \mathbf{s}, \tau)$	Return $\Pi.\mathsf{FVer}(sk_d, [\mathbf{c}], \tau, \pi)$
Return $ct := ([\mathbf{c}], [v], \pi)$	

Fig. 10. Construction of $\mathsf{FPKE}_{\mathsf{mcca}}$ from tag-based FV-NIZK Π. For the ease of reading, we emphasize the parts related to Π in gray boxes .

where Q_{enc}, Q_{sk} and Q_{dec} denote the total numbers of encryption, delegation and decryption queries, respectively.

Proof. We prove the theorem via a series of games $\mathsf{G}_0^\beta, ..., \mathsf{G}_5^\beta$ ($\beta \in \{0,1\}$), where the first two games G_0^β are the mCCA experiments $\mathsf{Exp}_{\mathsf{FPKE},\mathcal{A},\beta}^{mcca}(\lambda)$ (cf. Fig. 8), and G_5^0, G_5^1 are identical.

Game G_0^β. They are just the original experiments $\mathsf{Exp}_{\mathsf{FPKE},\mathcal{A},\beta}^{mcca}(\lambda)$, except that we use secret key $\mathbf{w}$ to do the encryption. Due to the equation $[\mathbf{w}^\top \mathbf{A}]\mathbf{s} = \mathbf{w}^\top[\mathbf{A}\mathbf{s}] = \mathbf{w}^\top[\mathbf{c}]$, we have that

$$\Pr[\mathsf{Exp}_{\mathsf{FPKE},\mathcal{A},\beta}^{mcca}(\lambda) \Rightarrow 1] = \Pr[\mathsf{G}_0^\beta \Rightarrow 1], \text{ for } \beta \in \{0,1\}.$$

Game G_1^β. In this two games, whenever there is an encryption or decryption query with tag τ' that collides with some τ used in encryption before, the experiment returns $\bot$ and aborts. By the collision resistance of $\mathcal{H}$, we have

$$|\Pr[\mathsf{G}_0^\beta \Rightarrow 1] - \Pr[\mathsf{G}_1^\beta \Rightarrow 1]| \leq \mathsf{Adv}_{\mathcal{H},\mathcal{B}_1}^{cr}(\lambda), \text{ for } \beta \in \{0,1\}.$$

Game G_2^β. In this two games, $\mathrm{ENC}(M^0, M^1)$ generates proofs π via $\Pi.\mathsf{Sim}(\mathrm{td}, \cdot, \cdot)$. G_1^β and G_2^β are the same due to the perfect zero-knowledge of Π, and we have

$$\Pr[\mathsf{G}_1^\beta \Rightarrow 1] = \Pr[\mathsf{G}_2^\beta \Rightarrow 1], \text{ for } \beta \in \{0,1\}.$$

Game G_3^β. In this two games, we sample $\mathbf{A}_0 \xleftarrow{\$} \mathbb{Z}_q^{2k \times k}$ in the beginning of the experiment. Meanwhile, $\mathrm{Enc}(M^0, M^1)$ computes $[\mathbf{c}] := [\mathbf{A}_0]\mathbf{s}$, instead of $[\mathbf{c}] := [\mathbf{A}]\mathbf{s}$ for $\mathbf{s} \xleftarrow{\$} \mathbb{Z}_q^k$. By the $\mathcal{D}_{2k,k}$-MDDH assumption and Lemma 1, we have

$$|\Pr[G_2^\beta \Rightarrow 1] - \Pr[G_3^\beta \Rightarrow 1]| \le (k+1)\mathsf{Adv}_{\mathcal{D}_{2k,k}, \mathbb{G}, \mathcal{B}_3}^{mddh} + \tfrac{2}{q-1}, \text{ for } \beta \in \{0,1\}.$$

Game G_4^β. In this two games, the decryption oracle $\mathrm{Dec}([\mathbf{c}^*], [v^*], \pi^*)$ returns $\perp$ directly if $([\mathbf{c}^*], [v^*], \pi^*) \notin \mathcal{Q}_{enc}$ and $[\mathbf{c}^*] \notin \mathscr{L}_{[\mathbf{A}]}$.

Define by bad the event that there exists a query $\mathrm{Dec}([\mathbf{c}^*], [v^*], \pi^*)$, such that $([\mathbf{c}^*], [v^*], \pi^*) \notin \mathcal{Q}_{enc}$, $[\mathbf{c}^*] \notin \mathscr{L}_{[\mathbf{A}]}$, and there is no hash collision, but $\Pi.\mathsf{MVer}(\widehat{msk}, [\mathbf{c}^*], \tau^*, \pi^*) = 1$, where $\tau^* := H(pk, [\mathbf{c}^*], [v^*])$. Obviously, G_3^β and G_4^β are identical unless bad happens. Thanks to the strong USS of Π, we have the following lemma.

Lemma 3 *For* $\beta \in \{0,1\}$, $|\Pr[G_3^\beta \Rightarrow 1] - \Pr[G_4^\beta \Rightarrow 1]| \le \Pr[\mathsf{bad}] \le \mathsf{Adv}_{\Pi, \mathcal{B}_4}^{uss}(\lambda)$.

Game G_5^β. In this two games, $\mathrm{Enc}(M^0, M^1)$ uniformly samples $[\mathbf{c}] \xleftarrow{\$} \mathbb{G}^{2k}$ and $[v] \xleftarrow{\$} \mathbb{G}$, instead of computing $[\mathbf{c}] := [\mathbf{A}_0]\mathbf{s}$ for $\mathbf{s} \xleftarrow{\$} \mathbb{Z}_q^k$ and $[v] := \mathbf{w}^\top[\mathbf{c}] + M^\beta$.

Lemma 4 *For* $\beta \in \{0,1\}$, $|\Pr[G_4^\beta \Rightarrow 1] - \Pr[G_5^\beta \Rightarrow 1]| \le \mathsf{Adv}_{\mathcal{U}_k, \mathbb{G}, \mathcal{B}_5}^{mddh} + \tfrac{1}{q-1}$.

Proof. First we argue that in G_4^β, $\mathbf{w}$ still contains some entropy which is not leaked via pk and $\mathrm{Dec}(\cdot, \cdot, \cdot)$. Then we show that the left entropy helps us change $[\mathbf{c}]$ from $[\mathbf{c}] := [\mathbf{A}_0]\mathbf{s}$ to $[\mathbf{c}] \xleftarrow{\$} \mathbb{G}^{2k}$, and change $[v]$ from $[v] := \mathbf{w}^\top[\mathbf{c}] + M^\beta$ to $[v] \xleftarrow{\$} \mathbb{G}$, based on the Q_{sim}-fold $\mathcal{U}_{2k+1,k}$-MDDH assumption.

To see this, we redefine $\mathbf{w}^\top$ as $\mathbf{w}^\top := \mathbf{w}'^\top + \mathbf{z}^\top \mathbf{A}^\perp$, where $\mathbf{w}' \xleftarrow{\$} \mathbb{Z}_q^{2k}$, $\mathbf{z} \xleftarrow{\$} \mathbb{Z}_q^k$, and $\mathbf{A}^\perp \xleftarrow{\$} \mathbb{Z}_q^{k \times 2k}$ s.t. $\mathbf{A}^\perp \mathbf{A} = \mathbf{0}$. We argue that the information of $\mathbf{z}$ is totally hidden to $\mathcal{A}$.

- pk hides the information of $\mathbf{z}$, due to

$$\mathbf{w}^\top \mathbf{A} = (\mathbf{w}'^\top + \mathbf{z}^\top \mathbf{A}^\perp)\mathbf{A} = \mathbf{w}'^\top \mathbf{A}.$$

- $\mathrm{Delegate}(\cdot)$ hides the information of $\mathbf{z}$, since it does not involve $\mathbf{w}$ at all.
- $\mathrm{Dec}([\mathbf{c}^*], [v^*], \pi^*)$ hides the information of $\mathbf{z}$. Thanks to the new rejection rule added in G_4, we have $[\mathbf{c}^*] \in \mathscr{L}_{[\mathbf{A}]}$ as otherwise $\mathrm{Dec}([\mathbf{c}^*], [v^*], \pi^*)$ returns $\perp$ immediately. Therefore, $\mathbf{A}^\perp[\mathbf{c}^*] = [\mathbf{0}]$, and

$$\mathbf{w}^\top[\mathbf{c}^*] = (\mathbf{w}'^\top + \mathbf{z}^\top \mathbf{A}^\perp)[\mathbf{c}^*] = \mathbf{w}'^\top[\mathbf{c}^*].$$

With overwhelming probability we have $\mathbf{A}^\perp \mathbf{A}_0 \ne \mathbf{0}$. That is, $\mathbf{z}^\top \mathbf{A}^\perp \mathbf{A}_0$ is a random value over $\mathbb{Z}_q^{1 \times k}$ from $\mathcal{A}$'s view. According to the Q_{sim}-fold $\mathcal{U}_{2k+1,k}$-MDDH assumption (equivalently the $\mathcal{U}_k$-MDDH assumption due to Lemma 1 and Lemma 2), we know the following two distributions are computationally indistinguishable:

$$\{[\mathbf{A}_0\mathbf{s}_j], [\mathbf{z}^\top\mathbf{A}^\perp\mathbf{A}_0\mathbf{s}_j]\}_{j\in[Q_{sim}]} \stackrel{c}{\approx} \{[\mathbf{c}'_j], [v'_j]\}_{j\in[Q_{sim}]},$$

where $\mathbf{s}_j \xleftarrow{\$} \mathbb{Z}_q^k, \mathbf{c}'_j \xleftarrow{\$} \mathbb{Z}_q^{2k}, v'_j \xleftarrow{\$} \mathbb{Z}_q$ for $1 \le j \le Q_{sim}$.

Recall that in G_4^β, $\mathrm{ENC}(M_0, M_1)$ computes $[\mathbf{c}], [v]$ as $[\mathbf{c}] := [\mathbf{A}_0]\mathbf{s}$ and $[v] := \mathbf{w}^\top[\mathbf{c}] + M^\beta = \mathbf{w}'^\top[\mathbf{c}] + M^\beta + \mathbf{z}^\top\mathbf{A}^\perp[\mathbf{A}_0\mathbf{s}]$, which are indistinguishable from $[\mathbf{c}] \xleftarrow{\$} \mathbb{G}^{2k}$ and $[v] \xleftarrow{\$} \mathbb{G}$ according to the formula above. Then by Lemma 1, Lemma 4 holds as a result.   □

Obviously G_5^0 and G_5^1 are identical. At last, thanks to Lemma 2, Theorem 8 follows by taking all things together.   □

Theorem 9 (Almost Tight Ciphertext Pseudorandomness of FPKE$_{\mathsf{mcca}}$). *If the $\mathcal{D}_{2k,k}$-MDDH assumption holds in $\mathbb{G}$, $\mathcal{H}$ is a family of collision resistant hash functions, and Π is a tag-based FV-NIZK with strong USS and proof pseudorandomness, then* FPKE$_{\mathsf{mcca}}$ *shown in Fig. 10 has ciphertext pseudorandomness. Concretely, for any PPT adversary $\mathcal{A}$, there exist PPT algorithms $\mathcal{B}_1, ..., \mathcal{B}_4$ s.t. $\max(Time(\mathcal{B}_1), ..., Time(\mathcal{B}_4)) \approx Time(\mathcal{A}) + (Q_{enc} + Q_{dec}) \cdot \mathsf{poly}(\lambda)$ with $\mathsf{poly}(\lambda)$ independent of $\mathcal{A}$, and*

$$\mathsf{Adv}_{\mathsf{FPKE}_{\mathsf{mcca}},\mathcal{A}}^{cp}(\lambda) \le 2\mathsf{Adv}_{\mathcal{H},\mathcal{B}_1}^{cr}(\lambda) + (2k+2)\mathsf{Adv}_{\mathcal{D}_{2k,k},\mathbb{G},\mathcal{B}_2}^{mddh}(\lambda) + 2\mathsf{Adv}_{\Pi,\mathcal{B}_3}^{uss}(\lambda)$$
$$+ \mathsf{Adv}_{\Pi,\mathcal{B}_4}^{pp}(\lambda) + \tfrac{4}{q-1},$$

where Q_{enc} and Q_{dec} denote the total numbers of encryption and decryption queries, respectively.

Proof. Theorem 9 is proved via a series of games $\mathsf{G}_0, ..., \mathsf{G}_8$, where G_0 is the ciphertext pseudorandomness experiment $\mathsf{Exp}_{\mathsf{FPKE},\mathcal{A},0}^{cp}(\lambda)$ (cf. Fig. 9), and G_8 is indistinguishable with $\mathsf{Exp}_{\mathsf{FPKE},\mathcal{A},1}^{cp}(\lambda)$.

Due to the page limitation, we safely omit the descriptions of games $\mathsf{G}_0, ..., \mathsf{G}_5$, since they are similar with those in the proof of Theorem 8.

Game G_6. In this game, we eliminate the additional check $[\mathbf{c}^*] \in \mathsf{Span}([\mathbf{A}])$. Similar to the change from G_3 to G_4, due to the strong USS of Π, we have that

$$|\Pr[\mathsf{G}_5 \Rightarrow 1] - \Pr[\mathsf{G}_6 \Rightarrow 1]| \le \mathsf{Adv}_{\Pi,\mathcal{B}_6}^{uss}(\lambda).$$

Game G_7. In this game, $\mathrm{ENC}(M)$ computes $[\mathbf{c}] := [\mathbf{A}]\mathbf{s}$ for $\mathbf{s} \xleftarrow{\$} \mathbb{Z}_q^k$, instead of $[\mathbf{c}] \xleftarrow{\$} \mathbb{G}^{2k}$. By the $\mathcal{D}_{2k,k}$-MDDH assumption and Lemma 1, we have

$$|\Pr[\mathsf{G}_6 \Rightarrow 1] - \Pr[\mathsf{G}_7 \Rightarrow 1]| \le k\mathsf{Adv}_{\mathcal{D}_{2k,k},\mathbb{G},\mathcal{B}_7}^{mddh} + \tfrac{1}{q-1}.$$

Game G_8. In this game, $\mathrm{ENC}(M)$ uniformly samples $[\mathbf{c}] \xleftarrow{\$} \mathbb{G}^{2k}$ and $\pi \xleftarrow{\$} \mathcal{P}$ instead of $[\mathbf{c}] := [\mathbf{A}]\mathbf{s}$ for $\mathbf{s} \xleftarrow{\$} \mathbb{Z}_q^k$ and $\pi \leftarrow \Pi.\mathsf{Sim}(\mathsf{td}, [\mathbf{c}], \tau)$, where $\mathcal{P}$ denotes the proof space of Π.

Lemma 5 $|\Pr[\mathsf{G}_7 \Rightarrow 1] - \Pr[\mathsf{G}_8 \Rightarrow 1]| \le \mathsf{Adv}^{pp}_{\Pi,\mathcal{B}_8}(\lambda)$.

Proof. We construct a reduction algorithm $\mathcal{B}_8$ to distinguish $\mathsf{Exp}^{pp}_{\Pi,\mathcal{B}_8,0}(\lambda)$ from $\mathsf{Exp}^{pp}_{\Pi,\mathcal{B}_8,1}(\lambda)$ for the proof pseudorandomness security of Π (cf. Fig. 3), as shown in Fig. 11. Recall that $\mathcal{B}_8$ has access to three oracles SAM, SIM, and VER in $\mathsf{Exp}^{pp}_{\Pi,\mathcal{B}_8,\beta}(\lambda)$.

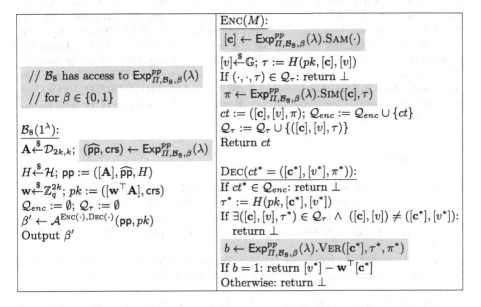

Fig. 11. $\mathcal{B}_8$'s reduction for the proof of Lemma 5.

Obviously, if $\mathcal{B}_8$ has access to $\mathsf{Exp}^{pp}_{\Pi,\mathcal{B}_8,0}(\lambda)$, then it simulates G_7 for $\mathcal{A}$; and if $\mathcal{B}_8$ has access to $\mathsf{Exp}^{pp}_{\Pi,\mathcal{B}_8,1}(\lambda)$, then it simulates G_8 for $\mathcal{A}$. Lemma 5 holds as a result.

From G_8 to $\mathsf{Exp}^{pp}_{\mathsf{FPKE},\mathcal{A},1}(\lambda)$, we eliminate the additional check of hash collisions in ENC(M) and DEC(ct^*). With the same analysis we have

$$|\Pr[\mathsf{G}_8 \Rightarrow 1] - \Pr[\mathsf{Exp}^{cp}_{\mathsf{FPKE},\mathcal{A},1}(\lambda) \Rightarrow 1]| \le \mathsf{Adv}^{cr}_{\mathcal{H},\mathcal{B}'_8}(\lambda).$$

Finally, taking Lemma 2 and all things together, Theorem 9 follows. $\square$

Remark 11 (Extension to the multi-user setting). For better readability, we prove the almost tight mCCA security and ciphertext pseudorandomness of $\mathsf{FPKE}_{\mathsf{mcca}}$ in the single-user setting in Theorems 8 and 9. Now we show how to extend the proof techniques to the multi-user setting. More precisely, the public parameter $\mathsf{pp} = ([\mathbf{A}], \widehat{\mathsf{pp}}, H)$ is shared among all users, and each user $i \in [\mu]$ samples its own master secret key $(\mathbf{w}^{(i)}, \widehat{msk}^{(i)})$. In all computational steps in the proof, we modify all samples of $[\mathbf{c}]$ simultaneously, based on the random self-reducibility of the MDDH assumption. Moreover, the underlying FV-NIZK scheme Π is required to have almost tight strong USS and proof pseudorandomness in the multi-user setting, which is satisfied by the first construction in Subsect. 4.1.

Acknowledgments. We would like to thank the anonymous reviewers for their valuable comments and suggestions. Shengli Liu and Xiangyu Liu were partially supported by National Natural Science Foundation of China (NSFC No. 61925207), Guangdong Major Project of Basic and Applied Basic Research (2019B030302008), and the National Key R&D Program of China under Grant 2022YFB2701500. Shuai Han was partially supported by National Natural Science Foundation of China (Grant No. 62002223), Shanghai Sailing Program (20YF1421100), Young Elite Scientists Sponsorship Program by China Association for Science and Technology (YESS20200185), and Ant Group through CCF-Ant Research Fund (CCF-AFSG RF20220224). Dawu Gu is partially supported by the National Key Research and Development Project (Grant No. 2020YFA0712302).

References

1. Abdalla, M., Bourse, F., Caro, A.D., Pointcheval, D.: Simple functional encryption schemes for inner products. In: PKC 2015, vol. 9020, pp. 733–751 (2015)
2. Abdalla, M., Bourse, F., Caro, A.D., Pointcheval, D.: Better security for functional encryption for inner product evaluations. IACR Cryptol. ePrint Arch. **2016**, 11 (2016)
3. Abe, M., David, B., Kohlweiss, M., Nishimaki, R., Ohkubo, M.: Tagged one-time signatures: tight security and optimal tag size. In: PKC 2013, vol. 7778, pp. 312–331 (2013)
4. Abe, M., Jutla, C.S., Ohkubo, M., Pan, J., Roy, A., Wang, Y.: Shorter QA-NIZK and SPS with tighter security. In: ASIACRYPT 2019, vol. 11923, pp. 669–699 (2019)
5. Abe, M., Jutla, C.S., Ohkubo, M., Roy, A.: Improved (almost) tightly-secure simulation-sound QA-NIZK with applications. In: ASIACRYPT 2018, pp. 627–656 (2018)
6. Agrawal, S., Libert, B., Stehlé, D.: Fully secure functional encryption for inner products, from standard assumptions. In: CRYPTO 2016, pp. 333–362 (2016)
7. Bellare, M., Goldwasser, S.: New paradigms for digital signatures and message authentication based on non-interactive zero knowledge proofs. In: CRYPTO 1989, vol. 435, pp. 194–211 (1989)
8. Blazy, O., Kakvi, S.A., Kiltz, E., Pan, J.: Tightly-secure signatures from chameleon hash functions. In: PKC 2015, pp. 256–279 (2015)
9. Blazy, O., Kiltz, E., Pan, J.: (Hierarchical) identity-based encryption from affine message authentication. In: CRYPTO 2014, pp. 408–425 (2014)
10. Boneh, D., Sahai, A., Waters, B.: Functional encryption: definitions and challenges. In: TCC 2011, vol. 6597, pp. 253–273 (2011)
11. Chen, J., Wee, H.: Fully, (almost) tightly secure IBE and dual system groups. In: CRYPTO 2013, vol. 8043, pp. 435–460 (2013)
12. Cramer, R., Shoup, V.: Universal hash proofs and a paradigm for adaptive chosen ciphertext secure public-key encryption. In: EUROCRYPT 2002, vol. 2332, pp. 45–64 (2002)

13. Dodis, Y., Ostrovsky, R., Reyzin, L., Smith, A.D.: Fuzzy extractors: Hhw to generate strong keys from biometrics and other noisy data. SIAM J. Comput. **38**(1), 97–139 (2008)
14. Dolev, D., Dwork, C., Naor, M.: Non-malleable cryptography (extended abstract). In: STOC 1991, pp. 542–552 (1991)
15. Escala, A., Herold, G., Kiltz, E., Ràfols, C., Villar, J.L.: An algebraic framework for Diffie-Hellman assumptions. In: CRYPTO 2013, vol. 8043, pp. 129–147 (2013)
16. Gay, R., Hofheinz, D., Kiltz, E., Wee, H.: Tightly CCA-secure encryption without pairings. In: EUROCRYPT 2016, vol. 9665, pp. 1–27 (2016)
17. Gay, R., Hofheinz, D., Kohl, L.: Kurosawa-desmedt meets tight security. In: CRYPTO 2017, vol. 10403, pp. 133–160 (2017)
18. Groth, J., Ostrovsky, R., Sahai, A.: New techniques for noninteractive zero-knowledge. J. ACM **59**(3), 1–35 (2012)
19. Han, S., et al.: Authenticated key exchange and signatures with tight security in the standard model. In: CRYPTO 2021, vol. 12828, pp. 670–700 (2021)
20. Han, S., Liu, S., Lyu, L., Gu, D.: Tight leakage-resilient CCA-security from quasi-adaptive hash proof system. In: CRYPTO 2019, vol. 11693, pp. 417–447 (2019)
21. Hofheinz, D., Jager, T.: Tightly secure signatures and public-key encryption. Des. Codes Cryptogr. **80**(1), 29–61 (2016)
22. Hofheinz, D., Jia, D., Pan, J.: Identity-based encryption tightly secure under chosen-ciphertext attacks. In: ASIACRYPT 2018, vol. 11273, pp. 190–220 (2018)
23. Jutla, C.S., Roy, A.: Shorter quasi-adaptive NIZK proofs for linear subspaces. In: ASIACRYPT 2013, vol. 8269, pp. 1–20 (2013)
24. Libert, B., Joye, M., Yung, M., Peters, T.: Concise multi-challenge CCA-secure encryption and signatures with almost tight security. In: ASIACRYPT 2014, pp. 1–21 (2014)
25. Libert, B., Peters, T., Joye, M., Yung, M.: Compactly hiding linear spans - tightly secure constant-size simulation-sound QA-NIZK proofs and applications. In: ASIACRYPT 2015, vol. 9452, pp. 681–707 (2015)
26. Liu, X., Liu, S., Han, S., Gu, D.: Tightly CCA-secure inner product functional encryption scheme. Theor. Comput. Sci. **898**, 1–19 (2022)
27. Naor, M., Yung, M.: Public-key cryptosystems provably secure against chosen ciphertext attacks. In: STOC 1990, pp. 427–437 (1990)
28. O'Neill, A.: Definitional issues in functional encryption. IACR Cryptol. ePrint Arch. **2010**, 556 (2010)
29. Ràfols, C.: Stretching Groth-Sahai: NIZK proofs of partial satisfiability. In: TCC 2015, vol. 9015, pp. 247–276 (2015)
30. Sahai, A.: Non-malleable non-interactive zero knowledge and adaptive chosen-ciphertext security. In: FOCS 1999, pp. 543–553 (1999)
31. Tomida, J.: Tightly secure inner product functional encryption: multi-input and function-hiding constructions. In: ASIACRYPT 2019, pp. 459–488 (2019)

Zero-Knowledge Arguments
for Subverted RSA Groups

Dimitris Kolonelos[1,2(✉)], Mary Maller[3], and Mikhail Volkhov[4]

[1] IMDEA Software Institute, Madrid, Spain
dimitris.kolonelos@imdea.org
[2] Universidad Politecnica de Madrid, Madrid, Spain
[3] Ethereum Foundation, London, UK
mary.maller@ethereum.org
[4] The University of Edinburgh, Edinburgh, UK
mikhail.volkhov@ed.ac.uk

Abstract. This work investigates zero-knowledge protocols in subverted RSA groups where the prover can choose the modulus and where the verifier does not know the group order. We introduce a novel technique for extracting the witness from a general homomorphism over a group of unknown order that does not require parallel repetitions. We then present a NIZK range proof for general homomorphisms as Paillier encryptions in the designated verifier model that works under a subverted setup. The key ingredient of our proof is a constant sized NIZK proof of knowledge for a plaintext. Security is proven in the ROM assuming an IND-CPA additively homomorphic encryption scheme. The verifier's public key can be maliciously generated and is reusable and linear in the number of proofs to be verified.

1 Introduction

A zero-knowledge proof consists of a prover that demonstrates to a verifier that a statement is true while revealing no information about the witness. Sigma protocols [28,58] are a special type of zero knowledge proof that avoid expensive NP encodings and work naturally with many popular non-general relations. Sigma protocols enjoy negligible soundness-error in groups of known order. The story is different in groups of hidden order where negligible soundness can only be achieved by running $O(\lambda)$ sigma protocols in parallel [6,60], thus multiplying the prover, proof size, and verifier costs by $O(\lambda)$.

In the common reference string model [11], a negligible soundness-error of hidden order group sigma protocols can be directly linked to hardness assumptions such as the strong-RSA [9,27,34,40]. However, relying on hardness assumptions introduces an avenue for subversion: we can make no guarantees about any hardness assumption when a malicious prover corrupts the parameters of the hidden

---

D. Kolonelos and M. Volkhov—Most of the work was done while the first and third authors were interns at Ethereum Foundation.

A. Boldyreva and V. Kolesnikov (Eds.): PKC 2023, LNCS 13941, pp. 512–541, 2023.
https://doi.org/10.1007/978-3-031-31371-4_18

order group. For the prominent case of RSA-groups, i.e., multiplicative groups over the ring $\mathbb{Z}_N$ with $N = p \times q$, subversion is easy because one can compute the order of the group given the factorization, p and q.

To date, no natural[1] protocol for general homomorphism-languages with hidden order co-domain has negligible soundness-error (without repetitions), and at the same time does not rely on computational assumptions over the co-domain. Indeed, the task of constructing zero-knowledge proofs over subverted RSA-groups is exceedingly challenging; strictly more so than over traditional hidden order groups that are correctly formed. One can make no guarantees about how the modulus was generated and the Fiat-Shamir challenges can be continuously sampled until one from a malicious distribution is found.

Our Question. We thus put forward the question:

Can one build a generalised sigma-protocol in subverted RSA-groups achieving negligible soundness-error without repetitions?

Our answer to this question is affirmative assuming a designated-verifier; we provide and prove secure a construction in the designated verifier model [33,55]. This is excellent news because currently the only known method to construct RSA-groups is via a trusted setup [45]. Generating secure RSA parameters with a MPC is an extremely challenging task to realise in practice and to date no large scale RSA-MPCs have ever been completed. Our work thus provides an exciting avenue for numerous results in RSA-groups to remain applicable in subverted settings.

Subverted RSA groups are primarily interesting because they are a rare instantiation for groups of unknown order. The only known alternative for building hidden order groups is class groups, that can also be used to build ZKPs (e.g. [26]). In high contrast to RSA groups, cryptanalysists have only recently started focusing on class groups and we are still learning the best practices for choosing the parameters for implementation [38,47,50].

Further, the potential for N to be subverted is a delicacy which is rarely considered when using the additively homomorphic Paillier [54] encryption scheme. Here subverted parameters should be considered the default because participants can choose their encryption modulus N. Nonetheless, the handling of subverted parameters is a detail that is often overlooked in protocols that use Paillier. For example, in the influential paper by Hazay et al. [45], we see that they require a subversion resistant zero-knowledge range proof to realise their multiparty MPC but that none of their suggestions are subversion resistant. For more detail see the full version of the paper. As a second example, in the Damgard-Jurik voting scheme [36], they assume that a modulus N is generated by a trusted third party. If it were instead chosen by an election authority—which is a likelihood in real world systems—then this modulus could certainly be subverted. By colluding

---

[1] By 'natural' we mean a protocol that works directly for the underlying language and does not involve NP-reductions.

with just a single voter, the authority could provide verifying proofs of faulty encryptions and thus entirely decide the election result.

1.1 Our Contributions

In this paper we investigate zero-knowledge proofs under subverted RSA parameters. This is an extremely adversarial setting where the modulus N can be factorised by the prover but not by the verifier. We make no assumptions about ideal properties of the modulus: for example we can have that N is smooth or even that the prover knows the factorisation of N.

Our first contribution is a *new extraction method* for extracting a witness inside general homomorphisms. This extraction technique is completely new to the literature. We reify this technique through a designated-verifier protocol, named $\mathsf{DV_{Prot}}$, which answers affirmatively the main question of this work introduced in the previous section. A substantial caveat for our extractor is that the challenges used by the sigma protocol are encrypted (under the designated verifiers secret key which importantly is independent from the potentially subverted N). Our extractor should fail if the adversary could decrypt the challenges, thus we describe the general extraction method and reduce the probability of the extractor failing to an adversary's advantage against IND-CPA. At the heart of our extraction method is an information-theoretical lemma about the distribution of the challenges extracted, which we prove to hold unconditionally. Exemplifying the extraction method, and as a stepping stone towards the second contribution, we explain how to make the $\mathsf{DV_{Prot}}$ protocol practical, with reusable and potentially maliciously generated verifier's public key. Our main results are in the random oracle model however we also provide an optimised version in the generic group model.

Using our extraction technique we arrive at our second contribution, namely a zero-knowledge designated verifier *range proof* for Paillier encryptions under subverted modulus with negligible soundness, which we call $\mathsf{DVRange_{Prot}}$. The protocol prevents a prover from encrypting a value outside the range even if the prover chooses the encryption key. Our proof is non-interactive (in the random oracle model) and has negligible soundness error without parallel repetitions. Security is proven in the RO model under the assumption that Paillier is IND-CPA. Our techniques for proving security are potentially of independent interest and described in more detail in Sect. 1.3. In the full version we show how our range proof can be applied for non-injective homomorphisms.

The verifier's public key has size $\mathcal{O}((\lambda + Q) \log N)$ for N a Paillier modulus, λ the security parameter, and Q the number of proofs the verifier will respond to. Our protocol does not require a common reference string; being DV the (designated) verifier inherently runs a setup to generate their potentially malicious key. To ensure zero-knowledge holds against all verifier keys we describe a non-interactive publicly verifiable key generation algorithm. In more detail, the verifier runs a publicly verifiable range proof to demonstrate that the verification public key (VPK) contains ciphertexts in the correct range. We apply amortisation techniques by Cramer et al. [30] (in Sect. 4.3) to minimise the cost of this range proof. The key generation process is relatively expensive and can be avoided in scenarios where the verifier only needs to retrospectively prove honest behaviour by revealing the secrets behind their public key. Such scenarios are common in applications such as MPC with identifiable abort (ID-MPC, [46]).

1.2 Related Work

In composite order groups the standard Σ-protocol has knowledge error of only $1/2$ [6]. For a negligibly small extraction error one needs to run the protocol λ times in parallel (for λ the security parameter). This induces an $O(\lambda)$ multiplicative overhead. There are many different approaches in the literature to proving composite group statements more efficiently which we summarise here.

Proofs over Groups of Unknown Order. An intensive line of work focuses on constructing efficient zero knowledge proofs for relations over groups where the order is unknown to all parties, however none would fit our context. The Fujisaki-Okamoto solution [27,34,40], the protocols of [8,18] and the solution by Boneh et al. [13] being computationally-sound are not sound in subverted RSA groups because having known (to the prover) group order prevents the underlying computational assumptions from holding. The protocol of [7] considers a model where the verifier has extra information about the witness[2]. The protocol from [5] was later cryptanalized [49]. For specific relations, [35,36] present efficient protocols where the prover knows the order of the group, however they are sound only when the RSA group is correctly formed. The work of Cramer et al. [29,30] presents a transformation that allows the protocol to have negligible soundness error, yet only when proving λ statements simultaneously. For a single proof it cannot be applied. Finally, Bangerter et al. [6] and Terelius et al. [60] show a lower bound on soundness error for constant round sigma-like protocols in the standard model (no CRS, no RO), that translates to $1/2$ for common parameters.

Proving RSA Relations with zk-SNARKs. Many zk-SNARK proof systems are both general enough to encode any NP circuit and efficient enough to be used in practice. Thus we can prove relations about subverted RSA groups by representing them with an arithmetic circuit or similar. Ozdemir et al. implement an RSA based accumulator inside a SNARK [53]. Their work improves upon xJsnark [48]. Using Ozdemir et al.'s BigNat library[3] we compute the size of the Paillier knowledge-of-plaintext circuit at 80 million gates for 2048 bit N. This is towards the upper end of what can feasibly be computed with a SNARK. To the best of our knowledge the biggest circuits currently in production have about 100-million constraints and take minutes to compute even on specialist hardware[4]. Our work does not require a reduction to NP and therefore we avoid

---

[2] For some relations (e.g. Paillier Encryptions) this can lead to fully reconstructing the witness.

[3] https://github.com/alex-ozdemir/bellman-bignat.

[4] https://research.protocol.ai/sites/snarks/.

this prover overhead. Our approach also avoids the significant challenge of auditing an 80 million gate circuit.

Range Proofs in the RSA Setting. In this work we present range proofs for RSA-like relations (e.g. Paillier encryption), or generally (additive) homomorphisms with unknown co-domain. Variations of basic Schnorr-like Σ-protocol exist for RSA-like range relations [12,18,20,25,27,34,39]. Boudot [14] presents the first range proof for general range $[L, R]$ with slackness 1 (i.e. the message lies exactly in $m \in [0 \dots R]$ as opposed to some extended range $m \in [0 \dots \delta R]$). Further [14] uses a so-called four-squares integer decomposition property, a technique which is later used and improved in [44,51,62]. None of these works consider a subverted modulus. In fact they are computationally sound and make assumptions about the RSA group, thus they do not work in subverted settings.

Proofs of Correct Form of Moduli. An orthogonal to the above line of work intends to prove that the group itself is not subverted [3,10,19,41,42,61], meaning that the modulus N of the RSA group has some beneficial property; for example is square-free, a product of two primes, a product of equally-sized primes, a Blum integer or a product of two safe primes, etc. Other works consider proving that moduli are correctly formed in the context of specific applications as password-based key agreement [23] or threshold ECDSA signatures [21]. All these solutions require repetitions to reach a negligible soundness-error. Furthermore, to apply computationally-sound protocols for general homomorphisms (such as Fujisaki-Okamoto) over the group afterwards, one needs to prove that the RSA group is a product of two safe primes. Only [19] ensures this, however it has high costs and does not avoid the $O(\lambda)$ parallel repetitions.

1.3   Overview of Techniques

In this work we design efficient designated-verifier ZK protocols for knowledge and range of RSA group homomorphisms, which have negligible soundness error without repetitions even when the group is maliciously chosen. The main unifying ideas of all our techniques are (1) an alternative approach to Σ-protocols' witness extraction and (2) a careful realisation through homomorphic encryption with respect to (also potentially subverted) verifier's modulus, which allows hiding protocol challenges from the prover in a way that prevents lower-bound attacks of [6,60].

Let $\psi : \mathcal{D} \to \mathbb{H}$ be a group homomorphism where $\mathbb{H}$ is an RSA-related group, such as exponentatiations $w \mapsto g^w$ over $\mathbb{H} = \mathbb{Z}_N^*$ (or multiexponentations), or Paillier encryption $(w, r) \mapsto (N+1)^w h^r$. We wish to design an efficient argument of knowledge of w such that $Y = \psi(w)$, and $w \in \{0 \dots R\}$ for $R \in \mathcal{D} \subset \mathbb{Z}$.

Σ-Protocol Soundness. The classic Σ-protocol for proving knowledge of w such that $Y = \psi(w)$, described in Sect. 1, is only secure if elements from $\mathcal{D}$ are invertible. The standard special-soundness extractor behaves as follows: given two successful transcripts with the same first message $(a, c, s), (a, c', s')$ such that $aY^c = \psi(s)$ and $aY^{c'} = \psi(s')$ and $c \neq c'$ it combines the two:

$$aY^c = \psi(s) \quad aY^{c'} = \psi(s')$$

from which it gets $Y = \psi(s-s')^{(c-c')^{-1}} = \psi((s-s')(c-c')^{-1})$. When $\mathbb{H}$ is a group of public prime order p, as in case of the Schnorr protocol, this strategy always succeeds, because $(c - c')^{-1} \bmod p$ is efficiently computable. However, when $\mathbb{H}$ is a maliciously chosen RSA group, the extractor has two problems. First, it does not know the order of the group and thus can only compute $(c - c')^{-1}$ when $c - c' = 1$ (in this trivial case $Y^1 = \psi(s - s')$, and $s - s'$ is the witness). This limitation is similar to the hardness of taking roots in groups of unknown order. Second, some inverses $(c - c')^{-1}$ do not exist because it is possible that $\gcd(c - c', \mathrm{ord}(\mathcal{D})) \neq 1$ for a maliciously chosen N.

In fact the impossibility results of [6,60] show that the above extractor fails for any group $\mathbb{H}$ whose order is not publicly known, such as RSA groups.

A Generalized Extraction Lemma. Towards constructing an efficient protocol with negligible soundness error, our starting point is a generalized extraction approach. Assume that our extractor has $M \geq 3$ successful transcripts[5] $\{(a, c_i, s_i)\}_{i=1}^{M}$ such that:

$$aY^{c_1} = \psi(s_1) \quad aY^{c_2} = \psi(s_2) \quad \ldots \quad aY^{c_M} = \psi(s_M)$$

then combining the first with the rest we get the equivalent:

$$Y^{c_2 - c_1} = \psi(s_2 - s_1) \quad \ldots \quad Y^{c_M - c_1} = \psi(s_M - s_1)$$

Now if $\gcd(c_2 - c_1, \ldots, c_M - c_1) = 1$ then we can always compute coefficients $\gamma_2, \ldots, \gamma_M$ such that $\gamma_2(c_2 - c_m) + \ldots + \gamma_M(c_2 - c_M) = 1$, which means:

$$Y^1 = Y^{\gamma_2(c_2 - c_1) + \ldots + \gamma_2(c_M - c_1)} = \psi(\gamma_2(s_2 - s_1) + \ldots + \gamma_M(s_M - s_1))$$

so $s^* = \gamma_2(s_2 - s_1) + \ldots + \gamma_M(s_M - s_1)$ is a valid pre-image.

This extraction technique succeeds as long as $\gcd(c_2 - c_1, \ldots, c_M - c_1) = 1$. If we had an honest prover and the c_i challenges were truly random and independent, then well-known results from mathematics show that this happens with probability $1/\zeta(M)$, for ζ being the zeta Riemann function. This probability is overwhelming (negligibly close to 1) as a function of M.

However, a malicious prover may choose not to respond upon receiving certain challenges c, so that $\gcd(c_2 - c_1, \ldots, c_M - c_1) \neq 1$. As an example they can choose only to answer even challenges. The natural conclusion is that for this generalized extraction to work we need the (adversarial) prover to be oblivious to the challenges it answers.

---

[5] Extracting k successful transcripts is no harder than extracting 2 [1].

Prover $\mathcal{P}(x)$		Verifier $\mathcal{V}(Y)$
$r \leftarrow\!\!\text{\$}\ \mathcal{D}; a = \psi(r)$	$\xrightarrow{\hspace{1cm} a \hspace{1cm}}$	
	$\xleftarrow{\hspace{1cm} c \hspace{1cm}}$	$c \leftarrow\!\!\text{\$}\ \{0,1\}^\lambda$
$s = r + cx$	$\xrightarrow{\hspace{1cm} s \hspace{1cm}}$	
		Return $aY^c \overset{?}{=} \psi(s)$

Fig. 1. A Σ-protocol for the relation containing elements (Y, w) such that $Y = \psi(w)$, where ψ is a general homomorphism. This protocol is only knowledge sound if elements from $\mathcal{D}$ are invertible.

Designated Verifier Techniques. We bootstrap the protocol of Fig. 1 to a secure one (with negligible soundness error) in the Designated-Verifier model.

One of our key observations is that in the Designated-Verifier setting we can hide the challenge c from the malicious prover by encrypting it with a homomorphic encryption scheme for verifier's public key. Then the prover computes the response to the challenge "blindly", using additive homomorphism of the encryption scheme. The verifier, who possesses the secret key of the encryption, decrypts the response normally in order to retrieve the plaintext response of the Σ-protocol. For this we need the verifier to hold the corresponding secret key, which must be kept secret from the prover. The public key of the designated verifier (VPK) is merely the pk of the encryption scheme and the ciphertext ct of the encrypted challenge. The idea of encrypting a (single) challenge in the designated-verifier public key appears in previous DV protocols [24, 33]

To prove the existence of an extractor we require M answers with different challenges from the prover. This is clearly not possible when we encrypt just a single challenge; but we also cannot do it even when we encrypt M challenges—the prover can potentially choose only to answer with respect to the first challenge. What we require is an exponential sized challenge space. For this, we encrypt λ sub-challenges that are chosen uniformly at random: $\mathsf{ct}_1 = \mathsf{Enc}(c_1), \ldots, \mathsf{ct}_\lambda = \mathsf{Enc}(c_\lambda)$ and add them to the public key. Then the value $\mathcal{P}$ responds to is a random $(0, 1)$ linear combination of $\{c_i\}$: $c = \sum_{i=1}^{\lambda} b_i c_i$ where $\boldsymbol{b} = (b_1, \ldots, b_\lambda)$ a random bitstring-challenge sampled by the verifier, which gives rise to exponential $\mathcal{C}$.

To prove soundness, the core of our security proof is an information-theoretical lemma showing that after $M = \mathsf{poly}(\lambda)$ linear combinations have been extracted, the probability of $\{\boldsymbol{b}_i \boldsymbol{c}^\top\}_{i=1}^M$ being coprime is overwhelming (assuming that c_i's were uniformly sampled and independent during the setup).

DV with a Reusable VPK. A common issue in the Designated-Verifier model is that a prover, after seeing whether some proofs of its choice verify or not, can learn information about the VPK's structure and break soundness. This is the analogue of IND-CCA security of encryption schemes. Intuitively, the verification oracle behaves in a similar manner to a decryption oracle. Additive homomorphic encryption schemes cannot be IND-CCA and thus an attacker could use a verification oracle to learn information about vpk. We overcome this by adding $Q = \mathsf{poly}(\lambda)$ statistical blinding factors $e_1, \ldots, e_Q$ encrypted in the VPK. At each proof one of these factors is added to the linear combination and thus statistically blinds it; thus Q is maximum number of verification queries the prover can ask. The CRS size is thus $O(1)$ per proof.

1.4   Comparison with Alternative Approaches

To the best of our knowledge, this work is the first that deals with the problem of constructing zero-knowledge proofs in subverted RSA groups. On the other hand, the literature provides numerous techniques on constructing zero-knowledge proofs in non-subverted RSA groups. It is challenging to compare the efficiency of our scheme directly against the state-of-the-art for non-subverted solutions because this would require fully researching how to convert multiple solutions into the subverted setting. Instead we here briefly justify our techniques against two possible alternative approaches that provide partial solutions to the problem.

Combine with an Auxiliary Group of Unknown Order. A possible approach to constructing a sound *proof of knowledge* in the subverted RSA setting would be to combine the simple protocol of Fig. 1 with a proof of a preimage in an established group of unknown order. That is, generate an unknown order group $\mathbb{G}$, commit to the same preimage $\mathsf{Commit}(w)$ and send the commitment to the verifier. Then compose in parallel a proof of knowledge for $\mathsf{Commit}(w)$ (over $\mathbb{G}$) and the protocol of Fig. 1 (over the subverted RSA group). The Fujisaki-Okamoto extraction technique [27, 34, 40] gives negligible knowledge error and avoids the need for λ repetitions. However, this solution either requires a private-coin trusted setup in case an RSA group is used as the auxiliary group of unknown order, or must rely on class groups [16]. Solutions relying on class groups are outside the scope of this work (see Introduction).

Range Proof with an Auxiliary Prime Order Group. For the *range proof* problem for the preimage w of a homomorphism, $Y = \psi(w)$ with $0 < w < R$, one possible approach is the following. Generate an auxiliary prime order group $\mathbb{G}$ and commit to the preimage, $\mathsf{Commit}(w)$ over this group (e.g. via Pedersen commitment). Then run in parallel the protocol of Fig. 1 for $\psi(w)$ in the subverted RSA group and a simple Schnorr protocol for the commitment on $\mathbb{G}$, to prove that $\mathsf{Commit}(w)$ and $\psi(w)$ contain the same value. Afterwards one can use a range proof protocol in the prime order group [17, 26] to prove the range of w. The main benefit here is that due to progress on range proofs over prime order groups, the actual range proof block is concretely efficient.

This solution, however, inherits the soundness-error (and thus the required iterations) of the protocol of Fig. 1. That is $1/2$ for general homomorphisms $1/\mathsf{poly}(\lambda)$ for some specific special homomorphisms such as the (original) Paillier Encryption [6]. This leads to an overhead of $O(\lambda)$ and $O(\lambda/\log(\lambda))$ respectively, due to the repetitions needed.

Our work concerns with the former category, general non-special homomorphisms (such as ElGamal-Paillier) where the overhead is $O(\lambda)$, and provides a truly unique perspective on how to decrease their asymptotic efficiency to $O(1)$ which was not previously known to be possible. We achieve this by providing and proving secure an alternative extraction technique together with an information theoretical lemma that have no dependence on parallel executions.

2   Preliminaries

2.1   Notation

We denote the security parameter with λ; $\mathsf{poly}(\lambda)$ is any positive $f(n) = O(\mathsf{poly}(n))$, and $\mathsf{negl}(\lambda)$ is a negligible positive function. With $[a, b]$ we denote the set $\{a, a + 1, \ldots, b\}$, and with $[n]$ we denote $[1, n]$. Similarly with $[\![n]\!]$ we denote the set $[-\lfloor \frac{n}{2} \rfloor \ldots \lfloor \frac{n}{2} \rfloor]$. Adversaries are assumed to be stateful unless stated otherwise.

$\mathbb{Z}_n$ is the additive group of order n. We often explicitly consider interval $[\![n]\!]$ as the integer encoding for $\mathbb{Z}_n$. $\mathbb{Z}_n^*$ is the multiplicative group of all integers in $[\![n]\!]$ coprime with n. With $\phi(\cdot)$ we denote the Euler's totient function. $\mathcal{U}_S$ stands for uniform distribution on S as a finite set (e.g. $\mathcal{U}_{\mathbb{Z}_p}$); $\mathcal{U}_{[L,R]}$ is a uniform distribution on $[L, R]$, and $\mathcal{U}_R$ is a shorthand for $\mathcal{U}_{[0,R]}$. In general we denote with capital letters, e.g. Y, elements of the RSA group. In bold we denote vectors (e.g. s) and matrices (e.g. $\boldsymbol{A}$).

2.2   Homomorphic Encryption Schemes

In this work we engage public-key encryption schemes that have additively homomorphic properties. That is an encryption scheme is called additively homomorphic if for every $\mathsf{pk} \in \mathcal{PK}$ and $m_1, m_2 \in \mathcal{M}$, $\mathsf{Enc}_{\mathsf{pk}}(m_1) \cdot \mathsf{Enc}_{\mathsf{pk}}(m_2) = \mathsf{Enc}_{\mathsf{pk}}(m_1 + m_2)$, where '$\cdot$' is a ciphertext space operation. In the rest we assume that the message space $\mathcal{M}$ of the additively homomorphic schemes we refer to forms a ring. Some known examples of additively homomorphic encryption are the Paillier cryptosystem and its variants [15,31,36,54] in the RSA setting, the Castagnos-Laguillaumie cryptosystem over class groups [22] and schemes from lattices [43,56]. Notably, no additively homomorphic public-key cryptosystems from groups of prime order exist.[6]

Paillier Encryption Scheme. We briefly recall the Paillier public key encryption scheme [54], and refer the reader to our full version for more details.

---

[6] Although the lifted ElGamal cryptosystem (alike ElGamal but the message is lifted in the exponent) is additively homomorphic, the decryption is not polynomial-time, unless one restricts the message space to polynomial size. This makes it unsuitable for most applications.

KeyGen(1^λ): sample p, q primes of the size λ and set $N = p \cdot q$. Compute $d = \phi(N)^{-1} \mod N^2$. Output pk $= N$ and sk $= (d, \phi(N))$.

Enc$_{\text{pk}}(m)$: sample uniformly $r \leftarrow_\$ \mathbb{Z}_N^*$ and output ct $= (N+1)^m r^N \mod N^2$.

Dec$_{\text{sk}}(\text{ct})$: compute $c = (\text{ct}^{\phi(N)} - 1)d \mod N^2$ and return $m = \frac{c}{N}$.

2.3 Homomorphisms and Efficient Σ-protocols

Let $\psi : \mathcal{D} \to \mathbb{H}$ be a homomorphism between a domain $\mathcal{D}$ (group or ring), and an output group $\mathbb{H}$ (e.g. RSA). When $Y = \psi(w)$, we call w a witness, and Y an instance.

A pair $(v, u) \in \mathbb{Z} \times \mathcal{D}$ is called a *pseudo-preimage* (PP) for instance $Y = \psi(x)$, if $Y^v = \psi(u)$ holds [5,7], where v is called a degree of a given PP. Pseudo-preimages naturally occur in Σ-protocols: the extractor usually transforms two transcripts for the same commitment a ($Y^{c_i} a = \psi(s_i)$, $i \in 1, 2$) into a single PP by dividing the equations: $Y^{c_1 - c_2} = \psi(s_1 - s_2)$, thus $(c_1 - c_2, s_1 - s_2)$ is a PP.

In prime-order groups ($|\mathbb{H}| = p$) knowledge of PP implies knowledge of preimage, since inverses in $\mathbb{Z}_p$ are efficiently computable. In groups where the order is not prime or even unknown to V (e.g. in Paillier $\mathbb{H} = \mathbb{Z}_{N^2}^*$) there is another way to extract a proper preimage, but from *two* pseudo-preimages: given (v_1, u_1), (v_2, u_2) with $\gcd(v_1, v_2) = 1$ for any Y we can use the so-called called "Shamir's trick". Given $(v_1, u_1), (v_2, u_2)$ s.t. $Y^{v_i} = \psi(u_i), i \in \{1, 2\}$, it first checks if $\gcd(v_1, v_2) \neq 1$ and aborts if not. Then it computes Bezout coefficients—integers γ, δ such that $\gamma v_1 + \delta v_2 = 1$, and returns $u := \gamma u_1 + \delta u_2$. This extractor succeeds, since given $Y^{v_i} = \psi(u_i)$, $Y = Y^{\gamma v_1 + \delta v_2} = \psi(u_1 \gamma + u_2 \delta) = \psi(u)$.

Special Homomorphisms. In [7], following Cramer [28], the homomorphism $\psi : \mathcal{D} \to \mathbb{H}$ is called *special* if for any instance Y one can easily find a *non-trivial* PP $(\hat{v}, \hat{u})$ of Y (non-trivial means $\hat{v} \neq 0 \mod |\mathbb{H}|$). Examples of special homomorphisms include Schnorr-like homomorphism[7] $\psi : \mathbb{Z}_q \to \mathbb{Z}_p^*$, $\psi : x \mapsto h^x$ with $\text{ord}(h) = q$, $q \mid (p - 1)$ and Paillier homomorphism[8].

For special homomorphisms it is sometimes possible to build Σ-protocols with non-binary challenge spaces (and thus small soundness error) by applying Shamir's trick to just one extracted PP, and the special PP. This is the best known method of extraction for Paillier in the honest setting. However, in the subverted N scenario it does not work, and binary challenges are still optimal. This is because of the GCD condition in Shamir's trick: $\mathcal{A}$ can choose N to maximize $\Pr[\gcd(c_1 - c_2, N) \neq 1]$ (N is a degree of Paillier special PP); with binary challenges $c_1 - c_2 = 1$, and GCD is always 1. Other variants of Paillier (e.g. ElGamal-Paillier [15,31]), are not known to be special, thus even the above extraction technique fails unless challenges are binary ($c_1 - c_2 = 1$).

---

[7] Its special PP is $(q, 0)$, since $Y^q = \psi(0)$; and the PP is non-trivial: $q \neq 0 \mod p$.

[8] From $Y = G^m r^N$ we can derive $Y^N = (G^m r^N)^N = G^0 (G^m r^N)^N$, so $(N, (0, Y))$ is a pseudo-preimage of degree N (and $N \neq 0 \mod \phi(N^2)$).

2.4   Designated-Verifier Arguments of Knowledge

We assume some familiarity with the notion of interactive arguments of knowledge and their standard security properties (completeness, knowledge-soundness, and zero-knowledge). In the *designated verifier* (DV) model, additionally to $\mathcal{P}, \mathsf{V}$ programs we claim existence of a KeyGen routine that the verifier uses to create verifier's public key (VPK). This public key is then used to interact with this verifier only, and can potentially be reused multiple times. The formal definitions of completeness, soundness with reusable VPK, and honest verifier zero-knowledge under a malicious VPK are deferred to the full version.

3   Our Extraction Technique

In this section we state and prove two lemmas about our novel extraction method. The first is a generalised extraction lemma, Lemma 1, that describes how to extract a witness given M accepting transcripts such that the gcd of the challenges is 1. Our second lemma, Lemma 2, is the core information-theoretical lemma behind the security of our construction, which argues about this probability of random challenges being coprime.

3.1   The Generalized Extraction Lemma

We consider the three-round public-coin protocol of Fig. 1 where transcripts have the form (a, c, s). In Lemma 1 we design an extractor that, given M valid transcripts on the same first message, always succeeds provided that $\gcd(c^{(2)} - c^{(1)}, \ldots, c^{(M)} - c^{(1)}) = 1$. The following is proven in the full version.

Lemma 1. *Let* $\mathcal{T} = \left\{ (a, c^{(i)}, s^{(i)}) \right\}_{i=1}^{M}$ *be a collection of* $M \geq 3$ *successful transcripts for the relation* $\mathcal{R}_{\mathsf{Hom}}$ *and input* Y, $aY^{c^{(i)}} = \psi(s^{(i)})$, *such that* $\gcd(c^{(2)} - c^{(1)}, \ldots, c^{(M)} - c^{(1)}) = 1$. *Then there exists a PPT extractor* Ext *that outputs* w *such that* $Y = \psi(w)$ *with probability 1.*

3.2   Our Core Coprimality Lemma

The above generalized extraction technique is effective conditioned on the fact that differences of the challenges in the extracted transcripts are coprime, $\gcd(c^{(2)} - c^{(1)}, \ldots, c^{(M)} - c^{(1)}) = 1$. However, this cannot be guaranteed for any malicious prover. This stems from the fact that an adversarial prover can manipulate the $c^{(i)}$'s by selectively choosing to answer successfully or not, after receiving $c^{(i)}$.

Intuitively, we would like the adversary to answer independently of $c^{(i)}$. Then for sufficiently large $M = \mathsf{poly}(\lambda)$, $\gcd(c^{(2)} - c^{(1)}, \ldots, c^{(M)} - c^{(1)}) = 1$ would hold. To this end we let the challenges consist of two factors: the challenge is $e = \boldsymbol{b}\boldsymbol{c}^T$ where $\boldsymbol{b}$ is sampled during the protocol execution and $\boldsymbol{c}$ is a vector that is uniformly random from the point of view of the adversary. The adversary can manipulate $\boldsymbol{b}$ because $\boldsymbol{b}$ is chosen during the protocol, but $\boldsymbol{c}$ cannot be manipulated. Looking ahead, in Sect. 4 we realize this technique in the designated-verifier setting.

In Lemma 2 we prove an information-theoretical statement which is at the core of our construction. The distribution of values output by our extractor depend nontrivially on some adversarial matrix B: the matrix of all b that the adversary chooses to answer successfully. Because there are no computational restrictions on how an adversary might choose B, we require that for any B the extractor will succeed with high probability. Lemma 2 is new to this work and as far as we are aware there are no similar results in the literature.

How to Interpret the Lemma. As previously noted, Lemma 2 aims to information-theoretically prove that M extracted accepting transcripts (on the same first message) have coprime challenges where each challenge is $b^{(i)}c^T$. From the point of view of the adversary b is known but c is not, and assumed uniformly random.

To make the applicability of the lemma more clear we briefly recall (omitting the non-relevant details) the extractor of [2] (that generalizes [32]) which obtains M accepting transcripts, with the same first message, for any Σ-protocol.

Let H be the binary matrix where the rows represent the first messages $\alpha_1 = \psi(r_1), \alpha_2 = \psi(r_2), \ldots, \alpha_{|\mathcal{D}|} = \psi(r_{|\mathcal{D}|})$ and the columns represent the different challenges $b_1, b_2, \ldots, b_{2^\lambda}$. The position $H_{i,j}$ is 1 if the adversary can answer successfully on α_i, b_j and 0 otherwise. The extractor works as follows:

- Probes different positions of H until it finds a 1.
- If it finds a first 1 it continues sampling uniformly in the same row until it finds $M - 1$ more 1's (or terminates with some specific probability).

Attema et al. [2] show that this extraction strategy outputs M accepting transcripts in expected polynomial time.

Assume that the extractor succeeds in outputting the M transcripts from some row i. Then B (in matrix form) represents all the b_j's of this row that have 1. Similarly, B' (also in matrix form) represents all the $b^{(j)}$'s of the row that were sampled (uniformly) by the extractor, contained 1 and thus gave an accepting transcript. Lastly, for the lemma to be applied we need that B has exponentially large number of rows $> 2^\lambda/\mathsf{poly}(\lambda)$. Conditioned on the fact that the extractor terminates in (expected) polynomial time this holds, otherwise the probability of the extractor to find M 1's in the row (in poly-time) would be negligible. Clearly then, B' is a polynomially sized sub-matrix of B.

We highlight that the matrix H represents the malicious prover's strategy and it is clearly adversarially chosen, thus so is B. For this it is important that the lemma holds for any arbitrary B. This makes the lemma and its proof highly non-trivial.

Lemma Statement. Lemma 2 proves the following. Assume *any* exponentially-large $(2^\lambda/\mathsf{poly}(\lambda))$ space B of binary vectors with λ coordinates. Then if we sample uniformly $M = \mathsf{poly}(\lambda)$ vectors from this space $b^{(1)}, \ldots, b^{(M)} \overset{\$}{\leftarrow}$

B and λ uniformly random values (from an exponentially large space) $c \;:=$
$(c_1, \ldots, c_\lambda) \leftarrow_\$ \left(\llbracket 2^\lambda \rrbracket\right)^\lambda$ we get that their inner products $b^{(1)} c^T, \ldots, b^{(M)} c^T$ are
coprime, except with negligible probability. This then generalizes to our final result
that concerns with the differences $\{b^{(i)} c^T - b^{(1)} c^T\}_{i=2}^M$ being coprime.

Crucially, this holds for any space B as long as it is sufficiently large.

Lemma 2. *Let B be any $(\epsilon' 2^\lambda) \times \lambda$ binary matrix consisting of $\epsilon' 2^\lambda$ distinct
binary rows, with $\epsilon' > 1/\mathsf{poly}(\lambda)$. Sample:*

- *$M = \mathsf{poly}(\lambda)$ rows of B, $i_k \leftarrow_\$ [1, \epsilon' 2^\lambda]$ for $k = 1, \ldots, M$, and set*

$$B' = (b^{(1)} \ b^{(2)} \ldots b^{(M)})^T := (b_{i_1} \ b_{i_2} \ldots b_{i_M})^T$$

- *λ uniformly random values, $c_i \leftarrow_\$ \llbracket 2^\lambda \rrbracket$ for $i = 1, \ldots, \lambda$, and set*

$$c = (c_1 \ c_2 \ \ldots \ c_\lambda)$$

and set $(e^{(1)} \ldots e^{(M)})^T = B' c$. Then:

$$\Pr[\gcd(e^{(2)} - e^{(1)}, \ldots, e^{(M)} - e^{(1)}) = 1] = 1 - \mathsf{negl}(\lambda)$$

the probability is over the choices of c, B'.

Due to space limitations the full proof is deferred to full version.

4   Designated Verifier Proofs of Knowledge for General Homomorphisms

In this section we design a designated verifier argument of knowledge for an
opening to a general homomorphisms. We prove that there is a negligible soundness error assuming an additively homomorphic encryption scheme that is CPA
secure. Zero-knowledge holds even under subverted parameters and it does not
require a common reference string. Our proofs consist of 6 elements and can be
made non-interactive using the Fiat-Shamir transform.

We show in Sect. 5 that knowledge of an opening for a general homomorphism is powerful enough to build range proofs for ciphertexts over a subverted
encryption key. For now we focus on the simpler general relation

$$\mathcal{R}_{\mathsf{Hom}} = \{\, \psi, A \,|\, w : Y = \psi(w) \,\}$$

where $\psi : \mathcal{D} \to \mathbb{H}$ and $\mathbb{H}$ is a group parametrized by a maliciously generated
RSA modulus N (for example $\mathbb{Z}_N^*$ or $\mathbb{Z}_{N^2}^*$). Although not directly in our scope,
the techniques of this sections also apply to any group of unknown order.

4.1   The Designated-Verifier Protocol

We are now ready to present our designated verifier zero-knowledge proof system for $\mathcal{R}_{\mathsf{Hom}}$ where ψ is any additive group homomorphism.

The public-coin interactive DV protocol for $\mathcal{R}_{\mathsf{Hom}}$ is run between a prover and the verifier. The protocol is a modification of the sigma protocol in Fig. 1 to ensure soundness even for subverted RSA groups. One of the key observations is that in the Designated-Verifier setting we can hide the challenge from the malicious prover. We can thus assume that *all* the challenges answered are independent, provided that they are sampled independently by the verifier. In order to hide the challenges from the prover they are encrypted with a public key homomorphic encryption scheme. These encrypted challenges are provided in advance inside the verifier's public key.

Then if these encrypted challenges are linearly combined with fresh (binary) challenges, sampled during the actual execution one can directly apply the extraction techniques of Sect. 3 (Lemma 1 and Lemma 2). The linear combination is performed homomorphically through the ciphertexts.

The full protocol is presented in $\mathsf{DV_{Prot}}$. For ease of presentation, we first describe our protocol incrementally: with respect to a trusted setup that always outputs $(\mathsf{vpk}, \mathsf{vsk})$ honestly and without allowing any reusability of it; then in the next sections we incrementally present how to achieve these properties.

Our construction makes use of any additive additively homomorphic encryption scheme with message space $\mathcal{M}$, randomness space $\mathcal{R}$, and ciphertext space $\mathcal{CT}$ such that $\mathcal{CT}$ forms a multiplicative group. For simplicity we will assume AHE to be standard Paillier w.r.t. N_{pk}, and $\mathcal{M}$ to be the ring $\mathbb{Z}_{N_{\mathsf{pk}}}$ for an integer N_{pk}, although our scheme works with any AHE and ring $\mathcal{M}$.[9]

First the key generation algorithm creates a verification key: it chooses an encryption key pair $(\mathsf{pk}, \mathsf{sk})$ and sets the verifier's secret key to $\mathsf{vsk} = \mathsf{sk}$. It then samples uniformly λ values, $c_1, \ldots, c_\lambda \stackrel{\$}{\leftarrow} [\![2^\lambda]\!]$ (denote $\boldsymbol{c} = (c_1, \ldots, c_\lambda)$) and encrypts them under pk, $\mathsf{ct}_1 = \mathsf{Enc}_{\mathsf{pk}}(c_1), \ldots, \mathsf{ct}_\lambda = \mathsf{Enc}_{\mathsf{pk}}(c_\lambda)$. In Sect. 4.3 we describe a protocol by which the verifier proves that their vpk is well formed, ensuring that we achieve zero-knowledge under subverted vpk (hence without trusting the designated verifier for the key setup).

The protocol then proceeds in 5 moves which we detail in Fig. 2. The prover essentially proves that $Y = \psi(w)$ by sending $a = \psi(r)$; an encryption S of $(r + cw)$; and a proof (T, u_1, u_2, u_3) that the prover knows the contents of S. The additional steps 4 and 5 that prove knowledge of the preimage of S are there so that we can technically avoid passing vsk to the extractor to compute s. Instead they can extract s from the additional protocol of these steps. This explains why d is sampled from the exponentially big challenge space – the modulus in question (chosen by the verifier and extractor) is trusted for soundness.

As usual in public-coin protocols, the interactive $\mathsf{DV_{Prot}}$ can be transformed into a non-interactive one applying the Fiat-Shamir transformation (in the random oracle model).

---

[9] As long as all elements in $[\![2^{\lambda+1}]\!]$ have a multiplicative inverse in $\mathcal{M}$.

$\mathcal{V}.\mathsf{KeyGen}(1^\lambda)$: Generate a VPK:

- Sample a key pair $(\mathsf{sk}, \mathsf{pk}) \leftarrow \mathsf{AHE}.\mathsf{KeyGen}(1^\lambda)$ with $|\mathcal{M}| > 2^{2\lambda + \log \lambda}|\mathcal{D}|$.
- Sample challenges uniformly: $c_1, \ldots, c_\lambda \xleftarrow{\$} [\![2^\lambda]\!]$
- Encrypt them: $\mathsf{ct}_i = \mathsf{Enc}_{\mathsf{pk}}(c_i)$ for each $i \in [1, \lambda]$.
- Return $\mathsf{vpk} = (\mathsf{pk}, \mathsf{ct}_1, \ldots, \mathsf{ct}_\lambda)$, $\mathsf{vsk} = \mathsf{sk}$.

$\mathcal{P} \leftrightarrow \mathcal{V}$: The prover and the verifier interact as follows.

$\mathcal{P}(\mathsf{vpk}, \psi, Y, w)$		$\mathcal{V}(\mathsf{vsk}, \mathsf{vpk}, \psi, Y)$
$r_1 \xleftarrow{\$} [\![2^{2\lambda + \log \lambda}|\mathcal{D}|]\!]$		
$a = \psi(r_1)$	$\xrightarrow{\quad a \quad}$	
	$\xleftarrow{\quad b \quad}$	$b \xleftarrow{\$} \{0,1\}^\lambda$
$C = \prod_{i=1}^{\lambda} \mathsf{ct}_i^{b_i}$		
$r_2 \xleftarrow{\$} \mathcal{R}$		
$S = C^w \cdot \mathsf{Enc}_{\mathsf{pk}}(r_1; r_2)$		
$t_1 \xleftarrow{\$} [\![2^{2\lambda}|\mathcal{D}|]\!]$		
$t_2 \xleftarrow{\$} \mathcal{M}, t_3 \xleftarrow{\$} \mathcal{R}$		
$T = C^{t_1} \cdot \mathsf{Enc}_{\mathsf{pk}}(t_2; t_3)$	$\xrightarrow{\quad S, T \quad}$	
	$\xleftarrow{\quad d \quad}$	$d \xleftarrow{\$} [\![2^\lambda]\!]$
$u_1 = t_1 + dw \in \mathbb{Z}$		
$u_2 = t_2 + dr_1 \in \mathcal{M}$		
$u_3 = t_3 \cdot r_2^d \in \mathcal{R}$	$\xrightarrow{\quad u_1, u_2, u_3 \quad}$	$s = \mathsf{Dec}_{\mathsf{sk}}(S)$
		$c = \sum c_i b_i; C = \prod \mathsf{ct}_i^{b_i}$
		$aY^c \stackrel{?}{=} \psi(s)$
		$TS^d \stackrel{?}{=} C^{u_1} \cdot \mathsf{Enc}_{\mathsf{pk}}(u_2; u_3)$

Fig. 2. $\mathsf{DV}_{\mathsf{Prot}}$: The designated-verifier Σ-protocol for $\mathcal{R}_{\mathsf{Hom}}$ demonstrating knowledge of a preimage of $\psi(\cdot)$. The additively homomorphic encryption scheme is instantiated with Paillier with $|\mathcal{M}| = |N_{\mathsf{pk}}|$. This scheme is knowledge sound for subverted RSA groups provided that the outputs of $\mathsf{KeyGen}(1^\lambda)$ are well-formed.

4.2 Security

We now argue the security of our $\mathsf{DV}_{\mathsf{Prot}}$. For correctness, we only need to make sure that the message space $\mathcal{M}$ of AHE is large enough to fit the largest possible $s = r_1 + cw$. That is we require an additively homomorphic IND-CPA secure Encryption Scheme with message space $|\mathcal{M}| > 2^{2\lambda + \log \lambda}|\mathcal{D}|$.

Knowledge Soundness. To demonstrate knowledge soundness we first describe an extractor that can rewind a malicious prover and aims to output the prover's witness. This extractor obtains $M(\lambda) = \mathsf{poly}(\lambda)$ different verifying transcripts from the prover and succeeds if the gcd of the challenges of these transcripts is equal to 1. We then describe a reduction $\mathcal{B}$ that succeeds at IND-CPA whenever the extractor fails at obtaining a valid witness. The reduction queries an encryption oracle to determine the vpk and therefore does not know the contents of the encryptions. It runs the prover and decides whether a transcript verifies or not based on whether the transcript verifies with *both* possible contents. We argue that if it verifies with one of the possible contents but not the other, then provided the domain space of $\psi()$ is bigger than 2^λ, then $\mathcal{B}$ can guess the contents of the ciphertexts with overwhelming probability. We further argue that the gcd of the challenges the prover does not see must equal 1 with overwhelming probability. Thus if the extractor fails then $\mathcal{B}$ can guess which challenges the ciphertexts contain based on whether the gcd is 1 or not.

The protocol and theorem currently do not give the prover oracle access to the verifier. In Sect. 4.4 we will describe an extension of our DV protocol that can give the prover this access.

Theorem 1 (Knowledge Soundness). *The* DV$_{\mathsf{Prot}}$ *protocol is knowledge-sound in the designated verifier model, provided that the* AHE *is IND-CPA secure.*[10]

Proof. Suppose that $(\mathsf{vpk}, \mathsf{vsk}, \tau) \xleftarrow{\$} \mathsf{KeyGen}(1^\lambda)$, where $\tau = \{c_1, \ldots, c_\lambda\}$ contains the challenges encrypted in vpk but not the secret key sk of AHE. Assume that $\mathcal{P}^*(\mathsf{vpk}, \psi, Y; \mathsf{coin})$ is a malicious prover that is run on random coins coin. We first describe an extractor Ext, that has rewindable black-box access to the prover $\mathcal{P}^*$, such that whenever $\mathcal{P}^*$ outputs verifying $(Y; (a, S, T, u_1, u_2, u_3))$ $\mathsf{Ext}^{\mathcal{P}^*}(\tau, \mathsf{vpk}, \psi, Y)$ outputs a witness w such that $Y = \psi(w)$. The Ext algorithm depends on two subalgorithms, Ext$_0$ and Ext$_1$ where Ext$_0$ is the extractor from Lemma 1, and Ext$_1$ we present below.

Ext$_1$, on input τ, vpk, ψ and Y, runs $\mathcal{P}^*(\mathsf{vpk}, \psi, Y; \mathsf{coin})$ (on challenges b, d of its choice) until it obtains a full $(M, 2)$-tree of accepting transcripts, for the same first message a. That is:

$$\mathcal{T} = \left\{ \left(a, b^{(j)}, S^{(j)}, T^{(j)}, d^{(j,k)}, u_1^{(j,k)}, u_2^{(j,k)}, u_3^{(j,k)}\right) \right\}_{j \in [M], k \in [2]}$$

and outputs $\mathcal{T}$. For Ext$_1$ we use the generic $(M, 2)$-special soundness extractor (see [2]), that efficiently finds such a tree. As we argue later we set $M = \mathsf{poly}(\lambda)$.

More specifically, Ext$_1$ proceeds as follows. It probes $\mathcal{P}^*$ on randomly sampled coin, b, d until it obtains $\left(a, b^{(1)}, S^{(1)}, T^{(1)}, d^{(1,1)}, u_1^{(1,1)}, u_2^{(1,1)}, u_3^{(1,1)}\right)$ such that

$$T^{(1)}(S^{(1)})^{d^{(1,1)}} = (C^{(1)})^{u_1^{(1,1)}} \mathsf{Enc}_{\mathsf{pk}}(u_2^{(1,1)}; u_3^{(1,1)}), \text{ where } C^{(1)} = \prod_{i=1}^\lambda \mathsf{ct}_i^{b_i^{(1)}}. \text{ Since}$$

it does not have vsk it cannot directly decrypt $S^{(1)}$ to $s^{(1)}$ and check whether

---

[10] We further assume that if $\mathbb{Z}_N$ is the message space, then the largest factor of N is larger than $2^{\lambda+1}$, which is the case for example in Paillier.

$aY^{c^{(1)}} = \psi(s^{(1)})$. For this it continues probing $\mathcal{P}^*$ on the same coin and $b^{(1)}$ until it obtains a second $\left(a, b^{(1)}, S^{(1)}, T^{(1)}, d^{(1,2)}, u_1^{(1,2)}, u_2^{(1,2)}, u_3^{(1,2)}\right)$ such that $T^{(1)}(S^{(1)})^{d^{(1,2)}} = (C^{(1)})^{u_1^{(1,2)}} \mathsf{Enc}_{\mathsf{pk}}(u_2^{(1,2)}; u_3^{(1,2)})$. So we have:

$$T^{(1)}(S^{(1)})^{d^{(1,1)}} = (C^{(1)})^{u_1^{(1,1)}} \mathsf{Enc}_{\mathsf{pk}}(u_2^{(1,1)}; u_3^{(1,1)})$$
$$T^{(1)}(S^{(1)})^{d^{(1,2)}} = (C^{(1)})^{u_1^{(1,2)}} \mathsf{Enc}_{\mathsf{pk}}(u_2^{(1,2)}; u_3^{(1,2)})$$

or

$$(S^{(1)})^{d^{(1,1)} - d^{(1,2)}} = \mathsf{Enc}_{\mathsf{pk}}(u_2^{(1,1)} + c^{(1)} u_1^{(1,1)} - u_2^{(1,2)} - c^{(1)} u_1^{(1,2)})$$

From assumption $\gcd(d^{(1,1)} - d^{(1,2)}, N) = 1$ (given that the largest prime factor of N is larger that $|d^{(1,1)} - d^{(1,2)}|$) so the inverse $(d^{(1,1)} - d^{(1,2)})^{-1}$ exists in $\mathcal{M}$ and Ext_1 extracts $s^{(1)} = s_2^{(1)} + c^{(1)} s_1^{(1)}$ such that $S^{(1)}$ encrypts $s^{(1)}$ (under some randomness unknown to the extractor) where

$$s_1^{(1)} = \left(u_1^{(1,1)} - u_1^{(1,2)}\right)\left(d^{(1,1)} - d^{(1,2)}\right)^{-1} \mod N$$
$$s_2^{(1)} = \left(u_2^{(1,1)} - u_2^{(1,2)}\right)\left(d^{(1,1)} - d^{(1,2)}\right)^{-1} \mod N$$

From here Ext_1 can verify $aY^{c^{(1)}} = \psi(s^{(1)})$ to confirm if the two transcripts are accepting or not. It continues in a similar manner until it obtains a full $(M, 2)$-tree of accepting transcripts $\mathcal{T}$. Whenever $\mathcal{P}^*$ convinces V with non-negligible probability Ext_1 computes the decryption of $S^{(1)}$ in polynomial time thus the probability that Ext_1 accepts a false transcript is negligible.[11]

Now, the extractor Ext behaves as follows. It runs $\mathcal{T} \leftarrow \mathsf{Ext}_1^{\mathcal{P}^*}(\tau, \mathsf{vpk}, \psi, Y)$ and computes $c^{(j)} = \boldsymbol{b}^{(j)} \boldsymbol{c}^T = \sum_{i=1}^{\lambda} c_i b_i^{(j)}$. If $\gcd(c^{(2)} - c^{(1)}, \ldots, c^{(\lambda)} - c^{(1)}) \neq 1$ it aborts. Else it computes $s^{(j)}$ as shown above (where it holds that $s^{(j)} = \mathsf{Dec}_{\mathsf{sk}}(S^{(j)})$) for each $j \in [M]$ and runs $w \leftarrow \mathsf{Ext}_0(\psi, Y; (a, c^{(1)}, s^{(1)}), \ldots, (a, c^{(M)}, s^{(M)}))$ and returns w.

We first see that Ext runs in polynomial time provided that the adversary $\mathcal{P}^*$ has non-negligible probability of success. So either $\epsilon(\lambda)$ is polynomial in λ or $\mathcal{P}^*$ only convinces V with negligible probability. Let $\epsilon(\lambda) > 1/\mathsf{poly}(\lambda)$ denote the probability that $\mathcal{P}^*$ convinces an honest verifier on input (ψ, Y). By Lemma 1 we have that Ext_0 runs in polynomial time. For the runtime of Ext_1 we rely on [2, Lemma 5] which shows that Ext_1 runs in expected time $O(\frac{\lambda}{\epsilon - (M-1)/2^\lambda})$, which is polynomial (since we assumed that ϵ is non-negligible).

We must now show that Ext only aborts with negligible probability. This occurs if and only if $\gcd(c^{(2)} - c^{(1)}, \ldots, c^{(M)} - c^{(1)}) \neq 1$ with non-negligible probability. In order to show this, we design an adversary $\mathcal{B}$ against IND-CPA that, using Ext, wins the IND-CPA game:

---

[11] For ease of exposition we keep the description simple. We omit the technical details of special soundness extractors related to aborting senarios, that ensure termination in polynomial time(see lemma 5, [2]).

$\underline{\mathcal{B}^{\mathcal{O}_{\mathsf{Enc}}}(\mathsf{pk})}$

$c_1, z_1, \ldots, c_\lambda, z_\lambda \xleftarrow{\$} [\![2^\lambda]\!]$

$\mathsf{ct}_i \xleftarrow{\$} \mathcal{O}_{\mathsf{Enc}}(c_i, z_i)$ for $i \in [\lambda]$;

$\mathsf{vpk} \leftarrow (\mathsf{pk}, \mathsf{ct}_1, \ldots, \mathsf{ct}_\lambda)$

$\mathsf{coin} \xleftarrow{\$} [1, 2^\lambda]; j \leftarrow 1$

while $j < M$: $(\mathsf{trans}_{j,1}, \mathsf{trans}_{j,2}) \leftarrow \mathcal{P}^*(\mathsf{vpk}, \psi, Y; \mathsf{coin})$

    if $aY^{c^{(j)}} = \psi(s_2^{(j)} + c^{(j)}s_1^{(j)})$ and $aY^{z^{(j)}} \neq \psi(s_2^{(j)} + z^{(j)}s_1^{(j)})$ return 0

    if $aY^{c^{(j)}} \neq \psi(s_2^{(j)} + c^{(j)}s_1^{(j)})$ and $aY^{z^{(j)}} = \psi(s_2^{(j)} + z^{(j)}s_1^{(j)})$ return 1

    if $aY^{c^{(j)}} = \psi(s_2^{(j)} + c^{(j)}s_1^{(j)})$ and $aY^{z^{(j)}} = \psi(s_2^{(j)} + z^{(j)}s_1^{(j)})$ $j \leftarrow j + 1$

if $\gcd(c^{(2)} - c^{(1)}, \ldots, c^{(M)} - c^{(1)}) \neq 1$ return 0

if $\gcd(z^{(2)} - z^{(1)}, \ldots, z^{(M)} - z^{(1)}) \neq 1$ return 1

where we denote $c^{(j)} = \boldsymbol{b}^{(j)}\boldsymbol{c}^T$ and $z^{(j)} = \boldsymbol{b}^{(j)}\boldsymbol{z}^T$.

Case 1. First we show that if $aY^{c^{(j)}} = \psi(s_2^{(j)} + c^{(j)}s_1^{(j)})$ and $aY^{z^{(j)}} \neq \psi(s_2^{(j)} + z^{(j)}s_1^{(j)})$, then with overwhelming probability the encryptions contain $c_1, \ldots, c_\lambda$ and $\mathcal{B}$ succeeds.

The fact that $aY^{c^{(j)}} = \psi(s_2^{(j)} + c^{(j)}s_1^{(j)})$ can be rewritten as:

$$\left(a\psi(-s_2^{(j)})\right) = \left(\psi(s_1^{(j)})Y^{-1}\right)^{c^{(j)}}$$

Assume that $\mathsf{ct}_i \neq \mathsf{Enc}_{\mathsf{pk}}(c_i)$ then $\mathcal{P}^*$ gets no information about $c_1, \ldots, c_\lambda$, so they are perfectly hidden. This means that from the point of view of $\mathcal{P}^*$ these are uniformly random over $[\![2^\lambda]\!]$, which makes the above happen with probability $2^{-\lambda}$ (considering also that $|\mathbb{H}| > 2^\lambda$), unless $a\psi(-s_2^{(j)}) = \psi(s_1^{(j)})Y^{-1} = 1$. Now, since $aY^{z^{(j)}} \neq \psi(s_2^{(j)} + z^{(j)}s_1^{(j)})$ then $a \neq \psi(s_2^{(j)})$ or $Y \neq \psi(s_1^{(j)})$.

We conclude then that, except with negligible probability $2^{-\lambda}$, $\{\mathsf{ct}_i\}_i$ contain encryptions of c_i.

Case 2. Second, we use the same argument as in the previous case to claim that if $aY^{c^{(j)}} \neq \psi(s_2^{(j)} + c^{(j)}s_1^{(j)})$ and $aY^{z^{(j)}} = \psi(s_2^{(j)} + z^{(j)}s_1^{(j)})$, then with overwhelming probability the encryptions contain $z_1, \ldots, z_\lambda$ and $\mathcal{B}$ succeeds.

Case 3. Third we argue that if the extractor Ext fails then $\mathcal{B}$ succeeds. Indeed we have from the first two cases that transcripts only verify if both $aY^{c^{(j)}} = \psi(s_2^{(j)} + c^{(j)}s_1^{(j)})$ and $aY^{z^{(j)}} = \psi(s_2^{(j)} + z^{(j)}s_1^{(j)})$. If the encryptions contain $c_1, \ldots, c_\lambda$ then Ext only fails if $\gcd(c^{(2)} - c^{(1)}, \ldots, c^{(M)} - c^{(1)}) \neq 1$. In this case $\mathcal{B}$ correctly guesses.

If the encryptions instead contain $z_1, \ldots, z_\lambda$ then Ext only fails if $\gcd(z^{(2)} - z^{(1)}, \ldots, z^{(M)} - z^{(1)}) \neq 1$. In this case $\mathcal{B}$ guesses correctly unless $\gcd(c^{(2)} - c^{(1)}, \ldots, c^{(M)} - c^{(1)}) \neq 1$. The $(c_1, \ldots, c_\lambda)$ are uniformly distributed values that are perfectly hidden from the prover and the extractor Indeed, the encryptions contain no information and, by the first two cases, the behaviour of the extractor is entirely determined by the verification with respect to $z_1, \ldots, z_\lambda$. So the probability that $\gcd(c^{(2)} - c^{(1)}, \ldots, c^{(M)} - c^{(1)}) = 1$ is overwhelming (see Lemma 2). We thus argue that if Ext fails then $\mathcal{B}$ succeeds with overwhelming probability.

Indeed Lemma 2 shows that $\Pr[\gcd(c^{(2)} - c^{(1)}, \ldots, c^{(M)} - c^{(1)}) = 1] = 1 - \mathsf{negl}(\lambda)$.

To see why Lemma 2 applies in our case, $\boldsymbol{B}$ corresponds to the matrix containing all the challenges b which the adversary can successfully answer, when the first message is a. Since the extractor was able to obtain M such challenges in (expected) polynomial time, this means that $\boldsymbol{B}$ is at most polynomially smaller than 2^λ: there exists $\epsilon' > 1/\mathsf{poly}(\lambda)$ such that $|\boldsymbol{B}| = \epsilon' 2^\lambda$. We can show this by contradiction, assume that $\epsilon' = 1/\omega(\mathsf{poly}(\lambda))$, then the expected time for Ext to find a successful answer would be non-polynomial $\omega(\mathsf{poly}(\lambda))$. Finally, $\boldsymbol{B}'$ corresponds to the matrix consisting of the challenges in $\mathcal{T}$.

Zero-Knowledge. To demonstrate zero-knowledge we will provide a simulator and argue that the simulators outputs are indistinguishable from the honest provers. We make use of a standard blinding lemma.

The main HVZK result is as follows (due to space limitations the proof is deferred to the full version of the paper):

Theorem 2 (Honest Verifier Zero Knowledge). $\mathsf{DV_{Prot}}$ *is statistical honest-verifier zero-knowledge for the relation* $\mathcal{R}_{\mathsf{Hom}}$.

Since our DV protocol is essentially Schnorr-like, the simulator is almost as usual: it samples response values uniformly (since they are properly blinded in the honest protocol), and generates (encrypted) challenges using verifier's equations. The only difference is that one challenge is an encryption value. Also the proof assumes honest CRS setup.

4.3 Malicious VPK Generation

The $\mathsf{DV_{Prot}}$ protocol in the previous section assumes that the verifier's public key is trusted. In particular, zero-knowledge only holds on the condition that ct_i contains plaintexts $c_i \in [\![2^\lambda]\!]$ for all i. In this section we explain how to generate a vpk in a way that prevents dishonest verifiers from breaking zero-knowledge of our DV construction.

For lack of space we defer the formal description of the malicious-verifier alternative key generation procedure is presented to the full version. We edit the setup algorithm such that the verifier must provide a range proof on the ciphertexts it generates for vpk.

In the full version we present a protocol proving range of the VPK ciphertext efficiently, together with a security proof. The protocol follows the transformation by Cramer et al. [29,30] allowing to increase performance when proving multiple instances simultaneously; however our instantiation has a number of differences from the original transformation. The range proof comes with a slack:

a verifying π on the prover's side guarantees that when $c_i \in [\![2^\lambda]\!]$, the resulting messages in the ciphertexts ct_i of vpk are in the extended interval $[\![2^{3\lambda+\log\lambda-1}]\!]$ (the slack is $2^{2\lambda+\log\lambda-1}$). Therefore the encrypted sum-challenge $\mathcal{P}$ replies to is in $[\![2^{3\lambda+2\log\lambda-1}]\!]$. To preserve zero-knowledge we must increase the blinding parameter r_1 on the prover's side to this value, multiplied by $|\mathcal{D}|$. This in turn requires us to increase AHE $|\mathcal{M}|$ to $|\mathcal{D}|2^{3\lambda+2\log\lambda}$, to be enough to fit the new $s = r_1 + cw \overset{s}{\approx} r_1$.

In addition to this, we also must prove that verifier's public key N_{pk} gives rise to an *injective* Paillier instantiation, since otherwise the statement of the range proof is not useful. For this we use [42, Protocol $\mathcal{P}_{\mathsf{Paillier-N}}$, Sect. 3.2]— it is public-coin, so can be executed non-interactively (using FS); it proves $\gcd(N_{\mathsf{pk}}, \phi(N_{\mathsf{pk}})) = 1$, which is enough to achieve injectivity of Paillier; and it is quite efficient, only taking a few percent of all KeyGen computations.

4.4 Reusable VPK

In this section we present $\mathsf{DVReusable}_{\mathsf{Prot}}$, a modification of $\mathsf{DV}_{\mathsf{Prot}}$, in which vpk is reusable $Q = \mathsf{poly}(\lambda)$ number of times. This means the prover can query the verifier to learn whether their response verifies up to Q times. We achieve this by adding Q encrypted challenges to the vpk. The result is that both the communication and the computation complexity related to vpk generation and verification can be amortized down to $O(1)$ per query.

For the basic $\mathsf{DV}_{\mathsf{Prot}}$ it is possible to show an attack in which an adversarial prover, interacting with the verifier many times, uses the information of whether a (malicious) proof of their choice verifies or not in order to learn plaintext challenges c_i in the vpk. This in turn defeats the purpose of hiding the challenges, and prevents extraction, breaking soundness.

To overcome this we introduce additional challenge blinders. First, we sample $\hat{c}_\kappa$ of size at least $\lambda 2^{2\lambda}$ per query, encrypt them to $\hat{\mathsf{ct}}_\kappa$, and add them all to the VPK. Then we use $\hat{\mathsf{ct}}_\kappa$ in the final challenge $C = \hat{\mathsf{ct}}_\kappa \prod_i \mathsf{ct}_i^{b_i}$ (for a challenge bit-vector b) so that $\hat{c}_\kappa$ statistically hides $\sum c_i b_i$ since $\hat{c}_\kappa$ is at least 2^λ larger. This means that the adversary statistically learns no information about $\{c_i\}$, but only about $\hat{c}_\kappa$. Each challenge $\hat{c}_\kappa$ must be used exactly once, which is enforced by V.

The final challenge size now grows to $\lambda 2^{2\lambda}$, which means r_1 must be sampled from $[\![\lambda 2^{3\lambda}|\mathcal{D}|]\!]$, and $|\mathcal{M}|$ of verifier's AHE must be bigger than this value.

Theorem 3. $\mathsf{DVReusable}_{\mathsf{Prot}}$ *is a complete, honest-verifier zero-knowledge protocol in the designated-verifier setting, that has knowledge-soundness with Q-times reusable VPK for any polynomial $Q(\lambda)$.*

Due to space limitations the proof is deffered to the full version.

4.5 Malicious and Reusable VPK

Techniques from the two previous sections can be combined. The *reusable* VPK from Sect. 4.4 can also be generated *maliciously* with the same technique from Sect. 4.3.

The batched range proof now must also cover new "bigger" challenges introduced for reusability. From the perspective of efficiency of amortized $\mathsf{SigmaRangeA_{Prot}}$ it is optimal to batch exactly $n = \lambda$ instances together. Thus we will prove challenge ranges of c_i in batches of size λ, where first batch uses range bound $R_1 = 2^\lambda$ (corresponding to small ciphertexts), and the following Q/λ batches use $R_2 = \lambda 2^{2\lambda}$. When $\lambda \nmid Q$, $\mathsf{SigmaRangeA_{Prot}}$ instance can be padded with dummy values.

Given $2^{\lambda + \log \lambda - 1}$ slack of the range proof, we must sample $r_1 \in [\![2^{5\lambda + 2 \log \lambda} |\mathcal{D}|]\!]$; and $|\mathcal{M}|$ must be chosen to be bigger than this r_1.

4.6   Efficiency Optimization in the Generic Group Model

Here we describe a variant of the $\mathsf{DV_{Prot}}$ protocol that consists of 3 rounds (instead of 5) and thus saves 4 elements from the proof size. The protocol transcript simply consists of (a, b, S) omitting T, d, u_1, u_2, u_3 together with the last two rounds.

In $\mathsf{DV_{Prot}}$ the last three messages T, d and (u_1, u_2, u_3) are used to prove that S is a well-formed ciphertext. Namely, the extractor of Theorem 1, at each accepting transcript should be able to obtain an $s^{(j)}$ such that $S^{(i)} = \mathsf{Enc_{pk}}(s^{(j)})$. We observe that if we instantiate the encryption scheme with the Paillier-with-randomness-in-the-exponent cryptosystem, $S^{(j)} = (N+1)^{s^{(j)}} h^r$ then our extractor can obtain $s^{(j)}$ for free in the generic group model [52,59] (GGM).

GGM for unknown order groups has been established [13,37] in a similar manner to the original model. For this optimization we make use of this model. For knowledge-soundness we assume that the group generated for the Paillier encryption is honest (it's part of VPK), thus the model applies normally.

The following proof is almost identical to that of Theorem 1 except that the extractor now uses whitebox access to the prover instead of the rewinding argument to find a representation for S.

Theorem 4 (Knowledge Soundness). *The optimised $\mathsf{DV_{Prot}}$ described above is knowledge-sound in the generic group model provided that the AHE is IND-CPA secure.*

Due to space limitations the proof is deffered to the full version.

5   Designated Verifier Range Proof

In this section we construct $\mathsf{DVRange_{Prot}}$—a zero-knowledge argument of knowledge for the range of the pre-image of general homomorphisms. Formally, we are interested in the relation:

$$\mathcal{R}_{\mathsf{HomRange}} = \big\{ (\psi, Y, R); x : Y = \psi(x) \ \wedge \ x \in [0, R] \big\}$$

where $\psi : \mathcal{D} \to \mathbb{G}$ and $\mathbb{G}$ is a group parameterised by a (possibly subverted) RSA modulus N. We use our designated-verifier protocol of Sect. 4, that is able to extract the witness using the extraction strategy of Theorem 1. On top of that, we use the range proof from [27] for RSA groups.

The protocol from [27] works over an integer commitment [34,40] $c = g^x h^r$ in an RSA group for which the order is unknown to the prover. Since we cannot assume that $\mathbb{G}$ is such a group (recall that the prover might know the order of $\mathbb{G}$) we let the verifier generate an RSA modulus N_{cm} together with the bases of the commitment g, h, which are included in the verification key. The prover first commits to the pre-image x in $\mathbb{Z}_{N_{cm}}$, $c = g^x h^r$ and sends c to the verifier. Then it performs the two protocols, the opening of ψ (Sect. 4.1) and the range proof of [27] (compiled with the same Designated-Verifier technique), in parallel.

For completeness, we recall the aforementioned integer commitment scheme used. It works over any group of unknown (to the committer) order such as an RSA group or a class group. In our case, we focus on the RSA instantiation, thus the underlying group is $\mathbb{Z}_{N_{cm}}$, where N_{cm} is an RSA modulus. The commitment key consists of two random elements $g, h \in \mathbb{Z}_{N_{cm}}$ such that $g \in \langle h \rangle$. In the key generation phase we sample uniformly $g \leftarrow_\$ \mathbb{Z}_{N_{cm}}$ and $f \leftarrow_\$ \phi(N_{cm})^{12}$ and output $(g, h) = (h^f, h)$. A commitment to x is merely $c = g^x h^r$ for a random $r \leftarrow_\$ [\![\frac{N_{cm}}{2}]\!]$. The opening values are (x, r) and the verification is $c = \pm g^x h^r$.[13] The scheme is binding under the factoring assumption for N_{cm} and statistically hiding.

We present $\mathsf{DVRange}_{\mathsf{Prot}}$ in Fig. 3(for lack of space we describe its key generation in the full version). For ease of presentation parts related to the range proof and the opening of ψ are visually separated, denoted as (1) and (2) respectively. We directly present our protocol with reusable and maliciously generated vpk, similarly to how these were presented for $\mathsf{DV}_{\mathsf{Prot}}$ in Sects. 4.3 and 4.4.

For the key generation, except for a secret/public key of the additively homomorphic encryption scheme (Paillier cryptosystem), we further need an RSA modulus N_{cm} and the group elements g, h to instantiate the integer commitment scheme. For zero-knowledge to hold even under maliciously generated vpk it is important that $g = h^f$ holds. Therefore we additionally include a zero-knowledge proof ensuring it.

Security. The above protocol consists of two sub-protocols: our protocol of Sect. 4.1 and the range proof by Couteau et al. [27] over RSA groups. Thus the security of the protocol can be proven in a straightforward way from the security of these subprotocols. For correctness, again we need to consider the size of the message space $\mathcal{M}$ of the encryption scheme AHE. Indeed $|\mathcal{M}|$ needs to be at least as large as the maximum value encrypted, which equals $\tau + \sum_{i=1}^3 x_i t_i - 4(R-x)t$, the content of U_4. Knowledge-Soundness follows directly from the knowledge-soundness of the two sub-protocols.

---

[12] In case $\phi(N_{cm})$ is unknown, sampling $f \leftarrow_\$ [\![\frac{N_{cm}}{2}]\!]$ is statistically close.

[13] The $\pm$ relaxation is artificially added in order to achieve a sound zero-knowledge proof of opening of c, which however does not affect the binding of the commitment scheme.

$\mathcal{P}(\mathsf{vpk}, \psi, Y, R, \kappa, x) \leftrightarrow \mathcal{V}(\mathsf{vsk}, \mathsf{vpk}, \psi, Y, R, \kappa)$:

$\mathcal{P}_1$: 1. Sample $t \leftarrow\!\!\$ \; [\![2^\lambda \frac{N_{\mathsf{cm}}}{2}]\!]$ and compute $\mathsf{cm} = g^x h^t \mod N_{\mathsf{cm}}$.

2. Sample $r \leftarrow\!\!\$ \; [\![2^{5\lambda+2\log\lambda} R]\!]$, $\sigma \leftarrow\!\!\$ \; [\![2^{6\lambda+2\log\lambda} \frac{N_{\mathsf{cm}}}{2}]\!]$ and compute $\beta = g^r h^\sigma$.

3. Find $x_1, x_2, x_3 \in \mathbb{Z}$ such that $4x(R-x)+1 = \sum_{i=1}^3 x_i^2$ (using e.g. [61]).

4. Sample $t_i \leftarrow\!\!\$ \; [\![2^\lambda \frac{N_{\mathsf{cm}}}{2}]\!]$ and compute $\mathsf{cm}_i = g^{x_i} h^{t_i}$, for $i \in [1,3]$.

5. Sample $r_i \leftarrow\!\!\$ \; [\![2^{5\lambda+2\log\lambda} R]\!]$, $\sigma_i \leftarrow\!\!\$ \; [\![2^{6\lambda+2\log\lambda} \frac{N_{\mathsf{cm}}}{2}]\!]$ and compute $\beta_i = g^{r_i} h^{\sigma_i}$, for $i \in [1,3]$.

6. Sample $\tau \leftarrow\!\!\$ \; [\![2^{6\lambda+2\log\lambda+4} \frac{N_{\mathsf{cm}}}{2} R]\!]$ and compute $\beta_4 = h^\tau \mathsf{cm}^{4r} \prod_{i=1}^3 \mathsf{cm}_i^{-r_i}$.

7. Compute $\alpha = \psi(r)$.

$\underline{\mathcal{P} \to \mathcal{V}}$: send $a = \left(\mathsf{cm}, \{\mathsf{cm}_i\}_{i\in[1,3]}, \alpha, \beta, \{\beta_i\}_{i\in[1,4]}\right)$

$\mathcal{V}_1$: Sample $b \xleftarrow{\$} \{0,1\}^\lambda$ (denote $(b_1, \ldots, b_\lambda) := b$).

$\underline{\mathcal{V} \to \mathcal{P}}$: send b

$\mathcal{P}_2$: 1. Compute challenge ciphertext $C = \mathsf{ct}_{\lambda+\kappa} \cdot \prod_{i=1}^\lambda \mathsf{ct}_i^{b_i}$

2. Compute:
   - $U = \mathsf{Enc}_{\mathsf{pk}}(r) \cdot C^{R-x}$, $V = \mathsf{Enc}_{\mathsf{pk}}(\sigma) \cdot C^{-t}$.
   - $U_i = \mathsf{Enc}_{\mathsf{pk}}(r_i) \cdot C^{x_i}$, $V_i = \mathsf{Enc}_{\mathsf{pk}}(\sigma_i) \cdot C^{t_i}$, for $i \in [1,3]$.
   - $U_4 = \mathsf{Enc}_{\mathsf{pk}}(\tau) \cdot C^{\sum_{i=1}^3 x_i t_i - 4(R-x)t}$.

$\underline{\mathcal{P} \to \mathcal{V}}$: send $S = (U, V, \{U_i\}_{i\in[1,3]}, \{V_i\}_{i\in[1,3]}, U_4)$

$\mathcal{V}_2$: 1. Compute plaintext challenge $c = c_{\lambda+\kappa} + \sum_{i=1}^\lambda c_i b_i$

2. Decrypt $U, V, \{U_i\}_{i\in[1,3]}, \{V_i\}_{i\in[1,3]}, U_4$: $u = \mathsf{Dec}_{\mathsf{sk}}(U)$, $v = \mathsf{Dec}_{\mathsf{sk}}(V)$, $u_i = \mathsf{Dec}_{\mathsf{sk}}(U_i)$, $v_i = \mathsf{Dec}_{\mathsf{sk}}(V_i)$ for $i \in [1,3]$ and $u_4 = \mathsf{Dec}_{\mathsf{sk}}(U_4)$

3. Perform the following checks:
   - $\beta(\mathsf{cm}^{-1}g^R)^c \stackrel{?}{=} g^u h^v$
   - $\beta_i \mathsf{cm}_i^c \stackrel{?}{=} g^{u_i} h^{v_i}$, for $i \in [1,3]$
   - $\beta_4 \prod_{i\in[1,3]} \mathsf{cm}_i^{u_i} \stackrel{?}{=} h^{u_4} g^c \mathsf{cm}^{4u}$
   - $u_i \stackrel{?}{\in} [\![2^{5\lambda+2\log\lambda} R]\!]$, for $i \in [1,3]$
   - $\alpha \left(Y^{-1}\psi(R)\right)^c \stackrel{?}{=} \psi(u)$

$\mathcal{P} \leftrightarrow \mathcal{V}$: (Non-GGM part:) For each ciphertext of the third message S perform a variant of the three-round $\mathsf{Sigma}_{\mathsf{Prot}}$ for the relation $\mathcal{R} = \left\{(S_i, C); (w_1, w_2, w_3) : S_i = \mathsf{Enc}_{\mathsf{pk}}(w_1; w_2) \cdot C^{w_3}\right\}$ with $|\mathcal{C}| = 2^\lambda$. This can be done in two extra rounds starting with $\mathcal{P}_2$, as in Fig. 2.

Fig. 3. DVRange$_{\mathsf{Prot}}$: The designated-verifier range proof of a preimage of ψ.

Table 1. Evaluation of our main protocols. Timings are in ms. "GGM" is GGM optimisation, and "M/T" stand for malicious or trusted setup.

	VPK Gen	VPK Verify	Prove	Verify	Proof size	VPK size
DV_{Prot} M	4754	12310	162	66	5.52 KB	741 KB
DV_{Prot} T	836	–	130	56	5.14 KB	159 KB
DV_{Prot} M GGM	4754	12310	84	32	2.32 KB	741 KB
DV_{Prot} T GGM	836	–	69	28	2.19 KB	159 KB
$DVRange_{Prot}$ M	13827	25900	1880	1120	34.32 KB	842 KB
$DVRange_{Prot}$ T	9106	–	1330	782	31.78 KB	188 KB
$DVRange_{Prot}$ M GGM	13827	25900	689	153	11.05 KB	842 KB
$DVRange_{Prot}$ T GGM	9106	–	490	111	10.41 KB	188 KB

Theorem 5. *Let* AHE *be an IND-CPA secure Encryption Scheme with message space* $|\mathcal{M}| > 2^{6\lambda+2\log\lambda+4}N_{cm}R$. *Then* $DVRange_{Prot}$ *is a designated verifier argument of knowledge for the relation* $\mathcal{R}_{HomRange}$ *that is: correct, Q-reusable knowledge-sound under the Factoring assumption for* N_{cm} *and IND-CPA security of* AHE *and statistically honest-verifier zero-knowledge under malicious VPK.*

Due to space limitations the proof is deffered to the full version.

$DVRange_{Prot}$ can be optimised in the generic group model similarly to how it is done in Sect. 4.6. In this case we can omit the final interaction between prover and verifier in Fig. 3 that proves knowledge of the plaintext inside S_i.

6   Evaluation and Performance

We implemented[14] and benchmarked our protocols, primarily focusing on evaluating and comparing DV_{Prot} and $DVRange_{Prot}$ (Table 1), proving knowledge of the ciphertext message, and its range correspondingly. As a baseline we also implemented several flavours of the basic Σ-protocol (Table 2). For simplicity here we only present non-interactive (Fiat-Shamir transformed) variants.

The evaluation indicates that our protocols is a strictly better choice for certain types of applications (e.g. ID-MPC such as RSA ceremonies), as they exhibit better verification time and communication size. For *generic* applications, our protocols are comparable to other solutions, providing different performance trade-offs.

Setup and Instantiation Details. We ran our benchmarks on the Intel i5-8500 @ 3.00 GHz processor. For illustrative purposes the protocol code runs in the single-core mode only, and no specifically tailored low-level optimisations are implemented. All the evaluations are presented for $\lambda = 128$, and $\log N = 2048$;

---

[14] The implementation is available publicly on Github: https://github.com/volhovm/rsa-zkps-impl.

Table 2. Performance for the baseline algorithms. Timings are in milliseconds. $\mathsf{Sigma}_{\mathsf{Prot}}$ is evaluated with different $p_{\max}$/number of repetition parameters. Note that $\mathsf{SigmaRange}_{\mathsf{Prot}}$ has range slack while $\mathsf{DVRange}_{\mathsf{Prot}}$ is tight.

	Prove	Pre-Verify	Verify	Proof size
$\mathsf{Sigma}_{\mathsf{Prot}}$ Paillier, $\lambda = 128$ reps	342	0	1161	134.00 KB
$\mathsf{Sigma}_{\mathsf{Prot}}$ Paillier, 8 reps	21	4	73	8.38 KB
$\mathsf{Sigma}_{\mathsf{Prot}}$ Paillier, 7 reps	19	36	64	7.33 KB
$\mathsf{Sigma}_{\mathsf{Prot}}$ Paillier, 6 reps	16	339	55	6.28 KB
$\mathsf{Sigma}_{\mathsf{Prot}}$ Paillier, 5 reps	14	6535	46	5.23 KB
$\mathsf{SigmaRange}_{\mathsf{Prot}}$ Paillier (with slack)	345	0	1157	108.00 KB

for the range proof we take $R = 2^{256}$; the maximum query number of VPK reuses is set to $Q = 128$. For Fiat-Shamir transformation we instantiate the random oracle with the Blake2b [4] hash function.

For $\mathsf{DV}_{\mathsf{Prot}}$ and $\mathsf{DVRange}_{\mathsf{Prot}}$ we use Paillier-ElGamal encryption as the target homomorphism (which is additively homomorphic in both message and randomness), and standard Paillier as the AHE scheme on the verifier's side. For each of our two protocols we evaluate four cases, depending on whether we use the GGM optimisation or not, and whether we consider malicious VPK or a trusted one (for the ID-MPC case). In the latter case we do not consider VPK verification time.

For the baseline $\mathsf{Sigma}_{\mathsf{Prot}}$ and $\mathsf{SigmaRange}_{\mathsf{Prot}}$ we use standard Paillier. We evaluate $\mathsf{Sigma}_{\mathsf{Prot}}$ with naive $\lambda = 128$ reps, and also with varying $\log p_{\max} \in \{16, 19, 22, 26\}$. The range proof $\mathsf{SigmaRange}_{\mathsf{Prot}}$ cannot use the $p_{\max}$ optimisation. Note, importantly, that $\mathsf{SigmaRange}_{\mathsf{Prot}}$ has multiplicative range slack $2^{\lambda+1}$, while our $\mathsf{DVRange}_{\mathsf{Prot}}$ is tight; this means comparing them directly is not even possible for all applications.

Performance Overview. Below we will mostly consider the GGM optimised variants of our protocols that assumes trusted setup, since it gives us best performance, and fits ID-MPC case well. The main advantage of our $\mathsf{DV}_{\mathsf{Prot}}$ and $\mathsf{DVRange}_{\mathsf{Prot}}$ is that they are single-shot, requiring no repetitions. It affects the two protocols non-proportionally, benefiting $\mathsf{DVRange}_{\mathsf{Prot}}$ more, since the baseline $\mathsf{SigmaRange}_{\mathsf{Prot}}$ cannot avoid λ repetitions. Our verification time is strictly less than the baseline: 1.5–2× for $\mathsf{DV}_{\mathsf{Prot}}$, and 10× for $\mathsf{DVRange}_{\mathsf{Prot}}$. Communication is more efficient too, since our proofs are strictly smaller. Even with our VPK being comparably heavy, its size together with $Q = 128$ proofs gives us 1.5–2× improvement for $\mathsf{DV}_{\mathsf{Prot}}$ and 6–9× improvement for $\mathsf{DVRange}_{\mathsf{Prot}}$. Our proving time is slightly higher for $\mathsf{DVRange}_{\mathsf{Prot}}$, and about 2× higher with $\mathsf{DV}_{\mathsf{Prot}}$.

Acknowledgements. The first author received funding from projects from the European Research Council (ERC) under the European Union's Horizon 2020 research and innovation program under project PICOCRYPT (grant agreement No. 101001283), from the Spanish Government under project PRODIGY (TED2021-132464B-I00), and from the Madrid Regional Government under project BLOQUES (S2018/TCS-4339). The last two projects are co-funded by European Union EIE, and NextGenerationEU/PRTR funds. The last author was partially funded by Input Output (iohk.io) through their funding of the Edinburgh Blockchain Technology Lab.

References

1. Attema, T., Cramer, R.: Compressed Σ-protocol theory and practical application to plug & play secure algorithmics. In: Micciancio, D., Ristenpart, T. (eds.) CRYPTO 2020, Part III, vol. 12172. LNCS, pp. 513–543. Springer, Heidelberg (2020). https://doi.org/10.1007/978-3-030-56877-1_18

2. Attema, T., Cramer, R., Kohl, L.: A compressed Σ-protocol theory for lattices. In: Malkin, T., Peikert, C. (eds.) Annual International Cryptology Conference, CRYPTO 2021. LNCS, vol. 12826, pp. 549–579. Springer, Cham (2021). https://doi.org/10.1007/978-3-030-84245-1_19

3. Auerbach, B., Poettering, B.: Hashing solutions instead of generating problems: on the interactive certification of RSA moduli. In: Abdalla, M., Dahab, R. (eds.) PKC 2018, Part II. LNCS, vol. 10770, pp. 403–430. Springer, Heidelberg (2018). https://doi.org/10.1007/978-3-319-76581-5_14

4. Aumasson, J.-P., Neves, S., Wilcox-O'Hearn, Z., Winnerlein, C.: BLAKE2: simpler, smaller, fast as MD5. In: Jacobson Jr., M.J., Locasto, M.E., Mohassel, P., Safavi-Naini, R. (eds.) ACNS 2013. LNCS, vol. 7954, pp. 119–135. Springer, Heidelberg (2013). https://doi.org/10.1007/978-3-642-38980-1_8

5. Bangerter, E.: Efficient zero knowledge proofs of knowledge for homomorphisms. Ph.D. thesis. Citeseer (2005)

6. Bangerter, E., Camenisch, J., Krenn, S.: Efficiency limitations for Σ-protocols for group homomorphisms. In: Micciancio, D. (ed.) TCC 2010. LNCS, vol. 5978, pp. 553–571. Springer, Heidelberg (2010). https://doi.org/10.1007/978-3-642-11799-2_33

7. Bangerter, E., Camenisch, J., Maurer, U.: Efficient proofs of knowledge of discrete logarithms and representations in groups with hidden order. In: Vaudenay, S. (ed.) PKC 2005. LNCS, vol. 3386, pp. 154–171. Springer, Heidelberg (2005). https://doi.org/10.1007/978-3-540-30580-4_11

8. Bangerter, E., Krenn, S., Sadeghi, A.-R., Schneider, T., Tsay, J.-K.: On the design and implementation of efficient zero-knowledge proofs of knowledge. In: Software Performance Enhancements Encryption Decryption Cryptographic Compilers-SPEED-CC, vol. 9, pp. 12–13 (2009)

9. Barić, N., Pfitzmann, B.: Collision-free accumulators and fail-stop signature schemes without trees. In: Fumy, W. (ed.) EUROCRYPT 1997. LNCS, vol. 1233, pp. 480–494. Springer, Heidelberg (1997). https://doi.org/10.1007/3-540-69053-0_33

10. Benhamouda, F., Ferradi, H., Géraud, R., Naccache, D.: Non-interactive provably secure attestations for arbitrary RSA prime generation algorithms. In: Foley, S.N., Gollmann, D., Snekkenes, E. (eds.) ESORICS 2017, Part I. LNCS, vol. 10492, pp. 206–223. Springer, Cham (2017). https://doi.org/10.1007/978-3-319-66402-6_13

11. Blum, M., Feldman, P., Micali, S.: Non-interactive zero-knowledge and its applications (extended abstract). In: 20th ACM STOC, pp. 103–112. ACM Press, May 1988. https://doi.org/10.1145/62212.62222
12. Böhl, F., Hofheinz, D., Jager, T., Koch, J., Seo, J.H., Striecks, C.: Practical signatures from standard assumptions. In: Johansson, T., Nguyen, P.Q. (eds.) EUROCRYPT 2013. LNCS, vol. 7881, pp. 461–485. Springer, Heidelberg (2013). https://doi.org/10.1007/978-3-642-38348-9_28
13. Boneh, D., Bünz, B., Fisch, B.: Batching techniques for accumulators with applications to IOPs and stateless blockchains. In: Boldyreva, A., Micciancio, D. (eds.) CRYPTO 2019, Part I. LNCS, vol. 11692, pp. 561–586. Springer, Cham (2019). https://doi.org/10.1007/978-3-030-26948-7_20
14. Boudot, F.: Efficient proofs that a committed number lies in an interval. In: Preneel, B. (ed.) EUROCRYPT 2000. LNCS, vol. 1807, pp. 431–444. Springer, Heidelberg (2000). https://doi.org/10.1007/3-540-45539-6_31
15. Bresson, E., Catalano, D., Pointcheval, D.: A simple public-key cryptosystem with a double trapdoor decryption mechanism and its applications. In: Laih, C.-S. (ed.) ASIACRYPT 2003. LNCS, vol. 2894, pp. 37–54. Springer, Heidelberg (2003). https://doi.org/10.1007/978-3-540-40061-5_3
16. Buchmann, J., Hamdy, S.: A survey on IQ cryptography (2001). http://tubiblio.ulb.tu-darmstadt.de/100933/
17. Bünz, D., Bootle, J., Boneh, D., Poelstra, A., Wuille, P., Maxwell, G.: Bulletproofs: short proofs for confidential transactions and more. In: 2018 IEEE Symposium on Security and Privacy, pp. 315–334. IEEE Computer Society Press, May 2018. https://doi.org/10.1109/SP.2018.00020
18. Camenisch, J., Kiayias, A., Yung, M.: On the portability of generalized Schnorr proofs. In: Joux, A. (ed.) EUROCRYPT 2009. LNCS, vol. 5479, pp. 425–442. Springer, Heidelberg (2009). https://doi.org/10.1007/978-3-642-01001-9_25
19. Camenisch, J., Michels, M.: Proving in zero-knowledge that a number is the product of two safe primes. In: Stern, J. (ed.) EUROCRYPT 1999. LNCS, vol. 1592, pp. 107–122. Springer, Heidelberg (1999). https://doi.org/10.1007/3-540-48910-X_8
20. Camenisch, J., Michels, M.: Separability and efficiency for generic group signature schemes. In: Wiener, M. (ed.) CRYPTO 1999. LNCS, vol. 1666, pp. 413–430. Springer, Heidelberg (1999). https://doi.org/10.1007/3-540-48405-1_27
21. Canetti, R., Gennaro, R., Goldfeder, S., Makriyannis, N., Peled, U.: UC non-interactive, proactive, threshold ECDSA with identifiable aborts. In: Ligatti, J., Ou, X., Katz, J., Vigna, G. (eds.) ACM CCS 2020, pp. 1769–1787. ACM Press, November 2020. https://doi.org/10.1145/3372297.3423367
22. Castagnos, G., Laguillaumie, F.: Linearly homomorphic encryption from DDH. In: Nyberg, K. (ed.) CT-RSA 2015. LNCS, vol. 9048, pp. 487–505. Springer, Cham (2015). https://doi.org/10.1007/978-3-319-16715-2_26
23. Catalano, D., Pointcheval, D., Pornin, T.: IPAKE: isomorphisms for password-based authenticated key exchange. In: Franklin, M. (ed.) CRYPTO 2004. LNCS, vol. 3152, pp. 477–493. Springer, Heidelberg (2004). https://doi.org/10.1007/978-3-540-28628-8_29
24. Chaidos, P., Couteau, G.: Efficient designated-verifier non-interactive zero-knowledge proofs of knowledge. In: Nielsen, J.B., Rijmen, V. (eds.) EUROCRYPT 2018, Part III. LNCS, vol. 10822, pp. 193–221. Springer, Cham (2018). https://doi.org/10.1007/978-3-319-78372-7_7
25. Chan, A., Frankel, Y., Tsiounis, Y.: Easy come—easy go divisible cash. In: Nyberg, K. (ed.) EUROCRYPT 1998. LNCS, vol. 1403, pp. 561–575. Springer, Heidelberg (1998). https://doi.org/10.1007/BFb0054154

26. Couteau, G., Klooß, M., Lin, H., Reichle, M.: Efficient range proofs with transparent setup from bounded integer commitments. In: Canteaut, A., Standaert, F.-X. (eds.) EUROCRYPT 2021. LNCS, vol. 12698, pp. 247–277. Springer, Cham (2021). https://doi.org/10.1007/978-3-030-77883-5_9

27. Couteau, G., Peters, T., Pointcheval, D.: Removing the strong RSA assumption from arguments over the integers. In: Coron, J.-S., Nielsen, J.B. (eds.) EUROCRYPT 2017, Part II. LNCS, vol. 10211, pp. 321–350. Springer, Cham (2017). https://doi.org/10.1007/978-3-319-56614-6_11

28. Cramer, R.: Modular design of secure yet practical cryptographic protocols. Ph.D. thesis, CWI and University of Amsterdam (1996)

29. Cramer, R., Damgård, I.: On the amortized complexity of zero-knowledge protocols. In: Halevi, S. (ed.) CRYPTO 2009. LNCS, vol. 5677, pp. 177–191. Springer, Heidelberg (2009). https://doi.org/10.1007/978-3-642-03356-8_11

30. Cramer, R., Damgård, I., Keller, M.: On the amortized complexity of zero-knowledge protocols. J. Cryptol. **27**(2), 284–316 (2013). https://doi.org/10.1007/s00145-013-9145-x

31. Cramer, R., Shoup, V.: Universal hash proofs and a paradigm for adaptive chosen ciphertext secure public-key encryption. In: Knudsen, L.R. (ed.) EUROCRYPT 2002. LNCS, vol. 2332, pp. 45–64. Springer, Heidelberg (2002). https://doi.org/10.1007/3-540-46035-7_4

32. Damgård, I.: On Σ-Protocols. Lecture Notes, University of Aarhus, Department for Computer Science, p. 84 (2002). Accessed: 16 Feb 2022

33. Damgård, I., Fazio, N., Nicolosi, A.: Non-interactive zero-knowledge from homomorphic encryption. In: Halevi, S., Rabin, T. (eds.) TCC 2006. LNCS, vol. 3876, pp. 41–59. Springer, Heidelberg (2006). https://doi.org/10.1007/11681878_3

34. Damgård, I., Fujisaki, E.: A statistically-hiding integer commitment scheme based on groups with hidden order. In: Zheng, Y. (ed.) ASIACRYPT 2002. LNCS, vol. 2501, pp. 125–142. Springer, Heidelberg (2002). https://doi.org/10.1007/3-540-36178-2_8

35. Damgård, I., Jurik, M.: A length-flexible threshold cryptosystem with applications. In: Safavi-Naini, R., Seberry, J. (eds.) ACISP 2003. LNCS, vol. 2727, pp. 350–364. Springer, Heidelberg (2003). https://doi.org/10.1007/3-540-45067-X_30

36. Damgård, I., Jurik, M.: A generalisation, a simplification and some applications of Paillier's probabilistic public-key system. In: Kim, K. (ed.) PKC 2001. LNCS, vol. 1992, pp. 119–136. Springer, Heidelberg (2001). https://doi.org/10.1007/3-540-44586-2_9

37. Damgård, I., Koprowski, M.: Generic lower bounds for root extraction and signature schemes in general groups. In: Knudsen, L.R. (ed.) EUROCRYPT 2002. LNCS, vol. 2332, pp. 256–271. Springer, Heidelberg (2002). https://doi.org/10.1007/3-540-46035-7_17

38. Dobson, S., Galbraith, S.D., Smith, B.: Trustless groups of unknown order with hyperelliptic curves. Cryptology ePrint Archive, Report 2020/196 (2020). https://eprint.iacr.org/2020/196

39. Fujisaki, E., Okamoto, T.: A practical and provably secure scheme for publicly verifiable secret sharing and its applications. In: Nyberg, K. (ed.) EUROCRYPT 1998. LNCS, vol. 1403, pp. 32–46. Springer, Heidelberg (1998). https://doi.org/10.1007/BFb0054115

40. Fujisaki, E., Okamoto, T.: Statistical zero knowledge protocols to prove modular polynomial relations. In: Kaliski, B.S. (ed.) CRYPTO 1997. LNCS, vol. 1294, pp. 16–30. Springer, Heidelberg (1997). https://doi.org/10.1007/BFb0052225

41. Gennaro, R., Micciancio, D., Rabin, T.: An efficient non-interactive statistical zero-knowledge proof system for quasi-safe prime products. In: Gong, L., Reiter, M.K. (eds.) ACM CCS 1998, pp. 67–72. ACM Press, November 1998. https://doi.org/10.1145/288090.288108

42. Goldberg, S., Reyzin, L., Sagga, O., Baldimtsi, F.: Efficient noninteractive certification of RSA moduli and beyond. In: Galbraith, S.D., Moriai, S. (eds.) ASIACRYPT 2019. LNCS, vol. 11923, pp. 700–727. Springer, Cham (2019). https://doi.org/10.1007/978-3-030-34618-8_24

43. Goldwasser, S., Kharchenko, D.: Proof of plaintext knowledge for the Ajtai-Dwork cryptosystem. In: Kilian, J. (ed.) TCC 2005. LNCS, vol. 3378, pp. 529–555. Springer, Heidelberg (2005). https://doi.org/10.1007/978-3-540-30576-7_29

44. Groth, J.: Non-interactive zero-knowledge arguments for voting. In: Ioannidis, J., Keromytis, A., Yung, M. (eds.) ACNS 2005. LNCS, vol. 3531, pp. 467–482. Springer, Heidelberg (2005). https://doi.org/10.1007/11496137_32

45. Hazay, C., Mikkelsen, G.L., Rabin, T., Toft, T., Nicolosi, A.A.: Efficient RSA key generation and threshold Paillier in the two-party setting. J. Cryptol. **32**(2), 265–323 (2018). https://doi.org/10.1007/s00145-017-9275-7

46. Ishai, Y., Ostrovsky, R., Zikas, V.: Secure multi-party computation with identifiable abort. In: Garay, J.A., Gennaro, R. (eds.) CRYPTO 2014, Part II. LNCS, vol. 8617, pp. 369–386. Springer, Heidelberg (2014). https://doi.org/10.1007/978-3-662-44381-1_21

47. Kirchner, P., Fouque, P.-A.: Getting rid of linear algebra in number theory problems. Cryptology ePrint Archive, Report 2020/1619 (2020). https://ia.cr/2020/1619

48. Kosba, A., Papamanthou, C., Shi, E.: xJsnark: a framework for efficient verifiable computation. In: 2018 IEEE Symposium on Security and Privacy (SP), pp. 944–961. IEEE (2018)

49. Kunz-Jacques, S., Martinet, G., Poupard, G., Stern, J.: Cryptanalysis of an efficient proof of knowledge of discrete logarithm. In: Yung, M., Dodis, Y., Kiayias, A., Malkin, T. (eds.) PKC 2006. LNCS, vol. 3958, pp. 27–43. Springer, Heidelberg (2006). https://doi.org/10.1007/11745853_3

50. Lee, J.: The security of groups of unknown order based on Jacobians of hyperelliptic curves. Cryptology ePrint Archive, Report 2020/289 (2020). https://eprint.iacr.org/2020/289

51. Lipmaa, H.: On diophantine complexity and statistical zero-knowledge arguments. In: Laih, C.-S. (ed.) ASIACRYPT 2003. LNCS, vol. 2894, pp. 398–415. Springer, Heidelberg (2003). https://doi.org/10.1007/978-3-540-40061-5_26

52. Maurer, U.M.: Abstract models of computation in cryptography (invited paper). In: Smart, N.P. (ed.) 10th IMA International Conference on Cryptography and Coding. LNCS, vol. 3796, pp. 1–12. Springer, Heidelberg (2005)

53. Ozdemir, A., Wahby, R., Whitehat, B., Boneh, D.: Scaling verifiable computation using efficient set accumulators. In: 29th USENIX Security Symposium (USENIX Security 2020), pp. 2075–2092 (2020)

54. Paillier, P.: Public-key cryptosystems based on composite degree residuosity classes. In: Stern, J. (ed.) EUROCRYPT 1999. LNCS, vol. 1592, pp. 223–238. Springer, Heidelberg (1999). https://doi.org/10.1007/3-540-48910-X_16

55. Pass, R., Shelat, A., Vaikuntanathan, V.: Construction of a non-malleable encryption scheme from any semantically secure one. In: Dwork, C. (ed.) CRYPTO 2006. LNCS, vol. 4117, pp. 271–289. Springer, Heidelberg (2006). https://doi.org/10.1007/11818175_16

56. Peikert, C., Waters, B.: Lossy trapdoor functions and their applications. In: Ladner, R.E., Dwork, C. (eds.) 40th ACM STOC, pp. 187–196. ACM Press, May 2008. https://doi.org/10.1145/1374376.1374406

57. Rabin, M.O., Shallit, J.O.: Randomized algorithms in number theory. Commun. Pure Appl. Math. **39**(S1), S239–S256 (1986)

58. Schnorr, C.P.: Efficient identification and signatures for smart cards. In: Brassard, G. (ed.) CRYPTO 1989. LNCS, vol. 435, pp. 239–252. Springer, New York (1990). https://doi.org/10.1007/0-387-34805-0_22

59. Shoup, V.: Lower bounds for discrete logarithms and related problems. In: Fumy, W. (ed.) EUROCRYPT 1997. LNCS, vol. 1233, pp. 256–266. Springer, Heidelberg (1997). https://doi.org/10.1007/3-540-69053-0_18

60. Terelius, B., Wikström, D.: Efficiency limitations of Σ-protocols for group homomorphisms revisited. In: Visconti, I., De Prisco, R. (eds.) SCN 2012. LNCS, vol. 7485, pp. 461–476. Springer, Heidelberg (2012). https://doi.org/10.1007/978-3-642-32928-9_26

61. van de Graaf, J., Peralta, R.: A simple and secure way to show the validity of your public key. In: Pomerance, C. (ed.) CRYPTO 1987. LNCS, vol. 293, pp. 128–134. Springer, Heidelberg (1988). https://doi.org/10.1007/3-540-48184-2_9

62. Yuen, T.H., Huang, Q., Mu, Y., Susilo, W., Wong, D.S., Yang, G.: Efficient noninteractive range proof. In: Ngo, H.Q. (ed.) COCOON 2009. LNCS, vol. 5609, pp. 138–147. Springer, Heidelberg (2009). https://doi.org/10.1007/978-3-642-02882-3_15

Dew: A Transparent Constant-Sized Polynomial Commitment Scheme

Arasu Arun[1], Chaya Ganesh[2], Satya Lokam[3], Tushar Mopuri[2(✉)], and Sriram Sridhar[4]

[1] New York University, New York, USA
arasu@nyu.edu
[2] Indian Institute of Science, Bengaluru, India
{chaya,tusharmopuri}@iisc.ac.in
[3] Microsoft Research India, Bengaluru, India
satya@microsoft.com
[4] University of California, Berkeley, USA
srirams@berkeley.edu

Abstract. We construct a polynomial commitment scheme with constant (i.e., independent of the degree) sized evaluation proofs and logarithmic (in the degree) verification time in the transparent setting. To the best of our knowledge, this is the first result achieving this combination of properties.

We build our scheme from an inner product commitment scheme with constant-sized proofs but with linear verification time. To improve the verification time to logarithmic for polynomial commitments, we prove a new extremal combinatorial bound. Our constructions rely on groups of unknown order instantiated by class groups. We prove security of our constructions in the Generic Group Model.

Compiling known information-theoretic proof systems using our polynomial commitment scheme yields transparent and constant-sized zkSNARKs (Zero-knowledge Succinct Non-interactive ARguments of Knowledge) with logarithmic verification.

1 Introduction

A Polynomial Commitment Scheme (PCS) [18] allows a prover to commit to a polynomial P of degree d so that, later. a verifier can query for $P(x)$ at an argument x of its choice and the prover can, together with its response, furnish an evaluation proof that its response is indeed consistent with its commitment. The commitment and the evaluation proof are required to be *succinct*, that is, of size independent of, or logarithmic, in d.

Polynomial commitments have applications in verifiable secret sharing [15], anonymous credentials [10], and zero-knowledge sets [22], among others. But by

---

S. Sridhar, T. Mopuri and A. Arun—Work partially done while at Microsoft Research India.

A. Boldyreva and V. Kolesnikov (Eds.): PKC 2023, LNCS 13941, pp. 542–571, 2023.
https://doi.org/10.1007/978-3-031-31371-4_19

far, their most dominant application is to constructions of zkSNARKs (zero-knowledge Succinct Non-interactive ARguments of Knowledge) for all of NP. Indeed, improvements to PCS imply improvements to SNARKs when combined with established modular approaches to SNARKs. On the other hand, a SNARK for all of NP in particular implies a succinct PCS by instantiating the SNARK for the NP-relation "$y = P(x)$ and the commitment C opens to P", where C is a succinct commitment to P. While this incidental corollary of a SNARK implies succinct PCS, we desire a "direct" construction of PCS without writing polynomial evaluation as a generic NP relation, since most SNARK constructions themselves use PCS as a crucial ingredient. PCS is therefore a core cryptographic construct and there is a strong motivation to construct one with the best possible parameters.

Transparent Setup. Non-interactive proof systems are typically in the Common Reference String (CRS) model where a CRS is generated during a setup phase which needs to be *trusted* if the CRS uses secret randomness. Constructions that do not involve a trusted setup phase and the verifier randomness consists of only *public coins* are called *transparent*. A recent line of work [11, 12, 17, 23] to construct SNARKs follows a modular approach: first, an information-theoretic component is constructed; then this is compiled into an argument using cryptographic tools, typically a PCS. Finally, this is made non-interactive to obtain a SNARK in the random oracle model (ROM). The resulting SNARK inherits the trusted setup assumption or the transparency property from the cryptographic tools used in the compilation process. Any resulting SNARK from compiling an information-theoretic protocol inherits the complexity of the PCS, that is, the proof size depends on the commitment size and evaluation proof size of the PCS. Unfortunately, all existing succinct PCS schemes either require trusted-setup assumptions [18], or are when they are transparent, only achieve logarithmic proof size [3, 9, 20][1]. We address this challenge in this work.

1.1 Our Contributions

We present the first PCS with constant size commitment, constant size evaluation proof[2] and logarithmic verification in the transparent setting. Our starting point is a construction of a transparent Inner Product Commitment (IPC) scheme (which is a more general object than PCS) that allows a prover to open a committed vector to inner products with a verifier's query vectors. Our IPC is succinct – that is, the size of the commitment and the proof of a correct opening are independent of the length of the vector and linear (in the length of the vector) time verification. Building on this IPC, we construct a succinct PCS,

---

[1] A flaw in the proof of security of the DARK scheme [9] was discovered by Block et al [3], who propose a different PCS with logarithmic proof size. We also note that a revised version of DARK [8] also proposes a fix by showing that the DARK PCS satisfies a property called almost-special-soundness which suffices for extraction.

[2] Constant is $O_\kappa(1)$. That is, independent of the size of the input, and polynomial only in the security parameter.

resulting in a *transparent constant-sized PCS* but, importantly, with *logarithmic time verification*. Our PCS is the *first* construction to achieve the above combination of properties to the best of our knowledge.

From a technical point of view, our contributions are summarized below.

Inner Product Commitment (IPC) and Polynomial Commitment Scheme (PCS). We construct a constant size transparent IPC scheme in Sect. 3. In Sect. 4, we present our transparent PCS construction that achieves constant sized proofs, constant sized public parameters, and verification in $O(\log n)$ field operations and a constant number of group operations for polynomials of degree n. Both the above constructions are in the GGM. We also show hiding and zero knowledge variants of our constructions. Using the now standard compilation process from information-theoretic proofs in idealized models to zkSNARKs via PCS [9,12], we obtain a *transparent constant-sized zkSNARK with constant-sized public parameters* (Sect. 5). The resulting zkSNARKs achieve $O_\kappa(1)$ communication and $O(\log n)$ verification[3], where n is the complexity of the NP relation (e.g., number of constraints of a Rank 1 Constraint System, or the number of gates in an arithmetic circuit). The only other transparent zkSNARKs with constant-sized proofs and public parameters are obtained by compiling constant-query PCPs using transparent vector commitment schemes with constant-sized opening proofs and public parameters. The VCs of [5,19] are such candidates.

A New Combinatorial Lemma. As noted above, we improve the verification time from linear (in length of vector) in our IPC to logarithmic (in degree of polynomial) in our PCS. We achieve this efficiency improvement using Kronecker products (details in Sect. 1.3.2 and Sect. 4.1); but their naive application breaks soundness. We recover soundness by solving a problem in extremal combinatorics. A special case of our problem asks: how many points can we choose in the discrete cube $[n]^d$ such that that set of points does not contain the corners of a d-dimensional hyper-rectangle (box)? When $d = 2$, this is the Zarankiewicz problem [4] in extremal graph theory for which an asymptotically tight bound of $\sim n^{3/2}$ is known. For higher d, the "Box Theorem" due to Rosenfeld [24] proves the bound $\sim n^{d-2^{-d+1}}$. We can use these bounds in the soundness proof of our PCS to obtain n^ϵ verification time for any constant $0 < \epsilon < 1$. While this improves on linear, our goal is to obtain *logarithmic* verification.

We achieve logarithmic verification by generalizing boxes in the extremal problem to "d-cancellation structures." With these d-cancellation structures, we can continue to exploit certain cancellation properties required for soundness (details in Sect. 4.2) similar to those for boxes but also, more importantly, succeed in proving much better bounds on the number of points in $[n]^d$ that do not contain a d-cancellation structure. Our bounds are $\sim dn^{d-1}$ and it is crucial for our soundness that this is a negligible fraction of the whole space (of size n^d); in contrast, as $d \to \infty$, the box theorem above gives a bound that approaches n^d – essentially filling the whole space.

---

[3] In the preprocessing setting.

To the best of our knowledge, our result is the first application of an extremal combinatorics theorem in the construction of PCS and SNARKs and we believe this to be of independent interest. We note that extremal combinatorics results like this have found applications in complexity theory and theoretical computer science in general.

Recovering the DARK [9] Result. We show that our PCS can be adapted to obtain logarithmic proof size and verification by employing the recursive evaluation protocol from DARK on our new commitment scheme. This recovers the flawed Lemmas 8, 9 from DARK thus recovering a transparent PCS with logarithmic proof size and logarithmic verification, *but* at the expense of an increased quadratic prover time. The DARK recovery does not require GGM; we achieve this result under the same assumptions made in DARK, i.e., the Adaptive Root and Strong RSA Assumptions. We note that [3] gives a construction that achieves similar results as DARK by modifying DARK's evaluation protocol, and a subsequent revision of DARK [8] shows that the DARK PCS satisfies a property called almost-special-soundness. In contrast, our construction is a commitment scheme that is syntactically close to DARK, has a similar evaluation protocol and recovers the flawed lemmas. We present this in the full version [1].

1.2   Related Work

Functional commitments were introduced by [21] as a generalization of vector commitments, where a prover can commit to a vector, and later open the commitment at functions of the committed vector with a succinct proof that the answer is consistent with the committed vector. The work of [21] also showed a construction for functional commitments for linear functions. Lai and Malavolta [19] put forth the notion of Linear Map Commitments (LMC) that allow a prover to open a commitment to the output of a linear map. The constructions from [19, 21] achieve succinctness - constant commitment and proof size, but require trusted setup.

In a recent concurrent work, [13] presents transparent inner product commitment schemes with constant size openings and constant size public parameters. Their scheme is also in groups of unknown order, however, the techniques they use are completely different. Their result relies on proofs of cardinality of RSA accumulated sets, whereas we rely on integer encoding of vectors and combinatorial techniques to show extraction. Though a PCS was not their goal, a PCS resulting from the inner product commitment scheme of [13] in the natural way results in a linear time verifier. In contrast, we achieve logarithmic verification time for our PCS.

Polynomial commitment schemes were introduced in [18], and have since led to several variants being used in recent SNARKs. The KZG scheme [18] gives constant-sized commitments and proofs, but require a trusted setup. In the transparent setting, Wahby et al. [25] constructed a polynomial commitment scheme for multilinear polynomials that has commitment size and evaluation proof size $O(\sqrt{d})$ for degree d polynomials. Zhang et al. [27] construct a polynomial commitment from FRI (Fast Reed Solomon IOPP) that is transparent, has constant size commitments, but evaluation proofs have size $O(\log^2 d)$.

As mentioned earlier, Bünz et al [9] used a Diophantine Argument of Knowledge (DARK), and constructed a polynomial commitment scheme with proof size $O(\log d)$ and $O(\log d)$ verification time for polynomials of degree d. Block et al. [3] identified a gap in the proof of security of the DARK scheme and propose a modification that sidesteps the gap in extraction, resulting in a PCS of polylogarithmic proof size and verification time.

1.3 Technical Overview

The intuitive starting point of our commitment schemes is a natural mapping from vectors to group elements *via* integers. Specifically, for a vector[4] $\mathbf{c}$, define $\mathsf{int}_\alpha(\mathbf{c}) := \langle \mathbf{c}, \boldsymbol{\alpha} \rangle := \sum_0^{l-1} c_i \alpha^i$, where $\boldsymbol{\alpha} := (1, \alpha, \alpha^2, \ldots, \alpha^{l-1})$ and α is sufficiently large. Let us also define $C := g^{\mathsf{int}_\alpha(\mathbf{c})}$ for a given group element $g \in \mathbb{G}$. When the group $\mathbb{G}$ is a *group of unknown order* and $g \in \mathbb{G}$ is random (but chosen during set up), we can show that a prover can prove knowledge of a unique positive exponent of C with base g and that the α-base representation $\mathbf{c}$ of that exponent must be a valid opening of C. This follows from a Proof of Knowledge of a *Positive* Exponent (PoKPE) protocol that builds on Wesolowski's Proof of Exponent (PoE) protocol [26] (details in Sect. 2.4).

We now wish to use the commitment C made by a Prover to vector c in a protocol for inner product $\langle \mathbf{c}, \mathbf{q} \rangle$, where $\mathbf{q}$ is the *query vector* from the Verifier. To that end, let us consider the integer product

$$\mathsf{int}_\alpha(\mathbf{c}) \cdot \mathsf{int}_\alpha(\mathsf{reverse}(\mathbf{q})) = \left(\sum_{i=0}^{l-1} c_i \alpha^i \right) \cdot \left(\sum_{i=0}^{l-1} q_{l-i} \alpha^i \right) = L + \alpha^l \langle \mathbf{c}, \mathbf{q} \rangle + H \quad (1)$$

where L and H are polynomials collecting powers of α of degree less than l and more than l respectively. Raising g to both sides of (1), we obtain

$$C^{\mathsf{int}_\alpha(\mathsf{reverse}(\mathbf{q}))} = (g^L) \cdot (g^{\alpha^l \langle \mathbf{c}, \mathbf{q} \rangle}) \cdot (g^H). \quad (2)$$

Note that the verifier can compute the l.h.s. of (2). Hence if the prover claims that the inner product $\langle \mathbf{c}, \mathbf{q} \rangle$ evaluates to v and *also* sends g^L and g^H to the verifier (and convinces the verifier of values L and H using a PoKPE protocol), then the verifier can check consistency of the prover's claim using (2) (with v in place of $\langle \mathbf{c}, \mathbf{q} \rangle$). While this intuition suffices for a completeness proof, it is by no means sufficient for a soundness proof. Our main contribution, outlined below, is to show that a check somewhat analogous to (2) with some additional machinery *suffices* for a verifier to catch a cheating prover with high probability. This intuition is essentially the basis for our inner product evaluation protocol **IPP** in Fig. 3 and the "additional machinery" appears as the **TEST** protocol in Fig. 2.

We remark that the above intuition is reminiscent of approaches in [9,19]. However, our approach below differs significantly from theirs to achieve *constant*

---

[4] Our vectors are over $\mathbb{Z}_p$ and we map elements of $\mathbb{Z}_p$ to integers $\{0, \ldots, p-1\}$.

sized proofs (unlike in [9] that uses recursion to obtain logarithmic size) and *transparent* setting where α is not secret (unlike the trusted setup in [19]).

1.3.1   A TEST Protocol and Extracting Structure from Overflows

A cheating prover could use a committed vector (derived by computing the α-base representation of exponent of g in C using the PoKPE extractor) with coordinate values that could cause "overflow" in the coefficients on the r.h.s. of (1). In that case, we can no longer guarantee the correctness of the inner product as the middle coefficient. We now describe ideas that help us overcome this challenge.

To control the issues caused by overflow, we intersperse 0's between coordinates of $\mathbf{c}$: we double the length of the vector to $2l$ and place the vector $\mathbf{c}$ to be committed in even positions $(0, 2, \ldots, 2l - 2)$ and 0's in odd positions. More generally, let $\mathbf{d}$ denote the subvector in the odd positions and let $\mathbf{c}\|\mathbf{d}$ denote the combined vector of length $2l$. Note first that completeness continues to hold with this change since an honest prover commits to $\mathbf{c}\|\mathbf{0}$, with $\mathbf{c} \in \mathbb{Z}_p^l$ and satisfy analogs of (1) and (2) for length-$2l$ vectors with 0's in odd positions, or equivalently, with α^2 replacing α. Second, and this is our next crucial step, note that the verifier can run a **TEST** protocol (cf. Fig 2) that queries for the inner product $\langle(\mathbf{c}\|\mathbf{d})\,,\,(\mathbf{0}\|\mathbf{z})\rangle$, where $\mathbf{z} \in \mathbb{Z}_p^l$ is a uniformly chosen *random* vector and the verifier can check if the middle coefficient of (generalization to $2l$-length vectors of) (2) is zero. *Assuming no overflows*, the middle coefficient would be $\langle\mathbf{d}, \mathbf{z}\rangle$. In this case, by the Schwartz-Zippel lemma, a cheating prover choosing nonzero $\mathbf{d}$ would be caught with high probability. However, a cheating prover could choose nonzero $\mathbf{d}$ and still pass the test for $\mathbf{z}$ by causing overflows from L in (1) (due to large products between $\mathbf{c}$ and $\mathbf{z}$ coordinates) to "cancel out" the non-zero value of $\langle\mathbf{d}, \mathbf{z}\rangle$. More precisely, it can be shown using (a generalization of) (1) and the PoKPE protocol relating (2) to (1) that if a prover can succeed in the **TEST** protocol with non-negligible probability, then

$$\langle\mathbf{d}, \mathbf{z}\rangle \bmod \alpha + \left\lfloor \frac{\langle\mathbf{c}, \mathbf{z}\rangle}{\alpha} \right\rfloor + u = 0 \mod \alpha, \tag{3}$$

for some $u \in \{0, 1\}$ must be satisfied (3) with non-negligible probability over a uniformly random $\mathbf{z} \in \mathbb{Z}_p^l$.

Call a test vector $\mathbf{z} \in \mathbb{Z}_p^l$ a *success point* for the prover if (3) is satisfied when verifier chooses $\mathbf{z}$ and prover's commitment C extracts – via a PoKPE protocol – to $\mathbf{c}\|\mathbf{d}$. Now, if a prover has two success points $\mathbf{z}$ and $\mathbf{z}'$ on a "line", i.e., $\mathbf{z}$ and $\mathbf{z}'$ agree on all coordinates except j-th, then $\langle\mathbf{d}, \mathbf{z}\rangle - \langle\mathbf{d}, \mathbf{z}'\rangle = d_j(z_j - z_j')$ because of cancellations in coordinates $\neq j$. Thus subtracting (3) for $\mathbf{z}'$ from that for $\mathbf{z}$, we obtain

$$d_j \cdot (z_j - z_j') = \left(\left\lfloor \frac{\langle\mathbf{c}, \mathbf{z}'\rangle}{\alpha} \right\rfloor - \left\lfloor \frac{\langle\mathbf{c}, \mathbf{z}\rangle}{\alpha} \right\rfloor + u' - u \right) \mod \alpha. \tag{4}$$

Using bounds on coordinates of $\mathbf{c}$ and $\mathbf{z}$, we conclude that d_j is $\theta_{1j}\alpha + \theta_{2j}$, where θ_1 and θ_2 are rationals with small denominators (a more detailed statement of this structure appears in Theorem 34). An easy combinatorial argument shows that if the prover succeeds with non-negligible probability, e.g., at least $1/p$ (p is $\exp(\kappa)$), then in *every* direction j, there must be a line in the j-th dimension with two success points $\mathbf{z}$ and $\mathbf{z}'$ on it. Hence, if the prover is accepted in the **TEST** protocol (Fig. 2) with non-negligible probability, every coordinate of $\mathbf{d}$ can be expressed as $d_j = \theta_{1j}\alpha + \theta_{2j}$ with θ's as above – *this is the structure we extract on $\mathbf{d}$ that we use to prove soundness.* This Structure Theorem 34 is a crucial technical ingredient of our results.

Armed with the structure theorem, we prove (Theorem 35) that if the inner product evaluation protocol **IPP** (Fig. 3) for $\langle(\mathbf{c}\|\mathbf{d}), (\mathbf{q}\|\mathbf{0})\rangle$ succeeds in satisfying (generalizations) of (1) and (2), with query vector $\mathbf{q}\|\mathbf{0}$, then we can extract a vector $\tilde{\mathbf{c}}$ that, while fractional over the integers, has invertible denominators modulo p. Using this $\tilde{\mathbf{c}}$ as the "opening hint" (cf. **Open()** in §3.1), we can then extract a unique $\mathbf{c}$ that is consistent with the claimed inner product.

1.3.2   Logarithmic Verification for Polynomial Commitments

Our IPC scheme above immediately yields a Polynomial Commitment Scheme (PCS), noting that, for a polynomial f given by its vector of coefficients $\mathbf{f} = (f_0, \ldots, f_{l-1})$, $f(x) = \langle\mathbf{f}, \mathbf{x}\rangle$, where $\mathbf{x} = (1, x, \ldots, x^{l-1})$. However, the verification complexity of the resulting PCS is much worse than what we want to achieve. Linear verification seems inherent for inner products (since the query vector $\mathbf{q}$ can be arbitrary and the verifier needs to at least read the statement, verifier's computation of $\text{int}_\alpha(\text{reverse}(\mathbf{q}))$ itself will take linear time). But, in a PCS, we can hope to achieve logarithmic verification time since the query vector $\mathbf{x}$ is parameterized by single variable x. In particular, we can compute $\text{int}_\alpha(\text{reverse}(\mathbf{x}))$ in only logarithmic time (cf. (5) below and (11)). This makes the verifier in **IPP** protocol (specialized to a PCS) logarithmic. However, we still have the bottleneck for verifier computation in the **TEST** protocol. Note that while the query vector $\mathbf{x}$ is parameterized by a single variable x, the *test vector* $\mathbf{z}$ is not and hence computing $\text{int}_\alpha(\text{reverse}(\mathbf{z}))$ in checking (2) in **TEST** protocol still seems to require linear verifier time.

To reduce verifier's computation in **TEST** protocol, we use the idea of **Kronecker products**[5]: instead of choosing $\mathbf{z}$ uniformly at random in $\mathbb{Z}_p^l$, we choose $\log l$ vectors $\mathbf{z}_0, \ldots, \mathbf{z}_{\log l - 1}$ uniformly at random from $\mathbb{Z}_p^2$ and define $\mathbf{z} = \mathbf{z}_0 \otimes \cdots \otimes \mathbf{z}_{\log l - 1}$ To illustrate how this helps, consider the following computation needed on the right hand side of (2), where $\mathbf{z}$ is as above and $i = (i_0, \ldots, i_{\log l - 1})$ the binary expansion of index $i \in [l]$.

$$\text{int}_\alpha(\text{reverse}(\mathbf{z})) = \sum_{i=0}^{l-1} \alpha^{l-i} \prod_{j=0}^{\log l - 1} z_{j,i_j} = \alpha^l \cdot \prod_{j=0}^{\log l - 1} (z_{j,0} + z_{j,1}\alpha^{-2^j}), \quad (5)$$

---

[5] We note that [2] and [20] also use Kronecker products in proof systems albeit with different motivations.

and note that the last product can be computed in logarithmic time. The new test protocol with Kronecker product test vectors is called **logTEST** (identical to **TEST** except with the query vector replaced as above).

While this helps improve verifier efficiency of **TEST**, it *breaks soundness!* The extractability proof of **TEST** in IPC relies on uniform randomness of the test vector $\mathbf{z} \in \mathbb{Z}_p^l$. So, we must now *improve the extractability proof to work with exponentially smaller randomness* in the $\log l$ vectors $\mathbf{z}_j$ of length 2. Specifically, it is crucial to recover an analog of the structure for the $\mathbf{d}$ vector as outlined in Sect. 1.3.1 but now from this vastly reduced space of verifier's randomness in **logTEST**. We outline how to do this next.

1.3.3   An Extremal Combinatorial Bound

We recover soundness with Kronecker product **TEST** vectors by proving a *new result in extremal combinatorics*. Informally, this theorem (Theorem 45) gives a tight upper bound on the number of points in the hypercube $[n]^d$ such that no subset of 2^d points in that set form a configuration that we call a d-cancellation structure. A d-cancellation structure generalizes the set of corners of a d-dimensional *box* or a hyper-rectangle. For instance, a 2-cancellation structure is a parallelogram generalizing a rectangle. In the case of a rectangle, this is the well-known Zarankiewicz problem [4] from extremal graph theory and has an asymptotically tight bound of $n^{3/2}$ points (out of n^2) that contain no four points as corners of a rectangle in $[n]^2$. Thus, our problem generalizes this in two ways: first, we consider high dimensions with growing d (but no more than $\log n$) and second, we generalize a rectangle/box to d-cancellation structure. A recursive definition is given in Definition 44. For $d > 2$ and in case of boxes, Rosenfeld [24] proved an upper bound of $\sim n^{d-2^{-d+1}}$ on the maximum number of points that do not contain the corners of a box. This bound, however, is insufficient for us to get logarithmic verification since as d grows, it tends to n^d almost entirely filling the space. Our main contribution is to obtain a significantly smaller upper bound by generalizing boxes to d-cancellation structure: a tight upper bound of $(n^d - (n-1)^d) \leq dn^{d-1}$, which is a vanishingly small fraction of n^d. For example, when the forbidden configurations are generalized from rectangles to parallelograms for $d = 2$, the upper bound improves to $\sim n$ from the $\sim n^{3/2}$ stated above for the Zarankiewicz problem.

We now tie back this combinatorial argument to the goal of extractability. As the name implies, a d-cancellation structure induces cancellations. Recall from Sect. 1.3.1 that cancellations between two success points (test vectors $\mathbf{z}$ and $\mathbf{z}'$ where the prover succeeds by satisfying (3)) allow us to deduce structural conditions on coordinates of $\mathbf{d}$ using (4). We now generalize that argument to Kronecker products as test vectors where a d-cancellation structure generalizes the role of a line, and cancellations between two points on a line generalize to recursive cancellations among 2^d points in a d-cancellation structure. Finally, the simple combinatorial argument outlined in Sect. 1.3.1 for **TEST** on the existence of at least one line in each dimension with at least two success points is replaced by the existence of a d-cancellation structure for every index $i = (i_0, \ldots, i_{\log l - 1})$

(corresponding to a **d**-coordinate d_i, cf. (5)) in the Kronecker product space for **logTEST**.

Specifically, each accepting run of **logTEST** corresponds to a chosen/success point in $[n]^d$ (this is our space of randomness, with $n = p$ and $d = \log l$). By suitable calibration of parameters, we can show that a prover that succeeds with a non-negligible probability gives rise to more than $n^d - (n-1)^d$ chosen points and then our combinatorial bound above implies the existence of a d-cancellation structure B, each of whose "corners" (for simplicity, think of a d-cancellation structure as a box) is a success point. Thus, we obtain 2^d equations like (3) at the corners of B; $\langle \mathbf{d}, \mathbf{z} \rangle$ is a multilinear polynomial with coefficients d_i (i-th coordinate of **d**, with bit representation of $i = (i_0, \dots, i_{\log l - 1})$) and variables z_{j,i_j} (cf. (5)) from the Kronecker product **TEST** vector $\mathbf{z} = \otimes_{j=0}^{\log l - 1} \mathbf{z_j}$. The recursive structure of B allows recursively combining these equations by folding, i.e., subtracting equations like (3) along "edges" of B in the same direction. Each successive folding reduces the number of equations by half and eliminates one of the free variables z_{j,i_j} to obtain a multilinear version of (4). After $\log l$ such folding steps, we obtain an equation generalizing (4) with one d_i on l.h.s, that yields the structure on coordinates of **d** that we seek. This helps us recover an analog of the structure theorem (Theorem 34) for **logTEST** (Theorem 42).

2 Preliminaries

Notation. A finite field is denoted by $\mathbb{F}$. We denote by κ a security parameter. When we explicitly specify the random tape for a randomized algorithm A, then we write $a \leftarrow A(\mathsf{pp}; \rho)$ to indicate that A outputs a given input pp and random tape ρ. We consider interactive arguments for relations, where a prover P convinces the verifier that it knows a witness w such that for a public statement $x, (x, w) \in \mathcal{R}$. For a pair of PPT interactive algorithms P, V, we denote by $\langle P(w), V \rangle(x)$, the output of V on its interaction with P where w is P's private input and x is a common input.

Fiat-Shamir transform. In this work, we consider *public coin* interactive arguments where the verifier's messages are uniformly random strings. Public coin protocols can heuristically be made non-interactive by applying the Fiat-Shamir [16] transform (FS) in the Random Oracle Model (ROM).

2.1 Inner Product Commitments

We define Inner Product Commitments (IPC) which is an extension of functional commitments introduced in [21]. IPC allows a prover to prove that the committed vector **f** satisfies $\langle \mathbf{f}, \mathbf{q} \rangle = v$, for some vector **q** and v.

An Inner Product Commitment scheme over $\mathbb{F}$ is a tuple
$\mathsf{IPC} = (\mathbf{Setup}, \mathbf{Com}, \mathbf{Open}, \mathbf{Eval})$ where:

- $\mathbf{Setup}(1^\kappa, D) \to \mathsf{pp}$. On input security parameter κ, and an upper bound D on accepted vector lengths, $\mathbf{Setup}$ generates public parameters pp.
- $\mathbf{Com}(\mathsf{pp}, f_0, \ldots, f_{l-1}, l) \to (C, \tilde{\mathbf{c}})$. On input the public parameters pp, the length of the vector $l \leq D$ and a vector of length l, given as $f_0, \ldots, f_{l-1} \in \mathbb{F}$, $\mathbf{Com}$ outputs a commitment C, and additionally an opening hint $\tilde{\mathbf{c}} \equiv (f_0 \ldots, f_{l-1})$.
- $\mathbf{Open}(\mathsf{pp}, \mathbf{f}, l, C, \tilde{\mathbf{c}}) \to b$. On input the public parameters pp, the opening hint $\tilde{\mathbf{c}}$, the length of the vector in the commitment l and the commitment C, the claimed committed vector $\mathbf{f}$, $\mathbf{Open}$ outputs a bit indicating accept or reject.
- $\mathbf{Eval}(\mathsf{pp}, C, l, \mathbf{q}, v; \mathbf{f}) \to b$. A public coin interactive protocol $\langle P_{\mathbf{Eval}}(\mathbf{f}), V_{\mathbf{Eval}} \rangle (\mathsf{pp}, C, l, \mathbf{q}, v)$ between a PPT prover and a PPT verifier. The parties have as common input public parameters pp, commitment C, the length of the vector in the commitment l, query vector $\mathbf{q} \in \mathbb{F}^l$, and claimed inner product v. The prover has, in addition, the vector committed to in C, $\mathbf{f}$. At the end of the protocol, the verifier outputs 1 indicating accepting the proof that $\langle \mathbf{f}, \mathbf{q} \rangle = v$, or outputs 0 indicating rejecting the proof.

Definition 21 (Completeness). *For all $l \leq D$, for all inputs $f_0, \ldots, f_{l-1} \in \mathbb{F}$, for query vectors $\mathbf{q} \in \mathbb{F}^l$,*

$$\Pr \left(b = 1 \; : \; \begin{array}{c} \mathsf{pp} \leftarrow \mathbf{Setup}(1^\kappa, D) \\ (C, \tilde{\mathbf{c}}) \leftarrow \mathbf{Com}(\mathsf{pp}, f_0, \ldots, f_{l-1}, l) \\ v \leftarrow \langle (f_0, \ldots, f_{l-1}), \mathbf{q} \rangle \\ b \leftarrow \mathbf{Eval}(\mathsf{pp}, C, l, \mathbf{q}, v; \mathbf{f}) \end{array} \right) = 1.$$

Definition 22 (Binding). *An Inner Product Commitment scheme PC is binding if for all PPT $\mathcal{A}$, the following probability is negligible in κ.*

$$\Pr \left(\begin{array}{l} \mathbf{Open}(\mathsf{pp}, \mathbf{f}_0, l, C, \tilde{\mathbf{c}}_0) = 1 \wedge \\ \mathbf{Open}(\mathsf{pp}, \mathbf{f}_1, l, C, \quad \tilde{\mathbf{c}}_1) = 1 \wedge \\ \tilde{\mathbf{c}}_0 \neq \tilde{\mathbf{c}}_1 \end{array} \; : \; \begin{array}{c} \mathsf{pp} \leftarrow \mathbf{setup}(1^\kappa, D) \\ (C, \mathbf{f}_0, \mathbf{f}_1, \tilde{\mathbf{c}}_0, \tilde{\mathbf{c}}_1, l) \leftarrow \mathcal{A}(\mathsf{pp}) \end{array} \right).$$

Definition 23 (Succinctness). *We require the commitments and the evaluation proofs to be of size independent of the length of the vector, that is the scheme is proof succinct if $|C|$ is $\mathsf{poly}(\kappa)$ and $|\pi|$ is $\mathsf{poly}(\kappa)$, where π is the transcript obtained by applying FS to $\mathbf{Eval}$.*

Definition 24 (Extractability). *For any PPT adversary $\mathcal{A} = (\mathcal{A}_1, \mathcal{A}_2)$, there exists a PPT algorithm Ext such that the following probability is negligible in κ:*

$$\Pr\left(b = 1 \wedge \mathcal{R}_{\mathbf{Eval}}(\mathsf{pp}, C, l, \mathbf{q}, v; \mathbf{f}, \tilde{\mathbf{c}}) = 0 \ : \ \begin{array}{c} \mathsf{pp} \leftarrow \mathbf{Setup}(1^\kappa, D) \\ (C, l, \mathbf{q}, v, \mathsf{st}) \leftarrow \mathcal{A}_1(\mathsf{pp}) \\ (\mathbf{f}, \tilde{\mathbf{c}}) = \mathsf{Ext}^{\mathcal{A}_2}(\mathsf{pp}) \\ b \leftarrow \langle \mathcal{A}_2(\mathsf{st}), V_{\mathbf{Eval}} \rangle(\mathsf{pp}, C, l, \mathbf{q}, v) \end{array} \right).$$

where the relation $\mathcal{R}_{\mathbf{Eval}}$ *is defined as follows:*

$$\mathcal{R}_{\mathbf{Eval}} = \{((\mathsf{pp}, C \in \mathbb{G}, \ l \in \mathbb{N}, \ \mathbf{q} \in \mathbb{F}^l, \ v \in \mathbb{F}); \ (\mathbf{f}, \tilde{\mathbf{c}})) :$$
$$(\mathbf{Open}(\mathsf{pp}, \mathbf{f}, l, C, \tilde{\mathbf{c}}) = 1) \wedge v = \langle \mathbf{f}, \mathbf{q} \rangle \mod p\}$$

2.2 Polynomial Commitment Scheme

The notion of a polynomial commitment scheme that allows the prover to open evaluations of the committed polynomial succinctly was introduced in [18] who gave a construction under the trusted setup assumption. A polynomial commitment scheme over $\mathbb{F}$ is a tuple $\mathsf{PC} = (\mathsf{setup}, \mathsf{commit}, \mathsf{open}, \mathsf{eval})$ where:

- $\mathsf{setup}(1^\kappa, D) \to \mathsf{pp}$. On input security parameter κ, and an upper bound $D \in \mathbb{N}$ on the degree, setup generates public parameters pp.
- $\mathsf{commit}(\mathsf{pp}, f(X), d) \to (C, \tilde{\mathbf{c}})$. On input the public parameters pp, and a univariate polynomial $f(X) \in \mathbb{F}[X]$ with degree at most $d \leq D$, commit outputs a commitment to the polynomial C, and additionally an opening hint $\tilde{\mathbf{c}}$.
- $\mathsf{open}(\mathsf{pp}, f(X), d, C, \tilde{\mathbf{c}}) \to b$. On input the public parameters pp, the commitment C and the opening hint $\tilde{\mathbf{c}}$, a polynomial $f(X)$ of degree $d \leq D$, open outputs a bit indicating accept or reject.
- $\mathsf{eval}(\mathsf{pp}, C, d, x, v; f(X)) \to b$. A public coin interactive protocol $\langle P_{\mathsf{eval}}(f(X)), V_{\mathsf{eval}} \rangle(\mathsf{pp}, C, d, z, v)$ between a PPT prover and a PPT verifier. The parties have as common input public parameters pp, commitment C, degree d, evaluation point x, and claimed evaluation v. The prover has, in addition, the opening $f(X)$ of C, with $\deg(f) \leq d$. At the end of the protocol, the verifier outputs 1 indicating accepting the proof that $f(x) = v$, or outputs 0 indicating rejecting the proof.

A polynomial commitment scheme must satisfy completeness, binding and extractability.

Definition 25 (Completeness). *For all polynomials* $f(X) \in \mathbb{F}[X]$ *of degree* $d \leq D$, *for all* $x \in \mathbb{F}$,

$$\Pr\left(b = 1 \ : \ \begin{array}{c} \mathsf{pp} \leftarrow \mathsf{setup}(1^\kappa, D) \\ (C, \tilde{\mathbf{c}}) \leftarrow \mathsf{commit}(\mathsf{pp}, f(X), d) \\ v \leftarrow f(x) \\ b \leftarrow \mathsf{eval}(\mathsf{pp}, C, d, x, v; f(X)) \end{array} \right) = 1.$$

Definition 26 (Binding). *A polynomial commitment scheme* PC *is binding if for all PPT* $\mathcal{A}$, *the following probability is negligible in* κ:

$$\Pr\left(\begin{array}{l} \mathsf{open}(\mathsf{pp}, f_0, d, C, \tilde{\mathbf{c}}_0) = 1 \wedge \\ \mathsf{open}(\mathsf{pp}, f_1, d, C, \tilde{\mathbf{c}}_1) = 1 \wedge \\ f_0 \neq f_1 \end{array} : \begin{array}{l} \mathsf{pp} \leftarrow \mathsf{setup}(1^\kappa, D) \\ (C, f_0, f_1, \tilde{\mathbf{c}}_0, \tilde{\mathbf{c}}_1, d) \leftarrow \mathcal{A}(\mathsf{pp}) \end{array}\right).$$

Definition 27 (Extractability). *For any PPT adversary* $\mathcal{A} = (\mathcal{A}_1, \mathcal{A}_2)$, *there exists a PPT algorithm* Ext *such that the following probability is negligible in* κ:

$$\Pr\left(b = 1 \wedge \mathcal{R}_{\mathsf{eval}}(\mathsf{pp}, C, x, v; \tilde{f}, \tilde{\mathbf{c}}) = 0 : \begin{array}{l} \mathsf{pp} \leftarrow \mathsf{setup}(1^\kappa, D) \\ (C, d, x, v, \mathsf{st}) \leftarrow \mathcal{A}_1(\mathsf{pp}) \\ (\tilde{f}, \tilde{\mathbf{c}}) \leftarrow \mathsf{Ext}^{\mathcal{A}_2}(\mathsf{pp}) \\ b \leftarrow \langle \mathcal{A}_2(\mathsf{st}), V_{\mathsf{eval}} \rangle(\mathsf{pp}, C, d, x, v) \end{array}\right).$$

where the relation $\mathcal{R}_{\mathsf{eval}}$ *is defined as follows:*

$$\mathcal{R}_{\mathsf{eval}} = \{((\mathsf{pp}, C \in \mathbb{G}, \ x \in \mathbb{F}, \ v \in \mathbb{F}); \ (f(X), \tilde{\mathbf{c}})) :$$
$$(\mathsf{open}(\mathsf{pp}, f, d, C, \tilde{\mathbf{c}}) = 1) \wedge v = f(x)\}$$

Definition 28 (Succinctness). *We require the commitments and the evaluation proofs to be of size independent of the degree of the polynomial, that is the scheme is* proof succinct *if* $|C|$ *is* $\mathsf{poly}(\kappa)$, $|\pi|$ *is* $\mathsf{poly}(\kappa)$ *where* π *is the transcript obtained by applying FS to* eval. *Additionally, the scheme is* verifier succinct *if* eval *runs in time* $\mathsf{poly}(\kappa) \cdot \log(d)$ *for the verifier.*

2.3 Assumptions

Groups of Unknown Order and GGM. Our constructions make use of groups of unknown order. A class group is a candidate group of unknown order. The *class group* of an imaginary quadratic order [6,7] is the quotient group of fractional ideals by principal ideals of an order of a number field with ideal multiplication. It is completely defined by its discriminant, which can be generated using only public randomness.

We use the generic group model (GGM) for groups of unknown order as defined by Damgård and Koprowski [14], and used in [5]. In this model, the group is parameterized by two integer public parameters A, B and the order of the group is sampled uniformly from $[A, B]$. The group $\mathbb{G}$ description consists of a random injective function $\sigma : \mathbb{Z}_{|\mathbb{G}|} \to \{0, 1\}^\ell$, for some ℓ where $2^\ell \gg |\mathbb{G}|$. The elements of the group are $\sigma(0), \sigma(1), \ldots, \sigma(|\mathbb{G}| - 1)$. A generic group algorithm $\mathcal{A}$ is a probabilistic algorithm with the following properties. Let $\mathcal{L}$ be a list that is initialized with the encodings (group elements) given to $\mathcal{A}$ as inputs. $\mathcal{A}$ can query two generic group oracles, $\mathcal{O}_1$ and $\mathcal{O}_2$. $\mathcal{O}_1$ samples a random $r \in \mathbb{Z}_{|\mathbb{G}|}$ and returns $\sigma(r)$ which is appended to $\mathcal{L}$. The second oracle $\mathcal{O}_2(i, j, \pm)$ takes two indices $i, j \in \{1, \ldots, q\}$, where q is the size of $\mathcal{L}$, and a sign bit and returns $\sigma(x_i \pm x_j)$, which is appended to $\mathcal{L}$. It should be noted that $\mathcal{A}$ is not given $|\mathbb{G}|$.

We use a group sampler GGen that on input a security parameter κ, samples a description of the group $\mathbb{G}$ of size $2^{\text{poly}(\kappa)}$. Note that GGen is public-coin.

We informally describe the rest of the assumptions – note that these problems are indeed intractable in the GGM. The formal definitions are deferred to the full version.

Adaptive root assumption. Computing random roots of arbitrary group elements g is hard for any PPT adversary.

Low order assumption. Computing the order of any non-trivial element in a group $\mathbb{G} \leftarrow$ GGen is hard for any PPT adversary.

2.4   Proofs about Exponents

PoE *(Proof of Exponentiation):* We use Wesolowski's proof of exponentiation (PoE) protocol [26] in it's slightly more generalized form as presented in [5] for the relation $\mathcal{R}_{\text{PoE}} = \{(u, w \in \mathbb{G}, x \in \mathbb{Z}; \bot) : w = u^x \in \mathbb{G}\}$.

PoKE *(Proof of Knowledge of Exponent):* We also use the PoKE protocol from [5] in our protocols. This protocol is an argument of knowledge in the GGM for the relation $\mathcal{R}_{\text{PoKE}} = \{(u, w \in \mathbb{G}; x \in \mathbb{Z}) : w = u^x \in \mathbb{G}\}$.

PoKPE *(Proof of Knowledge of* Positive *exponent):* Define the relation $\mathcal{R}_{\text{PoKPE}} = \{(w \in \mathbb{G}; x \in \mathbb{Z}) : (w = g^x) \wedge (x > 0)\}$. We construct an argument of knowledge for this relation called PoKPE using PoKE and Lagrange's four-square theorem. We also use the notation PoKPE$\{A, B, \dots\}$ to denote the combined protocol for the set, where the verifier outputs 1 iff PoKPE checks pass for all elements. More details about these protocols appear in the full version.

3   Inner Product Commitment Scheme with Constant-Sized Proof

In this section, we construct an inner product commitment (IPC) scheme that achieves constant-sized proof and linear time verification.

3.1   Construction

IPC $=$ (**Setup, Com, Open, Eval**) are as defined below:

- **Setup**$(1^\kappa, D)$: Here, κ is the security parameter and D is an upper bound on the length of the committed vectors. Sample a group of unknown order (we use class groups) $\mathbb{G} \leftarrow$ GGen(κ) and $g \leftarrow_\$ \mathbb{G}$. Define $\alpha = p^{2D}$ (p is a large prime such that $\text{len}(p) = \text{poly}(\kappa)$). Return pp $= (\kappa, \mathbb{G}, g, p)$ (α does not have to be explicitly returned; it is defined completely by p, D).

- **Com**$(pp, D, f_0, \ldots, f_{l-1}, l)$: Define the commitment to $\mathbf{f} = (f_0, \ldots, f_{l-1}) \in \mathbb{Z}_p^l$ as $C := g^{\sum_{i=0}^{l-1} f_i \alpha^{2i}}$, considering $f_i \in \mathbb{Z}_p$ as integers in $[0, p-1]$ and the sum in $\mathbb{Z}$. If $l \leq D$, return $(C, \mathbf{f})$, else return error.
- **Open**$(pp, \mathbf{f}, l, C, \tilde{\mathbf{c}})$: ($\mathbf{f}$ is the claimed opening and $\tilde{\mathbf{c}}$ is an opening hint) Return 1 if all the below conditions hold, else return 0.
  - $l \leq D, \tilde{\mathbf{c}} = \mathbf{f} \mod p$ [6]
  - $C = g^{\sum_{i=0}^{l-1} \tilde{c}_i \alpha^{2i}}$, exponent $\sum_{i=0}^{d} \tilde{c}_i \alpha^{2i} \in \mathbb{Z}$ and $\tilde{\mathbf{c}} \in \mathbb{Q}(2, 3)^l$, where

$$\mathbb{Q}(\beta_1, \beta_2) := \left\{ \frac{a}{b} : \gcd(b, p) = 1, \ 0 < b < p^{\beta_1}, \ |a/b| \leq \beta_2 \alpha \right\},$$

  where $|a|$ denotes the absolute value of $a \in \mathbb{Q}$. (*Note that $\mathbb{Q}(\beta_1, \beta_2)$ is a subset of $\mathbb{Q}(\beta_1', \beta_2')$ if $\beta_1 \leq \beta_1', \beta_2 \leq \beta_2'$*)
- **Eval**$(pp, C, l, \mathbf{q}, v; \mathbf{f})$: The **Eval** protocol consists of two sub-protocols **TEST** and **IPP** as described in Fig. 2 and 3 below.
  - $b_1 \leftarrow \textbf{TEST}(C, l; \mathbf{f})$, $b_2 \leftarrow \textbf{IPP}(C, l, \mathbf{q}, v; \mathbf{f})$. Return $b = (l \leq D) \wedge b_1 \wedge b_2$

3.2   Proofs of Security

We prove that our construction IPC satisfies the requirements of an inner product scheme as defined in §2.1.

Theorem 31 (Completeness). *The inner product commitment scheme* IPC *satisfies Completeness (Definition 21).*

Proof. Note that by definition of CoeffSplit and completeness of PoKPE, all the PoKPE checks will accept.

To show that the last checks in **TEST** and **IPP** hold, it suffices to show that $v = 0$ in **TEST** and $v = \langle \mathbf{f}, \mathbf{q} \rangle \mod p$ in **IPP**. We will show this by expanding the computations done in CoeffSplit.

In **TEST**, direct manipulation shows

$$\sum_{j=0}^{l-1} f_j \alpha^{2j} \times \sum_{j=0}^{l-1} \alpha^{2l-2-2j} z_j$$

$$= \alpha^{2l} \underbrace{\left(\sum_{j'>j} \alpha^{2(j'-j)-2} f_{j'} z_j \right)}_{\lambda} + \underbrace{\left(\sum_{j'<j} \alpha^{2l-2-2(j-j')} f_{j'} z_j + \sum_{j'=j} \alpha^{2l-2} f_j z_j \right)}_{\gamma}$$

and notice that since $\alpha > lp^2$, these are indeed the γ, λ returned by CoeffSplit, and $v = 0$ (Fig. 1).

---

[6] Treating any coordinate $\frac{a}{b}$ of $\tilde{\mathbf{c}} \mod p$ as $a' \cdot b'^{-1}$, where $a' = (a \mod p) \in \mathbb{Z}_p$ and $b' = (b \mod p) \in \mathbb{Z}_p$.

$$\boxed{\begin{array}{l} \text{CoeffSplit}(\alpha, a, b, i) \\[4pt] \hline \\[-6pt] \text{1. Write } a \cdot b \text{ in base } \alpha, \text{ call the resulting representation vector } \mathbf{c}. \\[4pt] \text{2. Set } v := c_i \ , \ \gamma := \sum_{j=0}^{i-1} c_j \alpha^j \ , \ \lambda := \sum_{j=i+1}^{\lceil \log_\alpha ab \rceil} c_j \alpha^j \\[6pt] \text{3. Output the tuple } (v', \gamma, \lambda). \end{array}}$$

Fig. 1. CoeffSplit

TEST

Prover		**Verifier**
$C := \text{commit}(\text{pp}, \mathbf{f} \in \mathbb{Z}_p^l)$	$\xrightarrow{\quad C \quad}$	
	$\xleftarrow{\quad \mathbf{z} \quad}$	$\mathbf{z} \leftarrow_{\$} \mathbb{Z}_p^l$ uniformly at random

Computations in **TEST**

$$\text{CoeffSplit}\left(\alpha, \sum_{j=0}^{l-1} f_j \alpha^{2j}, \right.$$
$$\left. \sum_{j=0}^{l-1} z_j \alpha^{2l-2-2j}, 2l-1 \right) \mapsto (v', \gamma, \lambda)$$

Define $\Lambda := g^\lambda, \ \Gamma := g^\gamma$

$\xrightarrow{\quad (\Lambda, \Gamma) \quad}$

Checks

$$\sigma := \sum_{j=0}^{l-1} \alpha^{2l-2-2j} z_j$$
$$E := \frac{g^{\alpha^{2l-1}}}{C}, \Delta := \frac{g^{\alpha^{2l-1}}}{\Gamma}$$

1: PoKPE$\{C, E, \Lambda, \Gamma, \Delta\}$ accepts

2: $C^\sigma \overset{?}{=} \Lambda^{\alpha^{2l}} \Gamma$

The blue colored parts will be replaced in subsequent versions of this protocol.

Fig. 2. The **TEST** Protocol

IPP

Prover		**Verifier**
	$\xleftarrow{\quad \mathbf{q} \quad}$	$\mathbf{q} \in \mathbb{Z}_p^l$ is the inner product vector

Computations in **IPP**

$$\text{CoeffSplit}\left(\alpha, \sum_{j=0}^{l-1} f_j \alpha^{2j}, \right.$$
$$\left. \sum_{j=0}^{l-1} q_j \alpha^{2l-1-2j}, 2l-1 \right) \mapsto (v', \gamma, \lambda)$$

Define $\Lambda := g^\lambda, \ \Gamma := g^\gamma$

$N := g^{\lfloor \frac{v}{p} \rfloor}, \ v := v' \mod p$

$\xrightarrow{\quad (v, N, \Lambda, \Gamma) \quad}$

Checks

$$\sigma := \sum_{j=0}^{l-1} \alpha^{2l-1-2j} q_j$$
$$\Delta := \frac{g^{\alpha^{2l-2}}}{\Gamma}$$

1: $v \in \mathbb{Z}_p$

2: PoKPE$\{\Lambda, \Gamma, \Delta, N\}$ accepts

3: $C^\sigma \overset{?}{=} (g^v N^p)^{\alpha^{2l-1}} \Lambda^{\alpha^{2l}} \Gamma$

The blue colored parts will be replaced in subsequent versions of this protocol.

Fig. 3. The **IPP** Protocol

And, in **IPP**,

$$\sum_{j=0}^{l-1} f_j \alpha^{2j} \times \sum_{j=0}^{l-1} \alpha^{2l-1-2j} q_j = \alpha^{2l-1} \left(\underbrace{\sum_{i=0}^{l-1} f_j q_j \mod p}_{v} + p \underbrace{\left\lfloor \frac{\sum_{i=0}^{l-1} f_j q_j}{p} \right\rfloor}_{n} \right)$$

$$+ \alpha^{2l-2}(0) + \alpha^{2l} \underbrace{\left(\sum_{j'>j} \alpha^{2(j'-j)-1} f_{j'} q_j \right)}_{\lambda} + \underbrace{\left(\sum_{j'<j} \alpha^{2l-1-2(j-j')} f_{j'} q_j \right)}_{\gamma}$$

Here, again since $\alpha > lp^2$, $(v + np, \lambda, \gamma)$ above coincide with the output of CoeffSplit, and $v = \langle \mathbf{f}, \mathbf{q} \rangle \mod p$.

Theorem 32 (Binding). *The inner product commitment scheme* IPC *Construction in Sect. 3.1 is binding (Definition 22) for opening hint vectors in* $\mathbb{Q}(\beta_1, \beta_2)$ *as long as* $\alpha > 4\beta_2 p^{2\beta_1}$ *and if the Order assumption holds for* GGen.

Proof. Suppose there exists an adversary $\mathcal{A}$ which breaks binding as defined in Definition 22, i.e., $\mathcal{A}(\mathsf{pp})$ outputs $(C, \mathbf{f}, \mathbf{f}', \mathbf{c}, \mathbf{c}', d)$ such that $\mathsf{open}(\mathsf{pp}, \mathbf{f}, d, C, \mathbf{c}) = 1$ and $\mathsf{open}(\mathsf{pp}, \mathbf{f}', d, C, \mathbf{c}') = 1$ but $\mathbf{f} \neq \mathbf{f}'$ (which also implies that $\mathbf{c} \neq \mathbf{c}'$ – we will use this condition to show a contradiction).

Then, since open outputs 1 for both $\mathbf{f}, \mathbf{f}'$ we know that the opening hints $\mathbf{c}, \mathbf{c}' \in \mathbb{Q}(\beta_1, \beta_2)^l$ and that $g^{\sum_{i=0}^{l-1} c_i \alpha^{2i}} = g^{\sum_{i=0}^{l-1} c_i' \alpha^{2i}} \iff g^{\sum_{i=0}^{l-1} (c_i - c_i') \alpha^{2i}} = 1$. If the exponent of g above were not zero, we could construct an adversary $\mathcal{A}_{Ord}$ that uses the above exponent to break the Low order assumption. Now, let the exponents be equal, and consider the largest index j such that $c_i' \neq c_i$ (WLOG, let $c_i' > c_i$). This implies that $\sum_{i=0}^{j-1}(c_i - c_i')\alpha^{2i} = (c_j' - c_j)\alpha^{2j}$.

We can now show that this equality is impossible given the conditions on α, β_1, β_2.

Notice that any difference $|c_i' - c_i|$ (if non-zero) can be bounded by $\frac{1}{p^{2\beta_1}} < |c_i' - c_i| < 2\beta_2 \alpha$, since $c_i, c_i' \in \mathbb{Q}(\beta_1, \beta_2)$. This gives a contradiction, since

$$\sum_{i=0}^{j-1}(c_i - c_i')\alpha^{2i} < 2\beta_2\alpha \sum_{i=0}^{j-1} \alpha^{2i} < 2\beta_2\alpha \cdot 2\alpha^{2j-2} < \frac{\alpha^{2j}}{p^{2\beta_1}} < (c_j' - c_j)\alpha^{2j},$$

Before proving extractability, we need a few definitions. Define

$$S := \left\{ \frac{m\alpha - n}{k} : m, n, k \in \mathbb{Z}, \gcd(m, k) = 1, 0 < m \leq k < p, -2 < n < k+2 \right\}$$

as a subset of $\mathbb{Z}$ and functions $\chi_m, \chi_n : S^q \to \mathbb{Q}^q$ which isolates the vector of fractions m/k and n/k from the elements of S^q:

$$\mathbf{v} \in S^q \implies \mathbf{v} = \left(\frac{m_i \alpha - n_i}{k_i} \right)_i, \quad \chi_m(\mathbf{v}) := \left(\frac{m_i}{k_i} \right)_i, \quad \text{and} \quad \chi_n(\mathbf{v}) := \left(\frac{n_i}{k_i} \right)_i.$$

These functions can be made well-defined by fixing a representation of elements of S: for any $d \in S$, consider the representation (m, n, k) as the one with the smallest denominator k and if there are multiple such representations, we pick the one with the smallest m.

Theorem 33 (Extractability). *The inner product commitment scheme* IPC *satisfies Extractability for* $(\beta_1, \beta_2) = (2, 3)$ *(Definition 24) in the Generic Group Model.*

Proof. We split the proof into two theorems; the first theorem (concerning **TEST**) will define a partial extractor and obtain conditions on the extracted objects, while the second theorem uses the results and the extractor of the first theorem and finishes the proof.

Suppose there exists a *generic* adversary $\mathcal{A}$ that makes the Verifier in eval accept with non-negligible probability (and hence both the **TEST** verifier and **IPP** verifier). We will construct a polynomial time extractor Ext that outputs $(\tilde{\mathbf{f}}, \tilde{\mathbf{c}})$ satisfying $\mathcal{R}_{\mathsf{eval}}$ (in Definition 27) with overwhelming probability.

Theorem 34 (TEST Extractor). *If the Verifier in* **TEST** *outputs accept with non-negligible probability, there exists an efficient extractor* Ext_T *in the GGM that outputs* $\mathbf{c}, \mathbf{d} \in [\alpha]^l$ *such that* $C = g^{\sum_{i=0}^{l-1}(c_i + \alpha d_i)\alpha^{2i}}$ *and* $\mathbf{d} \in S^l$.

Theorem 35 (IPP Extractor). *If the Verifier in* **IPP** *outputs accept with non-negligible probability (and given that the Verifier of* **TEST** *also did so), there exists an efficient extractor* Ext *in the GGM that outputs an opening* $\tilde{\mathbf{f}} \in \mathbb{Z}_p^l$ *and opening hint* $\tilde{\mathbf{c}} \in \mathbb{Q}(2, 3)$ *for* C *such that* $v = \langle \tilde{\mathbf{f}}, \mathbf{q} \rangle \mod p$ *and satisfies Extractability (Definition 24).*

3.3 Auxiliary Lemmas

Lemma 1. *Suppose* $K = \sum_{i=0}^{k} M_i \alpha^i$ *where* M_i's *are not necessarily* $< \alpha$, *but we have a bound* $M_i < \alpha(\alpha - 1) \; \forall i$. *Then, we can write* $K = \sum_{i=0}^{k+1} U_i \alpha^i$ *where each* $U_i < \alpha$, $u_i \in \{0, 1\}$, *and*

$$U_i := \begin{cases} (M_0 \mod \alpha + u_0) \mod \alpha & \text{if } i = 0 \\ (M_i \mod \alpha + \left\lfloor \frac{M_{i-1}}{\alpha} \right\rfloor + u_i) \mod \alpha & \text{if } 1 \leq i \leq k \\ (\left\lfloor \frac{M_k}{\alpha} \right\rfloor + u_{k+1}) & \text{if } i = k+1 \end{cases}$$

$$u_i := \begin{cases} 0 & \text{if } i = 0, 1 \\ \left\lfloor \frac{M_{i-1} \mod \alpha + \left\lfloor \frac{M_{i-2}}{\alpha} \right\rfloor + u_{i-1}}{\alpha} \right\rfloor & \text{if } 1 \leq i \leq k+1 \end{cases}$$

Lemma 2. *Suppose for some* α, $M'\alpha - N' = M\alpha - N$, *where* $M', N' \in \mathbb{Q}$ *and* $M, N \in \mathbb{Z}$. *If* $|N|, |N'| < B$, $M' = \frac{x}{y}$ *and* $y < \frac{\alpha}{2B}$, *then* $M' = M$ *and* $N' = N$.

3.4 Proof of Theorem 34 - TEST Extraction

First, we prove a lemma giving a partial extractor for the **TEST** protocol.

Lemma 3. *If the Verifier in* **TEST** *outputs accept with non-negligible probability, there exists an efficient extractor* Ext_T *in the GGM that outputs with high probability* $\mathbf{c}, \mathbf{d} \in \mathbb{Z}_p^l$ *(that only depends on the commitment C) such that*
$C = g^{\sum_{i=0}^{l-1}(c_i + \alpha d_i)\alpha^{2i}}$.
Moreover, if the random vector used in **TEST** *was* $\mathbf{z} \in \mathbb{Z}_p^l$, *then we also have the relation (for some* $u \in \{0,1\}$*):*

$$\langle \mathbf{d}, \mathbf{z} \rangle \mod \alpha + \left\lfloor \frac{\langle \mathbf{c}, \mathbf{z} \rangle}{\alpha} \right\rfloor + u = 0 \mod \alpha$$

Proof. We define an extractor Ext_T that invokes the PoKPE extractor for C, which outputs an exponent $c > 0$ such that $C = g^c$. Since E also passes the PoKPE protocol and $C \cdot E = g^{\alpha^{2l-1}}$, we can infer that $c < \alpha^{2l-1}$. Consider the base-α representation of c, which is a $2l$-length vector. Ext_T outputs the even indexed coordinates as $\mathbf{c}$ and the odd indexed coordinates as $\mathbf{d}$. By construction, $C = g^{\sum_{i=0}^{l-1}(c_i + \alpha d_i)\alpha^{2i}}$.

Notice that each PoKPE is essentially a range check as well as a proof of knowledge of the exponent. With overwhelming probability, we can assume that each of these statements are true (due to knowledge soundness of PoKPE). Hence, we get that the prover "knows" (formally, an extractor outputs) integers c, γ, λ such that $C = g^c$, $0 < c < \alpha^{2l-1}$, $\Gamma = g^\gamma$, $0 < \gamma < \alpha^{2l-1}$, and $\Lambda = g^\lambda$, $0 < \lambda$.

Now, notice that for any equality of group elements in a group of unknown order, we can (with overwhelming probability) equate their exponents when written with base g *over integers*. This follows from the Low order assumption as long as the prover knows all the exponents w.r.t. some fixed base g (else the prover could compute a multiple of the order of the group).

Hence, given an equation of the form $C^\sigma = \Gamma g^{v\alpha^{2l-1}} \Lambda^{\alpha^{2l}}$ (this is essentially Check 2 for the **TEST** verifier with $y = 0$), we can write

$$g^{c\sigma} = g^{\gamma + v\alpha^{2l-1} + \lambda\alpha^{2l}}$$
$$\implies c\sigma = \gamma + v\alpha^{2l-1} + \lambda\alpha^{2l}$$

Writing this in base α and using Lemma 1, we can compare the coefficients of α^{2l-1} on both sides:

$$v = \langle \mathbf{d}, \mathbf{z} \rangle \mod \alpha + \left\lfloor \frac{\langle \mathbf{c}, \mathbf{z} \rangle}{\alpha} \right\rfloor + u \mod \alpha$$

In **TEST**, we have $v = 0$, hence we prove the lemma.

Now, using the above lemma, we show that if the prover succeeds with non-negligible probability, we must have $d_i \in S$ for all i.

If the prover succeeds with non-negligible probability, it must hold that it also succeeds for a non-negligible probability over the choice of the random query $\mathbf{z} \in \mathbb{Z}_p^l$. Fix some index $0 \leq i \leq l - 1$.

Partition the randomness space $\mathbb{Z}_p^l$ into 1-dimensional "lines" of length p along the ith dimension:

$$T_{\mathbf{q}} := \{(z_i, \mathbf{q}) \; : \; z_i \in \mathbb{Z}_p\}$$

If the prover was only able to succeed for at most one value of $\mathbf{z}$ in all $T_{\mathbf{q}}$, the overall success probability of the prover is bounded by $\frac{1}{p}$, which is negligible and hence a contradiction. Hence, there must exist some $\mathbf{q}$ such that there exists two points $\mathbf{z_1}, \mathbf{z_2} \in T_{\mathbf{q}}$ such that the prover succeeds in convincing the verifier (for simplicity, we will use z_1, z_2 to denote the ith coordinate that differs in these two vectors. WLOG let $z_2 > z_1$).

Now, using Lemma 3, we get two equations:

$$\langle \mathbf{d}, \mathbf{z_1} \rangle \quad \mathrm{mod} \; \alpha + \left\lfloor \frac{\langle \mathbf{c}, \mathbf{z_1} \rangle}{\alpha} \right\rfloor + u_1 \quad \mathrm{mod} \; \alpha = 0 \quad \mathrm{mod} \; \alpha \tag{6}$$

$$\langle \mathbf{d}, \mathbf{z_2} \rangle \quad \mathrm{mod} \; \alpha + \left\lfloor \frac{\langle \mathbf{c}, \mathbf{z_2} \rangle}{\alpha} \right\rfloor + u_2 \quad \mathrm{mod} \; \alpha = 0 \quad \mathrm{mod} \; \alpha \tag{7}$$

where $u_1, u_2 \in \{0, 1\}$. Our aim is to isolate and prove conditions on a single coordinate d_i, and notice that the inner products $\langle \mathbf{d}, \mathbf{z_1} \rangle$ and $\langle \mathbf{d}, \mathbf{z_2} \rangle$ differ only in the ith term. Hence, subtracting the two equations, we get:

$$(z_2 - z_1)d_i = -\left(\left\lfloor \frac{\langle \mathbf{c}, \mathbf{z_2} \rangle}{\alpha} \right\rfloor - \left\lfloor \frac{\langle \mathbf{c}, \mathbf{z_1} \rangle}{\alpha} \right\rfloor + u_2 - u_1 \right) \quad \mathrm{mod} \; \alpha$$

Call the term in the brackets on the RHS n. Using the fact that $x - 1 \le \lfloor x \rfloor < x$ and $u_i \in \{0, 1\}$ for all i gives us trivial bounds $-2 < n < (z_2 - z_1) + 2$. We also know that $0 < z_2 - z_1 < p$. Letting $k := z_2 - z_1$,

$$kd_i = -n \quad \mathrm{mod} \; \alpha \implies d_i = \frac{m\alpha - n}{k}$$

where $-2 < n < k + 2$, $0 < k < p$ and $0 < m \le k$ since $d_i < \alpha$.
Hence $d_i \in S$. Since i was an arbitrary index, $\mathbf{d} \in S^l$.

3.5   Proof of Theorem 35 – IPP Extraction

We define the final extractor Ext for eval using the extractor Ext_T from **TEST** that outputs $\mathbf{c}, \mathbf{d} \in \mathbb{Z}_p^l$. Specifically, Ext invokes Ext_T and performs the following additional computations on $\mathbf{c}, \mathbf{d}$:

1. Compute m_i, n_i, k_i for every i such that $d_i = \frac{m_i \alpha - n_i}{k_i}$.
2. Let $m_{-1} := 0$, $k_{-1} := 1$ and define vectors $\mathbf{c'}, \mathbf{d'} \in \mathbb{Z}_p^l$ as
   $c_i' := c_i + \frac{m_{i-1}}{k_{i-1}}$ and $d_i' := -\frac{n_i}{k_i}$.
3. Output $\mathbf{c'} + \alpha \mathbf{d'}$ as the opening hint, and $(\mathbf{c'} + \alpha \mathbf{d'})$ $\mathrm{mod} \; p$ as the opening to the commitment.

Note that this extractor is indeed efficient as Ext_T is efficient and the only non-trivial computations done are in Step 1 above, which can be done efficiently (details in full version).

By construction, this is a valid opening hint, as $\mathbf{d} \in S^l \implies \mathbf{c}' + \alpha \mathbf{d}' \in \mathbb{Q}(2,3)$. This is just a rearrangement of the coordinates of $\mathbf{c}$ and $\mathbf{d}$ and keeps the sum $\sum_{i=0}^{l-1}(c_i' + \alpha d_i')\alpha^{2i}$ equal to the previous sum $\sum_{i=0}^{l-1}(c_i + \alpha d_i)\alpha^{2i}$ (since we just move the coefficient of α in d_i to c_{i+1}). Hence, $C = g^{\sum_{i=0}^{l-1}(c_i' + \alpha d_i')\alpha^{2i}}$ and the exponent $\in \mathbb{Z}$.

Now, since the verifier accepts in **IPP**, we can use similar arguments as made in Lemma 3 for the check equation in **IPP** to get

$$c\sigma = \gamma + 0\alpha^{2l-2} + (v + np)\alpha^{2l-1} + \lambda\alpha^{2l}$$

Focusing on the coefficients of α^{2l-2} and α^{2l-1}, we get two equations:

$$\langle \mathbf{d}, \mathbf{q}^+ \rangle \mod \alpha + \left\lfloor \frac{\langle \mathbf{c}, \mathbf{q}^+ \rangle}{\alpha} \right\rfloor + u' = 0 \mod \alpha \qquad (8)$$

$$\langle \mathbf{c}, \mathbf{q} \rangle \mod \alpha + \left\lfloor \frac{\langle \mathbf{d}, \mathbf{q}^+ \rangle}{\alpha} \right\rfloor + u = v + np \mod \alpha \qquad (9)$$

where $\mathbf{q}^+$ is defined as the vector with elements $q_i^+ := q_{i+1} \forall i \in \{0, \ldots, l-2\}$, $q_{l-1}^+ := 0$ and $u, u' \in \{0, 1\}$.

Due to the bounds on coefficients of $\mathbf{q}$ (chosen by the verifier $\in \mathbb{Z}_p$), we know that Eq. 8's LHS over integers must be either 0 or α. Also define

$$M' := \sum_{i=0}^{l-1} \frac{m_i}{k_i} q_i^+ , \quad \text{and} \quad N' := \sum_{i=0}^{l-1} \frac{n_i}{k_i} q_i^+$$

1. If the LHS is 0, then so are each of the terms in the LHS, as they are all non-negative. Hence, $\langle \mathbf{d}, \mathbf{q}^+ \rangle = 0 \mod \alpha$ which implies $u = 0$ (due to Lemma 1). Hence, we can simplify Eq. 9

$$v + np = \langle \mathbf{c}, \mathbf{q} \rangle \mod \alpha + \left\lfloor \frac{\langle \mathbf{d}, \mathbf{q}^+ \rangle}{\alpha} \right\rfloor + u \mod \alpha$$

$$= \langle \mathbf{c}, \mathbf{q} \rangle + \frac{\langle \mathbf{d}, \mathbf{q}^+ \rangle}{\alpha} \mod \alpha = \langle \mathbf{c}, \mathbf{q} \rangle + M' - \frac{N'}{\alpha} \mod \alpha$$

Since $M' - N'/\alpha$ must be an integer and $N' < \alpha \implies N' = 0$.

$$v + np = \langle \mathbf{c}, \mathbf{q} \rangle + M' \mod \alpha = \langle \mathbf{c}', \mathbf{q} \rangle \mod \alpha$$
$$\implies v = \langle \mathbf{c}', \mathbf{q} \rangle \mod p = \langle \mathbf{c}', \mathbf{q} \rangle + \alpha \langle \mathbf{d}', \mathbf{q} \rangle \mod p,$$

as $\alpha = 0 \mod p$ and $\langle \mathbf{d}', \mathbf{q} \rangle$ is invertible modulo p (or simply $0 \mod p$). In either case, $v = \langle \mathbf{c}' + \alpha \mathbf{d}', \mathbf{q} \rangle \mod p$.

2. If the LHS is α, we get $u = 1$. Now, write Eq. 8 in the form $\langle \mathbf{d}, \mathbf{q}^+ \rangle = M\alpha - N$ by moving all the terms but the inner product to the RHS and calling it

N. Now, we get $M'\alpha - N' = M\alpha - N$ where $|N|, |N'| < 3pl$ and M' has denominator at most the LCM of all the k_i, which is at most p^l.

We can apply Lemma 2 which implies that $M', N' \in \mathbb{Z}$ (since $\alpha > p^{2l}$). Then,

$$v + np = \langle \mathbf{c}, \mathbf{q} \rangle \quad \mathrm{mod}\ \alpha + \left\lfloor \frac{\langle \mathbf{d}, \mathbf{q}^+ \rangle}{\alpha} \right\rfloor + u \quad \mathrm{mod}\ \alpha$$

$$= \langle \mathbf{c}, \mathbf{q} \rangle \quad \mathrm{mod}\ \alpha + \left\lfloor M' - \frac{N'}{\alpha} \right\rfloor + 1 \quad \mathrm{mod}\ \alpha$$

$$= \langle \mathbf{c}, \mathbf{q} \rangle \quad \mathrm{mod}\ \alpha + M' - 1 + 1 \quad \mathrm{mod}\ \alpha$$

as $N' < \alpha$. Hence, as before, we get that $v = \langle \mathbf{c}' + \alpha \mathbf{d}', \mathbf{q} \rangle \quad \mathrm{mod}\ p$.

Thus, the extracted opening equals the claimed inner product v in both cases and we satisfy extractability.

Non-interactivity Using Fiat-Shamir. Protocol eval is public-coin and we can use the Fiat-Shamir heuristic [16] to obtain a non-interactive version in the ROM that has a constant-sized proof. The prover applies the RO on the commitment C to obtain the random query vector $\mathbf{z}$. Note that, the query vector $\mathbf{q}$ itself needs to be communicated, but the size of the proof is constant.

4   Dew – Constant-Sized PCS with Logarithmic Verifier

We prove our main result on PCS in this section. To go from IPC in Sect. 3 to a PCS of constant size and logarithmic verification time, we need two main ideas. First, we use Kronecker products test vectors to improve verification time from linear to logarithmic. But this breaks extractability of the new test. To recover extractability, we prove a new extremal combinatorial bound that enables us to prove a structure theorem despite the exponentially smaller randomness in the verifier's test vectors.

4.1   Dew: Our Polynomial Commitment Scheme

To construct Dew, we use ideas based on Kronecker products to define new query vectors in the **TEST** and **IPP** protocols from Sect. 3 and call the modified protocols **logTEST** and **logIPP**. These changes are to bring the verifier complexity down to logarithmic in the degree of the polynomial. For notational simplicity, let the degree of the polynomial $d = l - 1$. We change the blue messages in the **TEST, IPP** protocols as below. In the **logTEST** protocol, the query vector $\mathbf{z}$ in Fig. 2 is now redefined using just $2 \log l$ random elements in $\mathbb{Z}_p$:

1. Sample random $\mathbf{x}_1, \mathbf{x}_2, \ldots, \mathbf{x}_{\log l}$ from $\mathbb{Z}_p^2$ where $\mathbf{x}_j = (x_{j,0}, x_{j,1})$.
2. For $0 \le k \le l - 1$, let $(k_0, \ldots, k_{\log l - 1})$ be the base-2 representation of k so that $k = k_0 \cdot 2^0 + \cdots + k_{\log l - 1} \cdot 2^{\log l - 1}$. Then,

$$z_k \equiv z_{k_0, \ldots, k_{\log l - 1}} := \prod_{j=1}^{\log l} x_{j, k_{j-1}}. \tag{10}$$

For **logIPP**, the query vector **q** in Fig. 3 defined by the evaluation point $x \in \mathbb{Z}_p$ is modified as follows

$$q_k := \prod_{0 \leq j \leq \log l - 1} (x^{k_j 2^j} \mod p). \tag{11}$$

Note that $0 < z_k, q_k < p^{\log l}$ and $q_k \mod p = x^k \mod p$ for all k.

Our PCS Dew = (setup, commit, open, eval) is now constructed as follows:

- setup$(1^\kappa, D)$: Here, κ is the security parameter and D is an upper bound on the degree of the committed polynomial. Sample a group of unknown order (we use class groups) $\mathbb{G} \leftarrow \mathsf{GGen}(\kappa)$ and a random $g \leftarrow_\$ \mathbb{G}$. Define $\alpha := p^{2D \log D}$ (p is a large prime such that $\mathsf{len}(p) = \mathsf{poly}(\kappa)$). Return pp $= (\kappa, \mathbb{G}, g, p)$.
- commit$(\mathsf{pp}, D, f(X) \in \mathbb{Z}_p[X], l-1)$: Define the commitment $C := g^{\sum_{i=0}^{l-1} f_i \alpha^{2i}}$, where f_i are the coefficients of the degree $(l-1)$ polynomial $f(X)$ considered as integers from $[0, p-1]$ and the sum in $\mathbb{Z}$. If $l - 1 \leq D$, return $(C, \mathbf{f})$, else return error.
- open$(\mathsf{pp}, D, f(X) \in \mathbb{Z}_p[X], l-1, C, \tilde{\mathbf{f}})$: Check that
  (i) $l - 1 \leq D$, $\tilde{f}_i = f_i \mod p$ where $f_i \in \mathbb{Z}_p$ are the coefficients of $f(X)$.
  (ii) $C = g^{\sum_{i=0}^{l-1} \tilde{f}_i \alpha^{2i}}$, $\sum_{i=0}^{l-1} \tilde{f}_i \alpha^{2i} \in \mathbb{Z}$, and $\tilde{\mathbf{f}} \in \mathbb{Q}(\log l + 1, l + 1)^l$.
  Recall that

  $$\mathbb{Q}(\beta_1, \beta_2) := \left\{ \frac{a}{b} : \gcd(a, b) = \gcd(b, p) = 1, \ 0 < b < p^{\beta_1}, \ |a/b| \leq \beta_2 \alpha \right\},$$

  where $|a|$ denotes the absolute value of the integer a.
  return 1 if all checks (i)-(iii) above pass, else return 0.
- eval$(\mathsf{pp}, D, C, l-1, x, v; f(X))$: The eval protocol consists of two sub-protocols **logTEST** and **logIPP**:
  - If $l - 1 > D$, return 0
  - Else Run **logTEST**$(C, l-1; f(X))$ and **logIPP**$(C, l-1, x, v; f(X))$. return 1 if both these protocols accept else return 0.

The protocols **logTEST** and **logIPP** are simply variants of **TEST** and **IPP** in Figs. 2 and 3 by replacing the (blue messages) query vectors with Kronecker products of shorter vectors as in (10) and (11). We also replace all expensive group exponentiations for the verifier by invocations of Wesolowski's PoE protocol. The full protocols thus obtained are presented as figures in the Appendix of [1]. In the NI version, the random query vector is derived from the RO instead of being sent in **logTEST**.

Non-interactive Dew Using Fiat-Shamir. Note that even though **logTEST** and **logIPP** are described as separate protocols for ease of exposition, they are both run as part of eval. Protocol eval is public-coin and we can use the Fiat-Shamir heuristic [16] to obtain a non-interactive version in the ROM that has constant-sized proof and logarithmic verification. The prover applies the RO on the commitment C to obtain $\mathbf{x}_1, \ldots \mathbf{x}_{\log l}$, and the random query vector $\mathbf{z}$ is computed as described in Eq (10). The non-interactive (NI) transcript consists of all the elements communicated in both protocols along with the NI versions of PoE and PoKPE from both protocols. Hence, the transcript communicated is $\pi = ((C, A, \Lambda, \Gamma, R)_{\mathbf{logTEST}}, (B, N, \Lambda, \Gamma, R, S)_{\mathbf{logIPP}}, \pi_{\mathsf{PoE}}, \pi_{\mathsf{PoKPE}})$ where π_{PoE} consists of NI transcripts of steps $(4, 20, 21)$ and $(2, 16, 17, 18)$ in **logTEST** and **logIPP** respectively, and π_{PoKPE} consists of NI transcripts of steps $(13, 14, 15, 16, 17)$ and $(10, 11, 12, 13)$ in **logTEST** and **logIPP** respectively (from the figures in the appendix of [1]). It is easy to see that the Fiat-Shamir transformed NI transcript is succinct since the vectors $\mathbf{x}_1, \ldots, \mathbf{x}_{\log l}$ are now generated using the RO.

Proof of completeness is analogous (taking care of the new choices of parameters) to that of **IPP** in Theorem 31 and is deferred to the appendix of the full version [1]. Since the commitment scheme remains unchanged, the proof of binding remains as in Theorem 32. Proof of Extractability is shown in Sect. 4.2, and proof of succinctness is given in Sect. 4.3. The appendix of the full version contains concrete estimates of proof sizes. It also contains a section on how to achieve hiding and zero-knowledge evaluation for the commitment scheme.

4.2   Proof of Extractability of Dew

Define

$$S_{log} := \left\{ \frac{m\alpha - n}{k} : m, n, k \in \mathbb{Z}, \, gcd(m, k) = gcd(k, p) = 1, \, 0 < m \leq k < p^{\log l}, \right.$$

$$\left. -l < n < k + l \right\}$$

as a subset of $\mathbb{Z}$ and functions $\chi_m, \chi_n : S_{log}^q \to \mathbb{Q}^q$ which isolates the vector of fractions m/k and n/k from the elements of S_{log}^q:

$$\mathbf{v} \in S_{log} \implies \mathbf{v} = \left(\frac{m_i \alpha - n_i}{k_i} \right)_i, \quad \chi_m(\mathbf{v}) := \left(\frac{m_i}{k_i} \right)_i, \quad \text{and} \quad \chi_n(\mathbf{v}) := \left(\frac{n_i}{k_i} \right)_i.$$

Theorem 41. *The polynomial commitment scheme* Dew *satisfies Extractability (Def. 27) in the Generic Group Model.*

Proof. The proof of this theorem consists of two theorems about **logTEST** and **logIPP**. Both theorems rely on the fact that the adversary is *generic*.

Theorem 42. *If the Verifier in* **logTEST** *outputs accept with non-negligible probability over the choice of random* $\mathbf{z}_1, \ldots, \mathbf{z}_{\log 1} \in \mathbb{Z}_p^2$, *there exists an efficient extractor that outputs* $\mathbf{c}, \mathbf{d} \in [\alpha]^l$ *such that* $C = g^{\sum_{i=0}^{l-1}(c_i + \alpha d_i)\alpha^{2i}}$ *and* $\mathbf{d} \in S_{log}^l$.

Theorem 43. *If the Verifier in* **logIPP** *outputs accept with non-negligible probability and the Verifier of* **logTEST** *also did so, there exists an extractor that outputs an opening* $\tilde{f} \in \mathbb{Z}_p[x]$ *and an opening hint* $\tilde{\mathbf{c}}$ *in* $\mathbb{Q}(\log l + 1, l + 1)$ *for* C *such that* $v = \tilde{f}(x)$.

The proof of Theorem 42 is presented in Sect. 4.2.2. The proof of Theorem 43 is almost identical to that of Theorem 35 and we defer it to the full version. There are only two changes: $d_i \in S_{log}$ instead of S implies that the extracted vector $\in \mathbb{Q}(\log l + 1, l + 1)^l$ instead of $\mathbb{Q}(2, 3)^l$, and the bounds on N, N', M' are different, leading to a lower bound $\alpha > p^{2l(\log l)}$.

4.2.1   d-Cancellation Structures

Before we present the proof of Theorem 42 in Sect. 4.2.2, we define certain combinatorial structures and state an extremal bound about them that plays a crucial role in our extractability proof. These are d-cancellation structures and are generalizations of d-dimensional hyper-rectangles /boxes. For instance, a 2-cancellation structure is a parallelogram, while a 3-cancellation structure can be seen as two parallel parallelograms with the same base length and height (note that this is more general than a parallelepiped - in a parallelepiped, the two parallelograms have to be congruent). For general d, we have the following recursive definition.

Definition 44 (d-*cancellation structure*). *Given a d-tuple* $(a_1, \ldots, a_d) \in [n]^d$, *a* d-*cancellation structure is defined to be the set of* 2^d *points mapped to the leaves of a depth-d binary tree, where the mapping from* $[n]^d$ *to nodes of the tree is recursively defined as follows.*

- *Map* $(a_1, \ldots, a_d)$ *to the root (depth* 0*).*
- *Suppose* $(b_1, \ldots, b_d)$ *is mapped to a node* u *at depth* $d - j + 1$. *Then, for some* $y_{u,j} \in [n]$, *map* $(b_1, \ldots, b_{j-1}, y_{u,j} + b_j, \ldots, b_d)$ *to* u's *left child and* $(b_1, \ldots, b_{j-1}, y_{u,j}, \ldots, b_d)$ *to* u's *right child.*

Informally, when we start from the same d-tuple, we get "similar" d-cancellation structures (which form an equivalence class; see an equivalent definition in the full version [1]). This is useful in counting arguments about them such as the one below.

Our main result on d-cancellation structures states that in the $[n]^d$ integer lattice, we can choose at most $n^d - (n - 1)^d \leq dn^{d-1}$ points that do not contain a d-cancellation structure.

Theorem 45. *The maximum number of points in* $[n]^d$ *such that no subset of them forms a* d-*cancellation structure is* $N_d := n^d - (n - 1)^d$. *This bound is tight.*

In the extractability proof in the next section, we will argue that if the prover succeeds with non-negligible probability, then it must populate an appropriately chosen lattice with more points than this bound, leading to the existence of a log l-cancellation structure. We then use higher-dimensional/multilinear analogs of ideas in Theorem 34 to induce cancellations among the l equations at the points in this log l-cancellation structure to derive an equation with a single **d** coordinate, thereby deducing the required structure for it. Specifically, we traverse the corresponding tree bottom-up (from leaves to root) by "folding" equations from one level to the next – subtract them pairwise to reduce their number by half and eliminate half of the remaining terms in each of them. Details of this process appear in the next section and in the full version [1].

4.2.2 Proof of Theorem 42 – logTEST Extraction

Similar to the process in Lemma 3, we define the extractor Ext_T to first invoke the PoKPE extractor for C, which outputs $c > 0$ such that $C = g^c$. Since E also passes the PoKPE protocol and $C \cdot E = g^{\alpha^{2l-1}}$, we infer that $c < \alpha^{2l-1}$. Consider the base-α representation of c, which is a $2l$-length vector. Ext_T then outputs the even indexed coordinates as $\mathbf{c}$ and the odd indexed coordinates as $\mathbf{d}$.

Note that by definition, the first condition in the theorem is satisfied: $C = g^{\sum_{i=0}^{l-1}(c_i + \alpha d_i)\alpha^{2i}}$. An honest prover would clearly choose $d_i = 0$ and $c_i = x_i$, $0 \le c_i \le p-1$ for $i \in [l]$ to commit to a vector $\mathbf{x} \in \mathbb{Z}_p^l$. However, with a cheating prover, we are only guaranteed (at this point) that $0 \le c_i, d_i \le \alpha - 1$.

Now we use the checks done by the logTEST verifier to derive conditions on the above extracted vector and show the second part of the theorem – $\mathbf{d} \in S_{\log}^l$. Suppose the prover succeeds with a non-negligible probability over the random choice of $\mathbf{z}_1, \ldots, \mathbf{z}_{\log l}$ from $\mathbb{Z}_p^2$.

Fix an arbitrary index $0 \le k \le l - 1$, equivalently its binary representation $(k_1, \ldots k_{\log l})$. Consider the partition of the space $\mathbb{Z}_p^{2\log l}$ by sets of the form

$$T_{\mathbf{q}} := \{(x_{1,k_1}, \ldots, x_{\log l, k_{\log l}}, \mathbf{q}) : x_{j,k_j} \in \mathbb{Z}_p, \ 1 \le j \le \log l\} \text{ for } \mathbf{q} \in \mathbb{Z}_p^{\log l}.$$

Since the success probability of the prover is non-negligible, it is at least $\frac{\log l}{p}$. Hence, at least one of these sets (which are $\log l$-dimensional spaces) must have more than $\log l p^{\log l - 1} \ge p^{\log l} - (p-1)^{\log l}$ accepting points, which implies by Theorem 45 that there exists a $\log l$-cancellation structure in this space consisting of l accepting points.

For some fixed $1 < a_j < p$ and for all $g_1 g_2 \ldots g_\tau \in \{0,1\}^\tau$, let this $\log l$-cancellation structure be represented by

$$B := \{(y_{1,g_1,g_2,\ldots,g_{\log l - 1}} + g_{\log l} a_1, \ldots, y_{j,g_1,g_2,\ldots,g_{\log l - j}} +$$
$$g_{\log l - j + 1} a_j, \ldots, y_{\log l} + g_1 a_{\log l}) : 1 \le j \le \log l, \ y_{\ldots} \in \mathbb{Z}_p\}$$

All the points in B can be considered as the leaves of a binary tree, with leaves indexed as $g_1 g_2 \ldots g_{\log l}$. Starting from the root, at each node, the left child is labeled 1 and the right child is labeled 0. Thus the leftmost leaf would have index $11 \ldots 1$, and the rightmost leaf will have index $00 \ldots 0$.

Now, Lemma 3 gives us equations corresponding to each accepting point on the $\log l$-cancellation structure relating $\mathbf{c}, \mathbf{d}$ (given by Ext_T) and the random variables x_{j,i_j}. We recall the definition of the query vector $\mathbf{z}$ from Eq. (10), where for each coordinate z_i if the binary representation of $i = i_1 \ldots i_{\log l}$, then

$$z_i \equiv z_{i_1, i_2, \ldots, i_{\log l}} := \prod_{j=1}^{\log l} x_{j, i_j}$$

$$\langle \mathbf{d}, \mathbf{z} \rangle \mod \alpha + \left\lfloor \frac{\langle \mathbf{c}, \mathbf{z} \rangle}{\alpha} \right\rfloor + u_1 \mod \alpha = 0 \mod \alpha$$

The term $\langle \mathbf{d}, \mathbf{z} \rangle \mod \alpha$ can be expanded as follows:

$$\langle \mathbf{d}, \mathbf{z} \rangle \mod \alpha = \sum_{i_1, i_2, \ldots, i_{\log l} \in \{0,1\}} d_{i_1, i_2, \ldots, i_{\log l}} \cdot \prod_{j=1,}^{\log l} x_{j, i_j} \mod \alpha$$

$$= \sum_{i_1, \ldots, i_{\log l} \in \{0,1\}} d_{i_1, \ldots, i_{\log l}} \cdot \prod_{j=1}^{\log l} \left(y_{j, g_1, \ldots, g_{\log l - j}} + g_{\log l - j + 1} a_j \right) \cdot \prod_{\substack{j=1 \\ i_j \neq k_j}}^{\log l} x_{j, i_j} \mod \alpha$$

This expansion holds at height $\log l$ (for all leaves $g_1 g_2 \ldots g_{\log l}$). To obtain the required conditions on $\mathbf{d}$, we subtract the l equations in a specific order to cancel out all but one term. This is possible due to the fact that the coefficients of $d_{i_1 \ldots i_{\log l}}$ are multilinear in each of the randomly sampled variables.

More precisely, at any intermediate height in the binary tree, we obtain the equation at that node by subtracting the equation at the right child from the equation at the left child. For instance, at height $(\log l - 1)$, the first term takes the form :

$$a_1 \sum_{i_1, \ldots, i_{\log l - 1}} d_{k_1, i_2, \ldots, i_{\log l}} \cdot \prod_{j=2}^{\log l} \left(y_{j, g_1, \ldots, g_{\log l - j}} + g_{\log l - j + 1} a_j \right) \cdot \prod_{\substack{j=2 \\ i_j \neq k_j}}^{\log l} x_{j, i_j} \mod \alpha$$

In general, we get at height $0 \leq t < \log l$,

$$\prod_{j=1}^{\log l - t} a_i \sum_{i_1, i_2, \ldots, i_t \in \{0,1\}} d_{k_1, k_2, \ldots, k_{\log l - t}, i_{\log l - t + 1}, \ldots, i_{\log l}}$$

$$\cdot \prod_{j=\log l - t + 1}^{\log l} \left(y_{j, g_1, g_2, \ldots, g_{\log l - j}} + g_{\log l - j + 1} a_j \right) \cdot \prod_{\substack{j=\log l - t + 1 \\ i_j \neq k_j}}^{\log l} x_{j, i_j} \mod \alpha$$

Notice that at the root, i.e., at height 0, we are left with the single term $a_1 \ldots a_{\log l} \cdot d_{k_1, k_2, \ldots, k_{\log l}}$.

For the rest of the folded equation, we only use bounds on the other terms and not the exact expression. The actual expression is a symbolic subtraction of the floor terms and the 'u' terms. This is similar to what is done in Theorem 34 generalised to higher dimensions.

Specifically, indexing the l points/leaves by $\mathbf{z}_{g_1 g_2 \ldots g_{\log l}}$, we get the expression for the remaining two terms (call this expression n) as

$$\left(\sum_{g_1, g_2, \ldots, g_{\log l} \in \{0,1\}} (-1)^{\sum_{j=1}^{\log l} i_j} \cdot \left\lfloor \frac{\langle \mathbf{c}, \mathbf{z}_{\mathbf{g_1}, \mathbf{g_2}, \ldots, \mathbf{g}_{\log l}} \rangle}{\alpha} \right\rfloor + \right.$$

$$\left. \sum_{g_1, g_2, \ldots, g_{\log l} \in \{0,1\}} (-1)^{\sum_{j=1}^{\log l} i_j} \cdot u_{g_1, g_2, \ldots, g_{\log l}} \right) \mod \alpha$$

Since for all x, $x - 1 \leq \lfloor x \rfloor < x$ and $u \in \{0, 1\}$, we can bound the above expression n by

$$\frac{c_{k_1,\ldots,k_{\log l}} \cdot \prod_{i=1}^{\log l} a_i}{\alpha} - 2^{\log l} < n < \frac{c_{k_1,\ldots,k_{\log l}} \cdot \prod_{i=1}^{\log l} a_i}{\alpha} + 2^{\log l}$$

$$\implies -l < n < \prod_{i=1}^{\log l} a_i + l$$

Hence, there exists m such that $d_{k_1,\ldots,k_{\log l}} = \frac{m\alpha - n}{a_1 \cdots a_{\log l}}$ where $m \leq \prod_{i=1}^{\log l} a_i <$ $p^{\log l}$ (as $d_{k_1,\ldots,k_{\log l}} < \alpha$) and $-l < n < \prod_{i=1}^{\log l} a_i + l$ as shown above.

Hence, $d_{k_1,\ldots,k_{\log l}} \in S_{log}$. Since $(k_1, \ldots, k_{\log l})$ was arbitrary, $\mathbf{d} \in S_{log}^l$.

4.3 Succinctness of Dew

Theorem 46 (Proof and Verifier Succinctness). *In Dew, the commitment and evaluation proof sizes are* $\mathsf{poly}(\kappa)$ *and the Verifier runs in time* $\mathsf{poly}(\kappa) \cdot \log(l)$.

Proof. Proof succinctness is easy to see; the commitment is a single group element and the evaluation protocol only communicates a constant number of group elements (the PoE protocols are also constant-sized) and the query vector elements $\mathbf{x}_1, \ldots, \mathbf{x}_{\log l}$. However, as mentioned before, in the NI version, the $2 \log l$ *random* field elements are generated using a RO – this makes the proof size of the non-interactive version of the protocol constant.

To analyse the verifier computation, notice that the the only potentially expensive computations are the computation of σ and raising group elements to large powers (the PoKPE protocols consist of a constant number of PoKE protocols, which are efficient). The group exponentiations are made more efficient for the verifier by engaging in a constant number of PoE protocols with the prover. The only remaining bottleneck is the computation of σ mod q for some prime q in the invocation of Weslowski's PoE (for σ in both **logTEST** and **logIPP**).

In **logTEST**, using the definition of the test vector in (10) and direct manipulation implies that σ mod q can be computed in $O(\log l)$ time as follows

$$\sigma \mod q = \sum_{k=0}^{l-1} \alpha^{2l-2-2k} z_k \mod q = \alpha^{2l-2} \prod_{i=1}^{\log l} \left(x_{i,0} + x_{i,1} \alpha^{-2^{i+1}} \right) \mod q$$

In **logIPP**, by a similar manipulation as above using the definition of the the query vector in (11), we obtain

$$\sigma = \sum_{k=0}^{l-1} \alpha^{2l-1-2k} q_k \mod q = \alpha^{2l-1} \prod_{i=0}^{\log l - 1} \left(1 + (x^{2^i} \mod p) \alpha^{-2^{i+1}} \right) \mod q$$

Also note that for efficient computation, we need to compute α mod q and α^{-1} mod q (If α^{-1} mod q does not exist, then $\alpha = 0$ mod q and computing

σ becomes trivial). In this case, since $\alpha = p^L$ for some $L = O(l)$, computing $\alpha \mod q = p^L \mod q$ can be efficiently done in $O(\log l)$ time using repeated squaring. Once this is found, $\alpha^{-1} \mod q$ can also be efficiently found using the Extended Euclidean algorithm.

5 Transparent zkSNARKs via Dew

As a corollary of our PCS, we get concrete instantiations of new *transparent succinct arguments* by compiling an information theoretic proof in an idealized model into a succinct argument using a PCS.

The modular approach advocated for designing efficient arguments consists of two steps; constructing an information theoretic protocol in an abstract model (PCP, linear PCP, IOP etc.), and then compiling the information-theoretic protocol via a cryptographic compiler to obtain an argument system. Many recent constructions of zkSNARKs [9, 12, 17] follow this approach where the information theoretic object is an algebraic variant of IOP, and the cryptographic primitive in the compiler is a polynomial commitment scheme. Marlin [12] uses an IOP abstraction called algebraic holographic proofs (AHP), and [9] uses an abstraction called polynomial IOPs (PIOPs). In both these abstractions, the prover and the verifier interact where the prover provides oracle access to a set of polynomials, and the verifier sends random challenges. Then, the verifier asks for evaluations of these polynomials at these challenge points and decides to accept or reject based on the answers. PLONK [17] uses an abstraction called idealized low degree protocols (ILDPs) that proceeds in a similar way except that at the end of the protocol, the verifier checks a set of polynomial identities over the oracles sent by the prover. Polynomial Holographic IOP (PHP) [11] specializes the IOP notion in two ways (i) it is holographic – that is, the verifier has access to a set of oracle polynomials created during the setup phase that encode the relation, (ii) the verifier can directly check polynomial identities. The high level idea to build a zkSNARK with universal SRS starting from PIOPs/AHPs/ILDPs/PHPs is the following: the argument prover commits to the polynomials obtained from the information-theoretic prover, and then uses the evaluation opening property of the polynomial commitment scheme to respond to the evaluation queries of the verifier in a verifiable way.

We present concrete instantiations of zkSNARKs obtained by using our transparent PCS to cryptographically compile the AHP underlying the constructions of Sonic, Marlin and PLONK. We present the details and compare our zkSNARK Dew-SNARK to existing schemes in the full version [1].

References

1. Arun, A., Ganesh, C., Lokam, S., Mopuri, T., Sridhar, S.: Dew: Transparent constant-sized zkSNARKs. Cryptology ePrint Archive, Report 2022/419 (2022). https://eprint.iacr.org/2022/419

2. Ben-Sasson, E., Chiesa, A., Goldberg, L., Gur, T., Riabzev, M., Spooner, N.: Linear-size constant-query iops for delegating computation. In: Hofheinz, D., Rosen, A. (eds.) TCC 2019. LNCS, vol. 11892, pp. 494–521. Springer, Cham (2019). https://doi.org/10.1007/978-3-030-36033-7_19

3. Block, A.R., Holmgren, J., Rosen, A., Rothblum, R.D., Soni, P.: Time- and space-efficient arguments from groups of unknown order. In: Malkin, T., Peikert, C. (eds.) CRYPTO 2021. LNCS, vol. 12828, pp. 123–152. Springer, Cham (2021). https://doi.org/10.1007/978-3-030-84259-8_5

4. Bollobás, B.: Extremal Graph Theory. Reprint of the 1978 original. Dover Publications, Inc., Mineola, NY (2004) ISBN: 0-486-43596-2

5. Boneh, D., Bünz, B., Fisch, B.: Batching techniques for accumulators with applications to IOPs and stateless blockchains. In: Boldyreva, A., Micciancio, D. (eds.) CRYPTO 2019. LNCS, vol. 11692, pp. 561–586. Springer, Cham (2019). https://doi.org/10.1007/978-3-030-26948-7_20

6. Bosma, W., Stevenhagen, P.: On the computation of quadratic 2-class groups. Journal de Théorie des Nombres de Bordeaux 8(2), 283–313 (1996)

7. Buchmann. J., Hamdy, S.: A survey on iq cryptography. In: Proceedings of Public Key Cryptography and Computational Number Theory, pp. 1–15 (2001)

8. Bünz, B., Fisch, B., Szepieniec, A.: Transparent SNARKs from DARK compilers. Cryptology ePrint Archive, Report 2019/1229 (2019). https://eprint.iacr.org/2019/1229

9. Bünz, B., Fisch, B., Szepieniec, A.: Transparent SNARKs from DARK compilers. In: Canteaut, A., Ishai, Y. (eds.) EUROCRYPT 2020. LNCS, vol. 12105, pp. 677–706. Springer, Cham (2020). https://doi.org/10.1007/978-3-030-45721-1_24

10. Camenisch, J., Lysyanskaya, A.: Dynamic accumulators and application to efficient revocation of anonymous credentials. In: Yung, M. (ed.) CRYPTO 2002. LNCS, vol. 2442, pp. 61–76. Springer, Heidelberg (2002). https://doi.org/10.1007/3-540-45708-9_5

11. Campanelli, M., Faonio, A., Fiore, D., Querol, A., Rodríguez, H.: Lunar: a toolbox for more efficient universal and Updatable zkSNARKs and commit-and-prove extensions. In: Tibouchi, M., Wang, H. (eds.) ASIACRYPT 2021. LNCS, vol. 13092, pp. 3–33. Springer, Cham (2021). https://doi.org/10.1007/978-3-030-92078-4_1

12. Chiesa, A., Hu, Y., Maller, M., Mishra, P., Vesely, N., Ward, N.: Marlin: Preprocessing zkSNARKs with universal and updatable SRS. In: Canteaut, A., Ishai, Y. (eds.) EUROCRYPT 2020. LNCS, vol. 12105, pp. 738–768. Springer, Cham (2020). https://doi.org/10.1007/978-3-030-45721-1_26

13. Chu, H., Fiore, D., Kolonelos, D., Schröder, D.: Inner product functional commitments with constant-size public parameters and openings. In: Galdi, C., Jarecki, S., (eds.) Security and Cryptography for Networks, pp. 639–662. Springer International Publishing, Cham (2022). https://doi.org/10.1007/978-3-031-14791-3_28

14. Damgård, I., Koprowski, M.: Generic lower bounds for root extraction and signature schemes in general groups. In: Knudsen, L.R. (ed.) EUROCRYPT 2002. LNCS, vol. 2332, pp. 256–271. Springer, Heidelberg (2002). https://doi.org/10.1007/3-540-46035-7_17

15. Feldman, P.: A practical scheme for non-interactive verifiable secret sharing. In: 28th Annual Symposium on Foundations of Computer Science (sfcs 1987), pp. 427–438. IEEE (1987)

16. Fiat, A., Shamir, A.: How to prove yourself: practical solutions to identification and signature problems. In: Odlyzko, A.M. (ed.) CRYPTO 1986. LNCS, vol. 263, pp. 186–194. Springer, Heidelberg (1987). https://doi.org/10.1007/3-540-47721-7_12

17. Gabizon, A., Williamson, Z.J., Ciobotaru, O.: Plonk: Permutations over lagrange-bases for oecumenical noninteractive arguments of knowledge. Cryptology ePrint Archive, Report 2019/953 (2019). https://ia.cr/2019/953
18. Kate, A., Zaverucha, G.M., Goldberg, I.: Constant-size commitments to polynomials and their applications. In: Abe, M. (ed.) ASIACRYPT 2010. LNCS, vol. 6477, pp. 177–194. Springer, Heidelberg (2010). https://doi.org/10.1007/978-3-642-17373-8_11
19. Lai, R.W.F., Malavolta, G.: Subvector commitments with application to succinct arguments. In: Boldyreva, A., Micciancio, D. (eds.) CRYPTO 2019. LNCS, vol. 11692, pp. 530–560. Springer, Cham (2019). https://doi.org/10.1007/978-3-030-26948-7_19
20. Lee, J.: Dory: efficient, transparent arguments for generalised inner products and polynomial commitments. In: Nissim, K., Waters, B. (eds.) TCC 2021. LNCS, vol. 13043, pp. 1–34. Springer, Cham (2021). https://doi.org/10.1007/978-3-030-90453-1_1
21. Libert, B., Ramanna, S.C., Yung, M.: Functional commitment schemes: From polynomial commitments to pairing-based accumulators from simple assumptions. In: Chatzigiannakis, I., Mitzenmacher, M., Rabani, Y., Sangiorgi, D., (eds.) ICALP 2016, vol. 55 of LIPIcs, pp. 30:1–30:14. Schloss Dagstuhl, (July 2016)
22. Micali, S., Rabin, M., Kilian, J.: Zero-knowledge sets. In: 44th Annual IEEE Symposium on Foundations of Computer Science 2003, Proceedings, pp. 80–91. IEEE (2003)
23. Ràfols, C., Zapico, A.: An algebraic framework for universal and updatable SNARKs. In: Malkin, T., Peikert, C. (eds.) CRYPTO 2021. LNCS, vol. 12825, pp. 774–804. Springer, Cham (2021). https://doi.org/10.1007/978-3-030-84242-0_27
24. Rosenfeld, L.: The box problem in two and higher dimensions. Bachelor's thesis, University of Rochester (2016). https://www.sas.rochester.edu/mth/undergraduate/honorspaperspdfs/rosenfeldhonorsthesis16.pdf
25. Wahby, R.S., Tzialla, I., Shelat, A., Thaler, J., Walfish, M.: Doubly-efficient zkSNARKs without trusted setup. In: 2018 IEEE Symposium on Security and Privacy, pp. 926–943. IEEE Computer Society Press (May 2018)
26. Wesolowski, B.: Efficient verifiable delay functions. In: Ishai, Y., Rijmen, V. (eds.) EUROCRYPT 2019. LNCS, vol. 11478, pp. 379–407. Springer, Cham (2019). https://doi.org/10.1007/978-3-030-17659-4_13
27. Zhang, J., Xie, T., Zhang, Y., Song, D.: Transparent polynomial delegation and its applications to zero knowledge proof. In: 2020 IEEE Symposium on Security and Privacy, pp. 859–876. IEEE Computer Society Press (May 2020)

IO and ZK II

Non-Interactive Publicly-Verifiable Delegation of Committed Programs

Riddhi Ghosal[1]([✉]), Amit Sahai[1], and Brent Waters[2,3]

[1] UCLA, Los Angeles, USA
{riddhi,sahai}@cs.ucla.edu
[2] UT Austin, Austin, USA
bwaters@cs.utexas.edu
[3] NTT Research, Palo Alto, USA

Abstract. In this work, we present the first construction of a fully non-interactive publicly-verifiable delegation scheme for committed programs. More specifically, we consider a setting where Alice is a trusted author who delegates to an untrusted worker the task of hosting a program P, represented as a Boolean circuit. Alice also commits to a succinct value based on P. Any arbitrary user/verifier *without knowledge of* P should be convinced that they are receiving from the worker an actual computation of Alice's program on a given input x.

Before our work, the only object known to imply this challenging form of delegation was a SNARG/SNARK for $\mathcal{NP}$. This is because from the point of view of the user/verifier, the program P is an unknown witness to the computation. However, constructing a SNARG for $\mathcal{NP}$ from standard assumptions remains a major open problem.

In our work, we show how to achieve delegation in this challenging context assuming only the hardness of the Learning With Errors (LWE) assumption, bypassing the apparent need for a SNARG for $\mathcal{NP}$.

1 Introduction

We consider a scenario where a trusted software author Alice wishes to make it possible for a set of users to make use of her program P, which we treat as a (non-uniform) Boolean circuit. In particular, this program P may have embedded within it a large proprietary database that Alice's program makes use of. However, Alice neither wants to release her program P nor does she want to host and execute the program herself. Instead she wishes to delegate this computation to an untrusted Worker, and the User/Verifier wants to be certain that they are receiving an output obtained via a computation of Alice's actual program P. As illustrated in Fig. 1, the way this works is:

1. Alice sends the program P along with some computed state to the Worker, and Alice also publishes a succinct hash H_P of her program, which the User/Verifier obtains. This step is done once and for all.
2. An Input Provider chooses an input x, which is sent to both the Worker and the User/Verifier. Note that the input provider could be some public source

A. Boldyreva and V. Kolesnikov (Eds.): PKC 2023, LNCS 13941, pp. 575–605, 2023.
https://doi.org/10.1007/978-3-031-31371-4_20

of information like a news channel of bulletin board, and need not involve the User/Verifier.

3. Finally, the Worker computes the output $y = P(x)$ along with a succinct proof Π, and sends both of these to the User/Verifier. Steps 2 and 3 may be repeated polynomially many times.

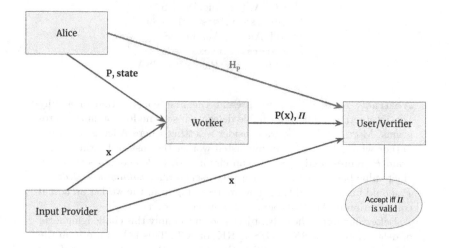

Fig. 1. The Delegation Setup

As illustrated in Fig. 1, this process involves no back–and–forth communication. The communication is entirely unidirectional – which we call non-interactive – from left to right. Furthermore, we say that this scenario is *succinct* if all communication to the User/Verifier, and the runtime of the User/Verifier, is $\mathsf{poly}(\log |P|, \lambda, |x|)$, where λ is a security parameter.

Remark 1. Note that on one hand, the Worker is trusted with the program P by Alice, whereas, it is not trusted by the verifier. This asymmetry of trust is inherent in our setup and is well motivated. In a typical real world situation, the verifier is typically a user on the internet who takes part in a one off interaction with a cloud service for some computation. The need to prove honesty in this situation is significant. On the other hand, Alice might be able to have an agreement with the cloud service before handing over her program, which would make it hard for their Worker to breach trust without consequences.

Comparison to Prior Work. What we have just described is one of the most challenging variants of the classical problem of *publicly verifiable delegation* which has been the subject of intense work for decades, for many relaxed variations of the model that we describe above.

Specifically, delegation schemes *without public verification* based on standard assumptions for deterministic and non-deterministic computations have been designed [1,6,7,11,12,22,24,25,37–39]. Restricting verification to a *designated* verifier implies that the worker needs to produce a fresh proof unique for each particular verifier for any computation, which is certainly not ideal. Another line of work [15] achieves public verification but does not achieve public delegation. In other words, the input provider needs to run a pre-processing algorithm corresponding to the program P before being able to delegate. Another model which has been extensively explored is when the User/Verifier is allowed to have interaction with the Worker, i.e., *interactive delegation*. Influenced by the first work on interactive efficient arguments by Kilian [27], there have been several works from standard assumptions [5,24,33,34] and some even unconditional soundness [17,36]. These are however not applicable in our setting where only one-way communication is permitted between the parties, as can be seen in the acyclic graph in Fig. 1.

With regard to *non-interactive publicly verifiable delegation*, Starting from the seminal work on computationally sound proofs by Micali [31] in the random oracle model, there have been several constructions on publicly verifiable non-interactive delegation schemes [2–4,13,16,18,28,32] based on the *Random Oracle Model* or non-standard *knowledge assumptions*. From more standard assumptions, there have been several works recently [1,6,7,23]. An illustrative example is the recent work of [23] that proposed the first publicly verifiable non-interactive delegation scheme from a falsifiable decisional assumption on groups with bilinear pairings. However, in contrast with the setting we describe above, they can only achieve succinct delegation when the Verifier *knows the program P*. In our setting of Boolean circuits, this trivializes the delegation problem, since reading P's description takes as long as evaluating P. Indeed, the case that we consider— where Alice's program is large—is extremely well motivated: the program P could be an ML model with billions of painstakingly learned parameters.

The SNARGs for $\mathcal{NP}$ barrier. Why has constructing a protocol that caters to the fully non-interactive setting which we have defined been so elusive? Note that in our problem, the User/Verifier and Input Provider do not know the program P. Hence, from User/Verifier's perspective, P is an $\mathcal{NP}$ witness. Thus, it certainly seems that finding a solution is intricately related to a major goal in the area of non interactive succinct proof systems, i.e., *SNARGs for $\mathcal{NP}$*. Unfortunately, the only known constructions of SNARGs for $\mathcal{NP}$ base their soundness on the *Random Oracle Model* or non-standard *knowledge assumptions*. Finding a solution solely relying on standard assumptions has been an open problem for over a decade. In fact, the closest that we have come is the very recent work achieving SNARGs for $\mathcal{P}$ [10] (see also [26]).

The major technical contribution in our work is to enable *Non-Interactive Publicly Verifiable Succinct Delegation for Committed Programs* without having to use SNARGs for $\mathcal{NP}$.

Our Contribution: We present the first complete solution to achieving succinct non interactive publicly verifiable delegation for committed programs. Indeed, furthermore, we can also achieve zero-knowledge guarantees as well. Our only computational assumption is the hardness of the *Learning with Errors* (LWE) problem. Somewhat surprisingly, we show that SNARGs for $\mathcal{NP}$ are not required to solve this problem, even though the statement being proved looks like an $\mathcal{NP}$ statement to the Verifier!

Instead, we show that many ideas from SNARGs for $\mathcal{P}$ [10] can in fact be applied here. Although P is unknown to the User/Verifier, we show that it suffices for Alice to communicate a tiny amount of information of size $\mathsf{poly}(\log |P|)$ about the program P (referred to as H_P) as shown in Fig. 1. Because Alice is the author of P, this H_P can be *trusted* as correctly generated. We stress that Alice does not need to know x to compute H_P, hence this achieves public delegation and public verification in the completely non-interactive model described above. This leads to our main theorem,

Theorem 1. *Assuming the hardness of the LWE problem, Fig. 2 gives a construction for publicly verifiable non-interactive succinct delegation for committed programs with CRS size, proof size and verifier time $\mathsf{poly}(\lambda, \log |P|, |x|)$ and prover run time being $\mathsf{poly}(\lambda, |P|)$.*

Finally, in order to get zero-knowledge, it suffices for Alice to commit to H_P rather than sending it out in the open. We then present a generic transformation to convert any delegation protocol of this form to attain zero-knowledge.

Theorem 2. *Assuming the hardness of the LWE problem and existence of a succinct delegation scheme, Fig. 5 gives a construction for publicly verifiable succinct delegation scheme with zero knowledge such that CRS size, proof size and verifier time are $\mathsf{poly}(\lambda, \log |P|)$ and prover run time is $\mathsf{poly}(\lambda, |P|)$.*

Finally, we also show how to achieve *zero knowledge* versions of our delegation scheme, meeting the same strong succinctness and efficiency goals, and under the same assumption (LWE).

We present a more detailed explanation in the Technical Overview.

2 Technical Overview

Our Delegation Scenario. Let us briefly recall the setup of our delegation scenario. There are 4 parties, namely, (1) Alice-the program author ProgAuth who sends a program P and some computed state state to a Worker, (2) an Input Provider I that outputs some value x, (3) Worker W that takes as input (P, state, x) and outputs $P(x)$ and a proof Π, and (4) User/Verifier V gets as inputs $(x, P(x), \Pi)$ and outputs 1 if and only if Π was a valid proof. Assume that all the parties get the security parameter λ as an input. An additional requirement is that $|\Pi|$ and runtime of V is $\mathsf{poly}(\lambda, \log |P|, |x|)$, and W runs in time $\mathsf{poly}(\lambda, |x|, |P|)$. Thus, any non-interactive publicly verifiable succinct delegation scheme can be viewed as a collection of 4 algorithms: $\mathsf{sDel} = (\mathsf{ProgAuth}, W, I, V)$ with the input output behaviour and efficiency guarantees as specified. Note that this is indeed a $\mathcal{P}$ computation for the Worker but the primary challenge is that the verifier does not have knowledge of the "witness" P, hence this is an $\mathcal{NP}$

computation from the verifier's point of view. In this work, we observe that it is indeed feasible to achieve our delegation scenario for all circuits without having to go through SNARGs for $\mathcal{NP}$. Our technique is based on the recent work of Choudhuri et al. [10] on SNARGs for $\mathcal{P}$. We begin by giving a brief overview of their approach and elaborate the challenges of directly incorporating their methodology for our setting.

Challenges of Implementing [10]. Roughly, the work of [10] uses Batch Arguments for $\mathcal{NP}$ (BARGs), which they build from LWE. BARGs allow an efficient prover to compute a non-interactive and publicly verifiable "batch proof" of many $\mathcal{NP}$ instances, with size $\mathsf{poly}(|w|\log T)$ for T-many $\mathcal{NP}$ statements with each witness of size $|w|$. They begin by looking at P as a Turing machine and the steps of P's computation are interpreted as an *Index Circuit* C_{index}. Say, P terminates in T steps. Formally, they construct a BARG for the *Index Language* $\mathcal{L}^{\mathsf{index}}$, where

$$\mathcal{L}^{\mathsf{index}} = \{(C_{\mathsf{index}}, i)|\exists w_i, \text{ such that } C(i, w_i) = 1\},$$

where $i \in [T]$ is an index. Let $s_0, s_1, \ldots, s_T$ denote the encoding of internal states of P along with its tape information, and let *Step* be its step function such that $Step(s_{i-1}) = s_i$ The witness for the ith intermediate computation is then defined as $w_i = (s_{i-1}, s_i)$. The index circuit is built such that $(C_{\mathsf{index}}, i) \in \mathcal{L}^{\mathsf{index}}$ essentially implies that the Turing machine step function was correctly computed on s_{i-1} to yield s_i. Note that this alone does not suffice as a proof because the BARG only confirms that (s_{i-1}, s_i) and (s'_i, s_{i+1}) are valid witnesses. If $s_{i-1}, s_i, s'_i, s_{i+1}$ are generated by the step function of the same Turing machine P, they must be consistent with each other, i.e., $s_i = s'_i$. However, this is not guaranteed by a BARG.

To resolve this issue, the prover also sends a *Somewhere Extractable Hash* *(SE)* to the witnesses $(s_0, \{s_{i-1}, s_i\}_{i\in[T]})$. The extraction property of this hash allows the verifier to check if the witness of two consecutive BARG instances are indeed consistent with each other. At this stage, we would like to remind the reader of their efficiency goals where crucially, they desire proof size and verification time to be $\mathsf{poly}(\lambda, \log T)$. However, note that $|C_{\mathsf{index}}|$ grows linearly with $|s_i|$ and the known constructions [20] of SE hashes can only produce hashes with size $\mathsf{poly}(|s_i|)$. This means that total communication and verifier run time will be at least $\mathsf{poly}(|s_i|)$. This is certainly no good if the Turing machine has massive states. To overcome this final barrier, they make use of Hash Trees which compress the states s_i to a short hash h_i such that $|h_i| = \mathsf{poly}(\lambda)$. Such trees [30] also have a soundness property where a Prover must produce a succinct proof Π_i that the hash tree was indeed implemented correctly at the ith step of the Turing machine computation. Once the succinctness guarantee is ensured, the prover then produces SE hashes corresponding to $(h_0, \Pi_0, \{h_{i-1}, \Pi_{i-1}, h_i, \Pi_i\}_{i\in[T]})$ along with the openings to these hashes. To summarise, the proof consists of two parts, (1) The BARG proof, and (2) A *somewhere extractable* hash of the witnesses. Relying on the soundness of BARG, extraction correctness property of SE hash and soundness of the Hash Tree, a User/Verifier can check if each of these T intermediate steps are indeed the correct states for P, i.e., the computation was done honestly.

However, this approach only works if User/Verifier can confirm that the inputs used for the computation by the Worker, i.e. (P, x) are indeed the correct starting values as provided by the Program Author and Input Provider. This works fine for [10] because in their setting, the User/Verifier actually knows (P, x). Unfortunately, this is not at all true in our scenario. Thus, the techniques of Choudhuri et al. [10] cannot be implemented directly as the soundness of the BARG proof cannot provide any guarantees if there is no way for to check that the initial inputs used by the Worker are correct.

Our Idea. We start with an alternate way of interpreting the computation of P on input x as the following: Consider a Circuit-Universal Turing Machine $\mathcal{TM}$ which takes as input P, x, y and accepts (P, x, y) in $T = \tilde{O}(|P|)$ steps if $P(x) = y$. We can assume without loss of generality that $P \in \{0,1\}^m$, $x \in \{0,1\}^n$ and $y \in \{0,1\}$, where $m, n \leq 2^\lambda$. Keeping this in mind, we introduce the notion of *Semi-Trusted SNARGs* for $\mathcal{NP}$. This new kind of SNARG is one that will work for general $\mathcal{NP}$ computations, but only with a little bit of extra help from a trusted party that knows the witness – which in our delegation scenario is Alice, who knows the witness P!

A Semi-Trusted SNARG is a tuple of algorithms: stSNARG = (Setup, TrustHash, P, V), where (1) Setup is a randomised algorithm that takes as input the security parameter and outputs a Common Random String (CRS). (2) a *trusted* deterministic TrustHash takes as input the (CRS, P) and outputs a digest H_P, (3) a deterministic prover P which takes as input CRS and (P, x, y), and outputs a proof Π, and (4) a deterministic verifier V which gets CRS,(H_P, x, y, Π) as input and outputs 1 iff Π is valid. It must be that $|\Pi|$ and run time of V is $\mathsf{poly}(\lambda, \log T)$, and P runs in time $\mathsf{poly}(\lambda, |x|, |P|, T)$. A simple reduction shows that in the CRS model (or alternatively in a model where Alice chooses the CRS), existence of stSNARG implies the existence of sDel. We show this formally in Lemma 11. Hence, from here onwards, our goal is to construct a *Semi-Trusted SNARG for $\mathcal{NP}$*.

We briefly provide an informal explanation of our construction.

Like [10], every intermediate state of the Universal Turing Machine is encoded into a succinct hash (call it $h_0, \ldots, h_T$) accompanied with succinct proofs $\{\Pi_i\}_{i \in [T]}$. The prover computes two independent copies of *Somewhere Extractable* (SE) hashes (c_1, c_2) of the encoding $\{h_0, \{(h_1, \Pi_1), \ldots, (h_T, \Pi_T)\}\}$ along with their corresponding openings. Here $h_0 = (\mathsf{st}_0, H_P, H_x, H_{work})$, where st_0 is that hash of $\mathcal{TM}$'s starting state which is publicly known, H_x denote the hash of x, and H_{work} is the hash of $\mathcal{TM}$'s blank work tape. The use of two independent SE hashes are pivotal for soundness which we elaborate later.

We point out that TrustHash computes H_P using the same hash tree which is used for hashing the Turing machine states by the Prover. This is crucial to ensure soundness of the protocol. We show in Fig. 3 that once the public hash is fixed by TrustHash, one can hard code $(y, c_1, c_2, T, H_P, H_x)$ to the index circuit

C_{index} for BARG. At this point, we can now follow the approach from [10]. V can rely upon the binding property/collision resistance of the hash to ensure that the prover has used P and x which were provided by Alice and the input provider respectively. The main observation here is that once a trusted party fixed a hash of the program P and V is convinced that computation was commenced with the correct inputs, the soundness of BARG, extraction correctness of the SE hash and soundness of hash tree ensures that the semi-trusted SNARG construction is sound.

While our proof of soundness closely follows the blueprint of [10], we choose to present our proof in a different, and arguably simpler, way. In [10], *No-Signaling Somewhere Extractable*(NSSE) hashes are used extensively. In our proof, we choose to omit explicit use of this notion, and instead we make direct use of two independent SE hashes as mentioned above. A simple hybrid argument then gives a straightforward proof for soundness. This shows that the "anchor and step" use of SE hashes, which dates to the introduction of somewhere-binding hashes [20] in 2015, is directly sufficient for this proof of soundness.

Zero-Knowledge. We have only discussed soundness guarantees thus far. However, in our delegation scenario, it might also be extremely important to ensure that no information about P leaked to V during the delegation process. Hence it is important to add *zero-knowledge* guarantees to our protocol. We finally give a generic transformation to modify a semi-trusted SNARG to add zero knowledge guarantees. In order to do so we make use of a statistically binding extractable commitment scheme and a NIZK[1], and roughly make the following modifications:

- We add an additional commitment to 0 in the CRS which is never used in the proof but helps in proving zero knowledge.
- The public hash output by TrustHash is a binding commitment C_P of H_P. It then sends (P, H_P) to the worker W only.
- The SE hashes c_1, c_2 are also committed as a part of the proof and not published in the open.
- The prover wraps the BARG Π with a NIZK which proves that that the BARG verification circuit indeed accepts the BARG proof.
- The Verifier then checks if the NIZK proof is valid.

The binding and hiding property of the commitment, and *witness indistinguishability* of NIZK guarantees zero knowledge.

3   Preliminaries

We use some standard tools as building blocks to perform the Succinct Delegation.

---

[1] Multi-theorem NIZK from LWE is possible by combining [35] and [14]. Note that the weaker notion NIWI would also suffice to achieve zero knowledge in our setting.

- **Somewhere Extractable Hash** [9,10,20]:
  SE =(SE.Gen, SE.TGen, SE.Hash, SE.Open, SE.Verify, SE.Ext)
- **Non Interactive Batch Arguments** (BARG) **for Index Language** [10]:
  BARG = (BARG.Gen, BARG.TGen, BARG.Prove, BARG.Verify)
- **Hash Tree** [23,30]:
  HT = HT.Gen, HT.Hash, HT.Read, HT.Write, HT.VerRead, HT.VerWrite
- **Non Interactive Zero Knowledge Argument** [8,19,35]:
  (NIZK = NIZK.Gen, NIZK.Prove, NIZK.V)
- **Statistically Binding Extractable Commitment** [29]:
  Com_{bind} = (Com.Gen, Com.TGen, Com.C, Com.Ext)

We use all the primitives in a standard way as prior works. The hash tree can be constructed from any collision resistant hash function. The others are known to be instantiated from LWE. Formal definitions and properties of the primitives can be found in the Supplementary Material.

4   Publicly Verifiable Non Interactive Succinct Delegation

We formally define the notion of Publicly Verifiable Non Interactive Succinct Delegation (sDel) which is similar to the definition proposed in prior works [21]. Such a delegation scheme in the CRS model involves the following PPT algorithms, (1)Software/Program Author ProgAuth (3)Cloud Worker W, and (3) Verifier V An sDel comprises of the following polynomial time algorithms:

- sDel.Setup(1^λ): A randomized setup algorithm which on input security parameter λ and outputs crs.
- sDel.ProgAuth(1^λ, crs): A program author which takes as input λ, outputs a (not public) program $P \in \{0,1\}^m$, $m \leq 2^\lambda \in \mathbb{N}$, state and a public digest H_P.
- sDel.W(crs, P, state, H_P, x): A deterministic cloud worker which on input crs, program P, input $x \in \{0,1\}^n$, $n \leq 2^\lambda \in \mathbb{N}$ outputs a value y and proof Π.
- sDel.V(crs, x, y, H_P, Π): A deterministic verifier which on input crs, digest H_P, x, y, Π either accepts or rejects.

A publicly verifiable succinct delegation scheme (sDel.Setup, sDel.ProgAuth, sDel.W, sDel.V) satisfies the following properties:

- **Completeness.** For every PPT program generating algorithm sDel. ProgAuth, every $\lambda, n, m \in \mathbb{N}$, and for all $x \in \{0,1\}^n$ such that $n, m < 2^\lambda$, we have

$$\Pr[\mathsf{sDel}.V(\mathsf{crs}, x, y, H_P, \Pi) = 1 \wedge P(x) = y | \mathsf{crs} \leftarrow \mathsf{sDel.Setup}(1^\lambda),$$
$$((P, \mathsf{state}), H_P) \leftarrow \mathsf{sDel.ProgAuth}(1^\lambda, \mathsf{crs}),$$
$$(y, \Pi) \leftarrow \mathsf{sDel}.W(\mathsf{crs}, P, \mathsf{state}, H_P, x)] = 1.$$

- **Efficiency.** sDel.Setup runs in time poly(λ), sDel.W runs in time poly(λ, $|P|$, $|x|$) and outputs a proofs of length poly(λ, $\log |P|$, $|x|$), and sDel.V runs in time poly(λ, $\log |P|$, $|x|$).

- **Soundness.** For every PPT adversary $\mathcal{A} := (\mathcal{A}_1, \mathcal{A}_2)$, every PPT program generating algorithm sDel.ProgAuth, and the tuple $n = n(\lambda)$, $m = m(\lambda)$, there exists a negligible function $\mathsf{negl}(\lambda)$ such that for every $\lambda \in \mathbb{N}$,

$$\Pr[\mathsf{sDel}.V(\mathsf{crs}, x, y, H_P, \Pi) = 1 \wedge P(x) \neq y \,|\, \mathsf{crs} \leftarrow \mathsf{sDel}.\mathsf{Setup}(1^\lambda),$$
$$((P, \mathsf{state}), H_P) \leftarrow \mathsf{sDel}.\mathsf{ProgAuth}(1^\lambda, \mathsf{crs}),$$
$$(x, \mathsf{aux}) \leftarrow \mathcal{A}_1(1^\lambda, \mathsf{crs}), (y, \Pi) \leftarrow \mathcal{A}_2(\mathsf{crs}, P, \mathsf{state}, H_P, x, \mathsf{aux})]$$
$$\leq \mathsf{negl}(\lambda).$$

To construct sDel, we introduce a notion of *Semi-Trusted Succinct Non-Interactive Arguments* stSNARG which we formally introduce and construct in Sect. 5. After that, we prove the following lemma (cf. Lemma 11) which shows how to construct sDel using stSNARG as a building block.

Lemma 1. *Assuming* $T = \mathsf{poly}(m, n)$, $T, m, n \leq 2^\lambda$, *the* stSNARG *protocol in Fig. 2 implies the unconditional existence of a publicly verifiable non interactive succinct delegation scheme* sDel *as defined above.*

4.1   sDel with Zero-Knowledge

A publicly verifiable non interactive succinct delegation scheme with zero knowledge zk − sDel is defined by the following efficient algorithms:

- zk − sDel.Setup(1^λ): A randomized setup algorithm which on input security parameter λ and outputs crs.
- zk − sDel.ProgAuth(1^λ, crs): A program author which takes as input λ, generates a program $P \in \{0, 1\}^m$, $m \leq 2^\lambda \in \mathbb{N}$. Additionally, it computes a digest H_P and creates a statistically binding and extractable commitment C_P of H_P under randomness r. Finally it sends a private output (P, state) and public output C_P. Here state contains the randomness r and H_P encoded in it along with any other state information.
- zk − sDel.W(crs, P, state, C_P, x): A deterministic cloud worker which on input crs, program P, commitment C_P, $x \in \{0, 1\}^n$, $n \leq 2^\lambda \in \mathbb{N}$ outputs a value y and proof Π.
- zk − sDel.V(crs, x, y, C_P, Π): A deterministic verifier which on input (crs, C_P, x, y, Π) either accepts or rejects.

Apart from the Completeness, Efficiency and Soundness guarantees mentioned above, a publicly verifiable succinct delegation scheme (zk − sDel.Setup, zk − sDel.ProgAuth, zk − sDel.W, zk − sDel.V) satisfies the following additional property:

Non Interactive Zero Knowledge. For all $\lambda, n, m \in \mathbb{N}$ such that $n, m \leq 2^\lambda$, $\forall, x \in \{0, 1\}^n$ and $y \in \{0, 1\}$, there exists a PPT simulator Sim := $(\mathsf{Sim}_1, \mathsf{Sim}_2, \mathsf{Sim}_3)$ such that the distributions of

$$(\mathsf{crs}, x, y, C_P, \Pi) | (\mathsf{crs}, \mathsf{aux}) \leftarrow \mathsf{Sim}_1(1^\lambda), (C_P, \mathsf{aux}') \leftarrow \mathsf{Sim}_2(\mathsf{crs}, \mathsf{aux}),$$
$$(y, \Pi) \leftarrow \mathsf{Sim}_3(\mathsf{aux}', \mathsf{crs}, x, C_P)$$

and

$$(\mathsf{crs}, x, y, C_P, \Pi) | \mathsf{crs} \leftarrow \mathsf{zk} - \mathsf{sDel}.\mathsf{Setup}(1^\lambda), ((P, \mathsf{state}), C_P) \leftarrow \mathsf{zk} - \mathsf{sDel}.\mathsf{ProgAuth}(1^\lambda, \mathsf{crs}),$$
$$(y := P(x), \Pi) \leftarrow \mathsf{zk} - \mathsf{sDel}.W(\mathsf{crs}, P, \mathsf{state}, x, C_P)$$

are indistinguishable.

In Sect. 6, we present a generic construction of a semi trusted non-interactive succinct arguments with zero-knowledge (ZKstSNARG) from stSNARG. Analogous to the previous lemma, we get the following corollary(cf. Corollary 2) from Lemma 11.

Corollary 1. *Assuming* $T = \mathsf{poly}(m, n)$, $T, m, n \leq 2^\lambda$, *the* ZKstSNARG *protocol in Fig. 5 implies the unconditional existence of a publicly verifiable non interactive succinct delegation scheme with zero knowledge.*

5   Semi-Trusted Succinct Non-Interactive Argument (stSNARG)

We introduce a notion of "Semi-Trusted" SNARGs which is similar to the general definition of SNARGs with an addition "trusted" polynomial time algorithm that outputs a hash for the witness. Further, we provide an explicit construction of an stSNARG for all of NP. Note that any SNARG for arbitrary NP language $\mathcal{L}$ can be reformulated as a Turing Machine which takes in as input an instance x along with witness w and accepts x, w in T steps if $x \in \mathcal{L}$ [10]. In this work, we modify the definition of [10] by using a Universal Turing Machine $\mathcal{TM}$ which takes as input an instance (x, y), a witness which is a program P and accepts (P, x, y) in T steps if $P(x) = y$. We formalise this notion as follows:

Let $\mathcal{TM}$ be a Universal Turing Machine which takes as input a program $P \in \{0, 1\}^m$ for some $m < 2^\lambda$, and $x \in \{0, 1\}^n$ for some $n < 2^\lambda$ and $y \in \{0, 1\}$ which serve as an input and output for P respectively. $\mathcal{TM}$ accepts (P, x, y) in T steps if $P(x) = y$. A prover produces a proof Π to convince a verifier that $\mathcal{TM}$ accepts P, x, y in T. A publicly verifiable semi-trusted SNARG (stSNARG) for $\mathcal{TM}$ has the following polynomial time algorithms:

- stSNARG.Setup$(1^\lambda, 1^T)$: A randomized setup algorithm which on input security parameter λ, and number of Turing Machine steps T, outputs crs.
- stSNARG.TrustHash(crs, P): A deterministic and honest algorithm which on input crs and a program $P \in \{0, 1\}^m$ for some $m < 2^\lambda$, outputs a succinct and public digest H_P of P corresponding to crs.

- stSNARG.P(crs, P, x, y, H_P): A deterministic prover algorithm which on input the crs, $P \in \{0,1\}^m$ for some $m < 2^\lambda$, $x \in \{0,1\}^n$ for some $n < 2^\lambda$, $y \in \{0,1\}$ and the digest H_P outputs a proof Π.
- stSNARG.V(crs, x, y, H_P, Π): A deterministic verification algorithm which on input crs, x, y, digest H_P and proof Π, either accepts(output 1) or rejects(output 0) it.

A Universal Turing Machine $\mathcal{TM}$ on input (P, x, y) outputs 1 if it accepts (P, x, y) within T steps. We define the NP language $\mathcal{L_{TM}}$ as,

$$\mathcal{L_{TM}} := \{(P, x, y, T, H_P, \text{crs}) | \mathcal{TM}(P, x, y) = 1 \land \text{stSNARG.TrustHash}(\text{crs}, P) = H_P\}.$$

Note that here P is not considered a part of the witness although it is unknown to the verifier because a typical NP statement puts a there exists constraint on the witness. In that case, the statement becomes trivial because there will always exist a program P which on input x ignores the input and outputs y. We need to ensure that P is the program output by the program author independent of x. Moreover, this is indeed a P statement for the prover.

A publicly verifiable stSNARG scheme stSNARG = (stSNARG.Setup, stSNARG.TrustHash, stSNARG.P, stSNARG.V) satisfies the following properties:

- **Completeness.** For every $\lambda, T, n, m \in \mathbb{N}$ such that $T, n, m < 2^\lambda$, program $P \in \{0,1\}^m$, input $x \in \{0,1\}^n$ and output $y \in \{0,1\}$ such that $(P, x, y, T, H_P, \text{crs}) \in \mathcal{L_{TM}}$, we have

$$\Pr[\text{stSNARG.V}(\text{crs}, x, y, H_P, \Pi) = 1 | \text{crs} \leftarrow \text{stSNARG.Setup}(1^\lambda, 1^T),$$
$$H_P \leftarrow \text{stSNARG.TrustHash}(\text{crs}, P), \Pi \leftarrow \text{stSNARG.P}(\text{crs}, P, x, y, H_P)] = 1.$$

- **Efficiency.** stSNARG.Setup runs in time poly(λ, T), stSNARG.TrustHash runs in time poly$(\lambda, |P|, T)$, stSNARG.P runs in time poly$(\lambda, |x|, |P|, T)$ and outputs a proofs of length poly$(\lambda, \log T)$, and stSNARG.V runs in time poly$(\lambda, \log T)$.
- **Soundness.** For every PPT adversary $\mathcal{A} := (\mathcal{A}_1, \mathcal{A}_2)$ and the tuple $T = T(\lambda), n = n(\lambda), m = m(\lambda)$, there exists a negligible function negl(λ) such that for every $\lambda \in \mathbb{N}$,

$$\Pr[\text{stSNARG.V}(\text{crs}, x, y, H_P, \Pi) = 1 \land (P, x, y, T, H_P, \text{crs}) \notin \mathcal{L_{TM}} |,$$
$$\text{crs} \leftarrow \text{stSNARG.Setup}(1^\lambda, 1^T), (P, \text{aux}) \leftarrow \mathcal{A}_1(1^\lambda, \text{crs}),$$
$$H_P \leftarrow \text{stSNARG.TrustHash}(\text{crs}, P), (x, y, \Pi) \leftarrow \mathcal{A}_2(\text{crs}, P, H_P, \text{aux})] \leq \text{negl}(\lambda).$$

Protocol 1 (Semi-Trusted SNARG)

- stSNARG.Setup($1^\lambda, 1^T$) :
  - SE.$K_{\text{even}} \leftarrow$ SE.Gen($1^\lambda, 1^{M_{\lambda,T}}, 1^{L_\lambda}$)[a]
  - SE.$K_{\text{odd}} \leftarrow$ SE.Gen($1^\lambda, 1^M, 1^L$)
  - BARG.crs $\leftarrow$ BARG.Gen($1^\lambda, 1^{T+1}, 1^{|C_{\text{index}}|}$)
  - dk $\leftarrow$ HT.Gen(1^λ)
  - *return* crs $:=$ (SE.K_{even}, SE.K_{odd}, BARG.crs, dk).
- stSNARG.TrustHash(crs, P)
  - (tree$_0^2$, rt$_0^2$) $\leftarrow$ HT.Hash(dk, P), $H_P \leftarrow$ rt$_0^2$
  - *return* H_P.
- stSNARG.P(crs, P, x, y, H_P) :
  - $\square := $ *empty string*
  - (tree$_0^1$, rt$_0^1$) $\leftarrow$ HT.Hash(dk, x), (tree$_0^2$, rt$_0^2$) $\leftarrow$ HT.Hash(dk, P), (tree$_0^3$, rt$_0^3$) $\leftarrow$ HT.Hash(dk, $\square$)
  - *initialize* s *with the* start *state of* $\mathcal{TM}$
  - st$_0 := (0, 0, 0, \mathsf{s})$
  - h$_0 := (\mathsf{st}_0, \mathsf{rt}_0^1, \mathsf{rt}_0^2, \mathsf{rt}_0^3)$
  - *for every* $i = 1$ *to* T,
    $$\mathsf{rt}_i^1 \leftarrow \mathsf{rt}_{i-1}^1, \mathsf{rt}_i^2 \leftarrow \mathsf{rt}_{i-1}^2$$
    $$(l_i^1, l_i^2, l_i^3) \leftarrow \mathsf{StepR}(\mathsf{st}_{i-1})$$
    $$\left\{(b_i^j, \mathit{\Pi}_i^j) \leftarrow \mathsf{HT.Read}(\mathsf{tree}_{i-1}^j, l_i^j)\right\}_{j \in [3]}$$
    $$(b_i', l_i', \mathsf{st}_i) \leftarrow \mathsf{StepW}(\mathsf{st}_{i-1}, b_i^1, b_i^2, b_i^3)$$
    $$(\mathsf{tree}_i^3, \mathsf{rt}_i^3, \mathit{\Pi}_i') \leftarrow \mathsf{HT.Write}(\mathsf{tree}_{i-1}^3, l_i'^3, b_i'^3)$$
    $$\mathsf{h}_i \leftarrow (\mathsf{st}_i, \mathsf{rt}_i^1, \mathsf{rt}_i^2, \mathsf{rt}_i^3)$$
  - $A := \left(\mathsf{h}_1, (\mathsf{h}_1, \{b_1^j, \mathit{\Pi}_1^j\}_{j \in [3]}, \mathit{\Pi}_1'), \ldots, (\mathsf{h}_T, \{b_T^j, \mathit{\Pi}_T^j\}_{j \in [3]}, \mathit{\Pi}_T')\right)$
  - $c_{\text{even}} \leftarrow$ SE.Hash(SE.K_{even}, A) *and* $c_{\text{odd}} \leftarrow$ SE.Hash(SE.K_{odd}, A)
  - $c := (c_{\text{even}}, c_{\text{odd}})$
  - $I_x \leftarrow \{[i_1, i_2] | A[i_1, i_2] = x\}$
  - $\rho_{\mathsf{h}_0} \leftarrow$ SE.Open(SE.$K_{\text{even}}, A, I_{\mathsf{h}_0}$)[b]
  - *for every* $i \leq \lfloor\lfloor T/2 \rfloor\rfloor$,
    for $B \in \{\mathsf{h}_{2i}, \{b_{2i}^j, \mathit{\Pi}_{2i}^j\}_{j \in [3]}, \mathit{\Pi}_{2i}'\}, \rho_B \leftarrow$ SE.Open(SE.K_{even}, A, I_B)
  - *for every* $i \leq \lfloor\lfloor T/2 \rfloor\rfloor$,
    for $B \in \{\mathsf{h}_{2i+1}, \{b_{2i+1}^j, \mathit{\Pi}_{2i+1}^j\}_{j \in [3]}, \mathit{\Pi}_{2i+1}'\}, \quad \rho_B \quad :=$ SE.Open(SE.K_{odd}, A, I_B)
  - *Let* C_{index} *be as defined in Figure 3*
  - $\mathit{\Pi} :=$ BARG.P$\Big($crs, C_{index}, h$_0$, $\{\mathsf{h}_{i-1}, \mathsf{h}_i, \{b_i^j, \mathit{\Pi}_i^j\}_{j \in [3]}, \mathit{\Pi}_i', \rho_{\mathsf{h}_{i-1}}, \rho_{\mathsf{h}_i},$
    $\{\rho_{b_i^j}, \rho_{\mathit{\Pi}_i^j}\}_{j \in [3]}, \rho_{\mathit{\Pi}_i'}\}_{i \in [T]}\Big)$
  - *return* $(c, \mathit{\Pi})$ [c].
- stSNARG.V(crs, $(x, y), H_P, (c, \mathit{\Pi})$) :
  - *Compute* C_{index}
  - *return* 1 *if and only if* BARG.V(BARG.crs, $C_{\text{index}}, \mathit{\Pi}$) = 1.

---

[a]$M_{\lambda,T} = O(T \, \mathsf{poly}(\lambda))$ and $L_\lambda = O(\mathsf{poly}(\lambda))$ are arbitrary and efficiently computable values which can be fixed in advance and hardcoded to the Setup algorithm during instantiation.

[b]Note that for simplification, we abuse notation here by specifying opening to more than a single bit.

[c] We often abuse notation and use $(c, \mathit{\Pi})$ to denote a proof. This can be done without loss of generality by defining a new proof $\mathit{\Pi}' = (c \| \mathit{\Pi})$.

Fig. 2. Semi-Trusted SNARG

Circuit 1 (Circuit C_{index})

- **Hard-coded:** $y, c, \text{start}, \phi, \text{SE}.K_{\text{even}}, \text{SE}.K_{\text{odd}}, T, H_P, H_x := \text{HT.Hash}(\text{dk}, x)$
- **Input:**
  $$\left(i, (h_i := (\text{st}_i, \text{rt}_i^1, \text{rt}_i^2, \text{rt}_i^3), \rho_{h_i})\right), \text{ if } i = 0$$
  $$\left(i, (\{h_{i-1}, h_i, \{b_i^j, \Pi_i^j\}_{j \in [3]}, \Pi_i', \rho_{h_{i-1}}, \rho_{h_i}, \{\rho_{b_i^j}, \rho_{\Pi_i^j}\}_{j \in [3]}, \rho_{\Pi_i'}\})\right), \forall i \in [T]$$
- **Output:** return 1 if and only if
  - if $i = 0$
    - $a.$ $\text{st}_0 = \text{start}$
    - $b.$ $H_x = \text{rt}_0^1$
    - $c.$ $H_P = \text{rt}_0^2$
    - $d.$ $\text{HT.Hash}(\text{dk}, \square)$ has rt_0^3 as root
  - else
    - * if i is even:
      - $a.$ $\text{SE.Verify}(\text{SE}.K_{\text{odd}}, c_{\text{odd}}, h_{i-1}, \rho_{h_{i-1}}) = 1$
      - $b.$ $\text{SE.Verify}(\text{SE}.K_{\text{even}}, c_{\text{even}}, h_i, \rho_{h_i}) = 1$
      - $c.$ $\left\{\text{SE.Verify}(\text{SE}.K_{\text{even}}, c_{\text{even}}, b_i^j, \rho_{b_i^j}) = 1\right\}_{j \in [3]}$
      - $d.$ $\left\{\text{SE.Verify}(\text{SE}.K_{\text{even}}, c_{\text{even}}, \Pi_i^j, \rho_{\Pi_i^j}) = 1\right\}_{j \in [3]}$
      - $e.$ $\text{SE.Verify}(\text{SE}.K_{\text{even}}, c_{\text{even}}, \Pi_i', \rho_{\Pi_i'}) = 1$
    - * if i is odd:
      - $a.$ $\text{SE.Verify}(\text{SE}.K_{\text{even}}, c_{\text{even}}, h_{i-1}, \rho_{h_{i-1}}) = 1$
      - $b.$ $\text{SE.Verify}(\text{SE}.K_{\text{odd}}, c_{\text{odd}}, h_i, \rho_{h_i}) = 1$
      - $c.$ $\left\{\text{SE.Verify}(\text{SE}.K_{\text{odd}}, c_{\text{odd}}, b_i^j, \rho_{b_i^j}) = 1\right\}_{j \in [3]}$
      - $d.$ $\left\{\text{SE.Verify}(\text{SE}.K_{\text{odd}}, c_{\text{odd}}, \Pi_i^j, \rho_{\Pi_i^j}) = 1\right\}_{j \in [3]}$
      - $e.$ $\text{SE.Verify}(\text{SE}.K_{\text{odd}}, c_{\text{odd}}, \Pi_i', \rho_{\Pi_i'}) = 1$
    - * $\phi(h_{i-1}, h_i, \{b_i^j, \Pi_i^j\}_{j \in [3]}, \Pi_i') = 1$
    - * if $i = T$
      - $a.$ $\text{HT.Hash}(\text{dk}, y)$ has rt_T^3 as root.
      - $b.$ st_T indeed encodes the **accept** state.

Fig. 3. Circuit C_{index}

5.1   Our Construction

Our construction is formulated similar to that of [10]. Specifically, we use the notion of non-interactive BARG for index language and SE Hash functions in our scheme.

Setup for Universal Turing Machine. For a cleaner analysis, we assume without loss of generality that $\mathcal{TM}$ consists of three tapes, namely, $\text{Tp}_1, \text{Tp}_2, \text{Tp}_3$. Tp_1 and Tp_2 are read only tapes that store x and P respectively. Tp_3 is the work tape which is initialized with $\square$ to denote an empty string.

Transition steps for $\mathcal{TM}$. $\mathcal{TM}$'s state information along with the head locations of the three tapes are encoded as st. To handle Turing Machines with arbitrarily long tapes, we encode $\{\mathsf{Tp}_i\}_{i\in[3]}$ using three Hash Trees as defined in previous sections and produce tree roots $\mathsf{rt}^1, \mathsf{rt}^2, \mathsf{rt}^3$ respectively.

Let the each intermediate transition state of $\mathcal{TM}$ be encoded as $h_i := (\mathsf{st}_i, \mathsf{rt}_i^1, \mathsf{rt}_i^2, \mathsf{rt}_i^3)$ for $i \in [T]$. A single step of $\mathcal{TM}$ can be interpreted in the manner described below which is similar to one described for a RAM in [23]. We break down the step function at the ith stage into two deterministic polynomial time algorithms:

- StepR: On input st_{i-1} of $\mathcal{TM}$, outputs head positions $l_{i-1}^1, l_{i-1}^2, l_{i-1}^3$ which denote the memory locations of $\mathsf{Tp}_1, \mathsf{Tp}_2, \mathsf{Tp}_3$ which $\mathcal{TM}$ in the current state st_{i-1} would read from.
- StepW: On input st_{i-1}, and bits $b_{i-1}^1, b_{i-1}^2, b_{i-1}^3$ outputs bit b', location l' and st_i such that $\mathcal{TM}$ upon reading $b_{i-1}^1, b_{i-1}^2, b_{i-1}^3$ at locations $l_{i-1}^1, l_{i-1}^2, l_{i-1}^3$ using HT.Read, would write b' at location l' of Tp_3, thereby transition to new state st_i.

Now, we translate the ith single step of $\mathcal{TM}$ to the circuit ϕ which is defined such that on input digests $h_{i-1} := (\mathsf{st}_{i-1}, \mathsf{rt}_{i-1}^1, \mathsf{rt}_{i-1}^2, \mathsf{rt}_{i-1}^3)$ and $h_i := (\mathsf{st}_i, \mathsf{rt}_i^1, \mathsf{rt}_i^2, \mathsf{rt}_i^3)$, bits b_i^1, b_i^2, b_i^3, and proofs $\Pi_i^1, \Pi_i^2, \Pi_i^3, \Pi_i'$, $\phi(h_{i-1}, h_i, b_i^1, b_i^2, b_i^3, \Pi_i^1, \Pi_i^2, \Pi_i^3, \Pi_i') = 1$ if and only if the following hold:

1. $(l_i^1, l_i^2, l_i^3) \leftarrow \mathsf{StepR}(\mathsf{st}_{i-1})$
2. $(b', l', \mathsf{st}') \leftarrow \mathsf{StepW}(\mathsf{st}_{i-1}, b_i^1, b_i^2, b_i^3)$
3. $\mathsf{st}' = \mathsf{st}_i$
4. $\mathsf{HT.VerRead}(\mathsf{dk}, \mathsf{rt}_{i-1}^1, l_i^1, b_i^1, \Pi_i^1) = 1$
5. $\mathsf{HT.VerRead}(\mathsf{dk}, \mathsf{rt}_{i-1}^2, l_i^2, b_i^2, \Pi_i^2) = 1$

6. $\mathsf{HT.VerRead}(\mathsf{dk}, \mathsf{rt}_{i-1}^3, l_i^3, b_i^3, \Pi_i^3) = 1$
7. $\mathsf{rt}_i^1 = \mathsf{rt}_{i-1}^1$
8. $\mathsf{rt}_i^2 = \mathsf{rt}_{i-1}^2$
9. $\mathsf{HT.VerWrite}(\mathsf{dk}, \mathsf{rt}_{i-1}^3, l', b', \mathsf{rt}_i^3, \Pi_i') = 1$

Here, dk denote the hash keys used to build the three hash trees. Note that the efficiency of hash tree implies that ϕ can be constructed such that it can represented as a formula in $L = \mathsf{poly}(\lambda)$ variables. For the T steps of $\mathcal{TM}$, we have the following formula over $M = O(L \cdot T)$ variables:

$$\Phi(h_0, \{h_i, b_i^1, b_i^2, b_i^3, \Pi_i^1, \Pi_i^2, \Pi_i^3, \Pi_i'\}_{i\in[T]}) = \bigwedge_{i\in[T]} \phi(h_{i-1}, h_i, b_i^1, b_i^2, b_i^3, \Pi_i^1, \Pi_i^2, \Pi_i^3, \Pi_i')$$

Following the techniques in [10], we use a combination of SE Hash along with ϕ to produce the circuit for index languages.

Our semi-trusted SNARG scheme is given in Fig. 2 and the corresponding index language circuit is shown as Fig. 3.

Theorem 3. *Assuming the existence of Somewhere Extractable Hash functions, non-interactive Batch Arguments for Index Languages, and Collision Resistant Hash Trees as described in Sect. 3, Fig. 2 is a publicly verifiable non-interactive semi-trusted SNARG with CRS size, proof size and verifier time $\mathsf{poly}(\lambda, \log T)$ and prover run time being $\mathsf{poly}(\lambda, T)$.*

Completeness. Here we give a sketch arguing completeness of our scheme. Our construction in Fig. 2 tells that

$$\Pr[\mathsf{stSNARG.V}(\mathsf{crs}, x, y, H_P, \Pi) = 1 \,|\, \mathsf{crs} \leftarrow \mathsf{stSNARG.Setup}(1^\lambda, 1^T),$$
$$H_P \leftarrow \mathsf{stSNARG.TrustHash}(\mathsf{crs}, P), \Pi \leftarrow \mathsf{stSNARG.P}(\mathsf{crs}, P, x, y, H_P)] =$$
$$\Pr[\mathsf{BARG.V}(\mathsf{BARG.crs}, C_{\mathsf{index}}, \Pi) = 1 \,|\, \mathsf{crs} \leftarrow \mathsf{stSNARG.Setup}(1^\lambda, 1^T),$$
$$H_P \leftarrow \mathsf{stSNARG.TrustHash}(\mathsf{crs}, P), \Pi \leftarrow \mathsf{stSNARG.P}(\mathsf{crs}, P, x, y, H_P)]$$

where C_{index} is the index circuit as shown in Fig. 3. Observing $\mathsf{stSNARG.P}$ algorithm in our scheme tells it is sufficient to show that if the prover is honest and uses a valid witness, then $(C_{\mathsf{index}}, i) \in \mathcal{L}_{\mathsf{index}}, \forall i \in \{0\} \cup [T]$. If we can argue that this is indeed the case, then the completeness of BARG gives the desired result.

If $(P, x, y, T, H_P, \mathsf{crs}) \in \mathcal{L}_{\mathcal{TM}}$, then $(C_{\mathsf{index}}, 0) \in \mathcal{L}_{\mathsf{index}}$ is trivially true by observation. Now, let us look at $(C_{\mathsf{index}}, 1)$. We start by analysing that $\phi(\mathsf{h}_0, \mathsf{h}_1, \{b_1^j, \Pi_1^j\}_{j \in [3]}, \Pi_1') = 1$ is true. $\{\mathsf{rt}_1^i = \mathsf{rt}_0^i\}_{i \in [2]}$ follow from the read-only nature of tapes $\mathsf{Tp}_1, \mathsf{Tp}_2$. Since, $\left\{ (b_1^j, \Pi_1^j) \leftarrow \mathsf{HT.Read}(\mathsf{tree}_0^j, l_1^j) \right\}_{j \in [3]}$, the hash tree completeness of read ensures that $\{\mathsf{HT.VerRead}(\mathsf{dk}, \mathsf{rt}_1^i, l_1^i, b_1^i, \Pi_1^i) = 1\}_{i \in [3]} = 1$ and $\{\mathsf{Tp}_i[l_1^i] = b_1^i\}_{i \in [3]}$. This along with the correctness of Turing Machine StepR function implies that b_1^1, b_1^2, b_1^3 are indeed the correct input for the StepW function of $\mathcal{TM}$. Finally, $(\mathsf{tree}_1^3, \mathsf{rt}_1^3, \Pi_1') \leftarrow \mathsf{HT.Write}(\mathsf{tree}_0^3, l_1', b_1')$ implies $\mathsf{HT.VerWrite}(\mathsf{dk}, \mathsf{rt}_0^3, l', b', \mathsf{rt}_1^3, \Pi_1') = 1$ from the hash tree completeness of write property. The same property also ensures that Tp_3 changes only at the l'^{th} memory location. When paired with the correctness of StepW, we get that $\mathsf{st}_1 = \mathsf{st}'$

The completeness of the SE hash implies that the verification algorithm certainly accepts all the local openings. Thus, $(C_{\mathsf{index}}, 1) \in \mathcal{L}^{\mathsf{index}}$. Now, $(C_{\mathsf{index}}, T) \in \mathcal{L}^{\mathsf{index}}$ because $\mathcal{TM}$ accept (P, x, y) in T steps. We can show in a similar manner that for all other i, $(C_{\mathsf{index}}, i) \in \mathcal{L}^{\mathsf{index}}$. This proves the completeness of the scheme in Fig. 2.

Efficiency.

- Runtime of $\mathsf{stSNARG.Setup}$ is $\mathsf{poly}(\lambda, T)$. This follows from the efficiency of underlying primitives.
- $\mathsf{stSNARG.TrustHash}$ computes H_P in time $|P| \cdot \mathsf{poly}(\lambda)$ which is $\mathsf{poly}(|P|, \lambda)$.
- $|C_{\mathsf{index}}| = \mathsf{poly}(\lambda, \log T)$. This follows from the efficiency of the SE hash and the efficiency of hash tree construction.
- CRS Size: By the corresponding properties of the underlying primitives, $|\mathsf{crs}| = \mathsf{poly}(\lambda, \log T)$.
- The prover's computation time is dominated by the hashes corresponding to x, P and the Turing Machine step functions that is run T times. This requires a total time of $\mathsf{poly}(\lambda, |x|) + \mathsf{poly}(\lambda, |P|) + \mathsf{poly}(\lambda, T) = \mathsf{poly}(\lambda, |x|, |P|, T)$.
- Proof Length: $|c| + |\Pi| = \mathsf{poly}(\lambda, \log T) + \mathsf{poly}(\lambda, \log T, |C_{\mathsf{index}}|) = \mathsf{poly}(\lambda, \log T)$.
- Verifier Time: Time taken to compute C_{index} and verify the BARG. This is $\mathsf{poly}(\lambda, \log T, |C_{\mathsf{index}}|) = \mathsf{poly}(\lambda, \log T)$.

Soundness. Let us assume for the sake of contradiction that our scheme in Fig. 2 is not sound, i.e., there exists a PPT adversary $\mathcal{A} := (\mathcal{A}_1, \mathcal{A}_2)$, a value T and a polynomial function $\mathsf{poly}(\lambda)$ such that for infinitely many values of $\lambda \in \mathbb{N}$,

$$\Pr[\mathsf{G}^{\mathcal{A}} = 1] \geq \frac{1}{\mathsf{poly}(\lambda)},$$

where $\mathcal{A}$ plays Game G described below

Real Game G
1. $\mathsf{crs} \leftarrow \mathsf{stSNARG.Setup}(1^\lambda, 1^T)$
2. $(P, \mathsf{aux}) \leftarrow \mathcal{A}_1(1^\lambda, \mathsf{crs})$
3. $H_P \leftarrow \mathsf{stSNARG.TrustHash}(\mathsf{crs}, P)$
4. $((x, y)(c, \Pi)) \leftarrow \mathcal{A}_2(\mathsf{crs}, P, H_P, \mathsf{aux})$
5. if $\mathsf{stSNARG.V}(\mathsf{crs}, (x, y), H_P, (c, \Pi)) = 1 \wedge ((x, y), T, P, H_P, \mathsf{crs}) \notin \mathcal{L}_{\mathcal{TM}}$, return 1
6. else return 0

Let S_i denote the following set:

$$S_i = \begin{cases} \mathsf{h}_0 & \text{if } i = 0 \\ \{\mathsf{h}_i, \{b_i\}_{j \in [3]}, \{\Pi_i\}_{j \in [3]}, \Pi'_i\} & \text{if } i \in [T] \end{cases}$$

Let D denote the string $\left(\mathsf{h}_0, \{\mathsf{h}_i, \{b_i\}_{j\in[3]}, \{\Pi_i\}_{j\in[3]}, \Pi'_i\}_{i\in[T]}\right)$. $I_{S_i} \subset |D|$ denotes the following:

$$I_{S_i} = \left\{[a, b] \,\middle|\, a, b \in |D|, D[a, b] = S_i\right\}.$$

In game G, say we have $(\mathsf{tree}_0^1, \mathsf{rt}_0^1) \leftarrow \mathsf{HT.Hash}(\mathsf{dk}, x)$, $(\mathsf{tree}_0^2, \mathsf{rt}_0^2) \leftarrow \mathsf{HT.Hash}(\mathsf{dk}, P)$, $(\mathsf{tree}_0^3, \mathsf{rt}_0^3) \leftarrow \mathsf{HT.Hash}(\mathsf{dk}, \square)$. Also, let $\mathsf{st}_0 := (0, 0, 0, \mathsf{s})$, where s is the start state of $\mathcal{TM}$. We say that $\bar{\mathsf{h}}_0 := (\mathsf{st}_0, \mathsf{rt}_0^1, \mathsf{rt}_0^2, \mathsf{rt}_0^3)$ defines a unique "true" digest for the starting step of $\mathcal{TM}$.

If $\mathsf{stSNARG.V}(\mathsf{crs}, x, H_P, c, \Pi) = 1$, then Algorithm $Step(x, P, \mathsf{crs}, i)$ in Fig. 4 computes the unique true digest $\bar{\mathsf{h}}_i$ after the ith Turing Machine Step along with the other uniquely correct values of the set $\bar{S}_i := \{\bar{\mathsf{h}}_i, \{\bar{b}_i\}_{j\in[3]}, \{\bar{\Pi}_i\}_{j\in[3]}, \bar{\Pi}'_i\}$. We use the notation $Step(x, P, \mathsf{crs}, i).x$ to denote $x \in \bar{S}_i$. We proceed by performing an induction on the following sequence outer hybrid games G_i, i from 1 to T. We use a sequence of inner hybrid games to transition between subsequent outer hybrids. Our induction hypothesis is that, under suitable assumptions, for all $i \in 1$ to T, there exists a negligible function λ such that,

$$\Pr[\mathsf{G}^{\mathcal{A}} = 1] \leq \Pr[\mathsf{G}_i^{\mathcal{A}} = 1] + \mathsf{negl}(\lambda).$$

Intuitively, the ith game G_i is similar to the real life soundness game with the following two changes: (1) The key generation for the SE hash and BARG is done in the trapdoor mode at the ith game. This allows for extractability of the ith block of the string D from the commitment c. (2) The adversary wins the game if they break the soundness assumption as the real life game G and the extracted block is indeed the correct one.

Algorithm $Step(x, y, P, \text{crs}, i)$

- $\Box := $ empty string
- $(\text{tree}_0^1, \text{rt}_0^1) := \text{HT.Hash}(\text{dk}, x)$, $(\text{tree}_0^2, \text{rt}_0^2) := \text{HT.Hash}(\text{dk}, P)$, $(\text{tree}_0^3, \text{rt}_0^3) := \text{HT.Hash}(\text{dk}, \Box)$
- initialize s with the start state of $\mathcal{TM}$
- $\mathsf{st}_0 := (0, 0, 0, \mathsf{s})$
- $\bar{\mathsf{h}}_0 := (\mathsf{st}_0, \text{rt}_0^1, \text{rt}_0^2, \text{rt}_0^3)$
- if $i = 0$, return $\bar{S}_0 := (\mathsf{st}_0, \text{rt}_0^1, \text{rt}_0^2, \text{rt}_0^3)$
- else
  - for $\text{count} = 1$ to i,
    $(l_{\text{count}}^1, l_{\text{count}}^2, l_{\text{count}}^3) \leftarrow \text{StepR}(\mathsf{st}_{\text{count}-1})$
    $\left\{ (b_{\text{count}}^k, \Pi_{\text{count}}^k) := \text{HT.Read}(\text{tree}_{\text{count}-1}^k, l_{\text{count}}^k) \right\}_{k \in [3]}$
    $(b_{\text{count}}'^3, l_{\text{count}}'^3, \mathsf{st}_{\text{count}}) := \text{StepW}(\mathsf{st}_{\text{count}-1}, b_{\text{count}}^1, b_{\text{count}}^2, b_{\text{count}}^3)$
    $(\text{tree}_{\text{count}}^3, \text{rt}_{\text{count}}^3, \Pi_{\text{count}}') := \text{HT.Write}(\text{tree}_{\text{count}-1}^3, l_{\text{count}}'^3, b_{\text{count}}'^3)$
  - $\bar{\mathsf{h}}_i := (\mathsf{st}_i, \text{rt}_i^1, \text{rt}_i^2, \text{rt}_i^3)$
  - $\bar{b}_i := (b_i^1, b_i^2, b_i^3)$
  - $\bar{l}_i := (l_i^1, l_i^2, l_i^3)$
  - $\bar{\text{rt}}_i := \text{rt}_{i-1}^1, \text{rt}_{i-1}^2, \text{rt}_i^3$
  - $\bar{\Pi}_i := (\Pi_i^1, \Pi_i^2, \Pi_i^3, \Pi_i')$
  - return $\bar{S}_i := (\bar{\mathsf{h}}_i, \bar{b}_i, \bar{\text{rt}}_i, \bar{\Pi}_i)$

Fig. 4. Turing Machine i^{th} step.

Outer Hybrid Game G_i

1. if i is even
   $\text{SE.}K_{\text{even}} \leftarrow \text{SE.TGen}(1^\lambda, 1^M, I_{S_i})$
   $\text{SE.}K_{\text{odd}} \leftarrow \text{SE.TGen}(1^\lambda, 1^M, I_{S_{i-1}})$
2. if i is odd
   $\text{SE.}K_{\text{even}} \leftarrow \text{SE.TGen}(1^\lambda, 1^M, I_{S_{i-1}})$
   $\text{SE.}K_{\text{odd}} \leftarrow \text{SE.TGen}(1^\lambda, 1^M, I_{S_i})$
3. $\text{BARG.crs} \leftarrow \text{BARG.TGen}(1^\lambda, 1^{T+1}, 1^{|C_{\text{index}}|}, i)$
4. $\text{dk} \leftarrow \text{HT.Gen}(1^\lambda)$
5. $\text{crs} := (\text{SE.}K_{\text{even}}, \text{SE.}K_{\text{odd}}, \text{BARG.crs}, \text{dk})$.
6. $(P, \text{aux}) \leftarrow \mathcal{A}_1(1^\lambda, \text{crs})$
7. $H_P \leftarrow \text{stSNARG.TrustHash}(\text{crs}, P)$
8. $((x, y), (c, \Pi)) \leftarrow \mathcal{A}_2(\text{crs}, P, \text{aux})$
9. Parse c as $(c_{\text{odd}}, c_{\text{even}})$
10. if i is even and $i \neq 0$
    - $(\mathsf{h}_i, \{b_i^k\}_{k \in [3]}, \{\Pi_i^k\}_{k \in [3]}, \Pi_i') \leftarrow \text{SE.Ext}_{\text{even}}(c_{\text{even}}, \text{SE.}K_{\text{even}})$
    - $(\mathsf{h}_{i-1}, \{b_{i-1}^k\}_{k \in [3]}, \{\Pi_{i-1}^k\}_{k \in [3]}, \Pi_{i-1}') \leftarrow \text{SE.Ext}_{\text{odd}}(c_{\text{odd}}, \text{SE.}K_{\text{odd}})$
11. if i is odd
    - $(\mathsf{h}_i, \{b_i^k\}_{k \in [3]}, \{\Pi_i^k\}_{k \in [3]}, \Pi_i') \leftarrow \text{SE.Ext}_{\text{odd}}(c_{\text{odd}}, \text{SE.}K_{\text{odd}})$
    - if $i - 1 > 0$ then $(\mathsf{h}_{i-1}, \{b_{i-1}^k\}_{k \in [3]}, \{\Pi_{i-1}^k\}_{k \in [3]}, \Pi_{i-1}') \leftarrow \text{SE.Ext}_{\text{even}}(c_{\text{even}}, \text{SE.}K_{\text{even}})$
    - if $i - 1 = 0$ then $\mathsf{h}_0 \leftarrow \text{SE.Ext}_{\text{even}}(c_{\text{even}}, \text{SE.}K_{\text{even}})$

12. if stSNARG.V $(\text{crs}, (x, y), H_P, (c, \Pi)) = 1 \wedge ((x, y), T, P, H_P, \text{crs}) \notin \mathcal{L}_{TM} \wedge$
    $h_i = Step(x, y, P, \text{crs}, i).\bar{h}_i$, return 1
13. else return 0

Base Case: Assuming key indistinguishability and soundness of SE hash and BARG, we need to show that $\Pr[G^{\mathcal{A}} = 1] \leq \Pr[G_1^{\mathcal{A}} = 1] + \text{negl}(\lambda)$.

We begin by using a sequence of hybrids to transition from G to an intermediate game G_0. The colored texts in the hybrids below indicate the steps in the hybrids exclusively appear in a particular game. We only present proof sketches for the intermediate lemmas in this section due to lack of space. Concrete proofs have been shifted to the Supplementary Material.

Hybrid Games G_a, G_b, G_{ab}, G_0
1. $\text{SE.}K_{\text{even}} \leftarrow \text{SE.TGen}(1^\lambda, 1^M, I_{S_0})$ ...(G_a, G_b, G_{ab}, G_0)
2. $\text{SE.}K_{\text{odd}} \leftarrow \text{SE.Gen}(1^\lambda, 1^M)$ ...(G_a)
3. $\text{SE.}K_{\text{odd}} \leftarrow \text{SE.TGen}(1^\lambda, 1^M, I_{S_1})$ ...(G_b, G_{ab}, G_0)
4. $\text{BARG.crs} \leftarrow \text{BARG.Gen}(1^\lambda, 1^{T+1}, 1^{|C_{\text{index}}|})$...$(G_a, G_b)$
5. $\text{BARG.crs} \leftarrow \text{BARG.TGen}(1^\lambda, 1^{T+1}, 1^{|C_{\text{index}}|}, 0)$...$(G_{ab}, G_0)$
6. $\text{dk} \leftarrow \text{HT.Gen}(1^\lambda)$
7. $\text{crs} := (\text{SE.}K_{\text{even}}, \text{SE.}K_{\text{odd}}, \text{BARG.crs}, \text{dk})$.
8. $(P, \text{aux}) \leftarrow \mathcal{A}_1(1^\lambda, \text{crs})$
9. $H_P \leftarrow \text{stSNARG.TrustHash}(\text{crs}, P)$
10. if stSNARG.V $(\text{crs}, (x, y), H_P, (c, \Pi)) = 1 \wedge ((x, y), T, P, H_P, \text{crs}) \notin \mathcal{L}_{TM}$,
    return 1
11. $h_0 \leftarrow \text{SE.Ext}_{\text{even}}(c_{\text{even}}, \text{SE.}K_{\text{even}})$...$(G_0)$...$(G_a, G_b, G_{ab})$
12. if stSNARG.V $(\text{crs}, (x, y), H_P, (c, \Pi)) = 1 \wedge ((x, y), T, P, H_P, \text{crs}) \notin \mathcal{L}_{TM} \wedge$
    $h_0 = Step(x, y, P, \text{crs}, 0).\bar{h}$, return 1 ...$(G_0)$
13. else return 0

Lemma 2. *Assuming key indistinguishability of* SE, $\left|\Pr[G^{\mathcal{A}} = 1] - \Pr[G_a^{\mathcal{A}} = 1]\right|$ $\leq \text{negl}(\lambda)$.

Proof. The only difference in Game G and G_a is that the key generation algorithm of the SE hash (SE.Gen) is replaced by the trapdoor key generation (SE.TGen).

If $\left|\Pr[G^{\mathcal{A}} = 1] - \Pr[G_a^{\mathcal{A}} = 1]\right| > \text{negl}(\lambda)$, then one can construct a PPT adversary $\mathcal{B}$ that breaks the key indistinguishability of SE using I_{S_0} with Key as input from the key generation algorithm of the SE hash and runs $\mathcal{A}$ on Key. Here, Key is either $\text{SE.Gen}(1^\lambda, 1^M)$ or $\text{SE.TGen}(1^\lambda, 1^M, I_{S_0})$ based on whether $\mathcal{A}$ is interacting with game G or G_a respectively. Note that the reduction can simulate the other steps of games G or G_a. Now, the probability that $\mathcal{B}$ returns 1 in either case is exactly equal to the probability that $\mathcal{A}$ wins the corresponding games, hence, $\mathcal{B}$ breaks if $\left|\Pr[G^{\mathcal{A}} = 1] - \Pr[G_a^{\mathcal{A}} = 1]\right| \geq \text{negl}(\lambda)$. This leads to a contradiction of our assumption.

Lemma 3. *Assuming key indistinguishability of* SE, $\left|\Pr[G_a^{\mathcal{A}} = 1] - \Pr[G_b^{\mathcal{A}} = 1]\right|$ $\leq \text{negl}(\lambda)$.

This again follows from the key-indistinguishability of SE as shown in the previous lemma as the only difference in these games is that the key generation algorithm for the SE hash has been changed to TGen, hence we skip the proof.

Lemma 4. *Assuming key indistinguishability of* BARG, $\left| \Pr[G_b^{\mathcal{A}} = 1] - \Pr[G_{ab}^{\mathcal{A}} = 1] \right| \leq \mathsf{negl}(\lambda)$.

Proof. The only difference in Game G_b and G_{ab} is that the key generation algorithm of the BARG (BARG.Gen) is replaced by the trapdoor key generation (BARG.TGen) at index 0.

If $\left| \Pr[G_b^{\mathcal{A}} = 1] - \Pr[G_{ab}^{\mathcal{A}} = 1] \right| > \mathsf{negl}(\lambda)$, then one can construct a PPT adversary $\mathcal{B}$ getting Key as input that breaks the key indistinguishability of BARG, where Key is either BARG.Gen$(1^\lambda, 1^{T+1}, 1^{|C_{\mathsf{index}}|})$ or BARG.TGen$(1^\lambda, 1^{T+1}, 1^{|C_{\mathsf{index}}|}, 0)$ based on whether $\mathcal{A}$ is interacting with game G_b or G_{ab} respectively. The reduction then following in a similar manner as the SE key indistinguishability adversary described above.

Lemma 5. *Assuming somewhere soundness of* BARG,

$$\left| \Pr[G_{ab}^{\mathcal{A}} = 1] - \Pr[G_0^{\mathcal{A}} = 1] \right| \leq \mathsf{negl}(\lambda).$$

Proof. The only difference in Games G_{ab} and G_0 is that there is an additional step which computes the true digest at index 0 and extracts at the 0th index from c_{even} using the extraction function of SE. Finally, the adversary wins if and only if the extracted value matches the true digest along with the usual win conditions in the previous game.

Note that,

$$\left| \Pr[G_{ab}^{\mathcal{A}} = 1] - \Pr[G_0^{\mathcal{A}} = 1] \right| \leq \Pr[\mathsf{BARG.V}(\mathsf{BARG.crs}, C_{\mathsf{index}}, \Pi) = 1 \wedge$$
$$((x,y), T, P, H_P, \mathsf{crs}) \notin \mathcal{L}_{\mathcal{TM}} \wedge h_0 \neq Step(x, P, \mathsf{crs}, 0).\bar{h}] \leq$$
$$\Pr[\mathsf{BARG.V}(\mathsf{BARG.crs}, C_{\mathsf{index}}, \Pi) = 1 \wedge h_0 \neq Step(x, P, \mathsf{crs}, 0).\bar{h}].$$

Let us assume that there exists a PPT adversary $\mathcal{A}$ such that for infinitely many values of $\lambda \in \mathbb{N}$,

$$\Pr[\mathsf{BARG.V}(\mathsf{BARG.crs}, C_{\mathsf{index}}, \Pi) = 1 \wedge h_0 \neq Step(x, y, P, \mathsf{crs}, 0).\bar{h}] \geq \frac{1}{\mathsf{poly}(\lambda)}.$$

Notice that $h_0 \neq Step(x, P, \mathsf{crs}, 0).\bar{h}$ implies that at least one of the conditions $st_0 = \mathsf{start}$, $H_x = rt_0^1$, $H_P = rt_0^2$ and HT.Hash$(\mathsf{dk}, \square)$ having rt_0^3 as root must not be true. If this is indeed true then our construction of C_{index} in Fig. 3 implies that $(C_{\mathsf{index}}, 0) \notin \mathcal{L}^{\mathsf{index}}$.

We now construct the following PPT adversary $\mathcal{B}$ playing the semi-adaptive somewhere soundness game of the BARG as follows

Adversary $\mathcal{B}$ playing semi adaptive somewhere soundness game of BARG.
- SE.$\mathcal{K}_{\mathsf{even}} \leftarrow$ SE.TGen$(1^\lambda, 1^M, I_{S_0})$
- SE.$\mathcal{K}_{\mathsf{odd}} \leftarrow$ SE.TGen$(1^\lambda, 1^M, I_{S_1})$

- BARG.crs ← BARG.TGen($1^\lambda, 1^{T+1}, 1^{|C_{\text{index}}|}, 0$)
- dk ← HT.Gen(1^λ)
- crs := (SE.K_{even}, SE.K_{odd}, BARG.crs, dk).
- (P, aux) ← $\mathcal{A}_1(1^\lambda, \text{crs})$
- H_P ← stSNARG.TrustHash(crs, P)
- ((x, y), (c, Π)) ← $\mathcal{A}_2$(crs, P, aux)
- return (C_{index}, Π)

By our assumption, it is clear that BARG.V(BARG.crs, C_{index}, Π) = 1 with non negligible probability but ($C_{\text{index}}, 0$) $\notin \mathcal{L}^{\text{index}}$. Thus, $\mathcal{B}$ will break the semi-adaptive somewhere soundness of BARG at index 0. Therefore, it must be the case that for every PPT adversary $\mathcal{A}$, there exists a negligible function negl(λ) such that for all $\lambda \in \mathbb{N}$,

$$\Pr[\text{BARG.V}(\text{BARG.crs}, C_{\text{index}}, \Pi) = 1 \wedge h_0 \neq Step(x, y, P, \text{crs}, 0).\bar{h}] \leq \text{negl}(\lambda)$$

$$\implies \left| \Pr[\mathsf{G}^{\mathcal{A}}_{ab} = 1] - \Pr[\mathsf{G}^{\mathcal{A}}_0 = 1] \right| \leq \text{negl}(\lambda)$$

Now, we transition from G_0 to the base case for our induction, G_1 using the following sequence of indistinguishable hybrids:

$\mathsf{G}_{0,a}$ Identical to G_0 except we add an extraction: ($h_1, \{b_1^k\}_{k \in [3]}, \{\Pi_1^k\}_{k \in [3]}, \Pi_i'$) ← SE.Ext$_{\text{odd}}$($c_{\text{odd}}$, SE.$K_{\text{odd}}$) which is not used in the hybrid, hence indistinguishability follows.

$\mathsf{G}_{0,b}$ The BARG key generation's trapdoor is changed from 0 to 1. This can be done due to key indistinguishability of BARG.

$\mathsf{G}_{0,c}$ The winning condition is changed to: if stSNARG.V (crs, (x, y), H_P, (c, Π)) = 1 $\wedge$ ((x, y), T, P, H_P, crs) $\notin \mathcal{L}_{TM} \wedge h_0 = Step(x, y, P, \text{crs}, 0).\bar{h} \wedge \{b_1^k\}_{k \in [3]} = Step(x, y, P, \text{crs}, 1).\bar{b} \wedge \{rt_1^k\}_{k \in [3]} = Step(x, y, P, \text{crs}, 1).\bar{rt} \wedge st_1 = Step(x, y, P, \text{crs}, 1).\bar{st}$, return 1

$\mathsf{G}_{0,d}$ The winning condition is changed to: if stSNARG.V (crs, (x, y), H_P, (c, Π)) = 1 $\wedge$ ((x, y), T, P, H_P, crs) $\notin \mathcal{L}_{TM} \wedge h_0 = Step(x, y, P, \text{crs}, 0).\bar{h} \wedge \{b_1^k\}_{k \in [3]} = Step(x, y, P, \text{crs}, 1).\bar{b} \wedge rt_1^3 = Step(x, y, P, \text{crs}, 1).\bar{rt} \wedge st_1 = Step(x, y, P, \text{crs}, 1).\bar{st} \wedge h_1 = Step(x, y, P, \text{crs}, 1).\bar{h}$, return 1

$\mathsf{G}_{0,e}$ The winning condition is changed to: if stSNARG.V (crs, (x, y), H_P, (c, Π)) = 1 $\wedge$ ((x, y), T, P, H_P, crs) $\notin \mathcal{L}_{TM} \wedge h_1 = Step(x, y, P, \text{crs}, 1).\bar{h}$, return 1

The indistinguishability of the last three hybrids follow from the following lemmas.

Lemma 6. *Assuming semi-adaptive somewhere soundness of* BARG, *extraction correctness of* SE, *read and write soundness of* HT,

$$\left| \Pr[\mathsf{G}^{\mathcal{A}}_{0,b} = 1] - \Pr[\mathsf{G}^{\mathcal{A}}_{0,c} = 1] \right| \leq \text{negl}(\lambda).$$

Proof. The only difference in Games $\mathsf{G}_{0,b}$ and $\mathsf{G}_{0,c}$ is that we have added some additional conditions for the adversary to win along with the ones in the previous game.

Note that,

$$\left|\Pr[\mathsf{G}_{0,b}^{\mathcal{A}} = 1] - \Pr[\mathsf{G}_{0,c}^{\mathcal{A}} = 1]\right| \leq \Pr[\mathsf{BARG.V}(\mathsf{BARG.crs}, C_{\mathsf{index}}, \Pi) = 1 \wedge$$

$$\mathsf{h}_0 = Step(x, P, \mathsf{crs}, 0).\bar{\mathsf{h}} \wedge \left(\{b_1^k\}_{k \in [3]} \neq Step(x, y, P, \mathsf{crs}, 1).\bar{b}\right.$$

$$\left.\vee \{\mathsf{rt}_1^k\}_{k \in [3]} \neq Step(x, y, P, \mathsf{crs}, 1).\bar{\mathsf{rt}} \vee \mathsf{st}_1 = Step(x, y, P, \mathsf{crs}, 1).\bar{\mathsf{st}}\right)].$$

Let us assume that there exists a PPT adversary $\mathcal{A}$ such that for infinitely many values of $\lambda \in \mathbb{N}$,

$$\Pr[\mathsf{BARG.V}(\mathsf{BARG.crs}, C_{\mathsf{index}}, \Pi) = 1 \wedge \mathsf{h}_0 = Step(x, y, P, \mathsf{crs}, 0).\bar{\mathsf{h}}$$

$$\wedge \left(\{b_1^k\}_{k \in [3]} \neq Step(x, y, P, \mathsf{crs}, 1).\bar{b} \vee \{\mathsf{rt}_1^k\}_{k \in [3]} \neq Step(x, y, P, \mathsf{crs}, 1).\bar{\mathsf{rt}}\right.$$

$$\left.\vee \mathsf{st}_1 = Step(x, y, P, \mathsf{crs}, 1).\bar{\mathsf{st}}\right)] \geq \frac{1}{\mathsf{poly}(\lambda)}.$$

Notice that $\mathsf{h}_0 = Step(x, P, \mathsf{crs}, 0).\bar{\mathsf{h}}$ implies that the conditions $\mathsf{st}_0 = \mathsf{start}$, $H_x = \mathsf{rt}_0^1$, $H_P = \mathsf{rt}_0^2$ and $\mathsf{HT.Hash}(\mathsf{dk}, \square)$ having rt_0^3 as root are true. In other words, h_0 is indeed the true digest at step 0.

Assuming extraction correctness of SE, read and write soundness of HT, we construct the following PPT adversary $\mathcal{B}$ playing the semi-adaptive somewhere soundness game of the BARG similar to the one in the proof of Lemma 5.

Thus, $\mathcal{B}$ will break the semi-adaptive somewhere soundness of BARG at index 1 if $(C_{\mathsf{index}}, 1) \notin \mathcal{L}^{\mathsf{index}}$.

It is now left to show that $(C_{\mathsf{index}}, 1) \notin \mathcal{L}^{\mathsf{index}}$.

Case 1 If the SE verifications in C_{index} do not all return 1, then by construction of C_{index}, we have that $(C_{\mathsf{index}}, 1) \notin \mathcal{L}^{\mathsf{index}}$.

Case 2 All SE verifications return 1. Extraction Correctness/ Somewhere binding property of SE hash implies that $\mathsf{h}_0 = (\mathsf{st}_0, \mathsf{rt}_0^1, \mathsf{rt}_0^2, \mathsf{rt}_0^3)$, $\mathsf{h}_1, \{b_1^k, \Pi_1^k\}_{k \in [3]}, \Pi_1'$ were indeed committed by the prover as the Turing machine output at step 0 and step 1. Now, let us analyze $\phi(\mathsf{h}_0, \mathsf{h}_1, \{b_1^k, \Pi_1^k\}_{k \in [3]}, \Pi_1')$. By assumption, we know that $\mathsf{h}_0 = \bar{\mathsf{h}}_0$, i.e., $\bar{\mathsf{st}}_0, \bar{\mathsf{rt}}_0^1, \bar{\mathsf{rt}}_0^2, \bar{\mathsf{rt}}_0^3 = \mathsf{st}_0, \mathsf{rt}_0^1, \mathsf{rt}_0^2, \mathsf{rt}_0^3$. StepR being a deterministic function ensures that (l_1^1, l_1^2, l_1^3) are indeed the correct Turing machine memory locations to be read at step 1. Thus $(\bar{l}_1^1, \bar{l}_1^2, \bar{l}_1^3) = (l_1^1, l_1^2, l_1^3)$. This along with the deterministic nature of hash tree read write operations means that we must have,

- $(\bar{l}_1^1, \bar{l}_1^2, \bar{l}_1^3) \leftarrow \mathsf{StepR}(\bar{\mathsf{st}}_0)$
- $\left\{(\bar{b}_1^j, \bar{\Pi}_1^k) := \mathsf{HT.Read}(\bar{\mathsf{tree}}_0^k, \bar{l}_1^k)\right\}_{k \in [3]}$

- $(\bar{b}_1'^3, \bar{l}_1'^3, \bar{\mathsf{st}}_1) := \mathsf{StepW}(\bar{\mathsf{st}}_0, \bar{b}_1^1, \bar{b}_1^2, \bar{b}_1^3)$
- $(\bar{\mathsf{tree}}_1^3, \bar{\mathsf{rt}}_1^3, \bar{\Pi}_1') := \mathsf{HT.Write}(\bar{\mathsf{tree}}_0^3, \bar{l}_1'^3, \bar{b}_1'^3)$

Read and Write Completeness of the hash tree implies

$\mathsf{HT}.\mathsf{VerRead}(\mathsf{dk}_1, \bar{\mathsf{rt}}_0^1, \bar{l}_1^1, \bar{b}_1^1, \bar{\varPi}_1^1) = 1$

$\mathsf{HT}.\mathsf{VerRead}(\mathsf{dk}_2, \bar{\mathsf{rt}}_0^2, \bar{l}_1^2, \bar{b}_1^2, \bar{\varPi}_1^2) = 1$

$\mathsf{HT}.\mathsf{VerRead}(\mathsf{dk}_3, \bar{\mathsf{rt}}_0^3, \bar{l}_1^3, \bar{b}_1^3, \bar{\varPi}_1^3) = 1$

$\mathsf{HT}.\mathsf{VerWrite}(\mathsf{dk}_3, \bar{\mathsf{rt}}_0^3, \bar{l}_1'^3, \bar{b}_1'^3, \bar{\mathsf{rt}}_1^3 \bar{\varPi}_1') = 1$

If $\{b_1^k\}_{k \in [3]} \neq Step(x, y, P, \mathsf{crs}, 1).\bar{b}$, then the read soundness assumption of HT implies that

$\left(\mathsf{HT}.\mathsf{VerRead}(\mathsf{dk}, \bar{\mathsf{rt}}_0^1, \bar{l}_1^k, b_1^k, \varPi_1^k) = 1\right)_{k \in [3]}$ happens with a negligible probability. Thus, with all but negligible probability we have that $(C_{\mathsf{index}}, 1) \notin \mathcal{L}^{\mathsf{index}}$ and we are done.

Let us say this is not the case, i.e., $\{b_1^k\}_{k \in [3]} = Step(x, y, P, \mathsf{crs}, 1).\bar{b}$, then the deterministic nature of the Turing machine write function StepW implies that $\mathsf{st}_1 = \bar{\mathsf{st}}_1$. Thus, for our assumption to be valid, it must be that $\{\mathsf{rt}_1^k\}_{k \in [3]} \neq Step(x, y, P, \mathsf{crs}, 1).\bar{\mathsf{rt}}$. If $\mathsf{rt}_1^1 \neq \bar{\mathsf{rt}}_1^1 = \mathsf{rt}_0^1$ or $\mathsf{rt}_1^2 \neq \bar{\mathsf{rt}}_1^2 = \mathsf{rt}_0^2$, then the definition of ϕ implies that $(C_{\mathsf{index}}, 1) \notin \mathcal{L}^{\mathsf{index}}$. If this is not the case, then the only other possible option is $\mathsf{rt}_1^3 \neq \bar{\mathsf{rt}}_1^3$. Now, the write soundness of HT implies that with all but negligible probability, $\mathsf{HT}.\mathsf{VerWrite}(\mathsf{dk}_3, \bar{\mathsf{rt}}_0^3, \bar{l}_1'^3, \bar{b}_1'^3, \mathsf{rt}_1^3, \varPi_1) \neq 1$ must hold. If this is indeed true then our construction of C_{index} in Fig. 3 implies that $(C_{\mathsf{index}}, 1) \notin \mathcal{L}^{\mathsf{index}}$.

Lemma 7.

$$\Pr[\mathsf{G}_{0,c}^{\mathcal{A}} = 1] = \Pr[\mathsf{G}_{0,d}^{\mathcal{A}} = 1].$$

Proof. Note that by definition, $h_1 = \mathsf{st}_1, \mathsf{rt}_1^1, \mathsf{rt}_1^2, \mathsf{rt}_1^3$. We already have that $\mathsf{rt}_1^1, \mathsf{rt}_1^2, \mathsf{rt}_1^3 = Step(x, y, P, \mathsf{crs}, 1).\bar{\mathsf{rt}}$ and $\mathsf{st}_1 = Step(x, y, P, \mathsf{crs}, 1).\bar{\mathsf{st}}$. Thus $h_1 = Step(x, y, P, \mathsf{crs}, 1).\bar{h}$ if and only if $\mathsf{rt}_1^3 = Step(x, y, P, \mathsf{crs}, 1).\bar{\mathsf{rt}} \wedge \mathsf{st}_1 = Step(x, y, P, \mathsf{crs}, 1).\bar{\mathsf{st}}$.

Lemma 8.

$$\Pr[\mathsf{G}_{0,d}^{\mathcal{A}} = 1] \leq \Pr[\mathsf{G}_{0,e}^{\mathcal{A}} = 1].$$

Proof. The number of conditions for the adversary to win simply decreases from Game $\mathsf{G}_{0,d}$ to Game $\mathsf{G}_{0,e}$, thus the probability of success must not increase.

A closer observation shows that $\mathsf{G}_{0,e}$ is indeed identical to the case when one puts $i = 1$ in game G_i.

Combining these together, we show the base case of the induction to be true. Thus,

$$\Pr[\mathsf{G}^{\mathcal{A}} = 1] \leq \Pr[\mathsf{G}_1^{\mathcal{A}} = 1] + \mathsf{negl}(\lambda).$$

Assuming that our induction hypothesis holds for some $j \in [T-1]$, we prove that it holds for $j + 1$ as well. We note that by chain rule, it suffices to show that $\Pr[\mathsf{G}_j^{\mathcal{A}} = 1] \leq \Pr[\mathsf{G}_{j+1}^{\mathcal{A}} = 1] + \mathsf{negl}(\lambda)$. We can show this by a sequence of indistinguishable inner hybrids to transition from Game G_j to G_{j+1} which look like the following:

$\mathsf{G}_{j,a}$ Identical to G_j except the SE hash extraction is done at S_{j+1} instead of S_j. Indistinguishability follows from the key indistinguishability of SE hash.

$\mathsf{G}_{j,b}$ Extraction for one of the SE hashes changes from $I_{S_{j-1}}$ to $I_{S_{j+1}}$. However, this does not affect the reduction in any way as extraction at indices $j - 1$ and $j + 1$ are not used by the reduction at any stage.

$\mathsf{G}_{j,c}$ The BARG key generation has a trapdoor at $j + 1$. This can be done due to key indistinguishability of BARG.

$\mathsf{G}_{j,d}$ The winning condition is changed to: if $\mathsf{stSNARG.V}$ ($\mathsf{crs}, (x,y), H_P, (c, \Pi)$) = $1 \wedge ((x,y), T, P, H_P, \mathsf{crs}) \notin \mathcal{L}_{TM} \wedge \mathsf{h}_j = Step(x, y, P, \mathsf{crs}, j).\bar{\mathsf{h}}_j \wedge \{b_{j+1}^k\}_{k \in [3]} = Step(x, y, P, \mathsf{crs}, j + 1).\bar{b}_{j+1} \wedge \mathsf{rt}_{j+1}^3 = Step(x, y, P, \mathsf{crs}, j + 1).\bar{\mathsf{rt}}_{j+1} \wedge \mathsf{st}_1 = Step(x, y, P, \mathsf{crs}, 1).\bar{\mathsf{st}}$, return 1.

$\mathsf{G}_{j,e}$ The winning condition is changed to: if $\mathsf{stSNARG.V}$ ($\mathsf{crs}, (x,y), H_P, (c, \Pi)$) = $1 \wedge ((x,y), T, P, H_P, \mathsf{crs}) \notin \mathcal{L}_{TM} \wedge \mathsf{h}_j = Step(x, y, P, \mathsf{crs}, j).\bar{\mathsf{h}}_j \wedge \{b_{j+1}^k\}_{k \in [3]} = Step(x, y, P, \mathsf{crs}, j + 1).\bar{b}_{j+1} \wedge \mathsf{rt}_{j+1}^3 = Step(x, P, \mathsf{crs}, j + 1).\bar{\mathsf{rt}}_{j+1} \wedge \mathsf{st}_1 = Step(x, y, P, \mathsf{crs}, 1).\bar{\mathsf{st}} \wedge \mathsf{h}_{j+1} = Step(x, y, P, \mathsf{crs}, j + 1).\bar{\mathsf{h}}$, return 1

$\mathsf{G}_{j,f}$ if $\mathsf{stSNARG.V}$ ($\mathsf{crs}, (x,y), H_P, (c, \Pi)$) = $1 \wedge ((x,y), T, P, H_P, \mathsf{crs}) \notin \mathcal{L}_{TM} \wedge \mathsf{h}_{j+1} = Step(x, y, P, \mathsf{crs}, j + 1).\bar{\mathsf{h}}$, return 1

The last three steps follow identically as Lemmas 6, 7, 8.

Observe $\mathsf{G}_{j,f}$ is identical to outer Game G_{j+1} with indices renamed.

Thus, combining the lemmas above, we get

Lemma 9. *Assuming extraction correctness of* SE, *semi-adaptive somewhere soundness of* BARG, *read and write soundness of* HT,

$$\Pr[\mathsf{G}_j^{\mathcal{A}} = 1] \leq \Pr[\mathsf{G}_{j+1}^{\mathcal{A}} = 1] + \mathsf{negl}(\lambda).$$

This follows from the combination of previous lemmas where we showed that the winning probability in the sequence of inner hybrids are either negligibly close to each other or increases (from Game $\mathsf{G}_{j,e}$ to Game $\mathsf{G}_{j,f}$).

Finally, we will show that the winning probability of $\mathcal{A}$ is 0 in the final game G_T.

Lemma 10. *Assuming extraction correctness of* SE *hash,*

$$\Pr[\mathsf{G}_T^{\mathcal{A}} = 1] = 0.$$

Proof. The extraction correctness of SE ensures that h_T was indeed the state committed by the prover. Now, $\mathsf{h}_T = \bar{\mathsf{h}}_T$ cannot be true since our assumption of $(x, y, T, P, H_P, \mathsf{crs}) \notin \mathcal{L}_{TM}$ means that Turing Machine state after T steps cannot be an accept state. Thus, the adversary's win conditions cannot be simultaneously satisfied.

Note that this step does not require us to resort to BARG soundness. Due to our specific construction of $\bar{\mathsf{h}}_T$, all we need ensure is that the state committed by the prover does not correspond to the correct state.

Compiling the lemmas together and using chain rule, it must be true that

$$\Pr[\mathsf{G}^{\mathcal{A}} = 1] \leq \mathsf{negl}(\lambda)$$

which is a contradiction to our assumption that the scheme is not sound.

Lemma 11. *Assuming $T = \mathsf{poly}(m, n)$, $T, m, n \leq 2^\lambda$, the stSNARG protocol in Fig. 2 implies the unconditional existence of a publicly verifiable non interactive succinct delegation scheme* sDel *as defined above.*

Proof. We provide an explicit construction of sDel assuming a semi-trusted SNARG stSNARG. Without loss of generality, we can assume that T is known a-priory.

- sDel.Setup(1^λ): Run stSNARG.Setup to generate crs.
- sDel.ProgAuth(1^λ, crs): Generate a program $P \in \{0,1\}^m$, state and run stSNARG.TrustHash(crs, P) to get H_P.
- sDel.$I(1^\lambda$, crs): Generate $x \in \{0,1\}^n$.
- sDel.W(crs, P, state, H_P, x): Generate $y \in \{0,1\}$ and run stSNARG.P(crs, P, x, y, H_P) to get Π.
- sDel.V(crs, x, y, H_P, Π): Run stSNARG.V(crs, x, y, H_P, Π) return V's output.

Completeness and soundness of sDel follows from the completeness of stSNARG in a straightforward way. Refer to Supplementary material for detailed analysis. The proof size and verifier run time of stSNARG is $\mathsf{poly}(\lambda, \log T) = \mathsf{poly}(\lambda, \log|P|, \log|x|)$. Similarly, the prover run time of sDel is also $\mathsf{poly}(\lambda, |P|, |x|)$.

6   Semi-Trusted Succinct Non-Interactive Argument with Zero Knowledge (ZK-stSNARG)

A publicly verifiable semi-trusted non interactive argument with zero-knowledge scheme ZKstSNARG : (ZKstSNARG.Setup, ZKstSNARG.TrustHash, ZKstSNARG.P, ZKstSNARG.V) is defined as

- ZKstSNARG.Setup(1^λ, 1^T): A randomized setup algorithm which on input security parameter λ, and number of Turing Machine steps T, outputs crs.
- ZKstSNARG.TrustHash(crs, P): A deterministic an honest algorithm which on input crs and a program $P \in \{0,1\}^m$ for some $m < 2^\lambda$, computes a succinct digest H_P of P. It then produces a statistically binding and extractable commitment C_P of H_P under randomness r_1. It then gives out a pair public output POut $= C_P$ and private output SOut $= (H_P, r)$. Here SOut is made available to the prover only.
- ZKstSNARG.P(crs, P, x, y, SOut, POut): A deterministic prover algorithm which on input the crs, $P \in \{0,1\}^m$ for some $m < 2^\lambda$, $x \in \{0,1\}^n$ for some $n < 2^\lambda$, $y \in \{0,1\}$, SOut, and POut outputs a proof Π.
- ZKstSNARG.V(crs, x, y, POut, Π): A deterministic verification algorithm which on input crs, x, y, public output POut of stSNARG.TrustHash and proof Π, either accepts(output 1) or rejects(output 0) it.

We define the following language

$$\mathcal{L}_{\mathcal{TM}} := \{(P, x, y, T, \mathsf{POut}, \mathsf{crs}) \, | \exists (H_P, r_1) \text{ such that } \mathcal{TM}(P, x, y) = 1 \wedge$$
$$(\mathsf{POut}, (H_P, r_1)) = \mathsf{ZKstSNARG.TrustHash}(\mathsf{crs}, P)\}.$$

A ZKstSNARG satisfies the standard completeness, soundness and efficiency properties as stSNARG. It also has an additional property:

Non Interactive Zero Knowledge. For all $(P, x, y, T, \mathsf{POut}, \mathsf{crs}) \in \mathcal{L}_{\mathcal{TM}}$, there exists a PPT simulator $\mathsf{Sim} := (\mathsf{Sim}_1, \mathsf{Sim}_2, \mathsf{Sim}_3)$ such that the distributions of

$$(\mathsf{crs}, x, y, \mathsf{POut}, \Pi) \big| (\mathsf{crs}, \mathsf{aux}) \leftarrow \mathsf{Sim}_1(1^\lambda, 1^T),$$
$$(\mathsf{POut}, \mathsf{aux}') \leftarrow \mathsf{Sim}_2(\mathsf{crs}, \mathsf{aux}),$$
$$\Pi \leftarrow \mathsf{Sim}_3(\mathsf{aux}', \mathsf{crs}, (x, y), \mathsf{POut})$$

and

$$(\mathsf{crs}, x, y, \mathsf{POut}, \Pi) \big| \mathsf{crs} \leftarrow \mathsf{ZKstSNARG.Setup}(1^\lambda, 1^T),$$
$$(\mathsf{POut}, \mathsf{SOut}) \leftarrow \mathsf{ZKstSNARG.TrustHash}(\mathsf{crs}, P),$$
$$\Pi \leftarrow \mathsf{ZKstSNARG.P}(\mathsf{crs}, P, x, y, \mathsf{POut}, \mathsf{SOut})$$

are indistinguishable.

To achieve non interactive zero knowledge, we use the following additional primitives, namely (1) a statistically binding extractable commitment scheme $\mathsf{Com}_{\mathsf{bind}}$ as defined in Sect. 3, and (2) a Non Interactive Zero Knowledge argument $\mathsf{NIZK} := (\mathsf{NIZK.Gen}, \mathsf{NIZK.P}, \mathsf{NIZK.V})$.

The protocol in Fig. 5 demonstrates the extension of stSNARG to achieve Zero-Knowledge. The CRS in Fig. 5 contains a statistically binding commitment to 0. This lets us extend $\mathcal{L}_{\mathcal{TM}}$ to the language,

$$\mathcal{L}_{\mathsf{hyb}} := \left\{ (P, x, y, T, C_P, \mathsf{crs}) \,\big|\, \exists (H_P, r_1) \text{ such that } \mathcal{TM}(P, x, y) = 1 \right.$$

$$\wedge (C_P, (H_P, r_1)) = \mathsf{ZKstSNARG.TrustHash}(\mathsf{crs}, P)$$

$$\left. \vee \Big(\exists r \text{ such that } \mathsf{crs} \text{ contains a commitment to 1 under randomness } r \Big). \right\}$$

such that any witness to $\mathcal{L}_{\mathcal{TM}}$ is vacuously a witness to $\mathcal{L}_{\mathsf{hyb}}$ due to binding property of the commitment. We use NIZK for the following NP language:

$$\mathcal{L} := \left\{ (c.\mathsf{com}, \Pi.\mathsf{com}, (\mathsf{crs}, x, y, T), C_P) \,\big|\, \exists r_1, r_2, r_3, r_4, c, \Pi, H_P \text{ such that} \right.$$

$$\Big(C_P = \mathsf{Com.C}(\mathsf{Com}_{\mathsf{bind}}.Key_1, H_P; r_1) \wedge c.\mathsf{com} = \mathsf{Com.C}(\mathsf{Com}_{\mathsf{bind}}.Key_2, c; r_2)$$

$$\wedge \Pi.\mathsf{com} = \mathsf{Com.C}(\mathsf{Com}_{\mathsf{bind}}.Key_3, \Pi; r_3) \wedge \mathsf{stSNARG.V}(\mathsf{crs}, ((x, y), T, H_P), (c, \Pi)) = 1 \Big)$$

$$\left. \vee \mathsf{crs} \text{ contains } \mathsf{Com.C}(\mathsf{Com}_{\mathsf{bind}}.Key_4, 1; r_4) \right\}$$

Also, note that in this construction, the underlying stSNARG is built for the index circuit C'_{index} which is identical to C_{index} except that H_P is a part of the input and not hard-coded in the circuit as it is not known to the verifier.

Theorem 4. *Assuming the existence of semi-trusted SNARGs and Extractable Statistically Binding Commitment Schemes, and NIZK as described in Sects. 3 and 5, Fig. 5 is a publicly verifiable non-interactive semi-trusted SNARG with zero knowledge such that CRS size, proof size and verifier time are* $\mathsf{poly}(\lambda, \log T)$ *and prover run time is* $\mathsf{poly}(\lambda, T)$.

Protocol 2 (stSNARG with Zero-Knowledge)

- ZKstSNARG.Setup($1^\lambda, T$) :
  - $\mathsf{crs}_1 \leftarrow \mathsf{stSNARG.Setup}(1^\lambda, 1^T)$
  - $\mathsf{Com}_{\mathsf{bind}}.Key_1 \leftarrow \mathsf{Com.Gen}(1^\lambda)$
  - $\mathsf{Com}_{\mathsf{bind}}.Key_2 \leftarrow \mathsf{Com.Gen}(1^\lambda)$
  - $\mathsf{Com}_{\mathsf{bind}}.Key_3 \leftarrow \mathsf{Com.Gen}(1^\lambda)$
  - $\mathsf{Com}_{\mathsf{bind}}.Key_4 \leftarrow \mathsf{Com.Gen}(1^\lambda)$
  - $r_4 \leftarrow_\$ \{0,1\}^\lambda, z \leftarrow \mathsf{Com.C}(\mathsf{Com}.Key_4, 0; r_4)$
  - $\mathsf{NIZK.crs} \leftarrow \mathsf{NIZK.Gen}(1^\lambda)$
  - *return* ($\mathsf{crs}_1, \mathsf{Com}_{\mathsf{bind}}.Key_1.\mathsf{Com}_{\mathsf{bind}}.Key_2, \mathsf{Com}_{\mathsf{bind}}.Key_3, z, \mathsf{NIZK.crs}$).
- ZKstSNARG.TrustHash(crs, P)
  - $H_P \leftarrow \mathsf{stSNARG.TrustHash}(\mathsf{crs}, P)$
  - $r_1 \leftarrow_\$ \{0,1\}^\lambda,\ C_P \leftarrow \mathsf{Com.C}(\mathsf{Com}_{\mathsf{bind}}.Key_1, H_P; r_1)$ *return* ($\mathsf{SOut} := (P, r_1), \mathsf{POut} := C_P$).
- ZKstSNARG.P($\mathsf{crs}, x, y, \mathsf{SOut}, \mathsf{POut}$) :
  - $(c, \Pi) \leftarrow \mathsf{stSNARG.P}(\mathsf{crs}, x, y, H_P)$
  - $r_2 \leftarrow_\$ \{0,1\}^\lambda, c.\mathsf{com} \leftarrow \mathsf{Com.C}(\mathsf{Com}_{\mathsf{bind}}.Key_2, c; r_2)$
  - $r_3 \leftarrow_\$ \{0,1\}^\lambda, \Pi.\mathsf{com} \leftarrow \mathsf{Com.C}(\mathsf{Com}_{\mathsf{bind}}.Key_3, \Pi; r_3)$
  - $\mathsf{NIZK}.\Pi \leftarrow \mathsf{NIZK.Prove}\big(\mathsf{NIZK.crs}, (c.\mathsf{com}, \Pi.\mathsf{com}, (\mathsf{crs}, x, y, T), C_P),$
    $((H_P, r_1), (c, r_2), (\Pi, r_3), \bot)\big)$
  - *return* ($c.\mathsf{com}, \Pi.\mathsf{com}, \mathsf{NIZK}.\Pi$).
- ZKstSNARG.V($\mathsf{crs}, (x, y), \mathsf{POut} = C_P, c.\mathsf{com}, \Pi.\mathsf{com}, \mathsf{NIZK}.\Pi$) :
  - *return* 1 *if and only if*
    $\mathsf{NIZK.V}(\mathsf{NIZK.crs}, (c.\mathsf{com}, \Pi.\mathsf{com}, (\mathsf{crs}, x, y, T), C_P), \mathsf{NIZK}.\Pi) = 1$.

Fig. 5. Semi-Trusted Universal Turing Machine Delegation with Non Interactive Zero-Knowledge

Completeness and Efficiency. Completeness follows from the completeness of the underlying stSNARG, NIZK and the binding property of the commitment. Similarly succinctness follows from the efficiency of stSNARG, NIZK, and the binding commitment $\mathsf{Com}_{\mathsf{bind}}$.

Soundness. The soundness following by a straightforward reduction using the CRS indistinguishability and Statistical Binding of $\mathsf{Com}_{\mathsf{bind}}$, and the soundness of the underlying stSNARG. We can construct an adversary that breaks the soundness of the underlying stSNARG using the following steps:

1 Change the keys for $\mathsf{Com}_{\mathsf{bind}}$ to be generated by TGen. This can be done due to CRS indistinguishability.

2 The reduction can now extract the committed proof from $c.\mathsf{com}$ and $\Pi.\mathsf{com}$. This is because the reduction has access to the trapdoor commitment key.

3 The stSNARG can now output the extracted proof. The extraction correctness of $\mathsf{Com_{bind}}$ ensures that if ZKstSNARG is not sound, then this adversary breaks the soundness of stSNARG.

A formal analysis is presented in the Supplementary Material.

Zero-Knowledge.

zk − stSNARG Simulator $\mathsf{NIZK.Sim} := (\mathsf{Sim_1}, \mathsf{Sim_2}, \mathsf{Sim_3})$

- $\mathsf{Sim_1}(1^\lambda, 1^T)$:
  1. $\mathsf{SE}.K_{\mathsf{even}} \leftarrow \mathsf{SE.Gen}(1^\lambda, 1^{M_{\lambda,T}}, 1^{L_\lambda})$
  2. $\mathsf{SE}.K_{\mathsf{odd}} \leftarrow \mathsf{SE.Gen}(1^\lambda, 1^M, 1^L)$
  3. $\mathsf{BARG.crs} \leftarrow \mathsf{BARG.Gen}(1^\lambda, 1^{T+1}, 1^{|C_{\mathsf{index}}|})$
  4. $\mathsf{dk} \leftarrow \mathsf{HT.Gen}(1^\lambda)$
  5. $\mathsf{Com_{bind}}.Key_1 \leftarrow \mathsf{Com.Gen}(1^\lambda)$
  6. $\mathsf{Com_{bind}}.Key_2 \leftarrow \mathsf{Com.Gen}(1^\lambda)$
  7. $\mathsf{Com_{bind}}.Key_3 \leftarrow \mathsf{Com.Gen}(1^\lambda)$
  8. $\mathsf{Com_{bind}}.Key_4 \leftarrow \mathsf{Com.Gen}(1^\lambda), r_4 \leftarrow_\$ \mathbb{N}, z \leftarrow \mathsf{Com.C}(\mathsf{Com}.Key_4, 1; r_4)$
  9. $\mathsf{NIZK.crs} \leftarrow \mathsf{NIZK.Gen}(1^\lambda)$
  10. return
     $\mathsf{crs} := (\mathsf{SE}.K_{\mathsf{even}}, \mathsf{SE}.K_{\mathsf{odd}}, \mathsf{BARG.crs}, \mathsf{dk}, \mathsf{Com_{bind}}.Key_1.\mathsf{Com_{bind}}.Key_2,$
     $\mathsf{Com_{bind}}.Key_3, z, \mathsf{NIZK.crs})$ and $\mathsf{aux} := r_4$
- $\mathsf{Sim_2}(\mathsf{crs}, \mathsf{aux})$:
  1. $r_1 \leftarrow_\$ \{0,1\}^\lambda, C_P \leftarrow \mathsf{Com.C}(\mathsf{Com_{bind}}.Key_1, 0; r_1)$ return $\mathsf{POut} := C_P$.
  2. return $(\mathsf{POut}, \mathsf{aux'} := \mathsf{aux})$
- $\mathsf{Sim_3}(\mathsf{crs}, \mathsf{aux'}, (x, y), \mathsf{POut} := C_P)$:
  1. $r_2 \leftarrow_\$ \{0,1\}^\lambda, c.\mathsf{com} \leftarrow \mathsf{Com.C}(\mathsf{Com_{bind}}.Key_2, 0; r_2)$
  2. Generate a dummy proof $\hat{\Pi}$
  3. $r_3 \leftarrow_\$ \{0,1\}^\lambda, \Pi.\mathsf{com} \leftarrow \mathsf{Com.C}(\mathsf{Com_{bind}}.Key_3, 0; r_3)$
  4. $\mathsf{NIZK}.\Pi \leftarrow \mathsf{NIZK.Prove}(\mathsf{NIZK.crs}, (c.\mathsf{com}, \Pi.\mathsf{com}, (\mathsf{crs}, x, y, T), C_P),$
     $(\bot, \bot, \bot, \mathsf{aux}))$
  5. return $(c.\mathsf{com}, \Pi.\mathsf{com}, \mathsf{NIZK}.\Pi)$.

The proof of zero-knowledge follows from a sequence of hybrids.

- We define a game $\mathsf{G'}$ which is identical to $\mathsf{G_0}$ except that crs has a commitment of 1 instead of 0. Note that an honest prover does not make use of this section of the crs in its proof. Consider $\mathsf{hyb'}$ as the output distribution of intermediate $\mathsf{G'}$. All other algorithms in $\mathsf{G'}$ remains identical as $\mathsf{G_0}$. $\mathsf{hyb_0}$ must be indistinguishable from $\mathsf{hyb'}$, otherwise we can construct an efficient adversary that breaks the computational hiding property of $\mathsf{Com_{bind}}$.
- The hybrid game $\mathsf{G''}$ with output distribution $\mathsf{hyb''}$ works like $\mathsf{G'}$ except stSNARG.P computes $(c.\mathsf{com}, \mathsf{NIZK}.\Pi)$ honestly and then ignores $c.\mathsf{com}$ and outputs $(c_1, \mathsf{NIZK}.\Pi)$ where c_1 is the statistical binding commitment to the 0 string using $\mathsf{Com_{bind}}$. The indistinguishability of $\mathsf{hyb'}$ and $\mathsf{hyb''}$ follows from the computational hiding property of $\mathsf{Com_{bind}}$.

- We now define another hybrid game G''' where everything remains identical as G'' but the NIZK proof NIZK.P proves that crs has a commitment of 1 using randomness r as a witness. This is indeed a valid witness for the same language $\mathcal{L}^*_{hyb}$. Observe that G'' and G''' have identical CRS. However, NIZK.P in each case uses different witnesses, namely r and $((c, r_{com_2}), \Pi)$ respectively. Thus, the Witness Indistinguishability of NIZK implies indistinguishability of G'' and G'''.
- In the next hybrid G'''', trusted commitment generator is replaced by Sim_2 which on input crs simply outputs a hiding commitment to the 0 string. Note that the output of Sim_2 is not used anywhere else in the proof and its output is computationally indistinguishable from the public output of ZKstSNARG.TrustHash(crs, P) because of the hiding property of commitment scheme.
- In the final game G_1, Sim_1 uses the same crs as the previous hybrid. Sim_3 ignores all operations performed by the prover and only outputs c_1 which is the statistical binding commitment to the 0 string using Com_{bind} and sends a NIZK proof as G''''. The output distributions of G'''' and G_1 are indeed identical as the output of Sim_3 solely depends on the output of Sim_1, Sim_2 and the commitment of the 0 string c_1.

Combining all the hybrids, we prove that G_0 and G_1 have output distributions which are computationally indistinguishable.

Public Verifiable Non Interactive Succinct Delegation with Zero Knowledge. A direct extension of Lemma 11 gives us the following corollary,

Corollary 2. *Assuming $T = poly(m, n)$, $T, m, n \leq 2^\lambda$, the ZKstSNARG protocol in Fig. 5 implies the unconditional existence of a publicly verifiable non interactive succinct delegation scheme with zero knowledge.*

The zero knowledge simulator for the delegation scheme $zk - sDel.Sim :=$ ($zk - sDel.Sim_1, zk - sDel.Sim_2$) can simply run the stSNARG ZK-simulator. More specifically, $zk - sDel.Sim_1$ and $zk - sDel.Sim_2$ call $zk - stSNARG.Sim_1$ and $zk - stSNARG.Sim_2$ respectively above. The proof follows in a straightforward manner, hence we skip the details.

Acknowledgements. This research was supported in part from a Simons Investigator Award, DARPA SIEVE award, NTT Research, BSF grant 2012378, a Xerox Faculty Research Award, a Google Faculty Research Award, and an Okawa Foundation Research Grant. This material is based upon work supported by the Defense Advanced Research Projects Agency through Award HR00112020024.

References

1. Badrinarayanan, S., Kalai, Y.T., Khurana, D., Sahai, A., Wichs, D.: Succinct delegation for low-space non-deterministic computation. In: Diakonikolas, I., Kempe, D., Henzinger, M. (eds.) 50th ACM STOC, pp. 709–721. ACM Press (2018)

2. Bitansky, N., et al.: The hunting of the snark. J. Cryptol. **30**(4), 989–1066 (2017)
3. Bitansky, N., Canetti, R., Chiesa, A., Tromer, E.: Recursive composition and bootstrapping for SNARKS and proof-carrying data. In: Boneh, D., Roughgarden, T., Feigenbaum, J. (eds.) 45th ACM STOC, pp. 111–120. ACM Press (2013)
4. Bitansky, N., Chiesa, A., Ishai, Y., Ostrovsky, R., Paneth, O.: Succinct noninteractive arguments via linear interactive proofs. In: Sahai, A. (ed.) TCC 2013. LNCS, vol. 7785, pp. 315–333. Springer, Heidelberg (Mar (2013). https://doi.org/10.1007/978-3-642-36594-2_18
5. Bitansky, N., Kalai, Y.T., Paneth, O.: Multi-collision resistance: a paradigm for keyless hash functions. In: Diakonikolas, I., Kempe, D., Henzinger, M. (eds.) 50th ACM STOC, pp. 671–684. ACM Press (2018)
6. Brakerski, Z., Holmgren, J., Kalai, Y.T.: Non-interactive delegation and batch NP verification from standard computational assumptions. In: Hatami, H., McKenzie, P., King, V. (eds.) 49th ACM STOC, pp. 474–482. ACM Press (2017)
7. Brakerski, Z., Kalai, Y.: Witness indistinguishability for any single-round argument with applications to access control. In: Kiayias, A., Kohlweiss, M., Wallden, P., Zikas, V. (eds.) PKC 2020, Part II. LNCS, vol. 12111, pp. 97–123. Springer, Heidelberg (May (2020). https://doi.org/10.1007/978-3-030-45388-6_4
8. Canetti, R., et al.: Fiat-Shamir: from practice to theory. In: Charikar, M., Cohen, E. (eds.) 51st ACM STOC, pp. 1082–1090. ACM Press (2019)
9. Choudhuri, A.R., Jain, A., Jin, Z.: Non-interactive batch arguments for NP from standard assumptions. In: Malkin, T., Peikert, C. (eds.) CRYPTO 2021, Part IV. LNCS, vol. 12828, pp. 394–423. Springer, Heidelberg, Virtual Event (Aug (2021). https://doi.org/10.1007/978-3-030-84259-8_14
10. Choudhuri, A.R., Jain, A., Jin, Z.: SNARGs for $\mathcal{P}$ from *lwe*. Cryptology ePrint Archive (2021)
11. Chung, K.M., Kalai, Y., Vadhan, S.P.: Improved delegation of computation using fully homomorphic encryption. In: Rabin, T. (ed.) CRYPTO 2010. LNCS, vol. 6223, pp. 483–501. Springer, Heidelberg (Aug (2010). https://doi.org/10.1007/978-3-642-14623-7_26
12. Cormode, G., Mitzenmacher, M., Thaler, J.: Practical verified computation with streaming interactive proofs. In: Proceedings of the 3rd Innovations in Theoretical Computer Science Conference, pp. 90–112 (2012)
13. Damgård, I., Faust, S., Hazay, C.: Secure two-party computation with low communication. In: Cramer, R. (ed.) TCC 2012. LNCS, vol. 7194, pp. 54–74. Springer, Heidelberg (Mar (2012). https://doi.org/10.1007/978-3-642-28914-9_4
14. Feige, U., Lapidot, D., Shamir, A.: Multiple non-interactive zero knowledge proofs based on a single random string. In: Proceedings [1990] 31st Annual Symposium on Foundations of Computer Science, pp. 308–317. IEEE (1990)
15. Gennaro, R., Gentry, C., Parno, B.: Non-interactive verifiable computing: Outsourcing computation to untrusted workers. In: Rabin, T. (ed.) CRYPTO 2010. LNCS, vol. 6223, pp. 465–482. Springer, Heidelberg (Aug (2010). https://doi.org/10.1007/978-3-642-14623-7_25
16. Gennaro, R., Gentry, C., Parno, B., Raykova, M.: Quadratic span programs and succinct NIZKs without PCPs. In: Johansson, T., Nguyen, P.Q. (eds.) EUROCRYPT 2013. LNCS, vol. 7881, pp. 626–645. Springer, Heidelberg (May (2013). https://doi.org/10.1007/978-3-642-38348-9_37
17. Goldwasser, S., Kalai, Y.T., Rothblum, G.N.: Delegating computation: interactive proofs for muggles. J. ACM (JACM) **62**(4), 1–64 (2015)

18. Groth, J.: Short pairing-based non-interactive zero-knowledge arguments. In: Abe, M. (ed.) ASIACRYPT 2010. LNCS, vol. 6477, pp. 321–340. Springer, Heidelberg (2010). https://doi.org/10.1007/978-3-642-17373-8_19

19. Holmgren, J., Lombardi, A., Rothblum, R.D.: Fiat-shamir via list-recoverable codes (or: parallel repetition of GMW is not zero-knowledge). In: Proceedings of the 53rd Annual ACM SIGACT Symposium on Theory of Computing, pp. 750–760 (2021)

20. Hubacek, P., Wichs, D.: On the communication complexity of secure function evaluation with long output. In: Roughgarden, T. (ed.) ITCS 2015, pp. 163–172. ACM (2015)

21. Kalai, Y., Paneth, O., Yang, L.: On publicly verifiable delegation from standard assumptions. Cryptology ePrint Archive (2018)

22. Kalai, Y.T., Paneth, O.: Delegating RAM computations. In: Hirt, M., Smith, A.D. (eds.) TCC 2016-B, Part II. LNCS, vol. 9986, pp. 91–118. Springer, Heidelberg (Oct / Nov (2016). https://doi.org/10.1007/978-3-662-53644-5_4

23. Kalai, Y.T., Paneth, O., Yang, L.: How to delegate computations publicly. In: Charikar, M., Cohen, E. (eds.) 51st ACM STOC, pp. 1115–1124. ACM Press (2019)

24. Kalai, Y.T., Raz, R., Rothblum, R.D.: Delegation for bounded space. In: Boneh, D., Roughgarden, T., Feigenbaum, J. (eds.) 45th ACM STOC, pp. 565–574. ACM Press (2013)

25. Kalai, Y.T., Raz, R., Rothblum, R.D.: How to delegate computations: the power of no-signaling proofs. In: Shmoys, D.B. (ed.) 46th ACM STOC, pp. 485–494. ACM Press (2014)

26. Kalai, Y.T., Vaikuntanathan, V., Zhang, R.Y.: Somewhere statistical soundness, post-quantum security, and SNARGs. In: Nissim, K., Waters, B. (eds.) TCC 2021. LNCS, vol. 13042, pp. 330–368. Springer, Cham (2021). https://doi.org/10.1007/978-3-030-90459-3_12

27. Kilian, J.: A note on efficient zero-knowledge proofs and arguments. In: Proceedings of the Twenty-Fourth Annual ACM Symposium on Theory of Computing, pp. 723–732 (1992)

28. Lipmaa, H.: Progression-free sets and sublinear pairing-based non-interactive zero-knowledge arguments. In: Cramer, R. (ed.) TCC 2012. LNCS, vol. 7194, pp. 169–189. Springer, Heidelberg (Mar (2012). https://doi.org/10.1007/978-3-642-28914-9_10

29. Lombardi, A., Schaeffer, L.: A note on key agreement and non-interactive commitments. Cryptology ePrint Archive (2019)

30. Merkle, R.C.: A digital signature based on a conventional encryption function. In: Pomerance, C. (ed.) CRYPTO'87. LNCS, vol. 293, pp. 369–378. Springer, Heidelberg (Aug (1988). https://doi.org/10.1007/3-540-48184-2_32

31. Micali, S.: Computationally sound proofs. SIAM J. Comput. **30**(4), 1253–1298 (2000)

32. Paneth, O., Rothblum, G.N.: On zero-testable homomorphic encryption and publicly verifiable non-interactive arguments. In: Kalai, Y., Reyzin, L. (eds.) TCC 2017, Part II. LNCS, vol. 10678, pp. 283–315. Springer, Heidelberg (Nov (2017). https://doi.org/10.1007/978-3-319-70503-3_9

33. Parno, B., Howell, J., Gentry, C., Raykova, M.: Pinocchio: Nearly practical verifiable computation. In: 2013 IEEE Symposium on Security and Privacy, pp. 238–252. IEEE (2013)

34. Parno, B., Raykova, M., Vaikuntanathan, V.: How to delegate and verify in public: verifiable computation from attribute-based encryption. In: Cramer, R. (ed.) TCC 2012. LNCS, vol. 7194, pp. 422–439. Springer, Heidelberg (Mar (2012). https://doi.org/10.1007/978-3-642-28914-9_24

35. Peikert, C., Shiehian, S.: Noninteractive zero knowledge for NP from (plain) learning with errors. In: Boldyreva, A., Micciancio, D. (eds.) CRYPTO 2019, Part I. LNCS, vol. 11692, pp. 89–114. Springer, Heidelberg (Aug (2019). https://doi.org/10.1007/978-3-030-26948-7_4

36. Reingold, O., Rothblum, G.N., Rothblum, R.D.: Constant-round interactive proofs for delegating computation. SIAM J. Comput. **50**(3), STOC16-255 (2019)

37. Setty, S., Vu, V., Panpalia, N., Braun, B., Blumberg, A.J., Walfish, M.: Taking $\{Proof - Based\}$ verified computation a few steps closer to practicality. In: 21st USENIX Security Symposium (USENIX Security 12), pp. 253–268 (2012)

38. Setty, S.T., McPherson, R., Blumberg, A.J., Walfish, M.: Making argument systems for outsourced computation practical (sometimes). In: NDSS, vol. 1, p. 17 (2012)

39. Thaler, J., Roberts, M., Mitzenmacher, M., Pfister, H.: $\{Verifiable\}$ computation with massively parallel interactive proofs. In: 4th USENIX Workshop on Hot Topics in Cloud Computing (HotCloud 12) (2012)

Laconic Function Evaluation for Turing Machines

Nico Döttling[1], Phillip Gajland[2,3($\boxtimes$)], and Giulio Malavolta[2]

[1] CISPA Helmoltz Center for Information Security, Saarbrücken, Germany
doettling@cispa.de
[2] Max Planck Institute for Security and Privacy, Bochum, Germany
{phillip.gajland,giulio.malavolta}@mpi-sp.org
[3] Ruhr-University Bochum, Bochum, Germany

Abstract. Laconic function evaluation (LFE) allows Alice to compress a large circuit $\mathbf{C}$ into a small digest d. Given Alice's digest, Bob can encrypt some input x under d in a way that enables Alice to recover $\mathbf{C}(x)$, without learning anything beyond that. The scheme is said to be *laconic* if the size of d, the runtime of the encryption algorithm, and the size of the ciphertext are all sublinear in the size of $\mathbf{C}$.

Until now, all known LFE constructions have ciphertexts whose size depends on the *depth* of the circuit $\mathbf{C}$, akin to the limitation of *levelled* homomorphic encryption. In this work we close this gap and present the first LFE scheme (for Turing machines) with asymptotically optimal parameters. Our scheme assumes the existence of indistinguishability obfuscation and somewhere statistically binding hash functions. As further contributions, we show how our scheme enables a wide range of new applications, including two previously unknown constructions:

- Non-interactive zero-knowledge (NIZK) proofs with optimal prover complexity.
- Witness encryption and attribute-based encryption (ABE) for Turing machines from falsifiable assumptions.

Nico Döttling—Funded by the European Union (ERC, LACONIC, 101041207). Views and opinions expressed are however those of the author(s) only and do not necessarily reflect those of the European Union or the European Research Council. Neither the European Union nor the granting authority can be held responsible for them.

Phillip Gajland—Funded by the Deutsche Forschungsgemeinschaft (DFG, German Research Foundation) under Germany's Excellence Strategy - EXC 2092 CASA - 390781972 and the European Union (ERC AdG REWORC - 101054911).

Giulio Malavolta—Funded by the German Federal Ministry of Education and Research BMBF (grant 16K15K042, project 6GEM) and the Deutsche Forschungsgemeinschaft (DFG, German Research Foundation) under Germany's Excellence Strategy - EXC 2092 CASA - 390781972 and by the German Federal Ministry of Education and Research (BMBF) in the course of the 6GEM research hub under grant number 16KISK038.

A. Boldyreva and V. Kolesnikov (Eds.): PKC 2023, LNCS 13941, pp. 606–634, 2023.
https://doi.org/10.1007/978-3-031-31371-4_21

1   Introduction

Laconic function evaluation (LFE) is a cryptographic primitive recently introduced by Quach, Wee, and Wichs [FOCS'18]. Using LFE, Alice can compress a large circuit **C** into a small digest d. Given Alice's digest, Bob can encrypt some input x under d in a way that enables Alice to recover $\mathbf{C}(x)$ without learning anything about Bob's input. The scheme is said to be *laconic* if the size of the digest d, the runtime of the encryption algorithm LFE.Enc, and the size of the ciphertext c are all sublinear in the size of **C**.

LFE is particularly interesting in the context of two-party and multi-party computation (2PC, MPC), since it enables the construction of protocols with novel properties. As an example, LFE enables a "Bob-optimised" two-round 2PC protocol in which Alice does all the work, while Bob's computation and communication are smaller than both the function being evaluated and Alice's input. However, for all known LFE constructions [QWW18, AR21, NRS21], the runtime of the encryption procedure and the size of Bob's ciphertext depend on the *depth* of the circuit being evaluated by Alice. This is a severe limitation which restricts the applicability of this primitive to "shallow" circuits. In some sense, this mirrors the efficiency gap between *levelled* and *fully* homomorphic encryption. This leaves us with the following open problem (also stated in [QWW18]):

Is it possible to construct LFE where Bob's work is independent of the circuit size?

1.1   Our Results

We answer this question in the affirmative and our main result is the construction of an asymptotically optimal LFE scheme assuming indistinguishability obfuscation [BGI+01] and somewhere statistically binding (SSB) hash functions [HW15]. Our construction enables the computation of any Turing machine M and, unlike all prior constructions [QWW18] [AR21] [NRS21], removes the dependency on the depth of the circuit (the runtime of the Turing machine in our case). In the standard simulation-security setting, we obtain the following result.

Theorem 1 (Informal). *Assuming indistinguishability obfuscation for circuits and somewhere statistically binding hash functions, there exists a simulation secure LFE scheme with the following parameters:*

- *The size of the digest* d *is* $\mathsf{poly}(\lambda)$.
- *The runtime of the encryption procedure is* $\mathcal{O}(|x| + |\mathsf{M}(x)|) \cdot \mathsf{poly}(\lambda)$.
- *The size of the ciphertext* c *is* $\mathcal{O}(|x| + |\mathsf{M}(x)|) \cdot \mathsf{poly}(\lambda)$.

If we relax the security to an indistinguishability-based notion, we can further improve the parameters by removing the dependency on the size of the output.

Theorem 2 (Informal). *Assuming indistinguishability obfuscation for circuits and somewhere statistically binding hash functions, there exists a LFE scheme with ciphertext indistinguishability and the following parameters:*

- *The size of the digest* d *is* poly(λ).
- *The runtime of the encryption procedure is* $\mathcal{O}(|x|) \cdot$ poly(λ).
- *The size of the ciphertext* c *is* $\mathcal{O}(|x|) \cdot$ poly(λ).

As for the underlying assumptions, SSB hash functions [OPWW15] can be constructed from a variety of standard assumptions (e.g. LWE or DDH), whereas indistinguishability obfuscation is a less understood primitive and currently the subject of a large body of research. Numerous recent works [BDGM20, GP20, JLS20, WW21] show provably-secure constructions of indistinguishability obfuscation for circuits under simple assumptions, some of which are regarded as well-founded.

We briefly describe some additional contributions which show how our construction enables a wide range of new results in cryptography.

(1) Witness Encryption for Turing Machines: We construct the first witness encryption where the size of the ciphertext depends only on the size of the witness and the security parameter (but not on the NP relation $\mathcal{R}$). Furthermore, the decryption runtime is only proportional to the runtime of the Turing machine computing $\mathcal{R}$, rather than its circuit representation. This implies the first ABE for Turing machines [GKP+13] from falsifiable assumptions. Prior to our work, Goldwasser et al. [GKP+13] constructed the same primitive from *extractable* witness encryption,[1] which is a considerably stronger and non-falsifiable assumption, whose validity has often been called into question [GGHW14, BP15, BSW16].

(2) NIZKs with Optimal Prover Complexity: By applying a known transformation [KNYY19], we construct the first *prover-optimal* NIZK proof system, where the prover's computational complexity depends only on the size of the witness and on the security parameter (and is otherwise independent of the size of the NP relation).

(3) MPC Compiler: By applying the transformation described in [QWW18] we obtain a compiler for multi-party computation (MPC) that reduces the communication complexity to be independent of the circuit size, *without introducing additional rounds of interaction*.

1.2 Technical Overview

Following is a brief overview of the techniques developed in this work. Before delving into our approach, we briefly discuss why trivial solutions fall short in constructing LFE.

---

[1] We should also mention a recent work of Ananth et al. [AFS19], which constructs ABE for RAM programs from LWE, although it achieves only a weaker form of efficiency where the public parameters and the ciphertexts grow with the runtime of the RAM program.

Why Trivial Solutions Fail. An astute reader may wonder why this is still a challenging problem, given iO for circuits. One plausible approach to constructing LFE via this route would be to place the hash of the circuit $d := H(\mathbf{C})$ in the common reference string. Bob could then obfuscate and send Alice the following universal circuit

$$\mathcal{U}(\mathbf{C}') : \text{if } d \stackrel{?}{=} H(\mathbf{C}') \text{ return } \mathbf{C}'(x).$$

Intuitively, Alice should only be able to run the obfuscated circuit on $\mathbf{C}$ unless she is able to find a collision for H. Unfortunately, this approach has two major flaws:

(1) Efficiency: The construction is *not laconic* since both the runtime of Bob and the size of the ciphertext depend on the size of $\mathbf{C}$. Even recent constructions of iO for Turing machines [AJS17] suffer from the drawback that the size of the obfuscated Turing machine depends on the maximum input size. An exception is the recent work of [BFK+19] which, however, requires a large shared random string or a random oracle. At present, constructing iO without input-size dependence remains an open problem.

(2) Provable Security: The above informal argument assumes the strong notion of virtual-blackbox obfuscation, which is known to be impossible [BGI+01]. Constructing a provably secure scheme requires a significant modification of the template in order to be able to leverage the weak *indistinguishability* security of iO.

Even if iO for Turing machines does not appear to be sufficient to construct LFE, it turns out that other techniques from the area [KLW15, CCHR15, CH16, CCC+16, ACC+16, GS18] will help us in building a provably-secure scheme, as we explain in the following.

To understand the challenge in more detail, it is useful to compare the notion of LFE with succinct randomized encodings (SRE) [BGL+15]: SRE allows one to encode an input x with respect to a public Turing machine M in such a way that nothing is revealed beyond M(x). However, the *runtime of the encoding algorithm and the size of the encoding* depend on the size of M, whereas in LFE Bob's ciphertext crucially only depends on the size of his input (and the security parameter). Furthermore, SRE do not allow Alice to privately hash her circuit/Turing machine.

Our Approach and Differences to [GS18]. Readers familiar with the work of [GS18] may wonder why their results cannot be used "off the shelf" as follows. Alice computes the digest of her encrypted input along with the circuit $\mathbf{C}$. Then she sends the resulting hash to Bob, who computes a succinct randomised encoding as specified in [GS18], except using Alice's digest. Then Alice can just load $\mathbf{C}$ into the memory of the Turing machine M, thus allowing us to use the result of [GS18] off-the-shelf. Unfortunately, this solution does not work, as [GS18] states that the hash is binding only for the *non-*⊥ locations of the database (whose length is denoted by the parameter n). This raises the question whether adding $\mathbf{C}$ to the database should result in a hash which is "binding for $\mathbf{C}$". - If yes, namely the hash is binding for $\mathbf{C}$, then the parameter

n will grow with the size of $|\mathbf{C}|$. In this case, the complexity of hash update (and consequently the runtime of Bob) will be $\mathsf{poly}(n, \lambda, \log M)$. Here, M denotes the size of the database. Since $n \geq |\mathbf{C}|$, this means that the runtime of Bob would depend on the size of $\mathbf{C}$, which nullifies Bob's efficiency. - If no, namely the hash is not binding for $\mathbf{C}$, then we do not see a direct way to prove the security of the construction, since we cannot rule out that Alice knows a different circuit $\mathbf{C}'$ that collides with $\mathbf{C}$, thus breaking the security of the encryption. Note that the hash is compressing, so collisions always exist even if the hash is computed honestly. The key observation here is that the size of [GS18]'s hash doesn't depend on the size of the unassigned $(= \bot)$ locations, but *does* depend on the number of specified locations $(= n)$. As such loading the circuit $\mathbf{C}$ into memory, would increase the number of specified locations.

Our construction builds on the techniques introduced in [GS18], and requires us to modify the construction in a non-blackbox manner, in order to constrain Alice to execute the Turing machine M on Bob's input while at the same time making Bob's runtime independent of it. To gain some intuition on the approach, we consider the simplified setting in which both parties know a public Turing machine M, where the transition function is denoted by $\mathbf{C}_\mathsf{M}$ and Bob holds an input x. Later in this overview, we show that this template can be lifted to the more generic setting where Alice evaluates a *private* Turing machine by letting M be a universal Turing machine with an additional input. To establish some notation, consider the insecure protocol where Bob sends his input x in plain: Alice can evaluate M by maintaining a database D that encodes x and the current state of the memory of M. Each operation of $\mathbf{C}_\mathsf{M}$ consists of reading the current state, one bit from Alice, and one from Bob.

Garbled Circuits. One possible way to secure this approach is to use Yao's garbled circuits [Yao82, Yao86], that allow for the secure computation of a circuit $\mathbf{C}$ by creating a *garbled* version $\widetilde{\mathbf{C}}$ and encoding the input $x = (x_1, \ldots, x_n)$ as a set of labels $(\mathsf{lbs}_1, \ldots, \mathsf{lbs}_n)$. Security is guaranteed as long as a *single* input encoding is revealed to the evaluator. If we were to garble the step circuit $\mathbf{C}_\mathsf{M}$, we immediately run into two problems: (1) From an efficiency perspective, Bob would need to garble one circuit for each step of the computation, which would be more expensive than just evaluating M locally. (2) With regards to functionality, the evaluator needs to receive the labels corresponding to an input encoding. This corresponds to a particular set of locations in D (depending on which bits $\mathbf{C}_\mathsf{M}$ needs to read). The difficulty here stems from the fact that the state of D evolves over the course of the computation, as it includes the memory tape of the Turing machines. Thus, we would need a way to *dynamically* select labels depending on the intermediate state of D. Fortunately, (1) can be solved using iO: Instead of garbling all step circuits explicitly, Bob sends an obfuscated circuit that, given an index i, returns the ith garbled step circuit. The remainder of this overview is devoted to solving (2).

Updatable Laconic Oblivious Transfer. Before explaining our solution, we recall the notion of updatable laconic oblivious transfer (ULOT) [CDG+17].

With an ULOT protocol, a large database D can be hashed to a small digest d offering the sender two operations.

Read: Given a pair of messages (m_0, m_1) and an index i, the sender can compute a ciphertext c such that the receiver (knowing D and d) can recover $m_{D[i]}$, where $D[i]$ is the value of the bit at the ith location of D.

Write: Given $|d|$-many pairs of messages $\{m_{0,i}, m_{1,i}\}_{i \in [|d|]}$, a bit b, and index i, the sender can compute a ciphertext c such that the receiver (knowing D and d) can recover $\left(m_{D'_1,1}, \ldots, m_{D'_{|d|},|d|} \right)$. Here, d' is the hash of D', the database D updated by writing b at index i.

Equipped with this functionality, we can now devise a mechanism to provide the evaluator with the appropriate input encodings. Bob compresses his input x, using the hashing procedure of the ULOT scheme and sends it to Alice, who will act as the evaluator. At each step of the computation, Alice is provided with the labels corresponding to the database locations needed by the current step circuit. She then uses these labels to evaluate the garbled step circuit, which performs the computation step and computes a ULOT ciphertext containing the pairs of labels for the next step of the computation. In the next step, Alice will be able to retrieve the set corresponding to the locations of the updated database, by running the receive algorithm of the ULOT. These include an encoding of the updated hash of D, as a result of the write operation of the step circuit.

Piecing It Together. Now only two problems remain. First, the state of D is given in clear to Alice, meaning the intermediate values of the computation are leaked. This is solved by adding a layer of symmetric encryption to the memory of the Turing machine. To ensure the correctness of the computation, we remove this layer before feeding the input into $\mathbf{C_M}$. The output is then re-encrypted using a new key that is only available in the next step circuit. As this happens within the garbled circuit, security is preserved. We can now lift the construction to the setting where Alice's M is not known to Bob. This is done by including an additional ULOT digest of the description of the Turing machine, which allows the step circuit to read the description (via ULOT read) and determines the next operation of the computation. Given the above procedure, the database lookup algorithm can be naturally extended to the case of an additional tape, encoding the machine's instructions. To ensure that the random coins used in the garbled circuits are *consistent* across different computations steps, we use a (puncturable) PRF to sample the labels.

The Final Scheme. We provide some intuition for the encryption and decryption procedures in Fig. 1. For the encryption procedure, Bob starts by obfuscating the Garbling Step Circuit and computing the first set of labels that will be needed to evaluate the garbled circuit. These are then sent along with his encrypted input to Alice. For the decryption procedure, Alice evaluates the garbled circuit using the first set of labels sent by Bob. The output from the Step Circuit is then used for receiving the updatable laconic oblivious transfer. This is repeated for all steps of the computation until the final output is returned by the decryption procedure.

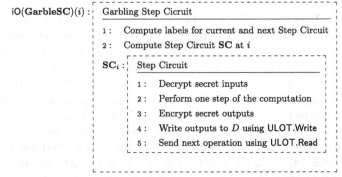

LFE.Enc(d, x)

1 : Block-wise encrypt x
2 : Obfuscate Garbling Step Circuit **GarbleSC**

iO(**GarbleSC**) : Garbling Step Cicruit

   1 : Computes labels for current and next Step Circuit
   2 : Computes Step Circuit **SC**

   SC : Step Circuit

     1 : Decrypts secret inputs
     2 : Performs one step of the computation
     3 : Encrypts secret outputs
     4 : Writes outputs to D using ULOT.Write
     5 : Sends next operation using ULOT.Read

3 : Compute initial labels for **GarbleSC**
4 : **return** encrypted x, iO(**GarbleSC**), initial labels

LFE.Dec(d, c)

1 : Compute **GarbleSC** at 1 using initial inputs
2 : **while** M is not done
  3 : Compute **GarbleSC** at i

    iO(**GarbleSC**)(i) : Garbling Step Cicruit

     1 : Compute labels for current and next Step Circuit
     2 : Compute Step Circuit **SC** at i

     SC$_i$: Step Circuit

       1 : Decrypt secret inputs
       2 : Perform one step of the computation
       3 : Encrypt secret outputs
       4 : Write outputs to D using ULOT.Write
       5 : Send next operation using ULOT.Read

  4 : Run ULOT.Receive to obtain labels used as inputs for iO(**GarbleSC**)($i + 1$)
  5 : **return** final output from Step Circuit

Fig. 1. High level overview of the encryption and decryption procedures.

Security Proof. Next, we provide some intuition about the security argument. To prove the security of our construction we use a similar proof strategy to that of [GS18]. In particular, our proof proceeds via a hybrid argument. In each hybrid we change the way the obfuscated circuit computes the garbled circuits for each step of the computation. Each garbled step circuit can be computed in three modes. The first mode is real, where the computations are just as in the real protocol. The second mode is dummy, where the output of the garbled circuit is constant and hardwired, but the same as in the real execution. The third mode is sim, which is similar to real mode, with the difference being that the garbled circuit only outputs dummy values which are not the same as in the real execution. We cannot change directly from real mode to sim mode because at each step of the computation the labels from the previous step are visible to the adversary. Hence, we first need to change to dummy mode and then to sim mode. We show a set of rules that define a pebbling game, where the pebbles are represented by simulation slots. The aim of the game is to switch the pebbles from real (white pebbles) to sim (black pebbles), while minimizing the number of nodes in dummy (grey pebbles). Our objective is to minimize the number of grey pebbles at any point in time because the size of the obfuscated circuit grows with the number of simulation slots in dummy mode. Finally, with help of a pebbling strategy [GS18], we prove that our LFE construction is secure while having only a poly-logarithmic number of grey pebbles at any point in the simulation.

Application: Witness Encryption for Turing Machines. We show how our newly constructed LFE scheme allows us to construct witness encryption for Turing machines. To encrypt a message m with respect to a relation $\mathcal{R}$, the witness encryption algorithm computes the crs of the LFE and hashes $\mathsf{d} \leftarrow \mathsf{LFE.Hash}(\mathsf{crs}, \mathbf{M}_{\mathcal{R}})$, where the Turing machine is defined as

$$\mathbf{M}_{\mathcal{R}}(m, w) := \begin{cases} \textbf{return } m & \text{if } \mathcal{R}(x, w) = 1 \\ \textbf{return } \bot & \text{else} \end{cases}.$$

Then it returns the obfuscation of a circuit $\mathsf{obC} \leftarrow \mathsf{iO}(\mathbf{C}_{x,m})$ where $\mathbf{C}_{x,m}$ is defined as

$$\mathbf{C}_{x,m}(w) := \textbf{return } \mathsf{LFE.Enc}(\mathsf{crs}, \mathsf{d}, (m, w)).$$

Given a witness w, one can recover m by querying the obfuscated circuit and evaluating the LFE decryption algorithm:

$$\begin{aligned} \mathsf{LFE.Dec}(\mathsf{crs}, \mathbf{M}_{\mathcal{R}}, \mathsf{obC}(w)) &= \mathsf{LFE.Dec}(\mathsf{crs}, \mathbf{M}_{\mathcal{R}}, \mathbf{C}_{x,m}(w)) \\ &= \mathsf{LFE.Dec}(\mathsf{crs}, \mathbf{M}_{\mathcal{R}}, \mathsf{LFE.Enc}(\mathsf{crs}, \mathsf{d}, (m, w))) \\ &= \mathbf{M}_{\mathcal{R}}(m, w) \\ &= m. \end{aligned}$$

Note that the size of the ciphertext is only dependent on the size of the witness w, the size of the message m, and the security parameter. Furthermore, the runtime of the decryption algorithm only depends on the runtime of the Turing machine computing $\mathbf{M}_{\mathcal{R}}$. Security follows via a standard puncturing argument.

Application: ABE for Turing Machines. We also sketch how to turn the above witness encryption into an ABE for Turing machines. This is a standard transformation [GGSW13] and therefore we only include an outline of the construction. To delegate a decryption key for a Turing machine M, the authority computes a signature σ on the tuple $(\mathsf{crs}, \mathsf{d_M})$, where $\mathsf{d_M} \leftarrow \mathsf{LFE.Hash}(\mathsf{crs}, \tilde{\mathsf{M}})$ and

$\tilde{\mathsf{M}}(x, m)$ returns m if and only if $\mathsf{M}(x) = 1$. Then encrypting a message m with respect to an attribute x can be done by obfuscating

$$\mathbf{C}_{x,m}(\mathsf{crs}, \mathsf{d}, \sigma, x) : \textbf{if } \mathsf{Verify}(\sigma, (\mathsf{crs}, \mathsf{d})) = 1; \textbf{return } \mathsf{LFE.Enc}(\mathsf{crs}, \mathsf{d}, (m, x)).$$

Note that the runtime of the encryption algorithm (and consequently the size of the ciphertext) only depends on the size of the attribute x and the message m. Furthermore, the runtime of the decryption algorithm is only proportional to the runtime of the Turing machine M.

For additional details and further applications, we refer the reader to the full version.

1.3 Related Works

The notion of LFE was introduced in the work of Quach et al. [QWW18], in which they presented a construction for depth-bounded polynomial-size circuits from the learning with errors problem. Work by Pang, Chen, Fan, and Tang [PCFT20] extended the notion of (single-input) LFE to the multi-input settings, by additionally assuming the existence of indistinguishability obfuscation. Their protocol uses single-input LFE (and in particular the scheme from [QWW18]) generically. Thus, our scheme can be plugged into their work to obtain improved parameters.

Recent work by Agrawal and Roşie [AR21] shows a new construction of LFE with adaptive security (based on the ring learning with errors assumption). However, the scheme is limited to the computation of NC^1 circuits. Another recent work by Naccache, Roşie, and Spignoli [NRS21] improves the concrete efficiency of LFE. In particular, the authors present a construction based on the LWE assumption with asymptotically smaller parameters than those used in [QWW18]. However, their construction is restricted to the class $\mathsf{L/poly}$, i.e., the class of circuits that can be represented by branching programs of polynomial length.

2 Definitions

Let $\lambda \in \mathbb{N}$ denote the security parameter. We say that a function $\mathsf{negl}(\cdot)$ is negligible if it vanishes faster than the inverse of any polynomial. Given a set S, we denote by $s \leftarrow_\$ S$ the uniform sampling from S. We say that an algorithm is PPT if it can be implemented by a probabilistic Turing machine running in time $\mathsf{poly}(\lambda)$. Let X and Y denote two random variables and let $\{X\}_{\lambda \in \mathbb{N}}$ and $\{Y\}_{\lambda \in \mathbb{N}}$ be two distribution ensembles. We say that these distributions are computationally indistinguishable if for all PPT algorithms $\mathcal{A}$, $|\Pr_{x \leftarrow X_\lambda}[\mathcal{A}(x) = 1] - \Pr_{x \leftarrow Y_\lambda}[\mathcal{A}(x) = 1]| \leq \mathsf{negl}(\lambda)$. We denote this by $X_\lambda \stackrel{c}{\approx} Y_\lambda$. Let G_{par} denote a game, defined relative to a set of parameters par, where an adversary $\mathcal{A}$ interacts with a challenger that answers oracle queries issued by $\mathcal{A}$. We denote the output of the game G_{par}, between a challenger and an adversary $\mathcal{A}$, as $\mathsf{G}_{par}^{\mathcal{A}}$. $\mathcal{A}$ is said to *win* the game if $\mathsf{G}_{par}^{\mathcal{A}} = 1$. We define the advantage of $\mathcal{A}$ in G_{par} as $\mathsf{Adv}_{par,\mathcal{A}}^{\mathsf{G}} := \Pr[\mathsf{G}_{par}^{\mathcal{A}} = 1]$.

2.1 Laconic Function Evaluation for Turing Machines

Here, we adapt the definition of laconic function evaluation (LFE), a primitive recently introduced by Quach, Wichs, and Wee [QWW18], to that of LFE for Turing machines. The runtime of the Turing machine, denoted T, is publicly known and available to all parties. Without loss of generality we assume the Turing machine to be oblivious.

Definition 1 (Laconic Function Evaluation for Turing Machines). *A laconic function evaluation scheme* LFE := (LFE.Gen, LFE.Hash, LFE.Enc, LFE.Dec) *for Turing machines is defined as the following tuple of* PPT *algorithms.*

crs ← LFE.Gen $(1^\lambda, 1^N)$**:** *Given the security parameter* 1^λ *and the block size* 1^N *(encoded in unary), the generation algorithm returns a common reference string* crs.

d ← LFE.Hash(crs, M)**:** *Given the common reference string* crs *and the description of a Turing machine* M, *the compression algorithm returns a digest* d.

c ← LFE.Enc(crs, d, x)**:** *Given the common reference string* crs, *a digest* d, *and a message* x, *the encoding algorithm returns a ciphertext* c.

y ← LFE.Dec(crs, M, c)**:** *Given the common reference string* crs, *the description of a Turing machine* M, *and a ciphertext* c, *the decoding algorithm returns a message* y.

For correctness, we require the encoding of an input with respect to the digest of a Turing machine, when decoded, to return the same result as evaluating the machine on the input. A more formal definition follows.

Definition 2 (Correctness). *A laconic function evaluation scheme* LFE := (LFE.Gen, LFE.Hash, LFE.Enc, LFE.Dec) *for Turing machines is correct if for all* $\lambda \in \mathbb{N}$, $N \in \mathbb{N}$, *for all Turing machines* M, *and all messages* x *it holds that*

$$
\Pr \left[M(x) = y \; \middle| \; \begin{array}{l} crs \leftarrow \mathsf{LFE.Gen}(1^\lambda, 1^N) \\ d \leftarrow \mathsf{LFE.Hash}(crs, M) \\ c \leftarrow \mathsf{LFE.Enc}(crs, d, x) \\ y \leftarrow \mathsf{LFE.Dec}(crs, M, c) \end{array} \right] = 1,
$$

where the probability is taken over the random coins of LFE.Gen *and* LFE.Enc.

The security notion captures the requirement that the encryption of a message x with respect to a compressed Turing machine M reveals nothing beyond $M(x)$.

Definition 3 (Security: Sender-Privacy Against Semi-Honestbreak Receivers). *A laconic function evaluation scheme* LFE := (LFE.Gen, LFE.Hash, LFE.Enc, LFE.Dec) *for Turing machines is secure if there exists a* PPT *simulator*

Sim_{LFE} *such that for any stateful* PPT *adversaries* $\mathcal{A} = (\mathcal{A}_1, \mathcal{A}_2)$ *and* $N \in \mathbb{N}$ *there exists a negligible function* $negl(\cdot)$ *such that*

$$\left| \Pr \left[\mathcal{A}_2(c, st) = 1 \middle| \begin{array}{l} crs \leftarrow LFE.Gen(1^\lambda, 1^N) \\ (x, M, st) \leftarrow \mathcal{A}_1(crs) \\ d \leftarrow LFE.Hash(crs, M) \\ c \leftarrow LFE.Enc(crs, d, x) \end{array} \right] \right.$$
$$\left. - \Pr \left[\mathcal{A}_2(c, st) = 1 \middle| \begin{array}{l} crs \leftarrow LFE.Gen(1^\lambda, 1^N) \\ (x, M, st) \leftarrow \mathcal{A}_1(crs) \\ d \leftarrow LFE.Hash(crs, M) \\ c \leftarrow Sim_{LFE}(crs, d, M, M(x), T) \end{array} \right] \right| \leq negl(\lambda),$$

where the probability is taken over the random coins of LFE.Gen, $\mathcal{A}_1$, LFE.Enc *and* Sim_{LFE}. *Here,* T *denotes the runtime of* $M(x)$ *and* st *the state of* $\mathcal{A}$.

An additional security property of an LFE scheme is that of *function hiding*, which captures the notion that the digest $d \leftarrow LFE.Hash(crs, M)$ should hide the description of the Turing machine M. We note that our scheme can be generically transformed to satisfy function-hiding using the transformation of [QWW18]. The transformation uses 2-round 2PC based on OT and garbled circuits, and maintains the same asymptotic efficiency.

3   Laconic Function Evaluation for Turing Machines

In this section we will construct a laconic function evaluation scheme Fig. 4 with asymptotically optimal parameters.

Notation. We consider the case where the protocol computes a function $F(m_A, m_B)$, where m_A and m_B are the inputs of Alice and Bob, respectively. We assume that the function $F(m_A, m_B)$ is computed by a Turing machine M, where m_A and m_B are given to M on two different input tapes. We assume without loss of generality that the Turing machine M is publicly known.[2] More formally, M denotes the 4-tape Turing machine consisting of two read-only input tapes, a read/write work tape, and a read/write output tape. M is described by the tuple (Γ, Q, δ), where Γ denotes the finite alphabet of M containing a blank symbol $\square$ as well as a start symbol $\triangleright$, and the numbers 0 and 1; Q denotes a finite set of states containing a start state q_{start} and a halting state q_{halt}; and $\delta : Q \times \Gamma^4 \to Q \times \Gamma^2 \times \{L, S, R\}^4$ denotes the transition function. We assume that the transition function δ of M is given by a circuit C_M. It is going to be convenient for us to load the input m_B onto the working tape of the Turing machine. For the remainder of this description, we consider the working tape and the input tape of m_B as a single tape. Furthermore, M is an oblivious Turing machine, meaning its head movements do not depend on the input but only on the input length. Note, that by a classical result of Pippinger and Fischer,

---

[2] One can always make the function F private by including an encoding of F in the input of Alice and computing LFE of a universal Turing machine.

Turing machines can be simulated by an oblivious (and deterministic) Turing machine with only a logarithmic slowdown [PF79]. For convenience, we denote by HeadPos(i) the function that outputs the state st′, the write location on the working tape I_w, and the read locations I_r, J_r on the input tapes m_B and m_A respectively; all at step i of $\mathbf{C_M}$'s computation.

Description. Our scheme assumes the existence of:

- A symmetric encryption scheme $\Pi := (\mathsf{Sym.Gen}, \mathsf{Sym.Enc}, \mathsf{Sym.Dec})$ that is IND-CPA secure.
- An updatable laconic oblivious transfer $\mathsf{ULOT} := (\mathsf{ULOT.Gen}, \mathsf{ULOT.Hash},$ $\mathsf{ULOT.Send}, \mathsf{ULOT.Receive},$ $\mathsf{ULOT.SendWriteRead}, \mathsf{ULOT.ReceiveWriteRead})$ with sender privacy against semi-honest receivers.
- An indistinguishability obfuscator iO.
- A garbling scheme $\mathsf{GC} := (\mathsf{GC.Garble}, \mathsf{GC.Eval}, \mathsf{GC.Input})$ with selective security.
- A puncturable pseudorandom function $\mathsf{PPRF} := (\mathsf{PPRF.Gen}, \mathsf{PPRF.Eval},$ $\mathsf{PPRF.Punc})$.

For convenience we make a few simplifying assumptions: (1) The Turing machine never writes to the same position twice (this does not affect its runtime, as we can just write to a new memory location every time) and (2) The input m_B is of length exactly N. Our scheme can be modified to handle the more general case but the description and the proof become somewhat more contrived.

The step circuit Fig. 2 handles the tasks performed at each step of M's computation. Namely, decrypting the secret input into $\mathbf{C_M}$, computing one step of $\mathbf{C_M}$ and encrypting the output with a new key. Furthermore, after each step, additional outputs are used to specify a location in the database where the encrypted data is to be written using the updatable laconic oblivious transfer. The garbling step circuit Fig. 3 garbles each step circuit and generates the relevant labels and keys so that the garbled circuit can be evaluated.

We define the step circuit $\mathbf{SC}_i$ as in Fig. 2. As inputs, $\mathbf{C_M}$ takes the state st $\in Q$ of the Turing machine M, as well as two input blocks $x_A \subseteq m_A$ and $x_B = m_B$ both of size N. After evaluating the circuit on its inputs, $\mathbf{C_M}$ returns a new state st′ $\in Q$; a write location I_w on the working tape, at which the next block of symbols y_B is written; a read location I_r on the input tape m_B; a read location J_r on the input tape m_A; and $q = \bot$, unless the halting state q_{halt} has been reached, in which case q is the only output of the computation.

Now we define the following circuit **GarbleSC**, which has the crs and a PRF seed s hardwired Fig. 3. It takes as input an index i and outputs a garbled circuit $\mathbf{GC}^{(i)}$.

We are now ready to present our laconic function evaluation protocol Fig. 4.

3.1 Correctness

The correctness of our LFE construction follows routinely from the correctness of its components, namely the indistinguishability obfuscator iO, the garbling

---

$SC_i [crs, k_i, k_{i+1}, lbs_{st}, lbs_A, lbs_B] (st, z_A, z_B):$
1. Parse $(d_A, x_A) := z_A$
2. Parse $(d_B, x'_B) := z_B$
3. Parse $(lbs_{B[0]}, lbs_{B[1]}) := lbs_B$
4. $x_B \leftarrow Sym.Dec(k_i, x'_B)$
5. $(st', I_w, y_B, I_r, J_r, q) \leftarrow C_M(st, x_A, x_B)$
6. $y'_B \leftarrow Sym.Enc(k_{i+1}, y_B)$
7. $e_A \leftarrow ULOT.Send(crs, d_A, J_r, lbs_A)$
8. $e_B \leftarrow ULOT.SendWriteRead(crs, d_B, I_w, y'_B, lbs_{B[0]}, I_r, lbs_{B[1]})$
9. $\widehat{st} \leftarrow GC.Input(st', lbs_{st})$
   return $(\widehat{st}, I_w, y'_B, I_r, J_r, e_A, e_B, q)$

Fig. 2. Step Circuit.

$GarbleSC[crs, s, k](i):$
1. $(lbs_{st} \| lbs_A \| lbs_B \| R) \leftarrow PPRF.Eval(s, i)$
2. $(lbs'_{st} \| lbs'_A \| lbs'_B \| \cdot) \leftarrow PPRF.Eval(s, i + 1)$
3. $(st, I_w, I_r, J_r) \leftarrow HeadPos(i)$
4. $(st', I'_w, I'_r, J'_r) \leftarrow HeadPos(i + 1)$
5. $k_i \leftarrow PPRF.Eval(k, I_w)$
6. $k_{i+1} \leftarrow PPRF.Eval(k, I'_w)$
7. $C' \leftarrow SC_i [crs, k_i, k_{i+1}, lbs'_{st}, lbs'_A, lbs'_B]$
8. $GC \leftarrow GC.Garble(1^\lambda, C', (lbs_{st} \| lbs_A \| lbs_B; R))$
   return GC

Fig. 3. Garbling Step Circuit. The circuit is padded to the maximum size of $Sim_{GarbleSC}$ [See proof of Theorem 3].

scheme GC, the updatable laconic oblivious transfer protocol ULOT, the symmetric encryption scheme Π and the puncturable pseudorandom function PPRF.

Proposition 1 (Correctness). *The Laconic Function Evaluation protocol in Fig. 4 is correct.*

Proof of Proposition 1. We prove the claim via an inductive argument. Let $c_B^{(i)}$ denote the contents of the databases at the beginning of the ith iteration of the while loop in LFE.Dec. Let tr'_i denote the transcript tr_i of M, except that we remove Alice's input tape m_A, and let T denote the runtime of M. We argue that $\forall i \in \{1, \ldots, T\}$, $c_B^{(i)}$ block-wise decrypts to the transcript tr'_i at step i of M's computation. We also show that at each i, the garbled input labels $\left(\widehat{st}^{(i)} \| \widehat{z}_A^{(i)} \| \widehat{z}_B^{(i)}\right)$ are a valid encoding of the state of the Turing machine M, d_A the block of m_A, and d_B the block of c_B all in step circuit SC_i.

LFE.Gen $\left(1^\lambda, 1^N\right)$:
1. Compute crs $\leftarrow$ ULOT.Gen $\left(1^\lambda, 1^N\right)$
   return crs
LFE.Hash(crs, m_A):
1. Compute $(d_A, \widehat{m_A}) \leftarrow$ ULOT.Hash(crs, m_A)
   return $(d_A, \widehat{m_A})$
LFE.Enc(crs, d_A, m_B):
1. Choose two uniformly random PRF seeds (s, k)
2. Compute $(\mathsf{lbs}_\mathsf{st} \,\|\, \mathsf{lbs}_A \,\|\, \mathsf{lbs}_B \,\|\, R) \leftarrow$ PPRF.Eval($s, 1$)
3. Compute $k_1 \leftarrow$ PPRF.Eval($k, 1$)
4. Compute obG $\leftarrow$ iO $(\mathbf{GarbleSC}[\text{crs}, s, k])$
5. Block-wise encrypt $c_B \leftarrow$ Sym.Enc(k_1, m_B)
6. Compute $(d_B, \widehat{c_B}) \leftarrow$ ULOT.Hash(crs, c_B)
7. Set st $\leftarrow 0^N$
8. Set $z_A \leftarrow \left(d_A, 0^N\right)$
9. Set $z_B \leftarrow \left(d_B, c_B\right)$
10. Compute $\widehat{\mathsf{st}} \leftarrow$ GC.Input(st, lbs_st)
11. Compute $\widehat{z}_A \leftarrow$ GC.Input(z_A, lbs_A)
12. Compute $\widehat{z}_B \leftarrow$ GC.Input(z_B, lbs_B)
13. Set $c \leftarrow \left(\widehat{c_B}, \text{obG}, \widehat{\mathsf{st}}, \widehat{z}_A, \widehat{z}_B\right)$
    return c
LFE.Dec(crs, m_A, c):
1. Parse $(\widehat{c_B}, \text{obG}, \widehat{\mathsf{st}}, \widehat{z}_A, \widehat{z}_B) := c$
2. Set $m_B^{(1)} \leftarrow \widehat{c_B}$, $\widehat{\mathsf{st}}^{(1)} \leftarrow \widehat{\mathsf{st}}$, $\widehat{z}_A^{(1)} \leftarrow \widehat{z}_A$, $\widehat{z}_B^{(1)} \leftarrow \widehat{z}_B$
3. Set $i := 1$
4. $q := \bot$
5. while true do
        if $q \neq \bot$ then
            return q
        Compute $\mathbf{GC}^{(i)} \leftarrow$ obG(i)
        Compute $\left(\widehat{\mathsf{st}}^{(i+1)} \,\middle\|\, I_w \,\middle\|\, m_B^{(i+1)} \,\middle\|\, I_r \,\middle\|\, J_r \,\middle\|\, e_A \,\middle\|\, e_B \,\middle\|\, q\right) \leftarrow$
        GC.Eval $\left(\mathbf{GC}^{(i)}, \left(\widehat{\mathsf{st}}^{(i)} \,\middle\|\, \widehat{z}_A^{(i)} \,\middle\|\, \widehat{z}_B^{(i)}\right)\right)$
        Compute $\widehat{z}_A^{(i+1)} \leftarrow$ ULOT.Receive^{m_A} (crs, e_A, J_r)
        Compute $\widehat{z}_B^{(i+1)} \leftarrow$ ULOT.ReceiveWriteRead$^{\widehat{c_B}}$ $\left(\text{crs}, I_w, m_B^{(i)}, e_B, I_r\right)$
        Set $i := i + 1$

Fig. 4. Laconic Function Evaluation Protocol.

The base case, when $i = 1$, follows trivially. Initially, the database $c_B^{(1)}$ contains a block-wise encryption of m_B [step 5 of LFE.Enc]. In step 9 of LFE.Enc x'_B is set to $c_B^{(1)}$, i.e. x'_B contains m_B and the content of the (empty) worktape. Similarly, x_A is also initialised to 0^N in step 8 of LFE.Enc. Hence, the transcript tr'_1 consists of the input tape m_B concatenated with an empty working tape and the state. Thus, $\text{Sym.Dec}\left(k_1, c_B^{(1)}\right) = \text{tr}'_1$. The garbled input labels $\left(\widehat{\text{st}}^{(1)} \,\|\, \widehat{z}_A^{(1)} \,\|\, \widehat{z}_B^{(1)}\right)$ are passed to LFE.Dec in the ciphertext.

By the inductive hypothesis we assume that the database $c_B^{(i-1)}$ block-wise decrypts to give tr'_{i-1}. We now show that $\text{Sym.Dec}\left(k_i, c_B^{(i)}\right) = \text{tr}'_i$. In the ith iteration of the while loop in LFE.Dec, $\mathbf{SC}_i$ is evaluated by $\mathbf{GC}^{(i)}$. Due to the correctness of the indistinguishability obfuscator iO, the obfuscated garbling step circuit obG can be correctly evaluated on input i, and $\mathbf{GC}^{(i)}$ is given by

$$\begin{aligned}
\mathbf{GC}^{(i)} &= \text{obG}(i) \\
&= \text{iO}\left(\mathbf{GarbleSC}[\text{crs}, \text{s}, k](i)\right) \\
&= \text{GC.Garble}\left(1^\lambda, \mathbf{SC}_i\left[\text{crs}, k_i, k_{i+1}, \text{lbs}'_{\text{st}}, \text{lbs}'_A, \text{lbs}'_B\right](\cdot, \cdot, \cdot), \text{lbs}_{\text{st}} \,\|\, \text{lbs}_A \,\|\, \text{lbs}_B; R\right).
\end{aligned}$$

By the induction hypothesis, the garbled input labels $\left(\widehat{\text{st}}^{(i)} \,\|\, \widehat{z}_A^{(i)} \,\|\, \widehat{z}_B^{(i)}\right)$ are a valid encoding of the state of the Turing machine M, d_A and the block of m_A, and d_B and the block of c_B all in step circuit $\mathbf{SC}_i$. In $\mathbf{SC}_i$, the decryption of $x'^{(i)}_B$ gives $x_B^{(i)}$. After running $\mathbf{C_M}$, $y_B^{(i)}$ is then written to the work tape at $I_w^{(i)}$, and encrypted to $y'^{(i)}_B$. By the correctness of updatable laconic oblivious transfer, ULOT.SendWriteRead specifies $y'^{(i)}_B$ to be written to a database and in step 5 of LFE.Dec, $y'^{(i)}_B$ is written to c_B at position $I_w^{(i)}$. Therefore, $\text{Sym.Dec}\left(k_i, c_B^{(i)}\right) = \text{tr}'_{i-1}$ with $y_B^{(i)}$ written on the work tape at $I_w^{(i)}$. I.e., $\text{Sym.Dec}\left(k_i, c_B^{(i)}\right) = \text{tr}'_i$. Furthermore, the garbled input labels $\widehat{z}_A^{(i+1)}$ and $\widehat{z}_B^{(i+1)}$ are given by

$$\begin{aligned}
\widehat{z}_A^{(i+1)} &= \text{ULOT.Receive}^{m_A^{(i)}}\left(\text{crs}, e_A^{(i)}, J_r^{(i)}\right) \\
&= \text{ULOT.Receive}^{m_A^{(i)}}\left(\text{crs}, \text{ULOT.Send}\left(\text{crs}, d_A, J_r^{(i)}, \text{lbs}_A\right), J_r^{(i)}\right),
\end{aligned}$$

and

$$\begin{aligned}
\widehat{z}_B^{(i+1)} &= \text{UL OT.ReceiveWriteRead}^{\widehat{c_B^{(i)}}}\left(\text{crs}, I_w^{(i)}, m_B^{(i)}, e_B^{(i)}, I_r^{(i)}\right) \\
&= \text{UL OT.ReceiveWriteRead}^{\widehat{c_B^{(i)}}}\left(\text{crs}, I_w^{(i)}, m_B^{(i)},\right. \\
&\qquad \left. \text{ULOT.SendWriteRead}\left(\text{crs}, d_B, I_w^{(i)}, y'^{(i)}_B, \text{lbs}_{B[0]}, I_r, \text{lbs}_{B[1]}\right), I_r^{(i)}\right),
\end{aligned}$$

respectively.

3.2 Proof of Security

We will now establish sender simulation security for our protocol, and start by stating the main security theorem.

Theorem 3 (Security). *Assume that* iO *is an indistinguishability obfuscator,* (GC.Garble, GC.Input, GC.Eval) *is simulation secure,* (ULOT.Gen, ULOT.Hash, ULOT.Send, ULOT.Receive, ULOT.SendWriteRead, ULOT.ReceiveWriteRead) *has sender privacy against semi-honest receivers,* (Sym.Gen, Sym.Enc, Sym.Dec) *is IND-CPA secure, and that* (PPRF.Gen, PPRF.Eval, PPRF.Punc) *is a puncturable pseudorandom function. Then* (LFE.Gen, LFE.Hash, LFE.Enc, LFE.Dec) *has sender privacy against semi-honest receivers.*

To prove the security of our construction we use a similar proof strategy to that of [GS18]. In particular, our proof will proceed via a hybrid argument. In each hybrid we change the way the circuit obG computes the garbled circuits $\mathbf{GC}^{(i)}$. Each garbled step circuit $\mathbf{GC}^{(i)}$ can be computed in three modes Fig. 8. The first mode is real, where the computations are just as in the real protocol. The second mode is dummy, where the output of the garbled circuit is constant and hardwired, but the same as in the real execution Fig. 5 and 6. The third mode is sim, which is similar to real mode, with the difference being that the garbled circuit only outputs dummy values which are not the same as in the real execution Fig. 2.

Both garbled circuits in real and dummy mode will keep the intermediate states and memory consistent (recall that the memory is accessed via an updatable laconic OT). On the other hand, a garbled circuit in sim mode will only output the dummy state and perform dummy read and writes to memory. Garbled circuits in real and sim mode are computed on-the-fly by obG, whereas circuits in dummy need to be hardwired into obG. As a result, the size of obG depends on the maximum number of dummy circuits needed in any given hybrid.

We will briefly discuss the necessary conditions under which we can switch the mode of a garbled step circuit. The first garbled circuit in the in line $\mathbf{GC}^{(1)}$ can always be switched from real to dummy or vice versa, provided there is a free simulation slot available, i.e., the number of currently simulated garbled circuits is less than some maximum amount t. For any other garbled circuit $\mathbf{GC}^{(i)}$, we can switch its mode from real to dummy or vice versa, given that the circuit $\mathbf{GC}^{(i-1)}$ is in dummy mode and a simulation slot is available. To switch a node into sim mode, we require that its successor node is in sim mode and that its predecessor is in dummy mode. In the case of the first node we only have the requirement for its successor node and for the last node we only have the requirement for its predecessor.

These rules define a pebbling game, where we identify pebbles as simulation slots. The goal of the game is to switch the nodes from real (white pebbles) to sim (black pebbles), while minimizing the number of nodes in dummy (grey pebbles). To win the game, we can use the same pebbling strategy as in [GS18], where $\mathcal{O}(\log(T))$ pebbles suffice to set a pebble at the last node (with index T) in poly(T) steps. Consequently, with this strategy we only need to simulate $\mathcal{O}(\log(T)) = \mathcal{O}(\lambda)$ nodes in any given hybrid. We refer the reader to the works of [GPSZ17] and [GS18] for an optimal strategy for the pebbling game. For the sake of completeness we state the main Lemmas here.

Lemma 1 ([GPSZ17]). *For any* $p \in \mathbb{Z}$, *such that* $n + 1 \leq p \leq n + 2^k - 1$, *it is possible to make* $\mathcal{O}\left((p - n)^{\log_2 3}\right) \approx \mathcal{O}\left((p - n)^{1.585}\right)$ *moves and get a black pebble at position* p *using* k *gray pebbles.*

Lemma 2 ([GS18]). *For any* $T \in \mathbb{N}$, *there exists a strategy for pebbling the line graph* $\{1, \ldots, T\}$ *according to rules* $\mathfrak{A}$ *and* $\mathfrak{B}$ *by using at most* $\log(T)$ *grey pebbles and making* $\mathsf{poly}(\lambda)$ *moves.*

Thus, our proof strategy will proceed as follows. First we will use the above pebbling argument to switch the last node, i.e. the node with index T to sim mode. This will take $\mathsf{poly}(T)$ steps. Next, we will again use the same pebbling argument to switch node $T-1$ to sim mode. This will take $\mathsf{poly}(T - 1) = \mathsf{poly}(T)$ steps. Consequently, we replace nodes $T - 2, T - 3, \ldots, 2, 1$ with sim nodes, in this order. In total, this will require $T \cdot \mathsf{poly}(T) = \mathsf{poly}(T)$ steps. In the very last hybrid, we will replace the encryption of that database m_B by an encryption of 0. Once all pebbles (step circuits) are in sim mode, and the encryption of m_B has been replaced with the encryption of 0, this corresponds to the simulator $\mathsf{Sim}_{\mathsf{LFE}}$, which takes as input the crs, d, the machine M, the output M(x) and the time bound T. The simulator then outputs the ciphertext c. As a result, the view of the adversary, in this last hybrid, is independent of the sender input m_B. Hence, we can use this hybrid to simulate the view of a semi-honest receiver by only using the receiver's output. The full proof of Theorem 3 follows from that of two lemmas [Lemma 3, Lemma 4].

Circuit Configuration. A circuit configuration conf consists of a subset of garbling step circuits in dummy mode as well as an index $i^* \in \{1, \ldots, T\}$ denoting the garbling step circuit to be changed by the rule.

Rules of Indistinguishability. We define the rules of indistinguishability (which determine the configurations in the pebbling game) below.

Rule $\mathfrak{A}$: Rule $\mathfrak{A}$ dictates when a garbling step circuit can be indistinguishably changed from real mode to dummy mode. Let conf and conf′ be two valid configurations and i^* be an index of the garbling step circuit, such that:
  – Index i^* is changed from real mode to dummy mode, and there are no indices in sim mode to the left of i^*.
  – Index i^* is either the first or its predecessor is in dummy mode.
  – The garbling step circuits in sim mode remain unchanged.
  In Lemma 3 we show that for two valid circuit configurations conf and conf′, satisfying the above constraints, the two distributions $\mathcal{H}_{\mathsf{conf}}$ and $\mathcal{H}_{\mathsf{conf}′}$ are computationally indistinguishable.

Rule $\mathfrak{B}$: Rule $\mathfrak{B}$ dictates when a step circuit can be indistinguishably changed from dummy mode to sim mode. Let conf and conf′ be two valid configurations and i^* be an index of the garbling step circuit, such that:
  – Index i^* is changed from dummy mode to sim mode.
  – Index i^* is either the last or its predecessor is in dummy mode.
  – The garbling step circuits in real mode remain unchanged.

$\mathbf{SC}_{i^*}^{\mathsf{dummy}}[\mathsf{crs}, \mathsf{k}_{i^*}, \mathsf{k}_{i^*+1}, \mathsf{lbs}_{\mathsf{st}}, \mathsf{lbs}_A, \mathsf{lbs}_B](\mathsf{st}, z_A, z_B)$:

1. Parse $(d_A, x_A) := z_A$
2. Parse $(d_B, x'_B) := z_B$
3. Parse $(\mathsf{lbs}_{B[0]}, \mathsf{lbs}_{B[1]}) := \mathsf{lbs}_B$
4. $x_B \leftarrow \mathsf{Sym.Dec}(\mathsf{k}_{i^*}, x'_B)$
5. $(\mathsf{st}', I_w, y_B, I_r, J_r, q) \leftarrow \mathbf{C}_\mathsf{M}(\mathsf{st}, x_A, x_B)$
6. $y'_B \leftarrow \mathsf{Sym.Enc}(\mathsf{k}_{i^*+1}, y_B)$
7. $d_B^* \leftarrow \mathsf{ULOT.Hash}(\mathsf{crs}, m_B^*)$
8. $e_A \leftarrow \mathsf{Sim}_{\mathsf{ULOT.S}}\left(\mathsf{crs}, m_A, J_r, \mathsf{GC.Input}\left(\mathsf{lbs}_A, m_{A[J_r]}\right)\right)$
9. $e_B \leftarrow \mathsf{Sim}_{\mathsf{ULOT.WR}}\Big(\mathsf{crs}, m_B, I_w, y'_B, \mathsf{GC.Input}\left(\mathsf{lbs}_{B[0]}, d_B^*\right), I_r,$

   $\quad\quad \mathsf{GC.Input}\left(\mathsf{lbs}_{B[1]}, m_{B[I_r]}^*\right)\Big)$
10. $\widehat{\mathsf{st}} \leftarrow \mathsf{GC.Input}(\mathsf{st}', \mathsf{lbs}_{\mathsf{st}})$
    $\mathbf{return}\ \left(\widehat{\mathsf{st}}, I_w, y'_B, I_r, J_r, e_A, e_B, q\right)$

Fig. 5. Step Circuit in dummy mode. Let m_B^* denote the database that is identical to m_B except that $m_B^*[I_w] = y'_B$.

In Lemma 4 we show that for two valid circuit configurations conf and conf', satisfying the above constraints, the two distributions $\mathcal{H}_\mathsf{conf}$ and $\mathcal{H}_{\mathsf{conf}'}$ are computationally indistinguishable.

$\mathbf{GC}_{i^*}^{\mathsf{dummy}}[\mathsf{crs}, \mathsf{s}, \mathsf{k}]$:

1. $(\mathsf{lbs}_{\mathsf{st}} \| \mathsf{lbs}_A \| \mathsf{lbs}_B \| R) \leftarrow \mathsf{PPRF.Eval}(\mathsf{s}, i)$
2. $(\mathsf{lbs}'_{\mathsf{st}} \| \mathsf{lbs}'_A \| \mathsf{lbs}'_B \| \cdot) \leftarrow \mathsf{PPRF.Eval}(\mathsf{s}, i+1)$
3. $(\mathsf{st}, I_w, I_r, J_r) \leftarrow \mathsf{HeadPos}(i)$
4. $(\mathsf{st}', I'_w, I'_r, J'_r) \leftarrow \mathsf{HeadPos}(i+1)$
5. $\mathsf{k}_i \leftarrow \mathsf{PPRF.Eval}(\mathsf{k}, I_w)$
6. $\mathsf{k}_{i+1} \leftarrow \mathsf{PPRF.Eval}(\mathsf{k}, I'_w)$
7. $\mathsf{L}_{\mathsf{st}} \leftarrow \mathsf{GC.Input}\left(\mathsf{lbs}_{\mathsf{st}}, \mathsf{st}^{(i^*)}\right)$
8. $\mathsf{L}_A \leftarrow \mathsf{GC.Input}\left(\mathsf{lbs}_A, z_A^{(i^*)}\right)$
9. $\mathsf{L}_B \leftarrow \mathsf{GC.Input}\left(\mathsf{lbs}_B, z_B^{(i^*)}\right)$
10. $\mathsf{out} \leftarrow \mathbf{SC}_{i^*}^{\mathsf{dummy}}[\mathsf{crs}, \mathsf{k}_{i^*}, \mathsf{k}_{i^*+1}, \mathsf{lbs}'_{\mathsf{st}}, \mathsf{lbs}'_A, \mathsf{lbs}'_B]\left(\mathsf{st}^{(i^*+1)}, z_A^{(i^*+1)}, z_B^{(i^*+1)}\right)$
11. $\mathbf{GC} \leftarrow \mathsf{Sim}_{\mathsf{GC}}\left(1^\lambda, 1^{|\mathbf{SC}_{i^*}^{\mathsf{dummy}}|}, \mathsf{out}, (\mathsf{L}_{\mathsf{st}} \| \mathsf{L}_A \| \mathsf{L}_B; R)\right)$
    $\mathbf{return}\ \mathbf{GC}$

Fig. 6. Garbling Step Circuit in dummy mode.

$\mathbf{SC}_{i^*}^{\text{sim}}[\text{crs}, k_{i^*}, k_{i^*+1}, \text{lbs}_{\text{st}}, \text{lbs}_A, \text{lbs}_B](\text{st}, z_A, z_B)$:

1. Parse $(d_A, x_A) := z_A$
2. Parse $(d_B, x'_B) := z_B$
3. Parse $(\text{lbs}_{B[0]}, \text{lbs}_{B[1]}) := \text{lbs}_B$
4. $(\text{st}', I_w, I_r, J_r) \leftarrow \text{HeadPos}(i^*)$
5. $y'_B \leftarrow \text{Sym.Enc}(k_{i^*+1}, 0)$
6. **if** $i^* = T$ **then**
   $q := \mathbf{C}(x)$
7. **else**
   $q := \bot$
8. $e_A \leftarrow \text{ULOT.Send}(\text{crs}, d_A, J_r, \text{lbs}_A)$
9. $e_B \leftarrow \text{ULOT.SendWriteRead}\left(\text{crs}, d_B, I_w, y'_B, \text{lbs}_{B[0]}, I_r, \text{lbs}_{B[1]}\right)$
10. $\widehat{\text{st}} \leftarrow \text{GC.Input}(\text{st}', \text{lbs}_{\text{st}})$
    return $\left(\widehat{\text{st}}, I_w, y'_B, I_r, J_r, e_A, e_B, q\right)$

Fig. 7. Step Circuit in sim mode.

$\text{Sim}_{\textbf{GarbleSC}}[\text{crs}, \textsf{s}](i^*)$:

1. **if** $i^* \in$ dummy **then**
   return $\mathbf{GC}_{i^*}^{\text{dummy}}[\text{crs}, \textsf{s}, k]$
2. **else**
   $(\text{lbs}_{\text{st}} \,||\, \text{lbs}_A \,||\, \text{lbs}_B \,||\, R) \leftarrow \text{PPRF.Eval}(\textsf{s}, i)$
   $(\text{lbs}'_{\text{st}} \,||\, \text{lbs}'_A \,||\, \text{lbs}'_B \,||\, \cdot) \leftarrow \text{PPRF.Eval}(\textsf{s}, i+1)$
   $(\text{st}, I_w, I_r, J_r) \leftarrow \text{HeadPos}(i)$
   $(\text{st}', I'_w, I'_r, J'_r) \leftarrow \text{HeadPos}(i+1)$
   $k_i \leftarrow \text{PPRF.Eval}(k, I_w)$
   $k_{i+1} \leftarrow \text{PPRF.Eval}(k, I'_w)$
3. **if** $i^* \in$ real **then**
   Set $\mathbf{C}' \leftarrow \mathbf{SC}_{i^*}[\text{crs}, k_{i^*}, k_{i^*+1}, \text{lbs}'_{\text{st}}, \text{lbs}'_A, \text{lbs}'_B]$
4. **if** $i^* \in$ sim **then**
   Set $\mathbf{C}' \leftarrow \mathbf{SC}_{i^*}^{\text{sim}}[\text{crs}, k_{i^*}, k_{i^*+1}, \text{lbs}'_{\text{st}}, \text{lbs}'_A, \text{lbs}'_B]$
   $\mathbf{GC} \leftarrow \text{GC.Garble}\left(1^\lambda, \mathbf{C}', (\text{lbs}_{\text{st}} \,||\, \text{lbs}_A \,||\, \text{lbs}_B; R)\right)$
   return $\mathbf{GC}$

Fig. 8. Garbling Step Circuit in real, dummy and sim mode.

3.3 Proof of Indistinguishability for the Rules

Implementing Rule $\mathfrak{A}$

Lemma 3 (Rule $\mathfrak{A}$). *Let* conf *and* conf' *be two valid circuit configurations satisfying the constraints of rule* $\mathfrak{A}$. *Assume that* iO *is an indistinguishability obfuscator,* GC *is simulation secure,* ULOT *has sender privacy against semi-honest receivers, and that* PPRF *is a puncturable pseudorandom function. Then,* *for the two distribution ensembles* $\{\mathcal{H}_{\mathsf{conf}_\lambda}\}_{\lambda \in \mathbb{N}}$ *and* $\{\mathcal{H}_{\mathsf{conf}'_\lambda}\}_{\lambda \in \mathbb{N}}$ *it holds that*

$$\left| \Pr_{c \leftarrow \mathcal{H}_{\mathsf{conf}_\lambda}} \left[\mathcal{A}\left(1^\lambda, c\right) = 1 \right] - \Pr_{c \leftarrow \mathcal{H}_{\mathsf{conf}'_\lambda}} \left[\mathcal{A}\left(1^\lambda, c\right) = 1 \right] \right| \leq \mathsf{negl}(\lambda).$$

Proof of Lemma 3. We prove this with help of a hybrid argument.

$\mathcal{H}_{\mathsf{conf}_\lambda}$: The garbling step circuit is in real mode.

$\mathcal{H}_1$: Instead of hardwiring the PPRF key s into $\mathsf{Sim}_{\mathbf{GarbleSC}}$, we hardwire the key $\mathsf{s}\{i^*\} \leftarrow \mathsf{PPRF.Punc}(\mathsf{s}, i^*)$, that is punctured at i^*. Since we cannot evaluate $\mathsf{PPRF.Eval}(\mathsf{s}\{i^*\}, i^*)$, we additionally hardwire the labels and key that are output by $\mathsf{PPRF.Eval}(\mathsf{s}, i^*)$ into $\mathsf{Sim}_{\mathbf{GarbleSC}}$.

$$(\mathsf{lbs}_{\mathsf{st}} \;||\; \mathsf{lbs}_A \;||\; \mathsf{lbs}_B \;||\; R) \leftarrow \mathsf{PPRF.Eval}(\mathsf{s}, i^*)$$

To be able to use the security of iO, the size of **GarbleSC** is padded to be the same size as $\mathsf{Sim}_{\mathbf{GarbleSC}}$.

Claim ($\mathcal{H}_{\mathsf{conf}} \rightarrow \mathcal{H}_1$*).* The advantage of any PPT adversary in distinguishing between $\mathcal{H}_{\mathsf{conf}}$ and $\mathcal{H}_1$ is:

$$\mathsf{Adv}_{\mathcal{A}_1}^{\mathcal{H}_{\mathsf{conf}} \rightarrow \mathcal{H}_1} \leq \mathsf{Adv}_{\mathsf{iO}, \mathcal{B}_1}^{\mathsf{iO\text{-}sec}}.$$

$\mathcal{H}_{\mathsf{conf}} \rightarrow \mathcal{H}_1$. The proof relies on the security of the indistinguishability obfuscator iO to be able to switch the PPRF key and hardwire the labels. The reduction $\mathcal{B}_1$ gets a bit b from the adversary $\mathcal{A}_1$, where $b = 0$ if the obfuscated circuit is as described in $\mathcal{H}_{\mathsf{conf}}$ and $b = 1$ if the obfuscated circuit is as described in $\mathcal{H}_1$. If $\mathcal{A}_1$ wins the game with advantage ϵ, $\mathcal{B}_1$ wins the iO-sec game with greater than ϵ probability. □

$\mathcal{H}_2$: As opposed to using the labels output by $\mathsf{PPRF.Eval}(\mathsf{s}, i^*)$, we sample a string u from the uniform distribution U_λ.

Claim ($\mathcal{H}_1 \rightarrow \mathcal{H}_2$*).* The advantage of any PPT adversary in distinguishing between $\mathcal{H}_1$ and $\mathcal{H}_2$ is:

$$\mathsf{Adv}_{\mathcal{A}_2}^{\mathcal{H}_1 \rightarrow \mathcal{H}_2} \leq \mathsf{Adv}_{\mathsf{PPRF}, \mathcal{B}_2}^{\mathsf{PPRF\text{-}rand}}.$$

$\mathcal{H}_1 \rightarrow \mathcal{H}_2$. The proof relies on the pseudorandomness property of PPRF, to be able to switch the output of $\mathsf{PPRF.Eval}(\mathsf{s}, i^*)$ with u. The reduction $\mathcal{B}_2$ gets a bit b from the adversary $\mathcal{A}_2$, where $b = 0$ if the output of $\mathsf{PPRF.Eval}(\mathsf{s}, i^*)$ is used, and $b = 1$ if the uniform string is used. If $\mathcal{A}_2$ wins the game with advantage ϵ, $\mathcal{B}_2$ wins the PPRF-rand game with greater than ϵ probability. □

$\mathcal{H}_3$: Since each label is computed twice, once in step $i^* - 1$ and once in step i^*, we now remove the following labels at step $i^* - 1$;

$$\mathsf{lbs}_{\mathsf{st}} \setminus \mathsf{GC.Input}\left(\mathsf{lbs}_{\mathsf{st}}, \mathsf{st}^{(i^* - 1)}\right)$$

$$\mathsf{lbs}_A \setminus \mathsf{GC.Input}\left(\mathsf{lbs}_A, z_A^{(i^* - 1)}\right)$$

$$\mathsf{lbs}_B \setminus \mathsf{GC.Input}\left(\mathsf{lbs}_B, z_B^{(i^* - 1)}\right).$$

I.e., those used in steps 8 –10 in $\mathbf{SC}^{\mathsf{dummy}}_{i^*-1}$. This is possible, since by the constraints of rule $\mathfrak{A}$, the previous step is known to be in dummy mode.

Claim ($\mathcal{H}_2 \rightarrow \mathcal{H}_3$). The distributions $\mathcal{H}_2$ and $\mathcal{H}_3$ are identical.

$\mathcal{H}_2 \rightarrow \mathcal{H}_3$. We note that $\mathbf{SC}^{\mathsf{dummy}}_{i^*}$ is not executed in the obfuscated circuit, but rather computed locally by the simulator. The output is hardwired in the obfuscated circuit, and we are simply removing unused variables.   □

$\mathcal{H}_4$: We hardwire the output out of

$$\mathsf{GC.Garble}\left(1^\lambda, \mathbf{SC}_{i^*}\left[\mathsf{crs}, \mathsf{k}_{i^*}, \mathsf{k}_{i^*+1}, \mathsf{lbs}', \mathsf{lbs}'_A, \mathsf{lbs}'_B\right], (\mathsf{lbs}_{\mathsf{st}} \mathbin{||} \mathsf{lbs}_A \mathbin{||} \mathsf{lbs}_B; R)\right)$$

into $\mathsf{Sim}_{\mathbf{GarbleSC}}$. iO reduction.

Claim ($\mathcal{H}_3 \rightarrow \mathcal{H}_4$). The advantage of any PPT adversary in distinguishing between $\mathcal{H}_3$ and $\mathcal{H}_4$ is:

$$\mathsf{Adv}^{\mathcal{H}_3 \rightarrow \mathcal{H}_4}_{\mathcal{A}_4} \leq \mathsf{Adv}^{\mathsf{iO\text{-}sec}}_{\mathsf{iO}, \mathcal{B}_4}.$$

$\mathcal{H}_3 \rightarrow \mathcal{H}_4$. The proof relies on the security of the indistinguishability obfuscator iO to be able to hardwire the output of the garbling scheme. The reduction $\mathcal{B}_4$ gets a bit b from the adversary $\mathcal{A}_4$, where $b = 0$ if the obfuscated circuit is as described in $\mathcal{H}_3$ and $b = 1$ if the obfuscated circuit is as described in $\mathcal{H}_4$. If $\mathcal{A}_4$ wins the game with advantage ϵ, $\mathcal{B}_4$ wins the iO-sec game with greater than ϵ probability.

□

$\mathcal{H}_5$: We simulate the garbling step circuit, as

$$\mathbf{GC} \leftarrow \mathsf{Sim}_{\mathsf{GC}}\left(1^\lambda, 1^{|\mathbf{SC}_{i^*}|}, \mathsf{out}, (\mathsf{L}_{\mathsf{st}} \mathbin{||} \mathsf{L}_A \mathbin{||} \mathsf{L}_B; R)\right),$$

where $\mathsf{out} \leftarrow \mathbf{SC}_{i^*}\left[\mathsf{crs}, \mathsf{k}_{i^*}, \mathsf{k}_{i^*+1}, \mathsf{lbs}'_{\mathsf{st}}, \mathsf{lbs}'_A, \mathsf{lbs}'_B\right]\left(\mathsf{st}^{(i^*+1)}, z_A^{(i^*+1)}, z_B^{(i^*+1)}\right)$, and $(\mathsf{lbs}'_{\mathsf{st}} \mathbin{||} \mathsf{lbs}'_A \mathbin{||} \mathsf{lbs}'_B \mathbin{||} R') \leftarrow \mathsf{PPRF.Eval}(\mathsf{s}\{i^*\}, i^* + 1)$. Recall that $\mathsf{st}^{(i^*+1)}, z_A^{(i^*+1)}$, and $z_B^{(i^*+1)}$ denote the state of the Turing machine M; the digest d_A and the input block x_A; as well as the digest d_B and the encrypted input block x_B, respectively, each at step $i^* + 1$ of the computation.

Claim ($\mathcal{H}_4 \rightarrow \mathcal{H}_5$). The advantage of any PPT adversary in distinguishing between $\mathcal{H}_4$ and $\mathcal{H}_5$ is:

$$\mathsf{Adv}^{\mathcal{H}_4 \rightarrow \mathcal{H}_5}_{\mathcal{A}_5} \leq \mathsf{Adv}^{\mathsf{GC\text{-}sec}}_{\mathsf{GC}, \mathcal{B}_5}.$$

$\mathcal{H}_4 \rightarrow \mathcal{H}_5$. The proof relies on the selective simulation security of the garbling scheme GC to be able to simulate the garbling step circuit. The reduction $\mathcal{B}_5$ gets a bit b from the adversary $\mathcal{A}_5$, where $b = 0$ if $\mathcal{A}_5$ identified

$$\Big\{ \mathsf{GC.Garble}\Big(1^\lambda, \mathbf{SC}_{i^*}\left[\mathsf{crs}, \mathsf{k}_{i^*}, \mathsf{k}_{i^*+1}, \mathsf{lbs}'_{\mathsf{st}}, \mathsf{lbs}'_A, \mathsf{lbs}'_B\right],$$

$$(\mathsf{lbs}_{\mathsf{st}} \mathbin{||} \mathsf{lbs}_A \mathbin{||} \mathsf{lbs}_B; R)\Big), (\mathsf{L}_{\mathsf{st}} \mathbin{||} \mathsf{L}_A \mathbin{||} \mathsf{L}_B; R) \Big\}$$

and $b = 1$ if $\mathcal{A}_5$ identified

$$\left\{ \mathsf{Sim}_{\mathsf{GC}} \left(1^\lambda, 1^{|\mathsf{SC}_{i^*}|}, \mathsf{out}, (\mathsf{L}_{\mathsf{st}} \parallel \mathsf{L}_A \parallel \mathsf{L}_B; R) \right), (\mathsf{L}_{\mathsf{st}} \parallel \mathsf{L}_A \parallel \mathsf{L}_B; R) \right\}.$$

If $\mathcal{A}_5$ wins the game with advantage ϵ, $\mathcal{B}_5$ wins the GC-sec game with greater than ϵ probability. $\qquad\square$

$\mathcal{H}_6$: We simulate the ULOT.Send ciphertext as $e_A \leftarrow \mathsf{Sim}_{\mathsf{ULOT.S}}$ $(\mathsf{crs}, m_A, J_r, \mathsf{GC.Input}\,(\mathsf{lbs}_A, m_{A[J_r]}))$. Recall that $m_{A[J_r]}$ denotes M's input tape m_A at read location J_r, all at step i^*.

Claim ($\mathcal{H}_5 \rightarrow \mathcal{H}_6$). The advantage of any PPT adversary in distinguishing between $\mathcal{H}_5$ and $\mathcal{H}_6$ is:

$$\mathsf{Adv}_{\mathcal{A}_6}^{\mathcal{H}_5 \rightarrow \mathcal{H}_6} \leq \mathsf{Adv}_{\mathsf{ULOT}, \mathcal{B}_6}^{\mathsf{SenPriExpt}}.$$

$\mathcal{H}_5 \rightarrow \mathcal{H}_6$. The proof relies on the semi-honest sender privacy of ULOT to be able to simulate the ciphertext. The reduction $\mathcal{B}_6$ gets a bit b from the adversary $\mathcal{A}_6$, where $b = 0$ if $\mathcal{A}_6$ identified the ciphertext as

$$\{\mathsf{ULOT.Send}\,(\mathsf{crs}, \mathsf{d}_A, J_r, \mathsf{lbs}_A)\}$$

and $b = 1$ if $\mathcal{A}_6$ identified the ciphertext as

$$\left\{ \mathsf{Sim}_{\mathsf{ULOT.S}}\,(\mathsf{crs}, m_A, J_r, \mathsf{GC.Input}\,(\mathsf{lbs}_A, m_{A[J_r]})) \right\}.$$

If $\mathcal{A}_6$ wins the game with advantage ϵ, $\mathcal{B}_6$ wins the SenPriExpt game with greater than ϵ probability. $\qquad\square$

$\mathcal{H}_7$: We simulate the ULOT.SendWriteRead ciphertext as $e_B \leftarrow \mathsf{Sim}_{\mathsf{ULOT.WR}}$ $\left(\mathsf{crs}, m_B, I_w, y'_B, \mathsf{GC.Input}\,(\mathsf{lbs}_{B[0]}, \mathsf{d}_B^*), I_r, \mathsf{GC.Input}\,\left(\mathsf{lbs}_{B[1]}, m_{B[I_r]}^*\right) \right)$. Here, m_B^* denotes the database that is identical to m_B except that $m_B^*[I_w] = y'_B$, and $\mathsf{d}_B^* \leftarrow \mathsf{ULOT.Hash}\,(\mathsf{crs}, m_B^*)$. Recall that I_w, I_r, and y'_B denote the write location on the working tape; the read location on the input tape m_B; and the encrypted block of symbols that are output by M, respectively, all step i^* of the computation.

Claim ($\mathcal{H}_6 \rightarrow \mathcal{H}_7$). The advantage of any PPT adversary in distinguishing between $\mathcal{H}_6$ and $\mathcal{H}_7$ is:

$$\mathsf{Adv}_{\mathcal{A}_7}^{\mathcal{H}_6 \rightarrow \mathcal{H}_7} \leq \mathsf{Adv}_{\mathsf{ULOT}, \mathcal{B}_7}^{\mathsf{WriReaSenPriExpt}}.$$

$\mathcal{H}_6 \rightarrow \mathcal{H}_7$. The proof relies on the semi-honest sender privacy for writes and reads of ULOT to be able to simulate the ciphertext. The reduction $\mathcal{B}_7$ gets a bit b from the adversary $\mathcal{A}_7$, where $b = 0$ if $\mathcal{A}_7$ identified the ciphertext as

$$\left\{ \mathsf{ULOT.SendWriteRead}\,(\mathsf{crs}, \mathsf{d}_B, I_w, y'_B, \mathsf{lbs}_{B[0]}, I_r, \mathsf{lbs}_{B[1]}) \right\}$$

and $b = 1$ if $\mathcal{A}_7$ identified the ciphertext as

$$\Big\{ \mathsf{Sim}_{\mathsf{ULOT.WR}} \Big(\mathsf{crs}, m_B, I_w, y'_B, \mathsf{GC.Input}\left(\mathsf{lbs}_{B[0]}, \mathsf{d}^*_B\right), I_r,$$

$$\mathsf{GC.Input}\left(\mathsf{lbs}_{B[1]}, m^*_{B[I_r]}\right) \Big) \Big\}.$$

If $\mathcal{A}_7$ wins the game with advantage ϵ, $\mathcal{B}_7$ wins the WriReaSenPriExpt game with greater than ϵ probability.

$\mathcal{H}_8 - \mathcal{H}_{10}$: Finally, we revert the changes made in $\mathcal{H}_1 - \mathcal{H}_3$. Here, the indistinguishability between $\mathcal{H}_8 - \mathcal{H}_{10}$ follows analogous to that of $\mathcal{H}_1 - \mathcal{H}_3$.
$\mathcal{H}_{\mathsf{conf}'_\lambda}$: The step circuit is in dummy mode.

■

This concludes the proof of Lemma 3.

Implementing Rule $\mathfrak{B}$

Lemma 4 Rule $\mathfrak{B}$). *Let* conf *and* conf' *be two valid circuit configurations satisfying the constraints of rule $\mathfrak{B}$. Assume that* iO *is an indistinguishability obfuscator,* GC *is simulation secure,* ULOT *has sender privacy against semi-honest receivers, and that* PPRF *is a puncturable pseudorandom function. Then, for the two distribution ensembles $\{\mathcal{H}_{\mathsf{conf}_\lambda}\}_{\lambda \in \mathbb{N}}$ and $\{\mathcal{H}_{\mathsf{conf}'_\lambda}\}_{\lambda \in \mathbb{N}}$ it holds that*

$$\left| \Pr_{c \leftarrow \mathcal{H}_{\mathsf{conf}_\lambda}} \left[\mathcal{A}\left(1^\lambda, c\right) = 1 \right] - \Pr_{c \leftarrow \mathcal{H}_{\mathsf{conf}'_\lambda}} \left[\mathcal{A}\left(1^\lambda, c\right) = 1 \right] \right| \leq \mathsf{negl}(\lambda).$$

Proof of Lemma. 4. We prove this with help of a hybrid argument. To keep the proof similar to that of Lemma 3, we start with hybrid $\mathcal{H}_{\mathsf{conf}'}$ and end with hybrid $\mathcal{H}_{\mathsf{conf}}$. □

$\mathcal{H}_{\mathsf{conf}'}$: The garbling step circuit is in sim mode.
$\mathcal{H}_1$: Same as $\mathcal{H}_1$ in Lemma 3.
$\mathcal{H}_2$: Same as $\mathcal{H}_2$ in Lemma 3.
$\mathcal{H}_3$: Same as $\mathcal{H}_3$ in Lemma 3.
$\mathcal{H}_4$: Instead of hardwiring the PPRF key k into $\mathsf{Sim}_{\mathbf{GarbleSC}}$, we hardwire the key $k\{i^*\} \leftarrow \mathsf{PPRF.Punc}(s, I_w)$, where I_w is the position of the writing head of the Turing Machine at step i^*. We additionally hardwire the labels and key that are output by $\mathsf{PPRF.Eval}(k, I_w)$ into $\mathsf{Sim}_{\mathbf{GarbleSC}}$.

$$k_{i^*} \leftarrow \mathsf{PPRF.Eval}(k, I_w)$$

To be able to use the security of iO, the size of **GarbleSC** is padded to be the same size as $\mathsf{Sim}_{\mathbf{GarbleSC}}$.

Claim ($\mathcal{H}_3 \to \mathcal{H}_4$). The advantage of any PPT adversary in distinguishing between $\mathcal{H}_3$ and $\mathcal{H}_4$ is:

$$\mathsf{Adv}_{\mathcal{A}_4}^{\mathcal{H}_3 \to \mathcal{H}_4} \le \mathsf{Adv}_{\mathsf{iO},\mathcal{B}_4}^{\mathsf{iO\text{-}sec}}.$$

$\mathcal{H}_3 \to \mathcal{H}_4$. The proof follows by a reduction to the security of the obfuscator, since the two circuits are functionally equivalent.
$\mathcal{H}_5$: As opposed to using the key output by $\mathsf{PPRF.Eval}(k, I_w)$, we sample a string u from the uniform distribution U_λ.

Claim ($\mathcal{H}_4 \to \mathcal{H}_5$). The advantage of any PPT adversary in distinguishing between $\mathcal{H}_4$ and $\mathcal{H}_5$ is:

$$\mathsf{Adv}_{\mathcal{A}_5}^{\mathcal{H}_4 \to \mathcal{H}_5} \le \mathsf{Adv}_{\mathsf{PPRF},\mathcal{B}_5}^{\mathsf{PPRF\text{-}rand}}.$$

$\mathcal{H}_4 \to \mathcal{H}_5$. Follows by the pseudorandomness of the puncturable PRF.
$\mathcal{H}_6$: We hardwire the output out of

$$\mathsf{GC.Garble}\left(1^\lambda, \mathsf{SC}_{i^*}^{\mathsf{sim}}\left[\mathsf{crs}, k_{i^*}, k_{i^*+1}, \mathsf{lbs}', \mathsf{lbs}'_A, \mathsf{lbs}'_B\right], (\mathsf{lbs}_{\mathsf{st}} \| \mathsf{lbs}_A \| \mathsf{lbs}_B; R)\right)$$

into $\mathsf{Sim}_{\mathsf{GarbleSC}}$.

Claim ($\mathcal{H}_5 \to \mathcal{H}_6$). The advantage of any PPT adversary in distinguishing between $\mathcal{H}_5$ and $\mathcal{H}_6$ is:

$$\mathsf{Adv}_{\mathcal{A}_6}^{\mathcal{H}_5 \to \mathcal{H}_6} \le \mathsf{Adv}_{\mathsf{iO},\mathcal{C}_6}^{\mathsf{iO\text{-}sec}}.$$

$\mathcal{H}_5 \to \mathcal{H}_6$. The proof relies on the security of the indistinguishability obfuscator iO to be able to hardwire the output of the garbling scheme. The reduction $\mathcal{C}_6$ gets a bit b from the adversary $\mathcal{A}_6$, where $b = 0$ if the obfuscated circuit is as described in $\mathcal{H}_5$ and $b = 1$ if the obfuscated circuit is as described in $\mathcal{H}_6$. If $\mathcal{A}_6$ wins the game with advantage ϵ, $\mathcal{B}_6$ wins the iO-sec game with greater than ϵ probability.   □
$\mathcal{H}_7$: We simulate the garbling step circuit, as

$$\mathbf{GC} \leftarrow \mathsf{Sim}_{\mathsf{GC}}\left(1^\lambda, 1^{|\mathsf{SC}_{i^*}^{\mathsf{sim}}|}, \mathsf{out}, (\mathsf{L}_{\mathsf{st}} \| \mathsf{L}_A \| \mathsf{L}_B; R)\right),$$

where $\mathsf{out} \leftarrow \mathsf{SC}_{i^*}^{\mathsf{sim}}[\mathsf{crs}, k_{i^*}, k_{i^*+1}, \mathsf{lbs}'_{\mathsf{st}}, \mathsf{lbs}'_A, \mathsf{lbs}'_B]\left(\mathsf{st}^{(i^*+1)}, z_A^{(i^*+1)}, z_B^{(i^*+1)}\right)$, and $(\mathsf{lbs}'_{\mathsf{st}} \| \mathsf{lbs}'_A \| \mathsf{lbs}'_B; R') \leftarrow \mathsf{PPRF.Eval}(s\{i^*\}, i^*+1)$. Recall that $\mathsf{st}^{(i^*+1)}, z_A^{(i^*+1)}$, and $z_B^{(i^*+1)}$ denote the state of the Turing machine M; the digest d_A and the input block x_A; as well as the digest d_B and the encrypted input block x_B, respectively, each at step i^*+1 of the computation.

Claim ($\mathcal{H}_6 \to \mathcal{H}_7$). The advantage of any PPT adversary in distinguishing between $\mathcal{H}_6$ and $\mathcal{H}_7$ is:

$$\mathsf{Adv}_{\mathcal{A}_7}^{\mathcal{H}_6 \to \mathcal{H}_7} \le \mathsf{Adv}_{\mathsf{GC},\mathcal{B}_7}^{\mathsf{GC\text{-}sec}}.$$

$\mathcal{H}_6 \to \mathcal{H}_7$. The proof relies on the selective simulation security of the garbling scheme GC to be able to simulate the garbling step circuit. The reduction $\mathcal{B}_7$ gets a bit b from the adversary $\mathcal{A}_7$, where $b = 0$ if $\mathcal{A}_7$ identified

$$\left\{ \mathsf{GC.Garble}\left(1^\lambda, \mathbf{SC}^{\mathrm{sim}}_{i^*} \left[\mathsf{crs}, \mathsf{k}_{i^*}, \mathsf{k}_{i^*+1}, \mathsf{lbs}'_{\mathsf{st}}, \mathsf{lbs}'_A, \mathsf{lbs}'_B \right], \right. \right.$$

$$\left. \left. (\mathsf{lbs}_{\mathsf{st}} \parallel \mathsf{lbs}_A \parallel \mathsf{lbs}_B; R) \right), (\mathsf{L}_{\mathsf{st}} \parallel \mathsf{L}_A \parallel \mathsf{L}_B; R) \right\}$$

and $b = 1$ if $\mathcal{A}_7$ identified

$$\left\{ \mathsf{Sim}_{\mathsf{GC}} \left(1^\lambda, 1^{|\mathbf{SC}^{\mathrm{sim}}_{i^*}|}, \mathsf{out}, (\mathsf{L}_{\mathsf{st}} \parallel \mathsf{L}_A \parallel \mathsf{L}_B; R) \right), (\mathsf{L}_{\mathsf{st}} \parallel \mathsf{L}_A \parallel \mathsf{L}_B; R) \right\}.$$

If $\mathcal{A}_7$ wins the game with advantage ϵ, $\mathcal{B}_7$ wins the GC-sec game with greater than ϵ probability. $\qquad\square$

$\mathcal{H}_8$: Same as $\mathcal{H}_6$ in Lemma 3.
$\mathcal{H}_9$: Same as $\mathcal{H}_7$ in Lemma 3.
$\mathcal{H}_{10}$: Instead of computing the state st', the write location I_w, the read locations I_r and J_r using $\mathsf{HeadPos}(i)$, as well as computing y'_B as $\mathsf{Sym.Enc}\,(\mathsf{k}_{i^*+1}, 0)$; we compute the output of $\mathbf{C_M}$, and y'_B as $\mathsf{Sym.Enc}\,(\mathsf{k}_{i^*+1}, y_B)$.

Claim ($\mathcal{H}_9 \to \mathcal{H}_{10}$). The advantage of any PPT adversary in distinguishing between $\mathcal{H}_9$ and $\mathcal{H}_{10}$ is:

$$\mathsf{Adv}^{\mathcal{H}_9 \to \mathcal{H}_{10}}_{\mathcal{A}_{10}} \leq \mathsf{Adv}_{\Pi, \mathcal{B}_{10}}.$$

$\mathcal{H}_9 \to \mathcal{H}_{10}$. The proof relies on the chosen plaintext attack security of the symmetric encryption scheme Π to be able to switch from encrypting 0 to y_B. We can do this, since the constraints of rule $\mathfrak{B}$ ensure that the next circuit is in sim mode and therefore the key k_{i^*+1} is not present in the view of the distinguisher. The reduction $\mathcal{C}_{10}$ gets a bit b from the adversary $\mathcal{A}_{10}$, where $b = 0$ if the plaintext is 0, and $b = 1$ if the plaintext is y_B. If $\mathcal{A}_{10}$ wins the game with advantage ϵ, $\mathcal{B}_{10}$ wins the symmetric encryption game with greater than ϵ probability. $\qquad\square$

$\mathcal{H}_{11} - \mathcal{H}_{13}$: Finally, we revert the changes made in $\mathcal{H}_1 - \mathcal{H}_3$. Here, the indistinguishability between $\mathcal{H}_{11} - \mathcal{H}_{13}$ follows analogously to that of $\mathcal{H}_1 - \mathcal{H}_3$.
$\mathcal{H}_{\mathsf{conf}}$: The garbling step circuit is in dummy mode.

This concludes the proof of Lemma 4. $\qquad\blacksquare$

Proof of Theorem 3. The sequence of hybrids shown in the proof of Lemma 3 and Lemma 4 are reversible, and imply an inverse of rule $\mathfrak{A}$ and rule $\mathfrak{B}$. Thus, the proof of Theorem 3 follows directly from the proofs of Lemma 3 and Lemma 4. $\qquad\blacksquare$

3.4 Removing the Output Dependency

We note that our whilst our construction Fig. 4 outputs only one bit, a generic transformation can be used to output multiple bits. Depending on the security definition that we want to achieve, there are two generic ways to carry out such a transformation.

Simulation Security. If we insist on simulation security (which is the same definition achieved by the protocol in Fig. 4) we can simply hash the circuit Φ as $d \leftarrow$ LFE.Hash(crs, Φ), where Φ takes as input an m_B and an index i and returns the i-th output bit of $\mathbf{C}(x)_i$. Then, for all output bits we let the sender compute

$$c := \big(c_1 \leftarrow \mathsf{LFE.Enc}(crs, d, (x, 1)), \ldots, c_{|y|} \leftarrow \mathsf{LFE.Enc}(crs, d, (x, |y|))\big)$$

where $|y|$ denotes the output size. The reciever can then recover the output bit-by-bit. Security follows from a standard hybrid argument.

Indistinguishability. If we relax the requirements to indistinguishability-based security, then it becomes possible to remove the output dependency entirely. Specifically, we require that LFE.Enc(crs, d, x) and LFE.Enc$(crs, d, \bar{x})$ are computationally indistinguishable, for pairs $(x, \bar{x})$ such that $\mathbf{C}(x) = \mathbf{C}(\bar{x})$.

Our scheme proceeds as described above except that the sender does not explicitly compute the ciphertexts $(c_1, \ldots, c_{|y|})$, instead the sender obfuscates a circuit that given an index $i \in \{1, \ldots, |y|\}$ returns

$$\mathsf{LFE.Enc}\big(crs, d, (x, i); \mathsf{PPRF.Eval}(k, i)\big)$$

where k is the key of a puncturable PRF. To compute the output, the receiver evaluates the obfuscated circuit on all possible indices to recover $(c_1, \ldots, c_{|y|})$, then she applies the LFE.Dec algorithm to recover the output bit-by-bit. Observe that now the size of the ciphertext depends on $|y|$ only logarithmically.

In terms of security, we can show indistinguishabilty by defining $(|y|+1)$-many intermediate distributions, where in the i^*-th distribution $\mathcal{H}_{i^*}$ we obfuscate the circuit that given an index $i \in \{1, \ldots, |y|\}$ returns

$$\mathsf{LFE.Enc}\big(crs, d, (\bar{x}, i); \mathsf{PPRF.Eval}(k, i)\big), \quad \text{if } i < i^*$$
$$\mathsf{LFE.Enc}\big(crs, d, (x, i); \mathsf{PPRF.Eval}(k, i)\big), \text{ otherwise.}$$

Note that $\mathcal{H}_0$ is functionally equivalent to the original obfuscated circuit, whereas $\mathcal{H}_{|y|+1}$ is functionally equivalent to the encryption of $\bar{x}$. Thus, it suffices to show that $\mathcal{H}_{i^*}$ and $\mathcal{H}_{i^*+1}$ are computationally indistinguishable. This is done with help of a five-steps argument:

- First we puncture the PRF key at point i^*, and indistinguishability follows from the security of iO.
- We switch PPRF.Eval(k, i^*) with a uniform string u, which is indistinguishable by the security of the puncturable PRF.

- We hardwire the output of $c^* \leftarrow \mathsf{LFE.Enc(crs, d}, (x, i^*); u)$ in the obfuscated circuit. Again, indistinguishability follows from the security of iO.
- We set $c^* \leftarrow \mathsf{LFE.Enc(crs, d}, (\bar{x}, i^*); u)$. Indistinguishability follows from the security of LFE.
- We undo the modifications done by the first three steps.

Note that the first distribution is identical to $\mathcal{H}_{i^*}$, whereas the latter is identical to $\mathcal{H}_{i^*+1}$.

References

[ACC+16] Ananth, P., Chen, Y.-C., Chung, K.-M., Lin, H., Lin, W.-K.: Delegating RAM computations with adaptive soundness and privacy. In: Hirt, M., Smith, A. (eds.) TCC 2016. LNCS, vol. 9986, pp. 3–30. Springer, Heidelberg (2016). https://doi.org/10.1007/978-3-662-53644-5_1

[AFS19] Ananth, P., Fan, X., Shi, E.: Towards attribute-based encryption for RAMs from LWE: sub-linear decryption, and more. In: Galbraith, S.D., Moriai, S. (eds.) ASIACRYPT 2019. LNCS, vol. 11921, pp. 112–141. Springer, Cham (2019). https://doi.org/10.1007/978-3-030-34578-5_5

[AJS17] Ananth, P., Jain, A., Sahai, A.: Indistinguishability obfuscation for turing machines: constant overhead and amortization. In: Katz, J., Shacham, H. (eds.) CRYPTO 2017. LNCS, vol. 10402, pp. 252–279. Springer, Cham (2017). https://doi.org/10.1007/978-3-319-63715-0_9

[AR21] Agrawal, S., Rosie, R.: Adaptively secure laconic function evaluation for NC1. E-prints/Working papers: ORBilu, 2021. https://orbilu.uni.lu/handle/10993/46493

[BDGM20] Brakerski, Z., Döttling, N., Garg, S., Malavolta, G.: Factoring and pairings are not necessary for iO: Circular-secure LWE suffices. Cryptology ePrint Archive, Report 2020/1024 (2020). https://eprint.iacr.org/2020/1024

[BFK+19] Badrinarayanan, S., Fernando, R., Koppula, V., Sahai, A., Waters, B.: Output compression, MPC, and iO for turing machines. In: Galbraith, S.D., Moriai, S. (eds.) ASIACRYPT 2019. LNCS, vol. 11921, pp. 342–370. Springer, Cham (2019). https://doi.org/10.1007/978-3-030-34578-5_13

[BGI+01] Barak, B., et al.: On the (Im)possibility of obfuscating programs. In: Kilian, J. (ed.) CRYPTO 2001. LNCS, vol. 2139, pp. 1–18. Springer, Heidelberg (2001). https://doi.org/10.1007/3-540-44647-8_1

[BGL+15] Bitansky, N., Garg, S., Lin, H., Pass, R., Telang, S.: Succinct randomized encodings and their applications. In: Servedio, R.A., Rubinfeld, R,M editors, 47th Annual ACM Symposium on Theory of Computing, pp. 439–448, Portland, OR, USA, June 14–17, ACM Press (2015)

[BP15] Boyle, E., Pass, R.: Limits of Extractability Assumptions with Distributional Auxiliary Input. In: Iwata, T., Cheon, J.H. (eds.) ASIACRYPT 2015. LNCS, vol. 9453, pp. 236–261. Springer, Heidelberg (2015). https://doi.org/10.1007/978-3-662-48800-3_10

[BSW16] Bellare, M., Stepanovs, I., Waters, B.: New Negative Results on Differing-Inputs Obfuscation. In: Fischlin, M., Coron, J.-S. (eds.) EUROCRYPT 2016. LNCS, vol. 9666, pp. 792–821. Springer, Heidelberg (2016). https://doi.org/10.1007/978-3-662-49896-5_28

[CCC+16] Chen, Y.C., Chow, S.S., Chung, K.M., Lai, R.W., Lin, W.K., Zhou, H.S.: Cryptography for parallel RAM from indistinguishability obfuscation. In Madhu Sudan, editor, ITCS 2016: 7th Conference on Innovations in Theoretical Computer Science, pp. 179–190, Cambridge, MA, USA, January 14–16, Association for Computing Machinery (2016)

[CCHR15] Canetti, R., Chen, Y., Holmgren, J., Raykova, M.: Succinct adaptive garbled RAM. Cryptology ePrint Archive, Report 2015/1074 (2015). https://eprint.iacr.org/2015/1074

[CDG+17] Cho, C., Döttling, N., Garg, S., Gupta, D., Miao, P., Polychroniadou, A.: Laconic oblivious transfer and its applications. In: Katz, J., Shacham, H. (eds.) CRYPTO 2017. LNCS, vol. 10402, pp. 33–65. Springer, Cham (2017). https://doi.org/10.1007/978-3-319-63715-0_2

[CH16] Canetti, R., Holmgren, J.: Fully succinct garbled RAM. In: Sudan, M., editor, ITCS 2016: 7th Conference on Innovations in Theoretical Computer Science, pp. 169–178, Cambridge, MA, USA, January 14–16, 2016. Association for Computing Machinery (2016)

[GGHW14] Garg, S., Gentry, C., Halevi, S., Wichs, D.: On the implausibility of differing-inputs obfuscation and extractable witness encryption with auxiliary input. Algorithmica 79(4), 1353–1373 (2017). https://doi.org/10.1007/s00453-017-0276-6

[GGSW13] Garg, S., Gentry, C., Sahai, A., Waters, B.: Witness encryption and its applications. In: Boneh, D., Roughgarden, T., Feigenbaum, J., editors, 45th Annual ACM Symposium on Theory of Computing, pp. 467–476, Palo Alto, CA, USA, June 1–4, 2013. ACM Press (2013)

[GKP+13] Goldwasser, S., Kalai, Y.T., Popa, R.A., Vaikuntanathan, V., Zeldovich, N.: How to run turing machines on encrypted data. In: Canetti, R., Garay, J.A. (eds.) CRYPTO 2013. LNCS, vol. 8043, pp. 536–553. Springer, Heidelberg (2013). https://doi.org/10.1007/978-3-642-40084-1_30

[GP20] Gay, R., Pass, R.: Indistinguishability obfuscation from circular security. Cryptology ePrint Archive, Report 2020/1010 (2020). https://eprint.iacr.org/2020/1010

[GPSZ17] Garg, S., Pandey, O., Srinivasan, A., Zhandry, M.: Breaking the subexponential barrier in obfustopia. In: Coron, J.-S., Nielsen, J.B. (eds.) EUROCRYPT 2017. LNCS, vol. 10212, pp. 156–181. Springer, Cham (2017). https://doi.org/10.1007/978-3-319-56617-7_6

[GS18] Garg, S., Srinivasan, A.: A simple construction of io for turing machines. In: Beimel, A., Dziembowski, S. (eds.) TCC 2018. LNCS, vol. 11240, pp. 425–454. Springer, Cham (2018). https://doi.org/10.1007/978-3-030-03810-6_16

[HW15] Hubacek, P., Wichs, D.: On the communication complexity of secure function evaluation with long output. In: Roughgarden, T., editor, ITCS 2015: 6th Conference on Innovations in Theoretical Computer Science, pp. 163–172, Rehovot, Israel, January 11–13, 2015. Association for Computing Machinery (2015)

[JLS20] Jain, A., Lin, H., Sahai, A.: Indistinguishability obfuscation from well-founded assumptions. Cryptology ePrint Archive, Report 2020/1003 (2020). https://eprint.iacr.org/2020/1003

[KLW15] Koppula, V., Lewko, A.B., Waters, B.: Indistinguishability obfuscation for turing machines with unbounded memory. In: Rocco A. Servedio and Ronitt Rubinfeld, editors, 47th Annual ACM Symposium on Theory of Computing, pp. 419–428, Portland, OR, USA, June 14–17, 2015. ACM Press (2015)

[KNYY19] Katsumata, S., Nishimaki, R., Yamada, S., Yamakawa, T.: Exploring constructions of compact NIZKs from various assumptions. In: Boldyreva, A., Micciancio, D. (eds.) CRYPTO 2019. LNCS, vol. 11694, pp. 639–669. Springer, Cham (2019). https://doi.org/10.1007/978-3-030-26954-8_21

[NRS21] Naccache, D., Rosie, R., Spignoli, L.: Post-quantum secure lfe for L/poly with smaller parameters. E-prints/Working papers: ORBilu, (2021). https://hdl.handle.net/10993/46725

[OPWW15] Okamoto, T., Pietrzak, K., Waters, B., Wichs, D.: New realizations of somewhere statistically binding hashing and positional accumulators. In: Iwata, T., Cheon, J.H. (eds.) ASIACRYPT 2015. LNCS, vol. 9452, pp. 121–145. Springer, Heidelberg (2015). https://doi.org/10.1007/978-3-662-48797-6_6

[PCFT20] Pang, B., Chen, L., Fan, X., Tang, Q.: Multi-input laconic function evaluation. In: Liu, J.K., Cui, H. (eds.) ACISP 2020. LNCS, vol. 12248, pp. 369–388. Springer, Cham (2020). https://doi.org/10.1007/978-3-030-55304-3_19

[PF79] Pippenger, N., Fischer, M.J.: Relations among complexity measures. J. ACM, 26(2), 361–381 (1979)

[QWW18] Quach, W., Wee, H., Wichs, D.: Laconic function evaluation and applications. In: Thorup, M., editor, 59th Annual Symposium on Foundations of Computer Science, pp. 859–870, Paris, France, October 7–9, 2018. IEEE Computer Society Press (2018)

[WW21] Wee, Hoeteck, Wichs, Daniel: Candidate obfuscation via oblivious LWE sampling. In: Canteaut, Anne, Standaert, François-Xavier. (eds.) EUROCRYPT 2021. LNCS, vol. 12698, pp. 127–156. Springer, Cham (2021). https://doi.org/10.1007/978-3-030-77883-5_5

[Yao82] Yao, A.C.C.: Protocols for secure computations (extended abstract). In: 23rd Annual Symposium on Foundations of Computer Science, pp. 160–164, Chicago, Illinois, November 3–5, 1982. IEEE Computer Society Press

[Yao86] Yao, A.C.C.: How to generate and exchange secrets (extended abstract). In 27th Annual Symposium on Foundations of Computer Science, pp. 162–167, Toronto, Ontario, Canada, October 27–29 (1986). IEEE Computer Society Press

A Map of Witness Maps: New Definitions and Connections

Suvradip Chakraborty[1]([✉]), Manoj Prabhakaran[2], and Daniel Wichs[3,4]

[1] Visa Research, Palo Alto, USA
suvradip1111@gmail.com
[2] Department of Computer Science, IIT Bombay, Mumbai, India
mp@cse.iitb.ac.in
[3] Northeastern University, Boston, USA
wichs@ccs.neu.edu
[4] NTT Research, Palo Alto, USA

Abstract. A *witness map* deterministically maps a witness w of some NP statement x into computationally sound proof that x is true, with respect to a public common reference string (CRS). In other words, it is a deterministic, non-interactive, computationally sound proof system in the CRS model. A *unique witness map* (UWM) ensures that for any fixed statement x, the witness map should output the same *unique* proof for x, no matter what witness w it is applied to. More generally a *compact witness map* (CWM) can only output one of at most 2^α proofs for any given statement x, where α is some compactness parameter. Such compact/unique witness maps were proposed recently by Chakraborty, Prabhakaran and Wichs (PKC '20) as a tool for building tamper-resilient signatures, who showed how to construct UWMs from indistinguishability obfuscation (iO). In this work, we study CWMs and UWMs as primitives of independent interest and present a number of interesting connections to various notions in cryptography.

- First, we show that UWMs lie somewhere between witness PRFs (Zhandry; TCC '16) and iO – they imply the former and are implied by the latter. In particular, we show that a relaxation of UWMs to the "designated verifier (dv-UWM)" setting is *equivalent* to witness PRFs. Moreover, we consider two flavors of such dv-UWMs, which correspond to two flavors of witness PRFs previously considered in the literature, and show that they are all in fact equivalent to each other in terms of feasibility.
- Next, we consider CWMs that are extremely compact, with $\alpha = O(\log \kappa)$, where κ is the security parameter. We show that such CWMs imply *pseudo-UWMs* where the witness map is allowed to be *pseudo-deterministic* – i.e., for every true statement x, there is a unique proof such that, on any witness w, the witness map outputs

---

S. Chakraborty—Work done while the author was at ETH Zurich.
M. Prabhakaran—Supported by the IITB Trust Lab.
D. Wichs—Research supported by NSF grant CNS-1750795, CNS-2055510, the Alfred P. Sloan Research Fellowship.

A. Boldyreva and V. Kolesnikov (Eds.): PKC 2023, LNCS 13941, pp. 635–662, 2023.
https://doi.org/10.1007/978-3-031-31371-4_22

this proof with $1 - 1/p(\lambda)$ probability, for a polynomial p that we can set arbitrarily large.

- Lastly, we consider CWMs that are mildly compact, with $\alpha = p(\lambda)$ for some a-priori fixed polynomial p, independent of the length of the statement x or witness w. Such CWMs are implied by succinct non-interactive arguments (SNARGs). We show that such CWMs imply NIZKs, and therefore lie somewhere between NIZKs and SNARGs.

1   Introduction

When several mathematicians prove the same theorem, it is unlikely that they would all write down the exact same proof. Similarly, in the context of NP, a true statement (e.g., that some graph is 3-colorable) will often have many different proofs/witnesses (e.g., 3-colorings of the vertices). Can we come up with a proof system for NP languages where the proofs are guaranteed to be unique?

This question was studied extensively in complexity theory, where the class of languages with unique proofs is known as UP [15]. It is believed to be unlikely that NP = UP, meaning that we do not believe that all NP languages have unique proof systems, and there are several results that separate the two classes relative to oracles [1,2,13]. Recently, the work of Chakraborty, Prabhakaran and Wichs [4] proposed unique proof systems with *computational soundness* (aka arguments). They defined the notion of a *unique witness map* (UWM) in the common reference string (CRS) model. This is a deterministic polynomial-time map that takes as input an NP statement x and some arbitrary witness w for x (and the CRS) and maps them to a unique proof w^* for x. Any other witness w' for x is mapped to the same unique proof w^*. There is also a polynomial time verifier that checks whether w^* is a good proof of the statement x. The computational soundness guarantee ensures that no polynomial time adversary can cause the verifier to accept a proof of a false statement x, except with negligible probability over the choice of the CRS. In other words, a UWM is a deterministic non-interactive computationally sound proof (aka argument) system with unique proofs. More generally, [4] also considered a relaxation of UWMs to *compact witness maps* (CWMs) where the number of possible proofs w^* that the map can output for any given statement x is bounded by 2^α, for some *compactness parameter* α. UWMs then naturally correspond to CWMs with $\alpha = 0$.

It is worth noting that UWMs/CWMs only impose a restriction on the number of proofs w^* that the prover outputs, but not on the number of proofs that the verifier accepts for a given statement x. It may be the case that we have a UWM where the prover outputs a unique proof w^* for a given statement x, but there are exponentially many alternate proofs that the verifier would accept as well. We also note that UWMs are easily seen to be a special case of a *witness-indistinguishable* proof system, since all witnesses are mapped to the same unique proof.

The work of [4] showed how to construct UWMs from indistinguishability obfuscation (iO) and one-way functions, closely following the construction of NIZKs due to [14]. They also showed that UWMs imply witness encryption. As their main result, they gave an application of UWMs to the problem of leakage and tamper-resilient signatures with a deterministic signer. However, not much else was known about UWMs/CWMs and how they relate to other notions in cryptography.

1.1 Our Results

In this work, we undertake the thorough study of UWMs/CWMs as primitives of interest in their own right. We provide a number of novel results to better understand these notions and discover surprising connections between UWM/CWM and other cryptographic objects of interest. Interestingly, we show that (quantitative) compression factor affects the (qualitative) cryptographic power, leading to a hierarchy of "worlds", depending on whether all of NP has α-CWM for, say, $\alpha = 0, O(1), \log n, n^c$ ($c < 1$), somewhat akin to Impagliazzo's worlds.

The study of UWMs/CWMs can be seen as part of a broader context of complexity theoretic study within cryptography, whose aim is to understand connections between primitives and their relative power. We also view the study of UWMs/CWMs as adding to the understanding of "functional compression" as a fundamental cryptographic feature. For example, functional compression plays a central role in obfuscation, where we can define variants (e.g., XiO vs iO [11]) depending on the level of compression provided. And (perhaps a bit further off), the complexity of computing Kolmogorov complexity, which is also about functional compression, is deeply related to the existence of one-way functions [12].

We now discuss each of our results, relating CWMs with various levels of compression to other cryptographic objects and to each other.

Relating UWMs and Witness PRFs. At its most compact end, witness maps take the form of UWMs. We show several results tightly relating flavors of UWMs and flavors of witness PRFs.

First, we show that UWMs imply witness PRFs [17], which lie somewhere between witness encryption and iO, but are believed to be strictly stronger than witness encryption. In particular, they were shown to imply multi-party key exchange without trusted setup, polynomially-many hardcore bits for any one-way function, and several other applications that are otherwise only known from iO, but not from witness encryption.

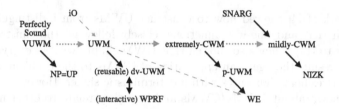

Fig. 1. A summary of the implications established (under standard cryptographic assumptions). The dotted lines correspond to trivial implications, and the dashed line are results from [4].

In a witness PRF, just like a standard PRF, there is a secret function key fk that allows the holder to evaluate the function on any input x. However, there is also a public evaluation key ek, that allows one to evaluate the function on any input x belonging to some NP language L, provided the evaluator also has the corresponding witness w. The basic security notion says that for any $x \notin L$, the output of the function looks uniform even given the public evaluation key. A stronger *interactive* security variant says that the above should hold even if the adversary can query the function on arbitrary other inputs $x \notin L$. It is trivial to construct witness encryption from witness PRFs (with basic security), but the other direction is not known.

We show that UWM and one-way functions imply witness PRFs. In fact, we show that witness PRFs are equivalent to a weaker form of designated-verifier UWMs (dv-UWMs), where the public CRS is generated together with a secret verification key needed to verify proofs. In this case we can define two flavors of soundness: A basic soundness guarantee when the adversarial prover does not get any information about the secret verification key, beyond seeing the CRS, and a *reusable soundness* guarantee for dv-UWMs, where the adversarial prover can make verification queries to check whether purported proofs for various (true or false) statements x would be accepted using the verification key. We show that all four notions are equivalent in terms of feasibility (assuming one-way functions): witness PRFs with interactive security imply reusable dv-UWMs, which imply basic dv-UWMs, which imply basic witness PRFs, which then imply interactive witness PRFs. In particular, the last result shows that it is possible to generically upgrade witness PRFs with basic security to interactive security.

The above results place UWMs on the map somewhere between witness PRFs (which are equivalent to dv-UWMs) and iO. We also believe that UWMs are likely stronger than witness PRFs and dv-UWMs, mainly since we do not know of any way to generically go from the designated verifier setting to public verifiability. Moreover, we show that UWMs imply non-interactive zero-knowledge (NIZKs) with a deterministic prover, which are currently only known from iO, but not from witness PRFs.

Extreme Compactness Implies Pseudo-Uniqueness. Next, we consider CWMs with "extreme compactness" $\alpha = O(\log \kappa)$ for security parameter κ. In other words, while we do not require the proofs to be unique, we require that the witness map can produce at most $2^\alpha = \mathsf{poly}(\kappa)$ many possible proofs for each statement $x \in L$. We show that such extreme compactness is almost as good as uniqueness. In particular, we show that one can generically transform an extremely compact CWM into a pseudo-unique witness map (pseudo-UWM), where the pseudo-uniqueness property says the following. For any statement $x \in L$ and any two witnesses w_1, w_2 for x, both witnesses will map to the same "pseudo-unique" proof w^* with high $1 - 1/p(\kappa)$ probability over the choice of the CRS, where we can choose $p(\kappa)$ to be an arbitrarily large polynomial.

We note that a pseudo-UWM remains a powerful primitive. It can be used instead of UWM in applications where the "error" (i.e., non-uniqueness) can be "corrected." In particular, it implies witness encryption. Indeed, in the construction of witness encryption using a UWM (from [4], or alternately, from a WPRF which is in turn constructed from a UWM as shown here), if we simply replace the UWM with a pseudo-UWM, it results in a small decryption error probability. This error probability can be made exponentially low by repeating the encryption process multiple times using independent keys and randomnes, and during decryption, outputting the majority.

To show that extremely compact WMs imply pseudo-UWM, we solve an abstract problem of potentially independent interest that we refer to as *pseudo-deterministic sampling*. Consider a sampler that has oracle access to some arbitrary distribution $\mathcal{D}$ whose support has polynomial size. The sampler can call the oracle polynomially many times and each call outputs a fresh random sample $x \leftarrow \mathcal{D}$. At the end, the sampler has to output some value x^* in the support of the distribution $\mathcal{D}$. Moreover, we want the sample x^* to be unique; if we run the sampler twice, with the oracle producing random/independent samples from $\mathcal{D}$ in each run, the sampler should output the same value x^* in both executions with high $1 - 1/p(\kappa)$ probability. This guarantee is similar to pseudo-deterministic algorithms [6,8], which are randomized algorithms that nevertheless output a unique value independent of their randomness with high probability. We show how to solve the pseudo-deterministic sampling problem in the CRS model. The sample x^* that the sampler outputs may depend on the CRS but, with high probability, should be the same for every execution of the sampler with the given CRS, no matter what samples it receives from its oracle.

Mild Compactness Implies NIZKs. We then turn our attention to CWMs with "mild compactness" where $\alpha = p(\kappa)$ for some fixed polynomial p, independent of the statement size $|x|$ or the witness size $|w|$. Such CWMs are implied by succinct non-interactive arguments (SNARGs) for NP, which are computationally sound proofs where the proof size is bounded by some fixed polynomial $p(\kappa)$, and independent of $|x|$ or $|w|$. The mild compactness of CWMs can be seen as a relaxation of the succinctness requirement for SNARGs, where the latter requires the proof to have small size $p(\kappa)$, while the former only requires the number of possible proofs that the prover outputs to be bounded by $2^{p(\kappa)}$ but allows the size of the proofs to be arbitrarily large. Although mildly compact

CWMs are weaker than SNARGs, we show that they nevertheless imply non-interactive zero knowledge (NIZK) proofs. We generalize the recent work of [10], who showed how to construct NIZKs from SNARGs, by showing that the same result holds if we replace SNARGs by mildly compact CWMs. The above shows that mildly compact CWMs lie somewhere between NIZKs and SNARGs.

UWMs with Statistical Soundness and UP. Lastly, we ask whether we can get UWMs with statistical/perfect soundness. This appears highly unlikely since it would imply a construction of witness PRFs (and hence witness encryption) from one-way functions. But can we rule out this possibility under some well-studied complexity assumption? Interestingly, we do not know the answer to this question. Intuitively, we'd like to say that perfectly sound UWMs for NP would imply NP = UP, where UP is the class of languages where every statement x has a unique witness w^*. However, a perfectly sound UWM only guarantees that the prover outputs a unique proof and that the verifier never accepts a proof for a false statement, but it may still be possible for the verifier to accept many possible proofs besides the one that the prover outputs. We define the stronger notion of verifier-unique witness maps (VUWM) where we also guarantee that the verifier only accepts a unique proof w^* for each x, and show that perfectly sound VUWMs for NP imply NP = UP.

1.2 Technical Overview

1.2.1 dv-UWM Is Equivalent to Witness PRFs

To show the equivalence between dv-UWM and witness PRF wPRF, we first show that wPRF implies dv-UWM.

Witness PRF Implies dv-UWM: This direction is rather straightforward and follows from the definition of wPRF. In particular, the dv-UWM proof w^* is computed by running the public evaluation algorithm using the evaluation key ek. The verification algorithm of dv-UWM is obtained by running the secret evaluation algorithm of wPRF using the secret function key fk and checking if the proof w^* is equal to the output of this algorithm. The correctness of the construction follows from the fact that the values computed in both the modes of wPRF are equal. Uniqueness is guaranteed since the private evaluation algorithm does not depend on the witness w and deterministically maps x to a unique output value. Finally, the soundness of dv-UWM follows from the interactive security of wPRF.

dv-UWM Implies Witness PRF: We show this result in two steps – (i) First, we show that a construction of non-interactive witness PRF for **NP** from any non-reusably sound dv-UWM for **NP**, (ii) next, we show a generic transformation from any non-interactive witness PRF for **NP** to an interactive witness PRF for **NP** additionally using one way function.

Non-reusably sound UWM Implies Non-interactive Witness PRF: To construct a non-interactive wPRF from a (non-reusable) dv-UWM, the key generation algorithm wPRF.Gen of wPRF samples a random seed z for a (length-doubling) pseudorandom generator G and sets $y = G(z)$. It then runs the setup algorithm of

DV-UWM, i.e., dv.setup to obtain $((\mathsf{K}, \mathsf{VK}))$. It then sets the evaluation key as $\mathsf{ek} = (\mathsf{K}, \mathsf{VK}, y)$ and the function key as $\mathsf{fk} = z$. To compute the function $\mathsf{F}(\mathsf{fk}, \cdot)$ on input $x \in L$, the evaluator uses DV-UWM to get a representative witness w^* for the statement $\hat{x}$ stating that "either x is true or y is pseudorandom", using z as the witness. It then outputs a hardcore bit (e.g., the Goldreich-Levin (GL) hardcore bit) of w^* as the pseudorandom bit b. In the public evaluation mode, on input (x, w) the algorithm wPRF.Eval uses the UWM to map the witness w for x into the unique witness w^* for the statement $\hat{x}$. It can then compute the pseudorandom bit b using the GL predicate. Intuitively, if an adversary can break wPRF security, then it can distinguish the bit 0 and 1 with non-negligible probability even if x is a false statement. This means that, using GL decoding, it can compute the correct value w^* given y with non-negligible probability. Furthermore this value w^* is a valid representative witness for the statement $\hat{x}$. Since the adversary cannot break the PRG, it must also compute a valid representative witness for $\hat{x}$ if we switch y to false. But this contradicts the soundness of dv-UWM.

Generic Transformation from Non-interactive to Interactive Witness PRF: To construct interactive witness PRF from non-interactive witness PRF (nI-wPRF) we need to carefully define the relation for the underlying nI-wPRF. In particular, the key generation algorithm of the interactive witness PRF wPRF runs the key generation algorithm of the non-interactive witness PRF nI-wPRF to obtain $(\hat{\mathsf{ek}}, \hat{\mathsf{fk}})$. It then uses a statistically binding commitment scheme to commit to a message $\mathbf{0}$ (using randomness r) such that $\mathbf{0}$ is not a valid statement of the underlying **NP** relation $\mathcal{R}$ for wPRF to obtain commitment c. In other words, $\mathbf{0} \notin \mathcal{X}$, where $\mathcal{X}$ is the statement space of $\mathcal{R}$. It then sets the evaluation key as $\mathsf{ek} = (\hat{\mathsf{ek}}, c)$ and the function key as $\mathsf{fk} = (\hat{\mathsf{fk}}, r)$. To compute the function $\mathsf{F}(\mathsf{fk}, \cdot)$ on input $x \in L$, the evaluator uses nI-wPRF to get a value y for the statement $\hat{x}$ stating that "either x is true or c is a commitment to some message x' such that $x \neq x'$". In the public evaluation mode, on input (x, w) the algorithm wPRF.Eval uses the public evaluation key of the underlying nI-wPRF to map the witness w for x into the value y for the statement $\hat{x}$. In the proof, when the adversary commits to a challenge $x^* \notin L$, we switch from a commitment to $\mathbf{0}$ to a commitment c^* to x^*. Hence, we have that the statement $\hat{x} = (x^*, c^*)$ is now false. The hiding property of the commitment allows us to make such a switch. On the other hand, for all other statement $x_i \neq x^*$, the statement (x_i, c^*) is still true, and hence we can simulate the queries of the wPRF adversary using the function nI-wPRF.F$(\hat{\mathsf{fk}}, \cdot)$.

1.2.2 Extremely Compact WM Implies Pseudo-Unique WM

As mentioned above, to construct a Pseudo-UWM from an extremely compact WM, we solve the abstract problem of *pseudo-deterministic sampling* from a distribution with polynomial-sized support. We briefly sketch our solution to the pseudo-deterministic sampling problem.

Solving Pseudo-Deterministic Sampling. As a first attempt, consider obtaining N samples from the distribution for a value N that is much larger than the size of the distribution's support, and then taking the lexicographically smallest one. This would indeed work if we could ensure that every element in the support gets sampled at least once. Unfortunately, this does not hold true for arbitrary distributions. For instance, if the lexicographically smallest element in the support has a probability $1/N$, then there is a constant probability for it to get sampled as well as to not get sampled. As a second attempt, one may consider using a hash function to define the lexicographic ordering to prevent the distribution from adversarially assigning such a probability to the smallest element; however, this does not help either, if a large fraction of the elements in the support have probability $1/N$. One may note that the difficulty here arises from (moderately) low probability elements; so to avoid such elements, we could try to pick a high probability element, which is guaranteed to occur many times in the sample. However neither picking the most frequent element (e.g., when there are multiple elements which have the maximum probability), nor picking the lexicographically smallest one from among a selected subset of frequent elements (e.g., when there are elements with probabilities that place them near the threshold used for selection) is sufficient to guarantee uniqueness. Our final solution combines ideas from all of these approaches: it obtains N samples and would choose one with the smallest hash value, but the hash is computed on *the element concatenated with a counter*. That is, if an element x occurs k times in the sample, then the hashes of all of $x\|1, x\|2, \ldots, x\|k$ are considered. This has the effect of picking an element from among the more frequent elements, but without creating a threshold for being considered frequent. Using elementary concentration bounds we show that the probability of two executions of this process yielding different outcomes (when using a N-wise independent hash function) goes down polynomially with $1/N$.

Pseudo-UWM from Pseudo-Deterministic Sampling. To reduce pseudo-UWM to pseudo-deterministic sampling, first we need to create a distribution over proofs that remains (essentially) the same for all witnesses. We achieve this using a Non-Interactive Witness Indistinguishable proof system (NIWI). Then we map this NIWI proof using the extremely compact WM (for the relation corresponding to NIWI verification) into a polynomial-sized support. The soundness of this proof depends on the fact that for any false statement, there should not *exist* a NIWI proof that gets accepted; this is guaranteed by using a statistically sound NIWI. At this point, we have a proof system that is sound, compact, and witness-indistinguishable. Now, pseudo-deterministic sampling from this distribution would result in a pseudo-UWM.

1.2.3   Mildly CWM Implies NIZK

We show that CWM with compactness level $\alpha = \mathsf{poly}(\kappa)$ for some fixed polynomial $\mathsf{poly}(\cdot)$, independent of the statement size $|x|$ or the witness size $|w|$ implies the existence of NIZK argument system. Our construction generalizes the recent work of [10] who constructed NIZKs from SNARG by replacing SNARG with CWM with the above compactness level. [10] shows how to compile any NIZK in the hidden-bits model (HBM) to NIZK in the CRS model using a primitive called *hidden-bits generator with subset-dependent proofs* (SDP-HBG). Then they they show how to construct such a SDP-HBG from any SNARG and bounded-leakage weak PRF (BLR-wPRF)[1]. Below we sketch the main idea of the construction and the proof of [10]. We then show how to modify their construction and proof technique when using CWM instead of SNARG. A SDP-HBG consists of the following algorithms:

- $\mathsf{HBG}^{\mathsf{sdp}}.\mathsf{Setup}(1^\kappa, 1^n)$ generates a CRS crs where n denotes the length of hidden-bits to be generated.
- $\mathsf{HBG}^{\mathsf{sdp}}.\mathsf{GenBits}(\mathsf{crs})$ generates "hidden-bits" $r \in \{0,1\}^n$ and a state st.
- $\mathsf{HBG}^{\mathsf{sdp}}.\mathsf{Prove}(\mathsf{st}, I)$ generates a proof π that certifies the sub-string r_I.
- $\mathsf{HBG}^{\mathsf{sdp}}.\mathsf{Verify}(\mathsf{crs}, I, r_I, \pi)$ verifies the proof π to ensure that the substring of r on the positions corresponding to subset I is indeed r_I.

The SDP-HBG is required to satisfy the following properties – (i) *Somewhat Computational Binding*, which requires that exists a "sparse" subset $\mathcal{V}^{\mathsf{crs}} \in \{0,1\}^n$ of size much smaller than 2^n such that no PPT malicious prover can generate a proof for bits that are not consistent with any element of $\mathcal{V}^{\mathsf{crs}}$, (ii) *Hiding*, which requires that for any subset $I \subseteq [n]$, no PPT adversary given can distinguish $r_{\bar{I}}$ from a uniformly random string $r'_{\bar{I}}$, where $r_{\bar{I}}$ denotes the substring of r on the positions corresponding to $\bar{I} = [n] \setminus I$. To construct SDP-HBG, the setup algorithm $\mathsf{HBG}^{\mathsf{sdp}}.\mathsf{Setup}(1^\kappa, 1^n)$ samples $\vec{x} = (x_1, \cdots, x_n) \in \{0,1\}^{m \times n}$ and sets $\mathsf{crs} = \vec{x}$. The algorithm $\mathsf{HBG}^{\mathsf{sdp}}.\mathsf{GenBits}(\mathsf{crs})$ derives the hidden bits $\vec{r} = (r_1, \cdots, r_n) \in \{0,1\}^n$ as $r_i = F_K(x_i)$, where $F_K : \{0,1\}^m \to \{0,1\}$ is a λ-BLR-wPRF and $K \in \{0,1\}^k$ for some polynomial $k = k(\kappa, \lambda)$, where κ is the security parameter. The algorithm $\mathsf{HBG}^{\mathsf{sdp}}.\mathsf{Prove}(\mathsf{st}, I)$ then uses the SNARG to generate a proof π for the statement that the values r_i for all $i \in [I]$ are correctly computed, using K as the witness. The verification then consists of verifying the SNARG proof.

The somewhat computational binding property of SDP-HBG easily follows from the soundness of SNARG as long as $k \ll n$ (where k is the size of the PRF key K and n is the length of the hidden bit string). The hiding property is easy to reduce to security of the underlying BLR-wPRF as long as $|\pi| \le \lambda$. In particular, the proof π corresponds to the subset I which does not depend on $x_{\bar{I}}$ (the bits of x in the positions $[n] \setminus I$), and thus we can think of $x_{\bar{I}}$ as the challenge inputs and π as the leakage.

Using CWM instead of SNARG. Our construction follows the same blueprint from [10], except that we use a α-CWM for $\alpha = \mathsf{poly}(\kappa)$ instead of a SNARG to generate the proof π and use a entropic leakage-resilient weak PRF[2] to generate

---

[1] Informally, a λ-BLR-wPRF $F_K(\cdot)$ guarantees pseudorandomness of the output of the PRF when evaluated on uniformly random inputs, even when the adversary can leak up to λ bits on K. [9] showed how to construct such BLR-wPRF from any OWF.

[2] Informally, a λ-entropic leakage-resilient PRF $F_K(\cdot)$ guarantees pseudorandomness of the output of the PRF when evaluated on uniformly random inputs, even when the adversary can get λ-entropic leakage on K. Roughly this means that the PRF key K still has $k - \lambda$ bits of average min-entropy, even conditioned on the leakage from K. [9] showed how to construct such entropic LR-wPRF from any OWF.

the hidden bits $r \in \{0, 1\}^n$, instead of a bounded leakage-resilient weak PRF. This is because, unlike SNARG the size of our CWM proofs π are *not* guaranteed to be succinct. However, we have the guarantee that the proof π is α-compact, for some $\alpha = \mathsf{poly}(\kappa)$, where $\mathsf{poly}(\kappa)$ is independent of n. This means the size of the CWM image is at most 2^α. Hence, as long as the underlying wPRF is resilient to λ-entropic leakage, where $\alpha \leq \lambda$, we can rely on the (entropic) leakage-resilience of ELR-wPRF to argue hiding of the SDP-HBG. We can then set the parameters appropriately to satisfy these two inequalities.

1.2.4   UWM Implies Deterministic-prover NIZK

We show that UWM implies deterministic prover NIZK arguments systems (DP-NIZK), where the prover and verifier are deterministic. In fact, we can achieve *perfect* zero-knowledge property. The main idea of our construction is similar to the construction of non-interactive witness PRF from dv-UWM. In particular, the setup algorithm of DP-NIZK chooses a pseudorandom string $y = G(z)$, where G is a length-doubling PRG. The CRS crs of DP-NIZK consists of the CRS K of UWM and the value y. The prover of DP-NIZK on input some (x, w) in the relation runs the UWM prover to get a representative witness w^* for the statement $\hat{x}$ stating that "either x is true or y is pseudorandom", using w as the witness. Note that the prover is deterministic. The verification of DP-NIZK simply uses the UWM verifier. To prove the soundness of this construction, we sample y uniformly at random and hence with very high probability there not exist any valid preimage of y with respect to G. Hence, if $x \notin L$, the statement $\hat{x} = (x, y)$ is also not in the (augmented) language with overwhelming probability. The soundness of the construction now follows from the soundness of UWM. To prove zero-knowledge property, the simulator uses the trapdoor z as the witness to simulate proofs of statements $x_i \in L$ queried by the adversary (note that z is a valid witness for the statements (x_i, y)). The uniqueness property of UWM guarantees that proofs computed by either of the witnesses result in the same proof. Hence, the zero-knowledge property follows. Finally, note that, we can achieve the stronger notion of perfect ZK since the CRS in both the real world and the simulation are identically distributed (both are computed by sampling the CRS K of UWM and the string y pseudorandomly).

1.2.5   Perfectly Sound Verifier UWM Implies NP = UP

Recall that a verifier UWM (VUWM) is similar to an UWM with the additional guarantee that the verifier also accepts a unique proof for each statement x. The complexity class **UP** consists of problems that are accepted by an unambiguous Turing machine with at most one accepting path for each input. It is easy to see that the verifier of a perfectly sound VUWM acts as a **UP** relation. Also, since we require the VUWM to be perfectly sound it does not require as setup. Hence, it shows that **NP** $\subseteq$ **UP**. The other direction is trivial and hence this shows that **NP** = **UP**.

2 Preliminaries

2.1 Notation

For $n \in \mathbb{N}$, we write $[n] = \{1, 2, \cdots, n\}$. If x is a string, we denote $|x|$ as the length of x. For a distribution or random variable X, we denote $x \leftarrow X$ the action of sampling an element x according to X. When A is an algorithm, we write $y \leftarrow A(x)$ to denote a run of A on input x and output y; if A is randomized, then y is a random variable and $A(x; r)$ denotes a run of A on input x and randomness r. An algorithm A is probabilistic polynomial-time (PPT) if A is randomized and for any input $x, r \in \{0, 1\}^*$; the computation of $A(x; r)$ terminates in at most $poly(|x|)$ steps. For a set S, we let U_S denote the uniform distribution over S. For an integer $\alpha \in \mathbb{N}$, let U_α denote the uniform distribution over $\{0, 1\}^\alpha$, the bit strings of length α. Throughout this paper, we denote the security parameter by κ. We refer the reader to the full version of the paper for some basic definitions and concepts related to information theory. We will need the following form of the Chernoff-Hoeffding inequality.

Lemma 1. *Let S_N be the sum of N independent samples of a Bernoulli random variable, which is 1 with probability p and 0 otherwise. Then $\Pr[|S_N - Np| > t] < e^{-t^2/N}$. In particular, $\Pr[|S_N - Np| > N^{2/3}] < e^{-N^{1/3}}$.*

2.2 Cryptographic Primitives

Next we summarize some of the cryptographic primitives from literature that we rely on.

2.2.1 Witness PRFs

A witness PRF [17] consists of triple of algorithms wPRF = (wPRF.Gen, F, wPRF.Eval) as follows:

1. wPRF.Gen(κ, R) : This is a randomized algorithm that takes as input the security parameter 1^κ and the description of a circuit $R : \mathcal{X} \times \mathcal{W} \rightarrow \{0, 1\}$ and outputs a function secret key fk along with a public evaluation key ek.
2. F(fk, x) : The private evaluation algorithm F is a deterministic algorithm that takes as input the function secret key fk and an input $x \in \mathcal{X}$ and produces some output $y \in \mathcal{Y}$ for some set $\mathcal{Y}$.
3. wPRF.Eval(ek, x, w) : The public evaluation algorithm wPRF.Eval is also a deterministic algorithm that takes as input the public evaluation key ek, an input $x \in \mathcal{X}$ and a witness $w \in \mathcal{W}$ to produce an output $y \in \mathcal{Y}$ or $\bot$.

* *Correctness.* The correctness of wPRF requires that for all $x \in \mathcal{X}$ and $w \in \mathcal{W}$, the following holds:

$$\text{wPRF.Eval}(\text{ek}, x, w) = \begin{cases} \text{F(fk}, x) & \text{if } R(x, w) = 1 \\ \bot & \text{if } R(x, w) = 0 \end{cases}$$

* *Security.* We recall the *adaptive instance interactive security* notion for witness PRFs from [17]. Consider the following experiment $\mathsf{Exp}^R_\mathcal{A}(\kappa, b)$ between an adversary $\mathcal{A}$ and a challenger $\mathcal{C}$, parameterized by a relation $R : \mathcal{X} \times \mathcal{W} \to \{0, 1\}$, a bit b and security parameter κ.

- The challenger $\mathcal{C}$ runs $(\mathsf{fk}, \mathsf{ek}) \leftarrow \mathsf{wPRF.Gen}(\kappa, R)$, and gives ek to $\mathcal{A}$.
- $\mathcal{A}$ can adaptively make queries on instances $x_i \in \mathcal{X}$ and receives the values $\mathsf{F}(\mathsf{fk}, x_i)$ from $\mathcal{C}$.
- At any point in the game, $\mathcal{A}$ can make a challenge query $x^* \in \mathcal{X}$. The challenger computes $y_0 \leftarrow \mathsf{F}(\mathsf{fk}, x^*)$ and $y_1 \xleftarrow{\$} \mathcal{Y}$. It then returns y_b to $\mathcal{A}$.
- $\mathcal{A}$ can make additional queries to F and finally $\mathcal{A}$ outputs a bit b'. The challenger $\mathcal{C}$ checks that $x^* \notin \{x_i\}$ and that $x^* \notin L_R$[3]. If either check fails, $\mathcal{C}$ outputs a random bit. Otherwise, it outputs b'.

Let W_b be the event that the challenger in experiment $\mathsf{Exp}^R_\mathcal{A}(\kappa, b)$ outputs 1. Define the advantage of $\mathcal{A}$ as $\mathsf{wPRF.Adv}^R_\mathcal{A}(\kappa) = |\Pr[W_0] - \Pr[W_1]|$.

Definition 1 (Adaptive instance Interactive security). wPRF $=$ (wPRF.Gen, F, wPRF.Eval) *is adaptive instance interactively secure for a NP relation R if for all PPT adversaries $\mathcal{A}$, the advantage $\mathsf{wPRF.Adv}^R_\mathcal{A}$ of $\mathcal{A}$ is negligible in the security parameter κ.*

One can also define *non-interactive* security for witness PRFs, where the adversary $\mathcal{A}$ in the above experiment is not allowed to make any F queries.

Definition 2 (Adaptive instance Non-Interactive security). wPRF $=$ (wPRF.Gen, F, wPRF.Eval) *is adaptive instance non-interactively secure for a NP relation R if for all PPT adversaries $\mathcal{A}$, the advantage $\mathsf{wPRF.Adv}^R_\mathcal{A}$ of $\mathcal{A}$ is negligible in the security parameter κ, and additionally the adversary $\mathcal{A}$ is not allowed to make any F queries in the above experiment.*

Finally, one can also define a weaker notion of security, called the *static instance interactive (non-interactive) security*, where the adversary needs to commit to the challenge x^* before seeing ek or before making any queries to the oracle F. We note that one can convert any static-instance interactive (resp. non-interactive) witness PRF to an adaptive instance one by relying on complexity leveraging when appropriate.

2.2.2   Generalized Goldreich-Levin Theorem

For our construction of witness PRF from witness maps we will need to use a generalized version of the Goldreich-Levin (GL) theorem [7], as stated below.

Lemma 2 (Generalized Goldreich-Levin Theorem). *There exists a PPT inverter $\mathcal{A}'$ and a non-zero polynomial $q(\cdot)$ such that, for any PPT algorithm $\mathcal{A}$ and any $(\alpha, \beta) \in \{0,1\}^k \times \{0,1\}^\ell$ such that $p(\alpha) := \Pr[\mathcal{A}(\alpha, r) = \langle \beta, r \rangle : r \xleftarrow{\$} \{0,1\}^\ell]$ (where $\langle \cdot, \cdot \rangle$ denotes the inner product over the binary field), then $\Pr[\mathcal{A}'^{\mathcal{A}(\alpha, \cdot)}(1^\ell, \alpha) = \beta] \geq q(p(\alpha) - \frac{1}{2}).$*

---

[3] Note that, the language $L_R := \{x \mid \exists w, (x, w) \in R\}$.

2.2.3   Leakage-resilient Weak PRF

A standard weak PRF (wPRF) requires that given arbitrarily many uniformly random inputs $x_1, \cdots, x_q$, the outputs of the wPRF $y_1, \cdots, y_q$ look pseudorandom. A leakage-resilient wPRF (LR-wPRF) requires wPRF security to hold even if the attacker can leak some information about the secret key. In particular, we will consider the entropy-bounded leakage model [3,5]. Following [5], we first recall the notion of λ-leaky functions.

Definition 3 (λ-leaky function). *A probabilistic function* $h : \{0,1\}^* \to \{0,1\}^*$ *is λ-leaky if, for all* $n \in \mathbb{N}$ *we have* $\widetilde{\mathrm{H}}_\infty(\mathcal{U}_n | h(\mathcal{U}_n)) \geq n - \lambda$, *where* $\mathcal{U}_n$ *is the uniform distribution over* $\{0,1\}^n$.

As shown in [5], if a function is λ-leaky (decreases the entropy of the uniform distribution by at most λ bits), then it decreases the entropy of every distribution by at most λ bits. Moreover, the definition composes nicely and an adversary that adaptively chooses several λ_i-leaky functions, only learns $\sum_i \lambda_i$ bits of information.

Informally, we say a function $\mathcal{F}_K(\$)$ is a $\lambda(\kappa)$-leakage-resilient weak PRF in the entropy-bounded leakage model, if the weak PRF security guarantee is maintained, even if the adversary can learn the output of a λ-leaky function on the key K. We refer to the full version for the formal definition.

We also rely on statistically-sound NIWI proof systems. We refer to the full version for the formal definition.

3   Different Notions of Witness Maps and Their Definitions

In this section, we present the definition of compact witness map from [4]. We then present different variations of their definition, namely designated-verifier witness maps and verifier-compact witness maps, which we introduce in this work. We start by recalling the definition of compact witness map (CWM) from [4].

3.1   Compact Witness Maps

We say that $R \subseteq \{0,1\}^* \times \{0,1\}^*$ is said to be an **NP** relation if membership in it can be computed in time polynomial in the length of the first input. Given an **NP** relation R, we define the **NP** language $L_R := \{x \mid \exists w, (x,w) \in R\}$. When referring to $(x,w) \in R$, where R is a given **NP** relation, x is called the statement and w the witness. It will be convenient for us to consider **NP** relations parametrized with their input length: Below we let $R_\ell := R \cap \{0,1\}^\ell \times \{0,1\}^*$.

Definition 4 (Compact Witness Map (CWM)). *For* $\alpha \geq 0$, *an* α-*CWM for an* **NP** *relation* R *is a triple* CWM $=$ (setup, map, check) *where* setup *is a PPT algorithm and the other two are deterministic polynomial time algorithms such that:*

- setup(κ, ℓ) *outputs a string* K *of length polynomial in the security parameter* κ *and* ℓ, *where* $\ell = \ell(\kappa)$ *is an upper bound on the length of the statements supported by* CWM.
- <u>*Completeness:*</u> *For any polynomial* ℓ, $\forall (x, w) \in R_{\ell(\kappa)}$, $\forall$K $\leftarrow$ setup$(\kappa, \ell(\kappa))$,

$$\mathsf{check}(\mathsf{K}, x, \mathsf{map}(\mathsf{K}, x, w)) = 1.$$

- <u>*Compactness:*</u> *For any polynomial* ℓ, $\forall$K $\leftarrow$ setup$(\kappa, \ell(\kappa))$, $\forall x \in \{0, 1\}^{\ell(\kappa)}$,

$$|\{\mathsf{map}(\mathsf{K}, x, w) \mid (x, w) \in R_{\ell(\kappa)}\}| \leq 2^{\alpha}.$$

- <u>*Soundness:*</u> *For any polynomial* ℓ *and any PPT adversary* $\mathcal{A}$, $\mathsf{Adv}^{\mathrm{CWM}}_{\mathcal{A}}(\kappa)$ *defined below is negligible:*

$$\Pr_{\substack{\mathsf{K} \leftarrow \mathsf{setup}(\kappa, \ell(\kappa)) \\ (x^*, w^*) \leftarrow \mathcal{A}(\mathsf{K})}} [\mathsf{check}(\mathsf{K}, x^*, w^*) = 1, x^* \notin L_R].$$

A 0-CWM is also called a **Unique Witness Map** *(UWM).*

The above definition has perfect security in the sense that the completeness and compactness conditions hold for *every possible* K that CWM.setup can output with positive probability. A statistical version, where this needs to hold with all but negligible probability over the choice of K will suffice for all our applications. But for simplicity, we shall use the perfect version above.

3.2   Designated-Verifier Witness Maps

In this section, we define (reusable/non-reusable) designated-verifier compact witness maps (dv-CWM).

Definition 5 (Reusable/Non-Reusable dv-CWM). *For* $\alpha \geq 0$, *a reusable (resp. non-reusable)* α-*dv-CWM for an* **NP** *relation* R *is a triple* DV-CWM $=$ (setup, map, check) *where* setup *is a PPT algorithm that on input the security parameter* κ *and the statement length* ℓ, *outputs a pair of strings* (K, VK), *and the other two are deterministic polynomial time algorithms that satisfy the completeness, compactness and reusable soundness (resp. non-reusable soundness) conditions below.*

- <u>*Completeness:*</u> *For any polynomial* ℓ, $\forall (x, w) \in R_{\ell(\kappa)}$, $\forall$(K, VK) $\leftarrow$ setup$(\kappa, \ell(\kappa))$,

$$\mathsf{check}(\mathsf{VK}, x, \mathsf{map}(\mathsf{K}, x, w)) = 1.$$

- *Compactness:* For any polynomial ℓ, $\forall (K, VK) \leftarrow \mathsf{setup}(\kappa, \ell(\kappa))$, $\forall x \in \{0,1\}^{\ell(\kappa)}$,

$$|\{\mathsf{map}(K, x, w) \mid (x, w) \in R_{\ell(\kappa)}\}| \leq 2^{\alpha}.$$

- *Reusable/Non-Reusable Soundness:* Reusable soundness requires that the advantage $\mathsf{Adv}_{\mathcal{A}}^{\mathrm{DV\text{-}CWM}}(\kappa)$ defined below is negligible for every polynomial ℓ and every PPT adversary $\mathcal{A}$ with oracle access to $\mathsf{check}(VK, \cdot, \cdot)$.

$$\mathsf{Adv}_{\mathcal{A}}^{\mathrm{DV\text{-}CWM}}(\kappa) = \Pr_{\substack{(K,VK) \leftarrow \mathsf{setup}(\kappa,\ell(\kappa)) \\ (x^*, w^*) \leftarrow \mathcal{A}^{\mathsf{check}(VK,\cdot,\cdot)}(K)}} [\mathsf{check}(VK, x^*, w^*) = 1 \wedge x^* \notin L_R].$$

Non-reusable soundness requires that $\mathsf{Adv}_{\mathcal{A}}^{\mathrm{DV\text{-}CWM}}(\kappa)$ *is negligible for every polynomial ℓ and every PPT adversary $\mathcal{A}$ which does not access its oracle.*

A 0-dv-CWM is also called a Designated-verifier UWM (dv-UWM).

Similar to CWM, one can also define a weaker notion of selective reusable (resp. non-reusable) soundness, in which the adversary is required to generate x^* first (given κ, ℓ) before it gets K and access to the verification oracle $\mathsf{check}(VK, \cdot, \cdot)$.

3.3 Verifier-Compact Witness Maps

Definition 6 (Verifier-Compact Witness Maps (VCWM)). *For $\alpha \geq 0$, an α-VCWM* (setup, map, check) *for an* **NP** *relation R is a CWM for R satisfying the following additional condition:*

- *Verifier-Compactness:* For any polynomial ℓ, $\forall K \leftarrow \mathsf{setup}(\kappa, \ell(\kappa))$, $\forall x \in \{0,1\}^{\ell(\kappa)}$,

$$|\{w^* \mid \mathsf{check}(K, x, w^*) = 1\}| \leq 2^{\alpha}.$$

*A 0-VCWM is also called a verifier-unique witness map (*VUWM*).*

Selective Soundness. The soundness condition for CWM and its variants (dv-CWM and VCWM) can be relaxed to obtain a *selectively sound* variant of the corresponding primitive. In the soundness conditions above, we considered an adversary $\mathcal{A}$ which outputs a statement x^* and a purported proof w^* at the end of the experiment. For selective soundness, we require $\mathcal{A}$ to output x^* at the beginning (given only κ, ℓ), before setup is executed. This level of soundness suffices for some applications (e.g., construction of a witness encryption scheme from a UWM), as shown in [4]. It also provides an intermediate target for constructions, as one can convert a selectively sound CWM to a standard CWM by relying on complexity leveraging.

4   Equivalence of Witness PRFs and dv-UWM

In this section, we explore the relationship between witness PRF (wPRF) and unique witness maps. In particular, we show that witness PRF and designated-verifier UWM (dv-UWM) are equivalent for **NP**. For these implications, we consider the static security variant of witness PRF and selective soundness of dv-UWM. Our implications can be adapted to the adaptive security variants of both these notions via complexity leveraging.

4.1   Witness PRF Imply dv-UWM

In this section, we present the construction of our (selective reusable sound) dv-UWM for any **NP** relation R. The main building block of our construction is a (static-instance secure) witness PRF for R.

Construction. Let wPRF = (wPRF.Gen, F, wPRF.Eval) be a *static-instance interactively secure* witness PRF for any **NP** relation R parametrized by statements of length at most $\ell(\kappa)$, where κ is the security parameter and ℓ is an arbitrary (but fixed) polynomial in the security parameter. We construct a (selective) *reusable* dv-UWM DV-UWM = (dv.setup, dv.map, dv.check) for R as follows:

- dv.setup(κ, ℓ) : Run (fk, ek) $\leftarrow$ wPRF.Gen(κ, R). Set K = ek and VK = fk.
- dv.map(K, x, w) : Parse K as ek. Run y = wPRF.Eval(ek, x, w). Output $w^* = y$
- dv.check(VK, x, w^*) : Parse VK as fk and compute $y' = F(fk, x)$ and check if $w^* \overset{?}{=} y'$. If the check is satisfied, output 1; else output $\bot$.

Theorem 1. *Let* wPRF *be an static-instance interactively secure witness PRF for* **NP** *with super-polynomial range* $|\mathcal{Y}| = \kappa^{\omega(1)}$. *Then the above construction of dv-UWM for* **NP** *satisfies selective reusable soundness.*

Proof. Firstly, we note that DV-UWM satisfies perfect completeness (assuming wPRF is perfectly correct). Also, it satisfies uniqueness, since (x, w) is deterministically mapped to the output of wPRF, regardless of the witness w. In particular, the correctness of wPRF guarantees that for all $(x, w) \in R$, wPRF.Eval(ek, x, w) = F(fk, x). The later function (i.e., F(fk, $\cdot$)) does not depend on w and deterministically maps x to a unique output value $y \in \mathcal{Y}$. Below, we shall prove that the construction satisfies selective reusable soundness as well.

Consider an adversary $\mathcal{A}$ in the definition of $\mathsf{Adv}_{\mathcal{A}}^{\text{DV-UWM}}(\kappa)$ (see Def. 5). Note that, in the (selective) reusable soundness experiment the adversary $\mathcal{A}$ first commits to the challenge x^* and then gets access to the public parameter K and the verification oracle, namely dv.check(VK, $\cdot, \cdot$). The oracle takes as input tuples of the form (x_i, w_i^*) and outputs either 1 or 0. We show how to construct another adversary $\mathcal{B}$ breaking the static-instance interactive security of wPRF using $\mathcal{A}$ in a black-box way. The adversary $\mathcal{B}$ simulates the environment of $\mathcal{A}$ as follows:

1. The adversary $\mathcal{B}$ first commits to a challenge x^* such that $x^* \notin L_R$. The adversary $\mathcal{A}$ forwards x^* to its own challenger and receives a value $y^* \in \mathcal{Y}$, which it stores in its memory.

2. The adversary $\mathcal{B}$ then receives ek from its challenger and sets $\mathsf{K} = \mathsf{ek}$. It gives K to $\mathcal{A}$.

3. When $\mathcal{A}$ queries a tuple (x_i, w_i^*) to $\mathsf{dv.check}(\mathsf{K}, \mathsf{VK}, \cdot, \cdot)$, the adversary $\mathcal{B}$ does the following:

   - Query the oracle $\mathsf{F}(\mathsf{fk}, \cdot)$ on input x_i to receive some output y_i.
   - Checks if $w_i^* \overset{?}{=} y_i$. If so, it outputs 1 to $\mathcal{A}'$ else it outputs 0.

4. Finally, at some point $\mathcal{A}$ outputs w^* corresponding to the challenge x^* (which it committed to before). The adversary $\mathcal{A}$ then retrieves the value y^* from its memory and checks if $y^* \overset{?}{=} w^*$. If the check passes, $\mathcal{B}$ outputs 0; else it outputs 1.

This completes the description of simulation of $\mathcal{A}'s$ environment by $\mathcal{B}$. Let us assume that $\mathcal{A}$ makes a total of $q = q(\kappa)$ queries to the verification oracle $\mathsf{dv.check}(\mathsf{VK}, \cdot, \cdot)$ (including the challenge query). Since $\mathcal{A}$ has some non-negligible advantage (say ϵ) in breaking the selective reusable soundness of DV-UWM, it must hold that $\mathsf{dv.check}(\mathsf{VK}, x^*, w^*) = 1$ holds with probability ϵ. According to the construction, the above check passes whenever $w^* = \mathsf{F}(\mathsf{fk}, x^*)$. If the value y^* received by $\mathcal{B}$ from its challenger was computed using the function $\mathsf{F}(\mathsf{fk}, \cdot)$, then it always holds that $y^* = w^*$. However, if y^* was randomly sampled, the probability that w^* is equal to y^* is $\frac{1}{|\mathcal{Y}|}$, which is negligible. Hence, the advantage of $\mathcal{B}$ in breaking the adaptive-instance interactive security of wPRF is $\epsilon - \frac{q}{|\mathcal{Y}|}$, which is non-negligible, thereby contradicting the security of wPRF. $\square$

4.2   dv-UWM Implies Witness PRF

Now, we present our implication in the other direction, namely that dv-UWM for **NP** implies witness PRF for **NP**. We split our transformation into two phases. First, we present a construction of a (static) non-interactive witness PRF for **NP** from any (selective) non-reusably sound dv-UWM for **NP**. Next, we show a generic transformation from any (static) non-interactive witness PRF for **NP** to an (static) interactive witness PRF for **NP** additionally using any one way function.

4.2.1   dv-UWM Implies Non-interactive Witness PRF

In this section, we show our first transformation from any (selective) non-reusably sound dv-UWM for **NP** to a (static-instance) non-interactive witness PRF for **NP**. The construction is shown in Fig. 2.

Theorem 2. *If* DV-UWM *is a selective non-reusably sound dv-UWM for the* **NP** *relation* $\mathfrak{R}$ *(defined in Fig. 2), then the construction shown in Fig. 2 is a static-instance non-interactively secure witness PRF for the* **NP** *relation* R.

Let R be a **NP** relation, and L_R be the corresponding **NP** language defined as $L_R :=$ $\{x \mid \exists w : (x, w) \in R\}$. Let R' be another **NP** relation defined as $(y, z) \in R'$ if and only if $y = G(z)$, where $G : \{0, 1\}^{\kappa} \to \{0, 1\}^{2\kappa}$ is a length-doubling pseudo-random generator. Also, let $L_{R'}$ be the corresponding **NP** language defined as $L_{R'} := \{y \mid \exists z : (y, z) \in R'\}$. Further, we assume that R and R' are parameterized with their input lengths. Define the following derived **NP** relation $\Re$ and language $L_{\Re}$ as:

$$\Re\big((x, y), (w, z)\big) = 1 \iff R(x, w) = 1 \vee R'(y, z) = 1, \text{ and}$$

$$L_{\Re} = \{(x, y) \mid \exists (w, z), ((x, y), (w, z)) \in \Re\}.$$

Note that, the relation $\Re$ is parameterized with statements of length at most $\ell' = \ell + 2\kappa$.

(a) Let DV-UWM $=$ (dv.setup, dv.map, dv.check) be a (selectively) sound dv-UWM for the language $L_{\Re}$. Further, let the length of the representative w^* of DV-UWM be $p(\kappa)$ bits, for some polynomial $p(\cdot)$.

(b) Let $\mathrm{GL}(\pi, r)$ denote the Goldreich-Levin (GL) hardcore bit [7] of π using randomness r. Recall that, the GL predicate is the bit-wise inner product of π and r.

1. wPRF.Gen(κ, R) : Takes as input an **NP** relation R (parametrized by its input length ℓ) as defined above. Run $(\mathsf{K}, \mathsf{VK}) \leftarrow$ dv.setup(κ, ℓ'), where ℓ' is defined as above. Sample $z \leftarrow \{0, 1\}^{\kappa}$ and $r \leftarrow \{0, 1\}^{p(\kappa)}$ uniformly at random, and compute $y = G(z)$. Set $\mathsf{ek} = (\mathsf{K}, y, r)$ and $\mathsf{fk} = z$.

2. F(fk, x) : Takes as input an instance $x \in L_R$. It does the following:
   - Computes the representative witness $w^* =$ dv.map$(\mathsf{K}, (x, y), (\perp, z))$, using $(\perp, z)$ as witness. Note that, $(x, y) \in L_{\Re}$.
   - Compute the GL hardcore bit $b = \mathrm{GL}(w^*, r)$.

3. wPRF.Eval(ek, x, w) : Takes as input an instance $x \in L_R$. It does the following:
   - Computes a representative witness $w^* =$ dv.map$(\mathsf{K}, (x, y), (w, \perp))$, using $(w, \perp)$ as witness. Note that, $(x, y) \in L_{\Re}$.
   - Compute the GL hardcore bit $b = \mathrm{GL}(w^*, r)$.

Fig. 2. Construction of Non-Interactive Witness PRF wPRF from DV-UWM

Proof. We show that any adversary $\mathcal{A}_{\mathsf{wprf}}$ breaking the static-instance non-interactive security of wPRF with a noticeable advantage can be transformed into an adversary $\mathcal{A}_{\mathsf{dv\text{-}uwm}}$ breaking the selective non-reusable soundness of DV-UWM. Note that, in the static-instance non-interactive security game of wPRF the adversary commits to the challenge x^* before seeing the evaluation key ek. At first, we show that the adversary $\mathcal{A}_{\mathsf{wprf}}$ breaking the security of wPRF can be converted into a predictor $\mathcal{A}_{\mathrm{GL}}$ for the generalized Goldreich-Levin theorem.

In more details, let the adversary $\mathcal{A}_{\mathsf{wprf}}$ can predict the bit b in the security experiment of wPRF on the challenge instance $x^* \notin L_R$ with non-negligible probability. Let, $\alpha = (\mathsf{K}, y)$, and $\beta = w^*$ from the generalized GL theorem (see Lemma 2). This implies that we can construct a distinguisher $\mathcal{A}$ that on input $(\alpha = (\mathsf{K}, y), r)$ can distinguish the bit b (in the above construction) from a random bit with non-negligible probability. Hence, by Lemma 2, we can use this distinguisher $\mathcal{A}$ to construct a predictor $\mathcal{A}'$, who given $\alpha = (\mathsf{K}, y)$ can predict the pre-image w^* with non-negligible probability. This implies that the predictor outputs w^* such that $w^* = \mathsf{dv.map}\big(\mathsf{K}, (x, y), (\bot, z)\big)$ with non-negligible probability. At this point, instead of computing $y = G(z)$, we sample a random $y \leftarrow \{0, 1\}^{2\kappa}$. The security of the PRG G ensures that this switch is indistinguishable to $\mathcal{A}'$. Hence the probability that $\mathcal{A}'$ outputs a "valid" w^* (w^* such that $\mathsf{dv.check}(\mathsf{K}, \mathsf{VK}, (x, y), w^*) = 1$) continues to hold, except with a negligible probability. However, note that, with very high probability it holds that $(x, y) \notin \mathfrak{R}$. This contradicts the selective non-reusable soundness property of dv-UWM, since the adversary $\mathcal{A}'$ outputs a valid representative witness corresponding to a false statement $(x, y) \notin \mathfrak{R}$. □

4.2.2 Equivalence of Non-Interactive and Interactive Witness PRF

In this section, we show that any (static-instance) non-interactive witness PRF for **NP** can be generically transformed to a (static-instance) interactive witness PRF for **NP**. The construction is given in Fig. 3.

Theorem 3. *Let nl-wPRF be a static-instance non-interactively secure witness PRF for the* **NP** *relation Ψ (defined in Fig. 3), and* (Com, Open) *be a statistically binding commitment scheme. Then the construction shown in Fig. 3 is a static-instance interactively secure witness PRF for the* **NP** *relation $\mathcal{R}$.*

The detailed proof of this theorem is presented in the full version of the paper. The intuition behind the proof is given in the technical overview.

5 Extremely Compact WM Implies Pseudo-UWM

In this section, we show that an *extremely compact* WM – i.e., a CWM with polynomial-sized image – implies a Pseudo-UWM (p-UWM) where the uniqueness may not hold with an inverse polynomial probability (that can be made arbitrarily small). In other words, we show that a α-CWM for $\alpha = O(\log \kappa)$ for security parameter κ implies a p-UWM as defined below.

Definition 7 (Pseudo Unique Witness Map (p-UWM)). *A Pseudo-UWM (p-UWM) for an* **NP** *relation R is a triple* CWM $=$ (setup, map, check) *where* setup *is a PPT algorithm, and* map *and* check *are deterministic polynomial time algorithms such that:*

Let $\mathcal{R} : \mathcal{X} \times \mathcal{W} \to \{0, 1\}$ be an **NP** relation restricted to inputs in $\mathcal{X} = \{0, 1\}^{\ell(\kappa)}$, and $L_\mathcal{R}$ be the corresponding **NP** language defined as $L_\mathcal{R} := \{x \mid \exists w, (x, w) \in \mathcal{R}\}$. Let $\mathcal{R}'$ be another **NP** relation defined as:

$$((x, c), (x', r)) \in \mathcal{R}' \iff (c = \mathsf{Com}(x'; r) \wedge (x \neq x')),$$

where Com is a polynomial-time statistically binding commitment scheme over a message space $\mathcal{X} \cup \{0\}$, where $0 \notin \mathcal{X}$. Also, let $L_{\mathcal{R}'}$ be the corresponding **NP** language. Finally, let us define the following **NP** relation Ψ and language L_Ψ as:

$$((x, c), (w, x', r)) \in \Psi \iff (x, w) \in \mathcal{R} \vee ((x, c), (x', r)) \in \mathcal{R}' \text{ and}$$

$$L_\Psi = \{(x, c) \mid \exists (w, x', r) \text{ s.t. } ((x, c), (w, x', r)) \in \Psi\}.$$

Note that, the relation Ψ is parameterized with the input length $\ell' = \ell + |c|$.

- Let nl-wPRF = (nl-wPRF.Gen, nl-wPRF.F, nl-wPRF.Eval) be a static-instance non-interactive witness PRF for the NP relation Ψ defined above.

We construct a static-instance interactively secure witness PRF wPRF = (wPRF.Gen, F, wPRF.Eval) as follows:

1. wPRF.Gen($\kappa, \mathcal{R}$) : Takes as input the **NP** relation $\mathcal{R}$ defined above. Run $(\hat{\mathsf{ek}}, \hat{\mathsf{fk}}) \leftarrow$ nl-wPRF.Gen(κ, Ψ), where the relation Ψ is defined as above. Sample a random tape r for the commitment scheme Com, and compute $c = \mathsf{Com}(0; r)$. Set $\mathsf{ek} = (\hat{\mathsf{ek}}, c)$ and $\mathsf{fk} = (\hat{\mathsf{fk}}, r)$.

2. F(fk, x) : Parse fk as $(\hat{\mathsf{fk}}, r)$, compute the commitment $c = \mathsf{Com}(0; r)$ and output $y = $ nl-wPRF.F($\hat{\mathsf{fk}}, (x, c)$).

3. wPRF.Eval(ek, x, w) : Takes as input an instance-witness pair $(x, w) \in \mathcal{R}$ and does the following: Parse ek as $(\hat{\mathsf{ek}}, c)$ and output nl-wPRF.Eval($\hat{\mathsf{ek}}, (x, c), (w, \perp, \perp)$). Note that $(x, c) \in L_\Psi$.

Fig. 3. Construction of an interactive wPRF wPRF from a non-interactive wPRF nl-wPRF

- setup(κ, ℓ, ϵ) *outputs a string* K *of length polynomial in* κ, ℓ *and* $1/\epsilon$.
- *Completeness: For any polynomials* $\ell, 1/\epsilon$, $\forall (x, w) \in R_{\ell(\kappa)}$,

$$\Pr_{\substack{\mathsf{K} \leftarrow \mathsf{setup}(\kappa, \ell(\kappa), \epsilon(\kappa)) \\ w^* \leftarrow \mathsf{map}(\mathsf{K}, x, w)}} [\mathsf{check}(\mathsf{K}, x, w^*) = 1] = 1.$$

- *Pseudo-Uniqueness: For any polynomial* ℓ, $\forall x \in \{0, 1\}^{\ell(\kappa)}$, $\forall w_1, w_2$ *such that* $(x, w_1), (x, w_2) \in R_{\ell(\kappa)}$ *(possibly* $w_1 = w_2$),

$$\Pr_{\substack{\mathsf{K} \leftarrow \mathsf{setup}(\kappa, \ell(\kappa), \epsilon(\kappa)) \\ w_1^* \leftarrow \mathsf{map}(\mathsf{K}, x, w_1) \\ w_2^* \leftarrow \mathsf{map}(\mathsf{K}, x, w_2)}} [w_1^* \neq w_2^*] \leq \epsilon(\kappa)$$

- *Soundness:* For any polynomials $\ell, 1/\epsilon$, and any PPT adversary $\mathcal{A}$, $\mathsf{Adv}_{\mathcal{A}}^{\mathrm{CWM}}(\kappa)$ defined below is negligible:

$$\Pr_{\substack{\mathsf{K}\leftarrow\mathsf{setup}(\kappa,\ell(\kappa),\epsilon(\kappa)) \\ (x^*,w^*)\leftarrow\mathcal{A}(\mathsf{K})}}[\mathsf{check}(\mathsf{K},x^*,w^*)=1, x^* \notin L_R].$$

We now present the construction below. The main building block of our construction is a statistically-sound NIWI (SNIWI) argument system NIWI. Before proceeding with the construction, let us try to solve a seemingly unrelated algorithmic problem, which we call the *pseudo-deterministic sampling* (PDS) problem over a polynomial-sized domain. We will later see how to use a solution for the PDS problem in our construction of p-UWM from CWM.

Pseudo-Deterministic Sampling for Small Domains. Let $\mathcal{D}$ be an arbitrary distribution over some set X with a support of size n. Our goal is to design an algorithm PDS.sam that is polynomial-time in n and with only sampling access to $\mathcal{D}$, can *pseudo-deterministically* output an element from the support of $\mathcal{D}$. PDS.sam takes a reference string crs, and the pseudo-determinism is required to hold with high probability over the choice of crs. More formally, (PDS.setup, PDS.sam) is said to be a PDS scheme if:

1. PDS.setup(n,ℓ,δ), with inputs the security parameter κ, a bound n on the support size of distributions over $\{0,1\}^\ell$ that are to be handled, and a probability $\delta > 0$, outputs a common reference string crs of length polynomial in n, ℓ and $1/\delta$.
2. PDS.sam$^{\mathcal{D}}$(crs) : Given an input crs and sampling access to a distribution $\mathcal{D}$ over $\{0,1\}^\ell$, the algorithm PDS.sam gets a polynomial number of samples from $\mathcal{D}$ (polynomial in $|\text{crs}|$) and outputs an element in the support of $\mathcal{D}$, such that the following holds:
   - **Pseudo-determinism:** For all distributions $\mathcal{D}$ over $\{0,1\}^\ell$ with support size at most n,

$$\Pr_{\substack{\mathsf{crs}\leftarrow\mathsf{PDS.setup}(n,\ell,\delta) \\ c_1\leftarrow\mathsf{PDS.sam}^{\mathcal{D}}(\mathsf{crs}), c_2\leftarrow\mathsf{PDS.sam}^{\mathcal{D}}(\mathsf{crs})}}[c_1 \neq c_2] \leq \delta$$

where the probability is over the choice of crs as well as the samples from $\mathcal{D}$.

We refer to an (n,ℓ,δ)-PDS as a PDS scheme setup with those parameters. We now present a construction of a PDS scheme in Fig. 4.

Let $\mathcal{D}$ be an arbitrary distribution over $\{0,1\}^\ell$ with a support of size at most n.

1. $\underline{\mathsf{PDS.setup}(n,\ell,\delta)}$: Let $\mathcal{H} = \{H_\kappa\}_{\kappa \in \mathbb{N}}$ be a family of $2N$-wise independent hash functions for $N = (2n/\delta)^3$. Sample a hash function $H \xleftarrow{\$} \mathcal{H}$, where $H : \{0,1\}^{\ell + \log N} \to \{0,1\}^\kappa$, κ is the security parameter. Set $\mathsf{crs} = H$.

2. $\mathsf{PDS.sam}^{\mathcal{D}}(\mathsf{crs})$:
   (a) Obtain a multi-set S of N samples from $\mathcal{D}$.
   (b) Define the set $Y = \{x \| i \mid i > 0 \text{ and } x \text{ has multiplicity at least } i \text{ in } S\}$.
   (c) Let $\mathsf{H} = \{H(y) \mid y \in Y\}$, where each $h \in \mathsf{H}$ is a bit string of length κ.
   (d) Return the lexicographically smallest element of H.

Fig. 4. A pseudo-deterministic sampling algorithm for a small support

Lemma 3. (PDS.setup, PDS.sam) *(Fig. 4) is a PDS scheme.*

Proof. Since PDS.sam satisfies the efficiency requirements, and always outputs an element in the support of $\mathcal{D}$, it remains to show that it satisfies the pseudo-determinism requirement.

Consider two independent runs of PDS.sam using the same H. Let S_i, Y_i denote the multi-set of samples and the set of count-appended samples in the two executions.

First, fix the sets Y_1 and Y_2. Note that if the lexicographically smallest element in $\{H(y) \mid y \in Y_1 \cup Y_2\}$ is an element $H(y)$ for $y \in Y_1 \cap Y_2$, then PDS.sam outputs the same value in both runs. Now, since $\mathcal{H}$ is $2N$-wise independent, H behaves identical to a random function over $Y_1 \cup Y_2$. Hence, over the choice of H, the probability of error – i.e., that the outputs of PDS.sam are different – is upper bounded by $\frac{|Y_1 \triangle Y_2|}{|Y_1 \cup Y_2|} \leq \frac{|Y_1 \triangle Y_2|}{N}$.

Now we define the following "Good" event for the choice of (S_1, S_2) over the samples from $\mathcal{D}$ (independent of H): For all x the support of $\mathcal{D}$, the multiplicity of x in S_1 and in S_2 are both in the range $[Np - N^{2/3}, Np + N^{2/3}]$, where p is the probability assigned to x by $\mathcal{D}$. When this condition holds, $|Y_1 \triangle Y_2| \leq n \cdot 2N^{2/3}$, where n is an upper bound on the size of the support of $\mathcal{D}$. Hence, conditioned on the Good event, the probability of error is at most $\frac{|n \cdot 2N^{2/3}|}{2N}$.

Finally, by Lemma 1 and union bound (for each x in the support of $\mathcal{D}$, and each of Y_1, Y_2), the probability of the Good event not occurring is at most $2ne^{-N^{1/3}}$. Hence the probability of error is at most $2ne^{-N^{1/3}} + nN^{-1/3}$. Letting $N = (2n/\delta)^3$, this is at most δ. $\qquad\square$

Now we present the p-UWM scheme for an NP relation R. For simplicity, first we present a randomized map, and then point out how to derandomize it using the CRS.

1. The p-UWM setup outputs $\mathsf{crs} = (\mathsf{crs}_{\mathrm{NIWI}}, \mathsf{crs}_{\mathrm{CWM}}, \mathsf{crs}_{\mathsf{PDS.sam}})$, which consists of the setup for a statistically sound NIWI proof system for the relation R, an α-CWM for the relation corresponding to the NIWI verifier, and a $(2^\alpha, \ell, \epsilon/2)$-PDS scheme (as given above).
2. The p-UWM, on input $(x, w) \in R$, defines the distribution $\mathcal{D}_{x,w}$ as the distribution of $\mathsf{map}(\mathrm{NIWI}(x, w; \mathsf{crs}_{\mathrm{NIWI}}); \mathsf{crs}_{\mathrm{CWM}})$. Then it outputs $\mathsf{PDS.sam}^{\mathcal{D}_{x,w}}$.
3. The p-UWM verifier is the same as check.

Completeness is easy to see. The soundness of this proof depends on the fact that for any false statement, there does not *exist* a NIWI proof that gets accepted (except with negligible probability, over the choice of $\mathsf{crs}_{\mathrm{NIWI}}$), and that CWM is (computationally) sound. For pseudo-uniqueness, first consider two runs of p-UWM (with the same setup) using the same witness w. In this case, from the compactness of CWM and the pseudo-determinism of the PDS scheme, the probability of the outputs differing is at most $\epsilon/2$. In the general case, when two different witnesses w_1, w_2 are used, we note that the distributions $\mathcal{D}_{x,w_1}$ and $\mathcal{D}_{x,w_2}$ are computationally indistinguishable from each other, thanks to the witness indistinguishability property of NIWI. Since PDS.sam is computationally efficient, this implies that the probability of the outputs differing given access to $\mathcal{D}_{x,w_1}$ and $\mathcal{D}_{x,w_2}$ (rather than two copies of $\mathcal{D}_{x,w_1}$) can only be negligibly more than $\epsilon/2$. Hence for any inverse polynomial ϵ, this error probability is bounded by ϵ, as required.

Finally, we address the fact the p-UWM mapping algorithm above was defined to be randomized, to carry out the implementation of (N samples from) $\mathcal{D}_{x,w}$, given (x, w). Since the definition of pseudo-uniqueness involves only two runs of the mapping algorithm, it is enough to include a pairwise independent hash function in the CRS which would be used to derive the required amount of randomness as a function of its input (x, w).

6   Mildly Compact WM Implies NIZK

In this section, we show that a mildly compact WM - i.e., a CWM with compactness level $\alpha = \mathsf{poly}(\kappa)$ for some fixed polynomial $\mathsf{poly}(\cdot)$, independent of the statement size $|x|$ or the witness size $|w|$ implies the existence of NIZK argument system. As mentioned in in the introduction, we generalize the recent work of [10] who constructed NIZKs from SNARG by replacing SNARG with CWM with the above compactness level. In particular, we show a construction of *hidden-bits generator with subset-dependent proofs* (SDP-HBG) from α-CWM. This result, along with the compiler of [10] that transforms any NIZK in the hidden-bits model (HBM-NIZK) to NIZK in the CRS model using SDP-HBG implies a construction of NIZK from any α-CWM as long as $\alpha = \mathsf{poly}(\kappa)$ as defined above. Following [10] we first provide the definition of SDP-HBG.

6.1   Hidden-Bits Generator with Subset-Dependent Proofs

Following [10], we recall the notion of hidden-bits generator with subset-dependent proofs (SDP-HBG).

Definition 8 (SDP-HBG). A hidden-bits generator with subset-dependent proofs (SDP-HBG) consists of four PPT algorithms (HBG^{sdp}.Setup, HBG^{sdp}.GenBits, HBG^{sdp}.Prove, HBG^{sdp}.Verify) defined as follows:

1. HBG^{sdp}.Setup($1^\kappa, 1^n$) : The setup algorithm takes the security parameter 1^κ and the length parameter 1^n as input, and outputs a CRS crs.
2. HBG^{sdp}.GenBits(crs) : The bits generation algorithm takes a CRS crs as input, and outputs a string $r \xleftarrow{\$} \{0,1\}^n$ and a state st.
3. HBG^{sdp}.Prove(st, I) : The proving algorithm takes a state st and a subset $I \subseteq [n]$ as input, and outputs a proof π.
4. HBG^{sdp}.Verify(crs, I, r_I, π) : The verification algorithm takes a CRS crs, a subset $I \subseteq [n]$, a string $r_I \in \{0,1\}^{|I|}$ and a proof π as input, and outputs either 1 or 0 indicating acceptance or rejection respectively.

A SDP-HBG is required to satisfy the following properties:

- **Correctness.** For any natural number n and $I \subseteq [n]$, we have:

$$
\Pr \left[\text{HBG}^{\mathsf{sdp}}.\text{Verify}(\text{crs}, I, r_I, \pi) = 1 : \begin{array}{l} \text{crs} \leftarrow \text{HBG}^{\mathsf{sdp}}.\text{Setup}(1^\kappa, 1^n); \\ (r, \text{st}) \leftarrow \text{HBG}^{\mathsf{sdp}}.\text{GenBits}(\text{crs}); \\ \pi \leftarrow \text{HBG}^{\mathsf{sdp}}.\text{Prove}(\text{st}, I) \end{array} \right] = 1
$$

- **Somewhat Computational Binding.** There exists a constant $\gamma < 1$ such that (1) for any polynomial $n = n(\kappa)$ and for all crs $\leftarrow$ HBG^{sdp}.Setup($1^\kappa, 1^n$), there exists a subset $\mathcal{V}^{\mathsf{crs}} \subseteq \{0,1\}^n$ such that $|\mathcal{V}^{\mathsf{crs}}| \leq 2^{n^\gamma} \mathsf{poly}(\kappa)$ holds, and (2) for any PPT adversary $\mathcal{A}$, we have:

$$
\Pr_{\text{crs} \leftarrow \text{HBG}^{\mathsf{sdp}}.\text{Setup}(1^\kappa, 1^n)} \left[r_I \notin \mathcal{V}_I^{\mathsf{crs}} \wedge \text{HBG}^{\mathsf{sdp}}.\text{Verify}(\text{crs}, I, r_I, \pi) = 1 : \right.
$$

$$
\left. (I, r_I, \pi) \leftarrow \mathcal{A}(\text{crs}) \right] = \mathsf{negl}(\kappa).
$$

where $\mathcal{V}_I^{\mathsf{crs}} = \{r_I : r \in \mathcal{V}^{\mathsf{crs}}\}$
- **Computational Hiding.** For any polynomial $n = n(\kappa)$, $I \subseteq [n]$, any PPT adversary $\mathcal{A}$, we have:

$$
\left| \Pr\left[\mathcal{A}(\text{crs}, I, r_I, \pi, r_{\bar{I}}) = 1 \right] - \Pr\left[\mathcal{A}(\text{crs}, I, r_I, \pi, r'_{\bar{I}}) = 1 \right] \right|
$$

where $r'_{\bar{I}}$ denotes the substring of r on the positions corresponding to $\bar{I} = [n] \setminus I$.

A SDP-HBG is a weaker primitive than HBG, and [10] showed how to construct a SDP-HBG generically starting from any HBG.

6.2 Construction of SDP-HBG

In this section, we show how to construct a SDP-HBG from CWM and OWF. Our construction requires the following ingredients:

- An λ-entropic leakage-resilient weak PRF (λ-LR-wPRF) $\mathcal{F} = \{F_K : \{0,1\}^m \to \{0,1\}\}_{K \in \{0,1\}^k}$ (see Sect. 2.2.3), with key length $k = k(\kappa, \lambda) = \lambda \cdot \mathsf{poly}(\kappa)$, input length $m = m(\kappa, \lambda) = \lambda \cdot \mathsf{poly}(\kappa)$, and output length 1 bit. Here λ denotes the leakage parameter of the ELR-wPRF $\mathcal{F}$.
- A α-CWM $\mathsf{CWM} = (\mathsf{setup}, \mathsf{map}, \mathsf{check})$ for $\alpha = \mathsf{poly}(\kappa)$ for an arbitrary polynomial $\mathsf{poly}(\kappa)$ (independent of the length of the statement or witness) for the language L associated with the following relation R:

$$\Big((k', \{x_i\}_{i \in [k']}, \{r_i\}_{i \in [k']}), K)\Big) \in R \iff r_i = F_K(x_i) \quad \forall i \in [k']$$

We now proceed to describe our construction.

1. $\mathsf{HBG^{sdp}}.\mathsf{Setup}(1^\kappa, 1^n)$: Do the following:
   (a) Run $K \leftarrow \mathsf{setup}(\kappa, \ell)$, where ℓ is the length of the statement mentioned in the relation above.
   (b) For all $i \in [n]$, sample $x_i \xleftarrow{\$} \{0,1\}^m$.
   Return $\mathsf{crs} = (K, \{x_i\}_{i \in [n]})$.
2. $\mathsf{HBG^{sdp}}.\mathsf{GenBits}(\mathsf{crs})$: Do the following:
   (a) Parse the CRS as $\mathsf{crs} = (K, \{x_i\}_{i \in [n]})$.
   (b) Sample key $K \xleftarrow{\$} \{0,1\}^k$, and compute $r_i = F_K(x_i)$ for all $i \in [n]$.
   Return $(r = \{r_i\}_{i \in [n]}, \mathsf{st} = (\mathsf{crs}, K, r))$.
3. $\mathsf{HBG^{sdp}}.\mathsf{Prove}(\mathsf{st}, I)$: Parse $\mathsf{st} = (\mathsf{crs}, K, r)$ and $\mathsf{crs} = ((K, \{x_i\}_{i \in [n]})$. Then compute $w^* \leftarrow \mathsf{map}(K, (|I|, x_I, r_I), K)$ and return $\pi := w^*$.
4. $\mathsf{HBG^{sdp}}.\mathsf{Verify}(\mathsf{crs}, I, r_I, \pi)$: Parse $\mathsf{crs} = ((K, \{x_i\}_{i \in [n]})$ and π as w^*. Return the output $\mathsf{check}(K, (|I|, x_I, r_I), w^*)$.

Theorem 4. *Let κ be the security parameter. If there exist a λ-entropic leakage-resilient weak PRF and a α-CWM for all NP languages for $\alpha = \mathsf{poly}(\kappa)$ (where $\mathsf{poly}(\kappa)$ is some polynomial) such that $\alpha \leq \lambda$ and that satisfies adaptive soundness, then there exists an SDP-HBG that satisfies somewhat computational binding and computational hiding.*

The detailed proof of this theorem is presented in the full version of the paper. The intuition behind the proof is given in the technical overview.

7 UWM Implies Deterministic-Prover NIZK

In this section we show that UWM implies *deterministic-prover* NIZK argument system (DP-NIZK) satisfying *perfect* zero-knowledge. Before this, we knew how to construct such a DP-NIZK argument system only from $i\mathcal{O}$. Below we briefly sketch the construction and defer to the full version of the paper for the details of the construction and proof.

A DP-NIZK argument system is NIZK argument system where the prover and verifier are both *deterministic*. Apart from completeness and soundness we require perfect zero-knowledge property to hold, i.e., the simulated proofs are identically distributed to the real proofs. The setup algorithm of our DP-NIZK chooses a random seed z for a length-doubling pseudorandom generator G and sets $y = G(z)$. The CRS crs of DP-NIZK consists of the CRS K of UWM and the value y. The prover of DP-NIZK on input some (x, w) in the relation runs the UWM prover to get a representative witness w^* for the statement $\hat{x}$ stating that "either x is true or y is pseudorandom", using w as the witness. Note that the prover is deterministic. In the proof of soundness, we sample y uniformly at random, so that y is not in the image of G, except with negligible probability. At this point the soundness of DP-NIZK follows from the soundness of UWM. To prove ZK, the simulator uses the witness z to simulate the proofs. The uniqueness property of UWM guarantees that proofs computed by either of the witnesses result in the same proof. Hence, the zero-knowledge property follows.

8   Perfectly Sound Verifier UWM Implies NP = UP

In this section, we show that if a perfect sound verifier unique witness map (VUWM) exists (see Definition 6) then the complexity class **NP** will be equal to the complexity class **UP**, where **UP** stands for unambiguous non-deterministic polynomial-time. Informally, the class **UP** is the complexity class of decision problems solvable in polynomial time on an *unambiguous* Turing machine with at most *one* accepting path for each input. Hence it is easy to see that **UP** contains the class **P** and is contained in **NP**. In the following we shall prove that **NP** $\subseteq$ **UP**, assuming perfect sound VUWM. Let us first formally define the class **UP**.

Definition 9 (Complexity class UP). *A language $L \in$ **UP** if there exists a two-input polynomial-time algorithm R and a constant c such that*

- *If $x \in L$, then there exists a* unique *certificate w with $|w| = O(|x|)^c$ such that $R(x, w) = 1$.*
- *If $x \notin L$, there is* no *certificate w with $|w| = O(|x|)^c$ such that $R(x, w) = 1$.*

Valiant and Vazirani [16] showed that **NP** $\subseteq$ **RP$^{\text{promise-UP}}$**, which means that that there is a randomized reduction from any problem in **NP** to a problem in **Promise-UP**.

Theorem 5. *If perfectly-sound VUWM exists for an **NP** relation R, then $L_R \in$ **UP**. In particular, if perfectly-sound VUWM exists for every **NP** relation, then **NP** = **UP**.*

The proof of this theorem is presented in the full version of the paper.

References

1. Beigel, R.: On the relativized power of additional accepting paths. In: Proceedings: Fourth Annual Structure in Complexity Theory Conference, University of Oregon, Eugene, Oregon, USA, 19–22 June 1989, pp. 216–224. IEEE Computer Society (1989)

2. Beigel, R., Buhrman, H., Fortnow, L.: NP might not be as easy as detecting unique solutions. In: Scott Vitter, J. (ed.) Proceedings of the Thirtieth Annual ACM Symposium on the Theory of Computing, Dallas, Texas, USA, 23–26 May 1998, pp. 203–208. ACM (1998)

3. Boyle, E., Segev, G., Wichs, D.: Fully leakage-resilient signatures. In: Paterson, K.G. (ed.) EUROCRYPT 2011. LNCS, vol. 6632, pp. 89–108. Springer, Heidelberg (2011). https://doi.org/10.1007/978-3-642-20465-4_7

4. Chakraborty, S., Prabhakaran, M., Wichs, D.: Witness maps and applications. In: Kiayias, A., Kohlweiss, M., Wallden, P., Zikas, V. (eds.) PKC 2020. Part I, volume 12110 of LNCS, pp. 220–246. Springer, Heidelberg (2020). https://doi.org/10.1007/978-3-030-45374-9_8

5. Dodis, Y., Haralambiev, K., López-Alt, A., Wichs, D.: Cryptography against continuous memory attacks. In: 51st FOCS, pp. 511–520. IEEE Computer Society Press (2010)

6. Gat, E., Goldwasser, S.: Probabilistic search algorithms with unique answers and their cryptographic applications. Electron. Colloquium Comput. Complex **TR11**, 136 (2011)

7. Goldreich, O., Levin, L.A.: A hard-core predicate for all one-way functions. In: 21st ACM STOC, pp. 25–32. ACM Press (1989)

8. Goldwasser, S., Grossman, O., Holden, D.: Pseudo-deterministic proofs. In: Karlin, A.R. (ed.) ITCS 2018, volume 94 of LIPIcs, pp. 1–18. Schloss Dagstuhl - Leibniz-Zentrum für Informatik (2018)

9. Hazay, C., López-Alt, A., Wee, H., Wichs, D.: Leakage-resilient cryptography from minimal assumptions. In: Johansson, T., Nguyen, P.Q. (eds.) EUROCRYPT 2013. LNCS, vol. 7881, pp. 160–176. Springer, Heidelberg (2013). https://doi.org/10.1007/978-3-642-38348-9_10

10. Kitagawa, F., Matsuda, T., Yamakawa, T.: NIZK from SNARG. In: Pass, R., Pietrzak, K. (eds.) TCC 2020. Part I, volume 12550 of LNCS, pp. 567–595. Springer, Heidelberg (2020). https://doi.org/10.1007/978-3-030-64375-1_20

11. Lin, H., Pass, R., Seth, K., Telang, S.: Indistinguishability obfuscation with nontrivial efficiency. In: Cheng, C.-M., Chung, K.-M., Persiano, G., Yang, B.-Y. (eds.) PKC 2016. Part II, volume 9615 of LNCS, pp. 447–462. Springer, Heidelberg (2016). https://doi.org/10.1007/978-3-662-49387-8_17

12. Liu, Y., Pass, R.: On one-way functions and Kolmogorov complexity. In: 61st FOCS, pp. 1243–1254. IEEE Computer Society Press (2020)

13. Rackoff, C.: Relativized questions involving probabilistic algorithms. J. ACM **29**(1), 261–268 (1982)

14. Sahai, A., Waters, B.: How to use indistinguishability obfuscation: deniable encryption, and more. In: Shmoys, D.B. (ed.) 46th ACM STOC, pp. 475–484. ACM Press (2014)

15. Valiant, L.G.: Relative complexity of checking and evaluating. Inf. Process. Lett. **5**(1), 20–23 (1976)

16. Valiant, L.G., Vazirani, V.V.: NP is as easy as detecting unique solutions. Theor. Comput. Sci. **47**(3), 85–93 (1986)
17. Zhandry, M.: How to avoid obfuscation using witness PRFs. In: Kushilevitz, E., Malkin, T. (eds.) TCC 2016-A. Part II, volume 9563 of LNCS, pp. 421–448. Springer, Heidelberg (2016). https://doi.org/10.1007/978-3-662-49099-0_16

Structure-Preserving Compilers from New Notions of Obfuscations

Matteo Campanelli[1], Danilo Francati[2($\boxtimes$)], and Claudio Orlandi[2]

[1] Protocol Labs, San Francisco, USA
matteo@protocol.ai
[2] Aarhus University, Aarhus, Denmark
{dfrancati,orlandi}@cs.au.dk

Abstract. The dream of software obfuscation is to take programs, *as they are*, and then generically compile them into obfuscated versions that hide their secret inner workings. In this work we investigate notions of obfuscations weaker than virtual black-box (VBB) but which still allow obfuscating cryptographic primitives preserving their original functionalities as much as possible.

In particular we propose two new notions of obfuscations, which we call *oracle-differing-input* obfuscation (odiO) and *oracle-indistinguishability* obfuscation (oiO). In a nutshell, odiO is a natural strengthening of *differing-input* obfuscation (diO) and allows obfuscating programs for which it is hard to find a *differing-input* when given only *oracle access* to the programs. An oiO obfuscator allows to obfuscate programs that are *hard to distinguish* when treated as oracles.

We then show applications of these notions, as well as positive and negative results around them. A few highlights include:

- Our new notions are weaker than VBB and stronger than diO.
- As it is the case for VBB, we show that there exist programs that cannot be obfuscated with odiO or oiO.
- Our new notions allow to generically compile several flavours of secret-key primitives (e.g., SKE, MAC, designated verifier NIZK) into their public-key equivalent (e.g., PKE, signatures, publicly verifiable NIZK) while preserving one of the algorithms of the original scheme (function-preserving), or the structure of their outputs (format-preserving).

1 Introduction

Obfuscation and Its (Dream) Applications. Obfuscation—the ability of running a program hiding its inner working—is a cryptographer's dream. This is especially true of its most powerful instantiation, virtual black-box (VBB) obfuscation: anything a VBB-obfuscated program leaks can be simulated through oracle access to the function it computes [8]. It follows that one important application of VBB is to *generically transform* secret-key cryptographic primitives into their public-key counterparts (an approach sometimes referred to as *white-box cryptography*). For example, the seminal work of Diffie and Hellman [25]

© International Association for Cryptologic Research 2023
A. Boldyreva and V. Kolesnikov (Eds.): PKC 2023, LNCS 13941, pp. 663–693, 2023.
https://doi.org/10.1007/978-3-031-31371-4_23

already imagined compiling secret key encryption (SKE) into public key encryption (PKE) by letting the public key consist of the obfuscated encryption program Enc(k, ·). Note that this compiler has the advantage of preserving the *format* of the underlying ciphertext, as well as the *function* used to perform decryption.

Transforming Primitives, Nicely. In this paper, we are interested in obfucators that allow generic *structure preserving* transformation of large classes of cryptographic primitives, i.e., obfuscators that allow to compile cryptographic primitives while *preserving* parts of the original primitive. In particular, with the term structure-preserving, we refer to two main classes of transformations (from secret-key to public-key primitives), dubbed *function-preserving* and *format-preserving* transformations:

- *Function-preserving.* This first type of transformation does not alter the algorithms (one of which is then obfuscated during the transformation) of the secret-key primitive. An example of such a transformation is the one described by Diffie and Hellman, i.e., compile a SKE into a PKE by obfuscating (without any modification) the encryption algorithm and keep the decryption one unchanged.
- *Format-preserving.* This other type of transformation modifies the algorithms of the original secret-key primitive but it preserves the format of the output.[1] For example, in order to convert a SKE into a PKE, a format-preserving transformation may require to modify both (before obfuscating) the encryption and decryption algorithm. However, these modifications do not alter the format of ciphertexts (i.e., the ciphertexts of the resulting PKE is of the same format as the original SKE one).

We see this as an interesting design approach to transformation of primitives, worth of study of its own. Structure-preserving compilers are desirable because of: *(i) reusability/retrocompatibility* and *(ii) efficiency*. First, with function-preserving transformations we can reuse existing code, programs, libraries, constructions and their cryptanalysis. Cryptographic primitives deployed in hardware could reuse that same hardware for the transformed primitive, instead of having to be redesigned from scratch and possibly replaced in a production environment. Moreover, transformations that preserve the *format* of their output allow to reuse parsing-related software and to be retrocompatible with older standards (particularly important for legacy systems). Also, function- and format-preserving transformations maintain some of the scheme's original efficiency guarantees such as preserving the running time of the (possibly heavily optimized) original function and its communication complexity, respectively.

Nice Transformations from *Weaker* Obfuscation? The seminal work in [7,8] has shown that the "dream version" of obfuscation, VBB, is in gen-

---

[1] Note that a function-preserving transformation is also format-preserving. This is because the former does not modify the algorithms of the original primitive. Hence, the format of the output is preserved by definition.

eral impossible, i.e., there exist programs that cannot be obfuscated through VBB. Since then cryptographers have defined new, weaker notions of obfuscations that could hopefully be constructed. One of the plausible weaker candidates in this sense is *indistinguishability obfuscation* (iO) that guarantees the indistinguishability of a pair obfuscated programs, only if the latter have the exact same input-output behavior. It is truly surprising that a notion of obfuscation as weak as iO has managed to generate so many applications [41]. However, most of the applications of iO are out of the spectrum of the "design once; obfuscate later"-approach that was dreamed in the beginning, i.e., generically compile an existing secret-key primitive that it has been designed without the intend of being obfuscated later in time. In fact, most iO-based constructions are quite involved and they are not generic since only carefully designed programs can be successfully obfuscated through iO. A clear example is [41] that leverages puncturable PRFs and pseudorandom generators (PRG) to build (from scratch) a SKE scheme that satisfies very specific properties (e.g., puncturability) which, in turn, allows iO to convert it into a PKE scheme. Intuitively, this is far from having a generic transformation since the SKE is built with the intent of being obfuscated through iO. It is therefore natural to ask the following question:

Can we obtain generic structure-preserving transformations from notions of obfuscation weaker than VBB?

Our Results: New Primitives, Compilers, Connections to Prior Notions. In this work we propose two new definitions of obfuscation, *oracle-differing-input* obfuscation (odiO) and *oracle-indistinguishability* obfuscation (oiO), and apply them to structure-preserving transformations for several classes of primitives.

Recall that iO [8] only guarantees indistinguishability of obfuscations between pair of programs that have the exact same input/output behaviour. *Differing-input obfuscation* (diO) [1,8,17] is a stronger kind of obfuscation which guarantees the same indistinguishability property of iO but for pair of programs which might have different input/output behaviour, as long as it is computationally hard to find inputs on which the output of the programs differ, even when looking at the code of the programs. Our first notion, odiO, enriches the class of programs that can be securely obfuscated including any pair of programs for which it is hard to find differing-inputs, but when the distinguisher is given only oracle access to the programs. oiO then takes it a step further and allows to obfuscate any pair of programs that are indistinguishable when given as oracle.

In the paper we formally study the relationship between our new notions of obfuscation and the existing one. Note that:

$$\text{VBB} > \text{oiO} > \text{odiO} > \text{diO} > \text{iO}$$

meaning that a VBB-obfuscator is also an oiO-obfuscator, and so on. Intuitively, the separation are strict. Again, focusing only on the first inequality: while a VBB-obfuscator cannot leak anything about the program that cannot be learned

dv-SNARG	pv-SNARG	MAC	Signature	SKE	PKE
Prove $- - \overset{\equiv}{-} - \to$ Prove		Tag $- - - \overset{\equiv}{-} \to$ Sign		Enc $\xrightarrow{\text{oiO}}$ Enc	
Verify $\xrightarrow{\text{odiO}}$ Verify		Verify $\xrightarrow{\text{odiO}}$ Verify		Dec $- - \overset{\equiv}{-} - \to$ Dec	
(1)		(2)		(5)	

MAC	Signature	SKE	PKE
Tag $- - - \overset{\cong}{-} - \to$ Sign		Enc $\xrightarrow{\text{odiO}_{(PPRF)}}$ Enc	
Verify $\xrightarrow{\text{odiO}_{(PPRF)}}$ Verify		Dec $- - - \overset{\cong}{-} - \to$ Dec	
(3)		(4)	

Fig. 1. The transformations (1)-(5) of this work: function-preserving on top row; format-preserving on bottom row. By odiO/oiO we denote an algorithm obtained through direct obfuscation of the one on the left; by $\equiv$ one that is completely unchanged; by $\cong$ one with minor changes but still able to take the same input; by (PPRF) we denote where we modify the algorithm through puncturable PRFs before obfuscation.

by the oracle version of the program, an oiO-obfuscator is allowed to leak any secret contained in its circuit, as long as these secrets do not allow to distinguish between the oracle programs. Focusing on oiO, odiO, diO, and iO, we have that all these notions provide the same flavor of security (i.e., two obfuscations are indistinguishable) but for different classes of circuits, each progressively contained into the other. For this reason, we have that oiO > odiO > diO > iO.

Note that odiO is stronger than diO. Hence, as considered by previous works for diO, this work assumes that current candidates of iO obfuscators are candidates obfuscators for odiO and oiO.

Still, since oiO and odiO are weaker than VBB, it is plausibly easier to build oiO and odiO obfuscators than VBB ones, at least for specific classes of programs: For example, it is known that point functions can be VBB-obfuscated, despite the general impossibility results for VBB; similarly, programs that differ in a single input (or polynomial number of inputs) can be diO-obfuscated, even if we believe that diO is unlikely to exist in general. In the same spirit, our results can be interpreted as showing that we can lift certain symmetric-key primitives to public-key primitives as long as specific functions (e.g., verification algorithms) can be odiO-obfuscated.

We then show that our new notions of obfuscation are enough for generic structure-preserving transformations of important cryptographic primitives. In particular we provide the following transformation (see also Fig. 1):

1. A *function-preserving* transformation from selectively sound succinct designated verifier non-interactive argument systems (dv-SNARG) into publicly verifiable ones (pv-SNARG) (Sect. 5.1); The same transformation allows transforming non-interactive argument systems that satisfy straight-line knowledge

soundness, i.e., it is possible to extract (through a trapdoor) a valid witness from verifying proofs without interacting with the adversary;[2]

2. A *function-preserving* transformation from strong existentially unforgeable MACs into digital signatures that remains strongly unforgeable only in the presence of adversaries that can ask signatures of arbitrary messages in a selective fashion;

3. A *format-preserving* transformation that leverages puncturable PRFs to convert selectively existentially unforgeable MACs into selectively existentially unforgeable digital signatures. In contrast to the previous (MACs to signatures) transformation, this is only format-preserving but achieves existential unforgeability under the standard notion of chosen message attacks (i.e., the adversary has adaptive oracle access to the signature algorithm);

4. A *format-preserving* transformation that leverages puncturable PRFs to convert IV-based selectively secure SKEs into selectively IND-CPA secure PKEs. Here, IV-based SKEs refer to encryption schemes of the form $\mathsf{Enc}(k, m; iv) = (iv, c)$ where iv is the initialization vector (i.e., randomness) used to encrypt a message m. Note that most SKE used in practice are IV-based e.g., those based on block ciphers mode operations such as AES-CBC-mode, AES-CTR-mode, and so on.

5. A *function-preserving* transformation from any semantically secure and key indistinguishable SKE into a selective IND-CPA PKE (Sect. 5.2). Here, the SKE's key indistinguishability property must hold under chosen message randomness attacks, i.e., it is infeasible to determine under which key a target message has been encrypted even if the adversary has oracle access to $\mathsf{Enc}(k, \cdot; \cdot)$ that accepts adversarially chosen messages and randomnesses.

Note that only the last transformation requires oiO (in order to use the key indistinguishability property of the SKE) whereas odiO is sufficient to achieve the other ones. Also, all the transformations that use puncturable PRFs are (only) *format-preserving*, i.e., the programs/algorithms of the compiled primitive are (slightly) modified but the format of the output is preserved.[3] We anticipate that all our transformations require odiO/oiO and they cannot be implemented using iO (or diO). In a nutshell, this is because we focus on generic transformations from secret-key to public-key primitives. In order to be generic, we need to eventually reduce the security of the transformation to the security of the original secret-key primitive. If we wish to accomplish this reduction using either iO or diO, we need to put, into the obfuscated circuit, the key sk of the original (secret-key)

---

[2] As for straight-line knowledge soundness, we do not consider succinctness (i.e., we do not cover dv-SNARG/pv-SNARG) since, in order to have a straight-line extraction, the size of the proof is proportional to the size of the witness.

[3] We will elaborate on this later, but intuitively this is because the obfuscated program will use the puncturable PRF to generate a fresh symmetric key for different input (e.g., messages, initialization vectors). Hence, on decryption/verification, the receiver needs to evaluate the same PRF in order to recompute the symmetric key used to decrypt/verify a particular ciphertext/signature.

primitive. However, this is not possible. During the reduction sk is sampled and kept secret by the challenger. We provide more details in Sect. 1.1.

Although both odiO and oiO are weaker than VBB, this does not tell us anything about the plausibility of these new notions of obfuscation (and their applications). As a last contribution, we investigate whether VBB's impossibility results of Barak et al. [7,8] extends to either odiO or oiO (or both). In particular, Barak et al. [7,8] shows the following two impossibility results regarding VBB. *(i)* The first states an *universal* VBB obfuscator does not exist, i.e. there exists (not necessarily natural) computations that cannot be obfuscated through VBB. *(ii)* The second states that even the specific applications/transformations of VBB we can naturally hope for are impossible (e.g., converting any SKE into a PKE).

What about the above and odiO/oiO? We answer this question as follows:

- Result *(i)* does apply to odiO and oiO. This does not say much about how useful they are, so in the paper we explore result (ii) as well (see Sect. 6.1).
- Result *(ii)* applies only to transformation (5) for oiO. Moreover, we need to rework the original result *(ii)* from [7,8] to extend it to transformation (5) since it does not apply as it is (see Sect. 6.2).
- Result *(ii)* does not apply at all to the applications/transformations we have for odiO and there seems no natural way to extend it to them. Hence, all our odiO-based transformations remain plausible.

Summing up, while the first result *(i)* applies to both our proposed notions, odiO is *not* at all subject to the second result *(ii)* (impossibility of applications), which is the most limiting one.

Expanding more about the above results, we provide two different negative results by adapting the techniques of [7,8] to the case of odiO and oiO. First, we show that there exists an ensemble of circuits that neither odiO nor oiO cannot obfuscate, unconditionally (Sect. 6.1). Second, we show that the oiO-based function-preserving transformation (5) from any semantically secure and key indistinguishable SKEs into selective IND-CPA secure PKEs is inherently impossible (no matter what type of obfuscator is used to implement it).[4] We elaborate further on this in the technical overview (Sect. 1.1) and in the related Sect. 6.

Why Study these New Notions if they are Still Subject to the [7,8] Impossibility Results? There are multiple responses to that (some of which we expand below):

1. The work of Barak et al. [7,8] does not really say much about how useful odiO/oiO are (see also technical overview). Indeed, [7,8] shows *two* types of impossibility results, i.e., impossibility of an universal obfuscator and impossibility of applications. As we mentioned above, these impossibilities do not

---

[4] Note that Barak et al. [8] demonstrates the impossibility of transforming a SKE into a PKE (through the obfuscation of its encryption algorithm $\mathsf{Enc}(\mathsf{k}, \cdot)$) by building a (contrived) secure SKE that, after applying the transformation, yields an insecure PKE. However, their contrived SKE is not key indistinguishable. For this reason, in order to prove the impossibility of our oiO-based transformation (5) (from key indistinguishable SKE to PKE) we need to rework their result.

equally extend to both notions, e.g., impossibility of applications do not extend to our odiO-based transformations.

2. It is still important to study foundational aspects of obfuscation. We think ours are natural questions and natural notions to propose and to turn our attention to. As it is often the case in theoretical research, these notions may be connected to others in the future in unexpected ways. They might also motivate further work on notions that will turn out to be achievable (the [7,8] prompted the quest for iO and other notions related to VBB).

3. Related to the above, both odiO and oiO might be useful for many "proof-of-concept" type of results that rely on VBB-obfuscation. In cases where these weaker definitions might suffice, the proposed notions could shed light on what security property is actually needed from the obfuscator to imply security of the overall construction.[5] As an example, our results can be interpreted as follows: If a particular circuit (e.g., secret-key verification/encryption algorithm) can be odiO-obfuscated (resp. oiO-obfuscated) then we can lift a particular secret-key primitive into its public-key flavor (e.g., MAC to signatures, SKE to PKE).

4. VBB and odiO/oiO are still distinct notions and with distinct flavors of security (simulation- vs indistinguishability-based). Moreover, nonetheless the known impossibility results, research on VBB is still active such as identifying specific and interesting class of circuits that can be securely VBB-obfuscated [33,43,45]. The same can be investigated for the case of odiO/oiO. For example, there could exist a specific class of circuits that can be oiO-/odiO-obfuscated but not VBB-obfuscated. Or there could exist circuit classes that are VBB-obfuscatable, but that can still be odiO/oiO-obfuscated more efficiently or from significantly weaker assumptions.

Lastly, we stress that odiO/oiO may have other interesting applications. This work focuses on secret-key to public-key transformations since these are most prominent applications of VBB and, we believe that studying odiO/oiO in the same context provides a better understanding about the relations between odiO/oiO and VBB, including their limitations.

1.1 Technical Overview

Oracle-Differing-Input Obfuscation (odiO). The notion of odiO is a variant of the notion of differing-input obfuscation, or diO. What is common with diO, for example, is that: *(i)* we are given a sampler S that outputs two circuits C_0 and C_1 and some auxiliary information α; *(ii)* the output of the sampler should satisfy some property P (we call such sampler "permissible"); *(iii)* if the sampler sastisfies property P then the obfuscated circuits $\mathsf{Obf}(C_0)$ and $\mathsf{Obf}(C_1)$ should look indistinguishable to a PPT adversary given also in input α. Also, in both diO and odiO, the property P corresponds to "no PPT D can find a *differing*

---

[5] This follows the same spirit of the UCE framework proposed by Bellare et al. [9] that allows to identify which property of the random oracle model (ROM) is needed to imply security of the (ROM-based) construction..

input x for C_0 and C_1 (given in input α)", that is an input x such that $C_0(x) \neq C_1(x)$. Where the two definitions diverge is that in diO algorithm D takes as input the *actual representation* (the code) of the two circuits, whereas in odiO D only has *oracle access* to the functions computed by C_0 and C_1.

An example of sampler that is permissible for odiO but not diO is the following: consider two programs C_0 and C_1 where their only (high-entropy) differing input is encoded as a comment in their code. Given their code it is easy to find such input, but not with oracle access to them. We provide more examples when we discuss our transformations below.

Public-key "Forgery-based" Transformations through odiO. We show that odiO is particularly suitable for transforming a general class of primitives—which we informally dub *forgery-based*—from their secret-key to their public-key version. By forgery-based we mean a primitive where the security is defined roughly as follows: "No adversary can produce (forge) a string passing a given test without knowledge of a certain secret (or if a certain condition does not hold)". Straightforward examples of this type of primitives include message-authentication codes (MACs) and digital signature, but non-interactive proof systems and signatures of knowledge [24] also capture this intuition.

The properties of odiO are sufficient for compiling the forgery-based primitives (1)-(3) listed above. We now give the main intuitions behind our transformations and their security. Our goal is to transform a primitive allowing us to verify a string through knowledge of secret into one that can do the same without such knowledge. Let us denote the first generic verification algorithm by Verify(sk, . . .);[6] we aim to transform it into a public key equivalent Verify'(pk, . . .). Our construction is straightforward: We define pk as the odiO-obfuscation of Verify(sk, . . .), and the program Verify'(pk, . . .) simply runs the program encoded in pk.

We now argue that the above is secure in a selective-security-flavored setting. In general, in such a setting, the adversary first claims some input (e.g., a message or an NP statement) for which it would like to forge a valid string (e.g., a signature or a proof). The rest of the intuition is better conveyed being specific. We thus focus on the setting of non-adaptive (selective) security in non-interactive proof systems where the verifier has the syntax Verify(vrs, x, π) and vrs is the (secret) verification key, x is a public statement (allegedly in a language $\mathcal{L}$), π is the proof. In this security game, for any input $\hat{x} \notin \mathcal{L}$, the adversary should not be able to forge a corresponding valid proof *after* seeing the public parameters (aka, common reference string or crs). We now show how to reduce the security of the publicly verifiable construction to that of the original (designated verifier) one applying odiO security. Recall that the security property of odiO must refer to a given sampler returning pairs of circuits. We require that our odiO obfuscator is secure against a sampler that returns (C_0, C_1) (we ignore the auxiliary input here) where:

---

[6] The rest of the input besides the key is irrelevant for this discussion.

- C_0 takes as input x and π and returns $\mathsf{Verify}(\mathsf{vrs}, x, \pi)$.
- C_1 behaves like C_0 *except* that it immediately returns 0 whenever $x = \hat{x}$.

The two circuits clearly satisfy the odiO permissibility notion since finding a differing input through oracle access to them would violate the original hypothesis of soundness (the only differing inputs are valid proofs for $\hat{x}$).[7]

Thus we can move to an hybrid where the crs is an obfuscation of C_1, and indistinguishability of the hybrids follows from the security of the odiO obfuscator. But now note that by construction of C_1, when $\mathsf{crs} = \mathsf{Obf}(C_1)$, an adversary by definition cannot produce a valid for $\hat{x}$. Moreover, we obtain (for free) that our transformation preserves zero-knowledge since it is function-preserving and the Prove algorithm is not modified (see Remark 5.3).

The blueprint for the construction and security proof above can be adapted (with the appropriate care) to the other forgery-settings (2)-(3) for which we propose transformations. For transformation (2)—which yields selectively-secure strongly unforgeable signatures—one technical challenge is that we need to simulate the queries to the signing oracle. Since these queries are selective we can embed them in one of the circuits we obfuscate during the hybrid arguments. Transformation (3) requires additional care since it yields a signature scheme secure against an adversary with *adaptive* queries to the signing oracle. To do so we slightly modify the signature algorithm and use a (puncturable) PRF to generate a fresh one-time symmetric-key used to sign a single message. The verification algorithm is similarly adapted and then obfuscated. Due to the use of the PRF, the transformation is not function-preserving but only format-preserving.

Compiling Extractable Argument Systems. We are able to extend our result for argument schemes satisfying *soundness* to arguments that satisfy *knowledge soundness*. This is achieved by the exact same function-preserving construction from odiO.[8] We are able to compile an adaptively-secure straight-line extractable designated verifier argument into an adaptively-secure straight-line extractable publicly verifiable argument. Note that, when considering straight-line extractability, proofs are not succinct anymore; hence, in this case we cover dv-NIZK and pv-NIZK. In contrast to soundness—which achieves only selective security—here we are able to preserve adaptive security. Again, the

---

[7] In particular, soundness (of underlying designated-verifier non-interactive proof system) must hold even if the adversary has oracle access to the verification algorithm. The latter is essential during the reduction to simulate the input-output behavior of the two circuits (treated as oracles). Hence, our transformation does not apply to non-interactive proofs systems that suffer from the so called verifier rejection problem, i.e., giving oracle access to the verifier allows the adversary to break soundness..

[8] Despite the construction is the same, the sampler required to prove knowledge soundness is different.

transformation is function-preserving and it does not alter the Prove algorithm. Hence, zero-knowledge is preserved (see also Remark 5.3). To the best of our knowledge ours is the first work applying obfuscation in the context of extractability in proof schemes.

Using odiO for Public-key Encryption through Puncturable PRFs.
So far we discussed how odiO is particularly useful for forgery-flavored primitives. We observe, however, that we are able to prove security of another type of primitive, encryption. In the full version of this work [21], we show how to compile IV-based selectively secure SKEs (whose ciphertexts have the form $\mathsf{Enc}(\mathsf{k}, m; \mathsf{iv}) = (\mathsf{iv}, c)$) into selectively IND-CPA secure PKEs. Our obfuscated circuit (that will be our pk) uses two puncturable PRFs: The first to generate the initialization vector iv from the randomness given to the PKE's Enc and, the second to generate a one-time fresh symmetric-key (used to encrypt) from iv.[9] The decryption algorithm has access to the key for the second PRF and takes as input the ciphertext (iv, c). It can then regenerate the key and thus decrypt. Note that this transformation is only format-preserving since we slightly modify both encryption and decryption algorithm to embed the evaluation of the PRF.

Oracle-Indistinguishability Obfuscation (oiO). The notion of oiO represents a natural strengthening of odiO. It has similar features to diO and odiO in that it requires samplers that output pairs of circuits satisfying some permissibility predicate P. While the permissibility predicate in diO and odiO requires hardness of finding a differing-input, in oiO we have a weaker permissibility predicate (which in turn makes oiO stronger than odiO): in oiO the sampler must output pairs of circuits such that an adversary (given also as input related auxiliary string α) cannot distinguish the circuits while having only oracle oracle access to them. An example of a sampler that is permissible for oiO but not odiO is the one where C_0 and C_1 are both PRFs but with different keys, since they differ on (almost) every input but their output distributions are indistinguishable.

Public-key "Indistinguishability-based" Transformations through oiO.
While odiO is suitable for transforming forgery-based primitives, oiO has synergies with indistinguishability-based primitives, i.e. where "No adversary can distinguish between two distributions without knowledge of a certain secret". Natural examples are encryption schemes where the distributions to distinguish are the encryption of different messages (e.g., IND-CPA security).

---

[9] If, instead of generating iv using the first PRF, we allow the circuit to take directly in input iv then the PKE (output by the transformation) is trivially broken. This is because (following the syntax of the IV-based SKE) iv is included into the ciphertext. Hence, an adversary can break the selective IND-CPA security of the compiled PKE by simply re-encrypting a message using the iv that is included into the challenge ciphertext.

Through oiO we are able to prove the security of a more general transformation (compared to (4)) from SKEs to PKEs. Starting from a symmetric encryption algorithm $\mathsf{Enc}(\mathsf{k}, \cdot; \cdot)$, our aim is to transform it into something with the following syntax $\mathsf{Enc}(\mathsf{pk}, \cdot; \cdot)$, where pk is a public key. Our transformation is identical to the one proposed by Diffie and Hellman [25]: We define pk as the oiO-obfuscation of $\mathsf{Enc}(\mathsf{k}, \cdot; \cdot)$ for some honestly chosen symmetric key k. To claim the IND-CPA security of the above transformation, we need to assume that the initial SKE is key indistinguishable under (adversarially) chosen message randomness attacks. The latter allows us to build a sampler that satisfies the permissibility predicate of oiO. In particular, the sampler returns (C_0, C_1) (again, we ignore the auxiliary input here) where:

- C_0 takes as input m and r and returns $\mathsf{Enc}(\mathsf{k}, m; r)$.
- C_1 is identical to the above except that it uses a different (honestly generated) symmetric key k'.

Intuitively, the circuits satisfy the oiO permissibility notion since any adversary that is able to distinguish between oracles C_0 and C_1 would also violates the key indistinguishability security of the SKE. Now, since the obfuscations of these two circuits are indistinguishable, we can reduce the security of the PKE to the security of the original SKE. Consider the standard IND-CPA experiment of PKE where pk is set to the obfuscation of C_0 and the challenge ciphertext c is computed as $c = \mathsf{pk}(m_b; r) = \mathsf{Enc}(\mathsf{k}, m_b; r)$ for r randomly chosen. We can now do an hybrid where pk is set to the obfuscation of C_1 whereas the challenge ciphertext is still computed as $c = \mathsf{Enc}(\mathsf{k}, m_b; r)$ where k is the key hardcoded in C_0. Since the ciphertext c is computed using a key k that is not the obfuscated one (recall C_1 uses an independent key k'), we can now conclude the proof by doing a reduction to the semantic security of the original SKE. We highlight that this proof technique works only if we consider selective IND-CPA security. This is because the sampler needs to output an auxiliary input that is an honest encryption of m_b under the key k (hardcoded into C_0). This is fundamental to simulate the challenge ciphertext (of the selective IND-CPA experiment) and concludes the hybrid argument.

Why aren't diO/iO Sufficient for these Transformations Above? We observe that each of the compilation described above would not be feasible with either iO or diO. Intuitively, this is because we would eventually need to reduce the security of our transformations (pv-SNARG, signature, PKE) to the security of the original secret-key primitive (dv-SNARG, MAC, SKE). However, in the latter experiment the secret-key sk (e.g., a vrs or a symmetric-key), that we need to obfuscate in order to conclude the reduction, is sampled and kept secret by the challenger. This makes iO and diO insufficient since we are not able to satisfy their permissibility notion during this reduction. For the case of iO, during the reduction, the only thing we could do is to to obfuscate different circuit C_1 that does not use the secret-key sk sampled by the challenger. However, this C_1 will have (with overwhelming probability) a different input/output behavior compared to C_0 (the original obfuscated circuit of the transformation that, in turn, contains sk).

A similar discussion applies to diO. For the sake of concreteness, consider transforming a dv-SNARG into a pv-SNARG by publishing an obfuscation of the circuit C_0 which implements the dv-SNARG verification algorithm using an hard-coded verification key vrs. During the reduction to the security of the underlying scheme we are not allowed to use the secret verification key vrs. Thus, during the reduction, we can only move to a hybrid where we obfuscate a circuit C_1 that does not use the vrs. But then we cannot argue that it is hard to find differing-inputs for C_0, C_1. In this specific case, the distinguisher could simply produce proofs π for true statements x and submit them to the circuits. While C_0 (using the vrs) returns 1, C_1 (without the vrs) is unable to verify the proof and cannot return a consistent output. Similar arguments apply to the other transformations.

The Landscape of Limitations of odiO/oiO. The seminal work of [7,8] explores the boundaries of obfuscation in several directions. As it is well known they show that there are (not necessarily natural) computations which are impossible to obfuscate using VBB. Moreover, [7,8] also shows that VBB-obfuscation cannot be used for securely performing certain structure-preserving transformations. In this direction, they show a (contrived but secure) SKE that turns into an insecure PKE scheme when compiled using obfuscation. We show that the results of [7,8] can be extended to the setting of odiO and oiO. In particular, we show that there (unconditionally) exist samplers that are odiO/oiO permissible but are not obfuscatable. Specifically we sample (somewhat contrived) circuits C_s with an embedded secret s that remains "hidden enough" when only oracle access is allowed (thus being odiO/oiO permissible). We then show that, once given access to the obfuscated circuit, it becomes possible to "partially extract" this secret s. Finally, we show that (since this sampler cannot be obfuscated) our oiO-based transformation (5) (from semantically secure and key indistinguishable SKE to selectively IND-CPA PKE) is inherently impossible, regardless of the strength of the obfuscator used. This is done by using the unobfuscatable circuits to build a contrived SKE (satisfying semantic security and key indistinguishability) that, once compiled, yields an insecure PKE. As mentioned, a similar impossibility result was given in [8, Theorem 4.10]. However their contrived SKE does not satisfy key indistinguishability and, for this reason, it cannot be directly used to show the infeasibility of our transformation (5). Thus, our negative result strengthens the one of [8] since ours apply to a smaller class of SKEs (i.e., SKEs with stronger notions of security) that satisfy key indistinguishability under chosen message randomness attacks. Note that while we just argued that the oiO-based transformation in (5) is inherently impossible, our odiO-based transformations (1)-(4) remain plausible as the impossibility results do not seem to extend. We elaborate further in Sect. 6.2.

1.2   Future Directions

Our work opens up several interesting future directions. How to generally formalize structure-preserving transformations? Can we characterize what type of games can be transformed (from "secret" to "public" key) through odiO? Several, but not all those we achieve, seem to have a "forgery" flavor to them (MAC, NIZKs, etc.). What are further connections between our proposed notions of obfuscation and VBB, iO and diO? While the techniques in [8] seem to fail to show that some of our transformations are paradoxical, what are other techniques that could shed light on further limitations of odiO oiO? Can we leverage our techniques for going from secret-key to public-key variants of different cryptographic primitives than those we consider here, e.g., proofs of retrievability [42]?

2   Related Work

Barak et al. [7,8] investigate the feasibility of obfuscation. They focus on virtual black-box (VBB) obfuscation, where an obfuscated program/circuit should leak no information except for its input-output behaviour. They show: 1) that a general VBB obfuscator cannot exist since there are circuits that cannot be unconditionally obfuscated in the VBB paradigm; 2) that most of the intriguing applications of VBB are impossible (including the suggestion of Diffie and Hellman's of building a PKE by obfuscating the SKE encryption algorithm with an embedded symmetric key). On the positive side, several works have shown that some restricted classes of circuits can be securely VBB-obfuscated [23,33,43,45] . Goldwasser and Kalai [30,31] and Bitansky et al. [13] extended VBB's impossibility results to the case of auxiliary information demonstrating that other "natural" circuits cannot be VBB obfuscated when some (dependent or independent) auxiliary information are available. In addition, [13] demonstrated that the availability of auxiliary information is equivalent to VBB with universal simulation. Goldwasser and Rothblum [32] proposed the notion of best-possible obfuscation that guarantees that the obfuscation of a circuit leaks as little information as any other circuit implementing the same functionality. They show that a separation between VBB and best-possible obfuscation and an impossibility result (for both) in the random oracle model. Other works [6,20,22,37,38,40] studied the (in)feasibility of VBB in different idealized models.

To avoid the VBB paradigm (and its impossibility results), [8] suggested two weaker security definitions of obfuscation: indistinguishability obfuscation (iO) and differing-input obfuscation (diO). The former has obtained a lot of interest thanks to its applications, as initially shown by Sahai and Waters [41]. The first work that proposed a candidate iO construction is by Garg et al. [26] that built iO via multilinear maps. Subsequent works [2–4,15,16,19,28,29,36,39] focused on both the relations of iO and other primitives (e.g., functional encryption) and new candidates construction from weaker assumptions. These works led to the recent works of Jain et al. [35] and Wee and Wichs [44]. [35] built (subexponentially secure) iO from the sub-exponential hardness of LWE, learning parity with noise, and boolean pseudorandom generators in NC^0. On the other hand, [44] proposed the first construction based solely on lattices and LWE. Their construction relies on a new falsifiable LWE assumption.

As for diO, [1,10,17,17] proposed different formalization of diO (for both circuits and Turing machines) and showed different applications. On the negative side, [11,18,27] showed that, in the presence of (some) auxiliary information (e.g., samplers), a general diO obfuscator may not exist. Notably, Bellare et al. [11] showed that if sub-exponentially secure one-way functions exist then a sub-exponentially secure general diO obfuscator for Turing machines does not exist, i.e., there exists a sampler that outputs two Turing machines and some auxiliary information that cannot be obfuscated through diO. Moreover, they show that the impossibility result extends to diO for circuits, if SNARKs exist. Garg et al. [27] showed a similar result for diO for circuits under the conjecture that a special-purpose obfuscator exists (i.e., an obfuscator that does not follow from diO). All the negative results of [11,18,27] rely on the fact that the sampler can silently provide a trapdoor that allows an adversary to distinguish between two obfuscations whereas the trapdoor does not help in finding a differing-input., Because of this, Ishai et al. [34] proposed the weaker notion of public-coin diO where the random coins of the sampler are public, i.e., a sampler cannot hide any trapdoor in the auxiliary information.

Among weaker notions of obfuscation, we also find virtual gray-box obfuscation (VGB) [12,14]. This notion is close to that of VBB but models the simulator as semi-bounded, i.e., unbounded in running time but limited to a polynomial number of oracle queries. VGB is equivalent to another notion, strong iO (siO), where it holds that $\mathsf{Obf}(C_0) \approx_c \mathsf{Obf}(C_1)$ whenever the pair (C_0, C_1) is sampled from a concentrated distribution $\mathbf{D}$: For every input x, the probability that $C_0(x)$ and $C_1(x)$ do not return to common output $maj_{\mathbf{D}}(x)$ is negligible (where $maj_{\mathbf{D}}(\cdot)$ is defined with respect to the concentrated distribution $\mathbf{D}$ taken into account). Observe that concentrated distributions are a generalization of evasive functions [5]. Intuitively, siO is weaker than odiO (and oiO) since circuits (sampled from concentrated distributions) are oracle-diffing-input even against semi-bounded adversaries. Also, note that siO is not powerful enough to achieve structure-preserving transformations. Intuitively, because siO is able to obfuscate distributions of circuits that "pass" an information theoretical test. This is a obstacle when trying to implement our structure-preserving transformations since our objective is to compile/obfuscate primitives whose security follows from computational assumptions.

3   Preliminaries on Obfuscation

We assume the reader to be familiar with standard cryptographic notation and definitions. Our notation and all the standard definitions used in the paper can be found in the full version.

Indistinguishability Obfuscation and Differing-input Obfuscation. Let $\mathcal{C} = \{\mathcal{C}_\lambda\}_{\lambda \in \mathbb{N}}$ be an ensemble of functionally equivalent circuits (of same size), i.e., $\forall \lambda \in \mathbb{N}, \forall C_0, C_1 \in \mathcal{C}_\lambda, \forall x \in \{0,1\}^{\ell_{in}}$, $C_0(x) = C_1(x)$ and $|C_0| = |C_1|$. Indistinguishability obfuscation (iO) [7] guarantees that the obfuscation of any two functionally equivalent circuits $C_0, C_1 \in \mathcal{C}_\lambda$ are computationally indistinguishable. The stronger notion of differing-input obfuscation (diO) [1,8,17] considers the larger class of differing-input circuits, i.e., circuits that differ on hard to find inputs. Below, we introduce the definition of diO with respect to samplers responsible of sampling two differing-input circuits and (some) auxiliary information.

Definition 3.1. *A sampler* S *for an ensemble of circuits* $\mathcal{C} = \{\mathcal{C}_\lambda\}_{\lambda \in \mathbb{N}}$ *is a PPT algorithm that, on input the security parameter* 1^λ, *it outputs two circuits* $C_0, C_1 \in \mathcal{C}_\lambda$ *such that* $|C_0| = |C_1|$ *and (possibly) some auxiliary information* α.

Definition 3.2. *(diO-sampler) We say a sampler* S *(Definition 3.1) is a* diO-*sampler if for every PPT adversary* A *we have*

$$\mathbb{P}\left[C_0(x) \neq C_1(x)\Big|(C_0, C_1, \alpha) \leftarrow\!\!{\scriptstyle\$}\, \mathsf{S}(1^\lambda), x \leftarrow\!\!{\scriptstyle\$}\, \mathsf{A}(1^\lambda, C_0, C_1, \alpha)\right] \leq \mathsf{negl}(\lambda).$$

Definition 3.3. [Differing-input obfuscation] *Let* $\mathcal{S}$ *be an ensemble of* diO-*samplers (Definition 3.2). For every* $\mathsf{S} \in \mathcal{S}$, *let* $\mathcal{C}^\mathsf{S} = \{\mathcal{C}^\mathsf{S}_\lambda\}_{\lambda \in \mathbb{N}}$ *be the ensemble of circuits output by* S. *A PPT algorithm* Obf *is a* $(\mathcal{S})$-diO-*obfuscator for the ensemble* $\mathcal{S}$ *if the following conditions are satisfied:*

Correctness. $\forall \mathsf{S} \in \mathcal{S}, \forall \lambda \in \mathbb{N}, \forall C \in \mathcal{C}^\mathsf{S}_\lambda, \forall x \in \{0,1\}^{\ell_{in}}$, *we have* $C'(x) = C(x)$ *where* $C' \leftarrow\!\!{\scriptstyle\$}\, \mathsf{Obf}(1^\lambda, C)$.

Polynomial slowdown. *There exists a polynomial* p *such that* $\forall \mathsf{S} \in \mathcal{S}, \forall C \in \mathcal{C}^\mathsf{S}_\lambda$, *we have* $|\mathsf{Obf}(1^\lambda, C)| \leq p(|C|)$.

Indistinguishability. *For every* $\mathsf{S} \in \mathcal{S}$, *every PPT adversary* D, *we have that*

$$\left|\mathbb{P}\left[\mathsf{D}(1^\lambda, \mathsf{Obf}(1^\lambda, C_0), \alpha) = 1\right] - \mathbb{P}\left[\mathsf{D}(1^\lambda, \mathsf{Obf}(1^\lambda, C_1), \alpha) = 1\right]\right| \leq \mathsf{negl}(\lambda),$$

where $(C_0, C_1, \alpha) \leftarrow\!\!{\scriptstyle\$}\, \mathsf{S}(1^\lambda)$.

The above definition is parametrized by an ensemble of diO-samplers since some negative results for diO are known [11,27] (see next). Because of this, an *universal* (general) diO-obfuscator may not exists, i.e., a diO-obfuscator that obfuscates any diO-sampler.

Negative Results. In the setting of Turing machines (not covered by this paper), Bellare et al. [11] show that if sub-exponentially secure one-way functions exist then a sub-exponentially secure diO-obfuscator Obf for any sampler for Turing machines does not exist (i.e., there exists a particular sampler that cannot be diO-obfuscated). We stress that the main impossibility result covers Turing machines but, as described by [11], if SNARKs exist the negative result can be extended to diO for circuits. Garg et al. [27] show that under the conjecture that a special-purpose obfuscator exists (i.e., an obfuscator that does not follow from the existence of a diO-obfuscator) then a diO-obfuscator Obf for any sampler for circuits does not exist. We highlight that both [11,27] show that only "some" diO-samplers cannot be obfuscated. Indeed, both works rely on samplers that output complex auxiliary information α (α is itself an obfuscation of contrived circuit/Turing machine). Hence, this does not rule out the possibility of obfuscating the same class of circuits/Turing machines under simpler auxiliary information.

Virtual Black-box Obfuscation. Virtual black-box obfuscation (VBB) [7], is the strongest known notion of obfuscation. In a nutshell, a VBB-obfuscator guarantees that having an obfuscation of a circuit C is "equivalent" to having oracle access to C. We consider the weakest notion of VBB that requires the adversary (and the simulator) to output a single bit. This is equivalent to asking the adversary/simulator to compute/determine an arbitrary predicate $\pi(C)$ of the original circuit [7]. Similarly to diO, we consider VBB with respect to samplers responsible to sample a circuit and (some) auxiliary information. This will allow us to provide a meaningful comparison between VBB and diO, odiO, oiO.

Definition 3.4. *(VBB-sampler) A VBB-sampler S for an ensemble of circuits $\mathcal{C} = \{\mathcal{C}_\lambda\}_{\lambda \in \mathbb{N}}$ is a PPT algorithm that, on input the security parameter 1^λ, it outputs a circuit $C \in \mathcal{C}_\lambda$ and some auxiliary information α.*

Definition 3.5 (Virtual black-box obfuscation). *Let $\mathcal{S}$ be an ensemble of VBB-samplers (Definition 3.4). For every $\mathsf{S} \in \mathcal{S}$, let $\mathcal{C}^\mathsf{S} = \{\mathcal{C}_\lambda^\mathsf{S}\}_{\lambda \in \mathbb{N}}$ be the ensemble of circuits output by S. A PPT algorithm Obf is a $(\mathcal{S})$-VBB-obfuscator for the ensemble $\mathcal{S}$ if the following conditions are satisfied:*

Correctness. $\forall \mathsf{S} \in \mathcal{S}, \forall \lambda \in \mathbb{N}, \forall C \in \mathcal{C}_\lambda^\mathsf{S}, \forall x \in \{0,1\}^{\ell_{in}}$, *we have $C'(x) = C(x)$ where $C' \leftarrow_\$ \mathsf{Obf}(1^\lambda, C)$.*
Polynomial slowdown. *There exists a polynomial p such that $\forall \mathsf{S} \in \mathcal{S}, \forall C \in \mathcal{C}_\lambda$, we have $|\mathsf{Obf}(1^\lambda, C)| \le p(|C|)$.*
Virtual black-box simulation. *For every PPT adversary A, there exists a PPT simulator Sim such that for every $\mathsf{S} \in \mathcal{S}$, we have*

$$\left| \mathbb{P}\left[\mathsf{A}(1^\lambda, \mathsf{Obf}(1^\lambda, C), \alpha) = 1 \right] - \mathbb{P}\left[\mathsf{Sim}^{C(\cdot)}(1^\lambda, 1^{|C|}, \alpha) = 1 \right] \right| \le \mathsf{negl}(\lambda),$$

where $(C, \alpha) \leftarrow_\$ \mathsf{S}(1^\lambda)$.

Note that VBB is a much stronger flavor of obfuscation than diO and iO for two reasons. First, VBB defines the concept of ideal/oracle obfuscation, i.e., an obfuscated circuit behaves as an oracle. Second, VBB is a simulation-based definition (whereas both iO and diO are indistinguishability-based), i.e., any bit of leakage (that can be retrieved from the obfuscation of a circuit) can be simulated (except with negligible probability) having only oracle access to the unobfuscated circuit.

Impossibility Results. VBB is a very interesting notion of obfuscation since it has several important applications (e.g., it permits to convert a SKE into PKE). However, VBB-obfuscation turned out to be impossible for several and reasonably simple class of circuits/samplers [7,8,13]. Moreover, also several applications of

VBB are impossible to achieve. As an example, Barak et al. [8, Theorem 4.10] have shown that there exist a SKE that cannot be transformed into a PKE by (simply) obfuscating the SKE's encryption algorithm (a similar impossibility result applies also to PRFs, MACs, and signatures). Still, VBB-obfuscation is still possible for other class of circuits/samplers. Examples are compute-and-compare programs [45] (also known as lockable obfuscation [33]) and point functions [43].

4   Oracle-Differing-Input and Oracle-Indistinguishability Obfuscation

In this section, we propose two new notions of obfuscation, dubbed *oracle-differing-input obfuscation* and *oracle-indistinguishability obfuscation* (odiO and oiO in short). Both odiO and oiO are the result of two natural extensions of diO (resp. iO): they introduce the notion of oracle circuits (as in VBB) while keeping the indistinguishability property of diO (resp. iO). In a nutshell, odiO requires that the obfuscations of two circuits C_0, C_1 are computationally indistinguishable if the latter two are differing-input circuits when treated as oracles, i.e., an adversary cannot find an input x such that $C_0(x) \neq C_1(x)$ when given oracle access to both C_0 and C_1. On the other hand, oiO provides the same indistinguishability guarantee with respect to circuits C_0, C_1 that are computationally indistinguishable when treated as oracles.

As usual, we define odiO and oiO with respect to an ensemble of samplers responsible of generating the circuits C_0, C_1 and (possibly) some auxiliary information α.

Definition 4.1. *(odiO- and oiO-sampler) Let* type $\in \{\text{odiO}, \text{oiO}\}$. *We say a sampler* S *(Definition 3.1) is an* type-*sampler if for every PPT adversary* A *we have*

If type = odiO: $\mathbb{P}\left[C_0(x) \neq C_1(x) \middle| x \leftarrow_{\$} \mathsf{A}^{C_0(\cdot), C_1(\cdot)}(1^\lambda, 1^{|C_0|}, \alpha)\right] \leq \mathsf{negl}(\lambda)$,

If type = oiO: $\left|\mathbb{P}\left[\mathsf{A}^{C_0(\cdot)}(1^\lambda, 1^{|C_0|}, \alpha) = 1\right] - \mathbb{P}\left[\mathsf{A}^{C_1(\cdot)}(1^\lambda, 1^{|C_1|}, \alpha) = 1\right]\right| \leq$ $\mathsf{negl}(\lambda)$,

where $(C_0, C_1, \alpha) \leftarrow_{\$} \mathsf{S}(1^\lambda).$[10]

Definition 4.2 (Oracle-differing-input and oracle-indistinguishability obfuscation). *For* type $\in \{\text{odiO}, \text{oiO}\}$, *let* S *be an ensemble of* type-*samplers (Definition 4.1). For every* S $\in S$, *let* $\mathcal{C}^{\mathsf{S}} = \{\mathcal{C}^{\mathsf{S}}_\lambda\}_{\lambda \in \mathbb{N}}$ *be the ensemble of circuits output by* S. *A PPT algorithm* Obf *is a* (S)-type-*obfuscator for the ensemble* S *if the following conditions are satisfied:*

Correctness. $\forall \mathsf{S} \in S, \forall \lambda \in \mathbb{N}, \forall C \in \mathcal{C}^{\mathsf{S}}_\lambda, \forall x \in \{0,1\}^{\ell_{in}}$, *we have* $C'(x) = C(x)$ *where* $C' \leftarrow_{\$} \mathsf{Obf}(1^\lambda, C)$.
Polynomial slowdown. *There exists a polynomial* p *such that* $\forall \mathsf{S} \in S, \forall C \in \mathcal{C}^{\mathsf{S}}_\lambda$, *we have* $|\mathsf{Obf}(1^\lambda, C)| \leq p(|C|)$.

---

[10] Recall that $|C_0| = |C_1|$ by definition of sampler (Definition 3.1).

Indistinguishability. *For every* $S \in \mathcal{S}$, *every PPT adversary* D, *we have that*

$$\left| \mathbb{P}\left[D(1^\lambda, \mathsf{Obf}(1^\lambda, C_0), \alpha) = 1\right] - \mathbb{P}\left[D(1^\lambda, \mathsf{Obf}(1^\lambda, C_1), \alpha) = 1\right] \right| \leq \mathsf{negl}(\lambda),$$

where $(C_0, C_1, \alpha) \leftarrow_\$ S(1^\lambda)$.

Comparing diO-, odiO-, oiO-, and VBB-obfuscation. We now study the relations between diO, odiO, oiO, and VBB. In order to provide a meaningful comparison, we work in terms of *best-possible universal* obfuscators, i.e., we compare the classes of circuits/samplers that each flavor of obfuscation is able to handle. We start by defining the notion of *best-possible universal* type-*obfuscator* Obf (for type $\in \{\mathsf{diO}, \mathsf{odiO}, \mathsf{oiO}, \mathsf{VBB}\}$) whose definition is tied with the (universal) set $\mathcal{S}_{\mathsf{type}}$ composed of all the type-samplers that can be securely type-obfuscated (as defined in Definitions 4.2 to 3.4).

Definition 4.3 (Best-possible universal type-obfuscator). *Let* type $\in \{\mathsf{diO}, \mathsf{odiO}, \mathsf{oiO}, \mathsf{VBB}\}$. *Consider the ensemble* $\mathcal{S}_{\mathsf{type}}$ *composed of every type-sampler* S *(Definitions 4.1, 3.2 and 3.4) that can be securely* type-*obfuscated (Definitions 4.2, 3.3 and 3.5), i.e.,*

$$\mathcal{S}_{\mathsf{type}} = \{\text{type-}sampler\ S \mid \exists\ \mathsf{Obf}\ s.t.\ \mathsf{Obf}\ is\ a\ (\{S\})\text{-}type\text{-}obfuscator\}.$$

A PPT algorithm Obf *is a* best-possible universal type-obfuscator *if* Obf *is a* $(\mathcal{S}_{\mathsf{type}})$-type-*obfuscator (Definitions 3.3, 4.2 and 3.5).*

Remark 4.4. There are two technical reasons behind the need of considering only best-possible universal obfuscators, while comparing diO, odiO, oiO, and VBB. First, for any notion of type-obfuscation, it is possible to find two contrived type-obfuscators Obf_0 and Obf_1 that result to be incomparable, even within the same flavor of obfuscation. As an example, we could have that Obf_0 (resp. Obf_1) is able to type-obfuscate S_0 (resp. S_1) but not S_1 (resp. S_0) where S_0, S_1 are two type-samplers.[11] The same argument holds between different notions. For example, if we consider diO and odiO, we could have that Obf_0 diO-obfuscates a diO-sampler S (that in turn, as we will see, is also a odiO-obfuscator) but Obf_1 does not odiO-obfuscate S. Also, we can have the symmetric case: there exist two obfuscators Obf_0' and Obf_1' such that Obf_1' odiO-obfuscates S but Obf_0' does not diO-obfuscate S. Hence by changing the obfuscator we could reach any conclusions: (i) odiO and diO are incomparable, (ii) odiO implies diO, or (iii) diO implies odiO. This clearly does not allow for a meaningful comparison. Definition 4.3 naturally solves the above problem since a best-possible universal type-obfuscator uniquely represents the power of a particular notion of obfuscation, i.e., the set $\mathcal{S}_{\mathsf{type}}$ of samplers that can be securely type-obfuscated. This allows us to have a meaninful (and unique) formal comparison between diO, odiO, oiO, and VBB.

---

[11] For instance, we can have that S_b only outputs circuits whose description starts with a bit b, and that Obf_b rejects any circuit whose description starts with the bit $1 - b$.

Second, Definition 4.3 allows us to exclude from the comparison the known impossibility results of VBB [7,13] (and odiO, oiO as we will show in Sect. 6). This is because, instead of quantifying over any possible type-sampler, best-possible universal type-obfuscation is defined over any possible type-sampler that can be type-obfuscated.

In the setting of best-possible universal obfuscation, odiO (resp. oiO) is stronger than diO since (i) any diO-sampler is also an odiO-sampler (resp. oiO-sampler) and (ii) both diO and odiO (resp. oiO) have the same indistinguishability-based security definition. The same argument applies to odiO and oiO, i.e., oiO is stronger than odiO.

Theorem 4.5 (oiO $\Rightarrow$ odiO $\Rightarrow$ diO). *For type $\in \{$diO, odiO, oiO$\}$, we have that* $\mathcal{S}_{\text{diO}} \subseteq \mathcal{S}_{\text{odiO}} \subseteq \mathcal{S}_{\text{oiO}}$ *where* $\mathcal{S}_{\text{type}}$ *as defined in Definition 4.3.*

The proof of this theorem is deferred to full version.

About (best-possible universal) odiO-, oiO-, and VBB-obfuscation, we have that VBB is stronger than odiO (resp. oiO) for two main reasons:

1. VBB leverages a simulation-based definition: any bit of information that can be leaked from an obfuscated circuit C can be simulated by only having oracle access to C. On the other hand, odiO (resp. oiO) provides a much weaker security guarantee: the obfuscation of two circuits C_0, C_1 (output by an odiO-sampler (resp. oiO-sampler)) are computationally indistinguishable. This implies that a odiO-obfuscator (resp. oiO-obfuscator) could leak significant information about the circuit, as long as the leaked information does not help in distinguishing (except with negligible probability) between the obfuscations of C_0 and C_1.

2. Both VBB and odiO (resp. oiO) incorporate the notion of oracle circuits in their definitions. However, oracles are used to define two different concepts. VBB uses oracle circuits to define the amount of information a VBB-obfuscator may leak. Since oracles leak no information (except their input-output behavior), this implies that a VBB-obfuscator does not leak any information, except with negligible probability.
   Conversely, odiO and oiO leverage the notion of oracle circuits to characterize the class of circuits (or samplers) that an odiO-/oiO-obfuscator can handle. The definition of security (i.e., the indistinguishability property of Definition 4.2) is independent from the oracles. Both odiO and oiO "only" guarantee that the information leaked by the obfuscation of two circuits are the same. This does not imply that the odiO-/oiO-obfuscated circuits must "behave" as oracles (as required by VBB (Definition 3.5)).

The relation between VBB, oiO, and odiO is formalized by the following theorem, whose proof is deferred to full version.

Theorem 4.6 (VBB $\Rightarrow$ oiO and VBB $\Rightarrow$ odiO). *Let* S *be a sampler (Definition 3.1). For* $b \in \{0, 1\}$, *let* S_b *be a sampler such that* $(C_b, \alpha) = S_b(1^\lambda; r)$ *where* $r \in \{0, 1\}^*$, *and* $(C_0, C_1, \alpha) = S(1^\lambda; r)$. *If* $S_0, S_1 \in \mathcal{S}_{\text{VBB}}$ *then* $S \in \mathcal{S}_{\text{type}}$ *where* $\mathcal{S}_{\text{VBB}}$ *and* $\mathcal{S}_{\text{type}}$ *are defined in Definition 4.3.*

By leveraging a similar argument to that used to prove Theorem 4.5, we can demonstrate that any negative result for diO extends to odiO. This because any diO-sampler S is also an odiO-sampler and, since diO and odiO leverage the same indistinguishability-based definition, if S $\notin S_{\text{diO}}$ then S $\notin S_{\text{odiO}}$.[12] The same applies between odiO and oiO, and between oiO and VBB (with respect to samplers as defined in Thoerem 4.6).

Corollary 4.7. *For* type $\in \{\text{diO}, \text{odiO}, \text{oiO}, \text{VBB}\}$, *let* S_{type} *be an ensemble of* type-*samplers as defined in Definition 4.3. The following conditions holds:*

1. *For every* diO-*sampler* S *such that* S $\notin S_{\text{diO}}$ *then* S $\notin S_{\text{odiO}}$.
2. *For every* odiO-*sampler* S *such that* S $\notin S_{\text{odiO}}$ *then* S $\notin S_{\text{oiO}}$.
3. *For every* oiO-*sampler* S *and every pair of* VBB-*samplers* (S_0, S_1) *such that* $(C_b, \alpha) = S_b(1^\lambda; r)$ *where* $r \in \{0,1\}^*$, $(C_0, C_1, \alpha) = S(1^\lambda; r)$ *and* $b \in \{0,1\}$ *(as defined in Theorem 4.6), if* S $\notin S_{\text{oiO}}$ *then* $S_0 \notin S_{\text{VBB}}$ *or* $S_1 \notin S_{\text{VBB}}$.

Lastly, odiO (resp. oiO) does not imply VBB, i.e., both odiO and oiO are strictly weaker than VBB. This follows by leveraging two observations. First, Barak et al. [7, Lemma 3.5, Corollary 3.8] have demonstrated that there (unconditionally) exists a distribution of circuits that cannot be VBB-obfuscated (see also Sect. 6.1). This, in turn, implies that there exists a VBB-sampler $S_0 \notin S_{\text{VBB}}$, i.e., S_0 outputs $(C, \perp)$ where C comes from the distribution of [7, Lemma 3.5]. Second, we have that any sampler S_1, that outputs $(C_0, C_1, \perp)$ such that $C_0 = C_1$, is an odiO-sampler (resp. oiO-sampler) that can be easily odiO-obfuscated (resp. oiO-obfuscated).[13] By combining these two observations, we conclude that if S_1 outputs $(C_0, C_1, \perp)$ where $C_0 = C_1$ and $(C_0, \perp) \leftarrow_\$ S_0(1^\lambda)$, it follows that neither C_0 nor C_1 (sampled by S_0) can be VBB-obfuscated but S_1 can be odiO-obfuscated (resp. oiO-obfuscated). While this counterexample might be trivial at first sight, it indeed captures the fact that an odiO-/oiO-obfuscator is allowed to reveal any information which is common to the two circuits, as long as this information does not allow to win the respective distinguishing game between the oracles.

Theorem 4.8 (odiO $\not\Rightarrow$ VBB **and** oiO $\not\Rightarrow$ VBB). *Let* S_0 *be a* VBB-*sampler (Definition 3.4). Consider the* odiO-*sampler (resp.* oiO-*sampler)* S_1 *defined as* $(C_0, C_1, \alpha) = S_1(1^\lambda; r)$ *where* $C_0 = C_1$ *and* $(C_0, \alpha) = S_0(1^\lambda; r)$ *for* $r \in \{0,1\}^*$. *For* type $\in \{\text{odiO}, \text{oiO}\}$, *there exists a* VBB-*sampler* S_0 *such that* $S_0 \notin S_{\text{VBB}}$ *and* $S_1 \in S_{\text{type}}$ *where* S_{VBB} *and* S_{type} *as defined in Definition 4.3.*

5   Applications of odiO and oiO

In this section, we show that odiO and oiO are able to compile several symmetric key primitives into their corresponding public key versions and designated verifier non-interactive argument systems into their public verifiable version. These

---

[12] Otherwise, if S $\in S_{\text{odiO}}$, there exists a ($\{S\}$)-odiO-obfuscator that in turn is also a ($\{S\}$)-diO-obfuscator.

[13] Indeed, any PPT obfuscator Obf that satisfies correctness and polynomial slowdown is a ($\{S\}$)-odiO-obfuscator (resp. ($\{S\}$)-oiO-obfuscator), e.g., Obf is the identity function or Obf is an iO-obfuscator.

transformations achieve (and use) different flavors of security whose definitions can be found in the full version of this paper. In more details, we demonstrate the following transformations:

Function-Preserving PV-NIZK from DV-NIZK: odiO is able to compile any designated verifier non-interactive argument system (that satisfies either selective soundness or straight-line knowledge soundness) into its public verifiable version (Sect. 5.1).

Function-Preserving Signatures from MACs: odiO is able to compile any (q)-sEUF-sel-CMA MAC into a (q)-sEUF-sel-CMA signature scheme (full version).

Format-Preserving Signatures from MACs: odiO is able to compile EUF MAC into a sel-EUF-CMA digital signature scheme, using puncturable PRF (full version).

Format-Preserving PKE from IV-based SKE: odiO is able to compile semantically secure IV-based SKE (i.e., SKE whose encryption algorithm has the following sintax $\mathsf{Enc}(\mathsf{k}, m; \mathsf{iv}) = (\mathsf{iv}, c)$) into a sel-IND-CPA PKE, using puncturable PRF (full version).

Function-Preserving PKE from SKE: oiO is able to compile any semantically and sel-IND-CPRA-key secure SKE into a sel-IND-CPA PKE (Sect. 5.2).

Note that transformations that use the puncturable PRFs are only format-preserving whereas the others are fully function-preserving.

We show the first and the last of our applications in detail in the main body; proofs and the remaining applications are deferred to the full version of this work.

5.1 From Designated Verifier to Public Verifiable Non-interactive Argument Systems

Construction 1. *Let $\Pi^* = (\mathsf{Setup}^*, \mathsf{Prove}^*, \mathsf{Verify}^*)$ and Obf be a DV non-interactive argument system for a relation $\mathcal{R}$ and an obfuscator, respectively. We compile Π^* into a PV non-interactive argument system $\Pi = (\mathsf{Setup}, \mathsf{Prove}, \mathsf{Verify})$ for the same relation $\mathcal{R}$ as follows:*

$\mathsf{Setup}(1^\lambda, \mathcal{R})$: *On input the security parameter 1^λ and a relation $\mathcal{R}$, the setup algorithm computes $(\mathsf{crs}^*, \mathsf{vrs}^*) \leftarrow_\$ \mathsf{Setup}^*(1^\lambda, \mathcal{R})$ and outputs $\mathsf{crs} = \mathsf{crs}^*$ and $\mathsf{vrs} = \widetilde{C}$ where $\widetilde{C} \leftarrow_\$ \mathsf{Obf}(1^\lambda, C_{\mathsf{vrs}^*}^{\mathsf{Verify}})$ and $C_{\mathsf{vrs}}^{\mathsf{Verify}}$ is depicted in Fig. 2.*

$\mathsf{Prove}(\mathsf{crs}, x, \omega)$: *On input the common reference string $\mathsf{crs} = \mathsf{crs}^*$, a statement x, and a witness ω, the prover algorithm outputs $\pi \leftarrow_\$ \mathsf{Prove}^*(\mathsf{crs}^*, x, \omega)$.*

$\mathsf{Verify}(\mathsf{vrs}, x, \pi)$: *On input the verification key $\mathsf{vrs} = \widetilde{C}$, a statement x, and a proof π, the verification algorithm returns $b = \widetilde{C}(x, \pi)$.*

Below we establish the following result.

$$
\begin{array}{l|l}
\hline
C_{\mathsf{vrs}}^{\mathsf{Verify}}(x, \pi) & \mathsf{S}_x(1^\lambda; r) \\
\hline
\mathbf{return}\ b = \mathsf{Verify}^*(\mathsf{vrs}, x, \pi) & (\mathsf{crs}, \mathsf{vrs}) = \mathsf{Setup}^*(1^\lambda; r) \\
 & \text{Set } C_0 = C_{\mathsf{vrs}}^{\mathsf{Verify}}, C_1 = C_{\mathsf{vrs}, x}^{\mathsf{Verify}}, \alpha = \mathsf{crs} \\
C_{\mathsf{vrs}, x^*}^{\mathsf{Verify}}(x, \pi) & \mathbf{return}\ (C_0, C_1, \alpha) \\
\hline
\mathbf{If}\ x = x^*,\ \mathbf{return}\ 0 & \\
\mathbf{return}\ b = \mathsf{Verify}^*(\mathsf{vrs}, x, \pi) & \mathsf{S}_{\mathsf{Ext}^*}(1^\lambda; r) \\
\hline
 & \text{Let } r = (r_0, r_1) \\
C_{\mathsf{vrs}, \mathsf{td}, r}^{\mathsf{Verify}}(x, \pi) & (\mathsf{crs}, \mathsf{vrs}, \mathsf{td}) = \mathsf{Ext}_0^*(1^\lambda, \mathcal{R}; r_0) \\
\hline
\omega = \mathsf{Ext}_1^*(1^\lambda, \mathsf{td}, x, \pi; r) & \text{Set } C_0 = C_{\mathsf{vrs}}^{\mathsf{Verify}}, C_1 = C_{\mathsf{vrs}, \mathsf{td}, r_1}^{\mathsf{Verify}}, \alpha = \mathsf{crs} \\
\mathbf{If}\ \mathsf{Verify}^*(\mathsf{vrs}, x, \pi) = 1\ \text{and} & \mathbf{return}\ (C_0, C_1, \alpha) \\
(x, \omega) \in \mathcal{R},\ \mathbf{return}\ 1 & \\
\mathbf{return}\ 0 & \\
\hline
\end{array}
$$

Fig. 2. The circuits $C_{\mathsf{vrs}}^{\mathsf{Verify}}$, $C_{\mathsf{vrs}, x^*}^{\mathsf{Verify}}$, $C_{\mathsf{vrs}, \mathsf{td}, r}^{\mathsf{Verify}}$, and the samplers $\mathsf{S}_x, \mathsf{S}_{\mathsf{Ext}^*}$. $C_{\mathsf{vrs}}^{\mathsf{Verify}}$ and $C_{\mathsf{vrs}, x^*}^{\mathsf{Verify}}$ (resp. $C_{\mathsf{vrs}}^{\mathsf{Verify}}$ and $C_{\mathsf{vrs}, \mathsf{td}, r}^{\mathsf{Verify}}$) are padded to match the size $\gamma = \max\{|C_{\mathsf{vrs}}^{\mathsf{Verify}}|, |C_{\mathsf{vrs}, x^*}^{\mathsf{Verify}}|\}$ (resp. $\gamma = \max\{|C_{\mathsf{vrs}}^{\mathsf{Verify}}|, |C_{\mathsf{vrs}, \mathsf{td}, r}^{\mathsf{Verify}}|\}$).

Theorem 5.1. *Let Π^* and Obf as defined in Construction 1. For every $x \notin \mathcal{L}$, consider the sampler S_x depicted in Fig. 2.*

1. *If Π^* satisfies selective soundness then, for every $x \notin \mathcal{L}$, S_x is an odiO-sampler (Definition 4.1), and*
2. *if Obf is a $(\{\mathsf{S}_x\}_{x \notin \mathcal{L}})$-odiO-obfuscator (Definition 4.2) then the publicly verifiable non-interactive argument system Π of Construction 1 satisfies selective soundness.*

We extend the above result to the case of straight-line knowledge soundness.

Theorem 5.2. *Let Π^* and Obf as defined in Construction 1.*

1. *If Π^* satisfies straight-line knowledge soundness then the sampler $\mathsf{S}_{\mathsf{Ext}^*}$ of Fig. 2 is an odiO-sampler (Definition 4.1) where $\mathsf{Ext}^* = (\mathsf{Ext}_0^*, \mathsf{Ext}_1^*)$ is the PPT extractor of Π^*, and*
2. *if Obf is a $(\{\mathsf{S}_{\mathsf{Ext}^*}\})$-odiO-obfuscator (Definition 4.2) then the publicly verifiable non-interactive argument system Π of Construction 1 satisfies straight-line knowledge soundness.*

Remark 5.3 (On zero-knowledge). Observe that Construction 1 preserves zero-knowledge if the underlying designated verifier non-interactive argument system Π^* is zero-knowledge. This is straightforward and follows intuitively because Construction 1 only obfuscates vrs (that it is known by a malicious verifier against zero-knowledge) and it does not alter Π^*'s Prove. A proof sketch of the zero-knowledge property would be as follows. The simulator for the publicly verifiable case is the same as the one for the designated verifier case. Now assume there exists an adversary A_{pv} distinguishing simulated proofs from honest ones. We could then design adversary A_{dv} breaking zero-knowledge of the

$C_k^{Enc}(m,r)$	$S_m(1^\lambda; r)$
return $c = Enc^*(k, m; r)$	Let $r = (r_0, r_1, r_2)$
	$k_0 = KGen^*(1^\lambda; r_0), k_1 = KGen^*(1^\lambda; r_1)$
	$c = Enc^*(k_0, m; r_2)$
	Set $C_0 = C_{k_0}^{Enc}, C_1 = C_{k_1}^{Enc}, \alpha = c$
	return (C_0, C_1, α)

Fig. 3. The circuit C_k^{Enc} and the sampler S_m. $C_{k_0}^{Enc}$ and $C_{k_1}^{Enc}$ (output by S_m) are padded to match the size $\gamma = \max\{|C_{k_0}^{Enc}|, |C_{k_1}^{Enc}|\}$)

original scheme. This adversary can in fact internally run A_{pv} passing to it the obfuscation $Obf(1^\lambda, C_{vrs}^{Verify})$. It can do that because the designated-verifier zero-knowledge has access to vrs.

5.2 From Semantically and sel-IND-CPRA-key SKEs to sel-IND-CPA PKEs

Construction 2. *Let* $\Pi^* = (KGen^*, Enc^*, Dec^*)$ *and* Obf *be a SKE with message space* $\mathcal{M}$ *and an obfuscator, respectively. We compile* Π^* *into a PKE scheme* $\Pi = (KGen, Enc, Dec)$ *with message space* $\mathcal{M}$ *as follows:*

$KGen(1^\lambda)$: *On input the security parameter* 1^λ, *the key generation algorithm computes* $k^* \leftarrow_\$ KGen^*(1^\lambda)$ *and outputs* $pk = \widetilde{C}$ *and* $sk = k^*$ *where* $\widetilde{C} \leftarrow_\$ Obf(1^\lambda, C_{k^*}^{Enc})$ *and* C_k^{Enc} *is depicted in Fig. 3.*

$Enc(pk, m; r)$: *On input the public key* $pk = \widetilde{C}$, *a message* $m \in \mathcal{M}$, *and randomness* $r \in \{0,1\}^*$, *the encryption algorithm outputs* $c = \widetilde{C}(m, r)$.

$Dec(sk, c)$: *On input the secret key* $sk = k^*$ *and a ciphertext* c, *the deterministic decryption algorithm returns* $m = Dec^*(k^*, c)$.

Below we establish the following result.

Theorem 5.4. *Let* Π^* *and* Obf *as defined in Construction 2. For every* $m \in \mathcal{M}$, *consider the sampler* S_m *depicted in Fig. 3.*

1. *If* Π^* *is sel-IND-CPRA-key then, for every* $m \in \mathcal{M}$, S_m *is an* oiO-*sampler (Definition 4.1), and*
2. *If* Π^* *is semantically secure and* Obf *is a* $(\{S_m\}_{m \in \mathcal{M}})$-oiO-*obfuscator (Definition 4.2) then the PKE scheme* Π *of Construction 2 is sel-IND-CPA.*

$$
\begin{array}{|l|l|l|}
\hline
C_{k,a,b}^0(x,r) & C_{k,a}^1(i,r) & C_k^2(c_1,c_2,\odot,r) \\
\hline
\text{If } x = a, \text{ return } b & \text{Let } a = a_1||\ldots||a_\lambda & x = \mathsf{Dec}_0(\mathsf{k},c_1)\odot\mathsf{Dec}_0(\mathsf{k},c_2) \\
\text{return } \mathsf{Enc}_0(\mathsf{k},0;r) & \text{return } \mathsf{Enc}_0(\mathsf{k},a_i;r) & \text{return } \mathsf{Enc}_0(\mathsf{k},x;r) \\
\hline
\end{array}
$$

Circuit definitions:

$C_{k,a,b,y,e}^3(d_1,\ldots,d_\lambda,r)$

Let $b = b_1||\ldots||b_\lambda$

For $i \in [\lambda]$ do:

   If $\mathsf{Dec}_0(\mathsf{k},d_i) \neq b_i$,

      return $\mathsf{Enc}_0(\mathsf{k},0;r)$

return (k,a,y,e)

$C_{\mathsf{s},(k,a,b,y,e)}^*(\ell,v,r)$

Let $v = (x,i,c_1,c_2,\odot,d_1,\ldots,d_\lambda)$

$r' = \mathsf{F}_1(\mathsf{s},(\ell,v,r))$

If $\ell = 0$, return $C_{k,a,b}^0(x,r')$

If $\ell = 1$, return $C_{k,a}^1(i,r')$

If $\ell = 2$, return $C_k^2(c_1,c_2,\odot,r')$

If $\ell = 3$, return $C_{k,a,b,y,e}^3(d_1,\ldots,d_\lambda,r')$

Fig. 4. The circuit $C_{\mathsf{s},(k,a,b,y,e)}^*$ where $(\mathsf{s},\mathsf{k},a,b,\mathsf{y},e) \in \{0,1\}^{5\lambda+1}$ and $\odot$ is the binary representation of a 2×2 table of an arbitrary binary operator (e.g., AND, OR, NOT).

6 Extending the Impossibility Results of Barak et al. [7,8] to the Setting of odiO and oiO

In Sect. 4, we have demonstrated that both odiO and oiO are weaker than VBB and, despite this, these new notions are enough to implement several of the most important applications of VBB (Sect. 5). At this point, the natural question is how weak odiO and oiO are, compared to VBB. In order to give an answer to this question, we investigate whether the impossibility results for VBB (of Barak et al. [7,8]) extend to either odiO or oiO (or both). Unfortunately, this turned out to be true: As we show in Sect. 6.1, for type $\in$ {odiO, oiO}, there exist a type-sampler that cannot be type-obfuscated (unconditionally).

In addition, Barak et al. [8, Theorem 4.10] have shown that converting an *arbitrary* SKE into a PKE (by simply obfuscating the SKE's encryption algorithm together with a symmetric key) is not possible: Indeed, there exists a contrived SKE Π that cannot be obfuscated (as described above) into a PKE. *However, such an impossibility result does not apply to our oiO-based transformation from semantically secure and sel-IND-CPRA-key secure SKEs into sel-IND-CPA PKEs (Sect. 5.2) since the contrived SKE Π of [8] is not sel-IND-CPRA-key.* Following the same spirit, we study whether a similar argument applies to our format-preserving (deferred to full version) and function-preserving transformations (Construction 2). In this case, we have a negative answer but only for the oiO-based function-preserving transformation (Construction 2): We demonstrate that there exists a SKE Π that is semantically and sel-IND-CPRA-key secure that cannot be converted into a sel-IND-CPA PKE by simply obfuscating the SKE's encryption algorithm together with a symmetric key, as done by our oiO-based Construction 2. On the other hand, it remains unclear how we can prove a similar impossibility result for our odiO-based format-preserving transformation from SKEs to PKEs (through puncturable PRFs). See full version of this work for more details.

We stress that both our impossibility results leverage similar techniques to that of Barak et al. [7,8] that we describe in the next sections.

Also, to meet space constraints, the formal proofs of the theorems that appear in next sections are deferred to full version.

6.1 Unobfuscatable odiO-samplers (Resp. oiO-samplers) Exist Unconditionally

We build an ensemble of circuits $\mathcal{C} = \{C^*_{s,(k,a,b,y,e)}\}$ (indexed by $(s, k, a, b, y, e) \in \{0,1\}^{5\lambda+1}$) that (i) $C^*_{s,(k,a,b,y,e)}$ leaks no information when treated as oracles, and (ii) the obfuscation of any $C^*_{s,(k,a,b,y,e)} \in \mathcal{C}$ allows to extract the hardcoded values (k, a, b, y, e). We anticipate that the value $e \in \{0,1\}$ will allow us to prove that a circuit $C^*_{s,(k,a,b,y,e)}$ cannot be odiO-obfuscated (resp. oiO-obfuscated) (see Sect. 6.1). On the other hand, the value y is a key of a PRF that is fundamental to build a contrived semantically and sel-IND-CPRA-key secure SKE that cannot be obfuscated (as described in Construction 2) into a sel-IND-CPA PKE (Sect. 6.2). We build such an ensemble $\mathcal{C}$ (depicted in Fig. 4) by using a similar technique to that of [7,8] (for more details, we refer the reader to [7,8]).

In a nutshell, $C^*_{s,(k,a,b,y,e)}$ (depicted in Fig. 4) is the composition of four circuits $(C^0_{k,a,b}, C^1_{k,a}, C^2_k, C^3_{k,a,b,y,e})$ and it is defined with respect to a SKE scheme $\Pi_0 = (\mathsf{KGen}_0, \mathsf{Enc}_0, \mathsf{Dec}_0)$ and a PRF $\Pi_1 = (\mathsf{Gen}_1, \mathsf{F}_1)$ (required to generate "fresh" randomnesses). On input (ℓ, v, r) where $v = (x, i, c_1, c_2, \odot, d_1, \ldots, d_\lambda)$, $C^*_{s,(k,a,b,y,e)}$ uses ℓ to select which circuit to execute:

1. If $\ell = 0$, $C^0_{k,a,b}(x, \mathsf{F}_1(s, (\ell, v, r)))$ is executed. This circuit presents a trigger input a. If $x = a$, $C^0_{k,a,b}(x, \mathsf{F}_1(s, (\ell, v, r)))$ returns b. Otherwise, it returns $\mathsf{Enc}_0(k, 0; \mathsf{F}_1(s, (\ell, v, r)))$.
2. If $\ell = 1$, $C^1_{k,a}(i, \mathsf{F}_1(s, (\ell, v, r)))$ is executed. This circuit simply outputs the encryption of the i-th bit of a, i.e., $\mathsf{Enc}_0(k, a_i; \mathsf{F}_1(s, (\ell, v, r)))$.
3. If $\ell = 2$, $C^2_k(c_1, c_2, \odot, \mathsf{F}_1(s, (\ell, v, r)))$ is executed. This circuit allows an evaluator to perform (gate by gate) computations over encrypted inputs. In more detail, it outputs the encryption of the evaluation of $w \odot z$ (i.e., $\mathsf{Enc}_0(k, w \odot z; \mathsf{F}_1(s, (\ell, v, r))))$ where $\odot$ is a binary operator, and w and z are the bits encrypted by c_1 and c_2, respectively.
4. If $\ell = 3$, $C^3_{k,a,b,y,e}(d_1, \ldots, d_\lambda, \mathsf{F}_1(s, (\ell, v, r)))$ is executed. This is another circuit that presents a trigger input b. In more detail, if each d_i is the encryption of the i-th of b, the circuit returns (k, a, y, e). Otherwise, it returns $\mathsf{Enc}_0(k, 0; \mathsf{F}_1(s, (\ell, v, r)))$.

Following [7,8], if the SKE scheme Π_0 is IND-CCA1 and Π_1 is a secure PRF, then oracle access to $C^*_{s,(k,a,b,y,e)}$ is computationally indistinguishable to oracle access to a circuit $\widetilde{C}_k$ that, on every input (ℓ, v, r), it always outputs a fresh encryption of 0. This is because an adversary only sees ciphertexts and, as a consequence, it cannot distinguish between $C^*_{s,(k,a,b,y,e)}$ and $\widetilde{C}_k$ unless it guesses the trigger inputs $a, b \in \{0,1\}^\lambda$. As a consequence, this implies that (i) an adversary cannot leak the hardcoded values (k, a, b, y, e) and, (ii) the pair of circuits $(C^*_{s,(k,a,b,y,0)}, C^*_{s,(k,a,b,y,1)})$ are both oracle-differing-input and oracle-indistinguishable circuits (Definition 4.1).

On the other hand, on input $\widetilde{C} \leftarrow_\$ \mathsf{Obf}(1^\lambda, C^*_{s,(k,a,b,y,e)})$, an adversary can easily extract (k, a, b, y, e), i.e., the circuit is partially reversible. This can be done as follows:

- Evaluate $\widetilde{C}(1, \cdot, \cdot)$ to get the encryptions $(c_1, \dots, c_\lambda)$ of the a's bits (see Item 2).
- Use $(c_1, \dots, c_\lambda)$ to compute $(d_1, \dots, d_\lambda)$ where d_i is the encryption of b's i-th bit. Observe that this can be done by leveraging $\widetilde{C}(2, \cdot, \cdot)$ to evaluate (gate by gate) $\widetilde{C}(0, \cdot, \cdot) = C^0_{k,a,b}(\cdot, \cdot)$ on a (see Item 3), and
- Compute (k, a, b, y, e) by $\widetilde{C}(3, \cdot, \cdot)$ on $(d_1, \dots, d_\lambda)$ (see Item 4).

The properties of the ensemble $\mathcal{C}$ are formalized in Theorem 6.1. We highlight that our technique of generating Enc_0's randomness as $\mathsf{F}_1(s, (\ell, v, r))$ (instead of $\mathsf{F}_1(s, (\ell, v))$ as done by Barak et al. [7,8]) permits to have multiple randomnesses for a fixed pair (ℓ, v). This is allows us to prove a new property (not achieved by [7,8]) named *input-indistinguishability* that, in turn, is fundamental to prove the impossibility (Sect. 6.2) of converting semantically and sel-IND-CPRA-key secure SKE into sel-IND-CPA PKE. We stress that the ensemble of circuits built by Barak et al. [7, Lemma 3.5] does not satisfy input-indistinguishability.

Theorem 6.1. *Let* $\Pi_0 = (\mathsf{KGen}_0, \mathsf{Enc}_0, \mathsf{Dec}_0)$, $\Pi_1 = (\mathsf{Gen}_1, \mathsf{F}_1)$, *and* $C^*_{s,(k,a,b,y,e)}$ *be a SKE scheme with key space* $\{0,1\}^\lambda$, *a PRF scheme with key space* $\{0,1\}^\lambda$, *and the circuit defined in Fig. 4 with respect to* Π_0 *and* Π_1, *respectively. Then, the ensemble* $\mathcal{C} = \{C^*_{s,(k,a,b,y,e)}\}_{s,k,a,b,y \in \{0,1\}^\lambda, e \in \{0,1\}}$ *satisfies the following properties:*

Oracle-differing-input: *If* Π_0 *is IND-CCA1 and* Π_1 *is secure then for every PPT adversary* D, *we have*

$$\mathbb{P}\left[C^*_{s,(k,a,b,y,0)}(\ell, v, r) \neq C^*_{s,(k,a,b,y,1)}(\ell, v, r)\right] \leq \mathsf{negl}(\lambda),$$

where $(\ell, v, r) \leftarrow_\$ \mathsf{A}^{C^*_{s,(k,a,b,y,0)}(\cdot,\cdot,\cdot), C^*_{s,(k,a,b,y,1)}(\cdot,\cdot,\cdot)}(1^\lambda)$, $\mathsf{k} \leftarrow_\$ \mathsf{KGen}_0(1^\lambda)$, $\mathsf{s} \leftarrow_\$ \mathsf{Gen}_1(1^\lambda)$, $\mathsf{y} \leftarrow_\$ \mathsf{Gen}_1(1^\lambda)$, *and* $(a, b) \leftarrow_\$ \{0,1\}^{2\lambda}$.

Input-indistinguishability: *If* Π_0 *is IND-CCA1 and IND-CPA-key, and* Π_1 *is secure, then for every* $\ell, v \in \{0,1\}^*$, *every PPT adversary* D, *we have*

$$\left| \mathbb{P}\left[\mathsf{D}^{C^*_{s_0,(k_0,a_0,b_0,y_0,0)}(\cdot,\cdot,\cdot), C^*_{s_1,(k_1,a_1,b_1,y_1,1)}(\cdot,\cdot,\cdot)}(1^\lambda, m_0) = 1\right] - \right.$$
$$\left. \mathbb{P}\left[\mathsf{D}^{C^*_{s_0,(k_0,a_0,b_0,y_0,0)}(\cdot,\cdot,\cdot), C^*_{s_1,(k_1,a_1,b_1,y_1,1)}(\cdot,\cdot,\cdot)}(1^\lambda, m_1) = 1\right] \right| \leq \mathsf{negl}(\lambda),$$

where $(a_0, b_0, a_1, b_1) \leftarrow_\$ \{0,1\}^{4\lambda}$, $k_j \leftarrow_\$ \mathsf{KGen}_0(1^\lambda)$ *for* $j \in \{0,1\}$, $s_j \leftarrow_\$ \mathsf{Gen}_1(1^\lambda)$ *for* $j \in \{0,1\}$, $y_j \leftarrow_\$ \mathsf{Gen}_1(1^\lambda)$ *for* $j \in \{0,1\}$, *and* $m_d = C^*_{s_d,(k_d,a_d,b_d,y_d,d)}(\ell, v, r_d)$ *for* $r_d \leftarrow_\$ \{0,1\}^*$ *and* $d \in \{0,1\}$.

$C_{r,b}^{\mathsf{owf}}(x)$	$\mathsf{S}_{\mathsf{owf}}(1^\lambda; r)$
If $x = r$, **return** b **return** 0	Set $C_0 = C_{r,0}^{\mathsf{owf}}, C_1 = C_{r,1}^{\mathsf{owf}}, \alpha = \bot$ **return** (C_0, C_1, α)

Fig. 5. The circuit $C_{r,b}^{\mathsf{owf}}$ and the sampler $\mathsf{S}_{\mathsf{owf}}$.

Partial reversibility: *There exists a PPT algorithm* Ext *such that for every* $(\mathsf{s}, \mathsf{k}, a, b, \mathsf{y}, e) \in \{0,1\}^{5\lambda+1}$ *and every circuit* $\widetilde{C}$ *such that* $\widetilde{C}(\ell, v, r) = C_{\mathsf{s},(\mathsf{k},a,b,\mathsf{y},e)}^*(\ell, v, r)$ *for all* $\ell, v, r \in \{0,1\}^*$, $\mathbb{P}\left[(\mathsf{k}, a, b, \mathsf{y}, e) \leftarrow_\$ \mathsf{Ext}(1^\lambda, \widetilde{C})\right] = 1$.

Theorem 6.1 implies that there exists an odiO-sampler (resp. oiO-sampler) $\widehat{\mathsf{S}}$ that cannot be odiO-obfuscated (resp. oiO-obfuscated), if OWFs exist (indeed, OWF implies both IND-CCA1 and IND-CPA-key security of SKE. See full version for more details).

Corollary 6.2. *For* type $\in \{\mathsf{odiO}, \mathsf{oiO}\}$, *if OWFs exist then there exists a* type-*sampler* $\widehat{\mathsf{S}}$ *(Definition 4.1) such that* $\widehat{\mathsf{S}} \notin \mathcal{S}_{\mathsf{type}}$ *where* $\mathcal{S}_{\mathsf{type}}$ *is defined in Definition 4.3.*

Similarly to VBB, both odiO and oiO imply the existence of OWFs. As a consequence, for type $\in \{\mathsf{odiO}, \mathsf{odiO}\}$, a type-unobfuscatable type-sampler exists *unconditionally.*

Theorem 6.3. *s Let* Obf *and* $\mathsf{S}_{\mathsf{owf}}$ *be an obfuscator and the sampler as defined in Fig. 5. Let* $p(\cdot)$ *and* $\mathcal{F} = \{\mathsf{F}_\lambda\}_{\lambda \in \mathbb{N}}$ *be a polynomial and an ensemble of functions such that* F_λ *is defined as* $\mathsf{F}_\lambda(b, r_0, r_1) = \mathsf{Obf}(1^\lambda, C_{r_0,b}^{\mathsf{owf}}; r_1)$ *where* $(b, r_0, r_1) \in \{0,1\} \times \{0,1\}^\lambda \times \{0,1\}^{p(\lambda)}$. *Then, the following statements hold:*

1. $\mathsf{S}_{\mathsf{owf}}$ *is an* odiO-*sampler (resp.* oiO-*sampler), and*
2. *if* Obf *is a* $(\{\mathsf{S}_{\mathsf{owf}}\})$-odiO-*obfuscator (resp.* $(\{\mathsf{S}_{\mathsf{owf}}\})$-oiO-*obfuscator) then* $\mathsf{F}_\lambda \in \mathcal{F}$ *is a OWF.*

Corollary 6.4. *For* type $\in \{\mathsf{odiO}, \mathsf{oiO}\}$, *there exists (unconditionally) a* type-*sampler* S *such that* $\mathsf{S} \notin \mathcal{S}_{\mathsf{type}}$ *where* $\mathcal{S}_{\mathsf{type}}$ *as defined in Definition 4.3.*

The above corollary follows by combining Corollary 6.2 and Theorem 6.3, i.e., either $\mathsf{S}_{\mathsf{owf}} \notin \mathcal{S}_{\mathsf{type}}$ or $\widehat{\mathsf{S}} \notin \mathcal{S}_{\mathsf{type}}$ (for type $\in \{\mathsf{odiO}, \mathsf{odiO}\}$) where $\mathsf{S}_{\mathsf{owf}}$ and $\widehat{\mathsf{S}}$ defined in Fig. 5 and Corollary 6.2, respectively.

6.2 Impossibility of Obfuscating Semantically and sel-IND-CPRA-key Secure SKE into sel-IND-CPA Secure PKE Schemes

We now demonstrate that it is inherently impossible to convert a semantically secure and sel-IND-CPRA-key SKEs into sel-IND-CPA PKEs by simply obfuscating the SKE's encryption algorithm, as described in our oiO-based Construction 2. We prove this by leveraging a similar technique to that of [8]: We construct a SKE Π^* that satisfies semantic and sel-IND-CPRA-key security that, when obfuscated into a PKE (as described in Sect. 5.2), the latter results to be completely insecure. By leveraging the ensemble $\mathcal{C}$ of Theorem 6.1, a PRF $\overline{\Pi} = (\overline{\mathsf{Gen}}, \overline{\mathsf{F}})$, and a semantically and sel-IND-CPRA-key secure SKE scheme $\widetilde{\Pi} = (\widetilde{\mathsf{KGen}}, \widetilde{\mathsf{Enc}}, \widetilde{\mathsf{Dec}})$, we build the contrived SKE Π^* as follows:

$$\mathsf{Enc}^*(\mathsf{k}^*, (\ell, v); r) = (\widetilde{\mathsf{Enc}}(\widetilde{\mathsf{k}}, (\ell, v); r), C^*_{\mathsf{s}, (\widehat{k}, a, b, \mathsf{y}, e)}(\ell, v, r), \overline{\mathsf{F}}(\mathsf{y}, (\ell, v, r)) \oplus \widetilde{\mathsf{k}}) \quad (1)$$

where $\mathsf{k}^* = (\widehat{\mathsf{k}}, \widetilde{\mathsf{k}}, \mathsf{s}, a, b, \mathsf{y}, e)$.

Π^* is a semantically and sel-IND-CPRA-key secure SKE for the following reasons. First, as described in Sect. 6.1, oracle access to the circuit $C^*_{\mathsf{s}, (\widehat{k}, a, b, \mathsf{y}, e)} \in \mathcal{C}$ is computationally indistinguishable from having oracle access to a circuit $\widetilde{C}_{\mathsf{k}}$ that always returns encryptions of 0. Hence, this implies that $C^*_{\mathsf{s}, (\widehat{k}, a, b, \mathsf{y}, e)}$ does not leak the message (ℓ, v) and that an adversary cannot leak any information about $(\widehat{\mathsf{k}}, a, b, \mathsf{y}, e)$. Second, conditioned to the above observation, the semantic security of Π^* easily follows from the semantic security of $\widetilde{\Pi}$ and the security of $\overline{\Pi}$. Third, as for the sel-IND-CPRA-key security of Π^*, it follows from sel-IND-CPRA-key security of $\widetilde{\Pi}$, the security of $\overline{\Pi}$, and the fact that $\mathcal{C}$ satisfies input-indistinguishability (see Theorem 6.1).

On the other hand, when Enc^* is obfuscated (as in Construction 2), an adversary can exploit the partial reversibility of $\mathcal{C}$ (Theorem 6.1) to extract y and, in turn, the key $\widetilde{\mathsf{k}}$ that is used to encrypt the message $m = (\ell, v)$. Below, we report the formal result.

Theorem 6.5. *If OWFs exist then the following statements hold:*

1. *there exist a SKE Π^* such that Π^* is semantically secure, sel-IND-CPRA-key, and*
2. *the PKE scheme $\Pi = (\mathsf{KGen}, \mathsf{Enc}, \mathsf{Dec})$ (output by applying to Π^* the transformation defined in Construction 2) is not sel-IND-CPA (Theorem 5.4).*

We stress that the above result improves the impossibility result of Barak et al. [8] since ours apply to the smaller class of SKEs (i.e., SKEs with stronger notions of security) that satisfy sel-IND-CPRA-key security.

Also, all our odiO-based transformations remain plausible as the impossibility result do not seem to extend. We provide more details in the full version of this work.

Acknowledgments. The authors would like to thank the anonymous reviewers for useful feedback. The research described in this paper received funding from: the Concordium Blockhain Research Center, Aarhus University, Denmark; the Carlsberg Foundation under the Semper Ardens Research Project CF18-112 (BCM); the European Research Council (ERC) under the European Unions's Horizon 2020 research and innovation programme under grant agreement No 803096 (SPEC).

References

1. Ananth, P., Boneh, D., Garg, S., Sahai, A., Zhandry, M.: Differing-inputs obfuscation and applications. IACR Cryptol. ePrint Arch. **2013**, 689 (2013)

2. Ananth, P., Jain, A., Lin, H., Matt, C., Sahai, A.: Indistinguishability obfuscation without multilinear maps: new paradigms via low degree weak pseudorandomness and security amplification. In: Boldyreva, A., Micciancio, D. (eds.) CRYPTO 2019. LNCS, vol. 11694, pp. 284–332. Springer, Cham (2019). https://doi.org/10.1007/978-3-030-26954-8_10

3. Ananth, P., Jain, A.: Indistinguishability obfuscation from compact functional encryption. In: Gennaro, R., Robshaw, M. (eds.) CRYPTO 2015. LNCS, vol. 9215, pp. 308–326. Springer, Heidelberg (2015). https://doi.org/10.1007/978-3-662-47989-6_15

4. Ananth, P., Jain, A., Sahai, A.: Indistinguishability obfuscation from functional encryption for simple functions. Cryptology ePrint Archive (2015)

5. Barak, B., Bitansky, N., Canetti, R., Kalai, Y.T., Paneth, O., Sahai, A.: Obfuscation for evasive functions. In: Lindell, Y. (ed.) TCC 2014. LNCS, vol. 8349, pp. 26–51. Springer, Heidelberg (2014). https://doi.org/10.1007/978-3-642-54242-8_2

6. Barak, B., Garg, S., Kalai, Y.T., Paneth, O., Sahai, A.: Protecting obfuscation against algebraic attacks. In: Nguyen, P.Q., Oswald, E. (eds.) EUROCRYPT 2014. LNCS, vol. 8441, pp. 221–238. Springer, Heidelberg (2014). https://doi.org/10.1007/978-3-642-55220-5_13

7. Barak, B., et al.: On the (Im)Possibility of obfuscating programs. In: Kilian, J. (ed.) CRYPTO 2001. LNCS, vol. 2139, pp. 1–18. Springer, Heidelberg (2001). https://doi.org/10.1007/3-540-44647-8_1

8. Barak, B., et al.: On the (im) possibility of obfuscating programs. J. ACM (JACM) 59(2), 1–48 (2012)

9. Bellare, M., Hoang, V.T., Keelveedhi, S.: Instantiating random oracles via UCEs. In: Canetti, R., Garay, J.A. (eds.) CRYPTO 2013. LNCS, vol. 8043, pp. 398–415. Springer, Heidelberg (2013). https://doi.org/10.1007/978-3-642-40084-1_23

10. Bellare, M., Stepanovs, I., Tessaro, S.: Poly-many hardcore bits for any one-way function and a framework for differing-inputs obfuscation. In: Sarkar, P., Iwata, T. (eds.) ASIACRYPT 2014. LNCS, vol. 8874, pp. 102–121. Springer, Heidelberg (2014). https://doi.org/10.1007/978-3-662-45608-8_6

11. Bellare, M., Stepanovs, I., Waters, B.: New negative results on differing-inputs obfuscation. In: Fischlin, M., Coron, J.-S. (eds.) EUROCRYPT 2016. LNCS, vol. 9666, pp. 792–821. Springer, Heidelberg (2016). https://doi.org/10.1007/978-3-662-49896-5_28

12. Bitansky, N., Canetti, R.: On strong simulation and composable point obfuscation. In: Rabin, T. (ed.) CRYPTO 2010. LNCS, vol. 6223, pp. 520–537. Springer, Heidelberg (2010). https://doi.org/10.1007/978-3-642-14623-7_28

13. Bitansky, N., et al.: The impossibility of obfuscation with auxiliary input or a universal simulator. In: Garay, J.A., Gennaro, R. (eds.) CRYPTO 2014. LNCS, vol. 8617, pp. 71–89. Springer, Heidelberg (2014). https://doi.org/10.1007/978-3-662-44381-1_5

14. Bitansky, N., Canetti, R., Kalai, Y.T., Paneth, O.: On virtual grey box obfuscation for general circuits. Algorithmica 79(4), 1014–1051 (2017)

15. Bitansky, N., Vaikuntanathan, V.: Indistinguishability obfuscation from functional encryption. In: 2015 IEEE 56th Annual Symposium on Foundations of Computer Science (FOCS), pp. 171–190. IEEE Computer Society (2015)

16. Bitansky, N., Vaikuntanathan, V.: Indistinguishability obfuscation from functional encryption. J. ACM (JACM) 65(6), 1–37 (2018)

17. Boyle, E., Chung, K.-M., Pass, R.: On extractability obfuscation. In: Lindell, Y. (ed.) TCC 2014. LNCS, vol. 8349, pp. 52–73. Springer, Heidelberg (2014). https://doi.org/10.1007/978-3-642-54242-8_3

18. Boyle, E., Pass, R.: Limits of extractability assumptions with distributional auxiliary input. In: Iwata, T., Cheon, J.H. (eds.) ASIACRYPT 2015. LNCS, vol. 9453, pp. 236–261. Springer, Heidelberg (2015). https://doi.org/10.1007/978-3-662-48800-3_10

19. Brakerski, Z., Döttling, N., Garg, S., Malavolta, G.: Candidate iO from homomorphic encryption schemes. In: Canteaut, A., Ishai, Y. (eds.) EUROCRYPT 2020. LNCS, vol. 12105, pp. 79–109. Springer, Cham (2020). https://doi.org/10.1007/978-3-030-45721-1_4

20. Brakerski, Z., Rothblum, G.N.: Virtual black-box obfuscation for all circuits via generic graded encoding. In: Lindell, Y. (ed.) TCC 2014. LNCS, vol. 8349, pp. 1–25. Springer, Heidelberg (2014). https://doi.org/10.1007/978-3-642-54242-8_1

21. Campanelli, M., Francati, D., Orlandi, C.: Structure-preserving compilers from new notions of obfuscations. Cryptology ePrint Archive, Paper 2022/732 (2022). https://eprint.iacr.org/2022/732

22. Canetti, R., Kalai, Y.T., Paneth, O.: On obfuscation with random oracles. In: Dodis, Y., Nielsen, J.B. (eds.) TCC 2015. LNCS, vol. 9015, pp. 456–467. Springer, Heidelberg (2015). https://doi.org/10.1007/978-3-662-46497-7_18

23. Canetti, R., Rothblum, G.N., Varia, M.: Obfuscation of hyperplane membership. In: Micciancio, D. (ed.) TCC 2010. LNCS, vol. 5978, pp. 72–89. Springer, Heidelberg (2010). https://doi.org/10.1007/978-3-642-11799-2_5

24. Chase, M., Lysyanskaya, A.: On signatures of knowledge. In: Dwork, C. (ed.) CRYPTO 2006. LNCS, vol. 4117, pp. 78–96. Springer, Heidelberg (2006). https://doi.org/10.1007/11818175_5

25. Diffie, W., Hellman, M.E.: New directions in cryptography. IEEE Trans. Inf. Theory **22**(6), 644–654 (1976)

26. Garg, S., Gentry, C., Halevi, S., Raykova, M., Sahai, A., Waters, B.: Candidate indistinguishability obfuscation and functional encryption for all circuits. In: 2013 IEEE 54th Annual Symposium on Foundations of Computer Science (FOCS), pp. 40–49. IEEE Computer Society (2013)

27. Garg, S., Gentry, C., Halevi, S., Wichs, D.: On the implausibility of differing-inputs obfuscation and extractable witness encryption with auxiliary input. Algorithmica **79**(4), 1353–1373 (2017)

28. Garg, S., Mahmoody, M., Mohammed, A.: When does functional encryption imply obfuscation? In: Kalai, Y., Reyzin, L. (eds.) TCC 2017. LNCS, vol. 10677, pp. 82–115. Springer, Cham (2017). https://doi.org/10.1007/978-3-319-70500-2_4

29. Gay, R., Pass, R.: Indistinguishability obfuscation from circular security. In: Proceedings of the 53rd Annual ACM SIGACT Symposium on Theory of Computing, pp. 736–749 (2021)

30. Goldwasser, S., Kalai, Y.T.: On the impossibility of obfuscation with auxiliary input. In: 46th Annual IEEE Symposium on Foundations of Computer Science (FOCS2005), pp. 553–562. IEEE (2005)

31. Goldwasser, S., Kalai, Y.T.: A note on the impossibility of obfuscation with auxiliary input. IACR Cryptol. ePrint Arch. **2013**, 665 (2013)

32. Goldwasser, S., Rothblum, G.N.: On best-possible obfuscation. In: Vadhan, S.P. (ed.) TCC 2007. LNCS, vol. 4392, pp. 194–213. Springer, Heidelberg (2007). https://doi.org/10.1007/978-3-540-70936-7_11

33. Goyal, R., Koppula, V., Waters, B.: Lockable obfuscation. In: 2017 IEEE 58th Annual Symposium on Foundations of Computer Science (FOCS), pp. 612–621. IEEE (2017)

34. Ishai, Y., Pandey, O., Sahai, A.: Public-coin differing-inputs obfuscation and its applications. In: Dodis, Y., Nielsen, J.B. (eds.) TCC 2015. LNCS, vol. 9015, pp. 668–697. Springer, Heidelberg (2015). https://doi.org/10.1007/978-3-662-46497-7_26

35. Jain, A., Lin, H., Sahai, A.: Indistinguishability obfuscation from well-founded assumptions. In: Proceedings of the 53rd Annual ACM SIGACT Symposium on Theory of Computing, pp. 60–73 (2021)

36. Lin, H., Pass, R., Seth, K., Telang, S.: Indistinguishability obfuscation with non-trivial efficiency. In: Cheng, C.-M., Chung, K.-M., Persiano, G., Yang, B.-Y. (eds.) PKC 2016. LNCS, vol. 9615, pp. 447–462. Springer, Heidelberg (2016). https://doi.org/10.1007/978-3-662-49387-8_17

37. Lynn, B., Prabhakaran, M., Sahai, A.: Positive results and techniques for obfuscation. In: Cachin, C., Camenisch, J.L. (eds.) EUROCRYPT 2004. LNCS, vol. 3027, pp. 20–39. Springer, Heidelberg (2004). https://doi.org/10.1007/978-3-540-24676-3_2

38. Mahmoody, M., Mohammed, A., Nematihaji, S.: On the impossibility of virtual black-box obfuscation in idealized models. In: Kushilevitz, E., Malkin, T. (eds.) TCC 2016. LNCS, vol. 9562, pp. 18–48. Springer, Heidelberg (2016). https://doi.org/10.1007/978-3-662-49096-9_2

39. Pass, R., Seth, K., Telang, S.: Indistinguishability obfuscation from semantically-secure multilinear encodings. In: Garay, J.A., Gennaro, R. (eds.) CRYPTO 2014. LNCS, vol. 8616, pp. 500–517. Springer, Heidelberg (2014). https://doi.org/10.1007/978-3-662-44371-2_28

40. Pass, R., Shelat, A.: Impossibility of VBB obfuscation with ideal constant-degree graded encodings. In: Kushilevitz, E., Malkin, T. (eds.) TCC 2016. LNCS, vol. 9562, pp. 3–17. Springer, Heidelberg (2016). https://doi.org/10.1007/978-3-662-49096-9_1

41. Sahai, A., Waters, B.: How to use indistinguishability obfuscation: deniable encryption, and more. In: Proceedings of the Forty-Sixth Annual ACM Symposium on Theory of Computing, pp. 475–484 (2014)

42. Shacham, H., Waters, B.: Compact proofs of retrievability. J. Cryptol. 26(3), 442–483 (2013)

43. Wee, H.: On obfuscating point functions. In: Proceedings of the Thirty-seventh Annual ACM Symposium on Theory of Computing, pp. 523–532 (2005)

44. Wee, H., Wichs, D.: Candidate obfuscation via oblivious LWE sampling. In: Canteaut, A., Standaert, F.-X. (eds.) EUROCRYPT 2021. LNCS, vol. 12698, pp. 127–156. Springer, Cham (2021). https://doi.org/10.1007/978-3-030-77883-5_5

45. Wichs, D., Zirdelis, G.: Obfuscating compute-and-compare programs under LWE. In: 2017 IEEE 58th Annual Symposium on Foundations of Computer Science (FOCS), pp. 600–611. IEEE (2017)

Author Index

© International Association for Cryptologic Research 2023
A. Boldyreva and V. Kolesnikov (Eds.): PKC 2023, LNCS 13941, pp. 695–697, 2023.
https://doi.org/10.1007/978-3-031-31371-4

Printed in the United States
by Baker & Taylor Publisher Services